Rob Tidrow
Jim Ness
Bob Retelle
Cheri Robinson

NEW RIDERS' OFFICIAL
COMPUSERVE®
YELLOW
PAGES

New Riders Publishing, Indianapolis, Indiana

New Riders' Official CompuServe Yellow Pages

By Rob Tidrow, Jim Ness, Bob Retelle, and Cheri Robinson

Published by:
New Riders Publishing
201 West 103rd Street
Indianapolis, IN 46290 USA

All rights reserved. No part of this book may be reproduced or transmitted in any form or by any means, electronic or mechanical, including photocopying, recording, or by any information storage and retrieval system, without written permission from the publisher, except for the inclusion of brief quotations in a review.

Copyright © 1994 by New Riders Publishing

Printed in the United States of America
1 2 3 4 5 6 7 8 9 0

```
New Riders' Official CompuServe yellow
pages / Rob Tidrow…[etal]
       p. cm.
   ISBN 1-56205-396-5
   1. CompuServe (Videotex system)--
   Directories.   I. Tidrow, Rob.
QA76.57.C65N49    1994w
384.3'54--dc20
                               94-37840
                                   CIP
```

Warning and Disclaimer

This book is designed to provide information about the CompuServe network. Every effort has been made to make this book as complete and as accurate as possible, but no warranty or fitness is implied.

The information is provided on an "as is" basis. The authors and New Riders Publishing shall have neither liability nor responsibility to any person or entity with respect to any loss or damages arising from the information contained in this book or from the use of the disks or programs that may accompany it.

Publisher	Lloyd J. Short
Associate Publisher	Tim Huddleston
Product Development Manager	Rob Tidrow
Marketing Manager	Ray Robinson
Director of Special Projects	Cheri Robinson
Managing Editor	Matthew Morrill

About the Authors

Rob Tidrow is the Product Development Manager for New Riders Publishing and specializes in operating systems, Windows-based applications, and online communications. Rob is a contributing author of several New Riders books, including *Windows for Non-Nerds, AutoCAD Student Workbook, Inside WordPerfect 6 for Windows, Inside Microsoft Office Professional,* and *Riding the Internet Highway, Deluxe Edition.* Rob has created technical documentation and instructional programs for use in a variety of industrial settings and has a degree in English literature from Indiana University. He resides in Indianapolis with his wife, Tammy, and his two boys, Adam and Wesley. He can be reached on CompuServe at 75250,1443.

Jim Ness is a sales engineer in the industrial programmable controls market. He has been a member of CompuServe and other online services since 1980, has been a SysOp since 1991, and has written several shareware telecom utilities for use online. Jim has been the CompuServe columnist for *Connect Magazine* since May 1993.

Bob Retelle has been involved in computers since the days of the KIM-1, the OSI C-IP, and the Radio Shack TRS-80. He wrote best-selling entertainment software for these early microcomputers, finally owning and operating Pretzell and Software during the heyday of the eight-bit computer. Since then, Bob has been professionally involved in the online community, working as a SysOp on both CompuServe and Delphi, and he created and managed one of the original roundtables on GEnie.

Bob has done some professional photography and now restores and rides motorcycles for fun. In his "spare time," Bob helps keep the mainframe computers humming for a major timeshare/payroll/banking services company, mostly on the midnight shift.

Cheri Robinson is the Director of Special Projects at New Riders Publishing. She has 15 years of experience in the publishing field. During her tenure at New Riders, she has edited and developed a number of titles, including *Inside Adobe Photoshop 2.5 for Windows, A Guide to CD-ROM,* and *Inside CorelDRAW!.* She also is the author of *The Fonts Coach,* also published by New Riders Publishing. Before joining New Riders, she was a Senior Editor for Que Corporation. Cheri also was employed as a graphics designer for several trade publications in the hardware industry.

Trademark Acknowledgments

All terms mentioned in this book that are known to be trademarks or service marks have been appropriately capitalized. New Riders Publishing cannot attest to the accuracy of this information. Use of a term in this book should not be regarded as affecting the validity of any trademark or service mark.

Product Director
Cheri Robinson

Production Editor
John Kane

Editors
Amy Bezek
Laura Frey
Sarah Kearns
Rob Lawson
Tad Ringo
Cliff Shubs
John Sleeva
Suzanne Snyder
Lisa Wilson
Lillian Yates

Senior Acquisitions Editor
Jim LeValley

Acquisitions Coordinator
Stacey Beheler

Editorial Assistant
Karen Opal

Publisher's Assistant
Melissa Lynch

Cover Designer
Jay Corpus

Book Designer
Roger S. Morgan

Graphics Image Specialists
Clint Lahnen
Dennis Sheehan

Production Imprint Manager
Juli Cook

Production Imprint Team Leader
Katy Bodenmiller

Production Analysts
Dennis Clay Hager
Mary Beth Wakefield

Production Team
Georgiana Briggs
Michael Brumitt
Elaine Brush
Mary Ann Cosby
Judy Everly
Rob Falco
Louisa Klucznik
Chad Poore
Brian-Kent Proffitt
Marc Shecter
Susan Shephard
Scott Tullis

Indexers
Johnna Vanhoose

TABLE OF CONTENTS

Introduction 1
What is the *CompuServe Yellow Pages*? 1
Anatomy of the Directory 2
    Subjects 3
    Audience 3
    Content Summary 3
    See Also 3
    Cost and User Guide 3
    Activity Level 3
    Address 3
Preparing for Access 3
    Phone Numbers 3
Using Plain-Vanilla Telecom Software 3
Your Best Software Options 4
WinCIM 5
MacCIM and DOS CIM 5
CompuServe Navigator for Windows 5
CompuServe Navigator for Macintosh 6
OzCIS and OzWIN 6
TAPCIS 6
AutoSig (ATO) 7
Software Summary 7
CompuServe Mail 7
Forums: Messages, Conferences, and Libraries 7
    Message Area 7
    Conference Area 8
    Libraries 8
What is ZiffNet? 8
New Riders Publishing 8
Alphabetical Directory Listing 11
Index 613

Introduction

Introduction

The CompuServe Information Service is the world's largest commercial online service, providing its members with information, entertainment, and access to the worldwide community of modem communicators—the information superhighway.

During 1994, CompuServe celebrated its 15th year of operation by surpassing the two million member mark and will enter 1995 with an estimated 2.5 million members worldwide. Online, CompuServe's product index contains in excess of 1,000 publicly available services. Most are based on the English language, but there also are several services presented in German and French. By any measure, CompuServe has become a huge entity, whose breadth of services is difficult to grasp.

What Is the CompuServe Yellow Pages?

The *New Riders Official CompuServe Yellow Pages* is designed to allow CompuServe members—novice or veteran—to locate quickly the services they need to visit or learn about. Readers familiar with an American phone book should have no trouble finding services by searching for subjects. A listed subject will include from one to several individual service listings, and a given service might appear several times in the directory, under different subject headings.

CompuServe provides several types of services, including forums, databases, and online games areas. The listings are designed with enough flexibility to describe them all.

The most popular CompuServe service is the forum. A *forum* consists of a message area, a library, and a conference area. In the *message area,* members post public messages to each other about the subjects covered by the forum. *Libraries* hold files pertinent to the forum topics. And in *conference areas,* members get together "live" to speak to each other in real time.

Each listing contains the service name, a short description, and information describing the service content and its typical audience. CompuServe forum listings include an activity dial to help the reader gauge how busy the area is. All listings also include a See Also section, referring the reader to other related areas on CompuServe. A detailed description of the listing format appears later in this Introduction.

Every attempt has been made to ensure that this guide includes all the publicly available services CompuServe provides, and that each listing is as accurate as possible. However, it is possible that a few errors crept in during the information gathering process. Our apologies in advance for any such errors.

Knowing where to look is only one part of getting to the information you need. You also will need appropriate and efficient telecommunications hardware and software, and knowledge of the sometimes intricate sequence of events needed to connect to CompuServe. Information on these topics has been included later in this Introduction. You also will find descriptive information on some of the more common CompuServe features, including CompuServe e-mail, forum messages, and software libraries.

You should find this directory a valuable tool in getting the most efficient use of CompuServe. New Riders Publishing maintains a support area in the Macmillan Computer Publishing Forum on CompuServe. If you have comments or questions on this directory, or on any New Riders publication, simply type **GO MACMILLAN**.

Anatomy of the Directory

The listings portion of the *CompuServe Yellow Pages* is organized alphabetically by topic and service name. You can look up an entry, therefore, by looking under the exact name of a forum or by browsing the topic in which you are interested. Suppose that you want to find information about a Microsoft program. You can look under Microsoft or under Computers. Each subject will have one or more individual listings describing CompuServe services. Services include databases, forums, various entertainment areas, and several areas that defy general description.

Each listing in the directory contains a number of useful bits of information about the service shown. Listings are headed by the name of the service being portrayed and a brief description of the service; the following is a sample listing.

Macmillan Publishing Forum

Description
Get up-to-date information, technical support, customer service, and files relating to Macmillan Computer Publishing books.

Subjects
Books, Computers

Audience
Management information specialists, computer users

Content Summary
Computer books published by New Riders Publishing, Que, SAMS, Hayden, Alpha, Que College, and Brady are supported in this forum. You can find files associated with specific books, graphics files, word processing templates, spreadsheets, and utilities to help you get the most out of your computer system. This forum has one of the best opening bitmaps on CompuServe.

See Also
Computer book publishers

User Guide
- ☑ Windows
- ☑ DOS
- ☑ Macintosh
- ☐ Terminal Emulation
- ☐ VMS
- ☐ UNIX
- ☑ OS/2
- ☑ Other platform

Cost
- ☐ Unknown
- ☐ Basic
- ☑ Extended
- ☐ Premium ($)
- ☐ Executive w/$

Activity Level
MEDIUM (LOW — HIGH)

Address
GO: **MACMILLAN**

Subjects

An extension of the Descriptions field, Subjects helps to further define the information covered by the listed service.

Audience

Each service has a typical audience: a group of people to whom the service appeals. This typical audience is described in the Audience section.

Content Summary

This area of the listing provides further insight into the types of information that the listing includes. The libraries and message areas are highlighted, along with any files of unusual interest.

See Also

This field refers the reader to other related forums or areas within the directory, helping to zero in on the desired CompuServe service.

Cost and User Guide

With a glance at the User Guide and Cost areas, you can learn several things about the service. Checkboxes are provided to tell you whether this area is free (Basic), on the clock (Extended), or charged on a premium basis of some kind (Premium). You also will be told whether it caters to Windows, Macintosh, or DOS users, if applicable.

Activity Level

A special gauge gives readers a visual indicator of the activity level of CompuServe forums.

Address

Movement from one CompuServe area to another is accomplished by using "GO: *words*". This part of the listing shows the GO word for the service.

PREPARING FOR ACCESS

Access to CompuServe requires several very basic items: First, a computer with an RS232 serial interface port. Second, a modem. (Note: Sometimes, particularly with laptop computers, the modem is built in and attaches to the serial port internally.) Third, a phone line to which you can attach the modem. And last, a software package that supports telecommunications via modem.

Your computer retailer can help make sure you have an appropriate computer and modem. You will have to talk to your local telephone company about the phone line. Access software is discussed later in this Introduction.

After the hardware and software is ready, all that is needed is a way to dial into CompuServe's host computers.

Phone Numbers

CompuServe is more than just an information service located in Columbus, Ohio. CompuServe also owns its own data network that provides local dial-up access to thousands of cities and towns in the United States and around the world.

During 1993 and 1994 CompuServe completely upgraded its network to provide higher access speeds and handle projected growth for the next several years. Most local access points now provide access to modems with speeds ranging from 300 to 14,400 bits per second (bps). As of late 1994, CompuServe is also testing 28,800 bps access for selected areas.

Members are provided with several ways to locate the nearest telephone connect point. While online, members can type **GO PHONES** to access the CompuServe database of connection information. As well as providing the location and phone number of its network access points, PHONES also provides connection information for other networks providing access to the service.

The PHONES database enables members to search by location or by modem speed, and also includes areas describing upcoming changes or additions to the network.

In addition to the PHONES database, CompuServe provides two toll-free numbers that can be used within the United States to locate a local access point. Dial (800) 63-LOCAL on a voice line to use a computer voice directory of connection points. This number also provides an option to be connected to a customer service representative. Or, dial (800) FINDCIS with a modem to be directly connected to a copy of the PHONES database.

Using Plain-Vanilla Telecom Software

Members who do not own one of the CompuServe-specific software packages will still be able to connect by using a generic telecommunications program, such as Windows Terminal (see fig. I.1).

To set up the program, you will need to get to Terminal's Settings area. Set the "baud" or "bps" rate to 2400 for your first call. The RS232 port parameters should be 7 data bits, 1 stop bit, Even parity. Flow control can be set to XON/XOFF, sometimes called "software flow control."

If a modem is properly connected and turned on, it now should be possible to test the connection by typing **AT** and pressing the Enter key. If all is well, modern modems will respond on-screen with "OK" to that command.

Now a first dialing attempt can be made by typing **ATDT** followed by the access phone number and the

Enter key. Your modem should dial the access number and attempt to connect with CompuServe.

There are several reasons this could fail initially, and most of them are due to different modem configurations and command sets among different brands. Study the modem manual and follow its directions for setting up the modem. Call the modem's support number if all else fails.

If the dial-up was successful, the modem should display CONNECT on-screen, possibly followed by additional text describing the connection. At this point, press Enter. CompuServe's network should respond with "Host Name:", to which you should respond with **CIS** and the Enter key.

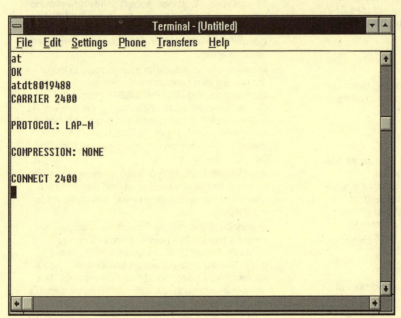

Figure I.1
Windows Terminal.

CIS will send "User ID:", expecting you to type your CIS User ID, followed by another press of the Enter key. You then will be asked for your password, which you should enter.

If all of this is successful, you will be logged in and should see CompuServe's main menu. If anything goes wrong, you should call CompuServe customer service, which will help you through the login process.

Several software packages include scripts to automate the CompuServe login process. Such packages generally include a long list of login scripts for use with different online services. These scripts automatically set up the telecom package for use with a particular service, and know how to respond to the various prompts.

Crosstalk for Windows and Procomm for Windows are two such products, but there are many more, for all computer platforms. Again, your local retailer will have suggestions for you.

YOUR BEST SOFTWARE OPTIONS

Due largely to the size of CompuServe's membership, members can use several CIS-specific software products to access the service.

There are two modes of access used by members: real-time and automated/offline modes. In the former, you use your software to log in to CompuServe and navigate from one area to another. In the latter, your software automatically logs in, travels to a preselected group of services, performs tasks you've given it, and then automatically logs out.

Because most of CompuServe is covered by a pay-by-the-minute plan, members can save significantly by using the automated software to gather messages and mail at computer-to-computer speeds. Gathered text is then read offline at the members' leisure. Replies and original messages can be created offline and later posted by the same software. Automated software also will download files for you.

CompuServe provides both types of software to its members who use DOS, Windows, or Macintosh software. For real-time access, you will want to obtain a copy of The CompuServe Information Manager. There are versions for MS-DOS, Windows, and Macintosh—DOS CIM, WinCIM, and MacCIM, respectively. You can order these either online (GO ORDER) or by phone to customer service.

It also is possible to log in using a simple telecommunications program such as Windows Terminal, as was explained in the preceding section. In fact, nearly half of all CompuServe members use such telecom programs to regularly access CompuServe. However, DOS CIM, WinCIM, and MacCIM provide a much simpler point-and-click interface, which greatly eases navigation around the system.

CompuServe also provides a second type of access software: automated access. CompuServe's automated access packages are available for Windows and Macintosh users—CIS Navigator for Windows and CIS Navigator for Macintosh. Again, these products are available online via GO ORDER, or by phone.

Third-party sources offer several rivals to CompuServe's software. CompuServe members are always looking for ways to reduce costs, and this provides an avid market for the automated style of access software.

Following are detailed descriptions of CompuServe's access software, as well as descriptions and availability information for several popular third-party applications.

WinCIM

For the last couple of years, WinCIM has been the most popular real-time access program for CompuServe members. CompuServe has experienced phenomenal membership growth over that period, and WinCIM lends itself particularly well to helping new members find their way around.

The CompuServe Information Manager concept is to enable members to find services by name and click on that name to get there (see fig. I.2). No command line is used, and the member rarely needs to type any information. Usually, a destination name (GO *word*) can simply be clicked on, via an index of online services.

members to use, and is much simpler to customize to user preferences.

WinCIM has a particularly good chat interface, used in the forum conference areas or in the CompuServe CB area. Members who use these areas regularly should give WinCIM a try.

The biggest problem with CIM packages is that the clock is running while the member is moving from destination to destination. Members tend to visit services, read information, perhaps read and write messages, and look through lists of available files. All this costs money, except in one of the limited number of free online areas. A better solution for members interested in reading and writing messages and e-mail is to use one of the automated programs detailed later in this section.

WinCIM is available for purchase at GO ORDER and for download at GO WINCIM. The program is essentially free of charge—members pay $10 and immediately receive a $10 usage credit. WinCIM is supported by CompuServe customer service personnel, both on the phone and at GO WCIMSUPPORT.

MacCIM and DOS CIM

Packages similar to WinCIM also are available for MS-DOS and Macintosh users. The point-and-click functionality is similar, the underlying protocol is identical, and the order cost is offset by an online credit.

The same negatives also apply. Users intending to spend a lot of time in online mail and message discussions should consider using one of the automated access programs discussed later in this section.

Free online support is available at GO MACCIMSUP for MacCIM and GO CIMSUP for DOS CIM.

CompuServe Navigator for Windows

CompuServe Navigator for Windows is CompuServe's late entry into the automated access field. In general, programs of this type will visit CIS Mail to send and receive mail, and will visit forums to send and receive forum messages and to upload or download files in the forum libraries (see fig. I.3).

Figure I.2
A service appears in the window after you click on its icon.

WinCIM is a second-generation product, behind DOS CIM, and further refines the ease of using CIM by implementing it in the Windows fashion. The interface is much more colorful and interesting for

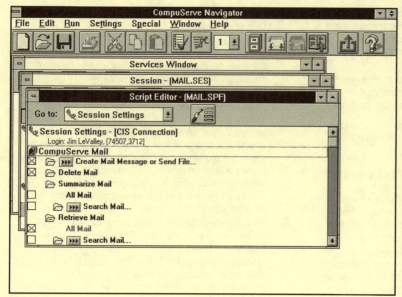

Figure I.3
The Script Editor within CompuServe Navigator enables you to download files for reading at your convenience.

CompuServe Navigator for Windows is available at GO ORDER, or by a phone call to customer service. An online credit is applied to partially defray the initial charge for the product. Online support is provided at GO CSNAVSUPPORT.

CompuServe Navigator for Macintosh

Mac Nav is similar in functionality and capability to the Windows version. Free support is provided at GO NAVSUP.

OzCIS and OzWIN

Ozarks West Software is the third-party source for OzCIS, a shareware auto-navigator for MSDOS. OzCIS is a do-everything navigator—it goes beyond simply capturing your mail and messages every day. Several ways are provided to save your messages permanently and sort them by several keys for easy lookup at a later date. OzCIS also creates catalogs of available library files, enabling the user to decide at a future date to download a file from a particular forum.

OzCIS is one of the most popular auto-navigators, due to strong customer support within its support forum and positive response to users' product suggestions. The program is available and supported at GO OZCIS. Perhaps the only knock on the program is that its potent functionality comes with a price in resources: the program requires lots of memory and a large hard disk.

Newly added to the OzCIS stable is a Windows version of the program, called OzWIN. OzWIN is available and supported in the same forum.

TAPCIS

TAPCIS is another popular DOS-based auto-navigator. Its online functionality is every bit as complete as that of OzCIS, but the offline message and library handling is less complete. Several secondary utilities are available to augment TAPCIS into a program every bit as capable as OzCIS, but without the bulk.

TAPCIS is shareware, and is available and supported at GO TAPCIS.

By doing all this at computer-to-computer speeds, and by enabling members to do their reading and writing while off the clock, such programs greatly increase online efficiencies. Members can choose to do the same things at greatly reduced costs, or to do more for the same costs.

CS-Nav's interface is somewhat unique. A forum template is set up with a list of possible activities that the program can perform. Users can choose forums from a supplied forum index, and then click on the template choices to tell CS-Nav what to do in each forum.

In most cases, the user will want to simply read all new messages posted since the last visit; however, several variations are available. Users can choose to read only certain message sections, certain subject groups, or even messages from certain writers. Because some forums receive over 1,000 new messages per day, such options narrowing the field can be very useful. CS-Nav also can be tasked to gather stock market information or news items as part of a member's daily update.

As each forum is chosen and its tasks assigned, a task list is built. This task list is then saved for all future calls.

CS-Nav has been designed to share setup files with WinCIM so that users will not have to reenter configuration data. Also shared are In Basket and Out Basket functions. Thus, it is possible to create outgoing messages within CS-Nav and later use WinCIM to post them with no special effort.

AutoSig (ATO)

Efficient functionality is also the key with ATO. This program provides all the same capabilities online as OzCIS and TAPCIS, and can run on a basic DOS computer.

ATO is a free program, available and supported at GO IBMCOM.

Software Summary

Table I.1 lists the most popular auto-navigator programs available to CompuServe members, including several not detailed in the text above.

CompuServe Mail

CompuServe Mail offers extensive links to outside e-mail systems, as well as offering internal e-mail for private communication among CompuServe members. CIS Mail's links to the outside world include access to the following mail systems:

- AT&T Mail 400
- Advantis
- BT Messaging Services
- FAX
- Postal Mail
- Infonet
- Internet
- MCI Mail
- CIS Mail Hub System
- NIFTY-Serve
- Sprint Mail
- Telex
- Unisource Business Networks
- Western Union 400
- X400

Several of the above systems simply provide businesses with a pathway through which to connect their own internal network to CompuServe's mail system. Such links enable business personnel to correspond with contacts around the world who use CompuServe Mail or any of the available links listed earlier.

CompuServe Mail also provides a one-way link to CompuServe forums by providing a way for forum members to post messages directly and privately from the forum message area to a member's CIS Mail mailbox.

CompuServe charges for CIS Mail are based on the amount of text transmitted. Members are always charged for outgoing mail, and in certain cases are charged for incoming mail. Commands are provided for sending mail "collect" and for splitting the costs with the recipient. Use GO MAILRATES for more details.

Binary files are supported, as are binary attachments to text messages. Additional information on CIS Mail is available at GO MAILHELP.

Forums: Messages, Conferences, and Libraries

Forums are the most popular services on CompuServe, providing members with a way to communicate with each other on shared interests. Each forum includes a message area, a conference area, and a group of software libraries.

Message Area

The message area, or BBS, is where members post public messages to one another on topics covered by the forum. Each forum has up to 24 subtopics into which messages are posted.

Message authors provide a Subject for new messages. Replies to existing messages retain the existing Subject, preserving a message thread. This

Table I.1
Auto-Navigator Programs

Operating Name	Supported At	System	Type
TAPCIS	GO TAPCIS	MS-DOS	Shareware
OzCIS	GO OZCIS	MS-DOS	Shareware
AutoSIG	GO IBMCOM	MS-DOS	Free
CISOP	GO XTALK *	MS-DOS	Shareware
NavCIS	GO DVORAK	Windows	Commercial
CSNav	GO CSNAVSUP	Windows	Commercial
AutoPilot	GO AMIGAVEN	Amiga	Shareware
QuickCIS	GO ATARICOMP	Atari ST	Free
Navigator	GO NAVSUPPORT	Macintosh	Commercial
Golden Compass	GO GCPSUPPORT	OS/2	Commercial
XC	GO UNIXFORUM	UNIX	Free

* REQUIRES A COPY OF CROSSTALK COMMUNICATOR, A DOS PROGRAM.

enables members to scan the message base for subjects of interest and to read only messages with that Subject.

Messages to a particular person are tracked by the forum software, so that when the person enters a forum, she is informed that messages are waiting. However, messages also can be addressed in general to "All" or "Anyone," as desired.

CompuServe has finite hardware resources and is careful in assigning those resources to each forum. Forums are given a number of message slots, based on the activity level. As new messages are posted, the oldest messages are automatically deleted to stay within the assigned resources.

Several CompuServe forums are so busy that even with the maximum number of slots, a message might survive only for a couple of days before being deleted to create space. It is important to check busy forums regularly to avoid missing a message you are awaiting. Check the Activity field in a forum's CYP listing for an idea of its activity level.

As a service, some forums are set up to automatically send your messages to your CIS Mail mailbox just as they are about to be deleted so that you will not miss them. In such cases, members are charged for the incoming message at standard CIS Mail rates.

Conference Area

All forums (except certain free customer service forums) have one or more conference areas. In these areas, members can chat in real time with other members who are present. It is possible to move off into private groups, whose conversations are invisible to members not in the group. Members also can be in one conference room while monitoring what's being said in another.

Forums often hold regularly scheduled formal conferences, in which guest speakers are available to be interviewed by forum members. In such formal conferences, members are expected to remain silent until called upon. Some members move to an adjacent conference room so they can talk freely while using the Monitor feature to monitor what is being said in the formal conference.

Libraries

For some forums, the forum libraries are the centers of attraction. Libraries hold files of interest to forum members. Files include simple text press releases, shareware utilities, popular games, application demos, and even operating-system upgrades from such industry giants as Microsoft and IBM. These files can be downloaded to members' computers, assuming the access software supports file transfers.

The Graphics forums on CompuServe (GO GRAPHICS) are examples of forums in which the libraries see much more action than the message or conference areas. The libraries of these forums are full of photographic-quality pictures and artwork, covering the entire spectrum of visual possibilities. With appropriate graphics viewing software, also available in the GO GRAPHICS area, members can view these pictures on their computers and print them to an appropriate printer.

Each forum can have up to 24 libraries, each of them covering a specific file topic. The Libraries field of a CYP forum listing contains information about library content.

What is ZiffNet?

As you use the *CompuServe Yellow Pages,* you will come across several services which are part of ZiffNet. *ZiffNet* is an independent online service that happens to share CompuServe's systems.

ZiffNet requires a separate membership, and if you join Ziff before joining CompuServe, your billing will be done through Ziff rather than through CompuServe. Such memberships are identified by a separate series of User ID numbers.

Members of either service are allowed to join the other quickly and easily by simply navigating across the "border" to the other side. GO ZIFFNET and GO CIS will take you across the respective borders. Billing for both will be done by the first online service that was joined.

Members also can put prefixes in front of GO words to indicate which online service the destination resides on. From the Ziff side, for instance, a member can travel to the CIS Macmillan Computer Publishing Forum by using GO CIS:MACMILLAN. Moving back to the ZiffNet Speakeasy Forum would then require GO ZNT:SPEAKEASY.

ZiffNet is primarily in place to enable subscribers of Ziff-Davis computer publications to meet the editors and writers, and to discuss issues presented in the publications. However, ZiffNet also contains several very useful database products, a wide range of shareware applications and utilities for downloading, and some forums unrelated to Ziff-Davis publications.

New Riders Publishing

The staff of New Riders Publishing is committed to bringing you the very best in computer reference material. Each New Riders book is the result of months of work by authors and staff who research and refine the information contained within its covers.

As part of this commitment to you, the NRP reader, New Riders invites your input. Please let us know if you enjoy this book, if you have trouble with the information and examples presented, or if you have a suggestion for the next edition.

Please note, though: New Riders staff cannot serve as a technical resource for CompuServe or for related questions about CompuServe problems. Please refer to the documentation that accompanies CompuServe or to CompuServe's Help systems.

If you have a question or comment about any New Riders book, there are several ways to contact New Riders Publishing. We will respond to as many

Introduction

readers as we can. Your name, address, and phone number will never become part of a mailing list or be used for any purpose other than to help us continue to bring you the best books possible. You can write us at the following address:

> New Riders Publishing
> Attn: Associate Publisher
> 201 W. 103rd Street
> Indianapolis, IN 46290

If you prefer, you can fax New Riders Publishing at (317) 581-4670.

You can send e-mail to New Riders from a variety of sources. NRP maintains several mailboxes organized by topic area. Mail in these mailboxes will be forwarded to the staff member who is best able to address your concerns. Substitute the appropriate mailbox name from the list below when addressing your e-mail. The mailboxes are as follows:

ADMIN	Comments and complaints for NRP's Publisher
APPS	Word, Excel, WordPerfect, other office applications
ACQ	Book proposal inquiries by potential authors
CAD	AutoCAD, 3D Studio, AutoSketch, and CAD products
DATABASE	Access, dBASE, Paradox, and other database products
GRAPHICS	CorelDRAW!, Photoshop, and other graphics products
INTERNET	Internet
NETWORK	NetWare, LANtastic, and other network-related topics
OS	MS-DOS, OS/2, all operating systems except UNIX and Windows
UNIX	UNIX
WINDOWS	Microsoft Windows (all versions)
OTHER	Anything that does not fit these categories

If you use an MHS e-mail system that routes through CompuServe, send your messages to:

> *mailbox* @ NEWRIDER

To send NRP mail from CompuServe, use the following to address:

> MHS: *mailbox* @ NEWRIDER

To send mail from the Internet, use the following address format:

> *mailbox*@newrider.mhs.compuserve.com

New Riders Publishing is an imprint of Macmillan Computer Publishing. To obtain a catalog or information, or to purchase any Macmillan Computer Publishing book, call (800) 428-5331.

Thank you for selecting *New Riders' Official CompuServe Yellow Pages*!

SYMBOLS

3Com Online Information Service Menu

Description
Access to Ask3Com services supporting users of 3Com Corporation products.

Subjects
Computers, Networking

Audience
Users of 3Com products

Content Summary
The library and message sections of this forum contain a list of new products, technical articles that contain troubleshooting tips, commonly asked questions, and release notes. Also available is a list of service centers.

User Guide
- ☑ Windows
- ☑ DOS
- ☐ Macintosh
- ☐ Terminal Emulation
- ☐ VMS
- ☐ UNIX
- ☐ OS/2
- ☐ Other platform

Cost
- ☐ Unknown
- ☐ Basic
- ☑ Extended
- ☐ Premium ($)
- ☐ Executive w/$

Activity Level

Address
GO: **THREECOM**

800 Flowers

Description
At 800-Flowers & 800-Gifthouse, the world's largest source of flowers & gifts, everyday is a holiday.

Subjects
Flowers, Gifts

Audience
Consumers

Content Summary
Order flowers and plants on-line for all occasions. You are billed through CompuServe.

See Also
Flower Stop

User Guide
- ☑ Windows
- ☑ DOS
- ☑ Macintosh
- ☐ Terminal Emulation
- ☐ VMS
- ☐ UNIX
- ☐ OS/2
- ☐ Other platform

Cost
- ☐ Unknown
- ☑ Basic
- ☐ Extended
- ☐ Premium ($)
- ☐ Executive w/$

Activity Level

Address
GO: **FGS**

ABC Worldwide Hotel Guide – Accounting

A

ABC Worldwide Hotel Guide

Description
The ABC Worldwide Hotel Guide provides up-to-date comprehensive listings of over 60,000 hotel properties worldwide.

Subjects
Hotels, Travel

Audience
Travelers

Content Summary
Within this forum, you can find information about the locations, addresses, services offered, and which credit cards are accepted at the member hotel and resorts.

See Also
Travel Forum

User Guide
- ☑ Windows
- ☑ DOS
- ☑ Macintosh
- ☐ Terminal Emulation
- ☐ VMS
- ☐ UNIX
- ☐ OS/2
- ☐ Other platform

Cost
- ☐ Unknown
- ☐ Basic
- ☑ Extended
- ☐ Premium ($)
- ☐ Executive w/$

Activity Level

Address
GO: **ABC**

ACADEMIC RESEARCH

The Sysop Forum

Description
Private forum hosted by CIS for the training of forum sysops and discussion of forum issues.

Subjects
Academic Research, Campus Activities and Student Newspaper

Audience
Administrators, accountants

Content Summary
This forum is not available to all users; only those members training to be Sysops.

See Also
Education Forum

User Guide
- ☑ Windows
- ☑ DOS
- ☑ Macintosh
- ☑ Terminal Emulation
- ☑ VMS
- ☑ UNIX
- ☑ OS/2
- ☐ Other platform

Cost
- ☐ Unknown
- ☐ Basic
- ☑ Extended
- ☐ Premium ($)
- ☐ Executive w/$

Activity Level

Address
GO: **ABC**

ACCOUNTING

Accounting Vendor Forum

Description
A place where accountants, people who need accounting help, vendors, and users of accounting software can meet and share information.

Subjects
Accounting, Business

Audience
Accountants

Content Summary
The libraries contain product demonstrations, news, and information on the products supported by the participating venders.

See Also
Business Forum

User Guide
- ☑ Windows
- ☑ DOS
- ☑ Macintosh
- ☐ Terminal Emulation
- ☐ VMS
- ☐ UNIX
- ☐ OS/2
- ☐ Other platform

Cost
- ☐ Unknown
- ☐ Basic
- ☑ Extended
- ☐ Premium ($)
- ☐ Executive w/$

Activity Level

(LOW ← MEDIUM → HIGH)

Address
GO: **ACCOUNTING**

ACIUS Forum

Description
The ACIUS Forum supports all ACIUS products with valuable technical support as well as an exchange of ideas from other users of ACIUS products.

Subjects
Accounting, Business, Software

Audience
Accountants

Content Summary
The libraries contain information on 4th Dimension, File Force, 4D Modules, time-saving programs, and sample databases.

See Also
Computer Directory, Computer Training Forum

User Guide
- ☑ Windows
- ☑ DOS
- ☐ Macintosh
- ☐ Terminal Emulation
- ☐ VMS
- ☐ UNIX
- ☐ OS/2
- ☐ Other platform

Cost
- ☐ Unknown
- ☐ Basic
- ☑ Extended
- ☐ Premium ($)
- ☐ Executive w/$

Activity level
LOW ← MEDIUM HIGH

Address
GO: **ACIUS**

ACTION REQUESTS DATABASE

Digitalk Database

Description
Since 1985, Digitalk, Inc. has been developing object-oriented programming environments for the PC with its Smalltalk/V product. The company has Smalltalk/V development environments worldwide for DOS, OS/2, Microsoft Windows, and the Apple Macintosh; the Team/V collaborative programming system; and PARTS Workbench for OS/2. The Digitalk Database contains problem reports on all Smalltalk/V and PARTS products.

Subjects
Action Requests Database, Computers, Object-Oriented Programming, Smalltalk/V

Audience
Consultants, object-oriented programmers, Smalltalk/V users, trainers

Content Summary
Select the "Search the Action Requests Database" option to search the Digitalk Action Requests database.

See Also
Digitalk Forum

User Guide
- ☑ Windows
- ☑ DOS
- ☑ Macintosh
- ☐ Terminal Emulation
- ☐ VMS
- ☐ UNIX
- ☑ OS/2
- ☐ Other platform

Cost
- ☐ Unknown
- ☐ Basic
- ☑ Extended
- ☐ Premium ($)
- ☐ Executive w/$

Activity Level
LOW MEDIUM HIGH — UNKNOWN

Address
GO: **DBDIGITALK**

ADD Forum

Description
Information and support for adults, parents and professionals interested in attention deficit disorder and other neurological conditions.

Subjects
Attention Deficit, Hyperactivity, Medicine

Audience
Medical personnel, parents

Content Summary
The libraries contain information on therapy, medication, parenting issues, family, conferences, schools, and learning.

See Also
Health and Fitness Forum

User Guide
- ☑ Windows
- ☑ DOS
- ☐ Macintosh
- ☐ Terminal Emulation
- ☐ VMS
- ☐ UNIX
- ☐ OS/2
- ☐ Other platform

Cost
- ☐ Unknown
- ☐ Basic
- ☑ Extended
- ☐ Premium ($)
- ☐ Executive w/$

ADD Forum - Adventures in Food

Activity Level MEDIUM (pointing toward HIGH)

Address
GO: **ADD**

Adobe Forum

Description
The Adobe Forum provides an area where users, dealers, service bureaus, third-party developers and others can communicate with Adobe.

Subjects
Computer Graphics, Computers, Software

Audience
Adobe products users

Content Summary
Libraries provide information on Adobe typefaces, Adobe Illustrator, PhotoShop, Acrobat, Transcript, and Premier.

See Also
Graphics Forum

User Guide
- ☑ Windows
- ☑ DOS
- ☑ Macintosh
- ☐ Terminal Emulation
- ☐ VMS
- ☐ UNIX
- ☐ OS/2
- ☐ Other platform

Cost
- ☐ Unknown
- ☐ Basic
- ☑ Extended
- ☐ Premium ($)
- ☐ Executive w/$

Activity Level MEDIUM (arrow pointing straight up)

Address
GO: **ADOBE**

Enhanced Adventure

Description
"Somewhere nearby is Colossal Cave. . . ." Are you ready for an online adventure? Have you experienced Classic Adventure already? Then this is the place for you.

Subjects
Electronic Games, Adventure Games

Audience
12 years and older

Content Summary
If you are new to ADVENTURE-Land, type Help for instructions. If you have experienced ADVENTURE-Land before, you're not going to get any hints here. A perfect ending gets you 751.

See Also
Classic Adventure, Entertainment Center

User Guide
- ☑ Windows
- ☑ DOS
- ☑ Macintosh
- ☐ Terminal Emulation
- ☐ VMS
- ☐ UNIX
- ☐ OS/2
- ☐ Other platform

Cost
- ☐ Unknown
- ☑ Basic
- ☐ Extended
- ☐ Premium ($)
- ☐ Executive w/$

Activity Level UNKNOWN

Address
GO: **ENADVENT**

Adventures in Food

Description
An online shop for discriminating food lovers.

Subjects
Food, Shopping

Audience
Gourmet enthusiasts

Content Summary
If you are looking for the unusual or hard-to-find food item, then this service is for you.

See Also
Omaha Steaks, Virginia Diner

User Guide
- ☑ Windows
- ☑ DOS
- ☑ Macintosh
- ☐ Terminal Emulation
- ☑ VMS
- ☑ UNIX
- ☑ OS/2
- ☑ Other platform

Cost
- ☐ Unknown
- ☑ Basic
- ☐ Extended
- ☐ Premium ($)
- ☐ Executive w/$

Activity Level UNKNOWN

Address
GO: **AIF**

Adventures in Travel

Description
Articles and stories about worldwide travels, prepared by professional travel writer Lee Foster.

Subjects
Travel

Audience
Travelers

Content Summary
Articles are updated every two weeks and contain information on every aspect of traveling.

See Also
Alaska Peddler, The Travel Club

User Guide
- ☑ Windows
- ☑ DOS
- ☑ Macintosh
- ☐ Terminal Emulation
- ☑ VMS
- ☑ UNIX
- ☑ OS/2
- ☑ Other platform

Cost
- ☐ Unknown
- ☐ Basic
- ☑ Extended
- ☐ Premium ($)
- ☐ Executive w/$

Activity Level

Address
GO: **AIT**

ADVERTISING

PR and Marketing Forum

Description
This forum is a gathering place for public relations, advertising, marketing, research, and public affairs professionals.

Subjects
Advertising, Marketing, Public Relations

Audience
Advertising professionals, market research specialists, public relations personnel

Content Summary
Members use the forum's message libraries to communicate on subjects of interest to the communications field. Other features include Jobs Online, from which members can review more than 100 job openings. Members can post resumes on as well as listing openings from their respective firms. Other sections include: starting up a business, marketing, media relations and crisis communications, new products and services, creativity, research, advertising and direct mail, electronic newsletters, desktop publishing, professional development, political campaigns and programming, creativity development, educational programs, and technology tools.

On-line college courses are offered in advertising, public relations, and print and electronic journalism.

See Also
Media Newsletter

User Guide
- ☑ Windows
- ☑ DOS
- ☑ Macintosh
- ☐ Terminal Emulation
- ☑ VMS
- ☑ UNIX
- ☑ OS/2
- ☐ Other platform

Cost
- ☐ Unknown
- ☐ Basic
- ☑ Extended
- ☐ Premium ($)
- ☐ Executive w/$

Activity Level

Address
GO: **PRSIG**

African American Art and Culture Forum

Description
This forum gives you the opportunity to experience the culture and art of African Americans. You can discuss current events and cultural issues.

Subjects
Art, Cultural Issues

Audience
Anyone interested in African American culture

Content Summary
The libraries include a wide range of topics, including art and artists, history, events, film and theater news, member profiles, and genealogy.

See Also
Genealogy Forum, Music and Performing Arts Forum

User Guide
- ☑ Windows
- ☑ DOS
- ☑ Macintosh
- ☐ Terminal Emulation
- ☐ VMS
- ☐ UNIX
- ☐ OS/2
- ☐ Other platform

Cost
- ☐ Unknown
- ☐ Basic
- ☑ Extended
- ☐ Premium ($)
- ☐ Executive w/$

African American Art and Culture Forum - AIDS

Activity Level

LOW — MEDIUM — HIGH

Address
GO: **AFRO**

Retirement Living Forum

Description
Managed by the Setting Priorities for Retirement Years (SPRY) Foundation, this forum is dedicated to making the retirement years happy and productive. Information and discussions on a wide range of topics are available to present and future retirees.

Subjects
Aging, Medicare, Social Security

Audience
Family of retirees, gerontologists, retirees

Content Summary
This forum's contributors include the Social Security Administration; the National Institute on Aging; the National Heart, Lung, and Blood Institute; the Traveling Healthy and Comfortably Newsletter; and the Pension Rights Center. Discussions can be found on eating right, housing, dealing with family, and Medicare.

See Also
Health/Fitness Forum

User Guide
- ☑ Windows
- ☑ DOS
- ☑ Macintosh
- ☐ Terminal Emulation
- ☑ VMS
- ☑ UNIX
- ☑ OS/2
- ☐ Other platform

Cost
- ☐ Unknown
- ☐ Basic
- ☑ Extended
- ☐ Premium ($)
- ☐ Executive w/$

Activity Level

LOW ← MEDIUM — HIGH

Address
GO: **RETIREMENT**

AI Expert Forum

Description
The electronic edition of *AI Expert* magazine serves as a forum for exchange of ideas and information on Artificial Intelligence research.

Subjects
Artificial Intelligence

Audience
Researchers

Content Summary
The libraries include articles and program listings. You also can consult the staff members of *AI Expert*.

See Also
CyberForum

User Guide
- ☑ Windows
- ☑ DOS
- ☐ Macintosh
- ☐ Terminal Emulation
- ☐ VMS
- ☐ UNIX
- ☐ OS/2
- ☐ Other platform

Cost
- ☐ Unknown
- ☐ Basic
- ☑ Extended
- ☐ Premium ($)
- ☐ Executive w/$

Activity Level

LOW ← MEDIUM — HIGH

Address
GO: **AIEXPERT**

CCML AIDS Articles

Description
Articles relating to AIDS from the Comprehensive Core Medical Library.

Subjects
AIDS, Health, Medicine

Audience
Medical personnel, researchers

Content Summary
The libraries contain full text articles from leading medical reference books, text books, and articles.

See Also
Rare Diseases Database

User Guide
- ☑ Windows
- ☑ DOS
- ☐ Macintosh
- ☐ Terminal Emulation
- ☐ VMS
- ☐ UNIX
- ☐ OS/2
- ☐ Other platform

Cost
- ☐ Unknown
- ☐ Basic
- ☐ Extended
- ☑ Premium ($)
- ☐ Executive w/$

AIDS – Air Flight

Activity Level

Address
GO: **CCMLAIDS**

Health/Fitness

Description
If you can't find the health-related forum that you want, use the Health/Fitness service to speed up your search.

Subjects
AIDS, Cancer, Disabilities, Health Care

Audience
Medical educators, medical professionals, medical researchers, general public

Content Summary
The main menu in this area lists all the health and fitness related forums and services available on CompuServe. Here you can choose from topics such as Consumer Reports Complete Drug Reference, HealthNet, AIDS Information, Attention Deficit Disorder Forum, Cancer Information, Diabetes Forum, Health & Fitness Forum, Human Sexuality, PaperChase (MEDLINE), and many more.

See Also
HealthNet, Holistic Health Forum, Health Database Plus($), Health and Vitamin Express, Health and Fitness Forum, Cancer Forum, AIDS News Clips, PaperChase MEDLINE($)

User Guide
- ☑ Windows
- ☑ DOS
- ☑ Macintosh
- ☐ Terminal Emulation
- ☑ VMS
- ☑ UNIX
- ☑ OS/2
- ☐ Other platform

Cost
- ☐ Unknown
- ☑ Basic
- ☐ Extended
- ☐ Premium ($)
- ☐ Executive w/$

Activity Level

Address
GO: **FITNESS**

Rare Diseases Database

Description
Developed and maintained by the National Organization for Rare Diseases (NORD), this database forum was constructed so that families and patients of rare disorders can understand the disorder and its implications.

Subjects
AIDS, Diseases, Health

Audience
AIDS suffers, health care providers, families of the ill

Content Summary
This forum contains a database that provides information on all rare diseases, their treatment, medicines, and implications. Newsletters from several national organizations, such as NORD, Parkinsons Foundation, and the Multiple Sclerosis Foundation, are available. Current information on AIDS and related illnesses also can be found. Also included is an orphan drug database.

See Also
Paperchase-MEDLINE

User Guide
- ☑ Windows
- ☑ DOS
- ☑ Macintosh
- ☑ Terminal Emulation
- ☑ VMS
- ☑ UNIX
- ☑ OS/2
- ☐ Other platform

Cost
- ☐ Unknown
- ☐ Basic
- ☐ Extended
- ☑ Premium ($)
- ☐ Executive w/$

Activity Level

Address
GO: **NORD**

AIR FLIGHT

Air France

Description
Information on Air France flights to Europe and other worldwide destinations.

Subjects
Travel

Audience
International travelers

Content Summary
Provides information on 216 flights worldwide. You also can receive information on hotels, car rentals, and restaurants.

See Also
Adventures in Travel, Air Information/Reservations

User Guide
- ☐ Windows
- ☐ DOS
- ☐ Macintosh
- ☑ Terminal Emulation
- ☐ VMS
- ☐ UNIX
- ☐ OS/2
- ☐ Other platform

Air Flight – Airlines

Cost
- ☐ Unknown
- ☑ Basic
- ☐ Extended
- ☐ Premium ($)
- ☐ Executive w/$

Activity Level

MEDIUM — arrow pointing between LOW and HIGH, toward HIGH

Address
GO: **AF**

EMI Aviation Services

Description
Designed for pilots and flight planners, the EMI Aviation Services area enables pilots of any aircraft to get flight plans, weather briefings, and flight plan filings from this service. The EMI database contains all public-use airports in the contiguous 48 states and southern Canada, except for Newfoundland.

Subjects
Air Flight, Travel Plans

Audience
Pilots, air traffic controllers

Content Summary
This is a full-featured aviation service that should help you plan and record your flights. The Pro-Plan Option, found in the EMI Descriptions and Instructions option on the main menu, gives you enhanced printouts of your top of climb and descent points, average ground speeds, calculated wind direction and speed, and ambient temperature and deviation from ISA. If you're familiar with all this terminology, this service might be just what you're looking for.

See Also
Travel Forum

User Guide
- ☑ Windows
- ☑ DOS
- ☑ Macintosh
- ☐ Terminal Emulation
- ☑ VMS
- ☑ UNIX
- ☑ OS/2
- ☐ Other platform

Cost
- ☐ Unknown
- ☐ Basic
- ☑ Extended
- ☑ Premium ($)
- ☐ Executive w/$

Activity Level

UNKNOWN

Address
GO: **EMI**

Air France

Description
Information on Air France flights to Europe and other worldwide destinations.

Subjects
Travel

Audience
International travelers

Content Summary
Provides information on 216 flights worldwide. You also can receive information on hotels, car rentals, and restaurants.

See Also
Adventures in Travel, Air Information/Reservations

User Guide
- ☐ Windows
- ☐ DOS
- ☐ Macintosh
- ☑ Terminal Emulation
- ☐ VMS
- ☐ UNIX
- ☐ OS/2
- ☐ Other platform

Cost
- ☐ Unknown
- ☑ Basic
- ☐ Extended
- ☐ Premium ($)
- ☐ Executive w/$

Activity Level

MEDIUM — arrow pointing toward HIGH

Address
GO: **AF**

AIRLINES

Official Airline Guide

Description
The Official Airline Guide is the most comprehensive, up-to-date source of travel-related information available online. This service also is easy to use and does not require you to know travel codes.

Subjects
Travel, Airline, Tourism

Audience
General public

Content Summary
From the Official Airline Guide main menu, you can read a description of the service, get a list of the commands, give feedback to the service, and access the service. Be sure to read the pricing instructions by selecting the Access option from the main menu.

Airlines – Air Traffic Controller

See Also
EAASY SABRE

User Guide
- ☑ Windows
- ☑ DOS
- ☑ Macintosh
- ☐ Terminal Emulation
- ☑ VMS
- ☑ UNIX
- ☑ OS/2
- ☑ Other platform

Cost
- ☐ Unknown
- ☐ Basic
- ☐ Extended
- ☑ Premium ($)
- ☐ Executive w/$

Activity Level
UNKNOWN (LOW — MEDIUM — HIGH)

Address
GO: OAG

Air France

Description
Information on Air France flights to Europe and other worldwide destinations.

Subjects
Travel

Audience
International travelers

Content Summary
Provides information on 216 flights worldwide. You also can receive information on hotels, car rentals, and restaurants.

See Also
Adventures in Travel, Air Information/Reservations

User Guide
- ☐ Windows
- ☐ DOS
- ☐ Macintosh
- ☑ Terminal Emulation
- ☐ VMS
- ☐ UNIX
- ☐ OS/2
- ☐ Other platform

Cost
- ☐ Unknown
- ☑ Basic
- ☐ Extended
- ☐ Premium ($)
- ☐ Executive w/$

Activity Level
HIGH (LOW — MEDIUM — HIGH)

Address
GO: AF

Air Line Pilots Association

Description
The Air Line Pilots Association is an AFL-CIO affiliated labor union representing most of the nation's commercial airline pilots.

Subjects
Labor Unions

Audience
Pilots

Content Summary
You can get all the up-to-date news about benefits, hot topics, and job openings.

See Also
NWS Aviation

User Guide
- ☑ Windows
- ☑ DOS
- ☐ Macintosh
- ☐ Terminal Emulation
- ☐ VMS
- ☐ UNIX
- ☐ OS/2
- ☐ Other platform

Cost
- ☐ Unknown
- ☑ Basic
- ☐ Extended
- ☐ Premium ($)
- ☐ Executive w/$

Activity Level
UNKNOWN (LOW — MEDIUM — HIGH)

Address
GO: ALPA

Air Traffic Controller

Description
An online game that simulates running the control tower at a major airport. The game can be played with multiple other CIS players.

Subjects
Entertainment, Games

Audience
Games enthusiasts

Content Summary
The object of the game is to keep your planes from running out of fuel or crashing.

See Also
Flight Simulation Forum

User Guide
- ☑ Windows
- ☑ DOS
- ☐ Macintosh
- ☐ Terminal Emulation
- ☐ VMS
- ☐ UNIX
- ☐ OS/2
- ☐ Other platform

Air Traffic Controller – Aldus Forum

Cost
- ☐ Unknown
- ☐ Basic
- ☐ Extended
- ☑ Premium ($)
- ☐ Executive w/$

Activity Level

LOW — UNKNOWN (MEDIUM) — HIGH

Address
GO: **ATCONTROL**

Airline Services Unlimited

Description
Order suitcases, totes, and garment bags online. "Trusted by Flight Crews for 25 Years."

Subjects
Shopping, Travel

Audience
Consumers

Content Summary
This online shopping service offers a wide variety of travel suitcases and accessories.

See Also
Travel Forum

User Guide
- ☑ Windows
- ☑ DOS
- ☐ Macintosh
- ☐ Terminal Emulation
- ☐ VMS
- ☐ UNIX
- ☐ OS/2
- ☐ Other platform

Cost
- ☐ Unknown
- ☐ Basic
- ☑ Extended
- ☐ Premium ($)
- ☐ Executive w/$

Activity Level

LOW — UNKNOWN (MEDIUM) — HIGH

Address
GO: **ASU-1**

Alaska Peddler

Description
Online shopping from a family-owned group of stores in Juneau, featuring unique Alaskan gifts.

Subjects
Gifts, Shopping

Audience
Consumers

Content Summary
This online shopping service provides unique gifts handcrafted in Alaska.

See Also
Adventures in Food

User Guide
- ☑ Windows
- ☑ DOS
- ☑ Macintosh
- ☐ Terminal Emulation
- ☑ VMS
- ☑ UNIX
- ☑ OS/2
- ☐ Other platform

Cost
- ☐ Unknown
- ☑ Basic
- ☐ Extended
- ☐ Premium ($)
- ☐ Executive w/$

Activity Level

LOW — UNKNOWN (MEDIUM) — HIGH

Address
GO: **ALASKA**

Aldus Forum

Description
The Aldus Forum provides technical support for issues encountered by both novice and experienced users of Aldus products.

Subjects
Computers, Software

Audience
Aldus products users

Content Summary
The libraries contain product updates and technical support for PageMaker, FreeHand, PhotoStyler, and Persuasion.

See Also
Aldus Special Programs Forum

User Guide
- ☑ Windows
- ☑ DOS
- ☐ Macintosh
- ☐ Terminal Emulation
- ☐ VMS
- ☐ UNIX
- ☐ OS/2
- ☐ Other platform

Cost
- ☐ Unknown
- ☐ Basic
- ☑ Extended
- ☐ Premium ($)
- ☐ Executive w/$

Activity Level

LOW — ↑ MEDIUM — HIGH

Address
GO: **ALDUSFORUM**

Aldus Online Customer Support

Description
Menu giving access to Aldus support services on CompuServe.

Subjects
Computers, Software

Audience
Aldus products users

Content Summary
The libraries provide information on product upgrades and new releases. Technical support is available for all Aldus products.

See Also
Aldus Special Programs Forum

User Guide
- ☑ Windows
- ☑ DOS
- ☑ Macintosh
- ☐ Terminal Emulation
- ☐ VMS
- ☐ UNIX
- ☐ OS/2
- ☐ Other platform

Cost
- ☐ Unknown
- ☐ Basic
- ☑ Extended
- ☐ Premium ($)
- ☐ Executive w/$

Activity Level
UNKNOWN

Address
GO: **ALDUS**

Aldus Special Programs Forum

Description
The ALSUSSP Forum provides support and service to various OEM, developer, training, and other special interest partners.

Subjects
Computers, Software

Audience
Computer programmers

Content Summary
Experts answer questions about Aldus Additions and TIFF specifications. Several areas are restricted and require access permission.

See Also
Aldus Online Customer Support

User Guide
- ☑ Windows
- ☑ DOS
- ☑ Macintosh
- ☐ Terminal Emulation
- ☐ VMS
- ☐ UNIX
- ☐ OS/2
- ☐ Other platform

Cost
- ☐ Unknown
- ☐ Basic
- ☑ Extended
- ☐ Premium ($)
- ☐ Executive w/$

Activity Level
UNKNOWN

Address
GO: **ALDUSSP**

All-Music Guide Forum

Description
The largest collection of music albums, ratings, and reviews open to public comment.

Subjects
Entertainment, Music

Audience
Musicians, music enthusiasts

Content Summary
The libraries contain biographies of artists, album reviews, and a list of the best works of specific artists.

See Also
Art/Music/Literature

User Guide
- ☑ Windows
- ☑ DOS
- ☐ Macintosh
- ☐ Terminal Emulation
- ☐ VMS
- ☐ UNIX
- ☐ OS/2
- ☐ Other platform

Cost
- ☐ Unknown
- ☐ Basic
- ☑ Extended
- ☐ Premium ($)
- ☐ Executive w/$

Activity Level
UNKNOWN

Address
GO: **AMGTOP**

American Heritage Dictionary

Description
The online version of the *American Heritage Dictionary*, with detailed definitions of over 303,000 words and phrases.

Subjects
Dictionary, Spelling

Audience
Students

Content Summary
Users can search the database by entering the word or part of the word, if the spelling is unknown.

See Also
Academic American Encyclopedia

User Guide
- ☑ Windows
- ☑ DOS
- ☐ Macintosh
- ☐ Terminal Emulation
- ☐ VMS
- ☐ UNIX
- ☐ OS/2
- ☐ Other platform

Cost
- ☐ Unknown
- ☑ Basic
- ☐ Extended
- ☐ Premium ($)
- ☐ Executive w/$

Activity Level
UNKNOWN

Address
GO: DICTIONARY

Americana Clothing

Description
Online shopping with a unique selection of clothing for men and women at everyday low prices.

Subjects
Clothing, Shopping

Audience
Consumers

Content Summary
This online shopping service specializes in Levi's and Lee jeans, Dockers, and Champion products.

See Also
Patagonia

User Guide
- ☐ Windows
- ☐ DOS
- ☐ Macintosh
- ☑ Terminal Emulation
- ☐ VMS
- ☐ UNIX
- ☐ OS/2
- ☐ Other platform

Cost
- ☐ Unknown
- ☑ Basic
- ☐ Extended
- ☐ Premium ($)
- ☐ Executive w/$

Activity Level
UNKNOWN

Address
GO:  AC

AMIGA

Amiga Arts Forum

Description
The Amiga Arts Forum is devoted to the artistically creative and entertainment-oriented Amiga computer users.

Subjects
Computers

Audience
Amiga users

Content Summary
The libraries contain programs, product reviews, conference updates, and message boards. Discussions range from beginning to advanced level.

See Also
Amiga File Finder

User Guide
- ☑ Windows
- ☑ DOS
- ☑ Macintosh
- ☐ Terminal Emulation
- ☑ VMS
- ☑ UNIX
- ☑ OS/2
- ☐ Other platform

Cost
- ☐ Unknown
- ☐ Basic
- ☑ Extended
- ☐ Premium ($)
- ☐ Executive w/$

Activity Level
 LOW

Address
GO: AMIGAARTS

Amiga File Finder

Description
File Finder is an online comprehensive keyword-searchable database of file descriptions from Amiga-related Forums.

Subjects
Computers

Audience
Amiga users

Content Summary
Using this database, users can search information by keyword, file date, forum name, file type, file name, or file originator.

See Also
Amiga User Forum

Amiga

User Guide
- ☑ Windows
- ☑ DOS
- ☐ Macintosh
- ☐ Terminal Emulation
- ☐ VMS
- ☐ UNIX
- ☐ OS/2
- ☐ Other platform

Cost
- ☐ Unknown
- ☐ Basic
- ☑ Extended
- ☐ Premium ($)
- ☐ Executive w/$

Activity Level: MEDIUM

Address
GO: **AMIGAFF**

Amiga Tech Forum

Description
This forum is dedicated to the technical and programming users of Amiga computers.

Subjects
Computers

Audience
Amiga users, Amiga programmers

Content Summary
The libraries contain public domain programs, help files, product reviews, and archived reference text.

See Also
Amiga User Forum

User Guide
- ☑ Windows
- ☑ DOS
- ☐ Macintosh
- ☐ Terminal Emulation
- ☐ VMS
- ☐ UNIX
- ☐ OS/2
- ☐ Other platform

Cost
- ☐ Unknown
- ☐ Basic
- ☑ Extended
- ☐ Premium ($)
- ☐ Executive w/$

Activity Level: LOW

Address
GO: **AMIGATECH**

Amiga User Forum

Description
This forum is dedicated to the everyday business and personal use of Amiga computers.

Subjects
Computers

Audience
Amiga users

Content Summary
The libraries and message areas promote Amiga news, hardware concerns, personal and business applications, and even include a classified ads section.

See Also
Amiga File Finder

User Guide
- ☑ Windows
- ☑ DOS
- ☐ Macintosh
- ☐ Terminal Emulation
- ☐ VMS
- ☐ UNIX
- ☐ OS/2
- ☐ Other platform

Cost
- ☐ Unknown
- ☐ Basic
- ☑ Extended
- ☐ Premium ($)
- ☐ Executive w/$

Activity Level: MEDIUM

Address
GO: **AMIGAUSER**

Amiga Vendor Forum

Description
This forum provides support for Amiga owners who use products from the vendors represented here.

Subjects
Computers

Audience
Amiga Users

Content Summary
Visit each vendor's library for information and technical support.

See Also
Amiga Arts Forum

User Guide
- ☑ Windows
- ☑ DOS
- ☐ Macintosh
- ☐ Terminal Emulation
- ☐ VMS
- ☐ UNIX
- ☐ OS/2
- ☐ Other platform

Cost
- ☐ Unknown
- ☐ Basic
- ☑ Extended
- ☐ Premium ($)
- ☐ Executive w/$

Amiga – Animals

Activity Level

Address
GO: **AMIGAVENDOR**

MIDI/Music Forum

Description
This forum is dedicated to supporting MIDI and computer music-related discussions and files. Also, it has the coolest forum logo. You have to see it!

Subjects
Amiga, Macintosh, Multimedia, Music

Audience
Musicians, computer game developers, computer users, Amiga users

Content Summary
Packed with files, discussions, tips and hints, and troubleshooting guidelines, the MIDI/Music Forum includes these and other library and message sections: Basics and Product Guides, General MIDI Songs, Atari Files, Macintosh Files, Patches/Samples, MS DOS Demos, and Windows Media Sound. You'll find items for sale in the Classified Ads library (Library 8).

See Also
MIDI A Vendor Forum, MIDI B Vendor Forum, MIDI C Vendor Forum

User Guide
- ☑ Windows
- ☑ DOS
- ☑ Macintosh
- ☐ Terminal Emulation
- ☐ VMS
- ☐ UNIX
- ☐ OS/2
- ☑ Other platform

Cost
- ☐ Unknown
- ☐ Basic
- ☑ Extended
- ☐ Premium ($)
- ☐ Executive w/$

Activity Level

Address
GO: **MIDIFORUM**

Pet Products/Reference Forum

Description
This forum provides customer support for those businesses that provide products or services to pet owners or pet professionals.

Subjects
Animals, Fish, Veterinarians

Audience
Aquarists, pet owners, veterinarians

Content Summary
This forum contains numerous libraries that include a complete list of all subscribing PetPro vendors and a description of their businesses. Also of interest are articles written by behavioral specialists and articles that have appeared in well-known animal publications.

See Also
Pets/Animal Forum

User Guide
- ☑ Windows
- ☑ DOS
- ☑ Macintosh
- ☐ Terminal Emulation
- ☐ VMS
- ☐ UNIX
- ☑ OS/2
- ☐ Other platform

Cost
- ☐ Unknown
- ☐ Basic
- ☑ Extended
- ☐ Premium ($)
- ☐ Executive w/$

Activity Level

Address
GO: **PETPRO**

Time Warner-Dogs & Cats Forum

Description
Forum sponsored by Time-Warner to discuss dogs, cats, and other household pets.

Subjects
Pets

Audience
Pet owners

Content Summary
The libraries include information on the care and feeding of pets, safety issues, and training.

See Also
Pets

User Guide
- ☑ Windows
- ☑ DOS
- ☐ Macintosh
- ☐ Terminal Emulation
- ☐ VMS
- ☐ UNIX
- ☐ OS/2
- ☐ Other platform

Cost
- ☐ Unknown
- ☐ Basic
- ☑ Extended
- ☐ Premium ($)
- ☐ Executive w/$

Animals – Apple

Activity Level: MEDIUM (arrow between low and high, pointing up)

Address
GO: **TWPETS**

APPC Info Exchange Forum

Description
The APPC Forum addresses many of the hot topics in networking today, to help you apply advanced networking in your own environment.

Subjects
Computers, Networking

Audience
Network Administrators

Content Summary
The libraries contain information on LAN/WAN integration, client/server development, downsizing, and rightsizing.

See Also
Novell

User Guide
- ☑ Windows
- ☑ DOS
- ☑ Macintosh
- ☐ Terminal Emulation
- ☑ VMS
- ☑ UNIX
- ☑ OS/2
- ☑ Other platform

Cost
- ☐ Unknown
- ☐ Basic
- ☑ Extended
- ☐ Premium ($)
- ☐ Executive w/$

Activity Level: MEDIUM (arrow pointing toward low)

Address
GO: **APPCFORUM**

Apple II Programmers' Forum

Description
The area for discussing programming Apple II computers, from BASIC to assembly language, to graphical interfaces like HyperStudio.

Subjects
Computers

Audience
Apple users, computer programmers

Content Summary
The libraries and message areas include information on programming tips and application ideas.

See Also
Apple II Users Forum

User Guide
- ☐ Windows
- ☐ DOS
- ☑ Macintosh
- ☐ Terminal Emulation
- ☐ VMS
- ☐ UNIX
- ☐ OS/2
- ☐ Other platform

Cost
- ☐ Unknown
- ☐ Basic
- ☑ Extended
- ☐ Premium ($)
- ☐ Executive w/$

Activity Level: MEDIUM (arrow pointing toward low)

Address
GO: **APPROG**

Apple II Users' Forum

Description
This is the place to discuss applications software and hardware for the Apple II computer.

Subjects
Computers

Audience
Apple users

Content Summary
The libraries inlcude information on the available programs, tips on choosing hardware and software, and expert advice from experienced users.

See Also
Apple II Vendor Forum

User Guide
- ☐ Windows
- ☐ DOS
- ☑ Macintosh
- ☐ Terminal Emulation
- ☐ VMS
- ☐ UNIX
- ☐ OS/2
- ☐ Other platform

Cost
- ☐ Unknown
- ☐ Basic
- ☑ Extended
- ☐ Premium ($)
- ☐ Executive w/$

Activity Level: MEDIUM (arrow pointing toward low)

Address
GO: **APUSER**

Apple – Application Development

Apple II Vendors' Forum

Description
Several vendors of Apple II related products offer online support for their users.

Subjects
Computers

Audience
Apple users

Content Summary
Vendors included in this forum are Applied Engineering, 1st Class Peripherals, Stone Edge Technology, Beagle Bros., Intrec Software, and TMS Peripherals.

See Also
Apple II Users' Forum

User Guide
- ☐ Windows
- ☐ DOS
- ☑ Macintosh
- ☐ Terminal Emulation
- ☐ VMS
- ☐ UNIX
- ☐ OS/2
- ☐ Other platform

Cost
- ☐ Unknown
- ☐ Basic
- ☑ Extended
- ☐ Premium ($)
- ☐ Executive w/$

Activity Level

Address
GO: **APIIVEN**

Newton Developers Forum

Description
This forum discusses the various aspects of Newton technology and how to design software and hardware for the Apple Newton PDA.

Subjects
Computers, Apple

Audience
Computer programmers

Content Summary
Use this forum to find files, technical issues, and other developer resources. The library and message sections include Mac Toolkit, Windows Toolkit, Other Languages, Book Maker, NewtonScipt, General Programming, Graphics, and more.

See Also
Apple Forum

User Guide
- ☑ Windows
- ☐ DOS
- ☑ Macintosh
- ☐ Terminal Emulation
- ☐ VMS
- ☐ UNIX
- ☐ OS/2
- ☑ Other platform

Cost
- ☐ Unknown
- ☐ Basic
- ☑ Extended
- ☐ Premium ($)
- ☐ Executive w/$

Activity Level

Address
GO: **NEWTDEV**

APPLICATION DEVELOPMENT

(Microsoft) Developers Relations Forums

Description
This forum is designed for high-level information exchange and tips about Microsoft Developer products. Section leaders from Microsoft Product Support Services monitor and participate in the forum. This area is for nontechnical information. See the Microsoft Developer Services Area (MSDS) for technical support questions and issues.

Subjects
Application Development, Computers, Microsoft

Audience
Advanced-level users, developers

Content Summary
This forum includes two libraries: General/Dev. Services, which includes files and information on job opportunities, general beta testing (non-Microsoft), and the Microsoft Support Network; and Strategic Issues, which includes information and tool kits for developers on different applications and operating systems.

See Also
Microsoft Developer Services Area, Microsoft Developer Network Forum, Microsoft Developer Knowledge Base, Microsoft Connection, Microsoft C and Other Languages Forum

User Guide
- ☑ Windows
- ☑ DOS
- ☐ Macintosh
- ☐ Terminal Emulation
- ☑ VMS
- ☑ UNIX
- ☑ OS/2
- ☐ Other platform

Application Development – Aquaria/Fish Forum

Cost
- ☐ Unknown
- ☐ Basic
- ☒ Extended
- ☐ Premium ($)
- ☐ Executive w/$

Activity Level: MEDIUM (arrow pointing up between LOW and HIGH)

Address
GO: **MSDR**

Digitalk Forum

Description
This forum provides a way to communicate with Digitalk and with other users of Smalltalk/V and PARTS products, including the latest information about Smalltalk/V and PARTS products, technical support answers, and how others are using Digitalk's development systems to create and deliver software.

Subjects
Application Development, Computers, Smalltalk/V

Audience
Application developers, PARTS users, Smalltalk/V users

Content Summary
The library and message areas contain various places to discuss several topics, including Digitalk news, product information, user contributions, third-party products, support, and miscellaneous information and products. If you're looking for source code or tips on Smalltalk/V, see library 5, "Support."

See Also
Digitalk Database

User Guide
- ☒ Windows
- ☒ DOS
- ☒ Macintosh
- ☐ Terminal Emulation
- ☐ VMS
- ☐ UNIX
- ☒ OS/2
- ☐ Other platform

Cost
- ☐ Unknown
- ☐ Basic
- ☒ Extended
- ☐ Premium ($)
- ☐ Executive w/$

Activity Level: MEDIUM (arrow pointing toward HIGH)

Address
GO: **DIGITALK**

APPLIED PHYSICS

Ei Compendex Plus

Description
The Ei Compendex Plus database contains abstracts and articles from engineering and technological literature. You can find literature from virtually all the engineering disciplines in this database.

Subjects
Applied Physics, Food Technology, Engineering, Pollution

Audience
Engineers

Content Summary
This database contains worldwide coverage of articles taken from journals, publications of engineering societies and organizations, conference papers and proceedings, and government reports and books. In a search, you can get the author, title, corporate source, conference title, publication year, language, and an abstract from the article. See the Pricing Information choice in the main menu for the various pricing charges.

See Also
ERIC, IQuest

User Guide
- ☒ Windows
- ☒ DOS
- ☒ Macintosh
- ☐ Terminal Emulation
- ☐ VMS
- ☒ UNIX
- ☐ OS/2
- ☐ Other platform

Cost
- ☐ Unknown
- ☐ Basic
- ☐ Extended
- ☒ Premium ($)
- ☐ Executive w/$

Activity Level: UNKNOWN

Address
GO: **COMPENDEX**

Aquaria/Fish Forum

Description
FISHNET is the place to meet for information dealing with all kinds of aquatic critters.

Subjects
Fish

Audience
Aquatic enthusiasts

Aquaria/Fish Forum – Art

Content Summary
The libraries contain information on equipment, disease, aquaculture, freshwater and marine aquaria, and a graphics library.

See Also
Travel Forum

User Guide
- ☑ Windows
- ☑ DOS
- ☐ Macintosh
- ☐ Terminal Emulation
- ☐ VMS
- ☐ UNIX
- ☐ OS/2
- ☐ Other platform

Cost
- ☐ Unknown
- ☐ Basic
- ☑ Extended
- ☐ Premium ($)
- ☐ Executive w/$

Activity Level

Address
GO: **FISHNET**

Archive Photos Forum

Description
Archive Photos is a leading source of historical engravings, drawings, and photographs, with over 1300 images available for download.

Subjects
History, Photography

Audience
History buffs, photographers, students

Content Summary
The libraries contain photographs of historical importance. Subjects include famous people, events, and disasters.

See Also
Photography Forum

User Guide
- ☑ Windows
- ☑ DOS
- ☐ Macintosh
- ☐ Terminal Emulation
- ☐ VMS
- ☐ UNIX
- ☐ OS/2
- ☐ Other platform

Cost
- ☐ Unknown
- ☐ Basic
- ☑ Extended
- ☐ Premium ($)
- ☐ Executive w/$

Activity Level

Address
GO: **ARCHIVE**

ART

African American Art and Culture Forum

Description
This forum gives you the opportunity to experience the culture and art of African Americans. You can discuss current events and cultural issues.

Subjects
Art, Cultural Issues

Audience
Anyone interested in African American culture

Content Summary
The libraries include a wide range of topics including art and artists, history, events, film and theater news, member profiles, and genealogy

See Also
Genealogy Forum

User Guide
- ☑ Windows
- ☑ DOS
- ☑ Macintosh
- ☐ Terminal Emulation
- ☐ VMS
- ☐ UNIX
- ☐ OS/2
- ☐ Other platform

Cost
- ☐ Unknown
- ☐ Basic
- ☑ Extended
- ☐ Premium ($)
- ☐ Executive w/$

Activity Level
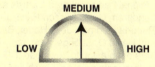

Address
GO: **AFRO**

Artist Forum

Description
The Artist Forum brings you the entire world of art.

Subjects
Hobbies

Audience
Artists, collectors, sculptors

Content Summary
Art of various types, such as cartoons, portraits, and landscapes, can be viewed. Also contains information on grants and scholarships.

See Also
Metropolitan Museum of Art

Artist Forum – Art History

User Guide
- ☑ Windows
- ☑ DOS
- ☑ Macintosh
- ☐ Terminal Emulation
- ☑ VMS
- ☑ UNIX
- ☑ OS/2
- ☑ Other platform

Cost
- ☐ Unknown
- ☐ Basic
- ☑ Extended
- ☐ Premium ($)
- ☐ Executive w/$

Activity Level
LOW ← (MEDIUM) HIGH

Address
GO: **ARTIST**

Fine Art Forum

Description
Michelangelo. Renoir. Matisse. DaVinci. Rembrandt. Montgomery. Montgomery? Find out about him and other artists in the Fine Arts Forum.

Subjects
Art, Art History, Classics, Modern Art

Audience
Art directors, art enthusiasts, art historians, artists, general interest

Content Summary
The Fine Art Forum focuses on the arts and techniques of the old masters, as well as local and regional traditional-media artists such as Carl Lundgren, Gunni Nilsson Price, Joe Bergeron, Roberta Laidman, Jess Hager, Barbara Johnson, and David O. Stillings. The many libraries offered here enable you to download .GIF files of many of your favorite paintings, such as Michelangelo's "The Fall of Man," DaVinci's "Last Supper," and Renoir's "Diana." You also can become familiar with modern artists and techniques by visiting Library 15, Modern Art.

See Also
Artist Forum, Graphics Forums, Graphics Gallery Forum, Graphics Plus Forum, Photography Forum

User Guide
- ☑ Windows
- ☑ DOS
- ☑ Macintosh
- ☐ Terminal Emulation
- ☐ VMS
- ☐ UNIX
- ☐ OS/2
- ☐ Other platform

Cost
- ☐ Unknown
- ☐ Basic
- ☐ Extended
- ☑ Premium ($)
- ☐ Executive w/$

Activity Level
LOW ← (MEDIUM) HIGH

Address
GO: **FINEARTS**

Metropolitan Museum of Art

Description
This service enables you order Metropolitan Museum of Art merchandise online, such as the Diamond-Shaped Celtic Bookmark or the Greek Horseman Relief Fragment.

Subjects
Art

Audience
Art enthusiasts, general public

Content Summary
The Metropolitan Museum is located at Fifth Avenue and 82 St, NYC, and is open till 8:45 on Friday and Saturday nights; closed Mondays. With this service, museum members receive a 10% discount on all purchases. The main menu enables you to choose options including Order from Our Catalogue, Store Locations, Become a Member of the Metropolitan Museum, and more.

See Also
Artist Forum

User Guide
- ☑ Windows
- ☑ DOS
- ☑ Macintosh
- ☐ Terminal Emulation
- ☐ VMS
- ☐ UNIX
- ☐ OS/2
- ☐ Other platform

Cost
- ☐ Unknown
- ☑ Basic
- ☐ Extended
- ☐ Premium ($)
- ☐ Executive w/$

Activity Level
LOW UNKNOWN HIGH

Address
GO: **MMA**

ART HISTORY

Fine Art Forum

Description
Michelangelo. Renoir. Matisse. DaVinci. Rembrandt. Montgomery. Montgomery? Find out about him and other artists in the Fine Arts Forum.

Subjects
Art, Art History, Classics, Modern Art

Audience
Art directors, art enthusiasts, art historians, artists, general interest

Content Summary
The Fine Art Forum focuses on the arts and techniques of the old masters, as well as local and regional traditional-media artists such as Carl Lundgren, Gunni Nilsson Price, Joe Bergeron, Roberta Laidman, Jess Hager, Barbara Johnson, and David O. Stillings. The many libraries offered here enable you to download .GIF files of many of your favorite paintings, such as Michelangelo's "The Fall of Man," DaVinci's "Last Supper," and Renoir's "Diana." You also can become familiar with modern artists and techniques by visiting Library 15, Modern Art.

See Also
Artist Forum, Graphics Forums, Graphics Gallery Forum, Graphics Plus Forum, Photography Forum

User Guide
- [x] Windows
- [x] DOS
- [x] Macintosh
- [ ] Terminal Emulation
- [ ] VMS
- [ ] UNIX
- [ ] OS/2
- [ ] Other platform

Cost
- [ ] Unknown
- [ ] Basic
- [ ] Extended
- [x] Premium ($)
- [ ] Executive w/$

Activity Level

MEDIUM
LOW — HIGH

Address
GO: **FINEARTS**

Artisoft Forum

Description
The Artisoft Forum provides online technical support for users of Artisoft products.

Subjects
Computers, Networking, Software

Audience
Network Administrators

Content Summary
Libraries include information on LANtastic products, Artisoft Sounding Board, Articom, and Netmedia products.

See Also
APPC Info Exchange Forum

User Guide
- [x] Windows
- [x] DOS
- [ ] Macintosh
- [ ] Terminal Emulation
- [ ] VMS
- [ ] UNIX
- [ ] OS/2
- [ ] Other platform

Cost
- [ ] Unknown
- [ ] Basic
- [x] Extended
- [ ] Premium ($)
- [ ] Executive w/$

Activity Level

MEDIUM
LOW — HIGH

Address
GO: **ARTISOFT**

Artist Forum

Description
The Artist Forum brings you the entire world of art.

Subjects
Hobbies

Audience
Artists, collectors, sculptors

Content Summary
Art of various types, such as cartoons, portraits, and landscapes, can be viewed. Also contains information on grants and scholarships.

See Also
Metropolitan Museum of Art

User Guide
- [x] Windows
- [x] DOS
- [x] Macintosh
- [ ] Terminal Emulation
- [x] VMS
- [x] UNIX
- [x] OS/2
- [x] Other platform

Cost
- [ ] Unknown
- [ ] Basic
- [x] Extended
- [ ] Premium ($)
- [ ] Executive w/$

Activity Level

MEDIUM
LOW ← HIGH

Address
GO: **ARTIST**

Ask Customer Service

Description
This forum provides commonly asked questions and answers about CompuServe.

Ask Customer Service – Associated Press Online

Subjects
CompuServe

Audience
CompuServe users

Content Summary
Questions about CompuServe Mail, billing, forums, and downloading software are answered by CompuServe personnel.

See Also
Billing Information

User Guide
- ☑ Windows
- ☑ DOS
- ☐ Macintosh
- ☐ Terminal Emulation
- ☐ VMS
- ☐ UNIX
- ☐ OS/2
- ☐ Other platform

Cost
- ☐ Unknown
- ☑ Basic
- ☐ Extended
- ☐ Premium ($)
- ☐ Executive w/$

Activity Level

LOW — UNKNOWN — MEDIUM — HIGH

Address
GO: **QUESTIONS**

Ask3Com Forum

Description
This forum is dedicated to the discussion of 3Com Corporation's networking products.

Subjects
Computers, Networking

Audience
3Com product users

Content Summary
The libraries contain patches and fixes, documentation, drivers, technical bulletins, and network management tips.

See Also
3Com Online Communication Forum

User Guide
- ☑ Windows
- ☑ DOS
- ☑ Macintosh
- ☐ Terminal Emulation
- ☑ VMS
- ☑ UNIX
- ☑ OS/2
- ☑ Other platform

Cost
- ☐ Unknown
- ☐ Basic
- ☑ Extended
- ☐ Premium ($)
- ☐ Executive w/$

Activity Level

LOW — MEDIUM (arrow points to LOW) — HIGH

Address
GO: **ASKFORUM**

ASP Shareware Forum

Description
Devoted to the general discussion of shareware, and to serve as a meeting place for members of the Association of Shareware Professionals.

Subjects
Computers, Shareware, Software

Audience
Computer programmers, software developers

Content Summary
The libraries contain program files you can download to your computer. You also can communicate with shareware developers.

See Also
Software Publishers Association Forum

User Guide
- ☑ Windows
- ☑ DOS
- ☑ Macintosh
- ☐ Terminal Emulation
- ☑ VMS
- ☑ UNIX
- ☑ OS/2
- ☑ Other platform

Cost
- ☐ Unknown
- ☐ Basic
- ☑ Extended
- ☐ Premium ($)
- ☐ Executive w/$

Activity Level

LOW — MEDIUM (arrow points up) — HIGH

Address
GO: **ASPFORUM**

Associated Press Online

Description
News stories from the Associated Press.

Subjects
Current Events, Entertainment, News

Audience
Consumers, journalists

Content Summary
Read up-to-date news stories of national and world interest.

See Also
The Business Wire

User Guide
- ☑ Windows
- ☑ DOS
- ☐ Macintosh
- ☐ Terminal Emulation
- ☐ VMS
- ☐ UNIX
- ☐ OS/2
- ☐ Other platform

Cost
- ☐ Unknown
- ☐ Basic
- ☑ Extended
- ☐ Premium ($)
- ☐ Executive w/$

Activity Level: UNKNOWN

Address
GO: **APO**

AST Forum

Description
The AST Forum serves as a means for technical support and discussion of the diverse line of AST products.

Subjects
Computers

Audience
AST Products Users

Content Summary
The libraries contain information on AST Fun Stuff, Bravo, Exec, GRiD Equipment, and servers.

See Also
Novell

User Guide
- ☑ Windows
- ☑ DOS
- ☐ Macintosh
- ☐ Terminal Emulation
- ☐ VMS
- ☐ UNIX
- ☐ OS/2
- ☐ Other platform

Cost
- ☐ Unknown
- ☐ Basic
- ☑ Extended
- ☐ Premium ($)
- ☐ Executive w/$

Activity Level: LOW

Address
GO: **ASTFORUM**

Astronomy Forum

Description
The Astronomy Forum is for anyone who shares a fascination with celestial happenings, whether at the amateur or professional level.

Subjects
Hobbies, Science

Audience
Astronomers, hobbyists

Content Summary
The libraries contain public domain software, reference articles, and graphics images.

See Also
Science Trivia Quiz

User Guide
- ☑ Windows
- ☑ DOS
- ☑ Macintosh
- ☐ Terminal Emulation
- ☑ VMS
- ☑ UNIX
- ☑ OS/2
- ☑ Other platform

Cost
- ☐ Unknown
- ☐ Basic
- ☑ Extended
- ☐ Premium ($)
- ☐ Executive w/$

Activity Level: MEDIUM

Address
GO: **ASTROFORUM**

Atari Computing Forum

Description
The forum supporting Atari 16- and 32-bit computers, peripherals, and productivity software.

Subjects
Computers, Software

Audience
Atari users

Content Summary
Libraries include downloadable programs on telecommunications, programming, utilities, applications, desktop accessories, and hardware.

See Also
Atari Users Network

User Guide
- ☐ Windows
- ☐ DOS
- ☐ Macintosh
- ☐ Terminal Emulation
- ☐ VMS
- ☐ UNIX
- ☐ OS/2
- ☑ Other platform

Atari Computing Forum – Autodesk Multimedia Forum

Cost
- ☐ Unknown
- ☐ Basic
- ☒ Extended
- ☐ Premium ($)
- ☐ Executive w/$

Activity Level

LOW ← MEDIUM HIGH

Address
GO: **ATARICOMP**

AUDIO/VIDEO

Sight And Sound Forum

Description
The forum covering all types of computerized audio and visual hardware.

Subjects
Audio/Video, Entertainment

Audience
Audio and video enthusiasts

Content Summary
Libraries include video techniques, audio techniques, graphics and sound files, and MIDI.

See Also
Audio Engineering Society, Video Games Forum

User Guide
- ☒ Windows
- ☒ DOS
- ☒ Macintosh
- ☐ Terminal Emulation
- ☐ VMS
- ☐ UNIX
- ☐ OS/2
- ☐ Other platform

Cost
- ☐ Unknown
- ☐ Basic
- ☒ Extended
- ☐ Premium ($)
- ☐ Executive w/$

Activity Level

LOW — UNKNOWN (MEDIUM) — HIGH

Address
GO: **SSFORUM**

Autodesk AutoCAD Forum

Description
An open forum for anyone with an interest in computer-aided design, with an emphasis on Autodesk products.

Subjects
CAD, Computers, Software

Audience
Autodesk products users

Content Summary
Libraries contain hints and techniques on Autodesk products, and discussions on operating systems and productivity.

See Also
Autodesk Software Forum

User Guide
- ☒ Windows
- ☒ DOS
- ☒ Macintosh
- ☐ Terminal Emulation
- ☐ VMS
- ☐ UNIX
- ☐ OS/2
- ☐ Other platform

Cost
- ☐ Unknown
- ☐ Basic
- ☒ Extended
- ☐ Premium ($)
- ☐ Executive w/$

Activity Level

LOW — MEDIUM ↑ — HIGH

Address
GO: **ACAD**

Autodesk Multimedia Forum

Description
Support for the Autodesk line of PC and workstation-based graphics programs.

Subjects
CAD, Computers, Multimedia

Audience
Autodesk products users

Content Summary
Libraries contain IPAS usage, 3D Studio updates, software developer news, animations, and education issues.

See Also
Autodesk AutoCAD Forum

User Guide
- ☒ Windows
- ☒ DOS
- ☐ Macintosh
- ☐ Terminal Emulation
- ☐ VMS
- ☐ UNIX
- ☐ OS/2
- ☐ Other platform

Autodesk Multimedia Forum – Automobiles

35

A

Cost
- ☐ Unknown
- ☐ Basic
- ☑ Extended
- ☐ Premium ($)
- ☐ Executive w/$

Activity Level: MEDIUM (arrow pointing up between LOW and HIGH)

Address
GO: **ASOFT**

Autodesk Retail Products Forum

Description
An open forum for anyone interested in low cost Precision Graphics software, with an emphasis on Autodesk Retail Division products.

Subjects
CAD, Computers, Software

Audience
Autodesk Products Users

Content Summary
Developments in the PC CADD industry are discussed. Questions are answered in 24 hours.

See Also
Autodesk AutoCAD Forum

User Guide
- ☑ Windows
- ☑ DOS
- ☐ Macintosh
- ☐ Terminal Emulation
- ☐ VMS
- ☐ UNIX
- ☐ OS/2
- ☐ Other platform

Cost
- ☐ Unknown
- ☐ Basic
- ☑ Extended
- ☐ Premium ($)
- ☐ Executive w/$

Activity Level: MEDIUM (arrow pointing up)

Address
GO: **ARETAIL**

AUTOMOBILES

Automobile Forum

Description
CARS covers all facets of the automotive world—from buying your first car to selling your last one, from fixing to the future.

Subjects
Cars

Audience
Automobile enthusiasts, mechanics

Content Summary
The libraries contain information on finance, insurance, safety issues, and what's new in the automobile industry.

See Also
New Car Showroom

User Guide
- ☑ Windows
- ☑ DOS
- ☐ Macintosh
- ☐ Terminal Emulation
- ☐ VMS
- ☐ UNIX
- ☐ OS/2
- ☐ Other platform

Cost
- ☐ Unknown
- ☐ Basic
- ☑ Extended
- ☐ Premium ($)
- ☐ Executive w/$

Activity Level:  (arrow pointing toward HIGH)

Address
GO: **CARS**

Ford Motor Company

The opening screen says: "Have you driven a Ford lately?" This service enables you to view the latest vehicles available from Ford.

Subjects
Automobiles, Ford Mustangs

Audience
Automobile enthusiasts, general public

Content Summary
Set up with a menu system, you can select to see the Welcome Center, Ford cars or Ford trucks, the World of Ford, the Ford Dealer Locator, Software, Video, or Sportswear, or the featured Ford vehicle (the 1994 Ford Escort at the time of this writing). The Ford Dealer Locator option enables you to find the nearest Ford dealer in your area. The Ford Motor Company service is free, but you are surcharged for items that you purchase.

See Also
Automobile Info Center (FREE), Automobile Forum, Automotive Information, AutoVantage OnLine (FREE), AutoQuot-R (FREE)

User Guide
- ☐ Windows
- ☐ DOS
- ☐ Macintosh
- ☑ Terminal Emulation
- ☐ VMS
- ☐ UNIX
- ☐ OS/2
- ☐ Other platform

Automobiles

Cost
- [ ] Unknown
- [x] Basic
- [ ] Extended
- [ ] Premium ($)
- [ ] Executive w/$

Activity Level

Address
GO: **FORD**

Motor Sports Forum

Description
Operated by Racing Information Systems of Redondo Beach, California, this news service provides an area for discussion of topics of interest to motor racing enthusiasts worldwide.

Subjects
Automobiles, Motor Racing, Motorcycles

Audience
Automobile enthusiasts

Content Summary
The library and message sections include racing topics such as IMSA Series Files, NASCAR/Stock Files, Indy Cars/Lite, USAC/WoO/Oval Track, NHRA/IHRA/Drags/LSR, Motorcycle Racing, Racing Graphics, and more.

See Also
Sports Forum

User Guide
- [x] Windows
- [x] DOS
- [x] Macintosh
- [ ] Terminal Emulation
- [x] VMS
- [x] UNIX
- [ ] OS/2
- [ ] Other platform

Cost
- [ ] Unknown
- [ ] Basic
- [x] Extended
- [ ] Premium ($)
- [ ] Executive w/$

Activity Level

Address
GO: **RACING**

New Car Showroom

Description
The New Car Showroom enables you to view and compare passenger car, van, special purpose, and truck features and specifications. Use this service when you are looking for a new car or truck.

Subjects
Automobiles

Audience
General public

Content Summary
You can enter two distinct Showrooms: one for cars, passenger vans, and special-purpose vehicles and one for trucks and cargo vans. In either Showroom, you can use the database to learn about models of interest to you. The Showrooms include data on over 1,000 passenger cars, vans, special-purpose vehicles, and light-duty trucks currently sold in the United States. You also can calculate monthly payments by using the Figure Your Monthly Payments option on the main menu.

See Also
Automobile Info Center, Automotive Information Forum

User Guide
- [x] Windows
- [x] DOS
- [x] Macintosh
- [ ] Terminal Emulation
- [x] VMS
- [x] UNIX
- [ ] OS/2
- [ ] Other platform

Cost
- [ ] Unknown
- [ ] Basic
- [x] Extended
- [ ] Premium ($)
- [ ] Executive w/$

Activity Level

Address
GO: **NEWCAR**

Worldwide Car Network

Description
This forum is the place to be for people interested in classic and later models of American, European, or Japanese cars, motorcycles, or trucks.

Subjects
Automobiles

Audience
Automobile enthusiasts

Content Summary
The libraries include information on cars, motorcycles, and trucks. Topics covered include price, finding parts, and shows.

See Also
Members interested in motor vehicles.

Automobiles – Aviation

User Guide
- ☑ Windows
- ☑ DOS
- ☑ Macintosh
- ☐ Terminal Emulation
- ☑ VMS
- ☑ UNIX
- ☐ OS/2
- ☐ Other platform

Cost
- ☐ Unknown
- ☐ Basic
- ☑ Extended
- ☐ Premium ($)
- ☐ Executive w/$

Activity Level
LOW ← MEDIUM — HIGH

Address
GO: **WCN**

AVIATION

Air Line Pilots Association

Description
The Air Line Pilots Association is an AFL-CIO affiliated labor union representing most of the nation's commercial airline pilots.

Subjects
Labor Unions

Audience
Pilots

Content Summary
You can get all the up-to-date news about benefits, hot topics, and job openings.

See Also
NWS Aviation Weather

User Guide
- ☑ Windows
- ☑ DOS
- ☑ Macintosh
- ☐ Terminal Emulation
- ☑ VMS
- ☑ UNIX
- ☑ OS/2
- ☐ Other platform

Cost
- ☐ Unknown
- ☑ Basic
- ☐ Extended
- ☐ Premium ($)
- ☐ Executive w/$

Activity Level

LOW — UNKNOWN — MEDIUM — HIGH

Address
GO: **ALPA**

Aviation Special Interest Group

Description
AVSIG, the oldest forum on CompuServe, brings together people who share an interest both in computers and in airplanes.

Subjects
Aircraft Safety, Airplanes

Audience
Aviators

Content Summary
The libraries include information on flying issues, safety, weather, balloons, air traffic control, and want ads.

See Also
NWS Aviation Weather

User Guide
- ☑ Windows
- ☑ DOS
- ☐ Macintosh
- ☐ Terminal Emulation
- ☐ VMS
- ☐ UNIX
- ☐ OS/2
- ☐ Other platform

Cost
- ☐ Unknown
- ☐ Basic
- ☑ Extended
- ☐ Premium ($)
- ☐ Executive w/$

Activity Level

LOW — MEDIUM — HIGH →

Address
GO: **AVSIG**

NWS Aviation Weather

Description
Get weather reports from various cities for aviation concerns.

Subjects
Aviation

Audience
Pilots

Content Summary
You can select to see Hourly Reports, Terminal Forecasts, Previous Hourly Reports, Winds Aloft Forecasts, Radar Summaries, and more.

See Also
Airline Pilots Association, Aviation Special Interest Group

Aviation

User Guide
- ☐ Windows
- ☐ DOS
- ☐ Macintosh
- ☑ Terminal Emulation
- ☐ VMS
- ☐ UNIX
- ☐ OS/2
- ☐ Other platform

Cost
- ☐ Unknown
- ☑ Basic
- ☐ Extended
- ☐ Premium ($)
- ☐ Executive w/$

Activity Level

LOW — UNKNOWN (MEDIUM) — HIGH

Address
GO: **AWX**

B

Bacchus Wine and Beer Forum

Description
The Wine Forum, operated by Bacchus Data Services, is the home for discussion of all the beverages that you enjoy.

Subjects
Food, Wine

Audience
General public, wine lovers

Content Summary
If you enjoy a good glass of wine or a cold beer, join this forum and visit the different libraries in it. Some of the library topics include wine tasting, wine shopping, beer, wine, brewing, recipes, spirits, coffee, and more.

See Also
The Absolut Museum

User Guide
- ☑ Windows
- ☑ DOS
- ☑ Macintosh
- ☐ Terminal Emulation
- ☑ VMS
- ☑ UNIX
- ☑ OS/2
- ☐ Other platform

Cost
- ☐ Unknown
- ☐ Basic
- ☑ Extended
- ☐ Premium ($)
- ☐ Executive w/$

Activity Level

Address
GO: **WINEFORUM**

BANYAN

Banyan Forum

Description
Help, information, and support for Banyan products, including Banyan VINES networking software.

Subjects
Computers, Networking

Audience
MIS people

Content Summary
Find out more about your Banyan products, including VINES, in this forum. Some of the library topics that you'll find include networking, servers, VINES, hardware, and more.

See Also
Other Ban Patch Forum

User Guide
- ☑ Windows
- ☑ DOS
- ☐ Macintosh
- ☐ Terminal Emulation
- ☐ VMS
- ☐ UNIX
- ☐ OS/2
- ☑ Other platform

Cost
- ☐ Unknown
- ☐ Basic
- ☑ Extended
- ☐ Premium ($)
- ☐ Executive w/$

Activity Level MEDIUM

Address
GO: **BANFORUM**

Vines 4.x Patchware Forum

Description
This vendor support forum offers software patches and support for Banyan's VINES 4.x networking products.

Subjects
Banyan, Computer Networking, Computers

Audience
VINES users

Content Summary
The libraries contain patches and upgrades to version 4.x products. Also included are technical documents for usage and support.

See Also
Software

User Guide
- ☑ Windows
- ☑ DOS
- ☐ Macintosh
- ☐ Terminal Emulation
- ☐ VMS
- ☐ UNIX
- ☐ OS/2
- ☐ Other platform

Cost
- ☐ Unknown
- ☐ Basic
- ☑ Extended
- ☐ Premium ($)
- ☐ Executive w/$

Activity Level

Address
GO: **VINES4**

Banyan – Beds

Vines 5.x Patchware Forum

Description
This vendor support forum offers software patches for Banyan's VINES 5.x networking products.

Subjects
Banyan, Computer Networking, Computers

Audience
Banyan users

Content Summary
Patches are available for version 5 products and technical bulletins provide documentation.

See Also
Vines 4.x Patchware Forum

User Guide
- ☑ Windows
- ☑ DOS
- ☐ Macintosh
- ☐ Terminal Emulation
- ☐ VMS
- ☐ UNIX
- ☐ OS/2
- ☐ Other platform

Cost
- ☐ Unknown
- ☐ Basic
- ☑ Extended
- ☐ Premium ($)
- ☐ Executive w/$

Activity Level

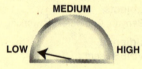

Address
GO: **VINES5**

BASIS International Forum

Description
The BASIS International Forum exists to support the business applications developer who uses BASIS supplied software development tools.

Subjects
Business, Computers

Audience
MIS people

Content Summary
You'll find library and message topics on BBxProgression/4, TAOS 4GL, TAOS/Views Report Writer, and more.

See Also
IBM File Finder

User Guide
- ☐ Windows
- ☑ DOS
- ☐ Macintosh
- ☐ Terminal Emulation
- ☐ VMS
- ☐ UNIX
- ☐ OS/2
- ☑ Other platform

Cost
- ☐ Unknown
- ☐ Basic
- ☑ Extended
- ☐ Premium ($)
- ☐ Executive w/$

Activity Level

Address
GO: **BASIS**

BEDS

Dial-A-Mattress

Description
Looking for a new bed or mattress? You can order or price premium bedding from Sealy, Simmons, and Serta from this service.

Subjects
Bedding, Beds, Mattresses

Audience
Consumers (anyone interested in bedding), gift givers

Content Summary
The Dial-A-Mattress service offers you several options from which to choose, including an order area, product listings, customer service and warranty information, and shipping information. If you want to talk to a "live" person, go to "Can I Speak To A Representative" (option 5) for more information. If you've never heard of Dial-A-Mattress, select option 2. Select option 3 for instructions on how to shop for a mattress or bed online.

See Also
JC Penney

User Guide
- ☑ Windows
- ☑ DOS
- ☑ Macintosh
- ☑ Terminal Emulation
- ☑ VMS
- ☑ UNIX
- ☑ OS/2
- ☐ Other platform

Cost
- ☐ Unknown
- ☑ Basic
- ☐ Extended
- ☐ Premium ($)
- ☐ Executive w/$

Activity Level

Address
GO: **BEDS**

Benchmarks and Standards Forum

Description
A place where individuals and companies can discuss aspects of PC performance, measurement technology, and productivity.

Subjects
Computers, Testing

Audience
MIS people

Content Summary
For discussions and support for benchmark performances and testing, this forum has library and message sections that contain topics such as standardizing, measurement, performance analysis, and the like.

See Also
Ziff-Davis Benchmark Operation Forum

User Guide
- ☑ Windows
- ☑ DOS
- ☑ Macintosh
- ☐ Terminal Emulation
- ☐ VMS
- ☐ UNIX
- ☑ OS/2
- ☑ Other platform

Cost
- ☐ Unknown
- ☐ Basic
- ☑ Extended
- ☐ Premium ($)
- ☐ Executive w/$

Activity Level

MEDIUM — LOW ← HIGH

Address
GO: **BENCHMARK**

BILINGUAL EDUCATION

Foreign Language Forum

Description
This forum is devoted to foreign languages, their study, teaching, use in the commercial world, or general interest items about foreign languages.

Subjects
Bilingual Education, Europe, Foreign News, French, International, Languages

Audience
General public, Europeans

Content Summary
As you can see from the various library headings, the Foreign Language forum offers a diverse cultural and languages experience. The libraries are listed as follows: Spanish/Portuguese, French, German/Germanic, Latin/Greek, Slavic/E. European, English, East Asian, Esperanto, Italian, FL Education, Translators, Computers/Languages, Resources/Careers, Semitic/Turkic, Others Using the Forum, and Sysops.

See Also
Education Forum

User Guide
- ☑ Windows
- ☑ DOS
- ☑ Macintosh
- ☐ Terminal Emulation
- ☐ VMS
- ☑ UNIX
- ☐ OS/2
- ☐ Other platform

Cost
- ☐ Unknown
- ☐ Basic
- ☑ Extended
- ☐ Premium ($)
- ☐ Executive w/$

Activity Level
MEDIUM — LOW → HIGH

Address
GO: **FLEF0**

BILLING

TIMESLIPS Forum

Description
Vendor support forum for Timeslips Corp. and its time tracking and billing software.

Subjects
Accounting

Audience
Accountants

Content Summary
The libraries include information on product usage, product information, and technical support.

See Also
Entrepreneur's Small Business Forum

User Guide
- ☑ Windows
- ☑ DOS
- ☐ Macintosh
- ☐ Terminal Emulation
- ☐ VMS
- ☐ UNIX
- ☐ OS/2
- ☐ Other platform

Cost
- ☐ Unknown
- ☐ Basic
- ☑ Extended
- ☐ Premium ($)
- ☐ Executive w/$

Billing – Boats

Activity Level

Address
GO: **PCVEND**

BIOLOGY

HSX Adult Forum

Description
The Human Sexuality (HSX) Support Groups are online self-help groups where you can freely discuss your feelings and relationships.

Subjects
Biology, General Interest, Human Behavior, Sexuality

Audience
General public

Content Summary
To gain access to the closed areas in this forum, see the text file CLOSED.TXT in the HSX Help Files library (Library 16). It's the one that has been downloaded over 60,000 times! If you don't want to join in the closed areas, see the HSX Open Forum (HSX100).

See Also
HSX Open Forum, Human Sexuality Databank

User Guide
- ☑ Windows
- ☑ DOS
- ☑ Macintosh
- ☐ Terminal Emulation
- ☐ VMS
- ☐ UNIX
- ☐ OS/2
- ☐ Other platform

Cost
- ☐ Unknown
- ☐ Basic
- ☑ Extended
- ☐ Premium ($)
- ☐ Executive w/$

Activity Level

Address
GO: **HSX200**

Blyth Software Forum

Description
This forum supplies technical support for users of Blyth software, as well as contact with others who have similar interests.

Subjects
Computers

Audience
Computer users, MIS people

Content Summary
This forum contains libraries and messages that discuss topics such as databases, Omnis, SQL, DAL, Extensions, and more.

See Also
Client Server Computing Forum

User Guide
- ☑ Windows
- ☑ DOS
- ☐ Macintosh
- ☐ Terminal Emulation
- ☐ VMS
- ☐ UNIX
- ☐ OS/2
- ☑ Other platform

Cost
- ☐ Unknown
- ☐ Basic
- ☑ Extended
- ☐ Premium ($)
- ☐ Executive w/$

Activity Level

Address
GO: **BLYTH**

BOATS

Sailing Forum

Description
This forum provides information and discussion groups to members who are avid sailors or who dream of sailing the seas.

Subjects
Boats, Yachts

Audience
Sailing enthusiasts

Content Summary
This forum provides open discussion of all types of sailing topics. Libraries include discussions of heavy weather survival tactics, sailor folklore, real-life sea stories of safety lessons, and classified ads for boating-related supplies.

See Also
Sports Forum

User Guide
- ☑ Windows
- ☑ DOS
- ☑ Macintosh
- ☐ Terminal Emulation
- ☑ VMS
- ☑ UNIX
- ☑ OS/2
- ☐ Other platform

Boats – Books

Cost
- ☐ Unknown
- ☐ Basic
- ☑ Extended
- ☐ Premium ($)
- ☐ Executive w/$

Activity Level
LOW ← MEDIUM   HIGH

Address
GO: **SAILING**

BOOKS

British Books in Print

Description
A database containing bibliographic references describing books published in the United Kingdom.

Subjects
Books

Audience
General public

Content Summary
From this database, you can get author, title, publisher, date of publication, edition, binding, list price, and other key information of various British books.

See Also
QPB

User Guide
- ☑ Windows
- ☑ DOS
- ☑ Macintosh
- ☐ Terminal Emulation
- ☑ VMS
- ☑ UNIX
- ☑ OS/2
- ☐ Other platform

Cost
- ☐ Unknown
- ☐ Basic
- ☐ Extended
- ☑ Premium ($)
- ☐ Executive w/$

Activity Level

LOW   UNKNOWN   HIGH (MEDIUM)

Address
GO: **BBIP**

Macmillan Publishing Forum

Description
Get up-to-date information, technical support, customer service, and files relating to Macmillan Computer Publishing books.

Subjects
Books, Computers

Audience
Management information specialists, computer users

Content Summary
Computer books published by New Riders Publishing, Que, SAMS, Hayden, Alpha, Que College, and Brady are supported in this forum. You can find files associated with specific books, graphics files, word processing templates, spreadsheets, and utilities to help you get the most out of your computer system. This forum has one of the best opening bitmaps on CompuServe.

See Also
Computer Directory

User Guide
- ☑ Windows
- ☑ DOS
- ☑ Macintosh
- ☐ Terminal Emulation
- ☐ VMS
- ☐ UNIX
- ☑ OS/2
- ☑ Other platform

Cost
- ☐ Unknown
- ☐ Basic
- ☑ Extended
- ☐ Premium ($)
- ☐ Executive w/$

Activity Level

LOW   MEDIUM ↑   HIGH

Address
GO: **MACMILLAN**

Quality Paperbacks

Description
This forum provides an online paperback book club. If you don't like leaving the comfort of home to shop, then this forum is for you. You can shop for all types of paperback books right from your home or office.

Subjects
Books, Online Shopping, Reading

Audience
Reading enthusiasts, students

Content Summary
Once you join this forum, you receive the QPB review every three-and-one-half weeks. The review contains book reviews and describes the current book selection. You can cancel your membership at any time. Membership is automatically cancelled if you do not purchase at least one book in any six-month period.

See Also
Book of the Month Club Forum, Book Review Digest Forum, Books in Print Forum, Books on Tape Forum

Books – British Books in Print

User Guide
- ☑ Windows
- ☑ DOS
- ☑ Macintosh
- ☑ Terminal Emulation
- ☑ VMS
- ☑ UNIX
- ☑ OS/2
- ☐ Other platform

Cost
- ☐ Unknown
- ☑ Basic
- ☐ Extended
- ☐ Premium ($)
- ☐ Executive w/$

Activity Level: UNKNOWN

Address
GO: **QPB1**

Small Computer Book Club

Description
This is an online shopping area for members of the Small Computer Book Club. Non-members can join online, with a purchase.

Subjects
Books

Audience
Readers

Content Summary
This online shopping forum enables members to order computer books of all types.

See Also
Quality Paperbacks Forum

User Guide
- ☐ Windows
- ☐ DOS
- ☐ Macintosh
- ☑ Terminal Emulation
- ☐ VMS
- ☐ UNIX
- ☐ OS/2
- ☐ Other platform

Cost
- ☐ Unknown
- ☑ Basic
- ☐ Extended
- ☐ Premium ($)
- ☐ Executive w/$

Activity Level: LOW

Address
GO: **BK**

Time Warner Bookstore

Description
Online shopping area offering Time Warner books.

Subjects
Books

Audience
General Public

Content Summary
This online shopping area contains the vast amount of published material offered by Time Warner.

See Also
Book-of-the-Month Club

User Guide
- ☑ Windows
- ☑ DOS
- ☑ Macintosh
- ☐ Terminal Emulation
- ☐ VMS
- ☐ UNIX
- ☐ OS/2
- ☐ Other platform

Cost
- ☐ Unknown
- ☑ Basic
- ☐ Extended
- ☐ Premium ($)
- ☐ Executive w/$

Activity Level: MEDIUM

Address
GO: **TWEP**

British Books in Print

Description
A database containing bibliographic references describing books published in the United Kingdom.

Subjects
Books

Audience
General public

Content Summary
From this database, you can get author, title, publisher, date of publication, edition, binding, list price, and other key information of various British books.

See Also
QPB

User Guide
- ☑ Windows
- ☑ DOS
- ☑ Macintosh
- ☐ Terminal Emulation
- ☑ VMS
- ☑ UNIX
- ☑ OS/2
- ☐ Other platform

Cost
- ☐ Unknown
- ☐ Basic
- ☐ Extended
- ☑ Premium ($)
- ☐ Executive w/$

British Books in Print – Broadcasting

Activity Level: UNKNOWN (LOW–MEDIUM–HIGH)

Address
GO: **BBIP**

British Trade Marks

Description
A database of all registered UK trademarks, pending applications, and lapsed trademarks and applications since 1976. Updated weekly.

Subjects
Business

Audience
Business analysts

Content Summary
The records from this service include trademark name, design description, owner name and address, types of goods, and other data.

See Also
UK Company Library

User Guide
- ☑ Windows
- ☑ DOS
- ☑ Macintosh
- ☐ Terminal Emulation
- ☑ VMS
- ☑ UNIX
- ☑ OS/2
- ☐ Other platform

Cost
- ☐ Unknown
- ☐ Basic
- ☐ Extended
- ☑ Premium ($)
- ☐ Executive w/$

Activity Level: UNKNOWN (LOW–MEDIUM–HIGH)

Address
GO: **UKTRADEMARK**

BROADCASTING

Broadcast Professionals Forum

Description
The BPFORUM is the place where professionals in radio, TV, Land Mobile Radio and Audio share news and views about the latest in the industry.

Subjects
Broadcasting, Television

Audience
Radio operators

Content Summary
You can find information and messages about television, cable TV, broadcast engineering, audio, talent, post production, the FCC, and more in this forum.

See Also
Ham Radio Forum

User Guide
- ☑ Windows
- ☑ DOS
- ☑ Macintosh
- ☐ Terminal Emulation
- ☑ VMS
- ☑ UNIX
- ☑ OS/2
- ☐ Other platform

Cost
- ☐ Unknown
- ☐ Basic
- ☑ Extended
- ☐ Premium ($)
- ☐ Executive w/$

Activity Level: MEDIUM–HIGH (LOW–MEDIUM–HIGH)

Address
GO: **BPFORUM**

Media Newsletters

Description
The Broadcast & Publishing section of PTS Newsletter Database contains articles from leading newsletters covering broadcasting and publishing industries.

Subjects
Broadcasting, Newsletters, Publishing

Audience
Researchers, general public

Content Summary
These newsletters are a unique source of facts, figures, analyses, and current information on changing market and company conditions, company activities, new products and technologies, and government policies and trade agreements. The information available for an article includes title, newsletter name, publisher, and date of publication, as well as the full text of the article. An individual article may not include all of this information. You can choose from Description, Search Guidelines, Pricing Information, Media Newsletters Example, and Access Media Newsletters.

See Also
IQuest($)

User Guide
- ☑ Windows
- ☑ DOS
- ☑ Macintosh
- ☐ Terminal Emulation
- ☑ VMS
- ☑ UNIX
- ☑ OS/2
- ☐ Other platform

Broadcasting – Brooks Brothers Online Store

Cost
- ☐ Unknown
- ☐ Basic
- ☐ Extended
- ☑ Premium ($)
- ☐ Executive w/$

Activity Level: UNKNOWN (LOW – MEDIUM – HIGH)

Address
GO: **MEDIANEWS**

Society of Broadcast Eng.

Description
This is the main menu for the Society of Broadcast Engineers area, featuring Society news and access to the Broadcast Professionals Forum (BPFORUM).

Subjects
Broadcasting, Television

Audience
Broadcasters

Content Summary
The areas of this forum include access to the Broadcast Professionals Forum, a list of upcoming conventions, and an information request area.

See Also
Broadcast Professionals Forum

User Guide
- ☑ Windows
- ☑ DOS
- ☑ Macintosh
- ☐ Terminal Emulation
- ☐ VMS
- ☐ UNIX
- ☐ OS/2
- ☐ Other platform

Cost
- ☐ Unknown
- ☐ Basic
- ☑ Extended
- ☐ Premium ($)
- ☐ Executive w/$

Activity Level: LOW (LOW – MEDIUM – HIGH)

Address
GO: **SBENET**

Broderbund Software

Description
Online software store featuring popular products from Broderbund Software.

Subjects
Computers

Audience
Game enthusiasts

Content Summary
Look for the library and message sections that interest you the most, including PrintShop, Carmen Sandiego, Prince of Persia, Automap, CD-ROM information, and more.

See Also
Entertainment Forum

User Guide
- ☑ Windows
- ☑ DOS
- ☑ Macintosh
- ☐ Terminal Emulation
- ☐ VMS
- ☐ UNIX
- ☐ OS/2
- ☐ Other platform

Cost
- ☐ Unknown
- ☑ Basic
- ☐ Extended
- ☐ Premium ($)
- ☐ Executive w/$

Activity Level: UNKNOWN (LOW – MEDIUM – HIGH)

Address
GO: **BB**

Brooks Brothers Online Store

Description
Online shopping at America's oldest retail store.

Subjects
Clothing, Shopping

Audience
General public

Content Summary
Looking for men's clothing and furnishings? Look no further. This service enables you to order your Brooks Brothers apparel, including contemporary and classic clothing for women and young men.

See Also
Figi's Inc., Omaha Steaks

User Guide
- ☑ Windows
- ☑ DOS
- ☑ Macintosh
- ☐ Terminal Emulation
- ☑ VMS
- ☑ UNIX
- ☑ OS/2
- ☐ Other platform

Cost
- ☐ Unknown
- ☑ Basic
- ☐ Extended
- ☐ Premium ($)
- ☐ Executive w/$

Activity Level: UNKNOWN (LOW – MEDIUM – HIGH)

Address
GO: **BR**

BUSINESS

Accounting Vendor Forum

Description
A place where accountants, people who need accounting help, vendors, and users of accounting software can meet and share information.

Subjects
Accounting, Business

Audience
Accountants

Content Summary
The libraries contain product demonstrations, news, and information on the products supported by the participating vendors.

See Also
Business Forum

User Guide
- [x] Windows
- [x] DOS
- [x] Macintosh
- [ ] Terminal Emulation
- [ ] VMS
- [ ] UNIX
- [ ] OS/2
- [ ] Other platform

Cost
- [ ] Unknown
- [ ] Basic
- [x] Extended
- [ ] Premium ($)
- [ ] Executive w/$

Activity Level

Address
GO: **ACCOUNTING**

BASIS International Forum

Description
The BASIS International Forum exists to support the business applications developer who uses BASIS supplied software development tools.

Subjects
Business, Computers

Audience
MIS people

Content Summary
You'll find library and message topics on BBxProgression/4, TAOS 4GL, TAOS/Views Report Writer, and more.

See Also
IBM File Finder

User Guide
- [ ] Windows
- [x] DOS
- [ ] Macintosh
- [ ] Terminal Emulation
- [ ] VMS
- [ ] UNIX
- [ ] OS/2
- [x] Other platform

Cost
- [ ] Unknown
- [ ] Basic
- [x] Extended
- [ ] Premium ($)
- [ ] Executive w/$

Activity Level

Address
GO: **BASIS**

British Trade Marks

Description
A database of all registered UK trademarks, pending applications, and lapsed trademarks and applications since 1976. Updated weekly.

Subjects
Business

Audience
Business analysts

Content Summary
The records from this service include trademark name, design description, owner name and address, types of goods, and other data.

See Also
UK Company Library

User Guide
- [x] Windows
- [x] DOS
- [x] Macintosh
- [ ] Terminal Emulation
- [x] VMS
- [x] UNIX
- [x] OS/2
- [ ] Other platform

Cost
- [ ] Unknown
- [ ] Basic
- [ ] Extended
- [x] Premium ($)
- [ ] Executive w/$

Activity Level

UNKNOWN

Address
GO: **UKTRADEMARK**

Census Bureau Online Service

Description
The United States Census Bureau provides a selection of its statistical reports on a wide variety of subjects, at no extra cost.

Business

Subjects
Business, Statistics

Audience
Researchers

Content Summary
Libraries include census reports, and reports on population, agriculture, business, construction, housing, foreign trade, and government.

See Also
Business Demographics

User Guide
- ☑ Windows
- ☑ DOS
- ☑ Macintosh
- ☐ Terminal Emulation
- ☐ VMS
- ☑ UNIX
- ☐ OS/2
- ☐ Other platform

Cost
- ☐ Unknown
- ☐ Basic
- ☑ Extended
- ☐ Premium ($)
- ☐ Executive w/$

Activity Level — UNKNOWN

Address
GO: **CENDATA**

Consumer Forum

Description
The place to find out how to make and save money, learn about your consumer rights, get buying advice, and read about scams and ripoffs.

Subjects
Business, Money

Audience
Consumers

Content Summary
Libraries include consumer information on automobiles, banking, bargains, coupons, complaints, rights, ripoffs, and money. You can even ask David Horowitz, a recognized expert, questions about products and consumer rights.

See Also
Consumer Reports

User Guide
- ☑ Windows
- ☑ DOS
- ☑ Macintosh
- ☐ Terminal Emulation
- ☐ VMS
- ☑ UNIX
- ☐ OS/2
- ☐ Other platform

Cost
- ☐ Unknown
- ☑ Basic
- ☑ Extended
- ☐ Premium ($)
- ☐ Executive w/$

Activity Level — MEDIUM (arrow pointing to LOW)

Address
GO: **CONSUMER**

D&B Dun's Canadian Market Identifiers

Description
The Canadian Dun's Market Identifiers database contains directory information on about 350,000 Canadian companies. You can see company name, address, and telephone number. You also can get sales figures, number of employees, and executives' names.

Subjects
Canadian Company Profiles, Business, Finance, Dun and Bradstreet

Audience
Accounting persons, businesspersons, executives, investors, journalists, management, researchers

Content Summary
Depending on the company listing, you might or might not see all the information detailed in the Description area. To retrieve records, enter the company name, geographic location, product or service, number of employees, or sales as your search criteria. For help on searching, select Choice 2, "Search Guidelines," from the main menu. The cost of this service is as follows:

- Search (retrieves up to 5 names): $7.50
- Additional names (in groups of 5): $7.50
- Full reference (selected from the names): $7.50

In addition to connect time charges, you are charged $1.00 for a search that retrieves no titles.

See Also
Company Information, Corporate Affiliations, D&B Dun's Electronic Business Directory, D&B Dun's Market Identifiers, Financial Forums, Investors' Forum, Tenderlink, TRW Business Profiles

User Guide
- ☑ Windows
- ☑ DOS
- ☑ Macintosh
- ☐ Terminal Emulation
- ☑ VMS
- ☑ UNIX
- ☑ OS/2
- ☐ Other platform

Cost
- ☐ Unknown
- ☐ Basic
- ☐ Extended
- ☑ Premium ($)
- ☐ Executive w/$

Activity Level
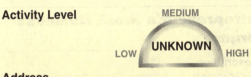

Address
GO: **DBCAN**

D&B Dun's Electronic Business Directory

Description
You can obtain a directory of over 8.5 million U.S. public and private businesses and professionals using this Dun and Bradstreet service. Available information includes name, address, phone number, type of business, its parent company, the industry it belongs to, the SIC code, number of employees, and the population of the city in which the business resides.

Subjects
Business, Finance, Investment, Dun and Bradstreet

Audience
Accounting persons, businesspersons, executives, investors, journalists, management, researchers

Content Summary
To search, select Choice 5, "Access Dun's Electronic Business Directory," from the main menu. Next, select the criterion for your search, such as company name or product or service; enter a name, word, or phrase that describes the company or product; and follow the on-screen instructions. See Choice 7, "Search Guidelines," for more help. The cost of this service is as follows:

- Search (retrieves up to 5 names): $7.50
- Additional names (in groups of 5): $7.50

In addition to connect time charges, you are charged $1.00 for a search that retrieves no titles.

See Also
Company Information, Corporate Affiliations, D&B Dun's Canadian Market Identifiers, D&B Dun's Market Identifiers, Financial Forums, Investors' Forum, Tenderlink, TRW Business Profiles

User Guide
- ☑ Windows
- ☑ DOS
- ☑ Macintosh
- ☐ Terminal Emulation
- ☑ VMS
- ☑ UNIX
- ☑ OS/2
- ☐ Other platform

Cost
- ☐ Unknown
- ☐ Basic
- ☐ Extended
- ☑ Premium ($)
- ☐ Executive w/$

Activity Level
UNKNOWN (LOW–MEDIUM–HIGH)

Address
GO: **DYP** or **DUNSEBD**

D&B Dun's Market Identifiers

Description
With this service, you can search three of Dun and Bradstreet's directories of business information, including information on over 6.7 million U.S. public and private businesses that have over $1 million in sales or more than five employees, information on over 350,000 Canadian companies, and information on over 2.1 million public, private, and government controlled international companies.

Subjects
Business, Finance, Investment, Dun and Bradstreet

Audience
Accounting persons, businesspersons, executives, investors, management, researchers

Content Summary
When you perform a search, you can get the company name, address, telephone number, sales figures, number of employees, parent company, and names of executives. The price of this service is as follows:

- Search (retrieves up to 5 names): $7.50
- Additional names (in groups of 5): $7.50
- Full reference (selected from the names): $7.50

In addition to connect time charges, you are charged $1.00 for a search that retrieves no titles.

See Also
Company Information, Corporate Affiliations, D&B Dun's Canadian Market Identifiers, Financial Forums, Investors' Forum, Tenderlink, TRW Business Profiles

User Guide
- ☑ Windows
- ☑ DOS
- ☑ Macintosh
- ☐ Terminal Emulation
- ☑ VMS
- ☑ UNIX
- ☑ OS/2
- ☐ Other platform

Cost
- ☐ Unknown
- ☐ Basic
- ☐ Extended
- ☑ Premium ($)
- ☐ Executive w/$

Activity Level

Address
GO: **DUNS** or **DMI**

Business

Entrepreneur's Small Business Forum

Description
Sponsored by Entrepreneur Group, the publishers of *Entrepreneur Magazine*, the Entrepreneur's Small Business Forum enables you to identify and communicate with other entrepreneurs in different cities and locales. This forum welcomes the sharing of information and helpful dialogue from all members.

Subjects
Business, Entrepreneurs, Free Enterprise, Small Business

Audience
Business owners, entrepreneurs, venture capitalists

Content Summary
The libraries contain information on business opportunities, start-up techniques, marketing and promotion files, financing, legal issues, planning files, and international issues. Check out the information in Library 13, "Homebased Business," if you are thinking about starting, or are maintaining, a business from your home. You also should take part in the message section if you have specific questions to ask.

See Also
Entrepreneur Small Business Square, Business Franchise and Opportunities Database

User Guide
- ☑ Windows
- ☑ DOS
- ☑ Macintosh
- ☐ Terminal Emulation
- ☑ VMS
- ☑ UNIX
- ☑ OS/2
- ☐ Other platform

Cost
- ☐ Unknown
- ☐ Basic
- ☑ Extended
- ☐ Premium ($)
- ☐ Executive w/$

Activity Level
MEDIUM (arrow pointing up between LOW and HIGH)

Address
GO: **USEN**

Executive News Service

Description
You can search the latest international news, weather, and sports from the world's major news agencies. This powerful news clipping service can scan many news sources for stories you specify and deliver them to you daily.

Subjects
Business, Financial News, International News, News

Audience
Business people

Content Summary
You can read about financial events in Reuters Financial Report and OTC NewsAlert, as well as in the daily headlines of The Washington Post. To use the News by Company Ticker option, enter a company ticker symbol and check on business news filed within the past 24 hours. For the News Clips option, you can read through special clipping folders set up by CompuServe to keep you up on specific news topics. You also can set up your own Personal area in which you specify the type of news you want to read by typing in key phrases. ENS then sends you electronic news "clippings" that you can read. ENS costs $15 per hour plus the base connect rates.

See Also
AP Sports($), Financial Forums, Global Crises Forum, NewsGrid, Newspaper Archives($), Reuter News Pictures Forum, United Press Int'l($), U.S. News Forum

User Guide
- ☑ Windows
- ☑ DOS
- ☐ Macintosh
- ☐ Terminal Emulation
- ☐ VMS
- ☐ UNIX
- ☐ OS/2
- ☐ Other platform

Cost
- ☐ Unknown
- ☐ Basic
- ☐ Extended
- ☑ Premium ($)
- ☐ Executive w/$

Activity Level
UNKNOWN (between LOW and HIGH, MEDIUM above)

Address
GO: **ENS**

Financial Forums

Description
From this service, you can access several financial forums and ask questions about financial concerns, investments, the economy, or financial software.

Subjects
Business

Audience
Accountants, investors

Content Summary
The Financial Forums main menu has the following options from which to choose: Investors Forum, NAIC Forum, MECA Software Forum, Intuit Forum, CA-Simply Forum, IRI Software Forum, The World of Lotus, Borland International, Consumer Forum. For more information on any of these forums, see the specific forum.

Business

See Also
Citibank's Global Report

User Guide
- ☑ Windows
- ☑ DOS
- ☑ Macintosh
- ☐ Terminal Emulation
- ☑ VMS
- ☑ UNIX
- ☑ OS/2
- ☐ Other platform

Cost
- ☐ Unknown
- ☑ Basic
- ☐ Extended
- ☐ Premium ($)
- ☐ Executive w/$

Activity Level UNKNOWN

Address
GO: FINFORUM

Global Report

Description
This is Citibank's online information resource database, where you can find data on a number of large corporations worldwide.

Subjects
Business, Databases, Financial News

Audience
Financial analysts, accountants, business researchers, business and financial researchers

Content Summary
Launched by Citibank in 1986, Global Report has become the primary information resource for a number of large corporations worldwide because it integrates and organizes news and financial data from well-respected sources, allowing for quick and easy information retrieval. For pricing information, see the Pricing/Sample Reports option on the Global Report main menu. If you're new to this service, be sure to choose the Important Pages option on the main menu to see a list of important searching criteria.

See Also
D&B Dun's Electronic Business Directory, TRW Bus. Credit Reports

User Guide
- ☑ Windows
- ☑ DOS
- ☑ Macintosh
- ☐ Terminal Emulation
- ☐ VMS
- ☑ UNIX
- ☑ OS/2
- ☐ Other platform

Cost
- ☐ Unknown
- ☐ Basic
- ☐ Extended
- ☑ Premium ($)
- ☐ Executive w/$

Activity Level UNKNOWN

Address
GO: GLOREP

OTC NewsAlert

Description
Search the latest international news, weather, and sports from the world's major news agencies. A powerful news clipping service that can scan many news sources for stories you specify and deliver them to you daily.

Subjects
Business, Financial News, International News, News

Audience
Associated Press Forum, Associated Press Online

Content Summary
You can read financial events through Reuters Financial Report and OTC NewsAlert, as well as read the day's headlines with The Washington Post. To use the News by Company Ticker option, enter a company ticker symbol and check on business news filed within the past 24 hours. For the News Clips option, you can read through special clipping folders set up by CompuServe to keep you up on specific news topics. You also set up your own Personal area in which you specify the type of news that you want to read by typing in key phrases. ENS then sends you electronic news clippings that you can read. ENS costs $15 per hour plus the base connect rates.

See Also
AP Sports, Financial Forums, Global Crises Forum, NewsGrid, Newspaper Archives, Reuters News Pictures Forum, United Press International, U.S. News Forum

User Guide
- ☑ Windows
- ☑ DOS
- ☐ Macintosh
- ☐ Terminal Emulation
- ☐ VMS
- ☐ UNIX
- ☐ OS/2
- ☐ Other platform

Cost
- ☐ Unknown
- ☐ Basic
- ☐ Extended
- ☑ Premium ($)
- ☐ Executive w/$

Activity Level UNKNOWN

Address
GO: ENS

Business

Standard Indus. Class.

Description
This is a database of SIC (industrial classification) codes, searchable by industry.

Subjects
Business, Databases

Audience
Researchers, business people

Content Summary
This database provides industrial information to business professionals.

See Also
IQuest Business Management

User Guide
- ☑ Windows
- ☑ DOS
- ☑ Macintosh
- ☐ Terminal Emulation
- ☐ VMS
- ☑ UNIX
- ☐ OS/2
- ☑ Other platform

Cost
- ☐ Unknown
- ☐ Basic
- ☑ Extended
- ☐ Premium ($)
- ☐ Executive w/$

Activity Level

Address
GO: **SICCODE**

The Absolut Museum

Description
Online area providing information and graphics files from Absolut Vodka.

Subjects
Entertainment, Hobbies

Audience
Absolut Vodka Enthusiasts

Content Summary
See famous artist's renditions of Absolut Vodka containers and read about upcoming events.

See Also
Bacchus Wine Forum

User Guide
- ☑ Windows
- ☑ DOS
- ☑ Macintosh
- ☐ Terminal Emulation
- ☑ VMS
- ☑ UNIX
- ☑ OS/2
- ☐ Other platform

Cost
- ☐ Unknown
- ☑ Basic
- ☐ Extended
- ☐ Premium ($)
- ☐ Executive w/$

Activity Level

Address
GO: **ABS**

The Business Wire

Description
News area offering press releases, news articles, and other information from the world of business.

Subjects
Business, Finance

Audience
Business People

Content Summary
The libraries include press releases, news articles, and information about specific companies. It is updated daily.

See Also
AP Online

User Guide
- ☑ Windows
- ☑ DOS
- ☐ Macintosh
- ☐ Terminal Emulation
- ☐ VMS
- ☐ UNIX
- ☐ OS/2
- ☐ Other platform

Cost
- ☐ Unknown
- ☐ Basic
- ☑ Extended
- ☐ Premium ($)
- ☐ Executive w/$

Activity Level

Address
GO: **TBW**

The Company Corporation

Description
The Company Corp. offers information on incorporating your business. You can even incorporate online.

Subjects
Business

Audience
Business People

Business

Content Summary
If you want to start a business, this forum can provide the answers to the legal questions of how to incorporate.

See Also
Company Analyzer

User Guide
- ☑ Windows
- ☑ DOS
- ☑ Macintosh
- ☐ Terminal Emulation
- ☑ VMS
- ☑ UNIX
- ☐ OS/2
- ☑ Other platform

Cost
- ☐ Unknown
- ☑ Basic
- ☐ Extended
- ☐ Premium ($)
- ☐ Executive w/$

Activity Level

Address
GO: **CORP**

The Entrepreneur's Forum

Description
Forum sponsored by *Entrepreneur Magazine* to meet with its readers around the world.

Subjects
Business

Audience
Entrepreneurs

Content Summary
Libraries include business start-up procedures and the development of your business.

See Also
Business

User Guide
- ☑ Windows
- ☑ DOS
- ☐ Macintosh
- ☐ Terminal Emulation
- ☐ VMS
- ☐ UNIX
- ☐ OS/2
- ☐ Other platform

Cost
- ☐ Unknown
- ☐ Basic
- ☑ Extended
- ☐ Premium ($)
- ☐ Executive w/$

Activity Level

Address
GO: **USEN**

TRADEMARKSCAN

Description
Two databases containing state and USA information on trademarks and applications currently on file.

Subjects
Trademarks

Audience
Businesspeople, attorneys

Content Summary
This database contains two sources of information. One provides the U.S. Patent and Trademark Office information. The other is the U.S. State database of trademark registration.

See Also
British Trademarks

User Guide
- ☑ Windows
- ☑ DOS
- ☐ Macintosh
- ☐ Terminal Emulation
- ☐ VMS
- ☐ UNIX
- ☐ OS/2
- ☐ Other platform

Cost
- ☐ Unknown
- ☐ Basic
- ☑ Extended
- ☐ Premium ($)
- ☐ Executive w/$

Activity Level

Address
GO: **TRADERC**

UK Company Library

Description
Database containing financial and other information on companies in the United Kingdom.

Subjects
Finance

Audience
Businesspeople

Content Summary
This database enables members to research British companies for information on business standing, products or services offered, and address.

See Also
Business Dateline

User Guide
- ☑ Windows
- ☑ DOS
- ☐ Macintosh
- ☐ Terminal Emulation
- ☐ VMS
- ☐ UNIX
- ☐ OS/2
- ☐ Other platform

Business

Cost
- ☐ Unknown
- ☐ Basic
- ☑ Extended
- ☐ Premium ($)
- ☐ Executive w/$

Activity Level: UNKNOWN (Low—High)

Address
GO:**UKLIB**

UK Historical Stock Pricing

Description
Database offering historical data on stock and bond issues from the United Kingdom. Updated daily.

Subjects
Investment

Audience
Investors

Contents Summary
This database offers members the capability to access historical data on stocks and bonds of the United Kingdom.

See Also
European Company Library

User Guide
- ☑ Windows
- ☑ DOS
- ☐ Macintosh
- ☐ Terminal Emulation
- ☐ VMS
- ☐ UNIX
- ☐ OS/2
- ☐ Other platform

Cost
- ☐ Unknown
- ☐ Basic
- ☑ Extended
- ☐ Premium ($)
- ☐ Executive w/$

Activity Level: UNKNOWN (Low—High)

Address
GO:**UKPRICE**

UK Professionals Forum

Description
UK Professionals deals with issues of interest to professionals living in the UK.

Subjects
UK

Audience
UK professionals

Content Summary
The libraries and message area include information about job opportunities, news, and professional groups.

See Also
European Company Library

User Guide
- ☑ Windows
- ☑ DOS
- ☐ Macintosh
- ☐ Terminal Emulation
- ☐ VMS
- ☐ UNIX
- ☐ OS/2
- ☐ Other platform

Cost
- ☐ Unknown
- ☐ Basic
- ☑ Extended
- ☐ Premium ($)
- ☐ Executive w/$

Activity Level: MEDIUM (Low—High)

Address
GO:**UKPROF**

Working-From-Home Forum

Description
This is a forum for those who work from their homes, uniting them with others in similar circumstances. Users can exchange info, share solutions, etc.

Subjects
Computers

Audience
Home-based workers

Content Summary
The libraries and message areas contain information on taxes, business setup, equipment recommendations, and areas to exchange information.

See Also
Entrepreneurs Forum

User Guide
- ☑ Windows
- ☑ DOS
- ☑ Macintosh
- ☐ Terminal Emulation
- ☑ VMS
- ☑ UNIX
- ☑ OS/2
- ☐ Other platform

Cost
- ☐ Unknown
- ☐ Basic
- ☑ Extended
- ☐ Premium ($)
- ☐ Executive w/$

Activity Level: MEDIUM (Low—High)

Address
GO: **WORK**

C- CAD

C

Cabletron Systems Forum

Description
Cabletron Forum provides help and information with questions or problems concerning Cabletron products or computer networking in general.

Subjects
Computers, Networking

Audience
Product users, network administrators

Content Summary
The libraries of this forum contain information about networking, Cabletron products, DNI cards, Ethernet, Token Ring, WAN, LANVIEW, and FDDI.

See Also
Cabletron Systems Menu

User Guide
- ☑ Windows
- ☑ DOS
- ☐ Macintosh
- ☐ Terminal Emulation
- ☐ VMS
- ☐ UNIX
- ☐ OS/2
- ☐ Other platform

Cost
- ☐ Unknown
- ☐ Basic
- ☑ Extended
- ☐ Premium ($)
- ☐ Executive w/$

Activity level

Address
GO: **CTRONFORUM**

Cabletron Systems Menu

Description
The menu provides access to information concerning Cabletron Systems, Inc.

Subjects
Computers, Networking

Audience
Network administrators

Content Summary
Included in the libraries are information on the corporate background of Cabletron, list of sales offices, training and presentation centers, and points of interest to users of Cabletron products.

See Also
Cabletron Systems Forum

User Guide
- ☑ Windows
- ☑ DOS
- ☑ Macintosh
- ☐ Terminal Emulation
- ☐ VMS
- ☑ UNIX
- ☐ OS/2
- ☐ Other platform

Cost
- ☐ Unknown
- ☐ Basic
- ☑ Extended
- ☐ Premium ($)
- ☐ Executive w/$

Activity Level

Address
GO: **CTRON**

CAD

Autodesk AutoCAD Forum

Description
An open forum for anyone with an interest in Computer Aided Design, with an emphasis on Autodesk products.

Subjects
CAD, Computers, Software

Audience
Autodesk products users

Content Summary
Discussions of Autodesk products: AutoCAD AME™, ADS™, AutoFlix™. Discusses applications software, hardware, operating systems and languages and CAD management and productivity. Also maintains sections where issues are discussed surrounding important applications markets: A/E/C, MCAD/MCAE, GIS, Civil Engineering. Libraries contain various utilites, add-ons, support files, and product information.

See Also
Autodesk Retail Products Forum, Autodesk Software Forum, CADD/CAM/CAE Vendor Forum, IBM CAD/CAM Forum

User Guide
- ☑ Windows
- ☑ DOS
- ☐ Macintosh
- ☐ Terminal Emulation
- ☐ VMS
- ☐ UNIX
- ☐ OS/2
- ☐ Other platform

Cost
- ☐ Unknown
- ☐ Basic
- ☑ Extended
- ☐ Premium ($)
- ☐ Executive w/$

CAD

Activity Level

Address
GO: **ACAD**

Autodesk Multimedia Forum

Description
Support for the Autodesk line of PC and workstation-based graphics programs.

Subjects
CAD, Computers, Multimedia

Audience
Autodesk products users

Content Summary
Provides an open forum for anyone who uses multimedia and Science Series products and more generally for those with an interest in computer graphics. Discusses Autodesk Animator, Autodesk 3D Studio, HyperChem, CA Lab and Chaos and related issues like hardware, operating systems and networks. Also maintains a wishlist section where you may suggest ways to improve products and policies. Libraries contain various utilites, add-ons, support files, and product information.

See Also
Autodesk Retail Products Forum

User Guide
- ☑ Windows
- ☑ DOS
- ☐ Macintosh
- ☐ Terminal Emulation
- ☐ VMS
- ☐ UNIX
- ☐ OS/2
- ☐ Other platform

Cost
- ☐ Unknown
- ☐ Basic
- ☑ Extended
- ☐ Premium ($)
- ☐ Executive w/$

Activity Level

Address
GO: **ASOFT**

Autodesk Retail Products Forum

Description
An open forum for anyone interested in low-cost Precision Graphics software, with an emphasis on Autodesk Retail Division products.

Subjects
CAD, Computers, Software

Audience
Autodesk products users

Content Summary
Provides an open forum for anyone with an interest in low-cost Precision Graphics software. The primary purpose of the Forum is to support users of the products marketed by the Retail Products division of Autodesk, Inc. At the same time it welcomes discussion of the issues and concerns of forum members as related to products, the company itself, and how to provide the best possible solutions to your CADD and Graphics needs. Libraries contain various utilites, add-ons, support files, and product information.

See Also
Autodesk Retail Products Forum, Autodesk Software Forum, CADD/CAM/CAE Vendor Forum, IBM CAD/CAM Forum

User Guide
- ☑ Windows
- ☑ DOS
- ☐ Macintosh
- ☐ Terminal Emulation
- ☐ VMS
- ☐ UNIX
- ☐ OS/2
- ☐ Other platform

Cost
- ☐ Unknown
- ☐ Basic
- ☑ Extended
- ☐ Premium ($)
- ☐ Executive w/$

Activity Level

Address
GO: **ARETAIL**

Cadence Forum

Description
The online electronic edition of *CADENCE* magazine, offering code listings and executable programs from each monthly issue.

Subjects
CAD/CAM, Computers

Audience
CAD professionals

See Also
CADD/CAM/CAE Vendor Forum, Autodesk AutoCAD Forum, Autodesk Software Forum

User Guide
- ☑ Windows
- ☑ DOS
- ☑ Macintosh
- ☐ Terminal Emulation
- ☐ VMS
- ☐ UNIX
- ☐ OS/2
- ☐ Other platform

Cost
- ☐ Unknown
- ☐ Basic
- ☑ Extended
- ☐ Premium ($)
- ☐ Executive w/$

CAD - CADD/CAM/CAE Vendor Forum

Activity Level

LOW ← MEDIUM — HIGH

Address
GO: **CADENCE**

MicroStation Forum

Description
This forum is devoted to the discussion and support of Bentley Systems Incorporated's MicroStation CAD product.

Subjects
CAD, Computers

Audience
Computer engineers

Content Summary
The library and message sections include MicroStation in General, 3rd Party Products, Programming, Input Devices, Printing/Plotting, Video/Graphics, Databases, Marketing, Change Requests, User Groups, What's New, and The Dialogue Box. Some of the libraries are empty. To download a copy of the Space Station image, see Library 1 for SPACE.JPG.

See Also
Autodesk AutoCAD Forum

User Guide
- ☑ Windows
- ☑ DOS
- ☐ Macintosh
- ☐ Terminal Emulation
- ☐ VMS
- ☑ UNIX
- ☐ OS/2
- ☐ Other platform

Cost
- ☐ Unknown
- ☐ Basic
- ☑ Extended
- ☐ Premium ($)
- ☐ Executive w/$

Activity Level

LOW — MEDIUM ↑ HIGH

Address
GO: **MSTATION**

Engineering Automation Forum

Description
LEAP (League for Engineering Productivity) sponsors this forum for discussions about CADD/CAM and other programs that are used by engineers, architects, and other professionals for design.

Subjects
CADD/CAM, Engineering, Computers, Computer-Aided Design

Audience
CADD/CAM engineers, engineers, designers

Content Summary
You can find discussions that will help you find the right CADD/CAM product for you, tips on using programs, information on new technologies, and management tools and utilities. Visit Library 9, "Classified/Jobs," for job opportunities and resumes.

See Also
IBM CAD/CAM Forum, CASE DCI Forum

User Guide
- ☑ Windows
- ☑ DOS
- ☑ Macintosh
- ☐ Terminal Emulation
- ☐ VMS
- ☐ UNIX
- ☐ OS/2
- ☐ Other platform

Cost
- ☐ Unknown
- ☐ Basic
- ☑ Extended
- ☐ Premium ($)
- ☐ Executive w/$

Activity Level

LOW — MEDIUM ↑ HIGH

Address
GO: **LEAP**

CADD/CAM/CAE Vendor Forum

Description
Discussion and support for users of products from the companies represented here.

Subjects
Computer Graphics, Computers

Audience
CAD professionals

Content Summary
Products represented in this forum include UTS/TK Solver!, EasyCAD/FastCAD, ISICAD, CADlink, CADKEY, ASHLAR, and IBM CAD to name just a few.

See Also
Cadence, Graphics Forum

User Guide
- ☑ Windows
- ☑ DOS
- ☐ Macintosh
- ☐ Terminal Emulation
- ☐ VMS
- ☐ UNIX
- ☐ OS/2
- ☐ Other platform

Cost
- ☐ Unknown
- ☐ Basic
- ☑ Extended
- ☐ Premium ($)
- ☐ Executive w/$

California Forum

Description
The California Forum is a wealth of information on California, its better-known residents, the history of California, and California today.

Subjects
Recreation

Audience
Californians

Content Summary
This Forum is dedicated to the people and places of the most densely populated state in the United States! The California Forum is divided into three parts: a library where data and text files are stored, a message board where members may send messages between each other, and a conference area where members may conduct real-time conversations with each other. Libraries contain information broken up by region along with some graphics files.

See Also
Travel Forum

User Guide
- ☑ Windows
- ☑ DOS
- ☑ Macintosh
- ☐ Terminal Emulation
- ☐ VMS
- ☑ UNIX
- ☐ OS/2
- ☐ Other platform

Cost
- ☐ Unknown
- ☐ Basic
- ☑ Extended
- ☐ Premium ($)
- ☐ Executive w/$

Activity Level

Address
GO: **CALFORUM**

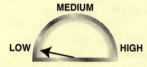

Photography Forum

Description
In this forum, photo enthusiasts of all expertise levels can meet and exchange ideas on topics ranging from tips on how to take good pictures to what type of equipment is needed.

Subjects
Cameras, Hobbies, Photography

Audience
Computer graphics, photographers

Content Summary
The Photography Forum offers many library areas of interest to photography enthusiasts of all levels. Of particular interest are conferences with famous photographers in which participants can ask questions or have their work critiqued. Also included are message areas on commonly asked questions, such as "What makes good photograph composition?". If you are looking for a camera or additional equipment, the numerous press releases on various equipment can be helpful.

See Also
Graphics Forum, Quick Picture Forum

User Guide
- ☑ Windows
- ☑ DOS
- ☑ Macintosh
- ☐ Terminal Emulation
- ☑ VMS
- ☑ UNIX
- ☑ OS/2
- ☐ Other platform

Cost
- ☐ Unknown
- ☐ Basic
- ☑ Extended
- ☐ Premium ($)
- ☐ Executive w/$

Activity Level

Address
GO: **PHOTOFORUM**

Recreational Vehicle Forum

Description
This forum is for all people who enjoy camping in tent trailers, travel trailers, fifth-wheels, and motor homes. If you are an experienced camper or are just looking for a motor home, this forum can help.

Subjects
Camping, Motor Homes, Travel

Audience
Camping enthusiasts, travel enthusiasts, RV enthusiasts

Content Summary
This forum not only provides up-to-date information about products and services for the travel trailer industry, but also provides articles and discussions

on where to go, where to stay, and what to do. Participants also state opinions and make recommendations on which RV to purchase and where to go for service. There's even a classified section if you are looking to purchase a recreational vehicle.

See Also
Travel Forum

User Guide
- ☑ Windows
- ☑ DOS
- ☑ Macintosh
- ☐ Terminal Emulation
- ☑ VMS
- ☑ UNIX
- ☑ OS/2
- ☐ Other platform

Cost
- ☐ Unknown
- ☐ Basic
- ☑ Extended
- ☐ Premium ($)
- ☐ Executive w/$

Activity Level
LOW ← MEDIUM HIGH

Address
GO: **RVFORUM**

CAMPUS ACTIVITIES AND STUDENT NEWSPAPER

The Sysop Forum

Description
Private forum hosted by CIS for the training of forum sysops and discussion of forum issues.

Subjects
Academic Research, Campus Activities and Student Newspaper

Audience
Administrators, adoptees, accountants

Content Summary
This forum is not available to all users; only those members training to be Sysops.

See Also
Practice Forum (FREE), CompuServe Help Forum (FREE), IBM Bulletin Board Forum

User Guide
- ☑ Windows
- ☑ DOS
- ☑ Macintosh
- ☑ Terminal Emulation
- ☑ VMS
- ☑ UNIX
- ☑ OS/2
- ☐ Other platform

Cost
- ☐ Unknown
- ☐ Basic
- ☑ Extended
- ☐ Premium ($)
- ☐ Executive w/$

Activity Level
LOW ↑ MEDIUM HIGH

Address
GO: **SYSOP**

CANCER

Health and Fitness Forum

Description
This forum provides health-related information and support groups for their members. Learn about exercise, nutrition, mental health, and other health items.

Subjects
Fitness, Health, Martial Arts

Audience
Anyone

Content Summary
The message library sections contain various health-related files and information and are divided into several topics, including Addiction/Recovery, Mental Health, Family Health, The Doctor's Inn, Exercise & Fitness, Master's Swimming, Running & Racing, Nutrition, Martial Arts, and Self Help. The Martial Arts library is very popular.

See Also
Health and Vitamin Express, Health Database Plus($), Health/Fitness, HealthNet, Holistic Health Forum

User Guide
- ☑ Windows
- ☑ DOS
- ☑ Macintosh
- ☐ Terminal Emulation
- ☐ VMS
- ☐ UNIX
- ☐ OS/2
- ☐ Other platform

Cost
- ☐ Unknown
- ☐ Basic
- ☑ Extended
- ☐ Premium ($)
- ☐ Executive w/$

Activity Level
LOW ← MEDIUM HIGH

Address
GO: **GOODHEALTH**

Canon Net Menu

Description
This menu provides access to services and information from Canon Computer Services, Inc.

Subjects
Hobbies, Photography

Audience
Product users

Content Summary
The libraries of this forum contain information about Canon, a list of regional offices, service facilities, and information on the Clean Earth Campaign.

See Also
Canon Support Forum

User Guide
- ☑ Windows
- ☑ DOS
- ☑ Macintosh
- ☐ Terminal Emulation
- ☐ VMS
- ☑ UNIX
- ☐ OS/2
- ☐ Other platform

Cost
- ☐ Unknown
- ☐ Basic
- ☑ Extended
- ☐ Premium ($)
- ☐ Executive w/$

Activity Level

Address
GO: **CANON**

Canon Support Forum

Description
Support for users of products from both Canon Computer Systems, Inc., and Canon USA.

Subjects
Hobbies, Photography

Audience
Product users

Content Summary
Product information contained in this libary includes laser printers, bubble jet printers, ImageScanners, digital copiers, and 35mm cameras.

See Also
Canon Net Menu

User Guide
- ☑ Windows
- ☑ DOS
- ☑ Macintosh
- ☐ Terminal Emulation
- ☐ VMS
- ☑ UNIX
- ☐ OS/2
- ☐ Other platform

Cost
- ☐ Unknown
- ☐ Basic
- ☑ Extended
- ☐ Premium ($)
- ☐ Executive w/$

Activity Level

Address
GO: **CAN-10**

Canopus Research Forum

Description
A place where computer and communications industry companies, products, technologies, markets, and trends can be freely discussed.

Subjects
Computers

Audience
Computer professionals

Content Summary
This forum provides open discussion on computer industry trends and technologies. Also included are discussions on operating system wars, hardware, and software.

See Also
IBM OS/2 Support Forum, Microsoft 32-bit Language Forum

User Guide
- ☑ Windows
- ☑ DOS
- ☑ Macintosh
- ☐ Terminal Emulation
- ☐ VMS
- ☑ UNIX
- ☐ OS/2
- ☐ Other platform

Cost
- ☐ Unknown
- ☐ Basic
- ☑ Extended
- ☐ Premium ($)
- ☐ Executive w/$

Activity Level

Address
GO: **CANOPUS**

CASE-DCI Forum

Description
CASEFORUM is a place where people interested in creating software in a more effective manner can meet and discuss concepts and tools.

Subjects
Computer Programming, Computers

Audience
Software developers

CASE-DCI Forum - Catalogs

Content Summary
Topics of interest to software developers include computer-aided software engineering and product details.

See Also
Borland C++ for Win/OS2 Forum, Borland C++/DOS Forum, Borland Pascal Forum, Programming MS Apps.

User Guide
- ☑ Windows
- ☑ DOS
- ☐ Macintosh
- ☐ Terminal Emulation
- ☐ VMS
- ☐ UNIX
- ☐ OS/2
- ☐ Other platform

Cost
- ☐ Unknown
- ☐ Basic
- ☑ Extended
- ☐ Premium ($)
- ☐ Executive w/$

Activity Level

Address
GO: **CASEFORUM**

CATALOGS

Omaha Steaks International

Description
Order thick, juicy steaks online from Omaha Steaks International, which has been in business since 1917.

Subjects
Food, Catalogs

Audience
General public

Content Summary
From the main menu, you can choose from several options, including Order From Our Online Catalog, Product QuickSearch, Customer Service, Welcome to Omaha Steaks International, Order Our Free Catalog, Order From Our Print Catalog, Join Our Electronic Mailing List, Recipe of the Month, and Special Offer.

See Also
Adventurees in Food Forum

User Guide
- ☑ Windows
- ☑ DOS
- ☑ Macintosh
- ☐ Terminal Emulation
- ☑ VMS
- ☑ UNIX
- ☐ OS/2
- ☐ Other platform

Cost
- ☐ Unknown
- ☑ Basic
- ☐ Extended
- ☐ Premium ($)
- ☐ Executive w/$

Activity Level

Address
GO: **OS**

PC Catalog

Description
PC Catalog features more than 2,000 product listings, spanning networking, microcomputers, and new technology.

Subjects
Computers, Catalogs

Audience
Computer users

Content Summary
From the PC Catalog main menu, you can select Shop Our Online Catalog, What is PC Catalog, What's New, Gif Images, Customer Service, Visit PC Publications, and more.

See Also
MicroWarehouse, IBM Personal Software Products, CompuServe Store

User Guide
- ☑ Windows
- ☑ DOS
- ☑ Macintosh
- ☐ Terminal Emulation
- ☑ VMS
- ☑ UNIX
- ☐ OS/2
- ☐ Other platform

Cost
- ☐ Unknown
- ☑ Basic
- ☐ Extended
- ☐ Premium ($)
- ☐ Executive w/$

Activity Level
UNKNOWN

Address
GO: **PCA**

PRC Publishing

Description
PRC's Database Publishing Services creates customized publications that reflect the specific information needs of their audiences. They are a leading publisher of database directories of all types.

Subjects
Catalogs, Computer Graphics, Database Publishing

Audience
Graphics professionals, publishers

Content Summary
PRC specializes in the combination of digital images and text data; in high volumes and at high speeds; and in customized layouts and electronic composition.

See Also
Graphics Forum

User Guide
- [x] Windows
- [x] DOS
- [x] Macintosh
- [ ] Terminal Emulation
- [x] VMS
- [x] UNIX
- [x] OS/2
- [ ] Other platform

Cost
- [ ] Unknown
- [x] Basic
- [ ] Extended
- [ ] Premium ($)
- [ ] Executive w/$

Activity Level

Address
GO: **PRC**

The Laser's Edge

Description
Online shopping area for The Laser's Edge and their laser disc products.

Subjects
Movies, Laser Disks, Catalogs

Audience
Movie buffs, laser disk player owners.

Content Summary
This online shopping service provides members access to the complete line of The Laser's Edge electronic products.

See Also
Viewers EDGE (FREE), Critics Choice Video (FREE), Entertainment Works (FREE)

User Guide
- [x] Windows
- [x] DOS
- [ ] Macintosh
- [x] Terminal Emulation
- [ ] VMS
- [ ] UNIX
- [ ] OS/2
- [ ] Other platform

Cost
- [x] Unknown
- [ ] Basic
- [ ] Extended
- [ ] Premium ($)
- [ ] Executive w/$

Activity Level

Address
GO: **LE**

The Mac Zone/PC Zone

Description
Online shopping area for Mac and PC hardware and software.

Subjects
Macintosh and PC parts, Catalogs

Audience
All computer users

Content Summary
This online shopping area enables members to purchase from a complete line of PC and Macintosh products often at reduced rates.

See Also
Micro Warehouse (FREE), JDR Microdevices (FREE)

User Guide
- [x] Windows
- [x] DOS
- [ ] Macintosh
- [x] Terminal Emulation
- [ ] VMS
- [ ] UNIX
- [ ] OS/2
- [ ] Other platform

Cost
- [ ] Unknown
- [x] Basic
- [ ] Extended
- [ ] Premium ($)
- [ ] Executive w/$

Activity Level

Address
GO: **MZ-1**

Time-Warner Bookstore

Description
Online shopping area offering Time-Warner books.

Subjects
Catalogs, Book orders

Audience
All users

Content Summary
This online shopping area contains the vast amount of published material offered by Time-Warner.

See Also
Ziff-Davis Press Booknet, Small Computer Bookclub (FREE), Prentice Hall PTR (FREE), Quality Paperbacks, McGraw-Hill Book Company (FREE), John

Wiley Book Store (FREE), Book of the Month Club (FREE), Books on Tape (FREE), CompuBooks (FREE), Detroit Free Press Store

User Guide
- ☑ Windows
- ☑ DOS
- ☐ Macintosh
- ☐ Terminal Emulation
- ☐ VMS
- ☐ UNIX
- ☐ OS/2
- ☐ Other platform

Cost
- ☑ Unknown
- ☐ Basic
- ☐ Extended
- ☐ Premium ($)
- ☐ Executive w/$

Activity Level

Address
GO: **TWEPB**

CBM Service Forum

Description
An area for the discussion of any and all aspects of Commodore computing, both with other members and with Commodore's in-house employees.

Subjects
Commodore Computers, Computers

Audience
Computer professionals

Content Summary
The libraries and message sections of this forum include product information on all Commodore products, information on user groups, and a list of service centers.

See Also
Commodore Users Network, Commodore Applications Forum, Commodore Arts/Games Forum, Amiga Tech Forum

User Guide
- ☑ Windows
- ☑ DOS
- ☐ Macintosh
- ☐ Terminal Emulation
- ☐ VMS
- ☐ UNIX
- ☐ OS/2
- ☐ Other platform

Cost
- ☐ Unknown
- ☐ Basic
- ☑ Extended
- ☐ Premium ($)
- ☐ Executive w/$

Activity Level

Address
GO: **CBMSERVICE**

CCML AIDS Articles

Description
Articles relating to AIDS from the Comprehensive Core Medical Library.

Subjects
AIDS, Health, Medicine

Audience
Medical personnel, researchers

Content Summary
The libraries contain full text articles from leading medical reference books, text books, and articles.

User Guide
- ☑ Windows
- ☑ DOS
- ☐ Macintosh
- ☐ Terminal Emulation
- ☐ VMS
- ☐ UNIX
- ☐ OS/2
- ☐ Other platform

Cost
- ☐ Unknown
- ☐ Basic
- ☐ Extended
- ☑ Premium ($)
- ☐ Executive w/$

Activity Level

Address
GO: **CCMLAIDS**

CD-ROM Forum

Description
The CD-ROM Forum deals with one of the most active and dynamic areas in the publishing/media field.

Subjects
Computers

Audience
CD-ROM developers, computer professionals

Content Summary
The libraries contain general information about CD-ROM technology, production, hardware, operating system concerns, and industry issues.

See Also
CD-ROM Vendor Forum, Multimedia Conference Forum, Kodak CD Forum

User Guide
- ☑ Windows
- ☑ DOS
- ☑ Macintosh
- ☐ Terminal Emulation
- ☐ VMS
- ☑ UNIX
- ☐ OS/2
- ☐ Other platform

CD-ROM Forum - Celebrities

Cost
- ☐ Unknown
- ☐ Basic
- ☑ Extended
- ☐ Premium ($)
- ☐ Executive w/$

Activity Level

MEDIUM / LOW / HIGH (arrow at medium)

Address
GO: **CDROM**

CD-ROM Vendors Forum

Description
Companies involved in creating and using CD-ROM products are represented here in the CD-ROM Vendors Forum.

Subjects
Computers

Audience
CD-ROM developers, computer professionals

Content Summary
This forum's libaries contain information about new products, product support, and message areas in which you can ask questions and receive answers on CD-ROM related topics.

See Also
CD-ROM Forum, Multimedia Conference Forum, Kodak CD Forum

User Guide
- ☑ Windows
- ☑ DOS
- ☑ Macintosh
- ☐ Terminal Emulation
- ☐ VMS
- ☑ UNIX
- ☐ OS/2
- ☐ Other platform

Cost
- ☐ Unknown
- ☐ Basic
- ☑ Extended
- ☐ Premium ($)
- ☐ Executive w/$

Activity Level

MEDIUM / LOW / HIGH (arrow pointing low)

Address
GO: **CDVEN**

CELEBRITIES

Entertainment Drive Center

Description
This is your backstage pass to the entertainment industry. You can get David Letterman Top 10 lists, O.J. Simpson trial transcripts, exclusive columns and reviews, and multimedia files.

Subjects
Celebrities, Entertainment, Multimedia

Audience
Journalists, photojournalists, anyone interested in the entertainment industry

Content Summary
Because of the nature of the entertainment industry, many of the files posted in this forum are removed on certain dates, including a collection of Lion King graphics that were posted until August 31, 1994. If you missed these, don't despair; other hot topics will be featured every month.

See Also
ShowBiz-Media Forum, Archive Films Forum, Hollywood Hotline, Movie Reviews, Roger Ebert's Movie Reviews, UK Entertainment Reviews

User Guide
- ☑ Windows
- ☑ DOS
- ☑ Macintosh
- ☐ Terminal Emulation
- ☐ VMS
- ☐ UNIX
- ☐ OS/2
- ☐ Other platform

Cost
- ☐ Unknown
- ☐ Basic
- ☑ Extended
- ☐ Premium ($)
- ☐ Executive w/$

Activity Level

MEDIUM / LOW / HIGH (arrow toward high)

Address
GO: **EDRIVE**

Stein Online

Description
This conference area is hosted by Eliot Stein, who interviews the stars online.

Subjects
Celebrities, Entertainment

Audience
Fans of celebrities

Content Summary
If you want to communicate online with famous celebrities, this forum provides online conferences.

See Also
Hollywood Hotline

User Guide
- ☑ Windows
- ☑ DOS
- ☑ Macintosh
- ☐ Terminal Emulation
- ☐ VMS
- ☑ UNIX
- ☐ OS/2
- ☑ Other platform

Cost
- ☐ Unknown
- ☐ Basic
- ☑ Extended
- ☐ Premium ($)
- ☐ Executive w/$

Activity Level

Address
GO: **STEIN**

Census Bureau Online Service

Description
The United States Census Bureau provides a selection of its statistical reports on a wide variety of subjects, at no extra cost.

Subjects
Business, Statistics

Audience
Researchers

Content Summary
Libraries include census reports and reports on population, agriculture, business, construction, housing, foreign trade, and government.

See Also
Business Demographics, Neighborhood Demographics, Supersite demographics, State-County Demographics

User Guide
- ☑ Windows
- ☑ DOS
- ☑ Macintosh
- ☐ Terminal Emulation
- ☐ VMS
- ☑ UNIX
- ☐ OS/2
- ☐ Other platform

Cost
- ☐ Unknown
- ☐ Basic
- ☑ Extended
- ☐ Premium ($)
- ☐ Executive w/$

Activity Level

Address
GO: **CENDATA**

Change Your Password

Description
Enables you to maintain the security of your CompuServe account by changing your password on a regular basis.

Subjects
CompuServe

Audience
CompuServe users

Content Summary
The libaries include information about passwords, CompuServe accounts, and security.

See Also
CompuServe Help Forum

User Guide
- ☑ Windows
- ☑ DOS
- ☑ Macintosh
- ☐ Terminal Emulation
- ☐ VMS
- ☑ UNIX
- ☐ OS/2
- ☑ Other platform

Cost
- ☐ Unknown
- ☑ Basic
- ☐ Extended
- ☐ Premium ($)
- ☐ Executive w/$

Activity Level

Address
GO: **PASSWORD**

Chess Forum

Description
The place to be if you love the game of chess or want to find out more about playing it.

Subjects
Games, Hobbies

Audience
Games enthusiasts

Content Summary
The libraries and message sections contain basic game playing theory, analysis of moves, chess tourneys, and a message area that enables you to ask chess masters questions.

See Also
Entertainment Center, Game Publishers C Forum, MTM Challenge Board, Modem Games Forum

User Guide
- ☑ Windows
- ☑ DOS
- ☑ Macintosh
- ☐ Terminal Emulation
- ☐ VMS
- ☑ UNIX
- ☐ OS/2
- ☐ Other platform

Cost
- ☐ Unknown
- ☐ Basic
- ☑ Extended
- ☐ Premium ($)
- ☐ Executive w/$

Activity Level

Address
GO: **CHESSFORUM**

Cheyenne Software Forum

Description
Support for all Cheyenne Software products. Technical support for questions and problems, file updates, and product information.

Subjects
Computers, Software

Audience
Product users

Content Summary
The libraries include information on ARCserv, ARCsolo, FAXserve, inocuLAN, Monitrix, IBM, and Macintosh related products.

User Guide
- ☑ Windows
- ☑ DOS
- ☑ Macintosh
- ☐ Terminal Emulation
- ☐ VMS
- ☑ UNIX
- ☐ OS/2
- ☐ Other platform

Cost
- ☐ Unknown
- ☐ Basic
- ☑ Extended
- ☐ Premium ($)
- ☐ Executive w/$

Activity Level

Address
GO: **CHEYENNE**

Missing Children Forum

Description
The primary purpose of this forum is to find missing and exploited children, support families whose children are missing, and offer child safety assistance.

Subjects
Children, Safety

Audience
General public

Content Summary
Note that his forum discourages the promotion of products and services, as well as contributions that are political or issues-oriented. The forum is sponsored by the National Center for Missing and Exploited Children (NCMEC). You can download GIF files of missing children from the Missing Children library (Library 2). Other libraries include Family Support, Child Safety, Resources, Recoveries, and State Clearinghouses.

See Also
Participate

User Guide
- ☑ Windows
- ☑ DOS
- ☑ Macintosh
- ☐ Terminal Emulation
- ☑ VMS
- ☑ UNIX
- ☑ OS/2
- ☐ Other platform

Cost
- ☐ Unknown
- ☑ Basic
- ☐ Extended
- ☐ Premium ($)
- ☐ Executive w/$

Activity Level

Address
GO: **MISSING**

Religion Forum

Description
People of all faiths and religions meet in this forum to discuss spiritual, ethical, and values issues. The discussions are open and courtesy is given to all.

Subjects
Christianity, Occult, Religions of the World

Audience
Clergy, religious, seminary students

Content Summary
The library and message areas contain various places to discuss religions of the world, study the Bible, research ministry issues, take part in an online prayer and bible study group, or read press releases on new religious products such as a CD-ROM–based Bible study guide.

See Also
Participate

Christianity - Classics

User Guide
- ☑ Windows
- ☑ DOS
- ☑ Macintosh
- ☐ Terminal Emulation
- ☐ VMS
- ☐ UNIX
- ☐ OS/2
- ☐ Other platform

Cost
- ☐ Unknown
- ☐ Basic
- ☑ Extended
- ☐ Premium ($)
- ☐ Executive w/$

Activity Level
MEDIUM (LOW — HIGH)

Address
GO: **RELIGION**

CIS Navigator Windows Support Forum

Description
The Forum supplies support for users of the Windows version of the CompuServe Navigator program.

Subjects
CS Navigator Software

Audience
CompuServe users

Content Summary
The libraries contain useful information on CompuServe, Windows, installation tips, problems and solutions, scripts, hardware, and modems.

See Also
CompuServe Navigator Mac (FREE), CompuServe (FREE), CompuServe Navigator Windows (FREE), MacNav Support Forum (FREE)

User Guide
- ☑ Windows
- ☑ DOS
- ☐ Macintosh
- ☐ Terminal Emulation
- ☐ VMS
- ☐ UNIX
- ☐ OS/2
- ☐ Other platform

Cost
- ☐ Unknown
- ☑ Basic
- ☐ Extended
- ☐ Premium ($)
- ☐ Executive w/$

Activity Level
MEDIUM (LOW — HIGH)

Address
GO: **WCSNAVSUP**

Clarion Software Forum

Description
This Forum is dedicated to the support and discussion of Clarion software products.

Subjects
Computers

Audience
Product users

Content Summary
Product support in the libraries include Clarion, Windows applications, TopSpeed, Application Generator, and Database Developer.

See Also
Graphics Forums, PC Vendor D Forum, PC File Finder

User Guide
- ☑ Windows
- ☑ DOS
- ☐ Macintosh
- ☐ Terminal Emulation
- ☐ VMS
- ☐ UNIX
- ☐ OS/2
- ☐ Other platform

Cost
- ☐ Unknown
- ☐ Basic
- ☑ Extended
- ☐ Premium ($)
- ☐ Executive w/$

Activity Level
MEDIUM (LOW — HIGH, pointing toward HIGH)

Address
GO: **CLARION**

CLASSICS

Fine Art Forum

Description
Michelangelo. Renoir. Matisse. DaVinci. Rembrandt. Montgomery. Montgomery? Find out about him and other artists in the Fine Art Forum.

Subjects
Art, Art History, Classics, Modern Art

Audience
Art directors, art enthusiasts, art historians, artists, general public

Content Summary
The Fine Art Forum focuses on the arts and techniques of the old masters, as well as local and regional traditional-media artists such as Carl Lundgren, Gunni Nilsson Price, Joe Bergeron, Roberta Laidman, Jess Hager, Barbara Johnson,

Classics - Client/Server

and David O. Stillings. The many libraries offered here enable you to download GIF files of many of your favorite paintings, such as Michelangelo's "The Fall of Man," DaVinci's "Last Supper," and Renoir's "Diana." You also can become familiar with modern artists and techniques by visiting Library 15, Modern Art.

See Also
Artist Forum, Graphics Forums, Graphics Gallery Forum, Graphics Plus Forum, Photography Forum

User Guide
- ☑ Windows
- ☑ DOS
- ☑ Macintosh
- ☐ Terminal Emulation
- ☐ VMS
- ☐ UNIX
- ☐ OS/2
- ☐ Other platform

Cost
- ☐ Unknown
- ☐ Basic
- ☐ Extended
- ☑ Premium ($)
- ☐ Executive w/$

Activity Level
MEDIUM (arrow pointing up)

Address
GO: **FINEARTS**

Classified Ads

Description
An online classified ads section where you can buy and sell most anything!

Subjects
Employment

Audience
Shoppers

Content Summary
You can find ads for employment, education, job searches, computer equipment, and business opportunities.

See Also
E-Span Online Job Listing

User Guide
- ☑ Windows
- ☑ DOS
- ☑ Macintosh
- ☐ Terminal Emulation
- ☐ VMS
- ☑ UNIX
- ☐ OS/2
- ☑ Other platform

Cost
- ☐ Unknown
- ☑ Basic
- ☐ Extended
- ☐ Premium ($)
- ☐ Executive w/$

Activity Level
MEDIUM — UNKNOWN

Address
GO: **CLASSIFIED**

CLIENT/SERVER

Digital Equipment Corporation

Description
This is the main area from which you can choose to enter one of several DEC forums or service areas. You can select Digital's Windows NT Support Forum, PC Integration Forum, or Digital-Related Forums. You also can go to Digital's PC Store from this menu.

Subjects
Computers, Client/Server, Multiprocessor Environments, Windows NT

Audience
DEC Alpha AXP users, support technicians, system integrators, VARs, Windows NT users

Content Summary
At the main menu, you can select from Digital NT Support Forum, Digital PC Integration Forum, and Digital's PC Store.

See Also
Digital NT Support Forum, Digital PC Integration Forum, Digital's PC Store

User Guide
- ☑ Windows
- ☑ DOS
- ☑ Macintosh
- ☐ Terminal Emulation
- ☑ VMS
- ☑ UNIX
- ☑ OS/2
- ☐ Other platform

Cost
- ☐ Unknown
- ☐ Basic
- ☑ Extended
- ☐ Premium ($)
- ☐ Executive w/$

Activity Level
MEDIUM — UNKNOWN

Address
GO: **DEC**

Digital NT Support Forum

Description
Dedicated to the user support of Windows NT, regardless of environment or platform, this forum is supported by Digital's Multi-Vendor Customer

Client/Server- Clothing

Services Group. You can find information here about DEC's Alpha AXP platform.

Subjects
Computers, Client/Server, Digital Equipment Corporation (DEC), Windows NT

Audience
DEC Alpha AXP users, support technicians, system integrators, VARs, Windows NT users

Content Summary
The library and message areas contain information about Digital and Digital's Multivendor Customer Services, including press releases and news on the Alpha AXP and Windows NT. You also can find specific areas devoted to NT user support, languages and application tools, hardware support, bug reporting, a "Wish List" area for what you want, and Alpha AXP support. You can find new BIOS files, Alpha Microcode, and utility programs in the "Patches & More" library.

See Also
DEC PC, DECPCI, PDP-11 Forum, VAX Forum

User Guide
- ☑ Windows
- ☑ DOS
- ☑ Macintosh
- ☐ Terminal Emulation
- ☐ VMS
- ☐ UNIX
- ☐ OS/2
- ☐ Other platform

Cost
- ☐ Unknown
- ☐ Basic
- ☑ Extended
- ☐ Premium ($)
- ☐ Executive w/$

Activity Level

Address
GO: **DECWNT**

CLOTHING

Americana Clothing

Description
Online shopping with a unique selection of clothing for men and women at everyday low prices.

Subjects
Clothing, Shopping

Audience
Consumers

Content Summary
Purchasing of clothing online.

See Also
JCPenney (FREE), Paul Fredick Shirts (FREE), Alaska Peddler (FREE), Austads Clothing (FREE), Brooks Brothers (FREE), Concord Direct (FREE)

User Guide
- ☑ Windows
- ☑ DOS
- ☐ Macintosh
- ☑ Terminal Emulation
- ☐ VMS
- ☐ UNIX
- ☐ OS/2
- ☐ Other platform

Cost
- ☐ Unknown
- ☑ Basic
- ☐ Extended
- ☐ Premium ($)
- ☐ Executive w/$

Activity Level
UNKNOWN

Address
GO: **AC**

Brooks Brothers Online Store

Description
Online shopping at America's oldest retail store.

Subjects
Clothing, Shopping

Audience
General public

Content Summary
Looking for men's clothing and furnishings? Look no further. This service enables you to order your Brooks Brothers apparel, including contemporary and classic clothing for women and young men.

See Also
JCPenney (FREE), Paul Fredick Shirts (FREE), Alaska Peddler (FREE), Austads Clothing (FREE), Concord Direct (FREE), Americana Clothing (FREE)

User Guide
- ☑ Windows
- ☑ DOS
- ☑ Macintosh
- ☐ Terminal Emulation
- ☑ VMS
- ☑ UNIX
- ☑ OS/2
- ☐ Other platform

Cost
- ☐ Unknown
- ☑ Basic
- ☐ Extended
- ☐ Premium ($)
- ☐ Executive w/$

Activity Level

Address
GO: **BR**

Shoppers Advantage Club

Description
This is America's largest discount electronic shopping service, with over 250,000 name brand items available.

Subjects
Clothing, Discount Shopping, Shopping

Audience
Consumers, shoppers

Content Summary
Shop 24 hours a day for over 250,000 different items.

See Also
Electronic Mall

User Guide
- ☑ Windows
- ☑ DOS
- ☑ Macintosh
- ☐ Terminal Emulation
- ☐ VMS
- ☑ UNIX
- ☐ OS/2
- ☐ Other platform

Cost
- ☐ Unknown
- ☑ Basic
- ☐ Extended
- ☐ Premium ($)
- ☐ Executive w/$

Activity Level: MEDIUM-HIGH

Address
GO: **SAC**

CoCo Forum

Description
This Forum specializes in support of the Tandy Color Computer and its users.

Subjects
Computers

Audience
Tandy users

Content Summary
The libraries include information on color computers, graphics, games, music, telecommunications, BBS systems, applications, utilities, operating systems, and hardware.

See Also
Tandy Model 100 Forum, Tandy Newsletter, Tandy Professional Forum, The Tandy Users Network, LDOS/TRSDOS6 Users Forum

User Guide
- ☑ Windows
- ☑ DOS
- ☐ Macintosh
- ☐ Terminal Emulation
- ☐ VMS
- ☐ UNIX
- ☐ OS/2
- ☐ Other platform

Cost
- ☐ Unknown
- ☐ Basic
- ☑ Extended
- ☐ Premium ($)
- ☐ Executive w/$

Activity Level: UNKNOWN

Address
GO: **COCO**

Collectibles Forum

Description
We are an electronic club for all collectors—and are a member of the ANA and APS.

Subjects
Dolls, Hobbies, Star Trek

Audience
Hobby enthusiasts

Content Summary
The library and message sections contain information on a wide variety of collectibles. Included are areas on stamps, coins, autographs, books, music, sports cards, dolls, figurines, Star Trek, and much more.

See Also
Comics/Animation Forum, Automobile Forum, Worldwide Car Network, Metropolitan Museum Of Art (FREE)

User Guide
- ☑ Windows
- ☑ DOS
- ☑ Macintosh
- ☐ Terminal Emulation
- ☐ VMS
- ☑ UNIX
- ☐ OS/2
- ☐ Other platform

Cost
- ☐ Unknown
- ☐ Basic
- ☑ Extended
- ☐ Premium ($)
- ☐ Executive w/$

Activity Level: MEDIUM

Address
GO: **COLLECT**

COMBAT

SNIPER!

Description
This online infantry combat game is set during World War II.

Subjects
Combat, Games, War

Audience
Games enthusiasts, military scenarios

Content Summary
You command a squad of soldiers in a mission against another squad. Actual wartime conditions are simulated. The game is over when a player has accomplished his or her mission. The game appears more lifelike if you download the SCOPE games software.

See Also
Games Forum

User Guide
- ☑ Windows
- ☑ DOS
- ☐ Macintosh
- ☐ Terminal Emulation
- ☐ VMS
- ☐ UNIX
- ☐ OS/2
- ☐ Other platform

Cost
- ☐ Unknown
- ☐ Basic
- ☑ Extended
- ☐ Premium ($)
- ☐ Executive w/$

Activity Level
UNKNOWN (LOW — MEDIUM — HIGH)

Address
Go: **SNIPER**

Comics/Animation Forum

Description
This Forum is for fans of comic books, comic strips, sequential art of all kinds, and animation.

Subjects
Hobbies

Audience
Comics enthusiasts

Content Summary
The libraries include information on comic books, Japanimation, animation, collecting, industry issues, newspaper strips, adult comics, and upcoming meetings.

See Also
Comics Publishers Forum, Generation X Comics Download, Graphics Corner Forum, Graphics Plus Forum, Quick Pictures Forum, Animation Vendor A Forum, Graphics Developers Forum, Multimedia Vendor Forum, Graphics Support Forum

User Guide
- ☑ Windows
- ☑ DOS
- ☑ Macintosh
- ☐ Terminal Emulation
- ☐ VMS
- ☑ UNIX
- ☐ OS/2
- ☐ Other platform

Cost
- ☐ Unknown
- ☐ Basic
- ☑ Extended
- ☐ Premium ($)
- ☐ Executive w/$

Activity Level
MEDIUM-HIGH (LOW — MEDIUM — HIGH)

Address
GO: **COMIC**

Commodore Applications Forum

Description
The Forum for Commodore 8-bit programming and discussions about hardware, utilities, and applications for the C64 and C128 computers.

Subjects
Computers

Audience
Commodore users

Content Summary
Libraries include information on Commodore 64/128, programming, hardware, telecommunications, BBSs, applications, and CP/M.

See Also
Commodore Users Network, Commodore Arts/Games Forum, Amiga Tech Forum, CBM Service Forum, Commodore Art/Games Forum, Amiga Vendor Forum, CP/M Users Group Forum

User Guide
- ☑ Windows
- ☑ DOS
- ☐ Macintosh
- ☐ Terminal Emulation
- ☐ VMS
- ☐ UNIX
- ☐ OS/2
- ☐ Other platform

Cost
Extended
- ☐ Unknown
- ☐ Basic
- ☑ Extended
- ☐ Premium ($)
- ☐ Executive w/$

Activity Level
LOW-MEDIUM (LOW — MEDIUM — HIGH)

Address
GO: **CBMAPP**

Commodore Art/Games Forum

Description
This forum features music, graphics, and games for the Commodore 8-bit computers.

Commodore Art/Games Forum - Commodore Computers

Subjects
Computers

Audience
Commodore users

Content Summary
Libraries include information about Commodore 64/128, music, graphics, games, GEOS, poetry, and SIDplayer.

See Also
Commodore Users Network, Commodore Applications Forum, Amiga Tech Forum, CBM Service Forum, Amiga Vendor Forum, CP/M Users Group Forum

User Guide
- [x] Windows
- [x] DOS
- [ ] Macintosh
- [ ] Terminal Emulation
- [ ] VMS
- [ ] UNIX
- [ ] OS/2
- [ ] Other platform

Cost
- [ ] Unknown
- [ ] Basic
- [x] Extended
- [ ] Premium ($)
- [ ] Executive w/$

Activity Level
LOW (arrow pointing low) MEDIUM HIGH

Address
GO: **CBMART**

Commodore Business Machines Menu

Description
Access to information and services for users of Commodore computers.

Subjects
Computers

Audience
Commodore users

Content Summary
Libraries include announcements, resources for education, user group information, forum conference schedule, software updates, service forum, and users network.

See Also
Commodore Users Network, Commodore Arts/Games Forum, Amiga Tech Forum, CBM Service Forum, Commodore Art/Games Forum, Amiga Vendor Forum, CP/M Users Group Forum

User Guide
- [x] Windows
- [x] DOS
- [ ] Macintosh
- [ ] Terminal Emulation
- [ ] VMS
- [ ] UNIX
- [ ] OS/2
- [ ] Other platform

Cost
- [ ] Unknown
- [ ] Basic
- [x] Extended
- [ ] Premium ($)
- [ ] Executive w/$

Activity Level
LOW MEDIUM (UNKNOWN) HIGH

Address
GO: **CBMNEWS**

COMMODORE COMPUTERS

CBM Service Forum

Description
An area for the discussion of any and all aspects of Commodore computing, both with other members and with Commodore's in-house employees.

Subjects
Commodore Computers, Computers

Audience
Computer professionals

Content Summary
The libraries and message sections of this forum include product information on all Commodore products, information on user groups, and a list of service centers.

See Also
Commodore Users Network, Commodore Arts/Games Forum, Amiga Tech Forum, Commodore Art/Games Forum, Amiga Vendor Forum, CP/M Users Group Forum

User Guide
- [x] Windows
- [x] DOS
- [ ] Macintosh
- [ ] Terminal Emulation
- [ ] VMS
- [ ] UNIX
- [ ] OS/2
- [ ] Other platform

Cost
- [ ] Unknown
- [ ] Basic
- [x] Extended
- [ ] Premium ($)
- [ ] Executive w/$

Activity Level
LOW (arrow pointing low) MEDIUM HIGH

Address
GO: **CBMSERVICE**

Commodore/Amiga Forums Menu

Description
Provides access to the Commodore and Amiga areas on CompuServe.

Subjects
Computers

Audience
Commodore and Amiga users

Content Summary
Libraries include information about arts, users, vendors, and File Finder for the Amiga. Included for Commodore users are libraries for arts and games, applications, service, and the newsletter.

See Also
Commodore Users Network, Commodore Arts/Games Forum, Amiga Tech Forum, CBM Service Forum, Commodore Art/Games Forum, Amiga Vendor Forum, CP/M Users Group Forum

User Guide
- ☑ Windows
- ☑ DOS
- ☐ Macintosh
- ☐ Terminal Emulation
- ☐ VMS
- ☐ UNIX
- ☐ OS/2
- ☐ Other platform

Cost
- ☐ Unknown
- ☐ Basic
- ☑ Extended
- ☐ Premium ($)
- ☐ Executive w/$

Activity Level

Address
GO: **CBMNET**

COMMUNICATIONS

Dataquest Online

Description
A private forum for Dataquest clients, or members of the Semiconductor Industry Association.

Subjects
Communications

Audience
MIS people

Content Summary
You can find information on technologies, communications, computers, document management, semiconductors, and various services.

See Also
Intel Forum

User Guide
- ☑ Windows
- ☑ DOS
- ☐ Macintosh
- ☐ Terminal Emulation
- ☐ VMS
- ☐ UNIX
- ☐ OS/2
- ☐ Other platform

Cost
- ☐ Unknown
- ☐ Basic
- ☑ Extended
- ☐ Premium ($)
- ☐ Executive w/$

Activity Level

Address
GO: **DATAQUEST**

IBM Communications Forum

Description
This forum is devoted to the topic of telecommunications on the IBM PC and compatible computers.

Subjects
Communications, Computers, IBM PCs, Modems

Audience
Computer users, management information specialists

Contents Summary
You can find various utilities, files, support Q&A, and other communications information for the PC in this forum. The libraries include Autosig (ATO), Communications Utilities, Communications Programs, FAX, Hot Topics, Modems/Communications Hardware, and more.

See Also
Hayes Forum, Modem Vendor Forum

User Guide
- ☑ Windows
- ☑ DOS
- ☐ Macintosh
- ☐ Terminal Emulation
- ☐ VMS
- ☐ UNIX
- ☑ OS/2
- ☑ Other platform

Cost
- ☐ Unknown
- ☐ Basic
- ☑ Extended
- ☐ Premium ($)
- ☐ Executive w/$

Activity Level

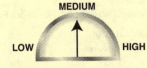

Address
GO: **IBMCOM**

Compaq Forum

Description
The forum provides technical support for Compaq Computer Corporation hardware products.

Subjects
Computers

Audience
Compaq users

Content Summary
Libraries include information on portables, laptops, notebooks, desktops, towers, networking, software, printers, and customer service.

See Also
PC Vendor C Forum, PC Industry Forum, Computing Support, Hardware Forums

User Guide
- ☑ Windows
- ☑ DOS
- ☐ Macintosh
- ☐ Terminal Emulation
- ☐ VMS
- ☐ UNIX
- ☐ OS/2
- ☐ Other platform

Cost
- ☐ Unknown
- ☐ Basic
- ☑ Extended
- ☐ Premium ($)
- ☐ Executive w/$

Activity Level

Address
GO: **CPQFORUM**

CompuAdd Forum

Description
The forum enables CompuAdd users to communicate with technical support and engineering staff, as well as each other.

Subjects
Computers

Audience
CompuAdd users

Content Summary
Libraries include information on systems, laptop computers, notebooks, networks, drives, peripherals, video, and SPARC/SS-2.

See Also
Computing Support, Hardware Forums

User Guide
- ☑ Windows
- ☑ DOS
- ☐ Macintosh
- ☐ Terminal Emulation
- ☐ VMS
- ☑ UNIX
- ☐ OS/2
- ☑ Other platform

Cost
- ☐ Unknown
- ☐ Basic
- ☑ Extended
- ☐ Premium ($)
- ☐ Executive w/$

Activity Level

Address
GO: **COMPUADD**

COMPUSERVE

Ask Customer Service

Description
This forum provides answers to commonly asked questions about CompuServe.

Subjects
CompuServe

Audience
CompuServe users

Content Summary
Service where you can ask questions about any part of the CompuServe service.

See Also
CompuServe Help Forum (FREE), Feedback To Customer Service (FREE), CompuServe Operating Rules (FREE), CompuServe Rates (FREE), Member Assistance (FREE)

User Guide
- ☑ Windows
- ☑ DOS
- ☐ Macintosh
- ☐ Terminal Emulation
- ☐ VMS
- ☐ UNIX
- ☐ OS/2
- ☐ Other platform

Cost
- ☐ Unknown
- ☑ Basic
- ☐ Extended
- ☐ Premium ($)
- ☐ Executive w/$

Activity Level

Address
GO: **QUESTIONS**

Change Your Password

Description
Enables you to maintain the security of your CompuServe account by changing your password on a regular basis.

CompuServe

Subjects
CompuServe

Audience
CompuServe users

Content Summary
The libaries include information about passwords, CompuServe accounts, and security.

See Also
Ask Customer Service, CompuServe Help Forum

User Guide
- ☑ Windows
- ☑ DOS
- ☑ Macintosh
- ☐ Terminal Emulation
- ☐ VMS
- ☑ UNIX
- ☐ OS/2
- ☑ Other platform

Cost
- ☐ Unknown
- ☑ Basic
- ☐ Extended
- ☐ Premium ($)
- ☐ Executive w/$

Activity Level
UNKNOWN (LOW — MEDIUM — HIGH)

Address
GO: **PASSWORD**

CompuServe Help Forum

Description
Free forum for all CIS members who need help using CompuServe or have questions about their membership.

Subjects
CompuServe, Help

Audience
CompuServe users

Content Summary
Libraries include information about CompuServe mail, reference services, news, sports, weather, financial, CB/Conferencing, pricing plans, and access to CompuServe.

See Also
Feedback To Customer Service (FREE), Commonly Asked Questions (FREE), CompuServe Operating Rules (FREE), CompuServe Rates (FREE), Member Assistance (FREE)

User Guide
- ☑ Windows
- ☑ DOS
- ☑ Macintosh
- ☐ Terminal Emulation
- ☐ VMS
- ☑ UNIX
- ☐ OS/2
- ☑ Other platform

Cost
- ☐ Unknown
- ☑ Basic
- ☐ Extended
- ☐ Premium ($)
- ☐ Executive w/$

Activity Level
UNKNOWN (LOW — MEDIUM — HIGH)

Address
GO: **HELPFORUM**

Member Assistance

Description
Need help while your on CompuServe? Type **GO HELP** and enter the Member Assistance service. From this main menu, you're assured to find what you're looking for.

Subjects
CompuServe

Audience
All CompuServe Users

Content Summary
The selections on the Member Assistance main menu include Tour/Find a Topic, Navigation/Commands, Ask Customer Service, Membership Changes, What's New, Missing Children Forum, Practice Forum, CompuServe Help Forum, Billing Information, Telephone Access Numbers, Order from CompuServe, Rules of Operation/Copyright, Member Directory, Special Events & Contests, and Member Support Services.

See Also
Feedback To Customer Service (FREE), Commonly Asked Questions (FREE), CompuServe Operating Rules (FREE), CompuServe Rates (FREE), CompuServe Help Forum (FREE)

User Guide
- ☑ Windows
- ☑ DOS
- ☑ Macintosh
- ☐ Terminal Emulation
- ☐ VMS
- ☐ UNIX
- ☐ OS/2
- ☐ Other platform

Cost
- ☐ Unknown
- ☑ Basic
- ☐ Extended
- ☐ Premium ($)
- ☐ Executive w/$

Activity Level
UNKNOWN (LOW — MEDIUM — HIGH)

Address
GO: **HELP**

CompuServe

Support Directory

Description
This is an online database of vendor support forums and services on CompuServe.

Subjects
CompuServe4

Audience
CompuServe users

Content Summary
This database enables CompuServe users to look up online vendors quickly and easily.

See Also
Support on Site Forum

User Guide
- [x] Windows
- [x] DOS
- [x] Macintosh
- [ ] Terminal Emulation
- [ ] VMS
- [x] UNIX
- [ ] OS/2
- [x] Other platform

Cost
- [ ] Unknown
- [ ] Basic
- [ ] Extended
- [x] Premium ($)
- [ ] Executive w/$

Activity Level

Address
GO: **SUPPORT**

Telephone Access Numbers

Description
Local CompuServe access numbers, information, and communications surcharges.

Subjects
Computers, CompuServe

Audience
Computer Users

Content Summary
Use this forum to look up the CompuServe access number or to get information about your account.

See Also
CompuServe Help

User Guide
- [x] Windows
- [x] DOS
- [x] Macintosh
- [ ] Terminal Emulation
- [x] VMS
- [x] UNIX
- [ ] OS/2
- [x] Other platform

Cost
- [ ] Unknown
- [x] Basic
- [ ] Extended
- [ ] Premium ($)
- [ ] Executive w/$

Activity Level

Address
GO: **PHONES**

The CompuServe Practice Forum

Description
Free forum for all CIS members.

Subjects
Aristitolian Texts, Chemical Engineering

Audience
Ada Repository users, collectors, accountants

Content Summary
Within this forum, you can practice creating forum messages or uploading/downloading files, or simply ask questions about using CIS forums

See Also
ABC Worldwide Hotel Guide, ABC Worldwide Hotel Guide, Access Numbers, Access Phone Numbers (FREE)

User Guide
- [x] Windows
- [x] DOS
- [x] Macintosh
- [x] Terminal Emulation
- [x] VMS
- [x] UNIX
- [x] OS/2
- [ ] Other platform

Cost
- [ ] Unknown
- [x] Basic
- [ ] Extended
- [ ] Premium ($)
- [ ] Executive w/$

Activity Level

Address
GO: **PRACTICE**

User Profile Program (FREE)

Description
Online area for users of the ASCII interface to set up their terminal parameters. This area is not useful to users of DOS CIM, WinCIM, or MacCIM software.

Subjects
Change your terminal type/parameters and/or service options.

Audience
All CompuServe Users

Contents Summary
Use the various options to change your CompuServe settings.

See Also
Member Directory (FREE), Member Assistance (FREE)

User Guide
- ☑ Windows
- ☑ DOS
- ☐ Macintosh
- ☐ Terminal Emulation
- ☐ VMS
- ☐ UNIX
- ☐ OS/2
- ☐ Other platform

Cost
Terminal Emulation
- ☐ Unknown
- ☑ Basic
- ☐ Extended
- ☐ Premium ($)
- ☐ Executive w/$

Activity Level
UNKNOWN (LOW – MEDIUM – HIGH)

Address
GO: **TERMINAL**

What's New

Description
This is CompuServe's menu of upcoming events and system changes, updated several times per week.

Subjects
CompuServe

Audience
CompuServe users

Content Summary
Find out what's happening on Compuserve by viewing this list of new topics.

See Also
CompuServe Help

User Guide
- ☑ Windows
- ☑ DOS
- ☑ Macintosh
- ☐ Terminal Emulation
- ☑ VMS
- ☑ UNIX
- ☑ OS/2
- ☐ Other platform

Cost
- ☐ Unknown
- ☑ Basic
- ☐ Extended
- ☐ Premium ($)
- ☐ Executive w/$

Activity Level
UNKNOWN (LOW – MEDIUM – HIGH)

Address
GO: **NEW**

WinCIM Support Forum

Description
This forum is sponsored by CompuServe as a "vendor support forum" covering WinCIM access software for Windows users.

Subjects
Support of the WinCIM software product, developed by CompuServe, which provides a simple but powerful interface to all of CompuServe's online features.

Audience
CompuServe users, WinCIM users

Content Summary
Contains information that enables users to navigate WinCIM better and faster. Topics include interface use, installation instructions, required hardware, and general usage.

See Also
WinCIM Information (FREE)

User Guide
- ☑ Windows
- ☐ DOS
- ☐ Macintosh
- ☐ Terminal Emulation
- ☐ VMS
- ☐ UNIX
- ☐ OS/2
- ☐ Other platform

Cost
- ☐ Unknown
- ☑ Basic
- ☐ Extended
- ☐ Premium ($)
- ☐ Executive w/$

Activity Level
HIGH (LOW – MEDIUM – HIGH)

Address
GO: **WCIMSUP**

CompuServe Help Forum

Description
Free forum for all CIS members who need help using CompuServe or have questions about their membership.

Subjects
CompuServe, Help

Audience
CompuServe users

Content Summary
Libraries include information about CompuServe mail, reference services, news, sports, weather, financial, CB/Conferencing, pricing plans, and access to CompuServe.

CompuServe Help Forum – Computer Applications

See Also
Feedback To Customer Service (FREE), Commonly Asked Questions (FREE), CompuServe Operating Rules (FREE), CompuServe Rates (FREE), Member Assistance (FREE)

User Guide
- ☑ Windows
- ☑ DOS
- ☑ Macintosh
- ☐ Terminal Emulation
- ☐ VMS
- ☑ UNIX
- ☐ OS/2
- ☑ Other platform

Cost
- ☐ Unknown
- ☑ Basic
- ☐ Extended
- ☐ Premium ($)
- ☐ Executive w/$

Activity Level
UNKNOWN (LOW – MEDIUM – HIGH)

Address
GO: **HELPFORUM**

COMPUSERVE NAVIGATIONAL TOOLS

Dvorak Development Forum

Description
If you use Dvorak Development's NavCIS programs, join this forum for technical support and product information. You also can download a free 30-day demo of the DOS and Windows products to see if you want to purchase the commercial versions.

Subjects
Computers, CompuServe Navigational Tools, NavCIS

Audience
CompuServe users, NavCIS users

Content Summary
If you want to try out NavCIS, see Library 1, "NavCIS Software," to download a 3-day demo of the DOS and Windows versions of NavCIS. Libraries 2–5 offer Windows and DOS support of the SE/TE and Pro versions of NavCIS. Library 7, "Modems and Hardware," contains information and files to help you configure and optimize your modem setup. You also should check out Library 8, "Tip and Techniques," for tips on using NavCIS.

See Also
NavCIS Download Area, CSNav-Win Support Forum, CompuServe Navigator Windows (FREE), CompuServe Navigator Mac (FREE), MacNav Support Forum

User Guide
- ☑ Windows
- ☑ DOS
- ☐ Macintosh
- ☐ Terminal Emulation
- ☐ VMS
- ☐ UNIX
- ☐ OS/2
- ☐ Other platform

Cost
- ☐ Unknown
- ☐ Basic
- ☑ Extended
- ☐ Premium ($)
- ☐ Executive w/$

Activity Level

MEDIUM (LOW – HIGH, arrow toward HIGH)

Address
GO: **DVORAK**

COMPUTER APPLICATIONS

IBM Applications Forum

Description
This forum is devoted to the topic of general applications on the IBM PC and any and all other compatible computers.

Subjects
Computer Applications, Computers, IBM PCs

Audience
Computer users

Content Summary
Find out information about IBM and IBM PC compatible software, including word processors, text editors, DBMS, accounting, general applications, graphics, education, desktop publishing, and more.

See Also
Microsoft Connection, Lotus Technical Library

User Guide
- ☑ Windows
- ☑ DOS
- ☐ Macintosh
- ☐ Terminal Emulation
- ☐ VMS
- ☐ UNIX
- ☑ OS/2
- ☑ Other platform

Cost
- ☐ Unknown
- ☐ Basic
- ☑ Extended
- ☐ Premium ($)
- ☐ Executive w/$

Activity Level

MEDIUM (LOW – HIGH, arrow toward HIGH)

Address
GO: **IBMAPP**

Computer Applications – Computer Books

Microsoft 32-bit Languages Forum

Description
This forum is designed as an area to exchange information, tips, and techniques concerning Microsoft languages.

Subjects
Computer Applications, Computer Programming Languages, Computer Users, Microsoft Corp.

Audience
Computer programmers

Content Summary
Some of the topics covered in this forum include Microsof C ++, Microsoft C, Assembler, QC/QCWin, FORTRAN, CodeView/IDE Debug, NonTech Cutomer Support, and others. This area is for the applications developer and programmer; be ready for high-level discussions if you join this forum.

See Also
Microsoft Languages Forum, Microsoft DevCast Forum, Microsoft WIN32 Forum

User Guide
☑	Windows	☐	VMS
☑	DOS	☐	UNIX
☑	Macintosh	☐	OS/2
☐	Terminal Emulation	☑	Other platform

Cost
☐	Unknown	☐	Premium ($)
☐	Basic	☐	Executive w/$
☑	Extended		

Activity Level MEDIUM (arrow pointing to HIGH side, between LOW and HIGH)

Address
GO: **MSLNG32**

Microsoft Software Library

Description
This area contains binary files, technical notes, utilities, and other files for various Microsoft applications.

Subjects
Computer Applications, Computer Users, Microsoft Corp.

Audience
Computer users, management information specialists, Macintosh users

Content Summary
Download the file you need by entering a keyword and searching for it. You can search on keyword, serial number, submission date, or file name.

See Also
MS WINFUN Forum, MS Windows Shareware Forum

User Guide
☑	Windows	☐	VMS
☑	DOS	☐	UNIX
☑	Macintosh	☑	OS/2
☑	Terminal Emulation	☑	Other platform

Cost
☐	Unknown	☐	Premium ($)
☐	Basic	☐	Executive w/$
☑	Extended		

Activity Level UNKNOWN (between LOW and HIGH, MEDIUM above)

Address
GO: **MSL**

COMPUTER BOOKS

Electronic Books

Description
This is a ZiffNet area. You must be a member of ZiffNet or apply for membership when you first go to the Electronic Books area. The cost of ZiffNet membership is $2.95 monthly. The Electronic Books area offers you an option to buy books directly from the Ziff-Davis Press at 20 percent discount by selecting the ZD Press Booknet option from the main menu.

Subjects
Computers, Computer Books, ZiffNet

Audience
Computer users

Content Summary
When you select the ZD Press Booknet option, you can order Ziff Davis Press books, get special discounts from their remainder table (40 percent off cover price sometimes), download any special offers, or talk to customer service. The Electronic Books service also features the Project Gutenburg Free Book Library, which has over 100 electronic books ranging from literature (such as *Moby Dick*) to Internet titles (such as the *Hitchhiker's Guide to the Internet*) that users can download.

See Also
Ziff-Davis Press Booknet, Time Warner Bookstore, Prentice Hall PTR (FREE), HarperCollins Online (FREE), John Wiley Book Store (FREE)

Computer Books – Computer Games

User Guide
- ☑ Windows
- ☑ DOS
- ☑ Macintosh
- ☑ Terminal Emulation
- ☑ VMS
- ☑ UNIX
- ☑ OS/2
- ☑ Other platform

Cost
- ☐ Unknown
- ☐ Basic
- ☐ Extended
- ☑ Premium ($)
- ☐ Executive w/$

Activity Level
UNKNOWN (LOW – MEDIUM – HIGH)

Address
GO: **ZNT:EBOOKS**

Computer Club Forum

Description
The Computer Club Forum is the home for users of computers no longer supported by their manufacturers or that have no other specific forum dedicated to them on CompuServe.

Subjects
Computers

Audience
Computer users

Content Summary
Libraries include information for users of Actrix, Adam, Amstrad, Apricot, Eagle, Kaypro, Ohio Scientific, Panasonic, Sanyo, Times/Sinclair, and Victor 9000.

See Also
Mac Community/Club Forum, Small Computer Book Club (FREE), Library Of Science Book Club (FREE), CB Club

User Guide
- ☑ Windows
- ☑ DOS
- ☐ Macintosh
- ☐ Terminal Emulation
- ☐ VMS
- ☐ UNIX
- ☐ OS/2
- ☐ Other platform

Cost
- ☐ Unknown
- ☐ Basic
- ☑ Extended
- ☐ Premium ($)
- ☐ Executive w/$

Activity Level
LOW (arrow pointing low) – MEDIUM – HIGH

Address
GO: **CLUB**

COMPUTER GAMES

Game Publishers Forums

Description
Access the numerous (way too many to list, in fact) game publishers forums and sections from this service.

Subjects
Computer Ethics, Computer Games, Games

Audience
Computer game enthusiasts, computer game developers, game players

Content Summary
To help answer the plethora of questions that CompuServe members have about games, including help and news releases, many game publishers (manufacturers) have online message sections. Game Publishers A Forum (GO GAMAPUB) includes Accolade, Bethesada Softworks, Cyberdreams, Sierra OnLine, and others. Game Publishers B Forum (GO GAMBPUB) includes Access, Activision, Disney/Buena Vista, Konami, and others. Game Publishers C Forum (GO GAMCPUB) includes Avalon Hill, Inline Software, Legend Entertainment, and others. Game Publishers D Forum (GO GAMDPUB) includes Megatech Software, Amtex Software, Crystal Dynamics, and many more. When you access the specific publishers forums, you are surcharged at the extended service charge.

See Also
Electronic Gamer™, Game Forums and News, Gamers Forum, Flight Simulation Forum

User Guide
- ☑ Windows
- ☑ DOS
- ☑ Macintosh
- ☐ Terminal Emulation
- ☐ VMS
- ☐ UNIX
- ☐ OS/2
- ☐ Other platform

Cost
- ☐ Unknown
- ☑ Basic
- ☐ Extended
- ☐ Premium ($)
- ☐ Executive w/$

Activity Level

LOW – MEDIUM – HIGH (arrow toward high)

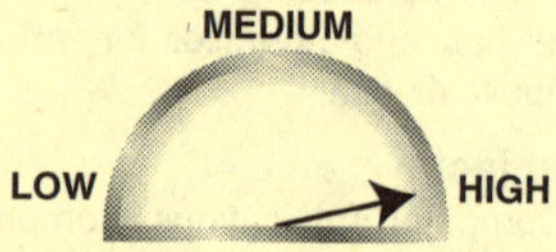

Address
GO: **GAMPUB**

Macintosh Entertainment Forum

Description
Sit back and relax. This forum has games, sound utilities, music, glamour graphics, and more—all for the Mac.

Subjects
Computer Games, Computers, Macintosh

Audience
Computer users, Macintosh users

Content Summary
This forum is full of files, discussions, suggestions, games, and other ways to help you get more enjoyment out of your Macintosh and computing life. You can also participate in the PlayMaker Football League, an online football simulation game for the Mac (see Library 10).

See Also
Macintosh Forums

User Guide
- [ ] Windows
- [ ] DOS
- [x] Macintosh
- [ ] Terminal Emulation
- [ ] VMS
- [ ] UNIX
- [ ] OS/2
- [ ] Other platform

Cost
- [ ] Unknown
- [ ] Basic
- [x] Extended
- [ ] Premium ($)
- [ ] Executive w/$

Activity Level
MEDIUM (gauge pointing HIGH)

Address
GO: **MACFUN**

COMPUTER GRAPHICS

Adobe Forum

Description
The Adobe Forum provides an area where users, dealers, service bureaus, third-party developers, and others can communicate with Adobe.

Subjects
Computer Graphics, Computers, Software

Audience
Adobe products users

Content Summary
Discussions and support of Adobe products. Discusses applications software, hardware, and operating systems . Libraries contain various utilities, add-ons, support files, and product information.

See Also
Graphics Forum

User Guide
- [x] Windows
- [x] DOS
- [x] Macintosh
- [ ] Terminal Emulation
- [ ] VMS
- [ ] UNIX
- [ ] OS/2
- [ ] Other platform

Cost
- [ ] Unknown
- [ ] Basic
- [x] Extended
- [ ] Premium ($)
- [ ] Executive w/$

Activity Level
MEDIUM (gauge pointing up)

Address
GO: **ADOBE**

CADD/CAM/CAE Vendor Forum

Description
Discussion and support for users of products from the companies represented here.

Subjects
Computer Graphics, Computers

Audience
CAD professionals

Content Summary
Products represented in this forum include UTS/TK Solver!, EasyCAD/FastCAD, ISICAD, CADlink, CADKEY, ASHLAR, and IBM CAD to name just a few.

See Also
Cadence, Graphics Forum

User Guide
- [x] Windows
- [x] DOS
- [ ] Macintosh
- [ ] Terminal Emulation
- [ ] VMS
- [ ] UNIX
- [ ] OS/2
- [ ] Other platform

Cost
- [ ] Unknown
- [ ] Basic
- [x] Extended
- [ ] Premium ($)
- [ ] Executive w/$

Activity Level
MEDIUM (gauge pointing LOW)

Address
GO: **CADVEN**

Corel Forum

Description
The Corel Forum is designed to provide support and information about Corel products.

Computer Graphics

Subjects
Computer Graphics, Computers

Audience
Corel uers

Content Summary
Libraries include information on CorelDRAW!, CorelPHOTO-PAINT, CorelSCSI, CorelGALLERY, printing, text, and graphics.

See Also
Ventura Software Forum, Windows 3rd Party B Forum, Graphics Forums

User Guide
- ☑ Windows
- ☑ DOS
- ☐ Macintosh
- ☐ Terminal Emulation
- ☐ VMS
- ☐ UNIX
- ☐ OS/2
- ☐ Other platform

Cost
- ☐ Unknown
- ☑ Basic
- ☑ Extended
- ☐ Premium ($)
- ☐ Executive w/$

Activity Level: MEDIUM (LOW — HIGH, arrow pointing toward HIGH)

Address
GO: **CORELAPPS**

Graphics Developers Forum

Description
If you are interested in computer graphics software, you should join the Graphics Developers Forum for various graphics-related news and information.

Subjects
Computer Graphics, Computers, Graphics

Audience
Computer graphics designers, graphics designers, graphics experts, graphics artists

Content Summary
The Graphics Developers Forum is devoted to the cutting edge of computer graphics software. Topics include fractal generation (using the Fractint software), raytracing (using POV-Ray and other programs), 3D/RDS images, the Virtual Art Gallery project, animation, morphing, motion video, and more. The Mythology library (Library 2) has several fantastic 3D images that you can download and use as wallpaper files. You also should check out the Demo Team library (Library 20) for software demos and routines.

See Also
Graphics Forums, Graphics Support Forum

User Guide
- ☑ Windows
- ☑ DOS
- ☑ Macintosh
- ☐ Terminal Emulation
- ☐ VMS
- ☐ UNIX
- ☐ OS/2
- ☐ Other platform

Cost
- ☐ Unknown
- ☐ Basic
- ☑ Extended
- ☐ Premium ($)
- ☐ Executive w/$

Activity Level: MEDIUM (LOW — HIGH, arrow pointing toward HIGH)

Address
GO: **GRAPHDEV**

Graphics File Finder

Description
If you're looking for a specific graphics file or just want to browse the graphics files that are available, use this service.

Subjects
Computer Graphics, Computers, Graphics

Audience
Graphic artists, graphics experts, graphic designers, computer users, computer graphics designers

Content Summary
Graphics File Finder is an online comprehensive keyword searchable database of file descriptions from graphics related forums, including the Computer Art Forum, Fine Art Forum, Graphics Corner Forum, Graphics Developers Forum, Graphics Gallery Forum, and the Quick Pictures Forum. It is designed to provide quick and easy reference to some of the best programs and files available. You can use seven common search criteria to find the location of a desired file or files quickly. You can search by topic, file submission date, forum name, file type, file extension, file name, or submitter's User ID. File descriptions, forum, and library location are displayed for the matched files.

See Also
Graphics Forums, Graphics Corner Forum

User Guide
- ☑ Windows
- ☑ DOS
- ☑ Macintosh
- ☐ Terminal Emulation
- ☐ VMS
- ☑ UNIX
- ☑ OS/2
- ☐ Other platform

Cost
- ☐ Unknown
- ☐ Basic
- ☑ Extended
- ☐ Premium ($)
- ☐ Executive w/$

Computer Graphics

Activity Level

Address
GO: **GRAPHFF**

Graphics Forums

Description
The Graphics Forums service provides access to several graphics-related forums, the Graphics File Finder, and an online tutorial.

Subjects
Computer Graphics, Computers, Graphic Arts, Graphics

Audience
Computer graphics designers, computer users, graphics designers, graphics artists, graphics experts

Content Summary
The Graphics Forums main menu consists of Introduction to Graphics, Graphics File Finder, Go Graphics News, Best of Go Graphics Directory, Graphics Support Forums, Image Collection Forums, Image Development Forums, Weather Maps, Nominate Image of the Month, and other forums with graphics. If you are looking for graphics to view or download, or information about graphics in general, you might want to start your search here. You're sure to find what you're looking for.

See Also
Graphics Plus Forum, Graphics File Finder

User Guide
☑	Windows	☐	VMS
☑	DOS	☑	UNIX
☑	Macintosh	☑	OS/2
☐	Terminal Emulation	☐	Other platform

Cost
☐	Unknown	☐	Premium ($)
☐	Basic	☐	Executive w/$
☑	Extended		

Activity Level

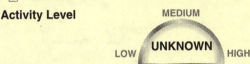

Address
GO: **GRAPHICS**

Graphics Gallery Forum

Description
This forum offers collections of graphics from NASA, the Smithsonian Institute, the Coast Guard, and tourism agencies.

Subjects
Computer Graphics, Computers, Graphics, Photography

Audience
Graphics artists, graphics designers, computer users, photographers

Content Summary
The Graphics Gallery Forum's libraries consist of the following topics: New Images, SI: Smithsonian Art, SI: Air/Space, SI: Science/Nature, SI: People/Places, NASA, Utah Shakespearean Festival, NAL/USDA, America! North, America! South, America! East, America! West, US Coast Guard, World Photography, Wisconsin Historical Society, and Civil War. The Utah Shakespearean Festival library (Library 9) contains a compilation of the best of moments from the 32 seasons of the Utah Shakespearean Festival's plays.

See Also
Graphics Forums, Graphics Corner Forum, Graphics File Finder

User Guide
☑	Windows	☐	VMS
☑	DOS	☐	UNIX
☑	Macintosh	☐	OS/2
☐	Terminal Emulation	☐	Other platform

Cost
☐	Unknown	☐	Premium ($)
☐	Basic	☐	Executive w/$
☑	Extended		

Activity Level
MEDIUM (arrow pointing LOW)

Address
GO: **GALLERY**

Graphics Plus Forum

Description
This forum contains true-color images in various formats. You can get graphics of cars, boats, people, landscapes, and much more.

Subjects
Computer Graphics, Graphics, Photography

Audience
Photographers, computer graphics designers, computer users, graphics artists, graphics designers, graphics experts

Content Summary
The Graphics Plus Forum has images in truecolor and vector formats such as TIFF, Targa, EPS, truecolor BMP and PCX, AI, PICT, and others. This forum also includes a section focusing on fractal and

Computer Graphics

raytraced images. The libraries include areas such as Cars-Boats-Planes, People & Portraits, Landscapes, World of Nature, Fantasy & Sci-Fi, Cartoons & Comics, Body Beautiful, Plain Brown Wrapper, Fractals/Raytracing, and more. Note that this forum contains files that have nudity. Those files that contain nudity have the following disclaimer: "Those offended by the artistic presentation of nudity should refrain from viewing."

See Also
Graphics File Finder, Graphics Forums, Graphics Gallery Forum, Photography Forum

User Guide
- ☑ Windows
- ☑ DOS
- ☑ Macintosh
- ☐ Terminal Emulation
- ☐ VMS
- ☑ UNIX
- ☑ OS/2
- ☐ Other platform

Cost
- ☐ Unknown
- ☐ Basic
- ☑ Extended
- ☐ Premium ($)
- ☐ Executive w/$

Activity Level
MEDIUM (arrow pointing toward HIGH)

Address
GO: **GRAPHPLUS**

Graphics Support Forum

Description
The GIF graphics specification, released by CompuServe, is featured in this forum, including file viewers, file converters, and GIF analysis tools.

Subjects
Computer Graphics, Graphics

Audience
Graphics experts, graphics artists, graphics designers, computer graphics designers

Content Summary
The Graphics Support Forum offers help and program files relating to viewing, downloading, converting, and printing graphics. You also can find animation and video players, specifications for many image formats, discussions on graphics-related issues, and help for programmers working with GIF and JPEG formats. If you need a DOS and Windows utility to print out graphics, check out the Printing Graphics library (Library 8).

See Also
Graphics Forums, Graphics File Finder

User Guide
- ☑ Windows
- ☑ DOS
- ☑ Macintosh
- ☐ Terminal Emulation
- ☐ VMS
- ☐ UNIX
- ☐ OS/2
- ☐ Other platform

Cost
- ☐ Unknown
- ☐ Basic
- ☑ Extended
- ☐ Premium ($)
- ☐ Executive w/$

Activity Level
MEDIUM (arrow pointing up)

Address
GO: **GRAPHSUPPORT**

Graphics Vendors C Forum

Description
The Graphics Vendor C Forum offers support from MicroFrontier, Clear Software, Artist Graphics, and Envisions.

Subjects
Computer Graphics, Computers, Graphics

Audience
Computer graphics designers, graphics artists, graphics designers, graphics experts

Content Summary
The library section contains these areas: Forum Information, MicroFrontier, Clear Software, Artist Graphics, and Envisions.

See Also
Graphics Forums, Graphics File Finder, Graphics Developers Forum

User Guide
- ☑ Windows
- ☑ DOS
- ☐ Macintosh
- ☐ Terminal Emulation
- ☐ VMS
- ☐ UNIX
- ☐ OS/2
- ☐ Other platform

Cost
- ☐ Unknown
- ☐ Basic
- ☑ Extended
- ☐ Premium ($)
- ☐ Executive w/$

Activity Level
MEDIUM (arrow pointing toward LOW)

Address
GO: **GRVENC**

IBM ImagePlus Forum

Description
You can get support for IBM's ImagePlus system for IP/2, IP/AS400, and IP/MVS.

Subjects
Computer Graphics, Computers, IBM

Audience
Computer users, management information specialists

Computer Graphics

Content Summary
The libraries in this forum include IP/2 Information, IP/2 General Questions, IP/2 Support, IP/AS400 Info, Visualinfo Info, and more.

See Also
Image Vendor A Forum, Graphics Forums, Graphics File Finder

User Guide
- [ ] Windows
- [ ] DOS
- [ ] Macintosh
- [ ] Terminal Emulation
- [ ] VMS
- [x] UNIX
- [x] OS/2
- [x] Other platform

Cost
- [ ] Unknown
- [ ] Basic
- [x] Extended
- [ ] Premium ($)
- [ ] Executive w/$

Activity Level
LOW → (arrow pointing left of MEDIUM)

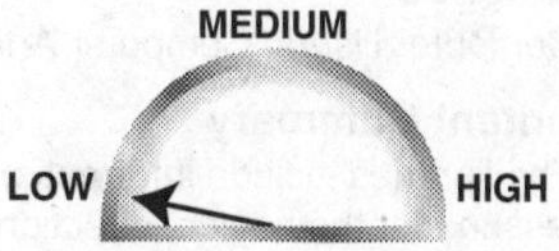

Address
GO: **IBMIMAGE**

LDC Words & Pixels Forum

Description
This Lotus Corporation forum discusses Magellan, Freelance, Freelance Plus, Graphwriter, Lotus Metro, and other graphics-related products.

Subjects
Computer Graphics, Computers

Audience
Computer users

Content Summary
You'll find information, discussions, questions, and other helpful insights for graphics-related products produced by Lotus Corporation. The library and message sections include Freelance/Windows, Multimedia Objects, Freelance OS/2, Freelance for DOS, ScreenCam, Agenda/Magellan, Symphony/LotusWorks, Oraganizer Technical, Approach, and others.

See Also
LDC Spreadsheets Forum, LDC Word Processing Forum, Lotus 123 For Windows Upgrade, Lotus Communications Forum, Lotus GmbH Forum, Lotus Press Release Forum, Lotus Technical Library

User Guide
- [x] Windows
- [x] DOS
- [ ] Macintosh
- [ ] Terminal Emulation
- [ ] VMS
- [ ] UNIX
- [x] OS/2
- [ ] Other platform

Cost
- [ ] Unknown
- [ ] Basic
- [x] Extended
- [ ] Premium ($)
- [ ] Executive w/$

Activity Level
UNKNOWN (LOW — HIGH)

Address
GO: **LOTUSB**

Micrografx Forum

Description
This forum is for anyone interested in Micrografx's professional and consumer graphics products. It provides technical support, contact with other Micrografx users, and a variety of other useful and entertaining things.

Subjects
Computer Graphics, Computers

Audience
Computer users, computer graphic designers

Content Summary
You can find press releases, comments, questions, support answers, clip art, and other graphics in the library and message sections. Some of the libraries include Utilities, Designer, ABC Flow/Toolkit, PhotoMagic, Charisma, and more.

See Also
Corel Forum, Graphics Forums, Graphics File Finder

User Guide
- [x] Windows
- [x] DOS
- [ ] Macintosh
- [ ] Terminal Emulation
- [ ] VMS
- [ ] UNIX
- [x] OS/2
- [ ] Other platform

Cost
- [ ] Unknown
- [ ] Basic
- [x] Extended
- [ ] Premium ($)
- [ ] Executive w/$

Activity Level
MEDIUM (arrow pointing up)

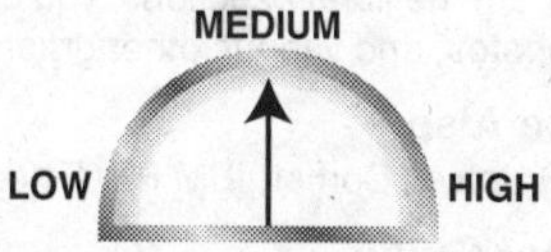

Address
GO: **MICROGRAFX**

PRC Publishing

Description
PRC's Database Publishing Services creates customized publications that reflect the specific information needs of their audiences. They are a leading publisher of database directories of all types.

Computer Graphics

Subjects
Catalogs, Computer Graphics, Database Publishing

Audience
Graphics professionals, publishers

Content Summary
PRC specializes in the combination of digital images and text data; in high volumes and at high speeds; and in customized layouts and electronic composition.

See Also
Graphics Forum

User Guide
- ☑ Windows
- ☑ DOS
- ☑ Macintosh
- ☐ Terminal Emulation
- ☑ VMS
- ☑ UNIX
- ☑ OS/2
- ☐ Other platform

Cost
- ☐ Unknown
- ☑ Basic
- ☐ Extended
- ☐ Premium ($)
- ☐ Executive w/$

Activity Level

Address
GO: **PRC**

Quick Picture Forum

Description
This forum provides images, clip art, missing children photos, and GIF images with fewer than 33 colors. These pictures tend to look better on PCs that have lower-resolution monitors.

Subjects
Computers, Computer Graphics

Audience
Computer graphics, graphics artists, photographers

Content Summary
From the library sections, you can download clip art, photos, and various other graphics files.

See Also
Graphics Corner, IBM File Finder

User Guide
- ☑ Windows
- ☑ DOS
- ☑ Macintosh
- ☐ Terminal Emulation
- ☐ VMS
- ☐ UNIX
- ☐ OS/2
- ☐ Other platform

Cost
- ☐ Unknown
- ☐ Basic
- ☑ Extended
- ☐ Premium ($)
- ☐ Executive w/$

Activity Level

Address
GO: **QPICS**

The 'GO GRAPHICS' Tutorial

Description
Online menu providing several helpful answers to commonly asked questions on CIS's GO GRAPHICS areas. Also, how to download pictures, how to view them, and so forth.

Subjects
Computers, Computer Graphics

Audience
Computer Users, Computer Artists

Content Summary
The libraries include information on file formats, lessons for the novice, directions for downloading graphics, converting images, and news.

See Also
Graphics Corner Forum

User Guide
- ☑ Windows
- ☑ DOS
- ☑ Macintosh
- ☐ Terminal Emulation
- ☐ VMS
- ☑ UNIX
- ☑ OS/2
- ☐ Other platform

Cost
- ☐ Unknown
- ☐ Basic
- ☑ Extended
- ☐ Premium ($)
- ☐ Executive w/$

Activity Level

Address
GO: **PIC**

Ventura Software Forum

Description
This is a vendor support forum for Ventura's Publisher, FormBase Database Publisher, and other software products.

Subjects
Computer Graphics, Computers

Audience
Ventura software users, desktop publishing users

Content Summary
Provides a place for users of Corel Ventura products to communicate with each other in order to get the

most out of their software. Libraries contain various utilities, add-ons, support files, and product information.

See Also
Software

User Guide
- ☑ Windows
- ☑ DOS
- ☐ Macintosh
- ☐ Terminal Emulation
- ☐ VMS
- ☐ UNIX
- ☐ OS/2
- ☐ Other platform

Cost
- ☐ Unknown
- ☐ Basic
- ☑ Extended
- ☐ Premium ($)
- ☐ Executive w/$

Activity Level

Address
GO: **VENTURA**

COMPUTER HARDWARE

Hayes Online

Description
This service gives you an introduction to Hayes Corporation, as well as product support.

Subjects
Computer Hardware, Computer Networking, Computers, Modems

Audience
Modem users, management information specialists

Content Summary
From the Online with Hayes main menu, you can select from About Online with Hayes, The Hayes Advantage, the Hayes Forum, LANstep, Product Descriptions, Special Support Forums, and Third Party Developers.

See Also
Hayes Forum, Modem Vendor Forum

User Guide
- ☑ Windows
- ☑ DOS
- ☑ Macintosh
- ☐ Terminal Emulation
- ☐ VMS
- ☐ UNIX
- ☐ OS/2
- ☐ Other platform

Cost
- ☐ Unknown
- ☐ Basic
- ☑ Extended
- ☐ Premium ($)
- ☐ Executive w/$

Activity Level

Address
GO: **HAYES**

HP Handhelds Forum

Description
This forum is designed to help you get the most out of your HP handheld computer, HP palmtop, or HP calculator.

Subjects
Computer Hardware, Computers, Field Computing

Audience
Computer programmers, computer professionals, computer users

Content Summary
You can get answers to your technical questions, exchange information with other users, take advantage of shareware and other files on the libraries, and stay in touch with the latest news from HP and 3rd-parties. The many libraries include areas for 1x,2x,3x calculators, 4x,6x,7x,9x calculators, the 95LX, the 100/200LX, HPHAND, and Palmtop programmers.

See Also
HP OmniBook Forum, HP Peripherals Forum, HP Specials

User Guide
- ☐ Windows
- ☐ DOS
- ☐ Macintosh
- ☐ Terminal Emulation
- ☐ VMS
- ☐ UNIX
- ☐ OS/2
- ☑ Other platform

Cost
- ☐ Unknown
- ☐ Basic
- ☑ Extended
- ☐ Premium ($)
- ☐ Executive w/$

Activity Level

Address
GO: **HPHAND**

Intel Corporation

Description
This service enables you to get to the Intel Forum and Intel Architecture Labs Forum.

Subjects
Computer Hardware, Computers, Microcomputers, Modems, Networking

Computer Hardware

Audience
Modem users, network users, computer users

Content Summary
The Intel Forum supports Intel's enhancement products for IBM PCs and any and all compatible computers. You can find information on Above Boards, SnapIn, Inboards, SatisFAXtion, and Connection CoProcessor FAX boards. Other products include Intel Math CoProcessors, modems, network-enhancement utilities, network-management tools, Visual Edge, Code Builder, Matched Memory, and NetPort. The Intel Architecture Labs Forum is an interactive, online service from which you can obtain the latest in technical and marketing information on the advanced Intel architectures.

See Also
Intal Access/iRUG Forum, The Intel Forum, PC Vendor J Forum, Palmtop B Forum

User Guide
- [x] Windows
- [x] DOS
- [ ] Macintosh
- [ ] Terminal Emulation
- [ ] VMS
- [ ] UNIX
- [x] OS/2
- [x] Other platform

Cost
- [ ] Unknown
- [ ] Basic
- [x] Extended
- [ ] Premium ($)
- [ ] Executive w/$

Activity Level MEDIUM (LOW – HIGH)

Address
GO: **INTEL**

Lexmark Forum

Description
This forum provides support and information for Lexmark products and services.

Subjects
Computer Hardware, Computers

Audience
Management information specialists, Macintosh users, computer hardware users, computer users

Content Summary
The libraries and message sections include Disk Images, Impact Drivers, Inkjet Drivers, Laser Drivers, Macintosh Drivers, Output Drivers, Thermal Drivers, and Utilities.

See Also
HP Peripherals Forum, Pacific Vendor Forum, Canon Support, Epson Forum, Support Directory

User Guide
- [x] Windows
- [x] DOS
- [x] Macintosh
- [ ] Terminal Emulation
- [ ] VMS
- [ ] UNIX
- [ ] OS/2
- [ ] Other platform

Cost
- [ ] Unknown
- [ ] Basic
- [x] Extended
- [ ] Premium ($)
- [ ] Executive w/$

Activity Level MEDIUM (LOW – HIGH)

Address
GO: **LEXMARK**

Logitech Forum

Description
This forum is devoted to Logitech products, including Scanman, FotoMan, 3D devices, mouse products, and others.

Subjects
Computer Hardware, Computers, Hardware/Software

Audience
Management information specialists, computer users, graphics designers

Content Summary
The Logitech Forum includes the following libraries: Mouse Products, Sound/Video, Scanman/FotoMan, Logitech OCR Software, MAC Products, Announcements, General Information, 3D Devices, and Top Q&A.

See Also
IBM Hardware Forum, PC Vendor B Forum, PC Vendor J Forum, Computer Buyers Guide, Computer Database Plus

User Guide
- [x] Windows
- [x] DOS
- [x] Macintosh
- [ ] Terminal Emulation
- [ ] VMS
- [x] UNIX
- [x] OS/2
- [x] Other platform

Cost
- [ ] Unknown
- [ ] Basic
- [x] Extended
- [ ] Premium ($)
- [ ] Executive w/$

Activity Level MEDIUM (LOW – HIGH)

Address
GO: **LOGITECH**

Computer Hardware

Lotus Communications Forum

Description
This forum is devoted to Lotus Corporation's communications products, including Notes and cc:Mail.

Subjects
Computer Communications, Computer Hardware, Computer Networking, Computers, E-mail, Networking

Audience
Management information specialists, network users

Content Summary
You can find a plethora of information, technical support solutions, hints and tips, and want ads in this forum. The library and message forums include Notes Tech Info, Notes Workstations/DB, Notes API Devlopment, cc:Mail Platform, cc:Mail Router, cc:Mail Admin, and many others.

See Also
Lotus Press Release Forum, Lotus Technical Library

User Guide
- ☑ Windows
- ☑ DOS
- ☑ Macintosh
- ☐ Terminal Emulation
- ☐ VMS
- ☐ UNIX
- ☑ OS/2
- ☑ Other platform

Cost
- ☐ Unknown
- ☐ Basic
- ☑ Extended
- ☐ Premium ($)
- ☐ Executive w/$

Activity Level

Address
GO: **LOTUSCOMM**

Macintosh Hardware Forum

Description
This forum discusses all types of Macintosh computers, including Classics, Quadras, Performas, Mac II, LC, Newton, and PDAs.

Subjects
Computer Hardware, Computers, Macintosh

Audience
Macintosh users, management information specialists

Content Summary
You can find several libraries in this forum that should satisfy your need for support and help for your Macintosh hardware, including Classic/Early Macs, Performas/Other, Quadras, Printers/Output, Scanners/Input, Monitors/Video, and more.

See Also
Macintosh Systems Forum, Macintosh Forums

User Guide
- ☐ Windows
- ☐ DOS
- ☑ Macintosh
- ☐ Terminal Emulation
- ☐ VMS
- ☐ UNIX
- ☐ OS/2
- ☐ Other platform

Cost
- ☐ Unknown
- ☐ Basic
- ☑ Extended
- ☐ Premium ($)
- ☐ Executive w/$

Activity Level

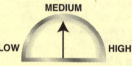

Address
GO: **MACHW**

Vobis AG Computer Forum

Description
This is a vendor support forum for Vobis AG products. Vobis AG is a German-speaking forum.

Subjects
Computer Hardware, Computers

Audience
Germans

Content Summary
You can find information and support for vobis AG products.

See Also
Hardware, Software Support

User Guide
- ☑ Windows
- ☑ DOS
- ☐ Macintosh
- ☐ Terminal Emulation
- ☐ VMS
- ☐ UNIX
- ☐ OS/2
- ☐ Other platform

Cost
- ☐ Unknown
- ☐ Basic
- ☑ Extended
- ☐ Premium ($)
- ☐ Executive w/$

Activity Level

Address
GO: **VOBIS**

Computer Library Online

Description
A family of information retrieval services designed to provide a complete reference and assistance resource for computer users.

Subjects
Computers, Databases

Audience
Computer users

Content Summary
Libraries include Computer Database Plus, Computer Buyers' Guide, Support on Site, articles, journals, recommendations, advice, and updates on products.

See Also
Information USA, MS Software Library, Ziff Software Center, Novell Library Forum, Lotus Technical Library

User Guide
- ☑ Windows
- ☑ DOS
- ☑ Macintosh
- ☐ Terminal Emulation
- ☐ VMS
- ☑ UNIX
- ☐ OS/2
- ☑ Other platform

Cost
- ☐ Unknown
- ☐ Basic
- ☐ Extended
- ☑ Premium ($)
- ☐ Executive w/$

Activity Level

Address
GO: **COMPLIB**

COMPUTER NETWORKING

Hayes Online

Description
This service gives you an introduction to Hayes Corporation, as well as product support.

Subjects
Computer Hardware, Computer Networking, Computers, Modems

Audience
Modem users, management information specialists

Content Summary
From the Online with Hayes main menu, you can select from About Online with Hayes, The Hayes Advantage, the Hayes Forum, LANstep, Product Descriptions, Special Support Forums, and Third Party Developers.

See Also
Hayes Forum, Modem Vendor Forum

User Guide
- ☑ Windows
- ☑ DOS
- ☑ Macintosh
- ☐ Terminal Emulation
- ☐ VMS
- ☐ UNIX
- ☐ OS/2
- ☐ Other platform

Cost
- ☐ Unknown
- ☐ Basic
- ☑ Extended
- ☐ Premium ($)
- ☐ Executive w/$

Activity Level

Address
GO: **HAYES**

LAN Magazine

Description
This forum is for network administrators, users, installers, and integrators to exchange information about computer networks.

Subjects
Computer Networking, Computers, Networking

Audience
Computer users, management information specialists

Content Summary
Sponsored by *LAN Magazine*, this forum is dedicated to help you solve LAN problems, stay in touch with the industry, and keep you informed of new products and services. The library and message sections include Reviews, Features, Guests & Interviews, Forum Member Bios, User-to-User, and others. For a story on salaries of network managers, see Library 3, Features.

See Also
LAN Technology Forum, LAN Vendor Forum

User Guide
- ☑ Windows
- ☑ DOS
- ☑ Macintosh
- ☐ Terminal Emulation
- ☐ VMS
- ☑ UNIX
- ☑ OS/2
- ☑ Other platform

Computer Networking – Computer Products

Cost
- [ ] Unknown
- [ ] Basic
- [x] Extended
- [ ] Premium ($)
- [ ] Executive w/$

Activity Level
MEDIUM (arrow pointing up between LOW and HIGH)

Address
GO: **LANMAG**

Vines 4.x Patchware Forum

Description
This vendor support forum offers software patches and support for Banyan's VINES 4.x networking products.

Subjects
Banyan, Computer Networking, Computers

Audience
Anyone using Banyan Vines Network

Content Summary
The primary purpose of this forum is to give users help, information, and support on Banyan and its product line. Libraries contain various add-ons, support files, patches, and product information.

See Also
Banyan Forum, Lan Magazine Forum

User Guide
- [x] Windows
- [x] DOS
- [ ] Macintosh
- [ ] Terminal Emulation
- [ ] VMS
- [ ] UNIX
- [ ] OS/2
- [ ] Other platform

Cost
- [ ] Unknown
- [ ] Basic
- [x] Extended
- [ ] Premium ($)
- [ ] Executive w/$

Activity Level
MEDIUM (arrow pointing toward LOW)

Address
GO: **VINES4**

Vines 5.x Patchware Forum

Description
This vendor support forum offers software patches for Banyan's VINES 5.x networking products.

Subjects
Banyan, Computer Networking, Computers

Audience
Anyone using Banyan Vines Network

Content Summary
The primary purpose of this forum is to give users help, information, and support on Banyan and its product line. Libraries contain various add-ons, support files, patches, and product information.

See Also
Banyan Forum, Other Ban Patchware Forum, LAN Magazine Forum

User Guide
- [x] Windows
- [x] DOS
- [ ] Macintosh
- [ ] Terminal Emulation
- [ ] VMS
- [ ] UNIX
- [ ] OS/2
- [ ] Other platform

Cost
- [ ] Unknown
- [ ] Basic
- [x] Extended
- [ ] Premium ($)
- [ ] Executive w/$

Activity Level
MEDIUM (arrow pointing toward LOW)

Address
GO: **VINES5**

COMPUTER PRODUCTS

Gateway 2000 Forum

Description
Moo! If you're like me, you can't live without your Gateway 2000 computer. This forum offers product support and information on Gateway's line of products.

Subjects
Computer, Computer Hardware, Computer Products, Computers, Hardware/Software

Audience
Computer hardware users, computer users

Content Summary
The libraries and message sections in this forum are devoted to help you use and service your Gateway 2000 product. You can download the latest drivers, patches, settings, prices, fixes, and utilities by visiting

the appropriate library. The Fun Files library (Library 13) is a must visit to get Gateway's latest bitmap for your wallpaper. Try the SpaceCow BMP or the COW.WAV file. The latter has been downloaded over 6,000 times! For more serious users, don't neglect looking in the various message sections for an answer to your hardware question. This is a very active message area.

See Also
Computer Buyers' Guide, Computing Support

User Guide
- ☑ Windows
- ☑ DOS
- ☐ Macintosh
- ☐ Terminal Emulation
- ☐ VMS
- ☐ UNIX
- ☐ OS/2
- ☐ Other platform

Cost
- ☐ Unknown
- ☐ Basic
- ☑ Extended
- ☐ Premium ($)
- ☐ Executive w/$

Activity Level

Address
GO: **GATEWAY**

JDR Microdevices

Description
This service enables you to order Microdevices products and get customer service. JDR specializes in high technology products.

Subjects
Computer Products, Computers

Audience
General public, computer users

See Also
PC Vendor C Forum, PC Industry Forum, Computing Support, Hardware Forums

Content Summary
From the JDR Microdevices main menu, you can choose from Shop Our Online Catalog, Product QuickSearch, Customer Service, Letter from the President, Request our Free Catalogs, Place An Order From Our Print Catalog, and Talk To Us. Browse the online catalog for items such as motherboards, memory, multimedia devices, books, and other products.

User Guide
- ☑ Windows
- ☑ DOS
- ☑ Macintosh
- ☐ Terminal Emulation
- ☐ VMS
- ☐ UNIX
- ☐ OS/2
- ☐ Other platform

Cost
- ☐ Unknown
- ☐ Basic
- ☐ Extended
- ☑ Premium ($)
- ☐ Executive w/$

Activity Level
UNKNOWN (LOW—HIGH)

Address
GO: **JDR**

MacWAREHOUSE

Description
Order products from MacWAREHOUSE online using this service.

Subjects
Computer Products, Macintosh

Audience
Computer users, Macintosh users

Content Summary
From the main menu, you can go to the MacWAREHOUSE Online Store to order products, view Best Selling Items, go to the QuickSearch area, Request or Order from the Online Catalog, talk to Customer Service, or play the MacWAREHOUSE Word Scramble game.

See Also
The Mac Zone/PC Zone (FREE), PC Industry Forum, Hardware Forums, Macintosh Hardware Forum

User Guide
- ☐ Windows
- ☐ DOS
- ☑ Macintosh
- ☑ Terminal Emulation
- ☐ VMS
- ☐ UNIX
- ☐ OS/2
- ☐ Other platform

Cost
- ☐ Unknown
- ☑ Basic
- ☐ Extended
- ☐ Premium ($)
- ☐ Executive w/$

Activity Level

Address
GO: **MW**

Computer Products – Computer Programming

MicroWarehouse

Description
MicroWarehouse is the "PC Superstore." Order printers, games, word processing software, and much more from this service.

Subjects
Computer Products, Computers

Audience
Computer users

Content Summary
Be sure to look at MicroWarehouses "Featured Products" by choosing MicroWAREHOUSE Online Store from the main menu. Other choices include Quicksearch, Request/Order from Free Online Catalog, Customer Service, and more.

See Also
PC Industry Forum, Hardware Forums

User Guide
- ☐ Windows
- ☐ DOS
- ☐ Macintosh
- ☑ Terminal Emulation
- ☐ VMS
- ☐ UNIX
- ☐ OS/2
- ☐ Other platform

Cost
- ☐ Unknown
- ☑ Basic
- ☐ Extended
- ☐ Premium ($)
- ☐ Executive w/$

Activity Level

Address
GO: **MCW**

COMPUTER PROGRAMMING

AI Expert Forum

Description
The electronic edition of AI EXPERT Magazine serves as a forum for exchange of ideas and information on Artificial Intelligence research.

Subjects
Artificial Intelligence

Audience
Researchers

Content Summary
The libraries are the heart of the Forum. You will find source code, executable programs, bibliographies, product reviews, bug reports, bug fixes, electronic versions of important papers and articles on AI, and more.

See Also
Mensa Forum, Knowledge Index, IQuest, Intelligence Test

User Guide
- ☑ Windows
- ☑ DOS
- ☐ Macintosh
- ☐ Terminal Emulation
- ☐ VMS
- ☐ UNIX
- ☐ OS/2
- ☐ Other platform

Cost
- ☐ Unknown
- ☐ Basic
- ☑ Extended
- ☐ Premium ($)
- ☐ Executive w/$

Activity Level

Address
GO: **AIEXPERT**

CASE-DCI Forum

Description
CASEFORUM is a place where people interested in creating software in a more effective manner can meet and discuss concepts and tools.

Subjects
Computer Programming, Computers

Audience
Software developers

Content Summary
Topics of interest to software developers include computer-aided software engineering and product details.

See Also
Mensa Forum, Knowledge Index, IQuest, Intelligence Test

User Guide
- ☑ Windows
- ☑ DOS
- ☐ Macintosh
- ☐ Terminal Emulation
- ☐ VMS
- ☐ UNIX
- ☐ OS/2
- ☐ Other platform

Cost
- ☐ Unknown
- ☐ Basic
- ☑ Extended
- ☐ Premium ($)
- ☐ Executive w/$

Activity Level

Address
GO: **CASEFORUM**

Computer Programming

CSI Forth Net Forum

Description
The Forth Forum supports the Forth language in general, as well as CSI Forth products.

Subjects
Computer Programming, Computers

Audience
Forth Programmers

Content Summary
Libraries include information on Forth, Programming, MOPS, MacForth Plus, CSI Hardware, and users groups.

User Guide
- ☑ Windows
- ☑ DOS
- ☑ Macintosh
- ☐ Terminal Emulation
- ☐ VMS
- ☑ UNIX
- ☐ OS/2
- ☐ Other platform

Cost
- ☐ Unknown
- ☐ Basic
- ☑ Extended
- ☐ Premium ($)
- ☐ Executive w/$

Activity Level

Address
GO: **FORTH**

PC MagNet Programming Forum

Description
The PC MagNet Programming Forum, part of ZiffNet, has the latest files from the programming sections of *PC Magazine*. Many of the authors can be found here as well.

Subjects
Computers, Computer Programming, ZiffNet

Audience
Computer users, computer programmers

Content Summary
The library and message sections include Utilities Code, Power Programming, Languages, Lab Notes, Environments, Toolkits, Corporate Developer, and more. If you are interested in computer-related trade shows, you can download a calendar of over 100 events from Library 1, General. The file name is ZCAL13.ZIP.

See Also
PC MagNet, PC MagNet Editorial Forum, PC MagNet Utilities/Tips Forum

User Guide
- ☑ Windows
- ☑ DOS
- ☑ Macintosh
- ☐ Terminal Emulation
- ☐ VMS
- ☐ UNIX
- ☑ OS/2
- ☑ Other platform

Cost
- ☐ Unknown
- ☐ Basic
- ☑ Extended
- ☐ Premium ($)
- ☐ Executive w/$

Activity Level

Address
GO: **PROGRAMMING**

Ziff Cobb Programming Forum

Description
The Cobb Programming Forum provides downloadable files and source code archived from the Cobb Programming Journals. C, C++, Pascal, Paradox, and dBASE are included.

Subjects
Computer Programming, Computers, ZiffNet

Audience
Computer users

Content Summary
If you are interested in programming, join this forum for information and files to help you with your programming needs.

See Also
Ziff Cobb Applications Forum

User Guide
- ☑ Windows
- ☑ DOS
- ☐ Macintosh
- ☐ Terminal Emulation
- ☐ VMS
- ☐ UNIX
- ☐ OS/2
- ☑ Other platform

Cost
- ☐ Unknown
- ☐ Basic
- ☑ Extended
- ☐ Premium ($)
- ☐ Executive w/$

Activity Level

Address
GO: **ZNT:COBBPR**

COMPUTER PROGRAMMING LANGUAGES

IBM Languages Forum

Description
This forum is for questions, answers, and discussion regarding IBM languages, including APL and APL2.

Subjects
Computer Programming Languages, Computers, IBM

Audience
Management information specialists, computer programmers

Content Summary
This forum contains the following libraries: General Library, APL2 Language, APL2 for OS/2 Demo, APL2 for OS/2 CSD, and APL2 User Files.

See Also
IBM OS/2 Developer 1 Forum, IBM OS/2 Developer 2 Forum, IBM Systems/Util. Forum

User Guide
- [ ] Windows
- [ ] DOS
- [ ] Macintosh
- [ ] Terminal Emulation
- [ ] VMS
- [ ] UNIX
- [x] OS/2
- [x] Other platform

Cost
- [ ] Unknown
- [ ] Basic
- [x] Extended
- [ ] Premium ($)
- [ ] Executive w/$

Activity Level MEDIUM

LOW ← HIGH

Address
GO: **IBMLANG**

IBM OS/2 Developers Forums

Description
The IBM OS/2 Developers 1 and 2 Forums contain information for OS/2 developers, including development tools, debugging, and other questions.

Subjects
Computer Programming Languages, Computers, IBM

Audience
Computer programmers, management information specialists

Content Summary
The IBM OS/2 Developers 1 Forum (GO OS2DF1) includes the following libraries: Base OS API's, PM API's, 2.x Workplace Shell, REXX/Other Languages, Device Drive Development, and more. The IBM OS/2 Developers 1 Forum (GO OS2DF1) includes the following libraries: Communications Manager, LAN Server, TCP/IP, CID Enablement, Pen Software, and more.

See Also
IBM OS/2 B Vendors Forum, IBM Object Technology Forum, IBM OS/2 Support Forum, IBM OS/2 Vendor Forum

User Guide
- [ ] Windows
- [ ] DOS
- [ ] Macintosh
- [ ] Terminal Emulation
- [ ] VMS
- [ ] UNIX
- [x] OS/2
- [ ] Other platform

Cost
- [ ] Unknown
- [ ] Basic
- [x] Extended
- [ ] Premium ($)
- [ ] Executive w/$

Activity Level MEDIUM

LOW → HIGH

Address
GO: **OS2DFI** or **OS2DF2**

IBM Programming Forum

Description
This forum is devoted to helping those interested in programming for the IBM or IBM PC compatible computers.

Subjects
Computer Programming Languages, Computers

Audience
Computer programmers

Content Summary
You can get assemblers, source code, tips, and techniques from this forum. The library and message sections include OS Services, C and C++, BASIC, Other Languages, Tools/Debuggers, Job Exchange, VESA, and more.

See Also
IBM Languages Forum, Microsoft Languages Forum

User Guide
- [x] Windows
- [x] DOS
- [x] Macintosh
- [ ] Terminal Emulation
- [ ] VMS
- [x] UNIX
- [x] OS/2
- [x] Other platform

Computer Programming Languages

Cost
- ☐ Unknown
- ☐ Basic
- ☑ Extended
- ☐ Premium ($)
- ☐ Executive w/$

Activity Level: MEDIUM

Address
GO: **IBMPRO**

Macintosh Developers Forum

Description
If you want to program your Macintosh—whether commercially or for your own use—the Mac Developers Forum is the right place for you.

Subjects
Computer Programming Languages, Computers, Macintosh

Audience
Macintosh users, computer programmers

Content Summary
The following libraries are found in this forum: BASIC, Assembly Language, C and Pascal, Object Oriented, Other Languages, Apple System Tools, Apple System Files, Development Environments, Scripting Month, Learn Programming, A/UX, Tools/Debuggers, and MacTech Magazine.

See Also
Macintosh Forums, Macintosh Systems Forum

User Guide
- ☐ Windows
- ☐ DOS
- ☑ Macintosh
- ☐ Terminal Emulation
- ☐ VMS
- ☐ UNIX
- ☐ OS/2
- ☐ Other platform

Cost
- ☐ Unknown
- ☐ Basic
- ☑ Extended
- ☐ Premium ($)
- ☐ Executive w/$

Activity Level: MEDIUM

Address
GO: **MACDEV**

Microsoft 32-bit Languages Forum

Description
This forum is designed as an area to exchange information, tips, and techniques concerning Microsoft Languages.

Subjects
Computer Applications, Computer Programming Languages, Computer Users, Microsoft Corp.

Audience
Computer programmers

Content Summary
Some of the topics covered in this forum include Microsoft C++, Microsoft C, Assembler, QC/QCWin, FORTRAN, CodeView/IDE Debug, NonTech Cutomer Support, and others. This area is for the applications developer and programmer; be ready for high-level discussions if you join this forum.

See Also
Microsoft Languages Forum, Microsoft DevCast Forum, Microsoft WIN32 Forum

User Guide
- ☑ Windows
- ☑ DOS
- ☑ Macintosh
- ☐ Terminal Emulation
- ☐ VMS
- ☐ UNIX
- ☐ OS/2
- ☑ Other platform

Cost
- ☐ Unknown
- ☐ Basic
- ☑ Extended
- ☐ Premium ($)
- ☐ Executive w/$

Activity Level: MEDIUM

Address
GO: **MSLNG32**

Microsoft BASIC Forum

Description
This forum is designed as an area to exchange information, tips, and techniques concerning Microsoft Basic products.

Subjects
Computer Programming Languages, Computers, Microsoft Corp.

Audience
Computer programmers, computer users

Content Summary
The MS BASIC forum contains several library and message sections, including MS Information and Index, Setup Wizard/Kit, Data Access Objects, Programming Issues, Calling APIs/DLLs, DOS Visual Basic, Mac Visual Basic, and more.

See Also
Microsoft Languages Forum, Microsoft DevCast Forum, Microsoft Connection

Computer Programming Languages

User Guide
- ☑ Windows
- ☑ DOS
- ☑ Macintosh
- ☐ Terminal Emulation
- ☐ VMS
- ☐ UNIX
- ☐ OS/2
- ☑ Other platform

Cost
- ☐ Unknown
- ☐ Basic
- ☑ Extended
- ☐ Premium ($)
- ☐ Executive w/$

Activity Level: HIGH (between MEDIUM and HIGH)

Address
GO: **MSBASIC**

Microsoft DevCast Forum

Description
This forum is designed to give conference attendees a temporary location for follow-up discussion regarding the Microsoft DevCast conference.

Subjects
Computer Programming Languages, Computers, Microsoft Corp.

Audience
Computer users, computer programmers

Content Summary
You can find files, information, and other useful material for upcoming DevCast conferences or from past conferences.

See Also
Microsoft Knowledge Base, Microsoft Languages Forum, MS 32bit Languages Forum

User Guide
- ☑ Windows
- ☑ DOS
- ☑ Macintosh
- ☐ Terminal Emulation
- ☐ VMS
- ☑ UNIX
- ☐ OS/2
- ☑ Other platform

Cost
- ☐ Unknown
- ☐ Basic
- ☑ Extended
- ☐ Premium ($)
- ☐ Executive w/$

Activity Level: MEDIUM

Address
GO: **DEVCAST**

Microsoft Foundation Classes Forum

Description
This forum is designed as an area to exchange information, tips, and techniques concerning Microsoft Foundation Classes.

Subjects
Computer Programming Languages, Computers, Microsoft Corp.

Audience
Computer programmers

Content Summary
This forum is for application developers interested in the Microsoft Foundation Classes. Some of the libraries include Beginners Library, Database Classes, OLE 2.0 Classes, VBX Usage, DLL & Memory, and Wizards/DDV/DDX. Also watch for online conferences and seminars, many of which feature Microsoft product managers.

See Also
MS Applications Forum, MS 32bit Languages Forum

User Guide
- ☑ Windows
- ☑ DOS
- ☑ Macintosh
- ☐ Terminal Emulation
- ☐ VMS
- ☐ UNIX
- ☐ OS/2
- ☐ Other platform

Cost
- ☐ Unknown
- ☐ Basic
- ☑ Extended
- ☐ Premium ($)
- ☐ Executive w/$

Activity Level: MEDIUM

Address
GO: **MSMFC**

Microsoft WIN32 Forum

Description
This forum is designed as an area to exchange information, tips, and techniques concerning Microsoft Win32 SDK.

Subjects
Computer Programming Languages, Computers, Microsoft Corp.

Audience
Computer users, computer professionals

Content Summary
You can find a plethora of information and tools for the WIN32 SDK. Library and message sections include API-User/GUI, API Graphics/GDI, API-Base/Console, API Security, Porting OS/2 & Unix, and more.

Computer Programming Languages

See Also
Microsoft Connection, Microsoft DevCast Forum, MS 32bit Languages Forum

User Guide
- [x] Windows
- [x] DOS
- [x] Macintosh
- [ ] Terminal Emulation
- [ ] VMS
- [x] UNIX
- [x] OS/2
- [ ] Other platform

Cost
- [ ] Unknown
- [ ] Basic
- [x] Extended
- [ ] Premium ($)
- [ ] Executive w/$

Activity Level

MEDIUM

Address
GO: **MSWIN32**

Microsoft Windows Extensions Forum

Description
This forum is designed as an area to exchange information, tips, and techniques concerning Microsoft Windows SDK extensions.

Subjects
Computer Programming Languages, Computers, Microsoft Corp.

Audience
Computer programmers

Content Summary
This forum includes these library and message sections: MS Info and Index, MS Test for Windows, TAPI SDK, WOSA/XRT, WOSA/XFS, MS Delta, Arabic/Hebrew SDK, Pen SDK, Far East SDK, ODBC, ODBC Desktop Drivers, LSAPI, MAPI/Schedule+ Libraries, and DSPRMI and SPEECH.

See Also
Microsoft Knowledge Base, Microsoft Languages Forum

User Guide
- [x] Windows
- [x] DOS
- [x] Macintosh
- [ ] Terminal Emulation
- [ ] VMS
- [ ] UNIX
- [ ] OS/2
- [x] Other platform

Cost
- [ ] Unknown
- [ ] Basic
- [x] Extended
- [ ] Premium ($)
- [ ] Executive w/$

Activity Level

MEDIUM

Address
GO: **WINEXT**

Microsoft Windows Objects Forum

Description
This forum is designed as an area to exchange information, tips, and techniques concerning Microsoft OLE.

Subjects
Computer Programming Languages, Computers, Microsoft Corp.

Audience
Computer users, computer programmers

Content Summary
Interested in finding information on OLE and how to use it in your programs? Look in the libraries and message sections in this forum for your answers. You'll find libraries such as Component Object Model, Structured Storage, OLE: User Interface, OLE: Automation, OLE: Mac Issues, and more.

See Also
MS Windows Extensions Forum, MS Windows SDK Forum, MS Foundation Classes Forum, Microsoft Languages Forum

User Guide
- [x] Windows
- [x] DOS
- [x] Macintosh
- [ ] Terminal Emulation
- [ ] VMS
- [ ] UNIX
- [ ] OS/2
- [ ] Other platform

Cost
- [ ] Unknown
- [ ] Basic
- [x] Extended
- [ ] Premium ($)
- [ ] Executive w/$

Activity Level

MEDIUM

Address
GO: **WINOBJECTS**

Microsoft Windows SDK Forum

Description
This forum is designed as an area to exchange information, tips, and techniques concerning the Microsoft Windows SDK.

Subjects
Computer Programming Languages, Computers, Microsoft Corp.

Computer PROGRAMMING Languages – Computer Software

Audience
Computer programmers

Content Summary
This forum includes several library and message sections, including Public Utilities, Training, USER, Common Dialogs, Printing, GDI, Kernel—Memory Management, WinHelp, and others.

See Also
Microsoft Languages Forum, MS Windows Objects Forum

User Guide
- ☑ Windows
- ☑ DOS
- ☑ Macintosh
- ☐ Terminal Emulation
- ☐ VMS
- ☐ UNIX
- ☑ OS/2
- ☑ Other platform

Cost
- ☐ Unknown
- ☐ Basic
- ☑ Extended
- ☐ Premium ($)
- ☐ Executive w/$

Activity Level

Address
GO: **WINSDK**

COMPUTER SECURITY

National Computer Security Association (NCSA)

Description
This service helps you understand the NCSA and the NCSA Ethics Committee, and go to the NCSA Forum.

Subjects
Computers, Computer Security

Audience
Computer users, MIS people

Content Summary
From the main menu, you can select these options: NCSA InfoSecurity Forum, About the NCSA, and About the NCSA Ethics Committee.

See Also
NCSA Forum

User Guide
- ☑ Windows
- ☑ DOS
- ☑ Macintosh
- ☐ Terminal Emulation
- ☑ VMS
- ☑ UNIX
- ☐ OS/2
- ☐ Other platform

Cost
- ☐ Unknown
- ☑ Basic
- ☐ Extended
- ☐ Premium ($)
- ☐ Executive w/$

Activity Level

Address
GO: **NCSA**

COMPUTER SOFTWARE

SOFTEX

Description
This CompuServe-sponsored forum enables you to purchase software for your personal computer often at a lower cost than if you purchased it through retail.

Subjects
Computer Software, Online Shopping

Audience
Computer users, software

Content Summary
You can purchase software by searching by type of software, publisher of the software, or by other criteria. If you choose to purchase the software, you get a description of the product, hardware and software requirements, and an estimate of download time. The charge appears on your monthly CompuServe bill.

See Also
Computer Buyers Guide Forum, Computer Shopper Forum, Shop-at-home Forum

User Guide
- ☑ Windows
- ☑ DOS
- ☑ Macintosh
- ☑ Terminal Emulation
- ☐ VMS
- ☑ UNIX
- ☐ OS/2
- ☑ Other platform

Cost
- ☐ Unknown
- ☐ Basic
- ☑ Extended
- ☐ Premium ($)
- ☐ Executive w/$

Activity Level

Address
GO: **SOFTEX**

Computer Training Forum

Description
The DPTRAIN Forum is dedicated to the question of how people learn to use computers and how to help them learn more effectively.

Subjects
Computers, Education

Audience
Computer trainers

Content Summary
Libraries include training techniques, technology, support, information centers, local groups, newsletters, and training software.

User Guide
- ☑ Windows
- ☑ DOS
- ☑ Macintosh
- ☐ Terminal Emulation
- ☐ VMS
- ☑ UNIX
- ☐ OS/2
- ☐ Other platform

Cost
- ☐ Unknown
- ☐ Basic
- ☑ Extended
- ☐ Premium ($)
- ☐ Executive w/$

Activity Level

MEDIUM / LOW / HIGH

Address
GO: **DPTRAIN**

COMPUTER USERS

IBM New User's Forum

Description
This forum is devoted to newer users of CompuServe and the PC as well as those who like to join in and share their experience with newcomers. In addition, you'll find an excellent selection of games and entertainment files.

Subjects
Computer Users, IBM PCs

Audience
Computer users

Content Summary
If you're new to using CompuServe or your PC (or both), use this forum to get comfortable downloading files, learn different applications, and have fun with your computer. The libraries include Download Help, Library Tools, Adventures, Music, Fun Graphics, Windows Fun, and more.

See Also
CompuServe Help Forum (FREE)

User Guide
- ☑ Windows
- ☑ DOS
- ☑ Macintosh
- ☐ Terminal Emulation
- ☐ VMS
- ☐ UNIX
- ☑ OS/2
- ☑ Other platform

Cost
- ☐ Unknown
- ☐ Basic
- ☑ Extended
- ☐ Premium ($)
- ☐ Executive w/$

Activity Level

MEDIUM / LOW / HIGH

Address
GO: **IBMNEW**

IBM OS/2 Support Forum

Description
Get general OS/2 support help from this forum directly from IBM and other members.

Subjects
Computer Users, IBM

Audience
Computer users, management information specialists, IBM users

Content Summary
The library and message sections include Installation Questions, H/W - I/O Media, H/W - Platform, REXX/Language Questions, Windows Application Questions, IBM Files, and much more.

See Also
IBM OS/2 Service Pak, IBM PowerPC Forum

User Guide
- ☐ Windows
- ☐ DOS
- ☐ Macintosh
- ☐ Terminal Emulation
- ☐ VMS
- ☐ UNIX
- ☑ OS/2
- ☐ Other platform

Cost
- ☐ Unknown
- ☐ Basic
- ☑ Extended
- ☐ Premium ($)
- ☐ Executive w/$

Activity Level

MEDIUM / LOW / HIGH

Address
GO: **OS2SUPPORT**

Computer Users

IBM OS/2 Users Forum

Description
Whether you're a new user to OS/2 or a seasoned OS/2 bigot, you should join this forum and its discussions on hardware and software issues as they relate to OS/2.

Subjects
Computer Users, IBM

Audience
IBM users, computer users

Content Summary
The library and message sections include OS/2 Public Image, OS/2 & Hardware, Application Questions, New User Questions, OS/2 User Groups, and more.

See Also
IBM OS/2 Support Forum

User Guide
- ☐ Windows
- ☐ DOS
- ☐ Macintosh
- ☐ Terminal Emulation
- ☐ VMS
- ☐ UNIX
- ☑ OS/2
- ☐ Other platform

Cost
- ☐ Unknown
- ☐ Basic
- ☑ Extended
- ☐ Premium ($)
- ☐ Executive w/$

Activity Level

Address
GO: **OS2USER**

Microsoft 32-bit Languages Forum

Description
This forum is designed as an area to exchange information, tips, and techniques concerning Microsoft Languages.

Subjects
Computer Applications, Computer Programming Languages, Computer Users, Microsoft Corp.

Audience
Computer programmers

Content Summary
Some of the topics covered in this forum include Microsoft C ++, Microsoft C, Assembler, QC/QCWin, FORTRAN, CodeView/IDE Debug, NonTech Cutomer Support, and others. This area is for the applications developer and programmer; be ready for high-level discussions if you join this forum.

See Also
Microsoft Languages Forum, Microsoft DevCast Forum, Microsoft WIN32 Forum

User Guide
- ☑ Windows
- ☑ DOS
- ☑ Macintosh
- ☐ Terminal Emulation
- ☐ VMS
- ☐ UNIX
- ☐ OS/2
- ☑ Other platform

Cost
- ☐ Unknown
- ☐ Basic
- ☑ Extended
- ☐ Premium ($)
- ☐ Executive w/$

Activity Level

Address
GO: **MSLNG32**

Microsoft DOS Forum

Description
Have questions about MS DOS? Do you just love to discuss DOS problems and features? You should join this forum then.

Subjects
Computer Users, Microsoft Corp., MS-DOS

Audience
Computer users, management information specialists

Content Summary
You can find out the latest about the newest release of MS DOS, troubleshooting suggestions, hardware issues, setup and installation problems and concerns, memory management concerns, and other topics. For information on DoubleSpace, DriveSpace, and Stacker, see the lively message section area.

See Also
Microsoft Connection, MS DOS 6.2 DLOAD (Microsoft)

User Guide
- ☐ Windows
- ☑ DOS
- ☐ Macintosh
- ☐ Terminal Emulation
- ☐ VMS
- ☐ UNIX
- ☐ OS/2
- ☐ Other platform

Cost
- ☐ Unknown
- ☐ Basic
- ☑ Extended
- ☐ Premium ($)
- ☐ Executive w/$

Activity Level

Address
GO: **MSDOS**

Microsoft Sales and Information Forum

Description
This forum is monitored by our Microsoft Sales and Information staff to respond to your product information, sales, registration, promotion, and pricing questions.

Subjects
Computer Users, Computers, Microsoft Corp.

Audience
Computer users

Content Summary
The two areas in this forum are library and messages. The message board is where you can post sales information questions or browse through previously posted questions and responses. The libraries of this forum contain files posted by Microsoft only.

See Also
Microsoft Connection

User Guide
- ☑ Windows
- ☑ DOS
- ☑ Macintosh
- ☐ Terminal Emulation
- ☐ VMS
- ☐ UNIX
- ☐ OS/2
- ☑ Other platform

Cost
- ☐ Unknown
- ☐ Basic
- ☑ Extended
- ☐ Premium ($)
- ☐ Executive w/$

Activity Level

Address
GO: **MSIC**

Microsoft Software Library

Description
This area contains binary files, technical notes, utilities, and other files for various Microsoft applications.

Subjects
Computer Applications, Computer Users, Microsoft Corp.

Audience
Computer users, management information specialists, Macintosh users

Content Summary
Download the file you need by entering a keyword and searching for it. You can search on keyword, serial number, submission date, or file name.

See Also
MS WINFUN Forum, MS Windows Shareware Forum

User Guide
- ☑ Windows
- ☑ DOS
- ☑ Macintosh
- ☑ Terminal Emulation
- ☐ VMS
- ☐ UNIX
- ☑ OS/2
- ☑ Other platform

Cost
- ☐ Unknown
- ☐ Basic
- ☑ Extended
- ☐ Premium ($)
- ☐ Executive w/$

Activity Level

Address
GO: **MSL**

COMPUTER VIRUSES

McAfee Virus Forum

Description
The purpose of this forum is to help you with any questions or problems you have related to anti-viral software and computer viruses.

Subjects
Computer Viruses, Computers

Audience
Computer users, management information specialists

Content Summary
Find information and updates for virus software and network tools in the libraries and in the message sections.

See Also
Symantic AntiVirus Prod. Forum, IBM Systems/Util. Forum, KAOS AntiVirus

User Guide
- ☑ Windows
- ☑ DOS
- ☐ Macintosh
- ☐ Terminal Emulation
- ☐ VMS
- ☐ UNIX
- ☐ OS/2
- ☑ Other platform

Cost
- ☐ Unknown
- ☐ Basic
- ☑ Extended
- ☐ Premium ($)
- ☐ Executive w/$

Activity Level

Address
GO: **NCSAVIRUS**

Microsoft Windows Forum

Description
News, files, tips, and other information related to MS Windows.

Subjects
Computer Viruses, Computers, Microsoft Corp., Windows

Audience
Computer users

Content Summary
Some of the library and message sections include Setup, Mouse, Display Drivers, Memory Optimization, MS-DOS Apps/PIFs, Printing/Fonts/WPS, and Terminal/Comm.

See Also
Microsoft Connection, Microsoft Knowledge Base

User Guide
- ☑ Windows
- ☑ DOS
- ☐ Macintosh
- ☐ Terminal Emulation
- ☐ VMS
- ☐ UNIX
- ☐ OS/2
- ☐ Other platform

Cost
- ☐ Unknown
- ☐ Basic
- ☑ Extended
- ☐ Premium ($)
- ☐ Executive w/$

Activity Level

Activity Level: HIGH

Address
GO: **MSWIN**

COMPUTER-AIDED DESIGN

Engineering Automation Forum

Description
LEAP (League for Engineering Productivity) sponsors this forum for discussions about CADD/CAM and other programs that are used by engineers, architects, and other professionals for design.

Subjects
CADD/CAM, Engineering, Computers, Computer-Aided Design

Audience
CADD/CAM engineers, engineers, designers

Content Summary
You can find discussions that will help you find the right CADD/CAM product for you, tips on using

programs, information on new technologies, and management tools and utilities. Visit Library 9, "Classified/Jobs," for job opportunities and resumes.

See Also
IBM CAD/CAM Forum, CASE DCI Forum

User Guide
- ☑ Windows
- ☑ DOS
- ☑ Macintosh
- ☐ Terminal Emulation
- ☐ VMS
- ☐ UNIX
- ☐ OS/2
- ☐ Other platform

Cost
- ☐ Unknown
- ☐ Basic
- ☑ Extended
- ☐ Premium ($)
- ☐ Executive w/$

Activity Level

Activity Level: MEDIUM

Address
GO: **LEAP**

COMPUTER-BASED COMMUNICATIONS

Electronic Frontier Foundation Forum

Description
The Electronic Frontier Foundation (EFF) was founded in July 1990 to assure freedom of expression in digital media, with a particular emphasis on applying the principles embodied in the Constitution and the Bill of Rights to computer-based communications.

Subjects
Computer-Based Communications, Digital Media Rights, Internet

Audience
Computer users, activists, civil libertarians, journalists

Content Summary
The libraries in this forum contain areas for EFF-related files, networking, communications, back issues of the EFF newsletter, Cyberlaw, Zines and the Net, Internet news, and maps and guides. You also can get freeware and shareware applications for DOS and Macintosh machines in libraries 9 and 10.

See Also
Internet Forum

Computer-Based Communications – Computers

User Guide
- ☑ Windows
- ☑ DOS
- ☑ Macintosh
- ☐ Terminal Emulation
- ☐ VMS
- ☐ UNIX
- ☐ OS/2
- ☐ Other platform

Cost
- ☐ Unknown
- ☐ Basic
- ☑ Extended
- ☐ Premium ($)
- ☐ Executive w/$

Activity Level: MEDIUM

Address
GO: **EFFSIG**

COMPUTERS

3Com Online Information Service Menu

Description
Access to Ask3Com services supporting users of 3Com Corporation products.

Subjects
Computers, Networking

Audience
Users of 3Com products

Content Summary
The library and message sections of this forum contain a list of new products, technical articles that contain troubleshooting tips, commonly asked questions, and release notes. Also available is a list of service centers.

See Also
Ask 3Com Forum, Lan Magazine Forum, Lan Vendor Forum, Lan Technology Forum

User Guide
- ☑ Windows
- ☑ DOS
- ☐ Macintosh
- ☐ Terminal Emulation
- ☐ VMS
- ☐ UNIX
- ☐ OS/2
- ☐ Other platform

Cost
- ☐ Unknown
- ☐ Basic
- ☑ Extended
- ☐ Premium ($)
- ☐ Executive w/$

Activity Level: MEDIUM (arrow pointing LOW)

Address
GO: **THREECOM**

ACI US Forum

Description
The ACI US Forum supports all ACI products with valuable technical support as well as an exchange of ideas from other users of ACI products.

Subjects
Accounting, Business, Software

Audience
Accountants

Content Summary
Libraries consist of example databases and externals. Many useful utilities can be found in these areas to help you with your 4th Dimension development.

See Also
Data Base Advisor Forum, Support Directory.

User Guide
- ☑ Windows
- ☑ DOS
- ☑ Macintosh
- ☐ Terminal Emulation
- ☐ VMS
- ☐ UNIX
- ☐ OS/2
- ☐ Other platform

Cost
- ☐ Unknown
- ☐ Basic
- ☑ Extended
- ☐ Premium ($)
- ☐ Executive w/$

Activity level: MEDIUM (arrow pointing LOW)

Address
GO: **ACIUS**

Adobe Forum

Description
The Adobe Forum provides an area where users, dealers, service bureaus, third-party developers and others can communicate with Adobe.

Subjects
Computer Graphics, Computers, Software

Audience
Adobe products users

Content Summary
Discussions and support of Adobe products. Discusses applications software, hardware, and operating systems. Libraries contain various utilities, add-ons, support files, and product information.

See Also
Graphics Forum

Computers

User Guide
- ☑ Windows
- ☑ DOS
- ☑ Macintosh
- ☐ Terminal Emulation
- ☐ VMS
- ☐ UNIX
- ☐ OS/2
- ☐ Other platform

Cost
- ☐ Unknown
- ☐ Basic
- ☑ Extended
- ☐ Premium ($)
- ☐ Executive w/$

Activity Level
MEDIUM (LOW — HIGH)

Address
GO: **ADOBE**

AI Expert Forum

Description
The electronic edition of AI EXPERT Magazine serves as a forum for exchange of ideas and information on Artificial Intelligence research.

Subjects
Artificial Intelligence

Audience
Researchers

Content Summary
The libraries are the heart of the Forum. You will find source code, executable programs, bibliographies, product reviews, bug reports, bug fixes, electronic versions of important papers and articles on AI, and more.

See Also
Mensa Forum, Knowledge Index, IQuest, Intelligence Test

User Guide
- ☑ Windows
- ☑ DOS
- ☐ Macintosh
- ☐ Terminal Emulation
- ☐ VMS
- ☐ UNIX
- ☐ OS/2
- ☐ Other platform

Cost
- ☐ Unknown
- ☐ Basic
- ☑ Extended
- ☐ Premium ($)
- ☐ Executive w/$

Activity Level
LOW

Address
GO: **AIEXPERT**

Aldus Forum

Description
The Aldus Forum provides technical support for issues encountered by both novice and experienced users of Aldus products.

Subjects
Computers, Software

Audience
Aldus products users

Content Summary
Discussions of Aldus products. Libraries contain various utilities, add-ons, support files, and product information.

See Also
Aldus Display, Aldus Software GmbH Forum, Aldus Special Programs Forum, Support On Site

User Guide
- ☑ Windows
- ☑ DOS
- ☐ Macintosh
- ☐ Terminal Emulation
- ☐ VMS
- ☐ UNIX
- ☐ OS/2
- ☐ Other platform

Cost
- ☐ Unknown
- ☐ Basic
- ☑ Extended
- ☐ Premium ($)
- ☐ Executive w/$

Activity Level
MEDIUM (LOW — HIGH)

Address
GO: **ALDUSFORUM**

Aldus Online Customer Support

Description
Menu giving access to Aldus support services on CompuServe.

Subjects
Computers, Software

Audience
Aldus products users

Content Summary
Menu for accessing various Aldus forums.

See Also
Aldus Forum, Aldus Software GmbH Forum, Aldus Special Programs Forum, Support On Site

User Guide
- ☑ Windows
- ☑ DOS
- ☐ Macintosh
- ☐ Terminal Emulation
- ☐ VMS
- ☐ UNIX
- ☐ OS/2
- ☐ Other platform

Computers

Cost
- ☐ Unknown
- ☐ Basic
- ☑ Extended
- ☐ Premium ($)
- ☐ Executive w/$

Activity Level: UNKNOWN (LOW — MEDIUM — HIGH)

Address
GO: **ALDUS**

Aldus Special Programs Forum

Description
The ALDUSSP Forum provides support and service to various OEM, developer, training, and other special interest partners.

Subjects
Computers, Software

Audience
Computer programmers

Content Summary
You can post questions directed to Aldus Developer Relations in regard to Aldus Additions and the Tagged Image File Format specifications (TIFF) which Aldus developed and maintains. Has one library containing various utilities, add-ons, support files, and product information.

See Also
Aldus Forum, Aldus Software GmbH Forum, Aldus Online Customer Support, Support On Site

User Guide
- ☑ Windows
- ☑ DOS
- ☐ Macintosh
- ☐ Terminal Emulation
- ☐ VMS
- ☐ UNIX
- ☐ OS/2
- ☐ Other platform

Cost
- ☐ Unknown
- ☐ Basic
- ☑ Extended
- ☐ Premium ($)
- ☐ Executive w/$

Activity Level: UNKNOWN (LOW — MEDIUM — HIGH)

Address
GO: **ALDUSSP**

Amiga Arts Forum

Description
The Amiga Arts Forum is devoted to the artistically creative and entertainment-oriented Amiga computer users.

Subjects
Computers

Audience
Amiga users

Content Summary
Libraries consist of various graphics and sound utilities, as well as a large collection of images.

See Also
Amiga File Finder, Amiga Tech Forum, Amiga Users Forum, Amiga Vendors Forum, Graphics Forums

User Guide
- ☑ Windows
- ☑ DOS
- ☐ Macintosh
- ☐ Terminal Emulation
- ☐ VMS
- ☐ UNIX
- ☐ OS/2
- ☐ Other platform

Cost
- ☐ Unknown
- ☐ Basic
- ☑ Extended
- ☐ Premium ($)
- ☐ Executive w/$

Activity Level: LOW (LOW — MEDIUM — HIGH)

Address
GO: **AMIGAARTS**

Amiga File Finder

Description
File Finder is an online comprehensive keyword-searchable database of file descriptions from Amiga-related Forums.

Subjects
Computers

Audience
Amiga users

Content Summary
Locates files that apply to the Amiga computer and its Forums.

See Also
Amiga Arts Forum, Amiga Tech Forum, Amiga Users Forum, Amiga Vendors Forum, Graphics Forums

User Guide
- ☑ Windows
- ☑ DOS
- ☐ Macintosh
- ☐ Terminal Emulation
- ☐ VMS
- ☐ UNIX
- ☐ OS/2
- ☐ Other platform

Cost
- ☐ Unknown
- ☐ Basic
- ☑ Extended
- ☐ Premium ($)
- ☐ Executive w/$

Computers

Activity Level

Address
GO: **AMIGAFF**

Amiga Tech Forum

Description
This forum is dedicated to the technical and programming users of Amiga computers.

Subjects
Computers

Audience
Amiga users, Amiga programmers

Content Summary
Provides an atmosphere of friendly learning and participation for users of Amiga computers. The forum is dedicated to the technical and programming use of Amiga computers. Libraries consist of programming utilities and add-ons.

See Also
Amiga Arts Forum, Amiga File Finder, Amiga Users Forum, Amiga Vendors Forum, Graphics Forums

User Guide
- ☑ Windows
- ☑ DOS
- ☐ Macintosh
- ☐ Terminal Emulation
- ☐ VMS
- ☐ UNIX
- ☐ OS/2
- ☐ Other platform

Cost
- ☐ Unknown
- ☐ Basic
- ☑ Extended
- ☐ Premium ($)
- ☐ Executive w/$

Activity Level (arrow pointing LOW)

Address
GO: **AMIGATECH**

Amiga User Forum

Description
This forum is dedicated to the everyday business and personal use of Amiga computers.

Subjects
Computers

Audience
Amiga users

Content Summary
The forum is dedicated to the everyday business and personal use of Amiga computers. Libraries consist of utilities, drivers, add-ons, software and hardware information.

See Also
Amiga Arts Forum, Amiga File Finder, Amiga Tech Forum, Amiga Vendors Forum, Graphics Forums

User Guide
- ☑ Windows
- ☑ DOS
- ☐ Macintosh
- ☐ Terminal Emulation
- ☐ VMS
- ☐ UNIX
- ☐ OS/2
- ☐ Other platform

Cost
- ☐ Unknown
- ☐ Basic
- ☑ Extended
- ☐ Premium ($)
- ☐ Executive w/$

Activity Level

Address
GO: **AMIGAUSER**

Amiga Vendor Forum

Description
This forum provides support for Amiga owners who use products from the vendors represented here.

Subjects
Computers

Audience
Amiga Users

User Guide
- ☑ Windows
- ☑ DOS
- ☐ Macintosh
- ☐ Terminal Emulation
- ☐ VMS
- ☐ UNIX
- ☐ OS/2
- ☐ Other platform

Cost
- ☐ Unknown
- ☐ Basic
- ☑ Extended
- ☐ Premium ($)
- ☐ Executive w/$

Activity Level (arrow pointing LOW)

Address
GO: **AMIGAVENDOR**

APPC Info Exchange Forum

Description
The APPC Forum addresses many of the hot topics in networking today, to help you apply advanced networking in your own environment.

Computers

Subjects
Computers, Networking

Audience
Network Administrators

Content Summary
Discussions of LAN/WAN integration, client/server development, multivendor networking, downsizing, and rightsizing. Libraries consist of sample programs and source code and utilities.

See Also
PC File Finder, Lan Technology Forum, Lan Vendor Forum, Lan Magazine Forum.

User Guide
- [x] Windows
- [x] DOS
- [ ] Macintosh
- [ ] Terminal Emulation
- [ ] VMS
- [ ] UNIX
- [ ] OS/2
- [ ] Other platform

Cost
- [ ] Unknown
- [ ] Basic
- [x] Extended
- [ ] Premium ($)
- [ ] Executive w/$

Activity Level

Address
GO: **APPCFORUM**

Apple II Programmers' Forum

Description
The area for discussing programming Apple II computers, from BASIC to assembly language, to graphical interfaces like HyperStudio.

Subjects
Computers

Audience
Apple users, computer programmers

Content Summary
Libraries consist of programming tools and utilities as well as sound tools and utilities.

See Also
Apple Feedback (FREE), Apple II Users Forum, Apple II Vendor Forum, Apple News Clips, Apple Support Forum, Apple Tech Info Library, Apple What's New Library

User Guide
- [x] Windows
- [x] DOS
- [ ] Macintosh
- [ ] Terminal Emulation
- [ ] VMS
- [ ] UNIX
- [ ] OS/2
- [ ] Other platform

Cost
- [ ] Unknown
- [ ] Basic
- [x] Extended
- [ ] Premium ($)
- [ ] Executive w/$

Activity Level

Address
GO: **APPROG**

Apple II Users' Forum

Description
This is the place to discuss applications software and hardware for the Apple II computer.

Subjects
Computers

Audience
Apple users

Content Summary
Libraries contain various utilities, applications, graphics, and games.

See Also
Apple Feedback (FREE), Apple II Programmers Forum, Apple II Vendor Forum, Apple News Clips, Apple Support Forum, Apple Tech Info Library, Apple What's New Library

User Guide
- [x] Windows
- [x] DOS
- [ ] Macintosh
- [ ] Terminal Emulation
- [ ] VMS
- [ ] UNIX
- [ ] OS/2
- [ ] Other platform

Cost
- [ ] Unknown
- [ ] Basic
- [x] Extended
- [ ] Premium ($)
- [ ] Executive w/$

Activity Level

Address
GO: **APUSER**

Apple II Vendors' Forum

Description
Several vendors of Apple II-related products offer online support for their users.

Subjects
Computers

Audience
Apple users

Content Summary
Libraries consist of various vendor utilities and product information.

See Also
Apple II Programmer's Forum, Apple II User's Forum, Apple News Clips

User Guide
- [x] Windows
- [x] DOS
- [ ] Macintosh
- [ ] Terminal Emulation
- [ ] VMS
- [ ] UNIX
- [ ] OS/2
- [ ] Other platform

Cost
- [ ] Unknown
- [ ] Basic
- [x] Extended
- [ ] Premium ($)
- [ ] Executive w/$

Activity Level

Address
GO: **APIIVEN**

Artisoft Forum

Description
The Artisoft Forum provides online technical support for users of Artisoft products.

Subjects
Computers, Networking, Software

Audience
Network Administrators

Content Summary
This forum is dedicated to the LANtastic Network Operating System, LANtastic for Windows, LANtastic for Netware, and LANtastic for MACs. In addition we will provide support for the Artisoft Sounding Board, Artisoft's Articom - Communications software and the new Netmedia Products. Libraries consist of demos, patches, utilities, and product information.

See Also
Lan Magazine Forum, Lan Vendor Forum, Lan Technology Forum

User Guide
- [x] Windows
- [x] DOS
- [ ] Macintosh
- [ ] Terminal Emulation
- [ ] VMS
- [ ] UNIX
- [ ] OS/2
- [ ] Other platform

Cost
- [ ] Unknown
- [ ] Basic
- [x] Extended
- [ ] Premium ($)
- [ ] Executive w/$

Activity Level

Address
GO: **ARTISOFT**

Ask3Com Forum

Description
This forum is dedicated to the discussion of 3Com Corporation's networking products.

Subjects
Computers, Networking

Audience
3Com product users

Content Summary
This forum is sponsored by 3Com Corporation's Customer Support Organization for use by all 3Com users and customers. Libraries consist of utilities, patches/fixes, drivers, and product information.

See Also
3Com Online Information Service, Lan Magazine Forum, Lan Vendor Forum, Lan Technology Forum

User Guide
- [x] Windows
- [x] DOS
- [ ] Macintosh
- [ ] Terminal Emulation
- [ ] VMS
- [ ] UNIX
- [ ] OS/2
- [ ] Other platform

Cost
- [ ] Unknown
- [ ] Basic
- [x] Extended
- [ ] Premium ($)
- [ ] Executive w/$

Activity Level
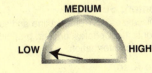

Address
GO: **ASKFORUM**

ASP Shareware Forum

Description
Devoted to the general discussion of shareware, this forum serves as a meeting place for members of the Association of Shareware Professionals.

Subjects
Computers, Shareware, Software

Audience
Computer programmers, software developers

Computers

Content Summary
Discussions and support of various Shareware product. Libraries consist of various files discussing Shareware issues and support.

See Also
Sharware Registration, PC File Finder, MS Windows Shareware Forum, Gamers Forum

User Guide
- [x] Windows
- [x] DOS
- [ ] Macintosh
- [ ] Terminal Emulation
- [ ] VMS
- [ ] UNIX
- [ ] OS/2
- [ ] Other platform

Cost
- [ ] Unknown
- [ ] Basic
- [x] Extended
- [ ] Premium ($)
- [ ] Executive w/$

Activity Level

Address
GO: **ASPFORUM**

AST Forum

Description
The AST Forum serves as a means for technical support and discussion of the diverse line of AST products.

Subjects
Computers

Audience
AST Products Users

Content Summary
Discusses AST product line and support. Libraries consist of updates, drivers, graphics, shareware, and product information.

See Also
IBM Hardware Forum, Computing Support

User Guide
- [x] Windows
- [x] DOS
- [ ] Macintosh
- [ ] Terminal Emulation
- [ ] VMS
- [ ] UNIX
- [ ] OS/2
- [ ] Other platform

Cost
- [ ] Unknown
- [ ] Basic
- [x] Extended
- [ ] Premium ($)
- [ ] Executive w/$

Activity Level

Address
GO: **ASTFORUM**

Atari Computing Forum

Description
This forum supports Atari 16- and 32-bit computers, peripherals, and productivity software.

Subjects
Computers, Software

Audience
Atari users

Content Summary
You will find information and downloadable programs relating to telecommunications, programming, utilities, applications, desktop accessories, hardware/peripherals, and more.

See Also
Atari File Finder, Atari GAMING Forum, Atari ST Prod. Forum, Atari Users Network, Atari Vendor Forum

User Guide
- [ ] Windows
- [ ] DOS
- [ ] Macintosh
- [ ] Terminal Emulation
- [ ] VMS
- [ ] UNIX
- [ ] OS/2
- [x] Other platform

Cost
- [ ] Unknown
- [ ] Basic
- [x] Extended
- [ ] Premium ($)
- [ ] Executive w/$

Activity Level

Address
GO: **ATARICOMP**

Autodesk AutoCAD Forum

Description
An open forum for anyone with an interest in Computer Aided Design, with an emphasis on Autodesk products.

Subjects
CAD, Computers, Software

Audience
Autodesk products users

Content Summary
Discussions of Autodesk products: AutoCAD®, AME™, AutoLISP™, ADS™, AutoFlix™. Discusses applications software, hardware, operating systems and languages, and CAD management and productivity. Also maintains sections where issues are discussed surrounding important applications

markets: A/E/C, MCAD/MCAE, GIS, Civil Engineering. Libraries contain various utilities, add-ons, support files, and product information.

See Also
Autodesk Retail Products Forum, Autodesk Software Forum, CADD/CAM/CAE Vendor Forum, IBM CAD/CAM Forum

User Guide
- ☑ Windows
- ☑ DOS
- ☐ Macintosh
- ☐ Terminal Emulation
- ☐ VMS
- ☐ UNIX
- ☐ OS/2
- ☐ Other platform

Cost
- ☐ Unknown
- ☐ Basic
- ☑ Extended
- ☐ Premium ($)
- ☐ Executive w/$

Activity Level MEDIUM (LOW — HIGH)

Address
GO: **ACAD**

Autodesk Multimedia Forum

Description
Support for the Autodesk line of PC and workstation-based graphics programs.

Subjects
CAD, Computers, Multimedia

Audience
Autodesk products users

Content Summary
Provides an open forum for anyone who uses multimedia and Science Series products and more generally for those with an interest in computer graphics. Discusses Autodesk Animator, Autodesk 3D Studio, HyperChem, CA Lab and Chaos and related issues like hardware, operating systems and networks. Also maintains a wishlist section where you may suggest ways to improve products and policies. Libraries contain various utilities, add-ons, support files, and product information.

See Also
Autodesk Retail Products Forum, Autodesk Software Forum, CADD/CAM/CAE Vendor Forum, IBM CAD/CAM Forum

User Guide
- ☑ Windows
- ☑ DOS
- ☐ Macintosh
- ☐ Terminal Emulation
- ☐ VMS
- ☐ UNIX
- ☐ OS/2
- ☐ Other platform

Cost
- ☐ Unknown
- ☐ Basic
- ☑ Extended
- ☐ Premium ($)
- ☐ Executive w/$

Activity Level MEDIUM (LOW — HIGH)

Address
GO: **ASOFT**

Autodesk Retail Products Forum

Description
An open forum for anyone interested in low cost Precision Graphics software, with an emphasis on Autodesk Retail Division products.

Subjects
CAD, Computers, Software

Audience
Autodesk Products Users

Content Summary
Provides an open forum for anyone with an interest in low-cost Precision Graphics software. The primary purpose of the forum is to support users of the products produced and marketed by the Retail Products division of Autodesk, Inc. At the same time, it welcomes discussion of the issues and concerns of forum members as relate to products, the company itself, and how to provide the best possible solutions to your CADD & Graphics needs. Libraries contain various utilities, add-ons, support files, and product information.

See Also
Autodesk Retail Products Forum, Autodesk Software Forum, CADD/CAM/CAE Vendor Forum, IBM CAD/CAM Forum

User Guide
- ☑ Windows
- ☑ DOS
- ☐ Macintosh
- ☐ Terminal Emulation
- ☐ VMS
- ☐ UNIX
- ☐ OS/2
- ☐ Other platform

Cost
- ☐ Unknown
- ☐ Basic
- ☑ Extended
- ☐ Premium ($)
- ☐ Executive w/$

Activity Level MEDIUM (LOW ← HIGH)

Activity level: Low

Address
GO: **ARETAIL**

Computers

Banyan Forum

Description
Help, information, and support for Banyan products, including Banyan VINES networking software.

Subjects
Computers, Networking

Audience
MIS people

Content Summary
Find out more about your Banyan products, including VINES, in this forum. Some of the library topics that you'll find include networking, servers, VINES, hardware, and more.

See Also
Other Ban Patch Forum

User Guide
- ☑ Windows
- ☑ DOS
- ☐ Macintosh
- ☐ Terminal Emulation
- ☐ VMS
- ☐ UNIX
- ☐ OS/2
- ☑ Other platform

Cost
- ☐ Unknown
- ☐ Basic
- ☑ Extended
- ☐ Premium ($)
- ☐ Executive w/$

Activity Level

Address
GO: BANFORUM

BASIS International Forum

Description
The BASIS International Forum exists to support the business applications developer who uses BASIS supplied software development tools.

Subjects
Business, Computers

Audience
MIS people

Content Summary
You'll find library and message topics on BBxProgression/4, TAOS 4GL, TAOS/Views Report Writer, and more.

See Also
IBM File Finder

User Guide
- ☐ Windows
- ☑ DOS
- ☐ Macintosh
- ☐ Terminal Emulation
- ☐ VMS
- ☐ UNIX
- ☐ OS/2
- ☑ Other platform

Cost
- ☐ Unknown
- ☐ Basic
- ☑ Extended
- ☐ Premium ($)
- ☐ Executive w/$

Activity Level

Address
GO: BASIS

Benchmarks and Standards Forum

Description
A place where individuals and companies can discuss aspects of PC performance, measurement technology, and productivity.

Subjects
Computers, Testing

Audience
MIS people

Content Summary
For discussions and support for benchmark performances and testing, this forum has library and message sections that contain topics such as standardizing, measurement, performance analysis, and the like.

See Also
Ziff-Davis Benchmark Operation Forum

User Guide
- ☑ Windows
- ☑ DOS
- ☑ Macintosh
- ☐ Terminal Emulation
- ☐ VMS
- ☐ UNIX
- ☑ OS/2
- ☑ Other platform

Cost
- ☐ Unknown
- ☐ Basic
- ☑ Extended
- ☐ Premium ($)
- ☐ Executive w/$

Activity Level

Address
GO: BENCHMARK

Blyth Software Forum

Description
This forum supplies technical support for users of Blyth software, as well as contact with others who have similar interests.

Computers

Subjects
Computers

Audience
Computer users, MIS people

Content Summary
This forum contains libraries and messages that discuss topics such as databases, Omnis, SQL, DAL, Extensions, and more.

See Also
Client Server Computing Forum

User Guide
- [x] Windows
- [x] DOS
- [ ] Macintosh
- [ ] Terminal Emulation
- [ ] VMS
- [ ] UNIX
- [ ] OS/2
- [x] Other platform

Cost
- [ ] Unknown
- [ ] Basic
- [x] Extended
- [ ] Premium ($)
- [ ] Executive w/$

Activity Level

Address
GO: **BLYTH**

Broderbund Software

Description
Online software store features popular products from Broderbund Software.

Subjects
Computers

Audience
Game enthusiasts

Content Summary
Look for the library and message sections that interest you the most, including PrintShop, Carmen Sandiego, Prince of Persia, Automap, CD-ROM information, and more.

See Also
Entertainment Forum

User Guide
- [x] Windows
- [x] DOS
- [x] Macintosh
- [ ] Terminal Emulation
- [ ] VMS
- [ ] UNIX
- [ ] OS/2
- [ ] Other platform

Cost
- [ ] Unknown
- [x] Basic
- [ ] Extended
- [ ] Premium ($)
- [ ] Executive w/$

Activity Level

Address
GO: **BB**

Cabletron Systems Forum

Description
Cabletron Forum provides help and information with questions or problems concerning Cabletron products or computer networking in general.

Subjects
Computers, Networking

Audience
Product users, network administrators

Content Summary
The libraries of this forum contain information about networking, Cabletron products, DNI cards, Ethernet, Token Ring, WAN, LANVIEW, and FDDI.

See Also
Cabletron Systems Menu

User Guide
- [x] Windows
- [x] DOS
- [ ] Macintosh
- [ ] Terminal Emulation
- [ ] VMS
- [ ] UNIX
- [ ] OS/2
- [ ] Other platform

Cost
- [ ] Unknown
- [ ] Basic
- [x] Extended
- [ ] Premium ($)
- [ ] Executive w/$

Activity level
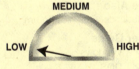

Address
GO: **CTRONFORUM**

Cabletron Systems Menu

Description
The menu provides access to information concerning Cabletron Systems, Inc.

Subjects
Computers, Networking

Audience
Network administrators

Content Summary
Included in the libraries are information on the corporate background of Cabletron, list of sales offices, training and presentation centers, and points of interest to users of Cabletron products.

Computers

See Also
Cabletron Systems Forum

User Guide
- ☑ Windows
- ☑ DOS
- ☑ Macintosh
- ☐ Terminal Emulation
- ☐ VMS
- ☑ UNIX
- ☐ OS/2
- ☐ Other platform

Cost
- ☐ Unknown
- ☐ Basic
- ☑ Extended
- ☐ Premium ($)
- ☐ Executive w/$

Activity Level: MEDIUM (arrow pointing toward LOW)

Address
GO: **CTRON**

CADD/CAM/CAE Vendor Forum

Description
Discussion and support for users of products from the companies represented here.

Subjects
Computer Graphics, Computers

Audience
CAD professionals

Content Summary
Products represented in this forum include UTS/TK Solver!, EasyCAD/FastCAD, ISICAD, CADlink, CADKEY, ASHLAR, and IBM CAD to name just a few.

See Also
Cadence, Graphics Forum

User Guide
- ☑ Windows
- ☑ DOS
- ☐ Macintosh
- ☐ Terminal Emulation
- ☐ VMS
- ☐ UNIX
- ☐ OS/2
- ☐ Other platform

Cost
- ☐ Unknown
- ☐ Basic
- ☑ Extended
- ☐ Premium ($)
- ☐ Executive w/$

Activity Level: MEDIUM (arrow pointing toward LOW)

Address
GO: **CADVEN**

Cadence Forum

Description
The online electronic edition of CADENCE magazine, offering code listings and executable programs from each monthly issue.

Subjects
CAD/CAM, Computers

Audience
CAD professionals

See Also
CADD/CAM/CAE Vendor Forum, Autodesk AutoCAD Forum, Autodesk Software Forum

User Guide
- ☑ Windows
- ☑ DOS
- ☑ Macintosh
- ☐ Terminal Emulation
- ☐ VMS
- ☐ UNIX
- ☐ OS/2
- ☐ Other platform

Cost
- ☐ Unknown
- ☐ Basic
- ☑ Extended
- ☐ Premium ($)
- ☐ Executive w/$

Activity Level: MEDIUM (arrow pointing toward LOW)

Address
GO: **CADENCE**

Canopus Research Forum

Description
A place where computer and communications industry companies, products, technologies, markets, and trends can be freely discussed.

Subjects
Computers

Audience
Computer professionals

Content Summary
This forum provides open discussion on computer industry trends and technologies. Also included are discussions on operating system wars, hardware, and software.

See Also
IBM OS/2 Support Forum, Microsoft 32-bit Language Forum

User Guide
- ☑ Windows
- ☑ DOS
- ☑ Macintosh
- ☐ Terminal Emulation
- ☐ VMS
- ☑ UNIX
- ☐ OS/2
- ☐ Other platform

Cost
- ☐ Unknown
- ☐ Basic
- ☑ Extended
- ☐ Premium ($)
- ☐ Executive w/$

Activity Level: MEDIUM (arrow pointing toward HIGH)

Address
GO: **CANOPUS**

CASE-DCI Forum

Description
CASEFORUM is a place where people interested in creating software in a more effective manner can meet and discuss concepts and tools.

Subjects
Computer Programming, Computers

Audience
Software developers

Content Summary
Topics of interest to software developers include computer-aided software engineering and product details.

See Also
Borland C++ for Win/OS2 Forum, Borland C++/DOS Forum, Borland Pascal Forum, Programming MS Apps.

User Guide
- ☑ Windows
- ☑ DOS
- ☐ Macintosh
- ☐ Terminal Emulation
- ☐ VMS
- ☐ UNIX
- ☐ OS/2
- ☐ Other platform

Cost
- ☐ Unknown
- ☐ Basic
- ☑ Extended
- ☐ Premium ($)
- ☐ Executive w/$

Activity Level: MEDIUM (arrow pointing toward LOW)

Address
GO: **CASEFORUM**

CBM Service Forum

Description
An area for the discussion of any and all aspects of Comodore computing, both with other members and with Commodore's in-house employees.

Subjects
Commodore Computers, Computers

Audience
Computer professionals

Content Summary
The libraries and message sections of this forum include product information on all Commodore products, information on user groups, and a list of service centers.

See Also
Commodore Users Network, Commodore Applications Forum, Commodore Arts/Games Forum, Amiga Tech Forum

User Guide
- ☑ Windows
- ☑ DOS
- ☐ Macintosh
- ☐ Terminal Emulation
- ☐ VMS
- ☐ UNIX
- ☐ OS/2
- ☐ Other platform

Cost
- ☐ Unknown
- ☐ Basic
- ☑ Extended
- ☐ Premium ($)
- ☐ Executive w/$

Activity Level: MEDIUM (arrow pointing toward LOW)

Address
GO: **CBMSERVICE**

CD-ROM Forum

Description
The CD-ROM Forum deals with one of the most active and dynamic areas in the publishing/media field.

Subjects
Computers

Audience
CD-ROM developers, computer professionals

Content Summary
The libraries contain general information about CD-ROM technology, production, hardware, operating system concerns, and industry issues.

See Also
CD-ROM Vendor Forum, Multimedia Conference Forum, Kodak CD Forum

User Guide
- ☑ Windows
- ☑ DOS
- ☑ Macintosh
- ☐ Terminal Emulation
- ☐ VMS
- ☑ UNIX
- ☐ OS/2
- ☐ Other platform

Cost
- ☐ Unknown
- ☐ Basic
- ☑ Extended
- ☐ Premium ($)
- ☐ Executive w/$

Computers

Activity Level

Address
GO: **CDROM**

CD-ROM Vendors Forum

Description
Companies involved in creating and using CD-ROM products are represented here in the CD-ROM Vendors Forum.

Subjects
Computers

Audience
CD-ROM developers, computer professionals

Content Summary
This forum's libaries contain information about new products, product support, and message areas in which you can ask questions and receive answers on CD-ROM related topics.

See Also
CD-ROM Forum, Multimedia Conference Forum, Kodak CD Forum

User Guide
- [x] Windows
- [x] DOS
- [x] Macintosh
- [ ] Terminal Emulation
- [ ] VMS
- [x] UNIX
- [ ] OS/2
- [ ] Other platform

Cost
- [ ] Unknown
- [ ] Basic
- [x] Extended
- [ ] Premium ($)
- [ ] Executive w/$

Activity Level

Address
GO: **CDVEN**

Clarion Software Forum

Description
This forum is dedicated to the support and discussion of Clarion software products.

Subjects
Computers

Audience
Product users

Content Summary
Product support in the libraries include Clarion, Windows applications, TopSpeed, Application Generator, and Database Developer.

See Also
Graphics Forums, PC Vendor D Forum, PC File Finder

User Guide
- [x] Windows
- [x] DOS
- [ ] Macintosh
- [ ] Terminal Emulation
- [ ] VMS
- [ ] UNIX
- [ ] OS/2
- [ ] Other platform

Cost
- [ ] Unknown
- [ ] Basic
- [x] Extended
- [ ] Premium ($)
- [ ] Executive w/$

Activity Level

Address
GO: **CLARION**

CoCo Forum

Description
This forum specializes in support of the Tandy Color Computer and its users.

Subjects
Computers

Audience
Tandy users

Content Summary
The libraries include information on color computers, graphics, games, music, telecommunications, BBS systems, applications, utilities, operating systems, and hardware.

User Guide
- [x] Windows
- [x] DOS
- [ ] Macintosh
- [ ] Terminal Emulation
- [ ] VMS
- [ ] UNIX
- [ ] OS/2
- [ ] Other platform

Cost
- [ ] Unknown
- [ ] Basic
- [x] Extended
- [ ] Premium ($)
- [ ] Executive w/$

Activity Level

UNKNOWN

Address
GO: **COCO**

Computers

Commodore Applications Forum

Description
The forum for Commodore 8-bit programming and discussions about hardware, utilities, and applications for the C64 and C128 computers.

Subjects
Computers

Audience
Commodore users

Content Summary
Libraries include information on Commodore 64/128, programming, hardware, telecommunications, BBSs, applications, and CP/M.

See Also
Commodore Users Network, Commodore Arts/Games Forum, Amiga Tech Forum, CBM Service Forum, Commodore Art/Games Forum, Amiga Vendor Forum, CP/M Users Group Forum

User Guide
- ☑ Windows
- ☑ DOS
- ☐ Macintosh
- ☐ Terminal Emulation
- ☐ VMS
- ☐ UNIX
- ☐ OS/2
- ☐ Other platform

Cost
- ☐ Unknown
- ☐ Basic
- ☑ Extended
- ☐ Premium ($)
- ☐ Executive w/$

Activity Level

Address
GO: **CBMAPP**

Commodore Art/Games Forum

Description
This forum features music, graphics, and games for the Commodore 8-bit computers.

Subjects
Computers

Audience
Commodore users

Content Summary
Libraries include information about Commodore 64/128, music, graphics, games, GEOS, poetry, and SIDplayer.

See Also
Commodore Users Network, Commodore Applications Forum, Amiga Tech Forum, CBM Service Forum, Amiga Vendor Forum, CP/M Users Group Forum

User Guide
- ☑ Windows
- ☑ DOS
- ☐ Macintosh
- ☑ Terminal Emulation
- ☐ VMS
- ☐ UNIX
- ☐ OS/2
- ☐ Other platform

Cost
- ☐ Unknown
- ☐ Basic
- ☑ Extended
- ☐ Premium ($)
- ☐ Executive w/$

Activity Level

Address
GO: **CBMART**

Commodore Business Machines Menu

Description
Access to information and services for users of Commodore computers.

Subjects
Computers

Audience
Commodore users

Content Summary
Libraries include announcements, resources for education, user group information, forum conference schedule, software updates, service forum, and users network.

See Also
Commodore Users Network, Commodore Arts/Games Forum, Amiga Tech Forum, CBM Service Forum, Commodore Art/Games Forum, Amiga Vendor Forum, CP/M Users Group Forum

User Guide
- ☑ Windows
- ☑ DOS
- ☐ Macintosh
- ☐ Terminal Emulation
- ☐ VMS
- ☐ UNIX
- ☐ OS/2
- ☐ Other platform

Cost
- ☐ Unknown
- ☐ Basic
- ☑ Extended
- ☐ Premium ($)
- ☐ Executive w/$

Activity Level

Address
GO: **CBMNEWS**

Commodore/Amiga Forums Menu

Description
Provides access to the Commodore and Amiga areas on CompuServe.

Subjects
Computers

Audience
Commodore and Amiga users

Content Summary
Libraries include information about arts, users, vendors, and File Finder for the Amiga. Included for Commodore users are libraries for arts and games, applications, service, and the newsletter.

See Also
Commodore Users Network, Commodore Arts/Games Forum, Amiga Tech Forum, CBM Service Forum, Commodore Art/Games Forum, Amiga Vendor Forum, CP/M Users Group Forum

User Guide
- ☑ Windows
- ☑ DOS
- ☐ Macintosh
- ☐ Terminal Emulation
- ☐ VMS
- ☐ UNIX
- ☐ OS/2
- ☐ Other platform

Cost
- ☐ Unknown
- ☐ Basic
- ☑ Extended
- ☐ Premium ($)
- ☐ Executive w/$

Activity Level

Address
GO: **CBMNET**

Compaq Forum

Description
The forum provides technical support for Compaq Computer Corporation hardware products.

Subjects
Computers

Audience
Compaq users

Content Summary
Libraries include information on portables, laptops, notebooks, desktops, towers, networking, software, printers, and customer service.

See Also
PC Vendor C Forum, PC Industry Forum, Computing Support, Hardware Forums

User Guide
- ☑ Windows
- ☑ DOS
- ☐ Macintosh
- ☐ Terminal Emulation
- ☐ VMS
- ☐ UNIX
- ☐ OS/2
- ☐ Other platform

Cost
- ☐ Unknown
- ☐ Basic
- ☑ Extended
- ☐ Premium ($)
- ☐ Executive w/$

Activity Level

Address
GO: **CPQFORUM**

CompuAdd Forum

Description
The forum enables CompuAdd users to communicate with technical support and engineering staff, as well as each other.

Subjects
Computers

Audience
CompuAdd users

Content Summary
Libraries include information on systems, laptop computers, notebooks, networks, drives, peripherals, video, and SPARC/SS-2.

See Also
Computing Support, Hardware Forums

User Guide
- ☑ Windows
- ☑ DOS
- ☐ Macintosh
- ☐ Terminal Emulation
- ☐ VMS
- ☑ UNIX
- ☐ OS/2
- ☑ Other platform

Cost
- ☐ Unknown
- ☐ Basic
- ☑ Extended
- ☐ Premium ($)
- ☐ Executive w/$

Activity Level — MEDIUM (arrow pointing toward LOW)

Address
GO: **COMPUADD**

Computer Club Forum

Description
The Computer Club Forum is the home for users of computers no longer supported by their manufactur-

ers or that have no other specific forum dedicated to them on CompuServe.

Subjects
Computers

Audience
Computer users

Content Summary
Libraries include information for users of Actrix, Adam, Amstrad, Apricot, Eagle, Kaypro, Ohio Scientific, Panasonic, Sanyo, Times/Sinclair, and Victor 9000.

See Also
Mac Community/Club Forum, Small Computer Book Club (FREE), Library Of Science Book Club (FREE), CB Club

User Guide
- ☑ Windows
- ☑ DOS
- ☐ Macintosh
- ☐ Terminal Emulation
- ☐ VMS
- ☐ UNIX
- ☐ OS/2
- ☐ Other platform

Cost
- ☐ Unknown
- ☐ Basic
- ☑ Extended
- ☐ Premium ($)
- ☐ Executive w/$

Activity Level

Address
GO: **CLUB**

Computer Library Online

Description
A family of information retrieval services designed to provide a complete reference and assistance resource for computer users.

Subjects
Computers, Databases

Audience
Computer users

Content Summary
Libraries include Computer Database Plus, Computer Buyers' Guide, Support on Site, articles, journals, recommendations, advice, and updates on products.

See Also
Information USA, MS Software Library, Ziff Software Center, Novell Library Forum, Lotus Technical Library

User Guide
- ☑ Windows
- ☑ DOS
- ☑ Macintosh
- ☐ Terminal Emulation
- ☐ VMS
- ☑ UNIX
- ☐ OS/2
- ☑ Other platform

Cost
- ☐ Unknown
- ☐ Basic
- ☐ Extended
- ☑ Premium ($)
- ☐ Executive w/$

Activity Level

Address
GO: **COMPLIB**

Computer Training Forum

Description
The DPTRAIN Forum is dedicated to the question of how people learn to use computers and how to help them learn more effectively.

Subjects
Computers, Education

Audience
Computer trainers

Content Summary
Libraries include training techniques, technology, support, information centers, local groups, newsletters, and training software.

User Guide
- ☑ Windows
- ☑ DOS
- ☑ Macintosh
- ☐ Terminal Emulation
- ☐ VMS
- ☑ UNIX
- ☐ OS/2
- ☐ Other platform

Cost
- ☐ Unknown
- ☐ Basic
- ☑ Extended
- ☐ Premium ($)
- ☐ Executive w/$

Activity Level

Address
GO: **DPTRAIN**

Computers/Technology Menu

Description
Access to forums and services dealing with computers and technology.

Subjects
Computers

Computers

Audience
Computer users

Content Summary
Libraries include software forums, hardware forums, connectivity, research, reference, magazines, shareware registration, electronic mall, science, and ZiffNet.

User Guide
- [x] Windows
- [x] DOS
- [x] Macintosh
- [ ] Terminal Emulation
- [ ] VMS
- [x] UNIX
- [ ] OS/2
- [ ] Other platform

Cost
- [ ] Unknown
- [ ] Basic
- [x] Extended
- [ ] Premium ($)
- [ ] Executive w/$

Activity Level

LOW — UNKNOWN — HIGH (MEDIUM)

Address
GO: **COMPUTERS**

Corel Forum

Description
The Corel Forum is designed to provide support and information about Corel products.

Subjects
Computer Graphics, Computers

Audience
Corel uers

Content Summary
Libraries include information on CorelDRAW!, CorelPHOTO-PAINT, CorelSCSI, CorelGALLERY, printing, text, and graphics.

See Also
Ventura Software Forum, Windows 3rd Party B Forum, Graphics Forums

User Guide
- [x] Windows
- [x] DOS
- [ ] Macintosh
- [ ] Terminal Emulation
- [ ] VMS
- [ ] UNIX
- [ ] OS/2
- [ ] Other platform

Cost
- [ ] Unknown
- [ ] Basic
- [x] Extended
- [ ] Premium ($)
- [ ] Executive w/$

Activity Level

LOW — HIGH (MEDIUM, arrow to HIGH)

Address
GO: **CORELAPPS**

CP/M Forum

Description
Support for users of the CP/M Operating System is the primary purpose of the CP/M Forum.

Subjects
Computers

Audience
CP/M Operating System Users

Content Summary
Libraries include information on CP/M, hardware, telecommunications, word processing, dBASE, languages, ZCPR, CP/M BBSs, CP/M-80, Commodore, Epson, and portables.

See Also
Commodore Users Network, Commodore Arts/Games Forum, Amiga Tech Forum, CBM Service Forum, Commodore Art/Games Forum, Amiga Vendor Forum, Commodore Applications Forum

User Guide
- [x] Windows
- [x] DOS
- [ ] Macintosh
- [ ] Terminal Emulation
- [ ] VMS
- [ ] UNIX
- [ ] OS/2
- [ ] Other platform

Cost
- [ ] Unknown
- [ ] Basic
- [x] Extended
- [ ] Premium ($)
- [ ] Executive w/$

Activity Level

LOW (arrow) — HIGH (MEDIUM)

Address
GO: **CPMFORUM**

Creative Labs

Description
This forum gives worldwide support to Creative Labs' and Creative Technologies' products, including the popular Sound Blaster line of cards.

Subjects
Computers, Music

Audience
Creative Labs users

Content Summary
Libraries include information about SoundBlaster, SB Pro, SB16, WaveBlaster, AWE-32, CDROM kits, Video Blaster, VideoSpigot, and Multimedia update kits.

Computers

See Also
MIDI Music Forum, Media Vision Forum, Multimedia Forum, Multimedia Vendor Forum, Music Industry Forum, Sight and Sound Forum, MS WINFUN Forum, Gamers Forum

User Guide
- ☑ Windows
- ☑ DOS
- ☑ Macintosh
- ☐ Terminal Emulation
- ☐ VMS
- ☑ UNIX
- ☐ OS/2
- ☐ Other platform

Cost
- ☐ Unknown
- ☐ Basic
- ☑ Extended
- ☐ Premium ($)
- ☐ Executive w/$

Activity Level

Address
GO: **BLASTER**

Crosstalk Forum

Description
Support for users of software products developed and marketed by DCA/Crosstalk Communications.

Subjects
Computers

Audience
Crosstalk users

Content Summary
Libraries include information on Crosstalk, Crossfax, Remote2, XTALK Communicator, client/server, and utilities.

See Also
DATASTORM Forum, IBM Communications Forum, Modem Vendor Forum, Hayes Forum, Mac Communications Forum, Practical Periph. Forum

User Guide
- ☑ Windows
- ☑ DOS
- ☑ Macintosh
- ☐ Terminal Emulation
- ☐ VMS
- ☑ UNIX
- ☐ OS/2
- ☐ Other platform

Cost
- ☐ Unknown
- ☐ Basic
- ☑ Extended
- ☐ Premium ($)
- ☐ Executive w/$

Activity Level

Address
GO: **XTALK**

CSI Forth Net Forum

Description
The Forth Forum supports the Forth language in general, as well as CSI Forth products.

Subjects
Computer Programming, Computers

Audience
Forth Programmers

Content Summary
Libraries include information on Forth, Programming, MOPS, MacForth Plus, CSI Hardware, and users groups.

See Also
PC File Finder, PC Vendor D Forum

User Guide
- ☑ Windows
- ☑ DOS
- ☑ Macintosh
- ☐ Terminal Emulation
- ☐ VMS
- ☑ UNIX
- ☐ OS/2
- ☐ Other platform

Cost
- ☐ Unknown
- ☐ Basic
- ☑ Extended
- ☐ Premium ($)
- ☐ Executive w/$

Activity Level

Address
GO: **FORTH**

CTOS/Pathway Forum

Description
The forum supports users of the UniSys CTOS Client/Server Operating System, and the Pathway series of Client/Server products and services.

Subjects
Computers, Networking

Audience
CTOS users

Content Summary
Libraries include information on CTOS product information, tips and tricks, shareware, developers, networking, and client/server topics.

See Also
Client-Server Computing Forum, Novell Client Forum, MS Client

User Guide
- ☑ Windows
- ☑ DOS
- ☐ Macintosh
- ☐ Terminal Emulation
- ☐ VMS
- ☐ UNIX
- ☐ OS/2
- ☐ Other platform

Computers

Cost
- ☐ Unknown
- ☐ Basic
- ☑ Extended
- ☐ Premium ($)
- ☐ Executive w/$

Activity Level: LOW (arrow pointing left of MEDIUM)

Address
GO: **CTOS**

Cyber Forum

Description
The future of computing is the subject of the Cyber Forum, from Virtual Reality to nanotechnology.

Subjects
Computers, Virtual Reality

Audience
Computer users

Content Summary
Libraries include virtual reality, gaming, entertainment, CyberArts, robotics, CyberLit, news, art, and PCVR magazine.

See Also
Speak Easy Forum

User Guide
- ☑ Windows
- ☑ DOS
- ☑ Macintosh
- ☐ Terminal Emulation
- ☐ VMS
- ☑ UNIX
- ☐ OS/2
- ☑ Other platform

Cost
- ☐ Unknown
- ☐ Basic
- ☑ Extended
- ☐ Premium ($)
- ☐ Executive w/$

Activity Level: HIGH (arrow pointing right toward HIGH)

Address
GO: **CYBERFORUM**

Da Vinci Forum

Description
This forum provides support for Da Vinci products and messaging in general.

Subjects
Computers

Audience
Computer users, MIS people

Content Summary
This forum contains library and message sections that discuss electronic mail, names services, Coordinator, and more. You also can find demos of products in this forum.

See Also
Novell Forums, IBM Forums, Microsoft Forums

User Guide
- ☑ Windows
- ☑ DOS
- ☐ Macintosh
- ☐ Terminal Emulation
- ☐ VMS
- ☐ UNIX
- ☐ OS/2
- ☑ Other platform

Cost
- ☐ Unknown
- ☐ Basic
- ☑ Extended
- ☐ Premium ($)
- ☐ Executive w/$

Activity Level: LOW (arrow pointing left of MEDIUM)

Address
GO: **DAVINCI**

Data Access Corp. Forum

Description
This forum provides support for Data Access software development tools and products.

Subjects
Computers

Audience
Computer users, computer programmers

Content Summary
The library and message sections contain several areas, including DataFlex, FlexQL/WinQL, Office Works, C Source, API, and more.

See Also
Microsoft Developers Forum

User Guide
- ☑ Windows
- ☑ DOS
- ☐ Macintosh
- ☐ Terminal Emulation
- ☐ VMS
- ☐ UNIX
- ☐ OS/2
- ☑ Other platform

Cost
- ☐ Unknown
- ☐ Basic
- ☑ Extended
- ☐ Premium ($)
- ☐ Executive w/$

Activity Level: LOW (arrow pointing left of MEDIUM)

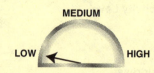

Address
GO: **DACCESS**

Computers

DataEase International Forum

Description
This forum provides support for all DataEase International products and services.

Subjects
Computers

Audience
Computer users, MIS people

Content Summary
You can find information and discussions about DataEase DQL, Express of Windows, Client-Server, DataEase user groups, and more.

See Also
Client Server Computer Forum

User Guide
- ☑ Windows
- ☑ DOS
- ☐ Macintosh
- ☐ Terminal Emulation
- ☐ VMS
- ☐ UNIX
- ☐ OS/2
- ☐ Other platform

Cost
- ☐ Unknown
- ☐ Basic
- ☑ Extended
- ☐ Premium ($)
- ☐ Executive w/$

Activity Level

Address
GO: DATAEASE

DEC PC Forum

Description
This forum provides independent support for the Digital Equipment line of PCs.

Subjects
Computers

Audience
Computer users, MIS people

Content Summary
You can find information on DECpc Hardware, DECpc Software, DECstation/VAXmate, and more in this forum.

See Also
Various Digital Equipment Corporation Forums

User Guide
- ☐ Windows
- ☐ DOS
- ☐ Macintosh
- ☐ Terminal Emulation
- ☐ VMS
- ☐ UNIX
- ☐ OS/2
- ☑ Other platform

Cost
- ☐ Unknown
- ☐ Basic
- ☑ Extended
- ☐ Premium ($)
- ☐ Executive w/$

Activity Level

Address
GO: DECPC

DEC Users Network Main Menu

Description
This forum provides access to several DEC (Digital EquipmentCorp)-related Forums.

Subjects
Computers

Audience
Computer users, MIS people

Content Summary
You can access the DEC PC Forum, DEC Windows NT Forum, DECPCI Forum, PDP-11 Forum, and VAX Forum from this main menu.

See Also
Various Digital Equipment Corporation Forums

User Guide
- ☐ Windows
- ☐ DOS
- ☐ Macintosh
- ☐ Terminal Emulation
- ☐ VMS
- ☐ UNIX
- ☐ OS/2
- ☑ Other platform

Cost
- ☐ Unknown
- ☐ Basic
- ☑ Extended
- ☐ Premium ($)
- ☐ Executive w/$

Activity Level

Address
GO: DECUNET

DECPCI Forum

Description
The DECPCI forum discusses aspects of Digital's PC Integration software and hardware.

Subjects
Computers

Audience
MIS people

Computers

Content Summary
You can find information on PATHWorks, DECpc, EtherWORKS, DOS, Macintosh, VMS, Ultrix, SCO, OS/2, networking, and other topics as they pertain to the DEC PC product line.

See Also
Various Digital Equipment Corporation Forums

User Guide
- ☐ Windows
- ☐ DOS
- ☐ Macintosh
- ☐ Terminal Emulation
- ☐ VMS
- ☐ UNIX
- ☐ OS/2
- ☑ Other platform

Cost
- ☐ Unknown
- ☐ Basic
- ☑ Extended
- ☐ Premium ($)
- ☐ Executive w/$

Activity Level: MEDIUM (LOW — HIGH)

Address
GO: **DECPCI**

DELL Forum

Description
The place to be for online support from Dell Computer Corporation.

Subjects
Computers

Audience
Computer users

Content Summary
The forum contains several library and message sections, including DELL Computers, Portable Systems, Operating Systems, Telecommunications, Customer Care, and more.

See Also
IBM File Finder

User Guide
- ☑ Windows
- ☑ DOS
- ☐ Macintosh
- ☐ Terminal Emulation
- ☐ VMS
- ☐ UNIX
- ☐ OS/2
- ☑ Other platform

Cost
- ☐ Unknown
- ☐ Basic
- ☑ Extended
- ☐ Premium ($)
- ☐ Executive w/$

Activity Level: MEDIUM (LOW — HIGH)

Address
GO: **DELL**

Delrina Forum

Description
This forum provides support for users of all Delrina products.

Subjects
Computers

Audience
Computer users

Content Summary
You can find information on various Delrina products in this forum, including WINFAX, DOSFAX, PerFORM, FormFlow, WinComm, and others.

See Also
Modem Forum, Hayes Forum

User Guide
- ☑ Windows
- ☑ DOS
- ☑ Macintosh
- ☐ Terminal Emulation
- ☐ VMS
- ☐ UNIX
- ☐ OS/2
- ☐ Other platform

Cost
- ☐ Unknown
- ☐ Basic
- ☑ Extended
- ☐ Premium ($)
- ☐ Executive w/$

Activity Level: MEDIUM (LOW — HIGH)

Address
GO: **DELRINA**

DiagSoft QAPlus Forum

Description
Provides support for DiagSoft QAPlus programs and discussions relating to these programs.

Subjects
Computers, Diagnostics, Service and Support, System Integration

Audience
Diagnostic personnel, DiagSoft Users, MIS personnel, service and support technicians, system integrators, VARs

Content Summary
Like the message area, the library area is divided into sections that discuss general information, customer support, QAPlus, QAPlus / FE (field engineers diagnostic software), Peace of Mind (DiagSoft's Macintosh product), and QAPlus for Windows information. You can find installation and compatibility information in Library 1, "General Information."

Computers

See Also
Lan Vendor Forum, PC Vendor H Forum, Thomas-Conrad Forum

User Guide
- ☑ Windows
- ☑ DOS
- ☑ Macintosh
- ☐ Terminal Emulation
- ☐ VMS
- ☐ UNIX
- ☐ OS/2
- ☐ Other platform

Cost
- ☐ Unknown
- ☐ Basic
- ☑ Extended
- ☐ Premium ($)
- ☐ Executive w/$

Activity Level — MEDIUM (arrow pointing to LOW)

Address
GO: **DIAGSOFT**

Digital Equipment Corporation

Description
This is the main area from which you can choose to enter one of several DEC forums or service areas. You can select Digital's Windows NT Support Forum, PC Integration Forum, or Digital-Related Forums. You also can go to Digital's PC Store from this menu.

Subjects
Computers, Client/Server, Multiprocessor Environments, Windows NT

Audience
DEC Alpha AXP users, support technicians, system integrators, VARs, Windows NT users

Content Summary
At the main menu, you can select from Digital NT Support Forum, Digital PC Integration Forum, and Digital's PC Store.

See Also
Digital NT Support Forum, Digital PC Integration Forum, Digital's PC Store

User Guide
- ☑ Windows
- ☑ DOS
- ☑ Macintosh
- ☐ Terminal Emulation
- ☑ VMS
- ☑ UNIX
- ☑ OS/2
- ☐ Other platform

Cost
- ☐ Unknown
- ☐ Basic
- ☑ Extended
- ☐ Premium ($)
- ☐ Executive w/$

Activity Level — MEDIUM / UNKNOWN

Address
GO: **DEC**

Digital NT Support Forum

Description
Dedicated to the user support of Windows NT, regardless of environment or platform, this forum is supported by Digital's Multi-Vendor Customer Services Group. You can find information here about DEC's Alpha AXP platform.

Subjects
Computers, Client/Server, Digital Equipment Corporation (DEC), Windows NT

Audience
DEC Alpha AXP users, support technicians, system integrators, VARs, Windows NT users

Content Summary
The library and message areas contain information about Digital and Digital's Multivendor Customer Services, including press releases and news on the Alpha AXP and Windows NT. You also can find specific areas devoted to NT user support, languages and application tools, hardware support, bug reporting, a "Wish List" area for what you want, and Alpha AXP support. You can find new BIOS files, Alpha Microcode, and utility programs in the "Patches & More" library.

See Also
DEC PC, DECPCI, PDP-11 Forum, VAX Forum

User Guide
- ☑ Windows
- ☑ DOS
- ☑ Macintosh
- ☐ Terminal Emulation
- ☐ VMS
- ☐ UNIX
- ☐ OS/2
- ☐ Other platform

Cost
- ☐ Unknown
- ☐ Basic
- ☑ Extended
- ☐ Premium ($)
- ☐ Executive w/$

Activity Level — MEDIUM

Address
GO: **DECWNT**

Digital PC Integration Forum

Description
The DECPCI Forum discusses aspects of Digital's PC Integration software and hardware, including PATHWORKS for DOS, Macintosh, VMS, Ultrix, SCO and OS/2, the DECpc family of personal computers and peripherals, and the EtherWORKS family of network connectivity products.

Computers

Subjects
Computers, DEC Integration Products, DEC PATHWORKS

Audience
DEC Alpha AXP users, support technicians, system integrators, VARs, Windows NT users

Content Summary
This message and library areas provide support and technical assistance to people who use or are interested in PATHWORKS and DEC's PC integration products. You can find technical assistance, product announcements, hints and tips, tuning guides, patches, drivers, workarounds, and other information in this forum. You can find a description of the PATHWORKS V5 Migration Guide in text or PostScript format.

See Also
DEC PC Forum, DEC Windows NT Support Forum, DECPCI Forum, PDP-11 Forum, VAX Forum

User Guide
- ☑ Windows
- ☑ DOS
- ☑ Macintosh
- ☐ Terminal Emulation
- ☑ VMS
- ☑ UNIX
- ☑ OS/2
- ☐ Other platform

Cost
- ☐ Unknown
- ☐ Basic
- ☑ Extended
- ☐ Premium ($)
- ☐ Executive w/$

Activity Level

Address
GO: **DECPCI**

Digital PC Store

Description
Order DEC products or browse its online catalog of products, including the Alpha AXP PC, networking products, and printers.

Subjects
Computers, DEC Equipment, Online Catalogs

Audience
DEC Alpha AXP users, support technicians, system integrators, VARs, Windows NT users

Content Summary
Several options enable you to browse DEC's online catalog of products, enter sweepstakes, order products, or join Digital's electronic store.

See Also
DEC PC Forum, DEC Windows NT Support Forum, DECPCI Forum, PDP-11 Forum, VAX Forum

User Guide
- ☑ Windows
- ☑ DOS
- ☑ Macintosh
- ☑ Terminal Emulation
- ☐ VMS
- ☐ UNIX
- ☐ OS/2
- ☐ Other platform

Cost
- ☐ Unknown
- ☐ Basic
- ☑ Extended
- ☐ Premium ($)
- ☐ Executive w/$

Activity Level

Address
GO: **DD-31**

Digitalk Database

Description
Since 1985, Digitalk, Inc. has been developing object-oriented programming environments for the PC with its Smalltalk/V product. The company has Smalltalk/V development environments worldwide for DOS, OS/2, Microsoft Windows, and the Apple Macintosh; the Team/V collaborative programming system; and PARTS Workbench for OS/2. The Digitalk Database contains problem reports on all Smalltalk/V and PARTS products.

Subjects
Action Requests Database, Computers, Object-Oriented Programming, Smalltalk/V

Audience
Consultants, object-oriented programmers, Smalltalk/V users, trainers

Content Summary
Select the "Search the Action Requests Database" option to search the Digitalk Action Requests database.

See Also
Digitalk Forum

User Guide
- ☑ Windows
- ☑ DOS
- ☑ Macintosh
- ☐ Terminal Emulation
- ☐ VMS
- ☐ UNIX
- ☑ OS/2
- ☐ Other platform

Cost
- ☐ Unknown
- ☐ Basic
- ☑ Extended
- ☐ Premium ($)
- ☐ Executive w/$

Activity Level

Computers

Address
GO: **DBDIGITALK**

Digitalk Forum

Description
This forum provides a way to communicate with Digitalk and with other users of Smalltalk/V and PARTS products, and includes the latest information about Smalltalk/V and PARTS products, technical support answers, and how others are using Digitalk's development systems to create and deliver software.

Subjects
Application Development, Computers, Smalltalk/V

Audience
Application developers, PARTS users, Smalltalk/V users

Content Summary
The library and message areas contain various places to discuss several topics, including Digitalk news, product information, user contributions, third-party products, support, and miscellaneous information and products. If you're looking for source code or tips on Smalltalk/V, see Library 5, "Support."

See Also
Digitalk Database

User Guide
- ☑ Windows
- ☑ DOS
- ☑ Macintosh
- ☐ Terminal Emulation
- ☐ VMS
- ☐ UNIX
- ☑ OS/2
- ☐ Other platform

Cost
- ☐ Unknown
- ☐ Basic
- ☑ Extended
- ☐ Premium ($)
- ☐ Executive w/$

Activity Level

Address
GO: **DIGITALK**

Dr. Dobb's Forum

Description
This is an "electronic" version of *Dr. Dobb's Journal*, a journal devoted to computer languages, tools, utilities, algorithms, and programming techniques. If you're interested in writing articles for the *Journal*, post them here for review. You might get published in the future.

Subjects
Computers, Programming, Utilities

Audience
Application developers, MIS personnel, system integrators

Content Summary
You can upload or download source code; find information on OS/2, UNIX, Macintosh, and Windows programming; and find listings (not text) of the articles and columns from the *Dr. Dobb's Journal* magazine. This forum is not intended to be a substitute for the magazine, but a complement to it.

See Also
MS Developers Relations Forum

User Guide
- ☑ Windows
- ☑ DOS
- ☑ Macintosh
- ☐ Terminal Emulation
- ☐ VMS
- ☑ UNIX
- ☑ OS/2
- ☐ Other platform

Cost
- ☐ Unknown
- ☐ Basic
- ☑ Extended
- ☐ Premium ($)
- ☐ Executive w/$

Activity Level
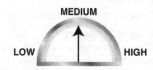

Address
GO: **DDJFORUM**

Dr. Neuhaus Forum

Description
This forum is devoted to German-speaking people interested in Dr. Neuhaus communications products. You can get technical support and information on products such as FURY modems, FAXY fax boards, and NICCY ISDN modems. You also can find information and support for Carbon Copy.

Subjects
Computers, Fax Boards, Modems, Remote Communications

Audience
All German-speaking computer users.

Content Summary
This forum is entirely in German.

See Also
Modem Vendor Forum, Palmtop Forum

User Guide
- ☑ Windows
- ☑ DOS
- ☑ Macintosh
- ☐ Terminal Emulation
- ☐ VMS
- ☐ UNIX
- ☐ OS/2
- ☐ Other platform

Cost
- ☐ Unknown
- ☐ Basic
- ☑ Extended
- ☐ Premium ($)
- ☐ Executive w/$

Activity Level

MEDIUM
UNKNOWN
LOW
HIGH

Address
GO: **NEUHAUS**

Dvorak Development Forum

Description
If you use Dvorak Development's NavCIS programs, join this forum for technical support and product information. You also can download a free 30-day demo of the DOS and Windows products to see if you want to purchase the commercial versions.

Subjects
Computers, CompuServe Navigational Tools, NavCIS

Audience
CompuServe users, NavCIS users

Content Summary
If you want to try out NavCIS, see Library 1, "NavCIS Software," to download a 3-day demo of the DOS and Windows versions of NavCIS. Libraries 2–5 offer Windows and DOS support of the SE/TE and Pro versions of NavCIS. Library 7, "Modems and Hardware," contains information and files to help you configure and optimize your modem setup. You also should check out Library 8, "Tip and Techniques," for tips on using NavCIS.

See Also
NavCIS Download Area, CSNav-Win Support Forum, CompuServe Navigator Windows (FREE), CompuServe Navigator Mac (FREE), MacNav Support Forum

User Guide

- [x] Windows
- [x] DOS
- [ ] Macintosh
- [ ] Terminal Emulation
- [ ] VMS
- [ ] UNIX
- [ ] OS/2
- [ ] Other platform

Cost

- [ ] Unknown
- [ ] Basic
- [x] Extended
- [ ] Premium ($)
- [ ] Executive w/$

Activity Level

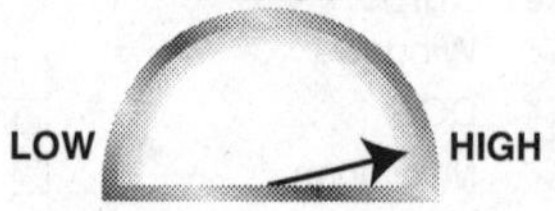
MEDIUM
LOW
HIGH

Address
GO: **DVORAK**

Eicon Technology Forum

Description
Sponsored by Eicon Technology, this forum helps users find answers to questions or problems concerning Eicon products. Eicon offers products of connectivity solutions for the X.25 and SNA environment.

Subjects
Computers, Connectivity, X.25, SNA

Audience
MIS people, Eicon consumers

Content Summary
The library and message sections contain information about Eicon products as well as technical support, press releases, utilities, help files, applications, demos, and Q&A. The libraries include sections for emulators, gateways, tool kits, international services, and WAN services.

See Also
Novell Connectivity Forum

User Guide

- [x] Windows
- [x] DOS
- [x] Macintosh
- [ ] Terminal Emulation
- [x] VMS
- [x] UNIX
- [x] OS/2
- [ ] Other platform

Cost

- [ ] Unknown
- [ ] Basic
- [x] Extended
- [ ] Premium ($)
- [ ] Executive w/$

Activity Level

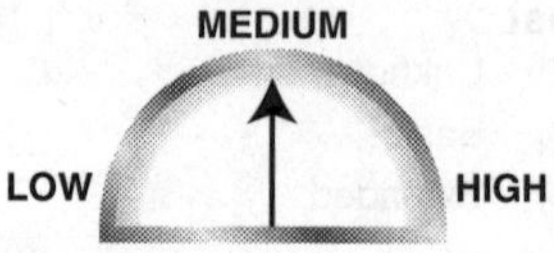
MEDIUM
LOW
HIGH

Address
GO: **EICON**

Electronic Books

Description
This is a ZiffNet area. You must be a member of ZiffNet or apply for membership when you first go to the Electronic Books area. The cost of ZiffNet membership is $2.95 monthly. The Electronic Books area offers you an option to buy books directly from the Ziff-Davis Press at 20 percent discount by selecting the ZD Press Booknet option from the main menu.

Subjects
Computers, Computer Books, ZiffNet

Audience
Computer users

Content Summary
When you select the ZD Press Booknet option, you can order Ziff Davis Press books, get special discounts from their remainder table (40 percent off cover price sometimes), download any special offers, or talk to customer service. The Electronic Books service also features the Project Gutenberg Free Book Library, which has over 100 electronic books ranging from literature (such as *Moby Dick*) to Internet titles (such as the *Hitchhiker's Guide to the Internet*) that users can download.

See Also
Ziff-Davis Press Booknet, Time-Warner Bookstore, Prentice Hall PTR (FREE), HarperCollins Online (FREE), John Wiley Book Store (FREE)

User Guide
- ☑ Windows
- ☑ DOS
- ☑ Macintosh
- ☑ Terminal Emulation
- ☑ VMS
- ☑ UNIX
- ☑ OS/2
- ☑ Other platform

Cost
- ☐ Unknown
- ☐ Basic
- ☐ Extended
- ☑ Premium ($)
- ☐ Executive w/$

Activity Level

Address
GO: **ZNT:EBOOKS**

Engineering Automation Forum

Description
LEAP (League for Engineering Productivity) sponsors this forum for discussions about CADD/CAM and other programs that are used by engineers, architects, and other professionals for design.

Subjects
CADD/CAM, Engineering, Computers, Computer-Aided Design

Audience
CADD/CAM engineers, engineers, designers

Content Summary
You can find discussions that will help you find the right CADD/CAM product for you, tips on using programs, information on new technologies, and management tools and utilities. Visit Library 9, "Classified/Jobs," for job opportunities and resumes.

See Also
IBM CAD/CAM Forum, CASE DCI Forum

User Guide
- ☑ Windows
- ☑ DOS
- ☑ Macintosh
- ☐ Terminal Emulation
- ☐ VMS
- ☐ UNIX
- ☐ OS/2
- ☐ Other platform

Cost
- ☐ Unknown
- ☐ Basic
- ☑ Extended
- ☐ Premium ($)
- ☐ Executive w/$

Activity Level
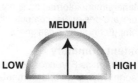

Address
GO: **LEAP**

Graphics A Vendor Forum

Description
This forum provides support from manufacturers of graphics hardware and software. You can post questions, read messages, and download files here.

Subjects
Computers, Graphics, Hardware/Software

Audience
Computer graphic designers, computer hardware users, management information specialists, hardware/software designers, handicapping enthusiasts

Content Summary
The Graphics A Vendor Forum offers support from Tempra, Grasp, STB, Jovian, Genus, RIX Softworks, Digital Vision, Global Softworks, Big_D, Pacific Motion (formerly Presidio), Metagraphics, Image-In, Inset Systems, VRLI Inc., TEGL, and ATI Technologies.

See Also
Graphics Forums, Graphics Developers Forum

User Guide
- ☑ Windows
- ☑ DOS
- ☑ Macintosh
- ☐ Terminal Emulation
- ☐ VMS
- ☑ UNIX
- ☑ OS/2
- ☐ Other platform

Cost
- ☐ Unknown
- ☐ Basic
- ☑ Extended
- ☐ Premium ($)
- ☐ Executive w/$

Activity Level

Address
GO: **GRAPHAVEN**

Graphics B Vendor Forum

Description
This forum provides support from manufacturers of graphics hardware and software. You can post questions, read messages, and download files here.

Computers

Subjects
Computers, Graphics, Hardware/Software

Audience
Management information specialists, hardware/software designers, computer hardware users, computer graphics designers

Content Summary
The Graphics B Vendor Forum offers support from Tseng Labs, Diamond Computer Systems, Animated Software, StereoGraphics, Sun Country Software, LEAD Technologies, Hercules, Genoa Systems, CrystalGraphics, Volante, Domark Software, DesignWare, Inc., HSC Software, Solana Software, Matrox, and Appian Technology.

See Also
Graphics Vendor Forum, Graphics Support Forum

User Guide
- ☑ Windows
- ☑ DOS
- ☑ Macintosh
- ☐ Terminal Emulation
- ☐ VMS
- ☑ UNIX
- ☑ OS/2
- ☐ Other platform

Cost
- ☐ Unknown
- ☐ Basic
- ☑ Extended
- ☐ Premium ($)
- ☐ Executive w/$

Activity Level

Address
GO: **GRAPHBVEN**

Graphics Corner Forum

Description
You can download and upload GIF and JPEG graphics images to this forum, such as people, portraits, animals, nature scenes, and landmarks.

Subjects
Computers, Graphics, Photography

Audience
Graphics artists, computer users, general public

Content Summary
The Graphics Corner Forum is the primary collection of user-contributed GIF and JPEG images that contain subjects such as Cars, Boats, Planes, People & Portraits, Landscapes, World of Nature, Fantasy & Sci-Fi, Space & Astronomy, Landmarks, and the Body Beautiful. This area has files that contain nudity. Those files include the following message: "This file contains nudity. Those offended by the artistic presentation of nudity should refrain from viewing."

See Also
Graphics Support Forum, Glamour Graphics Forum

User Guide
- ☑ Windows
- ☑ DOS
- ☑ Macintosh
- ☐ Terminal Emulation
- ☐ VMS
- ☑ UNIX
- ☑ OS/2
- ☐ Other platform

Cost
- ☐ Unknown
- ☐ Basic
- ☑ Extended
- ☐ Premium ($)
- ☐ Executive w/$

Activity Level

Address
GO: **CORNER**

Graphics Developers Forum

Description
If you are interested in computer graphics software, you should join the Graphics Developers Forum for various graphics-related news and information.

Subjects
Computer Graphics, Computers, Graphics

Audience
Computer graphics designers, graphics designers, graphics experts, graphics artists

Content Summary
The Graphics Developers Forum is devoted to the cutting edge of computer graphics software. Topics include fractal generation (using the Fractint software), raytracing (using POV-Ray and other programs), 3D/RDS images, the Virtual Art Gallery project, animation, morphing, motion video, and more. The Mythology library (Library 2) has several fantastic 3D images that you can download and use as wallpaper files. You also should check out the Demo Team library (Library 20) for software demos and routines.

See Also
Graphics Forums, Graphics Support Forum

User Guide
- ☑ Windows
- ☑ DOS
- ☑ Macintosh
- ☐ Terminal Emulation
- ☐ VMS
- ☐ UNIX
- ☐ OS/2
- ☐ Other platform

Cost
- ☐ Unknown
- ☐ Basic
- ☑ Extended
- ☐ Premium ($)
- ☐ Executive w/$

Computers

Activity Level

Address
GO: **GRAPHDEV**

Graphics File Finder

Description
If you're looking for a specific graphics file or just want to browse the graphics files that are available, use this service.

Subjects
Computer Graphics, Computers, Graphics

Audience
Graphic artists, graphics experts, graphic designers, computer users, computer graphics designers

Content Summary
Graphics File Finder is an online comprehensive keyword searchable database of file descriptions from graphics-related forums, including the Computer Art Forum, Fine Art Forum, Graphics Corner Forum, Graphics Developers Forum, Graphics Gallery Forum, and the Quick Pictures Forum. It is designed to provide quick and easy reference to some of the best programs and files available. You can use seven common search criteria to find the location of a desired file or files quickly. You can search by topic, file submission date, forum name, file type, file extension, file name, or submitter's User ID. File descriptions, forum, and library location are displayed for the matched files.

See Also
Graphics Forums, Graphics Corner Forum

User Guide
- [✓] Windows
- [✓] DOS
- [✓] Macintosh
- [ ] Terminal Emulation
- [ ] VMS
- [✓] UNIX
- [✓] OS/2
- [ ] Other platform

Cost
- [ ] Unknown
- [ ] Basic
- [✓] Extended
- [ ] Premium ($)
- [ ] Executive w/$

Activity Level

UNKNOWN

Address
GO: **GRAPHFF**

Graphics Forums

Description
The Graphics Forums service enables you to access several graphics-related forums, the Graphics File Finder, and an online tutorial.

Subjects
Computer Graphics, Computers, Graphic Arts, Graphics

Audience
Computer graphics designers, computer users, graphics designers, graphics artists, graphics experts

Content Summary
The Graphics Forums main menu consists of Introduction to Graphics, Graphics File Finder, Go Graphics News, Best of Go Graphics Directory, Graphics Support Forums, Image Collection Forums, Image Development Forums, Weather Maps, Nominate Image of the Month, and other forums with graphics. If you are looking for graphics to view, download, get information, or learn more about graphics in general, you might want to start your search here. You're sure to find what you're looking for.

See Also
Graphics Plus Forum, Graphics File Finder

User Guide
- [✓] Windows
- [✓] DOS
- [✓] Macintosh
- [ ] Terminal Emulation
- [ ] VMS
- [✓] UNIX
- [✓] OS/2
- [ ] Other platform

Cost
- [ ] Unknown
- [ ] Basic
- [✓] Extended
- [ ] Premium ($)
- [ ] Executive w/$

Activity Level

Address
GO: **GRAPHICS**

Graphics Gallery Forum

Description
This forum offers collections of graphics from NASA, the Smithsonian Institute, the Coast Guard, and tourism agencies.

Subjects
Computer Graphics, Computers, Graphics, Photography

Audience
Graphics artists, graphics designers, computer users, photographers

Content Summary
The Graphics Gallery Forum's libraries consist of the following topics: New Images, SI: Smithsonian Art, SI: Air/Space, SI: Science/Nature, SI: People/Places, NASA, Utah Shakespearean Festival, NAL/USDA, America! North, America! South, America! East, America! West, US Coast Guard, World Photography, Wisconsin Historical Society, and Civil War. The Utah Shakespearean Festival library (Library 9) contains a compilation of the best of moments from the 32 seasons of the Utah Shakespearean Festival's plays.

See Also
Graphics Forums, Graphics Corner Forum, Graphics File Finder

User Guide
- ☑ Windows
- ☑ DOS
- ☐ Macintosh
- ☐ Terminal Emulation
- ☐ VMS
- ☐ UNIX
- ☑ OS/2
- ☐ Other platform

Cost
- ☐ Unknown
- ☐ Basic
- ☑ Extended
- ☐ Premium ($)
- ☐ Executive w/$

Activity Level
LOW (arrow pointing low)

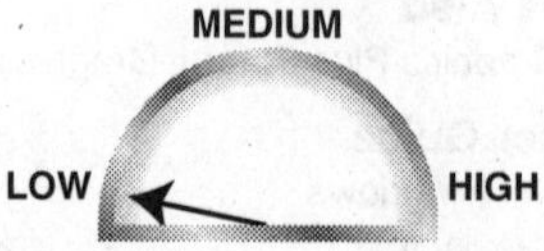

Address
GO: **GALLERY**

Graphics Plus Forum

Description
This forum contains true-color images in various formats. You can get graphics of cars, boats, people, landscapes, and much more.

Subjects
Computer Graphics, Graphics, Photography

Audience
Photographers, computer graphics designers, computer users, graphics artists, graphics designers, graphics experts

Content Summary
The Graphics Plus Forum has images in truecolor and vector formats such as TIFF, Targa, EPS, truecolor BMP and PCX, AI, PICT, and others. This forum also includes a section focusing on fractal and raytraced images. The libraries include areas such as Cars-Boats-Planes, People & Portraits, Landscapes, World of Nature, Fantasy & Sci-Fi, Cartoons & Comics, Body Beautiful, Plain Brown Wrapper, Fractals/Raytracing, and more. Note that this forum contains files that have nudity. Those files that contain nudity have the following disclaimer: "Those offended by the artistic presentation of nudity should refrain from viewing."

See Also
Graphics File Finder, Graphics Forums, Graphics Gallery Forum, Photography Forum

User Guide
- ☑ Windows
- ☑ DOS
- ☑ Macintosh
- ☐ Terminal Emulation
- ☐ VMS
- ☑ UNIX
- ☑ OS/2
- ☐ Other platform

Cost
- ☐ Unknown
- ☐ Basic
- ☑ Extended
- ☐ Premium ($)
- ☐ Executive w/$

Activity Level

MEDIUM-HIGH

Address
GO: **GRAPHPLUS**

Graphics C Vendor Forum

Description
The Graphics C Vendor Forum offers support from MicroFrontier, Clear Software, Artist Graphics, and Envisions.

Subjects
Computer Graphics, Computers, Graphics

Audience
Computer graphics designers, graphics artists, graphics designers, graphics experts

Content Summary
The library section contains these areas: Forum Information, MicroFrontier, Clear Software, Artist Graphics, and Envisions.

See Also
Graphics Forums, Graphics File Finder, Graphics Developers Forum

User Guide
- ☑ Windows
- ☑ DOS
- ☐ Macintosh
- ☐ Terminal Emulation
- ☐ VMS
- ☐ UNIX
- ☐ OS/2
- ☐ Other platform

Cost
- ☐ Unknown
- ☐ Basic
- ☑ Extended
- ☐ Premium ($)
- ☐ Executive w/$

Activity Level
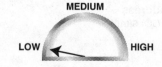
LOW

Address
GO: **GRAPHCVEN**

Computers

Gupta Forum

Description
This forum is a support forum sponsored by Gupta for its PC client/server system software and products, such as SQLBase and SQLWindows.

Subjects
Computers

Audience
Computer programmers, computer systems analysts, management information specialists

Content Summary
The libraries in this forum include topics on SQLBase, Connectivity/SQLNet, SQLWindows/TeamWin, Quest, Product Marketing, Third Party Products, User Groups, and Gupta JobNet.

See Also
Client Server Computing Forum

User Guide
- ☑ Windows
- ☑ DOS
- ☐ Macintosh
- ☐ Terminal Emulation
- ☐ VMS
- ☐ UNIX
- ☐ OS/2
- ☑ Other platform

Cost
- ☐ Unknown
- ☐ Basic
- ☑ Extended
- ☐ Premium ($)
- ☐ Executive w/$

Activity Level

Address
GO: **GUPTAFORUM**

Hayes Forum

Description
This forum contains press releases, technical support, tips, and much more. Some of the products include Smartmodems, ACCURA, and JT Fax.

Subjects
Computers, Modems

Audience
Management information specialists, computer hardware users

Content Summary
The library and message sections in this forum include discussions and files on high-speed modems, Smartmodems, Smartcom for DOS and Windows, Fax products, Hayes for the Mac, Hayes for LANS, and Hayes for ISDN.

See Also
Modem Vendor Forum, Hayes

User Guide
- ☑ Windows
- ☑ DOS
- ☑ Macintosh
- ☐ Terminal Emulation
- ☐ VMS
- ☐ UNIX
- ☐ OS/2
- ☐ Other platform

Cost
- ☐ Unknown
- ☐ Basic
- ☑ Extended
- ☐ Premium ($)
- ☐ Executive w/$

Activity Level
MEDIUM
LOW ← HIGH

Address
GO: **HAYFORUM**

Hayes Online

Description
This service gives you an introduction to Hayes Corporation, as well as product support.

Subjects
Computer Hardware, Computer Networking, Computers, Modems

Audience
Modem users, management information specialists

Content Summary
From the Online with Hayes main menu, you can select from About Online with Hayes, The Hayes Advantage, the Hayes Forum, LANstep, Product Descriptions, Special Support Forums, and Third Party Developers.

See Also
Hayes Forum, Modem Vendor Forum

User Guide
- ☑ Windows
- ☑ DOS
- ☑ Macintosh
- ☐ Terminal Emulation
- ☐ VMS
- ☐ UNIX
- ☐ OS/2
- ☐ Other platform

Cost
- ☐ Unknown
- ☐ Basic
- ☑ Extended
- ☐ Premium ($)
- ☐ Executive w/$

Activity Level

Address
GO: **HAYES**

Computers

HP Handhelds Forum

Description
This forum is designed to help you get the most out of your HP handheld computer, HP palmtop, or HP calculator.

Subjects
Computer Hardware, Computers, Field Computing

Audience
Computer programmers, computer professionals, computer users

Content Summary
You can get answers to your technical questions, exchange information with other users, take advantage of shareware and other files on the libraries, and stay in touch with the latest news from HP and 3rd-parties. The many libraries include areas for 1x,2x,3x calculators, 4x,6x,7x,9x calculators, the 95LX, the 100/200LX, HPHAND, and Palmtop programmers.

See Also
HP OmniBook Forum, HP Peripherals Forum, HP Specials

User Guide
- ☐ Windows
- ☐ DOS
- ☐ Macintosh
- ☐ Terminal Emulation
- ☐ VMS
- ☐ UNIX
- ☐ OS/2
- ☑ Other platform

Cost
- ☐ Unknown
- ☐ Basic
- ☑ Extended
- ☐ Premium ($)
- ☐ Executive w/$

Activity Level

Address
GO: **HPHAND**

HP Omnibook Forum

Description
Find out the latest on the HP Omnibook in this forum.

Subjects
Computers

Audience
Computer users

Content Summary
Not officially sponsored by HP, this forum can help you find the answers you might need for your HP Omnibook. This forum also will keep you up-to-date with the latest information from HP and other vendors, and let you access a collection of application notes, tips, and software for your OmniBook.

See Also
HP Specials, HP Peripherals Forum

User Guide
- ☑ Windows
- ☑ DOS
- ☐ Macintosh
- ☐ Terminal Emulation
- ☐ VMS
- ☐ UNIX
- ☐ OS/2
- ☐ Other platform

Cost
- ☐ Unknown
- ☐ Basic
- ☑ Extended
- ☐ Premium ($)
- ☐ Executive w/$

Activity Level

Address
GO: **HPOMNIBOOK**

HP Peripherals Forum

Description
This is Hewlett-Packard's forum for disseminating information about HP peripherals, such as its DeskJet and LaserJet printers.

Subjects
Computers

Audience
Management information specialists, computer users

Content Summary
This forum is sponsored by Hewlett-Packard as a distribution channel for information about HP peripherals. The forum may also be used to get assistance from other users. You should note, however, that HP does not respond to technical questions posted in this forum. You can find files, support questions and answers, and press releases about printers, fax products, and other HP peripherals. Don't miss their library and message areas on their TWAIN support.

See Also
HP Specials

User Guide
- ☑ Windows
- ☑ DOS
- ☑ Macintosh
- ☐ Terminal Emulation
- ☐ VMS
- ☐ UNIX
- ☐ OS/2
- ☐ Other platform

Cost
- ☐ Unknown
- ☐ Basic
- ☑ Extended
- ☐ Premium ($)
- ☐ Executive w/$

Computers

Activity Level

LOW — MEDIUM ↑ — HIGH

Address
GO: **HPPER**

HP Specials

Description
Can't find it in the other HP forums? Maybe it's in this area.

Subjects
Computers

Audience
Computer users, management information specialists

Content Summary
Files located in the HP Special Library differ from files located in HP forum libraries. Some of the files in the HP Special Library area may have licensing agreements that prevent distribution in HP forum libraries. Other files may have charges associated with them in addition to the normal CompuServe connect-time charges required to download the file. As new files become available in the HP Special Library, they will be announced in the HP Forums.

See Also
HP Handheld Forum, HP OmniBook Forum, HP Peripherals Forum, HP Systems Forum

User Guide
- ☑ Windows
- ☑ DOS
- ☑ Macintosh
- ☑ Terminal Emulation
- ☐ VMS
- ☐ UNIX
- ☐ OS/2
- ☑ Other platform

Cost
- ☐ Unknown
- ☐ Basic
- ☑ Extended
- ☐ Premium ($)
- ☐ Executive w/$

Activity Level

LOW — UNKNOWN — HIGH (MEDIUM)

Address
GO: **HPSPEC**

HP Systems Forum

Description
This forum, sponsored by Hewlett-Packard, is intended to provide support and services for HP products such as Dashboard, EtherTwist, and NewWave.

Subjects
Computers

Audience
Management information specialists, computer users

Content Summary
The several libraries in forum include topics such as HP mass storage, Vectra, NetServer PCs, Windows clients, EtherTwist, NewWave, and HP-UX systems. You can find patches, tips and hints, utilities, and other files for various HP products in the libraries. If you use Dashboard, download the Top Ten Tips file in the Dashboard/misc. apps library (Library 11).

See Also
HP Specials, HP Peripherals Forum, HP OmniBook Forum, HP Handheld Forum

User Guide
- ☑ Windows
- ☑ DOS
- ☐ Macintosh
- ☐ Terminal Emulation
- ☐ VMS
- ☑ UNIX
- ☐ OS/2
- ☑ Other platform

Cost
- ☐ Unknown
- ☐ Basic
- ☑ Extended
- ☐ Premium ($)
- ☐ Executive w/$

Activity Level

LOW — MEDIUM ↑ — HIGH

Address
GO: **HPSYS**

IBM Applications Forum

Description
This forum is devoted to the topic of general applications on the IBM PC and any and all other compatible computers.

Subjects
Computer Applications, Computers, IBM PCs

Audience
Computer users

Content Summary
Find out information about IBM and IBM PC compatible software, including word processors, text editors, DBMS, accounting, general applications, graphics, education, desktop publishing, and more.

See Also
Microsoft Connection, Lotus Technical Library

User Guide
- ☑ Windows
- ☑ DOS
- ☐ Macintosh
- ☐ Terminal Emulation
- ☐ VMS
- ☐ UNIX
- ☑ OS/2
- ☑ Other platform

Computers

Cost
- ☐ Unknown
- ☐ Basic
- ☒ Extended
- ☐ Premium ($)
- ☐ Executive w/$

Activity Level: HIGH

Address
GO: **IBMAPP**

IBM CAD/CAM Forum

Description
This forum is devoted to the users and/or potential users of IBM CAD/CAM application products. The products supported in this forum are CATIA, CADAM, and other products relating to CAD/CAM.

Subjects
Computers, IBM

Audience
Computer users, computer engineers

Contents Summary
The library and message sections include RLM Q&A, CAITIA AIX SYS Q&A, CADAM HOST SYS Q&A, CADAM How-To Guides, and more.

See Also
IBM Applications Forum

User Guide
- ☐ Windows
- ☐ DOS
- ☐ Macintosh
- ☐ Terminal Emulation
- ☐ VMS
- ☒ UNIX
- ☐ OS/2
- ☒ Other platform

Cost
- ☐ Unknown
- ☐ Basic
- ☒ Extended
- ☐ Premium ($)
- ☐ Executive w/$

Activity Level: LOW

Address
GO: **IBMENG**

IBM Communications Forum

Description
This forum is devoted to the topic of telecommunications on the IBM PC and compatible computers.

Subjects
Communications, Computers, IBM PCs, Modems

Audience
Computer users, management information specialists

Contents Summary
You can find various utilities, files, support Q&A, and other communications information for the PC in this forum. The libraries include Autosig (ATO), Communications Utilities, Communications Programs, FAX, Hot Topics, Modems/Communications Hardware, and more.

See Also
Hayes Forum, Modem Vendor Forum

User Guide
- ☒ Windows
- ☒ DOS
- ☐ Macintosh
- ☐ Terminal Emulation
- ☐ VMS
- ☐ UNIX
- ☒ OS/2
- ☒ Other platform

Cost
- ☐ Unknown
- ☐ Basic
- ☒ Extended
- ☐ Premium ($)
- ☐ Executive w/$

Activity Level: MEDIUM

Address
GO: **IBMCOM**

IBM DB2 Database Forum

Description
This forum is designed for people interested in or currently using the DB2/2, DB2/6000, DB2 Clients, DB2/VSE&VM (SQL/DS), DB2/MVS relational database products, as well as Visualizer and IMS products.

Subjects
Computers, Databases, IBM

Audience
Management information specialists, computer users, database managers

Content Summary
You can find the following libraries in this forum: DB2/2, DB2/6000, DB2/VSE&VM, DB2/MVS, DB2 Clients, Visualizer, IMS Family, and Open Forum.

See Also
Client Server Computing Forum

User Guide
- ☐ Windows
- ☒ DOS
- ☐ Macintosh
- ☐ Terminal Emulation
- ☐ VMS
- ☒ UNIX
- ☒ OS/2
- ☒ Other platform

Cost
- ☐ Unknown
- ☐ Basic
- ☒ Extended
- ☐ Premium ($)
- ☐ Executive w/$

Computers

Activity Level

Address
GO: **IBMDB2**

IBM File Finder

Description
If it's on CompuServe and in a computer-related forum, you should be able to find it with this service. This searchable database is useful if you are looking for a number of files that are in several known or unknown forums.

Subjects
Computers, Databases, IBM PCs

Audience
Computer users, management information specialists

Content Summary
With File Finder, you can use seven common search criteria for finding the location of a desired file or files. You can search by topic, file submission date, forum name, file type, file extension, file name, or submitter's User ID. File descriptions, forum, and library location are displayed for the matched files, giving instant information on where to find a most wanted file.

See Also
MS Software Library

User Guide
- ☑ Windows
- ☑ DOS
- ☑ Macintosh
- ☐ Terminal Emulation
- ☐ VMS
- ☑ UNIX
- ☑ OS/2
- ☑ Other platform

Cost
- ☐ Unknown
- ☐ Basic
- ☑ Extended
- ☐ Premium ($)
- ☐ Executive w/$

Activity Level

Address
GO: **IBMFF**

IBM Hardware Forum

Description
This forum is devoted to the topic of hardware on the IBM PC and any other compatible computers.

Subjects
Computers, Hardware, IBM PCs

Audience
Management information specialists, computer users

Content Summary
You can find library and message areas such as Disk/Disk Utilities, Printer Utilities, Video, PC-AT, Classifieds, PCJr, Tape, and more.

See Also
IBMNET, PC Vendor Forums

User Guide
- ☑ Windows
- ☑ DOS
- ☐ Macintosh
- ☐ Terminal Emulation
- ☐ VMS
- ☐ UNIX
- ☑ OS/2
- ☑ Other platform

Cost
- ☐ Unknown
- ☐ Basic
- ☑ Extended
- ☐ Premium ($)
- ☐ Executive w/$

Activity Level
MEDIUM LOW HIGH (high)

Address
GO: **IBMHW**

IBM ImagePlus Forum

Description
You can get support for IBM's ImagePlus system for IP/2, IP/AS400, and IP/MVS.

Subjects
Computer Graphics, Computers, IBM

Audience
Computer users, management information specialists

Content Summary
The libraries in this forum include IP/2 Info, IP/2 General Questions, IP/2 Support, IP/AS400 Info, Visualinfo Info, and more.

See Also
Graphics, Graphics Vendor Forums, PC Vendor Forums

User Guide
- ☐ Windows
- ☐ DOS
- ☐ Macintosh
- ☐ Terminal Emulation
- ☐ VMS
- ☑ UNIX
- ☑ OS/2
- ☑ Other platform

Cost
- ☐ Unknown
- ☐ Basic
- ☑ Extended
- ☐ Premium ($)
- ☐ Executive w/$

Activity Level
MEDIUM LOW HIGH (low)

Address
GO: **IBMIMAGE**

Computers

IBM Languages Forum

Description
This forum is for questions, answers, and discussion regarding IBM languages, including APL and APL2.

Subjects
Computer Programming Languages, Computers, IBM

Audience
Management information specialists, computer programmers

Content Summary
This forum contains the following libraries: General Library, APL2 Language, APL2 for OS/2 Demo, APL2 for OS/2 CSD, and APL2 User Files.

See Also
IBM OS/2 Developer 1 Forum, IBM OS/2 Developer 2 Forum, IBM Systems/Util. Forum

User Guide
- ☐ Windows
- ☐ DOS
- ☐ Macintosh
- ☐ Terminal Emulation
- ☐ VMS
- ☐ UNIX
- ☑ OS/2
- ☑ Other platform

Cost
- ☐ Unknown
- ☐ Basic
- ☑ Extended
- ☐ Premium ($)
- ☐ Executive w/$

Activity Level LOW ← MEDIUM HIGH

Address
GO: **IBMLANG**

IBM LMU2 Forum

Description
This forum is an open forum for the discussion of all topics related to LAN Management Utilities/2 (LMU/2).

Subjects
Computers, IBM, Networking

Audience
Computer users, management information specialists

See Also
IBM File Finder

Content Summary
This forum includes libraries named Common Questions, Tools/Samples, News/Announcements, LMU/2 V2 Updates, and LMU Updates.

See Also
IBM File Finder

User Guide
- ☐ Windows
- ☐ DOS
- ☐ Macintosh
- ☐ Terminal Emulation
- ☐ VMS
- ☐ UNIX
- ☑ OS/2
- ☐ Other platform

Cost
- ☐ Unknown
- ☐ Basic
- ☑ Extended
- ☐ Premium ($)
- ☐ Executive w/$

Activity Level LOW ← MEDIUM HIGH

Address
GO: **LMUFORUM**

IBM Object Technology Forum

Description
The IBMSOM Forum provides service and support for the IBM SOMobjects products.

Subjects
Computers, IBM

Audience
Computer users, computer programmers, IBM users

Content Summary
The products discussed in this forum include SOMobjects Developer Toolkit, Version 2.0, SOMobjects Workstation Enabler, Version 2.0, and SOMobjects Workgroup Enabler, Version 2.0.

See Also
IBM Languages Forum

User Guide
- ☐ Windows
- ☐ DOS
- ☐ Macintosh
- ☐ Terminal Emulation
- ☐ VMS
- ☐ UNIX
- ☑ OS/2
- ☐ Other platform

Cost
- ☐ Unknown
- ☐ Basic
- ☑ Extended
- ☐ Premium ($)
- ☐ Executive w/$

Activity Level LOW ↑ MEDIUM HIGH

Address
GO: **IBMOBJ**

IBM OS/2 Developers Forums

Description
The IBM OS/2 Developers 1 and 2 Forums contain information for OS/2 developers, including development tools, debugging, and other information.

Computers

Subjects
Computer Programming Languages, Computers, IBM

Audience
Computer programmers, management information specialists

Content Summary
The IBM OS/2 Developers 1 Forum (GO OS2DF1) includes the following libraries: Base OS API's, PM API's, 2.x Workplace Shell, REXX/Other Languages, Device Drive Development, and more. The IBM OS/2 Developers 1 Forum (GO OS2DF1) includes the following libraries: Communications Manager, LAN Server, TCP/IP, CID Enablement, Pen Software, and more.

See Also
IBM OS/2 B Vendors Forum, IBM Object Technology Forum, IBM OS/2 Support Forum, IBM OS/2 Vendor Forum

User Guide
- [ ] Windows
- [ ] DOS
- [ ] Macintosh
- [ ] Terminal Emulation
- [ ] VMS
- [ ] UNIX
- [x] OS/2
- [ ] Other platform

Cost
- [ ] Unknown
- [ ] Basic
- [x] Extended
- [ ] Premium ($)
- [ ] Executive w/$

Activity Level

Address
GO: **OS2DFI** or **OS2DF2**

IBM OS/2 Service Pak

Description
If you are having problems with OS/2, you should visit this service and download the ServicePaks, which offer fixes to common problems.

Subjects
Computers, IBM

Audience
Management information specialists, IBM users, computer users

Content Summary
The ServicePak contains OS/2 product fixes for reported customer problems and problems identified by IBM. The ServicePak also contains certain product enhancements, including additional video graphics adapter ship set support, and drivers. The version control number for this General Availability ServicePak product is XR06100. If you have not had problems with OS/2 2.0 or OS/2 2.0 with ServicePak 1 installed, you do not need to download Service Pak 2.

See Also
IBM OS/2 Support Forum, IBM OS/2 Users Forum

User Guide
- [ ] Windows
- [ ] DOS
- [ ] Macintosh
- [ ] Terminal Emulation
- [ ] VMS
- [ ] UNIX
- [x] OS/2
- [ ] Other platform

Cost
- [ ] Unknown
- [ ] Basic
- [x] Extended
- [ ] Premium ($)
- [ ] Executive w/$

Activity Level

Address
GO: **OS2SERV**

IBM OS/2 Vendor Forums

Description
The OS/2 A Vendor and OS/2 B Vendor Forums contain information from various vendors of OS/2 products and services.

Subjects
Computers, IBM

Audience
IBM users, computer users

Content Summary
The IBM OS/2 A Vendor Forum includes these vendors: OS/2 Magazine, One UP, JDS Publishing, Sundial Systems, and others. The IBM OS/2 B Vendor Forum includes these vendors: OS/2 Shareware, PCX, Carry Associates, MSR Development, and more.

See Also
IBM OS/2 Support Forum, IBM OS/2 Users Forum

User Guide
- [ ] Windows
- [ ] DOS
- [ ] Macintosh
- [ ] Terminal Emulation
- [ ] VMS
- [ ] UNIX
- [x] OS/2
- [ ] Other platform

Cost
- [ ] Unknown
- [ ] Basic
- [x] Extended
- [ ] Premium ($)
- [ ] Executive w/$

Activity Level
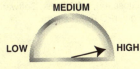

Computers

Address
GO: **OS2AVEN** or **OS2BVEN**

IBM Personal Software Products

Description
This is the IBM Personal Software Products online store. You can get products and product information, and join the electronic mailing list.

Subjects
Computers, IBM

Audience
IBM users, computer users

Content Summary
From the main menu, you can choose to shop the store, download an OS/2 demo, get OS/2 user tips, and get information on technical support. You also can get information on IBM's line of other products, including multimedia and networking.

See Also
IBM New Users Forum

User Guide
- ☐ Windows
- ☐ DOS
- ☐ Macintosh
- ☐ Terminal Emulation
- ☐ VMS
- ☐ UNIX
- ☑ OS/2
- ☑ Other platform

Cost
- ☐ Unknown
- ☑ Basic
- ☐ Extended
- ☐ Premium ($)
- ☐ Executive w/$

Activity Level

Address
GO: **IBMPSP**

IBM PowerPC Forum

Description
Interested in the PowerPC? If so, come to this forum and get up-to-date information on this new microprocessor.

Subjects
Computers, IBM

Audience
Computer users, management information specialists

Content Summary
Libraries include Press Releases/Announcements, General Information, Publication Index, What is? (Glossary), Q&A Bank, Software, Hardware, and PowerPC Ref Platform.

See Also
Computer Buyers Guide, Computer Database Plus

User Guide
- ☐ Windows
- ☐ DOS
- ☐ Macintosh
- ☐ Terminal Emulation
- ☐ VMS
- ☐ UNIX
- ☑ OS/2
- ☐ Other platform

Cost
- ☐ Unknown
- ☐ Basic
- ☑ Extended
- ☐ Premium ($)
- ☐ Executive w/$

Activity Level

Address
GO: **POWERPC**

IBM Programming Forum

Description
This forum is devoted to helping those interested in programming for the IBM or IBM PC-compatible computers.

Subjects
Computer Programming Languages, Computers

Audience
Computer programmers

Content Summary
You can get assemblers, source code, tips, and techniques from this forum. The library and message sections include OS Services, C and C++, BASIC, Other Languages, Tools/Debuggers, Job Exchange, VESA, and more.

See Also
IBM Languages Forum, Microsoft Languages Forum

User Guide
- ☑ Windows
- ☑ DOS
- ☑ Macintosh
- ☐ Terminal Emulation
- ☐ VMS
- ☑ UNIX
- ☑ OS/2
- ☑ Other platform

Cost
- ☐ Unknown
- ☐ Basic
- ☑ Extended
- ☐ Premium ($)
- ☐ Executive w/$

Activity Level

Address
GO: **IBMPRO**

IBM Software Forum

Description
This forum is devoted to users of or those interested in becoming users of IBM Software Solutions applications products.

Subjects
Computers

Audience
Computer programmers, management information specialists

Content Summary
The various library and message sections in this forum include the following: Calendar of Events, OV/VM, Current/OV, FormTalk, Tested and Approved, Time and Place/2, IntelliAgent, and more.

See Also
IBM New Users Forum

User Guide
- [ ] Windows
- [ ] DOS
- [ ] Macintosh
- [ ] Terminal Emulation
- [ ] VMS
- [ ] UNIX
- [ ] OS/2
- [x] Other platform

Cost
- [ ] Unknown
- [ ] Basic
- [x] Extended
- [ ] Premium ($)
- [ ] Executive w/$

Activity Level

MEDIUM (LOW – HIGH)

Address
GO: **IBMDESK**

IBM Storage Systems Forum

Description
This forum has information concerning IBM Storage Systems Division Software Products, including information for the ADSTAR Distributed Storage Manager.

Subjects
Computers, IBM, Multimedia

Audience
Management information apecialists, computer users

Content Summary
The sections in this forum include ADSTAR Distributed Storage Manager (ADSM), ADSM Special Programs, ADSM BETA Program (private), and ADSM Developers Program (private).

See Also
PC Vendors Forums, Stac Electronics

User Guide
- [ ] Windows
- [ ] DOS
- [ ] Macintosh
- [ ] Terminal Emulation
- [ ] VMS
- [ ] UNIX
- [x] OS/2
- [x] Other platform

Cost
- [ ] Unknown
- [ ] Basic
- [x] Extended
- [ ] Premium ($)
- [ ] Executive w/$

Activity Level

MEDIUM (LOW – HIGH)

Address
GO: **IBMSTORAGE**

IBM Systems/Utilities Forum

Description
Find the most current utilities for your IBM or IBM compatible PC, including files for Windows, MS-DOS, PC-DOS, and OS/2.

Subjects
Computers, IBM PCs

Audience
Computer users

Content Summary
The library and message sections include the following: DOS Utilities, OS/2 Utilities, General Utilities, Multitasking, DOS Shells/Managers, File Utilities, Desktop Utilities, Demos, and Disk Library.

See Also
IBM File Finder, MS Software Library

User Guide
- [x] Windows
- [x] DOS
- [ ] Macintosh
- [ ] Terminal Emulation
- [ ] VMS
- [ ] UNIX
- [x] OS/2
- [ ] Other platform

Cost
- [ ] Unknown
- [ ] Basic
- [x] Extended
- [ ] Premium ($)
- [ ] Executive w/$

Activity Level

MEDIUM (LOW – HIGH)

Address
GO: **IBMSYS**

Computers

IBM ThinkPad Forum

Description
This forum is designed to exchange information, experiences, and opinions on the IBM ThinkPad, including application development concerns and questions.

Subjects
Computers, IBM

Audience
Computer users

Content Summary
This forum contains the following libraries: Hardware, Software, Options/Accessories, Audio Central, and User Uploads. Be sure to join in on the message sections to share and receive ideas and experiences about the ThinkPad.

See Also
IBM New Users Forum

User Guide
☐ Windows		☐ VMS	
☐ DOS		☐ UNIX	
☐ Macintosh		☐ OS/2	
☐ Terminal Emulation		☑ Other platform	

Cost
☐ Unknown		☐ Premium ($)	
☐ Basic		☐ Executive w/$	
☑ Extended			

Activity Level

Address
GO: **THINKPAD**

IBM Users Network

Description
This service provides a place for people who have a special interest in the IBM and compatible family of computers.

Subjects
Computers, IBM PCs

Audience
Computer users, IBM users

Content Summary
From the IBM Users Network main menu, you can choose from several options, including Top 10 Utilities, File Finder, New Users/Fun Forum, Communications Forum, ASP/Shareware Forum, and several other forum options. Use this service as a starting point to learn more about the forums that are available for IBM and IBM PC-compatible computers.

See Also
MS Software Library, IBM File Finder

User Guide
☑ Windows		☐ VMS	
☑ DOS		☐ UNIX	
☐ Macintosh		☑ OS/2	
☐ Terminal Emulation		☑ Other platform	

Cost
☐ Unknown		☐ Premium ($)	
☐ Basic		☐ Executive w/$	
☑ Extended			

Activity Level

Address
GO: **IBMNET**

Information Management Forum

Description
This forum includes topics ranging from staff management and time management to technology management.

Subjects
Computers, Management

Audience
Management information specialists

Content Summary
This forum discusses issues that are currently scattered over numerous CompuServe forums, and offers the opportunity to concentrate on new issues as they emerge. Many forums often address the "how" for solving computing problems. This forum is also able to address the "why," and computing foundations. Although technical issues can be discussed, this forum focuses primarily on the management issues in the information processing community. The library and message sections include Professional Development, Desktop Issues, Network Issues, Host Issues, Professional Issues, and much more.

See Also
Business Database Plus, PC Vendors G Forum, Polaris Software

User Guide
☑ Windows		☐ VMS	
☑ DOS		☐ UNIX	
☐ Macintosh		☐ OS/2	
☐ Terminal Emulation		☐ Other platform	

Cost
☐ Unknown		☐ Premium ($)	
☐ Basic		☐ Executive w/$	
☑ Extended			

Computers

Activity Level

Address
GO: **INFOMANAGE**

Intel Corporation

Description
This service enables you to get to the Intel Forum and Intel Architecture Labs Forum.

Subjects
Computer Hardware, Computers, Microcomputers, Modems, Networking

Audience
Modem users, network users, computer users

Content Summary
The Intel Forum supports Intel's enhancement products for IBM PCs and any and all compatible computers. You can find information on Above Boards, SnapIn, Inboards, SatisFAXtion, and Connection CoProcessor FAX boards. Other products include Intel Math CoProcessors, modems, network-enhancement utilities, network-management tools, Visual Edge, Code Builder, Matched Memory, and NetPort. The Intel Architecture Labs Forum is an interactive, online service in which you can obtain the latest in technical and marketing information on the advanced Intel architectures.

See Also
IBM Users Network

User Guide
☑	Windows	☐	VMS
☑	DOS	☐	UNIX
☐	Macintosh	☑	OS/2
☐	Terminal Emulation	☑	Other platform

Cost
☐	Unknown	☐	Premium ($)
☐	Basic	☐	Executive w/$
☑	Extended		

Activity Level

Address
GO: **INTEL**

Internet Forum

Description
This forum is dedicated to the Internet. You can find information on "surfing" utilities, ftp and telnet sites, newsgroups, and World-Wide Web and Gopher sites.

Subjects
Computers, Internet

Audience
Computer users, Internet surfers

Content Summary
The forum's library and message sections include Getting Started, Internet Access, Directory Services, Electronic Mail, Mailing Lists, Gopher/WAIS/WWW, and more. Look in the Resources-Technical library (Library 15) for up-to-date information on Internet security and the latest virus. If you're new to the Internet, look in the Getting Started library for various files on how to start surfing on the 'Net.

See Also
Electronic Frontier Foundation

User Guide
☑	Windows	☑	VMS
☑	DOS	☑	UNIX
☑	Macintosh	☑	OS/2
☑	Terminal Emulation	☑	Other platform

Cost
☐	Unknown	☐	Premium ($)
☐	Basic	☐	Executive w/$
☑	Extended		

Activity Level

Address
GO: **INETFORUM**

Intuit Forum

Description
Do you use Quicken, Quickpay, or Quickbooks? If so, stop by the Intuit Forum and read tips, press releases, and support comments about these products.

Subjects
Computers, Finance

Audience
Computer users

Content Summary
The purpose of this forum is to provide technical support and discussion areas for all of the Intuit products. The Intuit Technical Support Staff monitor and participate in this forum regularly. The Intuit Forum provides support and information on all Intuit Products, including Quicken for DOS, Windows, and Macintosh, and Quickpay and Quickbooks for DOS and Windows.

See Also
IBM Applications Forum, Pacific Vendor Forum

Computers

User Guide
- [x] Windows
- [x] DOS
- [x] Macintosh
- [ ] Terminal Emulation
- [ ] VMS
- [ ] UNIX
- [ ] OS/2
- [ ] Other platform

Cost
- [ ] Unknown
- [ ] Basic
- [x] Extended
- [ ] Premium ($)
- [ ] Executive w/$

Activity Level
MEDIUM (LOW — HIGH)

Address
GO: **INTUIT**

JDR Microdevices

Description
This service enables you to order Microdevices products and get customer service. JDR specializes in high technology products.

Subjects
Computer Products, Computers

Audience
General public, computer users

See Also
IBM Hardware

Content Summary
From the JDR Microdevices main menu, you can choose from Shop Our Online Catalog, Product QuickSearch, Customer Service, Letter from the President, Request our Free Catalogs, Place An Order From Our Print Catalog, and Talk To Us. Browse the online catalog for items such as motherboards, memory, multimedia devices, books, and other products.

User Guide
- [x] Windows
- [x] DOS
- [x] Macintosh
- [ ] Terminal Emulation
- [ ] VMS
- [x] UNIX
- [ ] OS/2
- [ ] Other platform

Cost
- [ ] Unknown
- [ ] Basic
- [ ] Extended
- [x] Premium ($)
- [ ] Executive w/$

Activity Level
UNKNOWN (LOW — MEDIUM — HIGH)

Address
GO: **JDR**

Kodak CD Forum

Description
Maintained by Kodak, this forum is devoted to Kodak CD products and technology, as well as related products.

Subjects
Computers, Photo-CD, Printing

Audience
Computer users, computer graphics designers

Content Summary
The library and message sections include Kodak News, Photo CD General, Photo CD Software, Writable CD, International, Color Management, Member Uploads, and others. The Kodak Printer library (Library 8) contains drivers, information, and press releases relating to Kodak's line of high-quality printers.

See Also
Graphics Forums, Graphics Forums, Graphics File Finder, Photography Forum

User Guide
- [x] Windows
- [x] DOS
- [x] Macintosh
- [ ] Terminal Emulation
- [ ] VMS
- [ ] UNIX
- [ ] OS/2
- [ ] Other platform

Cost
- [ ] Unknown
- [ ] Basic
- [x] Extended
- [ ] Premium ($)
- [ ] Executive w/$

Activity Level
MEDIUM (LOW — HIGH)

Address
GO: **KODAK**

LAN Magazine

Description
This forum is for network administrators, users, installers, and integrators to exchange information about computer networks.

Subjects
Computer Networking, Computers, Networking

Audience
Computer users, management information specialists

Content Summary
Sponsored by *LAN Magazine,* this forum is dedicated to help you solve LAN problems, stay in touch with the industry, and keep you informed of new products and services. The library and message sections include Reviews, Features, Guest & Interviews,

Computers

Forum Member Bios, User-to-User, and others. For a story on salaries of network managers, see Library 3, Features.

See Also
LAN Technology, Lan Vendor

User Guide
- ☑ Windows
- ☑ DOS
- ☑ Macintosh
- ☐ Terminal Emulation
- ☐ VMS
- ☑ UNIX
- ☑ OS/2
- ☑ Other platform

Cost
- ☐ Unknown
- ☐ Basic
- ☑ Extended
- ☐ Premium ($)
- ☐ Executive w/$

Activity Level

Address
GO: **LANMAG**

Lan Technology Forum

Description
This is *Lan Technology* magazine's forum for network issues, products, and discussions.

Subjects
Computers, Networking

Audience
Management information specialists, Macintosh users, Computer users

Content Summary
The Lan Technology Forum is an online resource from *Lan Technology*, which is the leading independent monthly magazine devoted to the technical issues and problems faced by network specialists. The forum is a focal point for discovering how to work with the technologies and products in local and widearea networks. The library and message sections include E-Mail, To Stacks, NetWare, VINES, Macintosh, UNIX, Network Management, Servers, Demos, and others.

See Also
Lan Magazine Forum

User Guide
- ☑ Windows
- ☑ DOS
- ☑ Macintosh
- ☐ Terminal Emulation
- ☐ VMS
- ☑ UNIX
- ☑ OS/2
- ☑ Other platform

Cost
- ☐ Unknown
- ☐ Basic
- ☑ Extended
- ☐ Premium ($)
- ☐ Executive w/$

Activity Level

Address
GO: **LANTECH**

LAN Vendor Forum

Description
For support and discussions on various networking vendors, join this forum.

Subjects
Computers, Networking

Audience
Computer users, management information specialists

Content Summary
This forum has libraries and message sections for the following vendors: Synergy Solutions, AMD, Newport Systems, SilCom Technology, Robertson-Caruso, Horizons Technology, Impulse Technology, DE/CartesRecall-IT!, Aleph Takoma Systems, Olicom, Compatible Systems, Momentum Software, AG Group, and CACI Products.

See Also
Lan Magazine Forum, Lan Technology Forum

User Guide
- ☑ Windows
- ☑ DOS
- ☑ Macintosh
- ☐ Terminal Emulation
- ☐ VMS
- ☐ UNIX
- ☐ OS/2
- ☑ Other platform

Cost
- ☐ Unknown
- ☐ Basic
- ☑ Extended
- ☐ Premium ($)
- ☐ Executive w/$

Activity Level

Address
GO: **LANVEN**

LDC Spreadsheet Forum

Description
This forum is dedicated to Lotus Corporation's family of spreadsheet products, including 1-2-3 (DOS and Windows) and Improv.

Subjects
Computers

Audience
Computer users

Computers

Content Summary
You can find utilities, updates, press releases, help, and tips and hints in the library and message sections. Some of the libraries include 123 Release 2-4 for DOS, 1-2-3 Release 4-5 for Windows, 123 for OS/2, 123 for Macintosh, Improv for Windows, and more.

See Also
LDC Word Processing Forum, LDC Words & Pixels Forum, Lotus 1-2-3 For Windows Upgrade, Lotus Communications Forum, Lotus GmbH Forum, Lotus Technical Library, Lotus Press Release Forum

User Guide
- [x] Windows
- [x] DOS
- [x] Macintosh
- [ ] Terminal Emulation
- [ ] VMS
- [ ] UNIX
- [x] OS/2
- [ ] Other platform

Cost
- [ ] Unknown
- [ ] Basic
- [x] Extended
- [ ] Premium ($)
- [ ] Executive w/$

Activity Level

Address
GO: **LOTUSA**

LDC Word Processing Forum

Description
This forum is dedicated to Lotus Corporation's line of word processing applications, including Ami Pro, LotusWrite, and SmarText.

Subjects
Computers

Audience
Computer users

Content Summary
This forum is operated by the Word Processing Division Technical Support Department of Lotus Corporation, located in Atlanta, Georgia, and includes discussions and files relating to Lotus' word processors. The libraries include Product Info. Demos, Ami Pro /w Technotes, Contest, Ami Pro w/ Macros, Fun & Graphics, Ami Pro OS/2 Macros, and more.

See Also
Lotus Communications Forum, Lotus 123 For Windows Upgrade, Lotus GmbH Forum, Lotus Press Release Forum, Lotus Technical Library, LDC Words & Pixels Forum, LDC Spreadsheets Forum

User Guide
- [x] Windows
- [x] DOS
- [ ] Macintosh
- [ ] Terminal Emulation
- [ ] VMS
- [ ] UNIX
- [x] OS/2
- [ ] Other platform

Cost
- [ ] Unknown
- [ ] Basic
- [x] Extended
- [ ] Premium ($)
- [ ] Executive w/$

Activity Level

Address
GO: **LOTUSWP**

LDC Words & Pixels Forum

Description
This Lotus Corporation forum discusses Magellan, Freelance, Freelance Plus, Graphwriter, Lotus Metro, and other graphics-related products.

Subjects
Computer Graphics, Computers

Audience
Computer users

Content Summary
You'll find information, discussions, questions, and other helpful insights for graphics-related products produced by Lotus Corporation. The library and message sections include Freelance/Windows, Multimedia Objects, Freelance OS/2, Freelance for DOS, ScreenCam, Agenda/Magellan, Symphony/LotusWorks, Oraganizer Technical, Approach, and others.

See Also
LDC Spreadsheets Forum, LDC Word Processing Forum, Lotus 123 For Windows Upgrade, Lotus Communications Forum, Lotus GmbH Forum, Lotus Press Release Forum, Lotus Technical Library

User Guide
- [x] Windows
- [x] DOS
- [ ] Macintosh
- [ ] Terminal Emulation
- [ ] VMS
- [ ] UNIX
- [x] OS/2
- [ ] Other platform

Cost
- [ ] Unknown
- [ ] Basic
- [x] Extended
- [ ] Premium ($)
- [ ] Executive w/$

Activity Level

Address
GO: **LOTUSB**

Lexmark Forum

Description
This forum provides support and information for Lexmark products and services.

Subjects
Computer Hardware, Computers

Audience
Management information specialists, Macintosh users, computer hardware users, Computer users

Content Summary
The libraries and message sections include Disk Images, Impact Drivers, Inkjet Drivers, Laser Drivers, Macintosh Drivers, Output Drivers, Thermal Drivers, and Utilities.

See Also
IBM Hardware, PC Vendors Forums

User Guide
- ☑ Windows
- ☑ DOS
- ☑ Macintosh
- ☐ Terminal Emulation
- ☐ VMS
- ☐ UNIX
- ☐ OS/2
- ☐ Other platform

Cost
- ☐ Unknown
- ☐ Basic
- ☑ Extended
- ☐ Premium ($)
- ☐ Executive w/$

Activity Level

Address
GO: **LEXMARK**

Logitech Forum

Description
This forum is devoted to Logitech products, including Scanman, FotoMan, 3D devices, mouse products, and others.

Subjects
Computer Hardware, Computers, Hardware/Software

Audience
Management information specialists, Computer users, graphics designers

Content Summary
The Logitech Forum includes the following libraries: Mouse Products, Sound/Video, Scanman/FotoMan, Logitech OCR Software, MAC Products, Announcements, General Information, 3D Devices, and Top Q&A.

See Also
PC Vendors Forums

User Guide
- ☑ Windows
- ☑ DOS
- ☑ Macintosh
- ☐ Terminal Emulation
- ☐ VMS
- ☑ UNIX
- ☑ OS/2
- ☑ Other platform

Cost
- ☐ Unknown
- ☐ Basic
- ☑ Extended
- ☐ Premium ($)
- ☐ Executive w/$

Activity Level

MEDIUM — LOW / HIGH

Address
GO: **LOGITECH**

Lotus Communications Forum

Description
This forum is devoted to Lotus Corporation's communications products, including Notes and cc:Mail.

Subjects
Computer Communications, Computer Hardware, Computer Networking, Computers, E-mail, Networking

Audience
Management information specialists, network users

Content Summary
You can find a plethora of information, technical support solutions, hints and tips, and want ads in this forum. The library and message forums include Notes Tech Info, Notes Workstations/DB, Notes API Devloment, cc:Mail Platform, cc:Mail Router, cc:Mail Admin, and many others.

See Also
Lotus Press Release Forum, Lotus Technical Library

User Guide
- ☑ Windows
- ☑ DOS
- ☑ Macintosh
- ☐ Terminal Emulation
- ☐ VMS
- ☐ UNIX
- ☑ OS/2
- ☑ Other platform

Cost
- ☐ Unknown
- ☐ Basic
- ☑ Extended
- ☐ Premium ($)
- ☐ Executive w/$

Activity Level

Address
GO: **LOTUSCOMM**

Lotus Press Release Forum

Description
Want to find the official word from Lotus Corporation on their latest release? Check out this forum for press releases.

Subjects
Computers

Audience
Management information specialists, Computer users

Content Summary
This forum's libraries are divided into months so you can quickly find the most current PR material from Lotus.

See Also
Lotus Technical Library, Lotus Communications Forum, LDC Spreadsheets Forum, LDC Word Processing Forum, LDC Words & Pixels Forum

User Guide
- ☐ Windows
- ☐ DOS
- ☐ Macintosh
- ☐ Terminal Emulation
- ☐ VMS
- ☐ UNIX
- ☐ OS/2
- ☐ Other platform

Cost
- ☐ Unknown
- ☐ Basic
- ☒ Extended
- ☐ Premium ($)
- ☐ Executive w/$

Activity Level

Address
GO: **LOTUSNEWS**

Lotus Technical Library

Description
Need a quick answer to a question about a Lotus product? If so, this service should help you find the answer.

Subjects
Computers

Audience
Computer users

Content Summaary
The Lotus Technical Library is a comprehensive collection of Lotus product information. The Technical Library contains answers to common questions, tips and techniques for using Lotus products more effectively, and troubleshooting guidelines for identifying and resolving technical difficulties. The information in the Lotus Technical Library is researched and written by the Lotus Customer Support staff. Information is available for all Lotus products and releases.

See Also
LDC Spreadsheets Forum, LDC Word Processing Forum, LDC Words & Pixels Forum, Lotus Communications Forum, Lotus Press Release Forum

User Guide
- ☐ Windows
- ☐ DOS
- ☐ Macintosh
- ☐ Terminal Emulation
- ☐ VMS
- ☐ UNIX
- ☐ OS/2
- ☐ Other platform

Cost
- ☐ Unknown
- ☐ Basic
- ☒ Extended
- ☐ Premium ($)
- ☐ Executive w/$

Activity Level

Address
GO: **LOTUSTECH**

Macintosh Applications Forum

Description
This is the MAUG area for discussing all of the many application programs for the Macintosh.

Subjects
Computers, Macintosh

Audience
Macintosh users, Computer users

Content Summary
This forum's library and message sections include Word Processing, Databases, Spreadsheets/Models, Accounting/Finance, DTP Templates, Multimedia, Graphics Tools, and more.

See Also
Macintosh Forums

User Guide
- ☐ Windows
- ☐ DOS
- ☒ Macintosh
- ☐ Terminal Emulation
- ☐ VMS
- ☐ UNIX
- ☐ OS/2
- ☐ Other platform

Cost
- ☐ Unknown
- ☐ Basic
- ☒ Extended
- ☐ Premium ($)
- ☐ Executive w/$

Activity level

Address
GO: **MACAP**

Macintosh CIM Support Forum

Description
This forum offers support for MacCIM and is free of connect time charges.

Subjects
Computers, Macintosh

Audience
Computer users, Macintosh users

Content Summary
This message and library sections in this forum include Support Files, User Contributions, Scripts (CCL), Filing Cabinet, and more.

See Also
Macintosh Forums

User Guide
- [ ] Windows
- [ ] DOS
- [x] Macintosh
- [ ] Terminal Emulation
- [ ] VMS
- [ ] UNIX
- [ ] OS/2
- [ ] Other platform

Cost
- [ ] Unknown
- [x] Basic
- [ ] Extended
- [ ] Premium ($)
- [ ] Executive w/$

Activity Level MEDIUM (LOW — HIGH)

Address
GO: **MCIMSUP**

Macintosh Communications Forum

Description
You can find support, tips, files, and discussions concerning Mac communications topics that include fax, modems, and ISDN.

Subjects
Computers, Macintosh, Modem

Audience
Macintosh users, Computer users

Content Summary
The many library and message sections include CIS Navigator, Scripts/Tools, Communication Programs/Utilities, Hardware, FAX, Networking, Talking to PCs, BBS Systems, and more.

See Also
Macintosh Forums, Macintosh Hardware Forum

Macintosh Community Club Forum

Description
This is the MAUG lobby area, which includes informal discussions ranging from views on Apple's corporate policies to current events.

Subjects:
Computers, Macintosh

Audience
Computer users, Macintosh users

Content Summary
This forum includes several helpful libraries and has a lively message area. In these areas, you can find topics such as Help Files, Community Square, Parties/Cons, Resumes, Magazines/Review, and more. There's also a Classified area where you can post an ad or respond to one.

See Also
Macintosh Forums, Mac Entertainment Forum

User Guide
- [ ] Windows
- [ ] DOS
- [x] Macintosh
- [ ] Terminal Emulation
- [ ] VMS
- [ ] UNIX
- [ ] OS/2
- [ ] Other platform

Cost
- [ ] Unknown
- [ ] Basic
- [x] Extended
- [ ] Premium ($)
- [ ] Executive w/$

Activity Level MEDIUM (LOW — HIGH)

Address
GO: **MACCOM**

User Guide
- [ ] Windows
- [ ] DOS
- [x] Macintosh
- [ ] Terminal Emulation
- [ ] VMS
- [ ] UNIX
- [ ] OS/2
- [ ] Other platform

Cost
- [ ] Unknown
- [ ] Basic
- [x] Extended
- [ ] Premium ($)
- [ ] Executive w/$

Activity Level MEDIUM (LOW — HIGH)

Address
GO: **MACCLUB**

Macintosh Developers Forum

Description
If you want to program your Macintosh—whether commercially or for your own use—the Mac Developers Forum is the right place for you.

Subjects
Computer Programming Languages, Computers, Macintosh

Audience
Macintosh users, computer programmers

Content Summary
The following libraries are found in this forum: BASIC, Assembly Language, C and Pascal, Object Oriented, Other Languages, Apple System Tools, Apple System Files, Development Environments, Scripting Month, Learn Programming, A/UX, Tools/Debuggers, and MacTech Magazine.

See Also
Macintosh Forums, Macintosh Systems Forum

User Guide
- [ ] Windows
- [ ] DOS
- [x] Macintosh
- [ ] Terminal Emulation
- [ ] VMS
- [ ] UNIX
- [ ] OS/2
- [ ] Other platform

Cost
- [ ] Unknown
- [ ] Basic
- [x] Extended
- [ ] Premium ($)
- [ ] Executive w/$

Activity Level
MEDIUM (arrow pointing up)

Address
GO: **MACDEV**

Macintosh Entertainment Forum

Description
Sit back and relax. This forum has games, sound utilities, music, glamour graphics, and more—all for the Mac.

Subjects
Computer Games, Computers, Macintosh

Audience
Computer users, Macintosh users

Content Summary
This forum is full of files, discussions, suggestions, games, and other ways to help you get more enjoyment out of your Macintosh and computing life. You can also participate in the PlayMaker Football League, an online football simulation game for the Mac (see Library 10).

See Also
Macintosh Forums

User Guide
- [ ] Windows
- [ ] DOS
- [x] Macintosh
- [ ] Terminal Emulation
- [ ] VMS
- [ ] UNIX
- [ ] OS/2
- [ ] Other platform

Cost
- [ ] Unknown
- [ ] Basic
- [x] Extended
- [ ] Premium ($)
- [ ] Executive w/$

Activity Level
MEDIUM (arrow pointing toward HIGH)

Address
GO: **MACFUN**

Macintosh File Finder

Description
Use this service to find any file from Macintosh forums on CompuServe.

Subjects
Computers, Macintosh

Audience
Macintosh users, Computer users

Content Summary
MAC File Finder is an online comprehensive keyword searchable database of file descriptions from MAC-related forums. It is designed to provide quick and easy reference to some of the best programs and files available.

See Also
Macintosh Forums, Mac New Users Help Forum

User Guide
- [ ] Windows
- [ ] DOS
- [x] Macintosh
- [ ] Terminal Emulation
- [ ] VMS
- [ ] UNIX
- [ ] OS/2
- [ ] Other platform

Cost
- [ ] Unknown
- [ ] Basic
- [x] Extended
- [ ] Premium ($)
- [ ] Executive w/$

Activity Level
UNKNOWN

Address
GO: **MACFF**

Macintosh Forums

Description
Not sure which Mac-related forum to visit? Start from this service.

Subjects
Computers, Macintosh

Audience
Computer users, Macintosh users

Content Summary
You can choose from Apple Systems, Inc forums, MAUG (Micronetworked Apple Users Group) forums, and ZiffNet/MacUser/ZMAC forums.

See Also
Mac New Users Help Forum, Apple Support Forum

User Guide
- [ ] Windows
- [ ] DOS
- [x] Macintosh
- [ ] Terminal Emulation
- [ ] VMS
- [ ] UNIX
- [ ] OS/2
- [ ] Other platform

Cost
- [ ] Unknown
- [x] Basic
- [ ] Extended
- [ ] Premium ($)
- [ ] Executive w/$

Activity Level
UNKNOWN (LOW — HIGH)

Address
GO: **MACINTOSH**

Macintosh Hardware Forum

Description
This forum discusses all types of Macintosh computers, including Classics, Quadras, Performas, Mac II, LC, Newton, and PDAs.

Subjects
Computer Hardware, Computers, Macintosh

Audience
Macintosh users, management information specialists

Content Summary
You can find several libraries in this forum that should satisfy your need for support and help for your Macintosh hardware, including Classic/Early Macs, Performas/Other, Quadras, Printers/Output, Scanners/Input, Monitors/Video, and more.

See Also
Macintosh Systems Forum, Macintosh Forums

User Guide
- [ ] Windows
- [ ] DOS
- [x] Macintosh
- [ ] Terminal Emulation
- [ ] VMS
- [ ] UNIX
- [ ] OS/2
- [ ] Other platform

Cost
- [ ] Unknown
- [ ] Basic
- [x] Extended
- [ ] Premium ($)
- [ ] Executive w/$

Activity Level
MEDIUM (LOW — HIGH)

Address
GO: **MACHW**

Macintosh Hypertext Forum

Description
Whether you are a browser or are familiar with XCMNDS and Hypertalk, this forum is for you.

Subjects
Computers, Macintosh, Multimedia

Audience
Macintosh users

Content Summary
This forum includes libraries such as Games, Education, Music and Sound, Art: Clip and Fine!, Reference Stacks, and more. Also note that there is an R-Rated Stacks library that contains nudity and may be offensive to some people and should not be viewed by minors under the age of 18.

See Also
Macintosh Forums, Mac Entertainment Forum

User Guide
- [ ] Windows
- [ ] DOS
- [x] Macintosh
- [ ] Terminal Emulation
- [ ] VMS
- [ ] UNIX
- [ ] OS/2
- [ ] Other platform

Cost
- [ ] Unknown
- [ ] Basic
- [x] Extended
- [ ] Premium ($)
- [ ] Executive w/$

Activity Level
MEDIUM (LOW — HIGH)

Address
GO: **MACHYPER**

Macintosh Multimedia Forum

Description
This forum discusses the various uses of the Macintosh as a platform for multimedia development.

Subjects
Computers, Macintosh, Multimedia

Computers

Audience
Macintosh users

Content Summary
Loaded with multimedia clips, QuickTime movies and tools, HyperCard tools, and templates, this forum is for you if you are interested in multimedia, the creation of it, or the final results of multimedia. Check out these libraries: Video Clips, Sound Tools, Glamour Films, and Home Movies.

See Also
Macintosh Forums, Mac Entertainment Forum, Mac Hypertext Forum

User Guide
- [ ] Windows
- [ ] DOS
- [x] Macintosh
- [ ] Terminal Emulation
- [ ] VMS
- [ ] UNIX
- [ ] OS/2
- [ ] Other platform

Cost
- [ ] Unknown
- [ ] Basic
- [x] Extended
- [ ] Premium ($)
- [ ] Executive w/$

Activity Level

Address
GO: **MACMULTI**

Macintosh New Users Help Forum

Description
This forum is designed to aid the new user to the MAUG forums.

Subjects
Computers, Macintosh

Audience
Computer users, Macintosh users

Content Summary
You'll find many library and message sections in this forum, including Help Files, Using Forums, Using LIBs, MAUG Guide, Disk Tools, Anti-Virus Tools, System Tools, and Guest/CO Archives.

See Also
Macintosh Forums, Macintosh File Finder

User Guide
- [ ] Windows
- [ ] DOS
- [x] Macintosh
- [ ] Terminal Emulation
- [ ] VMS
- [ ] UNIX
- [ ] OS/2
- [ ] Other platform

Cost
- [ ] Unknown
- [ ] Basic
- [x] Extended
- [ ] Premium ($)
- [ ] Executive w/$

Activity Level

Address
GO: **MACNEW**

Macintosh Systems Forum

Description
Join this forum for discussions and support files for system-related topics about the Mac.

Subjects
Computers, Macintosh

Audience
Macintosh users, management information specialists

Content Summary
This is the MAUG area for discussing the many system-related areas of the Mac, both hardware (such as printers, disks, monitors) and software (such as System, Finder, INITs, cdevs and FKEYs). You can find topics such as System 6 Specific, Control Panels, Fonts, Utilities, Aliases/Icons, QuickTime, Emergency, and more.

See Also
Macintosh File Finder, Mac Community/Club Forum

User Guide
- [ ] Windows
- [ ] DOS
- [x] Macintosh
- [ ] Terminal Emulation
- [ ] VMS
- [ ] UNIX
- [ ] OS/2
- [ ] Other platform

Cost
- [ ] Unknown
- [ ] Basic
- [x] Extended
- [ ] Premium ($)
- [ ] Executive w/$

Activity Level

Address
GO: **MACSYS**

Macintosh Vendor Forums

Description
These forums include support from various Mac vendors.

Subjects
Computers, Macintosh

Computers

Audience
Computer users, Macintosh users

Content Summary
The Mac A Vendor Forum (GO MACAVEN) includes these vendors: Portfolio Software, Nisus Software, CE Software, DeltaPoint, DayStar Digital, and more. The Mac B Vendor Forum (GO MACBVEN) includes these vendors: GCC Technologies, Altsys Corporation, Jasik Designs, Software Ventures, Radius Corporation, Deneba Software, and more. The Mac C Vendor Forum (GO MACCVEN) includes these vendors: Alladin Systems, Baseline Publishing, Inline Software, Avator Corporation, Farallon, Virtus Corporation, and more. The Mac D Vendor Forum (GO MACDVEN) includes these vendors: MacTech Magazine, Atticus, TidBITS Magazine, Micronet, and more.

See Also
Mac Applications Forum, Macintosh Forums

User Guide
- [ ] Windows
- [ ] DOS
- [x] Macintosh
- [ ] Terminal Emulation
- [ ] VMS
- [ ] UNIX
- [ ] OS/2
- [ ] Other platform

Cost
- [ ] Unknown
- [ ] Basic
- [x] Extended
- [ ] Premium ($)
- [ ] Executive w/$

Activity Level

Address
GO: **MACxVEN**

Macmillan Computer Publishing USA Forum

Description
Get up-to-date information, technical support, customer service, and files relating to Macmillan Computer Publishing books.

Subjects
Books, Computers

Audience
Management information specialists, Computer users

Content Summary
Computer books published by New Riders Publishing, Que, SAMS, Hayden, Alpha, Que College, and Brady are supported in this forum. You can find files associated with specific books, graphics files, word processing templates, spreadsheets, and utilities to help you get the most out of your computer system. This forum has one of the best opening bitmaps on CompuServe.

See Also
COMPUBOOKS, Small Computer Book Club, Software, Hardware, Applications

User Guide
- [x] Windows
- [x] DOS
- [x] Macintosh
- [ ] Terminal Emulation
- [ ] VMS
- [ ] UNIX
- [x] OS/2
- [x] Other platform

Cost
- [ ] Unknown
- [ ] Basic
- [x] Extended
- [ ] Premium ($)
- [ ] Executive w/$

Activity Level

Address
GO: **MACMILLAN**

MacNav Support Forum

Description
Need help with MacNav? If so, head to this forum.

Subjects
Computers, Macintosh

Audience
Macintosh users, Computer users

Content Summary
This forum encourages discussions and helpful hints for using MacNav. You'll find these library and message sections on this forum: CompuServe Mail, Manual Mode/Scripts, Session Parameters, Navigator Tips, Suggestions, and Navigator Patches.

See Also
Macintosh Forums

User Guide
- [ ] Windows
- [ ] DOS
- [x] Macintosh
- [ ] Terminal Emulation
- [ ] VMS
- [ ] UNIX
- [ ] OS/2
- [ ] Other platform

Cost
- [ ] Unknown
- [x] Basic
- [ ] Extended
- [ ] Premium ($)
- [ ] Executive w/$

Activity Level

Address
GO: **MNAVSUPPORT**

Macromedia Forum

Description
This forum provides technical support and discussions on Macromedia products.

Subjects
Computers, Multimedia

Audience
Computer users

Content Summary
Macromedia topics discussed in this forum include Director, Authoware, Action/ClipMedia, 3D/Modeling/MMaker, sound products, and more.

See Also
Multimedia Forum, Multimedia Vendor Forum

User Guide
- ☑ Windows
- ☑ DOS
- ☑ Macintosh
- ☐ Terminal Emulation
- ☐ VMS
- ☐ UNIX
- ☐ OS/2
- ☑ Other platform

Cost
- ☐ Unknown
- ☐ Basic
- ☑ Extended
- ☐ Premium ($)
- ☐ Executive w/$

Activity Level

Address
GO: **MACROMEDIA**

McAfee Virus Forum

Description
The purpose of this forum is to help you with any questions or problems you have related to anti-viral software and computer viruses.

Subjects
Computer Viruses, Computers

Audience
Computer users, management information specialists

Content Summary
Find information and updates for virus software and network tools in the libraries and in the message sections.

See Also
KAOS Antivirus, Symantec Antivirus

User Guide
- ☑ Windows
- ☑ DOS
- ☐ Macintosh
- ☐ Terminal Emulation
- ☐ VMS
- ☐ UNIX
- ☐ OS/2
- ☑ Other platform

Cost
- ☐ Unknown
- ☐ Basic
- ☑ Extended
- ☐ Premium ($)
- ☐ Executive w/$

Activity Level

Address
GO: **NCSAVIRUS**

Media Vision Forum

Description
This forum is intended for technical support, general discussions of Media Vision products, and storage of files.

Subjects
Computers, Multimedia

Audience
Computer users, management information specialists

Content Summary
The library and message sections include Pro Audio Spectrum, Pro Audio Studio, ProSonic, Fusion Kits, Multimedia Kits, CD-ROM Drivere, ProGraphics, and more.

See Also
Multimedia Forum, Multimedia Conference Forum, Multimedia Vendor Forum

User Guide
- ☑ Windows
- ☑ DOS
- ☐ Macintosh
- ☐ Terminal Emulation
- ☐ VMS
- ☐ UNIX
- ☐ OS/2
- ☑ Other platform

Cost
- ☐ Unknown
- ☐ Basic
- ☑ Extended
- ☐ Premium ($)
- ☐ Executive w/$

Activity Level

Address
GO: **MEDIAVISION**

Micrografx Forum

Description
This forum is for anyone interested in Micrografx's professional and consumer graphics products. It provides technical support, contact with other Micrografx users, and a variety of other useful and entertaining things.

Subjects
Computer Graphics, Computers

Audience
Computer users, computer graphic designers

Content Summary
You can find press releases, comments, questions, support answers, clip art, and other graphics in the library and message sections. Some of the libraries include Utilities, Designer, ABC Flow/Toolkit, PhotoMagic, Charisma, and more.

See Also
Corel Forum, Graphics Forums, Graphics File Finder

User Guide
- [x] Windows
- [x] DOS
- [ ] Macintosh
- [ ] Terminal Emulation
- [ ] VMS
- [ ] UNIX
- [x] OS/2
- [ ] Other platform

Cost
- [ ] Unknown
- [ ] Basic
- [x] Extended
- [ ] Premium ($)
- [ ] Executive w/$

Activity Level
MEDIUM (LOW — HIGH)

Address
GO: **MICROGRAFX**

Microsoft Access Forum

Description
This forum is dedicated to the Microsoft Access database product.

Subjects
Computers, Databases, Microsoft Corp.

Audience
Computer users, database managers

Content Summary
Find out about designing forms, reports, queries, and other related questions. The library and message sections include Getting Started, Tables/DB Design, Queries, Forms, Import/Export, Multi-User Networks, Interop/OLE/DDE, and more.

See Also
MS SQL Server Forum, MS Applications Forum, Microsoft Knowledge Base

User Guide
- [x] Windows
- [ ] DOS
- [ ] Macintosh
- [ ] Terminal Emulation
- [ ] VMS
- [ ] UNIX
- [ ] OS/2
- [ ] Other platform

Cost
- [ ] Unknown
- [ ] Basic
- [x] Extended
- [ ] Premium ($)
- [ ] Executive w/$

Activity Level
MEDIUM (LOW → HIGH)

Address
GO: **MSACCESS**

Microsoft Applications Forum

Description
The Microsoft Applications Forum is designed for discussions and support of some of Microsoft's "end-user" programs, such as Encarta and Publisher.

Subjects
Computers, Microsoft Corp.

Audience
Computer users

Content Summary
This forum covers Microsoft programs such as PowerPoint, Video for Windows, Windows Sound System, Works for the Mac, Windows Project, Project of the Mac, Works for the PC, Works for Windows, Mouse/Paintbrush, Publisher, Money, and more. For those serious times, be sure to check out the Flight Simulator library and discussions.

See Also
Microsoft TechNet Services, Microsoft Knowledge Base, Microsoft Plus Services, Microsoft Press(FREE)

User Guide
- [x] Windows
- [x] DOS
- [x] Macintosh
- [ ] Terminal Emulation
- [ ] VMS
- [ ] UNIX
- [ ] OS/2
- [ ] Other platform

Cost
- [ ] Unknown
- [ ] Basic
- [x] Extended
- [ ] Premium ($)
- [ ] Executive w/$

Activity Level
MEDIUM (LOW → HIGH)

Address
GO: **MSAPP**

Microsoft BASIC Forum

Description
This forum is designed as an area to exchange information, tips, and techniques concerning Microsoft Basic products.

Computers

Subjects
Computer Programming Languages, Computers, Microsoft Corp.

Audience
Computer programmers, Computer users

Content Summary
The MS BASIC forum contains several library and message sections, including MS Info and Index, Setup Wizard/Kit, Data Access Objects, Programming Issues, Calling APIs/DLLs, DOS Visual Basic, Mac Visual Basic, and more.

See Also
Microsoft Languages Forum, Microsoft DevCast Forum, Microsoft Connection

User Guide
- ☑ Windows
- ☑ DOS
- ☑ Macintosh
- ☐ Terminal Emulation
- ☐ VMS
- ☐ UNIX
- ☐ OS/2
- ☑ Other platform

Cost
- ☐ Unknown
- ☐ Basic
- ☑ Extended
- ☐ Premium ($)
- ☐ Executive w/$

Activity Level

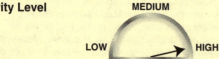

Address
GO: **MSBASIC**

Microsoft Connection

Description
Use this service to find the Microsoft-related forum of your choice, including international forums.

Subjects
Computers, Microsoft Corp.

Audience
Computer users

Content Summary
The main menu includes About the Microsoft Connection, Microsoft Benelux, Microsoft Central Europe, Microsoft France, Microsoft Italy, Microsoft Spain/Latin America, Microsoft Sweden, and Microsoft US.

See Also
MS Applications Forum, Microsoft Plus Services

User Guide
- ☐ Windows
- ☐ DOS
- ☐ Macintosh
- ☐ Terminal Emulation
- ☐ VMS
- ☐ UNIX
- ☐ OS/2
- ☐ Other platform

Cost
- ☑ Extended
- ☐ Unknown
- ☐ Basic
- ☐ Premium ($)
- ☐ Executive w/$

Activity Level

UNKNOWN (LOW - MEDIUM - HIGH)

Address
GO: **MICROSOFT**

Microsoft DevCast Forum

Description
This forum is designed to give conference attendees a temporary location for follow up discussion regarding the Microsoft DevCast conference.

Subjects
Computer Programming Languages, Computers, Microsoft Corp.

Audience
Computer users, computer programmers

Content Summary
You can find files, information, and other useful material for upcoming DevCast conferences or from past conferences.

See Also
Microsoft Knowledge Base, Microsoft Languages Forum, MS 32bit Languages Forum

User Guide
- ☑ Windows
- ☑ DOS
- ☑ Macintosh
- ☐ Terminal Emulation
- ☐ VMS
- ☑ UNIX
- ☐ OS/2
- ☑ Other platform

Cost
- ☐ Unknown
- ☐ Basic
- ☑ Extended
- ☐ Premium ($)
- ☐ Executive w/$

Activity Level

MEDIUM (LOW - HIGH)

Address
GO: **DEVCAST**

(Microsoft) Developers Relations Forums

Description
This forum is designed for high-level information exchange and tips about Microsoft Developer products. Section leaders from Microsoft Product Support Services monitor and participate in the

forum. This area is for nontechnical information. See the Microsoft Developer Services Area (MSDS) for technical support questions and issues.

Subjects
Application Development, Computers, Microsoft

Audience
Advanced-level users, developers

Content Summary
This forum includes two libraries: General/Dev. Services, which includes files and information on job opportunities, general beta testing (non-Microsoft), and the Microsoft Support Network; and Strategic Issues, which includes information and tool kits for developers on different applications and operating systems.

See Also
Microsoft Developer Services Area, Microsoft Developer Network Forum, Microsoft Developer Knowledge Base, Microsoft Connection, Microsoft C and Other Languages Forum

User Guide
- ☑ Windows
- ☑ DOS
- ☑ Macintosh
- ☐ Terminal Emulation
- ☑ VMS
- ☑ UNIX
- ☑ OS/2
- ☐ Other platform

Cost
- ☐ Unknown
- ☐ Basic
- ☑ Extended
- ☐ Premium ($)
- ☐ Executive w/$

Activity Level

Address
GO: **MSDR**

Microsoft Excel Forum

Description
Find out information about MS Excel for Windows and Mac, VBA topics, and other spreadsheet informormation.

Subjects
Computers, Microsoft Corp.

Audience
Computer users

Content Summary
The library and message sections include Index and Info, Excel for the Mac, Excel for the PC, VBA for Excel, Desktop III Products, and EIS Pak Mac/Win.

See Also
MS Applications Forum, MS Software Library, MS TechNet Forum

User Guide
- ☑ Windows
- ☑ DOS
- ☑ Macintosh
- ☐ Terminal Emulation
- ☐ VMS
- ☐ UNIX
- ☐ OS/2
- ☐ Other platform

Cost
- ☐ Unknown
- ☐ Basic
- ☑ Extended
- ☐ Premium ($)
- ☐ Executive w/$

Activity Level

Address
GO: **MSEXCEL**

Microsoft Foundation Classes Forum

Description
This forum is designed as an area to exchange information, tips, and techniques concerning Microsoft Foundation Classes.

Subjects
Computer Programming Languages, Computers, Microsoft Corp.

Audience
Computer programmers

Content Summary
This forum is for application developers interested in the Microsoft Foundation Classes. Some of the libraries include Beginners Library, Database Classes, OLE 2.0 Classes, VBX Usage, DLL & Memory, and Wizards/DDV/DDX. Also watch for online conferences and seminars, many of which feature Microsoft product managers.

See Also
MS Applications Forum, MS 32bit Languages Forum

User Guide
- ☑ Windows
- ☑ DOS
- ☑ Macintosh
- ☐ Terminal Emulation
- ☐ VMS
- ☐ UNIX
- ☐ OS/2
- ☐ Other platform

Cost
- ☐ Unknown
- ☐ Basic
- ☑ Extended
- ☐ Premium ($)
- ☐ Executive w/$

Activity Level

Address
GO: **MSMFC**

Microsoft Fox Users Forum

Description
This forum is designed as an area to exchange information, tips, and techniques concerning Microsoft Fox products.

Subjects
Computers, Databases, Microsoft Corp.

Audience
Computer system designers, database managers

Content Summary
Some of the areas in this forum include FOXGANG, Want Ads, Archive, and 3rd Party Products. Watch the message sections for discussions on development issues, Fox user groups, and conventions.

See Also
MS TechNet Forum, Microsoft Connection

User Guide
- ☑ Windows
- ☑ DOS
- ☑ Macintosh
- ☐ Terminal Emulation
- ☐ VMS
- ☐ UNIX
- ☐ OS/2
- ☐ Other platform

Cost
- ☐ Unknown
- ☐ Basic
- ☑ Extended
- ☐ Premium ($)
- ☐ Executive w/$

Activity Level

Address
GO: **FOXUSER**

Microsoft Knowledge Base

Description
The Knowledge Base is a database that provides you with access to information previously available only to the Microsoft support engineers.

Subjects
Computers, Microsoft Corp.

Audience
Computer users

Content Summary
Expand the usage of your Microsoft products by using this service. The selections on the Knowledge Base include What's New in the Knowledge Base, Description of Database, Online User's Guide, Search the Knowledge Base, Search Using Expert Mode, QuickSearch—By Document ID Number, and Microsoft Software Library.

See Also
MS TechNet Forum, Microsoft Connection

User Guide
- ☑ Windows
- ☑ DOS
- ☑ Macintosh
- ☐ Terminal Emulation
- ☐ VMS
- ☑ UNIX
- ☑ OS/2
- ☑ Other platform

Cost
- ☐ Unknown
- ☐ Basic
- ☑ Extended
- ☐ Premium ($)
- ☐ Executive w/$

Activity Level

Address
GO: **MSKB**

Microsoft Mail and Workgroups Forum

Description
This forum is designed as an area to exchange information, tips, and techniques concerning Microsoft Windows Workgroup Applications.

Subjects
Computers, E-mail, Microsoft Corp.

Audience
Computer users, management information specialists

Content Summary
If you have a problem with Microsoft's Windows Workgroup Applications, such as MS Schedule Plus and Mail, you probably can find the solution here. Some of the libraries and message sections include MS Mail for PC, Remote/Modems, MS Schedule Plus, MS Mail for Mac, MS Eforms, Workgroup Templates, and much more. The Microsoft Forms Designer Run Time file is available in Library 16, Workgroup Templates.

See Also
Microsoft Connection, Microsoft DevCast Forum, Microsoft Knowledge Base

User Guide
- ☑ Windows
- ☑ DOS
- ☑ Macintosh
- ☐ Terminal Emulation
- ☐ VMS
- ☐ UNIX
- ☐ OS/2
- ☐ Other platform

Cost
- ☐ Unknown
- ☑ Basic
- ☐ Extended
- ☐ Premium ($)
- ☐ Executive w/$

Activity Level

Address
GO: **MSWGA**

Microsoft Sales and Information Forum

Description
This forum is monitored by the Microsoft Sales and Information staff to respond to your product information, sales, registration, promotion, and pricing questions.

Subjects
Computer users, Computers, Microsoft Corp.

Audience
Computer users

Content Summary
The two areas in this forum are library and messages. The message board is where you can post sales information questions or browse through previously posted questions and responses. The libraries of this forum contain files posted by Microsoft only.

See Also
Microsoft Connection

User Guide
- ☑ Windows
- ☑ DOS
- ☑ Macintosh
- ☐ Terminal Emulation
- ☐ VMS
- ☐ UNIX
- ☐ OS/2
- ☑ Other platform

Cost
- ☐ Unknown
- ☐ Basic
- ☑ Extended
- ☐ Premium ($)
- ☐ Executive w/$

Activity Level

MEDIUM / LOW / HIGH

Address
GO: **MSIC**

Microsoft SQL Server Forum

Description
This forum is designed as an area to exchange information, tips, and techniques concerning Microsoft SQL products.

Subjects
Computers, Database Management

Audience
Management information specialists, computer programmers, database managers

Content Summary
The SQL Server Forum has several libraries that contain updates, libraries, and other supporting files for the SQL developer. Some of the libraries include MS SQL Server for Windows NT, MS SQL Server for OS/2, MS Program Toolkits, Non-MS SQL Front Ends, and others.

See Also
Microsoft Languages Forum, Microsoft Press(FREE), MS WinNT SNA Forum

User Guide
- ☑ Windows
- ☑ DOS
- ☐ Macintosh
- ☐ Terminal Emulation
- ☐ VMS
- ☐ UNIX
- ☑ OS/2
- ☑ Other platform

Cost
- ☐ Unknown
- ☐ Basic
- ☑ Extended
- ☐ Premium ($)
- ☐ Executive w/$

Activity Level

MEDIUM / LOW / HIGH

Address
GO: **MSSQL**

Microsoft TechNet Forum

Description
This forum supports Microsoft's TechNet products and services.

Subjects
Computers, Microsoft Corp.

Audience
Management information specialists, Computer users

Content Summary
This forum is designed to provide up-to-date information on special TechNet events, connections to the Microsoft TechNet community, and the capability to download the latest technical information from Microsoft TechNet. You'll find updates to the TechNet CDs, conventions, and press releases in the libraries.

See Also
MS Windows Forum, Microsoft Plus Services, Microsoft Knowledge Base

User Guide
- ☑ Windows
- ☑ DOS
- ☑ Macintosh
- ☐ Terminal Emulation
- ☐ VMS
- ☐ UNIX
- ☐ OS/2
- ☐ Other platform

Cost
- ☐ Unknown
- ☐ Basic
- ☑ Extended
- ☐ Premium ($)
- ☐ Executive w/$

Computers

Activity Level

Address
GO: **TNFORUM**

Microsoft WIN32 Forum

Description
This forum is designed as an area to exchange information, tips and techniques concerning Microsoft Win32 SDK.

Subjects
Computer Programming Languages, Computers, Microsoft Corp.

Audience
Computer users, computer professionals

Content Summary
You can find a plethora of information and tools for the the WIN32 SDK. Library and message sections include API-User/GUI, API Graphics/GDI, API-Base/ Console, API Security, Porting OS/2 & Unix, and more.

See Also
Microsoft Connection, Microsoft DevCast Forum, MS 32bit Languages Forum

User Guide
- ☑ Windows
- ☑ DOS
- ☑ Macintosh
- ☐ Terminal Emulation
- ☐ VMS
- ☑ UNIX
- ☑ OS/2
- ☐ Other platform

Cost
- ☐ Unknown
- ☐ Basic
- ☑ Extended
- ☐ Premium ($)
- ☐ Executive w/$

Activity Level

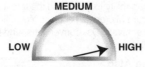

Address
GO: **MSWIN32**

Microsoft Windows Extensions Forum

Description
This forum is designed as an area to exchange information, tips and techniques concerning Microsoft Windows SDK extensions.

Subjects
Computer Programming Languages, Computers, Microsoft Corp.

Audience
Computer programmers

Content Summary
This forum includes these library and message sections: MS Info and Index, MS Test for Windows, TAPI SDK, WOSA/XRT, WOSA/XFS, MS Delta, Arabic/Hebrew SDK, Pen SDK, Far East SDK, ODBC, ODBC Desktop Drivers, LSAPI, MAPI/ Schedule+ Libraries, and DSPRMI and SPEECH.

See Also
Microsoft Knowledge Base, Microsoft Languages Forum

User Guide
- ☑ Windows
- ☑ DOS
- ☑ Macintosh
- ☐ Terminal Emulation
- ☐ VMS
- ☐ UNIX
- ☐ OS/2
- ☑ Other platform

Cost
- ☐ Unknown
- ☐ Basic
- ☑ Extended
- ☐ Premium ($)
- ☐ Executive w/$

Activity Level

Address
GO: **WINEXT**

Microsoft Windows Forum

Description
News, files, tips, and other related information to MS Windows.

Subjects
Computer Viruses, Computers, Microsoft Corp., Windows

Audience
Computer users

Content Summary
Some of the library and message sections include Setup, Mouse, Display Drivers, Memory Optimization, MS-DOS Apps/PIFs, Printing/Fonts/WPS, and Terminal/Comm.

See Also
Microsoft Connection, Microsoft Knowledge Base

User Guide
- ☑ Windows
- ☑ DOS
- ☐ Macintosh
- ☐ Terminal Emulation
- ☐ VMS
- ☐ UNIX
- ☐ OS/2
- ☐ Other platform

Cost
- ☐ Unknown
- ☐ Basic
- ☑ Extended
- ☐ Premium ($)
- ☐ Executive w/$

Computers

Activity Level

MEDIUM — arrow pointing between LOW and HIGH, toward HIGH

Address
GO: **MSWIN**

Microsoft Windows Fun Forum

Description
This forum is designed to allow Windows users a mechanism to discuss and obtain fun Windows files.

Subjects
Computers, Games, Microsoft Corp.

Audience
Computer users

Content Summary
You can find cool things on this forum, such as sound files from movies, screen saver utilities (see Library 4), graphics and graphics utilities (such as the one that changes the standard Windows startup .BMP) in Library 9, card games, a WinDominoes game (see Library 3), and other stuff. Have fun!

See Also
Entertainment Center, MS Software Library

User Guide
- [x] Windows
- [x] DOS
- [x] Macintosh
- [ ] Terminal Emulation
- [ ] VMS
- [ ] UNIX
- [ ] OS/2
- [ ] Other platform

Cost
- [ ] Unknown
- [ ] Basic
- [x] Extended
- [ ] Premium ($)
- [ ] Executive w/$

Activity Level

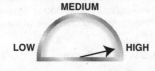

Address
GO: **WINFUN**

Microsoft Windows News Forum

Description
Find out up-to-date information on Windows and future Windows products.

Subjects
Computers, Microsoft Corp., Windows

Audience
Computer users

Content Summary
This forum essentially has one library: Hot News. Here, you can find press releases, articles, tips, speeches, and similar files associated with Windows.

See Also
MS Windows Forum

User Guide
- [x] Windows
- [x] DOS
- [ ] Macintosh
- [ ] Terminal Emulation
- [ ] VMS
- [ ] UNIX
- [ ] OS/2
- [ ] Other platform

Cost
- [ ] Unknown
- [x] Basic
- [ ] Extended
- [ ] Premium ($)
- [ ] Executive w/$

Activity Level

Address
GO: **WINNEWS**

Microsoft Windows NT SNA Forum

Description
This forum is designed as an area to exchange information, tips, and techniques concerning Microsoft SNA Server for Windows NT.

Subjects
Computers, Microsoft Corp.

Audience
Management information specialists, computer system designers, Computer users

Content Summary
Some of the library and message sections you might find on this forum include Fixes and Updates, Problem Reports, 3rd Party/Unsupported, MS SNA Archives, and Setup and Adminstration topics.

See Also
MS SQL Server Forum

User Guide
- [x] Windows
- [x] DOS
- [ ] Macintosh
- [ ] Terminal Emulation
- [ ] VMS
- [ ] UNIX
- [ ] OS/2
- [x] Other platform

Cost
- [ ] Unknown
- [ ] Basic
- [x] Extended
- [ ] Premium ($)
- [ ] Executive w/$

Activity Level

Address
GO: **MSSNA**

Microsoft Windows Objects Forum

Description
This forum is designed as an area to exchange information, tips and techniques concerning Microsoft OLE.

Subjects
Computer Programming Languages, Computers, Microsoft Corp.

Audience
Computer users, computer programmers

Content Summary
Interested in finding information on OLE and how to use it in your programs? Look in the libraries and message sections in this forum for your answers. You'll find libraries such as Component Object Model, Structured Storage, OLE: User Interface, OLE: Automation, OLE: Mac Issues, and more.

See Also
MS Windows Extensions Forum, MS Windows SDK Forum, MS Foundation Classes Forum, Microsoft Languages Forum

User Guide
- ☑ Windows
- ☑ DOS
- ☑ Macintosh
- ☐ Terminal Emulation
- ☐ VMS
- ☐ UNIX
- ☐ OS/2
- ☐ Other platform

Cost
- ☐ Unknown
- ☐ Basic
- ☑ Extended
- ☐ Premium ($)
- ☐ Executive w/$

Activity Level

Address
GO: **WINOBJECTS**

Microsoft Windows SDK Forum

Description
This forum is designed as an area to exchange information, tips, and techniques concerning the Microsoft Windows SDK.

Subjects
Computer Programming Languages, Computers, Microsoft Corp.

Audience
Computer programmers

Content Summary
This forum includes several library and message sections, including Public Utilities, Training, USER, Common Dialogs, Printing, GDI, Kernel—Memory Management, WinHelp, and others.

See Also
Microsoft Languages Forum, MS Windows Objects Forum

User Guide
- ☑ Windows
- ☑ DOS
- ☑ Macintosh
- ☐ Terminal Emulation
- ☐ VMS
- ☐ UNIX
- ☑ OS/2
- ☑ Other platform

Cost
- ☐ Unknown
- ☐ Basic
- ☑ Extended
- ☐ Premium ($)
- ☐ Executive w/$

Activity Level

Address
GO: **WINSDK**

Microsoft Windows Shareware Forum

Description
This forum is designed to allow Windows users a mechanism to discuss and obtain Windows files such as utilities, tools, and applications.

Subjects
Computers, Shareware & Freeware

Audience
Computer users

Content Summary
Download and share your experiences about Windows shareware. This forum includes these libraries: File Applications/Utilities, Communication/Fax Applications, Windows System Utilities, Font/Printing Applications, Disk Utilties, and more.

See Also
MS WINFUN Forum

User Guide
- ☑ Windows
- ☑ DOS
- ☑ Macintosh
- ☐ Terminal Emulation
- ☐ VMS
- ☐ UNIX
- ☐ OS/2
- ☑ Other platform

Cost
- ☐ Unknown
- ☐ Basic
- ☑ Extended
- ☐ Premium ($)
- ☐ Executive w/$

Activity Level

Address
GO: **WINSHARE**

Microsoft Word Forum

Description
This forum is designed as an area to exchange information, tips, and techniques concerning Microsoft Word.

Subjects
Computers, Microsoft Corp.

Audience
Computer users

Content Summary
Get the latest patches and updates from Microsoft for Word 6 in this forum. You also can find information on Word for Windows, Word for Macintosh, Word for DOS, and Word for OS/2.

See Also
MS Applications Forum, Microsoft TechNet Services, Microsoft Knowledge Base

User Guide
- ☑ Windows
- ☑ DOS
- ☑ Macintosh
- ☐ Terminal Emulation
- ☐ VMS
- ☐ UNIX
- ☑ OS/2
- ☐ Other platform

Cost
- ☐ Unknown
- ☐ Basic
- ☑ Extended
- ☐ Premium ($)
- ☐ Executive w/$

Activity Level

Address
GO: **MSWORD**

MicroStation Forum

Description
This forum is devoted to the discussion and support of Bentley Systems Incorporated's MicroStation CAD product.

Subjects
CAD, Computers

Audience
Computer engineers

Content Summary
The library and message sections include MicroStation in General, 3rd Party Products, Programming, Input Devices, Printing/Plotting, Video/Graphics, Databases, Marketing, Change Requests, User Groups, What's New, and The Dialogue Box. Some of the libraries are empty. To download a copy of the Space Station image, see Library 1 for SPACE.JPG.

See Also
Autodesk AutoCAD Forum

User Guide
- ☑ Windows
- ☑ DOS
- ☐ Macintosh
- ☐ Terminal Emulation
- ☐ VMS
- ☑ UNIX
- ☐ OS/2
- ☐ Other platform

Cost
- ☐ Unknown
- ☐ Basic
- ☑ Extended
- ☐ Premium ($)
- ☐ Executive w/$

Activity Level

MEDIUM (arrow pointing up) LOW HIGH

Address
GO: **MSTATION**

MicroWarehouse

Description
MicroWarehouse is the "PC Superstore." Order printers, games, word processing software, and much more from this service.

Subjects
Computer Products, Computers

Audience
Computer users

Content Summary
Be sure to look at MicroWarehouses "Featured Products" by choosing MicroWAREHOUSE Online Store from the main menu. Other choices include Quicksearch, Request/Order from Free Online Catalog, Customer Service, and more.

See Also
PC Vendor Forums

User Guide
- ☐ Windows
- ☐ DOS
- ☐ Macintosh
- ☑ Terminal Emulation
- ☐ VMS
- ☐ UNIX
- ☐ OS/2
- ☐ Other platform

Cost
- ☐ Unknown
- ☑ Basic
- ☐ Extended
- ☐ Premium ($)
- ☐ Executive w/$

Activity Level

Address
GO: **MCW**

MIDI Vendor Forums

Description
Supporting various MIDI vendors, the MIDI A, MIDI B, and MIDI C Vendor Forums help users with specific product problems and concerns.

Subjects
Computers, Multimedia, Music

Audience
Computer users, computer game developers, musicians

Content Summary
The MIDI A Vendor Forum (GO MIDIAVEN) includes these vendors: Turtle Beach, Twelve Tone, E-Mu, Big Noise, and many others. The MIDI B Vendor Forum (GO MIDIBVEN) includes these vendors: Midiman, Cool Shoes, Covox, Sweetwater Sound, Passport Designs, Windjammer Software, and others. The MIDI C Vendor Forum (GO MIDICVEN) includes these vendors: MediaTech, AVM, Blue Ribbon, Roland, Steinberg, and others.

See Also
PC Vendor Forums

User Guide
- ☑ Windows
- ☑ DOS
- ☐ Macintosh
- ☐ Terminal Emulation
- ☐ VMS
- ☐ UNIX
- ☐ OS/2
- ☐ Other platform

Cost
- ☐ Unknown
- ☐ Basic
- ☑ Extended
- ☐ Premium ($)
- ☐ Executive w/$

Activity Level MEDIUM

Address
GO: **MIDIAVEN** or **MIDIBVEN** or **MIDICVEN**

Mobile Computing

Description
The Mobile Computing Menu enables you to go to a number of vendor forums that offer support and discussions of their mobile computing products.

Subjects
Computers, Mobile Computing

Audience
Computer users, mobile computing users

Content Summary
From the main menu, you can select from a number of vendor forums, including Compaq Connection, CompuAdd Forum, Epson Forum, Gateway 2000 Forum, IBM Thinkpad Forum, Intel Forum, Toshiba Forum, and many more.

See Also
Various vendor forums

User Guide
- ☑ Windows
- ☑ DOS
- ☑ Macintosh
- ☐ Terminal Emulation
- ☑ VMS
- ☑ UNIX
- ☑ OS/2
- ☐ Other platform

Cost
- ☐ Unknown
- ☑ Basic
- ☐ Extended
- ☐ Premium ($)
- ☐ Executive w/$

Activity Level UNKNOWN

Address
GO: **MOBILE**

Modem Games Forum

Description
This forum is an electronic special interest group devoted to discussion of computer games capable of utilizing telecommunications and networking technology for play and competition.

Subjects
Computers, Games, Modems

Audience
Computer users, modem users, game enthusiasts

Content Summary
You can find a number of games, utilities, and other supporting files in the libraries in this forum. Some of the library areas include Modem Air Combat, Historic Air Combat, VGA Planets, Chess/Board/Card, DOOM, Network Games, and more.

See Also
Entertainment Forum, Multi-Player Games Forum

User Guide
- ☑ Windows
- ☑ DOS
- ☑ Macintosh
- ☐ Terminal Emulation
- ☑ VMS
- ☑ UNIX
- ☐ OS/2
- ☐ Other platform

Cost
- ☐ Unknown
- ☐ Basic
- ☑ Extended
- ☐ Premium ($)
- ☐ Executive w/$

Activity Level MEDIUM (HIGH)

Address
GO: **MODEMGAMES**

Modem Vendor Forum

Description
This forum is devoted to the support of products of the supporting vendors here, including direct assistance of software and hardware products.

Subjects
Computers, Modems

Audience
Computer users, modem users

Content Summary
In addition to discussions and support, you can find help files, programs, patches, and example files in the libraries. Some of the libraries include Supra Corporation, Boca Research, Global Village Communications, US Robotics, Zoom, Prometheus, and more.

See Also
Telecommunications Forum

User Guide
- [✓] Windows
- [✓] DOS
- [✓] Macintosh
- [ ] Terminal Emulation
- [ ] VMS
- [✓] UNIX
- [ ] OS/2
- [✓] Other platform

Cost
- [ ] Unknown
- [ ] Basic
- [✓] Extended
- [ ] Premium ($)
- [ ] Executive w/$

Activity Level

Address
GO: **MODEMVENDOR**

Multimedia Services

Description
If you use computers with audio, video, animation, and music, the multimedia services and forums are for you.

Subjects
Computers, Multimedia

Audience
Computer users, multimedia users

Content Summary
The Multimedia Vendor Forum (GO MULTIVEN) includes vendor support from BCD Associates, Lenel Systems, Voyager, Truevision, and others. The Multimedia B Vendor Forum (GO MULTIBVEN) includes vendor support from Adda Technologies, In Focus Systems, FAST Electronic, and others. The Multimedia Forum (GO MULTIMEDIA) includes files, advice, and technical support for topics such as Video and audio, Animation, Interface design, Education/training, and more.

See Also
Autodesk Multimedia Forum

User Guide
- [✓] Windows
- [✓] DOS
- [✓] Macintosh
- [ ] Terminal Emulation
- [ ] VMS
- [ ] UNIX
- [ ] OS/2
- [ ] Other platform

Cost
- [ ] Unknown
- [ ] Basic
- [✓] Extended
- [ ] Premium ($)
- [ ] Executive w/$

Activity Level

Address
GO: **MUTIBVEN**, **MULTIMEDIA**, **MULTIVEN**

National Computer Security Association (NCSA)

Description
This service helps you understand the NCSA and the NCSA Ethics Committee, and to go to the NCSA Forum.

Subjects
Computers, Computer Security

Audience
Computer users, MIS people

Content Summary
From the main menu, you can select these options: NCSA InfoSecurity Forum, About the NCSA, and About the NCSA Ethics Committee.

See Also
NCSA Forum

User Guide
- [✓] Windows
- [✓] DOS
- [✓] Macintosh
- [ ] Terminal Emulation
- [✓] VMS
- [✓] UNIX
- [ ] OS/2
- [ ] Other platform

Cost
- [ ] Unknown
- [✓] Basic
- [ ] Extended
- [ ] Premium ($)
- [ ] Executive w/$

Activity Level

LOW UNKNOWN HIGH

Address
GO: **NCSA**

NCR/ATT Forum

Description
Use this forum to find the latest drivers, news, and patches for NCR/ATT products.

Subjects
Computers

Audience
Computer users, MIS people

Content Summary
The library and message sections include The Info Shop, Windows NT, Desktop Computing, AT&T PC's, Portable Computing, Network Connections, and Cooperative FWS.

See Also
IBM File Finder

User Guide
- [x] Windows
- [x] DOS
- [ ] Macintosh
- [ ] Terminal Emulation
- [ ] VMS
- [ ] UNIX
- [ ] OS/2
- [x] Other platform

Cost
- [ ] Unknown
- [ ] Basic
- [x] Extended
- [ ] Premium ($)
- [ ] Executive w/$

Activity Level

Address
GO: **NCRATT**

NCSA InfoSecurity Forum

Description
This forum is devoted to the subject of information and data security.

Subjects
Computers, Security

Audience
Computer users, MIS people

Content Summary
If you're concerned about computer security, viruses, and firewalls, examine the various library and message sections in this forum. Some of the topics include Ethics/Privacy, Info Security News, Virus Tools/Info, PC/LAN Security, UNIX/Internet, Auditing, and others.

See Also
Internet Forum

User Guide
- [x] Windows
- [ ] VMS

- [x] DOS
- [x] Macintosh
- [ ] Terminal Emulation
- [x] UNIX
- [ ] OS/2
- [x] Other platform

Cost
- [ ] Unknown
- [ ] Basic
- [x] Extended
- [ ] Premium ($)
- [ ] Executive w/$

Activity Level

(MEDIUM, arrow pointing HIGH)

Address
GO: **NCSA Forum**

Newton Developers Forum

Description
This forum discusses the various aspects of Newton technology and how to design software and hardware for the Apple Newton PDA.

Subjects
Computers, Apple

Audience
Computer programmers

Content Summary
Use this forum to find files, technical issues, and other developer resources. The library and message sections include Mac Toolkit, Windows Toolkit, Other Languages, Book Maker, NewtonScipt, General Programming, Graphics, and more.

See Also
Apple Forum

User Guide
- [x] Windows
- [ ] DOS
- [x] Macintosh
- [ ] Terminal Emulation
- [ ] VMS
- [ ] UNIX
- [ ] OS/2
- [x] Other platform

Cost
- [ ] Unknown
- [ ] Basic
- [x] Extended
- [ ] Premium ($)
- [ ] Executive w/$

Activity Level

Address
GO: **NEWTDEV**

NeXT Forum

Description
Find solutions, technical support, and other information concerning the NeXT operating system.

Computers

Subjects
Computers

Audience
Computer users

Content Summary
The library and message areas contain several sections, including Recreation, NeXT/Misc. Info, Connectivity, Utilities, Applications, Sound, Graphics, and more.

See Also
UNIX Forum

User Guide
- ☐ Windows
- ☐ DOS
- ☑ Macintosh
- ☐ Terminal Emulation
- ☐ VMS
- ☐ UNIX
- ☐ OS/2
- ☑ Other platform

Cost
- ☐ Unknown
- ☐ Basic
- ☑ Extended
- ☐ Premium ($)
- ☐ Executive w/$

Activity Level

Address
GO: **NEXTFORUM**

Novell Client Forum

Description
A Novell NetWire forum that includes a message area for topics relating to client support.

Subjects
Computers, Novell Inc., Computer Networking

Audience
Computer users, MIS people

Content Summary
The message section contains the following topics: IPX/ODI Issues, NETX Issues, VLM Issues, ODINSUP Issues, NetBIOS Issues, and NetWare & Windows.

See Also
Novell NetWire, Novell User Library, Novell Files Database

User Guide
- ☑ Windows
- ☑ DOS
- ☑ Macintosh
- ☐ Terminal Emulation
- ☐ VMS
- ☑ UNIX
- ☐ OS/2
- ☑ Other platform

Cost
- ☐ Unknown
- ☐ Basic
- ☑ Extended
- ☐ Premium ($)
- ☐ Executive w/$

Activity Level

Address
GO: **NOVCLIENT**

Novell Connectivity Forum

Description
This Novell NetWire forum includes a message section devoted to connectivity issues.

Subjects
Computers, Novell Inc., Computer Networking

Audience
Computer users, MIS people

Content Summary
Some of the topics available in the message section include NACS, NW Connect, NW for SAA, AS/400 Connectivity, Host Printing, SNA Links, NetWare Macintosh, NW/IP NFS-TCP/IP, and others.

See Also
Novell NetWire, Novell Files Database, Novell Library Forum

User Guide
- ☑ Windows
- ☑ DOS
- ☑ Macintosh
- ☐ Terminal Emulation
- ☐ VMS
- ☑ UNIX
- ☐ OS/2
- ☑ Other platform

Cost
- ☐ Unknown
- ☐ Basic
- ☑ Extended
- ☐ Premium ($)
- ☐ Executive w/$

Activity Level

Address
GO: **NCONNECT**

Novell Developer Info Forum

Description
This Novell NetWire Forum includes information on development issues pertaining to Novell products.

Subjects
Computers, Novell Inc., Computer Networking

Audience
Computer programmers, MIS people

Content Summary
The message section includes topics such as Btrieve, NetWare Client SDK, NetWare Sever SDK, LAN Workplace SDK, Telephony SDK, Telephony PBX Dev, Embedded NetWare, and more.

Computers

See Also
Novell Developer Support Forum, Novell NetWire, Novell Files Database, Novell Library Forum

User Guide
- [x] Windows
- [x] DOS
- [x] Macintosh
- [ ] Terminal Emulation
- [ ] VMS
- [ ] UNIX
- [ ] OS/2
- [x] Other platform

Cost
- [ ] Unknown
- [ ] Basic
- [x] Extended
- [ ] Premium ($)
- [ ] Executive w/$

Activity Level
MEDIUM / LOW → HIGH

Address
GO: **NDEVINFO**

Novell Developer Support Forum

Description
This Novell NetWire forum provides technical support and a message section for Novell developers.

Subjects
Computers, Novell Inc., Computer Networking

Audience
Computer programmers, MIS people

Content Summary
The message section includes Btrieve, NetWare SQL, Client SDK, Server SDK, Macintosh SDK, Communication SDKs, NMS SDK, Personal NW SDK, and more.

See Also
Novell NetWire, Novell Files Database, Novell Library Forum

User Guide
- [x] Windows
- [x] DOS
- [x] Macintosh
- [ ] Terminal Emulation
- [ ] VMS
- [ ] UNIX
- [ ] OS/2
- [x] Other platform

Cost
- [ ] Unknown
- [ ] Basic
- [x] Extended
- [ ] Premium ($)
- [ ] Executive w/$

Activity Level
MEDIUM / LOW → HIGH

Address
GO: **NDEVSUPPORT**

Novell DSG Forum

Description
This forum is devoted to the Novell DOS operating system.

Subjects
Computers, Novell Inc., Computer Networking

Audience
Computer users, MIS people

Content Summary
This forum contains only two libraries: Provisional and NetWare NT Client. You'll find a great deal of information from the message sections, including NWDOS/DRDOS Applications, NWDOS/DRDOS Disk, NWDOS/DRDOS Memory, NWDOS/DRDOS Utilities, NetWare Lite, and more.

See Also
Novell NetWire, Novell Files Database, Novell Library Forum

User Guide
- [x] Windows
- [x] DOS
- [ ] Macintosh
- [ ] Terminal Emulation
- [ ] VMS
- [ ] UNIX
- [ ] OS/2
- [x] Other platform

Cost
- [ ] Unknown
- [ ] Basic
- [x] Extended
- [ ] Premium ($)
- [ ] Executive w/$

Activity Level
MEDIUM / LOW ↑ HIGH

Address
GO: **DRFORUM**

Novell Files Database

Description
The files in this area are heavily downloaded files that will be moved to the Novell Library Forum as soon as the number of downloads decreases to a manageable level.

Subjects
Computers, Novell Inc., Computer Networking

Audience
Computer users, MIS people, computer programmers

Content Summary
The files currently in this area are DOS, Windows, and OS/2 Client updates; Server Drivers for NetWare 3.11; and NetWare 3.11 updates. From the main menu, you can choose Client Kits, NetWare Lite Utility, NetWare 3.12 Operating System Patches (47k), and others.

Computers

See Also
Novell NetWire, Novell Library Forum

User Guide
- ☑ Windows
- ☑ DOS
- ☑ Macintosh
- ☐ Terminal Emulation
- ☐ VMS
- ☐ UNIX
- ☐ OS/2
- ☑ Other platform

Cost
- ☐ Unknown
- ☐ Basic
- ☑ Extended
- ☐ Premium ($)
- ☐ Executive w/$

Activity Level
MEDIUM (arrow pointing between LOW and HIGH, leaning toward HIGH)

Address
GO: **NOVFILES**

Novell Information Forum

Description
Find out general information about Novell products, services, and certifications using this Novell NetWire message forum.

Subjects
Computers, Novell Inc., Computer Networking

Audience
Computer users, MIS people, computer programmers

Content Summary
The message sections include Suggestion Box, Application/Utilities, User Groups/Training, CNEs, NPA, NSEPro, NUI, and more. If you are a CNE or planning to become one, be sure to join the CNE message section for help and questions pertaining to this certification program.

See Also
Novell Developer Support Forum, Novell NetWire, Novell Files Database, Novell Library Forum

User Guide
- ☑ Windows
- ☑ DOS
- ☑ Macintosh
- ☐ Terminal Emulation
- ☑ VMS
- ☑ UNIX
- ☐ OS/2
- ☑ Other platform

Cost
- ☐ Unknown
- ☐ Basic
- ☑ Extended
- ☐ Premium ($)
- ☐ Executive w/$

Activity Level
MEDIUM (arrow pointing toward HIGH)

Address
GO: **NGENERAL**

Novell Library Forum

Description
This Novell NetWire forum includes several library sections that contain various files for your Novell environment.

Subjects
Computers, Novell Inc., Computer Networking

Audience
Computer users, computer programmers, MIS people

Content Summary
The library section includes thousands of files in several areas, including New Uploads, NetWare 2.*x* Specific, NetWare 3.*x* Specific, Client/Shell Drivers, NetWare Utilities, Btrieve/NW APIs, NetWare Lite, NetWare 4.*x*, Novell Information, and more. You can post questions about the libraries in the message section.

See Also
Novell Files Database, Novell Information Forum

User Guide
- ☑ Windows
- ☑ DOS
- ☑ Macintosh
- ☐ Terminal Emulation
- ☐ VMS
- ☑ UNIX
- ☑ OS/2
- ☑ Other platform

Cost
- ☐ Unknown
- ☐ Basic
- ☑ Extended
- ☐ Premium ($)
- ☐ Executive w/$

Activity Level
MEDIUM (arrow pointing toward HIGH)

Address
GO: **NOVLIB**

Novell NetWare 2.x Forum

Description
This Novell NetWire forum includes discussions about the Novell NetWare 2.*x* family of networking products.

Subjects
Computers, Novell Inc., Computer Networking

Audience
MIS people

Content Summary
The message section includes discussion on Printing, NetWare Utilities, Disk Drive/Controls, LAN Cards/Drivers, 2.1*x* & Below/OS, and Operating System.

Computers

See Also
Novell NetWare 3.x Forum, Novell NetWare 4.x Forum, Novell Library Forum, Novell Files Database

User Guide
- ☑ Windows
- ☑ DOS
- ☑ Macintosh
- ☐ Terminal Emulation
- ☑ VMS
- ☑ UNIX
- ☐ OS/2
- ☐ Other platform

Cost
- ☐ Unknown
- ☐ Basic
- ☑ Extended
- ☐ Premium ($)
- ☐ Executive w/$

Activity Level: MEDIUM (LOW → HIGH)

Address
GO: **NETW2X**

Novell NetWare 3.x Forum

Description
This Novell NetWire forum includes discussions about the Novell NetWare 3.x family of networking products.

Subjects
Computers, Novell Inc., Computer Networking

Audience
MIS people

Content Summary
The message section includes these topics: Printing, NetWare Utilities, Disk Drives/CDs/Controls, LAN Cards/Drivers, Upgrade Migration, SFT III, and NLM/OS/Console Utilities.

See Also
Novell NetWare 2.x Forum, Novell NetWare 4.x Forum, Novell Files Database, Novell Library Forum

User Guide
- ☑ Windows
- ☑ DOS
- ☑ Macintosh
- ☐ Terminal Emulation
- ☑ VMS
- ☑ UNIX
- ☐ OS/2
- ☐ Other platform

Cost
- ☐ Unknown
- ☐ Basic
- ☑ Extended
- ☐ Premium ($)
- ☐ Executive w/$

Activity Level: MEDIUM (LOW → HIGH)

Address
GO: **NETW3X**

Novell NetWare 4.x Forum

Description
This Novell NetWire forum includes discussions about the Novell NetWare 4.x family of networking products.

Subjects
Computers, Novell Inc., Computer Networking

Audience
MIS people

Content Summary
The message section includes Printing, NetWare Utilities, Disk Drives/CDs/Controls, LAN Cards/Drivers, Upgrade/Migration, Electro Text/Docs, Directory Services, and NLM/OS/Console Utilities.

See Also
Novell Files Database, Novell Library Forum, Novell Information Library, Novell NetWare 2.x Forum, Novell NetWare 3.x Forum

User Guide
- ☑ Windows
- ☑ DOS
- ☑ Macintosh
- ☐ Terminal Emulation
- ☑ VMS
- ☑ UNIX
- ☐ OS/2
- ☐ Other platform

Cost
- ☐ Unknown
- ☐ Basic
- ☑ Extended
- ☐ Premium ($)
- ☐ Executive w/$

Activity Level: MEDIUM (LOW → HIGH)

Address
GO: **NETW4X**

Novell NetWire

Description
The Novell NetWire service enables you to utilize Novell's online support for most of the problems you might have with a Novell product. NetWire is an exceptional alternative to using Novell's telephone Hotline for technical support.

Subjects
Computers, Novell Inc., Computer Networking

Audience
Computer users, computer programmers, MIS people

Content Summary
Use the NetWire main menu to find what you need online. You can find out What's New, get Service and Support, find out about Sales and Marketing, see Novell Programs, and get other information. If you are new to NetWire, be sure to download the

WELCOME.EXE file from the Novell Library (GO NOVLIB), library 2. This will help you take advantage of this wide-reaching service.

See Also
Novell Files Database, Novell Library Forum, Novell Information Library

User Guide
- ☑ Windows
- ☑ DOS
- ☑ Macintosh
- ☐ Terminal Emulation
- ☑ VMS
- ☑ UNIX
- ☐ OS/2
- ☐ Other platform

Cost
- ☐ Unknown
- ☐ Basic
- ☑ Extended
- ☐ Premium ($)
- ☐ Executive w/$

Activity Level

Address
GO: **NOVELL**

Novell Network Management Forum

Description
This Novell NetWire forum includes a message section devoted to discussions about network management issues.

Subjects
Computers, Novell Inc., Computer Networking

Audience
MIS people

Content Summary
This forum contains only a message section. The message section includes Network Management, NetWare Management System, Lantern System Management, LANalyzer for Windows, and NetWare for SAA Management.

See Also
Novell Connectivity Forum, Novell Files Database, Novell Library Forum

User Guide
- ☑ Windows
- ☑ DOS
- ☑ Macintosh
- ☐ Terminal Emulation
- ☑ VMS
- ☑ UNIX
- ☐ OS/2
- ☐ Other platform

Cost
- ☐ Unknown
- ☐ Basic
- ☑ Extended
- ☐ Premium ($)
- ☐ Executive w/$

Activity Level

Address
GO: **NOVMAN**

Novell OS/2 Forum

Description
This Novell NetWire forum is designed for messages pertaining to using NetWare with OS/2.

Subjects
Computers, Novell Inc., OS/2

Audience
MIS people

Content Summary
The message section includes OS/2 Printing, Client/Server, OS/2 Requester, NSM (OS/2), NetWare 4.*x* for OS/2, GUI Tools, and WINOS2/DOS.

See Also
Novell Files Database, Novell Library Forum, Novell Information Library, Novell NetWare 2.*x* Forum, Novell NetWare 3.*x* Forum, Novell NetWare 4.*x* Forum

User Guide
- ☐ Windows
- ☐ DOS
- ☐ Macintosh
- ☐ Terminal Emulation
- ☐ VMS
- ☐ UNIX
- ☑ OS/2
- ☐ Other platform

Cost
- ☐ Unknown
- ☐ Basic
- ☑ Extended
- ☐ Premium ($)
- ☐ Executive w/$

Activity Level

Address
GO: **NOVOS2**

Novell Technical Bulletin Database

Description
The Technical Bulletin Database enables you to search for bulletins and articles by title, keywords, technical bulletin number, or by Novell products number.

Subjects
Computers, Novell Inc., Database, Computer Networking

Computers

Audience
MIS people, Computer users

Content Summary
When you use this terminal emulation database, you must know the division prefix for the technical bulletin. The prefixes are as follows: NetWare Products Division (NPD); Communication Product Division (CPD); Enhanced Products Division (EPD). For more information on searching criteria, be sure to read the Instructions for Searching the Technical Bulletins.

See Also
Novell Information Forum, Novell Files Database, Novell Library Forum

User Guide
- [ ] Windows
- [ ] DOS
- [ ] Macintosh
- [x] Terminal Emulation
- [ ] VMS
- [ ] UNIX
- [ ] OS/2
- [ ] Other platform

Cost
- [ ] Unknown
- [ ] Basic
- [x] Extended
- [ ] Premium ($)
- [ ] Executive w/$

Activity Level

Address
GO: **NTB**

Novell Vendor Forums

Description
This Novell NetWire service contains information, files, and support from various Novell vendors of NetWare-related products and services.

Subjects
Computers, Novell Inc., Computer Networking

Audience
Computer users, MIS people

Content Summary
The Novell Vendor A Forum (GO NVENA) contains several vendors, including Folio Corporation, BindView, Computer Tyme, Infinite Technologies, and more. The Novell Vendor B Forum (GO NVENB) contains several vendors, including Ontrack Data, NetWorth, gadget, Simware, Lantech, and more.

See Also
Novell Library Forum, Novell Files Database

User Guide
- [x] Windows
- [x] DOS
- [x] Macintosh
- [ ] Terminal Emulation
- [x] VMS
- [x] UNIX
- [ ] OS/2
- [ ] Other platform

Cost
- [ ] Unknown
- [ ] Basic
- [x] Extended
- [ ] Premium ($)
- [ ] Executive w/$

Activity Level

Address
GO: **NVENx**

Oracle Forum

Description
Sponsored by Oracle Corporation and administered by the International Oracle Users Group (IOUG), this forum provides online technical advice and libraries of helpful routines.

Subjects
Computers, Oracle

Audience
Computer users, MIS people

Content Summary
You can find tips, techniques, files, books, documentation, and other resources in the numerous library and message sections. Some of the library sections include User Groups, Mainframe, Minicomputer & UNIX, Desktop-PC, Mac, NLM, RDBMS, SQL & PL/SQL, Oracle Bookstore, Training, and more.

See Also
Client Server Computer Forum

User Guide
- [x] Windows
- [x] DOS
- [x] Macintosh
- [ ] Terminal Emulation
- [x] VMS
- [x] UNIX
- [ ] OS/2
- [x] Other platform

Cost
- [ ] Unknown
- [ ] Basic
- [x] Extended
- [ ] Premium ($)
- [ ] Executive w/$

Activity Level

MEDIUM — LOW / HIGH

Address
GO: **ORACLE**

Other Banyan Patchware Forum

Description
Sponsored by Banyan Systems, Inc., this forum provides an area for users to download patches and support files for products relating to Banyan products.

Computers

Subjects
Computers

Audience
Computer users, MIS people

Content Summary
This library stores patches related to Banyan Products outside of VINES such as ENS, as well as future products that will soon be released by Banyan. Patches are uploaded by Banyan's Customer Support organization and are kept up-to-date. The library section is called Misc. BanPatches. You also can leave or read messages for general help.

See Also
Banyan Forum

User Guide
- ☑ Windows
- ☑ DOS
- ☑ Macintosh
- ☐ Terminal Emulation
- ☑ VMS
- ☑ UNIX
- ☐ OS/2
- ☐ Other platform

Cost
- ☐ Unknown
- ☐ Basic
- ☑ Extended
- ☐ Premium ($)
- ☐ Executive w/$

Activity Level

Address
GO: **BANPATCH**

Packard Bell Forum

Description
This forum provides technical support and an area to communicate with people who own Packard Bell computers.

Subjects
Computers

Audience
Computer users, Packard Bell users

Content Summary
Libraries include areas to ask technical support questions, get information on shareware utilities, and to download mouse drivers, video card drivers, and virus scanning utilities. Also provided is a list of Packard Bell service centers arranged alphabetically by state.

See Also
Computer Buyers' Guide

User Guide
- ☑ Windows
- ☑ DOS
- ☐ Macintosh
- ☐ Terminal Emulation
- ☐ VMS
- ☐ UNIX
- ☐ OS/2
- ☐ Other platform

Cost
- ☐ Unknown
- ☐ Basic
- ☑ Extended
- ☐ Premium ($)
- ☐ Executive w/$

Activity Level

Address
GO: **PACKARDBELL**

PC Catalog

Description
PC Catalog features more than 2,000 product listings, spanning networking, microcomputers, and new technology.

Subjects
Computers, Catalogs

Audience
Computer users

Content Summary
From the PC Catalog main menu, you can select Shop Our Online Catalog, What is PC Catalog, What's New, Gif Images, Customer Service, Visit PC Publications, and more.

See Also
MicroWarehouse, IBM Personal Software Products, CompuServe Store

User Guide
- ☑ Windows
- ☑ DOS
- ☑ Macintosh
- ☐ Terminal Emulation
- ☑ VMS
- ☑ UNIX
- ☐ OS/2
- ☐ Other platform

Cost
- ☐ Unknown
- ☑ Basic
- ☐ Extended
- ☐ Premium ($)
- ☐ Executive w/$

Activity Level
UNKNOWN

Address
GO: **PCA**

PC Computing

Description
The PC Computing service (a ZiffNet service) enables you to go to the PC Contact Forum, take a poll, or communicate with *PC Computing* magazine.

Subjects
Computers, ZiffNet

Computers

Audience
Computer users

Content Summary
From the main menu, you can select PC/Contact Forum, Take a PC/Computing Poll, Tips and Tricks from PC/Computing, File Submissions to PC/Computing, and Letters to the Editor. This is a ZiffNet service.

See Also
PC Contact, PC Magazine

User Guide
- [ ] Windows
- [ ] DOS
- [ ] Macintosh
- [x] Terminal Emulation
- [ ] VMS
- [ ] UNIX
- [ ] OS/2
- [ ] Other platform

Cost
- [ ] Unknown
- [x] Basic
- [ ] Extended
- [ ] Premium ($)
- [ ] Executive w/$

Activity Level

Address
GO: **PCCOMP**

PC Contact Forum

Description
The PC Contact Forum, a service of ZiffNet, is devoted to discussions among PC Computing's editors and readers.

Subjects
Computers, ZiffNet

Audience
Computer users

Content Summary
In addition to exchanging ideas or getting questions answered from your favorite writers or editors online, you can contact the PC Advocate about problems with vendors or talk to the Phantom Shopper to share your experiences with computer dealers around the country. Plus you can browse through the library and download productivity files and tricks.

See Also
PC Computing

User Guide
- [x] Windows
- [x] DOS
- [x] Macintosh
- [ ] Terminal Emulation
- [ ] VMS
- [ ] UNIX
- [ ] OS/2
- [ ] Other platform

Cost
- [ ] Unknown
- [ ] Basic
- [x] Extended
- [ ] Premium ($)
- [ ] Executive w/$

Activity Level

Address
GO: **PCCONTACT**

PC Direct UK Magazine Forum

Description
PC Direct UK Magazine Forum, part of ZiffNet, mixes inside knowledge of the United Kingdom computer trade with specialist buyers guides while always keeping the consumer in mind.

Subjects
Computers, United Kingdom, ZiffNet

Audience
Computer users, UK residents

Content Summary
Download buyer guides, editorial contributions (download *Frankenstein,* for instance), and utilities. The library sections are called Buying Advice, Utilities, and Editorial Contributions.

See Also
PC Contact, PC Computing

User Guide
- [x] Windows
- [x] DOS
- [x] Macintosh
- [ ] Terminal Emulation
- [ ] VMS
- [ ] UNIX
- [ ] OS/2
- [ ] Other platform

Cost
- [ ] Unknown
- [ ] Basic
- [x] Extended
- [ ] Premium ($)
- [ ] Executive w/$

Activity Level

MEDIUM (LOW – HIGH)

Address
GO: **PCDUK**

PC Magazine UK Forum

Description
This ZiffNet service offers utilities, sound files, graphics, and other files for your general computing needs.

Subjects
Computers, ZiffNet, United Kingdom

Computers

Audience
Computer users, UK Computer users

Content Summary
The library sections contains several areas, including Bench Tests, Productivity, Utilities, Editorial Contributions, After Hours, DOS, Spreadsheets, Words, Online/Internet, and more.

See Also
IBM File Finder, PC MagNet Utilities/Tips Forum

User Guide
- ☑ Windows
- ☑ DOS
- ☑ Macintosh
- ☐ Terminal Emulation
- ☐ VMS
- ☐ UNIX
- ☑ OS/2
- ☑ Other platform

Cost
- ☐ Unknown
- ☐ Basic
- ☑ Extended
- ☐ Premium ($)
- ☐ Executive w/$

Activity Level

Address
GO: **PCUKFORUM**

PC Magazine UK Online

Description
PC Magazine UK Online (a ZiffNet service) is jointly run by *PC Direct UK,* the business computer buyer's magazine, and *PC Magazine UK,* the leader in PC technology analysis and reporting.

Subjects
Computers, ZiffNet, United Kingdom

Audience
Computer users

Content Summary
Each magazine has its own forum. In the PC Magazine UK Forum (GO PCUKFORUM), you can access the libraries to download reports and buyer's guides. Access the respective library for articles to download. You can access the PC Direct UK Forum by using the command GO PCDUK.

See Also
PC Direct UK Forum, PC MagNet

User Guide
- ☑ Windows
- ☑ DOS
- ☐ Macintosh
- ☐ Terminal Emulation
- ☐ VMS
- ☐ UNIX
- ☐ OS/2
- ☐ Other platform

Cost
- ☐ Unknown
- ☐ Basic
- ☑ Extended
- ☐ Premium ($)
- ☐ Executive w/$

Activity Level

Address
GO: **PCUKONLINE**

PC MagNet Editorial Forum

Description
The PC MagNet Editorial Forum, part of ZiffNet, enables you to communicate with the likes of Michael Miller, John Dvorak, and Winn Rosch.

Subjects
Computers, ZiffNet

Audience
Computer users

Content Summary
From the library and message sections contain several areas, including Features-Hardware, Features-Software, First Looks, Trends, Viewpoints-Dvorak, Viewpoints-Seymour, Viewpoints-Miller, After Hours, and more. You can download John Dvorak's winning chili recipe from library 6.

See Also
PC MagNet, PC Computing, PC Programming Forum, PC MagNet Utilities/Tips Forum

User Guide
- ☑ Windows
- ☑ DOS
- ☑ Macintosh
- ☐ Terminal Emulation
- ☐ VMS
- ☑ UNIX
- ☑ OS/2
- ☐ Other platform

Cost
- ☐ Unknown
- ☐ Basic
- ☑ Extended
- ☐ Premium ($)
- ☐ Executive w/$

Activity Level
MEDIUM / LOW / HIGH

Address
GO: **EDITORIAL**

PC MagNet Programming Forum

Description
The PC MagNet Programming Forum, part of ZiffNet, has the latest files from the programming sections of *PC Magazine.* Many of the authors can be found here as well.

Subjects
Computers, Computer Programming, ZiffNet

Audience
Computer users, computer programmers

Computers

Content Summary
The library and message sections include Utilities Code, Power Programming, Languages, Lab Notes, Environments, Toolkits, Corporate Developer, and more. If you are interested in computer-related trade shows, you can download a calendar of over 100 events from library 1, General. The file name is ZCAL13.ZIP.

See Also
PC MagNet, PC MagNet Editorial Forum, PC MagNet Utilities/Tips Forum

User Guide
- [x] Windows
- [x] DOS
- [x] Macintosh
- [ ] Terminal Emulation
- [ ] VMS
- [ ] UNIX
- [x] OS/2
- [x] Other platform

Cost
- [ ] Unknown
- [ ] Basic
- [x] Extended
- [ ] Premium ($)
- [ ] Executive w/$

Activity Level

Address
GO: **PROGRAMMING**

PC MagNet Utilities/Tips Forum

Description
You can find the latest utilities from *PC Magazine* here as well as files from various other sections of the magazine. Many of the authors of the utilities provide support here as well. This is part of ZiffNet.

Subjects
Computers, ZiffNet

Audience
Computer users

Content Summary
Numerous shareware utilities can be found throughout these libraries. Some of the library sections include PC Magazine Utilities, Tutor, User-to-User, Sol: Hardware, Driver Alert, Windows & OS/2 Utilities, and more.

See Also
IBM File Finder, PC MagNet

User Guide
- [x] Windows
- [x] DOS
- [x] Macintosh
- [ ] Terminal Emulation
- [ ] VMS
- [ ] UNIX
- [x] OS/2
- [x] Other platform

Cost
- [ ] Unknown
- [ ] Basic
- [x] Extended
- [ ] Premium ($)
- [ ] Executive w/$

Activity Level
MEDIUM, arrow pointing toward HIGH

Address
GO: **TIPS**

PC Plug and Play Forum

Description
This forum is for the discussion of the hardware and software issues of implementing plug and play on PCs. The Plug and Play forum is operated by several hardware and software manufacturers.

Subjects
Computers, Hardware

Audience
Computer users, MIS people

Content Summary
This forum is mainly under construction due to the infancy of this topic. However, you can find files and technical information in several of its libraries, including General Information, Plug and Play ISA, and PCMCIA.

See Also
IBM File Finder

User Guide
- [x] Windows
- [x] DOS
- [ ] Macintosh
- [ ] Terminal Emulation
- [ ] VMS
- [ ] UNIX
- [ ] OS/2
- [ ] Other platform

Cost
- [ ] Unknown
- [ ] Basic
- [x] Extended
- [ ] Premium ($)
- [ ] Executive w/$

Activity Level
MEDIUM, arrow pointing toward LOW

Address
GO: **PLUGPLAY**

PC Plus/PC Answers Online

Description
This service is devoted to readers of *PC Plus* and *PC Answers,* two UK magazines, to communicate with editors, download and upload files, and submit articles.

Subjects
Computers, UK

Audience
Computer users, UK Computer users

Computers

177

Content Summary
From the PC Plus Online main menu, you can choose from several options, including About PC Plus Online, Using the Service, Top 10 Downloads, Coverdisks, Letters to the Editor, and more.

See Also
PC MagNet, PC Computing, PC Direct UK Forum

User Guide
- ☑ Windows
- ☑ DOS
- ☑ Macintosh
- ☐ Terminal Emulation
- ☑ VMS
- ☑ UNIX
- ☐ OS/2
- ☐ Other platform

Cost
- ☐ Unknown
- ☐ Basic
- ☑ Extended
- ☐ Premium ($)
- ☐ Executive w/$

Activity Level

Address
GO: **PCPLUS**

PC Publications

Description
This service enables you to order a subscription of *PC Novice*, *PC Today*, and *PC Catalog*.

Subjects
Computers

Audience
Computer users

Content Summary
From the main menu, you can select Order a Subscription, About PC Novice/PC Today/PC Catalog, Shipping and Ordering Information, Table of Contents - Sample Articles, Customer Service, and more.

See Also
IBM File Finder

User Guide
- ☑ Windows
- ☑ DOS
- ☑ Macintosh
- ☐ Terminal Emulation
- ☑ VMS
- ☑ UNIX
- ☐ OS/2
- ☐ Other platform

Cost
- ☐ Unknown
- ☑ Basic
- ☐ Extended
- ☐ Premium ($)
- ☐ Executive w/$

Activity Level

Address
GO: **PCB**

PC Vendor Forums

Description
These forums are designed to offer support from various PC vendors of PC products.

Subjects
Computers

Audience
Computer users, MIS people

Content Summary
There are 10 PC Vendor forums: PC Vendor A Forum (GO PCVENA), PC Vendor B Forum (GO PCVENB), PC Vendor C Forum (GO PCVENC), PC Vendor D Forum (GO PCVEND), PC Vendor E Forum (GO PCVENE), PC Vendor F Forum (GO PCVENF), PC Vendor G Forum (GO PCVENG), PC Vendor H Forum (GO PCVENH), PC Vendor I Forum (GO PCVENI), and PC Vendor J Forum (GO PCVENJ).

See Also
IBM File Finder, Graphics Vendor Forums, DTP Vendor Forums, MIDI Vendor Forums, Multimedia Vendor Forums, Modem Vendor Forums

User Guide
- ☑ Windows
- ☑ DOS
- ☑ Macintosh
- ☐ Terminal Emulation
- ☐ VMS
- ☑ UNIX
- ☑ OS/2
- ☑ Other platform

Cost
- ☐ Unknown
- ☐ Basic
- ☑ Extended
- ☐ Premium ($)
- ☐ Executive w/$

Activity Level
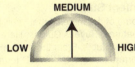

Address
GO: **PCVENx**

PC Week Forum

Description
PC Week is online as part of ZiffNet, enabling you to keep up with all the industry news. You can see headlines and full text of news stories the Friday before *PC Week* is published.

Computers

Subjects
Computers, ZiffNet

Audience
Computer users

Content Summary
See what the notorious Spender F. Katt has discovered this week or discuss the news and issues of the industry with the writers, editors, and other readers of the magazine.

See Also
PC MagNet, PC Computing

User Guide
- ☑ Windows
- ☑ DOS
- ☑ Macintosh
- ☐ Terminal Emulation
- ☐ VMS
- ☐ UNIX
- ☑ OS/2
- ☐ Other platform

Cost
- ☐ Unknown
- ☐ Basic
- ☑ Extended
- ☐ Premium ($)
- ☐ Executive w/$

Activity Level

Address
GO: **PCWEEK**

PC World Online

Description
This service is the online version of *PC World* magazine. You'll find timely and insightful information in this area that you also find in the print version of *PC World*.

Subjects
Computers, Magazine

Audience
Computer users

Content Summary
Some of the material that you'll find here includes Features, Buyer's Guides, Here's How, and news of new products. From the main menu, you can select Current Issue, PC WORLD forum, Online Exclusive, Exec/Direct Shop, News Wire, Press Release, and more.

See Also
PC Computing, PC Contact

User Guide
- ☑ Windows
- ☑ DOS
- ☑ Macintosh
- ☐ Terminal Emulation
- ☑ VMS
- ☑ UNIX
- ☑ OS/2
- ☐ Other platform

Cost
- ☐ Unknown
- ☐ Basic
- ☑ Extended
- ☐ Premium ($)
- ☐ Executive w/$

Activity Level

Address
GO: **PCWORLD**

Powersoft Forum

Description
This forum provides technical assistant to and a general discussion of Powersoft and WATCOM Corporation products.

Subjects
Computers, Database Consultants

Audience
Computer professionals, database professionals, Powersoft users

Content Summary
This forum's libraries and message areas contain information about PowerBuilder, PowerMaker, PowerViewer, PowerBuilder Desktop, WATCOM SQL, WATCOM C/C++, WATCOM VX-REXX, and WATCOM Fortran 77. Also included are bug fixes for products, user group lists, third-party vendors, and instructions on how to connect with other software.

See Also
Client Server Computing Forum

User Guide
- ☑ Windows
- ☑ DOS
- ☐ Macintosh
- ☐ Terminal Emulation
- ☐ VMS
- ☐ UNIX
- ☐ OS/2
- ☐ Other platform

Cost
- ☐ Unknown
- ☐ Basic
- ☑ Extended
- ☐ Premium ($)
- ☐ Executive w/$

Activity Level

Address
GO: **POWERSOFT**

Public Brand Software (PBS) Applications Forum

Description
This ZiffNet forum is a library of high-quality shareware, including DOS, Windows, and OS/2 applications, as well as communication programs.

Computers

Subjects
Computers, ZiffNet

Audience
Computer users

Content Summary
The library and message sections contain several areas for discussions and downloading PBS applications. The library sections include Hot Off the Presses, Reviewer's Picks, DOS, Windows, OS/2, Communications, WP and Text Editors, ZD Awards Nominees, and PBS Information.

See Also
Public Brand Software Home Forum

User Guide
- ☑ Windows
- ☑ DOS
- ☐ Macintosh
- ☐ Terminal Emulation
- ☐ VMS
- ☐ UNIX
- ☑ OS/2
- ☐ Other platform

Cost
- ☐ Unknown
- ☐ Basic
- ☑ Extended
- ☐ Premium ($)
- ☐ Executive w/$

Activity Level

Address
GO: **PBSAPPS**

Public Brand Software (PBS) Home Forum

Description
The Public Brand Software (PBS) Home Forum is a library of top-rated shareware programs for home, hobby, and education.

Subjects
Computers, ZiffNet

Audience
Computer users

Content Summary
Library sections include reference data and files in the news. Some of the library names include Hot Off the Presses, Reviewer's Picks, Home & Hobby, Education, Gutenburg, and more.

See Also
Public Brand Software Applications Forum

User Guide
- ☑ Windows
- ☑ DOS
- ☐ Macintosh
- ☐ Terminal Emulation
- ☐ VMS
- ☐ UNIX
- ☑ OS/2
- ☐ Other platform

Cost
- ☐ Unknown
- ☐ Basic
- ☑ Extended
- ☐ Premium ($)
- ☐ Executive w/$

Activity Level

Address
GO: **PBSHOME**

Shareware Depot

Description
This is an online shopping area offering shareware products for very low handling fees.

Subjects
Computers, Shareware

Audience
Computer users

Content Summary
This forum enables you to shop from home or office through many categories of computer shareware at attractive prices.

See Also
Computer Shopper, Shareware Registration

User Guide
- ☑ Windows
- ☑ DOS
- ☑ Macintosh
- ☐ Terminal Emulation
- ☐ VMS
- ☐ UNIX
- ☐ OS/2
- ☐ Other platform

Cost
- ☐ Unknown
- ☑ Basic
- ☐ Extended
- ☐ Premium ($)
- ☐ Executive w/$

Activity Level

Address
GO: **SD**

Shareware Registration

Description
This online area enables members to register for and pay for shareware software. The payment is added to members' CIS bill.

Subjects
Computers, Shareware

Audience
Computer users

Computers

Content Summary
This forum provides an easy way to register shareware. The registration fee is applied to your CompuServe bill.

See Also
Shareware Depot

User Guide
- ☑ Windows
- ☑ DOS
- ☑ Macintosh
- ☐ Terminal Emulation
- ☐ VMS
- ☑ UNIX
- ☐ OS/2
- ☐ Other platform

Cost
- ☐ Unknown
- ☑ Basic
- ☐ Extended
- ☐ Premium ($)
- ☐ Executive w/$

Activity Level

MEDIUM (LOW — HIGH)

Address
GO: **SWREG**

Sierra Online (FREE)

Description
This forum is an online shopping area for Sierra Online software products.

Subjects
Computers

Audience
Sierra software users

Content Summary
Within this forum, you can place orders for the entire product line offered by Sierra Software.

See Also
GAMAPUB, MODEMGAMES

User Guide
- ☑ Windows
- ☑ DOS
- ☐ Macintosh
- ☐ Terminal Emulation
- ☐ VMS
- ☐ UNIX
- ☐ OS/2
- ☐ Other platform

Cost
- ☐ Unknown
- ☐ Basic
- ☐ Extended
- ☐ Premium ($)
- ☐ Executive w/$

Activity Level

MEDIUM / UNKNOWN (LOW — HIGH)

Address
GO: **SI**

Smith Micro Forum

Description
This is the vendor support forum for Smith Micro products

Subjects
Computers

Audience
Smith Micro products users

Content Summary
Libraries include information about HotLine Windows/DOS, HotDisk, QLMC, QL GOLD, HotFax/QL DOS, and CrossConnection.

See Also
PC Vendors Forums

User Guide
- ☑ Windows
- ☑ DOS
- ☐ Macintosh
- ☐ Terminal Emulation
- ☐ VMS
- ☐ UNIX
- ☐ OS/2
- ☐ Other platform

Cost
- ☐ Unknown
- ☐ Basic
- ☑ Extended
- ☐ Premium ($)
- ☐ Executive w/$

Activity Level

MEDIUM (LOW — HIGH)

Address
GO: **SMITHMICRO**

Softdisk Publishing

Description
This is a online shopping area for Softdisk Publishing software products

Subjects
Computers

Audience
Shoppers, Computer users

Content Summary
This online shopping service enables you to choose from Softdisk's entire catalog of software products.

See Also
Small Computer Book Club

User Guide
- ☑ Windows
- ☑ DOS
- ☐ Macintosh
- ☐ Terminal Emulation
- ☐ VMS
- ☐ UNIX
- ☐ OS/2
- ☐ Other platform

Cost
- ☐ Unknown
- ☑ Basic
- ☐ Extended
- ☐ Premium ($)
- ☐ Executive w/$

Activity Level

[gauge: MEDIUM, arrow between LOW and HIGH]

Address
GO: **SP**

SOFTEX

Description
This CompuServe-sponsored forum enables you to purchase software for your personal computer often at a lower cost than if you purchased it through retail.

Subjects
Computer Software, Online Shopping

Audience
Computer users, software

Content Summary
You can purchase software by searching by type of software, publisher of the software, or by other criteria. If you choose to purchase the software, you get a description of the product, hardware and software requirements, and an estimate of download time. The charge appears on your monthly CompuServe bill.

See Also
Computer Buyers Guide Forum, Computer Shopper Forum, Shop-at-home Forum

User Guide
- ☑ Windows
- ☑ DOS
- ☑ Macintosh
- ☑ Terminal Emulation
- ☐ VMS
- ☑ UNIX
- ☐ OS/2
- ☑ Other platform

Cost
- ☐ Unknown
- ☐ Basic
- ☑ Extended
- ☐ Premium ($)
- ☐ Executive w/$

Activity Level

Address
GO: **SOFTEX**

Software Pub. Assoc. Forum

Description
This forum, sponsored by the Software Publishers Association, discusses how to publish software

Subjects
Computers

Audience
Computer users, computer programmers

Content Summary
Libraries include information about software publishing, software theft, and copyrights.

See Also
Software Development Forum

User Guide
- ☑ Windows
- ☑ DOS
- ☑ Macintosh
- ☐ Terminal Emulation
- ☐ VMS
- ☐ UNIX
- ☐ OS/2
- ☐ Other platform

Cost
- ☐ Unknown
- ☐ Basic
- ☑ Extended
- ☐ Premium ($)
- ☐ Executive w/$

Activity Level

Address
GO: **SPAFORUM**

Software Publisher Online

Description
This vendor forum supports the products of Software Publishing Corporation.

Subjects
Computers

Audience
SPA members, software developers

Content Summary
Libraries include news and information pertaining to SPAudit, business, consumers, education, and hot topics.

See Also
Software Pub. Assoc. Forum

User Guide
- ☑ Windows
- ☑ DOS
- ☑ Macintosh
- ☐ Terminal Emulation
- ☐ VMS
- ☐ UNIX
- ☐ OS/2
- ☐ Other platform

Cost
- ☐ Unknown
- ☐ Basic
- ☑ Extended
- ☐ Premium ($)
- ☐ Executive w/$

Computers

Activity Level

Address
GO: **SPC**

Speakeasy Forum

Description
This forum is for Ziffnet and/or CompuServe members looking for a relaxed, not-so-busy forum willing to allow general discussion on most any topic.

Subjects
Computers, Science Fiction

Audience
New Age enthusiasts

Content Summary
Libraries include information on science fiction, games, travel, sports, music, and After Hours.

See Also
Participate, Science Fiction Forum

User Guide
- ☑ Windows
- ☑ DOS
- ☑ Macintosh
- ☐ Terminal Emulation
- ☐ VMS
- ☑ UNIX
- ☐ OS/2
- ☑ Other platform

Cost
- ☐ Unknown
- ☐ Basic
- ☑ Extended
- ☐ Premium ($)
- ☐ Executive w/$

Activity Level

Address
GO: **SPEAKEASY**

Spinnaker Software Forum +

Description
This vendor forum supports all Spinnaker software products.

Subjects
Computers

Audience
Vendors who support Spinnaker software

Content Summary
Libraries include for PFS: products, Easyworking, Calendar Creator, and Express Publish.

See Also
Software Publishing Forum

User Guide
- ☑ Windows
- ☑ DOS
- ☑ Macintosh
- ☐ Terminal Emulation
- ☐ VMS
- ☐ UNIX
- ☐ OS/2
- ☐ Other platform

Cost
- ☐ Unknown
- ☐ Basic
- ☑ Extended
- ☐ Premium ($)
- ☐ Executive w/$

Activity Level

Address
GO: **SPINNAKER**

Standard Microsystems Forum

Description
This is a vendor support area for the networking products of Standard Microsystems Corp.

Subjects
Computers, Networking

Audience
Standard Microsystems users

Content Summary
Libraries include general information, Arcnet, Ethernet Elite, Ethernet 30XX, and Token Ring Elite.

See Also
PC Vendors Forums, Lan Vendors Forums, Lan Technology

User Guide
- ☑ Windows
- ☑ DOS
- ☑ Macintosh
- ☐ Terminal Emulation
- ☐ VMS
- ☐ UNIX
- ☐ OS/2
- ☐ Other platform

Cost
- ☐ Unknown
- ☐ Basic
- ☑ Extended
- ☐ Premium ($)
- ☐ Executive w/$

Activity Level

Address
GO: **SMC**

SunSoft Forum

Description
This is the vendor support area for SunSoft, the software unit of Sun Microsystems.

Subjects
Computers

Audience
Computer users, Sun Microsystems users

Content Summary
Libraries include Wabi & SWI, PC-NFS Family, SelectMAIL, SunPC, NetWare SunLink, Developers, Solaris X86, and Solaris Sparc.

See Also
UNIX Forum, UNIXWare

User Guide
- ☑ Windows
- ☑ DOS
- ☐ Macintosh
- ☐ Terminal Emulation
- ☐ VMS
- ☑ UNIX
- ☐ OS/2
- ☑ Other platform

Cost
- ☐ Unknown
- ☐ Basic
- ☑ Extended
- ☐ Premium ($)
- ☐ Executive w/$

Activity Level

Address
GO: **SUNSOFT**

Support On Site

Description
This database contains hints and helpful info on using some of the most popular software applications available today.

Subjects
Computers, Databases

Audience
Computer users

Content Summary
Libraries include technical information, user groups, SQL server, Sybase education, third party products, and PC products.

See Also
Computer Training Forum

User Guide
- ☑ Windows
- ☑ DOS
- ☑ Macintosh
- ☐ Terminal Emulation
- ☐ VMS
- ☑ UNIX
- ☐ OS/2
- ☑ Other platform

Cost
- ☐ Unknown
- ☐ Basic
- ☑ Extended
- ☐ Premium ($)
- ☐ Executive w/$

Activity Level

Address
GO: **ONSITE**

Sybase Forum

Description
This is a vendor support forum for Sybase networking and database products.

Subjects
Computers, Databases

Audience
Networking

Content Summary
Libraries include SW Treasure Chest, word processing, spreadsheets, databases, operating systems, programming, utilities, networking, and CAD.

See Also
Networking

User Guide
- ☑ Windows
- ☑ DOS
- ☐ Macintosh
- ☐ Terminal Emulation
- ☐ VMS
- ☐ UNIX
- ☐ OS/2
- ☐ Other platform

Cost
- ☐ Unknown
- ☐ Basic
- ☑ Extended
- ☐ Premium ($)
- ☐ Executive w/$

Activity Level

Address
GO: **SYBASE**

Symantec Applications Forum

Description
This is a vendor support forum for Symantec software applications such as GrandView, JustWrite, MORE II, OnTarget, Q&A, and TimeLine.

Subjects
Computers

Audience
Computer users

Content Summary
Libraries include general information, CP Backup for DOS, networking products, Commute, PC Tools, XTree Products, and accounting products.

Computers

See Also
Symantec AntiVirus Prod. Forum

User Guide
- ☑ Windows
- ☑ DOS
- ☐ Macintosh
- ☐ Terminal Emulation
- ☐ VMS
- ☐ UNIX
- ☐ OS/2
- ☐ Other platform

Cost
- ☐ Unknown
- ☐ Basic
- ☑ Extended
- ☐ Premium ($)
- ☐ Executive w/$

Activity Level: MEDIUM (LOW — HIGH)

Address
GO: **SYMAPPS**

Symantec CPS DOS Forum

Description
This is a vendor support area for Symantec's Central Point Software products for DOS.

Subjects
Computers

Audience
Computer users

Content Summary
Libraries include general information, Scrapbook, CPAV/Win-OS/2, ScriptTools, PC Tools, and XTree for Windows.

See Also
Symantec Forums

User Guide
- ☑ Windows
- ☑ DOS
- ☐ Macintosh
- ☐ Terminal Emulation
- ☐ VMS
- ☐ UNIX
- ☑ OS/2
- ☐ Other platform

Cost
- ☐ Unknown
- ☐ Basic
- ☑ Extended
- ☐ Premium ($)
- ☐ Executive w/$

Activity Level: MEDIUM (arrow pointing LOW)

Address
GO: **SYMCPDOS**

Symantec CPS WinMac Forum

Description
This is a vendor support area for Symantec's Central Point Software for Windows and Macintosh.

Subjects
Computers

Audience
Computer users

Content Summary
Libraries include Think C, Think Pascal, Power MAC, Multiscope, Optlink, and Think Reference.

See Also
Symantec Forums

User Guide
- ☑ Windows
- ☐ DOS
- ☑ Macintosh
- ☐ Terminal Emulation
- ☐ VMS
- ☐ UNIX
- ☐ OS/2
- ☐ Other platform

Cost
- ☐ Unknown
- ☐ Basic
- ☑ Extended
- ☐ Premium ($)
- ☐ Executive w/$

Activity Level: MEDIUM (LOW — HIGH)

Address
GO: **SYMCPWIN**

Symantec Dev. Tools Forum

Description
This is a vendor support forum for Symantec's development tools software, including Multiscope Debuggers, TCL, Think C, Think Pascal, and Zortech C++.

Subjects
Computers

Audience
Computer users

Content Summary
Libraries include orders and upgrades, Fastback, Fastback OS/2, Direct Access PC, and other PC products.

See Also
Symantech Forums

User Guide
- ☑ Windows
- ☑ DOS
- ☐ Macintosh
- ☐ Terminal Emulation
- ☐ VMS
- ☐ UNIX
- ☑ OS/2
- ☐ Other platform

Cost
- ☐ Unknown
- ☐ Basic
- ☑ Extended
- ☐ Premium ($)
- ☐ Executive w/$

Activity Level: MEDIUM (arrow pointing LOW)

Address
GO: **SYMDEVTOOL**

Symantec FGS Forum

Description
This is a vendor support forum for Symantec's Fifth Generation Systems products, such as Powerstation, Suitcase II, Copy Doubler, Disk Doubler, Pyro!, and DiskLock.

Subjects
Computers

Audience
Computer users

Content Summary
Libraries include upgrade information, Desktop for DOS, Desktop for Windows, Norton Disklock, Backup for DOS, and Backup for Windows.

See Also
Symantech Forums

User Guide
- ☑ Windows
- ☑ DOS
- ☐ Macintosh
- ☐ Terminal Emulation
- ☐ VMS
- ☐ UNIX
- ☐ OS/2
- ☐ Other platform

Cost
- ☐ Unknown
- ☐ Basic
- ☑ Extended
- ☐ Premium ($)
- ☐ Executive w/$

Activity Level: MEDIUM (arrow pointing LOW)

Address
GO: **SYMFGS**

Symantec Norton Util Forum

Description
This is a vendor support forum for Symantec's Norton Utilities, including Backup, Commander, and Utilities.

Subjects
Computers

Audience
Computer users

Content Summary
Libraries include Administrator (NAN), NAV/NetWare NAVNLM, Util/NetWare (NUA), and Enterprise Developer.

See Also
Symantech Forums

User Guide
- ☑ Windows
- ☑ DOS
- ☐ Macintosh
- ☐ Terminal Emulation
- ☐ VMS
- ☐ UNIX
- ☐ OS/2
- ☐ Other platform

Cost
- ☐ Unknown
- ☐ Basic
- ☑ Extended
- ☐ Premium ($)
- ☐ Executive w/$

Activity Level: MEDIUM (arrow pointing HIGH)

Address
GO: **SYMUTIL**

Symantec Ntwrk Products Forum

Description
This is a vendor support area for Symantec's network and enterprise software.

Subjects
Computers

Audience
Computer users

Content Summary
Libraries include Administrator (NAN), NAV/NetWare NAVNLM, Util/NetWare (NUA), and Enterprise Developer.

See Also
Symantec Forums

User Guide
- ☑ Windows
- ☑ DOS
- ☐ Macintosh
- ☐ Terminal Emulation
- ☐ VMS
- ☐ UNIX
- ☐ OS/2
- ☐ Other platform

Cost
- ☐ Unknown
- ☐ Basic
- ☑ Extended
- ☐ Premium ($)
- ☐ Executive w/$

Activity Level: MEDIUM (arrow pointing LOW)

Address
GO: **SYMNET**

SynOptics Forum

Description
This is a vendor support forum for Synoptic's intelligent LAN hubs and LAN management software.

Subjects
Computers, Networking

Audience
Network administrators

Content Summary
Libraries include product information, training information, and hot topics.

See Also
Lan Vendor, Lan Technology, Lan Magazine

User Guide
- ☑ Windows
- ☑ DOS
- ☐ Macintosh
- ☐ Terminal Emulation
- ☐ VMS
- ☐ UNIX
- ☐ OS/2
- ☐ Other platform

Cost
- ☐ Unknown
- ☐ Basic
- ☑ Extended
- ☐ Premium ($)
- ☐ Executive w/$

Activity Level

Address
GO: **SYNOPTICS**

Tandy Model 100 Forum

Description
This is a forum for users of Tandy nonDOS laptop computers.

Subjects
Computers

Audience
Computer users

Content Summary
The libraries include information on the Model 100, 200, 600 series. Also supports work-alikes such as NEC and Olivetti.

See Also
Tandy Users Network

User Guide
- ☑ Windows
- ☑ DOS
- ☐ Macintosh
- ☐ Terminal Emulation
- ☐ VMS
- ☐ UNIX
- ☐ OS/2
- ☐ Other platform

Cost
- ☐ Unknown
- ☐ Basic
- ☑ Extended
- ☐ Premium ($)
- ☐ Executive w/$

Activity Level

Address
GO: **Tandy Corporation Newsletter**

Tandy Professional Forum

Description
This is a forum for users of Tandy's "Professional" computers, such as the Tandy 2000, and Model 1/2/3/4 computers.

Subjects
Computers

Audience
Computer users

Content Summary
The libraries contain information on Tandy products and also contain software and utilities available for downloading.

See Also
Tandy Users Network

User Guide
- ☑ Windows
- ☑ DOS
- ☐ Macintosh
- ☐ Terminal Emulation
- ☐ VMS
- ☐ UNIX
- ☐ OS/2
- ☐ Other platform

Cost
- ☐ Unknown
- ☐ Basic
- ☑ Extended
- ☐ Premium ($)
- ☐ Executive w/$

Activity Level

Address
GO: **TRS80PRO**

TAPCIS Forum

Description
This is a vendor support forum for users of TAPCIS, the navigator and offline reader for CompuServe users.

Subjects
Computers

Audience
Computer users

Content Summary
The libraries contain basic information, information on usage, and tips on how to use TAPCIS internationally.

See Also
CIMSUPPORT, WCIM, OZCIS, NAVCIS

User Guide
- [x] Windows
- [x] DOS
- [ ] Macintosh
- [ ] Terminal Emulation
- [ ] VMS
- [ ] UNIX
- [ ] OS/2
- [ ] Other platform

Cost
- [ ] Unknown
- [ ] Basic
- [x] Extended
- [ ] Premium ($)
- [ ] Executive w/$

Activity Level

Address
GO: **TAPCIS**

Telecommunications Forum

Description
This is a forum that discusses telecommunications services and products, long distance services, and such things as protection of First Amendment rights.

Subjects
Computers

Audience
Computer users

Content Summary
Libraries include information about long distance services, First Amendment rights for electronic communication, and other related issues.

See Also
EFFSIG

User Guide
- [x] Windows
- [x] DOS
- [x] Macintosh
- [ ] Terminal Emulation
- [x] VMS
- [x] UNIX
- [ ] OS/2
- [ ] Other platform

Cost
- [ ] Unknown
- [ ] Basic
- [x] Extended
- [ ] Premium ($)
- [ ] Executive w/$

Activity Level

Address
GO: **TELECO**

Texas Instruments Forum

Description
This is a forum covering the TI-99/4a and TI Professional computers.

Subjects
Computers

Audience
Computer users

Content Summary
The libraries include information about user groups, product information, technical support, and more.

See Also
Texas Instrument Newsletter

User Guide
- [x] Windows
- [x] DOS
- [ ] Macintosh
- [ ] Terminal Emulation
- [ ] VMS
- [ ] UNIX
- [ ] OS/2
- [ ] Other platform

Cost
- [ ] Unknown
- [ ] Basic
- [x] Extended
- [ ] Premium ($)
- [ ] Executive w/$

Activity Level

Address
GO: **TIFORUM**

Texas Instruments News

Description
This is a menu-driven area containing news of the TI Forum and TI world in general.

Subjects
Computers

Audience
Computer users

Content Summary
The libraries contain information of help to new users, latest news, and new products and features of Texas Instrument.

See Also
TIFORUM

User Guide
- [x] Windows
- [x] DOS
- [ ] Macintosh
- [ ] Terminal Emulation
- [ ] VMS
- [ ] UNIX
- [ ] OS/2
- [ ] Other platform

Computers

Cost
- [ ] Unknown
- [ ] Basic
- [x] Extended
- [ ] Premium ($)
- [ ] Executive w/$

Activity Level

(gauge: UNKNOWN)

Address
GO: TINEWS

The 'GO GRAPHICS' Tutorial

Description
This is an online menu providing several helpful answers to commonly asked questions on CIS's GO GRAPHICS areas. Also, how to download pictures, how to view them, and so forth.

Subjects
Computers, Computer Graphics

Audience
Computer users, computer artists

Content Summary
The libraries include information on file formats, lessons for the novice, directions for downloading graphics, converting images, and news.

See Also
Graphics Corner Forum

User Guide
- [x] Windows
- [x] DOS
- [x] Macintosh
- [ ] Terminal Emulation
- [ ] VMS
- [x] UNIX
- [x] OS/2
- [ ] Other platform

Cost
- [ ] Unknown
- [ ] Basic
- [x] Extended
- [ ] Premium ($)
- [ ] Executive w/$

Activity Level

(gauge: UNKNOWN)

Address
GO: PIC

The Intel Forum

Description
This is a vendor support forum for Intel Corp and their computer-related hardware products.

Subjects
INTEL PCED/DTO Products

Audience
Computer programmers, computer users

Content Summary
The libraries contain information about product support, management and utility tools, fax/print servers, latest drivers, software revisions, troubleshooting documents.

See Also
Computer Hardware, Modems

User Guide
- [x] Windows
- [x] DOS
- [ ] Macintosh
- [ ] Terminal Emulation
- [ ] VMS
- [ ] UNIX
- [ ] OS/2
- [ ] Other platform

Cost
- [ ] Unknown
- [ ] Basic
- [ ] Extended
- [ ] Premium ($)
- [ ] Executive w/$

Activity Level

Address
GO: INTEL

The Laser's Edge

Description
Online shopping area for The Laser's Edge and their laser disc products.

Subjects
Laser Discs, Movies

Audience
General public

Content Summary
This online shopping service provides members access to the complete line of The Laser's Edge electronic products.

See Also
Shopping

User Guide
- [x] Windows
- [x] DOS
- [ ] Macintosh
- [ ] Terminal Emulation
- [ ] VMS
- [ ] UNIX
- [ ] OS/2
- [ ] Other platform

Cost
- [ ] Unknown
- [ ] Basic
- [ ] Extended
- [ ] Premium ($)
- [ ] Executive w/$

Activity Level

(gauge: UNKNOWN)

Address
GO: LE

The Mac Zone/PC Zone

Description
This is an online shopping area for Mac and PC hardware and software.

Subjects
IBM Compatibles, Macintosh Hardware & Software

Audience
Computer users

Content Summary
This online shopping area enables members to purchase from a complete line of PC and Macintosh products often at reduced rates.

See Also
PC Vendors Forums, Digitals PC Store

User Guide
- ☑ Windows
- ☑ DOS
- ☐ Macintosh
- ☐ Terminal Emulation
- ☐ VMS
- ☐ UNIX
- ☐ OS/2
- ☐ Other platform

Cost
- ☑ Unknown
- ☐ Basic
- ☐ Extended
- ☐ Premium ($)
- ☐ Executive w/$

Activity Level

Address
GO: MZ-1

TIMESLIPS Forum

Description
This is a vendor support forum for Timeslips Corp, and its time tracking and billing software.

Subjects
Tracking and Billing Software

Audience
Computer users, businesspeople

Content Summary
The libraries include information on product usage, product information, and technical support.

See Also
Accounting software

User Guide
- ☑ Windows
- ☑ DOS
- ☐ Macintosh
- ☐ Terminal Emulation
- ☐ VMS
- ☐ UNIX
- ☐ OS/2
- ☐ Other platform

Cost
- ☑ Unknown
- ☐ Basic
- ☐ Extended
- ☐ Premium ($)
- ☐ Executive w/$

Activity Level

Address
GO: TIMESLIPS

Toshiba Forum

Description
This is a vendor support forum for Toshiba laptop and notebook computers, and utility software.

Subjects
Help and Information for Toshiba Products

Audience
Computer users

Content Summary
The libraries include product information, technical support help, troubleshooting tips, and upcoming product releases.

See Also
Toshiba products

User Guide
- ☑ Windows
- ☑ DOS
- ☐ Macintosh
- ☐ Terminal Emulation
- ☐ VMS
- ☐ UNIX
- ☐ OS/2
- ☐ Other platform

Cost
- ☐ Unknown
- ☐ Basic
- ☑ Extended
- ☐ Premium ($)
- ☐ Executive w/$

Activity Level

(Medium, arrow pointing toward HIGH)

Address
GO: TOSHIBA

Toshiba GmbH Forum

Description
This is a vendor support forum for German users of Toshiba laptop and notebook computers

Subjects
German Help and Information for Toshiba Users

Audience
Computer users

Computers

Content Summary
The libraries include product information, technical support help, troubleshooting tips, and upcoming product releases.

See Also
Toshiba computers

User Guide
- [x] Windows
- [x] DOS
- [ ] Macintosh
- [ ] Terminal Emulation
- [ ] VMS
- [ ] UNIX
- [ ] OS/2
- [ ] Other platform

Cost
- [x] Unknown
- [ ] Basic
- [ ] Extended
- [ ] Premium ($)
- [ ] Executive w/$

Activity Level

Address
GO: **TOSHGER**

UK Computing Forum

Description
This is one of several UK forums covering topics important to members hailing from the United Kingdom. The UK Computing Forum covers computer hardware and software.

Subjects
United Kingdom computer related matters

Audience
Computer users

Content Summary
This forum's libraries contain information that pertains to computer hardware of software. Topics covered include product recommendations, usage, and press releases.

See Also
Computers and Software

User Guide
- [x] Windows
- [x] DOS
- [ ] Macintosh
- [ ] Terminal Emulation
- [ ] VMS
- [ ] UNIX
- [ ] OS/2
- [ ] Other platform

Cost
- [x] Unknown
- [ ] Basic
- [ ] Extended
- [ ] Premium ($)
- [ ] Executive w/$

Activity Level

Address
GO: **UKCOMP**

UKSHARE Forum

Description
In this forum, members discuss many of the most popular UK shareware programs and meet their authors.

Subjects
UK Shareware programs

Audience
Computer users

Content Summary
You can find files, utilities, and shareware programs from the United Kingdom in this forum. Find discussions and leave messages for shareware authors and developers.

See Also
Shareware

User Guide
- [x] Windows
- [x] DOS
- [ ] Macintosh
- [ ] Terminal Emulation
- [ ] VMS
- [ ] UNIX
- [ ] OS/2
- [ ] Other platform

Cost
- [ ] Unknown
- [ ] Basic
- [x] Extended
- [ ] Premium ($)
- [ ] Executive w/$

Activity Level

Address
GO: **UKSHARE**

Ultimedia Hardware Plus Forum

Description
This is a vendor support forum for Ultimedia's hardware products such as MWAVE System, ActionMedia, and V-Lan.

Subjects
Technical Suppor for all Ultimedia Tools Series products

Audience
Computer users, graphics artists

Content Summary
The library and message sections contain information and files for Ultimedia products. Be sure to check out the message sections for support questions and comments.

See Also
Multimedia

User Guide
- ☑ Windows
- ☑ DOS
- ☐ Macintosh
- ☐ Terminal Emulation
- ☐ VMS
- ☐ UNIX
- ☐ OS/2
- ☐ Other platform

Cost
- ☐ Unknown
- ☐ Basic
- ☑ Extended
- ☐ Premium ($)
- ☐ Executive w/$

Activity Level

Address
GO: **ULTIHW**

Ultimedia Tools Series A Forum

Description
This is one of three vendor support forums covering Ultimedia's software products.

Subjects
Technical Suppor for all Ultimedia Tools Series products

Audience
Computer users, graphics artists

Content Summary
The library and message sections contain information and files for Ultimedia products. Be sure to check out the message sections for support questions and comments.

See Also
Multimedia

User Guide
- ☑ Windows
- ☑ DOS
- ☐ Macintosh
- ☐ Terminal Emulation
- ☐ VMS
- ☐ UNIX
- ☐ OS/2
- ☐ Other platform

Cost
- ☐ Unknown
- ☐ Basic
- ☑ Extended
- ☐ Premium ($)
- ☐ Executive w/$

Activity Level

Address
GO: **ULTIATOOLS**

Ultimedia Tools Series B Forum

Description
This is one of three vendor support forums for Ultimedia's software products.

Subjects
Technical Suppor for all Ultimedia Tools Series products

Audience
Computer users

Content Summary
The library and message sections contain information and files for Ultimedia products. Be sure to check out the message sections for support questions and comments.

See Also
Multimedia

User Guide
- ☑ Windows
- ☑ DOS
- ☐ Macintosh
- ☐ Terminal Emulation
- ☐ VMS
- ☐ UNIX
- ☐ OS/2
- ☐ Other platform

Cost
- ☐ Unknown
- ☐ Basic
- ☑ Extended
- ☐ Premium ($)
- ☐ Executive w/$

Activity Level
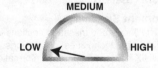

Address
GO: **ULTIBTOOLS**

Ultimedia Tools Series C Forum

Description
This is one of three vendor support forums for Ultimedia's software products.

Subjects
Technical Suppor for all Ultimedia Tools Series products

Audience
Computer users

Computers

Content Summary
The library and message sections contain information and files for Ultimedia products. Be sure to check out the message sections for support questions and comments.

See Also
Multimedia

User Guide
- ☑ Windows
- ☑ DOS
- ☐ Macintosh
- ☐ Terminal Emulation
- ☐ VMS
- ☐ UNIX
- ☐ OS/2
- ☐ Other platform

Cost
- ☐ Unknown
- ☐ Basic
- ☑ Extended
- ☐ Premium ($)
- ☐ Executive w/$

Activity Level

Address
GO: **ULTICTOOLS**

UNIX Forum

Description
In the UNIX Forum, users of the UNIX operating system discuss UNIX issues and exchange UNIX code.

Subjects
UNIX uses, implementations, networking, LINUX, communications

Audience
UNIX users, computer users

Content Summary
The library and message sections include numerous files, tips, techniques, discussions, and other related UNIX history and product information. Check out the discussions of the Linux operating system.

See Also
UNIX

User Guide
- ☑ Windows
- ☑ DOS
- ☐ Macintosh
- ☐ Terminal Emulation
- ☐ VMS
- ☑ UNIX
- ☐ OS/2
- ☐ Other platform

Cost
- ☐ Unknown
- ☐ Basic
- ☑ Extended
- ☐ Premium ($)
- ☐ Executive w/$

Activity Level

Address
GO: **UNIXFORUM**

Unix Vendor A Forum

Description
This is a vendor support forum for various UNIX vendors.

Subjects
Support sections for UNIX Vendors, Thoroughbred, GTR

Audience
UNIX users, computer users

Content Summary
You can find support from specific UNIX vendors in the library and message sections. Join this forum if you are an MIS professional or system analyst.

See Also
Software

User Guide
- ☑ Windows
- ☑ DOS
- ☐ Macintosh
- ☐ Terminal Emulation
- ☐ VMS
- ☑ UNIX
- ☐ OS/2
- ☐ Other platform

Cost
- ☐ Unknown
- ☐ Basic
- ☑ Extended
- ☐ Premium ($)
- ☐ Executive w/$

Activity Level

Address
GO: **UNIXAVEN**

UnixWare Forum

Description
This is a vendor support forum for Novell UnixWare software products.

Subjects
Technical Support & General Discussion of Novell's UNIXWare

Audience
UNIXWare users, computer users

Contents Summary
You can find information in the various library and message sections about the UnixWare operating system.

Computers

See Also
Software

User Guide
- [x] Windows
- [x] DOS
- [ ] Macintosh
- [ ] Terminal Emulation
- [ ] VMS
- [x] UNIX
- [ ] OS/2
- [ ] Other platform

Cost
- [ ] Unknown
- [ ] Basic
- [x] Extended
- [ ] Premium ($)
- [ ] Executive w/$

Activity Level: LOW (arrow pointing to low-medium)

Address
GO: **UNIXWARE**

UserLand Forum

Description
This is a vendor support forum for users of UserLand Software products.

Subjects
Frontier Scripting System for Macintosh

Audience
Macintosh users

Contents Summary
The library and message sections include files, tips, and supporting files for UserLand products.

See Also
Software

User Guide
- [ ] Windows
- [ ] DOS
- [x] Macintosh
- [ ] Terminal Emulation
- [ ] VMS
- [ ] UNIX
- [ ] OS/2
- [ ] Other platform

Cost
- [ ] Unknown
- [ ] Basic
- [x] Extended
- [ ] Premium ($)
- [ ] Executive w/$

Activity Level: LOW (arrow pointing to low-medium)

Address
GO: **USERLAND**

VAX Forum

Description
This forum provides support for users of the VAX series of computer systems from Digital Equip Corp. VAX Forum is sponsored by Professional Press.

Subjects
Computers, Digital Equipment

Audience
DEC users, computer users

Content Summary
VAX Hardware, ALPHA AXP, VMS System Software, VMS Applications, VMS Communications, VAX UNIX/ULTRIX, VMS Programming, Networking, VMS Entertainment

See Also
Computers, Software

User Guide
- [x] Windows
- [x] DOS
- [ ] Macintosh
- [ ] Terminal Emulation
- [x] VMS
- [x] UNIX
- [ ] OS/2
- [ ] Other platform

Cost
- [ ] Unknown
- [ ] Basic
- [x] Extended
- [ ] Premium ($)
- [ ] Executive w/$

Activity Level:  MEDIUM (arrow pointing to low-medium)

Address
GO: **VAXFORUM**

Ventura Software Forum

Description
This is a vendor support forum for Ventura's Publisher, FormBase Database Publisher, and other software products.

Subjects
Computer Graphics, Computers

Audience
Computer users

Content Summary
Ventura Software, Ventura Publisher for Gem, Ventura Publisher for Windows, Making Color work, Database Publisher Discussion, Fonts, Width Tables, printers, customer service.

See Also
Software

Computers

User Guide
- ☑ Windows
- ☑ DOS
- ☐ Macintosh
- ☐ Terminal Emulation
- ☐ VMS
- ☐ UNIX
- ☐ OS/2
- ☐ Other platform

Cost
- ☐ Unknown
- ☐ Basic
- ☑ Extended
- ☐ Premium ($)
- ☐ Executive w/$

Activity Level — LOW

Address
GO: **VENTURA**

Vines 4.x Patchware Forum

Description
This vendor support forum offers software patches and support for Banyan's VINES 4.x networking products.

Subjects
Banyan, Computer Networking, Computers

Audience
Banyon VINES users, network users

Content Summary
Banyan Vines 4.x patches

See Also
Software

User Guide
- ☑ Windows
- ☑ DOS
- ☐ Macintosh
- ☐ Terminal Emulation
- ☐ VMS
- ☐ UNIX
- ☐ OS/2
- ☐ Other platform

Cost
- ☑ Unknown
- ☐ Basic
- ☐ Extended
- ☐ Premium ($)
- ☐ Executive w/$

Activity Level — LOW

Address
GO: **VINES4**

Vines 5.x Patchware Forum

Description
This vendor support forum offers software patches for Banyan's VINES 5.x networking products.

Subjects
Banyan, Computer Networking, Computers

Audience
Banyon VINES users, network users

Content Summary
Banyan Vines 5.x patches

See Also
Software

User Guide
- ☑ Windows
- ☑ DOS
- ☐ Macintosh
- ☐ Terminal Emulation
- ☐ VMS
- ☐ UNIX
- ☐ OS/2
- ☐ Other platform

Cost
- ☑ Unknown
- ☐ Basic
- ☐ Extended
- ☐ Premium ($)
- ☐ Executive w/$

Activity Level — LOW

Address
GO: **VINES5**

Vobis AG Computer Forum

Description
This is a vendor support forum for Vobis AG products. Vobis AG is a German-speaking forum.

Subjects
Computer Hardware, Computers

Audience
German computer users

Content Summary
German VOBIS Microcomputer support

See Also
Hardware, Software Support

User Guide
- ☑ Windows
- ☑ DOS
- ☐ Macintosh
- ☐ Terminal Emulation
- ☐ VMS
- ☐ UNIX
- ☐ OS/2
- ☐ Other platform

Cost
- ☐ Unknown
- ☐ Basic
- ☑ Extended
- ☐ Premium ($)
- ☐ Executive w/$

Activity Level — LOW

Address
GO: **VOBIS**

Wang Support Forum

Description
This vendor forum supports Wang computer products.

Subjects
Computers

Audience
Computer users, Wang users

Content Summary
The libraries include information on products, training, services, and technical support.

See Also
PC Vendors Forums, WANG

User Guide
- [✓] Windows
- [✓] DOS
- [ ] Macintosh
- [ ] Terminal Emulation
- [ ] VMS
- [ ] UNIX
- [ ] OS/2
- [ ] Other platform

Cost
- [ ] Unknown
- [ ] Basic
- [✓] Extended
- [ ] Premium ($)
- [ ] Executive w/$

Activity Level

Address
GO: **WANGFORUM**

WinCIM Support Forum

Description
This forum is sponsored by CompuServe as a vendor support forum covering WinCIM access software for Windows users.

Subjects
Modems, Hardware, forums, solutions, upgrades, installation, printing, networks, terminal emulation

Audience
CompuServe users, WinCIM users

Content Summary
Contains information that enables users to navigate WinCIM better and faster. Topics include interface use, installation instructions, required hardware, and general usage.

See Also
Accessing CompuServe via WinCIM.

User Guide
- [✓] Windows
- [ ] DOS
- [ ] Macintosh
- [ ] Terminal Emulation
- [ ] VMS
- [ ] UNIX
- [ ] OS/2
- [ ] Other platform

Cost
- [ ] Unknown
- [✓] Basic
- [ ] Extended
- [ ] Premium ($)
- [ ] Executive w/$

Activity Level

Address
GO: **WCIMSUP**

Windows 3rd Party App. A Forum

Description
This is a vendor support forum for several Windows-based applications.

Subjects
Computers

Audience
Computer users, Windows users

Content Summary
Libraries include information about Access Softek, Arabesque Software, Asymetrix Corp., Future Soft Engineering, Geographix, hDC Computer Corp., Jensen-Jones, Lucid Corp., Micrografx, Playroom Software, Polaris Software, Premia Corp., 3-D Visions, and Wilson WindowWare.

See Also
Windows Vendor Forums

User Guide
- [✓] Windows
- [✓] DOS
- [ ] Macintosh
- [ ] Terminal Emulation
- [ ] VMS
- [ ] UNIX
- [ ] OS/2
- [ ] Other platform

Cost
- [ ] Unknown
- [ ] Basic
- [✓] Extended
- [ ] Premium ($)
- [ ] Executive w/$

Activity Level

MEDIUM
LOW   HIGH

Address
GO: **WINAPA**

Windows 3rd Party App. B Forum

Description
This is a vendor support forum for several Windows-based applications.

Subjects
Computers

Audience
Computer users, Windows users

Content Summary
The libraries include information about Computer Presentations, Connect Software, Frontier Technologies, InfoAccess, KASEWORKS, Kidasa Software, Knowledge Garden, Nu-Mega, Ocean Isle Software, Softbridge, SoftCraft, Window Craft, Wonderware, and Zenographics.

See Also
Windows Vendor Forums

User Guide
- ☑ Windows
- ☑ DOS
- ☐ Macintosh
- ☐ Terminal Emulation
- ☐ VMS
- ☐ UNIX
- ☐ OS/2
- ☐ Other platform

Cost
- ☐ Unknown
- ☐ Basic
- ☑ Extended
- ☐ Premium ($)
- ☐ Executive w/$

Activity Level

Address
GO: **WINAPB**

Windows 3rd Party App. D Forum

Description
This is a vendor support forum for several Windows-based applications.

Subjects
Computers

Audience
Computer users, Windows users

Content Summary
The libraries include information on ABC Systems and Development, Automated Design Systems, Baseline Publishing, DeltaPoint, Inmark, Okna Corp., Peachtree, Q+E Software, ShapeWare, SWFTE International, and WexTech.

See Also
Windows Vendor Forums

User Guide
- ☑ Windows
- ☑ DOS
- ☐ Macintosh
- ☐ Terminal Emulation
- ☐ VMS
- ☐ UNIX
- ☐ OS/2
- ☐ Other platform

Cost
- ☐ Unknown
- ☐ Basic
- ☑ Extended
- ☐ Premium ($)
- ☐ Executive w/$

Activity Level

Address
GO: **WINAPD**

Windows 3rd Party App. G Forum

Description
This is a vendor support forum for several Windows-based applications.

Subjects
Computers

Audience
Computer users, Windows users

Content Summary
Showcase Corp., AirTM, Pacific Crest Technology, First Floor Inc., Collabra Software, UnderWare Inc., Computer Knacks, Micro Frame Tech, Technical Tools, Crosswise Corp., Micromedium, Digital Workshop, ASNA, 20/20 Software

See Also
Windows Vendor Forums

User Guide
- ☑ Windows
- ☑ DOS
- ☐ Macintosh
- ☐ Terminal Emulation
- ☐ VMS
- ☐ UNIX
- ☐ OS/2
- ☐ Other platform

Cost
- ☐ Unknown
- ☐ Basic
- ☑ Extended
- ☐ Premium ($)
- ☐ Executive w/$

Activity Level
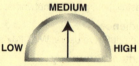

Address
GO: **WINAPG**

Windows 3rd Party App. E Forum +

Description
This is vendor support forum for several Windows-based applications.

Subjects
Computers

Computers

Audience
Computer users, Windows users

Content Summary
The libraries contain information about Andyne Computing, LaserTools, MapLinx, Scitor Corporation, and Systems Compatibility.

See Also
Windows Vendor Forums

User Guide
- [x] Windows
- [x] DOS
- [ ] Macintosh
- [ ] Terminal Emulation
- [ ] VMS
- [ ] UNIX
- [ ] OS/2
- [ ] Other platform

Cost
- [ ] Unknown
- [ ] Basic
- [x] Extended
- [ ] Premium ($)
- [ ] Executive w/$

Activity Level

Address
GO: **WINAPE**

Windows Sources Forum

Description
This enables the user to interact with the editors, columnists, writers, and reviewers of *Windows Sources Magazine*, and helps you find information on products you can buy directly from the manufacturer.

Subjects
Computers, Magazines

Audience
Computer users, Windows users

Content Summary
The libraries include product reviews, information on specific products, and issues affecting the computer industry.

See Also
Macmillan Computer Publishing Forum

User Guide
- [x] Windows
- [x] DOS
- [x] Macintosh
- [ ] Terminal Emulation
- [x] VMS
- [x] UNIX
- [x] OS/2
- [ ] Other platform

Cost
- [ ] Unknown
- [ ] Basic
- [x] Extended
- [ ] Premium ($)
- [ ] Executive w/$

Activity Level

Address
GO: **WINSOURCES**

WinNT Forum

Description
This is a vendor support forum for Microsoft Windows NT.

Subjects
Computers

Audience
Computer users, Windows NT users

Content Summary
This forum asks questions of Microsoft, reports bugs, discusses future releases, etc.

See Also
Windows Vendor Forums

User Guide
- [x] Windows
- [x] DOS
- [ ] Macintosh
- [ ] Terminal Emulation
- [ ] VMS
- [ ] UNIX
- [ ] OS/2
- [ ] Other platform

Cost
- [ ] Unknown
- [ ] Basic
- [x] Extended
- [ ] Premium ($)
- [ ] Executive w/$

Activity Level

Address
GO: **WINNT**

Wolfram Research Forum

Description
This is a vendor support forum for Wolfram Research's Mathematica software application.

Subjects
Mathematica

Audience
Computer users, educators

Content Summary
The libraries include papers from experts that outline the product's uses in specific applications.

See Also
GRAPHVEN, MULTIVEN

Computers

User Guide
- [x] Windows
- [x] DOS
- [ ] Macintosh
- [ ] Terminal Emulation
- [ ] VMS
- [ ] UNIX
- [ ] OS/2
- [ ] Other platform

Cost
- [ ] Unknown
- [ ] Basic
- [x] Extended
- [ ] Premium ($)
- [ ] Executive w/$

Activity Level
LOW ← MEDIUM HIGH

Address
Go: **WOLFRAM**

WordPerfect GmbH Forum

Description
This is a vendor support forum for WordPerfect's German software products.

Subjects
Computers

Audience
German computer users

Content Summary
The libraries include information on printers, graphics, desktop publishing, and training.

See Also
WordPerfect Users Forum

User Guide
- [x] Windows
- [x] DOS
- [ ] Macintosh
- [ ] Terminal Emulation
- [ ] VMS
- [ ] UNIX
- [ ] OS/2
- [ ] Other platform

Cost
- [ ] Unknown
- [ ] Basic
- [x] Extended
- [ ] Premium ($)
- [ ] Executive w/$

Activity Level
LOW MEDIUM HIGH — UNKNOWN

Address
GO: **WPGER**

WordPerfect Users Forum

Description
This is a user-sponsored forum for the discussion of any software produced by WordPerfect Corp.

Subjects
Computers

Audience
Computer users, WordPerfect users

Content Summary
The libraries include information on printers, graphics, desktop publishing, merges, training, file formats, and networking.

See Also
Desktop Publishing Forum

User Guide
- [x] Windows
- [x] DOS
- [ ] Macintosh
- [ ] Terminal Emulation
- [ ] VMS
- [ ] UNIX
- [ ] OS/2
- [ ] Other platform

Cost
- [ ] Unknown
- [ ] Basic
- [x] Extended
- [ ] Premium ($)
- [ ] Executive w/$

Activity Level
LOW MEDIUM ↑ HIGH

Address
GO: **WPUSERS**

WordStar Forum

Description
This is a forum for WordStar users sponsored by WordStar Int'l Technical Consulting Group.

Subjects
Computers

Audience
Computer users, WordStar users

Content Summary
The libraries and message areas include information on sample programs, usage articles and press releases, and printer drivers, templates, and utilities.

See Also
OnSite

User Guide
- [x] Windows
- [x] DOS
- [ ] Macintosh
- [ ] Terminal Emulation
- [ ] VMS
- [ ] UNIX
- [ ] OS/2
- [ ] Other platform

Cost
- [ ] Unknown
- [ ] Basic
- [x] Extended
- [ ] Premium ($)
- [ ] Executive w/$

Computers

Activity Level

Address:
Go: `WORDSTAR`

Working-From-Home Forum

Description
This is a forum for those who work from their homes, uniting them with others in similar circumstances. Users can exchange information, share solutions, etc.

Subjects
Computers

Audience
Home-based workers

Content Summary
The libraries and message areas contain information on taxes, business setup, equipment recommendations, and areas to exchange information.

See Also
Entrepreneur Magazine, Small Business

User Guide
- ☑ Windows
- ☑ DOS
- ☑ Macintosh
- ☐ Terminal Emulation
- ☑ VMS
- ☑ UNIX
- ☑ OS/2
- ☐ Other platform

Cost
- ☐ Unknown
- ☐ Basic
- ☑ Extended
- ☐ Premium ($)
- ☐ Executive w/$

Activity Level

Address
GO: `WORK`

WPCorp Files Forum

Description
This is a vendor support forum for WordPerfect drivers and macros, for such software as WordPerfect, Draw, DataPerfect, and PlanPerfect. This forum is supported by WPCorp.

Subjects
Computers

Audience
Computer users, WordPerfect users

Content Summary
The libraries include printer drivers, graphics drivers, macros, and information on related programs.

See Also
WordPerfect Corporation Forum

User Guide
- ☑ Windows
- ☑ DOS
- ☑ Macintosh
- ☐ Terminal Emulation
- ☐ VMS
- ☑ UNIX
- ☑ OS/2
- ☐ Other platform

Cost
- ☐ Unknown
- ☐ Basic
- ☑ Extended
- ☐ Premium ($)
- ☐ Executive w/$

Activity Level

Address
GO: `WPFILES`

WRQ/Reflection Forum

Description
This is a vendor support forum for Walker, Richer, and Quinn software products, such as their Reflection Series.

Subjects
Computers, Networking

Audience
Walker, Richer, Quinn software users

Content Summary
The libraries include discussions of terminal emulation, networking, office automation, and development applications products.

See Also
Telecommunications, LAN

User Guide
- ☑ Windows
- ☑ DOS
- ☑ Macintosh
- ☐ Terminal Emulation
- ☐ VMS
- ☐ UNIX
- ☐ OS/2
- ☐ Other platform

Cost
- ☐ Unknown
- ☐ Basic
- ☑ Extended
- ☐ Premium ($)
- ☐ Executive w/$

Activity Level
(Low–Medium)

Address
GO: `WRQFORUM`

WUGNET Forum

Description
The Windows User Group Network (WUGNET) forum supports Windows users around the world.

Subjects
Computers

Audience
Computer users, Windows users

Content Summary
The libraries include the bimonthly WUGNET Journal, information for developers, and an area to communicate with other Windows developers.

See Also
Windows Sources Forum

User Guide
- ☑ Windows
- ☑ DOS
- ☐ Macintosh
- ☐ Terminal Emulation
- ☐ VMS
- ☐ UNIX
- ☐ OS/2
- ☐ Other platform

Cost
- ☐ Unknown
- ☐ Basic
- ☑ Extended
- ☐ Premium ($)
- ☐ Executive w/$

Activity Level

Address
GO: **WUGNET**

Zenith Data Systems Forum

Description
This is an independent forum supporting the computer products of Zenith Data Systems.

Subjects
Computers

Audience
Computer users

Content Summary
This forum offers library and message section for members who own or are interested in Zenith computers.

See Also
IBM File Finder

User Guide
- ☑ Windows
- ☑ DOS
- ☐ Macintosh
- ☐ Terminal Emulation
- ☐ VMS
- ☐ UNIX
- ☐ OS/2
- ☐ Other platform

Cost
- ☐ Unknown
- ☐ Basic
- ☑ Extended
- ☐ Premium ($)
- ☐ Executive w/$

Activity Level

Address
GO: **ZENITH**

Ziff Bendata Forum

Description
This is a vendor support forum for Bendata's HEAT product.

Subjects:
Computers, ZiffNet

Audience
Computer users

Content Summary
This forum is ideal for members who use or are interested in Bendata products.

See Also
ZiffNet Free Utilities Forum

User Guide
- ☑ Windows
- ☑ DOS
- ☐ Macintosh
- ☐ Terminal Emulation
- ☐ VMS
- ☐ UNIX
- ☐ OS/2
- ☑ Other platform

Cost
- ☐ Unknown
- ☐ Basic
- ☑ Extended
- ☐ Premium ($)
- ☐ Executive w/$

Activity Level

Address
GO: **ZNT:BENDATA**

Ziff Cobb Applications Forum

Description
This forum provides problem-solving tips and downloadable software for users of Lotus 1-2-3, DOS, and Windows.

Subjects
Computers, ZiffNet

Audience
Computer users

Content Summary
If you are interested in problem solving for Lotus, DOS, and Windows, this forum's library and message sections contain information and files for you.

See Also
Ziff Software Center

User Guide
- ☑ Windows
- ☑ DOS
- ☐ Macintosh
- ☐ Terminal Emulation
- ☐ VMS
- ☐ UNIX
- ☐ OS/2
- ☐ Other platform

Cost
- ☐ Unknown
- ☐ Basic
- ☑ Extended
- ☐ Premium ($)
- ☐ Executive w/$

Activity Level

Address
GO: **ZNT:COBAPP**

Ziff Cobb Programming Forum

Description
The Cobb Programming Forum provides downloadable files and source code archived from the Cobb Programming Journals. C, C++, Pascal, Paradox, and dBASE are included.

Subjects
Computer Programming, Computers, ZiffNet

Audience
Computer users

Content Summary
If you are interested in programming, join this forum for information and files to help you with your programming needs.

See Also
Ziff Cobb Applications Forum

User Guide
- ☑ Windows
- ☑ DOS
- ☐ Macintosh
- ☐ Terminal Emulation
- ☐ VMS
- ☐ UNIX
- ☐ OS/2
- ☑ Other platform

Cost
- ☐ Unknown
- ☐ Basic
- ☑ Extended
- ☐ Premium ($)
- ☐ Executive w/$

Activity Level

Address
GO: **ZNT:COBBPR**

Ziff Computer Shopper Forum

Description
The forum for shoppers looking for information about buying computer systems, peripherals, and software.

Subjects
Computers, ZiffNet

Audience
Computers users

Content Summary
This forum is for members interested in getting information before they buy products.

See Also
Ziff Software Center

User Guide
- ☑ Windows
- ☑ DOS
- ☑ Macintosh
- ☐ Terminal Emulation
- ☐ VMS
- ☐ UNIX
- ☑ OS/2
- ☐ Other platform

Cost
- ☐ Unknown
- ☐ Basic
- ☑ Extended
- ☐ Premium ($)
- ☐ Executive w/$

Activity Level

Address
GO: **ZNT:COMPSHOPPER**

Ziff Editor's Choice

Description
This database of previous Editor Choice awards by *PC Magazine* helps members choose software and hardware.

Subjects
Computers, ZiffNet

Audience
Computer users

Content Summary
Looking for new hardware or software? This forum is for members looking for expert assistance in choosing hardware and software.

See Also
ZiffNet Reviews Index

User Guide
- ☑ Windows
- ☑ DOS
- ☑ Macintosh
- ☐ Terminal Emulation
- ☐ VMS
- ☐ UNIX
- ☑ OS/2
- ☑ Other platform

Computers

Cost
- ☐ Unknown
- ☑ Basic
- ☐ Extended
- ☐ Premium ($)
- ☐ Executive w/$

Activity Level: UNKNOWN

Address
GO: `ZNT:EDCHOICE`

Ziff Executives Online Forum

Description
The Executives Online Forum gives you direct access to industry leaders who visit to discuss products, strategies, and issues.

Subjects
Computers, ZiffNet

Audience
Computer users

Content Summary
Do you want to discuss topics with the likes of John Dvorak, Jim Seymour, and others? This forum is for members interested in discussing issues with executives in the computer industry.

See Also
ZiffNet Reviews Index

User Guide
- ☑ Windows
- ☑ DOS
- ☑ Macintosh
- ☐ Terminal Emulation
- ☐ VMS
- ☐ UNIX
- ☑ OS/2
- ☑ Other platform

Cost
- ☐ Unknown
- ☐ Basic
- ☑ Extended
- ☐ Premium ($)
- ☐ Executive w/$

Activity Level: MEDIUM

Address
GO: `ZNT:EXEC`

Ziff Newsbytes

Description
The Newsbytes News Network is an award-winning, global, daily newswire focused primarily on industry news.

Subjects
Computers, ZiffNet

Audience
Computer users

Content Summary
This service enables you to view up-to-date news and information concerning the top stories in the computer industry.

See Also
PC World, PC Contact

User Guide
- ☑ Windows
- ☑ DOS
- ☑ Macintosh
- ☐ Terminal Emulation
- ☐ VMS
- ☐ UNIX
- ☑ OS/2
- ☑ Other platform

Cost
- ☐ Unknown
- ☐ Basic
- ☑ Extended
- ☐ Premium ($)
- ☐ Executive w/$

Activity Level: UNKNOWN

Address
GO: `ZNT:NEWSBYTES`

Ziff Software Center

Description
The Software Center offers all kinds of high quality downloadable software, including ZiffNet utilities.

Subjects
Computers, ZiffNet

Audience
Computer users

Content Summary
This forum is ideal for users who are looking for utilities, files, and other resources.

See Also
Ziff Computer Shopper Forum

User Guide
- ☑ Windows
- ☑ DOS
- ☑ Macintosh
- ☐ Terminal Emulation
- ☐ VMS
- ☐ UNIX
- ☑ OS/2
- ☑ Other platform

Cost
- ☐ Unknown
- ☑ Basic
- ☐ Extended
- ☐ Premium ($)
- ☐ Executive w/$

Activity Level: UNKNOWN

203
Computers

Address
GO: ZNT:CENTER

Ziff-Davis Press Booknet

Description
This is an online shopping area for Ziff-Davis books, at a 20% discount.

Subjects
Computers, ZiffNet

Audience
Computer users, book buyers

Content Summary
This service enables you to order Ziff-Davis books online.

See Also
Macmillan Computer Publishing

User Guide
- [x] Windows
- [x] DOS
- [x] Macintosh
- [ ] Terminal Emulation
- [ ] VMS
- [ ] UNIX
- [ ] OS/2
- [x] Other platform

Cost
- [ ] Unknown
- [ ] Basic
- [x] Extended
- [ ] Premium ($)
- [ ] Executive w/$

Activity Level
UNKNOWN (LOW — MEDIUM — HIGH)

Address
GO: ZNT:BOOKNET

ZiffNet Designer Templates

Description
This is an online shopping area for spreadsheet and database templates.

Subjects
Computers, ZiffNet

Audience
Computer users

Content Summary
This service is for members wanting to make their spreadsheet and database work easier by buying pre-designed templates.

See Also
Microsoft Word Forum, Microsoft Excel Forum, IBM File Finder

User Guide
- [x] Windows
- [x] DOS
- [ ] Macintosh
- [ ] Terminal Emulation
- [ ] VMS
- [ ] UNIX
- [ ] OS/2
- [ ] Other platform

Cost
- [ ] Unknown
- [ ] Basic
- [x] Extended
- [ ] Premium ($)
- [ ] Executive w/$

Activity Level
UNKNOWN (LOW — MEDIUM — HIGH)

Address
GO: FORMS

ZiffNet File Finder

Description
Like all CompuServe File Finder databases, this one enables members to search for online software by keyword. ZFILEFINDER searches for ZiffNet software.

Subjects
Computers, ZiffNet

Audience
Computer users

Content Summary
Use this service to download utilities, software, and other files located in the ZiffNet area of CompuServe.

See Also
IBM File Finder, Novell File Finder

User Guide
- [x] Windows
- [x] DOS
- [x] Macintosh
- [ ] Terminal Emulation
- [ ] VMS
- [ ] UNIX
- [x] OS/2
- [x] Other platform

Cost
- [ ] Unknown
- [ ] Basic
- [x] Extended
- [ ] Premium ($)
- [ ] Executive w/$

Activity Level
UNKNOWN (LOW — MEDIUM — HIGH)

Address
GO: ZNT:ZFILEFINDER

ZiffNet FREE UTILS Forum

Description
This is a ZiffNet forum offering free utilities in the library, and discussions in the message area.

Subjects
Computers, ZiffNet

Audience
Computer users

Computers

Content Summary
This area is for members interested in downloading useful free utilities for the Macintosh and PCs.

See Also
ZiffNet File Finder, IBM File Finder

User Guide
- ☑ Windows
- ☑ DOS
- ☑ Macintosh
- ☐ Terminal Emulation
- ☐ VMS
- ☐ UNIX
- ☐ OS/2
- ☐ Other platform

Cost
- ☐ Unknown
- ☐ Basic
- ☑ Extended
- ☐ Premium ($)
- ☐ Executive w/$

Activity Level

Address
GO: `ZNT:FREEUTIL`

ZiffNet Membership & Benefits

Description
This is an online location in which members can change their membership data, or answer questions about their membership.

Subjects
Computers, ZiffNet

Audience
ZiffNet members

Content Summary
Use this service when you have concerns, customer support issues, or membership problems with ZiffNet.

See Also
ZiffNet Support Forum

User Guide
- ☑ Windows
- ☑ DOS
- ☑ Macintosh
- ☑ Terminal Emulation
- ☑ VMS
- ☑ UNIX
- ☑ OS/2
- ☑ Other platform

Cost
- ☐ Unknown
- ☑ Basic
- ☐ Extended
- ☐ Premium ($)
- ☐ Executive w/$

Activity Level

Address
GO: `ZNT:ZIFFMEM`

ZiffNet Reviews Index

Description
This database cites every product review published in a Ziff-Davis magazine since 1987.

Subjects
Computers

Audience
Computer users

Content Summary
This index is for members interested in locating product review articles on computer hardware and software.

See Also
PC World, PC Contact

User Guide
- ☑ Windows
- ☑ DOS
- ☑ Macintosh
- ☐ Terminal Emulation
- ☐ VMS
- ☐ UNIX
- ☑ OS/2
- ☑ Other platform

Cost
- ☐ Unknown
- ☑ Basic
- ☐ Extended
- ☐ Premium ($)
- ☐ Executive w/$

Activity Level

Address
GO: `ZIFFINDEX`

ZiffNet Support Forum

Description
This is a free forum offering help information on ZiffNet and ZiffNet services, help using ZiffNet, and support for Ziff database products.

Subjects
Computers, ZiffNet

Audience
Computer users, MIS

Content Summary
Use this forum for help in getting around ZiffNet.

See Also
ZiffNet Membership and Benefits

User Guide
- ☑ Windows
- ☑ DOS
- ☑ Macintosh
- ☑ Terminal Emulation
- ☑ VMS
- ☑ UNIX
- ☑ OS/2
- ☑ Other platform

Computers

Cost
- ☐ Unknown
- ☑ Basic
- ☐ Extended
- ☐ Premium ($)
- ☐ Executive w/$

Activity Level

MEDIUM (arrow pointing slightly above LOW toward HIGH)

Address
GO: **ZIFFHELP**

ZiffNet Surveys

Description
This is an area in which ZiffNet asks your opinion on various hardware and software products.

Subjects
Computers, ZiffNet

Audience
Computer users

Content Summary
This service enables ZiffNet members to respond to a product survey.

See Also
Speak Easy

User Guide
- ☑ Windows
- ☑ DOS
- ☑ Macintosh
- ☑ Terminal Emulation
- ☑ VMS
- ☑ UNIX
- ☑ OS/2
- ☑ Other platform

Cost
- ☐ Unknown
- ☑ Basic
- ☐ Extended
- ☐ Premium ($)
- ☐ Executive w/$

Activity Level

UNKNOWN

Address
GO: **ZNT:SURVEY**

Ziffnet Zshare Online Newsletter

Description
This is ZiffNet's monthly shareware review for shareware enthusiasts in a Windows Help file format.

Subjects
Computers, ZiffNet

Audience
Computer users

Content Summary
This newsletter is for members interested in shareware.

See Also
ZiffNet Reviews Index

User Guide
- ☑ Windows
- ☐ DOS
- ☐ Macintosh
- ☐ Terminal Emulation
- ☐ VMS
- ☐ UNIX
- ☐ OS/2
- ☐ Other platform

Cost
- ☐ Unknown
- ☐ Basic
- ☑ Extended
- ☐ Premium ($)
- ☐ Executive w/$

Activity Level

UNKNOWN

Address
GO: **ZNT:ZSHARE**

ZiffNet/Mac Download Forum

Description
This forum contains the top Macintosh shareware and freeware picks of the editors of *MacWEEK* and *MacUser* magazines.

Subjects
Computers, Macintosh, ZiffNet

Audience
Macintosh users

Content Summary
This forum is for members interested in discussing and downloading popular Macintosh freeware and shareware.

See Also
ZiffNet File Finder, IBM File Finder

User Guide
- ☐ Windows
- ☐ DOS
- ☑ Macintosh
- ☐ Terminal Emulation
- ☐ VMS
- ☐ UNIX
- ☐ OS/2
- ☐ Other platform

Cost
- ☐ Unknown
- ☐ Basic
- ☑ Extended
- ☐ Premium ($)
- ☐ Executive w/$

Activity Level

MEDIUM (arrow pointing toward LOW)

Address
GO: **ZMC:DOWNTECH**

Computers – Computers in Education

ZiffNet/Mac File Finder

Description
The ZMC File Finder database enables members to search through all files located in the ZMC forums.

Subjects
Computers, Macintosh, ZiffNet

Audience
Macintosh users

Content Summary
This service is for members wanting to search ZMC forums for specific file types.

See Also
ZiffNet/Mac Download Forum

User Guide
- [ ] Windows
- [ ] DOS
- [x] Macintosh
- [ ] Terminal Emulation
- [ ] VMS
- [ ] UNIX
- [ ] OS/2
- [ ] Other platform

Cost
- [ ] Unknown
- [ ] Basic
- [x] Extended
- [ ] Premium ($)
- [ ] Executive w/$

Activity Level UNKNOWN

Address
GO: `ZMC:FILEFINDER`

COMPUTERS IN EDUCATION

Education Forum

Description
This forum is designed to share and exchange information about all facets of the teaching and learning process. The use of computers and computer-related teaching methods is a hot topic in this forum.

Subjects
Computers in Education, Education, Teaching

Audience
Administrators, teachers, college and university faculty, product developers and publishers of educational material, librarians, school board members, counselors, principals

Content Summary
The Education Forum sponsors two weekly online meetings, including Tuesday evenings in Room 1 (General) at 9:30 p.m. Eastern and Thursday evenings in Room 5 (Homeschoolers) at 9:00 p.m. Eastern. This forum's libraries contain information on earning a degree online (Library 11), sex and AIDS education (Library 15), public domain and shareware software (Library 2), and lessons on how to participate in online conferences (Library 1, HOW2CO.TXT).

See Also
Education Research Forum, ERIC

User Guide
- [x] Windows
- [x] DOS
- [x] Macintosh
- [ ] Terminal Emulation
- [ ] VMS
- [ ] UNIX
- [ ] OS/2
- [ ] Other platform

Cost
- [ ] Unknown
- [ ] Basic
- [x] Extended
- [ ] Premium ($)
- [ ] Executive w/$

Activity Level MEDIUM

Address
GO: `EDFORUM`

Computers/Technology Menu

Description
Access to forums and services dealing with computers and technology.

Subjects
Computers

Audience
Computer users

Content Summary
Libraries include software forums, hardware forums, connectivity, research, reference, magazines, shareware registration, electronic mall, science, and ZiffNet.

User Guide
- [x] Windows
- [x] DOS
- [x] Macintosh
- [ ] Terminal Emulation
- [ ] VMS
- [x] UNIX
- [ ] OS/2
- [ ] Other platform

Cost
- [ ] Unknown
- [ ] Basic
- [x] Extended
- [ ] Premium ($)
- [ ] Executive w/$

Activity Level UNKNOWN

Address
GO: `COMPUTERS`

CONNECTIVITY

Eicon Technology Forum

Description
Sponsored by Eicon Technology, this forum helps users find answers to questions or problems concerning Eicon products. Eicon offers products of connectivity solutions for the X.25 and SNA environment.

Subjects
Computers, Connectivity, X.25, SNA

Audience
MIS people, Eicon consumers

Content Summary
The library and message sections contain information about Eicon products as well as technical support, press releases, utilities, help files, applications, demos, and Q&A. The libraries include sections for emulators, gateways, tool kits, international services, and WAN services.

User Guide
- ☑ Windows
- ☑ DOS
- ☑ Macintosh
- ☐ Terminal Emulation
- ☑ VMS
- ☑ UNIX
- ☑ OS/2
- ☐ Other platform

Cost
- ☐ Unknown
- ☐ Basic
- ☑ Extended
- ☐ Premium ($)
- ☐ Executive w/$

Activity Level
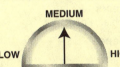

Address
GO: **EICON**

CONSUMER ELECTRONICS

The Escort Store

Description
This is an online shopping area for The Escort Store.

Subjects
Shopping, Top Rated Consumer Electronics

Audience
General public

Content Summary
The libraries include sources for top-rated consumer electronics products.

See Also
Shopping, The Heath Company

User Guide
- ☑ Windows
- ☑ DOS
- ☐ Macintosh
- ☐ Terminal Emulation
- ☐ VMS
- ☐ UNIX
- ☐ OS/2
- ☐ Other platform

Cost
- ☐ Unknown
- ☐ Basic
- ☐ Extended
- ☐ Premium ($)
- ☐ Executive w/$

Activity Level

Address
GO: **ESCORT**

The Heath Company

Description
This is an online shopping area for Heath Electronics, producers of Heathkit products.

Subjects
Heath Kit Electronics

Audience
Hobbyists, computer users

Content Summary
This online shopping service enables members to purchase electronic health products.

See Also
Shopping

User Guide
- ☑ Windows
- ☑ DOS
- ☐ Macintosh
- ☐ Terminal Emulation
- ☐ VMS
- ☐ UNIX
- ☐ OS/2
- ☐ Other platform

Cost
- ☑ Unknown
- ☐ Basic
- ☐ Extended
- ☐ Premium ($)
- ☐ Executive w/$

Activity Level

Address
GO: **HEATH**

Consumer Forum

Description
This is the place to find out how to make and save money, learn about your consumer rights, get buying advice, and read about scams and ripoffs.

Subjects
Business, Money

Audience
Consumers

Content Summary
The libraries include consumer information on automobiles, banking, bargains, coupons, complaints, rights, ripoffs, and money. You can even ask David Horowitz, a recognized expert, questions about products and consumer rights.

See Also
AUTO, DRUGS

User Guide
- ☑ Windows
- ☑ DOS
- ☑ Macintosh
- ☐ Terminal Emulation
- ☐ VMS
- ☑ UNIX
- ☐ OS/2
- ☐ Other platform

Cost
- ☐ Unknown
- ☐ Basic
- ☑ Extended
- ☐ Premium ($)
- ☐ Executive w/$

Activity Level

LOW ← MEDIUM HIGH

Address
GO: **CONSUMER**

CONVENTIONS

Electronic Convention Center

Description
The Electronic Convention Center enables you to access any of CompuServe's special conferences from your desktop. You can find out about upcoming conferences, make a reservation to attend one of them, and attend another all within a few minutes.

Subjects
Conventions

Audience
Anyone

Content Summary
The Convention Center has three types of conferences, including roundtable, moderated, and lecture conferences. A roundtable conference offers open chatter during the conference. A moderated conference is more formal than a roundtable and usually is hosted by an experienced individual on a topic. A lecture is a lecture—no chatter or questions are allowed. To make a reservation, type **RESERVE** *x*, where *x* is the number of the conference listing in the List Conference/Make Reservations option.

See Also
Meetings

User Guide
- ☐ Windows
- ☐ DOS
- ☐ Macintosh
- ☑ Terminal Emulation
- ☐ VMS
- ☐ UNIX
- ☐ OS/2
- ☐ Other platform

Cost
- ☑ Unknown
- ☐ Basic
- ☐ Extended
- ☐ Premium ($)
- ☐ Executive w/$

Activity Level

LOW MEDIUM HIGH — UNKNOWN

Address
GO: **CONVENTION**

Cook's Online Forum

Description
Everything dealing with cooking is what this forum is about, from appetizers to desserts, and a wine to go with the meal.

Subjects
Hobbies, Food

Audience
Cooks

Content Summary
Libraries include recipes and information about first courses, meat/poultry/fish, herbs and spices, desserts, ethnic recipes, breads, fruits, nutrition, and vegetarian cooking.

See Also
Chefs Catalog, Florida Fruit Shippers, Omaha Steaks

User Guide
- ☑ Windows
- ☑ DOS
- ☑ Macintosh
- ☐ Terminal Emulation
- ☐ VMS
- ☑ UNIX
- ☐ OS/2
- ☐ Other platform

Cost
- ☐ Unknown
- ☐ Basic
- ☑ Extended
- ☐ Premium ($)
- ☐ Executive w/$

Activity Level: MEDIUM (arrow pointing to LOW)

Address
GO: **COOKS**

Corel Forum

Description
The Corel Forum is designed to provide support and information about Corel products.

Subjects
Computer Graphics, Computers

Audience
Corel uers

Content Summary
Libraries include information on CorelDRAW!, CorelPHOTO-PAINT!, CorelSCSI, CorelGALLERY!, printing, text, and graphics.

See Also
Ventura, GRAPHICS

User Guide
- [x] Windows
- [x] DOS
- [ ] Macintosh
- [ ] Terminal Emulation
- [ ] VMS
- [ ] UNIX
- [ ] OS/2
- [ ] Other platform

Cost
- [ ] Unknown
- [ ] Basic
- [x] Extended
- [ ] Premium ($)
- [ ] Executive w/$

Activity Level: MEDIUM (arrow pointing to HIGH)

Address
GO: **CORELAPPS**

New Country Music

Description
If you like *Hee-Haw,* you'll love this place! *New Country Music Magazine* gives you an exclusive look into the world of Country. Enjoy intimate, friendly chats with superstars such as Alan Jackson, Trisha Yearwood, Travis Tritt, and others.

Subjects
Music, Country Music

Audience
Music enthusiasts, general public

Content Summary
From the main menu, you can choose from these options: What is New Country Music Service, To Sign Up, and Shipping and Billing Information. For a rate of $39.95 for 6 months or $69.95 for 12 months, you can sign for the *New Country Music Magazine* and get an exclusive CD every month.

See Also
Music Hall, Music Vendor Forum, Music Industry Forum

User Guide
- [ ] Windows
- [ ] DOS
- [ ] Macintosh
- [x] Terminal Emulation
- [ ] VMS
- [ ] UNIX
- [ ] OS/2
- [ ] Other platform

Cost
- [ ] Unknown
- [ ] Basic
- [x] Extended
- [ ] Premium ($)
- [ ] Executive w/$

Activity Level: MEDIUM / UNKNOWN

Address
GO: **COUNTRY**

CP/M Forum

Description
Support for users of the CP/M operating system is the primary purpose of the CP/M Forum.

Subjects
Computers

Audience
CP/M operating system users

Content Summary
The libraries include information on CP/M, hardware, telecommunications, word processing, dBASE, languages, ZCPR, CP/M BBSs, CP/M-80, Commodore, Epson, and portables.

See Also
Computer Club, Commodore Applications

User Guide
- [x] Windows
- [x] DOS
- [ ] Macintosh
- [ ] Terminal Emulation
- [ ] VMS
- [ ] UNIX
- [ ] OS/2
- [ ] Other platform

Cost
- [ ] Unknown
- [ ] Basic
- [x] Extended
- [ ] Premium ($)
- [ ] Executive w/$

CP/M Forum – Crime

Activity Level MEDIUM (arrow LOW)

Address
GO: **CPMFORUM**

Crafts

Description
This is a meeting place for folks worldwide who love to create with their hands; a resource for software, ideas, techniques and friends.

Subjects
Hobbies

Audience
Hobbyists

Content Summary
The libraries include information on crafting interests such as knitting, weaving, stitchery, glass, paper, woodworking, miniatures, lacemaking, quilting, jewelry making, and much more.

See Also
Garrett Wade Woodworking

User Guide
- ☑ Windows
- ☑ DOS
- ☑ Macintosh
- ☐ Terminal Emulation
- ☐ VMS
- ☑ UNIX
- ☐ OS/2
- ☑ Other platform

Cost
- ☐ Unknown
- ☐ Basic
- ☑ Extended
- ☐ Premium ($)
- ☐ Executive w/$

Activity Level MEDIUM (arrow HIGH)

Address
GO: **CRAFTS**

Creative Labs

Description
This forum gives world-wide support to Creative Labs' and Creative Technologies' products, including the popular Sound Blaster line of cards.

Subjects
Computers, Music

Audience
Creative Labs users

Content Summary
The libraries include information about SoundBlaster, SB Pro, SB16, WaveBlaster, AWE-32, CDROM kits, Video Blaster, VideoSpigot, Multimedia update kits.

See Also
MIDIFORUM, MEDIAVISION

User Guide
- ☑ Windows
- ☑ DOS
- ☑ Macintosh
- ☐ Terminal Emulation
- ☐ VMS
- ☑ UNIX
- ☐ OS/2
- ☐ Other platform

Cost
- ☐ Unknown
- ☐ Basic
- ☑ Extended
- ☐ Premium ($)
- ☐ Executive w/$

Activity Level MEDIUM (arrow HIGH)

Address
GO: **BLASTER**

CRIME

Safetynet Forum

Description
This forum provides and open communication channel for people and professionals interested in sharing information on any topic of public safety.

Subjects
Crime, Fire Fighting, Public Safety

Audience
Firefighters, health workers, police

Content Summary
This forum's libraries and message areas provide a wide assortment of information pertaining to public safety. A graphics library contains pictures of actual rescue attempts, crime scenes, and fires. Some of the pictures are graphic in nature. Of general interest are Red Cross disaster information, lists of public safety hotlines and bulletin boards, and copies of the Environmental Informer Newsletter. Separate libraries are available for firefighters, police, and public heath workers.

See Also
ZiffNet Crime and Violence Forum

User Guide
- ☑ Windows
- ☑ DOS
- ☐ Macintosh
- ☐ Terminal Emulation
- ☐ VMS
- ☐ UNIX
- ☐ OS/2
- ☐ Other platform

Cost
- ☐ Unknown
- ☐ Basic
- ☑ Extended
- ☐ Premium ($)
- ☐ Executive w/$

Crime – CSI Forth Net Forum

Activity Level

Address
GO: **SAFETYNET**

Time-Warner Crime Forum

Description
This is a forum sponsored by Time-Warner to discuss crime and violence worldwide.

Subjects
Crime of all types

Audience
General user

Content Summary
Vice, Violence, Murder, Theft, Fraud, Espionage, Genocide, Terrorism, Political Persecution, Safety/Protection, Spy, Bizarre/Unusual

See Also
Crime

User Guide
☑	Windows	☐	VMS
☑	DOS	☐	UNIX
☐	Macintosh	☐	OS/2
☐	Terminal Emulation	☐	Other platform

Cost
☐	Unknown	☐	Premium ($)
☐	Basic	☐	Executive w/$
☐	Extended		

Activity Level

Address
GO: **TWCRIME**

Crosstalk Forum

Description
This forum offers support for users of software products developed and marketed by DCA/Crosstalk Communications.

Subjects
Computers

Audience
Crosstalk users

Content Summary
The libraries include information on Crosstalk, Crossfax, Remote2, XTALK Communicator, client/server, and utilities.

See Also
Telecommunications, PC Vendor Forums

User Guide
☑	Windows	☐	VMS
☑	DOS	☑	UNIX
☑	Macintosh	☐	OS/2
☐	Terminal Emulation	☐	Other platform

Cost
☐	Unknown	☐	Premium ($)
☐	Basic	☐	Executive w/$
☑	Extended		

Activity Level

Address
GO: **XTALK**

CSI Forth Net Forum

Description
The Forth Forum supports the Forth language in general, as well as CSI Forth products.

Subjects
Computer Programming, Computers

Audience
Forth programmers

Content Summary
The libraries include information on Forth, Programming, MOPS, MacForth Plus, CSI Hardware, and users groups.

See Also
Programming

User Guide
☑	Windows	☐	VMS
☑	DOS	☑	UNIX
☑	Macintosh	☐	OS/2
☐	Terminal Emulation	☐	Other platform

Cost
☐	Unknown	☐	Premium ($)
☐	Basic	☐	Executive w/$
☑	Extended		

Activity Level

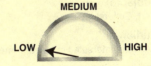

Address
GO: **FORTH**

CTOS/Pathway Forum

Description
The forum supports users of the UniSys CTOS Client/Server Operating System, and the Pathway series of Client/Server products and services.

Subjects
Computers, Networking

Audience
CTOS users

Content Summary
The libraries include information on CTOS product information, tips and tricks, shareware, developers, networking, and client/server topics.

See Also
Database, LAN

User Guide
- ☑ Windows
- ☑ DOS
- ☐ Macintosh
- ☐ Terminal Emulation
- ☐ VMS
- ☐ UNIX
- ☐ OS/2
- ☐ Other platform

Cost
- ☐ Unknown
- ☐ Basic
- ☑ Extended
- ☐ Premium ($)
- ☐ Executive w/$

Activity Level

Address
GO: **CTOS**

CULTURE

African American Art and Culture Forum

Description
This forum gives you the opportunity to experience the culture and art of African Americans. You can discuss current events and cultural issues.

Subjects
Art, Cultural Issues

Audience
Anyone interested in African American culture

Content Summary
Arts & Artists, History & Biography, Books & Writers, Cuisine, Film, Theatre/Dance, Music & Musicians, Geneaology, Travel, Education

See Also
Issues

User Guide
- ☑ Windows
- ☑ DOS
- ☑ Macintosh
- ☐ Terminal Emulation
- ☐ VMS
- ☐ UNIX
- ☐ OS/2
- ☐ Other platform

Cost
- ☐ Unknown
- ☐ Basic
- ☑ Extended
- ☐ Premium ($)
- ☐ Executive w/$

Activity Level

Address
GO: **AFRO**

CURRENT EVENTS

Global Crisis Forum

Description
This forum is devoted to the past, present, and future crises around the world, such as the Balkans, the former USSR, and other hot spots around the globe.

Subjects
Current Events, Global News, International Politics, Modern History, World View

Audience
Military historians, historians, general public, activists, writers, journalists

Content Summary
Because the world changes and some hot spots become cold spots and cold spots become hot spots, the library and message sections in this forum change often. Some of the recent hot spots on the forum have been the Asia/Pacific Rim, Africa, Russia, the Baltics, and the Americas. You'll also find HOTSPOT: areas denoted in the libraries and message areas for current topics. You'll find articles, theses, and other text files throughout the library sections for downloading.

See Also
Associated Press, Executive News Service, U.S. News & World Report

User Guide
- ☑ Windows
- ☑ DOS
- ☑ Macintosh
- ☐ Terminal Emulation
- ☑ VMS
- ☑ UNIX
- ☑ OS/2
- ☑ Other platform

Cost
- ☐ Unknown
- ☐ Basic
- ☑ Extended
- ☐ Premium ($)
- ☐ Executive w/$

Current Events

Activity Level

Address
GO: CRISIS

Issues Forum

Description
Devoted to current topics and issues, the Issues Forum discusses topics such as Afro-Americanism, parenting, human rights, and others.

Subjects
Current Events, Human Rights, Politics, Religion

Audience
General public

Content Summary
This special interest group is devoted to discussions of a wide variety of issues. Currently, there are sections for topics such as Afro-American issues, parenting issues, human rights, unexplained phenomena, men and women's issues, Asian-American issues, and others. The library and message sections include Culture & Society, Between the Sexes, Canadian Issues, Politics & Religion, and more. Look in Library 9, Rush H. Limbaugh, for summaries of Rush's show.

See Also
Entertainment Center, HSX Open Forum

User Guide
- ☑ Windows
- ☑ DOS
- ☑ Macintosh
- ☐ Terminal Emulation
- ☑ VMS
- ☑ UNIX
- ☑ OS/2
- ☑ Other platform

Cost
- ☐ Unknown
- ☐ Basic
- ☑ Extended
- ☐ Premium ($)
- ☐ Executive w/$

Activity Level

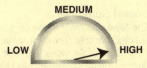

Address
GO: ISSUESFORUM

Reuters News Pictures Forum

Description
This forum contains the largest online source of news images from around the world. Also included are photographs of historical significance from the Bettman Archives.

Subjects
Current Events, News, Photographs

Audience
News enthusiasts, photographers

Content Summary
Photographs of interest to the United States, World, entertainment industry, and sports are featured. Note that photographs are protected by U.S. and International copyrights and are for personal use only.

See Also
AP Sports Forum, Associated Press Online Forum, Detroit Free Press

User Guide
- ☑ Windows
- ☑ DOS
- ☑ Macintosh
- ☐ Terminal Emulation
- ☑ VMS
- ☑ UNIX
- ☑ OS/2
- ☐ Other platform

Cost
- ☐ Unknown
- ☐ Basic
- ☑ Extended
- ☐ Premium ($)
- ☐ Executive w/$

Activity Level

UNKNOWN

Address
GO: NEWSPI

National Public Radio (NPR)

Description
Join with other CompuServe members as they listen to the *Talk of the Nation* radio program and share their comments with each other.

Subjects
Current Issues, General Issues

Audience
General public

Content Summary
Talk of the Nation radio program conferences are held every weekday from 2:00 p.m. till 4:00 p.m. EST in conference room 2 of the Issues Forum (GO ISSUES).

See Also
Issues Forum

User Guide
- ☑ Windows
- ☑ DOS
- ☑ Macintosh
- ☐ Terminal Emulation
- ☑ VMS
- ☑ UNIX
- ☐ OS/2
- ☐ Other platform

Cost
- ☐ Unknown
- ☑ Basic
- ☐ Extended
- ☐ Premium ($)
- ☐ Executive w/$

Current Events – Current Issues

Activity Level: UNKNOWN (LOW / MEDIUM / HIGH)

Address
GO: **NPR**

News Source USA

Description
News Source USA is a comprehensive collection of major U.S. magazines, newspapers, and special features to keep you up-to-date and informed about world events.

Subjects
News, Current Issues, Databases

Audience
General public

Content Summary
From the main menu, you can pick What is NEWS SOURCE USA, What's Available in NEWS SOURCE USA, Search/Scan Guidelines, Pricing Information, and Access NEWS SOURCE USA. See the Pricing Information for specific prices on searching this database.

See Also
IQUEST

User Guide
- ☑ Windows
- ☑ DOS
- ☑ Macintosh
- ☐ Terminal Emulation
- ☑ VMS
- ☑ UNIX
- ☐ OS/2
- ☐ Other platform

Cost
- ☐ Unknown
- ☐ Basic
- ☐ Extended
- ☑ Premium ($)
- ☐ Executive w/$

Activity Level: UNKNOWN (LOW / MEDIUM / HIGH)

Address
GO: **NEWSLIB**

NewsGrid

Description
NewsGrid captures thousands of stories from the world's leading news wire services and provides them to you online. You can read U.S. and world news headlines, business news headlines, regular market and economic updates, and hundreds of general news stories.

Subjects
News, Current Issues, Database

Audience
General public

Content Summary
From the main menu, you can select US/World Headline News, US Business Headline News, World Business Headline News, Market Update, Search by Keyword, and How To Use NewsGrid.

See Also
IQUEST

User Guide
- ☐ Windows
- ☐ DOS
- ☐ Macintosh
- ☑ Terminal Emulation
- ☐ VMS
- ☐ UNIX
- ☐ OS/2
- ☐ Other platform

Cost
- ☐ Unknown
- ☐ Basic
- ☑ Extended
- ☐ Premium ($)
- ☐ Executive w/$

Activity Level: UNKNOWN (LOW / MEDIUM / HIGH)

Address
GO: **NEWSGRID**

NewsNet

Description
NewsNet is the "Premier Current Awareness Resource." You can find more than 500 business newsletters and other important news services online in this service.

Subjects
Database, News, Current Issues

Audience
General public

Content Summary
The NewsNet main menu contains the following options: What Is NewsNet, What's Online—Take a Tour, Special Services*—Credit reports, stock quotes, airline schedules, and travel information, NewsFlash—The exclusive electronic clipping service, Using NewsNet, How Much Does NewsNet Cost, and Ask NewsNet. Be sure to read the pricing information before you use this service. The surcharges may be a little steep for general browsing.

See Also
IQUEST, News-A-Tron

Current Issues

User Guide
- ☑ Windows
- ☑ DOS
- ☑ Macintosh
- ☐ Terminal Emulation
- ☑ VMS
- ☑ UNIX
- ☐ OS/2
- ☐ Other platform

Cost
- ☐ Unknown
- ☐ Basic
- ☐ Extended
- ☑ Premium ($)
- ☐ Executive w/$

Activity Level

Address
GO: **NN**

Newspaper Archives

Description
Newspaper Archives gives you access to over 55 full-text U.S. and U.K. newspapers, including the ability to search each newspaper on any topic of interest and over a specific date range.

Subjects
News, Current Issues

Audience
General public

Content Summary
From the Newspaper Archives main menu, you can select Description, Search Guidelines, Pricing Information, Hours of Availability, Software Requirements, and Access Newspaper Archives. This service is not available on Sundays, between 2:00 a.m. and 10:00 a.m. Pacific Standard time. Be sure you understand the specific pricing information before you start your search.

See Also
IQUEST, NewsGrid, News-A-Tron

User Guide
- ☑ Windows
- ☑ DOS
- ☑ Macintosh
- ☐ Terminal Emulation
- ☑ VMS
- ☑ UNIX
- ☐ OS/2
- ☐ Other platform

Cost
- ☐ Unknown
- ☐ Basic
- ☐ Extended
- ☑ Premium ($)
- ☐ Executive w/$

Activity Level

Address
GO: **NEWSARCHIVE**

U.S. News & World Report

Description
This is an online version of the current *U.S. News & World Report* magazine, including text and pictures.

Subjects
News, World Reports, Business summaries, Science, Cover Stories

Audience
General users

Content Summary
This online magazine offers the full text of every issue of *U.S. News & World Report*.

See Also
News, Business

User Guide
- ☑ Windows
- ☑ DOS
- ☐ Macintosh
- ☐ Terminal Emulation
- ☐ VMS
- ☐ UNIX
- ☐ OS/2
- ☐ Other platform

Cost
- ☐ Unknown
- ☐ Basic
- ☑ Extended
- ☐ Premium ($)
- ☐ Executive w/$

Activity Level

Address
GO: **USNEWS**

U.S. News Forum

Description
Interact with the writers and editors of *U.S. News & World Report* in this forum.

Subjects
Background information on current events, discussions of current events

Audience
General Public

Content Summary
This forum enables members to send an online letter to the editor to the staff of *U.S. News & World Reports*. Also included are information about news articles appearing in the magazine.

See Also
News, Business

User Guide
- ☑ Windows
- ☑ DOS
- ☐ Macintosh
- ☐ Terminal Emulation
- ☐ VMS
- ☐ UNIX
- ☐ OS/2
- ☐ Other platform

Current Issues

Cost
- ☐ Unknown
- ☐ Basic
- ☑ Extended
- ☐ Premium ($)
- ☐ Executive w/$

Activity Level: MEDIUM (LOW—HIGH)

Address
GO: **USNFORUM**

U. S. News Women's Forum

Description
This forum is sponsored by *U.S. News*, covering women's issues.

Subjects
Working Women, Politics, Culture, Religion, Violence, Technology, Relationships, Population, Health, Children, Sexuality

Audience
All interested in womens topics

Content Summary
This forum includes a wide range of women's topics from information on families to job opportunities.

See Also
Women, Family

User Guide
- ☑ Windows
- ☑ DOS
- ☐ Macintosh
- ☐ Terminal Emulation
- ☐ VMS
- ☐ UNIX
- ☐ OS/2
- ☐ Other platform

Cost
- ☐ Unknown
- ☐ Basic
- ☑ Extended
- ☐ Premium ($)
- ☐ Executive w/$

Activity Level: MEDIUM (LOW—HIGH)

Address
GO: **WOMEN**

UK News Clips

Description
Realtime United Kingdom news, sports, and weather, provided by the PA News service.

Subjects
General, Financial, Sports, TV & Radio, Parliamentary, Law & Royal News

Audience
General public

Contents Summary
The libraries include the following topics: financial, political, economic, international news. Stories are held for 24 hours.

See Also
UK Newspaper Library

User Guide
- ☑ Windows
- ☑ DOS
- ☐ Macintosh
- ☐ Terminal Emulation
- ☐ VMS
- ☐ UNIX
- ☐ OS/2
- ☐ Other platform

Cost
- ☐ Unknown
- ☐ Basic
- ☑ Extended
- ☐ Premium ($)
- ☐ Executive w/$

Activity Level: UNKNOWN (LOW—MEDIUM—HIGH)

Address
GO: **UKNEWS**

UK Newspaper Library

Description
This is a database containing selected newspaper articles from the United Kingdom.

Subjects
Articles from UK Newspapers in a database

Audience
General public

Content Summary
This database offers articles from the *Daily Telegraph* and *Sunday Telegraph*, *The European*, *The Financial Times*, *The Guardian*, *The Times* and *Sunday Times*.

See Also
UK News Clips

User Guide
- ☑ Windows
- ☑ DOS
- ☐ Macintosh
- ☐ Terminal Emulation
- ☐ VMS
- ☐ UNIX
- ☐ OS/2
- ☐ Other platform

Cost
- ☐ Unknown
- ☐ Basic
- ☐ Extended
- ☐ Premium ($)
- ☑ Executive w/$

Activity Level: UNKNOWN (LOW—MEDIUM—HIGH)

Address
GO: **UKPAPERS**

Current Issues – Cyber Forum

White House Forum

Description
This independent political forum discusses what's happening in the USA White House. The libraries contain only files provided by official White House sources.

Subjects
Current Issues

Audience
General public

Content Summary
The libraries include information on the economy, the trade deficit, defense, education, social security, and international affairs.

See Also
Politics in America

User Guide
- [x] Windows
- [x] DOS
- [x] Macintosh
- [ ] Terminal Emulation
- [x] VMS
- [x] UNIX
- [x] OS/2
- [ ] Other platform

Cost
- [ ] Unknown
- [ ] Basic
- [x] Extended
- [ ] Premium ($)
- [ ] Executive w/$

Activity Level
MEDIUM (HIGH)

Address
GO: **WHITEHOUSE**

Detroit Free Press Store

Description
In this area, you can subscribe to the *Detroit Free Press* newspaper, order Detroit Free Press books, or leave a message for customer service.

Subjects
Customer Service, Subscriptions, Journalism

Audience
Anyone interested in the *Detroit Free Press* newspaper

Content Summary
The Store has areas in which you can shop for Detroit Free Press books, subscribe to the *Detroit Free Press* newspaper (including international subscriptions), and leave a message for customer service. If you want more information about this award-winning newspaper, see the "What is the Detroit Free Press?" area (number 4).

See Also
Detroit Free Press

User Guide
- [x] Windows
- [x] DOS
- [x] Macintosh
- [ ] Terminal Emulation
- [x] VMS
- [x] UNIX
- [x] OS/2
- [ ] Other platform

Cost
- [ ] Unknown
- [x] Basic
- [ ] Extended
- [ ] Premium ($)
- [ ] Executive w/$

Activity Level
UNKNOWN

Address
GO: **DFM-1**

Cyber Forum

The future of computing is the subject of the Cyber Forum, from Virtual Reality to nanotechnology.

Subjects
Computers, Virtual Reality

Audience
Computer users

Content Summary
The libraries include virtual reality, gaming, entertainment, CyberArts, robotics, CyberLit, news, art, and *PCVR* magazine.

See Also
Speak Easy Forum

User Guide
- [x] Windows
- [x] DOS
- [x] Macintosh
- [ ] Terminal Emulation
- [ ] VMS
- [x] UNIX
- [ ] OS/2
- [x] Other platform

Cost
- [ ] Unknown
- [ ] Basic
- [x] Extended
- [ ] Premium ($)
- [ ] Executive w/$

Activity Level
MEDIUM (HIGH)

Address
GO: **CYBERFORUM**

D

D&B Dun's Canadian Market Identifiers

Description
The Canadian Dun's Market Identifiers database contains directory information on about 350,000 Canadian companies. You can see company name, address, and telephone number. You also can get sales figures, number of employees, and executive's names.

Subjects
Canadian Company Profiles, Business, Finance, Dun and Bradstreet

Audience
Accounting persons, businesspersons, executives, investors, journalists, management, researchers

Content Summary
Depending on the company listing, you might or might not see all the information detailed in the Description area above. To retrieve records, enter the company name, geographic location, product or service, number of employees, or sales as your search criteria. For help on searching, select Choice 2, "Search Guidelines," from the main menu. The cost of this service is as follows:

- Search (retrieves up to 5 names): $7.50
- Additional names (in groups of 5): $7.50
- Full reference (selected from the names): $7.50

In addition to connect-time charges, you are charged $1.00 for a search that retrieves no titles.

See Also
Company Information, Corporate Affiliations, D&B Dun's Electronic Business Directory, D&B Dun's Market Identifiers, Financial Forums, Investors' Forum, Tenderlink, TRW Business Profiles

User Guide
- [✓] Windows
- [✓] DOS
- [✓] Macintosh
- [ ] Terminal Emulation
- [✓] VMS
- [✓] UNIX
- [✓] OS/2
- [✓] Other platform

Cost
- [ ] Unknown
- [ ] Basic
- [ ] Extended
- [✓] Premium ($)
- [ ] Executive w/$

Activity Level

Address
GO: **DBCAN**

D&B Dun's Electronic Business Directory

Description
You can obtain a directory of over 8.5 million U.S. public and private businesses and professionals using this Dun and Bradstreet service. Available information includes name, address, phone number, type of business, parent company, industry, the SIC code, number of employees, and the population of the city in which the business resides.

Subjects
Business, Finance, Investment, Dun and Bradstreet

Audience
Accounting persons, businesspersons, executives, investors, journalists, management, researchers

Content Summary
To search, select Choice 5, "Access Dun's Electronic Business Directory," from the main menu. Next, select the criterion for your search, such as company name or product or service; enter a name, word, or phrase that describes the company or product; and follow the on-screen instructions. See Choice 7, "Search Guidelines," for more help. The cost of this service is as follows:

- Search (retrieves up to 5 names): $7.50
- Additional names (in groups of 5): $7.50

In addition to connect-time charges, you are charged $1.00 for a search that retrieves no titles.

See Also
Company Information, Corporate Affiliations, D&B Dun's Canadian Market Identifiers, D&B Dun's Market Identifiers, Financial Forums, Investors' Forum, Tenderlink, TRW Business Profiles

User Guide
- [✓] Windows
- [✓] DOS
- [✓] Macintosh
- [ ] Terminal Emulation
- [✓] VMS
- [✓] UNIX
- [✓] OS/2
- [✓] Other platform

Cost
- [ ] Unknown
- [ ] Basic
- [ ] Extended
- [✓] Premium ($)
- [ ] Executive w/$

Activity Level

Address
GO: **DYP** or **DUNSEBD**

D&B Dun's Market Identifiers

Description
With this service, you can search three of Dun and Bradstreet's directories of business information, including information on over 6.7 million U.S. public and private businesses that have over $1 million in sales or more than five employees, information on over 350,000 Canadian companies, and information on over 2.1 million public, private, and government-controlled international companies.

Subjects
Business, Finance, Investment, Dun and Bradstreet

Audience
Accounting persons, businesspersons, executives, investors, management, researchers

Content Summary
When you perform a search, you can get the company name, address, telephone number, sales figures, number of employees, parent company, and names of executives. The price of this service is as follows:

- Search (retrieves up to 5 names): $7.50
- Additional names (in groups of 5): $7.50
- Full reference (selected from the names): $7.50

In addition to connect-time charges, you are charged $1.00 for a search that retrieves no titles.

See Also
Company Information, Corporate Affiliations, D&B Dun's Canadian Market Identifiers, Financial Forums, Investors' Forum, Tenderlink, TRW Business Profiles

User Guide
- ☑ Windows
- ☑ DOS
- ☑ Macintosh
- ☐ Terminal Emulation
- ☑ VMS
- ☑ UNIX
- ☑ OS/2
- ☑ Other platform

Cost
- ☐ Unknown
- ☐ Basic
- ☐ Extended
- ☑ Premium ($)
- ☐ Executive w/$

Activity Level

Address
GO: **DUNS** or **DMI**

Da Vinci Forum

Description
This forum provides support for Da Vinci products and messaging in general.

Subjects
Computers

Audience
Computer users, MIS people

Content Summary
This forum contains library and message sections that discuss electronic mail, names services, Coordinator, and more. You also can find demos of products in this forum.

See Also
Novell Forums, IBM Forums, Microsoft Forums

User Guide
- ☑ Windows
- ☑ DOS
- ☐ Macintosh
- ☐ Terminal Emulation
- ☐ VMS
- ☐ UNIX
- ☐ OS/2
- ☑ Other platform

Cost
- ☐ Unknown
- ☐ Basic
- ☑ Extended
- ☐ Premium ($)
- ☐ Executive w/$

Activity Level

Address
GO: **DAVINCI**

Data Access Corp. Forum

Description
This forum provides support for Data Access software development tools and products.

Subjects
Computers

Audience
Computer users, computer programmers

Content Summary
The library and message sections contain several areas, including DataFlex, FlexQL/WinQL, Office Works, C Source, API, and more.

See Also
Microsoft Developers Forum

User Guide
- ☑ Windows
- ☑ DOS
- ☐ Macintosh
- ☐ Terminal Emulation
- ☐ VMS
- ☐ UNIX
- ☐ OS/2
- ☑ Other platform

Cost
- ☐ Unknown
- ☐ Basic
- ☑ Extended
- ☐ Premium ($)
- ☐ Executive w/$

Data Access Corp. Forum – Database Publishing

Activity Level

Address
GO: **DACCESS**

DATABASE CONSULTANTS

Powersoft Forum

Description
This forum provides technical assistance and a general discussion of Powersoft and WATCOM Corporation products.

Subjects
Computers, Database Consultants

Audience
Computer professionals, database professionals, Powersoft users

Content Summary
This forum's libraries and message areas contain information about PowerBuilder, PowerMaker, PowerViewer, PowerBuilder Desktop, WATCOM SQL, WATCOM C/C++, WATCOM VX-REXX, and WATCOM Fortran 77. Also included are bug fixes for products, user group lists, third-party vendors, and instructions on how to connect with other software.

See Also
Client Server Computing Forum

User Guide
- ☑ Windows
- ☑ DOS
- ☐ Macintosh
- ☐ Terminal Emulation
- ☐ VMS
- ☐ UNIX
- ☐ OS/2
- ☐ Other platform

Cost
- ☐ Unknown
- ☐ Basic
- ☑ Extended
- ☐ Premium ($)
- ☐ Executive w/$

Activity Level

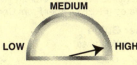

Address
GO: **POWERSOFT**

DATABASE MANAGEMENT

Microsoft SQL Server Forum

Description
This forum is designed as an area to exchange information, tips, and techniques concerning Microsoft SQL products.

Subjects
Computers, Database Management

Audience
Management information specialists, computer programmers, database managers

Content Summary
The SQL Server Forum has several libraries that contain updates, libraries, and other supporting files for the SQL developer. Some of the libraries include MS SQL Server for Windows NT, MS SQL Server for OS/2, MS Program Toolkits, Non-MS SQL Front Ends, and others.

See Also
Microsoft Languages Forum, Microsoft Press (FREE), MS WinNT SNA Forum

User Guide
- ☑ Windows
- ☑ DOS
- ☐ Macintosh
- ☐ Terminal Emulation
- ☐ VMS
- ☐ UNIX
- ☑ OS/2
- ☑ Other platform

Cost
- ☐ Unknown
- ☐ Basic
- ☑ Extended
- ☐ Premium ($)
- ☐ Executive w/$

Activity Level

Address
GO: **MSSQL**

DATABASE PUBLISHING

PRC Publishing

Description
PRC's Database Publishing Services creates customized publications that reflect the specific information needs of their audiences. They are a leading publisher of database directories of all types.

Database Publishing – Databases

Subjects
Catalogs, Computer Graphics, Database Publishing

Audience
Graphics professionals, publishers

Content Summary
PRC specializes in the combination of digital images and text data; in high volumes and at high speeds; and in customized layouts and electronic composition.

See Also
Graphics Forum

User Guide
- ☑ Windows
- ☑ DOS
- ☑ Macintosh
- ☐ Terminal Emulation
- ☑ VMS
- ☑ UNIX
- ☑ OS/2
- ☐ Other platform

Cost
- ☐ Unknown
- ☑ Basic
- ☐ Extended
- ☐ Premium ($)
- ☐ Executive w/$

Activity Level

Address
GO: **PRC**

DATABASES

Computer Library Online

Description
A family of information retrieval services designed to provide a complete reference and assistance resource for computer users.

Subjects
Computers, Databases

Audience
Computer users

Content Summary
Libraries include Computer Database Plus, Computer Buyers' Guide, Support on Site, articles, journals, recommendations, advice, and updates on products.

See Also
IBM File Finder

User Guide
- ☑ Windows
- ☑ DOS
- ☑ Macintosh
- ☐ Terminal Emulation
- ☐ VMS
- ☑ UNIX
- ☐ OS/2
- ☑ Other platform

Cost
- ☐ Unknown
- ☐ Basic
- ☐ Extended
- ☑ Premium ($)
- ☐ Executive w/$

Activity Level

Address
GO: **COMPLIB**

Executive Service Option

Description
This is a CompuServe service that enables you to access several value-added services, including databases, merchandise, and other online items.

Subjects
Databases, Financial News

Audience
General Public

Content Summary
When you select this option, you can access exclusive databases, including Company Analyzer, Disclosure II, Executive News Service, SuperSite, Institutional Broker's Estimate System, Securities Screening, Return Analysis, and Company Screening. You also get volume discounts on information retrieval from selected financial databases, a six-month storage period (rather than the standard 30 days) for personal files without charge, and a ten percent discount on most CompuServe products, excluding sale items. When you join the Executive Service Option, you are subject to a $10 monthly minimum usage level. Your monthly $8.95 CompuServe basic membership (Standard Pricing Plan) is applied to this minimum. All products associated with the Executive Service Option are considered wide-mode products. This means they display best on screens that allow widths of 80 columns.

See Also
CompuServe Help Forum (FREE), CompuServe Rates (FREE), Order From CompuServe (FREE)

User Guide
- ☑ Windows
- ☑ DOS
- ☑ Macintosh
- ☐ Terminal Emulation
- ☑ VMS
- ☑ UNIX
- ☑ OS/2
- ☑ Other platform

Cost
- ☐ Unknown
- ☐ Basic
- ☐ Extended
- ☑ Premium ($)
- ☐ Executive w/$

Databases

Global Report

Description
This is Citibank's online information resource database, where you can find data on a number of large corporations worldwide.

Subjects
Business, Databases, Financial News

Audience
Financial analysts, accountants, business and financial researchers

Content Summary
Launched by Citibank in 1986, Global Report has become the primary information resource for a number of large corporations worldwide because it integrates and organizes news and financial data from well-respected sources, allowing for quick and easy information retrieval. For pricing information, see the Pricing/Sample Reports option on the Global Report main menu. If you're new to this service, be sure to choose the Important Pages option on the main menu to see a list of important searching criteria.

See Also
Dun's Elect Business Dir, TRW Bus. Credit Reports

User Guide
- ☑ Windows
- ☑ DOS
- ☑ Macintosh
- ☐ Terminal Emulation
- ☑ VMS
- ☑ UNIX
- ☑ OS/2
- ☑ Other platform

Cost
- ☐ Unknown
- ☐ Basic
- ☐ Extended
- ☑ Premium ($)
- ☐ Executive w/$

Activity Level

Address
GO: **GLOREP**

IBM DB2 Database Forum

Description
This forum is designed for people interested in or currently using the DB2/2, DB2/6000, DB2 Clients, DB2/VSE&VM (SQL/DS), and DB2/MVS relational database products, as well as Visualizer and IMS products.

Subjects
Computers, Databases, IBM

Audience
Management information specialists, computer users, database managers

Content Summary
You can find the following libraries in this forum: DB2/2, DB2/6000, DB2/VSE&VM, DB2/MVS, DB2 Clients, Visualizer, IMS Family, and Open Forum.

See Also
Client Server Computing Forum

User Guide
- ☐ Windows
- ☑ DOS
- ☐ Macintosh
- ☐ Terminal Emulation
- ☐ VMS
- ☑ UNIX
- ☑ OS/2
- ☑ Other platform

Cost
- ☐ Unknown
- ☐ Basic
- ☑ Extended
- ☐ Premium ($)
- ☐ Executive w/$

Activity Level
MEDIUM / LOW ← / HIGH

Address
GO: **IBMDB2**

IBM File Finder

Description
If it's on CompuServe and in a computer-related forum, you should be able to find it with this service. This searchable database is useful if you are looking for a number of files that are in several known or unknown forums.

Subjects
Computers, Databases, IBM PCs

Audience
Computer users, management information specialists

Content Summary
With File Finder, you can use seven common search criteria for finding the location of a desired file or files. You can search by topic, file submission date, forum name, file type, file extension, file name, or submitter's User ID. File descriptions, forum, and library location are displayed for the matched files, giving instant information on where to find a most wanted file.

See Also
MS Software Library

Databases

User Guide
- ☑ Windows
- ☑ DOS
- ☑ Macintosh
- ☐ Terminal Emulation
- ☐ VMS
- ☑ UNIX
- ☑ OS/2
- ☑ Other platform

Cost
- ☐ Unknown
- ☐ Basic
- ☑ Extended
- ☐ Premium ($)
- ☐ Executive w/$

Activity Level
UNKNOWN (LOW–MEDIUM–HIGH)

Address
GO: **IBMFF**

InvesText

Description
This database has full-text research reports from the past two years compiled by over 50 Wall Street and other brokerage houses and research firms.

Subjects
Databases, Investments

Audience
Analysts, financial analysts, business analysts

Content Summary
This database provides the full-text of company and industry research reports compiled during the most recent two years by analysts in more than 50 Wall Street, regional, and international brokerage houses and research firms. Individual company reports are available for more than 8,200 U.S. public companies and over 2,300 publicly held foreign companies. Company reports include historical information, such as company profiles, revenues, earnings and other financial operating results, and stock performance. The reports can also include the brokerage's recommendations, with analysis and forecasts of the company's future performance. See the Pricing Information option on the InvesText main menu for the price of searches.

See Also
Dun's Canadian Mkt. Ident($), Dun's Elect Business Dir($), Dun's Market Identifiers($), E*TRADE Securities, Investors Forum

User Guide
- ☑ Windows
- ☑ DOS
- ☑ Macintosh
- ☐ Terminal Emulation
- ☑ VMS
- ☑ UNIX
- ☑ OS/2
- ☑ Other platform

Cost
- ☐ Unknown
- ☐ Basic
- ☐ Extended
- ☐ Premium ($)
- ☑ Executive w/$

Activity Level
UNKNOWN (LOW–MEDIUM–HIGH)

Address
GO: **INVTEXT**

IQuest

Description
With access to over 800 databases on topics such as accounting, aerospace, computers, and more, IQuest is one of the largest research services in the world.

Subjects
Databases, Information Retrieval, Research

Audience
General public, librarians, researchers

Content Summary
CompuServe members have seamless interaction with the IQuest reference and information service. IQuest provides access to over 800 databases, including business, government, research, news, popular entertainment, and sports. IQuest is a menu-based service that prompts you for your information, and then searches for you. Accessing databases from information suppliers such as Dialog Information Services, Inc., BRS Online Products, NewsNet, Inc., and Data-Star, IQuest executes the search and displays the results to you. IQuest can be expensive if you don't think out your searches beforehand, so be sure to read the Pricing Information on the main menu before you ask for too much.

See Also
Dun's Market Identifiers($), Executive News Service($), TRW Bus. Credit Reports($), Official Airline Guide EE($)

User Guide
- ☑ Windows
- ☑ DOS
- ☑ Macintosh
- ☐ Terminal Emulation
- ☑ VMS
- ☑ UNIX
- ☑ OS/2
- ☑ Other platform

Cost
- ☐ Unknown
- ☐ Basic
- ☐ Extended
- ☐ Premium ($)
- ☑ Executive w/$

Activity Level
MEDIUM–HIGH

Address
GO: **IQUEST**

Knowledge Index

Description
Access over 100 popular databases from the Knowledge Index service.

Subjects
Database, General Interest, Research

Audience
General interest, general public, researchers

Content Summary
Knowledge Index is a service that gives you evening and weekend access to over 100 popular full-text and bibliographic databases at reduced rates. With Knowledge Index, you can access over 50,000 journals on a wide variety of topics. Many of the Knowledge Index databases have the complete text of articles available online. You can order a hard-copy printout of those that have only a citation available. The price is $.40 per minute ($24 per hour) and includes CompuServe standard connect rates up to and including 9600 Baud.

See Also
IQuest

User Guide
- [x] Windows
- [x] DOS
- [x] Macintosh
- [ ] Terminal Emulation
- [x] VMS
- [x] UNIX
- [x] OS/2
- [ ] Other platform

Cost
- [ ] Unknown
- [ ] Basic
- [ ] Extended
- [x] Premium ($)
- [ ] Executive w/$

Activity Level

Address
GO: **KI**

Microsoft Access Forum

Description
This forum is dedicated to the Microsoft Access database product.

Subjects
Computers, Databases, Microsoft Corp.

Audience
Computer users, database managers

Content Summary
Find out about designing forms, reports, queries, and other related questions. The library and message sections include Getting Started, Tables/DB Design, Queries, Forms, Import/Export, Multi-User Networks, Interop/OLE/DDE, and more.

See Also
MS SQL Server Forum, MS Applications Forum, Microsoft Knowledge Base

User Guide
- [x] Windows
- [ ] DOS
- [ ] Macintosh
- [ ] Terminal Emulation
- [ ] VMS
- [ ] UNIX
- [ ] OS/2
- [ ] Other platform

Cost
- [ ] Unknown
- [ ] Basic
- [x] Extended
- [ ] Premium ($)
- [ ] Executive w/$

Activity Level

Address
GO: **MSACCESS**

Microsoft Fox Users Forum

Description
This forum is designed as an area to exchange information, tips, and techniques concerning Microsoft Fox products.

Subjects
Computers, Databases, Microsoft Corp.

Audience
Computer system designers, database managers

Content Summary
Some of the areas in this forum include FOXGANG, Want Ads, Archive, and 3rd Party Products. Watch the message sections for discussions on development issues, Fox user groups, and conventions.

See Also
MS TechNet Forum, Microsoft Connection

User Guide
- [x] Windows
- [x] DOS
- [x] Macintosh
- [ ] Terminal Emulation
- [ ] VMS
- [ ] UNIX
- [ ] OS/2
- [ ] Other platform

Cost
- [ ] Unknown
- [ ] Basic
- [x] Extended
- [ ] Premium ($)
- [ ] Executive w/$

Activity Level MEDIUM

Address
GO: **FOXUSER**

Databases

News Source USA

Description
News Source USA is a comprehensive collection of major U.S. magazines, newspapers, and special features to keep you up-to-date and informed about world events.

Subjects
News, Current Issues, Databases

Audience
General public

Content Summary
From the main menu, you can pick What is NEWS SOURCE USA, What's Available in NEWS SOURCE USA, Search/Scan Guidelines, Pricing Information, and Access NEWS SOURCE USA. See the Pricing Information for specific prices on searching this database.

See Also
IQuest

User Guide
- [✓] Windows
- [✓] DOS
- [✓] Macintosh
- [ ] Terminal Emulation
- [✓] VMS
- [✓] UNIX
- [ ] OS/2
- [ ] Other platform

Cost
- [ ] Unknown
- [ ] Basic
- [ ] Extended
- [✓] Premium ($)
- [ ] Executive w/$

Activity Level

Address
GO: **NEWSLIB**

NewsGrid

Description
NewsGrid captures thousands of stories from the world's leading news wire services and provides them to you online. You can read U.S. and world news headlines, business news headlines, regular market and economic updates, and hundreds of general news stories.

Subjects
News, Current Issues, Database

Audience
General public

Content Summary
From the main menu, you can select US/World Headline News, US Business Headline News, World Business Headline News, Market Update, Search by Keyword, and How To Use NewsGrid.

See Also
IQuest

User Guide
- [ ] Windows
- [ ] DOS
- [ ] Macintosh
- [✓] Terminal Emulation
- [ ] VMS
- [ ] UNIX
- [ ] OS/2
- [ ] Other platform

Cost
- [ ] Unknown
- [ ] Basic
- [✓] Extended
- [ ] Premium ($)
- [ ] Executive w/$

Activity Level

Address
GO: **NEWSGRID**

NewsNet

Description
NewsNet is the "Premier Current Awareness Resource." You can find more than 500 business newsletters and other important news services online in this service.

Subjects
Database, News, Current Issues

Audience
General public

Content Summary
The NewsNet main menu contains the following options: What Is NewsNet, What's Online—Take a Tour, Special Services*—Credit reports, stock quotes, airline schedules, and travel information, NewsFlash—The exclusive electronic clipping service, Using NewsNet, How Much Does NewsNet Cost, and Ask NewsNet. Be sure to read the pricing information before you use this service. The surcharges may be a little steep for general browsing.

See Also
IQuest, News-A-Tron

User Guide
- [✓] Windows
- [✓] DOS
- [✓] Macintosh
- [ ] Terminal Emulation
- [✓] VMS
- [✓] UNIX
- [ ] OS/2
- [ ] Other platform

Cost
- [ ] Unknown
- [ ] Basic
- [ ] Extended
- [✓] Premium ($)
- [ ] Executive w/$

Databases

Activity Level

LOW — UNKNOWN (MEDIUM) — HIGH

Address
GO: NN

Novell Technical Bulletin Database

Description
The Technical Bulletin Database enables you to search for bulletins and articles by title, keywords, technical bulletin number, or by Novell products number.

Subjects
Computers, Novell Inc., Database, Computer Networking

Audience
MIS people, Computer users

Content Summary
When you use this terminal emulation database, you must know the division prefix for the technical bulletin. The prefixes are as follows: NetWare Products Division (NPD), Communication Product Division (CPD), and Enhanced Products Division (EPD). For more information on searching criteria, be sure to read the Instructions for Searching the Technical Bulletins.

See Also
Novell Information Forum, Novell Files Database, Novell Library Forum

User Guide
- ☐ Windows
- ☐ DOS
- ☐ Macintosh
- ☑ Terminal Emulation
- ☐ VMS
- ☐ UNIX
- ☐ OS/2
- ☐ Other platform

Cost
- ☐ Unknown
- ☐ Basic
- ☑ Extended
- ☐ Premium ($)
- ☐ Executive w/$

Activity Level

LOW — UNKNOWN (MEDIUM) — HIGH

Address
GO: NTB

Standard Indus. Class.

Description
This is a database of SIC (industrial classification) codes, searchable by industry.

Subjects
Business, Databases

Audience
Researchers, businesspeople

Content Summary
This database provides industrial information to business professionals.

See Also
IQuest Business Management

User Guide
- ☑ Windows
- ☑ DOS
- ☑ Macintosh
- ☐ Terminal Emulation
- ☐ VMS
- ☑ UNIX
- ☐ OS/2
- ☑ Other platform

Cost
- ☐ Unknown
- ☐ Basic
- ☑ Extended
- ☐ Premium ($)
- ☐ Executive w/$

Activity Level

LOW — UNKNOWN (MEDIUM) — HIGH

Address
GO: SICCODE

State-County Demographics

Description
This database provides detailed summaries of the demographic makeup of states and counties in the U.S.

Subjects
Demographics, Statistics

Audience
Researchers, business people

Content Summary
This database contains demographic statistics on race, age, occupation, and further details of all the states and counties of the U.S.

See Also
SUPERSITE Demographics

User Guide
- ☑ Windows
- ☑ DOS
- ☑ Macintosh
- ☐ Terminal Emulation
- ☐ VMS
- ☑ UNIX
- ☐ OS/2
- ☑ Other platform

Cost
- ☐ Unknown
- ☐ Basic
- ☐ Extended
- ☑ Premium ($)
- ☐ Executive w/$

228
Databases

Activity Level

Address
GO: **DEMOGRAPHICS**

SUPERSITE Demographics

Description
This forum provides demographic reports for all of the United States, covering general demographics, income, housing, education, employment, and current and projected-year forecasts.

Subjects
Demographics, Market Research

Audience
Demographers, research analysts

Content Summary
This forum is available only to members who have the Executive Service Option. You obtain reports by indicating the type of geography you want to research, the geographic areas that form the market, and the reports you want.

See Also
State-County Demographics

User Guide
- [x] Windows
- [x] DOS
- [x] Macintosh
- [x] Terminal Emulation
- [x] VMS
- [x] UNIX
- [x] OS/2
- [x] Other platform

Cost
- [ ] Unknown
- [ ] Basic
- [ ] Extended
- [x] Premium ($)
- [ ] Executive w/$

Activity Level

Address
GO: **SUPERSITE**

Support On Site

Description
This database contains hints and helpful info on using some of the most popular software applications available today.

Subjects
Computers, Databases

Audience
Computer users

Content Summary
Libraries include technical information, user groups, SQL server, Sybase education, third-party products, and PC products.

See Also
Computer Training Forum

User Guide
- [x] Windows
- [x] DOS
- [x] Macintosh
- [ ] Terminal Emulation
- [ ] VMS
- [x] UNIX
- [ ] OS/2
- [x] Other platform

Cost
- [ ] Unknown
- [ ] Basic
- [x] Extended
- [ ] Premium ($)
- [ ] Executive w/$

Activity Level

(Unknown, Medium)

Address
GO: **ONSITE**

Thomas Register Online

Description
Database containing company info on almost 150,000 USA and Canadian manufacturers and service providers. Updated annually.

Subjects
Finance, Database

Audience
Financial analysts

Content Summary
Information for each entry includes company name, address, telephone number, and products or services offered.

User Guide
- [x] Windows
- [x] DOS
- [ ] Macintosh
- [ ] Terminal Emulation
- [ ] VMS
- [ ] UNIX
- [ ] OS/2
- [ ] Other platform

Cost
- [ ] Unknown
- [ ] Basic
- [ ] Extended
- [x] Premium ($)
- [ ] Executive w/$

Activity Level

(Unknown, Medium)

Address
GO: **THOMAS**

Databases – DEC Equipment

UK Company Library

Description
Database containing financial and other information on companies in the United Kingdom.

Subjects
Finance, Database

Audience
Financial analysts

Content Summary
This database enables members to research British companies for information on business standing, products or services offered, and address.

User Guide
- ☑ Windows
- ☑ DOS
- ☑ Macintosh
- ☐ Terminal Emulation
- ☑ VMS
- ☑ UNIX
- ☑ OS/2
- ☑ Other platform

Cost
- ☐ Unknown
- ☐ Basic
- ☑ Extended
- ☐ Premium ($)
- ☐ Executive w/$

Activity Level

Address
GO: **UKLIB**

DataEase International Forum

Description
This forum provides support for all DataEase International products and services.

Subjects
Computers

Audience
Computer users, MIS people

Content Summary
You can find information and discussions about DataEase DQL, Express of Windows, Client-Server, DataEase user groups, and more.

See Also
Client Server Computer Forum

User Guide
- ☑ Windows
- ☑ DOS
- ☐ Macintosh
- ☐ Terminal Emulation
- ☐ VMS
- ☐ UNIX
- ☐ OS/2
- ☐ Other platform

Cost
- ☐ Unknown
- ☐ Basic
- ☑ Extended
- ☐ Premium ($)
- ☐ Executive w/$

Activity Level

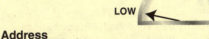

Address
GO: **DATAEASE**

Dataquest Online

Description
A private forum for Dataquest clients, or members of the Semiconductor Industry Association.

Subjects
Communications

Audience
MIS people

Content Summary
You can find information on technologies, communications, computers, document management, semiconductors, and various services.

See Also
Intel Forum

User Guide
- ☑ Windows
- ☑ DOS
- ☐ Macintosh
- ☐ Terminal Emulation
- ☐ VMS
- ☐ UNIX
- ☐ OS/2
- ☐ Other platform

Cost
- ☐ Unknown
- ☐ Basic
- ☑ Extended
- ☐ Premium ($)
- ☐ Executive w/$

Activity Level MEDIUM LOW ← HIGH

Address
GO: **DATAQUEST**

DEC EQUIPMENT

Digital PC Store

Description
Order DEC products or browse Digital's online catalog of products, including the Alpha AXP PC, networking products, and printers.

Subjects
Computers, DEC Equipment, Online Catalogs

DEC Equipment – DEC Pathworks

Audience
DEC Alpha AXP users, support technicians, system integrators, VARs, Windows NT users

Content Summary
Several options enable you to browse DEC's online catalog of products, enter sweepstakes, order products, or join Digital's electronic store.

See Also
DEC PC Forum, DEC Windows NT Support Forum, DECPCI Forum, PDP-11 Forum, VAX Forum

User Guide
- ☑ Windows
- ☑ DOS
- ☑ Macintosh
- ☑ Terminal Emulation
- ☐ VMS
- ☐ UNIX
- ☐ OS/2
- ☐ Other platform

Cost
- ☐ Unknown
- ☐ Basic
- ☑ Extended
- ☐ Premium ($)
- ☐ Executive w/$

Activity Level: UNKNOWN

Address
GO: DD-31

DEC INTEGRATION PRODUCTS

Digital PC Integration Forum

Description
The DECPCI Forum discusses aspects of Digital's PC Integration software and hardware, including PATHWORKS for DOS, Macintosh, VMS, Ultrix, SCO and OS/2, the DECpc family of personal computers and peripherals, and the EtherWORKS family of network connectivity products.

Subjects
Computers, DEC Integration Products, DEC PATHWORKS

Audience
DEC Alpha AXP users, support technicians, system integrators, VARs, Windows NT users

Content Summary
The message and library areas provide support and technical assistance to people who use or are interested in PATHWORKS and DEC's PC integration products. You can find technical assistance, product announcements, hints and tips, tuning guides, patches, drivers, workarounds, and other information in this forum. You can find a description of the PATHWORKS V5 Migration Guide in text or PostScript format.

See Also
DEC PC Forum, DEC Windows NT Support Forum, DECPCI Forum, PDP-11 Forum, VAX Forum

User Guide
- ☑ Windows
- ☑ DOS
- ☑ Macintosh
- ☐ Terminal Emulation
- ☑ VMS
- ☑ UNIX
- ☑ OS/2
- ☐ Other platform

Cost
- ☐ Unknown
- ☐ Basic
- ☑ Extended
- ☐ Premium ($)
- ☐ Executive w/$

Activity Level: MEDIUM

Address
GO: DECPCI

DEC PATHWORKS

Digital PC Integration Forum

Description
The DECPCI Forum discusses aspects of Digital's PC Integration software and hardware, including PATHWORKS for DOS, Macintosh, VMS, Ultrix, SCO and OS/2, the DECpc family of personal computers and peripherals, and the EtherWORKS family of network connectivity products.

Subjects
Computers, DEC Integration Products, DEC PATHWORKS

Audience
DEC Alpha AXP users, support technicians, system integrators, VARs, Windows NT users

Content Summary
The message and library areas provide support and technical assistance to people who use or are interested in PATHWORKS and DEC's PC integration products. You can find technical assistance, product announcements, hints and tips, tuning guides, patches, drivers, workarounds, and other information in this forum. You can find a description of the PATHWORKS V5 Migration Guide in text or PostScript format.

See Also
DEC PC Forum, DEC Windows NT Support Forum, DECPCI Forum, PDP-11 Forum, VAX Forum

User Guide
- ☑ Windows
- ☑ DOS
- ☑ Macintosh
- ☐ Terminal Emulation
- ☑ VMS
- ☑ UNIX
- ☑ OS/2
- ☐ Other platform

Cost
- ☐ Unknown
- ☐ Basic
- ☒ Extended
- ☐ Premium ($)
- ☐ Executive w/$

Activity Level: MEDIUM (LOW — HIGH)

Address
GO: **DECPCI**

DEC PC Forum

Description
This forum provides independent support for the Digital Equipment line of PCs.

Subjects
Computers

Audience
Computer users, MIS people

Content Summary
You can find information on DECpc Hardware, DECpc Software, DECstation/VAXmate, and more in this forum.

See Also
Various Digital Equipment Corporation Forums

User Guide
- ☐ Windows
- ☐ DOS
- ☐ Macintosh
- ☐ Terminal Emulation
- ☐ VMS
- ☐ UNIX
- ☐ OS/2
- ☒ Other platform

Cost
- ☐ Unknown
- ☐ Basic
- ☒ Extended
- ☐ Premium ($)
- ☐ Executive w/$

Activity Level: LOW (arrow pointing low)

Address
GO: **DECPC**

DEC Users Network Main Menu

Description
This forum provides access to several DEC-related Forums.

Subjects
Computers

Audience
Computer users, MIS people

Content Summary
You can access the DEC PC Forum, DEC Windows NT Forum, DECPCI Forum, PDP-11 Forum, and VAX Forum from this main menu.

See Also
Various Digital Equipment Corporation Forums

User Guide
- ☐ Windows
- ☐ DOS
- ☐ Macintosh
- ☐ Terminal Emulation
- ☐ VMS
- ☐ UNIX
- ☐ OS/2
- ☒ Other platform

Cost
- ☐ Unknown
- ☐ Basic
- ☒ Extended
- ☐ Premium ($)
- ☐ Executive w/$

Activity Level: UNKNOWN

Address
GO: **DECUNET**

DECPCI Forum

Description
The DECPCI forum discusses aspects of Digital's PC Integration software and hardware.

Subjects
Computers

Audience
MIS people

Content Summary
You can find information on PATHWorks, DECpc, EtherWORKS, DOS, Macintosh, VMS, Ultrix, SCO, OS/2, networking, and other topics as they pertain to the DEC PC product line.

See Also
Various Digital Equipment Corporation Forums

User Guide
- ☐ Windows
- ☐ DOS
- ☐ Macintosh
- ☐ Terminal Emulation
- ☐ VMS
- ☐ UNIX
- ☐ OS/2
- ☒ Other platform

Cost
- ☐ Unknown
- ☐ Basic
- ☒ Extended
- ☐ Premium ($)
- ☐ Executive w/$

Activity Level: MEDIUM

Address
GO: **DECPCI**

DELL Forum

Description
The place to be for online support from Dell Computer Corporation.

Subjects
Computers

Audience
Computer users

Content Summary
The forum contains several library and message sections, including DELL Computers, Portable Systems, Operating Systems, Telecommunications, Customer Care, and more.

See Also
IBM File Finder

User Guide
- ☑ Windows
- ☑ DOS
- ☐ Macintosh
- ☐ Terminal Emulation
- ☐ VMS
- ☐ UNIX
- ☐ OS/2
- ☑ Other platform

Cost
- ☐ Unknown
- ☐ Basic
- ☑ Extended
- ☐ Premium ($)
- ☐ Executive w/$

Activity Level

Address
GO: **DELL**

Delrina Forum

Description
This forum provides support for users of all Delrina products.

Subjects
Computers

Audience
Computer users

Content Summary
You can find information on various Delrina products in this forum, including WINFAX, DOSFAX, PerFORM, FormFlow, WinComm, and others.

See Also
Modem Forum, Hayes Forum

User Guide
- ☑ Windows
- ☑ DOS
- ☑ Macintosh
- ☐ Terminal Emulation
- ☐ VMS
- ☐ UNIX
- ☐ OS/2
- ☐ Other platform

Cost
- ☐ Unknown
- ☐ Basic
- ☑ Extended
- ☐ Premium ($)
- ☐ Executive w/$

Activity Level

(MEDIUM, arrow pointing toward HIGH)

Address
GO: **DELRINA**

DEMOGRAPHICS

State-County Demographics

Description
This database provides detailed summaries of the demographic makeup of states and counties in the U.S.

Subjects
Demographics, Statistics

Audience
Researchers, businesspeople

Content Summary
This database contains demographic statistics on race, age, occupation, and further details of all the states and counties of the U.S.

See Also
SUPERSITE Demographics Forum

User Guide
- ☑ Windows
- ☑ DOS
- ☑ Macintosh
- ☐ Terminal Emulation
- ☐ VMS
- ☑ UNIX
- ☐ OS/2
- ☑ Other platform

Cost
- ☐ Unknown
- ☐ Basic
- ☐ Extended
- ☑ Premium ($)
- ☐ Executive w/$

Activity Level

Address
GO: **DEMOGRAPHICS**

SUPERSITE Demographics Forum

Description
This forum provides demographic reports for all of the United States, covering general demographics, income, housing, education, employment, and current and projected-year forecasts.

Subjects
Demographics, Market Research

Audience
Demographers, research analysts

Content Summary
This forum is available only to members who have the Executive Service Option. You obtain reports by indicating the type of geography you want to research, the geographic areas that form the market, and the reports you want.

See Also
State-County Demographics

User Guide
- ☑ Windows
- ☑ DOS
- ☑ Macintosh
- ☑ Terminal Emulation
- ☑ VMS
- ☑ UNIX
- ☑ OS/2
- ☑ Other platform

Cost
- ☐ Unknown
- ☐ Basic
- ☐ Extended
- ☑ Premium ($)
- ☐ Executive w/$

Activity Level

Address
GO: **SUPERSITE**

Detroit Free Press

Description
This is the place to find news and information about the award-winning Detroit Free Press newspaper. And feel free to leave a letter to the editor while you're online.

Subjects
Journalism, National News, Photojournalism

Audience
Automobile enthusiasts, Detroit citizens, journalists, photojournalists, sports fans

Content Summary
In the message and library areas, you can find information on the auto industry (including photographs of cars), health tips, business news, Detroit metro news, computing, entertainment, sports, and cartoons. You also can find the top stories of the day in the "Today's Top Stories" library (Library 17).

See Also
Detroit Free Press Store

User Guide
- ☑ Windows
- ☑ DOS
- ☑ Macintosh
- ☐ Terminal Emulation
- ☑ VMS
- ☑ UNIX
- ☑ OS/2
- ☐ Other platform

Cost
- ☐ Unknown
- ☐ Basic
- ☑ Extended
- ☐ Premium ($)
- ☐ Executive w/$

Activity Level

Address
GO: **DETROIT**

Detroit Free Press Store

Description
In this area, you can subscribe to the Detroit Free Press newspaper, order Detroit Free Press books, or leave a message for customer service.

Subjects
Customer Service, Subscriptions, Journalism

Audience
Anyone interested in the Detroit Free Press newspaper

Content Summary
The Store has areas in which you can shop for Detroit Free Press books, subscribe to the Detroit Free Press newspaper (including international subscriptions), and leave a message for customer service. If you want more information about this award-winning newspaper, see the "What is the Detroit Free Press?" area (number 4).

See Also
Detroit Free Press

User Guide
- ☑ Windows
- ☑ DOS
- ☑ Macintosh
- ☐ Terminal Emulation
- ☑ VMS
- ☑ UNIX
- ☑ OS/2
- ☐ Other platform

Cost
- ☐ Unknown
- ☑ Basic
- ☐ Extended
- ☐ Premium ($)
- ☐ Executive w/$

Activity Level

Address
GO: **DFM-1**

(Microsoft) Developers Relations Forums

Description
This forum is designed for high-level information exchange and tips about Microsoft Developer products. Section leaders from Microsoft Product Support Services monitor and participate in the forum. This area is for nontechnical information. See the Microsoft Developer Services Area (MSDS) for technical support questions and issues.

Subjects
Application Development, Computers, Microsoft

Audience
Advanced-level users, developers

Content Summary
This forum includes two libraries: General/Dev. Services, which includes files and information on job opportunities, general beta testing (non-Microsoft), and the Microsoft Support Network; and Strategic Issues, which includes information and tool kits for developers on different applications and operating systems.

See Also
Microsoft Developer Services Area, Microsoft Developer Network Forum, Microsoft Developer Knowledge Base, Microsoft Connection, Microsoft C and Other Languages Forum

User Guide
- ☑ Windows
- ☑ DOS
- ☑ Macintosh
- ☐ Terminal Emulation
- ☑ VMS
- ☑ UNIX
- ☑ OS/2
- ☐ Other platform

Cost
- ☐ Unknown
- ☐ Basic
- ☑ Extended
- ☐ Premium ($)
- ☐ Executive w/$

Activity Level

Address
GO: **MSDR**

Diabetes Forum

Description
An online community for people with a common interest in diabetes, hypoglycemia, and related chronic metabolic disorders. Family members and friends of these people also are welcome to join and participate in this lively area.

Subjects
Diabetes, Health, Hypoglycemia

Audience
Diabetes patients, family and friends, hypoglycemia patients, medical personnel

Content Summary
The library and message areas are full of information about these disorders, including files on general diabetes information and explanations of diabetic terms. You also can find files and messages regarding friends and family, hypoglycemics, insulin information, oral medications, diet and exercise, complications associated with diabetes, pumping, various technologies and theories, and pregnancy and diabetes. Library 17, "Youth Connection," is devoted to young people with diabetes and includes graphics, games, and stories for the young.

See Also
Health and Fitness Forum, Health/Fitness, HealthNet, Health Database Plus, Physicians Data Query

User Guide
- ☑ Windows
- ☑ DOS
- ☑ Macintosh
- ☐ Terminal Emulation
- ☑ VMS
- ☑ UNIX
- ☑ OS/2
- ☐ Other platform

Cost
- ☐ Unknown
- ☐ Basic
- ☑ Extended
- ☐ Premium ($)
- ☐ Executive w/$

Activity Level

Address
GO: **DIABETES**

DIAGNOSTICS

DiagSoft QAPlus Forum

Description
Provides support for DiagSoft QAPlus programs and discussions relating to these programs.

Subjects
Computers, Diagnostics, Service and Support, System Integration

Audience
Diagnostic personnel, DiagSoft Users, MIS personnel, service and support technicians, system integrators, VARs

Content Summary
Like the message area, the library area is divided into sections that discuss general information, customer support, QAPlus, QAPlus / FE (field engineers diagnostic software), Peace of Mind

(DiagSoft's Macintosh product), and QAPlus for Windows information. You can find installation and compatibility information in Library 1, "General Information."

See Also
Nothing yet

User Guide
- [x] Windows
- [x] DOS
- [x] Macintosh
- [ ] Terminal Emulation
- [ ] VMS
- [ ] UNIX
- [ ] OS/2
- [ ] Other platform

Cost
- [ ] Unknown
- [ ] Basic
- [x] Extended
- [ ] Premium ($)
- [ ] Executive w/$

Activity Level

Address
GO: **DIAGSOFT**

DiagSoft QAPlus Forum

Description
Provides support for DiagSoft QAPlus programs and discussions relating to these programs.

Subjects
Computers, Diagnostics, Service and Support, System Integration

Audience
Diagnostic personnel, DiagSoft Users, MIS personnel, service and support technicians, system integrators, VARs

Content Summary
Like the message area, the library area is divided into sections that discuss general information, customer support, QAPlus, QAPlus / FE (field engineers diagnostic software), Peace of Mind (DiagSoft's Macintosh product), and QAPlus for Windows information. You can find installation and compatibility information in Library 1, "General Information."

See Also
Nothing yet

User Guide
- [x] Windows
- [x] DOS
- [x] Macintosh
- [ ] Terminal Emulation
- [ ] VMS
- [ ] UNIX
- [ ] OS/2
- [ ] Other platform

Cost
- [ ] Unknown
- [ ] Basic
- [x] Extended
- [ ] Premium ($)
- [ ] Executive w/$

Activity Level

Address
GO: **DIAGSOFT**

Dial-A-Mattress

Description
Looking for a new bed or mattress? You can order or price premium bedding from Sealy, Simmons, and Serta from this service.

Subjects
Bedding, Beds, Mattresses

Audience
Consumers (anyone interested in bedding), gift givers

Content Summary
The Dial-A-Mattress service offers you several options from which to choose, including an order area, product listings, customer service and warranty information, and shipping information. If you want to talk to a "live" person, go to "Can I Speak To A Representative" (option 5) for more information. If you've never heard of Dial-A-Mattress, select option 2. Select option 3 for instructions on how to shop for a mattress or bed online.

See Also
Sears

User Guide
- [x] Windows
- [x] DOS
- [x] Macintosh
- [x] Terminal Emulation
- [x] VMS
- [x] UNIX
- [x] OS/2
- [ ] Other platform

Cost
- [ ] Unknown
- [ ] Basic
- [ ] Extended
- [x] Premium ($)
- [ ] Executive w/$

Activity Level

Address
GO: **BEDS**

DICTIONARY

American Heritage Dictionary

Description
This is the online version of the American Heritage Dictionary, with detailed definitions of over 303,000 words and phrases.

Dictionary – Digital Equipment Corporation (DEC)

Subjects
Dictionary, Spelling

Audience
Students

Content Summary
This on-line dictionary conatins over 300,000 entries. You can look up words phonetically.

See Also
Academic American Encyclopedia

User Guide
- ☑ Windows
- ☑ DOS
- ☑ Macintosh
- ☐ Terminal Emulation
- ☑ VMS
- ☑ UNIX
- ☑ OS/2
- ☑ Other platform

Cost
- ☐ Unknown
- ☑ Basic
- ☐ Extended
- ☐ Premium ($)
- ☐ Executive w/$

Activity Level
UNKNOWN (LOW — MEDIUM — HIGH)

Address
GO: **DICTIONARY**

DIGITAL EQUIPMENT CORPORATION (DEC)

Digital Equipment Corporation

Description
This is the main area from which you can choose to enter one of several DEC forums or service areas. You can select Digital's Windows NT Support Forum, PC Integration Forum, or Digital-Related Forums. You also can go to Digital's PC Store from this menu.

Subjects
Computers, Client/Server, Multiprocessor Environments, Windows NT

Audience
DEC Alpha AXP users, support technicians, system integrators, VARs, Windows NT users

Content Summary
At the main menu, you can select from Digital NT Support Forum, Digital PC Integration Forum, and Digital's PC Store.

See Also
Digital NT Support Forum, Digital PC Integration Forum, Digital's PC Store

User Guide
- ☑ Windows
- ☑ DOS
- ☑ Macintosh
- ☐ Terminal Emulation
- ☑ VMS
- ☑ UNIX
- ☑ OS/2
- ☐ Other platform

Cost
- ☐ Unknown
- ☐ Basic
- ☑ Extended
- ☐ Premium ($)
- ☐ Executive w/$

Activity Level
UNKNOWN (LOW — MEDIUM — HIGH)

Address
GO: **DEC**

Digital NT Support Forum

Description
Dedicated to the user support of Windows NT, regardless of environment or platform, this forum is supported by Digital's Multi-Vendor Customer Services Group. You can find information here about DEC's Alpha AXP platform.

Subjects
Computers, Client/Server, Digital Equipment Corporation (DEC), Windows NT

Audience
DEC Alpha AXP users, support technicians, system integrators, VARs, Windows NT users

Content Summary
The library and message areas contain information about Digital and Digital's Multivendor Customer Services, including press releases and news on the Alpha AXP and Windows NT. You also can find specific areas devoted to NT user support, languages and application tools, hardware support, bug reporting, a "Wish List" area for what you want, and Alpha AXP support. You can find new BIOS files, Alpha Microcode, and utility programs in the "Patches & More" library.

See Also
DEC PC, DECPCI, PDP-11 Forum, VAX Forum

User Guide
- ☑ Windows
- ☑ DOS
- ☐ Macintosh
- ☐ Terminal Emulation
- ☐ VMS
- ☐ UNIX
- ☐ OS/2
- ☐ Other platform

Cost
- ☐ Unknown
- ☐ Basic
- ☑ Extended
- ☐ Premium ($)
- ☐ Executive w/$

Digital Equipment Corporation (DEC) – Digital NT Support Forum

Activity Level MEDIUM

Address
GO: **DECWNT**

VAX Forum

Description
This forum provides support for users of the VAX series of computer systems from Digital Equip Corp. VAX Forum is sponsored by Professional Press.

Subjects
Computers, Digital Equipment

Audience
Computer users

Content Summary
The libraries contain product information, support for VAX products, and press releases.

See Also
Computers, Software

User Guide
- ☑ Windows
- ☑ DOS
- ☐ Macintosh
- ☐ Terminal Emulation
- ☐ VMS
- ☐ UNIX
- ☐ OS/2
- ☐ Other platform

Cost
- ☐ Unknown
- ☐ Basic
- ☑ Extended
- ☐ Premium ($)
- ☐ Executive w/$

Activity Level LOW

Address
GO: **VAXFORUM**

DIGITAL MEDIA RIGHTS

Electronic Frontier Foundation Forum

Description
The Electronic Frontier Foundation (EFF) was founded in July 1990 to assure freedom of expression in digital media, with a particular emphasis on applying the principles embodied in the Constitution and the Bill of Rights to computer-based communications.

Subjects
Computer-Based Communications, Digital Media Rights, Internet

Audience
Computer users, activists, civil libertarians, journalists

Content Summary
The libraries in this forum contain areas for EFF-related files, networking, communications, back issues of the EFF newsletter, Cyberlaw, Zines and the Net, Internet news, and maps and guides. You also can get freeware and shareware applications for DOS and Macintosh machines in Libraries 9 and 10.

See Also
Internet Forum

User Guide
- ☑ Windows
- ☑ DOS
- ☑ Macintosh
- ☐ Terminal Emulation
- ☐ VMS
- ☐ UNIX
- ☐ OS/2
- ☐ Other platform

Cost
- ☐ Unknown
- ☐ Basic
- ☑ Extended
- ☐ Premium ($)
- ☐ Executive w/$

Activity Level MEDIUM

Address
GO: **EFFSIG**

Digital NT Support Forum

Description
Dedicated to the user support of Windows NT, regardless of environment or platform, this forum is supported by Digital's Multi-Vendor Customer Services Group. You can find information here about DEC's Alpha AXP platform.

Subjects
Computers, Client/Server, Digital Equipment Corporation (DEC), Windows NT

Audience
DEC Alpha AXP users, support technicians, system integrators, VARs, Windows NT users

Content Summary
The library and message areas contain information about Digital and Digital's Multivendor Customer Services, including press releases and news on the Alpha AXP and Windows NT. You also can find specific areas devoted to NT user support, languages and application tools, hardware support, bug reporting, a "Wish List" area for what you want, and Alpha AXP support. You can find new BIOS files, Alpha Microcode, and utility programs in the "Patches & More" library.

Digital NT Support Forum – Digitalk Database

See Also
DEC PC, DECPCI, PDP-11 Forum, VAX Forum

User Guide
- [x] Windows
- [x] DOS
- [ ] Macintosh
- [ ] Terminal Emulation
- [ ] VMS
- [ ] UNIX
- [ ] OS/2
- [ ] Other platform

Cost
- [ ] Unknown
- [ ] Basic
- [x] Extended
- [ ] Premium ($)
- [ ] Executive w/$

Activity Level: MEDIUM

Address
GO: DECWNT

Digital PC Integration Forum

Description
The DECPCI Forum discusses aspects of Digital's PC Integration software and hardware, including PATHWORKS for DOS, Macintosh, VMS, Ultrix, SCO and OS/2, the DECpc family of personal computers and peripherals, and the EtherWORKS family of network connectivity products.

Subjects
Computers, DEC Integration Products, DEC PATHWORKS

Audience
DEC Alpha AXP users, support technicians, system integrators, VARs, Windows NT users

Content Summary
The message and library areas provide support and technical assistance to people who use or are interested in PATHWORKS and DEC's PC integration products. You can find technical assistance, product announcements, hints and tips, tuning guides, patches, drivers, workarounds, and other information in this forum. You can find a description of the PATHWORKS V5 Migration Guide in text or PostScript format.

See Also
DEC PC Forum, DEC Windows NT Support Forum, DECPCI Forum, PDP-11 Forum, VAX Forum

User Guide
- [x] Windows
- [x] DOS
- [x] Macintosh
- [ ] Terminal Emulation
- [x] VMS
- [x] UNIX
- [x] OS/2
- [ ] Other platform

Cost
- [ ] Unknown
- [ ] Basic
- [x] Extended
- [ ] Premium ($)
- [ ] Executive w/$

Activity Level: MEDIUM

Address
GO: DECPCI

Digital PC Store

Description
Order DEC products or browse its online catalog of products, including the Alpha AXP PC, networking products, and printers.

Subjects
Computers, DEC Equipment, Online Catalogs

Audience
DEC Alpha AXP users, support technicians, system integrators, VARs, Windows NT users

Content Summary
Several options enable you to browse DEC's online catalog of products, enter sweepstakes, order products, or join Digital's electronic store.

See Also
DEC PC Forum, DEC Windows NT Support Forum, DECPCI Forum, PDP-11 Forum, VAX Forum

User Guide
- [x] Windows
- [x] DOS
- [x] Macintosh
- [x] Terminal Emulation
- [ ] VMS
- [ ] UNIX
- [ ] OS/2
- [ ] Other platform

Cost
- [ ] Unknown
- [ ] Basic
- [x] Extended
- [ ] Premium ($)
- [ ] Executive w/$

Activity Level: UNKNOWN

Address
GO: DD-31

Digitalk Database

Description
Since 1985, Digitalk, Inc. has been developing object-oriented programming environments for the PC with its Smalltalk/V product. The company has Smalltalk/V development environments worldwide for DOS, OS/2, Microsoft Windows, and the Apple Macintosh; the Team/V collaborative programming system; and PARTS Workbench for OS/2. The Digitalk Database contains problem reports on all Smalltalk/V and PARTS products.

Digitalk Database – Dinosaur Forum

Subjects
Action Requests Database, Computers, Object-Oriented Programming, Smalltalk/V

Audience
Consultants, object-oriented programmers, Smalltalk/V users, trainers

Content Summary
Select the "Search the Action Requests Database" option to search the Digitalk Action Requests database.

See Also
Digitalk Forum

User Guide
- ☑ Windows
- ☑ DOS
- ☑ Macintosh
- ☐ Terminal Emulation
- ☐ VMS
- ☐ UNIX
- ☑ OS/2
- ☐ Other platform

Cost
- ☐ Unknown
- ☐ Basic
- ☑ Extended
- ☐ Premium ($)
- ☐ Executive w/$

Activity Level: UNKNOWN (LOW – MEDIUM – HIGH)

Address
GO: **DBDIGITALK**

Digitalk Forum

Description
This forum provides a way to communicate with Digitalk and with other users of Smalltalk/V and PARTS products, including the latest information about Smalltalk/V and PARTS products, technical support answers, and how others are using Digitalk's development systems to create and deliver software.

Subjects
Application Development, Computers, Smalltalk/V

Audience
Application developers, PARTS users, Smalltalk/V users

Content Summary
The library and message areas contain various places to discuss several topics, including Digitalk news, product information, user contributions, third-party products, support, and miscellaneous information and products. If you're looking for source code or tips on Smalltalk/V, see Library 5, "Support."

See Also
Digitalk Database

User Guide
- ☑ Windows
- ☑ DOS
- ☑ Macintosh
- ☐ Terminal Emulation
- ☐ VMS
- ☐ UNIX
- ☑ OS/2
- ☐ Other platform

Cost
- ☐ Unknown
- ☐ Basic
- ☑ Extended
- ☐ Premium ($)
- ☐ Executive w/$

Activity Level: MEDIUM→HIGH (LOW – MEDIUM – HIGH)

Address
GO: **DIGITALK**

Dinosaur Forum

Description
If you like dinosaurs or know someone who does, you should visit or join this forum. This forum is devoted to information about dinosaurs, including scientific discussions, dinosaurs in popular culture (such as movies), and many other dinosaur-related topics.

Subjects
Dinosaurs, Science

Audience
Archaeologists, dinosaur lovers, paleontologists, scientists

Content Summary
The library and message forums contain information that any dinosaur lover would like, such as dinosaur facts and reports, drawings, sketches, FLI animations, conference information, and field reports. If you want some *Jurassic Park* sound samples, see Library 2, "Entertainment." If you are interested in visiting a dinosaur exhibition at a museum, look in "Museum Reports" (Library 9) for press releases from various museums.

See Also
Science Forum

User Guide
- ☑ Windows
- ☑ DOS
- ☑ Macintosh
- ☐ Terminal Emulation
- ☑ VMS
- ☑ UNIX
- ☑ OS/2
- ☐ Other platform

Cost
- ☐ Unknown
- ☐ Basic
- ☑ Extended
- ☐ Premium ($)
- ☐ Executive w/$

Dinosaur Forum – Disabilities

Activity Level

Address
GO: DINO

DIRECTORY

Member Directory

Description
Find another CompuServe member's account number by entering his/her name here. This service contains all CompuServe members, except for those asking to be excluded.

Subjects
Directory

Audience
General public

Content Summary
The CompuServe Information Service offers the Member Directory to facilitate the use of CompuServe's electronic mail. The Member Directory contains the first and last name, city, state, country, and User ID number of every CompuServe member except those who wish to be excluded. When searching for a member, you are prompted to enter the last name and first name. You are then prompted to enter the city, country, and state of residence for the member. The last name is required to be entered while the first name is optional. Also, you must answer at least one of the three prompts (city, country, and state) before a search will be conducted.

See Also
Member Assistance (FREE)

User Guide
- ☑ Windows
- ☑ DOS
- ☑ Macintosh
- ☐ Terminal Emulation
- ☑ VMS
- ☑ UNIX
- ☑ OS/2
- ☑ Other platform

Cost
- ☐ Unknown
- ☑ Basic
- ☐ Extended
- ☐ Premium ($)
- ☐ Executive w/$

Activity Level

Address
GO: DIRECTORY

DISABILITIES

Disabilities Forum

Description
This forum is designed to be an online support group and open communication facilitator for anyone interested in disabilities. You can find stories, reports, and information about disabled persons' daily lives, along with ideas and experiences of parents and friends of disabled people.

Subjects
Emotional Disturbances, Learning Disabilities, Multiple Sclerosis, Disabilities

Audience
Disabled persons, family and friends of disabled persons, professionals who work with disabled persons

Content Summary
Many message and library topics are available to choose from, including developmental disabilities, emotional disturbances, hearing impairments, multiple sclerosis, and mobility impairments. You can find the latest information on the Americans with Disabilities Act (ADA) in Library 7, "Government Activities." If you are looking for employment, see "Education/Employment," Library 8, for files designed for disabled persons searching for employment and education.

See Also
Handicapped Users Database, Health/Fitness, Healthnet

User Guide
- ☑ Windows
- ☑ DOS
- ☑ Macintosh
- ☐ Terminal Emulation
- ☑ VMS
- ☑ UNIX
- ☑ OS/2
- ☐ Other platform

Cost
- ☐ Unknown
- ☐ Basic
- ☑ Extended
- ☐ Premium ($)
- ☐ Executive w/$

Activity Level

MEDIUM (LOW – HIGH)

Address
GO: DISABILITIES

Health/Fitness

Description
If you can't find the health-related forum that you want, use the Health/Fitness service to speed up your search.

Disabilities – Diseases

Subjects
Aids, Cancer, Disabilities, Health Care

Audience
Medical educators, medical professionals, medical researchers, general public

Content Summary
The main menu in this area lists all the health and fitness related forums and services available on CompuServe. Here you can choose from topics such as Consumer Reports Complete Drug Reference, HealthNet, AIDS Information, Attention Deficit Disorder Forum, Cancer Information, Diabetes Forum, Health & Fitness Forum, Human Sexuality, PaperChase (MEDLINE), and many more.

See Also
HealthNet, Holistic Health Forum, Health Database Plus($), Health and Vitamin Express, Health and Fitness Forum, Cancer Forum, Aids News Clips, PaperChase MEDLINE($)

User Guide
- [x] Windows
- [x] DOS
- [x] Macintosh
- [ ] Terminal Emulation
- [x] VMS
- [x] UNIX
- [x] OS/2
- [x] Other platform

Cost
- [ ] Unknown
- [x] Basic
- [ ] Extended
- [ ] Premium ($)
- [ ] Executive w/$

Activity Level

Address
GO: **FITNESS**

DISCOUNT SHOPPING

Shoppers Advantage Club

Description
This is America's largest discount electronic shopping service, with over 250,000 name brand items available.

Subjects
Clothing, Discount Shopping, Shopping

Audience
Consumers, shoppers

Content Summary
Shop 24 hours a day for over 250,000 different items.

See Also
Electronic Mall

User Guide
- [x] Windows
- [x] DOS
- [x] Macintosh
- [ ] Terminal Emulation
- [ ] VMS
- [x] UNIX
- [ ] OS/2
- [ ] Other platform

Cost
- [ ] Unknown
- [x] Basic
- [ ] Extended
- [ ] Premium ($)
- [ ] Executive w/$

Activity Level

Address
GO: **SAC**

DISEASES

Rare Diseases Database

Description
Developed and maintained by the National Organization for Rare Diseases (NORD), this database forum was constructed so that patients of rare disorders and their families understand the disorder and its implications.

Subjects
AIDS, Diseases, Health

Audience
AIDS suffers, health care providers, families of the ill

Content Summary
This forum contains a database that provides information on all rare diseases, their treatment, medicines, and implications. Newsletters from several national organizations, such as NORD, Parkinsons Foundation, and the Multiple Sclerosis Foundation, are available. Current information on AIDS and related illnesses also can be found. Also included is an orphan drug database.

See Also
Paperchase-MEDLINE

User Guide
- [x] Windows
- [x] DOS
- [x] Macintosh
- [x] Terminal Emulation
- [x] VMS
- [x] UNIX
- [x] OS/2
- [ ] Other platform

Cost
- [ ] Unknown
- [ ] Basic
- [ ] Extended
- [x] Premium ($)
- [ ] Executive w/$

Activity Level: MEDIUM (UNKNOWN)

Address
GO: **NORD**

Florida Today Forum

This forum is the first international, interactive forum linking *Florida Today*, the Space Coast Newspaper, with newspaper readers everywhere.

Subjects
Disney Comics, Florida, Tourism

Audience
Tourists, Florida residents

Content Summary
The Florida Today Newslink forum is an electronic newspaper intended to give readers a way to get their news and information online. The libraries consist of sections devoted to space, sports, leisure and tourism, environment, gardening, weather, senior activities, politics, education, and many more areas. The Front Page Lounge (Library 15) is full of editorial cartoons for you to download and view.

See Also
Travel Forum, Florida Forum

User Guide
- ☑ Windows
- ☑ DOS
- ☑ Macintosh
- ☐ Terminal Emulation
- ☑ VMS
- ☑ UNIX
- ☑ OS/2
- ☑ Other platform

Cost
- ☐ Unknown
- ☐ Basic
- ☑ Extended
- ☐ Premium ($)
- ☐ Executive w/$

Activity Level: LOW (arrow pointing left from MEDIUM)

Address
GO: **FLATODAY**

Dissertation Abstracts

Description
Contains references to U.S. and Canadian Ph.D. dissertations since 1861 and master theses since 1962. Includes abstracts of dissertations from 1980 and on. Professional (such as MD) and honorary degrees are not included.

Subjects
Dissertations, Education, Research

Audience
Graduate students, historians, professors, researchers, students

Content Summary
Each dissertation includes author, title, date of publication, college, and degree for which the dissertation was submitted. Dissertation Abstracts is published and copyrighted by University Microfilms International and made available by BRS Information Technologies.

You should note that Dissertation Abstracts includes transaction charges in addition to CompuServe base connect rates. You can see a running total of transaction charges on the Dissertation Abstract menu pages. Connect charges are not included in the displayed total.

The following are rates for using Dissertation Abstracts:

- Search (retrieves up to 10 titles): $5
- Additional titles (in groups of 10): $5
- Full reference, with abstract where available (selected from the titles): $5 each

In addition to connect-time charges, there is a $1 charge for a search that retrieves no titles.

See Also
IQuest Database

User Guide
- ☑ Windows
- ☑ DOS
- ☑ Macintosh
- ☑ Terminal Emulation
- ☐ VMS
- ☐ UNIX
- ☑ OS/2
- ☐ Other platform

Cost
- ☐ Unknown
- ☐ Basic
- ☐ Extended
- ☑ Premium ($)
- ☐ Executive w/$

Scuba Forum

Description
Scuba forum is a forum for amateur and professional divers, discussing diving, diving equipment, and diving locations

Subjects
Divers, Hobbies

Audience
Divers, snorklers

Content Summary
The libraries of this forum contain information on diving in America, Europe, the Caribbean, and elsewhere. Also included is information on scuba

equipment, snorkling, and pictures of diving locations.

See Also
Sports Forum, Outdoor Forum, Photography Forum

User Guide
- [x] Windows
- [x] DOS
- [x] Macintosh
- [ ] Terminal Emulation
- [ ] VMS
- [x] UNIX
- [ ] OS/2
- [ ] Other platform

Cost
- [ ] Unknown
- [ ] Basic
- [x] Extended
- [ ] Premium ($)
- [ ] Executive w/$

Activity Level
MEDIUM (arrow pointing up, between LOW and HIGH)

Address
GO: DIVING

Dividends and Splits

Description
Gives information about dividends, bond interest, and splits over a selected period of time, to get a report that includes the exdate, record date, payment date, type of distribution, and rate of each distribution. You can find mutual fund distributions here that are otherwise difficult to obtain. You can specify the number of dividends you want to view or a period of time.

Subjects
Finance

Audience
Financial analysts

Content Summary
To sample this area without being surcharged, enter **HRP** at the prompt. To get information about a security or a market index, enter one or more securities or market indexes, a slash (/) followed by a navigation command, or press Enter (CR) to exit. If you enter more than one issue, place a comma between each entry, such as HRB,DEC,IBM. You can enter the ticker symbol or CUSIP number for each security. Enter an asterisk then the beginning of the issue or index name if you don't know the ticker symbol (such as *BLOCK for H&R Block).

See Also
Go Symbols

User Guide
- [ ] Windows
- [ ] DOS
- [ ] Macintosh
- [x] Terminal Emulation
- [ ] VMS
- [ ] UNIX
- [ ] OS/2
- [ ] Other platform

Cost
- [ ] Unknown
- [ ] Basic
- [x] Extended
- [ ] Premium ($)
- [ ] Executive w/$

Activity Level
UNKNOWN (between LOW and HIGH, MEDIUM above)

Address
GO: DIVIDENDS

DOLLS

Collectibles Forum

Description
We are an electronic club for all collectors—and are a member of the ANA and APS.

Subjects
Dolls, Hobbies, Star Trek

Audience
Hobby enthusiasts

Content Summary
The library and message sections contain information on a wide variety of collectibles. Included are areas on stamps, coins, autographs, books, music, sports cards, dolls, figurines, Star Trek, and much more.

See Also
Crafts Forum

User Guide
- [x] Windows
- [x] DOS
- [x] Macintosh
- [ ] Terminal Emulation
- [ ] VMS
- [x] UNIX
- [ ] OS/2
- [ ] Other platform

Cost
- [ ] Unknown
- [ ] Basic
- [x] Extended
- [ ] Premium ($)
- [ ] Executive w/$

Activity Level
MEDIUM (arrow pointing up, between LOW and HIGH)

Address
GO: COLLECT

Dr. Dobb's Forum

Description
This is an "electronic" version of *Dr. Dobb's Journal*, a journal devoted to computer languages, tools, utilities, algorithms, and programming techniques. If

you're interested in writing articles for the *Journal*, post them here for review. You might get published in the future.

Subjects
Computers, Programming, Utilities

Audience
Application developers, MIS personnel, system integrators

Content Summary
You can upload or download source code; find information on OS/2, UNIX, Macintosh, and Windows programming; and find listings (not text) of the articles and columns from the *Dr. Dobb's Journal* magazine. This forum is not intended to be a substitute for the magazine, but a complement to it.

See Also
MS Developers Relations Forum

User Guide
- ☑ Windows
- ☑ DOS
- ☑ Macintosh
- ☐ Terminal Emulation
- ☐ VMS
- ☑ UNIX
- ☑ OS/2
- ☐ Other platform

Cost
- ☐ Unknown
- ☐ Basic
- ☑ Extended
- ☐ Premium ($)
- ☐ Executive w/$

Activity Level

MEDIUM

Address
GO: **DDJFORUM**

Dr. Neuhaus Forum

Description
This forum is devoted to German-speaking people interested in Dr. Neuhaus communications products. You can get technical support and information on products such as FURY modems, FAXY fax boards, and NICCY ISDN modems. You also can find information and support for Carbon Copy.

Subjects
Computers, Fax Boards, Modems, Remote Communications

Audience
Computer users

Content Summary
This forum is entirely in German.

See Also
Modem Vendor Forum, Palmtop Forum

User Guide
- ☑ Windows
- ☑ DOS
- ☑ Macintosh
- ☐ Terminal Emulation
- ☑ VMS
- ☑ UNIX
- ☑ OS/2
- ☑ Other platform

Cost
- ☐ Unknown
- ☐ Basic
- ☑ Extended
- ☐ Premium ($)
- ☐ Executive w/$

Activity Level

UNKNOWN

Address
GO: **NEUHAUS**

Dreyfus Corporation

Description
Dreyfus Corporation has been the leader in the mutual funds field for over 40 years. In this area, you can start your investment portfolio with as little as $100, roll over your IRA and Keogh accounts, and look into other investment programs, such as the Investment Allocation Program.

Subjects
Investments, Mutual Funds

Audience
Investors

Content Summary
From the Dreyfus Corp. main menu, you can choose from several options. You can choose the Online Selection of Funds option to see how to select mutual funds, see the family of funds Dreyfus offers, and see the Featured Funds. To request a free Dreyfus prospectus online, select the Request a FREE Prospectus option from the main menu. Select the Minimum Investment Program option from the main menu for information on starting a mutual fund portfolio for as little as $100.

See Also
Thomas Register Online

User Guide
- ☐ Windows
- ☐ DOS
- ☐ Macintosh
- ☑ Terminal Emulation
- ☐ VMS
- ☐ UNIX
- ☐ OS/2
- ☐ Other platform

Cost
- ☐ Unknown
- ☑ Basic
- ☐ Extended
- ☐ Premium ($)
- ☐ Executive w/$

DUN AND BRADSTREET

Activity Level

Address
GO: **DR**

D&B Dun's Canadian Market Identifiers

Description
The Canadian Dun's Market Identifiers database contains directory information on about 350,000 Canadian companies. You can see company name, address, and telephone number. You also can get sales figures, number of employees, and executive's names.

Subjects
Canadian Company Profiles, Business, Finance, Dun and Bradstreet

Audience
Accounting persons, businesspersons, executives, investors, journalists, management, researchers

Content Summary
Depending on the company listing, you might or might not see all the information detailed in the Description area above. To retrieve records, enter the company name, geographic location, product or service, number of employees, or sales as your search criteria. For help on searching, select Choice 2, "Search Guidelines," from the main menu. The cost of this service is as follows:

- Search (retrieves up to 5 names): $7.50
- Additional names (in groups of 5): $7.50
- Full reference (selected from the names): $7.50

In addition to connect time-charges, you are charged $1.00 for a search that retrieves no titles.

See Also
Company Information, Corporate Affiliations, D&B Dun's Electronic Business Directory, D&B Dun's Market Identifiers, Financial Forums, Investors' Forum, Tenderlink, TRW Business Profiles

User Guide
- ☑ Windows
- ☑ DOS
- ☑ Macintosh
- ☐ Terminal Emulation
- ☑ VMS
- ☑ UNIX
- ☑ OS/2
- ☑ Other platform

Cost
- ☐ Unknown
- ☐ Basic
- ☐ Extended
- ☑ Premium ($)
- ☐ Executive w/$

Activity Level

Address
GO: **DBCAN**

D&B Dun's Electronic Business Directory

Description
You can obtain a directory of over 8.5 million U.S. public and private businesses and professionals using this Dun and Bradstreet service. Available information includes name, address, phone number, type of business, parent company, industry, the SIC code, number of employees, and the population of the city in which the business resides.

Subjects
Business, Finance, Investment, Dun and Bradstreet

Audience
Accounting persons, businesspersons, executives, investors, journalists, management, researchers

Content Summary
To search, select Choice 5, "Access Dun's Electronic Business Directory," from the main menu. Next, select the criterion for your search, such as company name or product or service; enter a name, word, or phrase that describes the company or product; and follow the on-screen instructions. See Choice 7, "Search Guidelines," for more help. The cost of this service is as follows:

- Search (retrieves up to 5 names): $7.50
- Additional names (in groups of 5): $7.50

In addition to connect-time charges, you are charged $1.00 for a search that retrieves no titles.

See Also
Company Information, Corporate Affiliations, D&B Dun's Canadian Market Identifiers, D&B Dun's Market Identifiers, Financial Forums, Investors' Forum, Tenderlink, TRW Business Profiles

User Guide
- ☑ Windows
- ☑ DOS
- ☑ Macintosh
- ☐ Terminal Emulation
- ☑ VMS
- ☑ UNIX
- ☑ OS/2
- ☑ Other platform

Cost
- ☐ Unknown
- ☐ Basic
- ☐ Extended
- ☑ Premium ($)
- ☐ Executive w/$

Activity Level

Dun and Bradstreet – Dvorak Development Forum

Address
GO: **DYP** or **DUNSEBD**

D&B Dun's Market Identifiers

Description
With this service, you can search three of Dun and Bradstreet's directories of business information, including information on over 6.7 million U.S. public and private businesses that have over $1 million in sales or more than five employees, information on over 350,000 Canadian companies, and information on over 2.1 million public, private, and government-controlled international companies.

Subjects
Business, Finance, Investment, Dun and Bradstreet

Audience
Accounting persons, businesspersons, executives, investors, management, researchers

Content Summary
When you perform a search, you can get the company name, address, telephone number, sales figures, number of employees, parent company, and names of executives. The price of this service is as follows:

- Search (retrieves up to 5 names): $7.50
- Additional names (in groups of 5): $7.50
- Full reference (selected from the names): $7.50

In addition to connect-time charges, you are charged $1.00 for a search that retrieves no titles.

See Also
Company Information, Corporate Affiliations, D&B Dun's Canadian Market Identifiers, Financial Forums, Investors' Forum, Tenderlink, TRW Business Profiles

User Guide
- ☑ Windows
- ☑ DOS
- ☑ Macintosh
- ☐ Terminal Emulation
- ☑ VMS
- ☑ UNIX
- ☑ OS/2
- ☑ Other platform

Cost
- ☐ Unknown
- ☐ Basic
- ☐ Extended
- ☑ Premium ($)
- ☐ Executive w/$

Activity Level
UNKNOWN

Address
GO: **DUNS** or **DMI**

Dvorak Development Forum

Description
If you use Dvorak Development's NavCIS programs, join this forum for technical support and product information. You also can download a free 30-day demo of the DOS and Windows products to see if you want to purchase the commercial versions.

Subjects
Computers, CompuServe Navigational Tools, NavCIS

Audience
CompuServe users, NavCIS users

Content Summary
If you want to try out NavCIS, see Library 1, "NavCIS Software," to download a 3-day demo of the DOS and Windows versions of NavCIS. Libraries 2–5 offer Windows and DOS support of the SE/TE and Pro versions of NavCIS. Library 7, "Modems and Hardware," contains information and files to help you configure and optimize your modem setup. You also should check out Library 8, "Tip and Techniques," for tips on using NavCIS.

See Also
WinCIM Forum

User Guide
- ☑ Windows
- ☑ DOS
- ☐ Macintosh
- ☐ Terminal Emulation
- ☐ VMS
- ☐ UNIX
- ☐ OS/2
- ☐ Other platform

Cost
- ☐ Unknown
- ☐ Basic
- ☑ Extended
- ☐ Premium ($)
- ☐ Executive w/$

Activity Level

MEDIUM / HIGH

Address
GO: **DVORAK**

E

E-MAIL

Lotus Communications Forum

Description
This forum is devoted to Lotus Corporation's communications products, including Notes and cc:Mail.

Subjects
Computer Communications, Computer Hardware, Computer Networking, Computers, E-mail, Networking

Audience
Management information specialists, network users

Content Summary
You can find a plethora of information, technical support solutions, hints and tips, and want ads in this forum. The library and message forums include Notes Tech Info, Notes Workstations/DB, Notes API Devlopment, cc:Mail Platform, cc:Mail Router, cc:Mail Admin, and many others.

See Also
Lotus Press Release Forum, Lotus Technical Library

User Guide
- ☑ Windows
- ☑ DOS
- ☑ Macintosh
- ☐ Terminal Emulation
- ☐ VMS
- ☐ UNIX
- ☑ OS/2
- ☑ Other platform

Cost
- ☐ Unknown
- ☐ Basic
- ☑ Extended
- ☐ Premium ($)
- ☐ Executive w/$

Activity Level

Address
GO: **LOTUSCOMM**

Microsoft Mail and Workgroups Forum

Description
This forum is designed as an area to exchange information, tips, and techniques concerning Microsoft Windows Workgroup Applications.

Subjects
Computers, E-mail, Microsoft Corp.

Audience
Computer users, management information specialists

Content Summary
If you have a problem with Microsoft's Windows Workgoup Applications, such as MS Schedule Plus and Mail, you probably can find the solution here. Some of the libraries and message sections include MS Mail for PC, Remote/Modems, MS Schedule Plus, MS Mail for Mac, MS Eforms, Workgroup Templates, and much more. The Microsoft Forms Designer Run Time file is available in Library 16, Workgroup Templates.

See Also
Microsoft Connection, Microsoft DevCast Forum, Microsoft Knowledge Base

User Guide
- ☑ Windows
- ☑ DOS
- ☑ Macintosh
- ☐ Terminal Emulation
- ☐ VMS
- ☐ UNIX
- ☐ OS/2
- ☐ Other platform

Cost
- ☐ Unknown
- ☑ Basic
- ☐ Extended
- ☐ Premium ($)
- ☐ Executive w/$

Activity Level

Address
GO: **MSWGA**

E*TRADE Securities

Description
Do you want to get a grip on your investments? This service enables you to do just that. E*TRADE handles individual, investment, margin, IRA, joint, KEOGH, and 401K accounts, and offers a stock market game that uses real stock market prices and data.

Subjects
Financial, Investments, Stock Market

Audience
Accountants, investors

Content Summary
This "around-the-clock" service offers you commissions of 1 1/2 cents per share, with a $35.00 minimum; Black-Sholes option analysis that uses current prices; investment management; and free checking accounts tied to your money market funds. The investment management offers you quotes, portfolio reports, limit orders, and news alerts.

See Also
ETGAME

E* TRADE Securities – Economy

User Guide
- ☐ Windows
- ☐ DOS
- ☐ Macintosh
- ☑ Terminal Emulation
- ☐ VMS
- ☐ UNIX
- ☐ OS/2
- ☐ Other platform

Cost
- ☐ Unknown
- ☐ Basic
- ☐ Extended
- ☑ Premium ($)
- ☐ Executive w/$

Activity Level

LOW — UNKNOWN — MEDIUM — HIGH

Address
GO: **ETRADE**

E*TRADE Stock Market Game

Description
Have you ever wondered what it would be like to be a Wall Street mover and shaker? Now's your chance to invest $100,000 in game accounts by playing the E*TRADE Stock Market Game. The game lets you play in stocks only, stocks and options, or both, and will track your performance—and commission rates—every month. If you have the right stuff and have the highest percentage increase of all the players, you can win a cash prize.

Subjects
Games, Finance, Wall Street

Audience
Financial persons, gamers, students

Content Summary
The E*TRADE Securities main menu offers you three choices: Game Instructions, Sign-up for the Game, and Play the E*TRADE Stock Market Game. Select Game Instructions to read directions on how to play and what you can win. You compete with other members to see who can become the wealthiest in a month. When you sign up for the game, you are given $100,000 in game money with which to start.

See Also
E*TRADE Securities

User Guide
- ☐ Windows
- ☐ DOS
- ☐ Macintosh
- ☑ Terminal Emulation
- ☐ VMS
- ☐ UNIX
- ☐ OS/2
- ☐ Other platform

Cost
- ☐ Unknown
- ☐ Basic
- ☑ Extended
- ☐ Premium ($)
- ☐ Executive w/$

Activity Level

LOW — UNKNOWN — MEDIUM — HIGH

Address
GO: **ETGAME**

Earth Forum

Description
Do you want to help solve environmental problems? If so, or if you're just interested in Earth-related issues, join this forum. Compare notes with other people and organizations concerned about the Earth and its environment.

Subjects
Environmental Issues

Audience
Environmentalists, scientists, biologists

Content Summary
The Earth Forum libraries contain topics such as air/climate, water, lands and forests, recycling, energy, population, and Greenpeace. Be sure to check out the graphics in Library 0, "Graphics/Animation," for some nice scenic photographs from around the world.

See Also
Gardening Forum, Humane Society of the United States Forum, Outdoors Forum, Space/Astronomy Forum

User Guide
- ☑ Windows
- ☑ DOS
- ☑ Macintosh
- ☐ Terminal Emulation
- ☑ VMS
- ☑ UNIX
- ☑ OS/2
- ☐ Other platform

Cost
- ☐ Unknown
- ☐ Basic
- ☑ Extended
- ☐ Premium ($)
- ☐ Executive w/$

Activity Level

LOW — MEDIUM — HIGH (arrow points to HIGH)

Address
GO: **EARTH**

ECONOMY

Finance

Description
The Finance service offers you a plethora of services for your financial concerns, including FundWatch Online by *Money Magazine*.

Subjects
Economy, Finance, Financial

Audience
Financial advisors, fitness enthusiasts, market researchers, accountants, businesspeople

Content Summary
From the Finance main menu, you can choose from several financial and investment services, including Basic Quotes, FundWatch Online by Money Magazine, Basic Company Snapshot, Issue/Symbol Lookup, Loan Analyzer, Market Quotes/Highlights, Company Information, Brokerage Services, Earnings/Economics Projections, Micro Software Interfaces, Personal Finance/Insurance, Financial Forums, MicroQuote II, Business News, Instructions/Fees, and Read Before Investing. When you select one of these options, you are sent to that specific area. Note that some of the areas are terminal emulation.

See Also
Commodity Pricing ($), Current Market Snapshot, Current Day Quotes ($), Financial Forums, Options Profile ($W)

User Guide
- ☑ Windows
- ☑ DOS
- ☑ Macintosh
- ☐ Terminal Emulation
- ☑ VMS
- ☑ UNIX
- ☑ OS/2
- ☐ Other platform

Cost
- ☐ Unknown
- ☑ Basic
- ☐ Extended
- ☐ Premium ($)
- ☐ Executive w/$

Activity Level UNKNOWN

Address
GO: **FINANCE**

EDUCATION

ADD Forum

Description
Information and support for adults, parents, and professionals interested in attention deficit disorder and other neurological conditions.

Subjects
Attention Deficit, Hyperactivity, Medicine

Audience
Medical personnel, parents

Content Summary
This forum's libraries include information for patients, parents, children, and other people interested in this disorder.

See Also
Information USA

User Guide
- ☑ Windows
- ☑ DOS
- ☐ Macintosh
- ☐ Terminal Emulation
- ☐ VMS
- ☐ UNIX
- ☐ OS/2
- ☐ Other platform

Cost
- ☐ Unknown
- ☐ Basic
- ☑ Extended
- ☐ Premium ($)
- ☐ Executive w/$

Activity Level MEDIUM (arrow pointing toward HIGH)

Address
GO: **ADD**

American Heritage Dictionary

Description
The online version of the American Heritage Dictionary, with detailed definitions of over 303,000 words and phrases.

Subjects
Dictionary, Spelling

Audience
Students

Content Summary
Users can search the database by entering the word or part of the word, if the spelling is unknown.

See Also
Academic American Enclopedia

User Guide
- ☑ Windows
- ☑ DOS
- ☐ Macintosh
- ☐ Terminal Emulation
- ☐ VMS
- ☐ UNIX
- ☐ OS/2
- ☐ Other platform

Cost
- ☐ Unknown
- ☑ Basic
- ☐ Extended
- ☐ Premium ($)
- ☐ Executive w/$

Activity Level UNKNOWN

Address
GO: **DICTIONARY**

Computer Training Forum

Description

The DPTRAIN Forum is dedicated to the question of how people learn to use computers and how to help them learn more effectively.

Subjects

Computers, Education

Audience

Computer trainers

Content Summary

Libraries include training techniques, technology, support, information centers, local groups, newsletters, and training software.

See Also

Computer Club Forum, Macmillan Publishing Forum

User Guide

- [x] Windows
- [x] DOS
- [x] Macintosh
- [ ] Terminal Emulation
- [ ] VMS
- [x] UNIX
- [ ] OS/2
- [ ] Other platform

Cost

- [ ] Unknown
- [ ] Basic
- [x] Extended
- [ ] Premium ($)
- [ ] Executive w/$

Activity Level

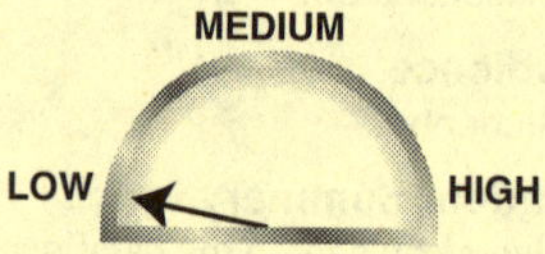

Address

GO: **DPTRAIN**

Dissertation Abstracts

Description

Contains references to U.S. and Canadian Ph.D. dissertations since 1861 and master theses since 1962. Includes abstracts of dissertations from 1980 and on. Professional (such as MD) and honorary degrees are not included.

Subjects

Dissertations, Education, Research

Audience

Graduate students, historians, professors, researchers, students

Content Summary

Each dissertation includes author, title, date of publication, college, and degree for which the dissertation was submitted. Dissertation Abstracts is published and copyrighted by University Microfilms International and made available by BRS Information Technologies.

You should note that Dissertation Abstracts includes transaction charges in addition to CompuServe base connect rates. You can see a running total of transaction charges on the Dissertation Abstract menu pages. Connect charges are not included in the displayed total.

The following are rates for using Dissertation Abstracts:

- Search (retrieves up to 10 titles): $5
- Additional titles (in groups of 10): $5
- Full reference, with abstract where available (selected from the titles): $5 each

In addition to connect time charges, there is a $1 charge for a search that retrieves no titles.

See Also

IQuest Database

User Guide

- [x] Windows
- [x] DOS
- [x] Macintosh
- [x] Terminal Emulation
- [x] VMS
- [x] UNIX
- [x] OS/2
- [ ] Other platform

Cost

- [ ] Unknown
- [ ] Basic
- [ ] Extended
- [x] Premium ($)
- [ ] Executive w/$

Activity Level

Address

GO: **DISSERTATION**

Education Forum

Description

This forum is designed to share and exchange information about all facets of the teaching and learning process. The use of computers and computer-related teaching methods is a hot topic in this forum.

Subjects

Computers in Education, Education, Teaching

Audience

Administrators, teachers, college and university faculty, product developers and publishers of educational material, librarians, school board members, counselors, principals

Content Summary

The Education Forum sponsors two weekly online meetings, including Tuesday evenings in Room 1 (General) at 9:30 p.m. Eastern and Thursday evenings in Room 5 (Homeschoolers) at 9:00 p.m. Eastern. This forum's libraries contain information on earning a degree online (Library 11), sex and AIDS education (Library 15), public domain and shareware software (Library 2), and lessons on how to participate in online conferences (Library 1, HOW2CO.TXT).

See Also
Education Research Forum, ERIC

User Guide
- [x] Windows
- [x] DOS
- [x] Macintosh
- [ ] Terminal Emulation
- [ ] VMS
- [ ] UNIX
- [ ] OS/2
- [ ] Other platform

Cost
- [ ] Unknown
- [ ] Basic
- [x] Extended
- [ ] Premium ($)
- [ ] Executive w/$

Activity Level

Address
GO: **EDFORUM**

Education Research Forum

Description
This forum is for people who are interested in research of products and topics in education, and is sponsored by the American Educational Research Association.

Subjects
Education, Education Research

Audience
Educators, researchers, principals

Content Summary
Libraries 1–11 correspond to the divisions of the American Educational Research Association, including programs, articles, and transcripts of conferences about the articles. You'll find libraries on curriculum studies, learning and instructions, methods, counseling, and virtual reality (Library 12). See Library 14 for information on employment opportunities.

See Also
ERIC, Education Forum

User Guide
- [x] Windows
- [x] DOS
- [x] Macintosh
- [ ] Terminal Emulation
- [ ] VMS
- [x] UNIX
- [ ] OS/2
- [ ] Other platform

Cost
- [ ] Unknown
- [ ] Basic
- [x] Extended
- [ ] Premium ($)
- [ ] Executive w/$

Activity Level

Address
GO: **EDRESEARCH**

ERIC—Education Resources Information Center

Description
This database contains abstracts of articles covering education, including vocational education, counseling, teacher education, and testing. ERIC is published by the U.S. Department of Education.

Subjects
Education

Audience
Educators, students, teachers, counselors, researchers

Content Summary
Information in this database goes back to 1966 and is updated monthly. Two subfiles are within ERIC: the Resources In Education (RIE) and the Current Index to Journals in Education (CIJE) files. The RIE contains reports on research and technical issues, conference papers and proceedings, program descriptions, opinions, bibliographies, reviews, dissertations, teaching and curriculum materials, lesson plans, and guides. The CIJE contains abstracts of articles from 750 education-related journals. Pricing varies depending on what you obtain. See the Pricing Information option in the ERIC main menu for more information.

See Also
IQUEST Education InfoCenter

User Guide
- [x] Windows
- [x] DOS
- [x] Macintosh
- [ ] Terminal Emulation
- [x] VMS
- [x] UNIX
- [x] OS/2
- [x] Other platform

Cost
- [ ] Unknown
- [ ] Basic
- [x] Extended
- [x] Premium ($)
- [ ] Executive w/$

Activity Level

UNKNOWN

Address
GO: **ERIC**

Education – Education Forum

Grolier's Academic American Encyclopedia

Description
Online edition of the *Grolier's Academic American Encyclopedia*.

Subjects
Education

Audience
Students, teachers, general public

Content Summary
Contains the complete text of the encyclopedia. Text is updated quarterly.

See Also
Information USA

User Guide
- ☑ Windows
- ☑ DOS
- ☐ Macintosh
- ☐ Terminal Emulation
- ☐ VMS
- ☐ UNIX
- ☐ OS/2
- ☐ Other platform

Cost
- ☐ Unknown
- ☐ Basic
- ☑ Extended
- ☐ Premium ($)
- ☐ Executive w/$

Activity Level

Address
GO: **GROLIERS**

Students' Forum

Description
A forum for students and teachers who wish to share their experiences and ideas in a friendly forum atmosphere.

Subjects
Education

Audience
Students, educators

Content Summary
Libraries include information on grade school, middle school, high school, college/university, and graduate and professional schools. Also included are conference areas for children and a Teen Club area.

See Also
Education Forum

User Guide
- ☑ Windows
- ☑ DOS
- ☑ Macintosh
- ☐ Terminal Emulation
- ☐ VMS
- ☐ UNIX
- ☐ OS/2
- ☐ Other platform

Cost
- ☐ Unknown
- ☐ Basic
- ☑ Extended
- ☐ Premium ($)
- ☐ Executive w/$

Activity Level

Address
GO: **STUFO**

Univ of Phoenix

Description
Online area providing information on the University of Phoenix' online curriculum. Students take courses via modem.

Subjects
Education

Audience
Students, teachers

Content Summary
This service enables you to view curriculum and take courses online.

See Also
Education Forum

User Guide
- ☑ Windows
- ☑ DOS
- ☐ Macintosh
- ☐ Terminal Emulation
- ☐ VMS
- ☐ UNIX
- ☐ OS/2
- ☐ Other platform

Cost
- ☐ Unknown
- ☐ Basic
- ☐ Extended
- ☐ Premium ($)
- ☑ Executive w/$

Activity Level

Address
GO: **UP**

Education Forum

Description
This forum is designed to share and exchange information about all facets of the teaching and learning process. The use of computers and computer-related teaching methods is a hot topic in this forum.

Subjects
Computers in Education, Education, Teaching

Education Forum (continued)

Audience
Administrators, teachers, college and university faculty, product developers and publishers of educational material, librarians, school board members, counselors, principals

Content Summary
The Education Forum sponsors two weekly online meetings, including Tuesday evenings in Room 1 (General) at 9:30 p.m. Eastern and Thursday evenings in Room 5 (Homeschoolers) at 9:00 p.m. Eastern. This forum's libraries contain information on earning a degree online (Library 11), sex and AIDS education (Library 15), public domain and shareware software (Library 2), and lessons on how to participate in online conferences (Library 1, HOW2CO.TXT).

See Also
Education Research Forum, ERIC

User Guide
- [x] Windows
- [x] DOS
- [x] Macintosh
- [ ] Terminal Emulation
- [ ] VMS
- [ ] UNIX
- [ ] OS/2
- [ ] Other platform

Cost
- [ ] Unknown
- [ ] Basic
- [x] Extended
- [ ] Premium ($)
- [ ] Executive w/$

Activity Level: MEDIUM (LOW — HIGH)

Address
GO: **EDFORUM**

Education Research Forum

Description
This forum is for people who are interested in research of products and topics in education, and is sponsored by the American Educational Research Association.

Subjects
Education, Education Research

Audience
Educators, researchers, principals

Content Summary
Libraries 1–11 correspond to the divisions of the American Educational Research Association, including programs, articles, and transcripts of conferences about the articles. You'll find libraries on curriculum studies, learning and instructions, methods, counseling, and virtual reality (Library 12). See Library 14 for information on employment opportunities.

See Also
ERIC, Education Forum

User Guide
- [x] Windows
- [x] DOS
- [x] Macintosh
- [ ] Terminal Emulation
- [ ] VMS
- [x] UNIX
- [ ] OS/2
- [ ] Other platform

Cost
- [ ] Unknown
- [ ] Basic
- [x] Extended
- [ ] Premium ($)
- [ ] Executive w/$

Activity Level: MEDIUM (LOW — HIGH)

Address
GO: **EDRESEARCH**

Ei Compendex Plus

Description
The Ei Compendex Plus database contains abstracts and articles from engineering and technological literature. You can find literature from virtually all the engineering disciplines in this database.

Subjects
Applied Physics, Food Technology, Engineering, Pollution

Audience
Engineers

Content Summary
This database contains worldwide coverage of articles taken from journals, publications of engineering societies and organizations, conference papers and proceedings, and government reports and books. In a search, you can get the author, title, corporate source, conference title, publication year, language, and an abstract from the article. See the Pricing Information choice in the main menu for the various pricing charges.

See Also
ERIC, IQuest

User Guide
- [x] Windows
- [x] DOS
- [x] Macintosh
- [ ] Terminal Emulation
- [x] VMS
- [x] UNIX
- [x] OS/2
- [x] Other platform

Cost
- [ ] Unknown
- [ ] Basic
- [ ] Extended
- [x] Premium ($)
- [ ] Executive w/$

Ei Compendex Plus – Electronic Convention Center

Activity Level

Address
GO: **COMPENDEX**

Eicon Technology Forum

Description
Sponsored by Eicon Technology, this forum helps users find answers to questions or problems concerning Eicon products. Eicon offers products of connectivity solutions for the X.25 and SNA environment.

Subjects
Computers, Connectivity, X.25, SNA

Audience
MIS people, Eicon consumers

Content Summary
The library and message sections contain information about Eicon products as well as technical support, press releases, utilities, help files, applications, demos, and Q&A. The libraries include sections for emulators, gateways, tool kits, international services, and WAN services.

See Also
Telacommunications Issues Forum

User Guide
- [x] Windows
- [x] DOS
- [x] Macintosh
- [ ] Terminal Emulation
- [x] VMS
- [x] UNIX
- [x] OS/2
- [ ] Other platform

Cost
- [ ] Unknown
- [ ] Basic
- [x] Extended
- [ ] Premium ($)
- [ ] Executive w/$

Activity Level

Address
GO: **EICON**

Electronic Books

Description
This is a ZiffNet area. You must be a member of ZiffNet or apply for membership when you first go to the Electronic Books area. The cost of ZiffNet membership is $2.95 monthly. The Electronic Books area offers you an option to buy books directly from the Ziff-Davis Press at 20 percent discount by selecting the ZD Press Booknet option from the main menu.

Subjects
Computers, Computer Books, ZiffNet

Audience
Computer users

Content Summary
When you select the ZD Press Booknet option, you can order Ziff Davis Press books, get special discounts from their remainder table (40 percent off cover price sometimes), download any special offers, or talk to customer service. The Electronic Books service also features the Project Gutenburg Free Book Library, which has over 100 electronic books ranging from literature (such as *Moby Dick*) to Internet titles (such as the *Hitchhiker's Guide to the Internet*) that users can download.

See Also
Macmillan Publishing Forum

User Guide
- [x] Windows
- [x] DOS
- [x] Macintosh
- [ ] Terminal Emulation
- [ ] VMS
- [ ] UNIX
- [ ] OS/2
- [ ] Other platform

Cost
- [ ] Unknown
- [ ] Basic
- [ ] Extended
- [x] Premium ($)
- [ ] Executive w/$

Activity Level

Address
GO: **ZNT:EBOOKS**

Electronic Convention Center

Description
The Electronic Convention Center enables you to access any of CompuServe's special conferences from your desktop. You can find out about upcoming conferences, make a reservation to attend one of them, and attend another all within a few minutes.

Subjects
Conventions

Audience
General public

Content Summary
The Convention Center has three types of conferences, including roundtable, moderated, and lecture conferences. A roundtable conference offers open chatter during the conference. A moderated conference is more formal than a roundtable and usually is hosted by an experienced individual on a topic. A lecture is a lecture—no chatter or questions

Electronic Convention Center – Electronics

are allowed. To make a reservation, type **RESERVE** *x,* where *x* is the number of the conference listing in the List Conference/Make Reservations option.

User Guide
- ☐ Windows
- ☐ DOS
- ☐ Macintosh
- ☑ Terminal Emulation
- ☐ VMS
- ☐ UNIX
- ☐ OS/2
- ☐ Other platform

Cost
- ☐ Unknown
- ☑ Basic
- ☐ Extended
- ☐ Premium ($)
- ☐ Executive w/$

Activity Level

Address
GO: **CONVENTION**

ELECTRONIC GAMES

Enhanced Adventure

Description
"Somewhere nearby is Colossal Cave. . . ." Are you ready for an online adventure? Have you experienced Classic Adventure already? Then this is the place for you.

Subjects
Electronic Games, Adventure Games

Audience
12 years and older

Content Summary
If you are new to ADVENTURE-Land, type **Help** for instructions. If you have experienced ADVENTURE-Land before, you're not going to get any hints here. A perfect ending gets you 751.

See Also
Classic Adventure, Entertainment Center

User Guide
- ☑ Windows
- ☑ DOS
- ☑ Macintosh
- ☐ Terminal Emulation
- ☐ VMS
- ☐ UNIX
- ☐ OS/2
- ☐ Other platform

Cost
- ☐ Unknown
- ☑ Basic
- ☐ Extended
- ☐ Premium ($)
- ☐ Executive w/$

Activity Level

Address
GO: **ENADVENT**

Electronic Tax Return Filing

Description
File your taxes online with this service.

Subjects
Electronic Filing, Taxes

Audience
Tax payers

Content Summary
During the off-season (which it was when this book was written), this service does not accept tax returns. You can, however, leave messages in the Member FEEDBACK option in the main menu.

See Also
Government Information

User Guide
- ☐ Windows
- ☐ DOS
- ☐ Macintosh
- ☑ Terminal Emulation
- ☐ VMS
- ☐ UNIX
- ☐ OS/2
- ☐ Other platform

Cost
- ☐ Unknown
- ☐ Basic
- ☑ Extended
- ☐ Premium ($)
- ☐ Executive w/$

Activity Level

Address
GO: **TAXRETURN**

ELECTRONICS

Siemens Automation

Description
This is the main menu for entrance to the product support forum and product database of Siemens AG, a German electronics manufacturer.

Subjects
Electronics

Audience
Siemens product users

Electronics – EMI Aviation Services

Content Summary
Libraries include new product uploads, animation library, graphics storeroom, sound clips library, and MIDI song library.

See Also
Stac Electronics Forum

User Guide
- ☑ Windows
- ☑ DOS
- ☑ Macintosh
- ☐ Terminal Emulation
- ☐ VMS
- ☑ UNIX
- ☐ OS/2
- ☑ Other platform

Cost
- ☐ Unknown
- ☐ Basic
- ☑ Extended
- ☐ Premium ($)
- ☐ Executive w/$

Activity Level

Address
GO: **SIEAUT**

Stac Electronics Forum

Description
This is the vendor support forum for products from Stac Electronics.

Subjects
Electronics

Audience
Stac users and vendors

Content Summary
Libraries include information on utilities, product information, tech notes, and developer products.

See Also
PC Catalog

User Guide
- ☑ Windows
- ☑ DOS
- ☑ Macintosh
- ☐ Terminal Emulation
- ☐ VMS
- ☐ UNIX
- ☐ OS/2
- ☐ Other platform

Cost
- ☐ Unknown
- ☐ Basic
- ☑ Extended
- ☐ Premium ($)
- ☐ Executive w/$

Activity Level

Address
GO: **STACKER**

EMI Aviation Services

Description
Designed for pilots and flight planners, the EMI Aviation Services area enables pilots of any aircraft to get flight plans, weather briefings, and flight plan filings from this service. The EMI database contains all public-use airports in the contiguous 48 states and southern Canada, except for Newfoundland.

Subjects
Air Flight, Travel Plans

Audience
Pilots, air traffic controllers

Content Summary
This is a full-featured aviation service that should help you plan and record your flights. The Pro-Plan Option, found in the EMI Descriptions and Instructions option on the main menu, gives you enhanced printouts of your top of climb and descent points, average ground speeds, calculated wind direction and speed, and ambient temperature and deviation from ISA. If you're familiar with all this terminology, this service might be just what you're looking for.

See Also
Air Line Pilots Association

User Guide
- ☑ Windows
- ☑ DOS
- ☑ Macintosh
- ☐ Terminal Emulation
- ☑ VMS
- ☑ UNIX
- ☑ OS/2
- ☑ Other platform

Cost
- ☐ Unknown
- ☐ Basic
- ☑ Extended
- ☑ Premium ($)
- ☐ Executive w/$

Activity Level

UNKNOWN

Address
GO: **EMI**

EMOTIONAL PROBLEMS

Disabilities Forum

Description
This forum is designed to be an online support group and open communication facilitator for anyone interested in disabilities. You can find stories, reports, and information about disabled persons' daily lives, along with ideas and experiences of parents and friends of disabled people.

Subjects
Emotional Problems, Learning Disabilities, Multiple Sclerosis, Disabilities

Audience
Disabled persons, family and friends of disabled persons, professionals who work with disabled persons

Content Summary
Many message and library topics are available to choose from, including developmental disabilities, emotional disturbances, hearing impairments, multiple sclerosis, and mobility impairments. You can find the latest information on the Americans with Disabilities Act (ADA) in Library 7, "Government Activities." If you are looking for employment, see "Education/Employment," Library 8, for files designed for disabled persons searching for employment and education.

See Also
Handicapped Users Database, Health/Fitness, Healthnet

User Guide
- ☑ Windows
- ☑ DOS
- ☑ Macintosh
- ☐ Terminal Emulation
- ☑ VMS
- ☑ UNIX
- ☑ OS/2
- ☐ Other platform

Cost
- ☐ Unknown
- ☐ Basic
- ☑ Extended
- ☐ Premium ($)
- ☐ Executive w/$

Activity Level

Address
GO: **DISABILITIES**

EMPLOYMENT

Classified Ads

Description
An online classified ads section where you can buy and sell most anything!

Subjects
Employment

Audience
Shoppers

Content Summary
You can find ads for employment, education, job searches, computer equipment, and business opportunities.

See Also
Career Track

User Guide
- ☑ Windows
- ☑ DOS
- ☑ Macintosh
- ☐ Terminal Emulation
- ☐ VMS
- ☑ UNIX
- ☐ OS/2
- ☑ Other platform

Cost
- ☐ Unknown
- ☑ Basic
- ☐ Extended
- ☐ Premium ($)
- ☐ Executive w/$

Activity Level

Address
GO: **CLASSIFIED**

ENCOUNTERS

Encounters Forum

Description
Have you ever experienced something paranormal? Spotted a UFO? Had an encounter that you cannot explain? If so, join this forum and discuss your encounter online. The FOX-TV *Encounters* television show producers plan frequent contact with Forum users via this service.

Subjects
Encounters, UFO, Paranormal Experiences

Audience
UFO researchers

Content Summary
The libraries in this forum offer AVI video clips of UFO sightings, interviews, news reports, multimedia files, and various software files. Check out Library 4, "Graphic Files," for graphics files of UFO sightings, aliens, and Mars photographs. You also can download the Roger Patterson photo of Bigfoot.

See Also
Participate

User Guide
- ☑ Windows
- ☑ DOS
- ☑ Macintosh
- ☐ Terminal Emulation
- ☐ VMS
- ☑ UNIX
- ☑ OS/2
- ☐ Other platform

Cost
- ☐ Unknown
- ☐ Basic
- ☑ Extended
- ☐ Premium ($)
- ☐ Executive w/$

Activity Level

Address
GO: **ENCOUNTERS**

ENGINEERING

Ei Compendex Plus

Description
The Ei Compendex Plus database contains abstracts and articles from engineering and technological literature. You can find literature from virtually all the engineering disciplines in this database.

Subjects
Applied Physics, Food Technology, Engineering, Pollution

Audience
Engineers

Content Summary
This database contains worldwide coverage of articles taken from journals, publications of engineering societies and organizations, conference papers and proceedings, and government reports and books. In a search, you can get the author, title, corporate source, conference title, publication year, language, and an abstract from the article. See the Pricing Information choice in the main menu for the various pricing charges.

See Also
ERIC, IQuest

User Guide
- ☑ Windows
- ☑ DOS
- ☑ Macintosh
- ☐ Terminal Emulation
- ☑ VMS
- ☑ UNIX
- ☑ OS/2
- ☑ Other platform

Cost
- ☐ Unknown
- ☐ Basic
- ☐ Extended
- ☑ Premium ($)
- ☐ Executive w/$

Activity Level

Address
GO: **COMPENDEX**

Engineering Automation Forum

Description
LEAP (League for Engineering Productivity) sponsors this forum for discussions about CADD/CAM and other programs that are used by engineers, architects, and other professionals for design.

Subjects
CADD/CAM, Engineering, Computers, Computer-Aided Design

Audience
CADD/CAM engineers, engineers, designers

Content Summary
You can find discussions that will help you find the right CADD/CAM product for you, tips on using programs, information on new technologies, and management tools and utilities. Visit Library 9, "Classified/Jobs," for job opportunities and resumes.

See Also
Autodesk AutoCAD Forum

User Guide
- ☑ Windows
- ☑ DOS
- ☑ Macintosh
- ☐ Terminal Emulation
- ☐ VMS
- ☐ UNIX
- ☐ OS/2
- ☐ Other platform

Cost
- ☐ Unknown
- ☐ Basic
- ☑ Extended
- ☐ Premium ($)
- ☐ Executive w/$

Activity Level MEDIUM (arrow pointing up)

Address
GO: **LEAP**

Enhanced Adventure

Description
"Somewhere nearby is Colossal Cave. . . ." Are you ready for an online adventure? Have you experienced Classic Adventure already? Then this is the place for you.

Subjects
Electronic Games, Adventure Games

Audience
12 years and older

Content Summary
If you are new to ADVENTURE-Land, type **Help** for instructions. If you have experienced ADVENTURE-Land before, you're not going to get any hints here. A perfect ending gets you 751.

See Also
Classic Adventure, Entertainment Center

User Guide
- ☑ Windows
- ☑ DOS
- ☑ Macintosh
- ☐ Terminal Emulation
- ☐ VMS
- ☐ UNIX
- ☐ OS/2
- ☐ Other platform

Cost
- ☐ Unknown
- ☑ Basic
- ☐ Extended
- ☐ Premium ($)
- ☐ Executive w/$

Activity Level

Address
GO: **ENADVENT**

ENTERTAINMENT

Associated Press Online

Description
News stories from the Associated Press.

Subjects
Current Events, Entertainment, News

Audience
Consumers, journalists

Content Summary
Read up-to-date news stories of national and world interest.

See Also
Information USA

(continued)

User Guide
- ☑ Windows
- ☑ DOS
- ☑ Macintosh
- ☐ Terminal Emulation
- ☑ VMS
- ☑ UNIX
- ☑ OS/2
- ☐ Other platform

Cost
- ☐ Unknown
- ☐ Basic
- ☑ Extended
- ☐ Premium ($)
- ☐ Executive w/$

Activity Level

(UNKNOWN, LOW–MEDIUM–HIGH)

Address
GO: **APO**

Entertainment Drive Center

Description
This is your backstage pass to the entertainment industry. You can get David Letterman Top 10 lists, O.J. Simpson trial transcripts, exclusive columns and reviews, and multimedia files.

Subjects
Celebrities, Entertainment, Multimedia

Audience
Journalists, photojournalists, anyone interested in entertainment industry

Content Summary
Because of the nature of the entertainment industry, many of the files posted in this forum are removed on certain dates, including a collection of Lion King graphics that were posted until August 31, 1994. If you missed these, don't despair; other hot topics will be featured every month.

See Also
Hollywood Hotline

User Guide
- ☑ Windows
- ☑ DOS
- ☑ Macintosh
- ☐ Terminal Emulation
- ☐ VMS
- ☐ UNIX
- ☐ OS/2
- ☐ Other platform

Cost
- ☐ Unknown
- ☐ Basic
- ☑ Extended
- ☐ Premium ($)
- ☐ Executive w/$

Activity Level

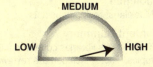

Address
GO: **EDRIVE**

Entertainment

Hollywood Hotline

Description
This service is devoted to the noteworthy events that happen in Hollywood and includes a Hollywood trivia quiz.

Subjects
Entertainment, Gossip

Audience
General public

Content Summary
If you want to find out what's going on in Hollywood or the movie business, stop by the Hollywood Hotline. You can read entertainment news, peruse an online entertainment encyclopedia, see film and TV ratings, read movie reviews, and take a quiz (in terminal emulation mode). The SHOWBIZQUIZ menu features games on Frank Sinatra, Judy Garland, Clint Eastwood, Wizard of Oz, TV Detective Puzzle, and many more.

See Also
Roger Ebert's Movie Reviews, SHOWBIZ Quiz, ShowBiz-Media Forum

User Guide
☑	Windows	☑	VMS
☑	DOS	☑	UNIX
☑	Macintosh	☑	OS/2
☑	Terminal Emulation	☐	Other platform

Cost
☐	Unknown	☐	Premium ($)
☑	Basic	☐	Executive w/$
☐	Extended		

Activity level

Address
GO: HOLLYWOOD

Rocknet Forum

Description
This forum provides the most up-to-date and accurate information on the rock community.

Subjects
Entertainment, Music, Rock Enthusiasts, Video

Audience
Musicians, rock enthusiasts

Content Summary
This forum's libraries cover the full range of rock topics. Topics included are reviews of concerts and music, lists of alternative radio stations, coverage of the musical group Grateful Dead, heavy metal, vintage rock, new music, online conversations with rock personalities, and graphics of musical group logos and photographs taken at concerts.

See Also
Rock Video Monthly

User Guide
☑	Windows	☐	VMS
☑	DOS	☐	UNIX
☑	Macintosh	☐	OS/2
☐	Terminal Emulation	☐	Other platform

Cost
☐	Unknown	☐	Premium ($)
☐	Basic	☐	Executive w/$
☑	Extended		

Activity Level — MEDIUM

Address
GO: ROCKNET

Showbiz Quiz

Description
Companion to the ShowBiz Forum and Hollywood Hotline, this area features trivia quizzes on several ShowBiz topics.

Subjects
Games, Movies, Television, Trivia

Audience
Movie enthusiasts

Content Summary
The libraries contain information about the forum, home entertainment, recent films, new films, classic films, television, celebrities, and Hollywood news.

See Also
Hollywood Hotline

User Guide
☑	Windows	☐	VMS
☑	DOS	☑	UNIX
☑	Macintosh	☐	OS/2
☐	Terminal Emulation	☐	Other platform

Cost
☐	Unknown	☐	Premium ($)
☐	Basic	☐	Executive w/$
☑	Extended		

Activity Level — UNKNOWN

Address
GO: SBQ

Entertainment

ShowBiz-Media Forum

Description
The oldest and largest entertainment forum on CIS, ShowBiz covers the entire spectrum of the world of show business and media.

Subjects
Entertainment

Audience
Trivia enthusiasts

Content Summary
Libraries include information on movies, radio, television, theater, celebrities, multimedia, music, soaps, screen writing

See Also
Showbiz Quiz Forum, Hollywood Hotline

User Guide
- ☑ Windows
- ☑ DOS
- ☑ Macintosh
- ☐ Terminal Emulation
- ☐ VMS
- ☑ UNIX
- ☐ OS/2
- ☐ Other platform

Cost
- ☐ Unknown
- ☐ Basic
- ☑ Extended
- ☐ Premium ($)
- ☐ Executive w/$

Activity Level

Address
GO: **SHOWBIZ**

Sight And Sound Forum

Description
The forum covering all types of computerized audio and visual hardware.

Subjects
Audio/Video, Entertainment

Audience
Audio and video enthusiasts

Content Summary
Libraries include video techniques, audio techniques, graphics and sound files, and MIDI.

See Also
Audio Engineering Society, Video Games Forum

User Guide
- ☑ Windows
- ☑ DOS
- ☑ Macintosh
- ☐ Terminal Emulation
- ☐ VMS
- ☐ UNIX
- ☐ OS/2
- ☐ Other platform

Cost
- ☐ Unknown
- ☐ Basic
- ☑ Extended
- ☐ Premium ($)
- ☐ Executive w/$

Activity Level

Address
GO: **SSFORUM**

Stein Online

Description
This conference area is hosted by Eliot Stein, who interviews the stars online.

Subjects
Celebrities, Entertainment

Audience
Fans of celebrities

Content Summary
If you want to communicate online with famous celebrities, this forum provides an online conferences.

See Also
Hollywood Hotline

User Guide
- ☑ Windows
- ☑ DOS
- ☑ Macintosh
- ☐ Terminal Emulation
- ☐ VMS
- ☑ UNIX
- ☐ OS/2
- ☑ Other platform

Cost
- ☐ Unknown
- ☐ Basic
- ☑ Extended
- ☐ Premium ($)
- ☐ Executive w/$

Activity Level

Address
GO: **STEIN**

UK Entertainment Reviews

Description
Database offering entertainment reviews of United Kingdom.

Subjects
News, Entertainment

Audience
Entertainment enthusiasts

Entertainment

Content Summary
Libraries include information on films, theatre, videos, and soap operas.

See Also
Hollywood Hotline

User Guide
- ☑ Windows
- ☑ DOS
- ☐ Macintosh
- ☐ Terminal Emulation
- ☐ VMS
- ☐ UNIX
- ☐ OS/2
- ☐ Other platform

Cost
- ☐ Unknown
- ☐ Basic
- ☑ Extended
- ☐ Premium ($)
- ☐ Executive w/$

Activity Level
UNKNOWN

Address
GO: **UKENT**

Video Game Publishers Forum

Description
This is a vendor support forum for the products of several video games publishers.

Subjects
Entertainment, Games, Video Games

Audience
Game enthusiasts

Content Summary
The libraries link you to fellow gamers and software developers and provide news relating to the industry.

See Also
Video Games Forum

User Guide
- ☑ Windows
- ☑ DOS
- ☑ Macintosh
- ☐ Terminal Emulation
- ☐ VMS
- ☐ UNIX
- ☐ OS/2
- ☐ Other platform

Cost
- ☐ Unknown
- ☐ Basic
- ☑ Extended
- ☐ Premium ($)
- ☐ Executive w/$

Activity Level
MEDIUM

Address
GO: **VIDPUB**

Video Games Forum

Description
The Video Games Forum is the place to go to discuss all of the available video games machines, and to argue over which offers the most entertainment.

Subjects
Entertainment, Games, Video Games

Audience
Games enthusiasts

Content Summary
Libraries include information on Sega, 3DO, Atari, Philips CD-i, games magazines, and new technologies.

See Also
Video Games

User Guide
- ☑ Windows
- ☑ DOS
- ☐ Macintosh
- ☐ Terminal Emulation
- ☐ VMS
- ☐ UNIX
- ☐ OS/2
- ☐ Other platform

Cost
- ☐ Unknown
- ☐ Basic
- ☑ Extended
- ☐ Premium ($)
- ☐ Executive w/$

Activity Level
MEDIUM-HIGH

Address
GO: **VIDGAM**

You Guessed It!

Description
This forum is an online multiplayer game in which players match their own answers against those of a previous "studio audience."

Subjects
Entertainment, Games

Audience
Members interested in multiplayer trivia games

Content Summary
Meet new friends and match skills with others in a multiplayer Trivia match.

See Also
The Whiz Quiz

Entertainment – Entrepreneurs

User Guide
- ☑ Windows
- ☑ DOS
- ☐ Macintosh
- ☐ Terminal Emulation
- ☐ VMS
- ☐ UNIX
- ☐ OS/2
- ☐ Other platform

Cost
- ☐ Unknown
- ☐ Basic
- ☑ Extended
- ☐ Premium ($)
- ☐ Executive w/$

Activity Level
UNKNOWN (LOW – MEDIUM – HIGH)

Address
GO: **YGI**

Entertainment Center

Description
Play a game online through the Entertainment Center. All you need is a PC with EGA graphics or better, and time. You can start your own game, play a game in progress, or watch a game. Save money by joining the CB Club.

Subjects
Games

Audience
Gamers

Content Summary
In the Download Games option on the main menu, you can download the available games, such as StarSprint, Backgammon, Chess, and Checkers. You are charged a surcharge depending on the game you download.

See Also
CDCLUB

User Guide
- ☑ Windows
- ☑ DOS
- ☑ Macintosh
- ☐ Terminal Emulation
- ☑ VMS
- ☑ UNIX
- ☑ OS/2
- ☐ Other platform

Cost
- ☐ Unknown
- ☐ Basic
- ☐ Extended
- ☑ Premium ($)
- ☐ Executive w/$

Activity Level

UNKNOWN (LOW – MEDIUM – HIGH)

Address
GO: **ECENTER**

Entertainment Drive Center

Description
This is your backstage pass to the entertainment industry. You can get David Letterman Top 10 lists, O.J. Simpson trial transcripts, exclusive columns and reviews, and multimedia files.

Subjects
Celebrities, Entertainment, Multimedia

Audience
Journalists, photojournalists, anyone interested in entertainment industry

Content Summary
Because of the nature of the entertainment industry, many of the files posted in this forum are removed on certain dates, including a collection of Lion King graphics that were posted until August 31, 1994. If you missed these, don't despair; other hot topics will be featured every month.

See Also
Hollywood Hotline

User Guide
- ☑ Windows
- ☑ DOS
- ☑ Macintosh
- ☐ Terminal Emulation
- ☐ VMS
- ☐ UNIX
- ☐ OS/2
- ☐ Other platform

Cost
- ☐ Unknown
- ☐ Basic
- ☑ Extended
- ☐ Premium ($)
- ☐ Executive w/$

Activity Level

MEDIUM (LOW → HIGH)

Address
GO: **EDRIVE**

ENTERPRENEURS

Entrepreneur Magazine

Description
This area is known also as the Small Business Emporium, from which you can find over 165 entrepreneur business guides. These guides will help you find businesses you can run from home, start in your spare time, and begin with little investment.

Subjects
Small Business, Home-Based Business, Entrepreneurs

Audience
Entrepreneurs, home-based business owners, small-business owners, venture capitalists

Entrepreneurs

Content Summary
After you get past the main menu in this area, you are given six choices from which to choose. From this menu, you can see the top 10 hottest businesses, see a directory of business guides, order a *Entrepreneur Magazine* subscription, and view a list of other business products such as videos and software products.

See Also
Entrepreneur's Small Business Forum, Entrepreneur Small Business Square

User Guide
- [ ] Windows
- [ ] DOS
- [ ] Macintosh
- [x] Terminal Emulation
- [ ] VMS
- [ ] UNIX
- [ ] OS/2
- [ ] Other platform

Cost
- [ ] Unknown
- [x] Basic
- [ ] Extended
- [ ] Premium ($)
- [ ] Executive w/$

Activity Level

Address
GO: **ENT**

Entrepreneur Small Business Square

Description
From this service, you can access the Entrepreneur's Small Business Forum, Franchise & Business Opportunities, Small Business Emporium, and the *Entrepreneur Magazine* Small Business Survey. The Franchise & Business Opportunities option is a database that lists company addresses, phone numbers, contact names, and descriptions of franchising and business opportunities.

Subjects
Entrepreneur, Small Business, Franchise

Audience
Entrepreneurs, small business owners, venture capitalists

Content Summary
To use the Franchise & Business Opportunities database, select that option from the Entrepreneur Small Business Square main menu and then select the Begin Your Search option. You then use search criteria from a list of 1,500 opportunities to find your results. The Small Business Emporium is a Terminal Emulation area that stores over 165 entrepreneur business guides to help you start and maintain a small business.

See Also
IQuest Business Management InfoCenter, Entrepreneur Small Business Forum

User Guide
- [ ] Windows
- [ ] DOS
- [ ] Macintosh
- [x] Terminal Emulation
- [ ] VMS
- [ ] UNIX
- [ ] OS/2
- [ ] Other platform

Cost
- [ ] Unknown
- [ ] Basic
- [x] Extended
- [ ] Premium ($)
- [ ] Executive w/$

Activity Level

Address
GO: **ENTMAGAZINE**

Entrepreneur's Small Business Forum

Description
Sponsored by Entrepreneur Group, the publishers of *Entrepreneur Magazine*, the Entrepreneur's Small Business Forum enables you to identify and communicate with other entrepreneurs in a different cities and locales. This forum welcomes the sharing of information and helpful dialogue from all members.

Subjects
Business, Entrepreneurs, Free Enterprise, Small Business

Audience
Business owners, entrepreneurs, venture capitalists

Content Summary
The libraries contain information on business opportunities, start-up techniques, marketing and promotion files, financing, legal issues, planning files, and international issues. Check out the information in Library 13, "Homebased Business," if you are thinking about starting, or are maintaining, a business from your home. You also should take part in the message section if you have specific questions to ask.

See Also
Entrepreneur Small Business Square, Business Franchise and Opportunities Database

User Guide
- [x] Windows
- [x] DOS
- [x] Macintosh
- [ ] Terminal Emulation
- [ ] VMS
- [ ] UNIX
- [ ] OS/2
- [ ] Other platform

Entrepreneurs – Epic MegaGames Forums

265

Cost
- ☐ Unknown
- ☐ Basic
- ☑ Extended
- ☐ Premium ($)
- ☐ Executive w/$

Activity Level: MEDIUM

Address
GO: **USEN**

ENVIRONMENTAL ISSUES

Earth Forum

Description
Do you want to help solve environmental problems? If so, or if you're just interested in Earth-related issues, join this forum. Compare notes with other people and organizations concerned about the Earth and its environment.

Subjects
Environmental Issues

Audience
Environmentalists, scientists, biologists

Content Summary
The Earth Forum libraries contain topics such as air/climate, water, lands and forests, recycling, energy, population, and Greenpeace. Be sure to check out the graphics in Library 0, "Graphics/Animation," for some nice scenic photographs from around the world.

See Also
Gardening Forum, Humane Society of the United States Forum, Outdoors Forum, Space/Astronomy Forum

User Guide
- ☑ Windows
- ☑ DOS
- ☑ Macintosh
- ☐ Terminal Emulation
- ☑ VMS
- ☑ UNIX
- ☑ OS/2
- ☐ Other platform

Cost
- ☐ Unknown
- ☐ Basic
- ☑ Extended
- ☐ Premium ($)
- ☐ Executive w/$

Activity Level: MEDIUM (arrow pointing toward HIGH)

Address
GO: **EARTH**

Epic MegaGames

Description
This area enables you download the Epic game of the month as well as other shareware games, including OverKill, Epic Pinball, Jill of the Jungle, and Zone 66. You also can access the Epic MegaGames Forum from this area.

Subjects
Games, Shareware Games

Audience
Gamers

Content Summary
From the EpicGames main menu, you can select the About Epic MegaGames option to see a synopsis of this game publisher. To read a description and download the game of the month, select the Download Game-of-the-Month choice. If you are interested in other Epic products, be sure to visit the terminal emulation area by selecting Purchase Epic Products from the main menu. Don't blame us if you become addicted.

See Also
Epic MegaGames Forum, The Electronic Gamer Archives, The Entertainment Center, The Modem Games Forum, The Gamers' Forum

User Guide
- ☑ Windows
- ☑ DOS
- ☑ Macintosh
- ☐ Terminal Emulation
- ☑ VMS
- ☑ UNIX
- ☑ OS/2
- ☐ Other platform

Cost
- ☐ Unknown
- ☐ Basic
- ☑ Extended
- ☐ Premium ($)
- ☐ Executive w/$

Activity Level: UNKNOWN

Address
GO: **EPIC**

Epic MegaGames Forums

Description
Download Epic's latest shareware games, previews, and support files; leave messages for the Epic staff; and chat with other members in this forum.

Subjects
Games

Audience
Gamers

Epic MegaGames Forums – Europe

Content Summary
The Epic Forum has several libraries from which you can download Epic's games, such as Jazz Jackrabbit, Heartlight, and Castle of the Winds. See Library 2, "Classic Epic Games," for some of Epic's older games. If you need a hint or tip, go to Library 3 or Library 4 for some useful utilities. You also can get the latest issues of *GameBytes Magazine* from Library 7, "GameBytes Magazine."

See Also
Epic MegaGames

User Guide
- ☐ Windows
- ☑ DOS
- ☐ Macintosh
- ☐ Terminal Emulation
- ☐ VMS
- ☐ UNIX
- ☐ OS/2
- ☐ Other platform

Cost
- ☐ Unknown
- ☐ Basic
- ☑ Extended
- ☐ Premium ($)
- ☐ Executive w/$

Activity Level
MEDIUM (LOW — HIGH)

Address
GO: **EPICFO**

ERIC—Education Resources Information Center

Description
This database contains abstracts of articles covering education, including vocational education, counseling, teacher education, and testing. ERIC is published by the U.S. Department of Education.

Subjects
Education

Audience
Educators, students, teachers, counselors, researchers

Content Summary
Information in this database goes back to 1966 and is updated monthly. Two subfiles are within ERIC: the Resources In Education (RIE) and the Current Index to Journals in Education (CIJE) files. The RIE contains reports on research and technical issues, conference papers and proceedings, program descriptions, opinions, bibliographies, reviews, dissertations, teaching and curriculum materials, lesson plans, and guides. The CIJE contains abstracts of articles from 750 education-related journals. Pricing varies depending on what you obtain. See the Pricing Information option in the ERIC main menu for more information.

See Also
Information USA

User Guide
- ☑ Windows
- ☑ DOS
- ☑ Macintosh
- ☐ Terminal Emulation
- ☐ VMS
- ☐ UNIX
- ☐ OS/2
- ☐ Other platform

Cost
- ☐ Unknown
- ☐ Basic
- ☑ Extended
- ☑ Premium ($)
- ☐ Executive w/$

Activity Level
UNKNOWN (LOW — MEDIUM — HIGH)

Address
GO: **ERIC**

EUROPE

Foreign Language Forum

Description
This forum is devoted to foreign languages, their study, teaching, use in the commercial world, or general interest items about foreign languages.

Subjects
Bilingual Education, Europe, Foreign News, French, International, Languages

Audience
General public, Europeans

Content Summary
As you can see from the various library headings, the Foreign Language forum offers a diverse cultural and languages experience. The libraries are listed as follows: Spanish/Portuguese, French, German/Germanic, Latin/Greek, Slavic/E. European, English, East Asian, Esperanto, Italian, FL Education, Translators, Computers/Languages, Resources/Careers, Semitic/Turkic, Others Using the Forum, and Sysops.

See Also
Education Forum

User Guide
- ☑ Windows
- ☑ DOS
- ☑ Macintosh
- ☐ Terminal Emulation
- ☑ VMS
- ☑ UNIX
- ☑ OS/2
- ☐ Other platform

Cost
- ☐ Unknown
- ☐ Basic
- ☑ Extended
- ☐ Premium ($)
- ☐ Executive w/$

267
Europe – Executive Service Option

Executive News Service

Activity Level

Address
GO: **FLEFO**

Description
You can search the latest international news, weather, and sports from the world's major news agencies. This powerful news clipping service can scan many news sources for stories you specify and deliver them to you daily.

Subjects
Business, Financial News, International News, News

Audience
Business professionals

Content Summary
You can read about financial events in Reuters Financial Report and OTC NewsAlert, as well as in the daily headlines of The Washington Post. To use the News by Company Ticker option, enter a company ticker symbol and check on business news filed within the past 24 hours. For the News Clips option, you can read through special clipping folders set up by CompuServe to keep you up on specific news topics. You also can set up your own Personal area in which you specify the type of news you want to read by typing in key phrases. ENS then sends you electronic news "clippings" that you can read. ENS costs $15 per hour plus the base connect rates.

See Also
AP Sports($), Financial Forums, Global Crises Forum, NewsGrid, Newspaper Archives($), Reuter News Pictures Forum, United Press Int'l($), U.S. News Forum

User Guide
- ☑ Windows
- ☑ DOS
- ☐ Macintosh
- ☐ Terminal Emulation
- ☐ VMS
- ☐ UNIX
- ☐ OS/2
- ☐ Other platform

Cost
- ☐ Unknown
- ☐ Basic
- ☐ Extended
- ☑ Premium ($)
- ☐ Executive w/$

Activity Level

Address
GO: **ENS**

Executive Service Option

Description
This is a CompuServe service that enables you to access several value-added services, including databases, merchandise, and other online items.

Subjects
Databases, Financial News

Audience
General public

Content Summary
When you select this option, you can access exclusive databases, including Company Analyzer, Disclosure II, Executive News Service, SuperSite, Institutional Broker's Estimate System, Securities Screening, Return Analysis, and Company Screening. You also get volume discounts on information retrieval from selected financial databases, a six month storage period (rather than the standard 30 days) for personal files without charge, and a ten percent discount on most CompuServe products, excluding sale items. When you join the Executive Service Option, you are subject to a $10 monthly minimum usage level. Your monthly $8.95 CompuServe basic membership (Standard Pricing Plan) is applied to this minimum. All products associated with the Executive Service Option are considered wide-mode products. This means they display best on screens that allow widths of 80 columns.

See Also
CompuServe Help Forum (free), CompuServe Rates (free), Order From CompuServe (free)

User Guide
- ☑ Windows
- ☑ DOS
- ☑ Macintosh
- ☐ Terminal Emulation
- ☑ VMS
- ☑ UNIX
- ☑ OS/2
- ☐ Other platform

Cost
- ☐ Unknown
- ☐ Basic
- ☐ Extended
- ☑ Premium ($)
- ☐ Executive w/$

Activity Level

Medium (Unknown)

Address
GO: **EXECUTIVE**

F

FAMILY

Family Handyman Forum

Description
This forum is for people who like to do home repairs and improvements, work with tools, do woodworking, or have questions about home repairs.

Subjects
Family, General Interest, Home Building

Audience
General public, general contractors, families

Content Summary
Sponsored by *Family Handyman* magazine, this forum is intended to help you find answers to your questions about tools, household repairs, and a variety of other topics. When you join this forum, you'll meet people with experience in home maintenance and repair, house building and remodeling, woodworking, painting, plumbing, tools, old houses, and electricity. You also have access to articles from *Family Handyman* magazine and a chance to interact with its editors. The Handy Hint section (Message section 15) is a great place to get and leave tips and hints for household problems.

See Also
Automobile Forum, Cook's Online Forum, Gardening Forum, Masonry Forum, Outdoor Forum

User Guide
- [✓] Windows
- [✓] DOS
- [✓] Macintosh
- [ ] Terminal Emulation
- [✓] VMS
- [✓] UNIX
- [✓] OS/2
- [✓] Other platform

Cost
- [ ] Unknown
- [ ] Basic
- [✓] Extended
- [ ] Premium ($)
- [ ] Executive w/$

Activity Level: LOW (arrow pointing toward LOW from MEDIUM)

Address
GO: **HANDYMAN**

Genealogy Forum

Description
Trying to find your great-great-grandmother's father's brother? Join the Genealogy Forum and start looking.

Subjects
Family, History

Audience
General public, families

Content Summary
This forum gives you access to a wide-range of members who are interested in genealogy and using their computers to help them. DOS, Windows, UNIX, Amiga, and Macintosh software is available in the libraries, as well as graphics and text files that might help you track down the hole in your family tree. Be sure to check out the message sections for leads to surnames or to post a query.

See Also
Military Forum

User Guide
- [✓] Windows
- [✓] DOS
- [✓] Macintosh
- [ ] Terminal Emulation
- [ ] VMS
- [✓] UNIX
- [ ] OS/2
- [✓] Other platform

Cost
- [ ] Unknown
- [ ] Basic
- [✓] Extended
- [ ] Premium ($)
- [ ] Executive w/$

Activity Level: HIGH (arrow pointing toward HIGH from MEDIUM)

Address
GO: **ROOTS**

Family Handyman Forum

Description
This forum is for people who like to do home repairs and improvements, work with tools, do woodworking, or have questions about home repairs.

Subjects
Family, General Interest, Home Building

Audience
General public, general contractors, families

Content Summary
Sponsored by *Family Handyman* magazine, this forum is intended to help you find answers to your questions about tools, household repairs, and a variety of other topics. When you join this forum, you'll meet people with experience in home maintenance and repair, house building and remodeling, woodworking, painting, plumbing, tools, old houses, and electricity. You also have access to articles from *Family Handyman* magazine and a chance to interact with its editors. The Handy Hint section (Message section 15) is a great place to get and leave tips and hints for household problems.

Family Handyman Forum – Fashion Merchandising

See Also
Automobile Forum, Cook's Online Forum, Gardening Forum, Masonry Forum, Outdoor Forum

User Guide
- ☑ Windows
- ☑ DOS
- ☑ Macintosh
- ☐ Terminal Emulation
- ☑ VMS
- ☑ UNIX
- ☑ OS/2
- ☑ Other platform

Cost
- ☐ Unknown
- ☐ Basic
- ☑ Extended
- ☐ Premium ($)
- ☐ Executive w/$

Activity Level: LOW (arrow pointing low)

Address
GO: **HANDYMAN**

Fantasy/Role-Playing Adventure

Description
Play role-playing games such as British Legends or Island of Kesmai, as well as access the Role-Playing Forum and Play-by-Mail Forum.

Subjects
Games, Role-Playing Games

Audience
Game players, game theorists, general public

Content Summary
From the Fantasy/Role-Playing Adventure main menu, you can select to play British Legends or Island of Kesmai. British Legends is a multi-player adventure game filled with mystery, dense forests, an island, a cottage, and much more. In Island of Kesmai, you encounter many computer-run characters as you travel across the many acres of land on the Island of Kesmai, where a group of magicians live to escape persecution. From the main menu, you also can choose to go to the Role-Playing or Play-by-Mail Forums.

See Also
Gamers Forum, Island of Kesmai, British Legends, Modem Games Forum

User Guide
- ☑ Windows
- ☑ DOS
- ☑ Macintosh
- ☐ Terminal Emulation
- ☑ VMS
- ☑ UNIX
- ☑ OS/2
- ☑ Other platform

Cost
- ☐ Unknown
- ☑ Basic
- ☐ Extended
- ☐ Premium ($)
- ☐ Executive w/$

Activity Level: UNKNOWN

Address
GO: **ADVENT**

FASHION MERCHANDISING

Glamour Graphics Forum

Description
Professional-quality images and photographs featuring fashion models can be found in this forum.

Subjects
Fashion Merchandising, Graphics, Photography

Audience
General public, photographers

Content Summary
The Glamour Graphics Forum offers fashion and glamour photography from stock photography agencies, including Len Kaltman Online, Texas Glamour, Richard Stevens Models, Classic Model Review, Imagine That, and Jade Creations. General sections, with subscriber uploads encouraged, show off high fashion, swimsuits, business attire, resort & sport, casual wear, and more. The file format of choice is GIF, but you might also find some JPG files as well.

See Also
Graphics Forums

User Guide
- ☑ Windows
- ☑ DOS
- ☑ Macintosh
- ☐ Terminal Emulation
- ☐ VMS
- ☐ UNIX
- ☑ OS/2
- ☑ Other platform

Cost
- ☐ Unknown
- ☐ Basic
- ☑ Extended
- ☐ Premium ($)
- ☐ Executive w/$

Activity Level: HIGH (arrow pointing high)

Address
GO: **GLAMOUR**

FAX BOARDS

Dr. Neuhaus Forum

Description
This forum is devoted to German-speaking people about Dr. Neuhaus communications products. You can get technical support and information on products such as FURY modems, FAXY fax boards, and NICCY ISDN modems. You also can find information and support for Carbon Copy.

Subjects
Computers, Fax Boards, Modems, Remote Communications

Audience
Computer Users

Content Summary
This forum is entirely in German.

See Also
Modem Vendor Forum, Palmtop Forum

User Guide
- ☑ Windows
- ☑ DOS
- ☐ Macintosh
- ☐ Terminal Emulation
- ☐ VMS
- ☐ UNIX
- ☐ OS/2
- ☑ Other platform

Cost
- ☐ Unknown
- ☐ Basic
- ☑ Extended
- ☐ Premium ($)
- ☐ Executive w/$

Activity Level

Address
GO: NEUHAUS

FICTION

Literary Forum

Description
Shakespeare. Plath. Milton. Twain. O'Conner. These and many other literary figures and discussions are in this forum.

Subjects
Fiction, Literature, Writing

Audience
Writers, educators, editors, literary critics, literary theorists

Content Summary
If you like to read and talk about it, join this forum. You'll also find discussions for writers and youth literature. Some of the libraries and message sections include Market Maneuvers, YouthLit/Learning, Journalism, Fiction, Science Fiction/Fantasy, Art of Writing, Romance/Historicals, and many more. The WotM! library (Library 3) is devoted to the Writer of the Month.

See Also
Journalism Forum

User Guide
- ☑ Windows
- ☑ DOS
- ☑ Macintosh
- ☐ Terminal Emulation
- ☑ VMS
- ☑ UNIX
- ☑ OS/2
- ☑ Other platform

Cost
- ☐ Unknown
- ☐ Basic
- ☑ Extended
- ☐ Premium ($)
- ☐ Executive w/$

Activity Level

Address
GO: LITFORUM

FIELD COMPUTING

HP Handhelds Forum

Description
This forum is designed to help you get the most out of your HP handheld computer, HP palmtop, or HP calculator.

Subjects
Computer Hardware, Computers, Field Computing

Audience
Computer programmers, computer professionals, computer users

Content Summary
You can get answers to your technical questions, exchange information with other users, take advantage of shareware and other files on the libraries, and stay in touch with the latest news from HP and 3rd-parties. The many libraries include areas for 1x,2x,3x calculators, 4x,6x,7x,9x calculators, the 95LX, the 100/200LX, HPHAND, and an area for Palmtop programmers.

See Also
HP OmniBook Forum, HP Peripherals Forum, HP Specials

User Guide
- ☐ Windows
- ☐ DOS
- ☐ Macintosh
- ☐ Terminal Emulation
- ☐ VMS
- ☐ UNIX
- ☐ OS/2
- ☑ Other platform

Field Computing – Finance

Cost
- ☐ Unknown
- ☐ Basic
- ☑ Extended
- ☐ Premium ($)
- ☐ Executive w/$

Activity Level

MEDIUM (LOW — HIGH)

Address
GO: **HPHAND**

Figi's Inc.

Description
For almost 50 years, Figi's has been giving people the most convenient way to order and give gifts—now they're online.

Subjects
Shopping

Audience
General public

Content Summary
From the main menu, you can read about Figi's history and shopping experience, order a catalog, shop the Figi store, order from the print catalog, and leave a message for customer service. Some of the products that you can order include cheese and sausage, oven-fresh bakery items, smokehouse favorites, and nuts. If you are looking for a light and low-fat gift, check out the Light 'n Healthy option under the >>Shop The Figi's Store<< selection on the main menu. Here you can find unsalted nuts, sugarfree fruit chews, and sugarfree cookies. You can use your American Express, Discover, VISA, and Master Card credit card to order. Delivery is usually within 72 hours, but you can get Express Delivery for $6.95 per household for delivery within 48 hours of your order. Shipping and handling charges vary depending on the total order amount. See the Shipping and Ordering Information option on the main menu for more information.

See Also
CompuServe Mail

User Guide
- ☐ Windows
- ☐ DOS
- ☐ Macintosh
- ☑ Terminal Emulation
- ☐ VMS
- ☐ UNIX
- ☐ OS/2
- ☐ Other platform

Cost
- ☐ Unknown
- ☑ Basic
- ☐ Extended
- ☐ Premium ($)
- ☐ Executive w/$

Activity Level

UNKNOWN (LOW — MEDIUM — HIGH)

Address
GO: **FIGIS**

FILM

Roger Ebert's Movie Reviews

Description
If you love movies, then this forum is for you. Get the thumbs up or thumbs down on recent movies by Roger Ebert himself.

Subjects
Film, Movies, Reviews

Audience
Film students, movie critics, movie enthusiasts

Content Summary
You can receive an alphabetical listing of recent movies with Roger Ebert's familiar star rating. You also can receive film reviews by searching by movie name, actor or actress name, or director name. Included in this forum are celebrity interviews with such well-known personalities as Oliver Stone. Other areas of interest include a glossary of movie terms, the 10 best films of the year, and a special area in which you can correspond with Roger Ebert.

See Also
Movie Reviews Forum, SHOWBIZ Quiz Forum

User Guide
- ☑ Windows
- ☑ DOS
- ☑ Macintosh
- ☐ Terminal Emulation
- ☑ VMS
- ☑ UNIX
- ☑ OS/2
- ☐ Other platform

Cost
- ☐ Unknown
- ☑ Basic
- ☐ Extended
- ☐ Premium ($)
- ☐ Executive w/$

Activity Level

MEDIUM (LOW — HIGH)

Address
GO: **EBERT**

FINANCE

D&B Dun's Canadian Market Identifiers

Description
The Canadian Dun's Market Identifiers database contains directory information on about 350,000 Canadian companies. You can see company name,

address, and telephone number. You also can get sales figures, number of employees, and executive's names.

Subjects
Canadian Company Profiles, Business, Finance, Dun and Bradstreet

Audience
Accounting persons, businesspersons, executives, investors, journalists, management, researchers

Content Summary
Depending on the company listing, you might or might not see all the information detailed in the Description area above. To retrieve records, enter the company name, geographic location, product or service, number of employees, or sales as your search criteria. For help on searching, select Choice 2, "Search Guidelines," from the main menu. The cost of this service is as follows:

- Search (retrieves up to 5 names): $7.50
- Additional names (in groups of 5): $7.50
- Full reference (selected from the names): $7.50

In addition to connect time charges, you are charged $1.00 for a search that retrieves no titles.

See Also
Company Information, Corporate Affiliations, D&B Dun's Electronic Business Directory, D&B Dun's Market Identifiers, Financial Forums, Investors' Forum, Tenderlink, TRW Business Profiles

User Guide
☑	Windows	☑	VMS
☑	DOS	☑	UNIX
☑	Macintosh	☑	OS/2
☑	Terminal Emulation	☑	Other platform

Cost
☐	Unknown	☑	Premium ($)
☐	Basic	☐	Executive w/$
☐	Extended		

Activity Level
MEDIUM (LOW — UNKNOWN — HIGH)

Address
GO: **DBCAN**

D&B Dun's Electronic Business Directory

Description
You can obtain a directory of over 8.5 million U.S. public and private businesses and professionals using this Dun and Bradstreet service. Available information includes name, address, phone number, type of business, its parent company, the industry it belongs to, the SIC code, number of employees, and the population of the city in which the business resides.

Subjects
Business, Finance, Investment, Dun and Bradstreet

Audience
Accounting persons, businesspersons, executives, investors, journalists, management, researchers

Content Summary
To search, select Choice 5, "Access Dun's Electronic Business Directory," from the main menu. Next, select the criterion for your search, such as company name or product or service; enter a name, word, or phrase that describes the company or product; and follow the on-screen instructions. See Choice 7, "Search Guidelines," for more help. The cost of this service is as follows:

- Search (retrieves up to 5 names): $7.50
- Additional names (in groups of 5): $7.50

In addition to connect time charges, you are charged $1.00 for a search that retrieves no titles.

See Also
Company Information, Corporate Affiliations, D&B Dun's Canadian Market Identifiers, D&B Dun's Market Identifiers, Financial Forums, Investors' Forum, Tenderlink, TRW Business Profiles

User Guide
☑	Windows	☑	VMS
☑	DOS	☑	UNIX
☑	Macintosh	☑	OS/2
☑	Terminal Emulation	☑	Other platform

Cost
☐	Unknown	☑	Premium ($)
☐	Basic	☐	Executive w/$
☐	Extended		

Activity Level
MEDIUM (LOW — UNKNOWN — HIGH)

Address
GO: **DYP** or **DUNSEBD**

D&B Dun's Market Identifiers

Description
With this service, you can search three of Dun and Bradstreet's directories of business information, including information on over 6.7 million U.S. public and private businesses that have over $1 million in sales or more than five employees, information on over 350,000 Canadian companies, and information on over 2.1 million public, private, and government controlled international companies.

Subjects
Business, Finance, Investment, Dun and Bradstreet

Audience
Accounting persons, businesspersons, executives, investors, management, researchers

Finance

Content Summary
When you perform a search, you can get the company name, address, telephone number, sales figures, number of employees, parent company, and names of executives. The price of this service is as follows:

- Search (retrieves up to 5 names): $7.50
- Additional names (in groups of 5): $7.50
- Full reference (selected from the names): $7.50

In addition to connect time charges, you are charged $1.00 for a search that retrieves no titles.

See Also
Company Information, Corporate Affiliations, D&B Dun's Canadian Market Identifiers, Financial Forums, Investors' Forum, Tenderlink, TRW Business Profiles

User Guide
- ☑ Windows
- ☑ DOS
- ☑ Macintosh
- ☑ Terminal Emulation
- ☑ VMS
- ☑ UNIX
- ☑ OS/2
- ☑ Other platform

Cost
- ☐ Unknown
- ☐ Basic
- ☐ Extended
- ☑ Premium ($)
- ☐ Executive w/$

Activity Level

Address
GO: **DUNS** or **DMI**

Dividends and Splits

Description
Information about dividends, bond interest, and splits over a selected period of time, to get a report that includes the exdate, record date, payment date, type of distribution, and rate of each distribution. You can find mutual fund distributions here that are otherwise difficult to obtain. You can specify the number of dividends you want to view or a period of time.

Subjects
Finance

Audience
Financial Analysts

Content Summary
To sample this area without being surcharged, enter **HRP** at the prompt. To get information about a security or a market index, enter one or more securities or market indexes, a slash (/) followed by a navigation command, or press Enter (CR) to exit. If you enter more than one issues, place a comma between each entry, such as HRB,DEC,IBM. You can enter the ticker symbol or CUSIP number for each security. Enter an asterisk then the beginning of the issue or index name if you don't know the ticker symbol (such as *BLOCK for H&R Block).

See Also
Go Symbols

User Guide
- ☐ Windows
- ☐ DOS
- ☐ Macintosh
- ☑ Terminal Emulation
- ☐ VMS
- ☐ UNIX
- ☐ OS/2
- ☐ Other platform

Cost
- ☐ Unknown
- ☐ Basic
- ☑ Extended
- ☐ Premium ($)
- ☐ Executive w/$

Activity Level

Address
GO: **DIVIDENDS**

E*TRADE Securities

Description
Do you want to get a grip on your investments? This service enables you to do just that. E*TRADE handles individual, investment, margin, IRA, joint, KEOGH, and 401K accounts, and offers a stock market game that uses real stock market prices and data.

Subjects
Financial, Investments, Stock Market

Audience
Accountants, investors

Content Summary
This "around-the-clock" service offers you commissions of 1 1/2 cents per share, with a $35.00 minimum; Black-Sholes option analysis that use current prices; investment management; and free checking accounts tied to your money market funds. The investment management offers you quotes, portfolio reports, limit orders, and news alerts.

See Also
ETGAME

User Guide
- ☐ Windows
- ☐ DOS
- ☐ Macintosh
- ☑ Terminal Emulation
- ☐ VMS
- ☐ UNIX
- ☐ OS/2
- ☐ Other platform

Cost
- ☐ Unknown
- ☐ Basic
- ☐ Extended
- ☑ Premium ($)
- ☐ Executive w/$

Finance

Activity Level

Address
GO: **ETRADE**

E*TRADE Stock Market Game

Description
Have you ever wondered what it would be like to be a Wall Street mover and shaker? Now's your chance to invest $100,000 in game accounts by playing the E*TRADE Stock Market Game. The game lets you play in stocks only, stocks and options, or both, and will track your performance—and commission rates—every month. If you have the right stuff and have the highest percentage increase of all the players, you can win a cash prize.

Subjects
Games, Finance, Wall Street

Audience
Financial persons, gamers, students

Content Summary
The E*TRADE Securities main menu offers you three choices: Game Instructions, Sign-up for the Game, and Play the E*TRADE Stock Market Game. Select Game Instructions to read directions on how to play and what you can win. You compete with other members to see who can become the wealthiest in a month. When you sign up for the game, you are given $100,000 in game money with which to start.

See Also
E*TRADE Securities

User Guide
- ☐ Windows
- ☐ DOS
- ☐ Macintosh
- ☑ Terminal Emulation
- ☐ VMS
- ☐ UNIX
- ☐ OS/2
- ☐ Other platform

Cost
- ☐ Unknown
- ☐ Basic
- ☑ Extended
- ☐ Premium ($)
- ☐ Executive w/$

Activity Level

Address
GO: **ETGAME**

Finance

Description
The Finance service offers you a plethora of services for your financial concerns, including FundWatch Online by *Money Magazine*.

Subjects
Economy, Finance, Financial

Audience
Financial advisors, fitness enthusiasts, market researchers, accountants, businesspeople

Content Summary
From the Finance main menu, you can choose from several financial and investment services, including Basic Quotes, FundWatch Online by Money Magazine, Basic Company Snapshot, Issue/Symbol Lookup, Loan Analyzer, Market Quotes/Highlights, Company Information, Brokerage Services, Earnings/Economics Projections, Micro Software Interfaces, Personal Finance/Insurance, Financial Forums, MicroQuote II, Business News, Instructions/Fees, Read Before Investing. When you select one of these options, you are sent to that specific area. Note that some of the areas are terminal emulation.

See Also
Commodity Pricing ($), Current Market Snapshot, Current Day Quotes ($), Financial Forums, Options Profile ($W)

User Guide
- ☑ Windows
- ☑ DOS
- ☑ Macintosh
- ☐ Terminal Emulation
- ☑ VMS
- ☑ UNIX
- ☑ OS/2
- ☑ Other platform

Cost
- ☐ Unknown
- ☑ Basic
- ☐ Extended
- ☐ Premium ($)
- ☐ Executive w/$

Activity Level

Address
GO: **FINANCE**

Financial Forecasts

Description
This area presents you with the Earnings/Economics Projections menu, from which you can choose five financial and investment services.

Subjects
Financial News, International Finance, Investments

Finance

Audience
Investors, market analysts, financial analysts, financial advisors, business and financial researchers

Content Summary
From the Earnings/Economics Projections main menu, you can select I/B/E/S Earnings Estimate, S&P Online, InvesText, MMS International Financial Reports, and CENDATA services (CENDATA is a Census Bureau service). For information and service fees associated with these services, select the Instructions/Fees option from the main menu. Some of the services require terminal emulation. I/B/E/S Earnings Estimate is a database that provides consensus earnings estimates on over 3,400 publicly traded corporations. S&P Online provides you with recent information on approximately 4,700 companies, including business summaries, recent market activity, and dividend information. The InvesText database provides company and industry research reports compiled during the most recent two years by analysts in more than 50 Wall Street, regional, and international brokerage houses and research firms. MMS International Financial Reports provides a calendar of economic events, daily market reports, debt market reports, and other information on international markets.

See Also
Dividends and Splits ($), Financial Forums, Dun's Market Identifiers ($), Dun's Elect Business Dir ($)

User Guide
☐ Windows	☐ VMS
☐ DOS	☐ UNIX
☐ Macintosh	☐ OS/2
☑ Terminal Emulation	☐ Other platform

Cost
☐ Unknown	☑ Premium ($)
☐ Basic	☐ Executive w/$
☐ Extended	

Activity Level

Address
GO: **EARNINGS**

Intuit Forum

Description
Do you use Quicken, Quickpay, or Quickbooks? If so, stop by the Intuit Forum and read tips, press releases, and support comments about these products.

Subjects
Computers, Finance

Audience
Computer users

Content Summary
The purpose of this forum is to provide technical support and discussion areas for all of the Intuit products. The Intuit Technical Support Staff monitor and participate in this forum regularly. The Intuit Forum provides support and information on all Intuit Products, including Quicken for DOS, Windows, and Macintosh, and Quickpay and Quickbooks for DOS and Windows.

See Also
IBM File Finder

User Guide
☑ Windows	☐ VMS
☑ DOS	☐ UNIX
☑ Macintosh	☐ OS/2
☐ Terminal Emulation	☐ Other platform

Cost
☐ Unknown	☐ Premium ($)
☐ Basic	☐ Executive w/$
☑ Extended	

Activity Level

Address
GO: **INTUIT**

Mortgage Calculator

Description
Do you need a quick and painless way to calculate a mortgage? If so, use the Mortgage Calculator service.

Subjects
Mortgage, Finance

Audience
General public

Content Summary
Type the amount of loan, interest rate, number of payments per year, and number of years, and see the results. You can display the payment schedule to see the breakdown of how much your monthly payment is paying on interest and principle, as well as see the balance of the loan each month.

See Also
Financial Forums

User Guide
☐ Windows	☐ VMS
☐ DOS	☐ UNIX
☐ Macintosh	☐ OS/2
☑ Terminal Emulation	☐ Other platform

Cost
☐ Unknown	☐ Premium ($)
☑ Basic	☐ Executive w/$
☐ Extended	

Finance

Activity Level

Address
GO: HOM-17

News-A-Tron

Description
News-A-Tron provides daily news, analytical features, and cash quotes for selected commodities, market indices, and financial instruments.

Subjects
Finance, News

Audience
Accountants, general public

Content Summary
From the main menu, you can select to see an introduction and sample of the service and price information, and use the Market Reports, Stock Indices, or Money Market Reports. Be sure to read the pricing information for specific costs for this service.

See Also
The Business Wire Forum

User Guide
- ☑ Windows
- ☑ DOS
- ☑ Macintosh
- ☐ Terminal Emulation
- ☑ VMS
- ☑ UNIX
- ☐ OS/2
- ☐ Other platform

Cost
- ☐ Unknown
- ☐ Basic
- ☐ Extended
- ☐ Premium ($)
- ☑ Executive w/$

Activity Level

(UNKNOWN)

Address
GO: NAT

Securities Screening

Description
This stock market issues screening area enables members to search through the Microquotes database for particular issue types.

Subjects
Finance, Stock Market

Audience
Business people

Content Summary
Members can search for specific types of information, such as price, earnings, dividends, and recent highs and lows of various stocks.

See Also
Business Dateline, Business Database Plus, IQuess Business Management

User Guide
- ☑ Windows
- ☑ DOS
- ☑ Macintosh
- ☐ Terminal Emulation
- ☐ VMS
- ☑ UNIX
- ☐ OS/2
- ☐ Other platform

Cost
- ☐ Unknown
- ☐ Basic
- ☐ Extended
- ☐ Premium ($)
- ☑ Executive w/$

Activity Level

Address
GO: SCREEN

Securities Symbols Lookup

Description
This is a stock market issues database that enables members to search for an issue by name or ticker symbol.

Subjects
Finance, Stock Market

Audience
Business people

Content Summary
This database enables users to perform searches on issues relating to the stock market by name or ticker symbol.

See Also
Securities Screening

User Guide
- ☑ Windows
- ☑ DOS
- ☑ Macintosh
- ☐ Terminal Emulation
- ☐ VMS
- ☑ UNIX
- ☐ OS/2
- ☐ Other platform

Cost
- ☐ Unknown
- ☐ Basic
- ☑ Extended
- ☐ Premium ($)
- ☐ Executive w/$

Activity Level

(MEDIUM-HIGH)

Finance

Address
GO: **SYMBOLS**

Single Issue Price Hist

Description
This online area quotes stock/bond issue pricing by name or ticker symbol.

Subjects
Finance, Stock Market

Audience
Business people

Content Summary
This forum enables you to find out pricing of particular stocks or bonds by looking up information in an alphabetical sort or by ticker symbol.

See Also
Securities Symbols Lookup Database

User Guide
- ☑ Windows
- ☑ DOS
- ☑ Macintosh
- ☐ Terminal Emulation
- ☐ VMS
- ☑ UNIX
- ☐ OS/2
- ☑ Other platform

Cost
- ☐ Unknown
- ☐ Basic
- ☐ Extended
- ☑ Premium ($)
- ☐ Executive w/$

Activity Level
UNKNOWN (LOW – MEDIUM – HIGH)

Address
GO: **PRICES**

Thomas Register Online

Description
This is a database containing company info on almost 150,000 US and Canadian manufacturers and service providers. It is updated annually.

Subjects
Finance, Database

Audience
Financial analysts

Content Summary
Information for each entry includes company name, address, telephone number, and products or services offered.

See Also
Thomas Conrad Forum

User Guide
- ☑ Windows
- ☑ DOS
- ☐ Macintosh
- ☐ Terminal Emulation
- ☐ VMS
- ☐ UNIX
- ☐ OS/2
- ☐ Other platform

Cost
- ☐ Unknown
- ☐ Basic
- ☐ Extended
- ☑ Premium ($)
- ☐ Executive w/$

Activity Level
UNKNOWN (LOW – MEDIUM – HIGH)

Address
GO: **THOMAS**

Ticker/Symbol Lookup

Description
This is an online database that provides financial information or various stocks.

Subjects
Finance

Audience
Financial analysts, general public

Content Summary
This database enables you to look up information by company name, ticker symbol, CUSIP number, CNUM, or primary SIC code.

See Also
Thomas Register Online

User Guide
- ☑ Windows
- ☑ DOS
- ☐ Macintosh
- ☐ Terminal Emulation
- ☐ VMS
- ☐ UNIX
- ☐ OS/2
- ☐ Other platform

Cost
- ☐ Unknown
- ☐ Basic
- ☐ Extended
- ☑ Premium ($)
- ☐ Executive w/$

Activity Level
UNKNOWN (LOW – MEDIUM – HIGH)

Address
GO: **LOOKUP**

Vestor Stock Recommendation

Description
This unique interactive system is comprised of over 30 systems that can help you in making investment decisions.

Finance – Financial Forums

Subjects
Finance, Stock Market

Audience
Financial analysts

Content Summary
The Vestor main menu includes Overviews/Sample Reports, Instructions, Surcharges, Terms and Conditions, and more.

See Also
Thomas Register Online

User Guide
- [x] Windows
- [x] DOS
- [ ] Macintosh
- [x] Terminal Emulation
- [ ] VMS
- [ ] UNIX
- [ ] OS/2
- [ ] Other platform

Cost
- [ ] Unknown
- [ ] Basic
- [x] Extended
- [ ] Premium ($)
- [ ] Executive w/$

Activity Level

Address
GO: **VESTOR**

Financial Forecasts

Description
This area presents you with the Earnings/Economics Projections menu, from which you can choose five financial and investment services.

Subjects
Financial News, International Finance, Investments, Investments, Investments

Audience
Investors, market analysts, financial analysts, financial advisors, business and financial researchers

Content Summary
From the Earnings/Economics Projections main menu, you can select I/B/E/S Earnings Estimate, S&P Online, InvesText, MMS International Financial Reports, and CENDATA services (CENDATA is a Census Bureau service). For information and service fees associated with these services, select the Instructions/Fees option from the main menu. Some of the services require terminal emulation. I/B/E/S Earnings Estimate is a database that provides consensus earnings estimates on over 3,400 publicly traded corporations. S&P Online provides you with recent information on approximately 4,700 companies, including business summaries, recent market activity, and dividend information. The InvesText database provides company and industry research reports compiled during the most recent two years by analysts in more than 50 Wall Street, regional, and international brokerage houses and research firms. MMS International Financial Reports provides a calendar of economic events, daily market reports, debt market reports, and other information on international markets.

See Also
Dividends and Splits ($), Financial Forums, Dun's Market Identifiers ($), Dun's Elect Business Dir ($)

User Guide
- [ ] Windows
- [ ] DOS
- [ ] Macintosh
- [x] Terminal Emulation
- [ ] VMS
- [ ] UNIX
- [ ] OS/2
- [ ] Other platform

Cost
- [ ] Unknown
- [ ] Basic
- [ ] Extended
- [x] Premium ($)
- [ ] Executive w/$

Activity Level

Address
GO: **EARNINGS**

Financial Forums

Description
From this service, you can access several financial forums and ask questions about financial concerns, investments, the economy, or financial software.

Subjects
Business

Audience
Financial analysts

Content Summary
The Financial Forums main menu has the following options from which to choose: Investors Forum, NAIC Forum, MECA Software Forum, Intuit Forum, CA-Simply Forum, IRI Software Forum, The World of Lotus, Borland International, Consumer Forum. For more information on any of these forums, see the specific forum.

See Also
Financial Forecasts

User Guide
- [x] Windows
- [x] DOS
- [x] Macintosh
- [ ] Terminal Emulation
- [x] VMS
- [x] UNIX
- [x] OS/2
- [x] Other platform

Financial Forums – Financial News

Cost
- ☐ Unknown
- ☑ Basic
- ☐ Extended
- ☐ Premium ($)
- ☐ Executive w/$

Activity Level: LOW — UNKNOWN (MEDIUM) — HIGH

Address
GO: **FINFORUM**

FINANCIAL NEWS

Executive News Service

Description
You can search the latest international news, weather, and sports from the world's major news agencies. This powerful news clipping service can scan many news sources for stories you specify and deliver them to you daily.

Subjects
Business, Financial News, International News, News

Audience
Financial analysts

Content Summary
You can read about financial events in Reuters Financial Report and OTC NewsAlert, as well as in the daily headlines of *The Washington Post*. To use the News by Company Ticker option, enter a company ticker symbol and check on business news filed within the past 24 hours. For the News Clips option, you can read through special clipping folders set up by CompuServe to keep you up on specific news topics. You also can set up your own Personal area in which you specify the type of news you want to read by typing in key phrases. ENS then sends you electronic news "clippings" that you can read. ENS costs $15 per hour plus the base connect rates.

See Also
AP Sports($), Financial Forums, Global Crises Forum, NewsGrid, Newspaper Archives($), Reuter News Pictures Forum, United Press Int'l($), U.S. News Forum

User Guide
- ☑ Windows
- ☑ DOS
- ☐ Macintosh
- ☐ Terminal Emulation
- ☐ VMS
- ☐ UNIX
- ☐ OS/2
- ☐ Other platform

Cost
- ☐ Unknown
- ☐ Basic
- ☐ Extended
- ☑ Premium ($)
- ☐ Executive w/$

Activity Level: LOW — UNKNOWN (MEDIUM) — HIGH

Address
GO: **ENS**

Executive Service Option

Description
This is a CompuServe service that enables you to access several value-added services, including databases, merchandise, and other online items.

Subjects
Databases, Financial News

Audience
General public

Content Summary
When you select this option, you can access exclusive databases, including Company Analyzer, Disclosure II, Executive News Service, SuperSite, Institutional Broker's Estimate System, Securities Screening, Return Analysis, and Company Screening. You also get volume discounts on information retrieval from selected financial databases, a six month storage period (rather than the standard 30 days) for personal files without charge, and a ten percent discount on most CompuServe products, excluding sale items. When you join the Executive Service Option, you are subject to a $10 monthly minimum usage level. Your monthly $8.95 CompuServe basic membership (Standard Pricing Plan) is applied to this minimum. All products associated with the Executive Service Option are considered wide-mode products. This means they display best on screens that allow widths of 80 columns.

See Also
CompuServe Help Forum (free), CompuServe Rates (free), Order From CompuServe (free)

User Guide
- ☐ Windows
- ☐ DOS
- ☐ Macintosh
- ☑ Terminal Emulation
- ☐ VMS
- ☐ UNIX
- ☐ OS/2
- ☐ Other platform

Cost
- ☐ Unknown
- ☐ Basic
- ☐ Extended
- ☑ Premium ($)
- ☐ Executive w/$

Activity Level: LOW — UNKNOWN (MEDIUM) — HIGH

Address
GO: **EXECUTIVE**

Financial Forecasts

Description
This area presents you with the Earnings/Economics Projections menu, from which you can choose five financial and investment services.

Subjects
Financial News, International Finance, Investments, Investments, Investments

Audience
Investors, market analysts, financial analysts, financial advisors, business and financial researchers

Content Summary
From the Earnings/Economics Projections main menu, you can select I/B/E/S Earnings Estimate, S&P Online, InvesText, MMS International Financial Reports, and CENDATA services (CENDATA is a Census Bureau service). For information and service fees associated with these services, select the Instructions/Fees option from the main menu. Some of the services require terminal emulation. I/B/E/S Earnings Estimate is a database that provides consensus earnings estimates on over 3,400 publicly traded corporations. S&P Online provides you with recent information on approximately 4,700 companies, including business summaries, recent market activity, and dividend information. The InvesText database provides company and industry research reports compiled during the most recent two years by analysts in more than 50 Wall Street, regional, and international brokerage houses and research firms. MMS International Financial Reports provides a calendar of economic events, daily market reports, debt market reports, and other information on international markets.

See Also
Dividends and Splits ($), Financial Forums, Dun's Market Identifiers ($), Dun's Elect Business Dir ($)

User Guide
- [ ] Windows
- [ ] DOS
- [ ] Macintosh
- [x] Terminal Emulation
- [ ] VMS
- [ ] UNIX
- [ ] OS/2
- [ ] Other platform

Cost
- [ ] Unknown
- [ ] Basic
- [ ] Extended
- [x] Premium ($)
- [ ] Executive w/$

Activity Level
UNKNOWN (LOW — MEDIUM — HIGH)

Address
GO: **EARNINGS**

Global Report

Description
This is Citibank's online information resource database, where you can find data on a number of large corporations worldwide.

Subjects
Business, Databases, Financial News

Audience
Financial analysts, accountants, business researchers, business and financial researchers

Content Summary
Launched by Citibank in 1986, Global Report has become the primary information resource for a number of large corporations worldwide because it integrates and organizes news and financial data from well-respected sources, allowing for quick and easy information retrieval. For pricing information, see the Pricing/Sample Reports option on the Global Report main menu. If you're new to this service, be sure to choose the Important Pages option on the main menu to see a list of important searching criteria.

See Also
Dun's Elect Business Dir, TRW Bus. Credit Reports

User Guide
- [ ] Windows
- [ ] DOS
- [ ] Macintosh
- [x] Terminal Emulation
- [ ] VMS
- [ ] UNIX
- [ ] OS/2
- [ ] Other platform

Cost
- [ ] Unknown
- [ ] Basic
- [ ] Extended
- [x] Premium ($)
- [ ] Executive w/$

Activity Level
UNKNOWN (LOW — MEDIUM — HIGH)

Address
GO: **GLOREP**

OTC NewsAlert

Description
Search the latest international news, weather, and sports from the world's major news agencies. A powerful news clipping service that can scan many news sources for stories you specify and deliver them to you daily.

Subjects
Business, Financial News, International News, News

Audience
Associated Press Forum, Associated Press Online

Content Summary
You can read financial events through Reuters Financial Report and OTC NewsAlert, as well as read the day's headlines with *The Washington Post*. To use the News by Company Ticker option, enter a company ticker symbol and check on business news filed within the past 24 hours. For the News Clips option, you can read through special clipping folders set up by CompuServe to keep you up on specific news topics. You also set up your own Personal area in which you specify the type of news that you want to read by typing in key phrases. ENS then sends you electronic news clippings that you can read. ENS costs $15 per hour plus the base connect rates.

See Also
AP Sports, Financial Forums, Global Crises Forum, NewsGrid, Newspaper Archives, Reuters News Pictures Forum, United Press International, U.S. News Forum

User Guide
- ☑ Windows
- ☑ DOS
- ☐ Macintosh
- ☐ Terminal Emulation
- ☐ VMS
- ☐ UNIX
- ☐ OS/2
- ☐ Other platform

Cost
- ☐ Unknown
- ☐ Basic
- ☐ Extended
- ☑ Premium ($)
- ☐ Executive w/$

Activity Level

Address
GO: **ENS**

Fine Arts Forum

Description
Michelangelo. Renoir. Matisse. DaVinci. Rembrandt. Montgomery. Montgomery? Find out about him and other artists in the Fine Arts Forum.

Subjects
Art, Art History, Classics, Modern Art

Audience
Art directors, art enthusiasts, art historians, artists, general interest

Content Summary
The Fine Arts Forum focuses on the arts and techniques of the old masters, as well as local and regional traditional-media artists such as Carl Lundgren, Gunni Nilsson Price, Joe Bergeron, Roberta Laidman, Jess Hager, Barbara Johnson, and David O. Stillings. The many libraries offered here enable you to download GIF files of many of your favorite paintings, such as Michelangelo's "The Fall of Man," DaVinci's "Last Supper," and Renoir's "Diana." You also can become familiar with modern artists and techniques by visiting Library 15, Modern Art.

See Also
Artist Forum, Graphics Forums, Graphics Gallery Forum, Graphics Plus Forum, Photography Forum

User Guide
- ☑ Windows
- ☑ DOS
- ☑ Macintosh
- ☐ Terminal Emulation
- ☑ VMS
- ☑ UNIX
- ☑ OS/2
- ☑ Other platform

Cost
- ☐ Unknown
- ☐ Basic
- ☐ Extended
- ☑ Premium ($)
- ☐ Executive w/$

Activity Level

Address
GO: **FINEARTS**

FIREFIGHTING

Safetynet Forum

Description
This forum provides and open communication channel for people and professionals interested in sharing information on any topic of public safety.

Subjects
Crime, Fire Fighting, Public Safety

Audience
Firefighters, health workers, police

Content Summary
This forum's libraries and message areas provide a wide assortment of information pertaining to public safety. A graphics library contains pictures of actual rescue attempts, crime scenes, and fires. Some of the pictures are graphic in nature. Of general interest are Red Cross disaster information, lists of public safety hotlines and bulletin boards, and copies of the Environmental Informer Newsletter. Separate libraries are available for firefighters, police, and public heath workers.

See Also
ZiffNet Crime and Violence Forum

User Guide
- ☑ Windows
- ☑ DOS
- ☐ Macintosh
- ☐ Terminal Emulation
- ☐ VMS
- ☐ UNIX
- ☐ OS/2
- ☐ Other platform

Cost
- ☐ Unknown
- ☐ Basic
- ☑ Extended
- ☐ Premium ($)
- ☐ Executive w/$

Activity Level: MEDIUM

Address
GO: **SAFETYNET**

FISH

Aquaria/Fish Forum

Description
FISHNET is the place to meet for information dealing with all kinds of aquatic critters.

Subjects
Fish

Audience
Aquatic enthusiasts

Content Summary
The libraries include Your First Aquarium, Equipment/Products, Graphics Library, and more.

See Also
Pet Products/Reference Forum

User Guide
- ☑ Windows
- ☑ DOS
- ☐ Macintosh
- ☐ Terminal Emulation
- ☐ VMS
- ☐ UNIX
- ☐ OS/2
- ☐ Other platform

Cost
- ☐ Unknown
- ☐ Basic
- ☑ Extended
- ☐ Premium ($)
- ☐ Executive w/$

Activity Level: MEDIUM (arrow toward HIGH)

Address
GO: **FISHNET**

Pet Products/Reference Forum

Description
This forum provides customer support for those businesses that provide products or services to pet owners or pet professionals.

Subjects
Animals, Fish, Veterinarians

Audience
Aquarists, pet owners, veterinarians

Content Summary
This forum contains numerous libraries that include a complete list of all subscribing PetPro vendors and a description of their businesses. Also of interest are articles written by behavioral specialists and articles that have appeared in well-known animal publications.

See Also
Pets/Animal Forum

User Guide
- ☑ Windows
- ☑ DOS
- ☑ Macintosh
- ☐ Terminal Emulation
- ☐ VMS
- ☐ UNIX
- ☑ OS/2
- ☐ Other platform

Cost
- ☐ Unknown
- ☐ Basic
- ☑ Extended
- ☐ Premium ($)
- ☐ Executive w/$

Activity Level: MEDIUM (arrow toward LOW)

Address
GO: **PETPRO**

FITNESS

Health and Fitness Forum

Description
This forum provides health-related information and support groups for their members. Learn about exercise, nutrition, mental health, and other health items.

Subjects
Fitness, Health, Martial Arts

Audience
General public

Content Summary
The message library sections contain various health-related files and information and are divided into several topics, including Addiction/Recovery, Mental Health, Family Health, The Doctor's Inn, Exercise & Fitness, Master's Swimming, Running & Racing, Nutrition, Martial Arts, and Self Help. The Martial Arts library is very popular.

Fitness

See Also
Health and Vitamin Express, Health Database Plus($), Health/Fitness, HealthNet, Holistic Health Forum

User Guide
- ☑ Windows
- ☑ DOS
- ☑ Macintosh
- ☐ Terminal Emulation
- ☑ VMS
- ☑ UNIX
- ☑ OS/2
- ☑ Other platform

Cost
- ☐ Unknown
- ☐ Basic
- ☑ Extended
- ☐ Premium ($)
- ☐ Executive w/$

Activity Level

(gauge: arrow pointing LOW)

Address
GO: **GOODHEALTH**

HealthNet

Description
Get health news, sports medicine, information on ailments and disorders, and other health-related information from this forum.

Subjects
Fitness, Health, Health Care, Sports

Audience
General public

Content Summary
The HealthNet main menu contains two options: HealthNet Reference Library and Sports Medicine. The HealthNet Reference Library contains several listings, including Disorders and Diseases, Symptoms, Drugs, Surgeries/Tests/Procedures, Home Care and First Aid, Obstetrics/Reproductive Medicine, and Ophthalmology/Eye Care. The Sports Medicine option contains General Aspects of Exercise, Nutrition and Exercise, and Some Specific Sports. Be sure to read the introduction to this service, and do not use this service as a substitute for your doctor or medical personnel.

See Also
Health/Fitness, Health Database Plus($), Health and Vitamin Express, Health & Fitness Forum, Holistic Health Forum, Sports Forum

User Guide
- ☑ Windows
- ☑ DOS
- ☑ Macintosh
- ☐ Terminal Emulation
- ☑ VMS
- ☑ UNIX
- ☑ OS/2
- ☑ Other platform

Cost
- ☐ Unknown
- ☑ Basic
- ☐ Extended
- ☐ Premium ($)
- ☐ Executive w/$

Activity Level

(gauge: UNKNOWN)

Address
GO: **HNT**

Holistic Health Forum

Description
The Holistic Health Forum tries to look at the whole person, stressing preventive measures an individual can take on his or her own behalf.

Subjects
Fitness, Health

Audience
General public

Content Summary
The libraries and message sections in this forum include such topics as herbs and plants, Chinese treatments, health graphics, diet and exercise, women's health, chiropractic, health politics, and the natural foods business. In the Healing & the Mind library (Library 10), you can learn about crystal healing and psychic holistic health. The Nutritional Therapy library (Library 3) contains a text file on antioxidants.

See Also
Health and Fitness Forum, Health and Vitamin Express, Health Database Plus($), Health/Fitness, HealthNet

User Guide
- ☑ Windows
- ☑ DOS
- ☑ Macintosh
- ☐ Terminal Emulation
- ☑ VMS
- ☑ UNIX
- ☑ OS/2
- ☑ Other platform

Cost
- ☐ Unknown
- ☐ Basic
- ☑ Extended
- ☐ Premium ($)
- ☐ Executive w/$

Activity Level

Address
GO: **HOLISTIC**

Flight Simulation Forum

Description
Are you interested in flight simulation software and scenery design? If so, check out this forum and download hundreds of support and help files.

Subjects
Flight Simulation, Simulation, Space Flight

Audience
General public, game players

Content Summary
This forum is packed with useful and up-to-date information and files for the flight simulation affionado. The libraries in this forum include General/Help, FS/General Aviation, Air Transport, Air Traffic Control, Aircraft/Adventures, Scenery Design, Historic Air Combat, as well as many others. You can get information and press releases on the latest and greatest hardware add-ons in Library 13, "Hardware." Also, be sure to visit "Hangar Talk" (Library 16) for miscellaneous events, reports, and graphics.

See Also
Space Flight Forum

User Guide
- ☑ Windows
- ☑ DOS
- ☑ Macintosh
- ☐ Terminal Emulation
- ☐ VMS
- ☐ UNIX
- ☐ OS/2
- ☐ Other platform

Cost
- ☐ Unknown
- ☐ Basic
- ☑ Extended
- ☐ Premium ($)
- ☐ Executive w/$

Activity Level
MEDIUM (LOW → HIGH)

Address
GO: **FSFORUM**

Florida Forum

Description
This forum provides a useful area of information to plan a Florida visit or vacation and about the sunny state in general.

Subjects
Florida, Florida History

Audience
Florida residents, general public, tourists

Content Summary
Regardless of why you are interested in Florida—a resident, tourist, visitor—this forum should help you find information about the best places to stay, the best restaurants, sporting events, or recreational areas. You also can find information out about Disney by visiting the DisneyMania library (Library 13). The libraries in this forum are divided into regions, cities (such as Ft. Lauderdale and Orlando), graphics, and other recreational/hobby areas.

See Also:
Florida Today Forum, Travel Forum

User Guide
- ☑ Windows
- ☑ DOS
- ☑ Macintosh
- ☐ Terminal Emulation
- ☑ VMS
- ☑ UNIX
- ☑ OS/2
- ☑ Other platform

Cost
- ☐ Unknown
- ☐ Basic
- ☑ Extended
- ☐ Premium ($)
- ☐ Executive w/$

Activity Level
MEDIUM (LOW → HIGH)

Address
GO: **FLORIDA**

Florida Today Forum

Description
This forum is the first international, interactive forum linking *Florida Today*, the Space Coast Newspaper, with newspaper readers everywhere.

Subjects
Disney Comics, Florida, Tourism

Audience
Tourists, Florida residents

Content Summary
The Florida Today Newslink forum is an electronic newspaper intended to give readers a way to get their news and information online. The libraries consist of sections devoted to space, sports, leisure and tourism, environment, gardening, weather, senior activities, politics, education, and many more areas. The Front Page Lounge (Library 15) is full of editorial cartoons for you to download and view.

See Also
Travel Forum, Florida Forum

User Guide
- ☑ Windows
- ☑ DOS
- ☑ Macintosh
- ☐ Terminal Emulation
- ☑ VMS
- ☑ UNIX
- ☑ OS/2
- ☑ Other platform

Florida – Flowers

Cost
- [ ] Unknown
- [ ] Basic
- [x] Extended
- [ ] Premium ($)
- [ ] Executive w/$

Activity Level

Address
GO: **FLATODAY**

FLOWERS

800 Flowers

Description
At 800-Flowers & 800-Gifthouse, the world's largest source of flowers & gifts, everyday is a holiday.

Subjects
Flowers, Gifts

Audience
Consumers

Content Summary
During your shopping experience, be sure to ask for assistance from the Gift Concierge Service.

See Also
CompuServe Mall

User Guide
- [x] Windows
- [x] DOS
- [x] Macintosh
- [ ] Terminal Emulation
- [ ] VMS
- [ ] UNIX
- [ ] OS/2
- [ ] Other platform

Cost
- [ ] Unknown
- [x] Basic
- [ ] Extended
- [ ] Premium ($)
- [ ] Executive w/$

Activity Level

Address
GO: **FGS**

FTD Online

Description
Order fresh, beautifiul flowers online through this FTD service. You can view your selection with online graphics.

Subjects
General interest

Audience
General Public

Content Summary
You have several options from which to choose in this service, including special offers, bithday arrangements, customer service, and contests (if applicable). After you make a choice, you can either view or download a graphic of the selections or read product descriptions and order the arrangements. Domestic deliveries are surcharged $4.95 for shipping and handling, and international orders are surcharged $10.00. Delivery times vary depending on the time you submit your order: Orders received before 12:00 noon EST can be delivered the same day; orders received after 12:00 noon EST are delivered the next day; orders received after 12:00 noon EST on Saturday are delivered the following Monday. Holidays are especially busy, so get your orders in early during those seasons.

See Also
Order From CompuServe (FREE), CompuServe Mail

User Guide
- [ ] Windows
- [ ] DOS
- [ ] Macintosh
- [x] Terminal Emulation
- [ ] VMS
- [ ] UNIX
- [ ] OS/2
- [ ] Other platform

Cost
- [ ] Unknown
- [ ] Basic
- [ ] Extended
- [x] Premium ($)
- [ ] Executive w/$

Activity Level

Address
GO: **FTD**

Walter Knoll Florist

Description
This is an online shopping area offering flowers and plants.

Subjects
Shopping

Audience
Consumers, shoppers

Content Summary
This shopping area offers the convenience of shopping for flowers or plants from your home or office.

See Also
Electronic Mall

Flowers – Food

User Guide
- ☑ Windows
- ☑ DOS
- ☑ Macintosh
- ☐ Terminal Emulation
- ☑ VMS
- ☑ UNIX
- ☑ OS/2
- ☐ Other platform

Cost
- ☐ Unknown
- ☑ Basic
- ☐ Extended
- ☐ Premium ($)
- ☐ Executive w/$

Activity Level
LOW — UNKNOWN — MEDIUM — HIGH

Address
GO: **WK**

FontBank Online

Description
Don't have enough fonts clogging up your hard drive? Stop by the FontBank Online service and get as many fonts as you want or can afford.

Subjects
Typography

Audience
Desktop publishers, designers, computer users, authors, artists, graphic artists, graphic designers, technical writers

Content Summary
FontBank Online is designed to deliver fonts, clip art, and graphics to the desktop publishing community. FontBank Online was designed for the entire desktop publishing community, from the desktop publishing professional to the novice. You can choose from several menu choices, such as Introduction to FontBank Online, Documentation/Tutorials, Download Font Catalog/Tutorials, FontFinder, Expert's Choice, New Fonts, and Feedback to FontBank. You can find the font you're looking for by several searching criteria, including scrolling through a list of the available fonts online. Prices for specific fonts vary, so see the online pricing structure for each font.

See Also
DTP Vendors Forum, DTPONLINE, Graphics Forums, Mac New Users Help Forum, Macintosh Forums, Macmillan Publishing Forum

User Guide
- ☑ Windows
- ☑ DOS
- ☑ Macintosh
- ☑ Terminal Emulation
- ☐ VMS
- ☐ UNIX
- ☐ OS/2
- ☐ Other platform

Cost
- ☐ Unknown
- ☐ Basic
- ☑ Extended
- ☐ Premium ($)
- ☐ Executive w/$

Activity Level
LOW — UNKNOWN — MEDIUM — HIGH

Address
GO: **FONTBANK**

FOOD

Adventures in Food

Description
An online shop for discriminating food lovers.

Subjects
Food, Shopping

Audience
Gourmet enthusiasts

Content Summary
Gourmet items, gift items, specialty cheeses, and more awaits you in this service area.

See Also
Bacchus Wine and Beer Forum

User Guide
- ☑ Windows
- ☑ DOS
- ☑ Macintosh
- ☐ Terminal Emulation
- ☐ VMS
- ☐ UNIX
- ☐ OS/2
- ☐ Other platform

Cost
- ☐ Unknown
- ☑ Basic
- ☐ Extended
- ☐ Premium ($)
- ☐ Executive w/$

Activity Level
LOW — UNKNOWN — MEDIUM — HIGH

Address
GO: **AIF**

Bacchus Wine and Beer Forum

Description
The Wine Forum, operated by Bacchus Data Services, is the home for discussion of all the beverages that you enjoy.

Subjects
Food, Wine

Audience
General public, wine lovers

Food

Content Summary
If you enjoy a good glass of wine or a cold beer, join this forum and visit the different libraries in it. Some of the library topics include wine tasting, wine shopping, beer, wine, brewing, recipes, spirits, coffee, and more.

See Also
The Absolut Museum

User Guide
- ☑ Windows
- ☑ DOS
- ☑ Macintosh
- ☐ Terminal Emulation
- ☑ VMS
- ☑ UNIX
- ☑ OS/2
- ☐ Other platform

Cost
- ☐ Unknown
- ☐ Basic
- ☑ Extended
- ☐ Premium ($)
- ☐ Executive w/$

Activity Level

Address
GO: **WINEFORUM**

Cook's Online Forum

Description
Everything dealing with cooking is what this forum is about, from appetizers to desserts, and a wine to go with the meal.

Subjects
Hobbies, Food

Audience
Cooks

Content Summary
The libraries include recipes and information about first courses, meat/poultry/fish, herbs and spices, desserts, ethnic recipes, breads, fruits, nutrition, and vegetarian cooking.

See Also
Omaha Steaks International

User Guide
- ☑ Windows
- ☑ DOS
- ☑ Macintosh
- ☐ Terminal Emulation
- ☐ VMS
- ☑ UNIX
- ☐ OS/2
- ☐ Other platform

Cost
- ☐ Unknown
- ☐ Basic
- ☑ Extended
- ☐ Premium ($)
- ☐ Executive w/$

Activity Level

Address
GO: **COOKS**

Home Forum

Description
This forum is about homes. What more can you say?

Subjects
Food, Hobbies, Home Building

Audience
General public, horticulture enthusiasts

Content Summary
You can find out information, tips, hints, and the like here, regardless of the type of home you live in, including apartments, condos, or older homes. Topics such as security, home building, interior furnishing, outdoor living, lighting, and the kitchen are included in the message and library sections. If you want to wire your house for a computer network, for example, look in the Conveniences library (Library 7) for a text file that explains it. You also might want to cut down on the amount of fat you serve at Thanksgiving, Christmas, or other holiday meals. The In the Kitchen library (Library 9) tells you how to substitute shrimp and crab meat for your hor d'oeuvres.

See Also
Family Handyman Forum, Gardening Forum

User Guide
- ☑ Windows
- ☑ DOS
- ☑ Macintosh
- ☐ Terminal Emulation
- ☑ VMS
- ☑ UNIX
- ☑ OS/2
- ☑ Other platform

Cost
- ☐ Unknown
- ☐ Basic
- ☑ Extended
- ☐ Premium ($)
- ☐ Executive w/$

Activity Level
MEDIUM (arrow pointing up, between LOW and HIGH)

Address
GO: **HOME**

Omaha Steaks International

Description
Order thick, juicy steaks online from Omaha Steaks International, which has been in business since 1917.

Subjects
Food, Catalogs

Audience
General public

Content Summary
From the main menu, you can choose from several options, including Order From Our Online Catalog, Product QuickSearch, Customer Service, Welcome to Omaha Steaks International, Order Our Free Catalog, Order From Our Print Catalog, Join Our Electronic Mailing List, Recipe of the Month, and Special Offer.

See Also
Adventures in Food Forum

User Guide
- ☑ Windows
- ☑ DOS
- ☑ Macintosh
- ☐ Terminal Emulation
- ☑ VMS
- ☑ UNIX
- ☐ OS/2
- ☐ Other platform

Cost
- ☐ Unknown
- ☑ Basic
- ☐ Extended
- ☐ Premium ($)
- ☐ Executive w/$

Activity Level

Address
GO: OS

Zagat Restaurant Guide

Description
This service features thousands of reviews based on annual surveys of restaurant patrons. Search for old and new restaurants in more than 20 cities and regions.

Subjects
Food

Audience
General interest

Content Summary
This guide is ideal for those members interested in looking up restaurant recommendations.

See Also
Home Forum

User Guide
- ☑ Windows
- ☑ DOS
- ☑ Macintosh
- ☑ Terminal Emulation
- ☑ VMS
- ☑ UNIX
- ☑ OS/2
- ☑ Other platform

Cost
- ☐ Unknown
- ☑ Basic
- ☐ Extended
- ☐ Premium ($)
- ☐ Executive w/$

Activity Level

(MEDIUM — UNKNOWN — LOW / HIGH)

Address
GO: ZAGAT

Ford Motor Company

Description
The opening screen says: "Have you driven a Ford lately?" This service enables you to view the latest vehicles available from Ford.

Subjects
Automobiles, Ford Mustangs

Audience
Automobile enthusiasts, general public

Content Summary
Set up with a menu system, you can select to see the Welcome Center, Ford cars or Ford trucks, the World of Ford, the Ford Dealer Locator, Software, Video, or Sportswear, or the featured Ford vehicle (the 1994 Ford Escort at the time of this writing). The Ford Dealer Locator option enables you to find the nearest Ford dealer in your area. The Ford Motor Company service is free, but you are surcharged for items that you purchase.

See Also
Automobile Info Center (FREE), Automobile Forum, Automotive Information, AutoVantage OnLine (FREE), AutoQuot-R (FREE)

User Guide
- ☐ Windows
- ☐ DOS
- ☐ Macintosh
- ☑ Terminal Emulation
- ☐ VMS
- ☐ UNIX
- ☐ OS/2
- ☐ Other platform

Cost
- ☐ Unknown
- ☑ Basic
- ☐ Extended
- ☐ Premium ($)
- ☐ Executive w/$

Activity Level

(MEDIUM — UNKNOWN — LOW / HIGH)

Address
GO: FORD

Foreign Language Forum

Description
This forum is devoted to foreign languages, their study, teaching, use in the commercial world, or general interest items about foreign languages.

Subjects
Bilingual Education, Europe, Foreign News, French, International, Languages

Audience
General public, Europeans

Content Summary
As you can see from the various library headings, the Foreign LanguageForum offers a diverse cultural and languages experience. The libraries are listed as follows: Spanish/Portuguese, French, German/Germanic, Latin/Greek, Slavic/E. European, English, East Asian, Esperanto, Italian, FL Education, Translators, Computers/Languages, Resources/Careers, Semitic/Turkic, Others Using the Forum, and Sysops.

See Also
Education Forum

User Guide
- ☑ Windows
- ☑ DOS
- ☑ Macintosh
- ☐ Terminal Emulation
- ☐ VMS
- ☐ UNIX
- ☐ OS/2
- ☑ Other platform

Cost
- ☐ Unknown
- ☐ Basic
- ☑ Extended
- ☐ Premium ($)
- ☐ Executive w/$

Activity Level
MEDIUM (LOW–HIGH)

Address
GO: **FLEFO**

Foreign Language Forum

Description
This forum is devoted to foreign languages, their study, teaching, use in the commercial world, or general interest items about foreign languages.

Subjects
Bilingual Education, Europe, Foreign News, French, International, Languages

Audience
General public, Europeans

Content Summary
As you can see from the various library headings, the Foreign Language Forum offers a diverse cultural and languages experience. The libraries are listed as follows: Spanish/Portuguese, French, German/Germanic, Latin/Greek, Slavic/E. European, English, East Asian, Esperanto, Italian, FL Education, Translators, Computers/Languages, Resources/Careers, Semitic/Turkic, Others Using the Forum, and Sysops.

See Also
Education Forum

User Guide
- ☑ Windows
- ☑ DOS
- ☑ Macintosh
- ☐ Terminal Emulation
- ☐ VMS
- ☐ UNIX
- ☐ OS/2
- ☑ Other platform

Cost
- ☐ Unknown
- ☐ Basic
- ☑ Extended
- ☐ Premium ($)
- ☐ Executive w/$

Activity Level
MEDIUM (LOW–HIGH)

Address
GO: **FLEFO**

Forums

Description
Need to find a forum on CompuServe? Do you just want to browse the different forums on CompuServe? Go to the Forums service to view all the available forums.

Subjects
Help

Audience
General public

Content Summary
The main menu lets you pick from a list of SIGS (Special Interest GroupS), which then lists specific forums relating to that SIG. You might, for instance, choose Aviation Forums which lists Aviation Forum and Model Aviation Forum as possible forums for you to visit or join. This area is helpful when you want to see the most up-to-date list of forums that CompuServe offers.

See Also
CompuServe Help Forum (free), CompuServe Operating Rules (free), CompuServe Tour (free)

User Guide
- [x] Windows
- [x] DOS
- [x] Macintosh
- [ ] Terminal Emulation
- [x] VMS
- [x] UNIX
- [x] OS/2
- [x] Other platform

Cost
- [ ] Unknown
- [x] Basic
- [ ] Extended
- [ ] Premium ($)
- [ ] Executive w/$

Activity Level
UNKNOWN

Address
GO: **FORUMS**

FRANCHISE

Entrepreneur Small Business Square

Description
From this service, you can access the Entrepreneur's Small Business Forum, Franchise & Business Opportunities, Small Business Emporium, and the *Entrepreneur Magazine* Small Business Survey. The Franchise & Business Opportunities option is a database that lists company addresses, phone numbers, contact names, and descriptions of franchising and business opportunities.

Subjects
Entrepreneur, Small Business, Franchise

Audience
Entrepreneurs, small business owners, venture capitalists

Content Summary
To use the Franchise & Business Opportunities database, select that option from the Entrepreneur Small Business Square main menu and then select the Begin Your Search option. You then use search criteria from a list of 1,500 opportunities to find your results. The Small Business Emporium is a terminal emulation area that stores over 165 entrepreneur business guides to help you start and maintain a small business.

See Also
IQuest Business Management InfoCenter, Entrepreneurs, Small Business Forum

User Guide
- [ ] Windows
- [ ] DOS
- [ ] Macintosh
- [x] Terminal Emulation
- [ ] VMS
- [ ] UNIX
- [ ] OS/2
- [ ] Other platform

Cost
- [ ] Unknown
- [ ] Basic
- [x] Extended
- [ ] Premium ($)
- [ ] Executive w/$

Activity Level
UNKNOWN

Address
GO: **ENTMAGAZINE**

FREE ENTERPRISE

Entrepreneur's Small Business Forum

Description
Sponsored by Entrepreneur Group, the publishers of *Entrepreneur Magazine,* the Entrepreneur's Small Business Forum enables you to identify and communicate with other entrepreneurs in a different cities and locales. This forum welcomes the sharing of information and helpful dialogue from all members.

Subjects
Business, Entrepreneurs, Free Enterprise, Small Business

Audience
Business owners, entrepreneurs, venture capitalists

Content Summary
The libraries contain information on business opportunities, start-up techniques, marketing and promotion files, financing, legal issues, planning files, and international issues. Check out the information in Library 13, "Homebased Business," if you are thinking about starting, or are maintaining, a business from your home. You also should take part in the message section if you have specific questions to ask.

See Also
Entrepreneur Small Business Square, Business Franchise and Opportunities Database

User Guide
- [ ] Windows
- [ ] DOS
- [ ] Macintosh
- [ ] Terminal Emulation
- [ ] VMS
- [ ] UNIX
- [ ] OS/2
- [ ] Other platform

Cost
- [ ] Unknown
- [ ] Basic
- [x] Extended
- [ ] Premium ($)
- [ ] Executive w/$

Free Enterprise

Activity Level: MEDIUM

Address
GO: **USEN**

G

Game Forums and News

Description
Access all the CompuServe forums relating to games by using this service.

Subjects
Games, Simulation

Audience
Game players

Content Summary
From the Games Forums/News main menu, you can choose to go to many forums or areas, such as The Electronic Gamer, The Gamer Forum, Multi-Player Games Forum, Role-Playing Games Forum, Play-by-Mail Games Forum, Game Publishers Forums, Modem Games Forum, Flight Simulation Forum, Chess Forum, Sports Simulation Forum, Epic Megagames Forum, Hot Games Download Area, Video Games Publishers Forum, and Video Games Forum.

See Also
Game Publishers Forums (free), Flight Simulation Forum, Entertainment Center, Electronic Gamer™

User Guide
- [x] Windows
- [x] DOS
- [x] Macintosh
- [ ] Terminal Emulation
- [x] VMS
- [x] UNIX
- [x] OS/2
- [x] Other platform

Cost
- [ ] Unknown
- [x] Basic
- [ ] Extended
- [ ] Premium ($)
- [ ] Executive w/$

Activity Level

MEDIUM
LOW
UNKNOWN
HIGH

Address
GO: **GAMECON**

Game Publishers Forums

Description
Access the numerous (way too many to list, in fact) game publishers forums and sections from this service.

Subjects
Computer Ethics, Computer Games, Games

Audience
Computer game enthusiasts, computer game developers, game players

Content Summary
To help answer the plethora of questions that CompuServe members have about games, including help and news releases, many game publishers (manufacturers) have online message sections. Game Publishers A Forum (GO GAMAPUB) includes Accolade, Bethesada Softworks, Cyberdreams, Sierra OnLine, and others. Game Publishers B Forum (GO GAMBPUB) includes Access, Activision, Disney/Buena Vista, Konami, and others. Game Publishers C Forum (GO GAMCPUB) includes Avalon Hill, Inline Software, Legend Entertainment, and others. Game Publishers D Forum (GO GAMDPUB) includes Megatech Software, Amtex Software, Crystal Dynamics, and many more. When you access the specific publishers forums, you are surcharged at the extended service charge.

See Also
Electronic Gamer™, Game Forums and News, Gamers Forum, Flight Simulation Forum

User Guide
- [x] Windows
- [x] DOS
- [x] Macintosh
- [ ] Terminal Emulation
- [x] VMS
- [x] UNIX
- [x] OS/2
- [x] Other platform

Cost
- [ ] Unknown
- [x] Basic
- [ ] Extended
- [ ] Premium ($)
- [ ] Executive w/$

Activity Level
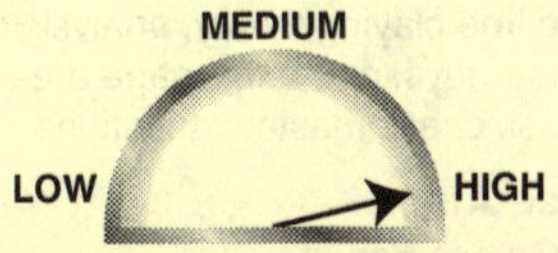
MEDIUM
LOW
HIGH

Address
GO: **GAMPUB**

GAMES

Air Traffic Controller

Description
An online game that simulates running the control towerat a major airport. The game can be played with multiple other CIS players.

Subjects
Entertainment, Games

Audience
Games enthusiasts

Content Summary
The object of the game is to keep your planes from running out of fuel or crashing.

See Also
Flight Simulation Forum

G

Games

User Guide
- ☑ Windows
- ☑ DOS
- ☑ Macintosh
- ☐ Terminal Emulation
- ☑ VMS
- ☑ UNIX
- ☑ OS/2
- ☑ Other platform

Cost
- ☐ Unknown
- ☐ Basic
- ☐ Extended
- ☑ Premium ($)
- ☐ Executive w/$

Activity Level
UNKNOWN (LOW — MEDIUM — HIGH)

Address
GO: **ATCONTROL**

Chess Forum

Description
The place to be if you love the game of Chess or want to find out more about playing it.

Subjects
Games, Hobbies

Audience
Games enthusiasts

Content Summary
The libraries and message sections contain basic game playing theory, analysis of moves, chess tourneys, and a message area that enables you to ask chess masters questions.

See Also
Games Forum

User Guide
- ☑ Windows
- ☑ DOS
- ☑ Macintosh
- ☐ Terminal Emulation
- ☐ VMS
- ☑ UNIX
- ☐ OS/2
- ☐ Other platform

Cost
- ☐ Unknown
- ☐ Basic
- ☑ Extended
- ☐ Premium ($)
- ☐ Executive w/$

Activity Level
MEDIUM-HIGH (LOW — MEDIUM — HIGH)

Address
GO: **CHESSFORUM**

E*TRADE Stock Market Game

Description
Have you ever wondered what it would be like to be a Wall Street mover and shaker? Now's your chance to invest $100,000 in game accounts by playing the E*TRADE Stock Market Game. The game lets you play in stocks only, stocks and options, or both, and will track your performance—and commission rates—every month. If you have the right stuff and have the highest percentage increase of all the players, you can win a cash prize.

Subjects
Games, Finance, Wall Street

Audience
Financial persons, gamers, students

Content Summary
The E*TRADE Securities main menu offers you three choices: Game Instructions, Sign-up for the Game, and Play the E*TRADE Stock Market Game. Select Game Instructions to read directions on how to play and what you can win. You compete with other members to see who can become the wealthiest in a month. When you sign up for the game, you are given $100,000 in game money with which to start.

See Also
E*TRADE Securities

User Guide
- ☐ Windows
- ☐ DOS
- ☐ Macintosh
- ☑ Terminal Emulation
- ☐ VMS
- ☐ UNIX
- ☐ OS/2
- ☐ Other platform

Cost
- ☐ Unknown
- ☐ Basic
- ☑ Extended
- ☐ Premium ($)
- ☐ Executive w/$

Activity Level
UNKNOWN (LOW — MEDIUM — HIGH)

Unknown

Address
GO: **ETGAME**

Entertainment Center

Description
Play a game online through the Entertainment Center. All you need is a PC with EGA graphics or better, and time. You can start your own game, play a game in progress, or watch a game. Save money by joining the CB Club.

Games

Subjects
Games

Audience
Gamers

Content Summary
In the Download Games option on the main menu, you can download the available games, such as StarSprint, Backgammon, Chess, and Checkers. You are charged a surcharge depending on the game you download.

See Also
CDCLUB

User Guide
- ☑ Windows
- ☑ DOS
- ☑ Macintosh
- ☐ Terminal Emulation
- ☑ VMS
- ☑ UNIX
- ☑ OS/2
- ☑ Other platform

Cost
- ☐ Unknown
- ☐ Basic
- ☐ Extended
- ☑ Premium ($)
- ☐ Executive w/$

Activity Level

Address
GO: **ECENTER**

Epic MegaGames

Description
This area enables you download the Epic game of the month as well as other shareware games, including OverKill, Epic Pinball, Jill of the Jungle, and Zone 66. You also can access the Epic MegaGames Forum from this area.

Subjects
Games, Shareware Games

Audience
Gamers

Content Summary
From the EpicGames main menu, you can select the About Epic MegaGames option to see a synopsis of this game publisher. To read a description and download the game of the month, select the Download Game-of-the-Month choice. If you are interested in other Epic products, be sure to visit the terminal emulation area by selecting Purchase Epic Products from the main menu. Don't blame us if you become addicted.

See Also
Epic MegaGames Forum, The Electronic Gamer Archives, The Entertainment Center, The Modem Games Forum, The Gamers' Forum

User Guide
- ☑ Windows
- ☑ DOS
- ☑ Macintosh
- ☐ Terminal Emulation
- ☑ VMS
- ☑ UNIX
- ☑ OS/2
- ☐ Other platform

Cost
- ☐ Unknown
- ☐ Basic
- ☑ Extended
- ☐ Premium ($)
- ☐ Executive w/$

Activity Level

Address
GO: **EPIC**

Epic MegaGames Forums

Description
Download Epic's latest shareware games, previews, and support files; leave messages for the Epic staff; and chat with other members in this forum.

Subjects
Games

Audience
Gamers

Content Summary
The Epic Forum has several libraries from which you can download Epic's games, such as Jazz Jackrabbit, Heartlight, and Castle of the Winds. See Library 2, "Classic Epic Games," for some of Epic's older games. If you need a hint or tip, go to Library 3 or Library 4 for some useful utilities. You also can get the latest issues of *GameBytes Magazine* from Library 7, "GameBytes Magazine."

See Also
Epic MegaGames (Go: EPIC)

User Guide
- ☐ Windows
- ☑ DOS
- ☐ Macintosh
- ☐ Terminal Emulation
- ☐ VMS
- ☐ UNIX
- ☐ OS/2
- ☐ Other platform

Cost
- ☐ Unknown
- ☐ Basic
- ☑ Extended
- ☐ Premium ($)
- ☐ Executive w/$

296 Games

Activity Level

MEDIUM (LOW — HIGH)

Address
GO: **EPICFO**

Fantasy/Role-Playing Adventure

Description
Play role-playing games such as British Legends or Island of Kesmai, as well as access the Role-Playing Forum and Play-by-Mail Forum.

Subjects
Games, Role-Playing Games

Audience
Game players, game theorists, general public

Content Summary
From the Fantasy/Role-Playing Adventure main menu, you can select to play British Legends or Island of Kesmai. British Legends is a multi-player adventure game filled with mystery, dense forests, an island, a cottage, and much more. In Island of Kesmai, you encounter many computer-run characters as you travel across the many acres of land on the Island of Kesmai, where a group of magicians live to escape persecution. From the main menu, you also can choose to go to the Role-Playing or Play-by-Mail Forums.

See Also
Gamers Forum, Island of Kesmai, British Legends, Modem Games Forum

User Guide
- [✓] Windows
- [✓] DOS
- [ ] Macintosh
- [ ] Terminal Emulation
- [ ] VMS
- [ ] UNIX
- [ ] OS/2
- [ ] Other platform

Cost
- [ ] Unknown
- [✓] Basic
- [ ] Extended
- [ ] Premium ($)
- [ ] Executive w/$

Activity Level
UNKNOWN (LOW — MEDIUM — HIGH)

Address
GO: **ADVENT**

Game Forums and News

Description
Access all the CompuServe forums relating to games by using this service.

Subjects
Games, Simulation

Audience
Game players

Content Summary
From the Games Forums/News main menu, you can choose to go to many forums or areas, such as The Electronic Gamer, The Gamer Forum, Multi-Player Games Forum, Role-Playing Games Forum, Play-by-Mail Games Forum, Game Publishers Forums, Modem Games Forum, Flight Simulation Forum, Chess Forum, Sports Simulation Forum, Epic Megagames Forum, Hot Games Download Area, Video Games Publishers Forum, and Video Games Forum.

See Also
Game Publishers Forums (free), Flight Simulation Forum, Entertainment Center, Electronic Gamer™

User Guide
- [✓] Windows
- [✓] DOS
- [✓] Macintosh
- [ ] Terminal Emulation
- [✓] VMS
- [✓] UNIX
- [✓] OS/2
- [✓] Other platform

Cost
- [ ] Unknown
- [✓] Basic
- [ ] Extended
- [ ] Premium ($)
- [ ] Executive w/$

Activity Level
UNKNOWN (LOW — MEDIUM — HIGH)

Address
GO: **GAMECON**

Game Publishers Forums

Description
Access the numerous (way too many to list, in fact) game publishers forums and sections from this service.

Subjects
Computer Ethics, Computer Games, Games

Audience
Computer game enthusiasts, computer game developers, game players

Games

Content Summary
To help answer the plethora of questions that CompuServe members have about games, including help and news releases, many game publishers (manufacturers) have online message sections. Game Publishers A Forum (GO GAMAPUB) includes Accolade, Bethesada Softworks, Cyberdreams, Sierra OnLine, and others. Game Publishers B Forum (GO GAMBPUB) includes Access, Activision, Disney/Buena Vista, Konami, and others. Game Publishers C Forum (GO GAMCPUB) includes Avalon Hill, Inline Software, Legend Entertainment, and others. Game Publishers D Forum (GO GAMDPUB) includes Megatech Software, Amtex Software, Crystal Dynamics, and many more. When you access the specific publishers forums, you are surcharged at the extended service charge.

See Also
Electronic Gamer™, Game Forums and News, Gamers Forum, Flight Simulation Forum

User Guide
- ☑ Windows
- ☑ DOS
- ☑ Macintosh
- ☐ Terminal Emulation
- ☑ VMS
- ☑ UNIX
- ☑ OS/2
- ☑ Other platform

Cost
- ☐ Unknown
- ☑ Basic
- ☐ Extended
- ☐ Premium ($)
- ☐ Executive w/$

Activity Level

Address
GO: **GAMPUB**

MegaWars I and III

Description
Play MegaWars I or MegaWars III by using this service.

Subjects
Games

Audience
Game players

Content Summary
The address for MegaWars I is MEGA1. The address for MegaWars III is MEGA3.

See Also
Fantasy/Role-Playing Adv., Epic MegaGames Forum

User Guide
- ☑ Windows
- ☑ DOS
- ☑ Macintosh
- ☐ Terminal Emulation
- ☑ VMS
- ☑ UNIX
- ☑ OS/2
- ☑ Other platform

Cost
- ☐ Unknown
- ☐ Basic
- ☑ Extended
- ☐ Premium ($)
- ☐ Executive w/$

Activity Level
UNKNOWN (LOW — MEDIUM — HIGH)

Address
GO: **MEGA1** or **MEGA3**

Microsoft Windows Fun Forum

Description
This forum is designed to allow Windows users a mechanism to discuss and obtain fun Windows files.

Subjects
Computers, Games, Microsoft Corp.

Audience
Computer users

Content Summary
You can find cool things on this forum, such as sound files from movies, screen saver utilities (see Library 4), graphics and graphics utilities (such as the one that changes the standard Windows startup .BMP) in Library 9, card games, a WinDominoes game (see Library 3), and other stuff. Have fun!

See Also
Entertainment Center, MS Software Library

User Guide
- ☑ Windows
- ☑ DOS
- ☑ Macintosh
- ☐ Terminal Emulation
- ☐ VMS
- ☐ UNIX
- ☐ OS/2
- ☐ Other platform

Cost
- ☐ Unknown
- ☐ Basic
- ☑ Extended
- ☐ Premium ($)
- ☐ Executive w/$

Activity Level

Address
GO: **WINFUN**

Microsoft Windows Multimedia Forum

Description
This forum offers many files, troubleshooting solutions, and technical support for your multimedia applications.

Games

Subjects
Games, Microsoft Corp., Multimedia

Audience
Computer users, computer game developers

Content Summary
The type of libraries and message sections you will see in this forum include MDK, MediaView, Video for Windows, Viewer 2.0, Windows Sound System, Multimedia (MM) Strategy, Third Party Software, and Windows Game Development. You can obtain a Viewer 2.0 compiler for Word 6.0 in the Viewer 2.0 library. Also, if you're looking for the Microsoft JumpStart CD, see Library 10, MM Strategy. This is the CD that Microsoft hands out at many of their conferences and seminars.

See Also
MS TechNet Forum, Multimedia Forum, Multimedia Conference Forum

User Guide
- ☑ Windows
- ☑ DOS
- ☑ Macintosh
- ☐ Terminal Emulation
- ☐ VMS
- ☐ UNIX
- ☐ OS/2
- ☐ Other platform

Cost
- ☐ Unknown
- ☐ Basic
- ☑ Extended
- ☐ Premium ($)
- ☐ Executive w/$

Activity Level

Address
GO: **WINMM**

Modem Games Forum

Description
This forum is an electronic special interest group devoted to discussion of computer games capable of utilizing telecommunications and networking technology for play and competition.

Subjects
Computers, Games, Modems

Audience
Computer users, modem users, game enthusiasts

Content Summary
You can find a number of games, utilities, and other supporting files in the libraries in this forum. Some of the library areas include Modem Air Combat, Historic Air Combat, VGA Planets, Chess/Board/Card, DOOM, Network Games, and more.

See Also
Entertainment Forum, Multi-Player Games Forum

User Guide
- ☑ Windows
- ☑ DOS
- ☑ Macintosh
- ☐ Terminal Emulation
- ☐ VMS
- ☑ UNIX
- ☐ OS/2
- ☐ Other platform

Cost
- ☐ Unknown
- ☐ Basic
- ☑ Extended
- ☐ Premium ($)
- ☐ Executive w/$

Activity Level

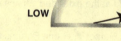

Address
GO: **MODEMGAMES**

Showbiz Quiz

Description
Companion to the ShowBiz Forum and Hollywood Hotline, this area features trivia quizzes on several ShowBiz topics.

Subjects
Games, Movies, Television, Trivia

Audience
Movie enthusiasts

Content Summary
The libraries contain information about the forum, home entertainment, recent films, new films, classic films, television, celebrities, and Hollywood news.

See Also
Hollywood Hotline

User Guide
- ☑ Windows
- ☑ DOS
- ☑ Macintosh
- ☐ Terminal Emulation
- ☐ VMS
- ☑ UNIX
- ☐ OS/2
- ☐ Other platform

Cost
- ☐ Unknown
- ☐ Basic
- ☑ Extended
- ☐ Premium ($)
- ☐ Executive w/$

Activity Level

Address
GO: **SBQ**

SNIPER!

Description
This online infantry combat game is set during World War II.

Subjects
Combat, Games, War

Audience
Games enthusiasts, military scenarios

Content Summary
You command a squad of soldiers in a mission against another squad. Actual wartime conditions are simulated. The game is over when a player has accomplished his or her mission. The game appears more lifelike if you download the SCOPE games software.

See Also
Games Forum

User Guide
- ☑ Windows
- ☑ DOS
- ☐ Macintosh
- ☐ Terminal Emulation
- ☐ VMS
- ☐ UNIX
- ☐ OS/2
- ☐ Other platform

Cost
- ☐ Unknown
- ☐ Basic
- ☑ Extended
- ☐ Premium ($)
- ☐ Executive w/$

Activity Level

UNKNOWN (LOW-MEDIUM-HIGH)

Address
Go: **SNIPER**

Sports Forum

Description
This forum covers sports from all angles—from yesterday's games to which referee blew the call.

Subjects
Games

Audience
Sports enthusiasts

See Also
Sports

User Guide
- ☑ Windows
- ☑ DOS
- ☑ Macintosh
- ☐ Terminal Emulation
- ☐ VMS
- ☐ UNIX
- ☐ OS/2
- ☐ Other platform

Cost
- ☐ Unknown
- ☐ Basic
- ☑ Extended
- ☐ Premium ($)
- ☐ Executive w/$

Activity Level

MEDIUM (LOW → HIGH)

Address
GO: **SPINNAKER**

Sports Simulation Forum

Description
This forum covers all of the various sports simulations software on the market. It also includes advice on how to beat the game, setting up your computer, etc.

Subjects
Games

Audience
Sports enthusiasts

Content Summary
Libraries included are football, basketball, hockey, baseball, fantasy sports, and other sports.

See Also
Sports Forum

User Guide
- ☑ Windows
- ☑ DOS
- ☑ Macintosh
- ☐ Terminal Emulation
- ☐ VMS
- ☐ UNIX
- ☐ OS/2
- ☐ Other platform

Cost
- ☐ Unknown
- ☐ Basic
- ☑ Extended
- ☐ Premium ($)
- ☐ Executive w/$

Activity Level

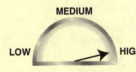

MEDIUM (LOW → HIGH)

Address
GO: **SPRTSIMS**

STAGEII

Description
This is an online multiplayer trivia game.

Subjects
Games

Audience
Games enthusiasts

300
Games

Content Summary
This online trivia game asks you three questions. After you answer the questions, you look for a common theme in the answers.

See Also
Games Forum

User Guide
- ☑ Windows
- ☑ DOS
- ☑ Macintosh
- ☐ Terminal Emulation
- ☐ VMS
- ☐ UNIX
- ☐ OS/2
- ☐ Other platform

Cost
- ☐ Unknown
- ☐ Basic
- ☑ Extended
- ☐ Premium ($)
- ☐ Executive w/$

Activity Level

Address
GO: **STAGEII**

Video Game Publishers Forum

Description
This is a vendor support forum for the products of several video games publishers.

Subjects
Entertainment, Games, Video Games

Audience
Game developers

Content Summary
The libraries contain information on Nintendo, Super Nintendo, Sega Genesis, Atari, and other video gaming systems.

See Also
Video Games Forum

User Guide
- ☑ Windows
- ☑ DOS
- ☐ Macintosh
- ☐ Terminal Emulation
- ☐ VMS
- ☐ UNIX
- ☐ OS/2
- ☐ Other platform

Cost
- ☐ Unknown
- ☐ Basic
- ☑ Extended
- ☐ Premium ($)
- ☐ Executive w/$

Activity Level

Address
GO: **VIDPUB**

Video Games Forum

Description
The Video Games Forum is the place to go to discuss all of the available video games machines, and to argue over which offers the most entertainment.

Subjects
Entertainment, Games, Video Games

Audience
Game enthusiats

Content Summary
The libraries and message areas contain product information and lively discussions about video game equipment.

See Also
Video Games Forum

User Guide
- ☑ Windows
- ☑ DOS
- ☑ Macintosh
- ☐ Terminal Emulation
- ☑ VMS
- ☑ UNIX
- ☑ OS/2
- ☑ Other platform

Cost
- ☐ Unknown
- ☐ Basic
- ☑ Extended
- ☐ Premium ($)
- ☐ Executive w/$

Activity Level

Address
GO: **VIDGAM**

You Guessed It!

Description
This forum is an online multiplayer game in which players match their own answers against those of a previous "studio audience."

Subjects
Entertainment, Games

Audience
Members interested in multiplayer trivia games

Content Summary
Meet new friends and match skills with others in a multi-player Trivia match.

See Also
The Whiz Quiz

Games – Genealogy Forum

User Guide
- ☑ Windows
- ☑ DOS
- ☑ Macintosh
- ☐ Terminal Emulation
- ☑ VMS
- ☑ UNIX
- ☑ OS/2
- ☑ Other platform

Cost
- ☐ Unknown
- ☐ Basic
- ☑ Extended
- ☐ Premium ($)
- ☐ Executive w/$

Activity Level — UNKNOWN

Address
GO: **YGI**

Gardening Forum

Description
This forum is dedicated to plants and gardening, and offers tips and ideas on ways to make your gardening and lawn maintenance experience more enjoyable.

Subjects
Genius, Horticulture, Plants

Audience
General public, horticulturists

Content Summary
If you're into vegetable, fruit, or flower gardening, exotic plants (such as orchids or bonsai), or just want to know the best way to make your grass grow, check out this forum's libraries and message sections. The forum managers are from *National Gardening Magazine*. You'll find libraries about herbs, bulbs, fruits, berries, nuts, tools, books, roses, and fertilizer.

See Also
Earth Forum, Outdoor Forum

User Guide
- ☑ Windows
- ☑ DOS
- ☑ Macintosh
- ☐ Terminal Emulation
- ☑ VMS
- ☑ UNIX
- ☑ OS/2
- ☑ Other platform

Cost
- ☐ Unknown
- ☐ Basic
- ☑ Extended
- ☐ Premium ($)
- ☐ Executive w/$

Activity — LOW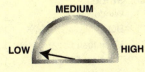

Address
GO: **GARDENING**

Gateway 2000 Forum

Description
Moo! If you're like me, you can't live without your Gateway 2000 computer. This forum offers product support and information on Gateway's line of products.

Subjects
Computer, Computer Hardware, Computer Products, Computers, Hardware/Software

Audience
Computer hardware users, computer users

Content Summary
The libraries and message sections in this forum are devoted to help you use and service your Gateway 2000 product. You can download the latest drivers, patches, settings, prices, fixes, and utilities by visiting the appropriate library. The Fun Files library (Library 13) is a must visit to get Gateway's latest bitmap for your wallpaper. Try the SpaceCow BMP or the COW.WAV file. The latter has been downloaded over 6000 times! For more serious users, don't neglect looking in the various message sections for an answer to your hardware question. This is a very active message area.

See Also
Computer Buyers' Guide, Computing Support

User Guide
- ☑ Windows
- ☑ DOS
- ☐ Macintosh
- ☐ Terminal Emulation
- ☐ VMS
- ☐ UNIX
- ☐ OS/2
- ☐ Other platform

Cost
- ☐ Unknown
- ☐ Basic
- ☑ Extended
- ☐ Premium ($)
- ☐ Executive w/$

Activity Level — HIGH

Address
GO: **GATEWAY**

Genealogy Forum

Description
Trying to find your great-great-grandmother's father's brother? Join the Genealogy Forum and start looking.

Subjects
Family, History

Audience
General public, families

Genealogy Forum – General Interest

Content Summary
This forum gives you access to a wide-range of members who are interested in genealogy and using their computers to help them. DOS, Windows, UNIX, Amiga, and Macintosh software is available in the libraries, as well as graphics and text files that might help you track down the hole in your family tree. Be sure to check out the message sections for leads to surnames or to post a query.

See Also
Military Forum

User Guide
- ☑ Windows
- ☑ DOS
- ☑ Macintosh
- ☐ Terminal Emulation
- ☐ VMS
- ☑ UNIX
- ☐ OS/2
- ☑ Other platform

Cost
- ☐ Unknown
- ☐ Basic
- ☑ Extended
- ☐ Premium ($)
- ☐ Executive w/$

Activity Level

Address
GO: **ROOTS**

GENERAL INTEREST

Family Handyman Forum

Description
This forum is for people who like to do home repairs and improvements, work with tools, do woodworking, or have questions about home repairs.

Subjects
Family, General Interest, Home Building

Audience
General public, general contractors, families

Content Summary
Sponsored by *Family Handyman* magazine, this forum is intended to help you find answers to your questions about tools, household repairs, and a variety of other topics. When you join this forum, you'll meet people with experience in home maintenance and repair, house building and remodeling, woodworking, painting, plumbing, tools, old houses, and electricity. You also have access to articles from The *Family Handyman* magazine and a chance to interact with its editors. The Handy Hint section (Message section 15) is a great place to get and leave tips and hints for household problems.

See Also
Automobile Forum, Cook's Online Forum, Gardening Forum, Masonry Forum, Outdoor Forum

User Guide
- ☑ Windows
- ☑ DOS
- ☑ Macintosh
- ☐ Terminal Emulation
- ☑ VMS
- ☑ UNIX
- ☑ OS/2
- ☑ Other platform

Cost
- ☐ Unknown
- ☐ Basic
- ☑ Extended
- ☐ Premium ($)
- ☐ Executive w/$

Activity Level

Address
GO: **HANDYMAN**

FTD Online

Description
Order fresh, beautiful flowers online through this FTD service. You can view your selection with online graphics.

Subjects
General interest

Audience
General Public

Content Summary
You have several options from which to choose in this service, including special offers, bithday arrangements, customer service, and contests (if applicable). After you make a choice, you can either view or download a graphic of the selections or read product descriptions and order the arrangements. Domestic deliveries are surcharged $4.95 for shipping and handling, and international orders are surcharged $10.00. Delivery times vary depending on the time you submit your order: Orders received before 12:00 noon EST can be delivered the same day; orders received after 12:00 noon EST are delivered the next day; orders received after 12:00 noon EST on Saturday are delivered the following Monday. Holidays are especially busy, so get your orders in early during those seasons.

See Also
Order From CompuServe (free), CompuServe Mail

User Guide
- ☐ Windows
- ☐ DOS
- ☐ Macintosh
- ☑ Terminal Emulation
- ☐ VMS
- ☐ UNIX
- ☐ OS/2
- ☐ Other platform

General Interest

Cost
- ☐ Unknown
- ☐ Basic
- ☐ Extended
- ☑ Premium ($)
- ☐ Executive w/$

Activity Level

UNKNOWN (LOW – MEDIUM – HIGH)

Address
GO: **FTD**

HSX Adult Forum

Description
The Human Sexuality (HSX) Support Groups are online self-help groups where you can freely discuss your feelings and relationships.

Subjects
Biology, General Interest, Human Behavior, Sexuality

Audience
General public

Content Summary
To gain access to the closed areas in this forum, see the text file CLOSED.TXT in the HSX Help Files library (Library 16). It's the one that has been downloaded over 60,000 times! If you don't want to join in the closed areas, see the HSX Open Forum (HSX100).

See Also
HSX Open Forum, Human Sexuality Databank

User Guide
- ☑ Windows
- ☑ DOS
- ☑ Macintosh
- ☐ Terminal Emulation
- ☑ VMS
- ☑ UNIX
- ☑ OS/2
- ☑ Other platform

Cost
- ☐ Unknown
- ☐ Basic
- ☑ Extended
- ☐ Premium ($)
- ☐ Executive w/$

Activity Level

MEDIUM (LOW – HIGH), arrow pointing to medium-high

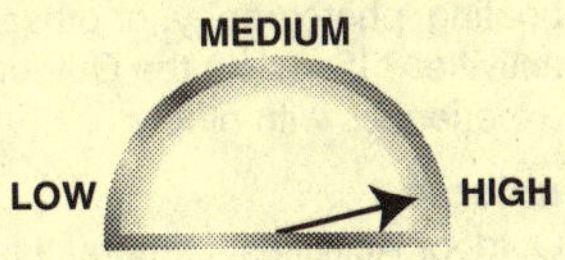

Address
GO: **HSX200**

HSX Open Forum

Description
The Human Sexuality (HSX) Support Groups are online self-help groups where you can freely discuss your feelings and relationships.

Subjects
General Interest, Human Behavior, Sexuality

Audience
General public

Content Summary
The following is the membership message in the HSX Open Forum: "The HSX Support Groups are online support (self-help) groups. Members share feelings and experiences, and provide one another with assistance and encouragement. Our goal is to create a compassionate community where members can freely discuss emotions and relationships. Here you can meet new friends and find sympathy and support. In the HSX forums, you'll find a warm place where people like you gather and talk about personal issues."

See Also
Human Sexuality Databank, HSX Adult Forum

User Guide
- ☑ Windows
- ☑ DOS
- ☑ Macintosh
- ☐ Terminal Emulation
- ☑ VMS
- ☑ UNIX
- ☑ OS/2
- ☑ Other platform

Cost
- ☐ Unknown
- ☐ Basic
- ☑ Extended
- ☐ Premium ($)
- ☐ Executive w/$

Activity level

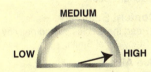

MEDIUM (LOW – HIGH)

Address
GO: **HSX100**

Knowledge Index

Description
Access over 100 popular databases from the Knowledge Index service.

Subjects
Database, General Interest, Research

Audience
General interest, general public, researchers

Content Summary
Knowledge Index is a service that gives you evening and weekend access to over 100 popular full-text and bibliographic databases at reduced rates. With Knowledge Index, you can access over 50,000 journals on a wide variety of topics. Many of the Knowledge Index databases have the complete text of articles available online. You can order a hard-copy printout of those that have only a citation available. The price is $.40 per minute ($24 per hour) and includes CompuServe standard connect rates up to and including 9600 Baud.

General Interest

See Also
IQuest

User Guide
- [x] Windows
- [x] DOS
- [x] Macintosh
- [ ] Terminal Emulation
- [x] VMS
- [x] UNIX
- [x] OS/2
- [ ] Other platform

Cost
- [ ] Unknown
- [ ] Basic
- [ ] Extended
- [x] Premium ($)
- [ ] Executive w/$

Activity Level: UNKNOWN (LOW–MEDIUM–HIGH)

Address
GO: **KI**

Marilyn Beck/Smith Hollywood

Description
Hot Hollywood news awaits you in this service.

Subjects
General Interest

Audience
General public

Content Summary
Read the articles posted daily by Marilyn Beck and Stacy Jenel Smith.

See Also
Entertainment Center, Entertainment Drive Forum

User Guide
- [x] Windows
- [x] DOS
- [x] Macintosh
- [ ] Terminal Emulation
- [x] VMS
- [x] UNIX
- [x] OS/2
- [x] Other platform

Cost
- [ ] Unknown
- [x] Basic
- [ ] Extended
- [ ] Premium ($)
- [ ] Executive w/$

Activity Level: UNKNOWN (LOW–MEDIUM–HIGH)

Address
GO: **BECK**

Online Surveys

Description
Take online surveys with this service. The surveys change frequently, so visit this area periodically to help in CompuServe research.

Subjects
Surveys, General Interest

Audience
General public

Content Summary
From the main menu, you can select Introduction, How To Take Online Surveys, Feedback/Comments, and the survey of your choice. You can take the New Member Survey if you have joined CompuServe within the past six months.

See Also
ZiffNet Surveys

User Guide
- [ ] Windows
- [ ] DOS
- [ ] Macintosh
- [x] Terminal Emulation
- [ ] VMS
- [ ] UNIX
- [ ] OS/2
- [ ] Other platform

Cost
- [ ] Unknown
- [x] Basic
- [ ] Extended
- [ ] Premium ($)
- [ ] Executive w/$

Activity Level: UNKNOWN (LOW–MEDIUM–HIGH)

Address
GO: **SURVEY**

Outdoor Forum

Description
Do you enjoy fishing, hunting, camping, scouting activities, cycling, birding, climbing, skiing, nudism, boating, photography, or other outdoor-related activities? If so, join the Outdoor Forum to share your experiences with others.

Subjects
Outdoor Activities, General Interest

Audience
General public

Content Summary
If you enjoy online magazines, you can get a copy of Outdoor Bytes, which is an electronic journal devoted to outdoor activities. You can get a Windows version or Replica version for Macintosh and Windows in library 16, Outdoor Bytes. Other library and message sections include General/Photography, Scouting, Power Boating, Fishing, Naturism/Nudism, and more.

General Interest

See Also
Gardening Forum

User Guide
- ☑ Windows
- ☑ DOS
- ☑ Macintosh
- ☐ Terminal Emulation
- ☑ VMS
- ☑ UNIX
- ☐ OS/2
- ☐ Other platform

Cost
- ☐ Unknown
- ☐ Basic
- ☑ Extended
- ☐ Premium ($)
- ☐ Executive w/$

Activity Level

Address
GO: **OUTDOORFORUM**

Participate

Description
This forum is a message base that uses Participate software to enable users to create and monitor discussions about any subject they choose.

Subjects
Music, Philosophy, Politics, General Interest

Audience
General public

Content Summary
In this forum, you will find numerous topic discussion areas that include politics, music, marketing, philosophy, and current events. If you don't find the topic of interest to you, you can start that topic area. Also of interest is The Arrow, which is an online newsletter that discusses this forum. If you want information on the most active discussions, you can join the Hot Points area, which is updated weekly. You also can join the New Points area, which provides you with a list of all new topic discussions.

See Also
Music/Arts Forum, Political Debate Forum

User Guide
- ☑ Windows
- ☑ DOS
- ☑ Macintosh
- ☑ Terminal Emulation
- ☑ VMS
- ☑ UNIX
- ☑ OS/2
- ☐ Other platform

Cost
- ☐ Unknown
- ☐ Basic
- ☑ Extended
- ☐ Premium ($)
- ☐ Executive w/$

Activity Level

Address
GO: **PARTI**

The Escort Store

Description
Online shopping area for The Escort Store.

Subjects
Shopping, general interest

Audience
Shoppers

Content Summary
Libraries include sources for top-rated consumer electronics products.

See Also
Electronic Mall

User Guide
- ☑ Windows
- ☑ DOS
- ☑ Macintosh
- ☐ Terminal Emulation
- ☑ VMS
- ☑ UNIX
- ☑ OS/2
- ☑ Other platform

Cost
- ☐ Unknown
- ☐ Basic
- ☑ Extended
- ☐ Premium ($)
- ☐ Executive w/$

Activity Level

Address
GO: **ESCORT**

The Gift Sender

Description
This online shopping area offers gifts from around the world.

Subjects
Shopping, general interest

Audience
Shoppers

Content Summary
This online shopping area gives you access to gifts from around the world, including clothing, food, and crafts.

See Also
Alaskan Peddler

General Interest

User Guide
- [x] Windows
- [x] DOS
- [x] Macintosh
- [ ] Terminal Emulation
- [x] VMS
- [x] UNIX
- [x] OS/2
- [x] Other platform

Cost
- [ ] Unknown
- [ ] Basic
- [x] Extended
- [ ] Premium ($)
- [ ] Executive w/$

Activity Level: UNKNOWN

Address
GO: **GIFT**

Travel Forum

Description
The Travel Forum allows CIS members to exchange stories, ideas, and information regarding travel experiences.

Subjects
General Interest, Travel

Audience
Travelers

Content Summary
Libraries include information on restaurants, hotels, customs in foreign countries, cruises, and rail travel.

See Also
Adventures in Travel

User Guide
- [x] Windows
- [x] DOS
- [x] Macintosh
- [ ] Terminal Emulation
- [x] VMS
- [x] UNIX
- [x] OS/2
- [x] Other platform

Cost
- [ ] Unknown
- [ ] Basic
- [x] Extended
- [ ] Premium ($)
- [ ] Executive w/$

Activity Level: MEDIUM (trending HIGH)

Address
GO: **TRAVSIG**

Virginia Diner

Description
This online shopping area offering specialty foods, gift baskets, tins, and so on.

Subjects
General Interest, Gifts

Audience
General public

Content Summary
Ordering on-line makes it convenient to order food gifts anytime. Products can be shipped anywhere.

See Also
Alaska Peddler

User Guide
- [x] Windows
- [x] DOS
- [x] Macintosh
- [ ] Terminal Emulation
- [x] VMS
- [x] UNIX
- [x] OS/2
- [x] Other platform

Cost
- [ ] Unknown
- [ ] Basic
- [x] Extended
- [ ] Premium ($)
- [ ] Executive w/$

Activity Level: UNKNOWN

Address
GO: **DINER**

What's New

Description
This is CompuServe's menu of upcoming events and system changes, updated several times per week.

Subjects
CompuServe

Audience
CompuServe users

Content Summary
Find out what's happening on Compuserve by viewing this list of new topics.

See Also
CompuServe Help

User Guide
- [x] Windows
- [x] DOS
- [x] Macintosh
- [ ] Terminal Emulation
- [x] VMS
- [x] UNIX
- [x] OS/2
- [ ] Other platform

Cost
- [ ] Unknown
- [x] Basic
- [ ] Extended
- [ ] Premium ($)
- [ ] Executive w/$

General Interest – Gifts

Activity Level

Address
GO: **NEW**

Working-From-Home Forum

Description
This is a forum for those who work from their homes, uniting them with others in similar circumstances. Users can exchange info, share solutions, etc.

Subjects
Computers

Audience
Home-based workers

Content Summary
The libraries and message areas contain information on taxes, business setup, equipment recommendations, and areas to exchange information.

User Guide
- ☑ Windows
- ☑ DOS
- ☑ Macintosh
- ☐ Terminal Emulation
- ☑ VMS
- ☑ UNIX
- ☑ OS/2
- ☐ Other platform

Cost
- ☐ Unknown
- ☐ Basic
- ☑ Extended
- ☐ Premium ($)
- ☐ Executive w/$

Activity Level

(MEDIUM — arrow pointing up)

Address
GO: **WORK**

GENERAL ISSUES

National Public Radio (NPR)

Description
Join with other CompuServe members as they listen to the *Talk of the Nation* radio program and share their comments with each other.

Subjects
Current Issues, General Issues

Audience
General public

Content Summary
Talk of the Nation radio program conferences are held every weekday from 2:00 p.m. till 4:00 p.m. EST in conference room 2 of the Issues Forum (GO ISSUES).

See Also
Issues Forum

User Guide
- ☑ Windows
- ☑ DOS
- ☑ Macintosh
- ☐ Terminal Emulation
- ☑ VMS
- ☑ UNIX
- ☐ OS/2
- ☐ Other platform

Cost
- ☐ Unknown
- ☑ Basic
- ☐ Extended
- ☐ Premium ($)
- ☐ Executive w/$

Activity Level

Address
GO: **NPR**

GIFTS

800 Flowers

Description
At 800-Flowers & 800-Gifthouse, the world's largest source of flowers & gifts, everyday is a holiday.

Subjects
Flowers, Gifts

Audience
Consumers

Content Summary
Order cut flowers or plants for any occasion and have them shipped anywhere in the U.S.

See Also
Flowers, FTD

User Guide
- ☑ Windows
- ☑ DOS
- ☑ Macintosh
- ☐ Terminal Emulation
- ☐ VMS
- ☐ UNIX
- ☐ OS/2
- ☐ Other platform

Cost
- ☐ Unknown
- ☑ Basic
- ☐ Extended
- ☐ Premium ($)
- ☐ Executive w/$

308
Gifts

Activity Level

Address
GO: **FGS**

Alaska Peddler

Description
Online shopping from a family-owned group of stores in Juneau, featuring unique Alaskan gifts.

Subjects
Gifts, Shopping

Audience
Consumers

Content Summary
If you are looking for a truly unique gift then this forum is for you. Handcrafted items are available.

See Also
The Gift Sender

User Guide
- [x] Windows
- [x] DOS
- [x] Macintosh
- [ ] Terminal Emulation
- [x] VMS
- [x] UNIX
- [x] OS/2
- [x] Other platform

Cost
- [ ] Unknown
- [x] Basic
- [ ] Extended
- [ ] Premium ($)
- [ ] Executive w/$

Activity Level

Address
GO: **ALASKA**

The Gift Sender

Description
This online shopping area offers gifts from around the world.

Subjects
Gifts

Audience
General public

Content Summary
This online shopping area gives you access to gifts from around the world, including clothing, food, and crafts.

See Also
Alaska Peddler

User Guide
- [x] Windows
- [x] DOS
- [x] Macintosh
- [ ] Terminal Emulation
- [x] VMS
- [x] UNIX
- [x] OS/2
- [x] Other platform

Cost
- [ ] Unknown
- [x] Basic
- [ ] Extended
- [ ] Premium ($)
- [ ] Executive w/$

Activity Level

UNKNOWN

Address
GO: **GIFT**

Virginia Diner

Description
This online shopping area offers specialty foods, gift baskets, tins, and so on.

Subjects
General Interest, Gifts

Audience
General public

Content Summary
Ordering on-line makes it convenient to order food gifts anytime. Products can be shipped anywhere.

See Also
Alaska Peddler

User Guide
- [x] Windows
- [x] DOS
- [x] Macintosh
- [ ] Terminal Emulation
- [x] VMS
- [x] UNIX
- [x] OS/2
- [x] Other platform

Cost
- [ ] Unknown
- [x] Basic
- [ ] Extended
- [ ] Premium ($)
- [ ] Executive w/$

Activity Level

UNKNOWN

Address
GO: **DINER**

Walter Knoll Florist

Description
This is an online shopping area offering flowers and plants.

Subjects
Shopping

Audience
Consumers, shoppers

Content Summary
This shopping area offers the convenience of shopping for flowers or plants from your home or office.

See Also
Electronic Mall

User Guide
- ☑ Windows
- ☑ DOS
- ☑ Macintosh
- ☐ Terminal Emulation
- ☑ VMS
- ☑ UNIX
- ☑ OS/2
- ☐ Other platform

Cost
- ☐ Unknown
- ☑ Basic
- ☐ Extended
- ☐ Premium ($)
- ☐ Executive w/$

Activity Level

Address
GO: WK

WORLDSPAN Travelshopper

Description
Travelshopper is your online travel agent, enabling you to search for and view airline flights and flight info.

Subjects
Travel

Audience
Travelers

Content Summary
Use this forum to obtain information about flights, make reservations, , book hotel reservations, or get cost of flights.

See Also
Travel Forum

User Guide
- ☑ Windows
- ☑ DOS
- ☑ Macintosh
- ☐ Terminal Emulation
- ☑ VMS
- ☑ UNIX
- ☐ OS/2
- ☑ Other platform

Cost
- ☐ Unknown
- ☑ Basic
- ☐ Extended
- ☐ Premium ($)
- ☐ Executive w/$

Activity Level

Address
GO: WORLDSPAN

Glamour Graphics Forum

Description
Professional-quality images and photographs featuring fashion models can be found in this forum.

Subjects
Fashion Merchandising, Graphics, Photography

Audience
General public, photographers

Content Summary
The Glamour Graphics Forum offers fashion and glamour photography from stock photography agencies, including Len Kaltman Online, Texas Glamour, Richard Stevens Models, Classic Model Review, Imagine That, and Jade Creations. General sections, with subscriber uploads encouraged, show off high fashion, swimsuits, business attire, resort & sport, casual wear, and more. The file format of choice is GIF, but you might also find some JPG files as well.

See Also
Graphics Forums

User Guide
- ☑ Windows
- ☑ DOS
- ☑ Macintosh
- ☐ Terminal Emulation
- ☑ VMS
- ☑ UNIX
- ☑ OS/2
- ☑ Other platform

Cost
- ☐ Unknown
- ☐ Basic
- ☑ Extended
- ☐ Premium ($)
- ☐ Executive w/$

Activity Level

MEDIUM — LOW → HIGH

Address
GO: GLAMOUR

Global Crisis Forum

Description
This forum is devoted to the past, present, and future crises around the world, such as the Balkans, the former USSR, and other hot spots around the globe.

Subjects
Current Events, Global News, International Politics, Modern History, World View

Audience
Military historians, historians, general public, activists, writers, journalists

Content Summary
Because the world changes and some hot spots become cold spots and cold spots become hot spots, the library and message sections in this forum change often. Some of the recent hot spots on the forum have been the Asia/Pacific Rim, Africa, Russia, the Baltics, and the Americas. You'll also find HOTSPOT: areas denoted in the libraries and message areas for current topics. You'll find articles, theses, and other text files throughout the library sections for downloading.

See Also
Associated Press, Executive News Service, U.S. News & World Report

User Guide
- ☑ Windows
- ☑ DOS
- ☑ Macintosh
- ☐ Terminal Emulation
- ☑ VMS
- ☑ UNIX
- ☑ OS/2
- ☑ Other platform

Cost
- ☐ Unknown
- ☐ Basic
- ☑ Extended
- ☐ Premium ($)
- ☐ Executive w/$

Activity Level
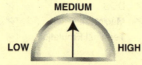
MEDIUM (LOW – HIGH)

Address
GO: **CRISIS**

GLOBAL NEWS

Global Crisis Forum

Description
This forum is devoted to the past, present, and future crises around the world, such as the Balkans, the former USSR, and other hot spots around the globe.

Subjects
Current Events, Global News, International Politics, Modern History, World View

Audience
Military historians, historians, general public, activists, writers, journalists

Content Summary
Because the world changes and some hot spots become cold spots and cold spots become hot spots, the library and message sections in this forum change often. Some of the recent hot spots on the forum have been the Asia/Pacific Rim, Africa, Russia, the Baltics, and the Americas. You'll also find HOTSPOT: areas denoted in the libraries and message areas for current topics. You'll find articles, theses, and other text files throughout the library sections for downloading.

See Also
Associated Press, Executive News Service, U.S. News & World Report

User Guide
- ☑ Windows
- ☑ DOS
- ☑ Macintosh
- ☐ Terminal Emulation
- ☑ VMS
- ☑ UNIX
- ☑ OS/2
- ☑ Other platform

Cost
- ☐ Unknown
- ☐ Basic
- ☑ Extended
- ☐ Premium ($)
- ☐ Executive w/$

Activity Level

MEDIUM (LOW – HIGH)

Address
GO: **CRISIS**

Global Report

Description
This is Citibank's online information resource database, where you can find data on a number of large corporations worldwide.

Subjects
Business, Databases, Financial News

Audience
Financial analysts, accountants, business researchers, business and financial researchers

Content Summary
Launched by Citibank in 1986, Global Report has become the primary information resource for a number of large corporations worldwide because it integrates and organizes news and financial data from well-respected sources, allowing for quick and easy information retrieval. For pricing information, see the Pricing/Sample Reports option on the Global Report main menu. If you're new to this service, be sure to choose the Important Pages option on the main menu to see a list of important searching criteria.

311
Global Report – Government

See Also
Dun's Elect Business Dir, TRW Bus. Credit Reports

User Guide
- ☑ Windows
- ☑ DOS
- ☑ Macintosh
- ☐ Terminal Emulation
- ☑ VMS
- ☑ UNIX
- ☑ OS/2
- ☑ Other platform

Cost
- ☐ Unknown
- ☐ Basic
- ☑ Extended
- ☑ Premium ($)
- ☐ Executive w/$

Activity Level

Address
GO: **GLOREP**

Golden CommPass Support

Description
This is the official support area of Golden CommPass, the only native OS/2 navigation program designed specifically for CompuServe.

Subjects
Computers, OS/2

Audience
OS2 users

Content Summary
Get support, the latest update, tips and hints, scripts, and other files associated with Golden CommPass. If you use OS/2 and have access to CompuServe, you've probably heard of Golden CommPass already. If not, join this forum and download the latest press release and demo of this navigator.

See Also
OS/2 Monthly

User Guide
- ☐ Windows
- ☐ DOS
- ☐ Macintosh
- ☐ Terminal Emulation
- ☐ VMS
- ☐ UNIX
- ☑ OS/2
- ☐ Other platform

Cost
- ☐ Unknown
- ☐ Basic
- ☑ Extended
- ☐ Premium ($)
- ☐ Executive w/$

Activity Level

Address
GO: **GCPSUPPORT**

GOSSIP

Hollywood Hotline

Description
This service is devoted to the noteworthy events that happen in Hollywood and includes a Hollywood trivia quiz.

Subjects
Entertainment, Gossip

Audience
General public

Content Summary
If you want to find out what's going on in Hollywood or the movie business, stop by the Hollywood Hotline. You can read entertainment news, peruse an online entertainment encyclopedia, see film and TV ratings, read movie reviews, and take a quiz (in terminal emulation mode). The SHOWBIZQUIZ menu features games on Frank Sinatra, Judy Garland, Clint Eastwood, Wizard of Oz, TV Detective Puzzle, and many more.

See Also
Roger Ebert's Movie Reviews, SHOWBIZ Quiz, ShowBiz-Media Forum

User Guide
- ☑ Windows
- ☑ DOS
- ☑ Macintosh
- ☐ Terminal Emulation
- ☑ VMS
- ☑ UNIX
- ☑ OS/2
- ☑ Other platform

Cost
- ☐ Unknown
- ☑ Basic
- ☐ Extended
- ☐ Premium ($)
- ☐ Executive w/$

Activity level
MEDIUM — UNKNOWN (LOW / HIGH)

Address
GO: **HOLLYWOOD**

GOVERNMENT

Information USA

Description
Are you looking for something? Do you need information but aren't sure where to get it? Start with the Information USA service. It will help you get started.

Subjects
Government, Information, Reference

Government

Audience
General public, researchers

Content Summary
This service, extracted from the *Information USA* reference book by Matthew Lesko, provides information and access to free or nearly free government publications in three areas: government publications and services; American Embassies and consulates; and travel information. From the main menu, you can select from several options, including Introduction/Talk to Mr. Lesko, Consumer Power, Careers and Workplace, Giveaways to Entrepreneurs, Selling to the Government, and much more. You have to see this service to believe it. It's full of very useful information.

See Also
Government Information

User Guide
- ☑ Windows
- ☑ DOS
- ☑ Macintosh
- ☐ Terminal Emulation
- ☑ VMS
- ☑ UNIX
- ☑ OS/2
- ☑ Other platform

Cost
- ☐ Unknown
- ☐ Basic
- ☑ Extended
- ☐ Premium ($)
- ☐ Executive w/$

Activity Level

Address

Members of Congress

Description
Need the address of your Congressperson? If so, use this service to find out name, address, party affiliation, and the committees he or she is on.

Subjects
Government

Audience
General public

Content Summary
You can select The White House, The Senate, House of Representatives, and Compose a CONGRESSGram. When you compose a CONGRESSGram, make sure you know the person's full name and what house he or she is in, such as President or Senator.

See Also
Issues Forum

User Guide
- ☑ Windows
- ☑ DOS
- ☑ Macintosh
- ☐ Terminal Emulation
- ☑ VMS
- ☑ UNIX
- ☑ OS/2
- ☑ Other platform

Cost
- ☐ Unknown
- ☐ Basic
- ☑ Extended
- ☐ Premium ($)
- ☐ Executive w/$

Activity Level

MEDIUM
LOW — UNKNOWN — HIGH

Address
GO: FCC-1

White House Forum

Description
This independent political forum discusses what's happening in the USA White House. The libraries contain only files provided by official White House sources.

Subjects
Current Issues

Audience
General public

Content Summary
Libraries include information on the economy, the trade deficit, defense, education, social security, and international affairs.

See Also
Politics in America

User Guide
- ☑ Windows
- ☑ DOS
- ☑ Macintosh
- ☐ Terminal Emulation
- ☑ VMS
- ☑ UNIX
- ☑ OS/2
- ☑ Other platform

Cost
- ☐ Unknown
- ☐ Basic
- ☑ Extended
- ☐ Premium ($)
- ☐ Executive w/$

Activity Level

Address
GO: WHITEHOUSE

GRAPHIC ARTS

Graphics Forums

Description
The Graphics Forums service enables you access several graphics-related forums, the Graphics File Finder, and an online tutorial.

Subjects
Computer Graphics, Computers, Graphic Arts, Graphics

Audience
Computer graphics designers, computer users, graphics designers, graphics artists, graphics experts

Content Summary
The Graphics Forums main menu consists of Introduction to Graphics, Graphics File Finder, Go Graphics News, Best of Go Graphics Directory, Graphics Support Forums, Image Collection Forums, Image Development Forums, Weather Maps, Nominate Image of the Month, Other Forums with Graphics. If you are looking for graphics to view, download, get information, or learn more about graphics in general, you might want to start your search here. You're sure to find what you're looking for.

See Also
Graphics Plus Forum, Graphics File Finder

User Guide
- [x] Windows
- [x] DOS
- [x] Macintosh
- [ ] Terminal Emulation
- [ ] VMS
- [x] UNIX
- [x] OS/2
- [ ] Other platform

Cost
- [ ] Unknown
- [ ] Basic
- [x] Extended
- [ ] Premium ($)
- [ ] Executive w/$

Activity Level

Address
GO: **GRAPHICS**

GRAPHICS

Glamour Graphics Forum

Description
Professional-quality images and photographs featuring fashion models can be found in this forum.

Subjects
Fashion Merchandising, Graphics, Photography

Audience
General public, photographers

Content Summary
The Glamour Graphics Forum offers fashion and glamour photography from stock photography agencies, including Len Kaltman Online, Texas Glamour, Richard Stevens Models, Classic Model Review, Imagine That, and Jade Creations. General sections, with subscriber uploads encouraged, show off high fashion, swimsuits, business attire, resort & sport, casual wear, and more. The file format of choice is GIF, but you might also find some JPG files as well.

See Also
Graphics Forums

User Guide
- [x] Windows
- [x] DOS
- [x] Macintosh
- [ ] Terminal Emulation
- [x] VMS
- [x] UNIX
- [x] OS/2
- [x] Other platform

Cost
- [ ] Unknown
- [ ] Basic
- [x] Extended
- [ ] Premium ($)
- [ ] Executive w/$

Activity Level

Address
GO: **GLAMOUR**

Graphics A Vendor Forum

Description
This forum provides support from manufacturers of graphics hardware and software. You can post questions, read messages, and download files here.

Subjects
Computers, Graphics, Hardware/Software

Audience
Computer graphic designers, computer hardware users, management information specialists, hardware/software designers, handicapping enthusiasts

Content Summary
The Graphics Vendor A Forum offers support from Tempra, Grasp, STB, Jovian, Genus, RIX Softworks, Digital Vision, Global Softworks, Big_D, Pacific Motion (formerly Presidio), Metagraphics, Image-In, Inset Systems, VRLI Inc., TEGL, and ATI Technologies.

See Also
Glamour Graphics Forum

Graphics

User Guide
- ☑ Windows
- ☑ DOS
- ☑ Macintosh
- ☐ Terminal Emulation
- ☐ VMS
- ☑ UNIX
- ☑ OS/2
- ☐ Other platform

Cost
- ☐ Unknown
- ☐ Basic
- ☑ Extended
- ☐ Premium ($)
- ☐ Executive w/$

Activity Level
LOW — HIGH (arrow pointing between MEDIUM and HIGH)

Address
GO: **GRAPHAVEN**

Graphics B Vendors Forum

Description
This forum provides support from manufacturers of graphics hardware and software. You can post questions, read messages, and download files here.

Subjects
Computers, Graphics, Hardware/Software

Audience
Management information specialists, hardware/software designers, computer hardware users, computer graphics designers

Content Summary
The Graphics Vendor B Forum offers support from Tseng Labs, Diamond Computer Systems, Animated Software, StereoGraphics, Sun Country Software, LEAD Technologies, Hercules, Genoa Systems, CrystalGraphics, Volante, Domark Software, DesignWare, Inc., HSC Software, Solana Software, Matrox, and Appian Technology.

See Also
Graphics Vendor Forum, Graphics Support Forum

User Guide
- ☑ Windows
- ☑ DOS
- ☑ Macintosh
- ☐ Terminal Emulation
- ☐ VMS
- ☑ UNIX
- ☑ OS/2
- ☐ Other platform

Cost
- ☐ Unknown
- ☐ Basic
- ☑ Extended
- ☐ Premium ($)
- ☐ Executive w/$

Activity Level
LOW — HIGH (arrow pointing between MEDIUM and HIGH)

Address
GO: **GRAPHBVEN**

Graphics Corner Forum

Description
You can download and upload GIF and JPEG graphics images to this forum, such as people, portraits, animals, nature scenes, and landmarks.

Subjects
Computers, Graphics, Photography

Audience
Graphics artists, computer users, general public

Content Summary
The Graphics Corner Forum is the primary collection of user-contributed GIF and JPEG images that contain subjects such as Cars, Boats, Planes, People & Portraits, Landscapes, World of Nature, Fantasy & Sci-Fi, Space & Astronomy, Landmarks, and the Body Beautiful. This area has files that contain nudity. Those files include the following message: "This file contains nudity. Those offended by the artistic presentation of nudity should refrain from viewing."

See Also
Graphics Support Forum, Glamour Graphics Forum

User Guide
- ☑ Windows
- ☑ DOS
- ☑ Macintosh
- ☐ Terminal Emulation
- ☐ VMS
- ☑ UNIX
- ☑ OS/2
- ☐ Other platform

Cost
- ☐ Unknown
- ☐ Basic
- ☑ Extended
- ☐ Premium ($)
- ☐ Executive w/$

Activity Level
LOW — HIGH (arrow pointing between MEDIUM and HIGH)

Address
GO: **CORNER**

Graphics Developers Forum

Description
If you are interested in computer graphics software, you should join the Graphics Developers Forum for various graphics-related news and information.

Subjects
Computer Graphics, Computers, Graphics

Audience
Computer graphics designers, graphics designers, graphics experts, graphics artists

Content Summary
The Graphics Developers Forum is devoted to the cutting edge of computer graphics software. Topics include fractal generation (using the Fractint software), raytracing (using POV-Ray and other programs), 3D/RDS images, the Virtual Art Gallery project, animation, morphing, motion video, and more. The Mythology library (Library 2) has several fantastic 3D images that you can download and use as wallpaper files. You also should check out the Demo Team library (Library 20) for software demos and routines.

See Also
Graphics Forums, Graphics Support Forum

User Guide
- ☑ Windows
- ☑ DOS
- ☑ Macintosh
- ☐ Terminal Emulation
- ☐ VMS
- ☐ UNIX
- ☐ OS/2
- ☐ Other platform

Cost
- ☐ Unknown
- ☐ Basic
- ☑ Extended
- ☐ Premium ($)
- ☐ Executive w/$

Activity Level

Address
GO: **GRAPHDEV**

Graphics File Finder

Description
If you're looking for a specific graphics file or just want to browse the graphics files that are available, use this service.

Subjects
Computer Graphics, Computers, Graphics

Audience
Graphic artists, graphics experts, graphic designers, computer users, computer graphics designers

Content Summary
Graphics File Finder is an online comprehensive keyword searchable database of file descriptions from graphics related forums, including the Computer Art Forum, Fine Art Forum, Graphics Corner Forum, Graphics Developers Forum, Graphics Gallery Forum, and the Quick Pictures Forum. It is designed to provide quick and easy reference to some of the best programs and files available. You can use seven common search criteria to find the location of a desired file or files quickly. You can search by topic, file submission date, forum name, file type, file extension, file name, or submitter's User ID. File descriptions, forum, and library location are displayed for the matched files.

See Also
Graphics Forums, Graphics Corner Forum

User Guide
- ☑ Windows
- ☑ DOS
- ☑ Macintosh
- ☐ Terminal Emulation
- ☐ VMS
- ☑ UNIX
- ☑ OS/2
- ☐ Other platform

Cost
- ☐ Unknown
- ☐ Basic
- ☑ Extended
- ☐ Premium ($)
- ☐ Executive w/$

Activity Level
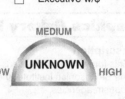

Address
GO: **GRAPHFF**

Graphics Forums

Description
The Graphics Forums service enables you access several graphics-related forums, the Graphics File Finder, and an online tutorial.

Subjects
Computer Graphics, Computers, Graphic Arts, Graphics

Audience
Computer graphics designers, computer users, graphics designers, graphics artists, graphics experts

Content Summary
The Graphics Forums main menu consists of Introduction to Graphics, Graphics File Finder, Go Graphics News, Best of Go Graphics Directory, Graphics Support Forums, Image Collection Forums, Image Development Forums, Weather Maps, Nominate Image of the Month, Other Forums with Graphics. If you are looking for graphics to view, download, get information, or learn more about graphics in general, you might want to start your search here. You're sure to find what you're looking for.

See Also
Graphics Plus Forum, Graphics File Finder

User Guide
- ☑ Windows
- ☑ DOS
- ☑ Macintosh
- ☐ Terminal Emulation
- ☐ VMS
- ☑ UNIX
- ☑ OS/2
- ☐ Other platform

Graphics

Cost
- [ ] Unknown
- [ ] Basic
- [x] Extended
- [ ] Premium ($)
- [ ] Executive w/$

Activity Level: UNKNOWN

Address
GO: GRAPHICS

Graphics Gallery Forum

Description
This forum offers collections of graphics from NASA, the Smithsonian Institute, the Coast Guard, and tourism agencies.

Subjects
Computer Graphics, Computers, Graphics, Photography

Audience
Graphics artists, graphics designers, computer users, photographers

Content Summary
The Graphics Gallery Forum's libraries consist of the following topics: New Images, SI: Smithsonian Art, SI: Air/Space, SI: Science/Nature, SI: People/Places, NASA, Utah Shakespearean Festival, NAL/USDA, America! North, America! South, America! East, America! West, US Coast Guard, World Photography, Wisconsin Historical Society, and Civil War. The Utah Shakespearean Festival library (Library 9) contains a compilation of the best of moments from the 32 seasons of the Utah Shakespearean Festival's plays.

See Also
Graphics Forums, Graphics Corner Forum, Graphics File Finder

User Guide
- [x] Windows
- [x] DOS
- [x] Macintosh
- [ ] Terminal Emulation
- [ ] VMS
- [x] UNIX
- [x] OS/2
- [ ] Other platform

Cost
- [ ] Unknown
- [ ] Basic
- [x] Extended
- [ ] Premium ($)
- [ ] Executive w/$

Activity Level: LOW

Address
GO: GALLERY

Graphics Plus Forum

Description
This forum contains true-color images in various formats. You can get graphics of cars, boats, people, landscapes, and much more.

Subjects
Computer Graphics, Graphics, Photography

Audience
Photographers, computer graphics designers, computer users, graphics artists, graphics designers, graphics experts

Content Summary
The Graphics Plus Forum has images in truecolor and vector formats such as TIFF, Targa, EPS, truecolor BMP and PCX, AI, PICT, and others. This forum also includes a section focusing on fractal and raytraced images. The libraries include areas such as Cars-Boats-Planes, People & Portraits, Landscapes, World of Nature, Fantasy & Sci-Fi, Cartoons & Comics, Body Beautiful, Plain Brown Wrapper, Fractals/Raytracing, and more. Note that this forum contains files that have nudity. Those files that contain nudity, have the following disclaimer: "Those offended by the artistic presentation of nudity should refrain from viewing."

See Also
Graphics File Finder, Graphics Forums, Graphics Gallery Forum, Photography Forum

User Guide
- [x] Windows
- [x] DOS
- [x] Macintosh
- [ ] Terminal Emulation
- [ ] VMS
- [x] UNIX
- [x] OS/2
- [ ] Other platform

Cost
- [ ] Unknown
- [ ] Basic
- [x] Extended
- [ ] Premium ($)
- [ ] Executive w/$

Activity Level: HIGH

Address
GO: GRAPHPLUS

Graphics Support Forum

Description
The GIF graphics specification, released by CompuServe, is featured in this forum, including file viewers, file converters, and GIF analysis tools.

Subjects
Computer Graphics, Graphics

Graphics – Grolier's Academic American Encyclopedia

Audience
Graphics experts, graphics artists, graphics designers, computer graphics designers

Content Summary
The Graphics Support Forum offers help and program files relating to viewing, downloading, converting, and printing graphics. You also can find animation and video players, specifications for many image formats, discussions on graphics-related issues, and help for programmers working with GIF and JPEG formats. If you need a DOS and Windows utility to print out graphics, check out the Printing Graphics library (Library 8).

See Also
Graphics Forums, Graphics File Finder

User Guide
- [x] Windows
- [x] DOS
- [x] Macintosh
- [ ] Terminal Emulation
- [ ] VMS
- [ ] UNIX
- [ ] OS/2
- [ ] Other platform

Cost
- [ ] Unknown
- [ ] Basic
- [x] Extended
- [ ] Premium ($)
- [ ] Executive w/$

Activity Level
MEDIUM (arrow pointing up, between LOW and HIGH)

Address
GO: **GRAPHSUPPORT**

Graphics Vendors C Forum

Description
The Graphics Vendor C Forum offers support from MicroFrontier, Clear Software, Artist Graphics, and Envisions.

Subjects
Computer Graphics, Computers, Graphics

Audience
Computer graphics designers, grass-roots organizers, graphics artists, graphics designers, graphics experts

Content Summary
The library section contains these areas: Forum Information, MicroFrontier, Clear Software, Artist Graphics, and Envisions.

See Also
Graphics Forums, Graphics File Finder, Graphics Developers Forum

User Guide
- [x] Windows
- [x] DOS
- [ ] Macintosh
- [ ] Terminal Emulation
- [ ] VMS
- [ ] UNIX
- [ ] OS/2
- [ ] Other platform

Cost
- [ ] Unknown
- [ ] Basic
- [x] Extended
- [ ] Premium ($)
- [ ] Executive w/$

Activity Level
MEDIUM (arrow pointing LOW)

Address
GO: **GRVENC**

Grolier's Academic American Encyclopedia

Description
This is an online edition of the *Grolier's Academic American Encyclopedia*.

Subjects
Education

Audience
Students, teachers, general public

Content Summary
The main menu contains the user's guide, feedback, Grolier's Backgroud on the News, and Search Encyclopedia.

See Also
Academic American Encyclopedia

User Guide
- [x] Windows
- [x] DOS
- [x] Macintosh
- [ ] Terminal Emulation
- [x] VMS
- [x] UNIX
- [x] OS/2
- [x] Other platform

Cost
- [ ] Unknown
- [ ] Basic
- [ ] Extended
- [ ] Premium ($)
- [x] Executive w/$

Activity Level
UNKNOWN

Address
GO: **GROLIERS**

Gupta Forum

Description
This forum is a support forum sponsored by Gupta for its PC client/server system software and products, such as SQLBase and SQLWindows.

Subjects
Computers

Audience
Computer programmers, computer systems analysts, management information specialists

Content Summary
The libraries in this forum include topics on SQLBase, Connectivity/SQLNet, SQLWindows/TeamWin, Quest, Product Marketing, Third Party Products, User Groups, Grupta JobNet.

See Also
Client Server Computing Forum

User Guide
- ☑ Windows
- ☑ DOS
- ☐ Macintosh
- ☐ Terminal Emulation
- ☐ VMS
- ☐ UNIX
- ☐ OS/2
- ☑ Other platform

Cost
- ☐ Unknown
- ☐ Basic
- ☑ Extended
- ☐ Premium ($)
- ☐ Executive w/$

Activity Level
MEDIUM (LOW — HIGH)

Address
GO: **GUPTAFORUM**

H – Handicapping

H

H&R Block

Description
Did you know that in 18th century England, taxes were based on the number of fireplaces and hearths a person had? You can get tax information in this service.

Subjects
Taxes

Audience
General public

Content Summary
This service offers a history of H&R Block (the parent company of CompuServe, Inc.), Executive Tax Service, Record Keeping Books, Important Tax Dates of 1994, Tax Trivia, H&R Block Financial News, and Income Tax Information by Category.

See Also
CompuServe Tax Connection

User Guide
- ☑ Windows
- ☑ DOS
- ☑ Macintosh
- ☐ Terminal Emulation
- ☑ VMS
- ☑ UNIX
- ☑ OS/2
- ☑ Other platform

Cost
- ☐ Unknown
- ☑ Basic
- ☐ Extended
- ☐ Premium ($)
- ☐ Executive w/$

Activity Level

Address
GO: **HRB**

HamNet Forum

Description
In this Forum, users can interact with other Ham Radio enthusiasts.

Subjects
Radios

Audience
Rave enthusiasts, radio enthusiasts (UK)

Content Summary
The HamNet Forum is dedicated to amateur radio and related topics, including shortwave listening, satellite television, and other related topics. If you are expert or an novice, this forum welcomes your questions, responses, and membership. Some of the specific libraries include the Scanning Library, Amateur Satellites, CW / Morse Code, FCC & Regulatory, and Vendor Support.

See Also

User Guide
- ☑ Windows
- ☑ DOS
- ☑ Macintosh
- ☐ Terminal Emulation
- ☑ VMS
- ☑ UNIX
- ☑ OS/2
- ☑ Other platform

Cost
- ☐ Unknown
- ☐ Basic
- ☑ Extended
- ☐ Premium ($)
- ☐ Executive w/$

Activity Level

Address
GO: **HAMNET**

HANDICAPPING

Handicapped User's Database

Description
The Handicapped User's Database contains articles, software and hardware reviews, lists of organizations, a reference library, and more.

Subjects
Handicapping

Audience
General public, health care professionals, health care providers

Content Summary
From the Handicapped User's Database main menu, select "Welcome" to find out more information about this database and how to search with it. An index is available on page HUD-7500, and a list of new additions on page HUD-1274. When you find an article you want to read in either of these sections, use the GO command and the listed page number to go that article.

See Also
Disabilities Forum

User Guide
- ☑ Windows
- ☑ DOS
- ☑ Macintosh
- ☐ Terminal Emulation
- ☑ VMS
- ☑ UNIX
- ☑ OS/2
- ☑ Other platform

Cost
- ☐ Unknown
- ☑ Basic
- ☐ Extended
- ☐ Premium ($)
- ☐ Executive w/$

Activity Level

Handicapping – Hardware/Software

HARDWARE/SOFTWARE

Gateway 2000 Forum

Description
Moo! If you're like me, you can't live without your Gateway 2000 computer. This forum offers product support and information on Gateway's line of products.

Subjects
Computer, Computer Hardware, Computer Products, Computers, Hardware/Software

Audience
Computer hardware users, computer users

Content Summary
The libraries and message sections in this forum are devoted to help you use and service your Gateway 2000 product. You can download the latest drivers, patches, settings, prices, fixes, and utilities by visiting the appropriate library. The Fun Files library (Library 13) is a must visit to get Gateway's latest bitmap for your wallpaper. Try the SpaceCow BMP or the COW.WAV file. The latter has been downloaded over 6000 times! For more serious users, don't neglect looking in the various message sections for an answer to your hardware question. This is a very active message area.

See Also
Computer Buyers' Guide, Computing Support

User Guide
- ☑ Windows
- ☑ DOS
- ☐ Macintosh
- ☐ Terminal Emulation
- ☐ VMS
- ☐ UNIX
- ☐ OS/2
- ☐ Other platform

Cost
- ☐ Unknown
- ☐ Basic
- ☑ Extended
- ☐ Premium ($)
- ☐ Executive w/$

Activity Level

Address
GO: **GATEWAY**

Graphics A Vendor Forum

Description
This forum provides support from manufacturers of graphics hardware and software. You can post questions, read messages, and download files here.

Subjects
Computers, Graphics, Hardware/Software

Audience
Computer graphic designers, computer hardware users, management information specialists, hardware/software designers

Content Summary
The Graphics Vendor A Forum offers support from Tempra, Grasp, STB, Jovian, Genus, RIX Softworks, Digital Vision, Global Softworks, Big_D, Pacific Motion (formerly Presidio), Metagraphics, Image-In, Inset Systems, VRLI Inc., TEGL, and ATI Technologies.

See Also

User Guide
- ☑ Windows
- ☑ DOS
- ☑ Macintosh
- ☐ Terminal Emulation
- ☐ VMS
- ☑ UNIX
- ☑ OS/2
- ☐ Other platform

Cost
- ☐ Unknown
- ☐ Basic
- ☑ Extended
- ☐ Premium ($)
- ☐ Executive w/$

Activity Level

(MEDIUM, LOW → HIGH)

Address
GO: **GRAPHAVEN**

Graphics B Vendors Forum

Description
This forum provides support from manufacturers of graphics hardware and software. You can post questions, read messages, and download files here.

Subjects
Computers, Graphics, Hardware/Software

Audience
Management information specialists, hardware/software designers, computer hardware users, computer graphics designers

Content Summary
The Graphics Vendor B Forum offers support from Tseng Labs, Diamond Computer Systems, Animated Software, StereoGraphics, Sun Country Software, LEAD Technologies, Hercules, Genoa Systems, CrystalGraphics, Volante, Domark Software,

Hardware/Software – Hardware

DesignWare, Inc., HSC Software, Solana Software, Matrox, and Appian Technology.

See Also
Graphics Vendor Forum, Graphics Support Forum

User Guide
- ☑ Windows
- ☑ DOS
- ☑ Macintosh
- ☐ Terminal Emulation
- ☐ VMS
- ☑ UNIX
- ☑ OS/2
- ☐ Other platform

Cost
- ☐ Unknown
- ☐ Basic
- ☑ Extended
- ☐ Premium ($)
- ☐ Executive w/$

Activity Level

Address
GO: **GRAPHBVEN**

Logitech Forum

Description
This forum is devoted to Logitech products, including Scanman, FotoMan, 3D devices, mouse products, and others.

Subjects
Computer Hardware, Computers, Hardware/Software

Audience
Management information specialists, computer users, graphics designers

Content Summary
The Logitech Forum includes the following libraries: Mouse Products, Sound/Video, Scanman/FotoMan, Logitech OCR Software, MAC Products, Announcements, General Information, 3D Devices, and Top Q&A.

See Also

User Guide
- ☑ Windows
- ☑ DOS
- ☑ Macintosh
- ☐ Terminal Emulation
- ☐ VMS
- ☑ UNIX
- ☑ OS/2
- ☑ Other platform

Cost
- ☐ Unknown
- ☐ Basic
- ☑ Extended
- ☐ Premium ($)
- ☐ Executive w/$

Activity Level

Address
GO: **LOGITECH**

HARDWARE

IBM Hardware Forum

Description
This forum is devoted to the topic of hardware on the IBM PC and any other compatible computers.

Subjects
Computers, Hardware, IBM PCs

Audience
Management information specialists, computer users

Content Summary
You can find library and message areas such as Disk/Disk Utilities, Printer Utilities, Video, PC-AT, Classifieds, PCJr, Tape, and more.

See Also

User Guide
- ☑ Windows
- ☑ DOS
- ☐ Macintosh
- ☐ Terminal Emulation
- ☐ VMS
- ☐ UNIX
- ☑ OS/2
- ☑ Other platform

Cost
- ☐ Unknown
- ☐ Basic
- ☑ Extended
- ☐ Premium ($)
- ☐ Executive w/$

Activity Level

Address
GO: **IBMHW**

PC Plug and Play Forum

Description
This forum is for the discussion of the hardware and software issues of implementing plug and play on PCs. The Plug and Play forum is operated by several hardware and software manufacturers.

Subjects
Computers, Hardware

Audience
Computer users, MIS people

Hardware – Health

Content Summary
This forum is mainly under construction due to the infancy of this topic. However, you can find files and technical information in several of its libraries, including General Information, Plug and Play ISA, and PCMCIA.

See Also
IBM File Finder

User Guide
- ☑ Windows
- ☑ DOS
- ☑ Macintosh
- ☐ Terminal Emulation
- ☐ VMS
- ☐ UNIX
- ☐ OS/2
- ☑ Other platform

Cost
- ☐ Unknown
- ☐ Basic
- ☑ Extended
- ☐ Premium ($)
- ☐ Executive w/$

Activity Level

Address
GO: **PLUGPLAY**

Hayes Forum

Description
This forum contains press releases, technical support, tips, and much more. Some of the products include Smartmodems, ACCURA, and JT Fax.

Subjects
Computers, Modems

Audience
Management information specialists, computer hardware users

Content Summary
The library and message sections in this forum include discussions and files on high speed modems, Smartmodems, Smartcom for DOS and Windows, Fax products, Hayes for the Mac, Hayes for LANS, and Hayes for ISDN.

See Also
Modem Vendor Forum, Hayes

User Guide
- ☑ Windows
- ☑ DOS
- ☑ Macintosh
- ☐ Terminal Emulation
- ☐ VMS
- ☐ UNIX
- ☐ OS/2
- ☐ Other platform

Cost
- ☐ Unknown
- ☐ Basic
- ☑ Extended
- ☐ Premium ($)
- ☐ Executive w/$

Activity Level

Address
GO: **HAYFORUM**

Hayes Online

Description
This service gives you an introduction to Hayes Corporation, as well as product support.

Subjects
Computer Hardware, Computer Networking, Computers, Modems

Audience
Modem users, management information specialists

Content Summary
From the Online with Hayes main menu, you can select from About Online with Hayes, The Hayes Advantage, the Hayes Forum, LANstep, Product Descriptions, Special Support Forums, and Third Party Developers.

See Also
Hayes Forum, Modem Vendor Forum

User Guide
- ☑ Windows
- ☑ DOS
- ☑ Macintosh
- ☐ Terminal Emulation
- ☐ VMS
- ☐ UNIX
- ☐ OS/2
- ☐ Other platform

Cost
- ☐ Unknown
- ☐ Basic
- ☑ Extended
- ☐ Premium ($)
- ☐ Executive w/$

Activity Level
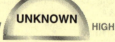

Address
GO:

HEALTH

CCML AIDS Articles

Description
This forum contains articles relating to AIDS from the Comprehensive Core Medical Library.

Subjects
AIDS, Health, Medicine

Audience
Medical personnel, researchers

Health

Content Summary
The libraries contain full text articles from leading medical reference books, text books, and articles.

See Also

User Guide
- ☑ Windows
- ☑ DOS
- ☐ Macintosh
- ☐ Terminal Emulation
- ☐ VMS
- ☐ UNIX
- ☐ OS/2
- ☐ Other platform

Cost
- ☐ Unknown
- ☐ Basic
- ☐ Extended
- ☑ Premium ($)
- ☐ Executive w/$

Activity Level

Address
GO: **CCMLAIDS**

Diabetes Forum

Description
An online community for people with a common interest in diabetes, hypoglycemia, and related chronic metabolic disorders. Family members and friends of these people also are welcome to join and participate in this lively area.

Subjects
Diabetes, Health, Hypoglycemia

Audience
Diabetes patients, family and friends, hypoglycemia patients, medical personnel

Content Summary
The library and message areas are full of information about these disorders, including files on general diabetes information and explanation of diabetic terms. You also can find files and messages for the friends and family, hypoglycemics, insulin information, oral medications, diet and exercise, complications associated with diabetes, pumping, various technologies and theories, and pregnancy and diabetes. Library 17, "Youth Connection," is devoted to young people with diabetes and includes graphics, games, and stories for the young.

See Also
Health and Fitness Forum, Health/Fitness, HealthNet, Health Database Plus, Physicians Data Query

User Guide
- ☑ Windows
- ☑ DOS
- ☑ Macintosh
- ☐ Terminal Emulation
- ☑ VMS
- ☑ UNIX
- ☑ OS/2
- ☐ Other platform

Cost
- ☐ Unknown
- ☐ Basic
- ☑ Extended
- ☐ Premium ($)
- ☐ Executive w/$

Activity Level

Address
GO: **DIABETES**

Health and Fitness Forum

Description
This forum provides health-related information and support groups for their members. Learn about exercise, nutrition, mental health, and other health items.

Subjects
Fitness, Health, Martial Arts

Audience

Content Summary
The message library sections contain various health-related files and information and are divided into several topics, including Addiction/Recovery, Mental Health, Family Health, The Doctor's Inn, Exercise & Fitness, Master's Swimming, Running & Racing, Nutrition, Martial Arts, and Self Help. The Martial Arts library is very popular.

See Also
Health and Vitamin Express, Health Database Plus($), Health/Fitness, HealthNet, Holistic Health Forum

User Guide
- ☑ Windows
- ☑ DOS
- ☑ Macintosh
- ☐ Terminal Emulation
- ☑ VMS
- ☑ UNIX
- ☑ OS/2
- ☑ Other platform

Cost
- ☐ Unknown
- ☐ Basic
- ☑ Extended
- ☐ Premium ($)
- ☐ Executive w/$

Activity Level
MEDIUM (LOW ← HIGH)

Address
GO: **GOODHEALTH**

Health

Health and Vitamin Express

Description
This forum enables you to shop online for your vitamin and nutrition needs. You can order amino acids, herbs, teas, energy packs, health candy, and much more.

Subjects
Health

Audience
General public, nutritionists

Content Summary
The Health and Vitamin Express main menu enables you shop by individual item, by category, or by a QuickSearch of items. You can even order your prescriptions from this service. Some of the other areas that you can choose from include Specials, Over the Counter Products, Receive a Free Catalog, Use the Electronic Order Form, read Health News, and Customer Service.

See Also
HealthNet, Health/Fitness, Health Database Plus($), Health & Fitness Forum

User Guide
- [✓] Windows
- [✓] DOS
- [✓] Macintosh
- [ ] Terminal Emulation
- [✓] VMS
- [✓] UNIX
- [✓] OS/2
- [✓] Other platform

Cost
- [ ] Unknown
- [ ] Basic
- [ ] Extended
- [ ] Premium ($)
- [✓] Executive w/$

Activity Level

Address
GO: HVE-1

Health Database Plus

Description
Search for health-related articles from consumer and professional publications using Health Database Plus.

Subjects
Health, Medical News, Medical Research, Medicine

Audience
Nutritionists, medical researchers, medical professionals, medical educators

Content Summary
Health Database Plus is a service that enables you to retrieve articles from consumer and professional publications on health care, disease prevention and treatment, fitness and nutrition, children and the elderly, substance abuse and smoking, and just about any health-related topic. The prices for searches vary, so be sure to read the pricing terms by choosing the Pricing option from the main menu.

See Also
Health & Fitness Forum, Health & Vitamin Express, Health/Fitness, HealthNet

User Guide
- [✓] Windows
- [✓] DOS
- [✓] Macintosh
- [ ] Terminal Emulation
- [✓] VMS
- [✓] UNIX
- [✓] OS/2
- [✓] Other platform

Cost
- [ ] Unknown
- [ ] Basic
- [ ] Extended
- [✓] Premium ($)
- [ ] Executive w/$

Activity Level

Address
GO: HLTDB

Holistic Health Forum

Description
The Holistic Health Forum tries to look at the whole person, stressing preventive measures an individual can take on his or her own behalf.

Subjects
Fitness, Health

Audience
General public

Content Summary
The libraries and message sections in this forum include such topics as herbs and plants, Chinese treatments, health graphics, diet and exercise, women's health, chiropractic, health politics, and the natural foods business. In the Healing & the Mind library (Library 10), you can learn about crystal healing and psychic holistic health. The Nutritional Therapy library (Library 3) contains a text file on antioxidants.

See Also
Health and Fitness Forum, Health and Vitamin Express, Health Database Plus($), Health/Fitness, HealthNet

User Guide
- [✓] Windows
- [✓] DOS
- [✓] Macintosh
- [ ] Terminal Emulation
- [✓] VMS
- [✓] UNIX
- [✓] OS/2
- [✓] Other platform

Cost
- [ ] Unknown
- [ ] Basic
- [x] Extended
- [ ] Premium ($)
- [ ] Executive w/$

Activity Level
MEDIUM (LOW — HIGH)

Address
GO: **HOLISTIC**

Human Sexuality Databank

Description
Presented by Howard and Martha Lewis, the Human Sexuality Databank provides information on topics such as gynecology, sexual therapy, and more.

Subjects
Health, Sexuality

Audience
Health care providers, general public

Content Summary
Because this area discusses sexually explicit topics, only people comfortable with all sex-related subjects and their frank treatment are advised to use this service. The Human Sexuality Databank main menu includes updates to the service, questions and answers posted by members and service administrators, a dictionary of sexual terms, hotline for your questions and comments, the 30 most-asked questions, and a letters sections. You also can enter forums where you can join in live talk with other members.

See Also
HSX Adult Forum, HSX Open Forum

User Guide
- [x] Windows
- [x] DOS
- [x] Macintosh
- [x] Terminal Emulation
- [x] VMS
- [x] UNIX
- [x] OS/2
- [x] Other platform

Cost
- [ ] Unknown
- [ ] Basic
- [x] Extended
- [ ] Premium ($)
- [ ] Executive w/$

Activity level

UNKNOWN (LOW — HIGH)

Address
GO: **HUMAN**

PaperChase-MEDLINE Forum

Description
This forum provides access to the world's largest biomedical database. The information is prepared by the National Library of Medicine and has more than seven million references from 4,000 journals.

Subjects
Health, Medicine, Research

Audience
Dentists, physicians, scientists

Content Summary
References are available from 1966. Updates to articles are added weekly. Because the database is so extensive, you should enter a very narrow topic of research. Cost can be prohibitive. The cost on weekdays from 7 p.m. until 8 a.m. or any time on weekends is $18 per hour. The cost on weekdays from 8 a.m. until 7 p.m. is $24 per hour. Photocopies are available for $10 by first-class mail or $25 by fax.

See Also
Rare Disease Database Forum

User Guide
- [x] Windows
- [x] DOS
- [x] Macintosh
- [ ] Terminal Emulation
- [x] VMS
- [x] UNIX
- [x] OS/2
- [ ] Other platform

Cost
- [ ] Unknown
- [ ] Basic
- [ ] Extended
- [x] Premium ($)
- [ ] Executive w/$

Activity Level
MEDIUM (arrow pointing to HIGH) (LOW — HIGH)

Address
GO: **PAPERCHASE**

Health and Fitness Forum

Description
This forum provides health-related information and support groups for their members. Learn about exercise, nutrition, mental health, and other health items.

Subjects
Fitness, Health, Martial Arts

Audience
General Public

Content Summary
The message library sections contain various health-related files and information and are divided into several topics, including Addiction/Recovery, Mental Health, Family Health, The Doctor's Inn, Exercise &

Health and Fitness Forum – Health Care

Fitness, Master's Swimming, Running & Racing, Nutrition, Martial Arts, and Self Help. The Martial Arts library is very popular.

See Also
Health and Vitamin Express, Health Database Plus($), Health/Fitness, HealthNet, Holistic Health Forum

User Guide
- ☑ Windows
- ☑ DOS
- ☑ Macintosh
- ☐ Terminal Emulation
- ☑ VMS
- ☑ UNIX
- ☑ OS/2
- ☑ Other platform

Cost
- ☐ Unknown
- ☐ Basic
- ☑ Extended
- ☐ Premium ($)
- ☐ Executive w/$

Activity Level

Address
GO: **GOODHEALTH**

Health and Vitamin Express

Description
This forum enables you to shop online for your vitamin and nutrition needs. You can order amino acids, herbs, teas, energy packs, health candy, and much more.

Subjects
Health

Audience
General public, nutritionists

Content Summary
The Health and Vitamin Express main menu enables you shop by individual item, by category, or by a QuickSearch of items. You can even order your prescriptions from this service. Some of the other areas that you can choose from include Specials, Over the Counter Products, Receive a Free Catalog, Use the Electronic Order Form, read Health News, and Customer Service.

See Also
HealthNet, Health/Fitness, Health Database Plus($), Health & Fitness Forum

User Guide
- ☑ Windows
- ☑ DOS
- ☑ Macintosh
- ☐ Terminal Emulation
- ☑ VMS
- ☑ UNIX
- ☑ OS/2
- ☑ Other platform

Cost
- ☐ Unknown
- ☐ Basic
- ☐ Extended
- ☐ Premium ($)
- ☑ Executive w/$

Activity Level

Address
GO: HVE-1

HEALTH CARE

Health/Fitness

Description
If you can't find the health-related forum that you want, use the Health/Fitness service to speed up your search.

Subjects
Aids, Cancer, Disabilities, Health Care

Audience
Medical educators, medical professionals, medical researchers, general public

Content Summary
The main menu in this area lists all the health and fitness related forums and services available on CompuServe. Here you can choose from topics such as Consumer Reports Complete Drug Reference, HealthNet, AIDS Information, Attention Deficit Disorder Forum, Cancer Information, Diabetes Forum, Health & Fitness Forum, Human Sexuality, PaperChase (MEDLINE), and many more.

See Also
HealthNet, Holistic Health Forum, Health Database Plus($), Health and Vitamin Express, Health and Fitness Forum, Cancer Forum, Aids News Clips, PaperChase MEDLINE($)

User Guide
- ☑ Windows
- ☑ DOS
- ☑ Macintosh
- ☐ Terminal Emulation
- ☑ VMS
- ☑ UNIX
- ☑ OS/2
- ☑ Other platform

Cost
- ☐ Unknown
- ☑ Basic
- ☐ Extended
- ☐ Premium ($)
- ☐ Executive w/$

Activity Level

Address
GO: **FITNESS**

Health Care – Health/Fitness

HealthNet

Description
Get health news, sports medicine, information on ailments and disorders, and other health-related information from this forum.

Subjects
Fitness, Health, Health Care, Sports

Audience
General public

Content Summary
The HealthNet main menu contains two options: HealthNet Reference Library and Sports Medicine. The HealthNet Reference Library contains several listings, including Disorders and Diseases, Symptoms, Drugs, Surgeries/Tests/Procedures, Home Care and First Aid, Obstetrics/Reproductive Medicine, and Ophthalmology/Eye Care. The Sports Medicine option contains General Aspects of Exercise, Nutrition and Exercise, and Some Specific Sports. Be sure to read the introduction to this service, and do not use this service as a substitute for your doctor or medical personnel.

See Also
Health/Fitness, Health Database Plus($), Health and Vitamin Express, Health & Fitness Forum, Holistic Health Forum, Sports Forum

User Guide
- ☑ Windows
- ☑ DOS
- ☑ Macintosh
- ☐ Terminal Emulation
- ☑ VMS
- ☑ UNIX
- ☑ OS/2
- ☑ Other platform

Cost
- ☐ Unknown
- ☑ Basic
- ☐ Extended
- ☐ Premium ($)
- ☐ Executive w/$

Activity Level

Address
GO: **HNT**

Health Database Plus

Description
Search for health-related articles from consumer and professional publications using Health Database Plus.

Subjects
Health, Medical News, Medical Research, Medicine

Audience
Nutritionists, medical researchers, medical professionals, medical educators

Content Summary
Health Database Plus is a service that enables you to retrieve articles from consumer and professional publications on health care, disease prevention and treatment, fitness and nutrition, children and the elderly, substance abuse and smoking, and just about any health-related topic. The prices for searches vary, so be sure to read the pricing terms by choosing the Pricing option from the main menu.

See Also
Health & Fitness Forum, Health & Vitamin Express, Health/Fitness, HealthNet

User Guide
- ☑ Windows
- ☑ DOS
- ☑ Macintosh
- ☑ Terminal Emulation
- ☑ VMS
- ☑ UNIX
- ☑ OS/2
- ☑ Other platform

Cost
- ☐ Unknown
- ☐ Basic
- ☐ Extended
- ☑ Premium ($)
- ☐ Executive w/$

Activity Level
LOW / UNKNOWN / MEDIUM / HIGH

Address
GO: **HLTDB**

Health/Fitness

Description
If you can't find the health-related forum that you want, use the Health/Fitness service to speed up your search.

Subjects
Aids, Cancer, Disabilities, Health Care

Audience
Medical educators, medical professionals, medical researchers, general public

Content Summary
The main menu in this area lists all the health and fitness related forums and services available on CompuServe. Here you can choose from topics such as Consumer Reports Complete Drug Reference, HealthNet, AIDS Information, Attention Deficit Disorder Forum, Cancer Information, Diabetes Forum, Health & Fitness Forum, Human Sexuality, PaperChase (MEDLINE), and many more.

See Also
HealthNet, Holistic Health Forum, Health Database Plus($), Health and Vitamin Express, Health and Fitness Forum, Cancer Forum, Aids News Clips, PaperChase MEDLINE($)

Health/Fitness – Help

User Guide
- ☑ Windows
- ☑ DOS
- ☑ Macintosh
- ☐ Terminal Emulation
- ☑ VMS
- ☑ UNIX
- ☑ OS/2
- ☑ Other platform

Cost
- ☐ Unknown
- ☑ Basic
- ☐ Extended
- ☐ Premium ($)
- ☐ Executive w/$

Activity Level

Address
GO: **FITNESS**

HealthNet

Description
Get health news, sports medicine, information on ailments and disorders, and other health-related information from this forum.

Subjects
Fitness, Health, Health Care, Sports

Audience
General public

Content Summary
The HealthNet main menu contains two options: HealthNet Reference Library and Sports Medicine. The HealthNet Reference Library contains several listings, including Disorders and Diseases, Symptoms, Drugs, Surgeries/Tests/Procedures, Home Care and First Aid, Obstetrics/Reproductive Medicine, and Ophthalmology/Eye Care. The Sports Medicine option contains General Aspects of Exercise, Nutrition and Exercise, and Some Specific Sports. Be sure to read the introduction to this service, and do not use this service as a substitute for your doctor or medical personnel.

See Also
Health/Fitness, Health Database Plus($), Health and Vitamin Express, Health & Fitness Forum, Holistic Health Forum, Sports Forum

User Guide
- ☑ Windows
- ☑ DOS
- ☑ Macintosh
- ☐ Terminal Emulation
- ☑ VMS
- ☑ UNIX
- ☑ OS/2
- ☑ Other platform

Cost
- ☐ Unknown
- ☑ Basic
- ☐ Extended
- ☐ Premium ($)
- ☐ Executive w/$

Activity Level

Address
GO: **HNT**

HELP

CompuServe Help Forum

Description
This is a free forum for all CIS members who need help using CompuServe or have questions about their membership

Subjects
CompuServe, Help

Audience
CompuServe users

Content Summary
Libraries include information about CompuServe mail, reference services, news, sports, weather, financial, CB/Conferencing, pricing plans, and access to CompuServe.

See Also
Computer Club Forum

User Guide
- ☑ Windows
- ☑ DOS
- ☑ Macintosh
- ☐ Terminal Emulation
- ☑ VMS
- ☑ UNIX
- ☑ OS/2
- ☑ Other platform

Cost
- ☐ Unknown
- ☐ Basic
- ☐ Extended
- ☐ Premium ($)
- ☐ Executive w/$

Activity Level

Address
GO: **HELPFORUM**

Computer Club Forum

Description
The Computer Club Forum is the home for users of computers no longer supported by their manufacturers or that have no other specific forum dedicated to them on CompuServe.

Subjects
Computers

Audience
Computer users

Content Summary
Libraries include information for users of Actrix, Adam, Amstrad, Apricot, Eagle, Kaypro, Ohio Scientific, Panasonic, Sanyo, Times/Sinclair, and Victor 9000.

See Also
CompuServe Help Forum

User Guide
- ☑ Windows
- ☑ DOS
- ☐ Macintosh
- ☐ Terminal Emulation
- ☐ VMS
- ☐ UNIX
- ☐ OS/2
- ☐ Other platform

Cost
- ☐ Unknown
- ☐ Basic
- ☑ Extended
- ☐ Premium ($)
- ☐ Executive w/$

Activity Level

Address
GO: **CLUB**

User Profile Program

Description
This is an online area for users of the ASCII interface to set up their terminal parameters. This area is not useful to users of DOSCIM, WinCIM, or MacCIM software.

Subjects
Help

Audience
General Public

Contents Summary
Use the various options to change your CompuServe settings.

See Also
CompuServe Help Forum

User Guide
- ☑ Windows
- ☑ DOS
- ☐ Macintosh
- ☑ Terminal Emulation
- ☐ VMS
- ☐ UNIX
- ☐ OS/2
- ☐ Other platform

Cost
- ☐ Unknown
- ☑ Basic
- ☐ Extended
- ☐ Premium ($)
- ☐ Executive w/$

Activity Level

Address
GO:

HISTORY

Archive Photos Forum

Description
Archive Photos is a leading source of historical engraving, drawings and photographs, with over 1300 images available for download.

Subjects
History, Photography

Audience
History buffs, photographers, students

Content Summary
This forum's libraries include Film/TV/ Stage/ Radio, Art/Literature, Vietnam War, and others.

See Also
Photography Forum

User Guide
- ☑ Windows
- ☑ DOS
- ☐ Macintosh
- ☐ Terminal Emulation
- ☐ VMS
- ☐ UNIX
- ☐ OS/2
- ☐ Other platform

Cost
- ☐ Unknown
- ☐ Basic
- ☑ Extended
- ☐ Premium ($)
- ☐ Executive w/$

Activity Level

Address
GO: **ARCHIVE**

Genealogy Forum

Description
Trying to find your great-great-grandmother's father's brother? Join the Genealogy Forum and start looking.

Subjects
Family, History

Audience
General public, families

Content Summary

History – Hobbies

This forum gives you access to a wide-range of members who are interested in genealogy and using their computers to help them. DOS, Windows, UNIX, Amiga, and Macintosh software is available in the libraries, as well as graphics and text files that might help you track down the hole in your family tree. Be sure to check out the message sections for leads to surnames or to post a query.

See Also
Military Forum

User Guide
- ☑ Windows
- ☑ DOS
- ☑ Macintosh
- ☐ Terminal Emulation
- ☐ VMS
- ☑ UNIX
- ☐ OS/2
- ☑ Other platform

Cost
- ☐ Unknown
- ☐ Basic
- ☑ Extended
- ☐ Premium ($)
- ☐ Executive w/$

Activity Level: MEDIUM-HIGH

Address
GO: **ROOTS**

JFK Assassination Forum

Description
Did Lee Harvey Oswald act alone or not? Search for answers in this forum.

Subjects
History

Audience
General public

Content Summary
The purpose of this forum is to facilitate research into the assassination of JFK, to work together as a cooperative community to determine the facts of the "crime of the century." The library and message sections include Transcripts/Threads, Books & Articles, Organized Crime, Oswald/Ruby/et al., and more. For photos and drawings, see the Photos & Documents library (Library 12).

See Also

User Guide
- ☑ Windows
- ☑ DOS
- ☑ Macintosh
- ☐ Terminal Emulation
- ☑ VMS
- ☑ UNIX
- ☑ OS/2
- ☑ Other platform

Cost
- ☐ Unknown
- ☐ Basic
- ☑ Extended
- ☐ Premium ($)
- ☐ Executive w/$

Activity Level: MEDIUM, LOW

Address
GO: **JFKFORUM**

HOBBIES

All-Music Guide

Description
The largest collection of music albums, ratings, and reviews open to public comment.

Subjects
Entertainment, Music

Audience
Musicians, music enthusiasts

Content Summary
This guide includes information and comments about music and related news.

See Also
All-Music Guide Forum

User Guide
- ☑ Windows
- ☑ DOS
- ☐ Macintosh
- ☐ Terminal Emulation
- ☐ VMS
- ☐ UNIX
- ☐ OS/2
- ☐ Other platform

Cost
- ☐ Unknown
- ☐ Basic
- ☑ Extended
- ☐ Premium ($)
- ☐ Executive w/$

Activity Level: UNKNOWN

Address
GO: **ALLMUSIC**

All-Music Guide Forum

Description
The AMGPOP Forum provides help in using the All-Music Guide Database, the largest collection of music albums, ratings, and reviews.

Hobbies

Subjects
Entertainment, Music

Audience
Musicians, music enthusiasts

Content Summary
This forum's libraries include AMG help, Resources/Reviews, Music Bibliography, and more.

See Also
All-Music Guide

User Guide
- ☑ Windows
- ☑ DOS
- ☐ Macintosh
- ☐ Terminal Emulation
- ☐ VMS
- ☐ UNIX
- ☐ OS/2
- ☐ Other platform

Cost
- ☐ Unknown
- ☐ Basic
- ☑ Extended
- ☐ Premium ($)
- ☐ Executive w/$

Activity Level

Address
GO: **AMGOP**

Aquaria/Fish Forum

Description
FISHNET is the place to meet for information dealing with all kinds of aquatic critters.

Subjects
Fish

Audience
Aquatic enthusiasts

Content Summary
The libraries contain information on equipment, disease, aquaculture, freshwater and marine aquaria, and a graphics library.

See Also
Travel Forum

User Guide
- ☑ Windows
- ☑ DOS
- ☑ Macintosh
- ☐ Terminal Emulation
- ☑ VMS
- ☑ UNIX
- ☑ OS/2
- ☑ Other platform

Cost
- ☐ Unknown
- ☐ Basic
- ☑ Extended
- ☐ Premium ($)
- ☐ Executive w/$

Activity Level

Address
GO: **FISHNET**

Artist Forum

Description
The Artist Forum brings you the entire world of art.

Subjects
Hobbies

Audience
Artists, collectors, sculptors

Content Summary
Art of various types such as cartoons, portraits, and landscapes can be viewed. Also contains information on grants and scholarships.

See Also
Metropolitan Museum of Art

User Guide
- ☑ Windows
- ☑ DOS
- ☑ Macintosh
- ☐ Terminal Emulation
- ☑ VMS
- ☑ UNIX
- ☑ OS/2
- ☑ Other platform

Cost
- ☐ Unknown
- ☐ Basic
- ☑ Extended
- ☐ Premium ($)
- ☐ Executive w/$

Activity Level

Address
GO: **ARTIST**

Astronomy Forum

Description
The Astronomy Forum is for anyone who shares a fascination with celestial happenings, whether at the amateur or professional level.

Subjects
Hobbies, Science

Audience
Astronomers, hobbyists

Hobbies

Content Summary
The libraries contain public domain software, reference articles, and graphics images.

See Also
Science Forum

User Guide
- ☑ Windows
- ☑ DOS
- ☐ Macintosh
- ☐ Terminal Emulation
- ☐ VMS
- ☐ UNIX
- ☐ OS/2
- ☐ Other platform

Cost
- ☐ Unknown
- ☐ Basic
- ☑ Extended
- ☐ Premium ($)
- ☐ Executive w/$

Activity Level
MEDIUM (LOW — HIGH)

Address
GO: **ASTROFORUM**

Canon Net Menu

Description
This menu provides access to services and information from Canon Computer Services, Inc.

Subjects
Hobbies, Photography

Audience
Product users

Content Summary
The libraries of this forum contain information about Canon, a list of regional offices, service facilities, and information on the Clean Earth Campaign.

See Also
Canon Support Forum

User Guide
- ☑ Windows
- ☑ DOS
- ☑ Macintosh
- ☐ Terminal Emulation
- ☐ VMS
- ☑ UNIX
- ☐ OS/2
- ☐ Other platform

Cost
- ☐ Unknown
- ☑ Basic
- ☐ Extended
- ☐ Premium ($)
- ☐ Executive w/$

Activity Level
UNKNOWN

Address
GO: **CANON**

Canon Support Forum

Description
This forum provides support for users of products from both Canon Computer Systems, Inc, and Canon USA.

Subjects
Hobbies, Photography

Audience
Product users

Content Summary
Product information contained in this library includes laser printers, bubble jet printers, ImageScanners, digital copiers, and 35mm cameras.

See Also
Canon Net Menu

User Guide
- ☑ Windows
- ☑ DOS
- ☑ Macintosh
- ☐ Terminal Emulation
- ☐ VMS
- ☑ UNIX
- ☐ OS/2
- ☐ Other platform

Cost
- ☐ Unknown
- ☐ Basic
- ☑ Extended
- ☐ Premium ($)
- ☐ Executive w/$

Activity Level
LOW

Address
GO: **CAN-10**

Chess Forum

Description
The place to be if you love the game of Chess or want to find out more about playing it.

Subjects
Games, Hobbies

Audience
Games enthusiasts

Content Summary
The libraries and message sections contain basic game playing theory, analysis of moves, chess tourneys, and a message area that enables you to ask chess masters questions.

See Also

User Guide
- ☑ Windows
- ☑ DOS
- ☑ Macintosh
- ☐ Terminal Emulation
- ☐ VMS
- ☑ UNIX
- ☐ OS/2
- ☐ Other platform

Hobbies

Cost
- [ ] Unknown
- [ ] Basic
- [x] Extended
- [ ] Premium ($)
- [ ] Executive w/$

Activity Level: MEDIUM (arrow pointing between medium and high)

Address
GO: **CHESSFORUM**

Collectibles Forum

Description
We are an electronic club for all collectors—and are a member of the ANA and APS.

Subjects
Dolls, Hobbies, Star Trek

Audience
Hobby enthusiasts

Content Summary
The library and message sections contain information on a wide variety of collectibles. Included are areas on stamps, coins, autographs, books, music, sports cards, dolls, figurines, Star Trek, and much more.

See Also
Fantasy Forum

User Guide
- [x] Windows
- [x] DOS
- [x] Macintosh
- [ ] Terminal Emulation
- [ ] VMS
- [x] UNIX
- [ ] OS/2
- [ ] Other platform

Cost
- [ ] Unknown
- [ ] Basic
- [x] Extended
- [ ] Premium ($)
- [ ] Executive w/$

Activity Level: MEDIUM (arrow pointing straight up to medium)

Address
GO: **COLLECT**

Comics/Animation Forum

Description
This forum is for fans of comic books, comic strips, sequential art of all kinds, and animation.

Subjects
Hobbies

Audience
Comics enthusiasts

Content Summary
The libraries include information on comic books, Japanimation, animation, collecting, industry issues, newspaper strips, adult comics, and upcoming meetings.

See Also
Artists Forum

User Guide
- [x] Windows
- [x] DOS
- [x] Macintosh
- [ ] Terminal Emulation
- [ ] VMS
- [x] UNIX
- [ ] OS/2
- [ ] Other platform

Cost
- [ ] Unknown
- [ ] Basic
- [x] Extended
- [ ] Premium ($)
- [ ] Executive w/$

Activity Level: MEDIUM (arrow pointing between medium and high)

Address
GO: **COMIC**

Cook's Online Forum

Description
Everything dealing with cooking is what this forum is about, from appetizers to desserts, and a wine to go with the meal.

Subjects
Hobbies, Food

Audience
Cooks

Content Summary
Libraries include recipes and information about first courses, meat/poultry/fish, herbs and spices, desserts, ethnic recipes, breads, fruits, nutrition, and vegetarian cooking.

See Also
Family Handyman Forum

User Guide
- [x] Windows
- [x] DOS
- [x] Macintosh
- [ ] Terminal Emulation
- [ ] VMS
- [x] UNIX
- [ ] OS/2
- [ ] Other platform

Cost
- [ ] Unknown
- [ ] Basic
- [x] Extended
- [ ] Premium ($)
- [ ] Executive w/$

Hobbies

Activity Level

Address
GO: COOKS

Crafts

Description
This forum is a meeting place for folks worldwide who love to create with their hands; a resource for software, ideas, techniques, and friends.

Subjects
Hobbies

Audience
Hobbyists

Content Summary
Libraries include information on crafting interests such as knitting, weaving, stitchery, glass, paper, woodworking, miniatures, lacemaking, quilting, jewelry making, and much more.

See Also
Family Handyman Forum

User Guide
☑	Windows	☐	VMS
☑	DOS	☑	UNIX
☑	Macintosh	☐	OS/2
☐	Terminal Emulation	☑	Other platform

Cost
☐	Unknown	☐	Premium ($)
☐	Basic	☐	Executive w/$
☑	Extended		

Activity Level

(arrow pointing to MEDIUM-HIGH)

Address
GO: CRAFTS

Home Forum

Description
This forum is about homes. What more can you say?

Subjects
Food, Hobbies, Home Building

Audience
General public, horticulture enthusiasts

Content Summary
You can find out information, tips, hints, and the like here, regardless of the type of home you live in, including apartments, condos, or older homes. Topics such as security, home building, interior furnishing, outdoor living, lighting, and the kitchen are included in the message and library sections. If you want to wire your house for a computer network, for example, look in the Conveniences library (Library 7) for a text file that explains it. You also might want to cut down on the amount of fat you serve at Thanksgiving, Christmas, or other holiday meals. The In the Kitchen library (Library 9) tells you how to substitute shrimp and crab meat for your hor d'oeuvres.

See Also
Family Handyman Forum, Gardening Forum

User Guide
☑	Windows	☑	VMS
☑	DOS	☑	UNIX
☑	Macintosh	☑	OS/2
☐	Terminal Emulation	☑	Other platform

Cost
☐	Unknown	☐	Premium ($)
☐	Basic	☐	Executive w/$
☑	Extended		

Activity Level

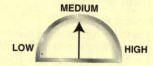

Address
GO: HOME

Photography Forum

Description
In this forum, photo enthusiasts of all expertise levels can meet and exchange ideas on topics ranging from tips on how to take good pictures to what type of equipment is needed.

Subjects
Cameras, Hobbies, Photography

Audience
Computer graphics, photographers

Content Summary
The Photography Forum offers many library areas of interest to photography enthusiasts of all levels. Of particular interest are conferences with famous photographers in which participants can ask questions or have their work critiqued. Also included are message areas on commonly asked questions, such as "What makes good photograph composition?". If you are looking for a camera or additional equipment, the numerous press released on various equipment can be helpful.

See Also
Graphics Forum, Quick Picture Forum

User Guide
☑	Windows	☑	VMS
☑	DOS	☑	UNIX
☑	Macintosh	☑	OS/2
☐	Terminal Emulation	☐	Other platform

Hobbies – Holistic Health Forum

Cost
- ☐ Unknown
- ☐ Basic
- ☑ Extended
- ☐ Premium ($)
- ☐ Executive w/$

Activity Level

(gauge: MEDIUM, pointing toward HIGH)

Address
GO: **PHOTOFORUM**

Scuba Forum

Description
This is a forum for amateur and professional divers, discussing diving, diving equipment, and diving locations.

Subjects
Divers, Hobbies

Audience
Divers, snorklers

Content Summary
The libraries of this forum contain information on diving in America, Europe, the Caribbean, and elsewhere. Also included is information on scuba equipment, snorkling, and pictures of diving locations.

See Also
Sports Forum, Outdoor Forum, Photography Forum

User Guide
- ☑ Windows
- ☑ DOS
- ☑ Macintosh
- ☐ Terminal Emulation
- ☑ VMS
- ☑ UNIX
- ☑ OS/2
- ☑ Other platform

Cost
- ☐ Unknown
- ☐ Basic
- ☑ Extended
- ☐ Premium ($)
- ☐ Executive w/$

Activity Level

(gauge: MEDIUM)

Address
GO: **DIVING**

TrainNet Forum

Description
The TrainNet Forum serves as a focal point for a wide range of railroad oriented subjects, from Amtrak employees to Z-Scale models.

Subjects
Hobbies

Audience
Train lovers

Content Summary
Libraries include information on hobby stores, historial and technical railroad societies, model railroad enthusiasts, and industry publications.

See Also
Trains, model trains, games/simulations, rail employees and unions, the rail industry

User Guide
- ☑ Windows
- ☑ DOS
- ☑ Macintosh
- ☐ Terminal Emulation
- ☑ VMS
- ☑ UNIX
- ☑ OS/2
- ☑ Other platform

Cost
- ☐ Unknown
- ☐ Basic
- ☑ Extended
- ☐ Premium ($)
- ☐ Executive w/$

Activity Level

(gauge: MEDIUM)

Address
GO:

Holistic Health Forum

Description
The Holistic Health Forum tries to look at the whole person, stressing preventive measures an individual can take on his or her own behalf.

Subjects
Fitness, Health

Audience
General public

Content Summary
The libraries and message sections in this forum include such topics as herbs and plants, Chinese treatments, health graphics, diet and exercise, women's health, chiropractic, health politics, and the natural foods business. In the Healing & the Mind library (Library 10), you can learn about crystal healing and psychic holistic health. The Nutritional Therapy library (Library 3) contains a text file on antioxidants.

See Also
Health and Fitness Forum, Health and Vitamin Express, Health Database Plus($), Health/Fitness, HealthNet

User Guide
- ☑ Windows
- ☑ DOS
- ☑ Macintosh
- ☐ Terminal Emulation
- ☑ VMS
- ☑ UNIX
- ☑ OS/2
- ☑ Other platform

336

Holistic Health Forum – Home Building

Cost
- ☐ Unknown
- ☐ Basic
- ☒ Extended
- ☐ Premium ($)
- ☐ Executive w/$

Activity Level — MEDIUM (arrow pointing up between LOW and HIGH)

Address
GO: **HOLISTIC**

Hollywood Hotline

Description
This service is devoted to the noteworthy events that happen in Hollywood and includes a Hollywood trivia quiz.

Subjects
Entertainment, Gossip

Audience
General public

Content Summary
If you want to find out what's going on in Hollywood or the movie business, stop by the Hollywood Hotline. You can read entertainment news, peruse an online entertainment encyclopedia, see film and TV ratings, read movie reviews, and take a quiz (in terminal emulation mode). The SHOWBIZQUIZ menu features games on Frank Sinatra, Judy Garland, Clint Eastwood, Wizard of Oz, TV Detective Puzzle, and many more.

See Also
Roger Ebert's Movie Reviews, SHOWBIZ Quiz, ShowBiz-Media Forum

User Guide
- ☒ Windows
- ☒ DOS
- ☒ Macintosh
- ☐ Terminal Emulation
- ☒ VMS
- ☒ UNIX
- ☒ OS/2
- ☒ Other platform

Cost
- ☐ Unknown
- ☒ Basic
- ☐ Extended
- ☐ Premium ($)
- ☐ Executive w/$

Activity level — UNKNOWN (MEDIUM, between LOW and HIGH)

Address
GO: **HOLLYWOOD**

HOME BUILDING

Family Handyman Forum

Description
This forum is for people who like to do home repairs and improvements, work with tools, do woodworking, or have questions about home repairs.

Subjects
Family, General Interest, Home Building

Audience
General public, general contractors, families

Content Summary
Sponsered by Family Handyman magazine, this forum is intended to help you find answers to your questions about tools, household repairs, and a variety of other topics. When you join this forum, you'll meet people with experience in home maintenance and repair, house building and remodeling, woodworking, painting, plumbing, tools, old houses, and electricity. You also have access to articles from The Family Handyman magazine and a chance to interact with its editors. The Handy Hint section (Message section 15) is a great place to get and leave tips and hints for household problems.

See Also
Automobile Forum, Cook's Online Forum, Gardening Forum, Masonry Forum, Outdoor Forum

User Guide
- ☒ Windows
- ☒ DOS
- ☒ Macintosh
- ☐ Terminal Emulation
- ☒ VMS
- ☒ UNIX
- ☒ OS/2
- ☒ Other platform

Cost
- ☐ Unknown
- ☐ Basic
- ☒ Extended
- ☐ Premium ($)
- ☐ Executive w/$

Activity Level — MEDIUM (arrow pointing toward LOW)

Address
GO: **HANDYMAN**

Home Forum

Description
This forum is about homes. What more can you say?

Subjects
Food, Hobbies, Home Building

Audience
General public, horticulture enthusiasts

Content Summary
You can find out information, tips, hints, and the like here, regardless of the type of home you live in, including apartments, condos, or older homes. Topics such as security, home building, interior furnishing, outdoor living, lighting, and the kitchen are included in the message and library sections. If you want to wire your house for a computer network, for example, look in the Conveniences library (Library 7) for a text file that explains it. You also might want to cut down on the amount of fat you serve at Thanksgiving, Christmas, or other holiday meals. The In the Kitchen library (Library 9) tells you how to substitute shrimp and crab meat for your hor d'oeuvres.

See Also
Family Handyman Forum, Gardening Forum

User Guide
- ☑ Windows
- ☑ DOS
- ☑ Macintosh
- ☐ Terminal Emulation
- ☑ VMS
- ☑ UNIX
- ☑ OS/2
- ☑ Other platform

Cost
- ☐ Unknown
- ☐ Basic
- ☑ Extended
- ☐ Premium ($)
- ☐ Executive w/$

Activity Level
MEDIUM (arrow pointing up between LOW and HIGH)

Address
GO: **HOME**

HOME-BASED BUSINESS

Entrepreneur Magazine

Description
This area is known also as the Small Business Emporium, from which you can find over 165 entrepreneur business guides. These guides will help you find businesses you can run from home, start in your spare time, and begin with little investment.

Subjects
Small Business, Home-Based Business, Entrepreneurs

Audience
Entrepreneurs, home-based business owners, small-business owners, venture capitalists

Content Summary
After you get past the main menu in this area, you are given six choices from which to choose. From this menu, you can see the top 10 hottest businesses, see a directory of business guides, order a *Entrepreneur Magazine* subscription, and view a list of other business products such as videos and software products.

See Also
Entrepreneur's Small Business Forum, Entrepreneur's Small Business Square

User Guide
- ☑ Windows
- ☑ DOS
- ☑ Macintosh
- ☑ Terminal Emulation
- ☑ VMS
- ☑ UNIX
- ☑ OS/2
- ☑ Other platform

Cost
- ☐ Unknown
- ☑ Basic
- ☐ Extended
- ☐ Premium ($)
- ☐ Executive w/$

Activity Level
UNKNOWN (between LOW and HIGH, MEDIUM above)

Address
GO: **ENT**

Home Forum

Description
This forum is about homes. What more can you say?

Subjects
Food, Hobbies, Home Building

Audience
General public, horticulture enthusiasts

Content Summary
You can find out information, tips, hints, and the like here, regardless of the type of home you live in, including apartments, condos, or older homes. Topics such as security, home building, interior furnishing, outdoor living, lighting, and the kitchen are included in the message and library sections. If you want to wire your house for a computer network, for example, look in the Conveniences library (Library 7) for a text file that explains it. You also might want to cut down on the amount of fat you serve at Thanksgiving, Christmas, or other holiday meals. The In the Kitchen library (Library 9) tells you how to substitute shrimp and crab meat for your hor d'oeuvres.

See Also
Family Handyman Forum, Gardening Forum

User Guide
- ☑ Windows
- ☑ DOS
- ☑ Macintosh
- ☐ Terminal Emulation
- ☑ VMS
- ☑ UNIX
- ☑ OS/2
- ☑ Other platform

Home Forum – Hotel Management

Cost
- ☐ Unknown
- ☐ Basic
- ☑ Extended
- ☐ Premium ($)
- ☐ Executive w/$

Activity Level

MEDIUM (arrow pointing to medium, between LOW and HIGH)

Address
GO: **HOME**

Homefinder By AMS

Description
Looking for a new home? Are you relocating to a new city? Use this service to help you find what you're looking for.

Subjects
Real Estate

Audience
General public, real estate brokers

Content Summary
From the Homefinder by AMS main menu, you can choose from several different options, including Community Information/Relocation Consultation, Schoolmatch - School System Evaluations, Right Choice, Inc. - Cost of Living Analysis, and Capability Corporation (CAPCO) - Job Search Services. You also can read testimonials from other users, make referrals, and leave messages to the service.

See Also
The Home Forum

User Guide
- ☑ Windows
- ☑ DOS
- ☑ Macintosh
- ☐ Terminal Emulation
- ☑ VMS
- ☑ UNIX
- ☑ OS/2
- ☑ Other platform

Cost
- ☐ Unknown
- ☑ Basic
- ☐ Extended
- ☐ Premium ($)
- ☐ Executive w/$

Activity Level

UNKNOWN (gauge)

Address
GO: **HF**

HORTICULTURE

Gardening Forum

Description
This forum is dedicated to plants and gardening, and offers tips and ideas on ways to make your gardening and lawn maintenance experience more enjoyable.

Subjects
Genius, Horticulture, Plants

Audience
General public, horticulturists

Content Summary
If you're into vegetable, fruit, or flower gardening, exotic plants (such as orchids or bonsai), or just want to know the best way to make your grass grow, check out this forum's libraries and message sections. The forum managers are from *National Gardening Magazine*. You'll find libraries about herbs, bulbs, fruits, berries, nuts, tools, books, roses, and fertilizer.

See Also
Earth Forum, Outdoor Forum

User Guide
- ☑ Windows
- ☑ DOS
- ☑ Macintosh
- ☐ Terminal Emulation
- ☑ VMS
- ☑ UNIX
- ☑ OS/2
- ☑ Other platform

Cost
- ☐ Unknown
- ☐ Basic
- ☑ Extended
- ☐ Premium ($)
- ☐ Executive w/$

Activity

(arrow between LOW and MEDIUM)

Address
GO: **GARDENING**

HOTEL MANAGEMENT

Inn and Lodging Forum

Description
This is the Lanier's Inn and Lodging forum, dedicated to discussions about alternative accommodations—places other than the chain hotels.

Subjects
Hotel Management, Travel

Hotel Management – HP Handhelds Forum

Audience
Tourists, General Public

Content Summary
Lanier's Inn and Lodging Forum is a place to talk about the places you've discovered off the beaten path, and learn about new ways to take advantage of what bed and breakfast inns, all-suite hotels, and other forms of alternative accommodations have to offer. It's also a place to meet the people behind the scenes—the professionals who make your business and leisure travel the success it is. You can use libraries and message sections such as Innkeeping Dreams, B&B Recipe Exchanges, Elegant Hotels, and more.

See Also
Travel Forum, Bed & Breakfast Database

User Guide
- ☑ Windows
- ☑ DOS
- ☑ Macintosh
- ☐ Terminal Emulation
- ☑ VMS
- ☑ UNIX
- ☑ OS/2
- ☑ Other platform

Cost
- ☐ Unknown
- ☐ Basic
- ☑ Extended
- ☐ Premium ($)
- ☐ Executive w/$

Activity Level

Address
GO: **INNFORUM**

HOTELS

ABC Worldwide Hotel Guide

Description
The ABC Worldwide Hotel Guide provides up-to-date comprehensive listings of over 60,000 hotel properties worldwide.

Subjects
Hotels, Travel

Audience
Travelers

Content Summary
Within this forum, you can find information about the locations, addresses, services offered, and which credit cards are accepted at the member hotel and resorts.

See Also
Travel Forum

User Guide
- ☑ Windows
- ☑ DOS
- ☑ Macintosh
- ☐ Terminal Emulation
- ☑ VMS
- ☑ UNIX
- ☑ OS/2
- ☑ Other platform

Cost
- ☐ Unknown
- ☐ Basic
- ☑ Extended
- ☐ Premium ($)
- ☐ Executive w/$

Activity Level

Address
GO: **ABC**

HP Handhelds Forum

Description
This forum is designed to help you get the most out of your HP handheld computer, HP palmtop, or HP calculator.

Subjects
Computer Hardware, Computers, Field Computing

Audience
Computer programmers, computer professionals, computer users

Content Summary
You can get answers to your technical questions, exchange information with other users, take advantage of shareware and other files on the libraries, and stay in touch with the latest news from HP and third-parties. The many libraries include areas for 1x,2x,3x calculators, 4x,6x,7x,9x calculators, the 95LX, the 100/200LX, HPHAND, and an area for Palmtop programmers.

See Also
HP OmniBook Forum, HP Peripherals Forum, HP Specials

User Guide
- ☐ Windows
- ☐ DOS
- ☐ Macintosh
- ☐ Terminal Emulation
- ☐ VMS
- ☐ UNIX
- ☐ OS/2
- ☑ Other platform

Cost
- ☐ Unknown
- ☐ Basic
- ☑ Extended
- ☐ Premium ($)
- ☐ Executive w/$

Activity Level
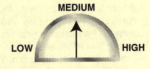

HP Handhelds Forum – HP Specials

Address
GO: **HPHAND**

HP Omnibook Forum

Description
Find out the latest on the HP Omnibook in this forum.

Subjects
Computers

Audience
Computer users

Content Summary
Not officially sponsored by HP, this forum can help you find the answers you might need for your HP Omnibook. This forum also will keep you up-to-date with the latest information from HP and other vendors, and let you access a collection of application notes, tips, and software for your OmniBook.

See Also
HP Specials, HP Peripherals Forum

User Guide
- ☑ Windows
- ☑ DOS
- ☐ Macintosh
- ☐ Terminal Emulation
- ☐ VMS
- ☐ UNIX
- ☐ OS/2
- ☐ Other platform

Cost
- ☐ Unknown
- ☐ Basic
- ☑ Extended
- ☐ Premium ($)
- ☐ Executive w/$

Activity Level MEDIUM

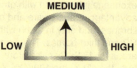

Address
GO: **HPOMNIBOOK**

HP Peripherals Forum

Description
This is Hewlett-Packard's forum for disseminating information about HP peripherals, such as its DeskJet and LaserJet printers.

Subjects
Computers

Audience
Management information specialists, computer users

Content Summary
This forum is sponsored by Hewlett-Packard as a distribution channel for information about HP peripherals. The forum may also be used to get assistance from other users. You should note, however, that HP does not respond to technical questions posted in this forum. You can find files, support questions and answers, and press releases about printers, fax products, and other HP peripherals. Don't miss the library and message areas on their TWAIN support.

See Also
HP Specials

User Guide
- ☑ Windows
- ☑ DOS
- ☑ Macintosh
- ☐ Terminal Emulation
- ☐ VMS
- ☐ UNIX
- ☐ OS/2
- ☐ Other platform

Cost
- ☐ Unknown
- ☐ Basic
- ☑ Extended
- ☐ Premium ($)
- ☐ Executive w/$

Activity Level MEDIUM

Address
GO: **HPPER**

HP Specials

Description
Can't find it in the other HP forums? Maybe it's in this area.

Subjects
Computers

Audience
Computer users, management information specialists

Content Summary
Files located in the HP Special Library differ from files located in HP forum libraries. Some of the files in the HP Special Library area may have licensing agreements that prevent distribution in HP forum libraries. Other files may have charges associated with them in addition to the normal CompuServe connect time charges required to download the file. As new files become available in the HP Special Library, they will be announced in the HP Forums.

See Also
HP Handheld Forum, HP OmniBook Forum, HP Peripherals Forum, HP Systems Forum

User Guide
- ☑ Windows
- ☑ DOS
- ☑ Macintosh
- ☑ Terminal Emulation
- ☐ VMS
- ☐ UNIX
- ☐ OS/2
- ☑ Other platform

Cost
- ☐ Unknown
- ☐ Basic
- ☑ Extended
- ☐ Premium ($)
- ☐ Executive w/$

HP Specials – HSX Open Forum

Activity Level: UNKNOWN (Low / Medium / High)

Address
GO: **HPSPEC**

HP Systems Forum

Description
This forum, sponsored by Hewlett-Packard, is intended to provide support and services for HP products such as Dashboard, EtherTwist, and NewWave.

Subjects
Computers

Audience
Management information specialists, computer users

Content Summary
The several libraries in forum include topics such as HP mass storage, Vectra, NetServer PCs, Windows clients, EtherTwist, NewWave, and HP-UX systems. You can find patches, tips and hints, utilities, and other files for various HP products in the libraries. If you use Dashboard, download the Top Ten Tips file in the Dashboard/misc. apps library (Library 11).

See Also
HP Specials, HP Peripherals Forum, HP OmniBook Forum, HP Handheld Forum

User Guide
- ☑ Windows
- ☑ DOS
- ☐ Macintosh
- ☐ Terminal Emulation
- ☐ VMS
- ☑ UNIX
- ☐ OS/2
- ☑ Other platform

Cost
- ☐ Unknown
- ☐ Basic
- ☑ Extended
- ☐ Premium ($)
- ☐ Executive w/$

Activity Level
MEDIUM (arrow pointing up)

Address
GO: **HPSYS**

HSX Adult Forum

Description
The Human Sexuality (HSX) Support Groups are online self-help groups where you can freely discuss your feelings and relationships.

Subjects
Biology, General Interest, Human Behavior, Sexuality

Audience
General public

Content Summary
To gain access to the closed areas in this forum, see the text file CLOSED.TXT in the HSX Help Files library (Library 16). It's the one that has been downloaded over 60,000 times! If you don't want to join in the closed areas, see the HSX Open Forum (HSX100).

See Also
HSX Open Forum, Human Sexuality Databank

User Guide
- ☑ Windows
- ☑ DOS
- ☑ Macintosh
- ☐ Terminal Emulation
- ☑ VMS
- ☑ UNIX
- ☑ OS/2
- ☑ Other platform

Cost
- ☐ Unknown
- ☐ Basic
- ☑ Extended
- ☐ Premium ($)
- ☐ Executive w/$

Activity Level
MEDIUM (arrow between Medium and High)

Address
GO: **HSX200**

HSX Open Forum

Description
The Human Sexuality (HSX) Support Groups are online self-help groups where you can freely discuss your feelings and relationships.

Subjects
General Interest, Human Behavior, Sexuality

Audience
General public

Content Summary
The following is the membership message in the HSX Open Forum: "The HSX Support Groups are online support (self-help) groups. Members share feelings and experiences, and provide one another with assistance and encouragement. Our goal is to create a compassionate community where members can freely discuss emotions and relationships. Here you can meet new friends and find sympathy and support. In the HSX forums, you'll find a warm place where people like you gather and talk about personal issues."

See Also
Human Sexuality Databank, HSX Adult Forum

User Guide
- ☑ Windows
- ☑ DOS
- ☑ Macintosh
- ☐ Terminal Emulation
- ☑ VMS
- ☑ UNIX
- ☑ OS/2
- ☑ Other platform

Cost
- ☐ Unknown
- ☐ Basic
- ☑ Extended
- ☐ Premium ($)
- ☐ Executive w/$

Activity level

Address

HUMAN RIGHTS

Issues Forum

Description
Devoted to current topics and issues, the Issues Forum discusses topics such as Afro-Americanism, parenting, human rights, and others.

Subjects
Current Events, Human Rights, Politics, Religion

Audience
General public

Content Summary
This special interest group is devoted to discussions of a wide variety of issues. Currently, there are sections for topics such as Afro-American issues, parenting issues, human rights, unexplained phenomena, men and women's issues, Asian-American issues, and others. The library and message sections include Culture & Society, Between the Sexes, Canadian Issues, Politics & Religion, and more. Look in Library 9, Rush H. Limbaugh, for summaries of Rush's show.

See Also
Entertainment Center, HSX Open Forum

User Guide
- ☑ Windows
- ☑ DOS
- ☑ Macintosh
- ☐ Terminal Emulation
- ☑ VMS
- ☑ UNIX
- ☑ OS/2
- ☑ Other platform

Cost
- ☐ Unknown
- ☐ Basic
- ☑ Extended
- ☐ Premium ($)
- ☐ Executive w/$

Activity Level

Address
GO: ISSUESFORUM

Human Sexuality Databank

Description
Presented by Howard and Martha Lewis, the Human Sexuality Databank provides information on topics such as gynecology, sexual therapy, and more.

Subjects
Health, Sexuality

Audience
Health care providers, general public

Content Summary
Because this area discusses sexually explicit topics, only people comfortable with all sex-related subjects and their frank treatment are advised to use this service. The Human Sexuality Databank main menu includes updates to the service, questions and answers posted by members and service administrators, a dictionary of sexual terms, hotline for your questions and comments, the 30 most-asked questions, and a letters sections. You also can enter forums where you can join in live talk with other members.

See Also
HSX Adult Forum, HSX Open Forum

User Guide
- ☑ Windows
- ☑ DOS
- ☑ Macintosh
- ☐ Terminal Emulation
- ☑ VMS
- ☑ UNIX
- ☑ OS/2
- ☑ Other platform

Cost
- ☐ Unknown
- ☐ Basic
- ☑ Extended
- ☐ Premium ($)
- ☐ Executive w/$

Activity level

Address
GO: HUMAN

HYPOGLYCEMIA

Diabetes Forum

Description
An online community for people with a common interest in diabetes, hypoglycemia, and related chronic metabolic disorders. Family members and friends of these people also are welcome to join and participate in this lively area.

Subjects
Diabetes, Health, Hypoglycemia

Audience
Diabetes patients, family and friends, hypoglycemia patients, medical personnel

Content Summary
The library and message areas are full of information about these disorders, including files on general diabetes information and explanation of diabetic terms. You also can find files and messages for the friends and family, hypoglycemics, insulin information, oral medications, diet and exercise, complications associated with diabetes, pumping, various technologies and theories, and pregnancy and diabetes. Library 17, "Youth Connection," is devoted to young people with diabetes and includes graphics, games, and stories for the young.

See Also
Health and Fitness Forum, Health/Fitness, HealthNet, Health Database Plus, Physicians Data Query

User Guide
- ☑ Windows
- ☑ DOS
- ☑ Macintosh
- ☐ Terminal Emulation
- ☑ VMS
- ☑ UNIX
- ☑ OS/2
- ☐ Other platform

Cost
- ☐ Unknown
- ☐ Basic
- ☑ Extended
- ☐ Premium ($)
- ☐ Executive w/$

Activity Level
MEDIUM

Address
GO: **DIABETES**

I — IBM

IBM Applications Forum

Description
This forum is devoted to the topic of general applications on the IBM PC and any and all other compatible computers.

Subjects
Computer Applications, Computers, IBM PCs

Audience
Computer users

Content Summary
Find out information about IBM and IBM PC compatible software, including word processors, text editors, DBMS, accounting, general applications, graphics, education, desktop publishing, and more.

See Also
Microsoft Connection, Lotus Technical Library

User Guide
- ☑ Windows
- ☑ DOS
- ☐ Macintosh
- ☐ Terminal Emulation
- ☐ VMS
- ☐ UNIX
- ☑ OS/2
- ☑ Other platform

Cost
- ☐ Unknown
- ☐ Basic
- ☑ Extended
- ☐ Premium ($)
- ☐ Executive w/$

Activity Level

Address
GO: **IBMAPP**

IBM CAD/CAM Forum

Description
This forum is devoted to the users and/or potential users of IBM CAD/CAM application products. The products supported in this forum are CATIA, CADAM, and other products relating to CAD/CAM.

Subjects
Computers, IBM

Audience
Computer users, computer engineers

Contents Summary
The library and message sections include RLM Q&A, CAITIA AIX SYS Q&A, CADAM HOST SYS Q&A, CADAM How-To Guides, and more.

See Also
IBM Applications Forum

User Guide
- ☐ Windows
- ☑ DOS
- ☐ Macintosh
- ☐ Terminal Emulation
- ☐ VMS
- ☑ UNIX
- ☐ OS/2
- ☑ Other platform

Cost
- ☐ Unknown
- ☐ Basic
- ☑ Extended
- ☐ Premium ($)
- ☐ Executive w/$

Activity Level

Address
GO: **IBMENG**

IBM DB2 Database Forum

Description
This forum is designed for people interested in or currently using the DB2/2, DB2/6000, DB2 Clients, DB2/VSE&VM (SQL/DS), DB2/MVS relational database products, as well as Visualizer and IMS products.

Subjects
Computers, Databases, IBM

Audience
Management information specialists, computer users, database managers

Content Summary
You can find the following libraries in this forum: DB2/2, DB2/6000, DB2/VSE&VM, DB2/MVS, DB2 Clients, Visualizer, IMS Family, and Open Forum.

See Also
Client Server Computing Forum

User Guide
- ☐ Windows
- ☑ DOS
- ☐ Macintosh
- ☐ Terminal Emulation
- ☐ VMS
- ☑ UNIX
- ☑ OS/2
- ☑ Other platform

Cost
- ☐ Unknown
- ☐ Basic
- ☑ Extended
- ☐ Premium ($)
- ☐ Executive w/$

Activity Level

Address
GO: **IBMDB2**

IBM

IBM File Finder

Description
If it's on CompuServe and in a computer-related forum, you should be able to find it with this service. This searchable database is useful if you are looking for a number of files that are in several known or unknown forums.

Subjects
Computers, Databases, IBM PCs

Audience
Computer users, management information specialists

Content Summary
With File Finder, you can use seven common search criteria for finding the location of a desired file or files. You can search by topic, file submission date, forum name, file type, file extension, file name, or submitter's User Id. File descriptions, forum, and library location are displayed for the matched files, giving instant information on where to find a most wanted file.

See Also
MS Software Library

User Guide
- ☑ Windows
- ☑ DOS
- ☑ Macintosh
- ☐ Terminal Emulation
- ☐ VMS
- ☑ UNIX
- ☑ OS/2
- ☑ Other platform

Cost
- ☐ Unknown
- ☐ Basic
- ☑ Extended
- ☐ Premium ($)
- ☐ Executive w/$

Activity Level

Address
GO: **IBMFF**

IBM Hardware Forum

Description
This forum is devoted to the topic of hardware on the IBM PC and any other compatible computers.

Subjects
Computers, Hardware, IBM PCs

Audience
Management information specialists, computer users

Content Summary
You can find library and message areas such as Disk/Disk Utilities, Printer Utilities, Video, PC-AT, Classifieds, PCJr, Tape, and more.

See Also
IBM Applications Forum

User Guide
- ☑ Windows
- ☑ DOS
- ☐ Macintosh
- ☐ Terminal Emulation
- ☐ VMS
- ☐ UNIX
- ☑ OS/2
- ☑ Other platform

Cost
- ☐ Unknown
- ☐ Basic
- ☑ Extended
- ☐ Premium ($)
- ☐ Executive w/$

Activity Level

Address
GO: **IBMHW**

IBM ImagePlus Forum

Description
You can get support for IBM's ImagePlus system for IP/2, IP/AS400, and IP/MVS.

Subjects
Computer Graphics, Computers, IBM

Audience
Computer users, management information specialists

Content Summary
The libraries in this forum include IP/2 Info, IP/2 General Questions, IP/2 Support, IP/AS400 Info, Visualinfo Info, and more.

See Also
IBM Applications Forum

User Guide
- ☐ Windows
- ☐ DOS
- ☐ Macintosh
- ☐ Terminal Emulation
- ☐ VMS
- ☑ UNIX
- ☑ OS/2
- ☑ Other platform

Cost
- ☐ Unknown
- ☐ Basic
- ☑ Extended
- ☐ Premium ($)
- ☐ Executive w/$

Activity Level
Medium, between low and high (arrow pointing left)

Address
GO: **IBMIMAGE**

IBM Languages Forum

Description
This forum is for questions, answers, and discussion regarding IBM languages, including APL and APL2.

Subjects
Computer Programming Languages, Computers, IBM

Audience
Management information specialists, computer programmers

Content Summary
This forum contains the following libraries: General Library, APL2 Language, APL2 for OS/2 Demo, APL2 for OS/2 CSD, and APL2 User Files.

See Also
IBM OS/2 Developer 1 Forum, IBM OS/2 Developer 2 Forum, IBM Systems/Util. Forum

User Guide
- [ ] Windows
- [ ] DOS
- [ ] Macintosh
- [ ] Terminal Emulation
- [ ] VMS
- [ ] UNIX
- [x] OS/2
- [x] Other platform

Cost
- [ ] Unknown
- [ ] Basic
- [x] Extended
- [ ] Premium ($)
- [ ] Executive w/$

Activity Level
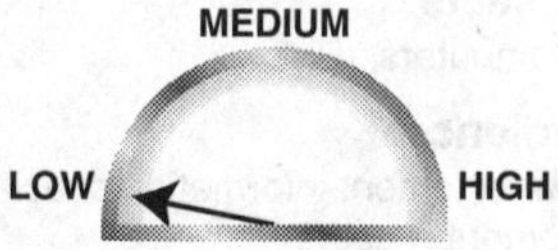
MEDIUM
LOW
HIGH

Address
GO: **IBMLANG**

IBM LMU2 Forum

Description
This forum is an open forum for the discussion of all topics related to LAN Management Utilities/2 (LMU/2).

Subjects
Computers, IBM, Networking

Audience
Computer users, management information specialists

See Also
IBM File Finder

Content Summary
This forum includes libraries named Common Questions, Tools/Samples, News/Announcements, LMU/2 V2 Updates, and LMU Updates.

See Also
IBM File Finder

User Guide
- [ ] Windows
- [ ] DOS
- [ ] Macintosh
- [ ] Terminal Emulation
- [ ] VMS
- [ ] UNIX
- [x] OS/2
- [ ] Other platform

Cost
- [ ] Unknown
- [ ] Basic
- [x] Extended
- [ ] Premium ($)
- [ ] Executive w/$

Activity Level
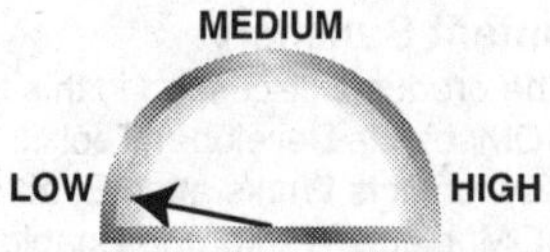
MEDIUM
LOW
HIGH

Address
GO: **LMUFORUM**

IBM New User's Forum

Description
This forum is devoted to newer users of CompuServe and the PC, as well as those who like to join in and share their experience with new comers. In addition, you'll find an excellent selection of games and entertainment files.

Subjects
Computer Users, IBM PCs

Audience
Computer users

Content Summary
If you're new to using CompuServe or your PC (or both), use this forum to get comfortable downloading files, learn different applications, and have fun with your computer. The libraries include Download Help, Library Tools, Adventures, Music, Fun Graphics, Windows Fun, and more.

See Also
CompuServe Help Forum (FREE)

User Guide
- [x] Windows
- [x] DOS
- [ ] Macintosh
- [ ] Terminal Emulation
- [ ] VMS
- [ ] UNIX
- [x] OS/2
- [x] Other platform

Cost
- [ ] Unknown
- [ ] Basic
- [x] Extended
- [ ] Premium ($)
- [ ] Executive w/$

Activity Level
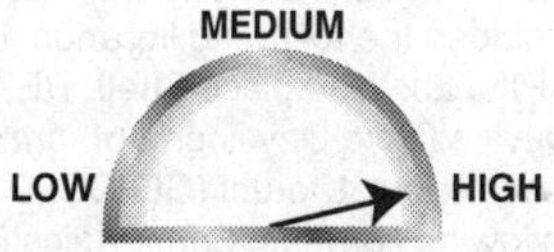
MEDIUM
LOW
HIGH

Address
GO: **IBMNEW**

IBM Object Technology Forum

Description
The IBMSOM Forum provides service and support for the IBM SOMobjects products.

Subjects
Computers, IBM

Audience
Computer users, computer programmers, IBM users

Content Summary
The products discussed in this forum include SOMobjects Developer Toolkit, Version 2.0, SOMobjects Workstation Enabler, Version 2.0, and SOMobjects Workgroup Enabler, Version 2.0.

See Also
IBM Languages Forum

User Guide
- [ ] Windows
- [ ] DOS
- [ ] Macintosh
- [ ] Terminal Emulation
- [ ] VMS
- [ ] UNIX
- [x] OS/2
- [ ] Other platform

Cost
- [ ] Unknown
- [ ] Basic
- [x] Extended
- [ ] Premium ($)
- [ ] Executive w/$

Activity Level
MEDIUM (arrow pointing up)

Address
GO: **IBMOBJ**

IBM OS/2 Developers Forums

Description
The IBM OS/2 Developers 1 and 2 forums contain information for OS/2 developers, including development tools, debugging, and other questions.

Subjects
Computer Programming Languages, Computers, IBM

Audience
Computer programmers, management information specialists

Content Summary
The IBM OS/2 Developers 1 forum (GO OS2DF1) includes the following libraries: Base OS API's, PM API's, 2.x Workplace Shell, REXX/Other Languages, Device Drive Development, and more. The IBM OS/2 Developers 1 forum (GO OS2DF1) includes the following libraries: Communications Manager, LAN Server, TCP/IP, CID Enablement, Pen Software, and more.

See Also
IBM OS/2 B Vendors Forum, IBM Object Technology Forum, IBM OS/2 Support Forum, IBM OS/2 Vendor Forum

User Guide
- [ ] Windows
- [ ] DOS
- [ ] Macintosh
- [ ] Terminal Emulation
- [ ] VMS
- [ ] UNIX
- [x] OS/2
- [ ] Other platform

Cost
- [ ] Unknown
- [ ] Basic
- [x] Extended
- [ ] Premium ($)
- [ ] Executive w/$

Activity Level
MEDIUM (arrow pointing toward HIGH)

Address
GO: **OS2DFI** or **OS2DF2**

IBM OS/2 Service Pak

Description
If you are having problems with OS/2, you should visit this service and download the ServicePaks, which offer fixes to common problems.

Subjects
Computers, IBM

Audience
Management information specialists, IBM users, computer users

Content Summary
The ServicePak contains OS/2 product fixes for reported customer problems and problems identified by IBM. The ServicePak also contains certain product enhancements, including additional video graphics adapter ship set support, and drivers. The version control number for this General Availability ServicePak product is XR06100. If you have not had problems with OS/2 2.0 or OS/2 2.0 with ServicePak 1 installed, you do not need to download ServicePak 2.

See Also
IBM OS/2 Support Forum, IBM OS/2 Users Forum

User Guide
- [ ] Windows
- [ ] DOS
- [ ] Macintosh
- [ ] Terminal Emulation
- [ ] VMS
- [ ] UNIX
- [x] OS/2
- [ ] Other platform

Cost
- [ ] Unknown
- [ ] Basic
- [x] Extended
- [ ] Premium ($)
- [ ] Executive w/$

Activity Level
UNKNOWN

Address
GO: **OS2SERV**

IBM OS/2 Support Forum

Description
Get general OS/2 support help from this forum directly from IBM and other members.

Subjects
Computer Users, IBM

Audience
Computer users, management information specialists, IBM users

Content Summary
The library and message sections include Installation Questions, H/W - I/O Media, H/W - Platform, REXX/Language Questions, Windows Application Questions, IBM Files, and much more.

See Also
IBM OS/2 Service Pak, IBM PowerPC Forum

User Guide
- ☐ Windows
- ☐ DOS
- ☐ Macintosh
- ☐ Terminal Emulation
- ☐ VMS
- ☐ UNIX
- ☑ OS/2
- ☐ Other platform

Cost
- ☐ Unknown
- ☐ Basic
- ☑ Extended
- ☐ Premium ($)
- ☐ Executive w/$

Activity Level
MEDIUM / HIGH

Address
GO: **OS2SUPPORT**

IBM OS/2 Users Forum

Description
Whether you're a new user to OS/2 or a seasoned OS/2 bigot, you should join this forum and its discussions on hardware and software issues as they relate to OS/2.

Subjects
Computer Users, IBM

Audience
IBM users, computer users

Content Summary
The library and message sections include OS/2 Public Image, OS/2 & Hardware, Application Questions, New User Questions, OS/2 User Groups, and more.

See Also
IBM OS/2 Support Forum

User Guide
- ☐ Windows
- ☐ DOS
- ☐ Macintosh
- ☐ Terminal Emulation
- ☐ VMS
- ☐ UNIX
- ☑ OS/2
- ☐ Other platform

Cost
- ☐ Unknown
- ☐ Basic
- ☑ Extended
- ☐ Premium ($)
- ☐ Executive w/$

Activity Level
MEDIUM

Address
GO: **OS2USER**

IBM OS/2 Vendor Forums

Description
The OS/2 A Vendor and OS/2 B Vendor forums contain information from various vendors of OS/2 products and services.

Subjects
Computers, IBM

Audience
IBM users, computer users

Content Summary
The IBM OS/2 A Vendor forum includes these vendors: OS/2 Magazine, One UP, JDS Publishing, Sundial Systems, and others. The IBM OS/2 B Vendor forum includes these vendors: OS/2 Shareware, PCX, Carry Associates, MSR Development, and more.

See Also
IBM OS/2 Support Forum, IBM OS/2 Users Forum

User Guide
- ☐ Windows
- ☐ DOS
- ☐ Macintosh
- ☐ Terminal Emulation
- ☐ VMS
- ☐ UNIX
- ☑ OS/2
- ☐ Other platform

Cost
- ☐ Unknown
- ☐ Basic
- ☑ Extended
- ☐ Premium ($)
- ☐ Executive w/$

Activity Level
MEDIUM / HIGH

Address
GO: **OS2AVEN** or **OS2BVEN**

IBM Personal Software Products

Description
This is the IBM Personal Software Products online store. You can get products and product information, and join the electronic mailing list.

Subjects
Computers, IBM

Audience
IBM users, computer users

Content Summary
From the main menu, you can select to shop the store, download an OS/2 demo, get OS/2 user tips and information on technical support. You also can get information on IBM's line of other products, including multimedia and networking.

See Also
IBM Apllications Forum

User Guide
- [ ] Windows
- [ ] DOS
- [ ] Macintosh
- [ ] Terminal Emulation
- [ ] VMS
- [ ] UNIX
- [x] OS/2
- [x] Other platform

Cost
- [ ] Unknown
- [x] Basic
- [ ] Extended
- [ ] Premium ($)
- [ ] Executive w/$

Activity Level

Address
GO: **IBMPSP**

IBM PowerPC Forum

Description
Interested in the PowerPC? If so, come to this forum and get up-to-date information on this new microprocessor.

Subjects
Computers, IBM

Audience
Computer users, management information specialists

Content Summary
Libraries include Press Releases/Announcements, General Information, Publication Index, What is? (Glossary), Q&A Bank, Software, Hardware, and PowerPC Ref Platform.

See Also
IBM Hardware Forum

User Guide
- [x] Windows
- [ ] DOS
- [x] Macintosh
- [ ] Terminal Emulation
- [ ] VMS
- [ ] UNIX
- [ ] OS/2
- [ ] Other platform

Cost
- [ ] Unknown
- [ ] Basic
- [x] Extended
- [ ] Premium ($)
- [ ] Executive w/$

Activity Level

Address
GO: **POWERPC**

IBM Programming Forum

Description
This forum is devoted to helping those interested in programming for the IBM or IBM PC compatible computers.

Subjects
Computer Programming Languages, Computers

Audience
Computer programmers

Content Summary
You can get assemblers, source code, tips, and techniques from this forum. The library and message sections include OS Services, C and C++, BASIC, Other Languages, Tools/Debuggers, Job Exchange, VESA, and more.

See Also
IBM Languages Forum, Microsoft Languages Forum

User Guide
- [x] Windows
- [x] DOS
- [x] Macintosh
- [ ] Terminal Emulation
- [ ] VMS
- [x] UNIX
- [x] OS/2
- [x] Other platform

Cost
- [ ] Unknown
- [ ] Basic
- [x] Extended
- [ ] Premium ($)
- [ ] Executive w/$

Activity Level

Address
GO: **IBMPRO**

IBM Software Solutions Forum

Description
This forum offers information, tips and techniques, and sometimes upgrades to IBM software products. This forum is managed by the Cary, NJ IBM Lab.

Subjects
IBM

Audience
Computer Users

Content Summary
The libraries included in this forum are BookManager, VisualAge, Install for Windows, WITT, ReDiscovery, TIRS, and VisualGen.

See Also
IBM OS/2 Vendor Forum

User Guide
- [x] Windows
- [x] DOS
- [ ] Macintosh
- [ ] Terminal Emulation
- [ ] VMS
- [ ] UNIX
- [x] OS/2
- [x] Other platform

Cost
- [ ] Unknown
- [ ] Basic
- [x] Extended
- [ ] Premium ($)
- [ ] Executive w/$

Activity Level

Address
GO: **SOFSOL**

IBM Storage Systems Forum

Description
This forum has information concerning IBM Storage Systems Division Software Products, including information for the ADSTAR Distributed Storage Manager.

Subjects
Computers, IBM, Multimedia

Audience
Management information apecialists, computer users

Content Summary
The sections in this forum include ADSTAR Distributed Storage Manager (ADSM), ADSM Special Programs, ADSM BETA Program (private), and ADSM Developers Program (private).

See Also
IBM Software Solutions Forum

User Guide
- [ ] Windows
- [ ] DOS
- [ ] Macintosh
- [ ] Terminal Emulation
- [ ] VMS
- [ ] UNIX
- [x] OS/2
- [x] Other platform

Cost
- [ ] Unknown
- [ ] Basic
- [x] Extended
- [ ] Premium ($)
- [ ] Executive w/$

Activity Level

Address
GO: **IBMSTORAGE**

IBM ThinkPad Forum

Description
This forum is designed to exchange information, experiences, and opinions on the IBM ThinkPad, including application development concerns and questions.

Subjects
Computers, IBM

Audience
Computer users

Content Summary
This forum contains the following libraries: Hardware, Software, Options/Accessories, Audio Central, and User Uploads. Be sure to join in on the message sections to share and receive ideas and experiences about the ThinkPad.

See Also
IBM Hardware Forum

User Guide
- [ ] Windows
- [ ] DOS
- [ ] Macintosh
- [ ] Terminal Emulation
- [ ] VMS
- [ ] UNIX
- [ ] OS/2
- [x] Other platform

Cost
- [ ] Unknown
- [ ] Basic
- [x] Extended
- [ ] Premium ($)
- [ ] Executive w/$

Activity Level

Address
GO: **THINKPAD**

IBM Users Network

Description
This service provides a place for people who have a special interest in the IBM and compatible family of computers.

Subjects
Computers, IBM PCs

Audience
Computer users, IBM users

Content Summary
From the IBM Users Network main menu, you can choose from several options, including Top 10 Utilities, File Finder, New Users/Fun Forum, Communications Forum, ASP/Shareware Forum, and several other forum options. Use this service as a starting point to learn more about the forums that are available for IBM and IBM PC compatible computers.

See Also
MS Software Library, IBM File Finder

User Guide
- [x] Windows
- [x] DOS
- [ ] Macintosh
- [ ] Terminal Emulation
- [ ] VMS
- [ ] UNIX
- [x] OS/2
- [x] Other platform

Cost
- [ ] Unknown
- [ ] Basic
- [x] Extended
- [ ] Premium ($)
- [ ] Executive w/$

Activity Level
UNKNOWN

Address
GO: **IBMNET**

IBM PCS

IBM Applications Forum

Description
This forum is devoted to the topic of general applications on the IBM PC and any and all other compatible computers.

Subjects
Computer Applications, Computers, IBM PCs

Audience
Computer users

Content Summary
Find out information about IBM and IBM PC compatible software, including word processors, text editors, DBMS, accounting, general applications, graphics, education, desktop publishing, and more.

See Also
Microsoft Connection, Lotus Technical Library

User Guide
- [x] Windows
- [x] DOS
- [ ] Macintosh
- [ ] Terminal Emulation
- [ ] VMS
- [ ] UNIX
- [x] OS/2
- [x] Other platform

Cost
- [ ] Unknown
- [ ] Basic
- [x] Extended
- [ ] Premium ($)
- [ ] Executive w/$

Activity Level

MEDIUM-HIGH

Address
GO: **IBMAPP**

IBM Communications Forum

Description
This forum is devoted to the topic of telecommunications on the IBM PC and compatible computers.

Subjects
Communications, Computers, IBM PCs, Modems

Audience
Computer users, management information specialists

Contents Summary
You can find various utilities, files, support Q&A, and other communications information for the PC in this forum. The libraries include Autosig (ATO), Communications Utilities, Communications Programs, FAX, Hot Topics, Modems/Communications Hardware, and more.

See Also
Hayes Forum, Modem Vendor Forum

User Guide
- [x] Windows
- [x] DOS
- [ ] Macintosh
- [ ] Terminal Emulation
- [ ] VMS
- [ ] UNIX
- [x] OS/2
- [x] Other platform

Cost
- [ ] Unknown
- [ ] Basic
- [x] Extended
- [ ] Premium ($)
- [ ] Executive w/$

Activity Level

MEDIUM

Address
GO: **IBMCOM**

IBM File Finder

Description
If it's on CompuServe and in a computer-related forum, you should be able to find it with this service. This searchable database is useful if you are looking for a number of files that are in several known or unknown forums.

Subjects
Computers, Databases, IBM PCs

Audience
Computer users, management information specialists

Content Summary
With File Finder, you can use seven common search criteria for finding the location of a desired file or files. You can search by topic, file submission date, forum name, file type, file extension, file name, or submitter's User Id. File descriptions, forum, and library location are displayed for the matched files, giving instant information on where to find a most wanted file.

See Also
MS Software Library

User Guide
- ☑ Windows
- ☑ DOS
- ☑ Macintosh
- ☐ Terminal Emulation
- ☐ VMS
- ☑ UNIX
- ☑ OS/2
- ☑ Other platform

Cost
- ☐ Unknown
- ☐ Basic
- ☑ Extended
- ☐ Premium ($)
- ☐ Executive w/$

Activity Level

Address
GO: **IBMFF**

IBM Hardware Forum

Description
This forum is devoted to the topic of hardware on the IBM PC and any other compatible computers.

Subjects
Computers, Hardware, IBM PCs

Audience
Management information specialists, computer users

Content Summary
You can find library and message areas such as Disk/Disk Utilities, Printer Utilities, Video, PC-AT, Classifieds, PCJr, Tape, and more.

See Also
IBM Users Network

User Guide
- ☑ Windows
- ☑ DOS
- ☐ Macintosh
- ☐ Terminal Emulation
- ☐ VMS
- ☐ UNIX
- ☑ OS/2
- ☑ Other platform

Cost
- ☐ Unknown
- ☐ Basic
- ☑ Extended
- ☐ Premium ($)
- ☐ Executive w/$

Activity Level

Address
GO: **IBMHW**

IBM New User's Forum

Description
This forum is devoted to newer users of CompuServe and the PC, as well as those who like to join in and share their experience with new comers. In addition, you'll find an excellent selection of games and entertainment files.

Subjects
Computer Users, IBM PCs

Audience
Computer users

Content Summary
If you're new to using CompuServe or your PC (or both), use this forum to get comfortable downloading files, learn different applications, and have fun with your computer. The libraries include Download Help, Library Tools, Adventures, Music, Fun Graphics, Windows Fun, and more.

See Also
CompuServe Help Forum (FREE)

User Guide
- ☑ Windows
- ☑ DOS
- ☑ Macintosh
- ☐ Terminal Emulation
- ☐ VMS
- ☐ UNIX
- ☑ OS/2
- ☑ Other platform

Cost
- ☐ Unknown
- ☐ Basic
- ☑ Extended
- ☐ Premium ($)
- ☐ Executive w/$

Activity Level

IBM Systems/Utilities Forum

Address
GO: **IBMNEW**

Description
Find the most current utilities for your IBM or IBM compatible PC, including files for Windows, MS-DOS, PC-DOS, and OS/2.

Subjects
Computers, IBM PCs

Audience
Computer users

Content Summary
The library and message sections include the following: DOS Utilities, OS/2 Utilities, General Utilities, Multitasking, DOS Shells/Managers, File Utilities, Desktop Utilities, Demos, and Disk Library.

See Also
IBM File Finder, MS Software Library

User Guide
- ☑ Windows
- ☑ DOS
- ☐ Macintosh
- ☐ Terminal Emulation
- ☐ VMS
- ☐ UNIX
- ☑ OS/2
- ☐ Other platform

Cost
- ☐ Unknown
- ☐ Basic
- ☑ Extended
- ☐ Premium ($)
- ☐ Executive w/$

Activity Level

Address
GO: **IBMSYS**

IBM Users Network

Description
This service provides a place for people who have a special interest in the IBM and compatible family of computers.

Subjects
Computers, IBM PCs

Audience
Computer users, IBM users

Content Summary
From the IBM Users Network main menu, you can choose from several options, including Top 10 Utilities, File Finder, New Users/Fun Forum, Communications Forum, ASP/Shareware Forum, and several other forum options. Use this service as a starting point to learn more about the forums that are available for IBM and IBM PC compatible computers.

See Also
MS Software Library, IBM File Finder

User Guide
- ☑ Windows
- ☑ DOS
- ☐ Macintosh
- ☐ Terminal Emulation
- ☐ VMS
- ☐ UNIX
- ☑ OS/2
- ☑ Other platform

Cost
- ☐ Unknown
- ☐ Basic
- ☑ Extended
- ☐ Premium ($)
- ☐ Executive w/$

Activity Level
MEDIUM
LOW UNKNOWN HIGH

Address
GO: **IBMNET**

Ideas and Inventions Forum

Description
Do you have a good idea or invention? Share your ideas and share in others' ideas in this forum. This forum is open for everyone.

Subjects
Inventors

Audience
Entrepreneurs, inventors

Content Summary
This forum is designed as a vehicle for discussion for inventors, innovators, those involved in technology transfer world-wide, management people, venture capitalists, investment bankers, new product managers, patent and trademark lawyers, or housewives. The purpose of the forum is networking, support, and development of new products or improvement of existing ones. You will find both experienced inventors and "wannabees" here. The libraries and message areas include Creativity Workshops, Source Locator, Research & New Technology, Funding Your Ideas, NASA Technical Briefs, and many more. If you're interested in online conferences, you can read threads of past ones or join in future ones. See the Creativity Workshop library (Library 5) for more information.

See Also
Legal Forum

User Guide
- ☑ Windows
- ☑ DOS
- ☑ Macintosh
- ☐ Terminal Emulation
- ☐ VMS
- ☐ UNIX
- ☐ OS/2
- ☐ Other platform

Ideas and Inventions Forum – Information Retrieval

INFORMATION RETRIEVAL

Cost
- [ ] Unknown
- [ ] Basic
- [x] Extended
- [ ] Premium ($)
- [ ] Executive w/$

Activity Level: MEDIUM (LOW – HIGH)

Address
GO: **INNOVATION**

Information Management Forum

Description
This forum includes topics ranging from staff management and time management to technology management.

Subjects
Computers, Management

Audience
Management information specialists

Content Summary
This forum discusses issues that are currently scattered over numerous CompuServe forums, and offers the opportunity to concentrate on new issues as they emerge. Many forums often address the "how" for solving computing problems. This forum is also able to address the "why" and computing foundations. Although technical issues can be discussed, this forum focuses primarily on the management issues in the information processing community. The library and message sections include Professional Development, Desktop Issues, Network Issues, Host Issues, Professional Issues, and much more.

See Also
Business Management

User Guide
- [x] Windows
- [x] DOS
- [ ] Macintosh
- [ ] Terminal Emulation
- [ ] VMS
- [ ] UNIX
- [ ] OS/2
- [ ] Other platform

Cost
- [ ] Unknown
- [ ] Basic
- [x] Extended
- [ ] Premium ($)
- [ ] Executive w/$

Activity Level: MEDIUM (LOW – HIGH)

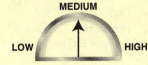

Address
GO: **INFOMANAGE**

IQuest

Description
With access to over 800 databases on topics such as accounting, aerospace, computers, and more, IQuest is one of the largest research services in the world.

Subjects
Databases, Information Retrieval, Research

Audience
General public, librarians, researchers

Content Summary
CompuServe members have seamless interaction with the IQuest reference and information service. IQuest provides access to over 800 databases, including business, government, research, news, popular entertainment, and sports. IQuest is a menu-based service that prompts you for your information, and then searches for you. Accessing databases from information suppliers such as Dialog Information Services, Inc., BRS Online Products, NewsNet, Inc., and Data-Star, IQuest executes the search and displays the results to you. IQuest can be expensive if you don't think out your searches beforehand, so be sure to read the Pricing Information on the main menu before you go asking for too much.

See Also
Dun's Market Identifiers($), Executive News Service($), TRW Bus. Credit Reports($), Official Airline Guide EE($)

User Guide
- [x] Windows
- [x] DOS
- [x] Macintosh
- [ ] Terminal Emulation
- [ ] VMS
- [x] UNIX
- [x] OS/2
- [ ] Other platform

Cost
- [ ] Unknown
- [ ] Basic
- [ ] Extended
- [ ] Premium ($)
- [x] Executive w/$

Activity Level: MEDIUM (LOW → HIGH)

Address
GO: **IQUEST**

Magazine Database Plus

Description
Magazine Database Plus is a service that lets you retrieve full-text articles from more than 140 general-interest magazines, journals, and reports.

Subjects
Information Retrieval, Magazines

Audience
Researchers, general public

Content Summary
The database contains a wealth of diverse publications, from *Time* to the *Atlantic*, *Forbes* to *Kiplinger's Personal Finance Magazine*, the *New Republic* to *National Review*, *Good Housekeeping* to *Cosmopolitan*. The main menu lets you choose from What Is Magazine Database Plus, Basic Instructions, Pricing, Terms and Conditions, and Database Customer Service, Access Magazine Database Plus.

See Also
IQuest($), MQDATA($)

User Guide
- ☑ Windows
- ☑ DOS
- ☑ Macintosh
- ☐ Terminal Emulation
- ☐ VMS
- ☑ UNIX
- ☐ OS/2
- ☐ Other platform

Cost
- ☐ Unknown
- ☐ Basic
- ☐ Extended
- ☑ Premium ($)
- ☐ Executive w/$

Activity Level

Address
GO: **MAGDB**

Information USA

Description
Are you looking for something? Do you need information but aren't sure where to get it? Start with the Information USA service. It will help you get started.

Subjects
Government, Information, Reference

Audience
General public, researchers

Content Summary
This service, extracted from the *Information USA* reference book by Matthew Lesko, provides information and access to free or nearly free government publications in three areas: government publications and services, American Embassies and consulates, and travel information. From the main menu, you can select from several options, including Introduction/Talk to Mr. Lesko, Consumer Power, Careers and Workplace, Giveaways to Entrepreneurs, Selling to the Government, and much more. You have to see this service to believe it. It's full of very useful information.

See Also
Government Publications

User Guide
- ☑ Windows
- ☑ DOS
- ☑ Macintosh
- ☐ Terminal Emulation
- ☐ VMS
- ☑ UNIX
- ☑ OS/2
- ☐ Other platform

Cost
- ☐ Unknown
- ☐ Basic
- ☑ Extended
- ☐ Premium ($)
- ☐ Executive w/$

Activity Level

Address
GO: **INFOUSA**

Inn and Lodging Forum

Description
This is the Lanier's Inn and Lodging forum, dedicated to discussions about alternative accommodations—places other than the chain hotels.

Subjects
Hotel Management, Travel

Audience
Tourists, General Public

Content Summary
Lanier's Inn and Lodging Forum is a place to talk about the places you've discovered off the beaten path, and learn about new ways to take advantage of what bed & breakfast inns, all-suite hotels, and other forms of alternative accommodations have to offer. It's also a place to meet the people behind the scenes—the professionals who make your business and leisure travel the success it is. You can use libraries and message sections such as Innkeeping Dreams, B&B Recipe Exchanges, Elegant Hotels, and more.

See Also
Travel Forum, Bed & Breakfast Database

User Guide
- ☑ Windows
- ☑ DOS
- ☑ Macintosh
- ☐ Terminal Emulation
- ☑ VMS
- ☑ UNIX
- ☑ OS/2
- ☐ Other platform

Cost
- ☐ Unknown
- ☐ Basic
- ☑ Extended
- ☐ Premium ($)
- ☐ Executive w/$

Inn and Lodging Forum – International

Activity Level: MEDIUM (arrow pointing LOW)

Address
GO: INNFORUM

Intel Corporation

Description
This service enables you to get to the Intel Forum and Intel Architecture Labs Forum.

Subjects
Computer Hardware, Computers, Microcomputers, Modems, Networking

Audience
Modem users, network users, computer users

Content Summary
The Intel Forum supports Intel's enhancement products for IBM PCs and any and all compatible computers. You can find information on Above Boards, SnapIn, Inboards, SatisFAXtion, and Connection CoProcessor FAX boards. Other products include Intel Math CoProcessors, modems, network enhancement utilities, network management tools, Visual Edge, Code Builder, Matched Memory, and NetPort. The Intel Architecture Labs Forum is an interactive, online service in which you can obtain the latest in technical and marketing information on the advanced Intel architectures.

See Also
Computer Club Forum

User Guide
- [x] Windows
- [x] DOS
- [ ] Macintosh
- [ ] Terminal Emulation
- [ ] VMS
- [ ] UNIX
- [x] OS/2
- [x] Other platform

Cost
- [ ] Unknown
- [ ] Basic
- [x] Extended
- [ ] Premium ($)
- [ ] Executive w/$

Activity Level: MEDIUM (arrow pointing HIGH)

Address
GO: INTEL

Intelligence Test

Description
So, you think you're smart? Take the CompuServe IQ test and prove it.

Subjects
Testing

Audience
General public

Content Summary
This is a terminal emulation service that enables you to take an IQ test that is formulated the same way that standardized tests are done. They advise you to take the test in a quiet room to get accurate results. The tests can take up to 32 minutes to complete.

See Also
MENSA Forum

User Guide
- [ ] Windows
- [ ] DOS
- [ ] Macintosh
- [x] Terminal Emulation
- [ ] VMS
- [ ] UNIX
- [ ] OS/2
- [ ] Other platform

Cost
- [ ] Unknown
- [ ] Basic
- [x] Extended
- [ ] Premium ($)
- [ ] Executive w/$

Activity Level: UNKNOWN

Address
GO: TMC-101

INTERNATIONAL

Japan Forum

Description
This forum is devoted to Japan, its culture, its history, and other aspects of Japanese life.

Subjects
International, Japan

Audience
General public, computer users, international travelers

Content Summary
The members from Japan and around the world are devoted to cross-cultural communications and learning about each others culture and history in this forum. They are interested in "all aspects of life in Japan, from Abe Seimei (A Japanese astronomer who lived in the year 1000) to Zen Buddhism." Other topics include karaoke, sushi, sumo, and the yen vs. the dollar, as well as other topics. The library and message sections include Travel, Software Macintosh, Software PC & Other, Hobbies & Pop Culture, Networks-J/Internet, and others.

International – International Finance

See Also
International Trade Forum, Travel Forum

User Guide
- ☑ Windows
- ☑ DOS
- ☑ Macintosh
- ☐ Terminal Emulation
- ☐ VMS
- ☐ UNIX
- ☐ OS/2
- ☑ Other platform

Cost
- ☐ Unknown
- ☐ Basic
- ☑ Extended
- ☐ Premium ($)
- ☐ Executive w/$

Activity Level
MEDIUM (arrow pointing LOW)

Address
GO: **JAPAN**

INTERNATIONAL EVENTS

Political Debate Forum

Description
This forum allows open discussion of political topics of all types. It is open to people of all political persuasions.

Subjects
International Events, News, U.S. Politics

Audience
Politicians, students

Content Summary
This forum provides debate areas for Democrats, Libertarians, and Republicans. Other libraries contain articles and information on topics ranging from the Crime Bill, health care, gun rights, gay rights, and international politics.

See Also
Democrat Forum, Participate, Republican Forum

User Guide
- ☑ Windows
- ☑ DOS
- ☑ Macintosh
- ☐ Terminal Emulation
- ☑ VMS
- ☑ UNIX
- ☑ OS/2
- ☐ Other platform

Cost
- ☐ Unknown
- ☐ Basic
- ☑ Extended
- ☐ Premium ($)
- ☐ Executive w/$

Activity Level
MEDIUM (arrow pointing HIGH)

Address
GO: **POLITICS**

INTERNATIONAL FINANCE

Financial Forecasts

Description
This area presents you with the Earnings/Economics Projections menu, from which you can choose five financial and investment services.

Subjects
Financial News, International Finance, Investments, Investments, Investments

Audience
Investors, market analysts, financial analysts, financial advisors, business and financial researchers

Content Summary
From the Earnings/Economics Projections main menu, you can select I/B/E/S Earnings Estimate, S&P Online, InvesText, MMS International Financial Reports, and CENDATA services (CENDATA is a Census Bureau service). For information and service fees associated with these services, select the Instructions/Fees option from the main menu. Some of the services require Terminal Emulation. I/B/E/S Earnings Estimate is a database that provides consensus earnings estimates on over 3,400 publicly traded corporations. S&P Online provides you with recent information on approximately 4,700 companies, including business summaries, recent market activity, and dividend information. The InvesText database provides company and industry research reports compiled during the most recent two years by analysts in more than 50 Wall Street, regional, and international brokerage houses and research firms. MMS International Financial Reports provides a calendar of economic events, daily market reports, debt market reports, and other information on international markets.

See Also
Dividends and Splits ($), Financial Forums, Dun's Market Identifiers ($), Dun's Elect Business Dir ($)

User Guide
- ☐ Windows
- ☐ DOS
- ☐ Macintosh
- ☑ Terminal Emulation
- ☐ VMS
- ☐ UNIX
- ☐ OS/2
- ☐ Other platform

Cost
- ☐ Unknown
- ☐ Basic
- ☐ Extended
- ☑ Premium ($)
- ☐ Executive w/$

International Finance – International News

Activity Level
MEDIUM / LOW / UNKNOWN / HIGH

Address
GO: **EARNINGS**

Foreign Language Forum

Description
This forum is devoted to foreign languages, their study, teaching, use in the commercial world, or general interest items about foreign languages.

Subjects
Bilingual Education, Europe, Foreign News, French, International, Languages

Audience
General public, Europeans

Content Summary
As you can see from the various library headings, the Foreign Language forum offers a diverse cultural and languages experience. The libraries are listed as follows: Spanish/Portuguese, French, German/Germanic, Latin/Greek, Slavic/E. European, English, East Asian, Esperanto, Italian, FL Education, Translators, Computers/Languages, Resources/Careers, Semitic/Turkic, Others Using the Forum, and Sysops.

See Also
Education Forum

User Guide
- ☑ Windows
- ☑ DOS
- ☑ Macintosh
- ☐ Terminal Emulation
- ☐ VMS
- ☑ UNIX
- ☐ OS/2
- ☐ Other platform

Cost
- ☐ Unknown
- ☐ Basic
- ☑ Extended
- ☐ Premium ($)
- ☐ Executive w/$

Activity Level
MEDIUM / LOW / HIGH

Address
GO: **FLEFO**

INTERNATIONAL NEWS

Executive News Service

Description
You can search the latest international news, weather, and sports from the world's major news agencies. This powerful news clipping service can scan many news sources for stories you specify and deliver them to you daily.

Subjects
Business, Financial News, International News, News

Audience
Business Professionals

Content Summary
You can read about financial events in Reuters Financial Report and OTC NewsAlert, as well as in the daily headlines of The Washington Post. To use the News by Company Ticker option, enter a company ticker symbol and check on business news filed within the past 24 hours. For the News Clips option, you can read through special clipping folders set up by CompuServe to keep you up on specific news topics. You also can set up your own Personal area in which you specify the type of news you want to read by typing in key phrases. ENS then sends you electronic news "clippings" that you can read. ENS costs $15 per hour plus the base connect rates.

See Also
AP Sports($), Financial Forums, Global Crises Forum, NewsGrid, Newspaper Archives($), Reuter News Pictures Forum, United Press Int'l($), U.S. News Forum

User Guide
- ☑ Windows
- ☑ DOS
- ☐ Macintosh
- ☐ Terminal Emulation
- ☐ VMS
- ☐ UNIX
- ☐ OS/2
- ☐ Other platform

Cost
- ☐ Unknown
- ☐ Basic
- ☐ Extended
- ☑ Premium ($)
- ☐ Executive w/$

Activity Level
MEDIUM / LOW / UNKNOWN / HIGH

Address
GO: **ENS**

OTC NewsAlert

Description
Search the latest international news, weather, and sports from the world's major news agencies. A

powerful news clipping service that can scan many news sources for stories you specify and deliver them to you daily.

Subjects
Business, Financial News, International News, News

Audience
Associated Press Forum, Associated Press Online

Content Summary
You can read financial events through Reuters Financial Report and OTC NewsAlert, as well as read the day's headlines with The Washington Post. To use the News by Company Ticker option, enter a company ticker symbol and check on business news filed within the past 24 hours. For the News Clips option, you can read through special clipping folders set up by CompuServe to keep you up on specific news topics. You also set up your own Personal area in which you specify the type of news that you want to read by typing in key phrases. ENS then sends you electronic news clippings that you can read. ENS costs $15 per hour plus the base connect rates.

See Also
AP Sports, Financial Forums, Global Crises Forum, NewsGrid, Newspaper Archives, Reuters News Pictures Forum, United Press International, U.S. News Forum

User Guide
☑ Windows	☐ VMS
☑ DOS	☐ UNIX
☐ Macintosh	☐ OS/2
☐ Terminal Emulation	☐ Other platform

Cost
☐ Unknown	☑ Premium ($)
☐ Basic	☐ Executive w/$
☐ Extended	

Activity Level
MEDIUM / LOW / UNKNOWN / HIGH

Address
GO: ENS

INTERNATIONAL POLITICS

Global Crisis Forum

Description
This forum is devoted to the past, present, and future crises around the world, such as the Balkans, the former USSR, and other hot spots around the globe.

Subjects
Current Events, Global News, International Politics, Modern History, World View

Audience
Military historians, historians, heneral hublic, hctivists, writers, journalists

Content Summary
Because the world changes and some hot spots become cold spots and cold spots become hot spots, the library and message sections in this forum change often. Some of the recent hot spots on the forum have been the Asia/Pacific Rim, Africa, Russia, the Baltics, and the Americas. You'll also find HOTSPOT: areas denoted in the libraries and message areas for current topics. You'll find articles, theses, and other text files throughout the library sections for downloading.

See Also
Associated Press, Executive News Service, U.S. News & World Report

User Guide
☑ Windows	☑ VMS
☑ DOS	☑ UNIX
☑ Macintosh	☑ OS/2
☐ Terminal Emulation	☑ Other platform

Cost
☐ Unknown	☐ Premium ($)
☐ Basic	☐ Executive w/$
☑ Extended	

Activity Level

MEDIUM / LOW / HIGH

Address
GO: CRISIS

INTERNET

Electronic Frontier Foundation Forum

Description
The Electronic Frontier Foundation (EFF) was founded in July 1990 to assure freedom of expression in digital media, with a particular emphasis on applying the principles embodied in the Constitution and the Bill of Rights to computer-based communications.

Subjects
Computer-Based Communications, Digital Media Rights, Internet

Audience
Computer users, activists, civil libertarians, journalists

Content Summary
The libraries in this forum contain areas for EFF-related files, networking, communications, back issues of the EFF newsletter, Cyberlaw, Zines and the Net, Internet news, and maps and guides. You also can get freeware and shareware applications for DOS and Macintosh machines in libraries 9 and 10.

See Also
Internet Forum

User Guide
- ☑ Windows
- ☑ DOS
- ☑ Macintosh
- ☐ Terminal Emulation
- ☐ VMS
- ☐ UNIX
- ☐ OS/2
- ☐ Other platform

Cost
- ☐ Unknown
- ☐ Basic
- ☑ Extended
- ☐ Premium ($)
- ☐ Executive w/$

Activity Level
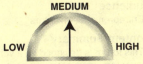

Address
GO: **EFFSIG**

Internet Forum

Description
This forum is dedicated to the Internet. You can find information on "surfing" utilities, ftp and telnet sites, newsgroups, and World-Wide Web and Gopher sites.

Subjects
Computers, Internet

Audience
Computer users, Internet surfers

Content Summary
The forum's library and message sections include Getting Started, Internet Access, Directory Services, Electronic Mail, Mailing Lists, Gopher/WAIS/WWW, and more. Look in the Resources-Technical library (Library 15) for up-to-date information on Internet security and the latest virus. If you're new to the Internet, look in the Getting Started library for various files on how to start surfing on the 'Net.

See Also
Electronic Frontier Foundation

User Guide
- ☑ Windows
- ☑ DOS
- ☑ Macintosh
- ☐ Terminal Emulation
- ☑ VMS
- ☑ UNIX
- ☑ OS/2
- ☑ Other platform

Cost
- ☐ Unknown
- ☐ Basic
- ☑ Extended
- ☐ Premium ($)
- ☐ Executive w/$

Activity Level

Address
GO: **INETFORUM**

Intuit Forum

Description
Do you use Quicken, Quickpay, or Quickbooks? If so, stop by the Intuit Forum and read tips, press releases, and support comments about these products.

Subjects
Computers, Finance

Audience
Computer users

Content Summary
The purpose of this forum is to provide technical support and discussion areas for all of the Intuit products. The Intuit Technical Support Staff monitor and participate in this forum regularly. The Intuit Forum provides support and information on all Intuit Products, including Quicken for DOS, Windows, and Macintosh, and Quickpay and Quickbooks for DOS and Windows.

See Also
Financial Forums

User Guide
- ☑ Windows
- ☑ DOS
- ☑ Macintosh
- ☐ Terminal Emulation
- ☐ VMS
- ☐ UNIX
- ☐ OS/2
- ☐ Other platform

Cost
- ☐ Unknown
- ☐ Basic
- ☑ Extended
- ☐ Premium ($)
- ☐ Executive w/$

Activity Level
MEDIUM (LOW — HIGH)

Address
GO: **INTUIT**

Intuit Personal Tax Forum

Description
This forum provides online support for Intuit products, including TurboTax for DOS, TurboTax for Windows, MacInTax, and more.

Subjects
Taxes

Audience
Accountants, computer users

Intuit Personal Tax Forum – Inventors

Content Summary
You can find fiiles, help files, and support questions and commands in the libraries.

See Also
IBM File Finder

User Guide
- ☑ Windows
- ☑ DOS
- ☑ Macintosh
- ☐ Terminal Emulation
- ☐ VMS
- ☐ UNIX
- ☐ OS/2
- ☐ Other platform

Cost
- ☐ Unknown
- ☐ Basic
- ☑ Extended
- ☐ Premium ($)
- ☐ Executive w/$

Activity Level
LOW — UNKNOWN (MEDIUM) — HIGH

Address
GO: **INVIT**

INVENTIONS

Patent Research Center

Description
This forum provides quick access to summaries of U.S. patents granted in chemical, mechanical, electrical, and design categories.

Subjects
Inventions, Legal Research, Research

Audience
Inventors, legal researchers, researchers

Content Summary
This forum contains summaries of patents granted internationally since the mid 1970s. Databases searched include the Claims/U.S. Patent Abstracts from 1950 to the present and the World Patents Index from 1963 to the present. You enter a search by typing a name, word, or phrase that describes the item you are searching for. The search can return up to 10 articles.

See Also
Legal Research Center

User Guide
- ☑ Windows
- ☑ DOS
- ☑ Macintosh
- ☐ Terminal Emulation
- ☑ VMS
- ☑ UNIX
- ☑ OS/2
- ☐ Other platform

Cost
- ☐ Unknown
- ☐ Basic
- ☐ Extended
- ☑ Premium ($)
- ☐ Executive w/$

Activity Level
LOW — UNKNOWN (MEDIUM) — HIGH

Address
GO: **PATENT**

INVENTORS

Ideas and Inventions Forum

Description
Do you have a good idea or invention? Share your ideas and share in others' ideas in this forum. This forum is open for everyone.

Subjects
Inventors

Audience
Entrepreneurs, inventors

Content Summary
This forum is designed as a vehicle for discussion for inventors, innovators, those involved in technology transfer world-wide, management people, venture capitalists, investment bankers, new product managers, patent and trademark lawyers, or housewives. The purpose of the forum is networking, support, and development of new products or improvement of existing ones. You will find both experienced inventors and "wannabees" here. The libraries and message areas include Creativity Workshops, Source Locator, Research & New Technology, Funding Your Ideas, NASA Technical Briefs, and many more. If your interested in online conferences, you can read threads of past ones or join in future ones. See the Creativity Workshop library (Library 5) for more information.

See Also
Legal Forum

User Guide
- ☑ Windows
- ☑ DOS
- ☑ Macintosh
- ☐ Terminal Emulation
- ☑ VMS
- ☑ UNIX
- ☑ OS/2
- ☑ Other platform

Cost
- ☐ Unknown
- ☐ Basic
- ☑ Extended
- ☐ Premium ($)
- ☐ Executive w/$

Activity Level
LOW — MEDIUM ↑ — HIGH

Address
GO: **INNOVATION**

InvesText

Description
This database has full-text research reports from the past two years compiled by over 50 Wall Street and other brokerage houses and research firms.

Subjects
Databases, Investments

Audience
Analysts, financial analysts, business analysts

Content Summary
This database provides the full-text of company and industry research reports compiled during the most recent two years by analysts in more than 50 Wall Street, regional, and international brokerage houses and research firms. Individual company reports are available for more than 8,200 U.S. public companies and over 2,300 publicly held foreign companies. Company reports include historical information, such as company profiles, revenues, earnings and other financial operating results, and stock performance. The reports can also include the brokerage's recommendations, with analysis and forecasts of the company's future performance. See the Pricing Information option on the InvesText main menu for the price of searches.

See Also
Dun's Canadian Mkt. Ident($), Dun's Elect Business Dir($), Dun's Market Identifiers($), E*TRADE Securities, Investors Forum

User Guide
- ☑ Windows
- ☑ DOS
- ☑ Macintosh
- ☐ Terminal Emulation
- ☑ VMS
- ☑ UNIX
- ☑ OS/2
- ☑ Other platform

Cost
- ☐ Unknown
- ☐ Basic
- ☐ Extended
- ☐ Premium ($)
- ☑ Executive w/$

Activity Level
UNKNOWN

Address
GO: **INVTEXT**

INVESTMENTS

D&B Duns Electronic Business Directory

Description
You can obtain a directory of over 8.5 million U.S. public and private businesses and professionals using this Dun and Bradstreet service. Available information includes name, address, phone number, type of business, its parent company, the industry it belongs to, the SIC code, number of employees, and the population of the city in which the business resides.

Subjects
Business, Finance, Investment, Dun and Bradstreet

Audience
Accounting persons, businesspersons, executives, investors, journalists, management, researchers

Content Summary
To search, select Choice 5, Access Duns Electronic Business Directory, from the main menu. Next, select the criterion for your search, such as company name or product or service, enter a name, word, or phrase that describes the company or product, and follow the on-screen instructions. See Choice 7, Search Guidelines, for more help. The cost of this service is as follows:
- Search (retrieves up to 5 names): $7.50
- Additional names (in groups of 5): $7.50

In addition to connect time charges, you are charged $1.00 for a search that retrieves no titles.

See Also
Company Information, Corporate Affiliations, D&B Duns Canadian Market Identifiers, D&B Duns Market Identifiers, Financial Forums, Investors Forum, Tenderlink, TRW Business Profiles

User Guide
- ☑ Windows
- ☑ DOS
- ☑ Macintosh
- ☑ Terminal Emulation
- ☑ VMS
- ☑ UNIX
- ☑ OS/2
- ☑ Other platform

Cost
- ☐ Unknown
- ☐ Basic
- ☐ Extended
- ☑ Premium ($)
- ☐ Executive w/$

Activity Level
UNKNOWN

Address
GO: **DYP** or **DUNSEBD**

D&B Duns Market Identifiers

Description
With this service, you can search three of Dun and Bradstreets directories of business information, including information on over 6.7 million U.S. public and private businesses that have over $1 million in sales or more than five employees, information on over 350,000 Canadian companies, and information on over 2.1 million public, private, and government controlled international companies.

Investments

Subjects
Business, Finance, Investment, Dun and Bradstreet

Audience
Accounting persons, businesspersons, executives, investors, management, researchers

Content Summary
When you perform a search, you can get the company name, address, telephone number, sales figures, number of employees, parent company, and names of executives. The price of this service is as follows:

- Search (retrieves up to 5 names): $7.50
- Additional names (in groups of 5): $7.50
- Full reference (selected from the names): $7.50

In addition to connect time charges, you are charged $1.00 for a search that retrieves no titles.

See Also
Company Information, Corporate Affiliations, D&B Duns Canadian Market Identifiers, Financial Forums, Investors Forum, Tenderlink, TRW Business Profiles

User Guide
- ☑ Windows
- ☑ DOS
- ☑ Macintosh
- ☐ Terminal Emulation
- ☑ VMS
- ☑ UNIX
- ☑ OS/2
- ☑ Other platform

Cost
- ☐ Unknown
- ☐ Basic
- ☐ Extended
- ☑ Premium ($)
- ☐ Executive w/$

Activity Level

Address
GO: **DUNS** or **DMI**

Dreyfus Corporation

Description
Dreyfus Corporation has been the leader in the mutual funds field for over 40 years. In this area, you can start your investment portfolio with as little as $100, roll over your IRA and Keogh accounts, and look into other investment programs, such as the Investment Allocation Program.

Subjects
Investments, Mutual Funds

Audience
Investors

Content Summary
From the Dreyfus Corp. main menu, you can choose from several options. You can choose the Online Selection of Funds option to see how to select mutual funds, see the family of funds Dreyfus offers, and see the Featured Funds. To request a free Dreyfus prospectus online, select the Request a FREE Prospectus option from the main menu. Select the Minimum Investment Program option from the main menu for information on starting a mutual fund portfolio for as little as $100.

See Also

User Guide
- ☐ Windows
- ☐ DOS
- ☐ Macintosh
- ☑ Terminal Emulation
- ☐ VMS
- ☐ UNIX
- ☐ OS/2
- ☐ Other platform

Cost
- ☐ Unknown
- ☑ Basic
- ☐ Extended
- ☐ Premium ($)
- ☐ Executive w/$

Activity Level

Address
GO: **DR**

E*TRADE Securities

Description
Do you want to get a grip on your investments? This service enables you to do just that. E*TRADE handles individual, investment, margin, IRA, joint, KEOGH, and 401K accounts, and offers a stock market game that uses real stock market prices and data.

Subjects
Financial, Investments, Stock Market

Audience
Accountants, investors

Content Summary
This around-the-clock service offers you commissions of 1 1/2 cents per share, with a $35.00 minimum; Black-Sholes option analysis that use current prices; investment management; and free checking accounts tied to your money market funds. The investment management offers you quotes, portfolio reports, limit orders, and news alerts.

See Also
ETGAME

User Guide
- ☐ Windows
- ☐ DOS
- ☐ Macintosh
- ☑ Terminal Emulation
- ☐ VMS
- ☐ UNIX
- ☐ OS/2
- ☐ Other platform

Cost
- [ ] Unknown
- [ ] Basic
- [ ] Extended
- [x] Premium ($)
- [ ] Executive w/$

Activity Level: UNKNOWN (LOW – MEDIUM – HIGH)

Address
GO: **ETRADE**

Financial Forecasts

Description
This area presents you with the Earnings/Economics Projections menu, from which you can choose five financial and investment services.

Subjects
Financial News, International Finance, Investments, Investments, Investments

Audience
Investors, market analysts, financial analysts, financial advisors, business and financial researchers

Content Summary
From the Earnings/Economics Projections main menu, you can select I/B/E/S Earnings Estimate, S&P Online, InvesText, MMS International Financial Reports, and CENDATA services (CENDATA is a Census Bureau service). For information and service fees associated with these services, select the Instructions/Fees option from the main menu. Some of the services require Terminal Emulation. I/B/E/S Earnings Estimate is a database that provides consensus earnings estimates on over 3,400 publicly traded corporations. S&P Online provides you with recent information on approximately 4,700 companies, including business summaries, recent market activity, and dividend information. The InvesText database provides company and industry research reports compiled during the most recent two years by analysts in more than 50 Wall Street, regional, and international brokerage houses and research firms. MMS International Financial Reports provides a calendar of economic events, daily market reports, debt market reports, and other information on international markets.

See Also
Dividends and Splits ($), Financial Forums, Dun's Market Identifiers ($), Dun's Elect Business Dir ($)

User Guide
- [ ] Windows
- [ ] DOS
- [ ] Macintosh
- [x] Terminal Emulation
- [ ] VMS
- [ ] UNIX
- [ ] OS/2
- [ ] Other platform

Cost
- [ ] Unknown
- [ ] Basic
- [ ] Extended
- [x] Premium ($)
- [ ] Executive w/$

Activity Level: UNKNOWN (LOW – MEDIUM – HIGH)

Address
GO: **EARNINGS**

InvesText

Description
This database has full-text research reports from the past two years compiled by over 50 Wall Street and other brokerage houses and research firms.

Subjects
Databases, Investments

Audience
Analysts, financial analysts, business analysts

Content Summary
This database provides the full-text of company and industry research reports compiled during the most recent two years by analysts in more than 50 Wall Street, regional, and international brokerage houses and research firms. Individual company reports are available for more than 8,200 U.S. public companies and over 2,300 publicly held foreign companies. Company reports include historical information, such as company profiles, revenues, earnings and other financial operating results, and stock performance. The reports can also include the brokerage's recommendations, with analysis and forecasts of the company's future performance. See the Pricing Information option on the InvesText main menu for the price of searches.

See Also
Dun's Canadian Mkt. Ident($), Dun's Elect Business Dir($), Dun's Market Identifiers($), E*TRADE Securities, Investors Forum

User Guide
- [x] Windows
- [x] DOS
- [x] Macintosh
- [ ] Terminal Emulation
- [x] VMS
- [x] UNIX
- [x] OS/2
- [x] Other platform

Cost
- [ ] Unknown
- [ ] Basic
- [ ] Extended
- [ ] Premium ($)
- [x] Executive w/$

Activity Level: UNKNOWN (LOW – MEDIUM – HIGH)

Investments – Issues Forum

Address
GO: **INVTEXT**

IQuest

Description
With access to over 800 databases on topics such as accounting, aerospace, computers, and more, IQuest is one of the largest research services in the world.

Subjects
Databases, Information Retrieval, Research

Audience
General public, librarians, researchers

Content Summary
CompuServe members have seamless interaction with the IQuest reference and information service. IQuest provides access to over 800 databases, including business, government, research, news, popular entertainment, and sports. IQuest is a menu-based service that prompts you for your information, and then searches for you. Accessing databases from information suppliers such as Dialog Information Services, Inc., BRS Online Products, NewsNet, Inc., and Data-Star, IQuest executes the search and displays the results to you. IQuest can be expensive if you don't think out your searches beforehand, so be sure to read the Pricing Information on the main menu before you go asking for too much.

See Also
Dun's Market Identifiers($), Executive News Service($), TRW Bus. Credit Reports($), Official Airline Guide EE($)

User Guide
- ☑ Windows
- ☑ DOS
- ☑ Macintosh
- ☐ Terminal Emulation
- ☑ VMS
- ☑ UNIX
- ☑ OS/2
- ☑ Other platform

Cost
- ☐ Unknown
- ☐ Basic
- ☐ Extended
- ☐ Premium ($)
- ☑ Executive w/$

Activity Level

Address
GO: **IQUEST**

IRS Tax Forms and Documents

Description
Save time and a stamp by doing your taxes online. This service explains how.

Subjects
Tax

Audience
General public

Content Summary
With over 450 documents online, this service offers every current IRS form and all instructions and publications that the IRS can provide. The file format that you use is Adobe Acrobat's Portable Document Format (PDF). The IRS-approved forms presented in PDF look nearly identical to the forms you get at the post office or library, or order from the IRS. The IRS Tax Documents main menu includes Overview, Searching for Documents, Contacting the IRS, Adobe Acrobat Reader, Member Feedback, and Access IRS Tax Documents.

See Also

User Guide
- ☑ Windows
- ☑ DOS
- ☑ Macintosh
- ☐ Terminal Emulation
- ☑ VMS
- ☑ UNIX
- ☑ OS/2
- ☑ Other platform

Cost
- ☐ Unknown
- ☐ Basic
- ☑ Extended
- ☐ Premium ($)
- ☐ Executive w/$

Activity Level

Address
GO: **TAXFORMS**

Issues Forum

Description
Devoted to current topics and issues, the Issues Forum discusses topics such as Afro-Americanism, parenting, human rights, and others.

Subjects
Current Events, Human Rights, Politics, Religion

Audience
General public

Content Summary
This special interest group is devoted to discussions of a wide variety of issues. Currently, there are sections for topics such as Afro-American issues, parenting issues, human rights, unexplained phenomena, men and women's issues, Asian-American issues, and others. The library and message sections include Culture & Society, Between the Sexes, Canadian Issues, Politics & Religion, and more. Look in Library 9, Rush H. Limbaugh, for summaries of Rush's show.

See Also
Entertainment Center, HSX Open Forum

User Guide
- ☑ Windows
- ☑ DOS
- ☑ Macintosh
- ☐ Terminal Emulation
- ☑ VMS
- ☑ UNIX
- ☑ OS/2
- ☑ Other platform

Cost
- ☐ Unknown
- ☐ Basic
- ☑ Extended
- ☐ Premium ($)
- ☐ Executive w/$

Activity Level

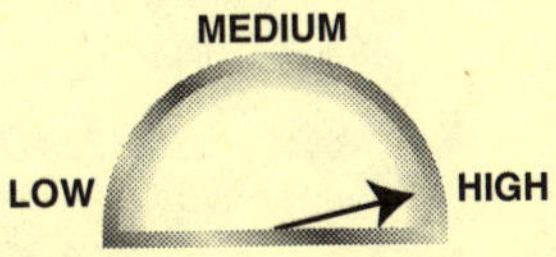

LOW / MEDIUM / HIGH (arrow pointing to HIGH)

Address
GO: **ISSUESFORUM**

J

Japan Forum

Description
This forum is devoted to Japan, its culture, its history, and other aspects of Japanese life.

Subjects
International, Japan

Audience
General public, computer users, international travelers

Content Summary
The members from Japan and around the world are devoted to cross-cultural communications and learning about each others culture and history in this forum. They are interested in "all aspects of life in Japan, from Abe Seimei (Japanese astronomer who lived in the year 1000) to Zen Buddhism." Other topics include karaoke, sushi, sumo, and the yen vs. the dollar, as well as other topics. The library and message sections include Travel, Software Macintosh, Software PC & Other, Hobbies & Pop Culture, Networks-J/Internet, and others.

See Also
International Trade Forum, Travel Forum

User Guide
- ☑ Windows
- ☑ DOS
- ☑ Macintosh
- ☐ Terminal Emulation
- ☐ VMS
- ☐ UNIX
- ☐ OS/2
- ☑ Other platform

Cost
- ☐ Unknown
- ☐ Basic
- ☑ Extended
- ☐ Premium ($)
- ☐ Executive w/$

Activity Level

Address
GO: **JAPAN**

JC Penney

Description
Shop JC Penney in the comfort of your own home by entering the JCPenney service. You can shop from their online store!

Subjects
Shopping

Audience
General public

Content Summary
The JCPenney main menu enables you to choose from Shop Our Online Store, Product QuickSearch, This Month's Specials, Catalog Ordering, Gift Certificates, Request Credit Card Application, U.S. Customer Service, Canadian Customer Service, and Join Our Mailing List.

See Also
Electronic Mall

User Guide
- ☑ Windows
- ☑ DOS
- ☑ Macintosh
- ☐ Terminal Emulation
- ☑ VMS
- ☑ UNIX
- ☑ OS/2
- ☐ Other platform

Cost
- ☐ Unknown
- ☑ Basic
- ☐ Extended
- ☐ Premium ($)
- ☐ Executive w/$

Activity Level

Address
GO: **JCPENNEY**

JDR Microdevices

Description
This service enables you to order Microdevices products and get customer service. JDR specializes in high-technology products.

Subjects
Computer Products, Computers

Audience
General public, computer users

See Also
IBM File Finder

Content Summary
From the JDR Microdevices main menu, you can choose from Shop Our Online Catalog, Product QuickSearch, Customer Service, Letter from the President, Request our Free Catalogs, Place An Order From Our Print Catalog, and Talk To Us. Browse the online catalog for items such as motherboards, memory, multimedia devices, books, and other products.

User Guide
- ☑ Windows
- ☑ DOS
- ☑ Macintosh
- ☐ Terminal Emulation
- ☐ VMS
- ☑ UNIX
- ☐ OS/2
- ☐ Other platform

JDR Microdevices – Journalism

Cost
- [ ] Unknown
- [ ] Basic
- [ ] Extended
- [x] Premium ($)
- [ ] Executive w/$

Activity Level: UNKNOWN

Address
GO: **JDR**

JFK Assassination Forum

Description
Did Lee Harvey Oswald act alone or not? Search for answers in this forum.

Subjects
History

Audience
General public

Content Summary
The purpose of this forum is to facilitate research into the assassination of JFK, to work together as a cooperative community to determine the facts of the "crime of the century." The library and message sections include Transcripts/Threads, Books & Articles, Organized Crime, Oswald/Ruby/et al., and more. For photos and drawings, see the Photos & Documents library (Library 12).

See Also
Participate

User Guide
- [x] Windows
- [x] DOS
- [x] Macintosh
- [ ] Terminal Emulation
- [x] VMS
- [x] UNIX
- [x] OS/2
- [ ] Other platform

Cost
- [ ] Unknown
- [ ] Basic
- [x] Extended
- [ ] Premium ($)
- [ ] Executive w/$

Activity Level: LOW

Address
GO: **JFKFORUM**

JOURNALISM

Detroit Free Press

Description
This is the place to find news and information about the award-winning Detroit Free Press newspaper. And feel free to leave a letter to the editor while you're online.

Subjects
Journalism, National News, Photojournalism

Audience
Automobile enthusiasts, Detroit citizens, journalists, photojournalists, sports fans

Content Summary
In the message and library areas, you can find information on the auto industry (including photographs of cars), health tips, business news, Detroit metro news, computing, entertainment, sports, and cartoons. You also can find the top stories of the day in the "Today's Top Stories" library (Library 17).

See Also
Detroit Free Press Store

User Guide
- [x] Windows
- [x] DOS
- [x] Macintosh
- [ ] Terminal Emulation
- [x] VMS
- [x] UNIX
- [x] OS/2
- [ ] Other platform

Cost
- [ ] Unknown
- [ ] Basic
- [x] Extended
- [ ] Premium ($)
- [ ] Executive w/$

Activity Level: HIGH

Address
GO: **DETROIT**

Detroit Free Press Store

Description
In this area, you can subscribe to the Detroit Free Press newspaper, order Detroit Free Press books, or leave a message for customer service.

Subjects
Customer Service, Subscriptions, Journalism

Audience
Anyone interested in the Detroit Free Press newspaper

Journalism

Content Summary
The Store has areas in which you can shop for Detroit Free Press books, subscribe to the Detroit Free Press newspaper (including international subscriptions), and leave a message for customer service. If you want more information about this award-winning newspaper, see the "What is the Detroit Free Press?" area (number 4).

See Also
Detroit Free Press

User Guide
- ☑ Windows
- ☑ DOS
- ☑ Macintosh
- ☐ Terminal Emulation
- ☑ VMS
- ☑ UNIX
- ☑ OS/2
- ☐ Other platform

Cost
- ☐ Unknown
- ☑ Basic
- ☐ Extended
- ☐ Premium ($)
- ☐ Executive w/$

Activity Level

Address
GO: **DFM-1**

Journalism Forum

Description
Since 1985, the Journalism Forum has been devoted to servicing the needs of journalists, photographers, and freelancers.

Subjects
Journalism, Writing

Audience
Journalists, writers

Content Summary
The Journalism Forum's library and message sections are full of files, writing guidelines, freelancing discussions, and other supporting files. Some of the libraries include Job/Stringers, Freelancers, Journalism Tools, Future Media, Newsroom Computers, Journalism Law, and other areas.

See Also
Entrepreneur Forum

User Guide
- ☑ Windows
- ☑ DOS
- ☑ Macintosh
- ☐ Terminal Emulation
- ☑ VMS
- ☑ UNIX
- ☑ OS/2
- ☑ Other platform

Cost
- ☐ Unknown
- ☐ Basic
- ☑ Extended
- ☐ Premium ($)
- ☐ Executive w/$

Activity Level

Address
GO: **JFORUM**

K

Knowledge Index

Description
Access over 100 popular databases from the Knowledge Index service.

Subjects
Database, General Interest, Research

Audience
General interest, general public, researchers

Content Summary
Knowledge Index is a service that gives you evening and weekend access to over 100 popular full-text and bibliographic databases at reduced rates. With Knowledge Index, you can access over 50,000 journals on a wide variety of topics. Many of the Knowledge Index databases have the complete text of articles available online. You can order a hard-copy printout of those that have only a citation available. The price is $.40 per minute ($24 per hour) and includes CompuServe standard connect rates up to and including 9600 Baud.

See Also
IQuest

User Guide
- ☑ Windows
- ☑ DOS
- ☑ Macintosh
- ☐ Terminal Emulation
- ☑ VMS
- ☑ UNIX
- ☑ OS/2
- ☐ Other platform

Cost
- ☐ Unknown
- ☐ Basic
- ☐ Extended
- ☑ Premium ($)
- ☐ Executive w/$

Activity Level

Address
GO: **KI**

Kodak CD Forum

Description
Maintained by Kodak, this forum is devoted to Kodak CD products and technology, as well as related products.

Subjects
Computers, Photo-CD, Printing

Audience
Computer users, computer graphics designers

Content Summary
The library and message sections include Kodak News, Photo CD General, Photo CD Software, Writable CD, International, Color Management, Member Uploads, and others. The Kodak Printer library (Library 8) contains drivers, information, and press releases relating to Kodak's line of high-quality printers.

See Also
Graphics Forums, Graphics File Finder, Photography Forum

User Guide
- ☑ Windows
- ☑ DOS
- ☑ Macintosh
- ☐ Terminal Emulation
- ☐ VMS
- ☐ UNIX
- ☐ OS/2
- ☐ Other platform

Cost
- ☐ Unknown
- ☐ Basic
- ☑ Extended
- ☐ Premium ($)
- ☐ Executive w/$

Activity Level

Address
GO: **KODAK**

L

LAN Magazine

Description
This forum is for network administrators, users, installers, and integrators to exchange information about computer networks.

Subjects
Computer Networking, Computers, Networking

Audience
Computer users, management information specialists

Content Summary
Sponsored by LAN Magazine, this forum is dedicated to help you solve LAN problems, stay in touch with the industry, and keep you informed of new products and services. The library and message sections include Reviews, Features, Guests & Interviews, Forum Member Bios, User-to-User, and others. For a story on salaries of network managers, see Library 3, Features.

See Also
LAN Technology Forum

User Guide
- ☑ Windows
- ☑ DOS
- ☑ Macintosh
- ☐ Terminal Emulation
- ☐ VMS
- ☑ UNIX
- ☑ OS/2
- ☑ Other platform

Cost
- ☐ Unknown
- ☐ Basic
- ☑ Extended
- ☐ Premium ($)
- ☐ Executive w/$

Activity Level

MEDIUM / LOW / HIGH

Address
GO: **LANMAG**

Lan Technology Forum

Description
This is *Lan Technology* magazine's forum for network issues, products, and discussions.

Subjects
Computers, Networking

Audience
Management information specialists, Macintosh users, computer users

Content Summary
The Lan Technology Forum is an online resource from Lan Technology, which is the leading independent monthly magazine devoted to the technical issues and problems faced by network specialists. The forum is a focal point for discovering how to work with the technologies and products in local and wide-area networks. The library and message sections include E-Mail, To Stacks, NetWare, VINES, Macintosh, UNIX, Network Management, Servers, Demos, and others.

See Also
LAN Magazine Forum

User Guide
- ☑ Windows
- ☑ DOS
- ☑ Macintosh
- ☐ Terminal Emulation
- ☐ VMS
- ☑ UNIX
- ☑ OS/2
- ☑ Other platform

Cost
- ☐ Unknown
- ☐ Basic
- ☑ Extended
- ☐ Premium ($)
- ☐ Executive w/$

Activity Level

MEDIUM / LOW / HIGH

Address
GO: **LANTECH**

LAN Vendor Forum

Description
For support and discussions on various networking vendors, join this forum.

Subjects
Computers, Networking

Audience
Computer users, management information specialists

Content Summary
This forum has libraries and message sections for the following vendors: Synergy Solutions, AMD, Newport Systems, SilCom Technology, Robertson-Caruso, Horizons Technology, Impulse Technology, DE/CartesRecall-IT!, Aleph Takoma Systems, Olicom, Compatible Systems, Momentum Software, AG Group, and CACI Products.

See Also
Lan Magazine Forum, Lan Technology Forum

User Guide
- ☑ Windows
- ☑ DOS
- ☑ Macintosh
- ☐ Terminal Emulation
- ☐ VMS
- ☐ UNIX
- ☐ OS/2
- ☑ Other platform

Cost
- ☐ Unknown
- ☐ Basic
- ☑ Extended
- ☐ Premium ($)
- ☐ Executive w/$

LAN Vendor Forum – Law

Activity Level: MEDIUM (arrow pointing toward LOW)

Address
GO: **LANVEN**

LAW

Legal Forum

Description
This forum is dedicated to legal and law discussions. The forum welcomes any CompuServe member to join this forum.

Subjects
Law, Legislation

Audience
Lawyers, legal professionals, general public

Content Summary
The Legal Forum includes various topics for attorneys and non-attorneys, including computer and technical law, law firm economics, legal research, Supreme Court discussions, related professions, and hot topics. For a basic primer on learning the process and procedures of the court, see the Hot Topic library (Library 9).

See Also
IQUEST, Legal Research Center

User Guide
- ☑ Windows
- ☑ DOS
- ☑ Macintosh
- ☐ Terminal Emulation
- ☑ VMS
- ☑ UNIX
- ☑ OS/2
- ☑ Other platform

Cost
- ☐ Unknown
- ☐ Basic
- ☑ Extended
- ☐ Premium ($)
- ☐ Executive w/$

Activity Level: MEDIUM (arrow pointing toward HIGH)

Address
GO: **LAWSIG**

Legal Research Center

Description
This database includes indexes to over 750 law journals, indexes to other law-related publications, summaries, and other topics.

Subjects
Law, Law Reviews, Legislation

Audience
Lawyers, legal professionals

Content Summary
You can use the Legal Research Center to search for legal topics from these databases: American Banker Full Text, Congressional Information Service, Criminal Justice Periodical Index, Legal Resource Index, National Criminal Justice Reference Service (NCJRS), and Tax Notes Today. See the description of pricing for specific searching prices.

See Also
Legal Forum

User Guide
- ☑ Windows
- ☑ DOS
- ☑ Macintosh
- ☐ Terminal Emulation
- ☑ VMS
- ☑ UNIX
- ☑ OS/2
- ☑ Other platform

Cost
- ☐ Unknown
- ☐ Basic
- ☐ Extended
- ☐ Premium ($)
- ☑ Executive w/$

Activity Level: UNKNOWN

Address
GO: **LEGALRC**

Patent Research Center

Description
This forum provides quick access to summaries of U.S. patents granted in chemical, mechanical, electrical, and design categories.

Subjects
Inventions, Legal Research, Research

Audience
Inventors, legal researchers, researchers

Content Summary
This forum contains summaries of patents granted internationally since the mid 1970s. Databases searched include the Claims/U.S. Patent Abstracts from 1950 to the present and the World Patents Index from 1963 to the present. You enter a search by typing a name, word, or phrase that describes the item you are searching for. The search can return up to 10 articles.

See Also
Legal Research Center, Legal Forum

User Guide
- ☑ Windows
- ☑ DOS
- ☑ Macintosh
- ☐ Terminal Emulation
- ☑ VMS
- ☑ UNIX
- ☑ OS/2
- ☐ Other platform

Cost
- ☐ Unknown
- ☐ Basic
- ☐ Extended
- ☑ Premium ($)
- ☐ Executive w/$

Activity Level

LOW — UNKNOWN (MEDIUM) — HIGH

Address
GO: **PATENT**

The Court Reporters Forum

Description
This forum is the headquarters for discussion of issues involving the court reporting profession worldwide.

Subjects
Law, Legislation

Audience
Lawers, legal professionals

Content Summary
The libraries include information on technology, litigation support, and marketing.

See Also
Legal Forum, Legal Research Center

User Guide
- ☑ Windows
- ☑ DOS
- ☐ Macintosh
- ☐ Terminal Emulation
- ☐ VMS
- ☐ UNIX
- ☐ OS/2
- ☐ Other platform

Cost
- ☐ Unknown
- ☐ Basic
- ☑ Extended
- ☐ Premium ($)
- ☐ Executive w/$

Activity Level

LOW — ↑MEDIUM — HIGH

Address
GO: **CRFORUM**

LDC Spreadsheet Forum

Description
This forum is dedicated to Lotus Corporation's family of spreadsheet products, including 1-2-3 (DOS and Windows) and Imrov.

Subjects
Computers

Audience
Computer users

Content Summary
You can find utilities, updates, press releases, help, and tips and hints in the library and message sections. Some of the libraries include 1-2-3 Release 2-4 for DOS, 1-2-3 Release 4-5 for Windows, 1-2-3 for OS/2, 1-2-3 for Macintosh, Improv for Windows, and more.

See Also
LDC Word Processing Forum, LDC Words & Pixels Forum, Lotus 123 For Windows Upgrade, Lotus Communications Forum, Lotus GmbH Forum, Lotus Technical Library, Lotus Press Release Forum

User Guide
- ☑ Windows
- ☑ DOS
- ☑ Macintosh
- ☐ Terminal Emulation
- ☐ VMS
- ☐ UNIX
- ☑ OS/2
- ☐ Other platform

Cost
- ☐ Unknown
- ☐ Basic
- ☑ Extended
- ☐ Premium ($)
- ☐ Executive w/$

Activity Level

LOW — MEDIUM → HIGH

Address
GO: **LOTUSA**

LDC Word Processing Forum

Description
This forum is dedicated to Lotus Corporation's line of word processing applications, including Ami Pro, LotusWrite, and SmarText.

Subjects
Computers

Audience
Computer users

Content Summary
This forum is operated by the Word Processing Division Technical Support Department of Lotus Corporation, located in Atlanta, Georgia, and includes discussions and files relating to Lotus' word processors. The libraries include Product Info. Demos, Ami Pro /w Technotes, Contest, Ami Pro w/ Macros, Fun & Graphics, Ami Pro OS/2 Macros, and more.

See Also
Lotus Communications Forum, Lotus 1-2-3 For Windows Upgrade, Lotus Press Release Forum, Lotus Technical Library, LDC Words & Pixels Forum, LDC Spreadsheet Forum

LCD Word Processing Forum – Learning Disabilities

User Guide
- ☑ Windows
- ☐ DOS
- ☐ Macintosh
- ☐ Terminal Emulation
- ☐ VMS
- ☐ UNIX
- ☑ OS/2
- ☐ Other platform

Cost
- ☐ Unknown
- ☐ Basic
- ☑ Extended
- ☐ Premium ($)
- ☐ Executive w/$

Activity Level: MEDIUM (LOW — HIGH)

Address
GO: **LOTUSWP**

LDC Words & Pixels Forum

Description
This Lotus Corporation forum discusses Magellan, Freelance, Freelance Plus, Graphwriter, Lotus Metro, and other graphics-related products.

Subjects
Computer Graphics, Computers

Audience
Computer users

Content Summary
You'll find information, discussions, questions, and other helpful insights for graphics-related products produced by Lotus Corporation. The library and message sections include Freelance/Windows, Multimedia Objects, Freelance OS/2, Freelance for DOS, ScreenCam, Agenda/Magellan, Symphony/LotusWorks, Oraganizer Technical, Approach, and others.

See Also
LDC Spreadsheet Forum, LDC Word Processing Forum, Lotus 1-2-3 For Windows Upgrade, Lotus Communications Forum, Lotus Press Release Forum, Lotus Technical Library

User Guide
- ☑ Windows
- ☑ DOS
- ☐ Macintosh
- ☐ Terminal Emulation
- ☐ VMS
- ☐ UNIX
- ☑ OS/2
- ☐ Other platform

Cost
- ☐ Unknown
- ☐ Basic
- ☑ Extended
- ☐ Premium ($)
- ☐ Executive w/$

Activity Level: MEDIUM (LOW — HIGH)

Address
GO: **LOTUSB**

LEARNING DISABILITIES

Disabilities Forum

Description
This forum is designed to be an online support group and open communication facilitator for anyone interested in disabilities. You can find stories, reports, and information about disabled persons' daily lives, along with ideas and experiences of parents and friends of disabled people.

Subjects
Emotional Disturbances, Learning Disabilities, Multiple Sclerosis, Disabilities

Audience
Disabled persons, family and friends of disabled persons, professionals who work with disabled persons

Content Summary
Many message and library topics are available to choose from, including developmental disabilities, emotional disturbances, hearing impairments, multiple sclerosis, and mobility impairments. You can find the latest information on the Americans with Disabilities Act (ADA) in Library 7, "Government Activities." If you are looking for employment, see "Education/Employment," Library 8, for files designed for disabled persons searching for employment and education.

See Also
Handicapped Users Database, Health/Fitness, Healthnet

User Guide
- ☑ Windows
- ☑ DOS
- ☑ Macintosh
- ☐ Terminal Emulation
- ☑ VMS
- ☑ UNIX
- ☑ OS/2
- ☐ Other platform

Cost
- ☐ Unknown
- ☐ Basic
- ☑ Extended
- ☐ Premium ($)
- ☐ Executive w/$

Activity Level: MEDIUM (LOW — HIGH)

Address
GO: **DISABILITIES**

Legal Forum

Description
This forum is dedicated to legal and law discussions. The forum welcomes any CompuServe member to join this forum.

Subjects
Law, Legislation

Audience
Lawyers, legal professionals, general public

Content Summary
The Legal Forum includes various topics for attorneys and non-attorneys, including computer and technical law, law firm economics, legal research, Supreme Court discussions, related professions, and hot topics. For a basic primer on learning the process and procedures of the court, see the Hot Topic library (Library 9).

See Also
IQUEST, Legal Research Center

User Guide
- [✓] Windows
- [✓] DOS
- [✓] Macintosh
- [ ] Terminal Emulation
- [✓] VMS
- [✓] UNIX
- [✓] OS/2
- [✓] Other platform

Cost
- [ ] Unknown
- [ ] Basic
- [✓] Extended
- [ ] Premium ($)
- [ ] Executive w/$

Activity Level

Address
GO: **LAWSIG**

Legal Research Center

Description
This database includes indexes to over 750 law journals, indexes to other law-related publications, summaries, and other topics.

Subjects
Law, Law Reviews, Legislation

Audience
Lawyers, legal professionals

Content Summary
You can use the Legal Research Center to search for legal topics from these databases: American Banker Full Text, Congressional Information Service, Criminal Justice Periodical Index, Legal Resource Index, National Criminal Justice Reference Service (NCJRS), and Tax Notes Today. See the description of pricing for specific searching prices.

See Also
Legal Forum

User Guide
- [✓] Windows
- [✓] DOS
- [✓] Macintosh
- [ ] Terminal Emulation
- [✓] VMS
- [✓] UNIX
- [✓] OS/2
- [✓] Other platform

Cost
- [ ] Unknown
- [ ] Basic
- [ ] Extended
- [ ] Premium ($)
- [✓] Executive w/$

Activity Level

Address
GO: **LEGALRC**

LEGISLATION

Legal Forum

Description
This forum is dedicated to legal and law discussions. The forum welcomes any CompuServe member to join this forum.

Subjects
Law, Legislation

Audience
Lawyers, legal professionals, general public

Content Summary
The Legal Forum includes various topics for attorneys and non-attorneys, including computer and technical law, law firm economics, legal research, Supreme Court discussions, related professions, and hot topics. For a basic primer on learning the process and procedures of the court, see the Hot Topic library (Library 9).

See Also
IQUEST, Legal Research Center

User Guide
- [✓] Windows
- [✓] DOS
- [✓] Macintosh
- [ ] Terminal Emulation
- [✓] VMS
- [✓] UNIX
- [✓] OS/2
- [✓] Other platform

Cost
- [ ] Unknown
- [ ] Basic
- [✓] Extended

Legislation – Literary Forum

Activity Level

Address
GO: **LAWSIG**

Legal Research Center

Description
This database includes indexes to over 750 law journals, indexes to other law-related publications, summaries, and other topics.

Subjects
Law, Law Reviews, Legislation

Audience
Lawyers, legal professionals

Content Summary
You can use the Legal Research Center to search for legal topics from these databases: American Banker Full Text, Congressional Information Service, Criminal Justice Periodical Index, Legal Resource Index, National Criminal Justice Reference Service (NCJRS), and Tax Notes Today. See the description of pricing for specific searching prices.

See Also
Legal Forum

User Guide
- ☑ Windows
- ☑ DOS
- ☑ Macintosh
- ☐ Terminal Emulation
- ☑ VMS
- ☑ UNIX
- ☑ OS/2
- ☑ Other platform

Cost
- ☐ Unknown
- ☐ Basic
- ☐ Extended
- ☐ Premium ($)
- ☑ Executive w/$

Activity Level

Address
GO: **LEGALRC**

Lexmark Support Forum

Description
This forum provides support and information for Lexmark products and services.

Subjects
Computer Hardware, Computers

Audience
Management information specialists, Macintosh users, computer hardware users, computer users

Content Summary
The libraries and message sections include Disk Images, Impact Drivers, Inkjet Drivers, Laser Drivers, Macintosh Drivers, Output Drivers, Thermal Drivers, and Utilities.

See Also
IBM File Finder

User Guide
- ☑ Windows
- ☑ DOS
- ☑ Macintosh
- ☐ Terminal Emulation
- ☐ VMS
- ☐ UNIX
- ☐ OS/2
- ☐ Other platform

Cost
- ☐ Unknown
- ☐ Basic
- ☑ Extended
- ☐ Premium ($)
- ☐ Executive w/$

Activity Level

MEDIUM (arrow pointing up to medium) LOW — HIGH

Address
GO: **LEXMARKFORUM**

Literary Forum

Description
Shakespeare. Plath. Milton. Twain. O'Conner. These and many other literary figures and related topics are discussed in this forum.

Subjects
Fiction, Literature, Writing

Audience
Writers, educators, editors, literary critics, literary theorists

Content Summary
If you like to read and talk about literature, join this forum. You'll also find discussions for writers and youth literature. Some of the libraries and message sections include Market Maneuvers, YouthLit/Learning, Journalism, Fiction, Science Fiction/Fantasy, Art of Writing, Romance/Historicals, and many more. The WotM! library (Library 3) is devoted to the Writer of the Month.

See Also
Journalism Forum

User Guide
- ☑ Windows
- ☑ DOS
- ☑ Macintosh
- ☐ Terminal Emulation
- ☑ VMS
- ☑ UNIX
- ☑ OS/2
- ☑ Other platform

Cost
- ☐ Unknown
- ☐ Basic
- ☑ Extended
- ☐ Premium ($)
- ☐ Executive w/$

LITERATURE

Literary Forum

Description
Shakespeare. Plath. Milton. Twain. O'Conner. These and many other literary figures and related topics are discussed in this forum.

Subjects
Fiction, Literature, Writing

Audience
Writers, educators, editors, literary critics, literary theorists

Content Summary
If you like to read and talk about literature, join this forum. You'll also find discussions for writers and youth literature. Some of the libraries and message sections include Market Maneuvers, YouthLit/Learning, Journalism, Fiction, Science Fiction/Fantasy, Art of Writing, Romance/Historicals, and many more. The WotM! library (Library 3) is devoted to the Writer of the Month.

See Also
Journalism Forum

User Guide
- ☑ Windows
- ☑ DOS
- ☑ Macintosh
- ☐ Terminal Emulation
- ☑ VMS
- ☑ UNIX
- ☑ OS/2
- ☑ Other platform

Cost
- ☐ Unknown
- ☐ Basic
- ☑ Extended
- ☐ Premium ($)
- ☐ Executive w/$

Activity Level
MEDIUM (arrow pointing to right of center, between LOW and HIGH)

Address
GO: **LITFORUM**

Logitech Forum

Description
This forum is devoted to Logitech products, including Scanman, FotoMan, 3D devices, mouse products, and others.

Subjects
Computer Hardware, Computers, Hardware/Software

Audience
Management information specialists, computer users, graphics designers

Content Summary
The Logitech Forum includes the following libraries: Mouse Products, Sound/Video, Scanman/FotoMan, Logitech OCR Software, MAC Products, Announcements, General Information, 3D Devices, and Top Q&A.

See Also
IBM File Finder

User Guide
- ☑ Windows
- ☑ DOS
- ☑ Macintosh
- ☐ Terminal Emulation
- ☐ VMS
- ☑ UNIX
- ☑ OS/2
- ☑ Other platform

Cost
- ☐ Unknown
- ☐ Basic
- ☑ Extended
- ☐ Premium ($)
- ☐ Executive w/$

Activity Level
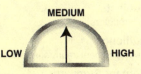
MEDIUM

Address
GO: **LOGITECH**

Lotus Communications Forum

Description
This forum is devoted to Lotus Corporation's communications products, including Notes and cc:Mail.

Subjects
Computer Communications, Computer Hardware, Computer Networking, Computers, E-mail, Networking

Audience
Management information specialists, network users

Content Summary
You can find a plethora of information, technical support solutions, hints and tips, and want ads in this forum. The library and message forums include Notes Tech Info, Notes Workstations/DB, Notes API Devlopment, cc:Mail Platform, cc:Mail Router, cc:Mail Admin, and many others.

See Also
Lotus Press Release Forum, Lotus Technical Library

Lotus Communications Forum – Lotus Technical Library

User Guide
- ☑ Windows
- ☑ DOS
- ☑ Macintosh
- ☐ Terminal Emulation
- ☐ VMS
- ☐ UNIX
- ☑ OS/2
- ☑ Other platform

Cost
- ☐ Unknown
- ☐ Basic
- ☑ Extended
- ☐ Premium ($)
- ☐ Executive w/$

Activity Level — MEDIUM (arrow pointing toward HIGH, between LOW and HIGH)

Address
GO: **LOTUSCOMM**

Lotus Press Release Forum

Description
Want to find the official word from Lotus Corporation on their latest release? Check out this forum for press releases.

Subjects
Computers

Audience
Management information specialists, computer users

Content Summary
This forum's libraries are divided into months so you can quickly find the most current PR material from Lotus.

See Also
Lotus Technical Library, Lotus Communications Forum, LDC Spreadsheets Forum, LDC Word Processing Forum, LDC Words & Pixels Forum

User Guide
- ☑ Windows
- ☑ DOS
- ☑ Macintosh
- ☐ Terminal Emulation
- ☐ VMS
- ☐ UNIX
- ☐ OS/2
- ☐ Other platform

Cost
- ☐ Unknown
- ☐ Basic
- ☑ Extended
- ☐ Premium ($)
- ☐ Executive w/$

Activity Level — MEDIUM (arrow pointing toward LOW)

Address
GO: **LOTUSNEWS**

Lotus Technical Library

Description
Need a quick answer to a question about a Lotus product? If so, this service should help you find the answer.

Subjects
Computers

Audience
Computer users

Content Summaary
The Lotus Technical Library is a comprehensive collection of Lotus product information. The Technical Library contains answers to common questions, tips and techniques for using Lotus products more effectively, and troubleshooting guidelines for identifying and resolving technical difficulties. The information in the Lotus Technical Library is researched and written by the Lotus Customer Support staff. Information is available for all Lotus products and releases.

See Also
LDC Spreadsheets Forum, LDC Word Processing Forum, LDC Words & Pixels Forum, Lotus Communications Forum, Lotus Press Release Forum

User Guide
- ☑ Windows
- ☑ DOS
- ☐ Macintosh
- ☐ Terminal Emulation
- ☐ VMS
- ☐ UNIX
- ☐ OS/2
- ☐ Other platform

Cost
- ☐ Unknown
- ☐ Basic
- ☑ Extended
- ☐ Premium ($)
- ☐ Executive w/$

Activity Level — MEDIUM / UNKNOWN

Address
GO: **LOTUSTECH**

M
MACINTOSH

Macintosh Applications Forum

Description
This is the MAUG area for discussing all of the many application programs for the Macintosh.

Subjects
Computers, Macintosh

Audience
Macintosh users, computer users

Content Summary
This forum's library and message sections include Word Processing, Databases, Spreadsheets/Models, Accounting/Finance, DTP Templates, Multimedia, Graphics Tools, and more.

See Also
Macintosh Forums

User Guide
- ☐ Windows
- ☐ DOS
- ☑ Macintosh
- ☐ Terminal Emulation
- ☐ VMS
- ☐ UNIX
- ☐ OS/2
- ☐ Other platform

Cost
- ☐ Unknown
- ☐ Basic
- ☑ Extended
- ☐ Premium ($)
- ☐ Executive w/$

Activity level

Address
GO: **MACAP**

Macintosh CIM Support Forum

Description
This forum offers support for MacCIM and is free of connect time charges.

Subjects
Computers, Macintosh

Audience
Computer users, Macintosh users

Content Summary
This message and library sections in this forum include Support Files, User Contributions, Scripts (CCL), Filing Cabinet, and more.

See Also
Macintosh Forums

User Guide
- ☐ Windows
- ☐ DOS
- ☑ Macintosh
- ☐ Terminal Emulation
- ☐ VMS
- ☐ UNIX
- ☐ OS/2
- ☐ Other platform

Cost
- ☐ Unknown
- ☑ Basic
- ☐ Extended
- ☐ Premium ($)
- ☐ Executive w/$

Activity Level

Address
GO: **MCIMSUP**

Macintosh Communications Forum

Description
You can find support, tips, files, and discussions concerning Mac communications topics that include fax, modems, and ISDN.

Subjects
Computers, Macintosh, Modems

Audience
Macintosh users, computer users

Content Summary
The many library and message sections include CIS Navigator, Scripts/Tools, Communication Programs/Utilities, Hardware, FAX, Networking, Talking to PCs, BBS Systems, and more.

See Also
Macintosh Forums, Macintosh Hardware Forum

User Guide
- ☐ Windows
- ☐ DOS
- ☑ Macintosh
- ☐ Terminal Emulation
- ☐ VMS
- ☐ UNIX
- ☐ OS/2
- ☐ Other platform

Cost
- ☐ Unknown
- ☐ Basic
- ☑ Extended
- ☐ Premium ($)
- ☐ Executive w/$

Activity Level

Address
GO: **MACCOM**

Macintosh

Macintosh Community Club Forum

Description
This is the MAUG lobby area, which includes informal discussions ranging from views on Apple's corporate policies to current events.

Subjects:
Computers, Macintosh

Audience
Computer users, Macintosh users

Content Summary
This forum includes several helpful libraries and has a lively message area. In these areas, you can find topics such as Help Files, Community Square, Parties/Cons, Resumes, Magazines/Review, and more. There's also a Classified area where you can post an ad or respond to one.

See Also
Macintosh Forums, Mac Entertainment Forum

User Guide
- [ ] Windows
- [ ] DOS
- [x] Macintosh
- [ ] Terminal Emulation
- [ ] VMS
- [ ] UNIX
- [ ] OS/2
- [ ] Other platform

Cost
- [ ] Unknown
- [ ] Basic
- [x] Extended
- [ ] Premium ($)
- [ ] Executive w/$

Activity Level

Address
GO: **MACCLUB**

Macintosh Developers Forum

Description
If you want to program your Macintosh—whether commercially or for your own use—the Mac Developers Forum is the right place for you.

Subjects
Computer Programming Languages, Computers, Macintosh

Audience
Macintosh users, computer programmers

Content Summary
The following libraries are found in this forum: BASIC, Assembly Language, C and Pascal, Object Oriented, Other Languages, Apple System Tools, Apple System Files, Development Environments, Scripting Month, Learn Programming, A/UX, Tools/Debuggers, and MacTech Magazine.

See Also
Macintosh Forums, Macintosh Systems Forum

User Guide
- [ ] Windows
- [ ] DOS
- [x] Macintosh
- [ ] Terminal Emulation
- [ ] VMS
- [ ] UNIX
- [ ] OS/2
- [ ] Other platform

Cost
- [ ] Unknown
- [ ] Basic
- [x] Extended
- [ ] Premium ($)
- [ ] Executive w/$

Activity Level

Address
GO: **MACDEV**

Macintosh Entertainment Forum

Description
Sit back and relax. This forum has games, sound utilities, music, glamour graphics, and more—all for the Mac.

Subjects
Computer Games, Computers, Macintosh

Audience
Computer users, Macintosh users

Content Summary
This forum is full of files, discussions, suggestions, games, and other ways to help you get more enjoyment out of your Macintosh and computing life. You can also participate in the PlayMaker Football League, an online football simulation game for the Mac (see Library 10).

See Also
Macintosh Forums

User Guide
- [ ] Windows
- [ ] DOS
- [x] Macintosh
- [ ] Terminal Emulation
- [ ] VMS
- [ ] UNIX
- [ ] OS/2
- [ ] Other platform

Cost
- [ ] Unknown
- [ ] Basic
- [x] Extended
- [ ] Premium ($)
- [ ] Executive w/$

Activity Level
MEDIUM — LOW / HIGH

Address
GO: **MACFUN**

Macintosh File Finder

Description
Use this service to find any file from Macintosh forums on CompuServe.

Subjects
Computers, Macintosh

Audience
Macintosh users, computer users

Content Summary
Mac File Finder is an online comprehensive keyword searchable database of file descriptions from Mac-related forums. It is designed to provide quick and easy reference to some of the best programs and files available.

See Also
Macintosh Forums, Mac New Users Help Forum

User Guide
- [ ] Windows
- [ ] DOS
- [x] Macintosh
- [ ] Terminal Emulation
- [ ] VMS
- [ ] UNIX
- [ ] OS/2
- [ ] Other platform

Cost
- [ ] Unknown
- [ ] Basic
- [x] Extended
- [ ] Premium ($)
- [ ] Executive w/$

Activity Level

Address
GO: **MACFF**

Macintosh Forums

Description
Not sure which Mac-related forum to visit? Start from this service.

Subjects
Computers, Macintosh

Audience
Computer users, Macintosh users

Content Summary
You can choose from Apple Systems, Inc forums, MAUG (Micronetworked Apple Users Group) forums, and ZiffNet/MacUser/ZMAC forums.

See Also
Mac New Users Help Forum, Apple Support Forum

User Guide
- [ ] Windows
- [ ] DOS
- [x] Macintosh
- [ ] Terminal Emulation
- [ ] VMS
- [ ] UNIX
- [ ] OS/2
- [ ] Other platform

Cost
- [ ] Unknown
- [x] Basic
- [ ] Extended
- [ ] Premium ($)
- [ ] Executive w/$

Activity Level

Address
GO: **MACINTOSH**

Macintosh Hardware Forum

Description
This forum discusses all types of Macintosh computers, including Classics, Quadras, Performas, Mac II, LC, Newton, and PDAs.

Subjects
Computer Hardware, Computers, Macintosh

Audience
Macintosh users, management information specialists

Content Summary
You can find several libraries in this forum that should satisfy your need for support and help for your Macintosh hardware, including Classic/Early Macs, Performas/Other, Quadras, Printers/Output, Scanners/Input, Monitors/Video, and more.

See Also
Macintosh Systems Forum, Macintosh Forums

User Guide
- [ ] Windows
- [ ] DOS
- [x] Macintosh
- [ ] Terminal Emulation
- [ ] VMS
- [ ] UNIX
- [ ] OS/2
- [ ] Other platform

Cost
- [ ] Unknown
- [ ] Basic
- [x] Extended
- [ ] Premium ($)
- [ ] Executive w/$

Activity Level

Address
GO: **MACHW**

Macintosh Hypertext Forum

Description
Whether you are a browser or are familiar with XCMNDS and Hypertalk, this Forum is for you.

Subjects
Computers, Macintosh, Multimedia

Macintosh

Audience
Macintosh users

Content Summary
This forum includes libraries such as Games, Education, Music and Sound, Art: Clip and Fine!, Reference Stacks, and more. Also note that there is an R-Rated Stacks library that contains nudity. This library may be offensive to some people and should not be viewed by minors under the age of 18.

See Also
Macintosh Forums, Mac Entertainment Forum

User Guide
- ☐ Windows
- ☐ DOS
- ☑ Macintosh
- ☐ Terminal Emulation
- ☐ VMS
- ☐ UNIX
- ☐ OS/2
- ☐ Other platform

Cost
- ☐ Unknown
- ☐ Basic
- ☑ Extended
- ☐ Premium ($)
- ☐ Executive w/$

Activity Level

Address
GO: **MACHYPER**

Macintosh Multimedia Forum

Description
This forum discusses the various uses of the Macintosh as a platform for multimedia development.

Subjects
Computers, Macintosh, Multimedia

Audience
Macintosh users

Content Summary
Loaded with multimedia clips, QuickTime movies and tools, HyperCard tools, and templates, this forum is for you if you are interested in multimedia, the creation of it, or the final results of multimedia. Check out these libraries: Video Clips, Sound Tools, Glamour Films, and Home Movies.

See Also
Macintosh Forums, Mac Entertainment Forum, Mac Hypertext Forum

User Guide
- ☐ Windows
- ☐ DOS
- ☑ Macintosh
- ☐ Terminal Emulation
- ☐ VMS
- ☐ UNIX
- ☐ OS/2
- ☐ Other platform

Cost
- ☐ Unknown
- ☐ Basic
- ☑ Extended
- ☐ Premium ($)
- ☐ Executive w/$

Activity Level

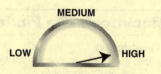

Address
GO: **MACMULTI**

Macintosh New Users Help Forum

Description
This forum is designed to aid the user new to the MAUG forums.

Subjects
Computers, Macintosh

Audience
Computer users, Macintosh users

Content Summary
You'll find many library and message sections in this forum, including Help Files, Using Forums, Using LIBs, MAUG Guide, Disk Tools, Anti-Virus Tools, System Tools, and Guest/CO Archives.

See Also
Macintosh Forums, Macintosh File Finder

User Guide
- ☐ Windows
- ☐ DOS
- ☑ Macintosh
- ☐ Terminal Emulation
- ☐ VMS
- ☐ UNIX
- ☐ OS/2
- ☐ Other platform

Cost
- ☐ Unknown
- ☐ Basic
- ☑ Extended
- ☐ Premium ($)
- ☐ Executive w/$

Activity Level

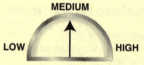

Address
GO: **MACNEW**

Macintosh Systems Forum

Description
Join this forum for discussions and support files for system-related topics about the Mac.

Subjects
Computers, Macintosh

Audience
Macintosh users, management information specialists

Content Summary
This is the MAUG area for discussing the many system-related areas of the Mac, both hardware

(such as printers, disks, and monitors) and software (such as System, Finder, INITs, cdevs, and FKEYs). You can find topics such as System 6 Specific, Control Panels, Fonts, Utilities, Aliases/Icons, QuickTime, Emergency, and more.

See Also
Macintosh File Finder, Mac Community/Club Forum

User Guide
- ☐ Windows
- ☐ DOS
- ☑ Macintosh
- ☐ Terminal Emulation
- ☐ VMS
- ☐ UNIX
- ☐ OS/2
- ☐ Other platform

Cost
- ☐ Unknown
- ☐ Basic
- ☑ Extended
- ☐ Premium ($)
- ☐ Executive w/$

Activity Level
MEDIUM (arrow pointing up)

Address
GO: **MACSYS**

Macintosh Vendor Forums

Description
These forums include support from various Mac vendors.

Subjects
Computers, Macintosh

Audience
Computer users, Macintosh users

Content Summary
The Mac A Vendor Forum (GO MACAVEN) includes these vendors: Portfolio Software, Nisus Software, CE Software, DeltaPoint, DayStar Digital, and more. The Mac B Vendor Forum (GO MACBVEN) includes these vendors: GCC Technologies, Altsys Corporation, Jasik Designs, Software Ventures, Radius Corporation, Deneba Software, and more. The Mac C Vendor Forum (GO MACCVEN) includes these vendors: Alladin Systems, Baseline Publishing, Inline Software, Avator Corporation, Farallon, Virtus Corporation, and more. The Mac D Vendor Forum (GO MACDVEN) includes these vendors: MacTech Magazine, Atticus, TidBITS Magazine, Micronet, and more.

See Also
Mac Applications Forum, Macintosh Forums

User Guide
- ☐ Windows
- ☐ DOS
- ☑ Macintosh
- ☐ Terminal Emulation
- ☐ VMS
- ☐ UNIX
- ☐ OS/2
- ☐ Other platform

Cost
- ☐ Unknown
- ☐ Basic
- ☑ Extended
- ☐ Premium ($)
- ☐ Executive w/$

Activity Level
LOW

Address
GO: **MACxVEN**

MacNav Support Forum

Description
Need help with MacNav? If so, head to this forum.

Subjects
Computers, Macintosh

Audience
Macintosh users, computer users

Content Summary
This forum encourages discussions and helpful hints for using MacNav. You'll find these library and message sections on this forum: CompuServe Mail, Manual Mode/Scripts, Session Parameters, Navigator Tips, Suggestions, and Navigator Patches.

See Also
Macintosh Forums

User Guide
- ☐ Windows
- ☐ DOS
- ☑ Macintosh
- ☐ Terminal Emulation
- ☐ VMS
- ☐ UNIX
- ☐ OS/2
- ☐ Other platform

Cost
- ☐ Unknown
- ☑ Basic
- ☐ Extended
- ☐ Premium ($)
- ☐ Executive w/$

Activity Level
MEDIUM

Address
GO: **MNAVSUPPORT**

MacWAREHOUSE

Description
Order products from MacWAREHOUSE online using this service.

Subjects
Computer Products, Macintosh

Audience
Computer users, Macintosh users

Macintosh

Content Summary
From the main menu, you can go to the MacWAREHOUSE Online Store to order products, view Best Selling Items, go to the QuickSearch area, Request or Order from the Online Catalog, talk to Customer Service, or play the MacWAREHOUSE Word Scramble game.

See Also
Macintosh Vender Forum

User Guide
- ☐ Windows
- ☐ DOS
- ☑ Macintosh
- ☑ Terminal Emulation
- ☐ VMS
- ☐ UNIX
- ☐ OS/2
- ☐ Other platform

Cost
- ☐ Unknown
- ☑ Basic
- ☐ Extended
- ☐ Premium ($)
- ☐ Executive w/$

Activity Level

Address
GO: **MW**

MIDI/Music Forum

Description
This forum is dedicated to supporting MIDI and computer music-related discussions and files. Also, it has the coolest forum logo. You have to see it!

Subjects
Amiga, Macintosh, Multimedia, Music

Audience
Musicians, computer game developers, computer users, Amiga users

Content Summary
Packed with files, discussions, tips and hints, and troubleshooting guidelines, the MIDI/Music Forum includes these and other library and message sections: Basics and Product Guides, General MIDI Songs, Atari Files, Macintosh Files, Patches/Samples, MS DOS Demos, and Windows Media Sound. You'll find items for sale in the Classified Ads library (Library 8).

See Also
MIDI A Vendor Forum, MIDI B Vendor Forum, MIDI C Vendor Forum

User Guide
- ☑ Windows
- ☑ DOS
- ☑ Macintosh
- ☐ Terminal Emulation
- ☐ VMS
- ☐ UNIX
- ☐ OS/2
- ☑ Other platform

Cost
- ☐ Unknown
- ☐ Basic
- ☑ Extended
- ☐ Premium ($)
- ☐ Executive w/$

Activity Level
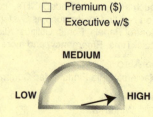

Address
GO: **MIDIFORUM**

The Mac Zone/PC Zone

Description
Online shopping area for Mac and PC hardware and software.

Subjects
Computer Products, Macintosh

Audience
Computer users, Macintosh users

Content Summary
This online shopping area enables members to purchase from a complete line of PC and Macintosh products often at reduced rates.

See Also

User Guide
- ☑ Windows
- ☑ DOS
- ☑ Macintosh
- ☐ Terminal Emulation
- ☐ VMS
- ☐ UNIX
- ☐ OS/2
- ☐ Other platform

Cost
- ☐ Unknown
- ☐ Basic
- ☐ Extended
- ☐ Premium ($)
- ☐ Executive w/$

Activity Level

Address
GO: **MPZ**

ZiffNet/Mac Download Forum

Description
This forum contains the top Macintosh shareware and freeware picks of the editors of *MacWEEK* and *MacUser* magazines.

Subjects
Computers, Macintosh, ZiffNet

Audience
Macintosh users

Content Summary
This forum is for members interested in discussing and downloading popular Macintosh freeware and shareware.

See Also
ZiffNet File Finder, IBM File Finder

User Guide
- ☐ Windows
- ☐ DOS
- ☑ Macintosh
- ☐ Terminal Emulation
- ☐ VMS
- ☐ UNIX
- ☐ OS/2
- ☐ Other platform

Cost
- ☐ Unknown
- ☐ Basic
- ☑ Extended
- ☐ Premium ($)
- ☐ Executive w/$

Activity Level
LOW (arrow pointing low-medium)

Address
GO: **ZMC:DOWNTECH**

ZiffNet/Mac File Finder

Description
The ZMC File Finder database enables members to search through all files located in the ZMC forums.

Subjects
Computers, Macintosh, ZiffNet

Audience
Macintosh users

Content Summary
This service is for members wanting to search ZMC forums for specific file types.

See Also
ZiffNet/Mac Download Forum

User Guide
- ☐ Windows
- ☐ DOS
- ☑ Macintosh
- ☐ Terminal Emulation
- ☐ VMS
- ☐ UNIX
- ☐ OS/2
- ☐ Other platform

Cost
- ☐ Unknown
- ☐ Basic
- ☑ Extended
- ☐ Premium ($)
- ☐ Executive w/$

Activity Level
UNKNOWN

Address
GO: **ZMC:FILEFINDER**

Macintosh Applications Forum

Description
This is the MAUG area for discussing all of the many application programs for the Macintosh.

Subjects
Computers, Macintosh

Audience
Macintosh users, computer users

Content Summary
This forum's library and message sections include Word Processing, Databases, Spreadsheets/Models, Accounting/Finance, DTP Templates, Multimedia, Graphics Tools, and more.

See Also
Macintosh Forums

User Guide
- ☐ Windows
- ☐ DOS
- ☑ Macintosh
- ☐ Terminal Emulation
- ☐ VMS
- ☐ UNIX
- ☐ OS/2
- ☐ Other platform

Cost
- ☐ Unknown
- ☐ Basic
- ☑ Extended
- ☐ Premium ($)
- ☐ Executive w/$

Activity level
MEDIUM-HIGH

Address
GO: **MACAP**

Macintosh CIM Support Forum

Description
This forum offers support for MacCIM and is free of connect-time charges.

Subjects
Computers, Macintosh

Audience
Computer users, Macintosh users

Content Summary
The message and library sections in this forum include Support Files, User Contributions, Scripts (CCL), Filing Cabinet, and more.

See Also
Macintosh Forums

User Guide
- ☐ Windows
- ☐ DOS
- ☑ Macintosh
- ☐ Terminal Emulation
- ☐ VMS
- ☐ UNIX
- ☐ OS/2
- ☐ Other platform

Cost
- ☐ Unknown
- ☑ Basic
- ☐ Extended
- ☐ Premium ($)
- ☐ Executive w/$

Activity Level: MEDIUM (arrow pointing up between LOW and HIGH)

Address
GO: **MCIMSUP**

Macintosh Communications Forum

Description
You can find support, tips, files, and discussions concerning Mac communications topics that include fax, modems, and ISDN.

Subjects
Computers, Macintosh, Modem

Audience
Macintosh users, computer users

Content Summary
The many library and message sections include CIS Navigator, Scripts/Tools, Communication Programs/Utilities, Hardware, FAX, Networking, Talking to PCs, BBS Systems, and more.

See Also
Macintosh Forums, Macintosh Hardware Forum

User Guide
- ☐ Windows
- ☐ DOS
- ☑ Macintosh
- ☐ Terminal Emulation
- ☐ VMS
- ☐ UNIX
- ☐ OS/2
- ☐ Other platform

Cost
- ☐ Unknown
- ☐ Basic
- ☑ Extended
- ☐ Premium ($)
- ☐ Executive w/$

Activity Level: MEDIUM (arrow pointing up)

Address
GO: **MACCOM**

Macintosh Community Club Forum

Description
This is the MAUG lobby area, which includes informal discussions ranging from views on Apple's corporate policies to current events.

Subjects:
Computers, Macintosh

Audience
Computer users, Macintosh users

Content Summary
This forum includes several helpful libraries and has a lively message area. In these areas, you can find topics such as Help Files, Community Square, Pros/Cons, Resumes, Magazines/Review, and more. There's also a Classified area where you can post an ad or respond to one.

See Also
Macintosh Forums, Mac Entertainment Forum

User Guide
- ☐ Windows
- ☐ DOS
- ☑ Macintosh
- ☐ Terminal Emulation
- ☐ VMS
- ☐ UNIX
- ☐ OS/2
- ☐ Other platform

Cost
- ☐ Unknown
- ☐ Basic
- ☑ Extended
- ☐ Premium ($)
- ☐ Executive w/$

Activity Level: MEDIUM (arrow pointing toward HIGH)

Address
GO: **MACCLUB**

Macintosh Developers Forum

Description
If you want to program your Macintosh—whether commercially or for your own use—the Mac Developers Forum is the right place for you.

Subjects
Computer Programming Languages, Computers, Macintosh

Audience
Macintosh users, computer programmers

Content Summary
The following libraries are found in this forum: BASIC, Assembly Language, C and Pascal, Object Oriented, Other Languages, Apple System Tools, Apple System Files, Development Environments, Scripting Month, Learn Programming, A/UX, Tools/Debuggers, and MacTech Magazine.

See Also
Macintosh Forums, Macintosh Systems Forum

User Guide
- ☐ Windows
- ☐ DOS
- ☑ Macintosh
- ☐ Terminal Emulation
- ☐ VMS
- ☐ UNIX
- ☐ OS/2
- ☐ Other platform

Macintosh Developers Forum – Macintosh Forums

Cost
- ☐ Unknown
- ☐ Basic
- ☑ Extended
- ☐ Premium ($)
- ☐ Executive w/$

Activity Level — MEDIUM (LOW / HIGH)

Address
GO: **MACDEV**

Macintosh Entertainment Forum

Description
Sit back and relax. This forum has games, sound utilities, music, glamour graphics, and more—all for the Mac.

Subjects
Computer Games, Computers, Macintosh

Audience
Computer users, Macintosh users

Content Summary
This forum is full of files, discussions, suggestions, games, and other ways to help you get more enjoyment out of your Macintosh and computing life. You can also participate in the PlayMaker Football League, an online football simulation game for the Mac (see Library 10).

See Also
Macintosh Forums

User Guide
- ☐ Windows
- ☐ DOS
- ☑ Macintosh
- ☐ Terminal Emulation
- ☐ VMS
- ☐ UNIX
- ☐ OS/2
- ☐ Other platform

Cost
- ☐ Unknown
- ☐ Basic
- ☑ Extended
- ☐ Premium ($)
- ☐ Executive w/$

Activity Level — MEDIUM (LOW / HIGH)

Address
GO: **MACFUN**

Macintosh File Finder

Description
Use this service to find any file from Macintosh forums on CompuServe.

Subjects
Computers, Macintosh

Audience
Macintosh users, computer users

Content Summary
Mac File Finder is an online comprehensive keyword searchable database of file descriptions from Mac-related forums. It is designed to provide quick and easy reference to some of the best programs and files available.

See Also
Macintosh Forums, Mac New Users Help Forum

User Guide
- ☐ Windows
- ☐ DOS
- ☑ Macintosh
- ☐ Terminal Emulation
- ☐ VMS
- ☐ UNIX
- ☐ OS/2
- ☐ Other platform

Cost
- ☐ Unknown
- ☐ Basic
- ☑ Extended
- ☐ Premium ($)
- ☐ Executive w/$

Activity Level — UNKNOWN

Address
GO: **MACFF**

Macintosh Forums

Description
Not sure which Mac-related forum to visit? Start from this service.

Subjects
Computers, Macintosh

Audience
Computer users, Macintosh users

Content Summary
You can choose from Apple Systems, Inc forums, MAUG (Micronetworked Apple Users Group) forums, and ZiffNet/MacUser/ZMAC forums.

See Also
Mac New Users Help Forum, Apple Support Forum

User Guide
- ☐ Windows
- ☐ DOS
- ☑ Macintosh
- ☐ Terminal Emulation
- ☐ VMS
- ☐ UNIX
- ☐ OS/2
- ☐ Other platform

Cost
- ☐ Unknown
- ☑ Basic
- ☐ Extended
- ☐ Premium ($)
- ☐ Executive w/$

M

Macintosh Forums – Macintosh Multimedia Forum

Activity Level

Address
GO: **MACINTOSH**

Macintosh Hardware Forum

Description
This forum discusses all types of Macintosh computers, including Classics, Quadras, Performas, Mac II, LC, Newton, and PDAs.

Subjects
Computer Hardware, Computers, Macintosh

Audience
Macintosh users, management information specialists

Content Summary
You can find several libraries in this forum that should satisfy your need for support and help for your Macintosh hardware, including Classic/Early Macs, Performas/Other, Quadras, Printers/Output, Scanners/Input, Monitors/Video, and more.

See Also
Macintosh Systems Forum, Macintosh Forums

User Guide
- ☐ Windows
- ☐ DOS
- ☑ Macintosh
- ☐ Terminal Emulation
- ☐ VMS
- ☐ UNIX
- ☐ OS/2
- ☐ Other platform

Cost
- ☐ Unknown
- ☐ Basic
- ☑ Extended
- ☐ Premium ($)
- ☐ Executive w/$

Activity Level

Address
GO: **MACHW**

Macintosh Hypertext Forum

Description
Whether you are a browser or are familiar with XCMNDS and Hypertalk, this forum is for you.

Subjects
Computers, Macintosh, Multimedia

Audience
Macintosh users

Content Summary
This forum includes libraries such as Games, Education, Music and Sound, Art: Clip and Fine!, Reference Stacks, and more. Also note that there is an R-Rated Stacks library that contains nudity and may be offensive to some people. This library should not be viewed by minors under the age of 18.

See Also
Macintosh Forums, Mac Entertainment Forum

User Guide
- ☐ Windows
- ☐ DOS
- ☑ Macintosh
- ☐ Terminal Emulation
- ☐ VMS
- ☐ UNIX
- ☐ OS/2
- ☐ Other platform

Cost
- ☐ Unknown
- ☐ Basic
- ☑ Extended
- ☐ Premium ($)
- ☐ Executive w/$

Activity Level

Address
GO: **MACHYPER**

Macintosh Multimedia Forum

Description
This forum discusses the various uses of the Macintosh as a platform for multimedia development.

Subjects
Computers, Macintosh, Multimedia

Audience
Macintosh users

Content Summary
Loaded with multimedia clips, QuickTime movies and tools, HyperCard tools, and templates, this forum is for you if you are interested in multimedia, the creation of it, or the final results of multimedia. Check out these libraries: Video Clips, Sound Tools, Glamour Films, and Home Movies.

See Also
Macintosh Forums, Mac Entertainment Forum, Mac Hypertext Forum

User Guide
- ☐ Windows
- ☐ DOS
- ☑ Macintosh
- ☐ Terminal Emulation
- ☐ VMS
- ☐ UNIX
- ☐ OS/2
- ☐ Other platform

Cost
- ☐ Unknown
- ☐ Basic
- ☑ Extended
- ☐ Premium ($)
- ☐ Executive w/$

Macintosh Multimedia Forum – Macintosh Vendor Forums

Activity Level

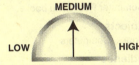

Address
GO: **MACMULTI**

Macintosh New Users Help Forum

Description
This forum is designed to aid the new user to the MAUG forums.

Subjects
Computers, Macintosh

Audience
Computer users, Macintosh users

Content Summary
You'll find many library and message sections in this forum, including Help Files, Using Forums, Using LIBs, MAUG Guide, Disk Tools, Anti-Virus Tools, System Tools, and Guest/CO Archives.

See Also
Macintosh Forums, Macintosh File Finder

User Guide
- ☐ Windows
- ☐ DOS
- ☑ Macintosh
- ☐ Terminal Emulation
- ☐ VMS
- ☐ UNIX
- ☐ OS/2
- ☐ Other platform

Cost
- ☐ Unknown
- ☐ Basic
- ☑ Extended
- ☐ Premium ($)
- ☐ Executive w/$

Activity Level

Address
GO: **MACNEW**

Macintosh Systems Forum

Description
Join this forum for discussions and support files for system-related topics about the Mac.

Subjects
Computers, Macintosh

Audience
Macintosh users, management information specialists

Content Summary
This is the MAUG area for discussing the many system-related areas of the Mac, both hardware (such as printers, disks, and monitors) and software (such as System, Finder, INITs, cdevs, and FKEYs). You can find topics such as System 6 Specific, Control Panels, Fonts, Utilities, Aliases/Icons, QuickTime, Emergency, and more.

See Also
Macintosh File Finder, Mac Community/Club Forum

User Guide
- ☐ Windows
- ☐ DOS
- ☑ Macintosh
- ☐ Terminal Emulation
- ☐ VMS
- ☐ UNIX
- ☐ OS/2
- ☐ Other platform

Cost
- ☐ Unknown
- ☐ Basic
- ☑ Extended
- ☐ Premium ($)
- ☐ Executive w/$

Activity Level

MEDIUM / LOW / HIGH

Address
GO: **MACSYS**

Macintosh Vendor Forums

Description
These forums include support from various Mac vendors.

Subjects
Computers, Macintosh

Audience
Computer users, Macintosh users

Content Summary
The Mac A Vendor Forum (GO MACAVEN) includes these vendors: Portfolio Software, Nisus Software, CE Software, DeltaPoint, DayStar Digital, and more. The Mac B Vendor Forum (GO MACBVEN) includes these vendors: GCC Technologies, Altsys Corporation, Jasik Designs, Software Ventures, Radius Corporation, Deneba Software, and more. The Mac C Vendor Forum (GO MACCVEN) includes these vendors: Alladin Systems, Baseline Publishing, Inline Software, Avator Corporation, Farallon, Virtus Corporation, and more. The Mac D Vendor Forum (GO MACDVEN) includes these vendors: MacTech Magazine, Atticus, TidBITS Magazine, Micronet, and more.

See Also
Mac Applications Forum, Macintosh Forums

User Guide
- ☐ Windows
- ☐ DOS
- ☑ Macintosh
- ☐ Terminal Emulation
- ☐ VMS
- ☐ UNIX
- ☐ OS/2
- ☐ Other platform

Macintosh Vendor Forums – Macromedia Forum

Cost
- ☐ Unknown
- ☐ Basic
- ☑ Extended
- ☐ Premium ($)
- ☐ Executive w/$

Activity Level: LOW (arrow pointing low-medium) MEDIUM HIGH

Address
GO: **MACxVEN**

Macmillan Publishing Forum

Description
Get up-to-date information, technical support, customer service, and files relating to Macmillan Computer Publishing books.

Subjects
Books, Computers

Audience
Management information specialists, computer users

Content Summary
Computer books published by New Riders Publishing, Que, SAMS, Hayden, Alpha, Que College, and Brady are supported in this forum. You can find files associated with specific books, graphics files, word processing templates, spreadsheets, and utilities to help you get the most out of your computer system. This forum has one of the best opening bitmaps on CompuServe.

See Also
Computer Club Forum

User Guide
- ☑ Windows
- ☑ DOS
- ☑ Macintosh
- ☐ Terminal Emulation
- ☐ VMS
- ☐ UNIX
- ☑ OS/2
- ☑ Other platform

Cost
- ☐ Unknown
- ☐ Basic
- ☑ Extended
- ☐ Premium ($)
- ☐ Executive w/$

Activity Level: LOW MEDIUM (arrow pointing medium) HIGH

Address
GO: **MACMILLAN**

MacNav Support Forum

Description
Need help with MacNav? If so, head to this forum.

Subjects
Computers, Macintosh

Audience
Macintosh users, computer users

Content Summary
This forum encourages discussions and helpful hints for using MacNav. You'll find these library and message sections on this forum: CompuServe Mail, Manual Mode/Scripts, Session Parameters, Navigator Tips, Suggestions, and Navigator Patches.

See Also
Macintosh Forums

User Guide
- ☐ Windows
- ☐ DOS
- ☑ Macintosh
- ☐ Terminal Emulation
- ☐ VMS
- ☐ UNIX
- ☐ OS/2
- ☐ Other platform

Cost
- ☐ Unknown
- ☑ Basic
- ☐ Extended
- ☐ Premium ($)
- ☐ Executive w/$

Activity Level: LOW MEDIUM (arrow pointing medium) HIGH

Address
GO: **MNAVSUPPORT**

Macromedia Forum

Description
This forum provides technical support and discussions on Macromedia products.

Subjects
Computers, Multimedia

Audience
Computer users

Content Summary
Macromedia topics discussed in this forum include Director, Authoware, Action/ClipMedia, 3D/Modeling/MMaker, sound products, and more.

See Also
Multimedia Forum, Multimedia Vendor Forum

User Guide
- ☑ Windows
- ☑ DOS
- ☑ Macintosh
- ☐ Terminal Emulation
- ☐ VMS
- ☐ UNIX
- ☐ OS/2
- ☑ Other platform

Cost
- ☐ Unknown
- ☐ Basic
- ☑ Extended
- ☐ Premium ($)
- ☐ Executive w/$

Macromedia Forum – Magazines

Activity Level

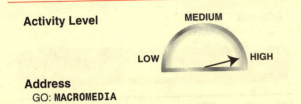

Address
GO: **MACROMEDIA**

MacWAREHOUSE

Description
Order products from MacWAREHOUSE online using this service.

Subjects
Computer Products, Macintosh

Audience
Computer users, Macintosh users

Content Summary
From the main menu, you can go to the MacWAREHOUSE Online Store to order products, view Best Selling Items, go to the QuickSearch area, Request or Order from the Online Catalog, talk to Customer Service, or play the MacWAREHOUSE Word Scramble game.

See Also
The Electronic Mall

User Guide
- ☐ Windows
- ☐ DOS
- ☑ Macintosh
- ☑ Terminal Emulation
- ☐ VMS
- ☐ UNIX
- ☐ OS/2
- ☐ Other platform

Cost
- ☐ Unknown
- ☑ Basic
- ☐ Extended
- ☐ Premium ($)
- ☐ Executive w/$

Activity Level
UNKNOWN

Address
GO: **MW**

MAGAZINES

Magazine Database Plus

Description
Magazine Database Plus is a service that lets you retrieve full-text articles from more than 140 general-interest magazines, journals, and reports.

Subjects
Information Retrieval, Magazines

Audience
Researchers, general public

Content Summary
The database contains a wealth of diverse publications, from *Time* to the *Atlantic*, *Forbes* to *Kiplinger's Personal Finance Magazine*, the *New Republic* to *National Review*, *Good Housekeeping* to *Cosmopolitan*. The main menu lets you choose from What Is Magazine Database Plus, Basic Instructions, Pricing, Terms and Conditions, Database Customer Service, and Access Magazine Database Plus.

See Also
IQuest($), MQDATA($)

User Guide
- ☑ Windows
- ☑ DOS
- ☑ Macintosh
- ☑ Terminal Emulation
- ☑ VMS
- ☑ UNIX
- ☑ OS/2
- ☑ Other platform

Cost
- ☐ Unknown
- ☐ Basic
- ☐ Extended
- ☑ Premium ($)
- ☐ Executive w/$

Activity Level

Address
GO: **MAGDB**

PC World Online

Description
This service is the online version of *PC World* magazine. You'll find timely and insightful information in this area that you also find in the print version of *PC World*.

Subjects
Computers, Magazine

Audience
Computer users

Content Summary
Some of the material that you'll find here includes Features, Buyer's Guides, Here's How, and news of new products. From the main menu, you can select Current Issue, PC WORLD forum, Online Exclusive, Exec/Direct Shop, News Wire, Press Release, and more.

See Also
PC Computing, PC Contact

User Guide
- ☑ Windows
- ☑ DOS
- ☑ Macintosh
- ☐ Terminal Emulation
- ☑ VMS
- ☑ UNIX
- ☑ OS/2
- ☐ Other platform

Cost
- [ ] Unknown
- [ ] Basic
- [x] Extended
- [ ] Premium ($)
- [ ] Executive w/$

Activity Level
MEDIUM / LOW / UNKNOWN / HIGH

Address
GO: **PCWORLD**

MANAGEMENT

Information Management Forum

Description
This forum includes topics ranging from staff management and time management to technology management.

Subjects
Computers, Management

Audience
Management information specialists

Content Summary
This forum discusses issues that are currently scattered over numerous CompuServe forums, and offers the opportunity to concentrate on new issues as they emerge. Many forums often address the "how" for solving computing problems. This forum is also able to address the "why" and computing foundations. Although technical issues can be discussed, this forum focuses primarily on the management issues in the information processing community. The library and message sections include Professional Development, Desktop Issues, Network Issues, Host Issues, Professional Issues, and much more.

See Also
Business Managment

User Guide
- [x] Windows
- [x] DOS
- [ ] Macintosh
- [ ] Terminal Emulation
- [ ] VMS
- [ ] UNIX
- [ ] OS/2
- [ ] Other platform

Cost
- [ ] Unknown
- [ ] Basic
- [x] Extended
- [ ] Premium ($)
- [ ] Executive w/$

Activity Level

MEDIUM / LOW / HIGH

Address
GO: **INFOMANAGE**

MAPS

Weather Maps

Description
This online area offers weather maps updated several times per day. With appropriate software, maps can be either viewed while online, or downloaded for later viewing.

Subjects
Maps, Weather

Audience
Weather forecasters, general public

Content Summary
The libraries include maps of North America, the United Kingdom, continental Europe, the Pacific Rim, and Australia.

See Also
Earth Forum

User Guide
- [x] Windows
- [x] DOS
- [ ] Macintosh
- [ ] Terminal Emulation
- [ ] VMS
- [ ] UNIX
- [ ] OS/2
- [ ] Other platform

Cost
- [ ] Unknown
- [x] Basic
- [ ] Extended
- [ ] Premium ($)
- [ ] Executive w/$

Activity Level
MEDIUM / LOW / UNKNOWN / HIGH

Address
GO: **MAPS**

Marilyn Beck/Smith Hollywood

Description
Hot Hollywood news awaits you in this service.

Subjects
General Interest

Audience
General public

Content Summary
Read the articles posted daily by Marilyn Beck and Stacy Jenel Smith.

See Also
Entertainment Center, Entertainment Drive Forum

Marilyn Beck/Smith Hollywood – Marketing

User Guide
- ☑ Windows
- ☑ DOS
- ☑ Macintosh
- ☑ Terminal Emulation
- ☐ VMS
- ☐ UNIX
- ☐ OS/2
- ☐ Other platform

Cost
- ☐ Unknown
- ☑ Basic
- ☐ Extended
- ☐ Premium ($)
- ☐ Executive w/$

Activity Level
UNKNOWN

Address
GO: **BECK**

Market Highlights

Description
You can find current quotes on stocks, options, market indexes, foreign currency exchange rates, net asset values for mutual funds, and more.

Subjects
Stock Market

Audience
General public, stockbrokers

Content Summary
Market Highlights is a full-featured database of market information. To use the service, choose from one of the three main menu options: New York Stock Exchange, American Exchange, and Over the Counter. You can get information on the most active stocks of the day, as well as other data. If you want to check the current price of a stock anytime, type **QUOTES** and a stock sticker symbol at the ! prompt.

See Also
MQDATA($), E*TRADE Securities, Dividends and Splits($), DISCLOSURE II($E)

User Guide
- ☐ Windows
- ☐ DOS
- ☐ Macintosh
- ☑ Terminal Emulation
- ☐ VMS
- ☐ UNIX
- ☐ OS/2
- ☐ Other platform

Cost
- ☐ Unknown
- ☐ Basic
- ☐ Extended
- ☑ Premium ($)
- ☐ Executive w/$

Activity Level

UNKNOWN

Address
GO: **MARKET**

MARKET RESEARCH

SUPERSITE Demographics Forum

Description
This forum provides demographic reports for all of the United States, covering general demographics, income, housing, education, employment, and current and projected-year forecasts.

Subjects
Demographics, Market Research

Audience
Demographers, research analysts

Content Summary
This forum is available only to members who have the Executive Service Option. You obtain reports by indicating the type of geography you want to research, the geographic areas that form the market, and the reports you want.

See Also
Business Demographics

User Guide
- ☑ Windows
- ☑ DOS
- ☑ Macintosh
- ☑ Terminal Emulation
- ☑ VMS
- ☑ UNIX
- ☑ OS/2
- ☑ Other platform

Cost
- ☐ Unknown
- ☐ Basic
- ☐ Extended
- ☑ Premium ($)
- ☐ Executive w/$

Activity Level

UNKNOWN

Address
GO: **SUPERSITE**

MARKETING

PR and Marketing Forum

Description
This forum is a gathering place for public relations, advertising, marketing, research, and public affairs professionals.

Subjects
Advertising, Marketing, Public Relations

Audience
Advertising professionals, market research specialists, public relations personnel

Marketing – Masonry Forum

Content Summary
Members use the forum's message libraries to communicate on subjects of interest to the communications field. Other features include Jobs Online, from which members can review more than 100 job openings. Members can post resumes as well as listing openings from their respective firms. Other sections include starting up a business, marketing, media relations and crisis communications, new products and services, creativity, research, advertising and direct mail, electronic newsletters, desktop publishing, professional development, political campaigns and programming, creativity development, educational programs, and technology tools.

Online college courses are offered in advertising, public relations, and print and electronic journalism.

See Also
Media Newsletter

User Guide
- ☑ Windows
- ☑ DOS
- ☑ Macintosh
- ☐ Terminal Emulation
- ☑ VMS
- ☑ UNIX
- ☑ OS/2
- ☐ Other platform

Cost
- ☐ Unknown
- ☐ Basic
- ☑ Extended
- ☐ Premium ($)
- ☐ Executive w/$

Activity Level
MEDIUM / LOW → HIGH

Address
GO: **PRSIG**

MARTIAL ARTS

Health and Fitness Forum

Description
This forum provides health-related information and support groups for their members. Learn about exercise, nutrition, mental health, and other health items.

Subjects
Fitness, Health, Martial Arts

Audience
Fitness Enthusiasts

Content Summary
The message library sections contain various health-related files and information and are divided into several topics, including Addiction/Recovery, Mental Health, Family Health, The Doctor's Inn, Exercise & Fitness, Master's Swimming, Running & Racing, Nutrition, Martial Arts, and Self Help. The Martial Arts library is very popular.

See Also
Health and Vitamin Express, Health Database Plus($), Health/Fitness, HealthNet, Holistic Health Forum

User Guide
- ☑ Windows
- ☑ DOS
- ☑ Macintosh
- ☑ Terminal Emulation
- ☑ VMS
- ☑ UNIX
- ☑ OS/2
- ☑ Other platform

Cost
- ☐ Unknown
- ☐ Basic
- ☑ Extended
- ☐ Premium ($)
- ☐ Executive w/$

Activity Level
MEDIUM / LOW ← HIGH

Address
GO: **GOODHEALTH**

Masonry Forum

Description
Are you a member of the Freemasonry? Are you just curious about the Masonry? If so, join this forum for discussions and topics of interest.

Subjects
Organizations

Audience
General public

Content Summary
This is the area to discuss and learn about all aspects of Freemasonry (which may be publicly discussed), including the history, symbolism, and concerns of Brothers and Lodges. For complete information read the Membership Information announcement after you have joined the forum. Some of the message and library sections that you might find in this forum include Masonic Programs, York Rite, Scottish Rite, Graphics/Art, and more.

See Also
Religion Forum

User Guide
- ☑ Windows
- ☑ DOS
- ☑ Macintosh
- ☐ Terminal Emulation
- ☑ VMS
- ☑ UNIX
- ☑ OS/2
- ☑ Other platform

Cost
- ☐ Unknown
- ☐ Basic
- ☑ Extended
- ☐ Premium ($)
- ☐ Executive w/$

399
Masonry Forum – Media Newsletters

Activity Level

Address
GO: **MASONRY**

MATTRESSES

Dial-A-Mattress

Description
Looking for a new bed or mattress? You can order or price premium bedding from Sealy, Simmons, and Serta from this service.

Subjects
Bedding, Beds, Mattresses

Audience
Consumers (anyone interested in bedding), gift givers

Content Summary
The Dial-A-Mattress service offers you several options from which to choose, including an order area, product listings, customer service and warranty information, and shipping information. If you want to talk to a "live" person, go to "Can I Speak To A Representative" (option 5) for more information. If you've never heard of Dial-A-Mattress, select option 2. Select option 3 for instructions on how to shop for a mattress or bed online.

See Also
Sears, JC Penney

User Guide
- ☑ Windows
- ☑ DOS
- ☑ Macintosh
- ☑ Terminal Emulation
- ☑ VMS
- ☑ UNIX
- ☑ OS/2
- ☐ Other platform

Cost
- ☐ Unknown
- ☑ Basic
- ☐ Extended
- ☐ Premium ($)
- ☐ Executive w/$

Activity Level

Address
GO: **BEDS**

McAfee Virus Forum

Description
The purpose of this forum is to help you with any questions or problems you have related to anti-viral software and computer viruses.

Subjects
Computer Viruses, Computers

Audience
Computer users, management information specialists

Content Summary
Find information and updates for virus software and network tools in the libraries and in the message sections.

See Also
Computer Club Forum

User Guide
- ☑ Windows
- ☑ DOS
- ☐ Macintosh
- ☐ Terminal Emulation
- ☐ VMS
- ☐ UNIX
- ☐ OS/2
- ☑ Other platform

Cost
- ☐ Unknown
- ☐ Basic
- ☑ Extended
- ☐ Premium ($)
- ☐ Executive w/$

Activity Level

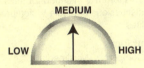

Address
GO: **NCSAVIRUS**

Media Newsletters

Description
The Broadcast & Publishing section of PTS Newsletter Database contains articles from leading newsletters covering broadcasting and publishing industries.

Subjects
Broadcasting, Newsletters, Publishing

Audience
Researchers, general public

Content Summary
These newsletters are a unique source of facts, figures, analyses, and current information on changing market and company conditions, company activities, new products and technologies, and government policies and trade agreements. The information available for an article includes title, newsletter name, publisher, and date of publication, as well as the full text of the article. An individual article may not include all of this information. You can choose from Description, Search Guidelines, Pricing Information, Media Newsletters Example, and Access Media Newsletters.

See Also
IQuest($)

Media Newsletters – Medicare

User Guide
- ☑ Windows
- ☑ DOS
- ☑ Macintosh
- ☑ Terminal Emulation
- ☑ VMS
- ☑ UNIX
- ☑ OS/2
- ☑ Other platform

Cost
- ☐ Unknown
- ☐ Basic
- ☐ Extended
- ☑ Premium ($)
- ☐ Executive w/$

Activity Level
UNKNOWN (LOW – MEDIUM – HIGH)

Address
GO: **MEDIANEWS**

Media Vision Forum

Description
This forum is intended for technical support, general discussions of Media Vision products, and storage of files.

Subjects
Computers, Multimedia

Audience
Computer users, management information specialists

Content Summary
The library and message sections include Pro Audio Spectrum, Pro Audio Studio, ProSonic, Fusion Kits, Multimedia Kits, CD-ROM Drivere, ProGraphics, and more.

See Also
Multimedia Forum, Multimedia Conference Forum, Multimedia Vendor Forum

User Guide
- ☑ Windows
- ☑ DOS
- ☐ Macintosh
- ☐ Terminal Emulation
- ☐ VMS
- ☐ UNIX
- ☐ OS/2
- ☑ Other platform

Cost
- ☐ Unknown
- ☐ Basic
- ☑ Extended
- ☐ Premium ($)
- ☐ Executive w/$

Activity Level
MEDIUM (LOW – HIGH)

Address
GO: **MEDIAVISION**

MEDICAL RESEARCH

Health Database Plus

Description
Search for health-related articles from consumer and professional publications using Health Database Plus.

Subjects
Health, Medical News, Medical Research, Medicine

Audience
Nutritionists, medical researchers, medical professionals, medical educators

Content Summary
Health Database Plus is a service that enables you to retrieve articles from consumer and professional publications on health care, disease prevention and treatment, fitness and nutrition, children and the elderly, substance abuse and smoking, and just about any health-related topic. The prices for searches vary, so be sure to read the pricing terms by choosing the Pricing option from the main menu.

See Also
Health & Fitness Forum, Health & Vitamin Express, Health/Fitness, HealthNet

User Guide
- ☑ Windows
- ☑ DOS
- ☑ Macintosh
- ☐ Terminal Emulation
- ☑ VMS
- ☑ UNIX
- ☑ OS/2
- ☑ Other platform

Cost
- ☐ Unknown
- ☐ Basic
- ☐ Extended
- ☑ Premium ($)
- ☐ Executive w/$

Activity Level
UNKNOWN (LOW – MEDIUM – HIGH)

Address
GO: **HLTDB**

MEDICARE

Retirement Living Forum

Description
Managed by the Setting Priorities for Retirement Years (SPRY) Foundation, this forum is dedicated to making the retirement years happy and productive. Information and discussions on a wide range of topics is available to present and future retirees.

Medicare – Medicine

Subjects
Aging, Medicare, Social Security

Audience
Families of retirees, gerontologists, retirees

Content Summary
This forum's contributors include the Social Security Administration; the National Institute on Aging; the National Heart, Lung, and Blood Institute; the Traveling Healthy and Comfortably Newsletter; and the Pension Rights Center. Discussions can be found on eating right, housing, dealing with family, and Medicare.

See Also
Health/Fitness Forum

User Guide
- ☑ Windows
- ☑ DOS
- ☑ Macintosh
- ☐ Terminal Emulation
- ☑ VMS
- ☑ UNIX
- ☑ OS/2
- ☐ Other platform

Cost
- ☐ Unknown
- ☐ Basic
- ☑ Extended
- ☐ Premium ($)
- ☐ Executive w/$

Activity Level

Address
GO: **RETIREMENT**

MEDICINE

Health Database Plus

Description
Search for health-related articles from consumer and professional publications using Health Database Plus.

Subjects
Health, Medical News, Medical Research, Medicine

Audience
Nutritionists, medical researchers, medical professionals, medical educators

Content Summary
Health Database Plus is a service that enables you to retrieve articles from consumer and professional publications on health care, disease prevention and treatment, fitness and nutrition, children and the elderly, substance abuse and smoking, and just about any health-related topic. The prices for searches vary, so be sure to read the pricing terms by choosing the Pricing option from the main menu.

See Also
Health & Fitness Forum, Health & Vitamin Express, Health/Fitness, HealthNet

User Guide
- ☑ Windows
- ☑ DOS
- ☑ Macintosh
- ☑ Terminal Emulation
- ☑ VMS
- ☑ UNIX
- ☑ OS/2
- ☑ Other platform

Cost
- ☐ Unknown
- ☐ Basic
- ☐ Extended
- ☑ Premium ($)
- ☐ Executive w/$

Activity Level

Address
GO: **HLTDB**

PaperChase-MEDLINE Forum

Description
This forum provides access to the world's largest biomedical database. The information is prepared by the National Library of Medicine and has more than seven million references from 4,000 journals.

Subjects
Health, Medicine, Research

Audience
Dentists, physicians, scientists

Content Summary
References are available from 1966. Updates to articles are added weekly. Because the database is so extensive, you should enter a very narrow topic of research. Cost can be prohibitive. The cost on weekdays from 7 p.m. until 8 a.m. or any time on weekends is $18 per hour. The cost on weekdays from 8 a.m. until 7 p.m. is $24 per hour. Photocopies are available for $10 by first-class mail or $25 by fax.

See Also
Rare Disease Database Forum

User Guide
- ☑ Windows
- ☑ DOS
- ☑ Macintosh
- ☐ Terminal Emulation
- ☑ VMS
- ☑ UNIX
- ☑ OS/2
- ☐ Other platform

Cost
- ☐ Unknown
- ☐ Basic
- ☐ Extended
- ☑ Premium ($)
- ☐ Executive w/$

Medicine – Member Directory

Activity Level

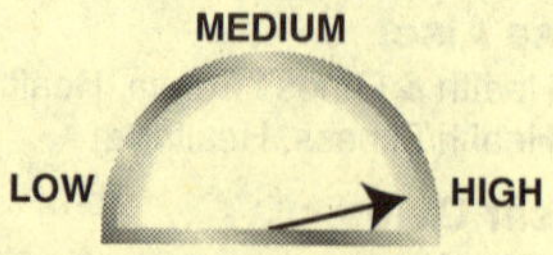

MEDIUM — LOW / HIGH (arrow pointing toward HIGH)

Address
GO: **PAPERCHASE**

MegaWars I and III

Description
Play MegaWars I or MegaWars III by using this service.

Subjects
Games

Audience
Game players

Content Summary
The address for MegaWars I is MEGA1. The address for MegaWars III is MEGA3.

See Also
Fantasy/Role-Playing Adv., Epic MegaGames Forum

User Guide
- ☑ Windows
- ☑ DOS
- ☐ Macintosh
- ☐ Terminal Emulation
- ☐ VMS
- ☐ UNIX
- ☐ OS/2
- ☐ Other platform

Cost
- ☐ Unknown
- ☐ Basic
- ☑ Extended
- ☐ Premium ($)
- ☐ Executive w/$

Activity Level

MEDIUM — LOW UNKNOWN HIGH

Address
GO: **MEGA1** or **MEGA3**

Member Assistance

Description
Need help while you're on CompuServe? Type **GO HELP** and enter the Member Assistance service. From this main menu, you're assured to find what you're looking for.

Subjects
CompuServe

Audience
CompuServe Users

Content Summary
The selections on the Member Assistance main menu include Tour/Find a Topic, Navigation/Commands, Ask Customer Service, Membership Changes, What's New, Missing Children Forum, Practice Forum, CompuServe Help Forum, Billing Information, Telephone Access Numbers, Order from CompuServe, Rules of Operation/Copyright, Member Directory, Special Events & Contests, and Member Support Services.

See Also
CompuServe Help Forum

User Guide
- ☑ Windows
- ☑ DOS
- ☑ Macintosh
- ☐ Terminal Emulation
- ☑ VMS
- ☑ UNIX
- ☑ OS/2
- ☑ Other platform

Cost
- ☐ Unknown
- ☑ Basic
- ☐ Extended
- ☐ Premium ($)
- ☐ Executive w/$

Activity Level

MEDIUM — LOW UNKNOWN HIGH

Address
GO: **HELP**

Member Directory

Description
Find another CompuServe member's account number by entering his/her name here. This service contains all CompuServe members, except for those asking to be excluded.

Subjects
Directory

Audience
General public

Content Summary
The CompuServe Information Service offers the Member Directory to facilitate the use of CompuServe's electronic mail. The Member Directory contains the first and last name, city, state, country, and User ID number of every CompuServe member except those who want to be excluded. When searching for a member, you are prompted to enter the last name and first name. You are then prompted to enter the city, country, and state of residence for the member. The last name is required to be entered, but the first name is optional. Also, you must answer at least one of the three prompts (city, country, and state) before a search will be conducted.

See Also
Member Assistance (FREE)

User Guide
- ☑ Windows
- ☑ DOS
- ☑ Macintosh
- ☑ Terminal Emulation
- ☑ VMS
- ☑ UNIX
- ☑ OS/2
- ☑ Other platform

Cost
- ☐ Unknown
- ☑ Basic
- ☐ Extended
- ☐ Premium ($)
- ☐ Executive w/$

Activity Level

LOW — UNKNOWN (MEDIUM) — HIGH

Address
GO: **DIRECTORY**

Member Recommendation

Description
Earn credit by recommending a friend to CompuServe.

Subjects
CompuServe

Audience
General public

Content Summary
This service enables you to give CompuServe names of people who you think would enjoy the service and who might want to join. You can earn a $25.00 usage credit when that person joins.

See Also
Member Directory(FREE)

User Guide
- ☑ Windows
- ☑ DOS
- ☑ Macintosh
- ☑ Terminal Emulation
- ☑ VMS
- ☑ UNIX
- ☑ OS/2
- ☑ Other platform

Cost
- ☐ Unknown
- ☑ Basic
- ☐ Extended
- ☐ Premium ($)
- ☐ Executive w/$

Activity Level

LOW — UNKNOWN (MEDIUM) — HIGH

Address
GO: **FRIEND**

Members of Congress

Description
Need the address of your Congress person? If so, use this service to find out name, address, party affiliation, and the committees they are on.

Subjects
Government

Audience
General public

Content Summary
You can select The White House, The Senate, House of Representatives, and Compose a CONGRESSGram. When you compose a CONGRESSGram, make sure you know the person's full name and what house they are in, such as President or Senator.

See Also
Issues Forum

User Guide
- ☑ Windows
- ☑ DOS
- ☑ Macintosh
- ☑ Terminal Emulation
- ☑ VMS
- ☑ UNIX
- ☑ OS/2
- ☑ Other platform

Cost
- ☐ Unknown
- ☐ Basic
- ☑ Extended
- ☐ Premium ($)
- ☐ Executive w/$

Activity Level

LOW — UNKNOWN (MEDIUM) — HIGH

Address
GO: **FCC-1**

Membership Changes

Description
This CompuServe service enables you to change information about your membership, such as billing address and display preference.

Subjects
Acts

Audience
General public

Content Summary
At the main menu, you can select these options: Change Your Billing Address, Change Your Billing Method, Change Your Password, Executive Service Option, Change Equipment/Display Profile, Cancel Your Membership, Mail Preference Service, Member Recommendation Program, CompuServe Pricing Plans, and ZiffNet Membership Information.

See Also
Member Assistance (FREE), Member Recommendation (FREE)

User Guide
- ☑ Windows
- ☑ DOS
- ☑ Macintosh
- ☑ Terminal Emulation
- ☑ VMS
- ☑ UNIX
- ☑ OS/2
- ☑ Other platform

Cost
- [ ] Unknown
- [x] Basic
- [ ] Extended
- [ ] Premium ($)
- [ ] Executive w/$

Activity Level
UNKNOWN (LOW – MEDIUM – HIGH)

Address
GO: **MEMBER**

Mensa Forum

Description
This forum is devoted to Mensa members and those living with gifted children.

Subjects
Mensa

Audience
General public, Mensa members

Content Summary
The Mensa Forum is intended to be the online counterpart to Mensa meetings. Here you'll find intelligent—and sometimes spirited—discussion, tips about living with gifted children, announcements about Regional Gatherings and Mensa's national Annual Gathering, and an assortment of interesting files in the Libraries.

See Also
Intelligence Test

User Guide
- [x] Windows
- [x] DOS
- [x] Macintosh
- [x] Terminal Emulation
- [x] VMS
- [x] UNIX
- [x] OS/2
- [x] Other platform

Cost
- [ ] Unknown
- [ ] Basic
- [x] Extended
- [ ] Premium ($)
- [ ] Executive w/$

Activity Level

MEDIUM (LOW – HIGH)

Address
GO: **MENSA**

Message Handling Service Hub

Description
The CompuServe Mail Hub offers global connectivity, which enables you to communicate with users all over the world. The Mail Hub is available to everyone who can access CompuServe.

Subjects
Networking, Networking, Networks

Audience
CompuServe users

Content Summary
Access to CompuServe gives the NetWare MHS user the capability to send messages to any other MHS user or CompuServe Mail address/gateways with an inexpensive local telephone call. The MHS user no longer must make an expensive long distance telephone call to send and receive messages. If you are using Remote MHS, or Global MHS, the CompuServe capability is built in. From the CompuServe Mail Hub main menu, you can choose from MHS Hub Service, Planning and Implementaion, Specific Mail Systems, Addressing, and Download File with all of the above.

See Also
Novell User Library

User Guide
- [x] Windows
- [x] DOS
- [x] Macintosh
- [x] Terminal Emulation
- [ ] VMS
- [x] UNIX
- [x] OS/2
- [x] Other platform

Cost
- [ ] Unknown
- [ ] Basic
- [x] Extended
- [ ] Premium ($)
- [ ] Executive w/$

Activity Level

UNKNOWN (LOW – MEDIUM – HIGH)

Address
GO: **MHSADMIN**

Metropolitan Museum of Art

Description
This service enables you to order Metropolitan Museum of Art merchandise online, such as the Diamond-Shaped Celtic Bookmark or the Greek Horseman Relief Fragment.

Subjects
Art

Audience
Art enthusiasts, general public

Content Summary
The Metropolitan Museum is located at Fifth Avenue & 82 St., NYC, and is open until 8:45 on Friday and Saturday nights; closed Mondays. With this service, museum members receive a 10% discount on all purchases. The main menu enables you to choose options including Order from Our Catalogue, Store Locations, Become a Member of the Metropolitan Museum, and more.

See Also
Art/Music/Literature

User Guide
- ☑ Windows
- ☑ DOS
- ☑ Macintosh
- ☐ Terminal Emulation
- ☑ VMS
- ☑ UNIX
- ☑ OS/2
- ☑ Other platform

Cost
- ☐ Unknown
- ☑ Basic
- ☐ Extended
- ☐ Premium ($)
- ☐ Executive w/$

Activity Level
UNKNOWN (LOW — MEDIUM — HIGH)

Address
GO: MMA

MICROCOMPUTERS

Intel Corporation

Description
This service enables you to get to the Intel Forum and Intel Architecture Labs Forum.

Subjects
Computer Hardware, Computers, Microcomputers, Modems, Networking

Audience
Modem users, network users, computer users

Content Summary
The Intel Forum supports Intel's enhancement products for IBM PCs and any and all compatible computers. You can find information on Above Boards, SnapIn, Inboards, SatisFAXtion, and Connection CoProcessor FAX boards. Other products include Intel Math CoProcessors, modems, network enhancement utilities, network management tools, Visual Edge, Code Builder, Matched Memory, and NetPort. The Intel Architecture Labs Forum is an interactive online service from which you can obtain the latest in technical and marketing information on the advanced Intel architectures.

See Also
Computer Club Forum

User Guide
- ☑ Windows
- ☑ DOS
- ☐ Macintosh
- ☐ Terminal Emulation
- ☐ VMS
- ☐ UNIX
- ☑ OS/2
- ☑ Other platform

Cost
- ☐ Unknown
- ☐ Basic
- ☑ Extended
- ☐ Premium ($)
- ☐ Executive w/$

Activity Level
MEDIUM (LOW — HIGH), arrow pointing toward HIGH

Address
GO: INTEL

Micrografx Forum

Description
This forum is for anyone interested in Micrografx's professional and consumer graphics products. It provides technical support, contact with other Micrografx users, and a variety of other useful and entertaining services.

Subjects
Computer Graphics, Computers

Audience
Computer users, computer graphic designers

Content Summary
You can find press releases, comments, questions, support answers, clip art, and other graphics in the library and message sections. Some of the libraries include Utilities, Designer, ABC Flow/Toolkit, PhotoMagic, Charisma, and more.

See Also
Corel Forum, Graphics Forums, Graphics File Finder

User Guide
- ☑ Windows
- ☑ DOS
- ☐ Macintosh
- ☐ Terminal Emulation
- ☐ VMS
- ☐ UNIX
- ☑ OS/2
- ☐ Other platform

Cost
- ☐ Unknown
- ☐ Basic
- ☑ Extended
- ☐ Premium ($)
- ☐ Executive w/$

Activity Level
MEDIUM (LOW — HIGH)

Address
GO: MICROGRAFX

MICROPROCESSORS

The Intel Forum

Description
Vendor support forum for Intel Corp and their computer-related hardware products.

Subjects
Computer Hardware, Computers, Modems, Networking

Audience
Modem users, network users, computer users

Content Summary
The libraries contain information about product support, management and utility tools, fax/print servers, latest drivers, software revisions, troubleshooting documents.

See Also
Computer Hardware, Modems

User Guide
- ☑ Windows
- ☑ DOS
- ☐ Macintosh
- ☐ Terminal Emulation
- ☐ VMS
- ☐ UNIX
- ☐ OS/2
- ☐ Other platform

Cost
- ☐ Unknown
- ☐ Basic
- ☑ Extended
- ☐ Premium ($)
- ☐ Executive w/$

Activity Level

MEDIUM (LOW — HIGH)

Address
GO: **INTEL**

MICROSOFT

(Microsoft) Developers Relations Forums

Description
This forum is designed for high-level information exchange and tips about Microsoft Developer products. Section leaders from Microsoft Product Support Services monitor and participate in the forum. This area is for nontechnical information. See the Microsoft Developer Services Area (MSDS) for technical support questions and issues.

Subjects
Application Development, Computers, Microsoft

Audience
Advanced-level users, developers

Content Summary
This forum includes two libraries: General/Dev. Services, which includes files and information on job opportunities, general beta testing (non-Microsoft), and the Microsoft Support Network; and Strategic Issues, which includes information and tool kits for developers on different applications and operating systems.

See Also
Microsoft Developer Services Area, Microsoft Developer Network Forum, Microsoft Developer Knowledge Base, Microsoft Connection, Microsoft C and Other Languages Forum

User Guide
- ☑ Windows
- ☑ DOS
- ☑ Macintosh
- ☐ Terminal Emulation
- ☑ VMS
- ☑ UNIX
- ☑ OS/2
- ☐ Other platform

Cost
- ☐ Unknown
- ☐ Basic
- ☑ Extended
- ☐ Premium ($)
- ☐ Executive w/$

Activity Level
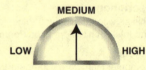
MEDIUM (LOW — HIGH)

Address
GO: **MSDR**

Windows 3rd Party App. A Forum

Description
This is a vendor support forum for several Windows-based applications.

Subjects
Computers

Audience
Computer users, Windows users

Content Summary
Libraries include information about Access Softek, Arabesque Software, Asymetrix Corp., Future Soft Engineering, Geographix, hDC Computer Corp., Jensen-Jones, Lucid Corp., Micrografx, Playroom Software, Polaris Software, Premia Corp., 3-D Visions, and Wilson WindowWare.

See Also
Windows Vendor Forums

Microsoft

User Guide
- ☑ Windows
- ☑ DOS
- ☐ Macintosh
- ☐ Terminal Emulation
- ☐ VMS
- ☐ UNIX
- ☐ OS/2
- ☐ Other platform

Cost
- ☐ Unknown
- ☐ Basic
- ☑ Extended
- ☐ Premium ($)
- ☐ Executive w/$

Activity Level: MEDIUM

Address
GO: **WINAPA**

Windows 3rd Party App. B Forum

Description
This is a vendor support forum for several Windows-based applications.

Subjects
Computers

Audience
Computer users, Windows users

Content Summary
Libraries include information about Computer Presentations, Connect Software, Frontier Technologies, InfoAccess, KASEWORKS, Kidasa Software, Knowledge Garden, Nu-Mega, Ocean Isle Software, Softbridge, SoftCraft, Window Craft, Wonderware, and Zenographics.

See Also
Windows Vendor Forums

User Guide
- ☑ Windows
- ☑ DOS
- ☐ Macintosh
- ☐ Terminal Emulation
- ☐ VMS
- ☐ UNIX
- ☐ OS/2
- ☐ Other platform

Cost
- ☐ Unknown
- ☐ Basic
- ☑ Extended
- ☐ Premium ($)
- ☐ Executive w/$

Activity Level: MEDIUM

Address
GO: **WINAPB**

Windows 3rd Party App. D Forum

Description
This is a vendor support forum for several Windows-based applications.

Subjects
Computers

Audience
Computer users, Windows users

Content Summary
The libraries include information on ABC Systems and Development, Automated Design Systems, Baseline Publishing, DeltaPoint, Inmark, Okna Corp., Peachtree, Q+E Software, ShapeWare, SWFTE International, and WexTech.

See Also
Windows Vendor Forums

User Guide
- ☑ Windows
- ☑ DOS
- ☐ Macintosh
- ☐ Terminal Emulation
- ☐ VMS
- ☐ UNIX
- ☐ OS/2
- ☐ Other platform

Cost
- ☐ Unknown
- ☐ Basic
- ☑ Extended
- ☐ Premium ($)
- ☐ Executive w/$

Activity Level: MEDIUM

Address
GO: **WINAPD**

Windows 3rd Party App. E Forum +

Description
This is vendor support forum for several Windows-based applications.

Subjects
Computers

Audience
Computer users, Windows users

Content Summary
The libraries contain information about Andyne Computing, LaserTools, MapLinx, Scitor Corporation, and Systems Compatibility.

See Also
Windows Vendor Forums

Microsoft – Microsoft Corp.

User Guide
- [x] Windows
- [x] DOS
- [ ] Macintosh
- [ ] Terminal Emulation
- [ ] VMS
- [ ] UNIX
- [ ] OS/2
- [ ] Other platform

Cost
- [ ] Unknown
- [ ] Basic
- [x] Extended
- [ ] Premium ($)
- [ ] Executive w/$

Activity Level: MEDIUM

Address
GO: **WINAPE**

Windows 3rd Party App. G Forum

Description
This is a vendor support forum for several Windows-based applications.

Subjects
Computers

Audience
Computer users, Windows users

Content Summary
Libraries include information on ShowCase, Air TM, Pacific Crest Tech, UnderWare, Zolzo Software, and others.

See Also
Windows Vendor Forums

User Guide
- [x] Windows
- [x] DOS
- [ ] Macintosh
- [ ] Terminal Emulation
- [ ] VMS
- [ ] UNIX
- [ ] OS/2
- [ ] Other platform

Cost
- [ ] Unknown
- [ ] Basic
- [x] Extended
- [ ] Premium ($)
- [ ] Executive w/$

Activity Level: MEDIUM

Address
GO: **WINAPG**

WinNT Forum

Description
This is a vendor support forum for Microsoft Windows NT.

Subjects
Computers

Audience
Computer users, Windows NT users

Content Summary
This forum asks questions of Microsoft, reports bugs, discusses future releases, etc.

See Also
Windows Vendor Forums

User Guide
- [x] Windows
- [x] DOS
- [ ] Macintosh
- [ ] Terminal Emulation
- [ ] VMS
- [ ] UNIX
- [ ] OS/2
- [ ] Other platform

Cost
- [ ] Unknown
- [ ] Basic
- [x] Extended
- [ ] Premium ($)
- [ ] Executive w/$

Activity Level: LOW–MEDIUM

Address
GO: **WINNT**

MICROSOFT CORP.

Microsoft 32-bit Languages Forum

Description
This forum is designed as an area to exchange information, tips, and techniques concerning Microsoft languages.

Subjects
Computer Applications, Computer Programming Languages, Computer Users, Microsoft Corp.

Audience
Computer programmers

Content Summary
Some of the topics covered in this forum include Microsof C ++, Microsoft C, Assembler, QC/QCWin, FORTRAN, CodeView/IDE Debug, NonTech Cutomer Support, and others. This area is for the applications developer and programmer; be ready for high-level discussions if you join this forum.

Microsoft Corp.

See Also
Microsoft Languages Forum, Microsoft DevCast Forum, Microsoft WIN32 Forum

User Guide
- ☑ Windows
- ☑ DOS
- ☑ Macintosh
- ☐ Terminal Emulation
- ☐ VMS
- ☐ UNIX
- ☐ OS/2
- ☑ Other platform

Cost
- ☐ Unknown
- ☐ Basic
- ☑ Extended
- ☐ Premium ($)
- ☐ Executive w/$

Activity Level MEDIUM (LOW — HIGH)

Address
GO: **MSLNG32**

Microsoft Access Forum

Description
This forum is dedicated to the Microsoft Access database product.

Subjects
Computers, Databases, Microsoft Corp.

Audience
Computer users, database managers

Content Summary
Find out about designing forms, reports, queries, and other related questions. The library and message sections include Getting Started, Tables/DB Design, Queries, Forms, Import/Export, Multi-User Networks, Interop/OLE/DDE, and more.

See Also
MS SQL Server Forum, MS Applications Forum, Microsoft Knowledge Base

User Guide
- ☑ Windows
- ☐ DOS
- ☐ Macintosh
- ☐ Terminal Emulation
- ☐ VMS
- ☐ UNIX
- ☐ OS/2
- ☐ Other platform

Cost
- ☐ Unknown
- ☐ Basic
- ☑ Extended
- ☐ Premium ($)
- ☐ Executive w/$

Activity Level MEDIUM (LOW — HIGH)

Address
GO: **MSACCESS**

Microsoft Applications Forum

Description
The Microsoft Applications Forum is designed for discussions and support of some of Microsoft's "end-user" programs, such as Encarta and Publisher.

Subjects
Computers, Microsoft Corp.

Audience
Computer users

Content Summary
This forum covers Microsoft programs such as PowerPoint, Video for Windows, Windows Sound System, Works for the Mac, Windows Project, Project of the Mac, Works for the PC, Works for Windows, Mouse/Paintbrush, Publisher, Money, and more. For those serious times, be sure to check out the Flight Simulator library and discussions.

See Also
Microsoft TechNet Services, Microsoft Knowledge Base, Microsoft Plus Services, Microsoft Press (FREE)

User Guide
- ☑ Windows
- ☑ DOS
- ☑ Macintosh
- ☐ Terminal Emulation
- ☐ VMS
- ☐ UNIX
- ☐ OS/2
- ☐ Other platform

Cost
- ☐ Unknown
- ☐ Basic
- ☑ Extended
- ☐ Premium ($)
- ☐ Executive w/$

Activity Level MEDIUM (LOW — HIGH)

Address
GO: **MSAPP**

Microsoft BASIC Forum

Description
This forum is designed as an area to exchange information, tips, and techniques concerning Microsoft Basic products.

Subjects
Computer Programming Languages, Computers, Microsoft Corp.

Audience
Computer programmers, computer users

Content Summary
The MS BASIC forum contains several library and message sections, including MS Info and Index, Setup Wizard/Kit, Data Access Objects, Programming Issues, Calling APIs/DLLs, DOS Visual Basic, Mac Visual Basic, and more.

Microsoft Corp.

See Also
Microsoft Languages Forum, Microsoft DevCast Forum, Microsoft Connection

User Guide
- ☑ Windows
- ☑ DOS
- ☑ Macintosh
- ☐ Terminal Emulation
- ☐ VMS
- ☐ UNIX
- ☐ OS/2
- ☑ Other platform

Cost
- ☐ Unknown
- ☐ Basic
- ☑ Extended
- ☐ Premium ($)
- ☐ Executive w/$

Activity Level: MEDIUM (LOW — HIGH, arrow pointing right of center)

Address
GO: **MSBASIC**

Microsoft Connection

Description
Use this service to find the Microsoft-related forum of your choice, including international forums.

Subjects
Computers, Microsoft Corp.

Audience
Computer users

Content Summary
The main menu includes About the Microsoft Connection, Microsoft Benelux, Microsoft Central Europe, Microsoft France, Microsoft Italy, Microsoft Spain/Latin America, Microsoft Sweden, and Microsoft US.

See Also
MS Applications Forum, Microsoft Plus Services

User Guide
- ☑ Windows
- ☑ DOS
- ☐ Macintosh
- ☐ Terminal Emulation
- ☐ VMS
- ☐ UNIX
- ☐ OS/2
- ☐ Other platform

Cost
- ☐ Unknown
- ☐ Basic
- ☑ Extended
- ☐ Premium ($)
- ☐ Executive w/$

Activity Level:

UNKNOWN (LOW — MEDIUM — HIGH)

Address
GO: **MICROSOFT**

Microsoft DevCast Forum

Description
This forum is designed to give conference attendees a temporary location for follow up discussion regarding the Microsoft DevCast conference.

Subjects
Computer Programming Languages, Computers, Microsoft Corp.

Audience
Computer users, computer programmers

Content Summary
You can find files, information, and other useful material for upcoming DevCast conferences or from past conferences.

See Also
Microsoft Knowledge Base, Microsoft Languages Forum, MS 32-bit Languages Forum

User Guide
- ☑ Windows
- ☑ DOS
- ☑ Macintosh
- ☐ Terminal Emulation
- ☐ VMS
- ☑ UNIX
- ☐ OS/2
- ☑ Other platform

Cost
- ☐ Unknown
- ☐ Basic
- ☑ Extended
- ☐ Premium ($)
- ☐ Executive w/$

Activity Level:

MEDIUM (LOW — HIGH, arrow pointing up/center)

Address
GO: **DEVCAST**

Microsoft DOS Forum

Description
Have questions about MS DOS? Do you just love to discuss DOS problems and features? You should join this forum then.

Subjects
Computer Users, Microsoft Corp., MS-DOS

Audience
Computer users, management information specialists

Content Summary
You can find out the latest about the newest release of MS DOS, troubleshooting suggestions, hardware issues, setup and installation problems and concerns, memory management concerns, and other topics. For information on DoubleSpace, DriveSpace, and Stacker, see the lively message section area.

See Also
Microsoft Connection, MS DOS 6.2 DLOAD (Microsoft)

Microsoft Corp.

User Guide
- [ ] Windows
- [x] DOS
- [ ] Macintosh
- [ ] Terminal Emulation
- [ ] VMS
- [ ] UNIX
- [ ] OS/2
- [ ] Other platform

Cost
- [ ] Unknown
- [ ] Basic
- [x] Extended
- [ ] Premium ($)
- [ ] Executive w/$

Activity Level
MEDIUM (arrow pointing up between LOW and HIGH)

Address
GO: **MSDOS**

Microsoft Excel Forum

Description
Find out information about MS Excel for Windows and Mac, VBA topics, and other spreadsheet informormation.

Subjects
Computers, Microsoft Corp.

Audience
Computer users

Content Summary
The library and message sections include Index and Info, Excel for the Mac, Excel for the PC, VBA for Excel, Desktop III Products, and EIS Pak Mac/Win.

See Also
MS Applications Forum, MS Software Library, MS TechNet Forum

User Guide
- [x] Windows
- [x] DOS
- [x] Macintosh
- [ ] Terminal Emulation
- [ ] VMS
- [ ] UNIX
- [ ] OS/2
- [ ] Other platform

Cost
- [ ] Unknown
- [ ] Basic
- [x] Extended
- [ ] Premium ($)
- [ ] Executive w/$

Activity Level
MEDIUM (arrow pointing toward HIGH)

Address
GO: **MSEXCEL**

Microsoft Foundation Classes Forum

Description
This forum is designed as an area to exchange information, tips, and techniques concerning Microsoft Foundation Classes.

Subjects
Computer Programming Languages, Computers, Microsoft Corp.

Audience
Computer programmers

Content Summary
This forum is for application developers interested in the Microsoft Foundation Classes. Some of the libraries include Beginners Library, Database Classes, OLE 2.0 Classes, VBX Usage, DLL & Memory, and Wizards/DDV/DDX. Also watch for online conferences and seminars, many of which feature Microsoft product managers.

See Also
MS Applications Forum, MS 32-bit Languages Forum

User Guide
- [x] Windows
- [x] DOS
- [x] Macintosh
- [ ] Terminal Emulation
- [ ] VMS
- [ ] UNIX
- [ ] OS/2
- [ ] Other platform

Cost
- [ ] Unknown
- [ ] Basic
- [x] Extended
- [ ] Premium ($)
- [ ] Executive w/$

Activity Level
MEDIUM (arrow pointing up between LOW and HIGH)

Address
GO: **MSMFC**

Microsoft Fox Users Forum

Description
This forum is designed as an area to exchange information, tips, and techniques concerning Microsoft Fox products.

Subjects
Computers, Databases, Microsoft Corp.

Audience
Computer system designers, database managers

Content Summary
Some of the areas in this forum include FOXGANG, Want Ads, Archive, and 3rd Party Products. Watch the message sections for discussions on development issues, Fox user groups, and conventions.

Microsoft Corp.

See Also
MS TechNet Forum, Microsoft Connection

User Guide
- ☑ Windows
- ☑ DOS
- ☑ Macintosh
- ☐ Terminal Emulation
- ☐ VMS
- ☐ UNIX
- ☐ OS/2
- ☐ Other platform

Cost
- ☐ Unknown
- ☐ Basic
- ☑ Extended
- ☐ Premium ($)
- ☐ Executive w/$

Activity Level: MEDIUM

Address
GO: **FOXUSER**

Microsoft Knowledge Base

Description
The Knowledge Base is a database that provides you with access to information previously available only to the Microsoft support engineers.

Subjects
Computers, Microsoft Corp.

Audience
Computer users

Content Summary
Expand the usage of your Microsoft products by using this service. The selections on the Knowledge Base include What's New in the Knowledge Base, Description of Database, Online User's Guide, Search the Knowledge Base, Search Using Expert Mode, QuickSearch—By Document ID Number, and Microsoft Software Library.

See Also
MS TechNet Forum, Microsoft Connection

User Guide
- ☑ Windows
- ☑ DOS
- ☑ Macintosh
- ☐ Terminal Emulation
- ☐ VMS
- ☑ UNIX
- ☑ OS/2
- ☑ Other platform

Cost
- ☐ Unknown
- ☐ Basic
- ☑ Extended
- ☐ Premium ($)
- ☐ Executive w/$

Activity Level: UNKNOWN

Address
GO: **MSKB**

Microsoft Languages Forum

Description
The Microsoft Plus Service Area and Forum are designed to complement membership in the Microsoft Plus program. The Microsoft Plus Service Area provides access to the Microsoft Plus Forum as well as other Microsoft services provided on CompuServe.

Subjects
Microsoft Corp.

Audience
Computer users

Content Summary
Before you join this forum, you are asked to fill out a registration by Microsoft and fill in the serial number from the CompuServe brochure that was included in your Microsoft Plus membership kit. Make sure you have this number handy.

See Also
Microsoft Knowledge Base

User Guide
- ☑ Windows
- ☑ DOS
- ☑ Macintosh
- ☐ Terminal Emulation
- ☐ VMS
- ☐ UNIX
- ☑ OS/2
- ☑ Other platform

Cost
- ☐ Unknown
- ☐ Basic
- ☑ Extended
- ☐ Premium ($)
- ☐ Executive w/$

Activity Level: UNKNOWN

Address
GO: **MSLANG**

Microsoft Mail and Workgroups Forum

Description
This forum is designed as an area to exchange information, tips, and techniques concerning Microsoft Windows Workgroup Applications.

Subjects
Computers, E-mail, Microsoft Corp.

Audience
Computer users, management information specialists

Content Summary
If you have a problem with Microsoft's Windows Workgoup Applications, such as MS Schedule Plus and Mail, you probably can find the solution here. Some of the libraries and message sections include

MS Mail for PC, Remote/Modems, MS Schedule Plus, MS Mail for Mac, MS Eforms, Workgroup Templates, and much more. The Microsoft Forms Designer Run Time file is available in Library 16, Workgroup Templates.

See Also
Microsoft Connection, Microsoft DevCast Forum, Microsoft Knowledge Base

User Guide
- [x] Windows
- [x] DOS
- [x] Macintosh
- [ ] Terminal Emulation
- [ ] VMS
- [ ] UNIX
- [ ] OS/2
- [ ] Other platform

Cost
- [ ] Unknown
- [x] Basic
- [ ] Extended
- [ ] Premium ($)
- [ ] Executive w/$

Activity Level
MEDIUM (arrow pointing up)

Address
GO: **MSWGA**

Microsoft Sales and Information Forum

Description
This forum is monitored by our Microsoft Sales and Information staff to respond to your product information, sales, registration, promotion, and pricing questions.

Subjects
Computer Users, Computers, Microsoft Corp.

Audience
Computer users

Content Summary
The two areas in this forum are library and messages. The message board is where you can post sales information questions or browse through previously posted questions and responses. The libraries of this forum contain files posted by Microsoft only.

See Also
Microsoft Connection

User Guide
- [x] Windows
- [x] DOS
- [x] Macintosh
- [ ] Terminal Emulation
- [ ] VMS
- [ ] UNIX
- [ ] OS/2
- [x] Other platform

Cost
- [ ] Unknown
- [ ] Basic
- [x] Extended
- [ ] Premium ($)
- [ ] Executive w/$

Activity Level
MEDIUM (arrow pointing left)

Address
GO: **MSIC**

Microsoft Software Library

Description
This area contains binary files, technical notes, utilities, and other files for various Microsoft applications.

Subjects
Computer Applications, Computer Users, Microsoft Corp.

Audience
Computer users, management information specialists, Macintosh users

Content Summary
Download the file you need by entering a keyword and searching for it. You can search on keyword, serial number, submission date, or file name.

See Also
MS WINFUN Forum, MS Windows Shareware Forum

User Guide
- [x] Windows
- [x] DOS
- [x] Macintosh
- [x] Terminal Emulation
- [ ] VMS
- [ ] UNIX
- [x] OS/2
- [x] Other platform

Cost
- [ ] Unknown
- [ ] Basic
- [x] Extended
- [ ] Premium ($)
- [ ] Executive w/$

Activity Level
UNKNOWN

Address
GO: **MSL**

Microsoft SQL Server Forum

Description
This forum is designed as an area to exchange information, tips, and techniques concerning Microsoft SQL products.

Subjects
Computers, Database Management

Microsoft Corp.

Audience
Management information specialists, computer programmers, database managers

Content Summary
The SQL Server Forum has several libraries that contain updates, libraries, and other supporting files for the SQL developer. Some of the libraries include MS SQL Server for Windows NT, MS SQL Server for OS/2, MS Program Toolkits, Non-MS SQL Front Ends, and others.

See Also
Microsoft Languages Forum, Microsoft Press (FREE), MS WinNT SNA Forum

User Guide
- [x] Windows
- [x] DOS
- [ ] Macintosh
- [ ] Terminal Emulation
- [ ] VMS
- [ ] UNIX
- [x] OS/2
- [x] Other platform

Cost
- [ ] Unknown
- [ ] Basic
- [x] Extended
- [ ] Premium ($)
- [ ] Executive w/$

Activity Level

Address
GO: MSSQL

Microsoft TechNet Forum

Description
This forum supports Microsoft's TechNet products and services.

Subjects
Computers, Microsoft Corp.

Audience
Management information specialists, computer users

Content Summary
This forum is designed to provide up-to-date information on special TechNet events, connections to the Microsoft TechNet community, and the capability to download the latest technical information from Microsoft TechNet. You'll find updates to the TechNet CDs, conventions, and press releases in the libraries.

See Also
MS Windows Forum, Microsoft Plus Services, Microsoft Knowledge Base

User Guide
- [x] Windows
- [x] DOS
- [x] Macintosh
- [ ] Terminal Emulation
- [ ] VMS
- [ ] UNIX
- [ ] OS/2
- [ ] Other platform

Cost
- [ ] Unknown
- [ ] Basic
- [x] Extended
- [ ] Premium ($)
- [ ] Executive w/$

Activity Level

Address
GO: TNFORUM

Microsoft WIN32 Forum

Description
This forum is designed as an area to exchange information, tips, and techniques concerning Microsoft Win32 SDK.

Subjects
Computer Programming Languages, Computers, Microsoft Corp.

Audience
Computer users, computer professionals

Content Summary
You can find a plethora of information and tools for the the WIN32 SDK. Library and message sections include API-User/GUI, API Graphics/GDI, API-Base/Console, API Security, Porting OS/2 & Unix, and more.

See Also
Microsoft Connection, Microsoft DevCast Forum, MS 32-bit Languages Forum

User Guide
- [x] Windows
- [x] DOS
- [x] Macintosh
- [ ] Terminal Emulation
- [ ] VMS
- [x] UNIX
- [x] OS/2
- [ ] Other platform

Cost
- [ ] Unknown
- [ ] Basic
- [x] Extended
- [ ] Premium ($)
- [ ] Executive w/$

Activity Level

Address
GO: MSWIN32

Microsoft Windows Extensions Forum

Description
This forum is designed as an area to exchange information, tips, and techniques concerning Microsoft Windows SDK extensions.

Microsoft Corp.

Subjects
Computer Programming Languages, Computers, Microsoft Corp.

Audience
Computer programmers

Content Summary
This forum includes these library and message sections: MS Info and Index, MS Test for Windows, TAPI SDK, WOSA/XRT, WOSA/XFS, MS Delta, Arabic/Hebrew SDK, Pen SDK, Far East SDK, ODBC, ODBC Desktop Drivers, LSAPI, MAPI/Schedule+ Libraries, and DSPRMI and SPEECH.

See Also
Microsoft Knowledge Base, Microsoft Languages Forum

User Guide
- [x] Windows
- [x] DOS
- [x] Macintosh
- [ ] Terminal Emulation
- [ ] VMS
- [ ] UNIX
- [ ] OS/2
- [x] Other platform

Cost
- [ ] Unknown
- [ ] Basic
- [x] Extended
- [ ] Premium ($)
- [ ] Executive w/$

Activity Level MEDIUM (LOW — HIGH, arrow pointing up/medium)

Address
GO: **WINEXT**

Microsoft Windows Forum

Description
News, files, tips, and other information related to MS Windows.

Subjects
Computer Viruses, Computers, Microsoft Corp., Windows

Audience
Computer users

Content Summary
Some of the library and message sections include Setup, Mouse, Display Drivers, Memory Optimization, MS-DOS Apps/PIFs, Printing/Fonts/WPS, and Terminal/Comm.

See Also
Microsoft Connection, Microsoft Knowledge Base

User Guide
- [x] Windows
- [x] DOS
- [ ] Macintosh
- [ ] Terminal Emulation
- [ ] VMS
- [ ] UNIX
- [ ] OS/2
- [ ] Other platform

Cost
- [ ] Unknown
- [ ] Basic
- [x] Extended
- [ ] Premium ($)
- [ ] Executive w/$

Activity Level MEDIUM (LOW — HIGH)

Address
GO: **MSWIN**

Microsoft Windows Fun Forum

Description
This forum is designed to allow Windows users a mechanism to discuss and obtain fun Windows files.

Subjects
Computers, Games, Microsoft Corp.

Audience
Computer users

Content Summary
You can find cool things on this forum, such as sound files from movies, screen saver utilities (see Library 4), graphics and graphics utilities (such as the one that changes the standard Windows startup BMP) in Library 9, card games, a WinDominoes game (see Library 3), and other stuff. Have fun!

See Also
Entertainment Center, MS Software Library

User Guide
- [x] Windows
- [x] DOS
- [x] Macintosh
- [ ] Terminal Emulation
- [ ] VMS
- [ ] UNIX
- [ ] OS/2
- [ ] Other platform

Cost
- [ ] Unknown
- [ ] Basic
- [x] Extended
- [ ] Premium ($)
- [ ] Executive w/$

Activity Level MEDIUM (LOW — HIGH)

Address
GO: **WINFUN**

Microsoft Windows Multimedia Forum

Description
This forum offers many files, troubleshooting solutions, and technical support for your multimedia applications.

Microsoft Corp.

Subjects
Games, Microsoft Corp., Multimedia

Audience
Computer users, computer game developers

Content Summary
The type of libraries and message sections you will see in this forum include MDK, MediaView, Video for Windows, Viewer 2.0, Windows Sound System, Multimedia (MM) Strategy, Third Party Software, and Windows Game Development. You can obtain a Viewer 2.0 compiler for Word 6.0 in the Viewer 2.0 library. Also, if you're looking for the Microsoft JumpStart CD, see Library 10, MM Strategy. This is the CD that Microsoft hands out at many of their conferences and seminars.

See Also
MS TechNet Forum, Multimedia Forum, Multimedia Conference Forum

User Guide
- ☑ Windows
- ☑ DOS
- ☑ Macintosh
- ☐ Terminal Emulation
- ☐ VMS
- ☐ UNIX
- ☐ OS/2
- ☐ Other platform

Cost
- ☐ Unknown
- ☐ Basic
- ☑ Extended
- ☐ Premium ($)
- ☐ Executive w/$

Activity Level

Address
GO: **WINMM**

Microsoft Windows News Forum

Description
Find out up-to-date information on Windows and future Windows products.

Subjects
Computers, Microsoft Corp., Windows

Audience
Computer users

Content Summary
This forum essentially has one library: Hot News. Here, you can find press releases, articles, tips, speeches, and similar files associated with Windows.

See Also
MS Windows Forum

User Guide
- ☑ Windows
- ☑ DOS
- ☐ Macintosh
- ☐ Terminal Emulation
- ☐ VMS
- ☐ UNIX
- ☐ OS/2
- ☐ Other platform

Cost
- ☐ Unknown
- ☑ Basic
- ☐ Extended
- ☐ Premium ($)
- ☐ Executive w/$

Activity Level

Address
GO: **WINNEWS**

Microsoft Windows NT SNA Forum

Description
This forum is designed as an area to exchange information, tips, and techniques concerning Microsoft SNA Server for Windows NT.

Subjects
Computers, Microsoft Corp.

Audience
Management information specialists, computer system designers, computer users

Content Summary
Some of the library and message sections you might find on this forum include Fixes and Updates, Problem Reports, 3rd Party/Unsupported, MS SNA Archives, and Setup and Adminstration topics.

See Also
MS SQL Server Forum

User Guide
- ☑ Windows
- ☑ DOS
- ☐ Macintosh
- ☐ Terminal Emulation
- ☐ VMS
- ☐ UNIX
- ☐ OS/2
- ☑ Other platform

Cost
- ☐ Unknown
- ☐ Basic
- ☑ Extended
- ☐ Premium ($)
- ☐ Executive w/$

Activity Level

Address
GO: **MSSNA**

Microsoft Windows Objects Forum

Description
This forum is designed as an area to exchange information, tips, and techniques concerning Microsoft OLE.

Microsoft Corp.

Subjects
Computer Programming Languages, Computers, Microsoft Corp.

Audience
Computer users, computer programmers

Content Summary
Interested in finding information on OLE and how to use it in your programs? Look in the libraries and message sections in this forum for your answers. You'll find libraries such as Component Object Model, Structured Storage, OLE: User Interface, OLE: Automation, OLE: Mac Issues, and more.

See Also
MS Windows Extensions Forum, MS Windows SDK Forum, MS Foundation Classes Forum, Microsoft Languages Forum

User Guide
- ☑ Windows
- ☑ DOS
- ☑ Macintosh
- ☐ Terminal Emulation
- ☐ VMS
- ☐ UNIX
- ☐ OS/2
- ☐ Other platform

Cost
- ☐ Unknown
- ☐ Basic
- ☑ Extended
- ☐ Premium ($)
- ☐ Executive w/$

Activity Level

Address
GO: **WINOBJECTS**

Microsoft Windows SDK Forum

Description
This forum is designed as an area to exchange information, tips, and techniques concerning the Microsoft Windows SDK.

Subjects
Computer Programming Languages, Computers, Microsoft Corp.

Audience
Computer programmers

Content Summary
This forum includes several library and message sections, including Public Utilities, Training, USER, Common Dialogs, Printing, GDI, Kernel—Memory Management, WinHelp, and others.

See Also
Microsoft Languages Forum, MS Windows Objects Forum

User Guide
- ☑ Windows
- ☑ DOS
- ☑ Macintosh
- ☐ Terminal Emulation
- ☐ VMS
- ☐ UNIX
- ☑ OS/2
- ☑ Other platform

Cost
- ☐ Unknown
- ☐ Basic
- ☑ Extended
- ☐ Premium ($)
- ☐ Executive w/$

Activity Level

Address
GO: **WINSDK**

Microsoft Windows Shareware Forum

Description
This forum is designed to allow Windows users a mechanism to discuss and obtain Windows files such as utilities, tools, and applications.

Subjects
Computers, Shareware & Freeware

Audience
Computer users

Content Summary
Download and share your experiences about Windows shareware. This forum includes these libraries: File Applications/Utilities, Communication/Fax Applications, Windows System Utilities, Font/Printing Applications, Disk Utilties, and more.

See Also
MS WINFUN Forum

User Guide
- ☑ Windows
- ☑ DOS
- ☑ Macintosh
- ☐ Terminal Emulation
- ☐ VMS
- ☐ UNIX
- ☐ OS/2
- ☑ Other platform

Cost
- ☐ Unknown
- ☐ Basic
- ☑ Extended
- ☐ Premium ($)
- ☐ Executive w/$

Activity Level

MEDIUM LOW HIGH

Address
GO: **WINSHARE**

Microsoft Corp. – MicroWarehouse

Microsoft Word Forum

Description
This forum is designed as an area to exchange information, tips, and techniques concerning Microsoft Word.

Subjects
Computers, Microsoft Corp.

Audience
Computer users

Content Summary
Get the latest patches and updates from Microsoft for Word 6 in this forum. You also can find information on Word for Windows, Word for Macintosh, Word for DOS, and Word for OS/2.

See Also
MS Applications Forum, Microsoft TechNet Services, Microsoft Knowledge Base

User Guide
- [x] Windows
- [x] DOS
- [x] Macintosh
- [ ] Terminal Emulation
- [ ] VMS
- [ ] UNIX
- [x] OS/2
- [ ] Other platform

Cost
- [ ] Unknown
- [ ] Basic
- [x] Extended
- [ ] Premium ($)
- [ ] Executive w/$

Activity Level

Address
GO: **MSWORD**

MicroStation Forum

Description
This forum is devoted to the discussion and support of Bentley Systems Incorporated's MicroStation CAD product.

Subjects
CAD, Computers

Audience
Computer engineers

Content Summary
The library and message sections include MicroStation in General, 3rd Party Products, Programming, Input Devices, Printing/Plotting, Video/Graphics, Databases, Marketing, Change Requests, User Groups, What's New, and The Dialogue Box. Some of the libraries are empty. To download a copy of the Space Station image, see Library 1 for SPACE.JPG.

See Also
Autodesk AutoCAD Forum

User Guide
- [x] Windows
- [x] DOS
- [ ] Macintosh
- [ ] Terminal Emulation
- [ ] VMS
- [x] UNIX
- [ ] OS/2
- [ ] Other platform

Cost
- [ ] Unknown
- [ ] Basic
- [x] Extended
- [ ] Premium ($)
- [ ] Executive w/$

Activity Level

Address
GO: **MICROSTATION**

MicroWarehouse

Description
This forum is devoted to the discussion and support of Bentley Systems Incorporated's MicroStation CAD product.

Subjects
CAD, Computers

Audience
Computer engineers

Content Summary
The library and message sections include MicroStation in General, 3rd Party Products, Programming, Input Devices, Printing/Plotting, Video/Graphics, Databases, Marketing, Change Requests, User Groups, What's New, and The Dialogue Box. Some of the libraries are empty. To download a copy of the Space Station image, see Library 1 for SPACE.JPG.

See Also
Autodesk AutoCAD Forum

User Guide
- [x] Windows
- [x] DOS
- [ ] Macintosh
- [ ] Terminal Emulation
- [ ] VMS
- [x] UNIX
- [ ] OS/2
- [ ] Other platform

Cost
- [ ] Unknown
- [x] Basic
- [ ] Extended
- [ ] Premium ($)
- [ ] Executive w/$

Activity Level

Address
GO: **MCW**

MIDI Vendor Forums

Description
Supporting various MIDI vendors, the MIDI A, MIDI B, and MIDI C Vendor Forums help users with specific product problems and concerns.

Subjects
Computers, Multimedia, Music

Audience
Computer users, computer game developers, musicians

Content Summary
The MIDI A Vendor Forum (GO MIDIAVEN) includes these vendors: Turtle Beach, Twelve Tone, E-Mu, Big Noise, and many others. The MIDI B Vendor Forum (GO MIDIBVEN) includes these vendors: Midiman, Cool Shoes, Covox, Sweetwater Sound, Passport Designs, Windjammer Software, and others. The MIDI C Vendor Forum (GO MIDICVEN) includes these vendors: MediaTech, AVM, Blue Ribbon, Roland, Steinberg, and others.

See Also
Autodesk Multimedia Forum

User Guide
- ☑ Windows
- ☑ DOS
- ☐ Macintosh
- ☐ Terminal Emulation
- ☐ VMS
- ☐ UNIX
- ☐ OS/2
- ☐ Other platform

Cost
- ☐ Unknown
- ☐ Basic
- ☑ Extended
- ☐ Premium ($)
- ☐ Executive w/$

Activity Level

Address
GO: **MIDIAVEN** or **MIDIBVEN** or **MIDICVEN**

MIDI/Music Forum

Description
This forum is dedicated to supporting MIDI and computer music-related discussions and files. Also, it has the coolest forum logo. You have to see it!

Subjects
Amiga, Macintosh, Multimedia, Music

Audience
Musicians, computer game developers, computer users, Amiga users

Content Summary
Packed with files, discussions, tips and hints, and troubleshooting guidelines, the MIDI/Music Forum includes these and other library and message sections: Basics and Product Guides, General MIDI Songs, Atari Files, Macintosh Files, Patches/Samples, MS DOS Demos, and Windows Media Sound. You'll find items for sale in the Classified Ads library (Library 8).

See Also
MIDI A Vendor Forum, MIDI B Vendor Forum, MIDI C Vendor Forum

User Guide
- ☑ Windows
- ☑ DOS
- ☑ Macintosh
- ☐ Terminal Emulation
- ☐ VMS
- ☐ UNIX
- ☐ OS/2
- ☑ Other platform

Cost
- ☐ Unknown
- ☐ Basic
- ☑ Extended
- ☐ Premium ($)
- ☐ Executive w/$

Activity Level
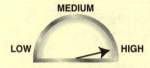

Address
GO: **MIDIFORUM**

MILITARY

Military Forum

Description
The forum is designed to address the various issues surrounding the military, including military history, current topics, and world issues.

Subjects
Collectibles, Military

Audience
Military enthusiasts, veterans

Content Summary
This forum does not propose to support veterans, but you can find files of recent legislation involving some veteran affairs. The library and message sections include topics such as Veterans Advocate, Vietnam, WWII/Commemorative, Military History, Reunions/Groups, Civil War, and much more.

See Also
Current Issues

User Guide
- ☑ Windows
- ☑ DOS
- ☑ Macintosh
- ☐ Terminal Emulation
- ☑ VMS
- ☑ UNIX
- ☑ OS/2
- ☐ Other platform

Military – Modems

Cost
- ☐ Unknown
- ☐ Basic
- ☑ Extended
- ☐ Premium ($)
- ☐ Executive w/$

Activity Level MEDIUM (LOW – HIGH)

Address
GO: `MILITARY`

Missing Children Forum

Description
The primary purpose of this forum is to find missing and exploited children, support families whose children are missing, and offer child safety assistance.

Subjects
Children, Safety

Audience
General public

Content Summary
Note that his forum discourages the promotion of products and services, as well as contributions that are political or issues-oriented. The forum is sponsored by the National Center for Missing and Exploited Children (NCMEC). You can download GIF files of missing children from the Missing Children library (Library 2). Other libraries include Family Support, Child Safety, Resources, Recoveries, and State Clearinghouses.

See Also
Participate

User Guide
- ☑ Windows
- ☑ DOS
- ☑ Macintosh
- ☐ Terminal Emulation
- ☑ VMS
- ☑ UNIX
- ☑ OS/2
- ☐ Other platform

Cost
- ☐ Unknown
- ☑ Basic
- ☐ Extended
- ☐ Premium ($)
- ☐ Executive w/$

Activity Level MEDIUM (LOW – HIGH)

Address
GO: `MISSING`

Mobile Computing

Description
The Mobile Computing Menu enables you to go to a number of vendor forums that offer support and discussions of their mobile computing products.

Subjects
Computers, Mobile Computing

Audience
Computer users, mobile computing users

Content Summary
From the main menu, you can select from a number of vendor forums, including Compaq Connection, CompuAdd Forum, Epson Forum, Gateway 2000 Forum, IBM Thinkpad Forum, Intel Forum, Toshiba Forum, and many more.

See Also
Various vendor forums

User Guide
- ☑ Windows
- ☑ DOS
- ☑ Macintosh
- ☐ Terminal Emulation
- ☑ VMS
- ☑ UNIX
- ☑ OS/2
- ☐ Other platform

Cost
- ☐ Unknown
- ☑ Basic
- ☐ Extended
- ☐ Premium ($)
- ☐ Executive w/$

Activity Level UNKNOWN (LOW – MEDIUM – HIGH)

Address
GO: `MOBILE`

MODEMS

Dr. Neuhaus Forum

Description
This forum is devoted to German-speaking people interested in Dr. Neuhaus communications products. You can get technical support and information on products such as FURY modems, FAXY fax boards, and NICCY ISDN modems. You also can find information and support for Carbon Copy.

Subjects
Computers, Fax Boards, Modems, Remote Communications

Audience
Computer users

Content Summary
This forum is entirely in German.

Modems

See Also
Modem Vendor Forum, Palmtop Forum

User Guide
- [x] Windows
- [x] DOS
- [x] Macintosh
- [ ] Terminal Emulation
- [x] VMS
- [x] UNIX
- [x] OS/2
- [x] Other platform

Cost
- [ ] Unknown
- [ ] Basic
- [x] Extended
- [ ] Premium ($)
- [ ] Executive w/$

Activity Level
UNKNOWN (MEDIUM, between LOW and HIGH)

Address
GO: **NEUHAUS**

Hayes Forum

Description
This forum contains press releases, technical support, tips, and much more. Some of the products include Smartmodems, ACCURA, and JT Fax.

Subjects
Computers, Modems

Audience
Management information specialists, computer hardware users

Content Summary
The library and message sections in this forum include discussions and files on high-speed modems, Smartmodems, Smartcom for DOS and Windows, Fax products, Hayes for the Mac, Hayes for LANS, and Hayes for ISDN.

See Also
Modem Vendor Forum, Hayes

User Guide
- [x] Windows
- [x] DOS
- [x] Macintosh
- [ ] Terminal Emulation
- [ ] VMS
- [ ] UNIX
- [ ] OS/2
- [ ] Other platform

Cost
- [ ] Unknown
- [ ] Basic
- [x] Extended
- [ ] Premium ($)
- [ ] Executive w/$

Activity Level
MEDIUM (arrow pointing toward LOW)

Address
GO: **HAYFORUM**

Hayes Online

Description
This service gives you an introduction to Hayes Corporation, as well as product support.

Subjects
Computer Hardware, Computer Networking, Computers, Modems

Audience
Modem users, management information specialists

Content Summary
From the Online with Hayes main menu, you can select from About Online with Hayes, The Hayes Advantage, the Hayes Forum, LANstep, Product Descriptions, Special Support Forums, and Third Party Developers.

See Also
Hayes Forum, Modem Vendor Forum

User Guide
- [x] Windows
- [x] DOS
- [x] Macintosh
- [ ] Terminal Emulation
- [ ] VMS
- [ ] UNIX
- [ ] OS/2
- [ ] Other platform

Cost
- [ ] Unknown
- [ ] Basic
- [x] Extended
- [ ] Premium ($)
- [ ] Executive w/$

Activity Level
UNKNOWN (MEDIUM, between LOW and HIGH)

Address
GO: **HAYES**

IBM Communications Forum

Description
This forum is devoted to the topic of telecommunications on the IBM PC and compatible computers.

Subjects
Communications, Computers, IBM PCs, Modems

Audience
Computer users, management information specialists

Contents Summary
You can find various utilities, files, support Q&A, and other communications information for the PC in this forum. The libraries include Autosig (ATO), Communications Utilities, Communications Programs, FAX, Hot Topics, Modems/Communications Hardware, and more.

See Also
Hayes Forum, Modem Vendor Forum

User Guide

- [x] Windows
- [x] DOS
- [ ] Macintosh
- [ ] Terminal Emulation
- [ ] VMS
- [ ] UNIX
- [x] OS/2
- [x] Other platform

Cost

- [ ] Unknown
- [ ] Basic
- [x] Extended
- [ ] Premium ($)
- [ ] Executive w/$

Activity Level

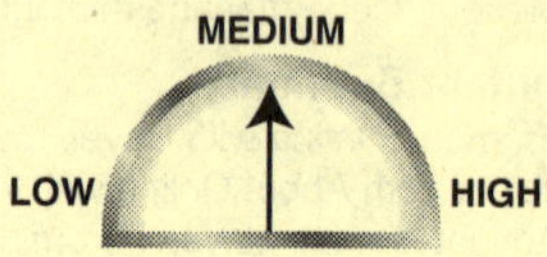
MEDIUM
LOW
HIGH

Address

GO: **IBMCOM**

Intel Corporation

Description

This service enables you to get to the Intel Forum and Intel Architecture Labs Forum.

Subjects

Computer Hardware, Computers, Microcomputers, Modems, Networking

Audience

Modem users, network users, computer users

Content Summary

The Intel Forum supports Intel's enhancement products for IBM PCs and any and all compatible computers. You can find information on Above Boards, SnapIn, Inboards, SatisFAXtion, and Connection CoProcessor FAX boards. Other products include Intel Math CoProcessors, modems, network enhancement utilities, network management tools, Visual Edge, Code Builder, Matched Memory, and NetPort. The Intel Architecture Labs Forum is an interactive, online service in which you can obtain the latest in technical and marketing information on the advanced Intel architectures.

See Also

Computer Club Forum

User Guide

- [x] Windows
- [x] DOS
- [ ] Macintosh
- [ ] Terminal Emulation
- [ ] VMS
- [ ] UNIX
- [x] OS/2
- [x] Other platform

Cost

- [ ] Unknown
- [ ] Basic
- [x] Extended
- [ ] Premium ($)
- [ ] Executive w/$

Activity Level

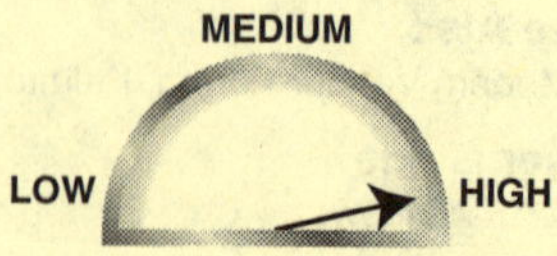
MEDIUM
LOW
HIGH

Address

GO: **INTEL**

Macintosh Communications Forum

Description

You can find support, tips, files, and discussions concerning Mac communications topics that include fax, modems, and ISDN.

Subjects

Computers, Macintosh, Modem

Audience

Macintosh users, computer users

Content Summary

The many library and message sections include CIS Navigator, Scripts/Tools, Communication Programs/ Utilities, Hardware, FAX, Networking, Talking to PCs, BBS Systems, and more.

See Also

Macintosh Forums, Macintosh Hardware Forum

User Guide

- [ ] Windows
- [ ] DOS
- [x] Macintosh
- [ ] Terminal Emulation
- [ ] VMS
- [ ] UNIX
- [ ] OS/2
- [ ] Other platform

Cost

- [ ] Unknown
- [ ] Basic
- [x] Extended
- [ ] Premium ($)
- [ ] Executive w/$

Activity Level

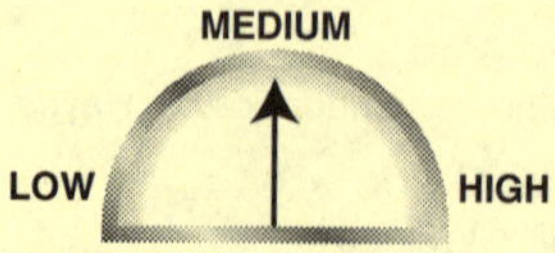
MEDIUM
LOW
HIGH

Address

GO: **MACCOM**

Modem Games Forum

Description

This forum is an electronic special interest group devoted to discussion of computer games capable of utilizing telecommunications and networking technology for play and competition.

Subjects

Computers, Games, Modems

Audience

Computer users, modem users, game enthusiasts

Content Summary
You can find a number of games, utilities, and other supporting files in the libraries in this forum. Some of the library areas include Modem Air Combat, Historic Air Combat, VGA Planets, Chess/Board/Card, DOOM, Network Games, and more.

See Also
Entertainment Forum, Multi-Player Games Forum

User Guide
- [x] Windows
- [x] DOS
- [x] Macintosh
- [ ] Terminal Emulation
- [x] VMS
- [x] UNIX
- [ ] OS/2
- [ ] Other platform

Cost
- [ ] Unknown
- [ ] Basic
- [x] Extended
- [ ] Premium ($)
- [ ] Executive w/$

Activity Level

Address
GO: **MODEMGAMES**

Modem Vendor Forum

Description
This forum is devoted to the support of products of the supporting vendors here, including direct assistance of software and hardware products.

Subjects
Computers, Modems

Audience
Computer users, modem users

Content Summary
In addition to discussions and support, you can find help files, programs, patches, and example files in the libraries. Some of the libraries include Supra Corporation, Boca Research, Global Village Communications, US Robotics, Zoom, Prometheus, and more.

See Also
Telecommunications Forum

User Guide
- [x] Windows
- [x] DOS
- [x] Macintosh
- [ ] Terminal Emulation
- [ ] VMS
- [x] UNIX
- [ ] OS/2
- [x] Other platform

Cost
- [ ] Unknown
- [ ] Basic
- [x] Extended
- [ ] Premium ($)
- [ ] Executive w/$

Activity Level

Address
GO: **MODEMVENDOR**

MODERN ART

Fine Art Forum

Description
Michelangelo. Renoir. Matisse. DaVinci. Rembrandt. Montgomery. Montgomery? Find out about him and other artists in the Fine Arts Forum.

Subjects
Art, Art History, Classics, Modern Art

Audience
Art directors, art enthusiasts, art historians, artists, general interest

Content Summary
The Fine Art Forum focuses on the arts and techniques of the old masters, as well as local and regional traditional-media artists such as Carl Lundgren, Gunni Nilsson Price, Joe Bergeron, Roberta Laidman, Jess Hager, Barbara Johnson, and David O. Stillings. The many libraries offered here enable you to download GIF files of many of your favorite paintings, such as Michelangelo's "The Fall of Man," DaVinci's "Last Supper," and Renoir's "Diana." You also can become familiar with modern artists and techniques by visiting Library 15, Modern Art.

See Also
Artist Forum, Graphics Forums, Graphics Gallery Forum, Graphics Plus Forum, Photography Forum

User Guide
- [x] Windows
- [x] DOS
- [x] Macintosh
- [ ] Terminal Emulation
- [ ] VMS
- [ ] UNIX
- [ ] OS/2
- [ ] Other platform

Cost
- [ ] Unknown
- [ ] Basic
- [ ] Extended
- [x] Premium ($)
- [ ] Executive w/$

Activity Level

Address
GO: **FINEARTS**

MODERN HISTORY

Global Crisis Forum

Description
This forum is devoted to the past, present, and future crises around the world, such as the Balkans, the former USSR, and other hot spots around the globe.

Subjects
Current Events, Global News, International Politics, Modern History, World View

Audience
Military historians, historians, general public, activists, writers, journalists

Content Summary
Because the world changes and some hot spots become cold spots and cold spots become hot spots, the library and message sections in this forum change often. Some of the recent hot spots on the forum have been the Asia/Pacific Rim, Africa, Russia, the Baltics, and the Americas. You'll also find HOTSPOT: areas denoted in the libraries and message areas for current topics. You'll find articles, theses, and other text files throughout the library sections for downloading.

See Also
Associated Press, Executive News Service, U.S. News & World Report

User Guide
- ☑ Windows
- ☑ DOS
- ☑ Macintosh
- ☑ Terminal Emulation
- ☑ VMS
- ☑ UNIX
- ☑ OS/2
- ☑ Other platform

Cost
- ☐ Unknown
- ☐ Basic
- ☑ Extended
- ☐ Premium ($)
- ☐ Executive w/$

Activity Level

Address
GO: CRISIS

MONEY

Consumer Forum

Description
The place to find out how to make and save money, learn about your consumer rights, get buying advice, and read about scams and ripoffs.

Subjects
Business, Money

Audience
Consumers

Content Summary
Libraries include consumer information on automobiles, banking, bargains, coupons, complaints, rights, ripoffs, and money. You can even ask David Horowitz, a recognized expert, questions about products and consumer rights.

See Also
Consumer Reports

User Guide
- ☑ Windows
- ☑ DOS
- ☑ Macintosh
- ☐ Terminal Emulation
- ☐ VMS
- ☑ UNIX
- ☐ OS/2
- ☐ Other platform

Cost
- ☐ Unknown
- ☐ Basic
- ☑ Extended
- ☐ Premium ($)
- ☐ Executive w/$

Activity Level

Address
GO: CONSUMER

MORTGAGE

Mortgage Calculator

Description
Do you need a quick and painless way to calculate a mortgage? If so, use the Mortgage Calculator service.

Subjects
Mortgage, Finance

Audience
General public

Content Summary
Type the amount of loan, interest rate, number of payments per year, and number of years, and see the results. You can display the payment schedule to see the breakdown of how much your monthly payment is paying on interest and principle, as well as see the balance of the loan each month.

See Also
Handyman Forum

User Guide
- [ ] Windows
- [ ] DOS
- [ ] Macintosh
- [x] Terminal Emulation
- [ ] VMS
- [ ] UNIX
- [ ] OS/2
- [ ] Other platform

Cost
- [ ] Unknown
- [x] Basic
- [ ] Extended
- [ ] Premium ($)
- [ ] Executive w/$

Activity Level
UNKNOWN

Address
GO: **HOM-17**

MOTOR HOMES

Recreational Vehicle Forum

Description
This forum is for all people who enjoy camping in tent trailers, travel trailers, fifth-wheels, and motor homes. If you are an experienced camper or are just looking for a motor home, this forum can help.

Subjects
Camping, Motor Homes, Travel

Audience
Camping enthusiasts, travel enthusiasts, RV enthusiasts

Content Summary
This forum not only provides up-to-date information about products and services for the travel trailer industry, but also provides articles and discussions on where to go, where to stay, and what to do. Participants also state opinions and make recommendations on which RV to purchase and where to go for service. There's even a classified section if you are looking to purchase a recreational vehicle.

See Also
Travel Forum

User Guide
- [x] Windows
- [x] DOS
- [x] Macintosh
- [ ] Terminal Emulation
- [x] VMS
- [x] UNIX
- [x] OS/2
- [ ] Other platform

Cost
- [ ] Unknown
- [ ] Basic
- [x] Extended
- [ ] Premium ($)
- [ ] Executive w/$

Activity Level
MEDIUM (arrow LOW)

Address
GO: **RVFORUM**

MOTOR RACING

Motor Sports Forum

Description
Operated by Racing Information Systems of Redondo Beach, California, this news service provides an area for discussion of topics of interest to motor racing enthusiasts worldwide.

Subjects
Automobiles, Motor Racing, Motorcycles

Audience
Automobile enthusiasts

Content Summary
The library and message sections include racing topics such as IMSA Series Files, NASCAR/Stock Files, Indy Cars/Lite, USAC/WoO/Oval Track, NHRA/IHRA/Drags/LSR, Motorcycle Racing, Racing Graphics, and more.

See Also
Sports Forum

User Guide
- [x] Windows
- [x] DOS
- [x] Macintosh
- [ ] Terminal Emulation
- [x] VMS
- [x] UNIX
- [ ] OS/2
- [ ] Other platform

Cost
- [ ] Unknown
- [ ] Basic
- [x] Extended
- [ ] Premium ($)
- [ ] Executive w/$

Activity Level
MEDIUM (arrow HIGH)

Address
GO: **RACING**

MOVIES

Movie Reviews

Description
Going to the movies? Use the Movie Reviews service to find the latest reviews on the hottest movies.

Subjects
Movies

Audience
General public

Content Summary
From the Movies Reviews menu, you can choose from Hollywood Hotline, HHL Movie Reviews, Roger Ebert's Movie Reviews, Magil's Survey of Cinema, and ShowBiz-Media Forum. The Magil's Survey of Cinema service carries additional surcharges.

See Also
Roger Ebert's Movie Reviews

User Guide
- ☑ Windows
- ☑ DOS
- ☑ Macintosh
- ☐ Terminal Emulation
- ☑ VMS
- ☑ UNIX
- ☐ OS/2
- ☐ Other platform

Cost
- ☐ Unknown
- ☐ Basic
- ☑ Extended
- ☐ Premium ($)
- ☐ Executive w/$

Activity Level

Address
GO: **MOVIES**

Roger Ebert's Movie Reviews

Description
If you love movies, then this forum is for you. Get the thumbs up or thumbs down on recent movies by Roger Ebert himself.

Subjects
Film, Movies, Reviews

Audience
Film students, movie critics, movie enthusiasts

Content Summary
You can receive an alphabetical listing of recent movies with Roger Ebert's familiar star rating. You also can receive film reviews by searching by movie name, actor or actress name, or director name. Included in this forum are celebrity interviews with such well-known personalities as Oliver Stone. Other areas of interest include a glossary of movie terms, the 10 best films of the year, and a special area in which you can correspond with Roger Ebert.

See Also
Movie Reviews Forum, SHOWBIZ Quiz Forum

User Guide
- ☑ Windows
- ☑ DOS
- ☑ Macintosh
- ☐ Terminal Emulation
- ☑ VMS
- ☑ UNIX
- ☑ OS/2
- ☐ Other platform

Cost
- ☐ Unknown
- ☑ Basic
- ☐ Extended
- ☐ Premium ($)
- ☐ Executive w/$

Activity Level

Address
GO: **EBERT**

Seattle Film Works

Description
This forum includes online shopping and film processing.

Subjects
Movies

Audience
Photographers

Content Summary
This shopping service enables you to shop online for film processing.

See Also
Photography Forum

User Guide
- ☑ Windows
- ☑ DOS
- ☑ Macintosh
- ☐ Terminal Emulation
- ☐ VMS
- ☐ UNIX
- ☐ OS/2
- ☐ Other platform

Cost
- ☐ Unknown
- ☑ Basic
- ☐ Extended
- ☐ Premium ($)
- ☐ Executive w/$

Activity Level

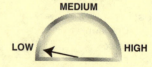

Address
GO: **SFW-1**

SHOWBIZ Quiz

Description
Companion to the ShowBiz Forum and Hollywood Hotline, this area features trivia quizzes on several ShowBiz topics.

Subjects
Games, Movies, Television, Trivia

Audience
Movie enthusiasts

Content Summary
The libraries contain information about the forum, home entertainment, recent films, new films, classic films, television, celebrities, and Hollywood news.

See Also
Hollywood Hotline

User Guide
- ☑ Windows
- ☑ DOS
- ☑ Macintosh
- ☐ Terminal Emulation
- ☐ VMS
- ☑ UNIX
- ☐ OS/2
- ☐ Other platform

Cost
- ☐ Unknown
- ☐ Basic
- ☑ Extended
- ☐ Premium ($)
- ☐ Executive w/$

Activity Level UNKNOWN

Address
GO: **SBQ**

MS-DOS

Microsoft DOS Forum

Description
Have questions about MS DOS? Do you just love to discuss DOS problems and features? You should join this forum then.

Subjects
Computer Users, Microsoft Corp., MS-DOS

Audience
Computer users, management information specialists

Content Summary
You can find out the latest about the newest release of MS DOS, troubleshooting suggestions, hardware issues, setup and installation problems and concerns, memory management concerns, and other topics. For information on DoubleSpace, DriveSpace, and Stacker, see the lively message section area.

See Also
Microsoft Connection, MS DOS 6.2 DLOAD (Microsoft)

User Guide
- ☐ Windows
- ☑ DOS
- ☐ Macintosh
- ☐ Terminal Emulation
- ☐ VMS
- ☐ UNIX
- ☐ OS/2
- ☐ Other platform

Cost
- ☐ Unknown
- ☐ Basic
- ☑ Extended
- ☐ Premium ($)
- ☐ Executive w/$

Activity Level MEDIUM

Address
GO: **MSDOS**

Multi-Player Games Forum

Description
Find files, support, and help for multiplayer computer games in this forum.

Subjects
Computers, Computer Games

Audience
Computer game enthusiasts

Content Summary
To find advice and assistance fast, be sure to post a message in one of the multiplayer game's sections, including MegaWars I, MegaWars III, Island of Kesmai, British Legends, You Guessed It!, Sniper!, ATC and Other Games, and ECenter Games (StarSprint, Backgammon, Checkers).

See Also
Modem Games Forum, Entertainment Forum

User Guide
- ☑ Windows
- ☑ DOS
- ☑ Macintosh
- ☐ Terminal Emulation
- ☑ VMS
- ☑ UNIX
- ☐ OS/2
- ☐ Other platform

Cost
- ☐ Unknown
- ☐ Basic
- ☑ Extended
- ☐ Premium ($)
- ☐ Executive w/$

Activity Level MEDIUM (toward HIGH)

Address
GO: **MPGAMES**

MULTIMEDIA

Autodesk Multimedia Forum

Description
Support for the Autodesk line of PC and workstation-based graphics programs.

Subjects
CAD, Computers, Multimedia

Audience
Autodesk products users

Content Summary
Libraries contain IPAS usage, 3D Studio updates, software developer news, animations, and education issues.

See Also
Autodesk AutoCAD Forum

User Guide
- ☑ Windows
- ☑ DOS
- ☐ Macintosh
- ☐ Terminal Emulation
- ☐ VMS
- ☐ UNIX
- ☐ OS/2
- ☐ Other platform

Cost
- ☐ Unknown
- ☐ Basic
- ☑ Extended
- ☐ Premium ($)
- ☐ Executive w/$

Activity Level

Address
GO: **ASOFT**

Entertainment Drive Center

Description
This is your backstage pass to the entertainment industry. You can get David Letterman Top 10 lists, O.J. Simpson trial transcripts, exclusive columns and reviews, and multimedia files.

Subjects
Celebrities, Entertainment, Multimedia

Audience
Journalists, photojournalists, anyone interested in the entertainment industry

Content Summary
Because of the nature of the entertainment industry, many of the files posted in this forum are removed on certain dates, including a collection of Lion King graphics that were posted until August 31, 1994. If you missed these, don't despair; other hot topics will be featured every month.

See Also
Holltwood Hotline

User Guide
- ☑ Windows
- ☑ DOS
- ☑ Macintosh
- ☐ Terminal Emulation
- ☐ VMS
- ☐ UNIX
- ☐ OS/2
- ☐ Other platform

Cost
- ☐ Unknown
- ☐ Basic
- ☑ Extended
- ☐ Premium ($)
- ☐ Executive w/$

Activity Level

Address
GO: **EDRIVE**

IBM Storage Systems Forum

Description
This forum has information concerning IBM Storage Systems Division Software Products, including information for the ADSTAR Distributed Storage Manager.

Subjects
Computers, IBM, Multimedia

Audience
Management information apecialists, computer users

Content Summary
The sections in this forum include ADSTAR Distributed Storage Manager (ADSM), ADSM Special Programs, ADSM BETA Program (private), and ADSM Developers Program (private).

See Also
Autodesk Multimedia Forum

User Guide
- ☑ Windows
- ☑ DOS
- ☐ Macintosh
- ☐ Terminal Emulation
- ☐ VMS
- ☐ UNIX
- ☑ OS/2
- ☑ Other platform

Cost
- ☐ Unknown
- ☐ Basic
- ☑ Extended
- ☐ Premium ($)
- ☐ Executive w/$

Activity Level

Address
GO: **IBMSTORAGE**

Macintosh Hypertext Forum

Description
Whether you are a browser or are familiar with XCMNDS and Hypertalk, this forum is for you.

Subjects
Computers, Macintosh, Multimedia

Audience
Macintosh users

Content Summary
This forum includes libraries such as Games, Education, Music and Sound, Art: Clip and Fine!, Reference Stacks, and more. Also note that there is an R-Rated Stacks library that contains nudity and may be offensive to some people and should not be viewed by minors under the age of 18.

See Also
Macintosh Forums, Mac Entertainment Forum

User Guide
- ☐ Windows
- ☐ DOS
- ☑ Macintosh
- ☐ Terminal Emulation
- ☐ VMS
- ☐ UNIX
- ☐ OS/2
- ☐ Other platform

Cost
- ☐ Unknown
- ☐ Basic
- ☑ Extended
- ☐ Premium ($)
- ☐ Executive w/$

Activity Level

Address
GO: **MACHYPER**

Macintosh Multimedia Forum

Description
This forum discusses the various uses of the Macintosh as a platform for multimedia development.

Subjects
Computers, Macintosh, Multimedia

Audience
Macintosh users

Content Summary
Loaded with multimedia clips, QuickTime movies and tools, HyperCard tools, and templates, this forum is for you if you are interested in multimedia, the creation of it, or the final results of multimedia. Check out these libraries: Video Clips, Sound Tools, Glamour Films, and Home Movies.

See Also
Macintosh Forums, Mac Entertainment Forum, Mac Hypertext Forum

User Guide
- ☐ Windows
- ☐ DOS
- ☑ Macintosh
- ☐ Terminal Emulation
- ☐ VMS
- ☐ UNIX
- ☐ OS/2
- ☐ Other platform

Cost
- ☐ Unknown
- ☐ Basic
- ☑ Extended
- ☐ Premium ($)
- ☐ Executive w/$

Activity Level

Address
GO: **MACMULTI**

Macromedia Forum

Description
This forum provides technical support and discussions on Macromedia products.

Subjects
Computers, Multimedia

Audience
Computer users

Content Summary
Macromedia topics discussed in this forum include Director, Authoware, Action/ClipMedia, 3D/Modeling/MMaker, sound products, and more.

See Also
Multimedia Forum, Multimedia Vendor Forum

User Guide
- ☑ Windows
- ☑ DOS
- ☑ Macintosh
- ☐ Terminal Emulation
- ☐ VMS
- ☐ UNIX
- ☐ OS/2
- ☑ Other platform

Cost
- ☐ Unknown
- ☐ Basic
- ☑ Extended
- ☐ Premium ($)
- ☐ Executive w/$

Activity Level

Address
GO: **MACROMEDIA**

Media Vision Forum

Description
This forum is intended for technical support, general discussions of Media Vision products, and storage of files.

Subjects
Computers, Multimedia

Audience
Computer users, management information specialists

Content Summary
The library and message sections include Pro Audio Spectrum, Pro Audio Studio, ProSonic, Fusion Kits, Multimedia Kits, CD-ROM Drivere, ProGraphics, and more.

See Also
Multimedia Forum, Multimedia Conference Forum, Multimedia Vendor Forum

User Guide
- ☑ Windows
- ☑ DOS
- ☐ Macintosh
- ☐ Terminal Emulation
- ☐ VMS
- ☐ UNIX
- ☐ OS/2
- ☑ Other platform

Cost
- ☐ Unknown
- ☐ Basic
- ☑ Extended
- ☐ Premium ($)
- ☐ Executive w/$

Activity Level: MEDIUM (LOW–HIGH)

Address
GO: `MEDIAVISION`

Microsoft Windows Multimedia Forum

Description
This forum offers many files, troubleshooting solutions, and technical support for your multimedia applications.

Subjects
Games, Microsoft Corp., Multimedia

Audience
Computer users, computer game developers

Content Summary
The type of libraries and message sections you will see in this forum include MDK, MediaView, Video for Windows, Viewer 2.0, Windows Sound System, Multimedia (MM) Strategy, Third Party Software, and Windows Game Development. You can obtain a Viewer 2.0 compiler for Word 6.0 in the Viewer 2.0 library. Also, if you're looking for the Microsoft JumpStart CD, see Library 10, MM Strategy. This is the CD that Microsoft hands out at many of their conferences and seminars.

See Also
MS TechNet Forum, Multimedia Forum, Multimedia Conference Forum

User Guide
- ☑ Windows
- ☑ DOS
- ☑ Macintosh
- ☐ Terminal Emulation
- ☐ VMS
- ☐ UNIX
- ☐ OS/2
- ☐ Other platform

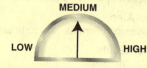

Cost
- ☐ Unknown
- ☐ Basic
- ☑ Extended
- ☐ Premium ($)
- ☐ Executive w/$

Activity Level: MEDIUM (LOW–HIGH)

Address
GO: `WINMM`

MIDI Vendor Forums

Description
Supporting various MIDI vendors, the MIDI A, MIDI B, and MIDI C Vendor Forums help users with specific product problems and concerns.

Subjects
Computers, Multimedia, Music

Audience
Computer users, computer game developers, musicians

Content Summary
The MIDI A Vendor Forum (GO MIDIAVEN) includes these vendors: Turtle Beach, Twelve Tone, E-Mu, Big Noise, and many others. The MIDI B Vendor Forum (GO MIDIBVEN) includes these vendors: Midiman, Cool Shoes, Covox, Sweetwater Sound, Passport Designs, Windjammer Software, and others. The MIDI C Vendor Forum (GO MIDICVEN) includes these vendors: MediaTech, AVM, Blue Ribbon, Roland, Steinberg, and others.

See Also
Macromedia Forum

User Guide
- ☑ Windows
- ☑ DOS
- ☐ Macintosh
- ☐ Terminal Emulation
- ☐ VMS
- ☐ UNIX
- ☐ OS/2
- ☐ Other platform

Cost
- ☐ Unknown
- ☐ Basic
- ☑ Extended
- ☐ Premium ($)
- ☐ Executive w/$

Multimedia

Activity Level

Address
GO: **MIDIAVEN** or **MIDIBVEN** or **MIDICVEN**

MIDI/Music Forum

Description
This forum is dedicated to supporting MIDI and computer music-related discussions and files. Also, it has the coolest forum logo. You have to see it!

Subjects
Amiga, Macintosh, Multimedia, Music

Audience
Musicians, computer game developers, computer users, Amiga users

Content Summary
Packed with files, discussions, tips and hints, and troubleshooting guidelines, the MIDI/Music Forum includes these and other library and message sections: Basics and Product Guides, General MIDI Songs, Atari Files, Macintosh Files, Patches/Samples, MS DOS Demos, and Windows Media Sound. You'll find items for sale in the Classified Ads library (Library 8).

See Also
MIDI A Vendor Forum, MIDI B Vendor Forum, MIDI C Vendor Forum

User Guide
☑	Windows	☐	VMS
☑	DOS	☐	UNIX
☑	Macintosh	☐	OS/2
☐	Terminal Emulation	☑	Other platform

Cost
☐	Unknown	☐	Premium ($)
☐	Basic	☐	Executive w/$
☑	Extended		

Activity Level

Address
GO: **MIDIFORUM**

Multimedia Services

Description
If you use computers with audio, video, animation, and music, the multimedia services and forums are for you.

Subjects
Computers, Multimedia

Audience
Computer users, multimedia users

Content Summary
The Multimedia Vendor Forum (GO MULTIVEN) includes vendor support from BCD Associates, Lenel Systems, Voyager, Truevision, and others. The Multimedia B Vendor Forum (GO MULTIBVEN) includes vendor support from Adda Technologies, In Focus Systems, FAST Electronic, and others. The Multimedia Forum (GO MULTIMEDIA) includes files, advice, and technical support for topics such as video and audio, animation, interface design, education/training, and more.

See Also
Autodesk Multimedia Forum

User Guide
☑	Windows	☐	VMS
☑	DOS	☐	UNIX
☑	Macintosh	☐	OS/2
☐	Terminal Emulation	☐	Other platform

Cost
☐	Unknown	☐	Premium ($)
☐	Basic	☐	Executive w/$
☑	Extended		

Activity Level

Medium/High

Address
GO: **MUTIBVEN**, **MULTIMEDIA**, **MULTIVEN**

Ultimedia Hardware Plus Forum

Description
Vendor support forum for Ultimedia's hardware products such as MWAVE System, ActionMedia, and V-Lan.

Subjects
Multimedia, Computers

Audience
Computer Users

Content Summary
The library and message sections contain information and files for Ultimedia products. Be sure to check out the message sections for support questions and comments.

See Also
Multimedia

User Guide
☑	Windows	☐	VMS
☑	DOS	☐	UNIX
☐	Macintosh	☐	OS/2
☐	Terminal Emulation	☐	Other platform

Multimedia

Cost
- ☐ Unknown
- ☐ Basic
- ☒ Extended
- ☐ Premium ($)
- ☐ Executive w/$

Activity Level: LOW (arrow pointing low), MEDIUM, HIGH

Address
GO: **ULTIHW**

Ultimedia Tools Series A Forum

Description
One of three vendor support forums covering Ultimedia's software products.

Subjects
Computers, Multimedia

Audience
Computer users

Content Summary
The library and message sections contain information and files for Ultimedia products. Be sure to check out the message sections for support questions and comments.

See Also
Multimedia Forum

User Guide
- ☒ Windows
- ☒ DOS
- ☐ Macintosh
- ☐ Terminal Emulation
- ☐ VMS
- ☐ UNIX
- ☐ OS/2
- ☐ Other platform

Cost
- ☐ Unknown
- ☐ Basic
- ☒ Extended
- ☐ Premium ($)
- ☐ Executive w/$

Activity Level: LOW (arrow), MEDIUM, HIGH

Address
GO: **ULTIATOOLS**

Ultimedia Tools Series B Forum

Description
One of three vendor support forums for Ultimedia's software products.

Subjects
Computers, Multimedia

Audience
Computer users

Content Summary
The library and message sections contain information and files for Ultimedia products. Be sure to check out the message sections for support questions and comments.

See Also
Multimedia Forum

User Guide
- ☒ Windows
- ☒ DOS
- ☐ Macintosh
- ☐ Terminal Emulation
- ☐ VMS
- ☐ UNIX
- ☐ OS/2
- ☐ Other platform

Cost
- ☐ Unknown
- ☐ Basic
- ☒ Extended
- ☐ Premium ($)
- ☐ Executive w/$

Activity Level: LOW (arrow), MEDIUM, HIGH

Address
GO: **ULTIBTOOLS**

Ultimedia Tools Series C Forum

Description
One of three vendor support forums for Ultimedia's software products.

Subjects
Computers, Multimedia

Audience
Computer users

Content Summary
The library and message sections contain information and files for Ultimedia products. Be sure to check out the message sections for support questions and comments.

See Also
Multimedia Forum

User Guide
- ☒ Windows
- ☒ DOS
- ☐ Macintosh
- ☐ Terminal Emulation
- ☐ VMS
- ☐ UNIX
- ☐ OS/2
- ☐ Other platform

Cost
- ☐ Unknown
- ☐ Basic
- ☒ Extended
- ☐ Premium ($)
- ☐ Executive w/$

Activity Level: LOW (arrow), MEDIUM, HIGH

Address
GO: **ULTICTOOLS**

Multimedia Services

Description
If you use computers with audio, video, animation, and music, the multimedia services and forums are for you.

Subjects
Computers, Multimedia

Audience
Computer users, multimedia users

Content Summary
The Multimedia Vendor Forum (GO MULTIVEN) includes vendor support from BCD Associates, Lenel Systems, Voyager, Truevision, and others. The Multimedia B Vendor Forum (GO MULTIBVEN) includes vendor support from Adda Technologies, In Focus Systems, FAST Electronic, and others. The Multimedia Forum (GO MULTIMEDIA) includes files, advice, and technical support for topics such as video and audio, animation, interface design, education/training, and more.

See Also
Autodesk Multimedia Forum

User Guide
- ☑ Windows
- ☑ DOS
- ☑ Macintosh
- ☐ Terminal Emulation
- ☐ VMS
- ☐ UNIX
- ☐ OS/2
- ☐ Other platform

Cost
- ☐ Unknown
- ☐ Basic
- ☑ Extended
- ☐ Premium ($)
- ☐ Executive w/$

Activity Level

Address
GO: **MUTIBVEN, MULTIMEDIA, MULTIVEN**

Disabilities Forum

Description
This forum is designed to be an online support group and open communication facilitator for anyone interested in disabilities. You can find stories, reports, and information about disabled persons' daily lives, along with ideas and experiences of parents and friends of disabled people.

Subjects
Emotional Disturbances, Learning Disabilities, Multiple Sclerosis, Disabilities

Audience
Disabled persons, family and friends of disabled persons, professionals who work with disabled persons

Content Summary
Many message and library topics are available to choose from, including developmental disabilities, emotional disturbances, hearing impairments, multiple sclerosis, and mobility impairments. You can find the latest information on the Americans with Disabilities Act (ADA) in Library 7, "Government Activities." If you are looking for employment, see "Education/Employment," Library 8, for files designed for disabled persons searching for employment and education.

See Also
Handicapped Users Database, Health/Fitness, Healthnet

User Guide
- ☑ Windows
- ☑ DOS
- ☑ Macintosh
- ☐ Terminal Emulation
- ☑ VMS
- ☑ UNIX
- ☑ OS/2
- ☐ Other platform

Cost
- ☐ Unknown
- ☐ Basic
- ☑ Extended
- ☐ Premium ($)
- ☐ Executive w/$

Activity Level

Address
GO: **DISABILITIES**

Digital Equipment Corporation

Description
This is the main area from which you can choose to enter one of several DEC forums or service areas. You can select Digital's Windows NT Support Forum, PC Integration Forum, or Digital-Related Forums. You also can go to Digital's PC Store from this menu.

Subjects
Computers, Client/Server, Multiprocessor Environments, Windows NT

Audience
DEC Alpha AXP users, support technicians, system integrators, VARs, Windows NT users

Content Summary
At the main menu, you can select from Digital NT Support Forum, Digital PC Integration Forum, and Digital's PC Store.

Multiprocessor Environments – Music

See Also
Digital NT Support Forum, Digital PC Integration Forum, Digital's PC Store

User Guide
- ☑ Windows
- ☑ DOS
- ☑ Macintosh
- ☐ Terminal Emulation
- ☑ VMS
- ☑ UNIX
- ☑ OS/2
- ☐ Other platform

Cost
- ☐ Unknown
- ☐ Basic
- ☑ Extended
- ☐ Premium ($)
- ☐ Executive w/$

Activity Level: UNKNOWN

Address
GO: **DEC**

MUSIC

All-Music Guide Forum

Description
The AMGPOP Forum provides help in using the All-Music Guide Database, the largest collection of music albums, ratings, and reviews.

Subjects
Entertainment, Music

Audience
Musicians, music enthusiasts

Content Summary
The libraries contain biographies of artists, album reviews, and a list of the best works of specific artists.

See Also
Art/Music/Literature

User Guide
- ☑ Windows
- ☑ DOS
- ☐ Macintosh
- ☐ Terminal Emulation
- ☐ VMS
- ☐ UNIX
- ☐ OS/2
- ☐ Other platform

Cost
- ☐ Unknown
- ☐ Basic
- ☑ Extended
- ☐ Premium ($)
- ☐ Executive w/$

Activity Level: LOW

Address
GO: **AMGOP**

Creative Labs

Description
This forum gives worldwide support to Creative Labs' and Creative Technologies' products, including the popular Sound Blaster line of cards.

Subjects
Computers, Music

Audience
Creative Labs users

Content Summary
Libraries include information about SoundBlaster, SB Pro, SB16, WaveBlaster, AWE-32, CDROM kits, Video Blaster, VideoSpigot, Multimedia update kits.

See Also
Multimedia Forum

User Guide
- ☑ Windows
- ☑ DOS
- ☑ Macintosh
- ☐ Terminal Emulation
- ☐ VMS
- ☑ UNIX
- ☐ OS/2
- ☐ Other platform

Cost
- ☐ Unknown
- ☐ Basic
- ☑ Extended
- ☐ Premium ($)
- ☐ Executive w/$

Activity Level: MEDIUM/HIGH

Address
GO: **BLASTER**

MIDI/Music Forum

Description
This forum is dedicated to supporting MIDI and computer music-related discussions and files. Also, it has the coolest forum logo. You have to see it!

Subjects
Amiga, Macintosh, Multimedia, Music

Audience
Musicians, computer game developers, computer users, Amiga users

Content Summary
Packed with files, discussions, tips and hints, and troubleshooting guidelines, the MIDI/Music Forum includes these and other library and message sections: Basics and Product Guides, General MIDI Songs, Atari Files, Macintosh Files, Patches/Samples, MS DOS Demos, and Windows Media Sound. You'll find items for sale in the Classified Ads library (Library 8).

See Also
MIDI A Vendor Forum, MIDI B Vendor Forum, MIDI C Vendor Forum

Music Hall

Description
From the Music Hall, you can access all the music areas on CompuServe to discuss, learn, network, and be entertained by others with your same interests.

Subjects
Music

Audience
Music enthusiasts

Content Summary
The Music Hall is an easy way to learn about and directly navigate a wide variety of forums, databases, contests, promotions, and Electronic Mall music merchants providing information, sound files, late-breaking industry news, prizes, and reviews to technical support, and the capability to order CDs, tapes, and musical equipment directly online.

See Also
Music Vendor Forum, Music Arts Forum

User Guide
- [✓] Windows
- [✓] DOS
- [✓] Macintosh
- [ ] Terminal Emulation
- [✓] VMS
- [✓] UNIX
- [ ] OS/2
- [ ] Other platform

Cost
- [ ] Unknown
- [ ] Basic
- [✓] Extended
- [ ] Premium ($)
- [ ] Executive w/$

Activity Level

Address
GO: **MUSIC**

Music Industry Forum

Description
Find files and information about the music industry in this forum. This forum evolved from the Music Vendor Forum to include various vendors and music news.

Subjects
Music, Rock Music, Musical Instruments

Audience
Music enthusiasts, general public

Content Summary
You can find library and message sections that include topics such as Music News, South by Southwest, CMC, Austin Music Chan, Gibson Guitar Corporation, Guitar World, Touring/Roadies, and DJs/Radio.

User Guide (previous entry)
- [✓] Windows
- [✓] DOS
- [✓] Macintosh
- [ ] Terminal Emulation
- [ ] VMS
- [ ] UNIX
- [ ] OS/2
- [✓] Other platform

Cost
- [ ] Unknown
- [ ] Basic
- [✓] Extended
- [ ] Premium ($)
- [ ] Executive w/$

Activity Level
MEDIUM (arrow pointing to HIGH)

Address
GO: **MIDIFORUM**

MIDI Vendor Forums

Description
Supporting various MIDI vendors, the MIDI A, MIDI B, and MIDI C Vendor Forums help users with specific product problems and concerns.

Subjects
Computers, Multimedia, Music

Audience
Computer users, computer game developers, musicians

Content Summary
The MIDI A Vendor Forum (GO MIDIAVEN) includes these vendors: Turtle Beach, Twelve Tone, E-Mu, Big Noise, and many others. The MIDI B Vendor Forum (GO MIDIBVEN) includes these vendors: Midiman, Cool Shoes, Covox, Sweetwater Sound, Passport Designs, Windjammer Software, and others. The MIDI C Vendor Forum (GO MIDICVEN) includes these vendors: MediaTech, AVM, Blue Ribbon, Roland, Steinberg, and others.

See Also
Macromedia Forum

User Guide
- [✓] Windows
- [✓] DOS
- [✓] Macintosh
- [ ] Terminal Emulation
- [✓] VMS
- [✓] UNIX
- [✓] OS/2
- [✓] Other platform

Cost
- [ ] Unknown
- [ ] Basic
- [✓] Extended
- [ ] Premium ($)
- [ ] Executive w/$

Activity Level

Address
GO: **MIDIAVEN** or **MIDIBVEN** or **MIDICVEN**

Music

See Also
Music Hall, Music Vendor Forum

User Guide
- ☑ Windows
- ☑ DOS
- ☑ Macintosh
- ☐ Terminal Emulation
- ☑ VMS
- ☑ UNIX
- ☐ OS/2
- ☐ Other platform

Cost
- ☐ Unknown
- ☐ Basic
- ☑ Extended
- ☐ Premium ($)
- ☐ Executive w/$

Activity Level

Address
GO: **INMUSIC**

Music Vendor Forum

Description
The Music Vendor Forum is known as the "Recording Industry Forum" that enables you to communicate directly with selected vendors. You can download sound files, graphics, tour dates, and various news reports about the music industry's hottest performers.

Subjects
Music, Rock Music

Audience
Music enthusiasts, general public

Content Summary
You can find information from several music vendors, including Warner Brothers, PolyGram, Virgin Records, Racer Records, Kudos Records, Geffen Records, RCA Records, and Arista Records.

See Also
Music Industry Forum

User Guide
- ☑ Windows
- ☑ DOS
- ☑ Macintosh
- ☐ Terminal Emulation
- ☑ VMS
- ☑ UNIX
- ☐ OS/2
- ☐ Other platform

Cost
- ☐ Unknown
- ☐ Basic
- ☑ Extended
- ☐ Premium ($)
- ☐ Executive w/$

Activity Level

Address
GO: **MUSICVEN**

Music/Arts Forum

Description
Whether you're a seasoned performer or an amateur—or a bystander with keen interests in the subject—you'll find the Music/Arts Forum a fun activity in which to participate.

Subjects
Music

Audience
Musicians, music enthusiasts, general public

Content Summary
This forum contains several library and message sections, including Classical/Opera, The Blues, Jazz/Big Bands, Shows & Soundtracks, Pop/Rock, Religious Music, Rap/Hiphop/Techno, and others.

See Also
Music Hall, Music Vendor Forum, Music Industry Forum

User Guide
- ☑ Windows
- ☑ DOS
- ☑ Macintosh
- ☐ Terminal Emulation
- ☑ VMS
- ☑ UNIX
- ☐ OS/2
- ☐ Other platform

Cost
- ☐ Unknown
- ☐ Basic
- ☑ Extended
- ☐ Premium ($)
- ☐ Executive w/$

Activity Level

Address
GO: **MUSICARTS**

New Country Music

Description
If you like *Hee-Haw,* you'll love this place! New Country Music Magazine gives you an exclusive look into the world of Country. Enjoy intimate, friendly chats with superstars such as Alan Jackson, Trisha Yearwood, Travis Tritt, and others.

Subjects
Music, Country Music

Audience
Music enthusiasts, general public

Content Summary
From the main menu, you can choose from these options: What is New Country Music Service, To Sign Up, and Shipping and Billing Information. For a rate of $39.95 for 6 months or $69.95 for 12 months, you can sign for the New Country Music Magazine and get an exclusive CD every month.

Music

See Also
Music Hall, Music Vendor Forum, Music Industry Forum

User Guide
- [ ] Windows
- [ ] DOS
- [ ] Macintosh
- [x] Terminal Emulation
- [ ] VMS
- [ ] UNIX
- [ ] OS/2
- [ ] Other platform

Cost
- [ ] Unknown
- [ ] Basic
- [x] Extended
- [ ] Premium ($)
- [ ] Executive w/$

Activity Level
UNKNOWN

Address
GO: **COUNTRY**

Participate

Description
This forum is a message base that uses Participate software to enable users to create and monitor discussions about any subject they choose.

Subjects
Music, Philosophy, Politics, General Interest

Audience
General public

Content Summary
In this forum, you will find numerous topic discussion areas that include politics, music, marketing, philosophy, and current events. If you don't find the topic of interest to you, you can insert that topic area. Also of interest is The Arrow, which is an online newsletter that discusses this forum. If you want information on the most active discussions, you can join the Hot Points area, which is updated weekly. You also can join the New Points area, which provides you with a list of all new topic discussions.

See Also
Music/Arts Forum, Political Debate Forum

User Guide
- [x] Windows
- [x] DOS
- [x] Macintosh
- [x] Terminal Emulation
- [x] VMS
- [x] UNIX
- [x] OS/2
- [ ] Other platform

Cost
- [ ] Unknown
- [ ] Basic
- [x] Extended
- [ ] Premium ($)
- [ ] Executive w/$

Activity Level

Address
GO: **PARTI**

Rocknet Forum

Description
This forum provides the most up-to-date and accurate information on the rock community.

Subjects
Entertainment, Music, Rock Enthusiasts, Video

Audience
Musicians, Rock Enthusiasts

Content Summary
This forum's libraries cover the full range of rock topics. Topics included are reviews of concerts and music, lists of alternative radio stations, coverage of the musical group Grateful Dead, heavy metal, vintage rock, new music, online conversations with rock personalities, and graphics of musical group logos and photographs taken at concerts.

See Also
Rock Video Monthly

User Guide
- [x] Windows
- [x] DOS
- [x] Macintosh
- [ ] Terminal Emulation
- [ ] VMS
- [ ] UNIX
- [ ] OS/2
- [ ] Other platform

Cost
- [ ] Unknown
- [ ] Basic
- [x] Extended
- [ ] Premium ($)
- [ ] Executive w/$

Activity Level

Address
GO: **ROCKNET**

Warner Bros. Song Preview

Description
This is an online area offering 30-second sound clips from some of Warner Bros. Records recent releases.

Subjects
Entertainment

Audience
Musicians, music enthusiasts

Content Summary
The sound clips enable users to review sound clips of popular recordings so that they can find the music

Music – Mutual Funds

they like. Users also can find out tour and release dates of popular artists.

See Also
Entertainment Center Forum

User Guide
- ☑ Windows
- ☑ DOS
- ☑ Macintosh
- ☐ Terminal Emulation
- ☑ VMS
- ☑ UNIX
- ☑ OS/2
- ☐ Other platform

Cost
- ☐ Unknown
- ☐ Basic
- ☑ Extended
- ☐ Premium ($)
- ☐ Executive w/$

Activity Level

Address
GO: **WBPREVIEW**

MUSICAL INSTRUMENTS

Music Industry Forum

Description
Find files and information about the music industry in this forum. This forum evolved from the Music Vendor Forum to include various vendors and music news.

Subjects
Music, Rock Music, Musical Instruments

Audience
Music enthusiasts, general public

Content Summary
You can find library and message sections that include topics such as Music News, South by Southwest, CMC, Austin Music Chan, Gibson Guitar Corporation, Guitar World, Touring/Roadies, and DJs/Radio.

See Also
Music Hall, Music Vendor Forum

User Guide
- ☑ Windows
- ☑ DOS
- ☑ Macintosh
- ☐ Terminal Emulation
- ☑ VMS
- ☑ UNIX
- ☐ OS/2
- ☐ Other platform

Cost
- ☐ Unknown
- ☐ Basic
- ☑ Extended
- ☐ Premium ($)
- ☐ Executive w/$

Activity Level

Address
GO: **INMUSIC**

MUTUAL FUNDS

Dreyfus Corporation

Description
Dreyfus Corporation has been the leader in the mutual funds field for over 40 years. In this area, you can start your investment portfolio with as little as $100, roll over your IRA and Keogh accounts, and look into other investment programs, such as the Investment Allocation Program.

Subjects
Investments, Mutual Funds

Audience
Investors

Content Summary
From the Dreyfus Corp. main menu, you can choose from several options. You can choose the Online Selection of Funds option to see how to select mutual funds, see the family of funds Dreyfus offers, and see the Featured Funds. To request a free Dreyfus prospectus online, select the Request a FREE Prospectus option from the main menu. Select the Minimum Investment Program option from the main menu for information on starting a mutual fund portfolio for as little as $100.

See Also
Investment Analysis

User Guide
- ☐ Windows
- ☐ DOS
- ☐ Macintosh
- ☑ Terminal Emulation
- ☐ VMS
- ☐ UNIX
- ☐ OS/2
- ☐ Other platform

Cost
- ☐ Unknown
- ☑ Basic
- ☐ Extended
- ☐ Premium ($)
- ☐ Executive w/$

Activity Level

Address
GO: **DR**

N

National Computer Security Association (NCSA)

Description
This service helps you understand the NCSA and the NCSA Ethics Committee, and to go to the NCSA Forum.

Subjects
Computers, Computer Security

Audience
Computer users, MIS people

Content Summary
From the main menu, you can select these options: NCSA InfoSecurity Forum, About the NCSA, and About the NCSA Ethics Committee.

See Also
NCSA Forum

User Guide
- ☑ Windows
- ☑ DOS
- ☑ Macintosh
- ☐ Terminal Emulation
- ☑ VMS
- ☑ UNIX
- ☐ OS/2
- ☐ Other platform

Cost
- ☐ Unknown
- ☑ Basic
- ☐ Extended
- ☐ Premium ($)
- ☐ Executive w/$

Activity Level

Address
GO: **NCSA**

NATIONAL NEWS

Detroit Free Press

Description
This is the place to find news and information about the award-winning Detroit Free Press newspaper. And feel free to leave a letter to the editor while you're online.

Subjects
Journalism, National News, Photojournalism

Audience
Automobile enthusiasts, Detroit citizens, journalists, photojournalists, sports fans

Content Summary
In the message and library areas, you can find information on the auto industry (including photographs of cars), health tips, business news, Detroit metro news, computing, entertainment, sports, and cartoons. You also can find the top stories of the day in the "Today's Top Stories" library (library 17).

See Also
Detroit Free Press Store

User Guide
- ☑ Windows
- ☑ DOS
- ☑ Macintosh
- ☐ Terminal Emulation
- ☑ VMS
- ☑ UNIX
- ☑ OS/2
- ☐ Other platform

Cost
- ☐ Unknown
- ☐ Basic
- ☑ Extended
- ☐ Premium ($)
- ☐ Executive w/$

Activity Level

Address
GO: **DETROIT**

National Public Radio (NPR)

Description
Join with other CompuServe members as they listen to the *Talk of the Nation* radio program and share their comments with each other.

Subjects
Current Issues, General Issues

Audience
General public

Content Summary
Talk of the Nation radio program conferences are held every weekday from 2:00 p.m. till 4:00 p.m. EST in conference room 2 of the Issues Forum (GO ISSUES).

See Also
Issues Forum

User Guide
- ☑ Windows
- ☑ DOS
- ☑ Macintosh
- ☐ Terminal Emulation
- ☑ VMS
- ☑ UNIX
- ☐ OS/2
- ☐ Other platform

Cost
- ☐ Unknown
- ☑ Basic
- ☐ Extended
- ☐ Premium ($)
- ☐ Executive w/$

National Public Radio – NCR/ATT Forum

Activity Level

Address
GO: **NPR**

Dvorak Development Forum

Description
If you use Dvorak Development's NavCIS programs, join this forum for technical support and product information. You also can download a free 30-day demo of the DOS and Windows products to see if you want to purchase the commercial versions.

Subjects
Computers, CompuServe Navigational Tools, NavCIS

Audience
CompuServe users, NavCIS users

Content Summary
If you want to try out NavCIS, see Library 1, "NavCIS Software," to download a 3-day demo of the DOS and Windows versions of NavCIS. Libraries 2–5 offer Windows and DOS support of the SE/TE and Pro versions of NavCIS. Library 7, "Modems and Hardware," contains information and files to help you configure and optimize your modem setup. You also should check out Library 8, "Tip and Techniques," for tips on using NavCIS.

See Also

User Guide
- ☑ Windows
- ☑ DOS
- ☐ Macintosh
- ☐ Terminal Emulation
- ☐ VMS
- ☐ UNIX
- ☐ OS/2
- ☐ Other platform

Cost
- ☐ Unknown
- ☐ Basic
- ☑ Extended
- ☐ Premium ($)
- ☐ Executive w/$

Activity Level

(MEDIUM, LOW, HIGH — arrow pointing to HIGH)

Address
GO: **DVORAK**

NCAA Collegiate Sports Network

Description
Need to satisfy your sports hunger? Go to this service for information on college football, basketball, and other sports.

Subjects
NCAA, Sports

Audience
General public

Content Summary
From the main menu, you can choose Statistics, Football Schedules and Scores, Men's Basketball Schedule Information, Women's Basketball Schedule Information, News Releases, Sports Polls, NCAA Basketball Final Four Championship Information, and NCAA Visitors Center Information.

See Also
Sports Forum

User Guide
- ☐ Windows
- ☐ DOS
- ☐ Macintosh
- ☑ Terminal Emulation
- ☐ VMS
- ☐ UNIX
- ☐ OS/2
- ☐ Other platform

Cost
- ☐ Unknown
- ☐ Basic
- ☑ Extended
- ☐ Premium ($)
- ☐ Executive w/$

Activity Level

Address
GO: **NCAA**

NCR/ATT Forum

Description
Use this forum to find the latest drivers, news, and patches for NCR/ATT products.

Subjects
Computers

Audience
Computer users, MIS people

Content Summary
The library and message sections include The Info Shop, Windows NT, Desktop Computing, AT&T PC's, Portable Computing, Network Connections, and Cooperative FWS.

See Also
IBM File Finder

NCR/ATT Forum – Networking

User Guide
- ☑ Windows
- ☑ DOS
- ☐ Macintosh
- ☐ Terminal Emulation
- ☐ VMS
- ☐ UNIX
- ☐ OS/2
- ☑ Other platform

Cost
- ☐ Unknown
- ☐ Basic
- ☑ Extended
- ☐ Premium ($)
- ☐ Executive w/$

Activity Level: MEDIUM

Address
GO: **NCRATT**

NCSA InfoSecurity Forum

Description
This forum is devoted to the subject of information and data security.

Subjects
Computers, Security

Audience
Computer users, MIS people

Content Summary
If you're concerned about computer security, viruses, and firewalls, examine the various library and message sections in this forum. Some of the topics include Ethics/Privacy, Info Security News, Virus Tools/Info, PC/LAN Security, UNIX/Internet, Auditing, and others.

See Also
Internet Forum

User Guide
- ☑ Windows
- ☑ DOS
- ☑ Macintosh
- ☐ Terminal Emulation
- ☐ VMS
- ☑ UNIX
- ☐ OS/2
- ☑ Other platform

Cost
- ☐ Unknown
- ☐ Basic
- ☑ Extended
- ☐ Premium ($)
- ☐ Executive w/$

Activity Level: MEDIUM (high)

Address
GO: **NCSA Forum**

NETWORKING

ACIUS Forum

Description
The ACI US Forum supports all ACI products with valuable technical support as well as an exchange of ideas from other users of ACI products.

Subjects
Accounting, Business, Software

Audience
Accountants

Content Summary
The libraries contain information on 4th Dimensions, File Force, 4D Modules, time-saving programs, and sample databases.

See Also
Computer Directory

User Guide
- ☑ Windows
- ☑ DOS
- ☐ Macintosh
- ☐ Terminal Emulation
- ☐ VMS
- ☐ UNIX
- ☐ OS/2
- ☐ Other platform

Cost
- ☐ Unknown
- ☐ Basic
- ☐ Extended
- ☐ Premium ($)
- ☐ Executive w/$

Activity level: MEDIUM (low)

Address
GO: **ACIUS**

APPC Info Exchange Forum

Description
The APPC Forum addresses many of the hot topics in networking today, to help you apply advanced networking in your own environment.

Subjects
Computers, Networking

Audience
Network administrators

Content Summary
The libraries contain information on LAN/WAN integration, client/server development, downsizing, and rightsizing.

See Also
Novell

Networking

User Guide
- ☑ Windows
- ☑ DOS
- ☐ Macintosh
- ☐ Terminal Emulation
- ☐ VMS
- ☐ UNIX
- ☐ OS/2
- ☐ Other platform

Cost
- ☐ Unknown
- ☐ Basic
- ☑ Extended
- ☐ Premium ($)
- ☐ Executive w/$

Activity Level — LOW (MEDIUM gauge, arrow pointing low)

Address
GO: **APPCFORUM**

Artisoft Forum

Description
The Artisoft Forum provides online technical support for users of Artisoft products.

Subjects
Computers, Networking, Software

Audience
Network administrators

Content Summary
Libraries include information on LANtastic products, Artisoft Sounding Board Articom, and Net-media products.

See Also
APPC Info Exchange Forum

User Guide
- ☑ Windows
- ☑ DOS
- ☐ Macintosh
- ☐ Terminal Emulation
- ☐ VMS
- ☐ UNIX
- ☐ OS/2
- ☐ Other platform

Cost
- ☐ Unknown
- ☐ Basic
- ☑ Extended
- ☐ Premium ($)
- ☐ Executive w/$

Activity Level — MEDIUM (arrow pointing up)

Address
GO: **ARTISOFT**

Banyan Forum

Description
Help, information, and support for Banyan products, including Banyan VINES networking software.

Subjects
Computers, Networking

Audience
MIS people

Content Summary
Find out more about your Banyan products, including VINES in this forum. Some of the library topics that you'll find include networking, servers, VINES, hardware, and more.

See Also
Other Ban Patch Forum

User Guide
- ☑ Windows
- ☑ DOS
- ☐ Macintosh
- ☐ Terminal Emulation
- ☐ VMS
- ☐ UNIX
- ☐ OS/2
- ☑ Other platform

Cost
- ☐ Unknown
- ☐ Basic
- ☑ Extended
- ☐ Premium ($)
- ☐ Executive w/$

Activity Level — MEDIUM (arrow pointing low)

Address
GO: **BANFORUM**

Cabletron Systems Forum

Description
Cabletron Systems Forum provides help and information with questions or problems concerning Cabletron products or computer networking in general.

Subjects
Computers, Networking

Audience
Product users, network administrators

Content Summary
The libraries of this forum contain information about networking, Cabletron products, DNI cards, Ethernet, Token Ring, WAN, LANVIEW, and FDDI.

See Also
Cabletron Systems Menu

User Guide
- ☑ Windows
- ☑ DOS
- ☐ Macintosh
- ☐ Terminal Emulation
- ☐ VMS
- ☐ UNIX
- ☐ OS/2
- ☐ Other platform

Networking

Cost
- ☐ Unknown
- ☐ Basic
- ☑ Extended
- ☐ Premium ($)
- ☐ Executive w/$

Activity level: LOW ← MEDIUM (HIGH)

Address
GO: **CTRONFORUM**

Cabletron Systems Menu

Description
The menu provides access to information concerning Cabletron Systems, Inc.

Subjects
Computers, Networking

Audience
Network administrators

Content Summary
Included in the libraries are information on the corporate background of Cabletron, list of sales offices, training and presentation centers, and points of interest to users of Cabletron products.

See Also
Cabletron Systems Forum

User Guide
- ☑ Windows
- ☑ DOS
- ☑ Macintosh
- ☐ Terminal Emulation
- ☐ VMS
- ☑ UNIX
- ☐ OS/2
- ☐ Other platform

Cost
- ☐ Unknown
- ☐ Basic
- ☑ Extended
- ☐ Premium ($)
- ☐ Executive w/$

Activity Level: LOW ← MEDIUM (HIGH)

Address
GO: **CTRON**

CTOS/Pathway Forum

Description
The Forum supports users of the UniSys CTOS Client/Server Operating System, and the Pathway series of Client/Server products and services.

Subjects
Computers, Networking

Audience
CTOS users

Content Summary
Libraries include information on CTOS product information, tips and tricks, shareware, developers, networking, and client/server topics.

See Also
Computer Directory

User Guide
- ☑ Windows
- ☑ DOS
- ☐ Macintosh
- ☐ Terminal Emulation
- ☐ VMS
- ☐ UNIX
- ☐ OS/2
- ☐ Other platform

Cost
- ☐ Unknown
- ☐ Basic
- ☑ Extended
- ☐ Premium ($)
- ☐ Executive w/$

Activity Level: LOW ← MEDIUM (HIGH)

Address
GO: **CTOS**

IBM LMU2 Forum

Description
This forum is an open forum for the discussion of all topics related to LAN Management Utilities/2 (LMU/2).

Subjects
Computers, IBM, Networking

Audience
Computer users, management information specialists

See Also
IBM File Finder

Content Summary
This forum includes libraries named Common Questions, Tools/Samples, News/Announcements, LMU/2 V2 Updates, and LMU Updates.

See Also
IBM File Finder

User Guide
- ☐ Windows
- ☐ DOS
- ☐ Macintosh
- ☐ Terminal Emulation
- ☐ VMS
- ☐ UNIX
- ☑ OS/2
- ☐ Other platform

Cost
- ☐ Unknown
- ☐ Basic
- ☑ Extended
- ☐ Premium ($)
- ☐ Executive w/$

Networking

Activity Level

Address
GO: **LMUFORUM**

LAN Magazine

Description
This forum is for network administrators, users, installers, and integrators to exchange information about computer networks.

Subjects
Computer Networking, Computers, Networking

Audience
Computer users, management information specialists

Content Summary
Sponsored by *LAN Magazine*, this forum is dedicated to help you solve LAN problems, stay in touch with the industry, and keep you informed of new products and services. The library and message sections include Reviews, Features, Guest & Interviews, Forum Member Bios, User-to-User, and others. For a story on salaries of network managers, see Library 3, Features.

See Also
LAN Technology Forum

User Guide
- ☑ Windows
- ☑ DOS
- ☑ Macintosh
- ☐ Terminal Emulation
- ☐ VMS
- ☑ UNIX
- ☑ OS/2
- ☑ Other platform

Cost
- ☐ Unknown
- ☐ Basic
- ☑ Extended
- ☐ Premium ($)
- ☐ Executive w/$

Activity Level

Address
GO: **LANMAG**

Lan Technology Forum

Description
This is *Lan Technology* magazine's forum for network issues, products, and discussions.

Subjects
Computers, Networking

Audience
Management information specialists, Macintosh users, computer users

Content Summary
The Lan Technology Forum is an on line resource from *Lan Technology*, which is the leading independent monthly magazine devoted to the technical issues and problems faced by network specialists. The forum is a focal point for discovering how to work with the technologies and products in local and wide-area networks. The library and message sections include E-Mail, To Stacks, NetWare, VINES, Macintosh, UNIX, Network Management, Servers, Demos, and others.

See Also
Lan Magazine Forum

User Guide
- ☑ Windows
- ☑ DOS
- ☑ Macintosh
- ☐ Terminal Emulation
- ☐ VMS
- ☑ UNIX
- ☑ OS/2
- ☑ Other platform

Cost
- ☐ Unknown
- ☐ Basic
- ☑ Extended
- ☐ Premium ($)
- ☐ Executive w/$

Activity Level

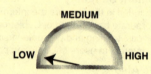

Address
GO: **LANTECH**

LAN Vendor Forum

Description
For support and discussions on various networking vendors, join this forum.

Subjects
Computers, Networking

Audience
Computer users, management information specialists

Content Summary
This forum has libraries and message sections for the following vendors: Synergy Solutions, AMD, Newport Systems, SilCom Technology, Robertson-Caruso, Horizons Technology, Impulse Technology, DE/CartesRecall-IT!, Aleph Takoma Systems, Olicom, Compatible Systems, Momentum Software, AG Group, and CACI Products.

See Also
Lan Magazine Forum, Lan Technology Forum

User Guide
- ☑ Windows
- ☑ DOS
- ☑ Macintosh
- ☐ Terminal Emulation
- ☐ VMS
- ☐ UNIX
- ☐ OS/2
- ☑ Other platform

Cost
- ☐ Unknown
- ☐ Basic
- ☒ Extended
- ☐ Premium ($)
- ☐ Executive w/$

Activity Level: LOW (arrow pointing low-medium), MEDIUM, HIGH

Address
GO: **LANVEN**

Lotus Communications Forum

Description
This forum is devoted to Lotus Corporation's communications products, including Notes and cc:Mail.

Subjects
Computer Communications, Computer Hardware, Computer Networking, Computers, E-mail, Networking

Audience
Management information specialists, network users

Content Summary
You can find a plethora of information, technical support solutions, hints and tips, and want ads in this forum. The library and message forums include Notes Tech Info, Notes Workstations/DB, Notes API Devlopment, cc:Mail Platform, cc:Mail Router, cc:Mail Admin, and many others.

See Also
Lotus Press Release Forum, Lotus Technical Library

User Guide
- ☒ Windows
- ☒ DOS
- ☒ Macintosh
- ☐ Terminal Emulation
- ☐ VMS
- ☐ UNIX
- ☒ OS/2
- ☒ Other platform

Cost
- ☐ Unknown
- ☐ Basic
- ☒ Extended
- ☐ Premium ($)
- ☐ Executive w/$

Activity Level: LOW, MEDIUM, HIGH (arrow pointing medium-high)

Address
GO: **LOTUSCOMM**

Message Handling Service Hub

Description
The CompuServe Mail Hub offers global connectivity, which enables you to communicate with users all over the world. The Mail Hub is available to everyone who can access CompuServe.

Subjects
Networking

Audience
Computer users, LAN administrators

Content Summary
Access to CompuServe gives the NetWare MHS user the capability to send messages to any other MHS user or CompuServe Mail address/gateways with an inexpensive local telephone call. The MHS user no longer must makan expensive long distance telephone call to send and receive messages. If you are using Remote MHS, or Global MHS, the CompuServe capability is built in. From the CompuServe Mail Hub main menu, you can choose from MHS Hub Service, Planning and Implementaion, Speeific Mail Systems, Addressing, and Download File with all of the above.

See Also
Novell User Library

User Guide
- ☒ Windows
- ☒ DOS
- ☒ Macintosh
- ☒ Terminal Emulation
- ☐ VMS
- ☒ UNIX
- ☒ OS/2
- ☒ Other platform

Cost
- ☐ Unknown
- ☐ Basic
- ☒ Extended
- ☐ Premium ($)
- ☐ Executive w/$

Activity Level: LOW, MEDIUM, HIGH — UNKNOWN

Address
GO: **MHSADMIN**

Standard Microsystems Forum

Description
This is a vendor support area for the networking products of Standard Microsystems Corp.

Subjects
Computers, Networking

Audience
Standard Microsystems users

Content Summary
Libraries include general information, Arcnet, Ethernet Elite, Ethernet 30XX, and Token Ring Elite.

See Also
Computer Directory

User Guide
- ☒ Windows
- ☒ DOS
- ☒ Macintosh
- ☐ Terminal Emulation
- ☐ VMS
- ☐ UNIX
- ☐ OS/2
- ☐ Other platform

Cost
- ☐ Unknown
- ☐ Basic
- ☑ Extended
- ☐ Premium ($)
- ☐ Executive w/$

Activity Level

LOW ← MEDIUM HIGH

Address
GO: **SMC**

SynOptics Forum

Description
This is a vendor support forum for Synoptic's intelligent LAN hubs and LAN management software.

Subjects
Computers, Networking

Audience
Network administrators

Content Summary
Libraries include product information, training information, and hot topics.

See Also
LAN Technology Forum

User Guide
- ☑ Windows
- ☑ DOS
- ☐ Macintosh
- ☐ Terminal Emulation
- ☐ VMS
- ☐ UNIX
- ☐ OS/2
- ☐ Other platform

Cost
- ☐ Unknown
- ☐ Basic
- ☑ Extended
- ☐ Premium ($)
- ☐ Executive w/$

Activity Level

LOW ← MEDIUM HIGH

Address
GO: **SYNOPTICS**

New Age Forum

Description
This is the area to discuss all aspects of the New Age including the theoretical, philosophical, and practical.

Subjects
New Age

Audience
New Age enthusiasts, general public

Content Summary
You can find several types of files and discussions in this forum, including diet programs, fortune-telling secrets, astrological wheelcharts, and more. Some of the library sections include Programs/IBM Compatible, Programs/MAC/Other, Magical Blend Magazine, New Age Books, Psychic Abilities, and more. Look for the various WAV files in these library—they are quite interesting.

See Also
Participate Forum, Speakeasy Forum

User Guide
- ☑ Windows
- ☑ DOS
- ☑ Macintosh
- ☐ Terminal Emulation
- ☑ VMS
- ☑ UNIX
- ☐ OS/2
- ☐ Other platform

Cost
- ☐ Unknown
- ☐ Basic
- ☑ Extended
- ☐ Premium ($)
- ☐ Executive w/$

Activity Level

LOW MEDIUM → HIGH

Address
GO: **NEWAGE**

New Car Showroom

Description
The New Car Showroom enables you to view and compare passenger car, van, special purpose, and truck features and specifications. Use this service when you are looking for a new car or truck.

Subjects
Automobiles

Audience
General public

Content Summary
You can enter two distinct Showrooms: one for cars, passenger vans, and special-purpose vehicles and one for trucks and cargo vans. In either Showroom, you can use the database to learn about models of interest to you. The Showrooms include data on over 1,000 passenger cars, vans, special-purpose vehicles, and light-duty trucks currently sold in the United States. You also can calculate monthly payments by using the Figure Your Monthly Payments option on the main menu.

See Also
Automobile Info Center, Automotive Information Forum

New Car Showroom – News

User Guide
- ☑ Windows
- ☑ DOS
- ☑ Macintosh
- ☐ Terminal Emulation
- ☑ VMS
- ☑ UNIX
- ☐ OS/2
- ☐ Other platform

Cost
- ☐ Unknown
- ☐ Basic
- ☑ Extended
- ☐ Premium ($)
- ☐ Executive w/$

Activity Level
UNKNOWN

Address
GO: **NEWCAR**

New Country Music

Description
If you like *Hee-Haw*, you'll love this place! *New Country Music Magazine* gives you an exclusive look into the world of Country. Enjoy intimate, friendly chats with superstars such as Alan Jackson, Trisha Yearwood, Travis Tritt, and others.

Subjects
Music, Country Music

Audience
Music enthusiasts, general public

Content Summary
From the main menu, you can choose from these options: What is New Country Music Service, To Sign Up, and Shipping and Billing Information. For a rate of $39.95 for 6 months or $69.95 for 12 months, you can sign for the *New Country Music Magazine* and get an exclusive CD every month.

See Also
Music Hall, Music Vendor Forum, Music Industry Forum

User Guide
- ☐ Windows
- ☐ DOS
- ☐ Macintosh
- ☑ Terminal Emulation
- ☐ VMS
- ☐ UNIX
- ☐ OS/2
- ☐ Other platform

Cost
- ☐ Unknown
- ☐ Basic
- ☑ Extended
- ☐ Premium ($)
- ☐ Executive w/$

Activity Level

UNKNOWN

Address
GO: **COUNTRY**

NEW YORK

New York NewsLink Forum

Description
New York NewsLink Forum is a forum for New Yorkers, ex-New Yorkers, visitors, and anyone with an interest in New York and things New York.

Subjects
New York

Audience
New Yorkers, general public

Content Summary
New York NewsLink is a service of Gannett Suburban Newspapers and includes resources of the daily newspapers that are available to members of the New York NewsLink forum. You can find Gannett Suburban reports, reviews, and columns that cover Broadway and off-Broadway theater and all of New York's professional sports teams.

See Also
Entertainment Center Forum

User Guide
- ☑ Windows
- ☑ DOS
- ☑ Macintosh
- ☐ Terminal Emulation
- ☑ VMS
- ☑ UNIX
- ☐ OS/2
- ☐ Other platform

Cost
- ☐ Unknown
- ☐ Basic
- ☑ Extended
- ☐ Premium ($)
- ☐ Executive w/$

Activity Level
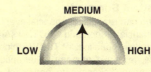
MEDIUM

Address
GO: **NEWYORK**

NEWS

Associated Press Online

Description
The Associated Press Online forum provides news stories from the Associated Press.

Subjects
Current Events, Entertainment, News

Audience
Consumers, journalists

News

Content Summary
Read up-to-date news stories of national and world interest.

User Guide
- ☑ Windows
- ☑ DOS
- ☐ Macintosh
- ☐ Terminal Emulation
- ☐ VMS
- ☐ UNIX
- ☐ OS/2
- ☐ Other platform

Cost
- ☐ Unknown
- ☐ Basic
- ☑ Extended
- ☐ Premium ($)
- ☐ Executive w/$

Activity Level
UNKNOWN (LOW — MEDIUM — HIGH)

Address
GO: **APO**

Executive News Service

Description
You can search the latest international news, weather, and sports from the world's major news agencies. This powerful news clipping service can scan many news sources for stories you specify and deliver them to you daily.

Subjects
Business, Financial News, International News, News

Audience
Business people

Content Summary
You can read about financial events in Reuters Financial Report and OTC NewsAlert, as well as in the daily headlines of The Washington Post. To use the News by Company Ticker option, enter a company ticker symbol and check on business news filed within the past 24 hours. For the News Clips option, you can read through special clipping folders set up by CompuServe to keep you up on specific news topics. You also can set up your own Personal area in which you specify the type of news you want to read by typing in key phrases. ENS then sends you electronic news "clippings" that you can read. ENS costs $15 per hour plus the base connect rates.

See Also
AP Sports($), Financial Forums, Global Crises Forum, NewsGrid, Newspaper Archives($), Reuter News Pictures Forum, United Press Int'l($), U.S. News Forum

User Guide
- ☑ Windows
- ☑ DOS
- ☐ Macintosh
- ☐ Terminal Emulation
- ☐ VMS
- ☐ UNIX
- ☐ OS/2
- ☐ Other platform

Cost
- ☐ Unknown
- ☐ Basic
- ☐ Extended
- ☑ Premium ($)
- ☐ Executive w/$

Activity Level
UNKNOWN (LOW — MEDIUM — HIGH)

Address
GO: **ENS**

News Source USA

Description
News Source USA is a comprehensive collection of major U.S. magazines, newspapers, and special features to keep you up-to-date and informed about world events.

Subjects
News, Current Issues, Databases

Audience
General public

Content Summary
From the main menu, you can pick What is NEWS SOURCE USA, What's Available in NEWS SOURCE USA, Search/Scan Guidelines, Pricing Information, and Access NEWS SOURCE USA. See the Pricing Information for specific prices on searching this database.

See Also
IQUEST

User Guide
- ☑ Windows
- ☑ DOS
- ☑ Macintosh
- ☐ Terminal Emulation
- ☑ VMS
- ☑ UNIX
- ☐ OS/2
- ☐ Other platform

Cost
- ☐ Unknown
- ☐ Basic
- ☐ Extended
- ☑ Premium ($)
- ☐ Executive w/$

Activity Level
UNKNOWN (LOW — MEDIUM — HIGH)

Address
GO: **NEWSLIB**

News-A-Tron

Description
News-A-Tron provides daily news, analytical features, and cash quotes for selected commodities, market indices, and financial instruments.

Subjects
Finance, News

Audience
Accountants, general public

Content Summary
From the main menu, you can select to see an introduction and sample of the service and price information, and use the Market Reports, Stock Indices, or Money Market Reports. Be sure to read the pricing information for specific costs for this service.

See Also
The Business Wire Forum

User Guide
- [x] Windows
- [x] DOS
- [x] Macintosh
- [ ] Terminal Emulation
- [x] VMS
- [x] UNIX
- [ ] OS/2
- [ ] Other platform

Cost
- [ ] Unknown
- [ ] Basic
- [ ] Extended
- [ ] Premium ($)
- [x] Executive w/$

Activity Level

Address
GO: **NAT**

NewsGrid

Description
NewsGrid captures thousands of stories from the world's leading news wire services and provides them to you online. You can read U.S. and world news headlines, business news headlines, regular market and economic updates, and hundreds of general news stories.

Subjects
News, Current Issues, Database

Audience
General public

Content Summary
From the main menu, you can select US/World Headline News, US Business Headline News, World Business Headline News, Market Update, Search by Keyword, and How To Use NewsGrid.

See Also
IQUEST

User Guide
- [ ] Windows
- [ ] DOS
- [ ] Macintosh
- [x] Terminal Emulation
- [ ] VMS
- [ ] UNIX
- [ ] OS/2
- [ ] Other platform

Cost
- [ ] Unknown
- [ ] Basic
- [x] Extended
- [ ] Premium ($)
- [ ] Executive w/$

Activity Level
LOW — UNKNOWN (MEDIUM) — HIGH

Address
GO: **NEWSGRID**

NewsNet

Description
NewsNet is the "Premier Current Awareness Resource." You can find more than 500 business newsletters and other important news services online in this service.

Subjects
Database, News, Current Issues

Audience
General public

Content Summary
The NewsNet main menu contains the following options: What Is NewsNet, What's Online—Take a Tour, Special Services*—Credit reports, stock quotes, airline schedules and travel information, NewsFlash—The exclusive electronic clipping service, Using NewsNet, How Much Does NewsNet Cost, and Ask NewsNet. Be sure to read the pricing information before you use this service. The surcharges may be a little steep for general browsing.

See Also
IQUEST, News-A-Tron

User Guide
- [x] Windows
- [x] DOS
- [x] Macintosh
- [ ] Terminal Emulation
- [x] VMS
- [x] UNIX
- [ ] OS/2
- [ ] Other platform

News

Cost
- [ ] Unknown
- [ ] Basic
- [ ] Extended
- [x] Premium ($)
- [ ] Executive w/$

Activity Level: UNKNOWN (Low / Medium / High)

Address
GO: **NN**

Newspaper Archives

Description
Newspaper Archives gives you access to over 55 full-text U.S. and U.K. newspapers, including the ability to search each newspaper on any topic of interest and over a specific date range.

Subjects
News, Current Issues

Audience
General public

Content Summary
From the Newspaper Archives main menu, you can select Description, Search Guidelines, Pricing Information, Hours of Availability, Software Requirements, and Access Newspaper Archives. This service is not available on Sundays, between 2:00 a.m. and 10:00 a.m. Pacific Standard time. Be sure you understand the specific pricing information before you start your search.

See Also
IQUEST, NewsGrid, News-A-Tron

User Guide
- [x] Windows
- [x] DOS
- [x] Macintosh
- [ ] Terminal Emulation
- [x] VMS
- [x] UNIX
- [ ] OS/2
- [ ] Other platform

Cost
- [ ] Unknown
- [ ] Basic
- [ ] Extended
- [x] Premium ($)
- [ ] Executive w/$

Activity Level: UNKNOWN (Low / Medium / High)

Address
GO: **NEWSARCHIVE**

OTC NewsAlert

Description
Search the latest international news, weather, and sports from the world's major news agencies. A powerful news clipping service that can scan many news sources for stories you specify and deliver them to you daily.

Subjects
Business, Financial News, International News, News

Audience
Associated Press Forum, Associated Press Online

Content Summary
You can read financial events through Reuters Financial Report and OTC NewsAlert, as well as read the day's headlines with The Washington Post. To use the News by Company Ticker option, enter a company ticker symbol and check on business news filed within the past 24 hours. For the News Clips option, you can read through special clipping folders set up by CompuServe to keep you up on specific news topics. You also set up your own Personal area in which you specify the type of news that you want to read by typing in key phrases. ENS then sends you electronic news clippings that you can read. ENS costs $15 per hour plus the base connect rates.

See Also
AP Sports, Financial Forums, Global Crises Forum, NewsGrid, Newspaper Archives, Reuters News Pictures Forum, United Press International, U.S. News Forum

User Guide
- [x] Windows
- [x] DOS
- [ ] Macintosh
- [ ] Terminal Emulation
- [ ] VMS
- [ ] UNIX
- [ ] OS/2
- [ ] Other platform

Cost
- [ ] Unknown
- [ ] Basic
- [ ] Extended
- [x] Premium ($)
- [ ] Executive w/$

Activity Level: UNKNOWN (Low / Medium / High)

Address
GO: **ENS**

Political Debate Forum

Description
This forum allows open discussion of political topics of all types. It is open to people of all political persuasions.

Subjects
International Events, News, U.S. Politics

Audience
Politicians, students

Content Summary
This forum provides debate areas for Democrats, Libertarians, and Republicans. Other libraries contain articles and information on topics ranging from the Crime Bill, health care, gun rights, gay rights, and international politics.

See Also
Democrat Forum, Participate, Republican Forum

User Guide
- ☑ Windows
- ☑ DOS
- ☑ Macintosh
- ☐ Terminal Emulation
- ☑ VMS
- ☑ UNIX
- ☑ OS/2
- ☐ Other platform

Cost
- ☐ Unknown
- ☐ Basic
- ☑ Extended
- ☐ Premium ($)
- ☐ Executive w/$

Activity Level

Address
GO: **POLITICS**

Reuters News Pictures Forum

Description
This forum contains the largest online source of news images from around the world. Also included are photographs of historical significance from the Bettman Archives.

Subjects
Current Events, News, Photographs

Audience
News enthusiasts, photographers

Content Summary
Photographs of interest to the United States, World, entertainment industry, and sports are featured. Note that photographs are protected by U.S. and International copyrights and are for personal use only.

See Also
AP Sports Forum, Associated Press Online Forum, Detroit Free Press

User Guide
- ☑ Windows
- ☑ DOS
- ☑ Macintosh
- ☐ Terminal Emulation
- ☑ VMS
- ☑ UNIX
- ☑ OS/2
- ☐ Other platform

Cost
- ☐ Unknown
- ☐ Basic
- ☑ Extended
- ☐ Premium ($)
- ☐ Executive w/$

Activity Level

Address
GO: **NEWSPI**

Syndicated Columns

Description
This is an online database containing recent columns from over a dozen well-known newspaper columnists

Subjects
News

Audience
Journalists, current events enthusiasts

See Also
Associated Press

Content Summary
This is a collection of syndicated columns covering a wide array of political opinions and present-day topics.

User Guide
- ☑ Windows
- ☑ DOS
- ☑ Macintosh
- ☐ Terminal Emulation
- ☐ VMS
- ☐ UNIX
- ☐ OS/2
- ☑ Other platform

Cost
- ☐ Unknown
- ☑ Basic
- ☐ Extended
- ☐ Premium ($)
- ☐ Executive w/$

Activity Level

Address
GO: **COLUMNS**

The Business Wire

Description
This is a news area offering press releases, news articles, and other information from the world of business.

Subjects
Business, Finance

Audience
Business people

News

Content Summary
The libraries include press releases, news articles, and information about specific companies. It is updated daily.

See Also
AP Online

User Guide
- ☑ Windows
- ☑ DOS
- ☑ Macintosh
- ☐ Terminal Emulation
- ☑ VMS
- ☑ UNIX
- ☑ OS/2
- ☐ Other platform

Cost
- ☐ Unknown
- ☐ Basic
- ☑ Extended
- ☐ Premium ($)
- ☐ Executive w/$

Activity Level

Address
GO: **TBW**

U.S. News & World Report

Description
This is an online version of the current *U.S. News & World Report* magazine, including text and pictures.

Subjects
News

Audience
General Public

Content Summary
This online magazine offers the full text of every issue of *U.S. News & World Report*.

See Also
U.S. News Forum

User Guide
- ☑ Windows
- ☑ DOS
- ☑ Macintosh
- ☐ Terminal Emulation
- ☑ VMS
- ☑ UNIX
- ☑ OS/2
- ☐ Other platform

Cost
- ☐ Unknown
- ☐ Basic
- ☑ Extended
- ☐ Premium ($)
- ☐ Executive w/$

Activity Level

Address
GO: **US NEWS**

U.S. News Forum

Description
You can interact with the writers and editors of *U.S. News & World Report* in this forum.

Subjects
News

Audience
General public

Content Summary
This forum enables members to send an online letter to the editor to the staff of *U.S. News & World Report*. Also included are information about news articles appearing in the magazine.

See Also
News, Business

User Guide
- ☑ Windows
- ☑ DOS
- ☑ Macintosh
- ☐ Terminal Emulation
- ☑ VMS
- ☑ UNIX
- ☑ OS/2
- ☑ Other platform

Cost
- ☐ Unknown
- ☐ Basic
- ☑ Extended
- ☐ Premium ($)
- ☐ Executive w/$

Activity Level

Address
GO: **USN FORUM**

U.S. News Women's Forum

Description
This is a forum sponsored by *U.S. News*, covering women's issues.

Subjects
News, women

Audience
General public, women

Content Summary
This forum includes a wide range of women's topics from information on families to job opportunities.

See Also
Women, Family

User Guide
- ☑ Windows
- ☑ DOS
- ☑ Macintosh
- ☐ Terminal Emulation
- ☑ VMS
- ☑ UNIX
- ☑ OS/2
- ☑ Other platform

Cost
- [ ] Unknown
- [ ] Basic
- [x] Extended
- [ ] Premium ($)
- [ ] Executive w/$

Activity Level
MEDIUM (arrow pointing to medium between LOW and HIGH)

Address
GO: **USNEWS**

UK News Clips

Description
This forum features realtime United Kingdom news, sports, and weather, provided by the PA News service.

Subjects
News

Audience
General public

Contents Summary
The libraries include the following topics: financial, political, economic, international news. Stores are held for 24 hours.

See Also
U.S. News and World Report

User Guide
- [x] Windows
- [x] DOS
- [x] Macintosh
- [ ] Terminal Emulation
- [x] VMS
- [x] UNIX
- [x] OS/2
- [ ] Other platform

Cost
- [ ] Unknown
- [ ] Basic
- [x] Extended
- [ ] Premium ($)
- [ ] Executive w/$

Activity Level
UNKNOWN (between LOW and HIGH, MEDIUM shown)

Address
GO: **UKCLIPS**

UK Newspaper Library

Description
This database contains selected newspaper articles from the United Kingdom.

Subjects
News

Audience
General public

Content Summary
This database offers articles from the Daily Telegraph and Sunday Telegraph, The European, The Financial Times, The Guardian, The Times and Sunday Time.

See Also
UK News Clips

User Guide
- [x] Windows
- [x] DOS
- [x] Macintosh
- [ ] Terminal Emulation
- [x] VMS
- [x] UNIX
- [x] OS/2
- [ ] Other platform

Cost
- [ ] Unknown
- [ ] Basic
- [x] Extended
- [ ] Premium ($)
- [ ] Executive w/$

Activity Level
UNKNOWN (between LOW and HIGH, MEDIUM shown)

Address
GO: **UKNL**

UK Sports Clips

Description
This service contains full-text sports clips provided by Reuters World news wire and is a comprehensive source for sports stories including cricket, soccer, snooker, and rugby.

Subjects
News

Audience
General public

Content Summary
The libraries include information on cricket, soccer, snooker, and rugby.

See Also
UK Newspaper Library

User Guide
- [x] Windows
- [x] DOS
- [x] Macintosh
- [ ] Terminal Emulation
- [x] VMS
- [x] UNIX
- [x] OS/2
- [ ] Other platform

Cost
- [ ] Unknown
- [x] Basic
- [ ] Extended
- [ ] Premium ($)
- [ ] Executive w/$

Activity Level

MEDIUM
LOW
UNKNOWN
HIGH

Address

GO: **UKSPORTS**

White House Forum

Description

This independent political forum discusses what's happening in the USA White House. The libraries contain only files provided by official White House sources.

Subjects

Current Issues

Audience

General public

Content Summary

The libraries include information on the economy, the trade deficit, defense, education, social security, and international affairs.

See Also

Politics in America

User Guide

- [x] Windows
- [x] DOS
- [x] Macintosh
- [ ] Terminal Emulation
- [x] VMS
- [x] UNIX
- [x] OS/2
- [ ] Other platform

Cost

- [ ] Unknown
- [ ] Basic
- [x] Extended
- [ ] Premium ($)
- [ ] Executive w/$

Activity Level

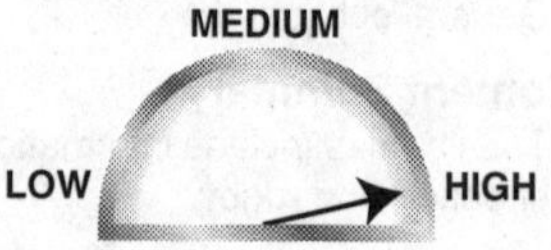
MEDIUM
LOW
HIGH

Address

GO: **WHITEHOUSE**

News Source USA

Description

News Source USA is a comprehensive collection of major U.S. magazines, newspapers, and special features to keep you up-to-date and informed about world events.

Subjects

News, Current Issues, Databases

Audience

General public

Content Summary

From the main menu, you can pick What is NEWS SOURCE USA, What's Available in NEWS SOURCE USA, Search/Scan Guidelines, Pricing Information, and Access NEWS SOURCE USA. See the Pricing Information for specific prices on searching this database.

See Also

IQUEST

User Guide

- [x] Windows
- [x] DOS
- [x] Macintosh
- [ ] Terminal Emulation
- [x] VMS
- [x] UNIX
- [ ] OS/2
- [ ] Other platform

Cost

- [ ] Unknown
- [ ] Basic
- [ ] Extended
- [x] Premium ($)
- [ ] Executive w/$

Activity Level

MEDIUM
LOW
UNKNOWN
HIGH

Address

GO: **NEWSLIB**

News-A-Tron

Description

News-A-Tron provides daily news, analytical features, and cash quotes for selected commodities, market indices, and financial instruments.

Subjects

Finance, News

Audience

Accountants, general public

Content Summary

From the main menu, you can select to see an introduction and sample of the service and price information, and use the Market Reports, Stock Indices, or Money Market Reports. Be sure to read the pricing information for specific costs for this service.

See Also

The Business Wire Forum

User Guide

- [x] Windows
- [x] DOS
- [x] Macintosh
- [ ] Terminal Emulation
- [x] VMS
- [x] UNIX
- [ ] OS/2
- [ ] Other platform

News-A-Tron – Newspaper Archives

Cost
- [ ] Unknown
- [ ] Basic
- [ ] Extended
- [ ] Premium ($)
- [x] Executive w/$

Activity Level

Address
GO: **NAT**

NewsGrid

Description
NewsGrid captures thousands of stories from the world's leading news wire services and provides them to you online. You can read U.S. and world news headlines, business news headlines, regular market and economic updates, and hundreds of general news stories.

Subjects
News, Current Issues, Database

Audience
General public

Content Summary
From the main menu, you can select US/World Headline News, US Business Headline News, World Business Headline News, Market Update, Search by Keyword, and How To Use NewsGrid.

See Also
IQUEST

User Guide
- [ ] Windows
- [ ] DOS
- [ ] Macintosh
- [x] Terminal Emulation
- [ ] VMS
- [ ] UNIX
- [ ] OS/2
- [ ] Other platform

Cost
- [ ] Unknown
- [ ] Basic
- [x] Extended
- [ ] Premium ($)
- [ ] Executive w/$

Activity Level

Address
GO: **NEWSGRID**

NewsNet

Description
NewsNet is the "Premier Current Awareness Resource." You can find more than 500 business newsletters and other important news services online in this service.

Subjects
Database, News, Current Issues

Audience
General public

Content Summary
The NewsNet main menu contains the following options: What Is NewsNet, What's Online—Take a Tour, Special Services*—Credit reports, stock quotes, airline schedules, and travel information, NewsFlash—The exclusive electronic clipping service, Using NewsNet, How Much Does NewsNet Cost, and Ask NewsNet. Be sure to read the pricing information before you use this service. The surcharges may be a little steep for general browsing.

See Also
IQUEST, News-A-Tron

User Guide
- [x] Windows
- [x] DOS
- [x] Macintosh
- [ ] Terminal Emulation
- [x] VMS
- [x] UNIX
- [ ] OS/2
- [ ] Other platform

Cost
- [ ] Unknown
- [ ] Basic
- [ ] Extended
- [x] Premium ($)
- [ ] Executive w/$

Activity Level

Address
GO: **NN**

Newspaper Archives

Description
Newspaper Archives gives you access to over 55 full-text U.S. and U.K. newspapers, including the ability to search each newspaper on any topic of interest and over a specific date range.

Subjects
News, Current Issues

Audience
General public

Content Summary
From the Newspaper Archives main menu, you can select Description, Search Guidelines, Pricing Information, Hours of Availability, Software Requirements, and Access Newspaper Archives. This service is not available on Sundays, between 2:00 a.m. and 10:00 a.m. Pacific Standard time. Be sure you understand the specific pricing information before you start your search.

Newspaper Archives – Novell Inc.

See Also
IQUEST, NewsGrid, News-A-Tron

User Guide
- ☑ Windows
- ☑ DOS
- ☑ Macintosh
- ☐ Terminal Emulation
- ☑ VMS
- ☑ UNIX
- ☐ OS/2
- ☐ Other platform

Cost
- ☐ Unknown
- ☐ Basic
- ☐ Extended
- ☑ Premium ($)
- ☐ Executive w/$

Activity Level

Address
GO: **NEWSARCHIVE**

Newton Developers Forum

Description
This forum discusses the various aspects of Newton technology and how to design software and hardware for the Apple Newton PDA.

Subjects
Computers, Apple

Audience
Computer programmers

Content Summary
Use this forum to find files, technical issues, and other developer resources. The library and message sections include Mac Toolkit, Windows Toolkit, Other Languages, Book Maker, NewtonScipt, General Programming, Graphics, and more.

See Also
Apple Forum

User Guide
- ☑ Windows
- ☐ DOS
- ☑ Macintosh
- ☐ Terminal Emulation
- ☐ VMS
- ☐ UNIX
- ☐ OS/2
- ☑ Other platform

Cost
- ☐ Unknown
- ☐ Basic
- ☑ Extended
- ☐ Premium ($)
- ☐ Executive w/$

Activity Level MEDIUM (arrow pointing up, between LOW and HIGH)

Address
GO: **NEWTDEV**

NeXT Forum

Description
With this service you can find solutions, technical support, and other information concerning the NeXT operating system.

Subjects
Computers

Audience
Computer users

Content Summary
The library and message areas contain several sections, including Recreation, NeXT/Misc. Info, Connectivity, Utilities, Applications, Sound, Graphics, and more.

See Also
UNIX Forum

User Guide
- ☐ Windows
- ☐ DOS
- ☑ Macintosh
- ☐ Terminal Emulation
- ☐ VMS
- ☐ UNIX
- ☐ OS/2
- ☑ Other platform

Cost
- ☐ Unknown
- ☐ Basic
- ☑ Extended
- ☐ Premium ($)
- ☐ Executive w/$

Activity Level MEDIUM (arrow pointing to LOW)

Address
GO: **NEXTFORUM**

Novell Client Forum

Description
This is a Novell NetWire forum that includes a message area for topics relating to client support.

Subjects
Computers, Novell Inc., Computer Networking

Audience
Computer users, MIS people

Content Summary
The message section contains the following topics: IPX/ODI Issues, NETX Issues, VLM Issues, ODINSUP Issues, NetBIOS Issues, and NetWare & Windows.

See Also
Novell NetWire, Novell User Library, Novell Files Database

User Guide
- ☑ Windows
- ☑ DOS
- ☑ Macintosh
- ☐ Terminal Emulation
- ☐ VMS
- ☑ UNIX
- ☐ OS/2
- ☑ Other platform

Cost
- ☐ Unknown
- ☐ Basic
- ☑ Extended
- ☐ Premium ($)
- ☐ Executive w/$

Activity Level
MEDIUM (arrow pointing between LOW and HIGH, toward HIGH)

Address
GO: **NOVCLIENT**

Novell Connectivity Forum

Description
This Novell NetWire forum includes a message section devoted to connectivity issues.

Subjects
Computers, Novell Inc., Computer Networking

Audience
Computer users, MIS people

Content Summary
Some of the topics available in the message section include NACS, NW Connect, NW for SAA, AS/400 Connectivity, Host Printing, SNA Links, NetWare Macintosh, NW/IP NFS-TCP/IP, and others.

See Also
Novell NetWire, Novell Files Database, Novell Library Forum

User Guide
- ☑ Windows
- ☑ DOS
- ☑ Macintosh
- ☐ Terminal Emulation
- ☐ VMS
- ☑ UNIX
- ☐ OS/2
- ☑ Other platform

Cost
- ☐ Unknown
- ☐ Basic
- ☑ Extended
- ☐ Premium ($)
- ☐ Executive w/$

Activity Level
MEDIUM (arrow pointing toward HIGH)

Address
GO: **NCONNECT**

Novell Developer Info Forum

Description
This Novell NetWire Forum includes information on development issues pertaining to Novell products.

Subjects
Computers, Novell Inc., Computer Networking

Audience
Computer programmers, MIS people

Content Summary
The message section includes topics such as Btrieve, NetWare Client SDK, NetWare Sever SDK, LAN Workplace SDK, Telephony SDK, Telephony PBX Dev, Embedded NetWare, and more.

See Also
Novell Developer Support Forum, Novell NetWire, Novell Files Database, Novell Library Forum

User Guide
- ☑ Windows
- ☑ DOS
- ☑ Macintosh
- ☐ Terminal Emulation
- ☐ VMS
- ☐ UNIX
- ☐ OS/2
- ☑ Other platform

Cost
- ☐ Unknown
- ☐ Basic
- ☑ Extended
- ☐ Premium ($)
- ☐ Executive w/$

Activity Level
MEDIUM (arrow pointing toward HIGH)

Address
GO: **NDEVINFO**

Novell Developer Support Forum

Description
This Novell NetWire forum provides technical support and a message section for Novell developers.

Subjects
Computers, Novell Inc., Computer Networking

Audience
Computer programmers, MIS people

Content Summary
The message section includes Btrieve, NetWare SQL, Client SDK, Server SDK, Macintosh SDK, Communication SDKs, NMS SDK, Personal NW SDK, and more.

See Also
Novell NetWire, Novell Files Database, Novell Library Forum

Novell Inc.

User Guide
- ☑ Windows
- ☑ DOS
- ☑ Macintosh
- ☐ Terminal Emulation
- ☐ VMS
- ☐ UNIX
- ☐ OS/2
- ☑ Other platform

Cost
- ☐ Unknown
- ☐ Basic
- ☑ Extended
- ☐ Premium ($)
- ☐ Executive w/$

Activity Level
MEDIUM (arrow pointing between MEDIUM and HIGH)

Address
GO: **NDEVSUPPORT**

Novell DSG Forum

Description
This forum is devoted to the Novell DOS operating system.

Subjects
Computers, Novell Inc., Computer Networking

Audience
Computer users, MIS people

Content Summary
This forum contains only two libraries: Provisional and NetWare NT Client. You'll find a great deal of information from the message sections, including NWDOS/DRDOS Applications, NWDOS/DRDOS Disk, NWDOS/DRDOS Memory, NWDOS/DRDOS Utilities, NetWare Lite, and more.

See Also
Novell NetWire, Novell Files Database, Novell Library Forum

User Guide
- ☑ Windows
- ☑ DOS
- ☐ Macintosh
- ☐ Terminal Emulation
- ☐ VMS
- ☐ UNIX
- ☐ OS/2
- ☑ Other platform

Cost
- ☐ Unknown
- ☐ Basic
- ☑ Extended
- ☐ Premium ($)
- ☐ Executive w/$

Activity Level
MEDIUM (arrow pointing straight up to MEDIUM)

Address
GO: **DRFORUM**

Novell Files Database

Description
The files in this area are heavily downloaded files that will be moved to the Novell Library Forum as soon as the number of downloads decreases to a manageable level.

Subjects
Computers, Novell Inc., Computer Networking

Audience
Computer users, MIS people, computer programmers

Content Summary
The files currently in this area are DOS, Windows, and OS/2 Client updates☐ Server Drivers for NetWare 3.11;1 and NetWare 3.11;1 updates. From the main menu, you can choose Client Kits, NetWare Lite Utility, NetWare 3.12 Operating System Patches (47k), and others.

See Also
Novell NetWire, Novell Library Forum

User Guide
- ☑ Windows
- ☑ DOS
- ☑ Macintosh
- ☐ Terminal Emulation
- ☐ VMS
- ☐ UNIX
- ☐ OS/2
- ☑ Other platform

Cost
- ☐ Unknown
- ☐ Basic
- ☑ Extended
- ☐ Premium ($)
- ☐ Executive w/$

Activity Level
MEDIUM (arrow pointing between MEDIUM and HIGH)

Address
GO: **NOVFILES**

Novell Information Forum

Description
Find out general information about Novell products, services, and certifications using this Novell NetWire message forum.

Subjects
Computers, Novell Inc., Computer Networking

Audience
Computer users, MIS people, computer programmers

Content Summary
The message sections include Suggestion Box, Application/Utilities, User Groups/Training, CNEs, NPA, NSEPro, NUI, and more. If you are a CNE or planning to become one, be sure to join the CNE message section for help and questions pertaining to this certification program.

See Also
Novell Developer Support Forum, Novell NetWire, Novell Files Database, Novell Library Forum

User Guide
- ☑ Windows
- ☑ DOS
- ☑ Macintosh
- ☐ Terminal Emulation
- ☑ VMS
- ☑ UNIX
- ☐ OS/2
- ☑ Other platform

Cost
- ☐ Unknown
- ☐ Basic
- ☑ Extended
- ☐ Premium ($)
- ☐ Executive w/$

Activity Level

MEDIUM (LOW → HIGH)

Address
GO: **NGENERAL**

Novell Library Forum

Description
This Novell NetWire forum includes several library sections that contain various files for your Novell environment.

Subjects
Computers, Novell Inc., Computer Networking

Audience
Computer users, computer programmers, MIS people

Content Summary
The library section includes thousands of files in several areas, including New Uploads, NetWare 2.x Specific, NetWare 3.x Specific, Client/Shell Drivers, NetWare Utilities, Btrieve/NW APIs, NetWare Lite, NetWare 4.x, Novell Information, and more. You can post questions about the libraries in the message section.

See Also
Novell Files Database, Novell Information Forum

User Guide
- ☑ Windows
- ☑ DOS
- ☑ Macintosh
- ☐ Terminal Emulation
- ☐ VMS
- ☑ UNIX
- ☑ OS/2
- ☑ Other platform

Cost
- ☐ Unknown
- ☐ Basic
- ☑ Extended

Activity Level

MEDIUM (LOW → HIGH)

Address
GO: **NOVLIB**

Novell NetWare 2.x Forum

Description
This Novell NetWire forum includes discussions about the Novell NetWare 2.x family of networking products.

Subjects
Computers, Novell Inc., Computer Networking

Audience
MIS people

Content Summary
The message section includes discussion on Printing, NetWare Utilities, Disk Drive/Controls, LAN Cards/Drivers, 2.1x & Below/OS, and Operating System.

See Also
Novell NetWare 3.x Forum, Novell NetWare 4.x Forum, Novell Library Forum, Novell Files Database

User Guide
- ☑ Windows
- ☑ DOS
- ☑ Macintosh
- ☐ Terminal Emulation
- ☑ VMS
- ☑ UNIX
- ☐ OS/2
- ☐ Other platform

Cost
- ☐ Unknown
- ☐ Basic
- ☑ Extended
- ☐ Premium ($)
- ☐ Executive w/$

Activity Level

MEDIUM (LOW → HIGH)

Address
GO: **NETW2X**

Novell NetWare 3.x Forum

Description
This Novell NetWire forum includes discussions about the Novell NetWare 3.x family of networking products.

Novell Inc.

Subjects
Computers, Novell Inc., Computer Networking

Audience
MIS people

Content Summary
The message section includes these topics: Printing, NetWare Utilities, Disk Drives/CDs/Controls, LAN Cards/Drivers, Upgrade Migration, SFT III, and NLM/OS/Console Utilities.

See Also
Novell NetWare 2.x Forum, Novell NetWare 4.x Forum, Novell Files Database, Novell Library Forum

User Guide
- [✓] Windows
- [✓] DOS
- [✓] Macintosh
- [ ] Terminal Emulation
- [✓] VMS
- [✓] UNIX
- [ ] OS/2
- [ ] Other platform

Cost
- [ ] Unknown
- [ ] Basic
- [✓] Extended
- [ ] Premium ($)
- [ ] Executive w/$

Activity Level

Address
GO: NETW3X

Novell NetWare 4.x Forum

Description
This Novell NetWire forum includes discussions about the Novell NetWare 4.x family of networking products.

Subjects
Computers, Novell Inc., Computer Networking

Audience
MIS people

Content Summary
The message section includes Printing, NetWare Utilities, Disk Drives/CDs/Controls, LAN Cards/Drivers, Upgrade/Migration, Electro Text/Docs, Directory Services, and NLM/OS/Console Utilities.

See Also
Novell Files Database, Novell Library Forum, Novell Information Library, Novell NetWare 2.x Forum, Novell NetWare 3.x Forum

User Guide
- [✓] Windows
- [✓] DOS
- [✓] Macintosh
- [ ] Terminal Emulation
- [✓] VMS
- [✓] UNIX
- [ ] OS/2
- [ ] Other platform

Cost
- [ ] Unknown
- [ ] Basic
- [✓] Extended
- [ ] Premium ($)
- [ ] Executive w/$

Activity Level

Address
GO: NETW4X

Novell NetWire

Description
The Novell NetWire service enables you to utilize Novell's online support for most of the problems you might have with a Novell product. NetWare is an exceptional alternative to using Novell's telephone Hotline for technical support.

Subjects
Computers, Novell Inc., Computer Networking

Audience
Computer users, computer programmers, MIS people

Content Summary
Use the NetWare main menu to find what you need online. You can find out What's New, get Service and Support, find out about Sales and Marketing, see Novell Programs, and get other information. If you are new to NetWare, be sure to download the WELCOME.EXE file from the Novell Library (GO NOVLIB), library 2. This will help you take advantage of this wide-reaching service.

See Also
Novell Files Database, Novell Library Forum, Novell Information Library

User Guide
- [✓] Windows
- [✓] DOS
- [ ] Macintosh
- [ ] Terminal Emulation
- [✓] VMS
- [✓] UNIX
- [ ] OS/2
- [ ] Other platform

Cost
- [ ] Unknown
- [ ] Basic
- [✓] Extended
- [ ] Premium ($)
- [ ] Executive w/$

Activity Level

Address
GO: NOVELL

Novell Inc.

Novell Network Management Forum

Description
This Novell NetWire forum includes a message section devoted to discussions about network management issues.

Subjects
Computers, Novell Inc., Computer Networking

Audience
MIS people

Content Summary
This forum contains only a message section. The message section includes Network Management, NetWare Management System, Lantern System Management, LANalyzer for Windows, and NetWare for SAA Management.

See Also
Novell Connectivity Forum, Novell Files Database, Novell Library Forum

User Guide
- [x] Windows
- [x] DOS
- [x] Macintosh
- [ ] Terminal Emulation
- [x] VMS
- [x] UNIX
- [ ] OS/2
- [ ] Other platform

Cost
- [ ] Unknown
- [ ] Basic
- [x] Extended
- [ ] Premium ($)
- [ ] Executive w/$

Activity Level
MEDIUM-HIGH (arrow pointing between MEDIUM and HIGH)

Address
GO: **NOVMAN**

Novell OS/2 Forum

Description
This Novell NetWire forum is designed for messages pertaining to using NetWare with OS/2.

Subjects
Computers, Novell Inc., OS/2

Audience
MIS people

Content Summary
The message section includes OS/2 Printing, Client/Server, OS/2 Requester, NSM (OS/2), NetWare 4.x for OS/2, GUI Tools, and WINOS2/DOS.

See Also
Novell Files Database, Novell Library Forum, Novell Information Library, Novell NetWare 2.x Forum, Novell NetWare 3.x Forum, Novell NetWare 4.x Forum

User Guide
- [ ] Windows
- [ ] DOS
- [ ] Macintosh
- [ ] Terminal Emulation
- [ ] VMS
- [ ] UNIX
- [x] OS/2
- [ ] Other platform

Cost
- [ ] Unknown
- [ ] Basic
- [x] Extended
- [ ] Premium ($)
- [ ] Executive w/$

Activity Level
MEDIUM (arrow pointing to MEDIUM, between LOW and HIGH)

Address
GO: **NOVOS2**

Novell Technical Bulletin Database

Description
The Technical Bulletin Database enables you to search for bulletins and articles by title, keywords, technical bulletin number, or by Novell products number.

Subjects
Computers, Novell Inc., Database, Computer Networking

Audience
MIS people, computer users

Content Summary
When you use this terminal emulation database, you must know the division prefix for the technical bulletin. The prefixes are as follows: NetWare Products Division (NPD), Communication Product Division (CPD), and Enhanced Products Division (EPD). For more information on searching criteria, be sure to read the Instructions for Searching the Technical Bulletins.

See Also
Novell Information Forum, Novell Files Database, Novell Library Forum

User Guide
- [ ] Windows
- [ ] DOS
- [ ] Macintosh
- [x] Terminal Emulation
- [ ] VMS
- [ ] UNIX
- [ ] OS/2
- [ ] Other platform

Novell Inc.

Cost
- ☐ Unknown
- ☐ Basic
- ☑ Extended
- ☐ Premium ($)
- ☐ Executive w/$

Activity Level

LOW — UNKNOWN — MEDIUM — HIGH

Address
GO: **NTB**

Novell Vendor Forums

Description
This Novell NetWire service contains information, files, and support from various Novell vendors of NetWare-related products and services.

Subjects
Computers, Novell Inc., Computer Networking

Audience
Computer users, MIS people

Content Summary
The Novell Vendor A Forum (GO NVENA) contains several vendors, including Folio Corporation, BindView, Computer Tyme, Infinite Technologies, and more. The Novell Vendor B Forum (GO NVENB) contains several vendors, including Ontrack Data, NetWorth, gadget, Simware, Lantech, and more.

See Also
Novell Library Forum, Novell Files Database

User Guide
- ☑ Windows
- ☑ DOS
- ☑ Macintosh
- ☐ Terminal Emulation
- ☑ VMS
- ☑ UNIX
- ☐ OS/2
- ☐ Other platform

Cost
- ☐ Unknown
- ☐ Basic
- ☑ Extended
- ☐ Premium($)
- ☐ Executive w$

Activity Level

LOW ← MEDIUM — HIGH

Address
GO: **NVENA** and **NVENB**

UnixWare Forum

Description
Vendor support forum for Novell UnixWare software products.

Subjects
Computers

Audience
Computer users

Contents Summary
You can find information in the various library and message sections about the UnixWare operating system.

See Also
Software

User Guide
- ☑ Windows
- ☑ DOS
- ☐ Macintosh
- ☐ Terminal Emulation
- ☐ VMS
- ☑ UNIX
- ☐ OS/2
- ☐ Other platform

Cost
- ☐ Unknown
- ☐ Basic
- ☑ Extended
- ☐ Premium ($)
- ☐ Executive w/$

Activity Level

LOW ← MEDIUM — HIGH

Address
GO: **UNIXWARE**

WordPerfect GmbH Forum

Description
This is a vendor support forum for WordPerfect's German software products.

Subjects
Computers

Audience
German computer users

Content Summary
Libraries include information on printers, graphics, desktop publishing, and training.

See Also
WordPerfect Users Forum

User Guide
- ☑ Windows
- ☑ DOS
- ☐ Macintosh
- ☐ Terminal Emulation
- ☐ VMS
- ☐ UNIX
- ☐ OS/2
- ☐ Other platform

Cost
- ☐ Unknown
- ☐ Basic
- ☑ Extended
- ☐ Premium ($)
- ☐ Executive w/$

Activity Level

Address
GO: **WPGER**

WordPerfect Users Forum

Description
This is a user-sponsored forum for the discussion of any software produced by WordPerfect Corp.

Subjects
Computers

Audience
Computer users, WordPerfect users

Content Summary
The libraries include information on printers, graphics, desktop publishing, merges, training, file formats, and networking.

See Also
Desktop Publishing Forum

User Guide
- [x] Windows
- [x] DOS
- [ ] Macintosh
- [ ] Terminal Emulation
- [ ] VMS
- [ ] UNIX
- [ ] OS/2
- [ ] Other platform

Cost
- [ ] Unknown
- [ ] Basic
- [x] Extended
- [ ] Premium ($)
- [ ] Executive w/$

Activity Level

(MEDIUM, arrow pointing up)

Address
GO: **WPUSERS**

WPCorp Files Forum

Description
This is a vendor support forum for WordPerfect drivers and macros, for such software as WordPerfect, Draw, DataPerfect, and PlanPerfect. This forum is supported by WPCorp.

Subjects
Computers

Audience
Computer users, WordPerfect users

Content Summary
The libraries include printer drivers, graphics drivers, macros, and information on related programs.

See Also
WordPerfect Corporation Forum

User Guide
- [x] Windows
- [x] DOS
- [x] Macintosh
- [ ] Terminal Emulation
- [ ] VMS
- [x] UNIX
- [x] OS/2
- [ ] Other platform

Cost
- [ ] Unknown
- [ ] Basic
- [x] Extended
- [ ] Premium ($)
- [ ] Executive w/$

Activity Level

Address
GO: **WPFILES**

NWS Aviation Weather

Description
This forum enables you to get weather reports from various cities for aviation concerns.

Subjects
Aviation

Audience
Pilots

Content Summary
You can select to see Hourly Reports, Terminal Forecasts, Previous Hourly Reports, Winds Aloft Forecasts, Radar Summaries, and more.

See Also
Airline Pilots Association

User Guide
- [ ] Windows
- [ ] DOS
- [ ] Macintosh
- [x] Terminal Emulation
- [ ] VMS
- [ ] UNIX
- [ ] OS/2
- [ ] Other platform

Cost
- [ ] Unknown
- [x] Basic
- [ ] Extended
- [ ] Premium ($)
- [ ] Executive w/$

Activity Level

Address
GO: **AWX**

465

O - Official Airline Guide

O

OBJECT-ORIENTED PROGRAMMING

Digitalk Database

Description
Since 1985, Digitalk, Inc. has been developing object-oriented programming environments for the PC with its Smalltalk/V product. The company has Smalltalk/V development environments worldwide for DOS, OS/2, Microsoft Windows, and the Apple Macintosh; the Team/V collaborative programming system; and PARTS Workbench for OS/2. The Digitalk Database contains problem reports on all Smalltalk/V and PARTS products.

Subjects
Action Requests Database, Computers, Object-Oriented Programming, Smalltalk/V

Audience
Consultants, object-oriented programmers, Smalltalk/V users, trainers

Content Summary
Select the "Search the Action Requests Database" option to search the Digitalk Action Requests database.

See Also
Digitalk Forum

User Guide
- ☑ Windows
- ☑ DOS
- ☑ Macintosh
- ☐ Terminal Emulation
- ☐ VMS
- ☐ UNIX
- ☑ OS/2
- ☐ Other platform

Cost
- ☐ Unknown
- ☐ Basic
- ☑ Extended
- ☐ Premium ($)
- ☐ Executive w/$

Activity Level

Address
GO: **DBDIGITALK**

OCCULT

Religion Forum

Description
People of all faiths and religions meet in this forum to discuss spiritual, ethical, and values issues. The discussions are open and courtesy is given to all.

Subjects
Christianity, Occult, Religions of the World

Audience
Clergy, religious, seminary students

Content Summary
The library and message areas contain various places to discuss religions of the world, study the Bible, research ministry issues, take part in an online prayer and bible study group, or read press releases on new religious products such as a CD-ROM–based Bible study guide.

See Also
Participate

User Guide
- ☑ Windows
- ☑ DOS
- ☑ Macintosh
- ☐ Terminal Emulation
- ☐ VMS
- ☐ UNIX
- ☐ OS/2
- ☐ Other platform

Cost
- ☐ Unknown
- ☐ Basic
- ☑ Extended
- ☐ Premium ($)
- ☐ Executive w/$

Activity Level

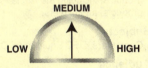

Address
GO: **RELIGION**

Official Airline Guide

Description
The Official Airline Guide is the most comprehensive, up-to-date source of travel-related information available online. This service also is easy to use and does not require you to know travel codes.

Subjects
Travel, Airline, Tourism

Audience
General public

Official Airline Guide – Online Shopping

Content Summary
From the Official Airline Guide main menu, you can read a description of the service, get a list of the commands, give feedback to the service, and access the service. Be sure to read the pricing instructions by selecting the Access option from the main menu.

See Also
EAASY SABRE

User Guide
- [x] Windows
- [x] DOS
- [x] Macintosh
- [ ] Terminal Emulation
- [x] VMS
- [x] UNIX
- [ ] OS/2
- [ ] Other platform

Cost
- [ ] Unknown
- [ ] Basic
- [ ] Extended
- [x] Premium ($)
- [ ] Executive w/$

Activity Level

Address
GO: **OAG**

ONLINE CATALOGS

Digital PC Store

Description
Order DEC products or browse its online catalog of products, including the Alpha AXP PC, networking products, and printers.

Subjects
Computers, DEC Equipment, Online Catalogs

Audience
DEC Alpha AXP users, support technicians, system integrators, VARs, Windows NT users

Content Summary
Several options enable you to browse DEC's online catalog of products, enter sweepstakes, order products, or join Digital's electronic store.

See Also
DEC PC Forum, DEC Windows NT Support Forum, DECPCI Forum, PDP-11 Forum, VAX Forum

User Guide
- [x] Windows
- [x] DOS
- [x] Macintosh
- [ ] Terminal Emulation
- [x] VMS
- [x] UNIX
- [x] OS/2
- [ ] Other platform

Cost
- [ ] Unknown
- [x] Basic
- [ ] Extended
- [ ] Premium ($)
- [ ] Executive w/$

Activity Level

Address
GO: **DD-31**

Omaha Steaks International

Description
Order thick, juicy steaks online from Omaha Steaks International, which has been in business since 1917.

Subjects
Food, Catalogs

Audience
General public

Content Summary
From the main menu, you can choose from several options, including Order From Our Online Catalog, Product QuickSearch, Customer Service, Welcome to Omaha Steaks International, Order Our Free Catalog, Order From Our Print Catalog, Join Our Electronic Mailing List, Recipe of the Month, and Special Offer.

See Also
Adventures in Food Forum

User Guide
- [x] Windows
- [x] DOS
- [x] Macintosh
- [ ] Terminal Emulation
- [x] VMS
- [x] UNIX
- [ ] OS/2
- [ ] Other platform

Cost
- [ ] Unknown
- [x] Basic
- [ ] Extended
- [ ] Premium ($)
- [ ] Executive w/$

Activity Level

Address
GO: **OS**

ONLINE SHOPPING

Quality Paperbacks

Description
This forum provides an online paperback book club. If you don't like leaving the comfort of home to shop, then this forum is for you. You can shop for all types of paperback books right from your home or office.

Subjects
Books, Online Shopping, Reading

Audience
Reading enthusiasts, students

Content Summary
Once you join this forum, you receive the QPB review every three-and-one-half weeks. The review contains book reviews and describes the current book selection. You can cancel your membership at any time. Membership is automatically cancelled if you do not purchase at least one book in any six-month period.

See Also
Book of the Month Club Forum, Book Review Digest Forum, Books in Print Forum, Books on Tape Forum

User Guide
- ☑ Windows
- ☑ DOS
- ☑ Macintosh
- ☑ Terminal Emulation
- ☑ VMS
- ☑ UNIX
- ☑ OS/2
- ☐ Other platform

Cost
- ☐ Unknown
- ☑ Basic
- ☐ Extended
- ☐ Premium ($)
- ☐ Executive w/$

Activity Level

Address
GO: **QPB1**

Online Surveys

Description
Take online surveys with this service. The surveys change frequently, so visit this area periodically to help in CompuServe research.

Subjects
Surveys, General Interest

Audience
General public

Content Summary
From the main menu, you can select Introduction, How To Take Online Surveys, Feedback/Comments, and the survey of your choice. You can take the New Member Survey if you have joined CompuServe within the past six months.

See Also
ZiffNet Surveys

User Guide
- ☐ Windows
- ☐ DOS
- ☐ Macintosh
- ☑ Terminal Emulation
- ☐ VMS
- ☐ UNIX
- ☐ OS/2
- ☐ Other platform

Cost
- ☐ Unknown
- ☑ Basic
- ☐ Extended
- ☐ Premium ($)
- ☐ Executive w/$

Activity Level

Address
GO: **SURVEY**

ORACLE

Oracle Forum

Description
Sponsored by Oracle Corporation and administered by the International Oracle Users Group (IOUG), this forum provides online technical advice and libraries of helpful routines.

Subjects
Computers, Oracle

Audience
Computer users, MIS people

Content Summary
You can find tips, techniques, files, books, documentation, and other resources in the numerous library and message sections. Some of the library sections include User Groups, Mainframe, Minicomputer & UNIX, Desktop-PC, Mac, NLM, RDBMS, SQL & PL/SQL, Oracle Bookstore, Training, and more.

See Also
Client Server Computer Forum

User Guide
- ☑ Windows
- ☑ DOS
- ☑ Macintosh
- ☐ Terminal Emulation
- ☑ VMS
- ☑ UNIX
- ☐ OS/2
- ☑ Other platform

Cost
- ☐ Unknown
- ☐ Basic
- ☑ Extended
- ☐ Premium ($)
- ☐ Executive w/$

Activity Level

Address
GO: **ORACLE**

OS/2

Golden CommPass Support

Description
This is the official support area of Golden CommPass, the only native OS/2 navigation program designed specifically for CompuServe.

Subjects
Computers, OS/2

Audience
OS/2 users

Content Summary
Get support, the latest update, tips and hints, scripts, and other files associated with Golden CommPass. If you use OS/2 and have access to CompuServe, you've probably heard of Golden CommPass already. If not, join this forum and download the latest press release and demo of this navigator.

See Also
OS/2 Monthly, OS/2 Vendor Forum

User Guide
- ☐ Windows
- ☐ DOS
- ☐ Macintosh
- ☐ Terminal Emulation
- ☐ VMS
- ☐ UNIX
- ☑ OS/2
- ☐ Other platform

Cost
- ☐ Unknown
- ☐ Basic
- ☑ Extended
- ☐ Premium ($)
- ☐ Executive w/$

Activity Level

Address
GO: **GCPSUPPORT**

Novell OS/2 Forum

Description
This Novell NetWire forum is designed for messages pertaining to using NetWare with OS/2.

Subjects
Computers, Novell Inc., OS/2

Audience
MIS people

Content Summary
The message section includes OS/2 Printing, Client/Server, OS/2 Requester, NSM (OS/2), NetWare 4.*x* for OS/2, GUI Tools, and WINOS2/DOS.

See Also
Novell Files Database, Novell Library Forum, Novell Information Library, Novell NetWare 2.*x* Forum, Novell NetWare 3.*x* Forum, Novell NetWare 4.*x* Forum

User Guide
- ☐ Windows
- ☐ DOS
- ☐ Macintosh
- ☐ Terminal Emulation
- ☐ VMS
- ☐ UNIX
- ☑ OS/2
- ☐ Other platform

Cost
- ☐ Unknown
- ☐ Basic
- ☑ Extended
- ☐ Premium ($)
- ☐ Executive w/$

Activity Level

Address
GO: **NOVOS2**

OTC NewsAlert

Description
Search the latest international news, weather, and sports from the world's major news agencies. A powerful news clipping service that can scan many news sources for stories you specify and deliver them to you daily.

Subjects
Business, Financial News, International News, News

Audience
Associated Press Forum, Associated Press Online

Content Summary
You can read financial events through Reuters Financial Report and OTC NewsAlert, as well as read the day's headlines with The Washington Post. To use the News by Company Ticker option, enter a company ticker symbol and check on business news filed within the past 24 hours. For the News Clips option, you can read through special clipping folders set up by CompuServe to keep you up on specific news topics. You also set up your own Personal area in which you specify the type of news that you want to read by typing in key phrases. ENS then sends you electronic news clippings that you can read. ENS costs $15 per hour plus the base connect rates.

See Also
AP Sports, Financial Forums, Global Crises Forum, NewsGrid, Newspaper Archives, Reuters News Pictures Forum, United Press International, U.S. News Forum

OTC NewsAlert – Outdoor Activities

469

User Guide
- ☑ Windows
- ☑ DOS
- ☐ Macintosh
- ☐ Terminal Emulation
- ☐ VMS
- ☐ UNIX
- ☐ OS/2
- ☐ Other platform

Cost
- ☐ Unknown
- ☐ Basic
- ☐ Extended
- ☑ Premium ($)
- ☐ Executive w/$

Activity Level
UNKNOWN

Address
GO: **ENS**

Other Banyan Patchware Forum

Description
Sponsored by Banyan Systems, Inc., this forum provides an area for users to download patches and support files for products relating to Banyan products.

Subjects
Computers

Audience
Computer users, MIS people

Content Summary
This library stores patches related to Banyan Products outside of VINES such as ENS, as well as future products that will soon be released by Banyan. Patches are uploaded by Banyan's Customer Support organization and are kept up-to-date. The library section is called Misc. BanPatches. You also can leave or read messages for general help.

See Also
Banyan Forum

User Guide
- ☑ Windows
- ☑ DOS
- ☑ Macintosh
- ☐ Terminal Emulation
- ☑ VMS
- ☑ UNIX
- ☐ OS/2
- ☐ Other platform

Cost
- ☐ Unknown
- ☐ Basic
- ☑ Extended
- ☐ Premium ($)
- ☐ Executive w/$

Activity Level

MEDIUM

Address
GO: **BANPATCH**

OUTDOOR ACTIVITIES

Outdoor Forum

Description
Do you enjoy fishing, hunting, camping, scouting activities, cycling, birding, climbing, skiing, nudism, boating, photography, or other outdoor-related activities? If so, join the Outdoor Forum to share your experiences with others.

Subjects
Outdoor Activities, General Interest

Audience
General public

Content Summary
If you enjoy online magazines, you can get a copy of Outdoor Bytes, which is an electronic journal devoted to outdoor activities. You can get a Windows version or Replica version for Macintosh and Windows in library 16, Outdoor Bytes. Other library and message sections include General/Photography, Scouting, Power Boating, Fishing, Naturism/Nudism, and more.

See Also
Gardening Forum

User Guide
- ☑ Windows
- ☑ DOS
- ☑ Macintosh
- ☐ Terminal Emulation
- ☑ VMS
- ☑ UNIX
- ☐ OS/2
- ☐ Other platform

Cost
- ☐ Unknown
- ☐ Basic
- ☑ Extended
- ☐ Premium ($)
- ☐ Executive w/$

Activity Level

MEDIUM-HIGH

Address
GO: **OUTDOORFORUM**

P

Packard Bell Forum

Description
This forum provides technical support and an area to communicate with people who own Packard Bell computers.

Subjects
Computers

Audience
Computer users, Packard Bell Users

Content Summary
Libraries include areas to ask technical support questions, get information on shareware utilities, and to download mouse drivers, video card drivers, and virus scanning utilities. Also provided is a list of Packard Bell service centers arranged alphabetically by state.

See Also
Computer Buyers' Guide

User Guide
- ☑ Windows
- ☑ DOS
- ☐ Macintosh
- ☐ Terminal Emulation
- ☐ VMS
- ☐ UNIX
- ☐ OS/2
- ☐ Other platform

Cost
- ☐ Unknown
- ☐ Basic
- ☑ Extended
- ☐ Premium ($)
- ☐ Executive w/$

Activity Level LOW ← MEDIUM HIGH

Address
GO: **PACKARDBELL**

PaperChase-MEDLINE Forum

Description
This forum provides access to the world's largest biomedical database. The information is prepared by the National Library of Medicine and has more than seven million references from 4,000 journals.

Subjects
Health, Medicine, Research

Audience
Dentists, physicians, scientists

Content Summary
References are available from 1966. Updates to articles are added weekly. Because the database is so extensive, you should enter a very narrow topic of research. Cost can be prohibitive. The cost on weekdays from 7 p.m. until 8 a.m. or any time on weekends is $18 per hour. The cost on weekdays from 8 a.m. until 7 p.m. is $24 per hour. Photocopies are available for $10 by first-class mail or $25 by fax.

See Also
Rare Disease Database Forum

User Guide
- ☑ Windows
- ☑ DOS
- ☑ Macintosh
- ☐ Terminal Emulation
- ☑ VMS
- ☑ UNIX
- ☑ OS/2
- ☐ Other platform

Cost
- ☐ Unknown
- ☐ Basic
- ☐ Extended
- ☑ Premium ($)
- ☐ Executive w/$

Activity Level LOW MEDIUM → HIGH

Address
GO: **PAPERCHASE**

PARANORMAL EXPERIENCES

Encounters Forum

Description
Have you ever experienced something paranormal? Spotted a UFO? Had an encounter that you cannot explain? If so, join this forum and discuss your encounter online. The FOX-TV [encounters:] television show producers plan frequent contact with Forum users via this service.

Subjects
Encounters, UFO, Paranormal Experiences

Audience
UFO researchers

Content Summary
The libraries in this forum offer AVI video clips of UFO sightings, interviews, news reports, multimedia files, and various software files. Check out Library 4, "Graphic Files," for graphics files of UFO sightings, aliens, and Mars photographs. You also can download the Roger Patterson photo of Bigfoot.

See Also

User Guide
- ☑ Windows
- ☑ DOS
- ☑ Macintosh
- ☐ Terminal Emulation
- ☑ VMS
- ☑ UNIX
- ☑ OS/2
- ☑ Other platform

Cost

- [ ] Unknown
- [ ] Basic
- [x] Extended
- [ ] Premium ($)
- [ ] Executive w/$

Activity Level

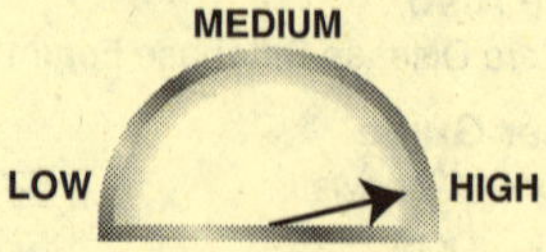
MEDIUM
LOW
HIGH

Address

GO: **ENCOUNTERS**

PARENTING

ADD Forum

Description

This forum provides information and support for adults, parents and professionals interested in attention deficit disorder and other neurological conditions.

Subjects

Attention Deficit, Hyperactivity, Medicine

Audience

Medical personnel, parents

Content Summary

This forum's libraries include Family/Social Life, Parenting Issues, Schools and Learning, Therapy/ Medication, and much more.

See Also

Medsig Forum

User Guide

- [x] Windows
- [x] DOS
- [ ] Macintosh
- [ ] Terminal Emulation
- [ ] VMS
- [ ] UNIX
- [ ] OS/2
- [ ] Other platform

Cost

- [ ] Unknown
- [ ] Basic
- [x] Extended
- [ ] Premium ($)
- [ ] Executive w/$

Activity Level

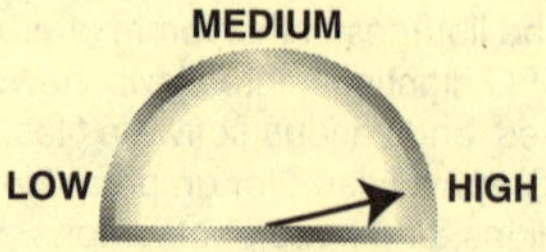
MEDIUM
LOW
HIGH

Address

GO: **ADD**

Participate

Description

This forum is a message base that uses Participate software to enable users to create and monitor discussions about any subject they choose.

Subjects

Music, Philosophy, Politics, General Interest

Audience

General public

Content Summary

In this forum, you will find numerous topic discussion areas that include politics, music, marketing, philosophy, and current events. If you don't find the topic of interest to you, you can start that topic area. Also of interest is The Arrow, which is an online newsletter that discusses this forum. If you want information on the most active discussions, you can join the Hot Points area, which is updated weekly. You also can join the New Points area, which provides you with a list of all new topic discussions.

See Also

Music/Arts Forum, Political Debate Forum

User Guide

- [x] Windows
- [x] DOS
- [x] Macintosh
- [x] Terminal Emulation
- [x] VMS
- [x] UNIX
- [x] OS/2
- [ ] Other platform

Cost

- [ ] Unknown
- [ ] Basic
- [x] Extended
- [ ] Premium ($)
- [ ] Executive w/$

Activity Level

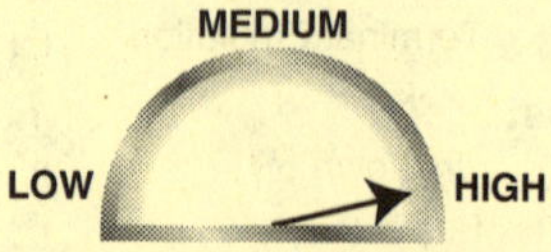
MEDIUM
LOW
HIGH

Address

GO: **PARTI**

PASSPORTS

VISA Advisors

Description

This service offers assistance in obtaining visas and passports. VISA Advisors hand-carries requests to the appropriate embassy in Washington, DC.

Subjects

Passports, Travel

Audience

General public

Content Summary

The VISA Advisors main menu contains Introduction to VISA Advisors, How to Use Us, How to Apply for a Passport, Look Up VISA Requirements, and Request Application Forms.

See Also

Travel Forum

Passports – PC Computing

User Guide
- ☑ Windows
- ☑ DOS
- ☑ Macintosh
- ☐ Terminal Emulation
- ☑ VMS
- ☑ UNIX
- ☑ OS/2
- ☑ Other platform

Cost
- ☐ Unknown
- ☑ Basic
- ☐ Extended
- ☐ Premium ($)
- ☐ Executive w/$

Activity Level
UNKNOWN (LOW – MEDIUM – HIGH)

Address
GO: **VISA**

Patent Research Center

Description
This forum provides quick access to summaries of U.S. patents granted in chemical, mechanical, electrical, and design categories.

Subjects
Inventions, Legal Research, Research

Audience
Inventors, legal researchers, researchers

Content Summary
This forum contains summaries of patents granted internationally since the mid 1970s. Databases searched include the Claims/U.S. Patent Abstracts from 1950 to the present and the World Patents Index from 1963 to the present. You enter a search by typing a name, word, or phrase that describes the item you are searching for. The search can return up to 10 articles.

See Also
Legal Research Center

User Guide
- ☑ Windows
- ☑ DOS
- ☑ Macintosh
- ☐ Terminal Emulation
- ☑ VMS
- ☑ UNIX
- ☑ OS/2
- ☐ Other platform

Cost
- ☐ Unknown
- ☐ Basic
- ☐ Extended
- ☑ Premium ($)
- ☐ Executive w/$

Activity Level
UNKNOWN (LOW – MEDIUM – HIGH)

Address
GO: **PATENT**

PC Catalog

Description
PC Catalog features more than 2,000 product listings, spanning networking, microcomputers, and new technology.

Subjects
Computers, Catalogs

Audience
Computer users

Content Summary
From the PC Catalog main menu, you can select Shop Our Online Catalog, What is PC Catalog, What's New, Gif Images, Customer Service, Visit PC Publications, and more.

See Also
MicroWarehouse, IBM Personal Software Products, CompuServe Store

User Guide
- ☑ Windows
- ☑ DOS
- ☑ Macintosh
- ☐ Terminal Emulation
- ☑ VMS
- ☑ UNIX
- ☐ OS/2
- ☐ Other platform

Cost
- ☐ Unknown
- ☑ Basic
- ☐ Extended
- ☐ Premium ($)
- ☐ Executive w/$

Activity Level
UNKNOWN (LOW – MEDIUM – HIGH)

Address
GO: **PCA**

PC Computing

Description
The PC Computing service (a ZiffNet service) enables you to go to the PC Contact Forum, take a poll, or communicate with *PC Computing* magazine.

Subjects
Computers, ZiffNet

Audience
Computer users

Content Summary
From the main menu, you can select PC/Contact Forum, Take a PC/Computing Poll, Tips and Tricks from PC/Computing, File Submissions to PC/Computing, and Letters to the Editor. This is a ZiffNet service.

See Also
PC Contact, PC Magazine

PC Computing – PC Magazine UK Forum

User Guide
- [ ] Windows
- [ ] DOS
- [ ] Macintosh
- [x] Terminal Emulation
- [ ] VMS
- [ ] UNIX
- [ ] OS/2
- [ ] Other platform

Cost
- [ ] Unknown
- [x] Basic
- [ ] Extended
- [ ] Premium ($)
- [ ] Executive w/$

Activity Level
UNKNOWN

Address
GO: **PCCOMP**

PC Contact Forum

Description
The PC Contact Forum, a service of ZiffNet, is devoted to discussions among PC Computing's editors and readers.

Subjects
Computers, ZiffNet

Audience
Computer users

Content Summary
In addition to exchanging ideas or getting questions answered from your favorite writers or editors online, you can contact the PC Advocate about problems with vendors or talk to the Phantom Shopper to share your experiences with computer dealers around the country. Plus you can browse through the library and download productivity files and tricks.

See Also
PC Computing

User Guide
- [x] Windows
- [x] DOS
- [x] Macintosh
- [ ] Terminal Emulation
- [ ] VMS
- [ ] UNIX
- [ ] OS/2
- [ ] Other platform

Cost
- [ ] Unknown
- [ ] Basic
- [x] Extended
- [ ] Premium ($)
- [ ] Executive w/$

Activity Level

MEDIUM (toward HIGH)

Address
GO: **PCCONTACT**

PC Direct UK Magazine Forum

Description
PC Direct UK Magazine Forum, part of ZiffNet, mixes inside knowledge of the United Kingdom computer trade with specialist buyers guides while always keeping the consumer in mind.

Subjects
Computers, United Kingdom, ZiffNet

Audience
Computer users, UK residents

Content Summary
Download buyer guides, editorial contributions (download *Frankenstein*, for instance), and utilities. The library sections are called Buying Advice, Utilities, and Editorial Contributions.

See Also
PC Contact, PC Computing

User Guide
- [x] Windows
- [x] DOS
- [x] Macintosh
- [ ] Terminal Emulation
- [ ] VMS
- [ ] UNIX
- [ ] OS/2
- [ ] Other platform

Cost
- [ ] Unknown
- [ ] Basic
- [x] Extended
- [ ] Premium ($)
- [ ] Executive w/$

Activity Level

MEDIUM

Address
GO: **PCDUK**

PC Magazine UK Forum

Description
This ZiffNet service offers utilities, sound files, graphics, and other files for your general computing needs.

Subjects
Computers, ZiffNet, United Kingdom

Audience
Computer users, UK computer users

Content Summary
The library sections contain several areas, including Bench Tests, Productivity, Utilities, Editorial Contributions, After Hours, DOS, Spreadsheets, Words, Online/Internet, and more.

See Also
IBM File Finder, PC MagNet Utilities/Tips Forum

User Guide
- ☑ Windows
- ☑ DOS
- ☑ Macintosh
- ☐ Terminal Emulation
- ☐ VMS
- ☐ UNIX
- ☑ OS/2
- ☑ Other platform

Cost
- ☐ Unknown
- ☐ Basic
- ☑ Extended
- ☐ Premium ($)
- ☐ Executive w/$

Activity Level
MEDIUM (LOW — HIGH)

Address
GO: **PCUKFORUM**

PC Magazine UK Online

Description
PC Magazine UK Online (a ZiffNet service) is jointly run by *PC Direct UK*, the business computer buyer's magazine, and *PC Magazine UK*, the leader in PC technology analysis and reporting.

Subjects
Computers, ZiffNet, United Kingdom

Audience
Computer users

Content Summary
Each magazine has its own forum. In the PC Magazine UK Forum (GO PCUKFORUM), you can access the libraries to download reports and buyer's guides. Access the respective library for articles to download. You can access the PC Direct UK Forum by using the command GO PCDUK.

See Also
PC Direct UK Forum, PC MagNet

User Guide
- ☑ Windows
- ☑ DOS
- ☑ Macintosh
- ☐ Terminal Emulation
- ☐ VMS
- ☐ UNIX
- ☑ OS/2
- ☐ Other platform

Cost
- ☐ Unknown
- ☐ Basic
- ☑ Extended
- ☐ Premium ($)
- ☐ Executive w/$

Activity Level

MEDIUM (LOW — HIGH)

Address
GO: **PCUKONLINE**

PC MagNet

Description
PC MagNet, part of ZiffNet, is the source for some of the finest utilities that meet the high standards of *PC Magazine*.

Subjects
Computers, ZiffNet

Audience
Computer users

Content Summary
Download utilities from the latest issue of *PC Magazine*. You can contact the staff at *PC Magazine* and ask for advice, tell the editors what you thought about their latest product review, debate the issues with the columnists, and get the answers to your specific questions.

See Also
PC Computing, PC Direct UK Forum, PC Contact Forum

User Guide
- ☑ Windows
- ☑ DOS
- ☑ Macintosh
- ☐ Terminal Emulation
- ☑ VMS
- ☑ UNIX
- ☐ OS/2
- ☐ Other platform

Cost
- ☐ Unknown
- ☐ Basic
- ☑ Extended
- ☐ Premium ($)
- ☐ Executive w/$

Extended

Activity Level

MEDIUM (LOW — HIGH)

Address
GO: **PCMAGNET**

PC MagNet Editorial Forum

Description
The PC MagNet Editorial Forum, part of ZiffNet, enables you to communicate with the likes of Michael Miller, John Dvorak, and Winn Rosch.

Subjects
Computers, ZiffNet

Audience
Computer users

Content Summary
From the library and message sections contain several areas, including Features-Hardware, Features-Software, First Looks, Trends, Viewpoints-Dvorak, Viewpoints-Seymour, Viewpoints-Miller, After Hours, and more. You can download John Dvorak's winning chili recipe from library 6.

See Also
PC MagNet, PC Computing, PC Programming Forum, PC MagNet Utilities/Tips Forum

User Guide
- [x] Windows
- [x] DOS
- [x] Macintosh
- [ ] Terminal Emulation
- [ ] VMS
- [x] UNIX
- [x] OS/2
- [ ] Other platform

Cost
- [ ] Unknown
- [ ] Basic
- [x] Extended
- [ ] Premium ($)
- [ ] Executive w/$

Activity Level
MEDIUM (arrow between LOW and HIGH, pointing toward HIGH)

Address
GO: **EDITORIAL**

PC MagNet Programming Forum

Description
The PC MagNet Programming Forum, part of ZiffNet, has the latest files from the programming sections of *PC Magazine*. Many of the authors can be found here as well.

Subjects
Computers, Computer Programming, ZiffNet

Audience
Computer users, computer programmers

Content Summary
The library and message sections include Utilities Code, Power Programming, Languages, Lab Notes, Environments, Toolkits, Corporate Developer, and more. If you are interested in computer-related trade shows, you can download a calendar of over 100 events from library 1, General. The file name is ZCAL13.ZIP.

See Also
PC MagNet, PC MagNet Editorial Forum, PC MagNet Utilities/Tips Forum

User Guide
- [x] Windows
- [x] DOS
- [x] Macintosh
- [ ] Terminal Emulation
- [ ] VMS
- [ ] UNIX
- [x] OS/2
- [x] Other platform

Cost
- [ ] Unknown
- [ ] Basic
- [x] Extended
- [ ] Premium ($)
- [ ] Executive w/$

Activity Level
MEDIUM (arrow pointing up)

Address
GO: **PROGRAMMING**

PC MagNet Utilities/Tips Forum

Description
You can find the latest utilities from *PC Magazine* here as well as files from various other sections of the magazine. Many of the authors of the utilities provide support here as well. This is part of ZiffNet.

Subjects
Computers, ZiffNet

Audience
Computer users

Content Summary
Numerous shareware utilities can be found throughout these libraries. Some of the library sections include PC Magazine Utilities, Tutor, User-to-User, Sol: Hardware, Driver Alert, Windows & OS/2 Utilities, and more.

See Also
IBM File Finder, PC MagNet

User Guide
- [x] Windows
- [x] DOS
- [x] Macintosh
- [ ] Terminal Emulation
- [ ] VMS
- [ ] UNIX
- [x] OS/2
- [x] Other platform

Cost
- [ ] Unknown
- [ ] Basic
- [x] Extended
- [ ] Premium ($)
- [ ] Executive w/$

Activity Level
MEDIUM (arrow between LOW and HIGH, pointing toward HIGH)

Address
GO: **TIPS**

PC Plug and Play Forum

Description
This forum is for the discussion of the hardware and software issues of implementing plug and play on PCs. The Plug and Play forum is operated by several hardware and software manufacturers.

Subjects
Computers, Hardware

Audience
Computer users, MIS people

Content Summary
This forum is mainly under construction due to the infancy of this topic. However, you can find files and technical information in several of its libraries, including General Information, Plug and Play ISA, and PCMCIA.

See Also
IBM File Finder

User Guide
- ☑ Windows
- ☑ DOS
- ☑ Macintosh
- ☐ Terminal Emulation
- ☐ VMS
- ☐ UNIX
- ☑ OS/2
- ☐ Other platform

Cost
- ☐ Unknown
- ☐ Basic
- ☑ Extended
- ☐ Premium ($)
- ☐ Executive w/$

Activity Level

Address
GO: **PLUGPLAY**

PC Plus/PC Answers Online

Description
This service is devoted to readers of *PC Plus* and *PC Answers,* two UK magazines, to communicate with editors, download and upload files, and submit articles.

Subjects
Computers, UK

Audience
Computer users, UK computer users

Content Summary
From the PC Plus Online main menu, you can choose from several options, including About PC Plus Online, Using the Service, Top 10 Downloads, Coverdisks, Letters to the Editor, and more.

See Also
PC MagNet, PC Computing, PC Direct UK Forum

User Guide
- ☑ Windows
- ☑ DOS
- ☑ Macintosh
- ☐ Terminal Emulation
- ☑ VMS
- ☑ UNIX
- ☐ OS/2
- ☐ Other platform

Cost
- ☐ Unknown
- ☐ Basic
- ☑ Extended
- ☐ Premium ($)
- ☐ Executive w/$

Activity Level

Address
GO: **PCPLUS**

PC Publications

Description
This service enables you to order a subscription of *PC Novice*, *PC Today*, and *PC Catalog*.

Subjects
Computers

Audience
Computer users

Content Summary
From the main menu, you can select Order a Subscription, About PC Novice/PC Today/PC Catalog, Shipping and Ordering Information, Table of Contents - Sample Articles, Customer Service, and more.

See Also
IBM File Finder

User Guide
- ☑ Windows
- ☑ DOS
- ☑ Macintosh
- ☐ Terminal Emulation
- ☑ VMS
- ☑ UNIX
- ☐ OS/2
- ☐ Other platform

Cost
- ☐ Unknown
- ☑ Basic
- ☐ Extended
- ☐ Premium ($)
- ☐ Executive w/$

Activity Level

Address
GO: **PCB**

PC Vendor Forums

Description
These forums are designed to offer support from various PC vendors of PC products.

Subjects
Computers

Audience
Computer users, MIS people

Content Summary
There are 10 PC Vendor forums: PC Vendor A Forum (GO PCVENA), PC Vendor B Forum (GO PCVENB), PC Vendor C Forum (GO PCVENC), PC

PC Vendor Forums – Personality Profile

Vendor D Forum (GO PCVEND), PC Vendor E Forum (GO PCVENE), PC Vendor F Forum (GO PCVENF), PC Vendor G Forum (GO PCVENG), PC Vendor H Forum (GO PCVENH), PC Vendor I Forum (GO PCVENI), and PC Vendor J Forum (GO PCVENJ).

See Also
IBM File Finder, Graphics Vendor Forums, DTP Vendor Forums, MIDI Vendor Forums, Multimedia Vendor Forums, Modem Vendor Forums

User Guide
- [x] Windows
- [x] DOS
- [x] Macintosh
- [ ] Terminal Emulation
- [ ] VMS
- [x] UNIX
- [x] OS/2
- [x] Other platform

Cost
- [ ] Unknown
- [ ] Basic
- [x] Extended
- [ ] Premium ($)
- [ ] Executive w/$

Activity Level

Address
GO: **PCVENx**

PC Week Forum

Description
PC Week is online as part of ZiffNet, enabling you to keep up with all the industry news. You can see headlines and full text of news stories the Friday before *PC Week* is published.

Subjects
Computers, ZiffNet

Audience
Computer users

Content Summary
See what the notorious Spender F. Katt has discovered this week or discuss the news and issues of the industry with the writers, editors, and other readers of the magazine.

See Also
PC MagNet, PC Computing

User Guide
- [x] Windows
- [x] DOS
- [x] Macintosh
- [ ] Terminal Emulation
- [ ] VMS
- [ ] UNIX
- [x] OS/2
- [ ] Other platform

Cost
- [ ] Unknown
- [ ] Basic
- [x] Extended
- [ ] Premium ($)
- [ ] Executive w/$

Activity Level

Address
GO: **PCWEEK**

PC World Online

Description
This service is the online version of *PC World* magazine. You'll find timely and insightful information in this area that you also find in the print version of *PC World*.

Subjects
Computers, Magazine

Audience
Computer users

Content Summary
Some of the material that you'll find here includes Features, Buyer's Guides, Here's How, and news of new products. From the main menu, you can select Current Issue, PC WORLD forum, Online Exclusive, Exec/Direct Shop, News Wire, Press Release, and more.

See Also
PC Computing, PC Contact

User Guide
- [x] Windows
- [x] DOS
- [x] Macintosh
- [ ] Terminal Emulation
- [x] VMS
- [x] UNIX
- [x] OS/2
- [ ] Other platform

Cost
- [ ] Unknown
- [ ] Basic
- [x] Extended
- [ ] Premium ($)
- [ ] Executive w/$

Activity Level
UNKNOWN

Address
GO: **PCWORLD**

Personality Profile

Description
This forum contains two personality quizzes. One quiz tests how well you know yourself; the other tests how well you know someone else.

Subjects
Psychology, Relationships

Audience
General public

Content Summary
The first area tests your knowledge of yourself. It contains questions about your psychological self, physical self, spiritual self, and your relationships and decision-making skills. After you finish this test, you see a graph that rates you in eight different areas. The other test rates how much you know about the people who are important to you. Tests are available for spouses, roommates, siblings, parents, and children.

See Also
Biorhythms

User Guide
- ☑ Windows
- ☑ DOS
- ☑ Macintosh
- ☑ Terminal Emulation
- ☑ VMS
- ☑ UNIX
- ☑ OS/2
- ☐ Other platform

Cost
- ☐ Unknown
- ☐ Basic
- ☑ Extended
- ☐ Premium ($)
- ☐ Executive w/$

Activity Level

Address
GO: **TMC-90**

Pet Products/Reference Forum

Description
This forum provides customer support for those businesses that provide products or services to pet owners or pet professionals.

Subjects
Animals, Fish, Veterinarians

Audience
Aquarists, pet owners, veterinarians

Content Summary
This forum contains numerous libraries that include a complete list of all subscribing PetPro vendors and a description of their businesses. Also of interest are articles written by behavioral specialists and articles that have appeared in well-known animal publications.

See Also
Pets/Animal Forum

User Guide
- ☑ Windows
- ☑ DOS
- ☑ Macintosh
- ☐ Terminal Emulation
- ☐ VMS
- ☐ UNIX
- ☑ OS/2
- ☐ Other platform

Cost
- ☐ Unknown
- ☐ Basic
- ☑ Extended
- ☐ Premium ($)
- ☐ Executive w/$

Activity Level

Address
GO: **PETPRO**

PHILOSOPHY

Participate

Description
This forum is a message base that uses Participate software to enable users to create and monitor discussions about any subject they choose.

Subjects
Music, Philosophy, Politics, General Interest

Audience
General public

Content Summary
In this forum, you will find numerous topic discussion areas that include politics, music, marketing, philosophy, and current events. If you don't find the topic of interest to you, you can start that topic area. Also of interest is The Arrow, which is an online newsletter that discusses this forum. If you want information on the most active discussions, you can join the Hot Points area, which is updated weekly. You also can join the New Points area, which provides you with a list of all new topic discussions.

See Also
Music/Arts Forum, Political Debate Forum

User Guide
- ☑ Windows
- ☑ DOS
- ☑ Macintosh
- ☑ Terminal Emulation
- ☑ VMS
- ☑ UNIX
- ☑ OS/2
- ☐ Other platform

Cost
- ☐ Unknown
- ☐ Basic
- ☑ Extended
- ☐ Premium ($)
- ☐ Executive w/$

Activity Level
MEDIUM (LOW → HIGH)

Address
GO: **PARTI**

PHOENIX

Univ of Phoenix

Description
Online area providing information on the University of Phoenix' online curriculum. Students take courses via modem.

Subjects
Phoenix, Universities

Audience
Students

Content Summary
This service enables you to view curriculum and take courses online.

See Also
Real Estate Forum

User Guide
- ☑ Windows
- ☑ DOS
- ☑ Macintosh
- ☐ Terminal Emulation
- ☑ VMS
- ☑ UNIX
- ☑ OS/2
- ☑ Other platform

Cost
- ☐ Unknown
- ☐ Basic
- ☐ Extended
- ☐ Premium ($)
- ☑ Executive w/$

Activity Level: UNKNOWN

Address
GO: **UP**

PHOTO-CD

Kodak CD Forum

Description
Maintained by Kodak, this forum is devoted to Kodak CD products and technology, as well as related products.

Subjects
Computers, Photo-CD, Printing

Audience
Computer users, computer graphics designers

Content Summary
The library and message sections include Kodak News, Photo CD General, Photo CD Software, Writable CD, International, Color Management, Member Uploads, and others. The Kodak Printer library (Library 8) contains drivers, information, and press releases relating to Kodak's line of high-quality printers.

See Also
Graphics Forums, Graphics Forums, Graphics File Finder, Photography Forum

User Guide
- ☑ Windows
- ☑ DOS
- ☑ Macintosh
- ☐ Terminal Emulation
- ☐ VMS
- ☐ UNIX
- ☐ OS/2
- ☐ Other platform

Cost
- ☐ Unknown
- ☐ Basic
- ☑ Extended
- ☐ Premium ($)
- ☐ Executive w/$

Activity Level: MEDIUM

Address
GO: **KODAK**

PHOTOGRAPHY

Archive Photos Forum

Description
Archive Photos is a leading source of historical engraving, drawings and photographs, with over 1,300 of images available for download.

Subjects
History, Photography

Audience
History buffs, photographers, students

Content Summary
The libraries include Focus: Elvis, Sex Symbols, People in History, Art/Literature, Nostalgia, and much more.

See Also
Graphics Gallery Forum

User Guide
- ☑ Windows
- ☑ DOS
- ☑ Macintosh
- ☐ Terminal Emulation
- ☐ VMS
- ☐ UNIX
- ☐ OS/2
- ☑ Other platform

Cost
- ☐ Unknown
- ☐ Basic
- ☑ Extended
- ☐ Premium ($)
- ☐ Executive w/$

Canon Net Menu

Activity Level: Low-Medium

Address
GO: ARCHIVE

Description
This menu provides access to services and information from Canon Computer Services, Inc.

Subjects
Hobbies, Photography

Audience
Product users

Content Summary
The libraries of this forum contain information about Canon, a list of regional offices, service facilities, and information on the Clean Earth Campaign.

See Also
Canon Support Forum

User Guide
- [x] Windows
- [x] DOS
- [x] Macintosh
- [ ] Terminal Emulation
- [ ] VMS
- [x] UNIX
- [ ] OS/2
- [ ] Other platform

Cost
- [ ] Unknown
- [ ] Basic
- [x] Extended
- [ ] Premium ($)
- [ ] Executive w/$

Activity Level: Unknown

Address
GO: CANON

Canon Support Forum

Description
This forum provides support for users of products from both Canon Computer Systems, Inc, and Canon USA.

Subjects
Hobbies, Photography

Audience
Product users

Content Summary
Product information contained in this libary includes laser printers, bubble jet printers, ImageScanners, digital copiers, and 35mm cameras.

See Also
Canon Net Menu

User Guide
- [x] Windows
- [x] DOS
- [x] Macintosh
- [ ] Terminal Emulation
- [ ] VMS
- [x] UNIX
- [ ] OS/2
- [ ] Other platform

Cost
- [ ] Unknown
- [ ] Basic
- [x] Extended
- [ ] Premium ($)
- [ ] Executive w/$

Activity Level: Low-Medium

Address
GO: CAN-10

Glamour Graphics Forum

Description
Professional-quality images and photographs featuring fashion models can be found in this forum.

Subjects
Fashion Merchandising, Graphics, Photography

Audience
General public, photographers

Content Summary
The Glamour Graphics Forum offers fashion and glamour photography from stock photography agencies, including Len Kaltman Online, Texas Glamour, Richard Stevens Models, Classic Model Review, Imagine That, and Jade Creations. General sections, with subscriber uploads encouraged, show off high fashion, swimsuits, business attire, resort & sport, casual wear, and more. The file format of choice is GIF, but you might also find some JPG files as well.

See Also
Graphics Forums

User Guide
- [x] Windows
- [x] DOS
- [x] Macintosh
- [ ] Terminal Emulation
- [ ] VMS
- [x] UNIX
- [x] OS/2
- [ ] Other platform

Cost
- [ ] Unknown
- [ ] Basic
- [x] Extended
- [ ] Premium ($)
- [ ] Executive w/$

Photography

Activity Level

Address
GO: **GLAMOUR**

Graphics Corner Forum

Description
You can download and upload GIF and JPEG graphics images to this forum, such as people, portraits, animals, nature scenes, and landmarks.

Subjects
Computers, Graphics, Photography

Audience
Graphics artists, computer users, general public

Content Summary
The Graphics Corner Forum is the primary collection of user-contributed GIF and JPEG images that contain subjects such as Cars, Boats, Planes, People & Portraits, Landscapes, World of Nature, Fantasy & Sci-Fi, Space & Astronomy, Landmarks, and the Body Beautiful. This area has files that contain nudity. Those files include the following message: "This file contains nudity. Those offended by the artistic presentation of nudity should refrain from viewing."

See Also
Graphics Support Forum, Glamour Graphics Forum

User Guide
- ☑ Windows
- ☑ DOS
- ☑ Macintosh
- ☐ Terminal Emulation
- ☐ VMS
- ☑ UNIX
- ☑ OS/2
- ☐ Other platform

Cost
- ☐ Unknown
- ☐ Basic
- ☑ Extended
- ☐ Premium ($)
- ☐ Executive w/$

Activity Level — MEDIUM (arrow pointing toward HIGH)

Address
GO: **CORNER**

Graphics Gallery Forum

Description
This forum offers collections of graphics from NASA, the Smithsonian Institute, the Coast Guard, and tourism agencies.

Subjects
Computer Graphics, Computers, Graphics, Photography

Audience
Graphics artists, graphics designers, computer users, photographers

Content Summary
The Graphics Gallery Forum's libraries consist of the following topics: New Images, SI: Smithsonian Art, SI: Air/Space, SI: Science/Nature, SI: People/Places, NASA, Utah Shakespearean Festival, NAL/USDA, America! North, America! South, America! East, America! West, US Coast Guard, World Photography, Wisconsin Historical Society, and Civil War. The Utah Shakespearean Festival library (Library 9) contains a compilation of the best of moments from the 32 seasons of the Utah Shakespearean Festival's plays.

See Also
Graphics Forums, Graphics Corner Forum, Graphics File Finder

User Guide
- ☑ Windows
- ☑ DOS
- ☑ Macintosh
- ☐ Terminal Emulation
- ☐ VMS
- ☑ UNIX
- ☑ OS/2
- ☐ Other platform

Cost
- ☐ Unknown
- ☐ Basic
- ☑ Extended
- ☐ Premium ($)
- ☐ Executive w/$

Activity Level — MEDIUM (arrow pointing toward LOW)

Address
GO: **GALLERY**

Graphics Plus Forum

Description
This forum contains true-color images in various formats. You can get graphics of cars, boats, people, landscapes, and much more.

Subjects
Computer Graphics, Graphics, Photography

Audience
Photographers, computer graphics designers, computer users, graphics artists, graphics designers, graphics experts

Content Summary
The Graphics Plus Forum has images in truecolor and vector formats such as TIFF, Targa, EPS, truecolor BMP and PCX, AI, PICT, and others. This forum also includes a section focusing on fractal and raytraced images. The libraries include areas such as Cars-Boats-Planes, People & Portraits, Landscapes, World of Nature, Fantasy & Sci-Fi, Cartoons & Comics, Body Beautiful, Plain Brown Wrapper, Fractals/Raytracing, and more. Note that this forum

Photography

contains files that have nudity. Those files that contain nudity, have the following disclaimer: "Those offended by the artistic presentation of nudity should refrain from viewing."

See Also
Graphics File Finder, Graphics Forums, Graphics Gallery Forum, Photography Forum

User Guide
- ☑ Windows
- ☑ DOS
- ☑ Macintosh
- ☐ Terminal Emulation
- ☐ VMS
- ☑ UNIX
- ☑ OS/2
- ☐ Other platform

Cost
- ☐ Unknown
- ☐ Basic
- ☑ Extended
- ☐ Premium ($)
- ☐ Executive w/$

Activity Level

Address
GO: **GRAPHPLUS**

Photography Forum

Description
In this forum, photo enthusiasts of all expertise levels can meet and exchange ideas on topics ranging from tips on how to take good pictures to what type of equipment is needed.

Subjects
Cameras, Hobbies, Photography

Audience
Computer graphics, photographers

Content Summary
The Photography Forum offers many library areas of interest to photography enthusiasts of all levels. Of particular interest are conferences with famous photographers in which participants can ask questions or have their work critiqued. Also included are message areas on commonly asked questions, such as "What makes good photograph composition?". If you are looking for a camera or additional equipment, the numerous press released on various equipment can be helpful.

See Also
Graphics Forum, Quick Picture Forum

User Guide
- ☑ Windows
- ☑ DOS
- ☑ Macintosh
- ☐ Terminal Emulation
- ☑ VMS
- ☑ UNIX
- ☑ OS/2
- ☐ Other platform

Cost
- ☐ Unknown
- ☐ Basic
- ☑ Extended
- ☐ Premium ($)
- ☐ Executive w/$

Activity Level

Address
GO: **PHOTOFORUM**

Reuters News Pictures Forum

Description
This forum contains the largest online source of news images from around the world. Also included are photographs of historical significance from the Bettman Archives.

Subjects
Current Events, News, Photographs

Audience
News enthusiasts, photographers

Content Summary
Photographs of interest to the United States, World, entertainment industry, and sports are featured. Note that photographs are protected by U.S. and International copyrights and are for personal use only.

See Also
AP Sports Forum, Associated Press Online Forum, Detroit Free Press

User Guide
- ☑ Windows
- ☑ DOS
- ☑ Macintosh
- ☐ Terminal Emulation
- ☑ VMS
- ☑ UNIX
- ☑ OS/2
- ☐ Other platform

Cost
- ☐ Unknown
- ☐ Basic
- ☑ Extended
- ☐ Premium ($)
- ☐ Executive w/$

Activity Level

Address
GO: **NEWSPI**

PHOTOJOURNALISM

Detroit Free Press

Description
This is the place to find news and information about the award-winning Detroit Free Press newspaper. And feel free to leave a letter to the editor while you're online.

Subjects
Journalism, National News, Photojournalism

Audience
Automobile enthusiasts, Detroit citizens, journalists, photojournalists, sports fans

Content Summary
In the message and library areas, you can find information on the auto industry (including photographs of cars), health tips, business news, Detroit metro news, computing, entertainment, sports, and cartoons. You also can find the top stories of the day in the "Today's Top Stories" library (library 17).

See Also
Detroit Free Press Store

User Guide
- ☑ Windows
- ☑ DOS
- ☑ Macintosh
- ☐ Terminal Emulation
- ☑ VMS
- ☑ UNIX
- ☑ OS/2
- ☐ Other platform

Cost
- ☐ Unknown
- ☐ Basic
- ☑ Extended
- ☐ Premium ($)
- ☐ Executive w/$

Activity Level

Address
GO: **DETROIT**

PILOTS

Air Line Pilots Association

Description
The Air Line Pilots Association is an AFL-CIO affiliated labor union representing most of the nation's commercial airline pilots.

Subjects
Labor Unions

Audience
Pilots

Content Summary
This service costs $6.00 per month for unlimited access to both ALPA National Forums and your MEC Forum.

See Also
Aviation Forum

User Guide
- ☑ Windows
- ☑ DOS
- ☑ Macintosh
- ☑ Terminal Emulation
- ☑ VMS
- ☑ UNIX
- ☑ OS/2
- ☑ Other platform

Cost
- ☐ Unknown
- ☑ Basic
- ☐ Extended
- ☐ Premium ($)
- ☐ Executive w/$

Activity Level

Address
GO: **ALPA**

PLANTS

Gardening Forum

Description
This forum is dedicated to plants and gardening, and offers tips and ideas on ways to make your gardening and lawn maintenance experience more enjoyable.

Subjects
Genius, Horticulture, Plants

Audience
General public, horticulturists

Content Summary
If you're into vegetable, fruit, or flower gardening, exotic plants (such as orchids or bonsai), or just want to know the best way to make your grass grow, check out this forum's libraries and message sections. The forum managers are from *National Gardening Magazine*. You'll find libraries about herbs, bulbs, fruits, berries, nuts, tools, books, roses, and fertilizer.

See Also
Earth Forum, Outdoor Forum

User Guide
- ☑ Windows
- ☑ DOS
- ☑ Macintosh
- ☐ Terminal Emulation
- ☑ VMS
- ☑ UNIX
- ☑ OS/2
- ☑ Other platform

Plants – Politics

Cost
- [ ] Unknown
- [ ] Basic
- [x] Extended
- [ ] Premium ($)
- [ ] Executive w/$

Activity

LOW ← MEDIUM HIGH

Address
GO: **GARDENING**

Political Debate Forum

Description
This forum allows open discussion of political topics of all types. It is open to people of all political persuasions.

Subjects
International Events, News, U.S. Politics

Audience
Politicians, students

Content Summary
This forum provides debate areas for Democrats, Libertarians, and Republicans. Other libraries contain articles and information on topics ranging from the Crime Bill, health care, gun rights, gay rights, and international politics.

See Also
Democrat Forum, Participate, Republican Forum

User Guide
- [x] Windows
- [x] DOS
- [x] Macintosh
- [ ] Terminal Emulation
- [x] VMS
- [x] UNIX
- [x] OS/2
- [ ] Other platform

Cost
- [ ] Unknown
- [ ] Basic
- [x] Extended
- [ ] Premium ($)
- [ ] Executive w/$

Activity Level

LOW MEDIUM → HIGH

Address
GO: **POLITICS**

Issues Forum

Description
Devoted to current topics and issues, the Issues Forum discusses topics such as Afro-Americanism, parenting, human rights, and others.

Subjects
Current Events, Human Rights, Politics, Religion

Audience
General public

Content Summary
This special interest group is devoted to discussions of a wide variety of issues. Currently, there are sections for topics such as Afro-American issues, parenting issues, human rights, unexplained phenomena, men and women's issues, Asian-American issues, and others. The library and message sections include Culture & Society, Between the Sexes, Canadian Issues, Politics & Religion, and more. Look in Library 9, Rush H. Limbaugh, for summaries of Rush's show.

See Also
Entertainment Center, HSX Open Forum

User Guide
- [x] Windows
- [x] DOS
- [x] Macintosh
- [ ] Terminal Emulation
- [x] VMS
- [x] UNIX
- [x] OS/2
- [x] Other platform

Cost
- [ ] Unknown
- [ ] Basic
- [x] Extended
- [ ] Premium ($)
- [ ] Executive w/$

Activity Level

LOW MEDIUM → HIGH

Address
GO: **ISSUESFORUM**

Participate

Description
This forum is a message base that uses Participate software to enable users to create and monitor discussions about any subject they choose.

Subjects
Music, Philosophy, Politics, General Interest

Audience
General public

Content Summary
In this forum, you will find numerous topic discussion areas that include politics, music, marketing, philosophy, and current events. If you don't find the topic of interest to you, you can start that topic area. Also of interest is The Arrow, which is an online newsletter that discusses this forum. If you want information on the most active discussions, you can join the Hot Points area, which is updated weekly. You also can join the New Points area, which provides you with a list of all new topic discussions.

Politics – Pollution

See Also
Music/Arts Forum, Political Debate Forum

User Guide
- ☑ Windows
- ☑ DOS
- ☑ Macintosh
- ☑ Terminal Emulation
- ☑ VMS
- ☑ UNIX
- ☑ OS/2
- ☐ Other platform

Cost
- ☐ Unknown
- ☐ Basic
- ☑ Extended
- ☐ Premium ($)
- ☐ Executive w/$

Activity Level

Address
GO: **PARTI**

POLLUTION

Ei Compendex Plus

Description
The Ei Compendex Plus database contains abstracts and articles from engineering and technological literature. You can find literature from virtually all the engineering disciplines in this database.

Subjects
Applied Physics, Food Technology, Engineering, Pollution

Audience
Engineers

Content Summary
This database contains worldwide coverage of articles taken from journals, publications of engineering societies and organizations, conference papers and proceedings, and government reports and books. In a search, you can get the author, title, corporate source, conference title, publication year, language, and an abstract from the article. See the Pricing Information choice in the main menu for the various pricing charges.

See Also
ERIC, IQuest

User Guide
- ☑ Windows
- ☑ DOS
- ☑ Macintosh
- ☐ Terminal Emulation
- ☑ VMS
- ☑ UNIX
- ☑ OS/2
- ☑ Other platform

Cost
- ☐ Unknown
- ☐ Basic
- ☐ Extended
- ☑ Premium ($)
- ☐ Executive w/$

Activity Level

Address
GO: **COMPENDEX**

Powersoft Forum

Description
This forum provides technical assistant to and a general discussion of Powersoft and WATCOM Corporation products.

Subjects
Computers, Database Consultants

Audience
Computer professionals, database professionals, Powersoft users

Content Summary
This forum's libraries and message areas contain information about PowerBuilder, PowerMaker, PowerViewer, PowerBuilder Desktop, WATCOM SQL, WATCOM C/C++, WATCOM VX-REXX, and WATCOM Fortran 77. Also included are bug fixes for products, user group lists, third-party vendors, and instructions on how to connect with other software.

See Also
Client Server Computing Forum

User Guide
- ☑ Windows
- ☑ DOS
- ☐ Macintosh
- ☐ Terminal Emulation
- ☐ VMS
- ☐ UNIX
- ☐ OS/2
- ☐ Other platform

Cost
- ☐ Unknown
- ☐ Basic
- ☑ Extended
- ☐ Premium ($)
- ☐ Executive w/$

Activity Level

Address
GO: **POWERSOFT**

PR and Marketing Forum

Description
This forum is a gathering place for public relations, advertising, marketing, research, and public affairs professionals.

Subjects
Advertising, Marketing, Public Relations

Audience
Advertising professionals, market research specialists, public relations personnel

Content Summary
Members use the forum's message libraries to communicate on subjects of interest to the communications field. Other features include Jobs Online, from which members can review more than 100 job openings. Members can post resumes on as well as listing openings from their respective firms. Other sections include: starting up a business, marketing, media relations and crisis communications, new products and services, creativity, research, advertising and direct mail, electronic newsletters, desktop publishing, professional development, political campaigns and programming, creativity development, educational programs, and technology tools.

Online college courses are offered in advertising, public relations, and print and electronic journalism.

See Also
Media Newsletter

User Guide
- [x] Windows
- [x] DOS
- [x] Macintosh
- [ ] Terminal Emulation
- [x] VMS
- [x] UNIX
- [x] OS/2
- [ ] Other platform

Cost
- [ ] Unknown
- [ ] Basic
- [x] Extended
- [ ] Premium ($)
- [ ] Executive w/$

Activity Level

MEDIUM (LOW — HIGH)

Address
GO: PRSIG

PRC Publishing

Description
PRC's Database Publishing Services creates customized publications that reflect the specific information needs of their audiences. They are a leading publisher of database directories of all types.

Subjects
Catalogs, Computer Graphics, Database Publishing

Audience
Graphics professionals, publishers

Content Summary
PRC specializes in the combination of digital images and text data; in high volumes and at high speeds; and in customized layouts and electronic composition.

See Also
Graphics Forum

User Guide
- [x] Windows
- [x] DOS
- [x] Macintosh
- [ ] Terminal Emulation
- [x] VMS
- [x] UNIX
- [x] OS/2
- [ ] Other platform

Cost
- [ ] Unknown
- [x] Basic
- [ ] Extended
- [ ] Premium ($)
- [ ] Executive w/$

Activity Level
MEDIUM UNKNOWN (LOW — HIGH)

Address
GO: PRC

PRINTING

Kodak CD Forum

Description
Maintained by Kodak, this forum is devoted to Kodak CD products and technology, as well as related products.

Subjects
Computers, Photo-CD, Printing

Audience
Computer users, computer graphics designers

Content Summary
The library and message sections include Kodak News, Photo CD General, Photo CD Software, Writable CD, International, Color Management, Member Uploads, and others. The Kodak Printer library (Library 8) contains drivers, information, and press releases relating to Kodak's line of high-quality printers.

See Also
Graphics Forums, Graphics Forums, Graphics File Finder, Photography Forum

User Guide
- [x] Windows
- [x] DOS
- [x] Macintosh
- [ ] Terminal Emulation
- [ ] VMS
- [ ] UNIX
- [ ] OS/2
- [ ] Other platform

Cost
- [ ] Unknown
- [ ] Basic
- [x] Extended
- [ ] Premium ($)
- [ ] Executive w/$

Activity Level: MEDIUM

Address
GO: KODAK

PROGRAMMING

Dr. Dobb's Forum

Description
This is an "electronic" version of *Dr. Dobb's Journal*, a journal devoted to computer languages, tools, utilities, algorithms, and programming techniques. If you're interested in writing articles for the *Journal*, post them here for review. You might get published in the future.

Subjects
Computers, Programming, Utilities

Audience
Application developers, MIS personnel, system integrators

Content Summary
You can upload or download source code; find information on OS/2, UNIX, Macintosh, and Windows programming; and find listings (not text) of the articles and columns from the *Dr. Dobb's Journal* magazine. This forum is not intended to be a substitute for the magazine, but a complement to it.

See Also
MS Developers Relations Forum

User Guide
- ☑ Windows
- ☑ DOS
- ☑ Macintosh
- ☐ Terminal Emulation
- ☐ VMS
- ☑ UNIX
- ☑ OS/2
- ☐ Other platform

Cost
- ☐ Unknown
- ☐ Basic
- ☑ Extended
- ☐ Premium ($)
- ☐ Executive w/$

Activity Level: MEDIUM

Address
GO: DDJFORUM

PSYCHOLOGY

Personality Profile

Description
This forum contains two personality quizzes. One quiz tests how well you know yourself; the other tests how well you know someone else.

Subjects
Psychology, Relationships

Audience
General public

Content Summary
The first area tests your knowledge of yourself. It contains questions about your psychological self, physical self, spiritual self, and your relationships and decision-making skills. After you finish this test, you see a graph that rates you in eight different areas. The other test rates how much you know about the people who are important to you. Tests are available for spouses, roommates, siblings, parents, and children.

See Also
Biorhythms

User Guide
- ☑ Windows
- ☑ DOS
- ☑ Macintosh
- ☑ Terminal Emulation
- ☑ VMS
- ☑ UNIX
- ☑ OS/2
- ☐ Other platform

Cost
- ☐ Unknown
- ☐ Basic
- ☑ Extended
- ☐ Premium ($)
- ☐ Executive w/$

Activity Level: UNKNOWN

Address
GO: TMC-90

Public Brand Software (PBS) Applications Forum

Description
This ZiffNet forum is a library of high-quality shareware, including DOS, Windows, and OS/2 applications, as well as communication programs.

Subjects
Computers, ZiffNet

Audience
Computer users

Content Summary
The library and message sections contain several areas for discussions and downloading PBS applications. The library sections include Hot Off the Presses, Reviewer's Picks, DOS, Windows, OS/2, Communications, WP and Text Editors, ZD Awards Nominees, and PBS Information.

See Also
Public Brand Software Home Forum

User Guide
- ☑ Windows
- ☑ DOS
- ☐ Macintosh
- ☐ Terminal Emulation
- ☐ VMS
- ☐ UNIX
- ☑ OS/2
- ☐ Other platform

Cost
- ☐ Unknown
- ☐ Basic
- ☑ Extended
- ☐ Premium ($)
- ☐ Executive w/$

Activity Level

Address
GO: **PBSAPPS**

Public Brand Software (PBS) Home Forum

Description
The Public Brand Software (PBS) Home Forum is a library of top-rated shareware programs for home, hobby, and education.

Subjects
Computers, ZiffNet

Audience
Computer users

Content Summary
Library sections include reference data and files in the news. Some of the library names include Hot Off the Presses, Reviewer's Picks, Home & Hobby, Education, Gutenburg, and more.

See Also
Public Brand Software Applications Forum

User Guide
- ☑ Windows
- ☑ DOS
- ☐ Macintosh
- ☐ Terminal Emulation
- ☐ VMS
- ☐ UNIX
- ☑ OS/2
- ☐ Other platform

Cost
- ☐ Unknown
- ☐ Basic
- ☑ Extended
- ☐ Premium ($)
- ☐ Executive w/$

Activity Level

Address
GO: **PBSHOME**

PUBLIC RELATIONS

PR and Marketing Forum

Description
This forum is a gathering place for public relations, advertising, marketing, research, and public affairs professionals.

Subjects
Advertising, Marketing, Public Relations

Audience
Advertising professionals, market research specialists, public relations personnel

Content Summary
Members use the forum's message libraries to communicate on subjects of interest to the communications field. Other features include Jobs Online, from which members can review more than 100 job openings. Members can post resumes on as well as listing openings from their respective firms. Other sections include: starting up a business, marketing, media relations and crisis communications, new products and services, creativity, research, advertising and direct mail, electronic newsletters, desktop publishing, professional development, political campaigns and programming, creativity development, educational programs, and technology tools.

Online college courses are offered in advertising, public relations, and print and electronic journalism.

See Also
Media Newsletter

User Guide
- ☑ Windows
- ☑ DOS
- ☑ Macintosh
- ☐ Terminal Emulation
- ☑ VMS
- ☑ UNIX
- ☑ OS/2
- ☐ Other platform

Cost
- ☐ Unknown
- ☐ Basic
- ☑ Extended
- ☐ Premium ($)
- ☐ Executive w/$

Activity Level

Address
GO: **PRSIG**

PUBLIC SAFETY

Safetynet Forum

Description
This forum provides and open communication channel for people and professionals interested in sharing information on any topic of public safety.

Subjects
Crime, Fire Fighting, Public Safety

Audience
Firefighters, health workers, police

Content Summary
This forum's libraries and message areas provide a wide assortment of information pertaining to public safety. A graphics library contains pictures of actual rescue attempts, crime scenes, and fires. Some of the pictures are graphic in nature. Of general interest are Red Cross disaster information, lists of public safety hotlines and bulletin boards, and copies of the Environmental Informer Newsletter. Separate libraries are available for firefighters, police, and public heath workers.

See Also
ZiffNet Crime and Violence Forum

User Guide
- ☑ Windows
- ☑ DOS
- ☐ Macintosh
- ☐ Terminal Emulation
- ☐ VMS
- ☐ UNIX
- ☐ OS/2
- ☐ Other platform

Cost
- ☐ Unknown
- ☐ Basic
- ☑ Extended
- ☐ Premium ($)
- ☐ Executive w/$

Activity Level
MEDIUM (LOW — HIGH)

Address
GO: **SAFETYNET**

PUBLISHING

Media Newsletters

Description
The Broadcast & Publishing section of PTS Newsletter Database contains articles from leading newsletters covering broadcasting and publishing industries.

Subjects
Broadcasting, Newsletters, Publishing

Audience
Researchers, general public

Content Summary
These newsletters are a unique source of facts, figures, analyses, and current information on changing market and company conditions, company activities, new products and technologies, and government policies and trade agreements. The information available for an article includes title, newsletter name, publisher, and date of publication, as well as the full text of the article. An individual article may not include all of this information. You can choose from Description, Search Guidelines, Pricing Information, Media Newsletters Example, and Access Media Newsletters.

See Also
IQuest($)

User Guide
- ☑ Windows
- ☑ DOS
- ☑ Macintosh
- ☐ Terminal Emulation
- ☑ VMS
- ☑ UNIX
- ☑ OS/2
- ☑ Other platform

Cost
- ☐ Unknown
- ☐ Basic
- ☐ Extended
- ☑ Premium ($)
- ☐ Executive w/$

Activity Level
UNKNOWN (LOW — MEDIUM — HIGH)

Address
GO: **MEDIANEWS**

Q

Quality Paperbacks

Description
This forum provides an online paperback book club. If you don't like leaving the comfort of home to shop, then this forum is for you. You can shop for all types of paperback books right from your home or office.

Subjects
Books, Online Shopping, Reading

Audience
Reading enthusiasts, students

Content Summary
Once you join this forum, you receive the QPB review every three-and-one-half weeks. The review contains book reviews and describes the current book selection. You can cancel your membership at any time. Membership is automatically cancelled if you do not purchase at least one book in any six-month period.

See Also
Book of the Month Club Forum, Book Review Digest Forum, Books in Print Forum, Books on Tape Forum

User Guide
- ☑ Windows
- ☑ DOS
- ☑ Macintosh
- ☑ Terminal Emulation
- ☑ VMS
- ☑ UNIX
- ☑ OS/2
- ☐ Other platform

Cost
- ☐ Unknown
- ☑ Basic
- ☐ Extended
- ☐ Premium ($)
- ☐ Executive w/$

Activity Level

Address
GO: **QPB1**

Quick Picture Forum

Description
This forum provides images, clip art, missing children photos, and GIF images with fewer than 33 colors. These pictures tend to look better on PCs that have lower-resolution monitors.

Subjects
Computers, Computer Graphics

Audience
Computer graphics, graphics artists, photographers

Content Summary
From the library sections, you can download clip art, photos, and various other graphics files.

See Also
Graphics Corner, IBM File Finder

User Guide
- ☑ Windows
- ☑ DOS
- ☑ Macintosh
- ☐ Terminal Emulation
- ☐ VMS
- ☐ UNIX
- ☐ OS/2
- ☐ Other platform

Cost
- ☐ Unknown
- ☐ Basic
- ☑ Extended
- ☐ Premium ($)
- ☐ Executive w/$

Activity Level

Address
GO: **QPICS**

R

RADIO

HamNet Forum

Description
In this forum, users can interact with other Ham Radio enthusiasts.

Subjects
Radios

Audience
Rave enthusiasts, radio enthusiasts (UK)

Content Summary
The HamNet forum is dedicated to amateur radio and related topics, including shortwave listening, satellite television, and other related topics. If you are an expert or a novice, this forum welcomes your questions, responses, and membership. Some of the specific libraries include the Scanning Library, Amateur Satellites, CW / Morse Code, FCC & Regulatory, and Vendor Support.

See Also
Broadcast Professionals Area

User Guide
- ☑ Windows
- ☑ DOS
- ☑ Macintosh
- ☐ Terminal Emulation
- ☑ VMS
- ☑ UNIX
- ☑ OS/2
- ☑ Other platform

Cost
- ☐ Unknown
- ☐ Basic
- ☑ Extended
- ☐ Premium ($)
- ☐ Executive w/$

Activity Level

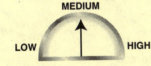

MEDIUM (LOW — HIGH)

Address
GO: **HAMNET**

Rare Diseases Database

Description
Developed and maintained by the National Organization for Rare Diseases (NORD), this database forum was constructed so that patients with rare disorders and their families can understand the disorder and its implications.

Subjects
AIDS, Diseases, Health

Audience
AIDS suffers, health care providers, families of the ill

Content Summary
This forum contains a database that provides information on all rare diseases, their treatment, medicines, and implications. Newsletters from several national organizations, such as NORD, Parkinsons Foundation, and the Multiple Sclerosis Foundation, are available. Current information on AIDS and related illnesses also can be found.

See Also
Paperchase-MEDLINE

User Guide
- ☑ Windows
- ☑ DOS
- ☑ Macintosh
- ☑ Terminal Emulation
- ☑ VMS
- ☑ UNIX
- ☑ OS/2
- ☐ Other platform

Cost
- ☐ Unknown
- ☐ Basic
- ☐ Extended
- ☑ Premium ($)
- ☐ Executive w/$

Activity Level

UNKNOWN (LOW — MEDIUM — HIGH)

Address
GO: **NORD**

READING

Quality Paperbacks

Description
This forum provides an online paperback book club. If you don't like leaving the comfort of home to shop, then this forum is for you. You can shop for all types of paperback books right from your home or office.

Subjects
Books, Online Shopping, Reading

Audience
Reading enthusiasts, students

Content Summary
Once you join this forum, you receive the QPB review every three-and-one-half weeks. The review contains book reviews and describes the current book selection. You can cancel your membership at any time. Membership is automatically cancelled if you do not purchase at least one book in any six-month period.

See Also
Book of the Month Club Forum, Book Review Digest Forum, Books in Print Forum, Books on Tape Forum

User Guide
- ☑ Windows
- ☑ DOS
- ☑ Macintosh
- ☑ Terminal Emulation
- ☑ VMS
- ☑ UNIX
- ☑ OS/2
- ☐ Other platform

Cost
- ☐ Unknown
- ☑ Basic
- ☐ Extended
- ☐ Premium ($)
- ☐ Executive w/$

Activity Level
UNKNOWN (LOW – MEDIUM – HIGH)

Address
GO: QPB1

REAL ESTATE

Homefinder By AMS

Description
Looking for a new home? Are you relocating to a new city? Use this service to help you find what you're looking for.

Subjects
Real Estate

Audience
General public, real estate brokers

Content Summary
From the Homefinder by AMS main menu, you can choose from several different options, including Community Information/Relocation Consultation, Schoolmatch - School System Evaluations, Right Choice, Inc. - Cost of Living Analysis, and Capability Corporation (CAPCO) - Job Search Services. You also can read testimonials from other users, make referrals, and leave messages to the service.

See Also
Family Handyman Forum

User Guide
- ☑ Windows
- ☑ DOS
- ☑ Macintosh
- ☐ Terminal Emulation
- ☑ VMS
- ☑ UNIX
- ☑ OS/2
- ☑ Other platform

Cost
- ☐ Unknown
- ☑ Basic
- ☐ Extended
- ☐ Premium ($)
- ☐ Executive w/$

Activity Level
UNKNOWN (LOW – MEDIUM – HIGH)

Address
GO: HF

RECREATION

Adventures in Travel

Description
Articles and stories about worldwide travels, prepared by professional travel writer Lee Foster.

Subjects
Travel

Audience
Travelers

Content Summary
This forum's main menu contains the current article, Earlier Adventures in Travel articles, questions and comments area, and more.

See Also
Travel Forum

User Guide
- ☑ Windows
- ☑ DOS
- ☑ Macintosh
- ☐ Terminal Emulation
- ☑ VMS
- ☑ UNIX
- ☑ OS/2
- ☑ Other platform

Cost
- ☐ Unknown
- ☐ Basic
- ☑ Extended
- ☐ Premium ($)
- ☐ Executive w/$

Activity Level
UNKNOWN (LOW – MEDIUM – HIGH)

Address
GO: AIT

California Forum

Description
The California Forum contains a wealth of information on California, its better known residents, the history of California, and California today.

Subjects
Recreation

Audience
Californians

Recreation – Reference

Content Summary
Some of the libraries that you'll find in this forum include San Diego, Southern California, LA Basin, SF Bay Area, and more.

See Also
Travel Forum

User Guide
- ☑ Windows
- ☑ DOS
- ☑ Macintosh
- ☐ Terminal Emulation
- ☐ VMS
- ☑ UNIX
- ☐ OS/2
- ☐ Other platform

Cost
- ☐ Unknown
- ☐ Basic
- ☑ Extended
- ☐ Premium ($)
- ☐ Executive w/$

Activity Level
MEDIUM (arrow pointing up)

Address
GO: **CALFORUM**

Warner Bros. Song Preview

Description
This is an online area offering 30-second sound clips from some of Warner Bros. Records' recent releases.

Subjects
Entertainment, Recreation

Audience
Musicians, music enthusiasts

Content Summary
The sound clips enable users to review sound clips of popular recordings so that they can find the music they like. Users also can find out tour and release dates of popular artists.

See Also
Entertainment Center Forum

User Guide
- ☑ Windows
- ☑ DOS
- ☑ Macintosh
- ☐ Terminal Emulation
- ☑ VMS
- ☑ UNIX
- ☑ OS/2
- ☐ Other platform

Cost
- ☐ Unknown
- ☐ Basic
- ☑ Extended
- ☐ Premium ($)
- ☐ Executive w/$

Activity Level

UNKNOWN

Address
GO: **WBPREVIEW**

Recreational Vehicle Forum

Description
This forum is for all people who enjoy camping in tent trailers, travel trailers, fifth-wheels, and motor homes. If you are an experienced camper or are just looking for a motor home, this forum can help.

Subjects
Camping, Motor Homes, Travel

Audience
Camping enthusiasts, travel enthusiasts, RV enthusiasts

Content Summary
This forum not only provides up-to-date information about products and services for the travel trailer industry, but also provides articles and discussions on where to go, where to stay, and what to do. Participants also state opinions and make recommendations on which RV to purchase and where to go for service. There's even a classified section if you are looking to purchase a recreational vehicle.

See Also
Travel Forum

User Guide
- ☑ Windows
- ☑ DOS
- ☑ Macintosh
- ☐ Terminal Emulation
- ☑ VMS
- ☑ UNIX
- ☑ OS/2
- ☐ Other platform

Cost
- ☐ Unknown
- ☐ Basic
- ☑ Extended
- ☐ Premium ($)
- ☐ Executive w/$

Activity Level
MEDIUM (arrow pointing to LOW)

Address
GO: **RVFORUM**

REFERENCE

Information USA

Description
Are you looking for something? Do you need information but aren't sure where to get it? Start with the Information USA service. It will help you get started.

Subjects
Government, Information, Reference

Audience
General public, researchers

Reference – Religion

Content Summary
This service, extracted from the *Information USA* reference book by Matthew Lesko, provides information and access to free or nearly free government publications in three areas: government publications and services; American Embassies and consulates; and travel information. From the main menu, you can select from several options, including Introduction/Talk to Mr. Lesko, Consumer Power, Careers and Workplace, Giveaways to Entrepreneurs, Selling to the Government, and much more. You have to see this service to believe it. It's full of very useful information.

See Also
IQuest($)

User Guide
- ☑ Windows
- ☑ DOS
- ☑ Macintosh
- ☐ Terminal Emulation
- ☑ VMS
- ☑ UNIX
- ☑ OS/2
- ☑ Other platform

Cost
- ☐ Unknown
- ☐ Basic
- ☑ Extended
- ☐ Premium ($)
- ☐ Executive w/$

Activity Level
UNKNOWN (LOW – MEDIUM – HIGH)

Address
GO: **INFOUSA**

RELATIONSHIPS

Personality Profile

Description
This forum contains two personality quizzes. One quiz tests how well you know yourself; the other tests how well you know someone else.

Subjects
Psychology, Relationships

Audience
General public

Content Summary
The first area tests your knowledge of yourself. It contains questions about your psychological self, physical self, spiritual self, and your relationships and decision-making skills. After you finish this test, you see a graph that rates you in eight different areas. The other test rates how much you know about the people who are important to you. Tests are available for spouses, roommates, siblings, parents, and children.

See Also
Biorhythms

User Guide
- ☑ Windows
- ☑ DOS
- ☑ Macintosh
- ☑ Terminal Emulation
- ☑ VMS
- ☑ UNIX
- ☑ OS/2
- ☐ Other platform

Cost
- ☐ Unknown
- ☐ Basic
- ☑ Extended
- ☐ Premium ($)
- ☐ Executive w/$

Activity Level
UNKNOWN (LOW – MEDIUM – HIGH)

Address
GO: **TMC-90**

RELIGION

Issues Forum

Description
Devoted to current topics and issues, the Issues Forum discusses topics such as Afro-Americanism, parenting, human rights, and others.

Subjects
Current Events, Human Rights, Politics, Religion

Audience
General public

Content Summary
This special interest group is devoted to discussions of a wide variety of issues. Currently, there are sections for topics such as Afro-American issues, parenting issues, human rights, unexplained phenomena, men and women's issues, Asian-American issues, and others. The library and message sections include Culture & Society, Between the Sexes, Canadian Issues, Politics & Religion, and more. Look in Library 9, Rush H. Limbaugh, for summaries of Rush's show.

See Also
Entertainment Center, HSX Open Forum

User Guide
- ☑ Windows
- ☑ DOS
- ☑ Macintosh
- ☐ Terminal Emulation
- ☑ VMS
- ☑ UNIX
- ☑ OS/2
- ☑ Other platform

Cost
- ☐ Unknown
- ☐ Basic
- ☑ Extended
- ☐ Premium ($)
- ☐ Executive w/$

Activity Level

Address
GO: **ISSUESFORUM**

Religion Forum

Description
People of all faiths and religions meet in this forum to discuss spiritual, ethical, and values issues. The discussions are open and courtesy is given to all.

Subjects
Christianity, Occult, Religions of the World

Audience
Clergy, religious, seminary students

Content Summary
The library and message areas contain various places to discuss religions of the world, study the Bible, research ministry issues, take part in an online prayer and bible study group, or read press releases on new religious products such as a CD-ROM–based Bible study guide.

See Also
Participate

User Guide
- ☑ Windows
- ☑ DOS
- ☑ Macintosh
- ☐ Terminal Emulation
- ☑ VMS
- ☑ UNIX
- ☑ OS/2
- ☑ Other platform

Cost
- ☐ Unknown
- ☐ Basic
- ☑ Extended
- ☐ Premium ($)
- ☐ Executive w/$

Activity Level

Address
GO: **RELIGION**

SDAs On-Line

Description
This is a forum for Seventh-Day Adventists around the world. (Prospective members must order a special version of CIM from (800)268-7171 to join the forum.)

Subjects
Religion

Audience
Seventh-Day Adventists

Content Summary
The libraries include Adventist news, Bible and theology discussions, pastoral practices, church resources, missions, and women's ministries.

See Also
Religion Forum

User Guide
- ☑ Windows
- ☑ DOS
- ☑ Macintosh
- ☐ Terminal Emulation
- ☐ VMS
- ☐ UNIX
- ☐ OS/2
- ☐ Other platform

Cost
- ☐ Unknown
- ☐ Basic
- ☑ Extended
- ☐ Premium ($)
- ☐ Executive w/$

Activity Level

Address
GO: **SDA**

REMOTE COMMUNICATIONS

Dr. Neuhaus Forum

Description
This forum is devoted to German-speaking people interested in Dr. Neuhaus communications products.

Subjects
Computers, Fax Boards, Modems, Remote Communications

Audience
MIS personnel

Content Summary
This forum is entirely in German. You can get technical support and information on products such as FURY modems, FAXY fax boards, and NICCY ISDN modems. You also can find information and support for Carbon Copy.

See Also
Modem Vendor Forum, Palmtop Forum

User Guide
- ☑ Windows
- ☑ DOS
- ☐ Macintosh
- ☐ Terminal Emulation
- ☐ VMS
- ☐ UNIX
- ☐ OS/2
- ☐ Other platform

Cost
- ☐ Unknown
- ☐ Basic
- ☑ Extended
- ☐ Premium ($)
- ☐ Executive w/$

498

Remote Communications – Research

Activity Level

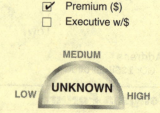

Address
GO: **NEUHAUS**

RESEARCH

Dissertation Abstracts

Description
Contains references to U.S. and Canadian Ph.D. dissertations since 1861 and master theses since 1962. Includes abstracts of dissertations from 1980 and on. Professional (such as MD) and honorary degrees are not included.

Subjects
Dissertations, Education, Research

Audience
Graduate students, historians, professors, researchers, students

Content Summary
Each dissertation includes author, title, date of publication, college, and degree for which the dissertation was submitted. Dissertation Abstracts is published and copyrighted by University Microfilms International and made available by BRS Information Technologies.

You should note that Dissertation Abstracts includes transaction charges in addition to CompuServe base connect rates. You can see a running total of transaction charges on the Dissertation Abstract menu pages. Connect charges are not included in the displayed total.

The following are rates for using Dissertation Abstracts:

- Search (retrieves up to 10 titles): $5
- Additional titles (in groups of 10): $5
- Full reference, with abstract where available (selected from the titles): $5 each

In addition to connect time charges, there is a $1 charge for a search that retrieves no titles.

See Also
IQuest Database

User Guide
- ☑ Windows
- ☑ DOS
- ☑ Macintosh
- ☑ Terminal Emulation
- ☑ VMS
- ☑ UNIX
- ☑ OS/2
- ☐ Other platform

Cost
- ☐ Unknown
- ☐ Basic
- ☐ Extended
- ☑ Premium ($)
- ☐ Executive w/$

Activity Level

(UNKNOWN)

Address
GO: **DISSERTATION**

IQuest

Description
With access to over 800 databases on topics such as accounting, aerospace, computers, and more, IQuest is one of the largest research services in the world.

Subjects
Databases, Information Retrieval, Research

Audience
General public, librarians, researchers

Content Summary
CompuServe members have seamless interaction with the IQuest reference and information service. IQuest provides access to over 800 databases, including business, government, research, news, popular entertainment, and sports. IQuest is a menu-based service that prompts you for your information, and then searches for you. Accessing databases from information suppliers such as Dialog Information Services, Inc., BRS Online Products, NewsNet, Inc., and Data-Star, IQuest executes the search and displays the results to you. IQuest can be expensive if you don't think out your searches beforehand, so be sure to read the Pricing Information on the main menu before you ask for too much.

See Also
Dun's Market Identifiers($), Executive News Service($), TRW Bus. Credit Reports($), Official Airline Guide EE($)

User Guide
- ☑ Windows
- ☑ DOS
- ☑ Macintosh
- ☑ Terminal Emulation
- ☑ VMS
- ☑ UNIX
- ☑ OS/2
- ☑ Other platform

Cost
- ☐ Unknown
- ☐ Basic
- ☐ Extended
- ☐ Premium ($)
- ☑ Executive w/$

Activity Level

Address
GO: **IQUEST**

Knowledge Index

Description
Access over 100 popular databases from the Knowledge Index service.

Subjects
Database, General Interest, Research

Audience
General interest, general public, researchers

Content Summary
Knowledge Index is a service that gives you evening and weekend access to over 100 popular full-text and bibliographic databases at reduced rates. With Knowledge Index, you can access over 50,000 journals on a wide variety of topics. Many of the Knowledge Index databases have the complete text of articles available online. You can order a hard-copy printout of those that have only a citation available. The price is $.40 per minute ($24 per hour) and includes CompuServe standard connect rates up to and including 9600 Baud.

See Also
IQuest

User Guide
- [x] Windows
- [x] DOS
- [x] Macintosh
- [ ] Terminal Emulation
- [x] VMS
- [x] UNIX
- [x] OS/2
- [ ] Other platform

Cost
- [ ] Unknown
- [ ] Basic
- [ ] Extended
- [x] Premium ($)
- [ ] Executive w/$

Activity Level

Address
GO: **KI**

PaperChase-MEDLINE Forum

Description
This forum provides access to the world's largest biomedical database. The information is prepared by the National Library of Medicine and has more than seven million references from 4,000 journals.

Subjects
Health, Medicine, Research

Audience
Dentists, physicians, scientists

Content Summary
References are available from 1966. Updates to articles are added weekly. Because the database is so extensive, you should enter a very narrow topic of research. Cost can be prohibitive. The cost on weekdays from 7 p.m. until 8 a.m. or any time on weekends is $18 per hour. The cost on weekdays from 8 a.m. until 7 p.m. is $24 per hour. Photocopies are available for $10 by first-class mail or $25 by fax.

See Also
Rare Disease Database Forum

User Guide
- [x] Windows
- [x] DOS
- [x] Macintosh
- [ ] Terminal Emulation
- [x] VMS
- [x] UNIX
- [x] OS/2
- [ ] Other platform

Cost
- [ ] Unknown
- [ ] Basic
- [ ] Extended
- [x] Premium ($)
- [ ] Executive w/$

Activity Level

Address
GO: **PAPERCHASE**

Patent Research Center

Description
This forum provides quick access to summaries of U.S. patents granted in chemical, mechanical, electrical, and design categories.

Subjects
Inventions, Legal Research, Research

Audience
Inventors, legal researchers, researchers

Content Summary
This forum contains summaries of patents granted internationally since the mid 1970s. Databases searched include the Claims/U.S. Patent Abstracts from 1950 to the present and the World Patents Index from 1963 to the present. You enter a search by typing a name, word, or phrase that describes the item you are searching for. The search can return up to 10 articles.

See Also
Legal Research Center

User Guide
- [x] Windows
- [x] DOS
- [x] Macintosh
- [ ] Terminal Emulation
- [x] VMS
- [x] UNIX
- [x] OS/2
- [ ] Other platform

500 Research – Reviews

Cost
- [ ] Unknown
- [ ] Basic
- [ ] Extended
- [x] Premium ($)
- [ ] Executive w/$

Activity Level

Address
GO: **PATENT**

Retirement Living Forum

Description
Managed by the Setting Priorities for Retirement Years (SPRY) Foundation, this forum is dedicated to making the retirement years happy and productive. Information and discussions on a wide range of topics is available to present and future retirees.

Subjects
Aging, Medicare, Social Security

Audience
Family of retirees, gerontologists, retirees

Content Summary
This forum's contributors include the Social Security Administration; the National Institute on Aging; the National Heart, Lung, and Blood Institute; the Traveling Healthy and Comfortably Newsletter; and the Pension Rights Center. Discussions can be found on eating right, housing, dealing with family, and Medicare.

See Also
Health/Fitness Forum

User Guide
- [x] Windows
- [x] DOS
- [x] Macintosh
- [ ] Terminal Emulation
- [x] VMS
- [x] UNIX
- [x] OS/2
- [ ] Other platform

Cost
- [ ] Unknown
- [ ] Basic
- [x] Extended
- [ ] Premium ($)
- [ ] Executive w/$

Activity Level

Address
GO: **RETIREMENT**

Reuters News Pictures Forum

Description
This forum contains the largest online source of news images from around the world. Also included are photographs of historical significance from the Bettman Archives.

Subjects
Current Events, News, Photographs

Audience
News enthusiasts, photographers

Content Summary
Photographs of interest to the United States, world, entertainment industry, and sports are featured. Note that photographs are protected by U.S. and international copyrights and are for personal use only.

See Also
AP Sports Forum, Associated Press Online Forum, Detroit Free Press

User Guide
- [x] Windows
- [x] DOS
- [x] Macintosh
- [ ] Terminal Emulation
- [x] VMS
- [x] UNIX
- [x] OS/2
- [ ] Other platform

Cost
- [ ] Unknown
- [ ] Basic
- [x] Extended
- [ ] Premium ($)
- [ ] Executive w/$

Activity Level

Address
GO: **NEWSPI**

REVIEWS

Roger Ebert's Movie Reviews

Description
If you love movies, then this forum is for you. Get the thumbs up or thumbs down on recent movies by Roger Ebert himself.

Subjects
Film, Movies, Reviews

Audience
Film students, movie critics, movie enthusiasts

Content Summary
You can receive an alphabetical listing of recent movies with Roger Ebert's familiar star rating. You also can receive film reviews by searching by movie name, actor or actress name, or director name. Included in this forum are celebrity interviews with such well-known personalities as Oliver Stone. Other areas of interest include a glossary of movie terms, the 10 best films of the year, and a special area in which you can correspond with Roger Ebert.

See Also
Movie Reviews Forum, SHOWBIZ Quiz Forum

User Guide
- ☑ Windows
- ☑ DOS
- ☑ Macintosh
- ☐ Terminal Emulation
- ☑ VMS
- ☑ UNIX
- ☑ OS/2
- ☐ Other platform

Cost
- ☐ Unknown
- ☑ Basic
- ☐ Extended
- ☐ Premium ($)
- ☐ Executive w/$

Activity Level
MEDIUM (arrow pointing up)

Address
GO: **EBERT**

ROCK ENTHUSIASTS

Rocknet Forum

Description
This forum provides the most up-to-date and accurate information on the rock community.

Subjects
Entertainment, Music, Rock Enthusiasts, Video

Audience
Musicians, rock enthusiasts

Content Summary
This forum's libraries cover the full range of rock topics. Topics included are reviews of concerts and music, lists of alternative radio stations, coverage of the musical group Grateful Dead, heavy metal, vintage rock, new music, online conversations with rock personalities, and graphics of musical group logos and photographs taken at concerts.

See Also
Rock Video Monthly

User Guide
- ☑ Windows
- ☑ DOS
- ☑ Macintosh
- ☐ Terminal Emulation
- ☐ VMS
- ☐ UNIX
- ☐ OS/2
- ☐ Other platform

Cost
- ☐ Unknown
- ☐ Basic
- ☑ Extended
- ☐ Premium ($)
- ☐ Executive w/$

Activity Level
MEDIUM (arrow pointing up)

Address
GO: **ROCKNET**

ROCK MUSIC

Music Industry Forum

Description
Find files and information about the music industry in this forum. This forum evolved from the Music Vendor Forum to include various vendors and music news.

Subjects
Music, Rock Music, Musical Instruments

Audience
Music enthusiasts, general public

Content Summary
You can find library and message sections that include topics such as Music News, South by Southwest, CMC, Austin Music Chan, Gibson Guitar Corporation, Guitar World, Touring/Roadies, and DJs/Radio.

See Also
Music Hall, Music Vendor Forum

User Guide
- ☑ Windows
- ☑ DOS
- ☑ Macintosh
- ☐ Terminal Emulation
- ☑ VMS
- ☑ UNIX
- ☑ OS/2
- ☑ Other platform

Cost
- ☐ Unknown
- ☐ Basic
- ☑ Extended
- ☐ Premium ($)
- ☐ Executive w/$

Activity Level
MEDIUM (arrow pointing toward HIGH)

Address
GO: **INMUSIC**

Music Vendor Forum

Description
The Music Vendor Forum is known as the "Recording Industry Forum" that enables you to communicate directly with selected vendors. You can download sound files, graphics, tour dates, and various news reports about the music industry's hottest performers.

502 Rock Music – Roger Ebert's Movie Reviews

Subjects
Music, Rock Music

Audience
Music enthusiasts, general public

Content Summary
You can find information from several music vendors, including Warner Brothers, PolyGram, Virgin Records, Racer Records, Kudos Records, Geffen Records, RCA Records, and Arista Records.

See Also
Music Industry Forum

User Guide
- ☑ Windows
- ☑ DOS
- ☑ Macintosh
- ☐ Terminal Emulation
- ☑ VMS
- ☑ UNIX
- ☑ OS/2
- ☑ Other platform

Cost
- ☐ Unknown
- ☐ Basic
- ☑ Extended
- ☐ Premium ($)
- ☐ Executive w/$

Activity Level

Address
GO: MUSICVEN

Rocknet Forum

Description
This forum provides the most up-to-date and accurate information on the rock community.

Subjects
Entertainment, Music, Rock Enthusiasts, Video

Audience
Musicians, rock enthusiasts

Content Summary
This forum's libraries cover the full range of rock topics. Topics included are reviews of concerts and music, lists of alternative radio stations, coverage of the musical group Grateful Dead, heavy metal, vintage rock, new music, online conversations with rock personalities, and graphics of musical group logos and photographs taken at concerts.

See Also
Rock Video Monthly

User Guide
- ☑ Windows
- ☑ DOS
- ☑ Macintosh
- ☐ Terminal Emulation
- ☐ VMS
- ☐ UNIX
- ☐ OS/2
- ☐ Other platform

Cost
- ☐ Unknown
- ☐ Basic
- ☑ Extended
- ☐ Premium ($)
- ☐ Executive w/$

Activity Level

Address
GO: ROCKNET

Roger Ebert's Movie Reviews

Description
If you love movies, then this forum is for you. Get the thumbs up or thumbs down on recent movies by Roger Ebert himself.

Subjects
Film, Movies, Reviews

Audience
Film students, movie critics, movie enthusiasts

Content Summary
You can receive an alphabetical listing of recent movies with Roger Ebert's familiar star rating. You also can receive film reviews by searching by movie name, actor or actress name, or director name. Included in this forum are celebrity interviews with such well-known personalities as Oliver Stone. Other areas of interest include a glossary of movie terms, the 10 best films of the year, and a special area in which you can correspond with Roger Ebert.

See Also
Movie Reviews Forum, SHOWBIZ Quiz Forum

User Guide
- ☑ Windows
- ☑ DOS
- ☑ Macintosh
- ☐ Terminal Emulation
- ☑ VMS
- ☑ UNIX
- ☑ OS/2
- ☑ Other platform

Cost
- ☐ Unknown
- ☑ Basic
- ☐ Extended
- ☐ Premium ($)
- ☐ Executive w/$

Activity Level MEDIUM

Address
GO: EBERT

ROLE-PLAYING GAMES

Fantasy/Role-Playing Adventure

Play role-playing games such as British Legends or Island of Kesmai, as well as access the Role-Playing Forum and Play-by-Mail Forum.

Subjects
Games, Role-Playing Games

Audience
Game players, game theorists, general public

Content Summary
From the Fantasy/Role-Playing Adventure main menu, you can select to play British Legends or Island of Kesmai. British Legends is a multi-player adventure game filled with mystery, dense forests, an island, a cottage, and much more. In Island of Kesmai, you encounter many computer-run characters as you travel across the many acres of land on the Island of Kesmai, where a group of magicians live to escape persecution. From the main menu, you also can choose to go to the Role-Playing or Play-by-Mail Forums.

See Also
Gamers Forum, Island of Kesmai, British Legends, Modem Games Forum

User Guide
- [ ] Windows
- [ ] DOS
- [ ] Macintosh
- [x] Terminal Emulation
- [ ] VMS
- [ ] UNIX
- [ ] OS/2
- [ ] Other platform

Cost
- [ ] Unknown
- [x] Basic
- [ ] Extended
- [ ] Premium ($)
- [ ] Executive w/$

Activity Level
UNKNOWN (LOW / MEDIUM / HIGH)

Address
GO: **ADVENT**

S

Safetynet Forum

Description
This forum provides and open communication channel for people and professionals interested in sharing information on any topic of public safety.

Subjects
Crime, Fire Fighting, Public Safety

Audience
Firefighters, health workers, police

Content Summary
This forum's libraries and message areas provide a wide assortment of information pertaining to public safety. A graphics library contains pictures of actual rescue attempts, crime scenes, and fires. Some of the pictures are graphic in nature. Of general interest are Red Cross disaster information, lists of public safety hotlines and bulletin boards, and copies of the Environmental Informer Newsletter. Separate libraries are available for firefighters, police, and public heath workers.

See Also
ZiffNet Crime and Violence Forum

User Guide
- ☑ Windows
- ☑ DOS
- ☐ Macintosh
- ☐ Terminal Emulation
- ☐ VMS
- ☐ UNIX
- ☐ OS/2
- ☐ Other platform

Cost
- ☐ Unknown
- ☐ Basic
- ☑ Extended
- ☐ Premium ($)
- ☐ Executive w/$

Activity Level

Address
GO: **SAFETYNET**

Sailing Forum

Description
This forum provides information and discussion groups to members who are avid sailors or who dream of sailing the seas.

Subjects
Boats, Yachts

Audience
Sailing enthusiasts

Content Summary
This forum provides open discussion of all types of sailing topics. Libraries include discussions of heavy weather survival tactics, sailor folklore, real-life sea stories of safety lessons, and classified ads for boating-related supplies.

See Also
Sports Forum

User Guide
- ☑ Windows
- ☑ DOS
- ☑ Macintosh
- ☐ Terminal Emulation
- ☑ VMS
- ☑ UNIX
- ☑ OS/2
- ☐ Other platform

Cost
- ☐ Unknown
- ☐ Basic
- ☑ Extended
- ☐ Premium ($)
- ☐ Executive w/$

Activity Level

Address
GO: **SAILING**

Santa Cruz Operation Forum

Description
This forum supports all SCO end users, resellers, developers, and SCO partners. It is supported by Santa Cruz Operations (SCO).

Subjects
Computers, SCO, UNIX

Audience
Computer programmers, SCO users, UNIX users

Content Summary
The library and message areas contain information about SCO's product information, bug fixes, and advice to users. Libraries include topics on UNIX binaries, Xenix binaries, Non-UNIX files, source code, third-party products, SCO product press releases, and SCO training and certification.

See Also
Computing Support Forum, UNIX Forum

User Guide
- ☑ Windows
- ☑ DOS
- ☐ Macintosh
- ☐ Terminal Emulation
- ☐ VMS
- ☐ UNIX
- ☐ OS/2
- ☐ Other platform

Cost
- ☐ Unknown
- ☐ Basic
- ☑ Extended
- ☐ Premium ($)
- ☐ Executive w/$

Activity Level

LOW — MEDIUM — HIGH

Address
GO: **SCOFORUM**

SCIENCE

Dinosaur Forum

Description
If you like dinosaurs or know someone who does, you should visit or join this forum. This forum is devoted to information about dinosaurs, including scientific discussions, dinosaurs in popular culture (such as movies), and many other dinosaur-related topics.

Subjects
Dinosaurs, Science

Audience
Archaeologists, dinosaur lovers, paleontologists, scientists

Content Summary
The library and message forums contain information that any dinosaur lover would like, such as dinosaur facts and reports, drawings, sketches, FLI animations, conference information, and field reports. If you want some *Jurassic Park* sound samples, see Library 2, "Entertainment." If you are interested in visiting a dinosaur exhibition at a museum, look in "Museum Reports" (Library 9) for press releases from various museums.

See Also
Science/Math Forum

User Guide
- ☑ Windows
- ☑ DOS
- ☑ Macintosh
- ☐ Terminal Emulation
- ☑ VMS
- ☑ UNIX
- ☑ OS/2
- ☐ Other platform

Cost
- ☐ Unknown
- ☐ Basic
- ☑ Extended
- ☐ Premium ($)
- ☐ Executive w/$

Activity Level

LOW — MEDIUM — HIGH

Address
GO: **DINO**

SCIENCE FICTION

Speakeasy Forum

Description
This forum is for Ziffnet and/or CompuServe members looking for a relaxed, not-so-busy forum willing to allow general discussion on most any topic.

Subjects
Computers, Science Fiction

Audience
New Age enthusiasts

Content Summary
The libraries include information on science fiction, games, travel, sports, music, and After Hours.

See Also
Participate, Science Fiction Forum

User Guide
- ☑ Windows
- ☑ DOS
- ☑ Macintosh
- ☐ Terminal Emulation
- ☐ VMS
- ☑ UNIX
- ☐ OS/2
- ☑ Other platform

Cost
- ☐ Unknown
- ☐ Basic
- ☑ Extended
- ☐ Premium ($)
- ☐ Executive w/$

Activity Level

LOW — MEDIUM — HIGH

Address
GO: **SPEAKEASY**

Scuba Forum

Description
This is a forum for amateur and professional divers, discussing diving, diving equipment, and diving locations

Subjects
Divers, Hobbies

Audience
Divers, snorklers

Content Summary
The libraries of this forum contain information on diving in America, Europe, the Caribbean, and elsewhere. Also included is information on scuba equipment, snorkling, and pictures of diving locations.

See Also
Sports Forum, Outdoor Forum, Photography Forum

User Guide
- ☑ Windows
- ☑ DOS
- ☑ Macintosh
- ☐ Terminal Emulation
- ☐ VMS
- ☑ UNIX
- ☐ OS/2
- ☐ Other platform

Cost
- ☐ Unknown
- ☐ Basic
- ☑ Extended
- ☐ Premium ($)
- ☐ Executive w/$

Activity Level: MEDIUM (arrow pointing up between LOW and HIGH)

Address
GO: **DIVING**

SDAs On-Line

Description
This is a forum for Seventh-Day Adventists around the world. (Prospective members must order a special version of CIM from (800) 268-7171, to join the forum.)

Subjects
Religion

Audience
Seventh-Day Adventists

Content Summary
The libraries include Adventist news, Bible and theology discussions, pastoral practices, church resources, missions, and women's ministries.

See Also
Religion Forum

User Guide
- ☑ Windows
- ☑ DOS
- ☑ Macintosh
- ☐ Terminal Emulation
- ☐ VMS
- ☐ UNIX
- ☐ OS/2
- ☐ Other platform

Cost
- ☐ Unknown
- ☐ Basic
- ☑ Extended
- ☐ Premium ($)
- ☐ Executive w/$

Activity Level: MEDIUM (arrow pointing up between LOW and HIGH)

Address
GO: **SDA**

Sears

Description
This is Sears Catalog, online shopping.

Subjects
Shopping

Audience
Shoppers

Content Summary
A wide array of Sears products are available for purchase. Featured products include Craftsman tools, toys and games, and special values. You also can request a catalog or reach customer service.

See Also
Electronic Mall

User Guide
- ☑ Windows
- ☑ DOS
- ☑ Macintosh
- ☐ Terminal Emulation
- ☐ VMS
- ☐ UNIX
- ☐ OS/2
- ☐ Other platform

Cost
- ☐ Unknown
- ☑ Basic
- ☐ Extended
- ☐ Premium ($)
- ☐ Executive w/$

Activity Level: MEDIUM (arrow pointing toward LOW)

Address
GO: **SEARS**

Seattle Film Works

Description
This forum includes online shopping and film processing.

Subjects
Movies, Photography

Audience
Photographers

Content Summary
This shopping service enables you to shop online for film processing.

See Also
Photography Forum

User Guide
- ☑ Windows
- ☑ DOS
- ☑ Macintosh
- ☐ Terminal Emulation
- ☐ VMS
- ☐ UNIX
- ☐ OS/2
- ☐ Other platform

Cost
- ☐ Unknown
- ☑ Basic
- ☐ Extended
- ☐ Premium ($)
- ☐ Executive w/$

508

Seattle Film Works – Security

Activity Level

 LOW → (arrow pointing left)

Address
GO: **SFW-1**

Securities Screening

Description
This stock market issues screening area enables members to search through the Microquotes database for particular issue types.

Subjects
Finance, Stock Market

Audience
Business people

Content Summary
Members can search for specific types of information, such as price, earnings, dividends, and recent highs and lows of various stocks.

See Also
Business Dateline, Business Database Plus, IQuess Business Management

User Guide
- ☑ Windows
- ☑ DOS
- ☑ Macintosh
- ☐ Terminal Emulation
- ☐ VMS
- ☑ UNIX
- ☐ OS/2
- ☐ Other platform

Cost
- ☐ Unknown
- ☐ Basic
- ☐ Extended
- ☐ Premium ($)
- ☑ Executive w/$

Activity Level

(gauge pointing toward HIGH)

Address
GO: **SCREEN**

Securities Symbols Lookup

Description
This is a stock market issues database that enables members to search for an issue by name or ticker symbol.

Subjects
Finance, Stock Market

Audience
Business people

Content Summary
This database enables users to perform searches on issues relating to the stock market by name or ticker symbol.

See Also
Securities Screening

User Guide
- ☑ Windows
- ☑ DOS
- ☑ Macintosh
- ☐ Terminal Emulation
- ☐ VMS
- ☑ UNIX
- ☐ OS/2
- ☐ Other platform

Cost
- ☐ Unknown
- ☐ Basic
- ☑ Extended
- ☐ Premium ($)
- ☐ Executive w/$

Activity Level

Address
GO: **SYMBOLS**

SECURITY

NCSA InfoSecurity Forum

Description
This forum is devoted to the subject of information and data security.

Subjects
Computers, Security

Audience
Computer users, MIS people

Content Summary
If you're concerned about computer security, viruses, and firewalls, examine the various library and message sections in this forum. Some of the topics include Ethics/Privacy, Info Security News, Virus Tools/Info, PC/LAN Security, UNIX/Internet, Auditing, and others.

See Also
Internet Forum

User Guide
- ☑ Windows
- ☑ DOS
- ☑ Macintosh
- ☐ Terminal Emulation
- ☐ VMS
- ☑ UNIX
- ☐ OS/2
- ☑ Other platform

Cost
- ☐ Unknown
- ☐ Basic
- ☑ Extended
- ☐ Premium ($)
- ☐ Executive w/$

Activity Level

Address
GO: **NCSA Forum**

SERVICE AND SUPPORT

DiagSoft QAPlus Forum

Description
This forum provides support for DiagSoft QAPlus programs and discussions relating to these programs.

Subjects
Computers, Diagnostics, Service and Support, System Integration

Audience
Diagnostic personnel, DiagSoft users, MIS personnel, service and support technicians, system integrators, VARs

Content Summary
Like the message area, the library area is divided into sections that discuss general information, customer support, QAPlus, QAPlus / FE (field engineers diagnostic software), Peace of Mind (DiagSoft's Macintosh product), and QAPlus for Windows information. You can find installation and compatibility information in Library 1, "General Information."

See Also
IBM File Finder

User Guide
- ☑ Windows
- ☑ DOS
- ☑ Macintosh
- ☐ Terminal Emulation
- ☐ VMS
- ☐ UNIX
- ☐ OS/2
- ☐ Other platform

Cost
- ☐ Unknown
- ☐ Basic
- ☑ Extended
- ☐ Premium ($)
- ☐ Executive w/$

Activity Level

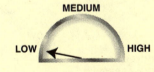

Address
GO: **DIAGSOFT**

SEXUALITY

HSX Adult Forum

Description
The Human Sexuality (HSX) Support Groups are online self-help groups where you can freely discuss your feelings and relationships.

Subjects
Biology, General Interest, Human Behavior, Sexuality

Audience
General public

Content Summary
To gain access to the closed areas in this forum, see the text file CLOSED.TXT in the HSX Help Files library (Library 16). It's the one that has been downloaded over 60,000 times! If you don't want to join in the closed areas, see the HSX Open Forum (HSX100).

See Also
HSX Open Forum, Human Sexuality Databank

User Guide
- ☑ Windows
- ☑ DOS
- ☑ Macintosh
- ☐ Terminal Emulation
- ☑ VMS
- ☑ UNIX
- ☑ OS/2
- ☑ Other platform

Cost
- ☐ Unknown
- ☐ Basic
- ☑ Extended
- ☐ Premium ($)
- ☐ Executive w/$

Activity Level

Address
GO: **HSX200**

HSX Open Forum

Description
The Human Sexuality (HSX) Support Groups are online self-help groups where you can freely discuss your feelings and relationships.

Subjects
General Interest, Human Behavior, Sexuality

Audience
General public

Content Summary
The following is the membership message in the HSX Open Forum: "The HSX Support Groups are online support (self-help) groups. Members share feelings and experiences, and provide one another with assistance and encouragement. Our goal is to create a compassionate community where members can freely discuss emotions and relationships. Here you can meet new friends and find sympathy and support. In the HSX forums, you'll find a warm place where people like you gather and talk about personal issues."

See Also
Human Sexuality Databank, HSX Adult Forum

510
Sexuality – Shareware

User Guide
- ☑ Windows
- ☑ DOS
- ☑ Macintosh
- ☐ Terminal Emulation
- ☑ VMS
- ☑ UNIX
- ☑ OS/2
- ☑ Other platform

Cost
- ☐ Unknown
- ☐ Basic
- ☑ Extended
- ☐ Premium ($)
- ☐ Executive w/$

Activity level
MEDIUM (LOW – HIGH)

Address
GO: **HSX100**

Human Sexuality Databank

Description
Presented by Howard and Martha Lewis, the Human Sexuality Databank provides information on topics such as gynecology, sexual therapy, and more.

Subjects
Health, Sexuality

Audience
Health care providers, general public

Content Summary
Because this area discusses sexually explicit topics, only people comfortable with all sex-related subjects and their frank treatment are advised to use this service. The Human Sexuality Databank main menu includes updates to the service, questions and answers posted by members and service administrators, a dictionary of sexual terms, hotline for your questions and comments, the 30 most-asked questions, and a letters sections. You also can enter forums where you can join in live talk with other members.

See Also
HSX Adult Forum, HSX Open Forum

User Guide
- ☑ Windows
- ☑ DOS
- ☑ Macintosh
- ☐ Terminal Emulation
- ☑ VMS
- ☑ UNIX
- ☑ OS/2
- ☑ Other platform

Cost
- ☐ Unknown
- ☐ Basic
- ☑ Extended
- ☐ Premium ($)
- ☐ Executive w/$

Activity level
UNKNOWN (LOW – MEDIUM – HIGH)

Address
GO: **HUMAN**

SHAREWARE

ASP Shareware Forum

Description
This forum is devoted to the general discussion of shareware and serves as a meeting place for members of the Association of Shareware Professionals.

Subjects
Computers, Shareware, Software

Audience
Computer programmers, software developers

Content Summary
The libraries and message areas contain programs that you can download. Also included are message areas, which provide open communication with developers.

See Also
Computer Club Forum

User Guide
- ☑ Windows
- ☑ DOS
- ☑ Macintosh
- ☐ Terminal Emulation
- ☑ VMS
- ☑ UNIX
- ☑ OS/2
- ☑ Other platform

Cost
- ☐ Unknown
- ☐ Basic
- ☑ Extended
- ☐ Premium ($)
- ☐ Executive w/$

Activity Level
MEDIUM (LOW – HIGH)

Address
GO: **ASPFORUM**

Shareware Depot

Description
This is an online shopping area offering shareware products for very low handling fees.

Subjects
Computers, Shareware

Audience
Computer users

Content Summary
This forum enables you to shop from home or office through many categories of computer shareware at attractive prices.

See Also
Computer Shopper, Shareware Registration

User Guide
- ☑ Windows
- ☑ DOS
- ☑ Macintosh
- ☐ Terminal Emulation
- ☐ VMS
- ☐ UNIX
- ☐ OS/2
- ☐ Other platform

Cost
- ☐ Unknown
- ☑ Basic
- ☐ Extended
- ☐ Premium ($)
- ☐ Executive w/$

Activity Level

Address
GO: **SD**

Shareware Registration

Description
This online area enables members to register for and pay for shareware software. The payment is added to members' CIS bill.

Subjects
Computers, Shareware

Audience
Computer users

Content Summary
This forum provides an easy way to register shareware. The registration fee is applied to your CompuServe bill.

See Also
Shareware Depot

User Guide
- ☑ Windows
- ☑ DOS
- ☑ Macintosh
- ☐ Terminal Emulation
- ☐ VMS
- ☑ UNIX
- ☐ OS/2
- ☐ Other platform

Cost
- ☐ Unknown
- ☑ Basic
- ☐ Extended
- ☐ Premium ($)
- ☐ Executive w/$

Activity Level

Address
GO: **SWREG**

UKSHARE Forum

Description
In this forum, members discuss many of the most popular UK shareware programs and meet their authors.

Subjects
Computers, Computer Software

Audience
Computer users

Content Summary
You can find files, utilities, and shareware programs from the United Kingdom in this forum. Find discussions and leave messages for shareware authors and developers.

See Also
Shareware

User Guide
- ☑ Windows
- ☑ DOS
- ☐ Macintosh
- ☐ Terminal Emulation
- ☐ VMS
- ☐ UNIX
- ☐ OS/2
- ☐ Other platform

Cost
- ☐ Unknown
- ☐ Basic
- ☑ Extended
- ☐ Premium ($)
- ☐ Executive w/$

Activity Level

Address
GO: **UKSHARE**

Shop-at-home

Description
This is CompuServe's Electronic Mall—an area containing dozens of online "stores" offering a variety of goods.

Subjects
Shopping

Audience
Shoppers

Content Summary
Visit this forum to make purchases ranging from food and clothing to books and computer software.

See Also
Sears, Americana Clothing

User Guide
- ☑ Windows
- ☑ DOS
- ☑ Macintosh
- ☐ Terminal Emulation
- ☐ VMS
- ☑ UNIX
- ☐ OS/2
- ☐ Other platform

Shop-at-home – Shareware Depot

Cost
- [ ] Unknown
- [x] Basic
- [ ] Extended
- [ ] Premium ($)
- [ ] Executive w/$

Activity Level: UNKNOWN (LOW – MEDIUM – HIGH)

Address
GO: **SHOPPING**

SHOPPERS ADVANTAGE Club

Description
This is America's largest discount electronic shopping service, with over 250,000 name brand items available.

Subjects
Clothing, Discount Shopping, Shopping

Audience
Consumers, shoppers

Content Summary
Shop 24 hours a day for over 250,000 different items.

See Also
Electronic Mall

User Guide
- [x] Windows
- [x] DOS
- [x] Macintosh
- [ ] Terminal Emulation
- [ ] VMS
- [x] UNIX
- [ ] OS/2
- [ ] Other platform

Cost
- [ ] Unknown
- [x] Basic
- [ ] Extended
- [ ] Premium ($)
- [ ] Executive w/$

Activity Level: HIGH (LOW – MEDIUM – HIGH)

Address
GO: **SAC**

SHAREWARE & FREEWARE

Microsoft Windows Shareware Forum

Description
This forum is designed to allow Windows users a mechanism to discuss and obtain Windows files such as utilities, tools, and applications.

Subjects
Computers, Shareware & Freeware

Audience
Computer users

Content Summary
Download and share your experiences about Windows shareware. This forum includes these libraries: File Applications/Utilities, Communication/Fax Applications, Windows System Utilities, Font/Printing Applications, Disk Utilties, and more.

See Also
MS WINFUN Forum

User Guide
- [x] Windows
- [x] DOS
- [x] Macintosh
- [ ] Terminal Emulation
- [ ] VMS
- [ ] UNIX
- [ ] OS/2
- [x] Other platform

Cost
- [ ] Unknown
- [ ] Basic
- [x] Extended
- [ ] Premium ($)
- [ ] Executive w/$

Activity Level: MEDIUM (LOW – MEDIUM – HIGH)

Address
GO: **WINSHARE**

Shareware Depot

Description
This is an online shopping area offering shareware products for very low handling fees.

Subjects
Computers, Shareware

Audience
Computer users

Content Summary
This forum enables you to shop from home or office through many categories of computer shareware at attractive prices.

See Also
Computer Shopper, Shareware Registration

User Guide
- [x] Windows
- [x] DOS
- [x] Macintosh
- [ ] Terminal Emulation
- [ ] VMS
- [ ] UNIX
- [ ] OS/2
- [ ] Other platform

Cost
- [ ] Unknown
- [x] Basic
- [ ] Extended
- [ ] Premium ($)
- [ ] Executive w/$

Shareware Depot – Shopping

Activity Level

Address
GO: **SD**

SHAREWARE GAMES

Epic MegaGames

Description
This area enables you download the Epic game of the month as well as other shareware games, including OverKill, Epic Pinball, Jill of the Jungle, and Zone 66. You also can access the Epic MegaGames Forum from this area.

Subjects
Games, Shareware Games

Audience
Gamers

Content Summary
From the EpicGames main menu, you can select the About Epic MegaGames option to see a synopsis of this game publisher. To read a description and download the game of the month, select the Download Game-of-the-Month choice. If you are interested in other Epic products, be sure to visit the terminal emulation area by selecting Purchase Epic Products from the main menu. Don't blame us if you become addicted.

See Also
Epic MegaGames Forum, The Electronic Gamer Archives, The Entertainment Center, The Modem Games Forum, The Gamers' Forum

User Guide
- ☑ Windows
- ☑ DOS
- ☑ Macintosh
- ☐ Terminal Emulation
- ☑ VMS
- ☑ UNIX
- ☑ OS/2
- ☐ Other platform

Cost
- ☐ Unknown
- ☐ Basic
- ☑ Extended
- ☐ Premium ($)
- ☐ Executive w/$

Activity Level

Address
GO: **EPIC**

SHOPPING

Adventures in Food

Description
This is an online shop for discriminating food lovers.

Subjects
Food, Shopping

Audience
Gourmet enthusiasts

Content Summary
This online shopping service contains gourmet food items, including specialty cheeses.

See Also
Bacchus Wine Forum

User Guide
- ☑ Windows
- ☑ DOS
- ☑ Macintosh
- ☐ Terminal Emulation
- ☑ VMS
- ☑ UNIX
- ☑ OS/2
- ☑ Other platform

Cost
- ☐ Unknown
- ☑ Basic
- ☐ Extended
- ☐ Premium ($)
- ☐ Executive w/$

Activity Level

Address
GO: **AIF**

Airline Services Unlimited

Description
Order suitcases, totes and garment bags online. "Trusted by Flight Crews for 25 Years."

Subjects
Shopping, Travel

Audience
Consumers

Content Summary
This online shopping service offers a complete line of travel suitcases and totes.

See Also
Air France

User Guide
- ☑ Windows
- ☑ DOS
- ☐ Macintosh
- ☐ Terminal Emulation
- ☐ VMS
- ☐ UNIX
- ☐ OS/2
- ☐ Other platform

Shopping

Cost
- ☐ Unknown
- ☐ Basic
- ☒ Extended
- ☐ Premium ($)
- ☐ Executive w/$

Activity Level

LOW — UNKNOWN — MEDIUM — HIGH

Address
GO: **ASU-1**

Alaska Peddler

Description
This forum offers online shopping from a family-owned group of stores in Juneau, featuring unique Alaskan gifts.

Subjects
Gifts, Shopping

Audience
Consumers

Content Summary
This online shopping service offers unique food and gift items handcrafted in Alaska.

See Also
Adventures in Food

User Guide
- ☒ Windows
- ☒ DOS
- ☐ Macintosh
- ☐ Terminal Emulation
- ☐ VMS
- ☐ UNIX
- ☐ OS/2
- ☐ Other platform

Cost
- ☐ Unknown
- ☒ Basic
- ☐ Extended
- ☐ Premium ($)
- ☐ Executive w/$

Activity Level

LOW — UNKNOWN — MEDIUM — HIGH

Address
GO: **ALASKA**

Americana Clothing

Description
This forum offers online shopping with a unique selection of clothing for men and women at everyday low prices.

Subjects
Clothing, Shopping

Audience
Consumers

Content Summary
This online shopping service offers a wide variety of clothing for men and women. Popular brands include Dockers and Lee.

See Also
Patagonia

User Guide
- ☒ Windows
- ☒ DOS
- ☐ Macintosh
- ☐ Terminal Emulation
- ☐ VMS
- ☐ UNIX
- ☐ OS/2
- ☐ Other platform

Cost
- ☐ Unknown
- ☒ Basic
- ☐ Extended
- ☐ Premium ($)
- ☐ Executive w/$

Activity Level

LOW — UNKNOWN — MEDIUM — HIGH

Address
GO: **AC**

Brooks Brothers Online Store

Description
This service offers online shopping at America's oldest retail store.

Subjects
Clothing, Shopping

Audience
Consumers, General public

Content Summary
Looking for men's clothing and furnishings? Look no further. This service enables you to order your Brooks Brothers apparel, including contemporary and classic clothing for women and young men.

See Also
Figi's Inc.

User Guide
- ☒ Windows
- ☒ DOS
- ☒ Macintosh
- ☐ Terminal Emulation
- ☒ VMS
- ☒ UNIX
- ☒ OS/2
- ☐ Other platform

Cost
- ☐ Unknown
- ☒ Basic
- ☐ Extended
- ☐ Premium ($)
- ☐ Executive w/$

Activity Level

LOW — UNKNOWN — MEDIUM — HIGH

Address
GO: **BR**

JC Penney

Description
Shop JC Penney in the comfort of your own home by entering the JCPenney service. You can shop from their Online Store!

Subjects
Shopping

Audience
General public, Shoppers

Content Summary
The JCPenney main menu enables you to choose from Shop Our Online Store, Product QuickSearch, This Month's Specials, Catalog Ordering, Gift Certificates, Request Credit Card Application, U.S. Customer Service, Canadian Customer Service, and Join Our Mailing List.

See Also
Americana Clothing, Sears

User Guide
- ☑ Windows
- ☑ DOS
- ☑ Macintosh
- ☐ Terminal Emulation
- ☑ VMS
- ☑ UNIX
- ☑ OS/2
- ☑ Other platform

Cost
- ☐ Unknown
- ☑ Basic
- ☐ Extended
- ☐ Premium ($)
- ☐ Executive w/$

Activity Level

Address
GO: **JCPENNEY**

Sears

Description
This is Sears Catalog, online shopping.

Subjects
Shopping

Audience
Shoppers

Content Summary
A wide array of Sears products are available for purchase. Featured products include Craftsman tools, toys and games, and special values. You also can request a catalog or reach customer service.

See Also
Electronic Mall

User Guide
- ☑ Windows
- ☑ DOS
- ☑ Macintosh
- ☐ Terminal Emulation
- ☐ VMS
- ☐ UNIX
- ☐ OS/2
- ☐ Other platform

Cost
- ☐ Unknown
- ☑ Basic
- ☐ Extended
- ☐ Premium ($)
- ☐ Executive w/$

Activity Level

Address
GO: **SEARS**

Shop-at-home

Description
This is CompuServe's Electronic Mall—an area containing dozens of online "stores" offering a variety of goods.

Subjects
Shopping

Audience
Shoppers

Content Summary
Visit this forum to make purchases ranging from food and clothing to books and computer software.

See Also
Sears, Americana Clothing

User Guide
- ☑ Windows
- ☑ DOS
- ☑ Macintosh
- ☐ Terminal Emulation
- ☐ VMS
- ☑ UNIX
- ☐ OS/2
- ☐ Other platform

Cost
- ☐ Unknown
- ☑ Basic
- ☐ Extended
- ☐ Premium ($)
- ☐ Executive w/$

Activity Level

Address
GO: **SHOPPING**

SHOPPERS ADVANTAGE Club

Description
This is America's largest discount electronic shopping service, with over 250,000 name brand items available.

Shopping – SHOWBIZ Quiz

Subjects
Clothing, Discount Shopping, Shopping

Audience
Consumers, shoppers

Content Summary
Shop 24 hours a day for over 250,000 different items.

See Also
Electronic Mall

User Guide
- ☑ Windows
- ☑ DOS
- ☑ Macintosh
- ☐ Terminal Emulation
- ☐ VMS
- ☑ UNIX
- ☐ OS/2
- ☐ Other platform

Cost
- ☐ Unknown
- ☑ Basic
- ☐ Extended
- ☐ Premium ($)
- ☐ Executive w/$

Activity Level

Address
GO: **SAC**

Sundown Vitamins

Description
This is an online shopping area offering vitamins at wholesale prices.

Subjects
Shopping, Vitamins

Audience
Health enthusiasts

Content Summary
A complete assortment of vitamins and food supplements is available for online purchase.

See Also
Health and Fitness Forum

User Guide
- ☑ Windows
- ☑ DOS
- ☑ Macintosh
- ☐ Terminal Emulation
- ☐ VMS
- ☑ UNIX
- ☐ OS/2
- ☐ Other platform

Cost
- ☐ Unknown
- ☑ Basic
- ☐ Extended
- ☐ Premium ($)
- ☐ Executive w/$

Activity Level

Address
GO: **SDV**

Sunglasses/Shavers & More

Description
This online shopping area offers such gifts as sunglasses and shavers.

Subjects
Shopping

Audience
Consumers, shoppers

Content Summary
This online shopping service provides product information, and a complete line of sunglasses, shavers, and related products.

See Also
Electronic Mall

User Guide
- ☑ Windows
- ☑ DOS
- ☑ Macintosh
- ☐ Terminal Emulation
- ☐ VMS
- ☑ UNIX
- ☐ OS/2
- ☑ Other platform

Cost
- ☐ Unknown
- ☑ Basic
- ☐ Extended
- ☐ Premium ($)
- ☐ Executive w/$

Activity Level

Address
GO: **SN**

SHOWBIZ Quiz

Description
Companion to the ShowBiz Forum and Hollywood Hotline, this area features trivia quizzes on several ShowBiz topics.

Subjects
Games, Movies, Television, Trivia

Audience
Movie enthusiasts

Content Summary
The libraries contain information about the forum, home entertainment, recent films, new films, classic films, television, celebrities, and Hollywood news.

See Also
Hollywood Hotline

User Guide
- ☑ Windows
- ☑ DOS
- ☑ Macintosh
- ☐ Terminal Emulation
- ☐ VMS
- ☑ UNIX
- ☐ OS/2
- ☐ Other platform

Cost
- ☐ Unknown
- ☐ Basic
- ☑ Extended
- ☐ Premium ($)
- ☐ Executive w/$

Activity Level: MEDIUM (LOW — UNKNOWN — HIGH)

Address
GO: **SBQ**

ShowBiz-Media Forum

Description
The oldest and largest entertainment forum on CIS, ShowBiz covers the entire spectrum of the world of show business and media.

Subjects
Entertainment

Audience
Trivia enthusiasts

Content Summary
The libraries include information on movies, radio, television, theater, celebrities, multimedia, music, soaps, screen writing.

See Also
Showbiz Quiz Forum, Hollywood Hotline

User Guide
- ☑ Windows
- ☑ DOS
- ☑ Macintosh
- ☐ Terminal Emulation
- ☐ VMS
- ☑ UNIX
- ☐ OS/2
- ☐ Other platform

Cost
- ☐ Unknown
- ☐ Basic
- ☑ Extended
- ☐ Premium ($)
- ☐ Executive w/$

Activity Level: MEDIUM (LOW — UNKNOWN — HIGH)

Address
GO: **SHOWBIZ**

Siemens Automation

Description
This is the main menu for entrance to the product support forum and product database of Siemens AG, a German electronics manufacturer.

Subjects
Electronics

Audience
Siemens product users

Content Summary
The libraries include new product uploads, animation library, graphics storeroom, sound clips library, and MIDI song library.

See Also
Hermacher Schlemmer

User Guide
- ☑ Windows
- ☑ DOS
- ☑ Macintosh
- ☐ Terminal Emulation
- ☐ VMS
- ☑ UNIX
- ☐ OS/2
- ☑ Other platform

Cost
- ☐ Unknown
- ☐ Basic
- ☑ Extended
- ☐ Premium ($)
- ☐ Executive w/$

Activity Level: MEDIUM (LOW ← HIGH)

Address
GO: **SIEAUT**

Sierra Online

Description
This forum is an online shopping area for Sierra Online software products.

Subjects
Computers

Audience
Sierra software users

Content Summary
Within this forum, you can place orders for the entire product line offered by Sierra Software.

See Also
Computer Express

User Guide
- ☑ Windows
- ☑ DOS
- ☐ Macintosh
- ☐ Terminal Emulation
- ☐ VMS
- ☐ UNIX
- ☐ OS/2
- ☐ Other platform

Sierra Online – Simulation

Cost
- ☐ Unknown
- ☒ Basic
- ☐ Extended
- ☐ Premium ($)
- ☐ Executive w/$

Activity Level: UNKNOWN (Low–Medium–High)

Address
GO: SI

Sight And Sound Forum

Description
This forum covers all types of computerized audio and visual hardware.

Subjects
Audio/Video, Entertainment

Audience
Audio and video enthusiasts

Content Summary
The libraries include video techniques, audio techniques, graphics and sound files, and MIDI.

See Also
Audio Engineering Society, Video Games Forum

User Guide
- ☒ Windows
- ☒ DOS
- ☒ Macintosh
- ☐ Terminal Emulation
- ☐ VMS
- ☐ UNIX
- ☐ OS/2
- ☐ Other platform

Cost
- ☐ Unknown
- ☐ Basic
- ☒ Extended
- ☐ Premium ($)
- ☐ Executive w/$

Activity Level: UNKNOWN (Low–Medium–High)

Address
GO: SSFORUM

SIMULATION

Flight Simulation Forum

Description
Are you interested in flight simulation software and scenery design? If so, check out this forum and download hundreds of support and help files.

Subjects
Flight Simulation, Simulation, Space Flight

Audience
General public, game players

Content Summary
This forum is packed with useful and up-to-date information and files for the flight simulation afficionado. The libraries in this forum include General/Help, FS/General Aviation, Air Transport, Air Traffic Control, Aircraft/Adventures, Scenery Design, Historic Air Combat, as well as many others. You can get information and press releases on the latest and greatest hardware add-ons in Library 13, "Hardware." Also, be sure to visit "Hangar Talk" (Library 16) for miscellaneous events, reports, and graphics.

See Also
Space Flight Forum

User Guide
- ☒ Windows
- ☒ DOS
- ☒ Macintosh
- ☐ Terminal Emulation
- ☐ VMS
- ☐ UNIX
- ☐ OS/2
- ☐ Other platform

Cost
- ☐ Unknown
- ☐ Basic
- ☒ Extended
- ☐ Premium ($)
- ☐ Executive w/$

Activity Level: High (Low–Medium–High)

Address
GO: FSFORUM

Game Forums and News

Description
Access all the CompuServe forums relating to games by using this service.

Subjects
Games, Simulation

Audience
Game players

Content Summary
From the Games Forums/News main menu, you can choose to go to many forums or areas, such as The Electronic Gamer, The Gamer Forum, Multi-Player Games Forum, Role-Playing Games Forum, Play-by-Mail Games Forum, Game Publishers Forums, Modem Games Forum, Flight Simulation Forum, Chess Forum, Sports Simulation Forum, Epic Megagames Forum, Hot Games Download Area, Video Games Publishers Forum, and Video Games Forum.

See Also
Game Publishers Forums (free), Flight Simulation Forum, Entertainment Center, Electronic Gamer™

Simulation – Small Business

SMALL BUSINESS

Entrepreneur Magazine

Description
This area is known also as the Small Business Emporium, from which you can find over 165 entrepreneur business guides. These guides will help you find businesses you can run from home, start in your spare time, and begin with little investment.

Subjects
Small Business, Home-Based Business, Entrepreneurs

Audience
Entrepreneurs, home-based business owners, small-business owners, venture capitalists

Content Summary
After you get past the main menu in this area, you are given six choices from which to choose. From this menu, you can see the top 10 hottest businesses, see a directory of business guides, order a *Entrepreneur Magazine* subscription, and view a list of other business products such as videos and software products.

See Also
Entrepreneur's Small Business Forum, Entrepreneur's Small Business Square

User Guide
- [x] Windows
- [x] DOS
- [x] Macintosh
- [ ] Terminal Emulation
- [x] VMS
- [x] UNIX
- [x] OS/2
- [x] Other platform

Cost
- [ ] Unknown
- [x] Basic
- [ ] Extended
- [ ] Premium ($)
- [ ] Executive w/$

Activity Level: UNKNOWN (LOW – MEDIUM – HIGH)

Address
GO: **GAMECON**

Single Issue Price Hist.

Description
This online area quotes stock/bond issue pricing by name or ticker symbol.

Subjects
Finance, Stock Market

Audience
Business people

Content Summary
This forum enables you to find out pricing of particular stocks or bonds by looking up information in an alphabetical sort or by ticker symbol.

See Also
Securities Symbols Lookup Database

User Guide
- [x] Windows
- [x] DOS
- [x] Macintosh
- [ ] Terminal Emulation
- [ ] VMS
- [x] UNIX
- [ ] OS/2
- [x] Other platform

Cost
- [ ] Unknown
- [ ] Basic
- [ ] Extended
- [x] Premium ($)
- [ ] Executive w/$

Activity Level: UNKNOWN (LOW – MEDIUM – HIGH)

Address
GO: **PRICES**

Entrepreneur Small Business Square

Description
From this service, you can access the Entrepreneur's Small Business Forum, Franchise & Business Opportunities, Small Business Emporium, and the *Entrepreneur Magazine* Small Business Survey. The Franchise & Business Opportunities option is a database that lists company addresses, phone numbers, contact names, and descriptions of franchising and business opportunities.

User Guide
- [ ] Windows
- [ ] DOS
- [ ] Macintosh
- [x] Terminal Emulation
- [ ] VMS
- [ ] UNIX
- [ ] OS/2
- [ ] Other platform

Cost
- [ ] Unknown
- [x] Basic
- [ ] Extended
- [ ] Premium ($)
- [ ] Executive w/$

Activity Level: UNKNOWN (LOW – MEDIUM – HIGH)

Address
GO: **ENT**

Small Business – Small Computer Book Club

Subjects
Entrepreneur, Small Business, Franchise

Audience
Entrepreneurs, small business owners, venture capitalists

Content Summary
To use the Franchise & Business Opportunities database, select that option from the Entrepreneur Small Business Square main menu and then select the Begin Your Search option. You then use search criteria from a list of 1,500 opportunities to find your results. The Small Business Emporium is a terminal emulation area that stores over 165 entrepreneur business guides to help you start and maintain a small business.

See Also
IQuest Business Management InfoCenter, Entrepreneur Small Business Forum

User Guide
- ☐ Windows
- ☐ DOS
- ☐ Macintosh
- ☑ Terminal Emulation
- ☐ VMS
- ☐ UNIX
- ☐ OS/2
- ☐ Other platform

Cost
- ☐ Unknown
- ☐ Basic
- ☑ Extended
- ☐ Premium ($)
- ☐ Executive w/$

Activity Level

Address
GO: **ENTMAGAZINE**

Entrepreneur's Small Business Forum

Description
Sponsored by Entrepreneur Group, the publishers of *Entrepreneur Magazine,* the Entrepreneur's Small Business Forum enables you to identify and communicate with other entrepreneurs in a different cities and locales. This forum welcomes the sharing of information and helpful dialogue from all members.

Subjects
Business, Entrepreneurs, Free Enterprise, Small Business

Audience
Business owners, entrepreneurs, venture capitalists

Content Summary
The libraries contain information on business opportunities, start-up techniques, marketing and promotion files, financing, legal issues, planning files, and international issues. Check out the information in Library 13, "Homebased Business," if you are thinking about starting, or are maintaining, a business from your home. You also should take part in the message section if you have specific questions to ask.

See Also
Entrepreneur Small Business Square, Business Franchise and Opportunities Database

User Guide
- ☑ Windows
- ☑ DOS
- ☑ Macintosh
- ☐ Terminal Emulation
- ☑ VMS
- ☑ UNIX
- ☑ OS/2
- ☑ Other platform

Cost
- ☐ Unknown
- ☐ Basic
- ☑ Extended
- ☐ Premium ($)
- ☐ Executive w/$

Activity Level

Address
GO: **USEN**

Small Computer Book Club

Description
This is an online shopping area for members of the Small Computer Book Club. Non-members can join online, with a purchase.

Subjects
Books

Audience
Readers

Content Summary
This online shopping forum enables members to order computer books of all types.

See Also
Quality Paperbacks Forum, Macmillan Computer Publishing

User Guide
- ☐ Windows
- ☐ DOS
- ☐ Macintosh
- ☑ Terminal Emulation
- ☐ VMS
- ☐ UNIX
- ☐ OS/2
- ☐ Other platform

Cost
- ☐ Unknown
- ☑ Basic
- ☐ Extended
- ☐ Premium ($)
- ☐ Executive w/$

Activity Level

Address
GO: **BK**

SMALLTALK/V

Digitalk Database

Description
Since 1985, Digitalk, Inc. has been developing object-oriented programming environments for the PC with its Smalltalk/V product. The company has Smalltalk/V development environments worldwide for DOS, OS/2, Microsoft Windows, and the Apple Macintosh; the Team/V collaborative programming system; and PARTS Workbench for OS/2. The Digitalk Database contains problem reports on all Smalltalk/V and PARTS products.

Subjects
Action Requests Database, Computers, Object-Oriented Programming, Smalltalk/V

Audience
Consultants, object-oriented programmers, Smalltalk/V users, trainers

Content Summary
Select the "Search the Action Requests Database" option to search the Digitalk Action Requests database.

See Also
Digitalk Forum

User Guide
- ☑ Windows
- ☑ DOS
- ☑ Macintosh
- ☐ Terminal Emulation
- ☐ VMS
- ☐ UNIX
- ☑ OS/2
- ☐ Other platform

Cost
- ☐ Unknown
- ☐ Basic
- ☑ Extended
- ☐ Premium ($)
- ☐ Executive w/$

Activity Level

Address
GO: **DBDIGITALK**

Digitalk Forum

Description
This forum provides a way to communicate with Digitalk and with other users of Smalltalk/V and PARTS products, including the latest information about Smalltalk/V and PARTS products, technical support answers, and how others are using Digitalk's development systems to create and deliver software.

Subjects
Application Development, Computers, Smalltalk/V

Audience
Application developers, PARTS users, Smalltalk/V users

Content Summary
The library and message areas contain various places to discuss several topics, including Digitalk news, product information, user contributions, third-party products, support, and miscellaneous information and products. If you're looking for source code or tips on Smalltalk/V, see library 5, "Support."

See Also
Digitalk Database

User Guide
- ☑ Windows
- ☑ DOS
- ☑ Macintosh
- ☐ Terminal Emulation
- ☐ VMS
- ☐ UNIX
- ☑ OS/2
- ☐ Other platform

Cost
- ☐ Unknown
- ☐ Basic
- ☑ Extended
- ☐ Premium ($)
- ☐ Executive w/$

Activity Level

Address
GO: **DIGITALK**

Smith Micro Forum

Description
This is the vendor support forum for Smith Micro products

Subjects
Computers

Audience
Smith Micro products users

Content Summary
The libraries include information about HotLine Windows/DOS, HotDisk, QLMC, QL GOLD, HotFax/QL DOS, and CrossConnection.

See Also
Computer Shopper Forum

User Guide
- ☑ Windows
- ☑ DOS
- ☐ Macintosh
- ☐ Terminal Emulation
- ☐ VMS
- ☐ UNIX
- ☐ OS/2
- ☐ Other platform

Cost
- ☐ Unknown
- ☐ Basic
- ☑ Extended
- ☐ Premium ($)
- ☐ Executive w/$

522 Smith Micro Forum – Soap Opera Summaries

Activity Level

LOW ← MEDIUM HIGH

Address
GO: **SMITHMICRO**

SNA

Eicon Technology Forum

Description
Sponsored by Eicon Technology, this forum helps users find answers to questions or problems concerning Eicon products. Eicon offers products of connectivity solutions for the X.25 and SNA environment.

Subjects
Computers, Connectivity, X.25, SNA

Audience
MIS people, Eicon consumers

Content Summary
The library and message sections contain information about Eicon products as well as technical support, press releases, utilities, help files, applications, demos, and Q&A. The libraries include sections for emulators, gateways, tool kits, international services, and WAN services.

See Also
Computer Shopper

User Guide
- ☑ Windows
- ☑ DOS
- ☑ Macintosh
- ☐ Terminal Emulation
- ☑ VMS
- ☑ UNIX
- ☑ OS/2
- ☐ Other platform

Cost
- ☐ Unknown
- ☐ Basic
- ☑ Extended
- ☐ Premium ($)
- ☐ Executive w/$

Activity Level

LOW MEDIUM ↑ HIGH

Address
GO: **EICON**

SNIPER!

Description
This online infantry combat game is set during World War II.

Subjects
Combat, Games, War

Audience
Games enthusiasts, military buffs

Content Summary
You command a squad of soldiers in a mission against another squad. Actual wartime conditions are simulated. The game is over when a player has accomplished his or her mission. The game appears more lifelike if you download the SCOPE games software.

See Also
Games Forum

User Guide
- ☑ Windows
- ☑ DOS
- ☐ Macintosh
- ☐ Terminal Emulation
- ☐ VMS
- ☐ UNIX
- ☐ OS/2
- ☐ Other platform

Cost
- ☐ Unknown
- ☐ Basic
- ☑ Extended
- ☐ Premium ($)
- ☐ Executive w/$

Activity Level

LOW MEDIUM UNKNOWN HIGH

Address
Go: **SNIPER**

Soap Opera Summaries

Description
This forum includes daily summaries of TV soap operas, including information on the stars and fan clubs.

Subjects
Television

Audience
Television viewers

Content Summary
The libraries include information about the celebrities who appear in soap operas, news about specific shows, and lists of fan clubs.

See Also
Hollywood Hotline, Showbiz Forum

User Guide
- ☑ Windows
- ☑ DOS
- ☑ Macintosh
- ☐ Terminal Emulation
- ☐ VMS
- ☐ UNIX
- ☐ OS/2
- ☐ Other platform

SOCIAL SECURITY

Retirement Living Forum

Description
Managed by the Setting Priorities for Retirement Years (SPRY) Foundation, this forum is dedicated to making the retirement years happy and productive. Information and discussions on a wide range of topics are available to present and future retirees.

Subjects
Aging, Medicare, Social Security

Audience
Family of retirees, gerontologists, retirees

Content Summary
This forum's contributors include the Social Security Administration; the National Institute on Aging; the National Heart, Lung, and Blood Institute; the Traveling Healthy and Comfortably Newsletter; and the Pension Rights Center. Discussions can be found on eating right, housing, dealing with family, and Medicare.

See Also
Health/Fitness Forum

User Guide
- ☑ Windows
- ☑ DOS
- ☑ Macintosh
- ☐ Terminal Emulation
- ☑ VMS
- ☑ UNIX
- ☑ OS/2
- ☐ Other platform

Cost
- ☐ Unknown
- ☐ Basic
- ☑ Extended
- ☐ Premium ($)
- ☐ Executive w/$

Activity Level: LOW (arrow pointing toward LOW)

Address
GO: **RETIREMENT**

(top left entry, continued)

Cost
- ☐ Unknown
- ☑ Basic
- ☐ Extended
- ☐ Premium ($)
- ☐ Executive w/$

Activity Level: MEDIUM

Address
GO: **SOAPS**

Society of Broadcast Eng.

Description
This is the main menu for the Society of Broadcast Engineers area, featuring Society news and access to the Broadcast Professionals Forum (BPFORUM).

Subjects
Broadcasting, Television

Audience
Broadcasters

Content Summary
The areas of this forum include access to the Broadcast Professionals Forum, a list of upcoming conventions, and an information request area.

See Also
Broadcast Professionals Forum

User Guide
- ☑ Windows
- ☑ DOS
- ☑ Macintosh
- ☐ Terminal Emulation
- ☐ VMS
- ☐ UNIX
- ☐ OS/2
- ☐ Other platform

Cost
- ☐ Unknown
- ☐ Basic
- ☑ Extended
- ☐ Premium ($)
- ☐ Executive w/$

Activity Level: MEDIUM (arrow pointing toward LOW)

Address
GO: **SBENET**

Softdisk Publishing

Description
This is a online shopping area for Softdisk Publishing software products.

Subjects
Computers

Audience
Shoppers, computer users

Content Summary
This online shopping service enables you to choose from Softdisk's entire catalog of software products.

See Also
Small Computer Book Club

User Guide
- ☑ Windows
- ☑ DOS
- ☐ Macintosh
- ☐ Terminal Emulation
- ☐ VMS
- ☐ UNIX
- ☐ OS/2
- ☐ Other platform

Softdisk Publishing – Software

Cost
- [ ] Unknown
- [x] Basic
- [ ] Extended
- [ ] Premium ($)
- [ ] Executive w/$

Activity Level: MEDIUM (arrow pointing up between LOW and HIGH)

Address
GO: **SP**

SOFTEX

Description
This CompuServe-sponsored forum enables you to purchase software for your personal computer often at a lower cost than if you purchased it through retail.

Subjects
Computer Software, Online Shopping

Audience
Computer users, software

Content Summary
You can purchase software by searching by type of software, publisher of the software, or by other criteria. If you choose to purchase the software, you get a description of the product, hardware and software requirements, and an estimate of download time. The charge appears on your monthly CompuServe bill.

See Also
Computer Buyers Guide Forum, Computer Shopper Forum, Shop-at-home Forum

User Guide
- [x] Windows
- [x] DOS
- [x] Macintosh
- [x] Terminal Emulation
- [ ] VMS
- [x] UNIX
- [ ] OS/2
- [x] Other platform

Cost
- [ ] Unknown
- [ ] Basic
- [x] Extended
- [ ] Premium ($)
- [ ] Executive w/$

Activity Level: UNKNOWN

Address
GO: **SOFTEX**

SOFTWARE

Adobe Forum

Description
The Adobe Forum provides an area where users, dealers, service bureaus, third-party developers, and others can communicate with Adobe.

Subjects
Computer Graphics, Computers, Software

Audience
Adobe products users

Content Summary
The libraries and message areas contain technical support and news of all Adobe products including PhotoShop, Illustrator, and Type Manager.

See Also
Graphics Forum

User Guide
- [x] Windows
- [x] DOS
- [x] Macintosh
- [ ] Terminal Emulation
- [ ] VMS
- [ ] UNIX
- [ ] OS/2
- [ ] Other platform

Cost
- [ ] Unknown
- [ ] Basic
- [x] Extended
- [ ] Premium ($)
- [ ] Executive w/$

Activity Level: MEDIUM (arrow pointing up between LOW and HIGH)

Address
GO: **ADOBE**

Aldus Forum

Description
The Aldus Forum provides technical support for issues encountered by both novice and experienced users of Aldus products.

Subjects
Computers, Software

Audience
Aldus products users

Content Summary
The libraries contain technical support and new about all Aldus products including PageMaker, Freehand, and Gallery Effects!

See Also
Aldus Special Programs Fund

User Guide
- ☑ Windows
- ☑ DOS
- ☐ Macintosh
- ☐ Terminal Emulation
- ☐ VMS
- ☐ UNIX
- ☐ OS/2
- ☐ Other platform

Cost
- ☐ Unknown
- ☐ Basic
- ☑ Extended
- ☐ Premium ($)
- ☐ Executive w/$

Activity Level: MEDIUM

Address
GO: **ALDUSFORUM**

Aldus Online Customer Support

Description
Menu giving access to Aldus support services on CompuServe.

Subjects
Computers, Software

Audience
Aldus products users

Content Summary
This online customer support service provides answers to users' questions within two working business days.

See Also

User Guide
- ☑ Windows
- ☑ DOS
- ☑ Macintosh
- ☐ Terminal Emulation
- ☐ VMS
- ☐ UNIX
- ☐ OS/2
- ☐ Other platform

Cost
- ☐ Unknown
- ☐ Basic
- ☑ Extended
- ☐ Premium ($)
- ☐ Executive w/$

Activity Level: UNKNOWN

Address
GO: **ALDUS**

Aldus Special Programs Forum

Description
The ALSUSSP Forum provided support and service to various OEM, developer, training, and other special interest partners.

Subjects
Computers, Software

Audience
Computer programmers

Content Summary
The libraries and message areas contain technical support for developers, trainers, and beta testers.

See Also
Aldus Online Customer Support

User Guide
- ☑ Windows
- ☑ DOS
- ☐ Macintosh
- ☐ Terminal Emulation
- ☐ VMS
- ☐ UNIX
- ☐ OS/2
- ☐ Other platform

Cost
- ☐ Unknown
- ☐ Basic
- ☑ Extended
- ☐ Premium ($)
- ☐ Executive w/$

Activity Level: UNKNOWN

Address
GO: **ALDUSSP**

Software Development Forum

Readers of *SOFTWARE DEVELOPMENT* magazine can interact with the writers and editors of the magazine, and obtain magazine code listings.

Subjects
Computers

Audience
Computer users

Content Summary
Libraries include information on C language and tools, debugging techniques, and software engineering.

See Also
Software Publishers Association Forum

User Guide
- ☑ Windows
- ☑ DOS
- ☑ Macintosh
- ☐ Terminal Emulation
- ☐ VMS
- ☐ UNIX
- ☐ OS/2
- ☐ Other platform

Cost
- ☐ Unknown
- ☐ Basic
- ☑ Extended
- ☐ Premium ($)
- ☐ Executive w/$

526

Software Development Forum – Solar System

Activity Level: LOW (arrow pointing toward LOW, between LOW and MEDIUM)

Address
GO: **SDFORUM**

Software Pub. Assoc. Forum

Description
This forum, sponsored by the Software Publishers Association, discusses how to publish software products, obtain copyrights, etc.

Subjects
Computers

Audience
Computer users, computer programmers

Content Summary
The libraries include information about software publishing, software theft, and copyrights.

See Also
Software Development Forum

User Guide
- ☑ Windows
- ☑ DOS
- ☑ Macintosh
- ☐ Terminal Emulation
- ☐ VMS
- ☐ UNIX
- ☐ OS/2
- ☐ Other platform

Cost
- ☐ Unknown
- ☐ Basic
- ☑ Extended
- ☐ Premium ($)
- ☐ Executive w/$

Activity Level: MEDIUM (arrow pointing up to MEDIUM)

Address
GO: **SPAFORUM**

Software Publisher Online

Description
This vendor forum supports the products of Software Publishing Corporation.

Subjects
Computers

Audience
SPA members, software developers

Content Summary
The libraries include news and information pertaining to SPAudit, business, consumers, education, and hot topics.

See Also
Software Pub. Assoc. Forum

User Guide
- ☑ Windows
- ☑ DOS
- ☑ Macintosh
- ☐ Terminal Emulation
- ☐ VMS
- ☐ UNIX
- ☐ OS/2
- ☐ Other platform

Cost
- ☐ Unknown
- ☐ Basic
- ☑ Extended
- ☐ Premium ($)
- ☐ Executive w/$

Activity Level: LOW (arrow pointing toward LOW)

Address
GO: **SPO**

SOLAR SYSTEM

Space Exploration Forum

Description
This forum is used to discuss all aspects of space exploration. It is a companion forum to the Space Flight Forum.

Subjects
Solar System, Space

Audience
Space enthusiasts

Content Summary
Libraries include information on earth observation, the sun and moon, Mercury, Venus, Mars, and meteors, just to name a few.

See Also
Space Flight Forum

User Guide
- ☑ Windows
- ☑ DOS
- ☐ Macintosh
- ☐ Terminal Emulation
- ☐ VMS
- ☐ UNIX
- ☐ OS/2
- ☐ Other platform

Cost
- ☐ Unknown
- ☐ Basic
- ☑ Extended
- ☐ Premium ($)
- ☐ Executive w/$

Activity Level: MEDIUM (arrow pointing up to MEDIUM)

Address
GO: **SPACEX**

SPACE FLIGHT

Flight Simulation Forum

Description
Are you interested in flight simulation software and scenery design? If so, check out this forum and download hundreds of support and help files.

Subjects
Flight Simulation, Simulation, Space Flight

Audience
General public, game players, space enthusiasts

Content Summary
This forum is packed with useful and up-to-date information and files for the flight simulation affionado. The libraries in this forum include General/Help, FS/General Aviation, Air Transport, Air Traffic Control, Aircraft/Adventures, Scenery Design, Historic Air Combat, as well as many others. You can get information and press releases on the latest and greatest hardware add-ons in Library 13, "Hardware." Also, be sure to visit "Hangar Talk" (Library 16) for miscellaneous events, reports, and graphics.

See Also
Space Flight Forum

User Guide
- ☑ Windows
- ☑ DOS
- ☑ Macintosh
- ☐ Terminal Emulation
- ☐ VMS
- ☐ UNIX
- ☐ OS/2
- ☐ Other platform

Cost
- ☐ Unknown
- ☐ Basic
- ☑ Extended
- ☐ Premium ($)
- ☐ Executive w/$

Activity Level

MEDIUM (arrow pointing toward HIGH)

Address
GO: **FSFORUM**

Space Exploration Forum

Description
This forum is used to discuss all aspects of space exploration. It is a companion forum to the Space Flight Forum.

Subjects
Solar System, Space

Audience
Space enthusiasts

Content Summary
The libraries include information on earth observation, the sun and moon, Mercury, Venus, Mars, and meteors, just to name a few.

See Also
Space Flight Forum

User Guide
- ☑ Windows
- ☑ DOS
- ☐ Macintosh
- ☐ Terminal Emulation
- ☐ VMS
- ☐ UNIX
- ☐ OS/2
- ☐ Other platform

Cost
- ☐ Unknown
- ☐ Basic
- ☑ Extended
- ☐ Premium ($)
- ☐ Executive w/$

Activity Level

MEDIUM

Address
GO: **SPACEX**

Space Flight Forum

Description
This forum is used to discuss all aspects of manned space flight. It is a companion forum to the Space Exploration Forum.

Subjects
Solar System, Space

Audience
Space enthusiasts

Content Summary
The libraries include information on the Space Shuttle, space stations, involvement of private enterprise, new technology, and general topics.

See Also
Space Exploration Forum

User Guide
- ☑ Windows
- ☑ DOS
- ☐ Macintosh
- ☐ Terminal Emulation
- ☐ VMS
- ☐ UNIX
- ☐ OS/2
- ☐ Other platform

Cost
- ☐ Unknown
- ☐ Basic
- ☑ Extended
- ☐ Premium ($)
- ☐ Executive w/$

Activity Level
MEDIUM

Address
GO: **SPACEFLIGHT**

Speakeasy Forum

Description
This forum is for Ziffnet and/or CompuServe members looking for a relaxed, not-so-busy forum willing to allow general discussion on most any topic.

Subjects
Computers, Science Fiction

Audience
New Age enthusiasts

Content Summary
The libraries include information on science fiction, games, travel, sports, music, and After Hours.

See Also
Participate, Science Fiction Forum

User Guide
- ☑ Windows
- ☑ DOS
- ☑ Macintosh
- ☐ Terminal Emulation
- ☐ VMS
- ☑ UNIX
- ☐ OS/2
- ☑ Other platform

Cost
- ☐ Unknown
- ☐ Basic
- ☑ Extended
- ☐ Premium ($)
- ☐ Executive w/$

Activity Level: LOW (arrow pointing low)

Address
GO: **SPEAKEASY**

Spinnaker Software Forum

Description
This vendor forum supports all Spinnaker software products.

Subjects
Computers

Audience
Vendors who support Spinnaker software

Content Summary
The libraries include for PFS: products, Easyworking, Calendar Creator, and Express Publish.

See Also
Desktop Publishing Forum

User Guide
- ☑ Windows
- ☑ DOS
- ☑ Macintosh
- ☐ Terminal Emulation
- ☐ VMS
- ☐ UNIX
- ☐ OS/2
- ☐ Other platform

Cost
- ☐ Unknown
- ☐ Basic
- ☑ Extended
- ☐ Premium ($)
- ☐ Executive w/$

Activity Level: LOW (arrow pointing low)

Address
GO: **SPINNAKER**

SPORTS

HealthNet

Description
Get health news, sports medicine, information on ailments and disorders, and other health-related information from this forum.

Subjects
Fitness, Health, Health Care, Sports

Audience
General public

Content Summary
The HealthNet main menu contains two options: HealthNet Reference Library and Sports Medicine. The HealthNet Reference Library contains several listings, including Disorders and Diseases, Symptoms, Drugs, Surgeries/Tests/Procedures, Home Care and First Aid, Obstetrics/Reproductive Medicine, and Ophthalmology/Eye Care. The Sports Medicine option contains General Aspects of Exercise, Nutrition and Exercise, and Some Specific Sports. Be sure to read the introduction to this service, and do not use this service as a substitute for your doctor or medical personnel.

See Also
Health/Fitness, Health Database Plus($), Health and Vitamin Express, Health & Fitness Forum, Holistic Health Forum, Sports Forum

User Guide
- ☑ Windows
- ☑ DOS
- ☑ Macintosh
- ☐ Terminal Emulation
- ☑ VMS
- ☑ UNIX
- ☑ OS/2
- ☑ Other platform

Cost
- ☐ Unknown
- ☑ Basic
- ☐ Extended
- ☐ Premium ($)
- ☐ Executive w/$

Activity Level: UNKNOWN

Sports Forum

Address
GO: **HNT**

Description
This forum covers sports from all angles—from yesterday's games to which referee blew the call.

Subjects
Games

Audience
Sports enthusiasts, general public

See Also
Sports

User Guide
- ☑ Windows
- ☑ DOS
- ☑ Macintosh
- ☐ Terminal Emulation
- ☐ VMS
- ☐ UNIX
- ☐ OS/2
- ☐ Other platform

Cost
- ☐ Unknown
- ☐ Basic
- ☑ Extended
- ☐ Premium ($)
- ☐ Executive w/$

Activity Level
MEDIUM (arrow pointing between LOW and HIGH, toward HIGH)

Address
GO: **SPINNAKER**

Sports Simulation Forum

Description
This forum covers all of the various sports simulations software on the market. It also includes advice on how to beat the game, setting up your computer, etc.

Subjects
Games

Audience
Sports enthusiasts

Content Summary
The libraries included are football, basketball, hockey, baseball, fantasy sports, and other sports.

See Also
Sports Forum

User Guide
- ☑ Windows
- ☑ DOS
- ☑ Macintosh
- ☐ Terminal Emulation
- ☐ VMS
- ☐ UNIX
- ☐ OS/2
- ☐ Other platform

Cost
- ☐ Unknown
- ☐ Basic
- ☑ Extended
- ☐ Premium ($)
- ☐ Executive w/$

Activity Level
MEDIUM (arrow pointing between LOW and HIGH, toward HIGH)

Address
GO: **SPRTSIMS**

UK Sports Clips

Description
This service contains full-text sports clips provided by Reuters World news wire and is a comprehensive source for sports stories including cricket, soccer, snooker, and rugby.

Subjects
Sports, News

Audience
General public, sports enthusiasts

Content Summary
The libraries include information on cricket, soccer, snooker, and rugby.

See Also
UK News Clips

User Guide
- ☑ Windows
- ☑ DOS
- ☐ Macintosh
- ☐ Terminal Emulation
- ☐ VMS
- ☐ UNIX
- ☐ OS/2
- ☐ Other platform

Cost
- ☐ Unknown
- ☐ Basic
- ☑ Extended
- ☐ Premium ($)
- ☐ Executive w/$

Activity Level
UNKNOWN

Address
GO: **UKSPORTS**

Stac Electronics Forum

Description
This is the vendor support forum for products from Stac Electronics.

Subjects
Electronics

Audience
Stac users and vendors

StacElectronics Forum – Standard Microsystems Forum

Content Summary
The libraries include information on utilities, product information, tech notes, and developer products.

See Also
Consumer Electronics

User Guide
- ☑ Windows
- ☑ DOS
- ☑ Macintosh
- ☐ Terminal Emulation
- ☑ VMS
- ☑ UNIX
- ☑ OS/2
- ☑ Other platform

Cost
- ☐ Unknown
- ☐ Basic
- ☑ Extended
- ☐ Premium ($)
- ☐ Executive w/$

Activity Level

Address
GO: **STACKER**

STAGEII

Description
This is an online multiplayer trivia game.

Subjects
Games

Audience
Games enthusiasts

Content Summary
This online trivia game asks you three questions. After you answer the questions, you look for a common theme in the answers.

See Also
Games Forum

User Guide
- ☑ Windows
- ☑ DOS
- ☑ Macintosh
- ☐ Terminal Emulation
- ☐ VMS
- ☐ UNIX
- ☐ OS/2
- ☐ Other platform

Cost
- ☐ Unknown
- ☐ Basic
- ☑ Extended
- ☐ Premium ($)
- ☐ Executive w/$

Activity Level

Address
GO: **STAGEII**

Standard Indus. Class.

Description
This is a database of SIC (industrial classification) codes, searchable by industry.

Subjects
Business, Databases

Audience
Researchers, business people

Content Summary
This database provides industrial information to business professionals.

See Also
IQuest Business Management

User Guide
- ☑ Windows
- ☑ DOS
- ☑ Macintosh
- ☐ Terminal Emulation
- ☐ VMS
- ☑ UNIX
- ☐ OS/2
- ☑ Other platform

Cost
- ☐ Unknown
- ☐ Basic
- ☑ Extended
- ☐ Premium ($)
- ☐ Executive w/$

Activity Level
UNKNOWN

Address
GO: **SICCODE**

Standard Microsystems Forum

Description
This is a vendor support area for the networking products of Standard Microsystems Corp.

Subjects
Computers, Networking

Audience
Standard Microsystems users

Content Summary
The libraries include general information, Arcnet, Ethernet Elite, Ethernet 30XX, and Token Ring Elite.

See Also
Computer Consultants Forum

User Guide
- ☑ Windows
- ☑ DOS
- ☑ Macintosh
- ☐ Terminal Emulation
- ☑ VMS
- ☑ UNIX
- ☑ OS/2
- ☑ Other platform

Standard Microsystems Forum – Statistics

Cost
- ☐ Unknown
- ☐ Basic
- ☒ Extended
- ☐ Premium ($)
- ☐ Executive w/$

Activity Level: LOW (arrow pointing low, MEDIUM / HIGH scale)

Address
GO: **SMC**

STAR TREK

Collectibles Forum

Description
We are an electronic club for all collectors—and are a member of the ANA and APS.

Subjects
Dolls, Hobbies, Star Trek

Audience
Hobby enthusiasts

Content Summary
The library and message sections contain information on a wide variety of collectibles. Included are areas on stamps, coins, autographs, books, music, sports cards, dolls, figurines, Star Trek, and much more.

See Also
Crafts Forum

User Guide
- ☒ Windows
- ☒ DOS
- ☒ Macintosh
- ☐ Terminal Emulation
- ☐ VMS
- ☒ UNIX
- ☐ OS/2
- ☐ Other platform

Cost
- ☐ Unknown
- ☐ Basic
- ☒ Extended
- ☐ Premium ($)
- ☐ Executive w/$

Activity Level: MEDIUM (arrow pointing medium)

Address
GO: **COLLECT**

State-County Demographics

Description
This database provides detailed summaries of the demographic makeup of states and counties in the USA.

Subjects
Demographics, Statistics

Audience
Researchers, business people

Content Summary
This database contains demographic statistics on race, age, occupation, and further details of all the states and counties of the U.S.

See Also
SUPERSITE Demographics

User Guide
- ☒ Windows
- ☒ DOS
- ☒ Macintosh
- ☐ Terminal Emulation
- ☐ VMS
- ☒ UNIX
- ☐ OS/2
- ☒ Other platform

Cost
- ☐ Unknown
- ☐ Basic
- ☐ Extended
- ☒ Premium ($)
- ☐ Executive w/$

Activity Level: UNKNOWN

Address
GO: **DEMOGRAPHICS**

STATISTICS

Census Bureau Online Service

Description
The United States Census Bureau provides a selection of its statistical reports on a wide variety of subjects, at no extra cost.

Subjects
Business, Statistics

Audience
Researchers

Content Summary
The libraries include census reports, and reports on population, agriculture, business, construction, housing, foreign trade, and government.

See Also
D&B Dun's Electronic Business Directory

User Guide
- ☒ Windows
- ☒ DOS
- ☒ Macintosh
- ☐ Terminal Emulation
- ☐ VMS
- ☒ UNIX
- ☐ OS/2
- ☐ Other platform

Statistics – Stock Market

Cost
- [ ] Unknown
- [ ] Basic
- [x] Extended
- [ ] Premium ($)
- [ ] Executive w/$

Activity Level: MEDIUM / UNKNOWN (LOW–HIGH)

Address
GO: **CENDATA**

State-County Demographics

Description
This database provides detailed summaries of the demographic makeup of states and counties in the USA.

Subjects
Demographics, Statistics

Audience
Researchers, business people

Content Summary
This database contains demographic statistics on race, age, occupation, and further details of all the states and counties of the U.S.

See Also
SUPERSITE Demographics

User Guide
- [x] Windows
- [x] DOS
- [x] Macintosh
- [ ] Terminal Emulation
- [ ] VMS
- [x] UNIX
- [ ] OS/2
- [x] Other platform

Cost
- [ ] Unknown
- [ ] Basic
- [ ] Extended
- [x] Premium ($)
- [ ] Executive w/$

Activity Level: MEDIUM / UNKNOWN (LOW–HIGH)

Address
GO: **DEMOGRAPHICS**

Stein Online

Description
This conference area is hosted by Eliot Stein, who interviews the stars online.

Subjects
Celebrities, Entertainment

Audience
Fans of celebrities

Content Summary
If you want to communicate online with famous celebrities, this forum provides an online conferences.

See Also
Hollywood Hotline

User Guide
- [x] Windows
- [x] DOS
- [x] Macintosh
- [ ] Terminal Emulation
- [ ] VMS
- [x] UNIX
- [ ] OS/2
- [x] Other platform

Cost
- [ ] Unknown
- [ ] Basic
- [x] Extended
- [ ] Premium ($)
- [ ] Executive w/$

Activity Level: MEDIUM / UNKNOWN (LOW–HIGH)

Address
GO: **STEIN**

STOCK MARKET

E*TRADE Securities

Description
Do you want to get a grip on your investments? This service enables you to do just that. E*TRADE handles individual, investment, margin, IRA, joint, KEOGH, and 401K accounts, and offers a stock market game that uses real stock market prices and data.

Subjects
Financial, Investments, Stock Market

Audience
Accountants, investors

Content Summary
This "around-the-clock" service offers you commissions of 1 1/2 cents per share, with a $35.00 minimum; Black-Sholes option analysis that use current prices; investment management; and free checking accounts tied to your money market funds. The investment management offers you quotes, portfolio reports, limit orders, and news alerts.

See Also
ETGAME

User Guide
- [ ] Windows
- [ ] DOS
- [ ] Macintosh
- [x] Terminal Emulation
- [ ] VMS
- [ ] UNIX
- [ ] OS/2
- [ ] Other platform

Stock Market

Cost
- ☐ Unknown
- ☐ Basic
- ☐ Extended
- ☑ Premium ($)
- ☐ Executive w/$

Activity Level: UNKNOWN

Address
GO: **ETRADE**

Market Highlights

Description
You can find current quotes on stocks, options, market indexes, foreign currency exchange rates, net asset values for mutual funds, and more.

Subjects
Stock Market

Audience
General public, stockbrokers

Content Summary
Market Highlights is a full-featured database of market information. To use the service, choose from one of the three main menu options: New York Stock Exchange, American Exchange, and Over the Counter. You can get information on the most active stocks of the day, as well as other data. If you want to check the current price of a stock anytime, type **QUOTES** and a stock sticker symbol at the ! prompt.

See Also
MQDATA($), E*TRADE Securities, Dividends and Splits($), DISCLOSURE II($E)

User Guide
- ☐ Windows
- ☐ DOS
- ☐ Macintosh
- ☑ Terminal Emulation
- ☐ VMS
- ☐ UNIX
- ☐ OS/2
- ☐ Other platform

Cost
- ☐ Unknown
- ☐ Basic
- ☐ Extended
- ☑ Premium ($)
- ☐ Executive w/$

Activity Level: UNKNOWN

Address
GO: **MARKET**

Securities Screening

Description
This stock market issues screening area enables members to search through the Microquotes database for particular issue types.

Subjects
Finance, Stock Market

Audience
Business people

Content Summary
Members can search for specific types of information, such as price, earnings, dividends, and recent highs and lows of various stocks.

See Also
Business Dateline, Business Database Plus, IQuess Business Management

User Guide
- ☑ Windows
- ☑ DOS
- ☑ Macintosh
- ☐ Terminal Emulation
- ☐ VMS
- ☑ UNIX
- ☐ OS/2
- ☐ Other platform

Cost
- ☐ Unknown
- ☐ Basic
- ☐ Extended
- ☐ Premium ($)
- ☑ Executive w/$

Activity Level: MEDIUM-HIGH

Address
GO: **SCREEN**

Securities Symbols Lookup

Description
This is a stock market issues database that enables members to search for an issue by name or ticker symbol.

Subjects
Finance, Stock Market

Audience
Business people

Content Summary
This database enables users to perform searches on issues relating to the stock market by name or ticker symbol.

See Also
Securities Screening

User Guide
- ☑ Windows
- ☑ DOS
- ☑ Macintosh
- ☐ Terminal Emulation
- ☐ VMS
- ☑ UNIX
- ☐ OS/2
- ☐ Other platform

Cost
- ☐ Unknown
- ☐ Basic
- ☑ Extended
- ☐ Premium ($)
- ☐ Executive w/$

Stock Market – Students' Forum

Activity Level

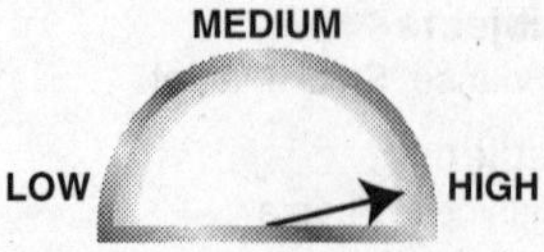

MEDIUM / LOW / HIGH (arrow pointing to HIGH side)

Address
GO: **SYMBOLS**

Single Issue Price Hist.

Description
This online area quotes stock/bond issue pricing by name or ticker symbol.

Subjects
Finance, Stock Market

Audience
Business people

Content Summary
This forum enables you to find out pricing of particular stocks or bonds by looking up information in an alphabetical sort or by ticker symbol.

See Also
Securities Symbols Lookup Database

User Guide
- ☑ Windows
- ☑ DOS
- ☑ Macintosh
- ☐ Terminal Emulation
- ☐ VMS
- ☑ UNIX
- ☐ OS/2
- ☑ Other platform

Cost
- ☐ Unknown
- ☐ Basic
- ☐ Extended
- ☑ Premium ($)
- ☐ Executive w/$

Activity Level

Address
GO: **PRICES**

Vestor Stock Recommendation

Description
This unique interactive system is comprised of over 30 systems that can help you in making investment decisions.

Subjects
Finance, Stock Market

Audience
Business people

Content Summary
This service enables you to evaluate stock portfolios by making changes in the portfolio to play out various scenarios.

See Also
Investors' Forum

User Guide
- ☑ Windows
- ☑ DOS
- ☐ Macintosh
- ☐ Terminal Emulation
- ☐ VMS
- ☐ UNIX
- ☐ OS/2
- ☐ Other platform

Cost
- ☐ Unknown
- ☐ Basic
- ☐ Extended
- ☐ Premium ($)
- ☑ Executive w/$

Activity Level

Address
GO: **VESTOR**

Students' Forum

Description
A forum for students and teachers who wish to share their experiences and ideas in a friendly forum atmosphere.

Subjects
Education

Audience
Students, educators

Content Summary
The libraries include information on grade school, middle school, high school, college/university, and graduate and professional schools. Also included are conference areas for children and a Teen Club area.

See Also
Education Forum

User Guide
- ☑ Windows
- ☑ DOS
- ☑ Macintosh
- ☐ Terminal Emulation
- ☐ VMS
- ☐ UNIX
- ☐ OS/2
- ☐ Other platform

Cost
- ☐ Unknown
- ☐ Basic
- ☑ Extended
- ☐ Premium ($)
- ☐ Executive w/$

Activity Level

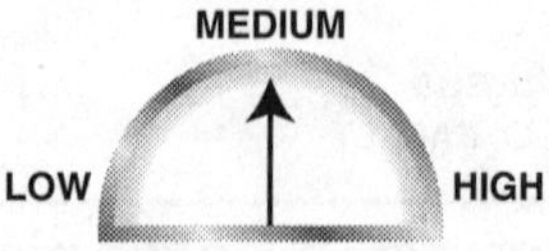

Address
GO: **STUFO**

SUBSCRIPTIONS

Detroit Free Press

Description
This is the place to find news and information about the award-winning *Detroit Free Press* newspaper. And feel free to leave a letter to the editor while you're online.

Subjects
Journalism, National News, Photojournalism

Audience
Automobile enthusiasts, Detroit citizens, journalists, photojournalists, sports fans

Content Summary
In the message and library areas, you can find information on the auto industry (including photographs of cars), health tips, business news, Detroit metro news, computing, entertainment, sports, and cartoons. You also can find the top stories of the day in the "Today's Top Stories" library (library 17).

See Also
Detroit Free Press Store

User Guide
- ☑ Windows
- ☑ DOS
- ☑ Macintosh
- ☐ Terminal Emulation
- ☑ VMS
- ☑ UNIX
- ☑ OS/2
- ☐ Other platform

Cost
- ☐ Unknown
- ☐ Basic
- ☑ Extended
- ☐ Premium ($)
- ☐ Executive w/$

Activity Level
MEDIUM (arrow pointing between MEDIUM and HIGH)

Address
GO: **DETROIT**

Sundown Vitamins

Description
This is an online shopping area offering vitamins at wholesale prices.

Subjects
Shopping, Vitamins

Audience
Health enthusiasts

Content Summary
A complete assortment of vitamins and food supplements is available for online purchase.

See Also
Health and Fitness Forum

User Guide
- ☑ Windows
- ☑ DOS
- ☑ Macintosh
- ☐ Terminal Emulation
- ☐ VMS
- ☑ UNIX
- ☐ OS/2
- ☐ Other platform

Cost
- ☐ Unknown
- ☑ Basic
- ☐ Extended
- ☐ Premium ($)
- ☐ Executive w/$

Activity Level
UNKNOWN

Address
GO: **SDV**

Sunglasses/Shavers & More

This online shopping area offers such gifts as sunglasses and shavers.

Subjects
Shopping

Audience
Consumers, shoppers

Content Summary
This online shopping service provides product information, and a complete line of sunglasses, shavers, and related products.

See Also
Electronic Mall

User Guide
- ☑ Windows
- ☑ DOS
- ☑ Macintosh
- ☐ Terminal Emulation
- ☐ VMS
- ☑ UNIX
- ☐ OS/2
- ☑ Other platform

Cost
- ☐ Unknown
- ☑ Basic
- ☐ Extended
- ☐ Premium ($)
- ☐ Executive w/$

Activity Level
UNKNOWN

Address
GO: **SN**

SunSoft Forum

Description
This is the vendor support area for SunSoft, the software unit of Sun Microsystems.

Subjects
Computers

SunSoft Forum – Support On Site

Audience
Computer users, Sun Microsystems users

Content Summary
The libraries include Wabi & SWI, PC-NFS Family, SelectMAIL, SunPC, NetWare SunLink, Developers, Solaris X86, and Solaris Sparc.

See Also
SunSelect Forum

User Guide
- ☑ Windows
- ☑ DOS
- ☐ Macintosh
- ☐ Terminal Emulation
- ☐ VMS
- ☑ UNIX
- ☐ OS/2
- ☑ Other platform

Cost
- ☐ Unknown
- ☐ Basic
- ☑ Extended
- ☐ Premium ($)
- ☐ Executive w/$

Activity Level

Address
GO: SUNSOFT

SUPERSITE Demographics

Description
This forum provides demographic reports for all of the United States, covering general demographics, income, housing, education, employment, and current and projected-year forecasts.

Subjects
Demographics, Market Research

Audience
Demographers, research analysts

Content Summary
This forum is available only to members who have the Executive Service Option. You obtain reports by indicating the type of geography you want to research, the geographic areas that form the market, and the reports you want.

See Also
Demographics

User Guide
- ☑ Windows
- ☑ DOS
- ☑ Macintosh
- ☑ Terminal Emulation
- ☑ VMS
- ☑ UNIX
- ☑ OS/2
- ☑ Other platform

Cost
- ☐ Unknown
- ☐ Basic
- ☐ Extended
- ☑ Premium ($)
- ☐ Executive w/$

Activity Level

Address
GO: SUPERSITE

Support Directory

Description
This is an online database of vendor support forums and services on CompuServe.

Subjects
CompuServe

Audience
CompuServe users

Content Summary
This database enables CompuServe users to look up online vendors quickly and easily.

See Also
Support on Site Forum

User Guide
- ☑ Windows
- ☑ DOS
- ☑ Macintosh
- ☐ Terminal Emulation
- ☐ VMS
- ☑ UNIX
- ☐ OS/2
- ☑ Other platform

Cost
- ☐ Unknown
- ☐ Basic
- ☐ Extended
- ☑ Premium ($)
- ☐ Executive w/$

Activity Level

Address
GO: SUPPORT

Support On Site

Description
This database contains hints and helpful info on using some of the most popular software applications available today.

Subjects
Computers, Databases

Audience
Computer users

Content Summary
The libraries include technical information, user groups, SQL server, Sybase education, third-party products, and PC products.

See Also
Computer Training Forum, Support Directory

User Guide
- ☑ Windows
- ☑ DOS
- ☑ Macintosh
- ☐ Terminal Emulation
- ☐ VMS
- ☑ UNIX
- ☐ OS/2
- ☑ Other platform

Cost
- ☐ Unknown
- ☐ Basic
- ☑ Extended
- ☐ Premium ($)
- ☐ Executive w/$

Activity Level: UNKNOWN (LOW — MEDIUM — HIGH)

Address
GO: **ONSITE**

SURVEYS

Online Surveys

Description
Take online surveys with this service. The surveys change frequently, so visit this area periodically to help in CompuServe research.

Subjects
Surveys, General Interest

Audience
General public

Content Summary
From the main menu, you can select Introduction, How To Take Online Surveys, Feedback/Comments, and the survey of your choice. You can take the New Member Survey if you have joined CompuServe within the past six months.

See Also
ZiffNet Surveys

User Guide
- ☐ Windows
- ☐ DOS
- ☐ Macintosh
- ☑ Terminal Emulation
- ☐ VMS
- ☐ UNIX
- ☐ OS/2
- ☐ Other platform

Cost
- ☐ Unknown
- ☑ Basic
- ☐ Extended
- ☐ Premium ($)
- ☐ Executive w/$

Activity Level: UNKNOWN (LOW — MEDIUM — HIGH)

Address
GO: **SURVEY**

Sybase Forum

Description
This is a vendor support forum for Sybase networking and database products.

Subjects
Computers

Audience
Networking enthusiasts

Content Summary
The libraries include SW Treasure Chest, word processing, spreadsheets, databases, operating systems, programming, utilities, networking, and CAD.

See Also
Networking

User Guide
- ☑ Windows
- ☑ DOS
- ☐ Macintosh
- ☐ Terminal Emulation
- ☐ VMS
- ☐ UNIX
- ☐ OS/2
- ☐ Other platform

Cost
- ☐ Unknown
- ☐ Basic
- ☑ Extended
- ☐ Premium ($)
- ☐ Executive w/$

Activity Level: LOW (LOW — MEDIUM — HIGH)

Address
GO: **SYBASE**

Symantec AntiVirus Prod. Forum

Description
This is a vendor support forum for Symantec and Norton anti-virus software products.

Subjects
Computers

Audience
Computer users

Content Summary
The libraries include information on upgrades, Q&A 4.0 for DOS, Q&A 4.0 for Windows, project management software, GrandView, and GreatWorks.

See Also
Symantec Applications Forum

User Guide
- ☑ Windows
- ☑ DOS
- ☐ Macintosh
- ☐ Terminal Emulation
- ☐ VMS
- ☐ UNIX
- ☐ OS/2
- ☐ Other platform

Cost
- ☐ Unknown
- ☐ Basic
- ☑ Extended
- ☐ Premium ($)
- ☐ Executive w/$

Activity Level: LOW (arrow pointing low)

Address
GO: **SYMVIRUS**

Symantec Applications Forum

Description
This is a vendor support forum for Symantec software applications such as GrandView, JustWrite, MORE II, OnTarget, Q&A, and TimeLine.

Subjects
Computers

Audience
Computer users

Content Summary
The libraries include general information, CP Backup for DOS, networking products, Commute, PC Tools, XTree Products, and accounting products.

See Also
Symantec AntiVius Prod. Forum

User Guide
- ☑ Windows
- ☑ DOS
- ☐ Macintosh
- ☐ Terminal Emulation
- ☐ VMS
- ☐ UNIX
- ☐ OS/2
- ☐ Other platform

Cost
- ☐ Unknown
- ☐ Basic
- ☑ Extended
- ☐ Premium ($)
- ☐ Executive w/$

Activity Level: MEDIUM

Address
GO: **SYMAPPS**

Symantec CPS DOS Forum

Description
This is a vendor support area for Symantec's Central Point Software products for DOS.

Subjects
Computers

Audience
Computer users

Content Summary
The libraries include general information, Scrapbook, CPAV/Win-OS/2, ScriptTools, PC Tools, and XTree for Windows.

See Also
Symantec Forums

User Guide
- ☑ Windows
- ☑ DOS
- ☐ Macintosh
- ☐ Terminal Emulation
- ☐ VMS
- ☐ UNIX
- ☑ OS/2
- ☐ Other platform

Cost
- ☐ Unknown
- ☐ Basic
- ☑ Extended
- ☐ Premium ($)
- ☐ Executive w/$

Activity Level: LOW

Address
GO: **SYMCPDOS**

Symantec CPS WinMac Forum

Description
This is a vendor support area for Symantec's Central Point Software for Windows and Macintosh.

Subjects
Computers

Audience
Computer users

Content Summary
The libraries include Think C, Think Pascal, Power MAC, Multiscope, Optlink, and Think Reference.

See Also
Symantec Forums

User Guide
- ☑ Windows
- ☐ DOS
- ☑ Macintosh
- ☐ Terminal Emulation
- ☐ VMS
- ☐ UNIX
- ☐ OS/2
- ☐ Other platform

Cost
- ☐ Unknown
- ☐ Basic
- ☑ Extended
- ☐ Premium ($)
- ☐ Executive w/$

Activity Level: MEDIUM

Address
GO: **SYMCPWIN**

Symantec Dev. Tools Forum

Description
This is a vendor support forum for Symantec's development tools software, including Multiscope Debuggers, TCL, Think C, Think Pascal, and Zortech C++.

Subjects
Computers

Audience
Computer users

Content Summary
The libraries include orders and upgrades, Fastback, Fastback OS/2, Direct Access PC, and other PC products.

See Also
Symantech Forums

User Guide
- ☑ Windows
- ☑ DOS
- ☐ Macintosh
- ☐ Terminal Emulation
- ☐ VMS
- ☐ UNIX
- ☑ OS/2
- ☐ Other platform

Cost
- ☐ Unknown
- ☐ Basic
- ☑ Extended
- ☐ Premium ($)
- ☐ Executive w/$

Activity Level

Address
GO: **SYMDEVTOOL**

Symantec FGS Forum

Description
This is a vendor support forum for Symantec's Fifth Generation Systems products, such as Powerstation, Suitcase II, Copy Doubler, Disk Doubler, Pyro!, and DiskLock.

Subjects
Computers

Audience
Computer users

Content Summary
The libraries include upgrade information, Desktop for DOS, Desktop for Windows, Norton Disklock, Backup for DOS, and Backup for Windows.

See Also
Symantech Forums

User Guide
- ☑ Windows
- ☑ DOS
- ☐ Macintosh
- ☐ Terminal Emulation
- ☐ VMS
- ☐ UNIX
- ☐ OS/2
- ☐ Other platform

Cost
- ☐ Unknown
- ☐ Basic
- ☑ Extended
- ☐ Premium ($)
- ☐ Executive w/$

Activity Level

Address
GO: **SYMFGS**

Symantec Norton Util Forum

Description
This is a vendor support forum for Symantec's Norton Utilities, including Backup, Commander, and Utilities.

Subjects
Computers

Audience
Computer users

Content Summary
The libraries include Administrator (NAN), NAV/NetWare NAVNLM, Util/NetWare (NUA), and Enterprise Developer.

See Also
Symantech Forums

User Guide
- ☑ Windows
- ☑ DOS
- ☐ Macintosh
- ☐ Terminal Emulation
- ☐ VMS
- ☐ UNIX
- ☐ OS/2
- ☐ Other platform

Cost
- ☐ Unknown
- ☐ Basic
- ☑ Extended
- ☐ Premium ($)
- ☐ Executive w/$

Activity Level

MEDIUM
LOW → HIGH

Address
GO: **SYMUTIL**

Symantec Ntwrk Products Forum

Description
This is a vendor support area for Symantec's network and enterprise software.

Symantec Ntwrk Products Forum – System Integration

Subjects
Computers

Audience
Computer users

Content Summary
The libraries include Administrator (NAN), NAV/NetWare NAVNLM, Util/NetWare (NUA), and Enterprise Developer.

See Also
Symantec Forums

User Guide
- ☑ Windows
- ☑ DOS
- ☐ Macintosh
- ☐ Terminal Emulation
- ☐ VMS
- ☐ UNIX
- ☐ OS/2
- ☐ Other platform

Cost
- ☐ Unknown
- ☐ Basic
- ☑ Extended
- ☐ Premium ($)
- ☐ Executive w/$

Activity Level
LOW (arrow pointing low) MEDIUM HIGH

Address
GO: SYMNET

Syndicated Columns

Description
This is an online database containing recent columns from over a dozen well-known newspaper columnists

Subjects
News

Audience
Journalists, current events enthusiasts

See Also
Associated Press

Content Summary
This service enables you search on news stories and current events.

User Guide
- ☑ Windows
- ☑ DOS
- ☑ Macintosh
- ☐ Terminal Emulation
- ☐ VMS
- ☐ UNIX
- ☐ OS/2
- ☑ Other platform

Cost
- ☐ Unknown
- ☑ Basic
- ☐ Extended
- ☐ Premium ($)
- ☐ Executive w/$

Activity Level
LOW UNKNOWN MEDIUM HIGH

Address
GO: COLUMNS

SynOptics Forum

Description
This is a vendor support forum for Synoptic's intelligent LAN hubs and LAN management software.

Subjects
Computers, Networking

Audience
Network administrators

Content Summary
The libraries include product information, training information, and hot topics.

See Also
IBM File Finder

User Guide
- ☑ Windows
- ☑ DOS
- ☐ Macintosh
- ☐ Terminal Emulation
- ☐ VMS
- ☐ UNIX
- ☐ OS/2
- ☐ Other platform

Cost
- ☐ Unknown
- ☐ Basic
- ☑ Extended
- ☐ Premium ($)
- ☐ Executive w/$

Activity Level
LOW (arrow pointing low) MEDIUM HIGH

Address
GO: SYNOPTICS

SYSTEM INTEGRATION

DiagSoft QAPlus Forum

Description
This service provides support for DiagSoft QAPlus programs and discussions relating to these programs.

Subjects
Computers, Diagnostics, Service and Support, System Integration

Audience
Diagnostic personnel, DiagSoft Users, MIS personnel, service and support technicians, system integrators, VARs

Content Summary
Like the message area, the library area is divided into sections that discuss general information, customer support, QAPlus, QAPlus / FE (field engineers diagnostic software), Peace of Mind (DiagSoft's Macintosh product), and QAPlus for Windows information. You can find installation and compatibility information in Library 1, "General Information."

See Also
IBM File Finder

User Guide
- [x] Windows
- [x] DOS
- [x] Macintosh
- [ ] Terminal Emulation
- [ ] VMS
- [ ] UNIX
- [ ] OS/2
- [ ] Other platform

Cost
- [ ] Unknown
- [ ] Basic
- [x] Extended
- [ ] Premium ($)
- [ ] Executive w/$

Activity Level
LOW

Address
GO: **DIAGSOFT**

T

Tandy Model 100 Forum

Description
This is a forum for users of Tandy nonDOS laptop computers.

Subjects
Computers

Audience
Computer users

Content Summary
The libraries include information on the Model 100, 200, 600 series and also support work-alikes such as NEC and Olivetti.

See Also
Tandy Users Network

User Guide
- [✓] Windows
- [ ] DOS
- [ ] Macintosh
- [ ] Terminal Emulation
- [ ] VMS
- [ ] UNIX
- [ ] OS/2
- [✓] Other platform

Cost
- [ ] Unknown
- [ ] Basic
- [✓] Extended
- [ ] Premium ($)
- [ ] Executive w/$

Activity Level

Address
GO: **Tandy Corporation Newsletter**

Tandy Professional Forum

Description
This is a forum for users of Tandy's "Professional" computers, such as the Tandy 2000, and Model 1/2/3/4 computers.

Subjects
Computers

Audience
Computer users

Content Summary
The libraries contain information on Tandy products and also contain software and utilities available for downloading.

See Also
Tandy Users Network

User Guide
- [✓] Windows
- [✓] DOS
- [ ] Macintosh
- [ ] Terminal Emulation
- [ ] VMS
- [ ] UNIX
- [ ] OS/2
- [ ] Other platform

Cost
- [ ] Unknown
- [ ] Basic
- [✓] Extended
- [ ] Premium ($)
- [ ] Executive w/$

Activity Level

Address
GO: **TRS80PRO**

TAPCIS Forum

Description
This is a vendor support forum for users of TAPCIS, the navigator and offline reader for CompuServe users.

Subjects
Computers

Audience
Computer users

Content Summary
The libraries contain basic information, information on usage, and tips on how to use TAPCIS internationally.

See Also
WinCim

User Guide
- [✓] Windows
- [✓] DOS
- [ ] Macintosh
- [ ] Terminal Emulation
- [ ] VMS
- [ ] UNIX
- [ ] OS/2
- [ ] Other platform

Cost
- [ ] Unknown
- [ ] Basic
- [✓] Extended
- [ ] Premium ($)
- [ ] Executive w/$

Activity Level

Address
GO: **TAPCIS**

544 Taxes

TAXES

Electronic Tax Return Filing

Description
File your taxes online with this service.

Subjects
Electronic Filing, Taxes

Audience
Accountants, Taxpayers

Content Summary
During the off-season (which it was when this book was written), this service does not accept tax returns. You can, however, leave messages in the Member FEEDBACK option in the main menu.

See Also
H&R Block

User Guide
- ☐ Windows
- ☐ DOS
- ☐ Macintosh
- ☑ Terminal Emulation
- ☐ VMS
- ☐ UNIX
- ☐ OS/2
- ☐ Other platform

Cost
- ☐ Unknown
- ☐ Basic
- ☑ Extended
- ☐ Premium ($)
- ☐ Executive w/$

Activity Level

Address
GO: **TAXRETURN**

H&R Block

Description
Did you know that in 18th century England, taxes were based on the number of fireplaces and hearths a person had? You can get tax information in this service.

Subjects
Taxes

Audience
General public

Content Summary
This service offers a history of H&R Block (the parent company of CompuServe, Inc.), Executive Tax Service, Record Keeping Books, Important Tax Dates of 1994, Tax Trivia, H&R Block Financial News, and Income Tax Information by Category.

See Also
CompuServe Tax Connection

User Guide
- ☑ Windows
- ☑ DOS
- ☑ Macintosh
- ☐ Terminal Emulation
- ☑ VMS
- ☑ UNIX
- ☑ OS/2
- ☐ Other platform

Cost
- ☐ Unknown
- ☑ Basic
- ☐ Extended
- ☐ Premium ($)
- ☐ Executive w/$

Activity Level

Address
GO: **HRB**

Intuit Personal Tax Forum

Description
This forum provides online support for Intuit products, including TurboTax for DOS, TurboTax for Windows, MacInTax, and more.

Subjects
Taxes

Audience
General public

Content Summary
Libraries include information on TurboTax for both DOS and Windows and MacInTax.

See Also
IRS Tax Forms & Documents

User Guide
- ☑ Windows
- ☑ DOS
- ☑ Macintosh
- ☐ Terminal Emulation
- ☐ VMS
- ☐ UNIX
- ☐ OS/2
- ☐ Other platform

Cost
- ☐ Unknown
- ☐ Basic
- ☐ Extended
- ☐ Premium ($)
- ☐ Executive w/$

Activity Level

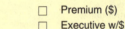

Address
GO: **INTUIT**

IRS Tax Forms and Documents

Description
Save time and a stamp by doing your taxes online. This service explains how.

Subjects
Tax

Audience
General public

Content Summary
With over 450 documents online, this service offers every current IRS form and all instructions and publications that the IRS can provide. The file format that you use is Adobe Acrobat's Portable Document Format (PDF). The IRS-approved forms presented in PDF look nearly identical to the forms you get at the post office or library, or order from the IRS. The IRS Tax Documents main menu includes Overview, Searching for Documents, Contacting the IRS, Adobe Acrobat Reader, Member Feedback, and Access IRS Tax Documents.

See Also
H&R Block

User Guide
- ☑ Windows
- ☑ DOS
- ☑ Macintosh
- ☐ Terminal Emulation
- ☑ VMS
- ☑ UNIX
- ☑ OS/2
- ☐ Other platform

Cost
- ☐ Unknown
- ☐ Basic
- ☑ Extended
- ☐ Premium ($)
- ☐ Executive w/$

Activity Level

Address
GO: **TAXFORMS**

TEACHING

Education Forum

Description
This forum is designed to share and exchange information about all facets of the teaching and learning process. The use of computers and computer-related teaching methods is a hot topic in this forum.

Subjects
Computers in Education, Education, Teaching

Audience
Administrators, teachers, college and university faculty, product developers and publishers of educational material, librarians, school board members, counselors, principals

Content Summary
The Education Forum sponsors two weekly online meetings, including Tuesday evenings in Room 1 (General) at 9:30 p.m. Eastern and Thursday evenings in Room 5 (Homeschoolers) at 9:00 p.m. Eastern. This forum's libraries contain information on earning a degree online (Library 11), sex and AIDS education (Library 15), public domain and shareware software (Library 2), and lessons on how to participate in online conferences (Library 1, HOW2CO.TXT).

See Also
Education Research Forum, ERIC

User Guide
- ☑ Windows
- ☑ DOS
- ☑ Macintosh
- ☐ Terminal Emulation
- ☑ VMS
- ☑ UNIX
- ☑ OS/2
- ☑ Other platform

Cost
- ☐ Unknown
- ☐ Basic
- ☑ Extended
- ☐ Premium ($)
- ☐ Executive w/$

Activity Level

Address
GO: **EDFORUM**

Telecommunications Forum

Description
This forum discusses telecommunications services and products, long distance services, and such things as protection of 1st Amendment rights.

Subjects
Computers

Audience
Computer users

Content Summary
The libraries include information about long distance services, First Amendment rights for electronic communication, and other related issues.

See Also
Computer Directory

Telecommunications Forum – Television

User Guide
- ☑ Windows
- ☑ DOS
- ☑ Macintosh
- ☐ Terminal Emulation
- ☑ VMS
- ☑ UNIX
- ☐ OS/2
- ☐ Other platform

Cost
- ☐ Unknown
- ☐ Basic
- ☑ Extended
- ☐ Premium ($)
- ☐ Executive w/$

Activity Level
MEDIUM

Address
GO: **TELECO**

Telephone Access Numbers

Description
This forum provides local CompuServe access numbers, information, and communications surcharges.

Subjects
Computers, CompuServe

Audience
Computer users

Content Summary
Use this forum to look up the CompuServe access number or to get information about your account.

See Also
CompuServe Help

User Guide
- ☑ Windows
- ☑ DOS
- ☑ Macintosh
- ☐ Terminal Emulation
- ☑ VMS
- ☑ UNIX
- ☐ OS/2
- ☑ Other platform

Cost
- ☐ Unknown
- ☑ Basic
- ☐ Extended
- ☐ Premium ($)
- ☐ Executive w/$

Activity Level

UNKNOWN

Address
GO: **PHONES**

TELESCOPES

Astronomy Forum

Description
The Astronomy Forum is for anyone who shares a fascination with celestial happenings, whether at the amateur or professional level.

Subjects
Hobbies, Science

Audience
Astronomers, hobbyists

Content Summary
The libraries contain public domain software, reference articles, and graphic images.

See Also
Participate

User Guide
- ☑ Windows
- ☑ DOS
- ☑ Macintosh
- ☐ Terminal Emulation
- ☑ VMS
- ☑ UNIX
- ☑ OS/2
- ☑ Other platform

Cost
- ☐ Unknown
- ☐ Basic
- ☑ Extended
- ☐ Premium ($)
- ☐ Executive w/$

Activity Level
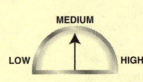
MEDIUM

Address
GO: **ASTROFORUM**

TELEVISION

Broadcast Professionals Forum

Description
The BPFORUM is the place where professionals in radio, TV, Land Mobile Radio and Audio share news and views about the latest in the industry.

Subjects
Broadcasting, Television

Audience
Radio operators

Content Summary
You can find information and messages about television, cable TV, broadcast engineering, audio, talent, post production, the FCC, and more in this forum.

Television

See Also
Ham Radio Forum

User Guide
- ☑ Windows
- ☑ DOS
- ☑ Macintosh
- ☐ Terminal Emulation
- ☑ VMS
- ☑ UNIX
- ☑ OS/2
- ☐ Other platform

Cost
- ☐ Unknown
- ☐ Basic
- ☑ Extended
- ☐ Premium ($)
- ☐ Executive w/$

Activity Level

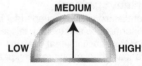

Address
GO: **BPFORUM**

Showbiz Quiz

Description
Companion to the ShowBiz Forum and Hollywood Hotline, this area features trivia quizzes on several ShowBiz topics.

Subjects
Games, Movies, Television, Trivia

Audience
Movie enthusiasts

Content Summary
The libraries contain information about the forum, home entertainment, recent films, new films, classic films, television, celebrities, and Hollywood news.

See Also
Hollywood Hotline

User Guide
- ☑ Windows
- ☑ DOS
- ☑ Macintosh
- ☐ Terminal Emulation
- ☐ VMS
- ☑ UNIX
- ☐ OS/2
- ☐ Other platform

Cost
- ☐ Unknown
- ☐ Basic
- ☑ Extended
- ☐ Premium ($)
- ☐ Executive w/$

Activity Level

Address
GO: **SBQ**

Soap Opera Summaries

Description
This forum includes daily summaries of TV soap operas, including information on the stars and fan clubs.

Subjects
Television

Audience
Television viewers

Content Summary
The libraries include information about the celebrities who appear in soap operas, news about specific shows, and lists of fan clubs.

See Also
Hollywood Hotline, Showbiz Forum

User Guide
- ☑ Windows
- ☑ DOS
- ☑ Macintosh
- ☐ Terminal Emulation
- ☑ VMS
- ☑ UNIX
- ☑ OS/2
- ☑ Other platform

Cost
- ☐ Unknown
- ☑ Basic
- ☐ Extended
- ☐ Premium ($)
- ☐ Executive w/$

Activity Level

Address
GO: **SOAPS**

Society of Broadcast Eng.

Description
This is the main menu for the Society of Broadcast Engineers area, featuring Society news and access to the Broadcast Professionals Forum (BPFORUM).

Subjects
Broadcasting, Television

Audience
Broadcasters

Content Summary
The areas of this forum include access to the Broadcast Professionals Forum, a list of upcoming conventions, and an information request area.

See Also
Broadcast Professionals Forum

User Guide
- ☑ Windows
- ☑ DOS
- ☑ Macintosh
- ☐ Terminal Emulation
- ☑ VMS
- ☑ UNIX
- ☑ OS/2
- ☑ Other platform

Television – Testing

Cost
- [ ] Unknown
- [ ] Basic
- [x] Extended
- [ ] Premium ($)
- [ ] Executive w/$

Activity Level
LOW ← MEDIUM HIGH

Address
GO: **SBENET**

TESTING

Benchmarks and Standards Forum

Description
This is a place where individuals and companies can discuss aspects of PC performance, measurement technology, and productivity.

Subjects
Computers, Testing

Audience
MIS people

Content Summary
For discussions and support for benchmark performances and testing, this forum has library and message sections that contain topics such as standardizing, measurement, performance analysis, and the like.

See Also
Ziff-Davis Benchmark Operation Forum

User Guide
- [x] Windows
- [x] DOS
- [x] Macintosh
- [ ] Terminal Emulation
- [ ] VMS
- [ ] UNIX
- [x] OS/2
- [x] Other platform

Cost
- [ ] Unknown
- [ ] Basic
- [x] Extended
- [ ] Premium ($)
- [ ] Executive w/$

Activity Level

LOW ← MEDIUM HIGH

Address
GO: **BENCHMARK**

Intelligence Test

Description
So, you think you're smart? Take the CompuServe IQ and prove it.

Subjects
Testing

Audience
General public

Content Summary
This is a terminal emulation service that enables you to take an IQ test that is formulated the same way that standardized tests are done. They advise you to take the test in a quiet room to get accurate results. The tests can take up to 32 minutes to complete.

See Also
The Whiz Quiz

User Guide
- [ ] Windows
- [ ] DOS
- [ ] Macintosh
- [x] Terminal Emulation
- [ ] VMS
- [ ] UNIX
- [ ] OS/2
- [ ] Other platform

Cost
- [ ] Unknown
- [ ] Basic
- [x] Extended
- [ ] Premium ($)
- [ ] Executive w/$

Activity Level

LOW UNKNOWN MEDIUM HIGH

Address
GO: **TMC-101**

The Whiz Quiz

Description
This is an online trivia quiz, using categories and questions supplied by Grolier.

Subjects
Games, Testing

Audience
General public

Content Summary
Trivia quizzes include geography, literature, current events, movies, sports, music, science, and many more.

See Also
Intelligence Test

User Guide
- [x] Windows
- [x] DOS
- [x] Macintosh
- [ ] Terminal Emulation
- [x] VMS
- [x] UNIX
- [x] OS/2
- [ ] Other platform

Cost
- ☐ Unknown
- ☐ Basic
- ☑ Extended
- ☐ Premium ($)
- ☐ Executive w/$

Activity Level

MEDIUM — UNKNOWN (LOW / HIGH)

Address
GO: **WHIZ**

Texas Instruments Forum

Description
This is a forum covering the TI-99/4a and TI Professional computers.

Subjects
Computers

Audience
Computer users

Content Summary
The libraries include information about user groups, product information, technical support, and more.

See Also
Texas Instrument Newsletter

User Guide
- ☑ Windows
- ☑ DOS
- ☐ Macintosh
- ☐ Terminal Emulation
- ☐ VMS
- ☐ UNIX
- ☐ OS/2
- ☐ Other platform

Cost
- ☐ Unknown
- ☐ Basic
- ☑ Extended
- ☐ Premium ($)
- ☐ Executive w/$

Activity Level

MEDIUM — arrow pointing LOW

Address
GO: **TIFORUM**

Texas Instruments News

Description
This is a menu-driven area containing news of the TI Forum and TI world in general.

Subjects
Computers

Audience
Computer users

Content Summary
The libraries contain information of help to new users, latest news, and new products and features of Texas Instruments.

See Also
The Computer Directory

User Guide
- ☑ Windows
- ☑ DOS
- ☐ Macintosh
- ☐ Terminal Emulation
- ☐ VMS
- ☐ UNIX
- ☐ OS/2
- ☐ Other platform

Cost
- ☐ Unknown
- ☐ Basic
- ☑ Extended
- ☐ Premium ($)
- ☐ Executive w/$

Activity Level

MEDIUM — UNKNOWN (LOW / HIGH)

Address
GO: **TINEWS**

The 'GO GRAPHICS' Tutorial

Description
This is an online menu providing several helpful answers to commonly asked questions on CIS's GO GRAPHICS areas. Also, how to download pictures, how to view them, and so forth.

Subjects
Computers, Computer Graphics

Audience
Computer users, computer artists

Content Summary
The libraries include information on file formats, lessons for the novice, directions for downloading graphics, converting images, and news.

See Also
Graphics Corner Forum

User Guide
- ☑ Windows
- ☑ DOS
- ☑ Macintosh
- ☐ Terminal Emulation
- ☐ VMS
- ☑ UNIX
- ☑ OS/2
- ☐ Other platform

Cost
- ☐ Unknown
- ☐ Basic
- ☑ Extended
- ☐ Premium ($)
- ☐ Executive w/$

Activity Level

MEDIUM — UNKNOWN (LOW / HIGH)

Address
GO: **PIC**

The Absolut Museum

Description
This online area provides information and graphics files from Absolut Vodka.

Subjects
Entertainment, Hobbies

Audience
Absolut Vodka enthusiasts

Content Summary
The libraries contain upcoming events and award-winning artwork from around the country.

See Also
Bacchus Wine Forum

User Guide
- ☑ Windows
- ☑ DOS
- ☑ Macintosh
- ☐ Terminal Emulation
- ☑ VMS
- ☑ UNIX
- ☑ OS/2
- ☐ Other platform

Cost
- ☐ Unknown
- ☑ Basic
- ☐ Extended
- ☐ Premium ($)
- ☐ Executive w/$

Activity Level

Address
GO: **ABS**

The Business Wire

Description
This is a news area offering press releases, news articles, and other information from the world of business.

Subjects
Business, Finance

Audience
Business people

Content Summary
The libraries include press releases, news articles, and information about specific companies. It is updated daily.

See Also
AP Online

User Guide
- ☑ Windows
- ☑ DOS
- ☑ Macintosh
- ☐ Terminal Emulation
- ☑ VMS
- ☑ UNIX
- ☑ OS/2
- ☑ Other platform

The Absolut Museum

Cost
- ☐ Unknown
- ☐ Basic
- ☑ Extended
- ☐ Premium ($)
- ☐ Executive w/$

Activity Level

Address
GO: **TBW**

The Company Corporation

Description
The Company Corporation offers information on incorporating your business. You can even incorporate online.

Subjects
Business

Audience
Business people

Content Summary
If you want to start a business, this forum can provide the answers to the legal questions of how to incorporate.

See Also
Company Analyzer

User Guide
- ☑ Windows
- ☑ DOS
- ☑ Macintosh
- ☐ Terminal Emulation
- ☑ VMS
- ☑ UNIX
- ☐ OS/2
- ☑ Other platform

Cost
- ☐ Unknown
- ☑ Basic
- ☐ Extended
- ☐ Premium ($)
- ☐ Executive w/$

Activity Level

Address
GO: **CORP**

The CompuServe Help Forum

Description
This is a free forum for all CIS members who need help using CompuServe or have questions about their membership.

Subjects
CompuServe

The CompuServe Help Forum – The Entrepreneur's Forum

Audience
CompuServe users

Content Summary
You can find information about billing, forums, usage, or general interest.

See Also
Feedback to CompuServe

User Guide
- ☑ Windows
- ☑ DOS
- ☑ Macintosh
- ☑ Terminal Emulation
- ☑ VMS
- ☑ UNIX
- ☑ OS/2
- ☐ Other platform

Cost
- ☐ Unknown
- ☑ Basic
- ☐ Extended
- ☐ Premium ($)
- ☐ Executive w/$

Activity Level

Address
GO: **HELPFORUM**

The CompuServe Practice Forum

Description
This is a free forum for all CIS members.

Subjects
Aristitolian Texts, Chemical Engineering

Audience
Ada Repository users, collectors, accountants

Content Summary
Within this forum, you can practice creating forum messages, or uploading/downloading files, or simply ask questions about using CIS forums.

See Also
Access Numbers, Access Phone Numbers(FREE)

User Guide
- ☑ Windows
- ☑ DOS
- ☑ Macintosh
- ☑ Terminal Emulation
- ☑ VMS
- ☑ UNIX
- ☑ OS/2
- ☐ Other platform

Cost
- ☐ Unknown
- ☑ Basic
- ☐ Extended
- ☐ Premium ($)
- ☐ Executive w/$

Activity Level

Address
GO: **PRACTICE**

The Court Reporters Forum

Description
This is the headquarters for discussion of issues involving the court reporting profession worldwide.

Subjects
Court reporting

Audience
Court reporters

Content Summary
The libraries include information on technology, litigation support, and marketing.

See Also
Legal Forum

User Guide
- ☑ Windows
- ☑ DOS
- ☑ Macintosh
- ☐ Terminal Emulation
- ☑ VMS
- ☑ UNIX
- ☑ OS/2
- ☐ Other platform

Cost
- ☐ Unknown
- ☐ Basic
- ☑ Extended
- ☐ Premium ($)
- ☐ Executive w/$

Activity Level

Address
GO: **CRF**

The Entrepreneur's Forum

Description
This forum is sponsored by *Entrepreneur Magazine* to meet with its readers around the world.

Subjects
Business

Audience
Entrepreneurs, business people

Content Summary
The libraries include business start-up procedures and the development of your business.

See Also
Business

The Entrepreneur's Forum – The Heath Company

User Guide
- ☑ Windows
- ☑ DOS
- ☐ Macintosh
- ☐ Terminal Emulation
- ☑ VMS
- ☑ UNIX
- ☑ OS/2
- ☐ Other platform

Cost
- ☐ Unknown
- ☐ Basic
- ☑ Extended
- ☐ Premium ($)
- ☐ Executive w/$

Activity Level: MEDIUM

Address
GO: **ENT**

The Escort Store

Description
This is an online shopping area for The Escort Store.

Subjects
Shopping

Audience
General public

Content Summary
The libraries include sources for top-rated consumer electronics products.

See Also
Electronic Mall

User Guide
- ☑ Windows
- ☑ DOS
- ☐ Macintosh
- ☐ Terminal Emulation
- ☑ VMS
- ☑ UNIX
- ☑ OS/2
- ☑ Other platform

Cost
- ☐ Unknown
- ☑ Basic
- ☐ Extended
- ☐ Premium ($)
- ☐ Executive w/$

Activity Level: UNKNOWN

Address
GO: **ESCORT**

The Gift Sender

Description
This is an online shopping area offering gifts from around the world.

Subjects
Gifts

Audience
General public

Content Summary
This online shopping area gives you access to gifts from around the world, including clothing, food, and crafts.

See Also
Alaskan Peddler

User Guide
- ☐ Windows
- ☐ DOS
- ☐ Macintosh
- ☑ Terminal Emulation
- ☐ VMS
- ☐ UNIX
- ☐ OS/2
- ☐ Other platform

Cost
- ☐ Unknown
- ☐ Basic
- ☑ Extended
- ☐ Premium ($)
- ☐ Executive w/$

Activity Level: UNKNOWN

Address
GO: **GIFT**

The Heath Company

Description
This is an online shopping area for Heath Electronics, producers of Heathkit products.

Subjects
Shopping

Audience
General public

Content Summary
This online shopping service enables members to purchase electronic health products.

See Also
The Escort Store

User Guide
- ☑ Windows
- ☑ DOS
- ☑ Macintosh
- ☐ Terminal Emulation
- ☑ VMS
- ☑ UNIX
- ☑ OS/2
- ☐ Other platform

Cost
- ☐ Unknown
- ☐ Basic
- ☑ Extended
- ☐ Premium ($)
- ☐ Executive w/$

Activity Level: UNKNOWN

Address
GO: **HEATH**

The Intel Forum

Description
This is a vendor support forum for Intel Corp. and their computer-related hardware products.

Subjects
Computers

Audience
Computer users

Content Summary
The libraries contain information about product support, management and utility tools, fax/print servers, latest drivers, software revisions, troubleshooting documents.

See Also
Computer Hardware, Modems

User Guide
- ☑ Windows
- ☑ DOS
- ☐ Macintosh
- ☐ Terminal Emulation
- ☐ VMS
- ☐ UNIX
- ☐ OS/2
- ☐ Other platform

Cost
- ☐ Unknown
- ☐ Basic
- ☑ Extended
- ☐ Premium ($)
- ☐ Executive w/$

Activity Level

Address
GO: **INTEL**

The Laser's Edge

Description
This is an online shopping area for The Laser's Edge, and their laser disc products.

Subjects
Shopping

Audience
General public

Content Summary
This online shopping service provides members access to the complete line of The Laser's Edge electronic products.

See Also
Electronic Mall

User Guide
- ☑ Windows
- ☑ DOS
- ☑ Macintosh
- ☐ Terminal Emulation
- ☑ VMS
- ☑ UNIX
- ☑ OS/2
- ☐ Other platform

Cost

Activity Level

Address
GO: **EDGE**

The Mac Zone/PC Zone

Description
This is an online shopping area for Mac and PC hardware and software.

Subjects
Shopping, Computers

Audience
General public

Content Summary
This online shopping area enables members to purchase from a complete line of PC and Macintosh products often at reduced rates.

See Also
MacFun forum

User Guide
- ☑ Windows
- ☑ DOS
- ☑ Macintosh
- ☐ Terminal Emulation
- ☐ VMS
- ☐ UNIX
- ☑ OS/2
- ☐ Other platform

Cost
- ☐ Unknown
- ☐ Basic
- ☑ Extended
- ☐ Premium ($)
- ☐ Executive w/$

Activity Level

Address
GO: **M2**

The Store

Description
You can purchase and download exciting commercial software, including Star Wars audio clips, Terminator 2 Screen Saver collections, and more.

Subjects
Computer Software

Audience
Computer users

The Store

Content Summary
This online shopping service enables members to purchase everything from screen savers to commercial software.

See Also
The Computer Forum

User Guide
- ☑ Windows
- ☑ DOS
- ☐ Macintosh
- ☐ Terminal Emulation
- ☐ VMS
- ☐ UNIX
- ☐ OS/2
- ☐ Other platform

Cost
- ☐ Unknown
- ☐ Basic
- ☑ Extended
- ☐ Premium ($)
- ☐ Executive w/$

Activity Level: UNKNOWN

Address
GO: **STORE**

The Sysop Forum

Description
This is a private forum hosted by CIS for the training of forum Sysops and discussion of forum issues.

Subjects
Academic Research, Campus Activities and Student Newspaper

Audience
Administrators

Content Summary
This forum is not available to all users—only to those members training to be Sysops.

See Also
Membership Support Services

User Guide
- ☑ Windows
- ☑ DOS
- ☑ Macintosh
- ☑ Terminal Emulation
- ☑ VMS
- ☑ UNIX
- ☑ OS/2
- ☐ Other platform

Cost
- ☐ Unknown
- ☐ Basic
- ☑ Extended
- ☐ Premium ($)
- ☐ Executive w/$

Activity Level: MEDIUM

Address
GO: **SYSOP**

The Whiz Quiz

Description
This is an online trivia quiz, using categories and questions supplied by Grolier.

Subjects
Games, Testing

Audience
General public

Content Summary
Trivia quizzes include geography, literature, current events, movies, sports, music, science, and many more.

See Also
Intelligence Test

User Guide
- ☑ Windows
- ☑ DOS
- ☐ Macintosh
- ☐ Terminal Emulation
- ☐ VMS
- ☐ UNIX
- ☐ OS/2
- ☐ Other platform

Cost
- ☐ Unknown
- ☐ Basic
- ☑ Extended
- ☐ Premium ($)
- ☐ Executive w/$

Activity Level: UNKNOWN

Address
GO: **WHIZ**

Thomas Register Online

Description
This database contains company information on almost 150,000 USA and Canadian manufacturers and service providers. It is updated annually.

Subjects
Business

Audience
Business people

Content Summary
Information for each entry includes company name, address, telephone number, and products or services offered.

See Also
Financial Forums

User Guide
- ☑ Windows
- ☑ DOS
- ☑ Macintosh
- ☐ Terminal Emulation
- ☑ VMS
- ☑ UNIX
- ☑ OS/2
- ☐ Other platform

Thomas Register Online – Time-Warner

555

Cost
- [ ] Unknown
- [ ] Basic
- [ ] Extended
- [x] Premium ($)
- [ ] Executive w/$

Activity Level
LOW — UNKNOWN (MEDIUM) — HIGH

Address
GO: **THOMAS**

Thomas-Conrad Forum

Description
This is a vendor supported forum for Thomas-Conrad, manufacturer of network adapters, hub concentrators, and other products for ARCnet, Ethernet, Token Ring and TCNS systems.

Subjects
Computers

Audience
Computer users

Content Summary
Libraries and message areas include answers to technical questions, product information, and news on development of products.

See Also
Networks

User Guide
- [x] Windows
- [x] DOS
- [x] Macintosh
- [ ] Terminal Emulation
- [ ] VMS
- [ ] UNIX
- [ ] OS/2
- [ ] Other platform

Cost
- [ ] Unknown
- [ ] Basic
- [x] Extended
- [ ] Premium ($)
- [ ] Executive w/$

Activity Level
LOW ← (MEDIUM) — HIGH

Address
GO: **TCC FORUM**

Ticker/Symbol Lookup

Description
This is an online database that provides financial information for various stocks.

Subjects
Finances, Investment

Audience
Business people

Content Summary
This database enables you to look up information by company name, ticker symbol, CUSIP number, CNUM, or primary SIC code.

See Also
Financial Forums

User Guide
- [x] Windows
- [x] DOS
- [x] Macintosh
- [ ] Terminal Emulation
- [x] VMS
- [x] UNIX
- [x] OS/2
- [ ] Other platform

Cost
- [ ] Unknown
- [ ] Basic
- [x] Extended
- [ ] Premium ($)
- [ ] Executive w/$

Activity Level
LOW — UNKNOWN (MEDIUM) — HIGH

Address
GO: **LOOKUP**

TIME-WARNER

Time-Warner Electronic Bookstore

Description
This is an online shopping area offering Time-Warner books.

Subjects
Shopping

Audience
General public

Content Summary
This online shopping area contains the vast amount of published material offered by Time-Warner.

See Also
Book-of-the-Month Club

User Guide
- [x] Windows
- [x] DOS
- [x] Macintosh
- [ ] Terminal Emulation
- [x] VMS
- [x] UNIX
- [x] OS/2
- [ ] Other platform

Cost
- [ ] Unknown
- [x] Basic
- [ ] Extended
- [ ] Premium ($)
- [ ] Executive w/$

Time-Warner – TIMESLIPS Forum

Activity Level

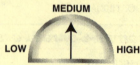

Address
GO: **TWB-12**

Time-Warner Crime Forum

Description
This is a forum sponsored by Time-Warner to discuss crime and violence worldwide.

Subjects
Crime, Time-Warner

Audience
General public

Content Summary
This forum contains information, facts, and discussions about crime and criminals.

See Also
Crime

User Guide
☑	Windows	☐	VMS
☑	DOS	☐	UNIX
☐	Macintosh	☐	OS/2
☐	Terminal Emulation	☐	Other platform

Cost
☐	Unknown	☐	Premium ($)
☐	Basic	☐	Executive w/$
☑	Extended		

Activity Level

Address
GO: **CRIME**

Time-Warner-Dogs & Cats Forum

Description
Forum sponsored by Time-Warner to discuss dogs, cats, and other household pets.

Subjects
Pets

Audience
Pet owners

Content Summary
If you own a pet, this forum provides information on the care and feeding of cats and dogs.

See Also
Pets Forum

User Guide
☑	Windows	☐	VMS
☑	DOS	☐	UNIX
☐	Macintosh	☐	OS/2
☐	Terminal Emulation	☐	Other platform

Cost
☐	Unknown	☐	Premium ($)
☐	Basic	☐	Executive w/$
☑	Extended		

Activity Level

Address
GO: **TWPETS**

TIMESLIPS Forum

Description
This is a vendor supported forum for Timeslips Corp., and its time tracking and billing software.

Subjects
Accounting

Audience
Computer users

Content Summary
The libraries include information on product usage, product information, and technical support.

See Also
Accounting software

User Guide
☑	Windows	☐	VMS
☑	DOS	☐	UNIX
☐	Macintosh	☐	OS/2
☐	Terminal Emulation	☐	Other platform

Cost
☐	Unknown	☐	Premium ($)
☐	Basic	☐	Executive w/$
☑	Extended		

Activity Level

Address
GO: **TIMESLIPS**

TOSHIBA

Toshiba Forum

Description
This is a vendor supported forum for Toshiba laptop and notebook computers, and utility software.

Subjects
Computers, Toshiba

Audience
Computer users

Content Summary
The libraries include product information, technical support help, troubleshooting tips, and upcoming product releases.

See Also
Toshiba products

User Guide
- ☑ Windows
- ☑ DOS
- ☐ Macintosh
- ☐ Terminal Emulation
- ☐ VMS
- ☐ UNIX
- ☐ OS/2
- ☐ Other platform

Cost
- ☐ Unknown
- ☐ Basic
- ☑ Extended
- ☐ Premium ($)
- ☐ Executive w/$

Activity Level

Address
GO: **TOSHIBA**

Toshiba GmbH Forum

Description
This is a vendor supported forum for German users of Toshiba laptop and notebook computers.

Subjects
Computers, Toshiba

Audience
Computer users

Content Summary
The libraries include product information, technical support help, troubleshooting tips, and upcoming product releases.

See Also
Toshiba computers

User Guide
- ☑ Windows
- ☑ DOS
- ☐ Macintosh
- ☐ Terminal Emulation
- ☐ VMS
- ☐ UNIX
- ☐ OS/2
- ☐ Other platform

Cost
- ☐ Unknown
- ☐ Basic
- ☑ Extended
- ☐ Premium ($)
- ☐ Executive w/$

Activity Level

Address
GO: **TOSHGER**

TOURISM

Florida Today Forum

Description
This forum is the first international, interactive forum linking *Florida Today*, the Space Coast Newspaper, with newspaper readers everywhere.

Subjects
Disney Comics, Florida, Tourism

Audience
Tourists, Florida residents

Content Summary
The Florida Today Newslink forum is an electronic newspaper intended to give readers a way to get their news and information online. The libraries consist of sections devoted to space, sports, leisure and tourism, environment, gardening, weather, senior activities, politics, education, and many more areas. The Front Page Lounge (Library 15) is full of editorial cartoons for you to download and view.

See Also
Travel Forum, Florida Forum

User Guide
- ☑ Windows
- ☑ DOS
- ☑ Macintosh
- ☐ Terminal Emulation
- ☑ VMS
- ☑ UNIX
- ☑ OS/2
- ☑ Other platform

Cost
- ☐ Unknown
- ☐ Basic
- ☑ Extended
- ☐ Premium ($)
- ☐ Executive w/$

Tourism – Trains

Activity Level: LOW (arrow pointing to LOW)

Address
GO: **FLATODAY**

Official Airline Guide

Description
The Official Airline Guide is the most comprehensive, up-to-date source of travel-related information available online. This service also is easy to use and does not require you to know travel codes.

Subjects
Travel, Airline, Tourism

Audience
General public

Content Summary
From the Official Airline Guide main menu, you can read a description of the service, get a list of the commands, give feedback to the service, and access the service. Be sure to read the pricing instructions by selecting the Access option from the main menu.

See Also
EAASY SABRE

User Guide
- ☑ Windows
- ☑ DOS
- ☑ Macintosh
- ☐ Terminal Emulation
- ☑ VMS
- ☑ UNIX
- ☐ OS/2
- ☐ Other platform

Cost
- ☐ Unknown
- ☐ Basic
- ☐ Extended
- ☑ Premium ($)
- ☐ Executive w/$

Activity Level: UNKNOWN

Address
GO: **OAG**

TRADE MARKS

TRADEMARKSCAN

Description
Two databases containing state and USA information on trademarks and applications currently on file.

Subjects
Trade marks

Audience
Business people

Content Summary
This database contains two sources of information. One provides the U.S. Patent and Trademark Office information. The other is the U.S. State database of trademark registration.

See Also
Patent Research Center

User Guide
- ☑ Windows
- ☑ DOS
- ☑ Macintosh
- ☐ Terminal Emulation
- ☑ VMS
- ☑ UNIX
- ☑ OS/2
- ☑ Other platform

Cost
- ☐ Unknown
- ☐ Basic
- ☐ Extended
- ☑ Premium ($)
- ☐ Executive w/$

Activity Level: UNKNOWN

Address
GO: **TRADERC**

TRAINS

TrainNet Forum

Description
The TrainNet Forum serves as a focal point for a wide range of railroad oriented subjects, from Amtrak employees to Z-Scale models.

Subjects
Hobbies, Trains

Audience
Train enthusiasts

Content Summary
Libraries include information on hobby stores, historial and technical railroad societies, model railroad enthusiasts, and industry publications.

See Also
Trains, model trains, games/simulations, rail employees and unions, the rail industry

User Guide
- ☑ Windows
- ☑ DOS
- ☑ Macintosh
- ☐ Terminal Emulation
- ☑ VMS
- ☑ UNIX
- ☑ OS/2
- ☑ Other platform

Cost
- ☐ Unknown
- ☐ Basic
- ☑ Extended
- ☐ Premium ($)
- ☐ Executive w/$

Trains – Travel

Activity Level

Address
GO: **TRAINS**

TRAVEL

ABC Worldwide Hotel Guide

Description
The ABC Worldwide Hotel Guide provides up-to-date comprehensive listings of over 60,000 hotel properties worldwide.

Subjects
Hotels, Travel

Audience
Travelers

Content Summary
Within this forum, you can find information about the locations, addresses, services offered, and which credit cards are accepted at the member hotel and resorts.

See Also
Travel Forum

User Guide
- ☑ Windows
- ☑ DOS
- ☑ Macintosh
- ☐ Terminal Emulation
- ☐ VMS
- ☐ UNIX
- ☐ OS/2
- ☐ Other platform

Cost
- ☐ Unknown
- ☐ Basic
- ☑ Extended
- ☐ Premium ($)
- ☐ Executive w/$

Activity Level

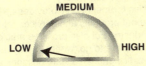

Address
GO: **ABC**

Air France

Description
This forum provides information on Air France flights to Europe and other world wide destinations.

Subjects
Travel

Audience
International travelers

Content Summary
This forum provides schedules and accommodations for destinations to Europe and other areas of the world.

See Also
Travel Forum

User Guide
- ☑ Windows
- ☑ DOS
- ☐ Macintosh
- ☐ Terminal Emulation
- ☐ VMS
- ☐ UNIX
- ☐ OS/2
- ☐ Other platform

Cost
- ☐ Unknown
- ☑ Basic
- ☐ Extended
- ☐ Premium ($)
- ☐ Executive w/$

Activity Level

Address
GO: **AF**

Airline Services Unlimited

Description
You can order suitcases, totes, and garment bags online. "Trusted by Flight Crews for 25 Years."

Subjects
Shopping, Travel

Audience
Consumers

Content Summary
This on-line shopping service offers all types of luggage and totes of all prices.

See Also
Travel Forum

User Guide
- ☑ Windows
- ☑ DOS
- ☐ Macintosh
- ☐ Terminal Emulation
- ☐ VMS
- ☐ UNIX
- ☐ OS/2
- ☐ Other platform

Cost
- ☐ Unknown
- ☐ Basic
- ☑ Extended
- ☐ Premium ($)
- ☐ Executive w/$

Activity Level

Address
GO: **ASU-1**

Inn and Lodging Forum

Description
This is the Lanier's Inn and Lodging forum, dedicated to discussions about alternative accommodations—places other than the chain hotels.

Subjects
Hotel Management, Travel

Audience
Tourists, general public

Content Summary
Lanier's Inn and Lodging Forum is a place to talk about the places you've discovered off the beaten path, and learn about new ways to take advantage of what bed and breakfast inns, all-suite hotels, and other forms of alternative accommodations have to offer. It's also a place to meet the people behind the scenes—the professionals who make your business and leisure travel the success it is. You can use libraries and message sections such as Innkeeping Dreams, B&B Recipe Exchanges, Elegant Hotels, and more.

See Also
Travel Forum, Bed & Breakfast Database

User Guide
☑	Windows	☑	VMS
☑	DOS	☑	UNIX
☑	Macintosh	☑	OS/2
☐	Terminal Emulation	☐	Other platform

Cost
☐	Unknown	☐	Premium ($)
☐	Basic	☐	Executive w/$
☑	Extended		

Activity Level

Address
GO: **INNFORUM**

Official Airline Guide

Description
The Official Airline Guide is the most comprehensive, up-to-date source of travel-related information available online. This service also is easy to use and does not require you to know travel codes.

Subjects
Travel, Airline, Tourism

Audience
General public

Content Summary
From the Official Airline Guide main menu, you can read a description of the service, get a list of the commands, give feedback to the service, and access the service. Be sure to read the pricing instructions by selecting the Access option from the main menu.

See Also
EAASY SABRE

User Guide
☑	Windows	☑	VMS
☑	DOS	☑	UNIX
☑	Macintosh	☐	OS/2
☐	Terminal Emulation	☐	Other platform

Cost
☐	Unknown	☑	Premium ($)
☐	Basic	☐	Executive w/$
☐	Extended		

Activity Level

Address
GO: **OAG**

Recreational Vehicle Forum

Description
This forum is for all people who enjoy camping in tent trailers, travel trailers, fifth-wheels, and motor homes. If you are an experienced camper or are just looking for a motor home, this forum can help.

Subjects
Camping, Motor Homes, Travel

Audience
Camping enthusiasts, travel enthusiasts, RV enthusiasts

Content Summary
This forum not only provides up-to-date information about products and services for the travel trailer industry, but also provides articles and discussions on where to go, where to stay, and what to do. Participants also state opinions and make recommendations on which RV to purchase and where to go for service. There's even a classified section if you are looking to purchase a recreational vehicle.

See Also
Travel Forum

User Guide
☑	Windows	☑	VMS
☑	DOS	☑	UNIX
☑	Macintosh	☑	OS/2
☐	Terminal Emulation	☐	Other platform

Travel

Cost
- [ ] Unknown
- [ ] Basic
- [x] Extended
- [ ] Premium ($)
- [ ] Executive w/$

Activity Level
LOW ← MEDIUM — HIGH

Address
GO: **RVFORUM**

Travel Britain Online

Description
This forum provides travelers' information on Great Britain.

Subjects
Travel

Audience
Travelers

Content Summary
The libraries include information on upcoming events, the latest tourist news, and an electronic guide to London.

See Also
Travel Forum

User Guide
- [x] Windows
- [x] DOS
- [ ] Macintosh
- [ ] Terminal Emulation
- [ ] VMS
- [ ] UNIX
- [ ] OS/2
- [ ] Other platform

Cost
- [ ] Unknown
- [ ] Basic
- [x] Extended
- [ ] Premium ($)
- [ ] Executive w/$

Activity Level
LOW — UNKNOWN — HIGH

Address
GO: **TBONLINE**

Travel Forum

Description
The Travel Forum allows CIS members to exchange stories, ideas, and information regarding travel experiences.

Subjects
Travel

Audience
General public

Content Summary
The libraries include information on restaurants, hotels, customs in foreign countries, cruises, and rail travel.

See Also
Travel

User Guide
- [x] Windows
- [x] DOS
- [x] Macintosh
- [ ] Terminal Emulation
- [x] VMS
- [x] UNIX
- [x] OS/2
- [x] Other platform

Cost
- [ ] Unknown
- [ ] Basic
- [x] Extended
- [ ] Premium ($)
- [ ] Executive w/$

Activity Level
LOW — MEDIUM → HIGH

Address
GO: **TRAVEL**

Travelers Advantage

Description
This is an online travel club, offering savings on travel, cruise, and hotel packages.

Subjects
Travel

Audience
Travelers

Content Summary
The libraries include information on travel savings, cruises, hotel packages, and general travel information.

See Also
Travel Forum

User Guide
- [x] Windows
- [x] DOS
- [x] Macintosh
- [ ] Terminal Emulation
- [x] VMS
- [x] UNIX
- [x] OS/2
- [x] Other platform

Cost
- [ ] Unknown
- [ ] Basic
- [x] Extended
- [ ] Premium ($)
- [ ] Executive w/$

Activity Level
LOW — UNKNOWN — HIGH

Address
GO: **TRAVADV**

UK Accommodation & Travel Services

Description
This forum provides travel and accomodations services from the UK Automobile Association.

Subjects
Travel

Audience
Travelers

Content Summary
This forum provides information about traveling in the United Kingdom. You can find destination information, reviews of restaurants and accommodations, and travel arrangements.

See Also
UK Forum

User Guide
- ☑ Windows
- ☑ DOS
- ☑ Macintosh
- ☐ Terminal Emulation
- ☑ VMS
- ☑ UNIX
- ☑ OS/2
- ☑ Other platform

Cost
- ☐ Unknown
- ☐ Basic
- ☑ Extended
- ☐ Premium ($)
- ☐ Executive w/$

Activity Level
UNKNOWN

Address
GO: **UKACCOMODATION**

UK Forum

Description
The UK Forum covers general issues not covered in UKCOMMS, UKCOMP, and UKPROF.

Subjects
Travel

Audience
Travelers

Content Summary
The forum contains a discussion area that simulates the lively discussions held in British pubs.

See Also
United Kingdom

User Guide
- ☑ Windows
- ☑ DOS
- ☑ Macintosh
- ☐ Terminal Emulation
- ☑ VMS
- ☑ UNIX
- ☑ OS/2
- ☑ Other platform

Cost
- ☐ Unknown
- ☐ Basic
- ☑ Extended
- ☐ Premium ($)
- ☐ Executive w/$

Activity Level

MEDIUM (arrow pointing HIGH)

Address
GO: **UKFORUM**

VISA Advisors

Description
This service offers assistance in obtaining visas and passports. VISA Advisors hand-carries requests to the appropriate embassy in Washington, DC.

Subjects
Passports, Travel

Audience
Travelers

Content Summary
If you are planning overseas travel, this forum can help you. VISA and passport requirements updated monthly.

See Also
Travel Forum

User Guide
- ☑ Windows
- ☑ DOS
- ☐ Macintosh
- ☐ Terminal Emulation
- ☐ VMS
- ☐ UNIX
- ☐ OS/2
- ☐ Other platform

Cost
- ☐ Unknown
- ☑ Basic
- ☐ Extended
- ☐ Premium ($)
- ☐ Executive w/$

Activity Level
UNKNOWN

Address
GO: **VISA**

Weather Maps

Description
This online area offers weather maps updated several times per day. With appropriate software, maps can be either viewed while online, or downloaded for later viewing.

Subjects
Maps, Weather

Audience
Weather forecasters, general public

Content Summary
The libraries include maps of North America, the United Kingdom, continental Europe, the Pacific Rim, and Australia.

See Also
Earth Forum

User Guide
- ☑ Windows
- ☑ DOS
- ☐ Macintosh
- ☐ Terminal Emulation
- ☐ VMS
- ☐ UNIX
- ☐ OS/2
- ☐ Other platform

Cost
- ☐ Unknown
- ☑ Basic
- ☐ Extended
- ☐ Premium ($)
- ☐ Executive w/$

Activity Level

Address
GO: **MAPS**

Weather Reports

Description
This online area enables members to retrieve text weather reports for specific regions.

Subjects
Weather

Audience
Weather forecasters, general public

Content Summary
The weather reports include state, zone, and local forecasts. Also included are forecasts for the nation, including severe weather reports, rain forecasts, and state summaries.

See Also
Weather Forum

User Guide
- ☑ Windows
- ☑ DOS
- ☐ Macintosh
- ☐ Terminal Emulation
- ☐ VMS
- ☐ UNIX
- ☐ OS/2
- ☐ Other platform

Cost
- ☐ Unknown
- ☑ Basic
- ☐ Extended
- ☐ Premium ($)
- ☐ Executive w/$

Activity Level

Address
GO: **WEA**

West Coast Travel

Description
This is a travel guide by Lee Foster that describes travel destinations throughout the western USA (updated weekly).

Subjects
Travel

Audience
Travelers

Content Summary
The libraries contain information on each destination's history, attractions, and where to go to get more information. Also included are articles on special travel interests.

See Also
Travel Forum

User Guide
- ☑ Windows
- ☑ DOS
- ☑ Macintosh
- ☐ Terminal Emulation
- ☑ VMS
- ☑ UNIX
- ☑ OS/2
- ☐ Other platform

Cost
- ☐ Unknown
- ☐ Basic
- ☑ Extended
- ☐ Premium ($)
- ☐ Executive w/$

Activity Level

Address
GO: **WESTCOAST**

WORLDSPAN Travelshopper

Description
Travelshopper is your online travel agent, enabling you to search for and view airline flights and flight information.

Subjects
Travel

Audience
Travelers

Content Summary
Use this forum to obtain information about flights, make reservations, book hotel reservations, or get the cost of flights.

Travel – Trivia

See Also
Travel Forum

User Guide
- ☑ Windows
- ☑ DOS
- ☑ Macintosh
- ☐ Terminal Emulation
- ☑ VMS
- ☑ UNIX
- ☐ OS/2
- ☑ Other platform

Cost
- ☐ Unknown
- ☑ Basic
- ☐ Extended
- ☐ Premium ($)
- ☐ Executive w/$

Activity Level

(gauge pointing HIGH)

Address
GO: **WORLDSPAN**

TRAVEL PLANS

EMI Aviation Services

Description
Designed for pilots and flight planners, the EMI Aviation Services area enables pilots of any aircraft to get flight plans, weather briefings, and flight plan filings from this service. The EMI database contains all public-use airports in the contiguous 48 states and southern Canada, except for Newfoundland.

Subjects
Air Flight, Travel Plans

Audience
Pilots, air traffic controllers

Content Summary
This is a full-featured aviation service that should help you plan and record your flights. The Pro-Plan Option, found in the EMI Descriptions and Instructions option on the main menu, gives you enhanced printouts of your top of climb and descent points, average ground speeds, calculated wind direction and speed, and ambient temperature and deviation from ISA. If you're familiar with all this terminology, this service might be just what you're looking for.

See Also
Travelers Advantage

User Guide
- ☑ Windows
- ☑ DOS
- ☑ Macintosh
- ☐ Terminal Emulation
- ☑ VMS
- ☑ UNIX
- ☑ OS/2
- ☑ Other platform

Cost
- ☐ Unknown
- ☐ Basic
- ☐ Extended
- ☑ Premium ($)
- ☐ Executive w/$

Activity Level

Address
GO: **EMI**

Travelers Advantage

Description
This is an online travel club, offering savings on travel, cruise, and hotel packages.

Subjects
Travel

Audience
General public

Content Summary
The libraries include information on travel savings, cruises, hotel packages, and general travel information.

See Also
Travel Forum

User Guide
- ☑ Windows
- ☑ DOS
- ☐ Macintosh
- ☐ Terminal Emulation
- ☐ VMS
- ☐ UNIX
- ☐ OS/2
- ☐ Other platform

Cost
- ☐ Unknown
- ☐ Basic
- ☑ Extended
- ☐ Premium ($)
- ☐ Executive w/$

Activity Level

Address
GO: **TRAVADV**

TRIVIA

Showbiz Quiz

Description
Companion to the ShowBiz Forum and Hollywood Hotline, this area features trivia quizzes on several ShowBiz topics.

Subjects
Games, Movies, Television, Trivia

Audience
Movie enthusiasts

Content Summary
The libraries contain information about the forum, home entertainment, recent films, new films, classic films, television, celebrities, and Hollywood news.

See Also
Hollywood Hotline

User Guide
- ☑ Windows
- ☑ DOS
- ☑ Macintosh
- ☐ Terminal Emulation
- ☐ VMS
- ☑ UNIX
- ☐ OS/2
- ☐ Other platform

Cost
- ☐ Unknown
- ☐ Basic
- ☑ Extended
- ☐ Premium ($)
- ☐ Executive w/$

Activity Level

Address
GO: **SBQ**

The Whiz Quiz

Description
This is an online trivia quiz, using categories and questions supplied by Grolier.

Subjects
Games, Trivia

Audience
General public

Content Summary
Trivia quizzes include geography, literature, current events, movies, sports, music, science, and many more.

See Also
Intelligence Test

User Guide
- ☑ Windows
- ☑ DOS
- ☑ Macintosh
- ☐ Terminal Emulation
- ☐ VMS
- ☐ UNIX
- ☐ OS/2
- ☐ Other platform

Cost
- ☐ Unknown
- ☐ Basic
- ☑ Extended
- ☐ Premium ($)
- ☐ Executive w/$

Activity Level

Address
GO: **WHIZ**

TRW Bus. Credit Reports

Description
This database is provided by TRW, and contains credit and business information on more than 13 million organizations.

Subjects
Business

Audience
Business people

Content Summary
Information includes credit histories, financial information, key business facts, executive summaries, and judgments and bankruptcies.

See Also
Thomas Register

User Guide
- ☑ Windows
- ☑ DOS
- ☑ Macintosh
- ☐ Terminal Emulation
- ☑ VMS
- ☑ UNIX
- ☑ OS/2
- ☐ Other platform

Cost
- ☐ Unknown
- ☐ Basic
- ☑ Extended
- ☐ Premium ($)
- ☐ Executive w/$

Activity Level

Address
GO: **TRW REPORTS**

TYPOGRAPHY

FontBank Online

Description
Don't have enough fonts clogging up your hard drive? Stop by the FontBank Online service and get as many fonts as you want or can afford.

Subjects
Typography

Audience
Desktop publishers, designers, computer users, authors, artists, graphic artists, graphic designers, technical writers

Content Summary
FontBank Online is designed to deliver fonts, clip art, and graphics to the desktop publishing community. FontBank Online was designed for the entire desktop publishing community, from the desktop publishing professional to the novice. You can choose from several menu choices, such as Introduction to FontBank Online, Documentation/Tutorials, Download Font Catalog/Tutorials, FontFinder, Expert's Choice, New Fonts, and Feedback to FontBank. You can find the font you're looking for by several searching criteria, including scrolling through a list of the available fonts online. Prices for specific fonts vary, so see the online pricing structure for each font.

See Also
DTP Vendors Forum, DTPONLINE, Graphics Forums, Mac New Users Help Forum, Macintosh Forums, Macmillan Publishing Forum

User Guide
- [x] Windows
- [x] DOS
- [x] Macintosh
- [x] Terminal Emulation
- [ ] VMS
- [ ] UNIX
- [ ] OS/2
- [ ] Other platform

Cost
- [ ] Unknown
- [ ] Basic
- [x] Extended
- [ ] Premium ($)
- [ ] Executive w/$

Activity Level
UNKNOWN

Address
GO: **FONTBANK**

U

U.S. News & World Report

Description
Online version of the current *U.S. News & World Report* magazine, including text and pictures.

Subjects
News, Current Events

Audience
General public

Content Summary
This online magazine offers the full text of every issue of *U.S. News & World Report*.

See Also
U.S. News Forum

User Guide
- ☑ Windows
- ☑ DOS
- ☐ Macintosh
- ☐ Terminal Emulation
- ☐ VMS
- ☐ UNIX
- ☐ OS/2
- ☐ Other platform

Cost
- ☐ Unknown
- ☐ Basic
- ☑ Extended
- ☐ Premium ($)
- ☐ Executive w/$

Activity Level

Address
GO: **USNEWS**

U.S. News Forum

Description
Interact with the writers and editors of *U.S. News & World Report* in this forum.

Subjects
News, Current Events

Audience
General public

Content Summary
This forum enables members to send an online letter to the editor to the staff of *U.S. News & World Report*. Also included is information about news articles appearing in the magazine.

See Also
News, Business

User Guide
- ☑ Windows
- ☑ DOS
- ☐ VMS
- ☐ UNIX

U – U.S. Politics

- ☐ Macintosh
- ☐ Terminal Emulation
- ☐ OS/2
- ☐ Other platform

Cost
- ☐ Unknown
- ☐ Basic
- ☑ Extended
- ☐ Premium ($)
- ☐ Executive w/$

Activity Level

Address
GO: **USNFORUM**

U.S. POLITICS

Political Debate Forum

Description
This forum allows open discussion of political topics of all types. It is open to people of all political persuasions.

Subjects
International Events, News, U.S. Politics

Audience
Politicians, students

Content Summary
This forum provides debate areas for Democrats, Libertarians, and Republicans. Other libraries contain articles and information on topics ranging from the Crime Bill, health care, gun rights, gay rights, and international politics.

See Also
Democrat Forum, Participate, Republican Forum

User Guide
- ☑ Windows
- ☑ DOS
- ☑ Macintosh
- ☐ Terminal Emulation
- ☑ VMS
- ☑ UNIX
- ☑ OS/2
- ☐ Other platform

Cost
- ☐ Unknown
- ☐ Basic
- ☑ Extended
- ☐ Premium ($)
- ☐ Executive w/$

Activity Level

Address
GO: **POLITICS**

UFO

Encounters Forum

Description
Have you ever experienced something paranormal? Spotted a UFO? Had an encounter that you cannot explain? If so, join this forum and discuss your encounter online. The FOX-TV [encounters:] television show producers plan frequent contact with Forum users via this service.

Subjects
Encounters, UFO, Paranormal Experiences

Audience
UFO researchers

Content Summary
The libraries in this forum offer AVI video clips of UFO sightings, interviews, news reports, multimedia files, and various software files. Check out Library 4, "Graphic Files," for graphics files of UFO sightings, aliens, and Mars photographs. You also can download the Roger Patterson photo of Bigfoot.

See Also
Space Forum

User Guide
- ☑ Windows
- ☑ DOS
- ☑ Macintosh
- ☐ Terminal Emulation
- ☑ VMS
- ☑ UNIX
- ☑ OS/2
- ☑ Other platform

Cost
- ☐ Unknown
- ☐ Basic
- ☑ Extended
- ☐ Premium ($)
- ☐ Executive w/$

Activity Level

HIGH

Address
GO: **ENCOUNTERS**

UK

PC Direct UK Magazine Forum

Description
PC Direct UK Magazine Forum, part of ZiffNet, mixes inside knowledge of the United Kingdom computer trade with specialist buyer guides while always keeping the consumer in mind.

Subjects
Computers, United Kingdom, ZiffNet

Audience
Computer users, UK residents

Content Summary
Download buyer guides, editorial contributions (download *Frankenstein,* for instance), and utilities. The library sections are called Buying Advice, Utilities, and Editorial Contributions.

See Also
PC Contact, PC Computing

User Guide
- ☑ Windows
- ☑ DOS
- ☑ Macintosh
- ☐ Terminal Emulation
- ☐ VMS
- ☐ UNIX
- ☐ OS/2
- ☐ Other platform

Cost
- ☐ Unknown
- ☐ Basic
- ☑ Extended
- ☐ Premium ($)
- ☐ Executive w/$

Activity Level

MEDIUM — LOW / HIGH

Address
GO: **PCDUK**

PC Magazine UK Forum

Description
This ZiffNet service offers utilities, sound files, graphics, and other files for your general computing needs.

Subjects
Computers, ZiffNet, United Kingdom

Audience
Computer users, UK computer users

Content Summary
The library sections contains several areas, including Bench Tests, Productivity, Utilities, Editorial Contributions, After Hours, DOS, Spreadsheets, Words, Online/Internet, and more.

See Also
IBM File Finder, PC MagNet Utilities/Tips Forum

User Guide
- ☑ Windows
- ☑ DOS
- ☑ Macintosh
- ☐ Terminal Emulation
- ☐ VMS
- ☐ UNIX
- ☑ OS/2
- ☑ Other platform

Cost
- ☐ Unknown
- ☐ Basic
- ☑ Extended
- ☐ Premium ($)
- ☐ Executive w/$

UK

Activity Level

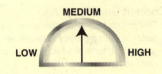

Address
GO: **PCUKFORUM**

PC Magazine UK Online

Description
PC Magazine UK Online (a ZiffNet service) is jointly run by *PC Direct UK,* the business computer buyers magazine, and *PC Magazine UK,* the leader in PC technology analysis and reporting.

Subjects
Computers, ZiffNet, United Kingdom

Audience
Computer users

Content Summary
Each magazine has its own forum. In the PC Magazine UK Forum (GO PCUKFORUM), you can access the libraries to download reports and buyers guides. Access the respective library for articles to download. You can access the PC Direct UK Forum by using the command GO PCDUK.

See Also
PC Direct UK Forum, PC MagNet

User Guide
- ☑ Windows
- ☑ DOS
- ☑ Macintosh
- ☐ Terminal Emulation
- ☐ VMS
- ☐ UNIX
- ☐ OS/2
- ☐ Other platform

Cost
- ☐ Unknown
- ☐ Basic
- ☑ Extended
- ☐ Premium ($)
- ☐ Executive w/$

Activity Level

Address
GO: **PCUKONLINE**

PC Plus/PC Answers Online

Description
This service is devoted to readers of *PC Plus* and *PC Answers,* two UK magazines, to communicate with editors, download and upload files, and submit articles.

Subjects
Computers, UK

Audience
Computer users, UK computer users

Content Summary
From the PC Plus Online main menu, you can choose from several options, including About PC Plus Online, Using the Service, Top 10 Downloads, Coverdisks, Letters to the Editor, and more.

See Also
PC MagNet, PC Computing, PC Direct UK Forum

User Guide
- ☑ Windows
- ☑ DOS
- ☑ Macintosh
- ☐ Terminal Emulation
- ☑ VMS
- ☑ UNIX
- ☐ OS/2
- ☐ Other platform

Cost
- ☐ Unknown
- ☐ Basic
- ☑ Extended
- ☐ Premium ($)
- ☐ Executive w/$

Activity Level

Address
GO: **PCPLUS**

UK Accommodation & Travel Services

Description
Travel and Accomodations services from the UK Automobile Association.

Subjects
UK, Travel

Audience
Travelers

Content Summary
This forum provides information about traveling in the United Kingdom. Find destination information, reviews of restaurants and accommodations, and tips on how to make travel arrangements.

See Also
Travel Forum

User Guide
- ☑ Windows
- ☑ DOS
- ☐ Macintosh
- ☐ Terminal Emulation
- ☐ VMS
- ☐ UNIX
- ☐ OS/2
- ☐ Other platform

Cost
- ☐ Unknown
- ☐ Basic
- ☑ Extended
- ☐ Premium ($)
- ☐ Executive w/$

UK

Activity Level

Address
GO: **UKACCOMMODATION**

UK Company Library

Description
This forum is a database containing financial and other information on companies in the United Kingdom.

Subjects
UK, Business

Audience
Businesspeople

Content Summary
This database enables members to research British companies for information on business standing, products or services offered, and address.

See Also
British Trade Marks

User Guide
- ☑ Windows
- ☑ DOS
- ☑ Macintosh
- ☐ Terminal Emulation
- ☐ VMS
- ☑ UNIX
- ☑ OS/2
- ☐ Other platform

Cost
- ☐ Unknown
- ☐ Basic
- ☐ Extended
- ☑ Premium ($)
- ☐ Executive w/$

Activity Level

Address
GO: **UKLIB**

UK Computing Forum

Description
One of several UK forums covering topics important to members hailing from the United Kingdom. The UK Computing Forum covers computer hardware and software.

Subjects
United Kingdom

Audience
Computer users

Content Summary
This forum's libraries contain information that pertains to computer hardware and software. Topics covered include product recommendations, usage, and press releases.

See Also
Computers and Software

User Guide
- ☑ Windows
- ☑ DOS
- ☑ Macintosh
- ☐ Terminal Emulation
- ☑ VMS
- ☑ UNIX
- ☑ OS/2
- ☑ Other platform

Cost
- ☐ Unknown
- ☐ Basic
- ☑ Extended
- ☐ Premium ($)
- ☐ Executive w/$

Activity Level

Address
GO: **UKCOMP**

UK Entertainment Reviews

Description
This forum is a database offering entertainment reviews of United Kingdom.

Subjects
Movies, Entertainment

Audience
General public

Content Summary
The main menu includes information on films, theatre, videos, and soap operas.

See Also
Classic Adventure, Music Hall

User Guide
- ☑ Windows
- ☑ DOS
- ☑ Macintosh
- ☐ Terminal Emulation
- ☑ VMS
- ☑ UNIX
- ☑ OS/2
- ☑ Other platform

Cost
- ☐ Unknown
- ☑ Basic
- ☐ Extended
- ☐ Premium ($)
- ☐ Executive w/$

Activity Level

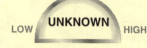

Address
GO: **UKREVIEWS**

UK Forum

Description
The UK Forum covers general issues not covered in UKCOMMS, UKCOMP, and UKPROF.

Subjects
United Kingdom

Audience
General public

Content Summary
The forum contains a discussion area that simulates the lively discussions held in British pubs.

See Also
United Kingdom

User Guide
- ☑ Windows
- ☑ DOS
- ☑ Macintosh
- ☐ Terminal Emulation
- ☑ VMS
- ☑ UNIX
- ☑ OS/2
- ☑ Other platform

Cost
- ☐ Unknown
- ☐ Basic
- ☑ Extended
- ☐ Premium ($)
- ☐ Executive w/$

Activity Level

Address
GO: **UKFORUM**

UK Historical Stock Pricing

Description
This forum is a database offering historical data on stock and bond issues from the United Kingdom. Updated daily.

Subjects
United Kingdom

Audience
Financial analysts

Contents Summary
This database offers members the capability to access historical data on stocks and bonds of the United Kingdom.

See Also
D & B Dun's Canadian

User Guide
- ☑ Windows
- ☑ DOS
- ☑ Macintosh
- ☐ Terminal Emulation
- ☑ VMS
- ☑ UNIX
- ☑ OS/2
- ☑ Other platform

Cost
- ☐ Unknown
- ☑ Basic
- ☐ Extended
- ☐ Premium ($)
- ☐ Executive w/$

Activity Level

UNKNOWN

Address
GO: **UKPRICING**

UK News Clips

Description
This forum provides realtime United Kingdom news, sports, and weather, provided by the PA News service.

Subjects
News, United Kingdom

Audience
General public

Contents Summary
Libraries include the following topics: financial, political, economic, and international news. Stores are held for 24 hours.

See Also
UK Sports Clips

User Guide
- ☑ Windows
- ☑ DOS
- ☑ Macintosh
- ☐ Terminal Emulation
- ☑ VMS
- ☑ UNIX
- ☑ OS/2
- ☑ Other platform

Cost
- ☐ Unknown
- ☑ Basic
- ☐ Extended
- ☐ Premium ($)
- ☐ Executive w/$

Activity Level

Address
GO: **UKNEWS**

UK Newspaper Library

Description
This forum is a database containing selected newspaper articles from the United Kingdom.

Subjects
United Kingdom

Audience
General public

UK

Content Summary
This database offers articles from the Daily Telegraph and Sunday Telegraph, The European, The Financial Times, The Guardian, The Times, and Sunday Times.

See Also
UK News Clips

User Guide
- ☑ Windows
- ☑ DOS
- ☑ Macintosh
- ☐ Terminal Emulation
- ☑ VMS
- ☑ UNIX
- ☑ OS/2
- ☑ Other platform

Cost
- ☐ Unknown
- ☑ Basic
- ☐ Extended
- ☐ Premium ($)
- ☐ Executive w/$

Activity Level

Address
GO: **UKNEWS**

UK Professionals Forum

Description
UK Professionals deals with issues of interest to professionals living in the UK.

Subjects
United Kingdom

Audience
Attorneys, doctors, general public

Content Summary
The libraries and message area include information about job opportunities, news, and professional groups.

See Also
United Kingdom

User Guide
- ☑ Windows
- ☑ DOS
- ☑ Macintosh
- ☐ Terminal Emulation
- ☑ VMS
- ☑ UNIX
- ☑ OS/2
- ☑ Other platform

Cost
- ☐ Unknown
- ☐ Basic
- ☑ Extended
- ☐ Premium ($)
- ☐ Executive w/$

Activity Level

Address
GO: **UKPROFESSIONAL**

UK Sports Clips

Description
Contains full-text sports clips provided by Reuters World news wire. A comprehensive source for sports stories including cricket, soccer, snooker, and rugby.

Subjects
News, United Kingdom

Audience
General public

Content Summary
Libraries include information on cricket, soccer, snooker, and rugby.

See Also
UK News

User Guide
- ☑ Windows
- ☑ DOS
- ☑ Macintosh
- ☐ Terminal Emulation
- ☑ VMS
- ☑ UNIX
- ☑ OS/2
- ☑ Other platform

Cost
- ☐ Unknown
- ☑ Basic
- ☐ Extended
- ☐ Premium ($)
- ☐ Executive w/$

Activity Level

Address
GO: **UKSPORTS**

UKSHARE Forum

Description
In this forum, members discuss many of the most popular UK shareware programs and meet their authors.

Subjects
Computers, United Kingdom

Audience
Computer users

Content Summary
You can find files, utilities, and shareware programs from the United Kingdom in this forum. Find discussions and leave messages for shareware authors and developers.

See Also
Shareware

UK – Ultimedia

User Guide
- ☑ Windows
- ☑ DOS
- ☐ Macintosh
- ☐ Terminal Emulation
- ☐ VMS
- ☐ UNIX
- ☐ OS/2
- ☑ Other platform

Cost
- ☐ Unknown
- ☐ Basic
- ☑ Extended
- ☐ Premium ($)
- ☐ Executive w/$

Activity Level
LOW ← MEDIUM → HIGH

Address
GO: **UKSHARE**

ULTIMEDIA

Ultimedia Hardware Plus Forum

Description
Vendor support forum for Ultimedia's hardware products such as MWAVE System, ActionMedia, and V-Lan.

Subjects
Computers, Ultimedia

Audience
Computer users, MIS personnel

Content Summary
The library and message sections contain information and files for Ultimedia products. Be sure to check out the message sections for support questions and comments.

See Also
Multimedia

User Guide
- ☑ Windows
- ☑ DOS
- ☐ Macintosh
- ☐ Terminal Emulation
- ☐ VMS
- ☐ UNIX
- ☑ OS/2
- ☑ Other platform

Cost
- ☐ Unknown
- ☐ Basic
- ☑ Extended
- ☐ Premium ($)
- ☐ Executive w/$

Activity Level
LOW ← MEDIUM → HIGH

Address
GO: **ULTIHW**

Ultimedia Tools Series A Forum

Description
One of three vendor support forums covering Ultimedia's software products.

Subjects
Computers, Ultimedia

Audience
Computer users

Content Summary
The library and message sections contain information and files for Ultimedia products. Be sure to check out the message sections for support questions and comments.

See Also
Multimedia

User Guide
- ☑ Windows
- ☑ DOS
- ☐ Macintosh
- ☐ Terminal Emulation
- ☐ VMS
- ☐ UNIX
- ☑ OS/2
- ☑ Other platform

Cost
- ☐ Unknown
- ☐ Basic
- ☑ Extended
- ☐ Premium ($)
- ☐ Executive w/$

Activity Level
LOW ← MEDIUM → HIGH

Address
GO: **IBMULTI**

Ultimedia Tools Series B Forum

Description
One of three vendor support forums for Ultimedia's software products.

Subjects
Computers, Ultimedia

Audience
Computer users

Content Summary
The library and message sections contain information and files for Ultimedia products. Be sure to check out the message sections for support questions and comments.

See Also
Multimedia

User Guide
- ☑ Windows
- ☑ DOS
- ☐ Macintosh
- ☐ Terminal Emulation
- ☐ VMS
- ☐ UNIX
- ☑ OS/2
- ☑ Other platform

Ultimedia – UNIX

Cost
- [ ] Unknown
- [ ] Basic
- [x] Extended
- [ ] Premium ($)
- [ ] Executive w/$

Activity Level: LOW (arrow pointing to low)

Address
GO: **IBMULTI**

Ultimedia Tools Series C Forum

Description
One of three vendor support forums for Ultimedia's software products.

Subjects
Computers, Ultimedia

Audience
Computer users

Content Summary
The library and message sections contain information and files for Ultimedia products. Be sure to check out the message sections for support questions and comments.

See Also
Multimedia

User Guide
- [x] Windows
- [x] DOS
- [ ] Macintosh
- [ ] Terminal Emulation
- [ ] VMS
- [ ] UNIX
- [x] OS/2
- [x] Other platform

Cost
- [ ] Unknown
- [ ] Basic
- [x] Extended
- [ ] Premium ($)
- [ ] Executive w/$

Activity Level: LOW (arrow pointing to low)

Address
GO: **IBMULTI**

UNIVERSITIES

University of Phoenix

Description
Online area providing information on the University of Phoenix' online curriculum. Students take courses via modem.

Subjects
Universities

Audience
Students

Content Summary
This service enables you to view curriculum and take courses online.

See Also
Real Estate Forum

User Guide
- [x] Windows
- [x] DOS
- [x] Macintosh
- [ ] Terminal Emulation
- [x] VMS
- [x] UNIX
- [x] OS/2
- [x] Other platform

Cost
- [ ] Unknown
- [ ] Basic
- [ ] Extended
- [ ] Premium ($)
- [x] Executive w/$

Activity Level: UNKNOWN

Address
GO: **UP**

UNIX

UNIX Forum

Description
In the UNIX Forum, users of the UNIX operating system discuss UNIX issues and exchange UNIX code.

Subjects
Computers, UNIX

Audience
Computer users

Content Summary
The library and message sections include numerous files, tips, techniques, discussions, and other related UNIX history and product information. Check out the discussions of the Linux operating system.

See Also
UNIX

User Guide
- [x] Windows
- [x] DOS
- [ ] Macintosh
- [ ] Terminal Emulation
- [ ] VMS
- [ ] UNIX
- [ ] OS/2
- [ ] Other platform

Cost
- [ ] Unknown
- [ ] Basic
- [x] Extended
- [ ] Premium ($)
- [ ] Executive w/$

UNIX – User Groups 575

Activity Level: MEDIUM (arrow pointing up)

Address
GO: **UNIXFORUM**

Unix Vendor A Forum

Description
Vendor support forum for various UNIX vendors.

Subjects
Computers

Audience
Computer users

Content Summary
You can find support from specific UNIX vendors in the library and message sections. Join this forum if you are an MIS professional or system analyst.

See Also
Software

User Guide
- [ ] Windows
- [ ] DOS
- [ ] Macintosh
- [ ] Terminal Emulation
- [ ] VMS
- [x] UNIX
- [ ] OS/2
- [ ] Other platform

Cost
- [ ] Unknown
- [ ] Basic
- [x] Extended
- [ ] Premium ($)
- [ ] Executive w/$

Activity Level: LOW (arrow pointing left)

Address
GO: **UNIXAFOR**

UnixWare Forum

Description
Vendor support forum for Novell UnixWare software products.

Subjects
Computers, Novell, UNIX

Audience
Computer users

Contents Summary
You can find information in the various library and message sections about the UnixWare operating system.

See Also
Software

User Guide
- [ ] Windows
- [ ] DOS
- [ ] Macintosh
- [ ] Terminal Emulation
- [ ] VMS
- [x] UNIX
- [ ] OS/2
- [ ] Other platform

Cost
- [ ] Unknown
- [ ] Basic
- [x] Extended
- [ ] Premium ($)
- [ ] Executive w/$

Activity Level: LOW (arrow pointing left)

Address
GO: **UNIXWARE**

USER GROUPS

WUGNET Forum

Description
The Windows User Group Network (WUGNET) forum supports Windows users around the world.

Subjects
Computers

Audience
Computer users, Windows users

Content Summary
Libraries include the bimonthly WUGNET Journal, information for developers, and an area to communicate with other Windows developers.

See Also
Windows Sources Forum

User Guide
- [x] Windows
- [x] DOS
- [ ] Macintosh
- [ ] Terminal Emulation
- [ ] VMS
- [ ] UNIX
- [ ] OS/2
- [x] Other platform

Cost
- [ ] Unknown
- [ ] Basic
- [x] Extended
- [ ] Premium ($)
- [ ] Executive w/$

Activity Level: MEDIUM (arrow pointing up)

Address
GO: **WUGNET**

User Profile Program – Utilities

User Profile Program

Description
Online area for users of the ASCII interface to set up their terminal parameters. This area is not useful to users of DOS CIM, WinCIM, or MacCIM software.

Subjects
Help

Audience
General public

Contents Summary
Use the various options to change your CompuServe settings.

See Also
CompuServe Help Forum

User Guide
- ☑ Windows
- ☑ DOS
- ☑ Macintosh
- ☑ Terminal Emulation
- ☑ VMS
- ☑ UNIX
- ☑ OS/2
- ☑ Other platform

Cost
- ☐ Unknown
- ☑ Basic
- ☐ Extended
- ☐ Premium ($)
- ☐ Executive w/$

Activity Level

Address
GO: **TERMINAL**

UserLand Forum

Description
Vendor support forum for users of UserLand Software products.

Subjects
Computers

Audience
Computer users

Contents Summary
The library and message sections include files, tips, and supporting files for UserLand products.

See Also
Software

User Guide
- ☑ Windows
- ☑ DOS
- ☐ Macintosh
- ☐ Terminal Emulation
- ☐ VMS
- ☐ UNIX
- ☐ OS/2
- ☐ Other platform

Cost
- ☐ Unknown
- ☐ Basic
- ☑ Extended
- ☐ Premium ($)
- ☐ Executive w/$

Activity Level

Address
GO: **USERLAND**

UTILITIES

Dr. Dobb's Forum

Description
This is an "electronic" version of *Dr. Dobb's Journal*, a journal devoted to computer languages, tools, utilities, algorithms, and programming techniques. If you're interested in writing articles for the *Journal*, post them here for review. You might get published in the future.

Subjects
Computers, Programming, Utilities

Audience
Application developers, MIS personnel, system integrators

Content Summary
You can upload or download source code; find information on OS/2, UNIX, Macintosh, and Windows programming; and find listings (not text) of the articles and columns from the *Dr. Dobb's Journal* magazine. This forum is not intended to be a substitute for the magazine, but a complement to it.

See Also
MS Developers Relations Forum

User Guide
- ☑ Windows
- ☑ DOS
- ☑ Macintosh
- ☐ Terminal Emulation
- ☐ VMS
- ☑ UNIX
- ☑ OS/2
- ☑ Other platform

Cost
- ☐ Unknown
- ☐ Basic
- ☑ Extended
- ☐ Premium ($)
- ☐ Executive w/$

Activity Level

Address
GO: **DDJFORUM**

V

VAX Forum

Description
This forum provides support for users of the VAX series of computer systems from Digital Equip Corp. VAX Forum is sponsored by Professional Press.

Subjects
Computers, Digital Equipment

Audience
Computer users, VAX users

Content Summary
Libraries include information about new and reviews of VAX products, DECUS Happenings, VAX Hardware, Alpha AXP, VMS systems software, and system management.

See Also
Computers, Software

User Guide
- ☑ Windows
- ☑ DOS
- ☑ Macintosh
- ☐ Terminal Emulation
- ☑ VMS
- ☑ UNIX
- ☑ OS/2
- ☑ Other platform

Cost
- ☐ Unknown
- ☐ Basic
- ☑ Extended
- ☐ Premium ($)
- ☐ Executive w/$

Activity Level

Address
GO: **VAXFORUM**

Ventura Software Forum

Description
This is a vendor support forum for Ventura's Publisher, FormBase Database Publisher, and other software products.

Subjects
Computer Graphics, Computers

Audience
Computer users, CorelDRAW! users, Ventura users

Content Summary
The libraries and message areas include information about Ventura applications, Gem Ventura, Windows Ventura, OS/2 and Macintosh Ventura, and third-party utilities.

See Also
Software

User Guide
- ☑ Windows
- ☑ DOS
- ☐ Macintosh
- ☐ Terminal Emulation
- ☐ VMS
- ☐ UNIX
- ☐ OS/2
- ☐ Other platform

Cost
- ☐ Unknown
- ☐ Basic
- ☑ Extended
- ☐ Premium ($)
- ☐ Executive w/$

Activity Level

Address
GO: **VENTURA**

Vestor Stock Recommendation

Description
This unique interactive system is comprised of over 30 systems that can help you in making investment decisions.

Subjects
Finance, Stock Market

Audience
Business people, investors

Content Summary
This service has over 30 different services to which you can connect to get the investment research you need to make strong decisions.

See Also
Securities Screening Forum, Portfolio Valuation Forum

User Guide
- ☑ Windows
- ☑ DOS
- ☑ Macintosh
- ☐ Terminal Emulation
- ☑ VMS
- ☑ UNIX
- ☑ OS/2
- ☑ Other platform

Cost
- ☐ Unknown
- ☐ Basic
- ☑ Extended
- ☐ Premium ($)
- ☐ Executive w/$

Activity Level

UNKNOWN

Address
GO: **VESTOR**

VETERINARIANS

Pet Products/Reference Forum

Description
This forum provides customer support for those businesses that provide products or services to pet owners or pet professionals.

Subjects
Animals, Fish, Veterinarians

Audience
Aquarists, pet owners, veterinarians

Content Summary
This forum contains numerous libraries that include a complete list of all subscribing PetPro vendors and a description of their businesses. Also of interest are articles written by behavioral specialists and articles that have appeared in well-known animal publications.

See Also
Pets/Animal Forum

User Guide
- ☑ Windows
- ☑ DOS
- ☑ Macintosh
- ☐ Terminal Emulation
- ☐ VMS
- ☐ UNIX
- ☑ OS/2
- ☐ Other platform

Cost
- ☐ Unknown
- ☐ Basic
- ☑ Extended
- ☐ Premium ($)
- ☐ Executive w/$

Activity Level
LOW ← MEDIUM   HIGH

Address
GO: **PETPRO**

VIDEO

Rocknet Forum

Description
This forum provides the most up-to-date and accurate information on the rock community.

Subjects
Entertainment, Music, Rock Enthusiasts, Video

Audience
Musicians, rock enthusiasts

Content Summary
This forum's libraries cover the full range of rock topics. Topics included are reviews of concerts and music, lists of alternative radio stations, coverage of the musical group The Grateful Dead, heavy metal, vintage rock, new music, online conversations with rock personalities, and graphics of musical group logos and photographs taken at concerts.

See Also
Rock Video Monthly

User Guide
- ☑ Windows
- ☑ DOS
- ☑ Macintosh
- ☐ Terminal Emulation
- ☐ VMS
- ☐ UNIX
- ☐ OS/2
- ☐ Other platform

Cost
- ☐ Unknown
- ☐ Basic
- ☑ Extended
- ☐ Premium ($)
- ☐ Executive w/$

Activity Level
LOW   MEDIUM ↑   HIGH

Address
GO: **ROCKNET**

VIDEO GAMES

Video Game Publishers Forum

Description
This is a vendor support forum for the products of several video games publishers.

Subjects
Entertainment, Games, Video Games

Audience
Games developers, games enthusiasts

Content Summary
The libraries contain forum help files and information specific to the following games manufacturers: Nintendo, 3DO Multiplayer, Atari Jaguar, and Philips CD-I. Also available is information on portables and product comparisons.

See Also
Video Games

User Guide
- ☑ Windows
- ☑ DOS
- ☐ Macintosh
- ☐ Terminal Emulation
- ☐ VMS
- ☐ UNIX
- ☐ OS/2
- ☐ Other platform

Cost
- ☐ Unknown
- ☐ Basic
- ☑ Extended
- ☐ Premium ($)
- ☐ Executive w/$

579
Video Games – Vines 5.x Patchware Forum

Activity Level

Address
GO: **VIDPUB**

Video Games Forum

Description
The Video Games Forum is the place to go to discuss all of the available video games machines, and to argue over which offers the most entertainment.

Subjects
Entertainment, Games, Video Games

Audience
Games developers, games enthusiasts

Content Summary
The message areas provide discussions about all sorts of game topics—from which games are best to tips on playing certain games.

See Also
Video Games

User Guide
- ☑ Windows
- ☑ DOS
- ☑ Macintosh
- ☐ Terminal Emulation
- ☑ VMS
- ☑ UNIX
- ☑ OS/2
- ☑ Other platform

Cost
- ☐ Unknown
- ☐ Basic
- ☑ Extended
- ☐ Premium ($)
- ☐ Executive w/$

Activity Level

Address
GO: **VIDGAM**

Vines 4.x Patchware Forum

Description
This vendor support forum offers software patches and support for Banyan's VINES 4.x networking products.

Subjects
Banyan, Computer Networking, Computers

Audience
Banyan users

Content Summary
The libraries contain new upleads for patches and support for Banyan 4.x.

See Also
Software

User Guide
- ☑ Windows
- ☑ DOS
- ☐ Macintosh
- ☐ Terminal Emulation
- ☐ VMS
- ☐ UNIX
- ☐ OS/2
- ☐ Other platform

Cost
- ☐ Unknown
- ☐ Basic
- ☑ Extended
- ☐ Premium ($)
- ☐ Executive w/$

Activity Level

Address
GO: **VINES4**

Vines 5.x Patchware Forum

Description
This vendor support forum offers software patches for Banyan's VINES 5.x networking products.

Subjects
Banyan, Computer Networking, Computers

Audience
Banyan users

Content Summary
The libraries contain new uploads for patches and support for Banyan 5.x.

See Also
Software

User Guide
- ☑ Windows
- ☑ DOS
- ☐ Macintosh
- ☐ Terminal Emulation
- ☐ VMS
- ☐ UNIX
- ☐ OS/2
- ☐ Other platform

Cost
- ☐ Unknown
- ☐ Basic
- ☑ Extended
- ☐ Premium ($)
- ☐ Executive w/$

Activity Level

Address
GO: **VINES5**

VIOLENCE

Time-Warner Crime Forum

Description
This is a forum sponsored by Time-Warner to discuss crime and violence worldwide.

Subjects
Crime, violence

Audience
General public

Content Summary
On-line discussion group provides forum for law enforcement profession.

See Also
Crime

User Guide
- [x] Windows
- [x] DOS
- [x] Macintosh
- [ ] Terminal Emulation
- [x] VMS
- [x] UNIX
- [x] OS/2
- [x] Other platform

Cost
- [ ] Unknown
- [ ] Basic
- [x] Extended
- [ ] Premium ($)
- [ ] Executive w/$

Activity Level

Address
GO: **CRIME**

Virginia Diner

Description
This online shopping area offering specialty foods, gift baskets, tins, and so on.

Subjects
General Interest, Gifts

Audience
Consumers, shoppers

Content Summary
You can purchase a great number of items ranging from food, gifts, and specialty products.

See Also
Electronic Mall

User Guide
- [x] Windows
- [x] DOS
- [x] Macintosh
- [ ] Terminal Emulation
- [x] VMS
- [x] UNIX
- [x] OS/2
- [x] Other platform

Cost
- [ ] Unknown
- [x] Basic
- [ ] Extended
- [ ] Premium ($)
- [ ] Executive w/$

Activity Level

Address
GO: **DINER**

VIRTUAL REALITY

Cyber Forum

Description
The future of computing is the subject of the Cyber Forum, from Virtual Reality to nanotechnology.

Subjects
Computers, Virtual Reality

Audience
Computer users

Content Summary
Libraries include virtual reality, gaming, entertainment, CyberArts, robotics, CyberLit, news, art, and *PCVR* magazine.

See Also
Speak Easy Forum

User Guide
- [x] Windows
- [x] DOS
- [x] Macintosh
- [ ] Terminal Emulation
- [ ] VMS
- [x] UNIX
- [ ] OS/2
- [x] Other platform

Cost
- [ ] Unknown
- [ ] Basic
- [x] Extended
- [ ] Premium ($)
- [ ] Executive w/$

Activity Level

Address
GO: **CYBERFORUM**

VISA Advisors

Description
This service offers assistance in obtaining visas and passports. VISA Advisors hand-carries requests to the appropriate embassy in Washington, DC.

Subjects
Passports, Travel

Audience
Travelers

Content Summary
You can receive information on obtaining visas and passports.

See Also
Travel Forum

User Guide
- ☑ Windows
- ☑ DOS
- ☑ Macintosh
- ☐ Terminal Emulation
- ☑ VMS
- ☑ UNIX
- ☐ OS/2
- ☐ Other platform

Cost
- ☐ Unknown
- ☐ Basic
- ☑ Extended
- ☐ Premium ($)
- ☐ Executive w/$

Activity Level

Address
GO: **VISA**

VITAMINS

Sundown Vitamins

Description
This is an online shopping area offering vitamins at wholesale prices.

Subjects
Shopping, Vitamins

Audience
Health enthusiasts

Content Summary
A complete assortment of vitamins and food supplements is available for online purchase.

See Also
Health and Fitness Forum

User Guide
- ☑ Windows
- ☑ DOS
- ☑ Macintosh
- ☐ Terminal Emulation
- ☐ VMS
- ☑ UNIX
- ☐ OS/2
- ☐ Other platform

Cost
- ☐ Unknown
- ☑ Basic
- ☐ Extended
- ☐ Premium ($)
- ☐ Executive w/$

Activity Level

Address
GO: **SDV**

Vobis AG Computer Forum

Description
This is a vendor support forum for Vobis AG products. Vobis AG is a German-speaking forum.

Subjects
Computer Hardware, Computers

Audience
German Vobis AG Product users

Content Summary
The libraries contain support for hardware and software.

See Also
Hardware, Software Support

User Guide
- ☑ Windows
- ☑ DOS
- ☑ Macintosh
- ☐ Terminal Emulation
- ☑ VMS
- ☑ UNIX
- ☑ OS/2
- ☑ Other platform

Cost
- ☐ Unknown
- ☐ Basic
- ☑ Extended
- ☐ Premium ($)
- ☐ Executive w/$

Activity Level

Address
GO: **VNUBA**

W

WALL STREET

E*TRADE Stock Market Game

Description
Have you ever wondered what it would be like to be a Wall Street mover and shaker? Now's your chance to invest $100,000 in game accounts by playing the E*TRADE Stock Market Game. The game lets you play in stocks only, stocks and options, or both, and will track your performance—and commission rates—every month. If you have the right stuff and have the highest percentage increase of all the players, you can win a cash prize.

Subjects
Games, Finance, Wall Street

Audience
Financial persons, gamers, students

Content Summary
The E*TRADE Securities main menu offers you three choices: Game Instructions, Sign-up for the Game, and Play the E*TRADE Stock Market Game. Select Game Instructions to read directions on how to play and what you can win. You compete with other members to see who can become the wealthiest in a month. When you sign up for the game, you are given $100,000 in game money with which to start.

See Also
E*TRADE Securities

User Guide
- ☐ Windows
- ☐ DOS
- ☐ Macintosh
- ☑ Terminal Emulation
- ☐ VMS
- ☐ UNIX
- ☐ OS/2
- ☐ Other platform

Cost
- ☐ Unknown
- ☐ Basic
- ☑ Extended
- ☐ Premium ($)
- ☐ Executive w/$

Activity Level
UNKNOWN (LOW / MEDIUM / HIGH)

Address
GO: **ETGAME**

Ticker/Symbol Lookup

Description
Online database that provides financial information on various stocks.

Subjects
Finance, Wall Street

Audience
Financial persons, accountants

Content Summary
This database enables you to look up information by company name, ticker symbol, CUSIP number, CNUM, or primary SIC code.

See Also
Basic Quotes, Financial Forums

User Guide
- ☑ Windows
- ☑ DOS
- ☐ Macintosh
- ☐ Terminal Emulation
- ☐ VMS
- ☐ UNIX
- ☐ OS/2
- ☐ Other platform

Cost
- ☐ Unknown
- ☐ Basic
- ☑ Extended
- ☐ Premium ($)
- ☐ Executive w/$

Activity Level
UNKNOWN (LOW / MEDIUM / HIGH)

Address
GO: **LOOKUP**

Walter Knoll Florist

Description
This is an online shopping area offering flowers and plants.

Subjects
Shopping

Audience
Consumers, shoppers

Content Summary
This shopping area offers the convenience of shopping for flowers or plants from your home or office.

See Also
Electronic Mall

User Guide
- ☑ Windows
- ☑ DOS
- ☑ Macintosh
- ☐ Terminal Emulation
- ☑ VMS
- ☑ UNIX
- ☑ OS/2
- ☐ Other platform

Cost
- ☐ Unknown
- ☑ Basic
- ☐ Extended
- ☐ Premium ($)
- ☐ Executive w/$

Activity Level

Address
GO: **WK**

Wang Support Forum

Description
This vendor forum supports Wang computer products.

Subjects
Computers

Audience
Computer users, Wang users

Content Summary
The libraries include information on products, training, services, and technical support.

See Also
IBM File Finder

User Guide

- ☑ Windows
- ☑ DOS
- ☐ Macintosh
- ☐ Terminal Emulation
- ☐ VMS
- ☐ UNIX
- ☐ OS/2
- ☐ Other platform

Cost

- ☐ Unknown
- ☐ Basic
- ☑ Extended
- ☐ Premium ($)
- ☐ Executive w/$

Activity Level

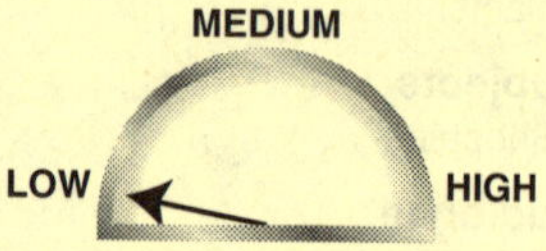

Address
GO: **WANGFORUM**

WAR

SNIPER!

Description
This online infantry combat game is set during World War II.

Subjects
Combat, Games, War

Audience
Games enthusiasts, military scenarios

Content Summary
You command a squad of soldiers in a mission against another squad. Actual wartime conditions are simulated. The game is over when a player has accomplished his or her mission. The game appears more lifelike if you download the SCOPE games software.

See Also
Games Forum

User Guide

- ☑ Windows
- ☑ DOS
- ☐ Macintosh
- ☐ Terminal Emulation
- ☐ VMS
- ☐ UNIX
- ☐ OS/2
- ☐ Other platform

Cost

- ☐ Unknown
- ☐ Basic
- ☑ Extended
- ☐ Premium ($)
- ☐ Executive w/$

Activity Level

Address
GO: **SNIPER**

Warner Bros. Song Preview

Description
This is an online area offering 30-second sound clips from some of Warner Bros. Records recent releases.

Subjects
Entertainment

Audience
Musicians, music enthusiasts

Content Summary
The sound clips enable users to review sound clips of popular recordings so that they can find the music they like. Users also can find out tour and release dates of popular artists.

See Also
Entertainment Center Forum

User Guide

- ☑ Windows
- ☑ DOS
- ☑ Macintosh
- ☐ Terminal Emulation
- ☑ VMS
- ☑ UNIX
- ☑ OS/2
- ☐ Other platform

Cost

- ☐ Unknown
- ☐ Basic
- ☑ Extended
- ☐ Premium ($)
- ☐ Executive w/$

Activity Level

Address
GO: **WBPREVIEW**

Weather – What's New

WEATHER

Weather Maps

Description
This online area offers weather maps updated several times per day. With appropriate software, maps can either be viewed while online, or downloaded for later viewing.

Subjects
Maps, Weather

Audience
Weather forecasters, general public

Content Summary
The libraries include maps of North America, the United Kingdom, continental Europe, the Pacific Rim, and Australia.

See Also
Earth Forum

User Guide
- ☑ Windows
- ☑ DOS
- ☐ Macintosh
- ☐ Terminal Emulation
- ☐ VMS
- ☐ UNIX
- ☐ OS/2
- ☐ Other platform

Cost
- ☐ Unknown
- ☑ Basic
- ☐ Extended
- ☐ Premium ($)
- ☐ Executive w/$

Activity Level

Address
GO: **MAPS**

Weather Reports

Description
This online area enables members to retrieve text weather reports for specific regions.

Subjects
Weather

Audience
Weather forecasters, general public

Content Summary
The weather reports include state, zone, and local forecasts. Also included are forecasts for the nation, including severe weather reports, rain forecasts, and state summaries.

See Also
Weather Forum

User Guide
- ☑ Windows
- ☑ DOS
- ☐ Macintosh
- ☐ Terminal Emulation
- ☐ VMS
- ☐ UNIX
- ☐ OS/2
- ☐ Other platform

Cost
- ☐ Unknown
- ☑ Basic
- ☐ Extended
- ☐ Premium ($)
- ☐ Executive w/$

Activity Level

Address
GO: **WEA**

West Coast Travel

Description
This is a travel guide by Lee Foster that describes travel destinations throughout the western USA (updated weekly).

Subjects
Travel

Audience
Travelers

Content Summary
The libraries contain information on each destination's history, attractions, and where to go to get more information. Also included are articles on special travel interests.

See Also
Travel Forum

User Guide
- ☑ Windows
- ☑ DOS
- ☑ Macintosh
- ☐ Terminal Emulation
- ☑ VMS
- ☑ UNIX
- ☑ OS/2
- ☐ Other platform

Cost
- ☐ Unknown
- ☐ Basic
- ☑ Extended
- ☐ Premium ($)
- ☐ Executive w/$

Activity Level

Address
GO: **WESTCOAST**

What's New

Description
This is CompuServe's menu of upcoming events and system changes, updated several times per week.

What's New – Windows

Subjects
CompuServe

Audience
CompuServe users

Content Summary
Find out what's happening on Compuserve by viewing this list of new topics.

See Also
CompuServe Help

User Guide
- ☑ Windows
- ☑ DOS
- ☑ Macintosh
- ☐ Terminal Emulation
- ☑ VMS
- ☑ UNIX
- ☑ OS/2
- ☐ Other platform

Cost
- ☐ Unknown
- ☑ Basic
- ☐ Extended
- ☐ Premium ($)
- ☐ Executive w/$

Activity Level

Address
GO: **NEW**

White House Forum

Description
This independent political forum discusses what's happening in the U.S. White House. The libraries contain only files provided by official White House sources.

Subjects
Current Issues

Audience
General public

Content Summary
Libraries include information on the economy, the trade deficit, defense, education, social security, and international affairs.

See Also
Politics in America

User Guide
- ☑ Windows
- ☑ DOS
- ☑ Macintosh
- ☐ Terminal Emulation
- ☑ VMS
- ☑ UNIX
- ☑ OS/2
- ☐ Other platform

Cost
- ☐ Unknown
- ☐ Basic
- ☑ Extended
- ☐ Premium ($)
- ☐ Executive w/$

Activity Level

Address
GO: **WHITEHOUSE**

WINCIM

WinCIM Support Forum

Description
This forum is sponsored by CompuServe as a "vendor support forum" covering WinCIM access software for Windows users.

Subjects
CompuServe, WinCIM

Audience
CompuServe users, WinCIM users

Content Summary
Contains information that enables users to navigate WinCIM better and faster. Topics include interface use, installation instructions, required hardware, and general usage.

See Also
CompuServe Help Forum

User Guide
- ☑ Windows
- ☐ DOS
- ☐ Macintosh
- ☐ Terminal Emulation
- ☐ VMS
- ☐ UNIX
- ☐ OS/2
- ☐ Other platform

Cost
- ☐ Unknown
- ☑ Basic
- ☐ Extended
- ☐ Premium ($)
- ☐ Executive w/$

Activity Level

Address
GO: **WCIMSUP**

WINDOWS

Microsoft Windows Forum

Description
News, files, tips, and other related information to MS Windows.

Windows

Subjects
Computer Viruses, Computers, Microsoft Corp., Windows

Audience
Computer users

Content Summary
Some of the library and message sections include Setup, Mouse, Display Drivers, Memory Optimization, MS-DOS Apps/PIFs, Printing/Fonts/WPS, and Terminal/Comm.

See Also
Microsoft Connection, Microsoft Knowledge Base

User Guide
- ☑ Windows
- ☑ DOS
- ☐ Macintosh
- ☐ Terminal Emulation
- ☐ VMS
- ☐ UNIX
- ☐ OS/2
- ☐ Other platform

Cost
- ☐ Unknown
- ☐ Basic
- ☑ Extended
- ☐ Premium ($)
- ☐ Executive w/$

Activity Level
MEDIUM-HIGH

Address
GO: **MSWIN**

Microsoft Windows News Forum

Description
Find out up-to-date information on Windows and future Windows products.

Subjects
Computers, Microsoft Corp., Windows

Audience
Computer users

Content Summary
This forum essentially has one library: Hot News. Here, you can find press releases, articles, tips, speeches, and similar files associated with Windows.

See Also
MS Windows Forum

User Guide
- ☑ Windows
- ☑ DOS
- ☐ Macintosh
- ☐ Terminal Emulation
- ☐ VMS
- ☐ UNIX
- ☐ OS/2
- ☐ Other platform

Cost
- ☐ Unknown
- ☑ Basic
- ☐ Extended
- ☐ Premium ($)
- ☐ Executive w/$

Activity Level
MEDIUM-HIGH

Address
GO: **WINNEWS**

Windows 3rd Party App. A Forum

Description
This is a vendor support forum for several Windows-based applications.

Subjects
Computers

Audience
Computer users, Windows users

Content Summary
Libraries include information about Access Softek, Arabesque Software, Asymetrix Corp., Future Soft Engineering, Geographix, hDC Computer Corp., Jensen-Jones, Lucid Corp., Micrografx, Playroom Software, Polaris Software, Premia Corp., 3-D Visions, and Wilson WindowWare.

See Also
Windows Vendor Forums

User Guide
- ☑ Windows
- ☑ DOS
- ☐ Macintosh
- ☐ Terminal Emulation
- ☐ VMS
- ☐ UNIX
- ☐ OS/2
- ☐ Other platform

Cost
- ☐ Unknown
- ☐ Basic
- ☑ Extended
- ☐ Premium ($)
- ☐ Executive w/$

Activity Level
MEDIUM

Address
GO: **WINAPA**

Windows 3rd Party App. B Forum

Description
This is a vendor support forum for several Windows-based applications.

Subjects
Computers

Audience
Computer users, Windows users

Windows

Content Summary
Libraries include information about Computer Presentations, Connect Software, Frontier Technologies, InfoAccess, KASEWORKS, Kidasa Software, Knowledge Garden, Nu-Mega, Ocean Isle Software, Softbridge, SoftCraft, Window Craft, Wonderware, and Zenographics.

See Also
Windows Vendor Forums

User Guide
- ☑ Windows
- ☑ DOS
- ☐ Macintosh
- ☐ Terminal Emulation
- ☐ VMS
- ☐ UNIX
- ☐ OS/2
- ☐ Other platform

Cost
- ☐ Unknown
- ☐ Basic
- ☑ Extended
- ☐ Premium ($)
- ☐ Executive w/$

Activity Level

Address
GO: **WINAPB**

Windows 3rd Party App. D Forum

Description
This is a vendor support forum for several Windows-based applications.

Subjects
Computers

Audience
Computer users, Windows users

Content Summary
The libraries include information on ABC Systems and Development, Automated Design Systems, Baseline Publishing, DeltaPoint, Inmark, Okna Corp., Peachtree, Q+E Software, ShapeWare, SWFTE International, and WexTech.

See Also
Windows Vendor Forums

User Guide
- ☑ Windows
- ☑ DOS
- ☐ Macintosh
- ☐ Terminal Emulation
- ☐ VMS
- ☐ UNIX
- ☐ OS/2
- ☐ Other platform

Cost
- ☐ Unknown
- ☐ Basic
- ☑ Extended
- ☐ Premium ($)
- ☐ Executive w/$

Activity Level

Address
GO: **WINAPD**

Windows 3rd Party App. E Forum +

Description
This is vendor support forum for several Windows-based applications.

Subjects
Computers

Audience
Computer users, Windows users

Content Summary
The libraries contain information about Andyne Computing, LaserTools, MapLinx, Scitor Corporation, and Systems Compatibility.

See Also
Windows Vendor Forums

User Guide
- ☑ Windows
- ☑ DOS
- ☐ Macintosh
- ☐ Terminal Emulation
- ☐ VMS
- ☐ UNIX
- ☐ OS/2
- ☐ Other platform

Cost
- ☐ Unknown
- ☐ Basic
- ☑ Extended
- ☐ Premium ($)
- ☐ Executive w/$

Activity Level

Address
GO: **WINAPE**

Windows 3rd Party App. G Forum

Description
This is a vendor support forum for several Windows-based applications.

Subjects
Computers

Audience
Computer users, Windows users

Content Summary
Libraries include information about ShowCase, Air TM, First Floor, Underware, and others.

Windows – Windows NT

See Also
Windows Vendor Forums

User Guide
- ☑ Windows
- ☑ DOS
- ☐ Macintosh
- ☐ Terminal Emulation
- ☐ VMS
- ☐ UNIX
- ☐ OS/2
- ☐ Other platform

Cost
- ☐ Unknown
- ☐ Basic
- ☑ Extended
- ☐ Premium ($)
- ☐ Executive w/$

Activity Level
MEDIUM (LOW – HIGH)

Address
GO: **WINAPG**

WUGNET Forum

Description
The Windows User Group Network (WUGNET) forum supports Windows users around the world.

Subjects
Computers

Audience
Computer users, Windows users

Content Summary
Libraries include the bimonthly WUGNET Journal, information for developers, and an area to communicate with other Windows developers.

See Also
Windows Sources Forum

User Guide
- ☑ Windows
- ☑ DOS
- ☐ Macintosh
- ☐ Terminal Emulation
- ☐ VMS
- ☐ UNIX
- ☐ OS/2
- ☐ Other platform

Cost
- ☐ Unknown
- ☐ Basic
- ☑ Extended
- ☐ Premium ($)
- ☐ Executive w/$

Activity Level
MEDIUM (LOW – HIGH)

Address
GO: **WUGNET**

Windows Sources Forum

Description
This enables the user to interact with the editors, columnists, writers, and reviewers of Windows Sources Magazine, and helps you find information on products you can buy directly from the manufacturer.

Subjects
Computers, Magazines

Audience
Computer users, Windows users

Content Summary
Libraries include product reviews, information on specific products, and issues affecting the computer industry.

See Also
Macmillan Computer Publishing Forum

User Guide
- ☑ Windows
- ☑ DOS
- ☑ Macintosh
- ☐ Terminal Emulation
- ☑ VMS
- ☑ UNIX
- ☑ OS/2
- ☐ Other platform

Cost
- ☐ Unknown
- ☐ Basic
- ☑ Extended
- ☐ Premium ($)
- ☐ Executive w/$

Activity Level
MEDIUM (LOW – HIGH)

Address
GO: **WINSOURCES**

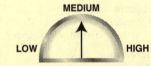

WINDOWS NT

Digital Equipment Corporation

Description
This is the main area from which you can choose to enter one of several DEC forums or service areas. You can select Digital's Windows NT Support Forum, PC Integration Forum, or Digital-Related Forums. You also can go to Digital's PC Store from this menu.

Subjects
Computers, Client/Server, Multiprocessor Environments, Windows NT

Audience
DEC Alpha AXP users, support technicians, system integrators, VARs, Windows NT users

Content Summary
At the main menu, you can select from Digital NT Support Forum, Digital PC Integration Forum, and Digital's PC Store.

Windows NT – WinNT Forum

See Also
Digital NT Support Forum, Digital PC Integration Forum, Digital's PC Store

User Guide
- ☑ Windows
- ☑ DOS
- ☑ Macintosh
- ☐ Terminal Emulation
- ☑ VMS
- ☑ UNIX
- ☑ OS/2
- ☐ Other platform

Cost
- ☐ Unknown
- ☐ Basic
- ☑ Extended
- ☐ Premium ($)
- ☐ Executive w/$

Activity Level
UNKNOWN

Address
GO: **DEC**

Digital NT Support Forum

Description
Dedicated to the user support of Windows NT, regardless of environment or platform, this forum is supported by Digital's Multi-Vendor Customer Services Group. You can find information here about DEC's Alpha AXP platform.

Subjects
Computers, Client/Server, Digital Equipment Corporation (DEC), Windows NT

Audience
DEC Alpha AXP users, support technicians, system integrators, VARs, Windows NT users

Content Summary
The library and message areas contain information about Digital and Digital's Multivendor Customer Services, including press releases and news on the Alpha AXP and Windows NT. You also can find specific areas devoted to NT user support, languages and application tools, hardware support, bug reporting, a "Wish List" area for what you want, and Alpha AXP support. You can find new BIOS files, Alpha Microcode, and utility programs in the "Patches & More" library.

See Also
DEC PC, DECPCI, PDP-11 Forum, VAX Forum

User Guide
- ☐ Windows
- ☐ DOS
- ☐ Macintosh
- ☐ Terminal Emulation
- ☐ VMS
- ☐ UNIX
- ☐ OS/2
- ☑ Other platform

Cost
- ☐ Unknown
- ☐ Basic
- ☑ Extended
- ☐ Premium ($)
- ☐ Executive w/$

Activity Level
MEDIUM

Address
GO: **DECWNT**

Bacchus Wine and Beer Forum

Description
The Wine Forum, operated by Bacchus Data Services, is the home for discussion of all the beverages that you enjoy.

Subjects
Food, Wine

Audience
General public, wine lovers

Content Summary
If you enjoy a good glass of wine or a cold beer, join this forum and visit the different libraries in it. Some of the library topics include wine tasting, wine shopping, beer, wine, brewing, recipes, spirits, coffee, and more.

See Also
The Absolut Museum

User Guide
- ☑ Windows
- ☑ DOS
- ☑ Macintosh
- ☐ Terminal Emulation
- ☑ VMS
- ☑ UNIX
- ☑ OS/2
- ☐ Other platform

Cost
- ☐ Unknown
- ☐ Basic
- ☑ Extended
- ☐ Premium ($)
- ☐ Executive w/$

Activity Level
MEDIUM

Address
GO: **WINEFORUM**

WinNT Forum

Description
This is a vendor support forum for Microsoft Windows NT.

Subjects
Computers

Audience
Computer users, Windows NT users

Content Summary
This forum asks questions of Microsoft, reports bugs, discusses future releases, etc.

See Also
Windows Vendor Forums

User Guide
- ☑ Windows
- ☑ DOS
- ☐ Macintosh
- ☐ Terminal Emulation
- ☐ VMS
- ☐ UNIX
- ☐ OS/2
- ☐ Other platform

Cost
- ☐ Unknown
- ☐ Basic
- ☑ Extended
- ☐ Premium ($)
- ☐ Executive w/$

Activity Level

Address
GO: **WINNT**

Wolfram Research Forum

Description
This is a vendor support forum for Wolfram Research's Mathematica software application.

Subjects
Computers

Audience
Computer users, educators

Content Summary
The libraries include papers from experts that outline the product's uses in specific applications.

See Also
IBM File Finder

User Guide
- ☑ Windows
- ☑ DOS
- ☐ Macintosh
- ☐ Terminal Emulation
- ☐ VMS
- ☐ UNIX
- ☐ OS/2
- ☐ Other platform

Cost
- ☐ Unknown
- ☐ Basic
- ☑ Extended
- ☐ Premium ($)
- ☐ Executive w/$

Activity Level

Address
Go: **WOLFRAM**

WOMEN

U. S. News Women's Forum

Description
Forum sponsored by *U.S. News*, covering women's issues.

Subjects
Women

Audience
Women, General Public

Content Summary
This forum includes a wide range of women's topics from information on families to job opportunities.

See Also
Women, Family

User Guide
- ☑ Windows
- ☑ DOS
- ☐ Macintosh
- ☐ Terminal Emulation
- ☐ VMS
- ☐ UNIX
- ☐ OS/2
- ☐ Other platform

Cost
- ☐ Unknown
- ☐ Basic
- ☑ Extended
- ☐ Premium ($)
- ☐ Executive w/$

Activity Level

Address
GO: **USNFORUM**

WORDPERFECT

WordPerfect GmbH Forum

Description
Vendor support forum for WordPerfect's German software products.

Subjects
Computers

Audience
German computer users

Content Summary
Libraries include information on printers, graphics, desktop publishing, and training.

See Also
WordPerfect Users Forum

Wordperfect – WordStar Forum

User Guide
- ☑ Windows
- ☑ DOS
- ☐ Macintosh
- ☐ Terminal Emulation
- ☐ VMS
- ☐ UNIX
- ☐ OS/2
- ☐ Other platform

Cost
- ☐ Unknown
- ☐ Basic
- ☑ Extended
- ☐ Premium ($)
- ☐ Executive w/$

Activity Level: UNKNOWN

Address
GO: **WPGER**

WordPerfect Users Forum

Description
This is a user-sponsored forum for the discussion of any software produced by WordPerfect Corp.

Subjects
Computers

Audience
Computer users, WordPerfect users

Content Summary
The libraries include information on printers, graphics, desktop publishing, merges, training, file formats, and networking.

See Also
Desktop Publishing Forum

User Guide
- ☑ Windows
- ☑ DOS
- ☐ Macintosh
- ☐ Terminal Emulation
- ☐ VMS
- ☐ UNIX
- ☐ OS/2
- ☐ Other platform

Cost
- ☐ Unknown
- ☐ Basic
- ☑ Extended
- ☐ Premium ($)
- ☐ Executive w/$

Activity Level: MEDIUM

Address
GO: **WPUSERS**

WPCorp Files Forum

Description
This is a vendor support forum for WordPerfect drivers and macros, for such software as WordPerfect, Draw, DataPerfect, and PlanPerfect. This forum is supported by WPCorp.

Subjects
Computers

Audience
Computer users, WordPerfect users

Content Summary
Libraries include printer drivers, graphics drivers, macros, and information on related programs.

See Also
WordPerfect Corporation Forum

User Guide
- ☑ Windows
- ☑ DOS
- ☑ Macintosh
- ☐ Terminal Emulation
- ☐ VMS
- ☑ UNIX
- ☑ OS/2
- ☐ Other platform

Cost
- ☐ Unknown
- ☐ Basic
- ☑ Extended
- ☐ Premium ($)
- ☐ Executive w/$

Activity Level: LOW

Address
GO: **WPFILES**

WordStar Forum

Description
This is a forum for WordStar users sponsored by WordStar Int'l Technical Consulting Group.

Subjects
Computers

Audience
Computer users, WordStar users

Content Summary
Libraries and message areas include information on sample programs, usage articles and press releases, and printer drivers, templates, and utilities.

See Also
IBM File Finder

User Guide
- ☑ Windows
- ☑ DOS
- ☐ Macintosh
- ☐ Terminal Emulation
- ☐ VMS
- ☐ UNIX
- ☐ OS/2
- ☐ Other platform

Cost
- ☐ Unknown
- ☐ Basic
- ☑ Extended
- ☐ Premium ($)
- ☐ Executive w/$

Activity Level

Address:
Go: WORDSTAR

Working-From-Home Forum

Description
This is a forum for those who work from their homes, uniting them with others in similar circumstances. Users can exchange info, share solutions, etc.

Subjects
Computers

Audience
Home-based workers

Content Summary
The libraries and message areas contain information on taxes, business setup, equipment recommendations, and areas to exchange information.

See Also
Family Handyman Forum

User Guide
- ☑ Windows
- ☑ DOS
- ☑ Macintosh
- ☐ Terminal Emulation
- ☑ VMS
- ☑ UNIX
- ☑ OS/2
- ☐ Other platform

Cost
- ☐ Unknown
- ☐ Basic
- ☑ Extended
- ☐ Premium ($)
- ☐ Executive w/$

Activity Level

Address
GO: WORK

WORLDSPAN Travelshopper

Description
Travelshopper is your online travel agent, enabling you to search for and view airline flights and flight info.

Subjects
Travel

Audience
Travelers

Content Summary
Use this forum to obtain information about flights, make reservations, book hotel reservations, or get costs of flights.

See Also
Travel Forum

User Guide
- ☑ Windows
- ☑ DOS
- ☑ Macintosh
- ☐ Terminal Emulation
- ☑ VMS
- ☑ UNIX
- ☐ OS/2
- ☑ Other platform

Cost
- ☐ Unknown
- ☑ Basic
- ☐ Extended
- ☐ Premium ($)
- ☐ Executive w/$

Activity Level

LOW → HIGH (MEDIUM)

Address
GO: WORLDSPAN

Worldwide Car Network

Description
This forum is the place to be for people interested in classic and later models of American, European, or Japanese cars, motorcycles, or trucks.

Subjects
Automobiles

Audience
Automobile enthusiasts

Content Summary
The libraries include information on cars, motorcycles, and trucks. Topics covered include price, finding parts, and shows.

See Also
Automobile Forum

User Guide
- ☑ Windows
- ☑ DOS
- ☑ Macintosh
- ☐ Terminal Emulation
- ☑ VMS
- ☑ UNIX
- ☐ OS/2
- ☐ Other platform

Cost
- ☐ Unknown
- ☐ Basic
- ☑ Extended
- ☐ Premium ($)
- ☐ Executive w/$

Activity Level

Address
GO: WCN

WPCorp Files Forum

Description
This is a vendor support forum for WordPerfect drivers and macros, for such software as WordPerfect, Draw, DataPerfect, and PlanPerfect. This forum is supported by WPCorp.

Subjects
Computers

Audience
Computer users, WordPerfect users

Content Summary
Libraries include printer drivers, graphics drivers, macros, and information on related programs.

See Also
WordPerfect Corporation Forum

User Guide
- ☑ Windows
- ☑ DOS
- ☑ Macintosh
- ☐ Terminal Emulation
- ☐ VMS
- ☑ UNIX
- ☑ OS/2
- ☐ Other platform

Cost
- ☐ Unknown
- ☐ Basic
- ☑ Extended
- ☐ Premium ($)
- ☐ Executive w/$

Activity Level

Address
GO: **WPFILES**

WRITING

Journalism Forum

Description
Since 1985, the Journalism Forum has been devoted to servicing the needs of journalists, photographers, and freelancers.

Subjects
Journalism, Writing

Audience
Journalists, writers

Content Summary
The Journalism Forum's library and message sections are full of files, writing guidelines, freelancing discussions, and other supporting files. Some of the libraries include Job/Stringers, Freelancers, Journalism Tools, Future Media, Newsroom Computers, Journalism Law, and other areas.

See Also
Literary Forum

User Guide
- ☑ Windows
- ☑ DOS
- ☑ Macintosh
- ☐ Terminal Emulation
- ☑ VMS
- ☑ UNIX
- ☑ OS/2
- ☑ Other platform

Cost
- ☐ Unknown
- ☐ Basic
- ☑ Extended
- ☐ Premium ($)
- ☐ Executive w/$

Activity Level

Address
GO: **JFORUM**

Literary Forum

Description
Shakespeare. Plath. Milton. Twain. O'Conner. These and many other literary figures and related discussions are in this forum.

Subjects
Fiction, Literature, Writing

Audience
Writers, educators, editors, literary critics, literary theorists

Content Summary
If you like to read and talk about literature, join this forum. You'll also find discussions for writers and youth literature. Some of the libraries and message sections include Market Maneuvers, YouthLit/Learning, Journalism, Fiction, Science Fiction/Fantasy, Art of Writing, Romance/Historicals, and many more. The WotM! library (Library 3) is devoted to the Writer of the Month.

See Also
Journalism Forum

User Guide
- ☑ Windows
- ☑ DOS
- ☑ Macintosh
- ☐ Terminal Emulation
- ☑ VMS
- ☑ UNIX
- ☑ OS/2
- ☑ Other platform

Cost
- ☐ Unknown
- ☐ Basic
- ☑ Extended
- ☐ Premium ($)
- ☐ Executive w/$

Activity Level

Address
GO: **LITFORUM**

WRQ/Reflection Forum

Description
This is a vendor support forum for Walker, Richer, and Quinn software products, such as their Reflection Series.

Subjects
Computers, Networking

Audience
Walker, Richer, Quinn software users

Content Summary
The libraries include discussions of terminal emulation, networking, office automation, and development applications products.

See Also
IBM File Finder

User Guide
- [x] Windows
- [x] DOS
- [x] Macintosh
- [ ] Terminal Emulation
- [ ] VMS
- [ ] UNIX
- [ ] OS/2
- [ ] Other platform

Cost
- [ ] Unknown
- [ ] Basic
- [x] Extended
- [ ] Premium ($)
- [ ] Executive w/$

Activity Level
LOW (arrow pointing toward LOW)

Address
GO: **WRQFORUM**

WUGNET Forum

Description
The Windows User Group Network (WUGNET) forum supports Windows users around the world.

Subjects
Computers

Audience
Computer users, Windows users

Content Summary
Libraries include the bimonthly WUGNET Journal, information for developers, and an area to communicate with other Windows developers.

See Also
Windows Sources Forum

User Guide
- [x] Windows
- [x] DOS
- [ ] Macintosh
- [ ] Terminal Emulation
- [ ] VMS
- [ ] UNIX
- [ ] OS/2
- [ ] Other platform

Cost
- [ ] Unknown
- [ ] Basic
- [x] Extended
- [ ] Premium ($)
- [ ] Executive w/$

Activity Level
MEDIUM

Address
GO: **WUGNET**

XYZ

X.25

Eicon Technology Forum

Description
Sponsored by Eicon Technology, this forum helps users find answers to questions or problems concerning Eicon products. Eicon offers products of connectivity solutions for the X.25 and SNA environment.

Subjects
Computers, Connectivity, X.25, SNA

Audience
MIS people, Eicon consumers

Content Summary
The library and message sections contain information about Eicon products as well as technical support, press releases, utilities, help files, applications, demos, and Q&A. The libraries include sections for emulators, gateways, tool kits, international services, and WAN services.

See Also

User Guide
- ☑ Windows
- ☑ DOS
- ☑ Macintosh
- ☐ Terminal Emulation
- ☑ VMS
- ☑ UNIX
- ☑ OS/2
- ☐ Other platform

Cost
- ☐ Unknown
- ☐ Basic
- ☑ Extended
- ☐ Premium ($)
- ☐ Executive w/$

Activity Level

Address
GO: EICON

YACHTS

Sailing Forum

Description
This forum provides information and discussion groups to members who are avid sailors or who dream of sailing the seas.

Subjects
Boats, Yachts

Audience
Sailing enthusiasts

Content Summary
This forum provides open discussion of all types of sailing topics. Libraries include discussions of heavy weather survival tactics, sailor folklore, real-life sea stories of safety lessons, and classified ads for boating-related supplies.

See Also
Sports Forum

User Guide
- ☑ Windows
- ☑ DOS
- ☑ Macintosh
- ☐ Terminal Emulation
- ☑ VMS
- ☑ UNIX
- ☑ OS/2
- ☐ Other platform

Cost
- ☐ Unknown
- ☐ Basic
- ☑ Extended
- ☐ Premium ($)
- ☐ Executive w/$

Activity Level

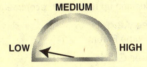

Address
GO: SAILING

You Guessed It!

Description
This forum is an online multiplayer game in which players match their own answers against those of a previous "studio audience."

Subjects
Entertainment, Games

Audience
Members interested in multiplayer trivia games

Content Summary
"... Out of nowhere there appear the stately columns, gleaming lights, ..." Now you add your comments and questions.

See Also

User Guide
- ☑ Windows
- ☑ DOS
- ☐ Macintosh
- ☑ Terminal Emulation
- ☐ VMS
- ☐ UNIX
- ☐ OS/2
- ☐ Other platform

Cost
- ☐ Unknown
- ☐ Basic
- ☑ Extended
- ☐ Premium ($)
- ☐ Executive w/$

You Guessed It! – Ziff Cobb Applications Forum

Activity Level: UNKNOWN (LOW / MEDIUM / HIGH)

Address
GO: **YGI**

Zagat Restaurant Guide

Description
This service features thousands of reviews based on annual surveys of restaurant patrons. Search for old and new restaurants in more than 20 cities and regions.

Subjects
Food

Audience
General interest

Content Summary
This guide is ideal for those members interested in looking up restaurant recommendations.

See Also
Home Forum

User Guide
- ☑ Windows
- ☑ DOS
- ☑ Macintosh
- ☑ Terminal Emulation
- ☑ VMS
- ☑ UNIX
- ☑ OS/2
- ☑ Other platform

Cost
- ☐ Unknown
- ☑ Basic
- ☐ Extended
- ☐ Premium ($)
- ☐ Executive w/$

Activity Level: UNKNOWN (LOW / MEDIUM / HIGH)

Address
GO: **ZAGAT**

Zenith Data Systems Forum

Description
This is an independent forum supporting the computer products of Zenith Data Systems.

Subjects
Computers

Audience
Computer users

Content Summary
This forum offers library and message section for members who own or are interested in Zenith computers.

See Also
IBM File Finder

User Guide
- ☑ Windows
- ☑ DOS
- ☐ Macintosh
- ☐ Terminal Emulation
- ☐ VMS
- ☐ UNIX
- ☐ OS/2
- ☐ Other platform

Cost
- ☐ Unknown
- ☐ Basic
- ☑ Extended
- ☐ Premium ($)
- ☐ Executive w/$

Activity Level: LOW (arrow pointing to LOW)

Address
GO: **ZENITH**

Ziff Bendata Forum

Description
This is a vendor support forum for Bendata's HEAT product.

Subjects:
Computers, ZiffNet

Audience
Computer users

Content Summary
This forum is ideal for members who use or are interested in Bendata products.

See Also
ZiffNet Free Utilities Forum

User Guide
- ☑ Windows
- ☑ DOS
- ☐ Macintosh
- ☐ Terminal Emulation
- ☐ VMS
- ☐ UNIX
- ☐ OS/2
- ☑ Other platform

Cost
- ☐ Unknown
- ☐ Basic
- ☑ Extended
- ☐ Premium ($)
- ☐ Executive w/$

Activity Level: MEDIUM (arrow pointing up to MEDIUM)

Address
GO: **ZNT:BENDATA**

Ziff Cobb Applications Forum

Description
This forum provides problem-solving tips and downloadable software for users of Lotus 1-2-3, DOS, and Windows.

Ziff Cobb Applications Forum – Ziff Editor's Coice

Subjects
Computers, ZiffNet

Audience
Computer users

Content Summary
If you are interested in problem solving for Lotus, DOS, and Windows, this forum's library and message sections contain information and files for you.

See Also
Ziff Software Center

User Guide
- ☑ Windows
- ☑ DOS
- ☐ Macintosh
- ☐ Terminal Emulation
- ☐ VMS
- ☐ UNIX
- ☐ OS/2
- ☐ Other platform

Cost
- ☐ Unknown
- ☐ Basic
- ☑ Extended
- ☐ Premium ($)
- ☐ Executive w/$

Activity Level

Address
GO: **ZNT:COBAPP**

Ziff Cobb Programming Forum

Description
The Cobb Programming Forum provides downloadable files and source code archived from the Cobb Programming Journals, including C, C++, Pascal, Paradox, and dBASE files.

Subjects
Computer Programming, Computers, ZiffNet

Audience
Computer users

Content Summary
If you are interested in programming, join this forum for information and files to help you with your programming needs.

See Also
Ziff Cobb Applications Forum

User Guide
- ☑ Windows
- ☑ DOS
- ☐ Macintosh
- ☐ Terminal Emulation
- ☐ VMS
- ☐ UNIX
- ☐ OS/2
- ☑ Other platform

Cost
- ☐ Unknown
- ☐ Basic
- ☑ Extended
- ☐ Premium ($)
- ☐ Executive w/$

Activity Level

Address
GO: **ZNT:COBBPR**

Ziff Computer Shopper Forum

Description
The forum for shoppers looking for information about buying computer systems, peripherals, and software.

Subjects
Computers, ZiffNet

Audience
Computers users

Content Summary
This forum is for members interested in getting information before they buy products.

See Also
Ziff Software Center

User Guide
- ☑ Windows
- ☑ DOS
- ☑ Macintosh
- ☐ Terminal Emulation
- ☐ VMS
- ☐ UNIX
- ☑ OS/2
- ☐ Other platform

Cost
- ☐ Unknown
- ☐ Basic
- ☑ Extended
- ☐ Premium ($)
- ☐ Executive w/$

Activity Level

Address
GO: **ZNT:COMPSHOPPER**

Ziff Editor's Choice

Description
This database of previous Editor Choice awards by *PC Magazine* helps members choose software and hardware.

Subjects
Computers, ZiffNet

Audience
Computer users

Content Summary
Looking for new hardware or software? This forum is for members looking for expert assistance in choosing hardware and software.

See Also
ZiffNet Reviews Index

Ziff Editor's Choice – Ziff Software Center

User Guide
- ☑ Windows
- ☑ DOS
- ☑ Macintosh
- ☐ Terminal Emulation
- ☐ VMS
- ☐ UNIX
- ☑ OS/2
- ☑ Other platform

Cost
- ☐ Unknown
- ☑ Basic
- ☐ Extended
- ☐ Premium ($)
- ☐ Executive w/$

Activity Level

Address
GO: ZNT:EDCHOICE

Ziff Executives Online Forum

Description
The Executives Online Forum gives you direct access to industry leaders who visit to discuss products, strategies, and issues.

Subjects
Computers, ZiffNet

Audience
Computer users

Content Summary
Do you want to discuss topics with the likes of John Dvorak, Jim Seymour, and others? This forum is for members interested in discussing issues with executives in the computer industry.

See Also
ZiffNet Reviews Index

User Guide
- ☑ Windows
- ☑ DOS
- ☑ Macintosh
- ☐ Terminal Emulation
- ☐ VMS
- ☐ UNIX
- ☑ OS/2
- ☑ Other platform

Cost
- ☐ Unknown
- ☐ Basic
- ☑ Extended
- ☐ Premium ($)
- ☐ Executive w/$

Activity Level

Address
GO: ZNT:EXEC

Ziff Newsbytes

Description
The Newsbytes News Network is an award-winning, global, daily newswire focused primarily on industry news.

Subjects
Computers, ZiffNet

Audience
Computer users

Content Summary
This service enables you to view up-to-date news and information concerning the top stories in the computer industry.

See Also
PC World, PC Contact

User Guide
- ☑ Windows
- ☑ DOS
- ☑ Macintosh
- ☐ Terminal Emulation
- ☐ VMS
- ☐ UNIX
- ☑ OS/2
- ☑ Other platform

Cost
- ☐ Unknown
- ☐ Basic
- ☑ Extended
- ☐ Premium ($)
- ☐ Executive w/$

Activity Level

Address
GO: ZNT:NEWSBYTES

Ziff Software Center

Description
The Software Center offers all kinds of high quality downloadable software, including ZiffNet utilities.

Subjects
Computers, ZiffNet

Audience
Computer users

Content Summary
This forum is ideal for users who are looking for utilities, files, and other resources.

See Also
Ziff Computer Shopper Forum

User Guide
- ☑ Windows
- ☑ DOS
- ☑ Macintosh
- ☐ Terminal Emulation
- ☐ VMS
- ☐ UNIX
- ☑ OS/2
- ☑ Other platform

Cost
- [ ] Unknown
- [x] Basic
- [ ] Extended
- [ ] Premium ($)
- [ ] Executive w/$

Activity Level: UNKNOWN

Address
GO: `ZNT:CENTER`

Ziff-Davis Press Booknet

Description
This is an online shopping area for Ziff-Davis books, at a 20% discount.

Subjects
Computers, ZiffNet

Audience
Computer users, book buyers

Content Summary
This service enables you to order Ziff-Davis books online.

See Also
Macmillan Computer Publishing

User Guide
- [x] Windows
- [x] DOS
- [x] Macintosh
- [ ] Terminal Emulation
- [ ] VMS
- [ ] UNIX
- [ ] OS/2
- [x] Other platform

Cost
- [ ] Unknown
- [ ] Basic
- [x] Extended
- [ ] Premium ($)
- [ ] Executive w/$

Activity Level: UNKNOWN

Address
GO: `ZNT:BOOKNET`

ZIFFNET

Electronic Books

Description
This is a ZiffNet area. You must be a member of ZiffNet or apply for membership when you first go to the Electronic Books area. The cost of ZiffNet membership is $2.95 monthly. The Electronic Books area offers you an option to buy books directly from the Ziff-Davis Press at 20 percent discount by selecting the ZD Press Booknet option from the main menu.

Subjects
Computers, Computer Books, ZiffNet

Audience
Computer users

Content Summary
When you select the ZD Press Booknet option, you can order Ziff Davis Press books, get special discounts from their remainder table (40 percent off cover price sometimes), download any special offers, or talk to customer service. The Electronic Books service also features the Project Gutenburg Free Book Library, which has over 100 electronic books ranging from literature (such as *Moby Dick*) to Internet titles (such as the *Hitchhiker's Guide to the Internet*) that users can download.

See Also
Macmillan Computer Publishing

User Guide
- [x] Windows
- [x] DOS
- [x] Macintosh
- [ ] Terminal Emulation
- [x] VMS
- [x] UNIX
- [x] OS/2
- [x] Other platform

Cost
- [ ] Unknown
- [ ] Basic
- [ ] Extended
- [x] Premium ($)
- [ ] Executive w/$

Activity Level: UNKNOWN

Address
GO: `ZNT:EBOOKS`

PC Computing

Description
The PC Computing service (a ZiffNet service) enables you to go to the PC Contact Forum, take a poll, or communicate with *PC Computing* magazine.

Subjects
Computers, ZiffNet

Audience
Computer users

Content Summary
From the main menu, you can select PC/Contact Forum, Take a PC/Computing Poll, Tips and Tricks from PC/Computing, File Submissions to PC/Computing, and Letters to the Editor. This is a ZiffNet service.

See Also
PC Contact, PC Magazine

User Guide

- [ ] Windows
- [ ] DOS
- [ ] Macintosh
- [x] Terminal Emulation
- [ ] VMS
- [ ] UNIX
- [ ] OS/2
- [ ] Other platform

Cost

- [ ] Unknown
- [x] Basic
- [ ] Extended
- [ ] Premium ($)
- [ ] Executive w/$

Activity Level

MEDIUM
LOW
UNKNOWN
HIGH

Address

GO: **PCCOMP**

PC Contact Forum

Description

The PC Contact Forum, a service of ZiffNet, is devoted to discussions among PC Computing's editors and readers.

Subjects

Computers, ZiffNet

Audience

Computer users

Content Summary

In addition to exchanging ideas or getting questions answered from your favorite writers or editors online, you can contact the PC Advocate about problems with vendors or talk to the Phantom Shopper to share your experiences with computer dealers around the country. Plus you can browse through the library and download productivity files and tricks.

See Also

PC Computing

User Guide

- [x] Windows
- [x] DOS
- [x] Macintosh
- [ ] Terminal Emulation
- [ ] VMS
- [ ] UNIX
- [ ] OS/2
- [ ] Other platform

Cost

- [ ] Unknown
- [ ] Basic
- [x] Extended
- [ ] Premium ($)
- [ ] Executive w/$

Activity Level

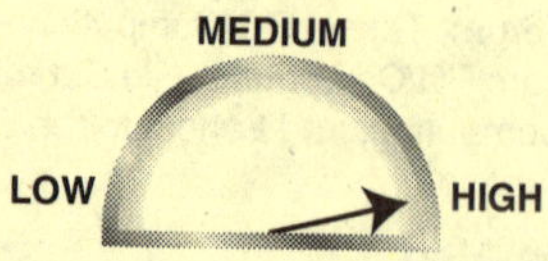
MEDIUM
LOW
HIGH

Address

GO: **PCCONTACT**

PC Direct UK Magazine Forum

Description

PC Direct UK Magazine Forum, part of ZiffNet, mixes inside knowledge of the United Kingdom computer trade with specialist buyers guides while always keeping the consumer in mind.

Subjects

Computers, United Kingdom, ZiffNet

Audience

Computer users, UK residents

Content Summary

Download buyer guides, editorial contributions (download *Frankenstein*, for instance), and utilities. The library sections are called Buying Advice, Utilities, and Editorial Contributions.

See Also

PC Contact, PC Computing

User Guide

- [x] Windows
- [x] DOS
- [x] Macintosh
- [ ] Terminal Emulation
- [ ] VMS
- [ ] UNIX
- [ ] OS/2
- [ ] Other platform

Cost

- [ ] Unknown
- [ ] Basic
- [x] Extended
- [ ] Premium ($)
- [ ] Executive w/$

Activity Level

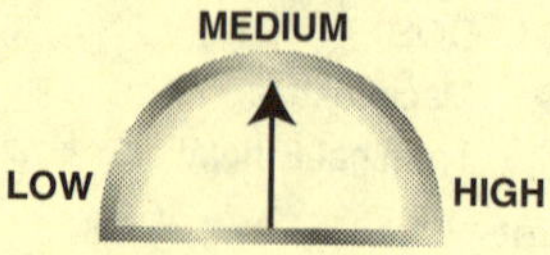
MEDIUM
LOW
HIGH

Address

GO: **PCDUK**

PC Magazine UK Forum

Description

This ZiffNet service offers utilities, sound files, graphics, and other files for your general computing needs.

Subjects

Computers, ZiffNet, United Kingdom

Audience

Computer users, UK computer users

Content Summary

The library sections contains several areas, including Bench Tests, Productivity, Utilities, Editorial Contributions, After Hours, DOS, Spreadsheets, Words, Online/Internet, and more.

See Also

IBM File Finder, PC MagNet Utilities/Tips Forum

User Guide
- ☑ Windows
- ☑ DOS
- ☑ Macintosh
- ☐ Terminal Emulation
- ☐ VMS
- ☐ UNIX
- ☑ OS/2
- ☑ Other platform

Cost
- ☐ Unknown
- ☐ Basic
- ☑ Extended
- ☐ Premium ($)
- ☐ Executive w/$

Activity Level
MEDIUM (LOW — HIGH)

Address
GO: **PCUKFORUM**

PC Magazine UK Online

Description
PC Magazine UK Online (a ZiffNet service) is jointly run by *PC Direct UK*, the business computer buyer's magazine, and *PC Magazine UK*, the leader in PC technology analysis and reporting.

Subjects
Computers, ZiffNet, United Kingdom

Audience
Computer users

Content Summary
Each magazine has its own forum. In the PC Magazine UK Forum (GO PCUKFORUM), you can access the libraries to download reports and buyer's guides. Access the respective library for articles to download. You can access the PC Direct UK Forum by using the command GO PCDUK.

See Also
PC Direct UK Forum, PC MagNet

User Guide
- ☑ Windows
- ☑ DOS
- ☑ Macintosh
- ☐ Terminal Emulation
- ☐ VMS
- ☐ UNIX
- ☐ OS/2
- ☐ Other platform

Cost
- ☐ Unknown
- ☐ Basic
- ☑ Extended
- ☐ Premium ($)
- ☐ Executive w/$

Activity Level
MEDIUM (LOW — HIGH)

Address
GO: **PCUKONLINE**

PC MagNet

Description
PC MagNet, part of ZiffNet, is the source for some of the finest utilities that meet the high standards of *PC Magazine*.

Subjects
Computers, ZiffNet

Audience
Computer users

Content Summary
Download utilities from the latest issue of *PC Magazine*. You can contact the staff at *PC Magazine* and ask for advice, tell the editors what you thought about their latest product review, debate the issues with the columnists, and get the answers to your specific questions.

See Also
PC Computing, PC Direct UK Forum, PC Contact Forum

User Guide
- ☑ Windows
- ☑ DOS
- ☑ Macintosh
- ☐ Terminal Emulation
- ☑ VMS
- ☑ UNIX
- ☐ OS/2
- ☐ Other platform

Cost
- ☐ Unknown
- ☐ Basic
- ☑ Extended
- ☐ Premium ($)
- ☐ Executive w/$

Activity Level
MEDIUM (LOW — HIGH)

Address
GO: **PCMAGNET**

PC MagNet Editorial Forum

Description
The PC MagNet Editorial Forum, part of ZiffNet, enables you to communicate with the likes of Michael Miller, John Dvorak, and Winn Rosch.

Subjects
Computers, ZiffNet

Audience
Computer users

Content Summary
From the library and message sections contain several areas, including Features-Hardware, Features-Software, First Looks, Trends, Viewpoints-Dvorak, Viewpoints-Seymour, Viewpoints-Miller, After Hours, and more. You can download John Dvorak's winning chili recipe from library 6.

ZIFFNET

See Also
PC MagNet, PC Computing, PC Programming Forum, PC MagNet Utilities/Tips Forum

User Guide
- ☑ Windows
- ☑ DOS
- ☑ Macintosh
- ☐ Terminal Emulation
- ☐ VMS
- ☑ UNIX
- ☑ OS/2
- ☐ Other platform

Cost
- ☐ Unknown
- ☐ Basic
- ☑ Extended
- ☐ Premium ($)
- ☐ Executive w/$

Activity Level
MEDIUM–HIGH

Address
GO: **EDITORIAL**

PC MagNet Programming Forum

Description
The PC MagNet Programming Forum, part of ZiffNet, has the latest files from the programming sections of *PC Magazine*. Many of the authors can be found here as well.

Subjects
Computers, Computer Programming, ZiffNet

Audience
Computer users, computer programmers

Content Summary
The library and message sections include Utilities Code, Power Programming, Languages, Lab Notes, Environments, Toolkits, Corporate Developer, and more. If you are interested in computer-related trade shows, you can download a calendar of over 100 events from library 1, General. The file name is ZCAL13.ZIP.

See Also
PC MagNet, PC MagNet Editorial Forum, PC MagNet Utilities/Tips Forum

User Guide
- ☑ Windows
- ☑ DOS
- ☑ Macintosh
- ☐ Terminal Emulation
- ☐ VMS
- ☐ UNIX
- ☑ OS/2
- ☑ Other platform

Cost
- ☐ Unknown
- ☐ Basic
- ☑ Extended
- ☐ Premium ($)
- ☐ Executive w/$

Activity Level
MEDIUM

Address
GO: **PROGRAMMING**

PC MagNet Utilities/Tips Forum

Description
You can find the latest utilities from *PC Magazine* here as well as files from various other sections of the magazine. Many of the authors of the utilities provide support here as well. This is part of ZiffNet.

Subjects
Computers, ZiffNet

Audience
Computer users

Content Summary
Numerous shareware utilities can be found throughout these libraries. Some of the library sections include PC Magazine Utilities, Tutor, User-to-User, Sol: Hardware, Driver Alert, Windows & OS/2 Utilities, and more.

See Also
IBM File Finder, PC MagNet

User Guide
- ☑ Windows
- ☑ DOS
- ☑ Macintosh
- ☐ Terminal Emulation
- ☐ VMS
- ☐ UNIX
- ☑ OS/2
- ☑ Other platform

Cost
- ☐ Unknown
- ☐ Basic
- ☑ Extended
- ☐ Premium ($)
- ☐ Executive w/$

Activity Level
MEDIUM–HIGH

Address
GO: **TIPS**

PC Week Forum

Description
PC Week is online as part of ZiffNet, enabling you to keep up with all the industry news. You can see headlines and full text of news stories the Friday before *PC Week* is published.

Subjects
Computers, ZiffNet

Audience
Computer users

Content Summary
See what the notorious Spender F. Katt has discovered this week or discuss the news and issues of the industry with the writers, editors, and other readers of the magazine.

See Also
PC MagNet, PC Computing

User Guide
- [x] Windows
- [x] DOS
- [x] Macintosh
- [ ] Terminal Emulation
- [ ] VMS
- [ ] UNIX
- [x] OS/2
- [ ] Other platform

Cost
- [ ] Unknown
- [ ] Basic
- [x] Extended
- [ ] Premium ($)
- [ ] Executive w/$

Activity Level
MEDIUM (LOW — HIGH)

Address
GO: **PCWEEK**

Public Brand Software (PBS) Applications Forum

Description
This ZiffNet forum is a library of high-quality shareware, including DOS, Windows, and OS/2 applications, as well as communication programs.

Subjects
Computers, ZiffNet

Audience
Computer users

Content Summary
The library and message sections contain several areas for discussions and downloading PBS applications. The library sections include Hot Off the Presses, Reviewer's Picks, DOS, Windows, OS/2, Communications, WP and Text Editors, ZD Awards Nominees, and PBS Information.

See Also
Public Brand Software Home Forum

User Guide
- [x] Windows
- [x] DOS
- [ ] Macintosh
- [ ] Terminal Emulation
- [ ] VMS
- [ ] UNIX
- [x] OS/2
- [ ] Other platform

Cost
- [ ] Unknown
- [ ] Basic
- [x] Extended
- [ ] Premium ($)
- [ ] Executive w/$

Activity Level
MEDIUM — HIGH

Address
GO: **PBSAPPS**

Public Brand Software (PBS) Home Forum

Description
The Public Brand Software (PBS) Home Forum is a library of top-rated shareware programs for home, hobby, and education.

Subjects
Computers, ZiffNet

Audience
Computer users

Content Summary
THe library sections include reference data and files in the news. Some of the library names include Hot Off the Presses, Reviewer's Picks, Home & Hobby, Education, Gutenburg, and more.

See Also
Public Brand Software Applications Forum

User Guide
- [x] Windows
- [x] DOS
- [ ] Macintosh
- [ ] Terminal Emulation
- [ ] VMS
- [ ] UNIX
- [x] OS/2
- [ ] Other platform

Cost
- [ ] Unknown
- [ ] Basic
- [x] Extended
- [ ] Premium ($)
- [ ] Executive w/$

Activity Level
MEDIUM — HIGH

Address
GO: **PBSHOME**

Ziff Bendata Forum

Description
This is a vendor support forum for Bendata's HEAT product.

Subjects:
Computers, ZiffNet

Audience
Computer users

Content Summary
This forum is ideal for members who use or are interested in Bendata products.

See Also
ZiffNet Free Utilities Forum

User Guide
- [x] Windows
- [x] DOS
- [ ] Macintosh
- [ ] Terminal Emulation
- [ ] VMS
- [ ] UNIX
- [ ] OS/2
- [x] Other platform

ZIFFNET

Cost
- ☐ Unknown
- ☐ Basic
- ☑ Extended
- ☐ Premium ($)
- ☐ Executive w/$

Activity Level: MEDIUM (arrow between LOW and HIGH, pointing up)

Address
GO: **ZNT:BENDATA**

Ziff Cobb Applications Forum

Description
This forum provides problem-solving tips and downloadable software for users of Lotus 1-2-3, DOS, and Windows.

Subjects
Computers, ZiffNet

Audience
Computer users

Content Summary
If you are interested in problem solving for Lotus, DOS, and Windows, this forum's library and message sections contain information and files for you.

See Also
Ziff Software Center

User Guide
- ☑ Windows
- ☑ DOS
- ☐ Macintosh
- ☐ Terminal Emulation
- ☐ VMS
- ☐ UNIX
- ☐ OS/2
- ☐ Other platform

Cost
- ☐ Unknown
- ☐ Basic
- ☑ Extended
- ☐ Premium ($)
- ☐ Executive w/$

Activity Level: MEDIUM (arrow pointing toward LOW)

Address
GO: **ZNT:COBAPP**

Ziff Cobb Programming Forum

Description
The Cobb Programming Forum provides downloadable files and source code archived from the Cobb Programming Journals, including C, C++, Pascal, Paradox, and dBASE files.

Subjects
Computer Programming, Computers, ZiffNet

Audience
Computer users

Content Summary
If you are interested in programming, join this forum for information and files to help you with your programming needs.

See Also
Ziff Cobb Applications Forum

User Guide
- ☑ Windows
- ☑ DOS
- ☐ Macintosh
- ☐ Terminal Emulation
- ☐ VMS
- ☐ UNIX
- ☐ OS/2
- ☑ Other platform

Cost
- ☐ Unknown
- ☐ Basic
- ☑ Extended
- ☐ Premium ($)
- ☐ Executive w/$

Activity Level: MEDIUM (arrow pointing toward LOW)

Address
GO: **ZNT:COBBPR**

Ziff Computer Shopper Forum

Description
The forum is for shoppers looking for information about buying computer systems, peripherals, and software.

Subjects
Computers, ZiffNet

Audience
Computers users

Content Summary
This forum is for members interested in getting information before they buy products.

See Also
Ziff Software Center

User Guide
- ☑ Windows
- ☑ DOS
- ☑ Macintosh
- ☐ Terminal Emulation
- ☐ VMS
- ☐ UNIX
- ☑ OS/2
- ☐ Other platform

Cost
- ☐ Unknown
- ☐ Basic
- ☑ Extended
- ☐ Premium ($)
- ☐ Executive w/$

Activity Level: MEDIUM (arrow pointing toward LOW)

Address
GO: ZNT:COMPSHOPPER

Ziff Editor's Choice

Description
This database of previous Editor Choice awards by *PC Magazine* helps members choose software and hardware.

Subjects
Computers, ZiffNet

Audience
Computer users

Content Summary
Looking for new hardware or software? This forum is for members looking for expert assistance in choosing hardware and software.

See Also
ZiffNet Reviews Index

User Guide
- ☑ Windows
- ☑ DOS
- ☑ Macintosh
- ☐ Terminal Emulation
- ☐ VMS
- ☐ UNIX
- ☑ OS/2
- ☑ Other platform

Cost
- ☐ Unknown
- ☑ Basic
- ☐ Extended
- ☐ Premium ($)
- ☐ Executive w/$

Activity Level

Address
GO: ZNT:EDCHOICE

Ziff Executives Online Forum

Description
The Executives Online Forum gives you direct access to industry leaders who visit to discuss products, strategies, and issues.

Subjects
Computers, ZiffNet

Audience
Computer users

Content Summary
Do you want to discuss topics with the likes of John Dvorak, Jim Seymour, and others? This forum is for members interested in discussing issues with executives in the computer industry.

See Also
ZiffNet Reviews Index

User Guide
- ☑ Windows
- ☑ DOS
- ☑ Macintosh
- ☐ Terminal Emulation
- ☐ VMS
- ☐ UNIX
- ☑ OS/2
- ☑ Other platform

Cost
- ☐ Unknown
- ☐ Basic
- ☑ Extended
- ☐ Premium ($)
- ☐ Executive w/$

Activity Level
MEDIUM (arrow pointing up) LOW — HIGH

Address
GO: ZNT:EXEC

Ziff Newsbytes

Description
The Newsbytes News Network is an award-winning, global, daily newswire focused primarily on industry news.

Subjects
Computers, ZiffNet

Audience
Computer users

Content Summary
This service enables you to view up-to-date news and information concerning the top stories in the computer industry.

See Also
PC World, PC Contact

User Guide
- ☑ Windows
- ☑ DOS
- ☑ Macintosh
- ☐ Terminal Emulation
- ☐ VMS
- ☐ UNIX
- ☑ OS/2
- ☑ Other platform

Cost
- ☐ Unknown
- ☐ Basic
- ☑ Extended
- ☐ Premium ($)
- ☐ Executive w/$

Activity Level
UNKNOWN

Address
GO: ZNT:NEWSBYTES

Ziff Software Center

Description
The Software Center offers all kinds of high quality downloadable software, including ZiffNet utilities.

ZIFFNET

Subjects
Computers, ZiffNet

Audience
Computer users

Content Summary
This forum is ideal for users who are looking for utilities, files, and other resources.

See Also
Ziff Computer Shopper Forum

User Guide
- [x] Windows
- [x] DOS
- [x] Macintosh
- [ ] Terminal Emulation
- [ ] VMS
- [ ] UNIX
- [x] OS/2
- [x] Other platform

Cost
- [ ] Unknown
- [x] Basic
- [ ] Extended
- [ ] Premium ($)
- [ ] Executive w/$

Activity Level

Address
GO: ZNT:CENTER

Ziff-Davis Press Booknet

Description
This is an online shopping area for Ziff-Davis books, at a 20% discount.

Subjects
Computers, ZiffNet

Audience
Computer users, book buyers

Content Summary
This service enables you to order Ziff-Davis books online.

See Also
Macmillan Computer Publishing

User Guide
- [x] Windows
- [x] DOS
- [x] Macintosh
- [ ] Terminal Emulation
- [ ] VMS
- [ ] UNIX
- [ ] OS/2
- [x] Other platform

Cost
- [ ] Unknown
- [ ] Basic
- [x] Extended
- [ ] Premium ($)
- [ ] Executive w/$

Activity Level

ZiffNet Designer Templates

Description
This is an online shopping area for spreadsheet and database templates.

Subjects
Computers, ZiffNet

Audience
Computer users

Content Summary
This service is for members wanting to make their spreadsheet and database work easier by buying pre-designed templates.

See Also
Microsoft Word Forum, Microsoft Excel Forum, IBM File Finder

User Guide
- [x] Windows
- [x] DOS
- [ ] Macintosh
- [ ] Terminal Emulation
- [ ] VMS
- [ ] UNIX
- [ ] OS/2
- [ ] Other platform

Cost
- [ ] Unknown
- [ ] Basic
- [x] Extended
- [ ] Premium ($)
- [ ] Executive w/$

Activity Level

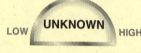

Address
GO: FORMS

ZiffNet File Finder

Description
Like all CompuServe File Finder databases, this one enables members to search for online software by keyword. ZFILEFINDER searches for ZiffNet software.

Subjects
Computers, ZiffNet

Audience
Computer users

Content Summary
Use this service to download utilities, software, and other files located in the ZiffNet area of CompuServe.

See Also
IBM File Finder, Novell File Finder

Address
GO: ZNT:BOOKNET

User Guide
- ☑ Windows
- ☑ DOS
- ☑ Macintosh
- ☐ Terminal Emulation
- ☐ VMS
- ☐ UNIX
- ☑ OS/2
- ☑ Other platform

Cost
- ☐ Unknown
- ☐ Basic
- ☑ Extended
- ☐ Premium ($)
- ☐ Executive w/$

Activity Level
UNKNOWN

Address
GO: `ZNT:ZFILEFINDER`

ZiffNet FREE UTILS Forum

Description
This is a ZiffNet forum offering free utilities in the library, and discussions in the message area.

Subjects
Computers, ZiffNet

Audience
Computer users

Content Summary
This area is for members interested in downloading useful free utilities for the Macintosh and PCs.

See Also
ZiffNet File Finder, IBM File Finder

User Guide
- ☑ Windows
- ☑ DOS
- ☑ Macintosh
- ☐ Terminal Emulation
- ☐ VMS
- ☐ UNIX
- ☐ OS/2
- ☐ Other platform

Cost
- ☐ Unknown
- ☐ Basic
- ☑ Extended
- ☐ Premium ($)
- ☐ Executive w/$

Activity Level
LOW

Address
GO: `ZNT:FREEUTIL`

ZiffNet Membership & Benefits

Description
Online location in which members can change their membership data or answer questions about their membership.

Subjects
Computers, ZiffNet

Audience
ZiffNet members

Content Summary
Use this service when you have concerns, customer support issues, or membership problems with ZiffNet.

See Also
ZiffNet Support Forum

User Guide
- ☑ Windows
- ☑ DOS
- ☑ Macintosh
- ☑ Terminal Emulation
- ☑ VMS
- ☑ UNIX
- ☑ OS/2
- ☑ Other platform

Cost
- ☐ Unknown
- ☑ Basic
- ☐ Extended
- ☐ Premium ($)
- ☐ Executive w/$

Activity Level
UNKNOWN

Address
GO: `ZNT:ZIFFMEM`

ZiffNet Reviews Index

Description
This database cites every product review published in a Ziff-Davis magazine since 1987.

Subjects
Computers

Audience
Computer users

Content Summary
This index is for members interested in locating product review articles on computer hardware and software.

See Also
PC World, PC Contact

User Guide
- ☑ Windows
- ☑ DOS
- ☑ Macintosh
- ☐ Terminal Emulation
- ☐ VMS
- ☐ UNIX
- ☑ OS/2
- ☑ Other platform

Cost
- ☐ Unknown
- ☑ Basic
- ☐ Extended
- ☐ Premium ($)
- ☐ Executive w/$

ZIFFNET

Activity Level

Address
GO: ZIFFINDEX

ZiffNet Support Forum

Description
This is a free forum offering help information on ZiffNet and ZiffNet services, help using ZiffNet, and support for Ziff database products.

Subjects
Computers, ZiffNet

Audience
Computer users, MIS

Content Summary
Use this forum for help in getting around ZiffNet.

See Also
ZiffNet Membership and Benefits

User Guide
- ☑ Windows
- ☑ DOS
- ☑ Macintosh
- ☑ Terminal Emulation
- ☑ VMS
- ☑ UNIX
- ☑ OS/2
- ☑ Other platform

Cost
- ☐ Unknown
- ☑ Basic
- ☐ Extended
- ☐ Premium ($)
- ☐ Executive w/$

Activity Level

Address
GO: ZIFFHELP

ZiffNet Surveys

Description
This is an area in which ZiffNet asks your opinion on various hardware and software products.

Subjects
Computers, ZiffNet

Audience
Computer users

Content Summary
This service enables ZiffNet members to respond to a product survey.

See Also
Speak Easy

User Guide
- ☑ Windows
- ☑ DOS
- ☑ Macintosh
- ☑ Terminal Emulation
- ☑ VMS
- ☑ UNIX
- ☑ OS/2
- ☑ Other platform

Cost
- ☐ Unknown
- ☑ Basic
- ☐ Extended
- ☐ Premium ($)
- ☐ Executive w/$

Activity Level

Address
GO: ZNT:SURVEY

Ziffnet Zshare Online Newsletter

Description
This is ZiffNet's monthly shareware review for shareware enthusiasts in a Windows Help file format.

Subjects
Computers, ZiffNet

Audience
Computer users

Content Summary
This newsletter is for members interested in shareware.

See Also
ZiffNet Reviews Index

User Guide
- ☑ Windows
- ☐ DOS
- ☐ Macintosh
- ☐ Terminal Emulation
- ☐ VMS
- ☐ UNIX
- ☐ OS/2
- ☐ Other platform

Cost
- ☐ Unknown
- ☐ Basic
- ☑ Extended
- ☐ Premium ($)
- ☐ Executive w/$

Activity Level

Address
GO: ZNT:ZSHARE

ZiffNet/Mac Download Forum

Description
This forum contains the top Macintosh shareware and freeware picks of the editors of *MacWEEK* and *MacUser* magazines.

Subjects
Computers, Macintosh, ZiffNet

Audience
Macintosh users

Content Summary
This forum is for members interested in discussing and downloading popular Macintosh freeware and shareware.

See Also
ZiffNet File Finder, IBM File Finder

User Guide
- ☐ Windows
- ☐ DOS
- ☒ Macintosh
- ☐ Terminal Emulation
- ☐ VMS
- ☐ UNIX
- ☐ OS/2
- ☐ Other platform

Cost
- ☐ Unknown
- ☐ Basic
- ☒ Extended
- ☐ Premium ($)
- ☐ Executive w/$

Activity Level
LOW / MEDIUM / HIGH

Address
GO: `ZMC:DOWNTECH`

ZiffNet/Mac File Finder

Description
The ZMC File Finder database enables members to search through all files located in the ZMC forums.

Subjects
Computers, Macintosh, ZiffNet

Audience
Macintosh users

Content Summary
This service is for members wanting to search ZMC forums for specific file types.

See Also
ZiffNet/Mac Download Forum

User Guide
- ☐ Windows
- ☐ DOS
- ☒ Macintosh
- ☐ Terminal Emulation
- ☐ VMS
- ☐ UNIX
- ☐ OS/2
- ☐ Other platform

Cost
- ☐ Unknown
- ☐ Basic
- ☒ Extended
- ☐ Premium ($)
- ☐ Executive w/$

Activity Level
UNKNOWN (LOW / MEDIUM / HIGH)

Address
GO: `ZMC:FILEFINDER`

INDEX

Symbols

3Com Online Information Service Menu, 11, 104
800 Flowers, 11, 286, 307-308

A

ABC Worldwide Hotel Guide, 13, 339, 559
The Absolut Museum, 550
academic research (The Sysop Forum), 13, 59
accounting
    Accounting Vendor Forum, 13, 47
    ACI US Forum, 14, 104, 441
Accounting Vendor Forum, 13, 47
ACI US Forum, 14, 104, 441
action requests database (Digitalk Database), 14, 126-127
ADD Forum, 14-15, 249, 472
Adobe Forum, 15, 81, 104-105, 524
adventure games (Enhanced Adventure), 15
Adventures in Food, 15, 513, 287
Adventures in Travel, 16, 494
advertising
    Classified Ads, 68, 257
    PR and Marketing Forum, 16, 397-398, 486-489
African American Art and Culture Forum, 16-17, 29, 212

aging (Retirement Living Forum), 17, 400-401, 500, 523
AI Expert Forum, 17, 93, 105
AIDS
    CCML AIDS Articles, 17-18, 63, 322-323
    Health/Fitness, 18
    Rare Diseases Database, 18
Air France, 18-19, 20, 559
Air Line Pilots Association, 20, 37, 484
Air Traffic Controller game, 20-21, 293-294
Airline Services Unlimited, 21, 513-514, 559
air travel
    Air France, 18-20, 559
    Air Line Pilots Association, 20, 37, 484
    Airline Services Unlimited, 21, 513-514, 559
    Aviation Special Interest Group, 37
    EMI Aviation Services, 19, 256, 564
    NWS Aviation Weather, 37-38, 463
    Official Airline Guide, 19-20, 465-466, 558, 560
    WORLDSPAN Travelshopper, 309
Alaska Peddler, 21, 308, 514
alcoholic beverages
    The Absolut Museum, 52
    Bacchus Wine and Beer Forum, 39
Aldus Forum, 21, 105, 524-525
Aldus Online Customer Support, 22, 105-106, 525

Aldus Special Programs Forum, 22, 106, 525
All-Music Guide Forum, 22, 330-331, 434
American Heritage Dictionary, 22-23, 235-236, 249
Americana Clothing, 23, 69, 514
Amiga Arts Forum, 23, 106
Amiga File Finder, 23-24, 106-107
Amiga Tech Forum, 24, 107
Amiga User Forum, 24, 107
Amiga Vendor Forum, 24-25, 107
animals
    Aquaria/Fish Forum, 28-29, 283, 331
    Dinosaur Forum, 239-240
    Pet Products/Reference Forum, 25, 283, 479, 578
    Time Warner-Dogs & Cats Forum, 25-26, 556
APPC Info Exchange Forum, 26, 107-108, 441-442
Apple computers
    Apple II Programmers' Forum, 26
    Apple II User's Forum, 26, 108
    Apple II Vendor's Forum, 27, 109
    Newton Developers's Forum, 27, 166, 456
Apple II
    Apple II Programmer's Forum, 26, 108
    Apple II User's Forum, 26, 108
    Apple II Vendor's Forum, 27, 109
applied physics (Ei Compendex Plus), 28, 253-254, 258, 486
Aquaria/Fish Forum, 28-29, 283, 331
archaeology (Dinosaur Forum), 239-240
Archive Photos Forum, 29, 329, 480-481
art
    African American Art and Culture Forum, 16-17, 29, 212
    Amiga Arts Forum, 23
    Artisoft Forum, 31
    Artist Forum, 29-31, 331
    Commodore Art/Games Forum, 71
    Fine Art Forum, 30-31, 67, 282, 423
    Literary Forum, 594-595
    Metropolitan Museum of Art, 30, 404-405
    Music/Arts Forum, 436
    see also photography
artificial intelligence
    AI Expert Forum, 17, 93, 105
Artisoft Forum, 31, 109, 442
Artist Forum, 29-31, 331
ASCII User Profile Program, 76-77
Ask Customer Service, 31-32, 74
Ask3Com Forum, 32, 109
ASP Shareware Forum, 32, 109-110, 510
Associated Press Online, 32-33, 259, 447-448
AST Forum, 33, 110
Astronomy Forum, 33, 331-332, 546
Atari Computing Forum, 33-34, 110
attention deficit disorder (ADD Forum), 14-15, 249, 472

audio/video (Sight And Sound Forum), 34, 261, 518
Autodesk AutoCAD Forum, 34, 55-56, 110-111
Autodesk Multimedia Forum, 34-35, 111, 428
Autodesk Retail Products Forum, 35-56, 111
automobiles
    Automobile Forum, 35
    Ford Motor Company, 35, 36
    Motor Sports Forum, 36
    New Car Showroom, 36, 446-447
    Worldwide Car Network, 36-37, 593
aviation, *see* air travel
Aviation Special Interest Group, 37

B

Bacchus Wine and Beer Forum, 39, 590
Banyan
    Banyan Forum, 39, 112, 442
    Other Banyan Patchware Forum, 172, 173, 469
    Vines 4.x Patchware Forum, 39, 91, 194, 579
    Vines 5.x Patchware Forum, 40, 91, 194, 579
Banyan Forum, 39, 112, 442
BASIS International Forum, 40, 47, 112
beds, *see* furniture
beer and wine
    The Absolut Museum, 550
    Bacchus Wine and Beer Forum, 39
Benchmarks and Standards Forum, 41, 112, 548
Bilingual Education, 41
billing CompuServe (TIMESLIPS Forum), 41-42
biology (HSX Adult Forum), 42
Blyth Software Forum, 42, 112-113
boating (Sailing Forum), 42-43, 597
books
    British Books in Print, 43-45
    Electronic Books, 79, 128-129, 254, 601
    Macmillan Publishing Forum, 43, 153, 394
    Quality Paperbacks, 43-44, 466-467, 491-494
    Small Computer Book Club, 44, 520
    Time Warner Bookstore, 44, 62, 555-556
    Ziff-Davis Press Booknet, 203, 601, 608
British Books in Print, 43-45
British Trade Marks, 45, 47
Broadcast Professionals Forum, 45, 546-547
broadcasting
    Broadcast Professionals Forum, 45, 546-547
    Media Newsletters, 45-46, 399-400
    Society of Broadcast Eng., 46, 523, 547-548
Brøderbund Software, 46, 113
Brooks Brothers Online Store, 46, 69, 514
business
    Accounting Vendor Forum, 13, 47
    ACI US Forum, 14, 104, 441
    BASIS International Forum, 40, 47, 112
    British Trade Marks, 45, 47

business – collectors

The Business Wire, 52, 451-452, 550
Census Bureau Online Service, 47-48, 65
The Company Corporation, 52-53, 550
Consumer Forum, 48, 208, 424
D&B Dun's Canadian Market, 219
D&B Dun's Canadian Market Identifiers, 48-49, 245, 272-273
D&B Dun's Electronic Business Directory, 49, 219, 245-246, 273, 363
D&B Dun's Market Identifiers, 49, 220, 246, 273-274, 363-364
Entrepreneur Magazine, 263-264, 519
Entrepreneur Small Business Square, 264, 519-520
The Entrepreneur's Forum, 53, 551-552
Entrepreneur's Small Business Forum, 50, 264-265, 520
Executive News Service, 50, 267, 280, 359, 448
Financial Forums, 50-51, 279-280
Global Report, 51, 223, 281, 310-311
Home-Based Business, 337
Information Management Forum, 142-143, 355, 396
OTC NewsAlert, 51, 281-282, 359-360, 450, 468-469
Standard Indus. Class., 52, 227, 530
Thomas Register Online, 228, 278, 554-555
TRADEMARKSCAN, 53
TRW Bus. Credit Reports, 565
UK Company Library, 229, 570
UK Professionals Forum, 572
Working-From-Home Forum, 307, 593
The Business Wire, 52, 451-452, 550

C

Cabletron Systems Forum, 55, 113, 442-443
Cabletron Systems Menu, 55, 113-114, 443
CAD
    Autodesk AutoCAD Forum, 34, 55-56, 110-111
    Autodesk Multimedia Forum, 34-35, 56, 111, 428
    Autodesk Retail Products Forum, 35, 56, 111
    CADD/CAM/CAE Vendor Forum, 114
    Cadence Forum, 56-57, 114
    Engineering Automation Forum, 57, 103, 129, 258
    IBM CAD/CAM Forum, 136, 345
    MicroStation Forum, 57, 163, 418
    MicroWarehouse, 418
CADD/CAM/CAE Vendor Forum, 57-58, 81, 114
Cadence Forum, 56-57, 114
California Forum, 58, 494-495
cameras
    Canon Net Menu, 59
    Canon Support Forum, 60
    Photography Forum, 58

camping (Recreational Vehicle Forum), 58-59
campus activities (The Sysop Forum), 13, 59, 554
Canada
    D&B Dun's Canadian Market, 219
    D&B Dun's Canadian Market Identifiers, 48-49, 245, 272-273
cancer
    Health and Fitness Forum, 59
    Health/Fitness, 18
Canon Net Menu, 59, 332, 481
Canon Support Forum, 60, 332, 481
Canopus Research Forum, 60, 114-115
cars, see **automobiles**
CASE-DCI Forum, 60, 93, 115
catalogs
    Digital PC Store, 126, 229-230, 238, 466
    Omaha Steaks International, 61, 466
    PC Catalog, 61, 173, 473
    PRC Publishing, 61, 85, 487
    Sears, 507
CBM Service Forum, 63, 72, 115
CCML AIDS Articles, 17, 18, 63, 322-323
CD-ROMs
    CD-ROM Forum, 63, 115-116
    CD-ROM Vendors Forum, 64, 116
    Kodak CD Forum, 144, 373, 480, 487-488
celebrities
    Entertainment Drive Center, 64, 259, 263, 428
    Hollywood Hotline, 260
    Stein Online, 64, 261, 532
    see also entertainment
Census Bureau Online Service, 47-48, 65, 531-532
Change Your Password, 65, 74
Chess Forum, 65, 294, 332-333
Cheyenne Software Forum, 66
childrens issues
    ADD Forum, 472
    Missing Children Forum, 66, 420
CIS Navigator Windows Support Forum, 67
Clarion Software Forum, 67, 116
Classified Ads, 68, 257
client/server
    Digital Equipment Corporation, 68, 125, 236, 433-434, 589-590
    Digital NT Support Forum, 68, 125, 236-238, 590
    Novell Client Forum, 167
clothing
    Americana Clothing, 23, 69
    Brooks Brothers Online Store, 46, 69
    Shoppers Advantage Club, 70
CoCo Forum, 70, 116
Collectibles Forum, 70, 243, 333, 531
collectors
    Artist Forum, 31
    Collectibles Forum, 70, 243, 333, 531

colleges (Univ of Phoenix), 252, 480, 574
Comaq Forum, 118
Comics/Animation Forum, 71, 333
Commodore Applications Forum, 71, 117
Commodore Art/Games Forum, 71, 117
Commodore Business Machines Menu, 72, 117
Commodore/Amiga Forums Menu, 73, 118
communications
    Crosstalk Forum, 121
    Dataquest Online, 73, 229
    Dr. Neuhaus Forum, 271, 497-498
    Electronic Frontier Foundation Forum, 103-104, 237, 360-361
    Hayes Forum, 133
    Hayes Online, 133
    IBM Communications Forum, 73, 136, 352-353, 421-422
    Lotus Communications Forum, 89, 147, 247, 381-382, 445
    Macintosh Communications Forum, 149, 383, 390, 422
    Modem Games Forum, 164
    Telecommunications Forum, 187, 545-546
The Company Corporation, 52-53, 550
Compaq Forum, 74
CompuAdd Forum, 74, 118
CompuServe
    Ask Customer Service, 31-32, 74
    Change Your Password, 65, 74
    The CompuServe Practice Forum, 76
    Dvorak Development Forum, 78
    Member Assistance, 75
    Support Directory, 76
    Telephone Access Numbers, 76
    What's New, 77, 585-586
    WinCIM Support Forum, 77
The CompuServe Practice Forum, 76, 551
The CompuServe Help Forum, 75, 77, 328, 550-551
Computer Club Forum, 80, 118-119, 328-329
Computer Library Online, 90, 119, 222
Computer Training Forum, 100, 119, 250
computers
    Aldus Forum, 21
    Aldus Online Customer Support, 22
    Aldus Special Programs Forum, 22
    Amiga Arts Forum, 23, 106
    Amiga File Finder, 23, 24, 106-107
    Amiga Tech Forum, 24, 107
    Amiga User Forum, 24, 107
    APPC Info Exchange Forum, 26, 107-108
    Apple II Programmers' Forum, 26, 108
    Apple II Users' Forum, 26, 108
    applications development
        Digitalk Forum, 28, 127, 239, 521
        Graphics Developers Forum, 314, 315

        IBM Applications Forum, 135-136, 345, 352
        Macintosh Applications Forum, 148, 155, 383, 389, 409
        Macintosh Developers Forum, 384, 390-391
        Microsoft Developers Relations Forum, 27-28, 156-157, 234, 406
        Ziff Cobb Applications Forum, 598-599
    Artisoft Forum, 31, 109, 442
    Ask3Com Forum, 32, 109
    ASP Shareware Forum, 32, 109-110
    AST Forum, 33, 110
    Atari Computing Forum, 33, 34, 110
    Autodesk Multimedia Forum, 34, 35-56, 111, 428
    Autodesk Retail Products Forum, 35, 56, 111
    Banyan Forum, 39, 112
    BASIS International Forum, 47, 112
    Benchmarks and Standards Forum, 41, 112, 548
    books (Electronic Books), 79
    Cabletron Systems Forum, 55, 113
    Cabletron Systems Menu, 55, 113-114
    Cadence Forum, 56-57, 114
    Canopus Research Forum, 60, 114-115
    CBM Service Forum, 63, 72, 115
    CD-ROM Forum, 63, 115-116
    CoCo Forum, 70
    Comaq Forum, 118
    Commodore Applications Forum, 71, 117
    Commodore Art/Games Forum, 71, 117
    Commodore Business Machines Menu, 72, 117
    Commodore/Amiga Forums Menu, 73, 118
    Compaq Forum, 74
    CompuAdd Forum, 74, 118
    Computer Club Forum, 80, 118-119, 328-329
    Computer Library Online, 222
    Computer Training Forum, 250
    Computers/Technology Menu, 119-120
    CP/M Forum, 120, 209-210
    Creative Labs, 120-121, 210
    Crosstalk Forum, 121, 211
    CTOS/Pathway Forum, 121-122, 212
    Cyber Forum, 122, 217, 580
    Da Vinci Forum, 122, 220
    Data Access Corp. Forum, 122, 220-221
    DataEase International Forum, 123, 229
    DEC PC Forum, 123, 231
    DEC Users Network Main Menu, 123, 231
    DECPCI Forum, 123-124, 231
    DELL Forum, 124, 232
    Delrina Forum, 124, 232
    DiagSoft QAPlus Forum, 124-125, 234-235, 509
    Digital Equipment Corporation, 68, 125, 236
        Digital NT Support Forum, 125, 236-238
        Digital PC Integration Forum, 125-126, 230-231, 238
        Digital PC Store, 126, 229-230, 238

Digitalk Database, 14, 238-239, 521
Digitalk Forum, 28, 239, 521
Dr. Dobb's Forum, 127, 243-244, 576
Dr. Neuhaus Forum, 127-128, 244, 271, 420-421, 497-498
Dvorak Development Forum, 78, 246, 440
education
    Education Forum, 206, 250-253, 545
    Education Research Forum, 207
Eicon Technology Forum, 128, 254, 522
Electronic Books, 128-129, 254
electronics
    The Escort Store, 207
    The Heath Company, 207
Engineering Automation Forum, 57, 129, 258
Gateway 2000 Forum, 91, 301, 320
The 'GO GRAPHICS' Tutorial, 188, 549
Golden CommPass Support, 311
graphics
    Adobe Forum, 15
    Autodesk AutoCAD Forum, 34, 55-56, 110-111
    Corel Forum, 81, 120, 209
    The 'GO GRAPHICS' Tutorial, 549
    Graphics A Vendor Forum, 129, 313-314, 320
    Graphics B Vendors Forum, 129-130, 314, 320-321
    Graphics Corner Forum, 130, 314, 482
    Graphics Developers Forum, 82, 130-131, 314-315
    Graphics File Finder, 82, 131, 315
    Graphics Forums, 83, 131, 313, 315-316
    Graphics Gallery Forum, 83, 131-132, 316, 482
    Graphics Plus Forum, 83-84, 132, 316, 482, 483
    Graphics Support Forum, 84, 316-317
    Graphics Vendors C Forum, 84, 132, 317
    IBM CAD/CAM Forum, 136, 345
    PRC Publishing, 61
    Quick Picture Forum, 491
Gupta Forum, 318
Hayes Forum, 133, 322, 421
Hayes Online, 87, 133, 322, 421
HP Handhelds Forum, 87, 134, 271-272, 339-340
HP Omnibook Forum, 134, 340
HP Peripherals Forum, 134-135, 340
HP Specials, 135, 340, 341
HP Systems Forum, 135, 341
IBM Applications Forum, 78, 345, 352
IBM CAD/CAM Forum, 136, 345
IBM Communications Forum, 73, 136, 352-353, 421-422
IBM DB2 Database Forum, 136-137, 223, 345
IBM File Finder, 137, 223-224, 346, 353
IBM Hardware Forum, 137, 321, 346, 353
IBM ImagePlus Forum, 137, 346
IBM LMU2 Forum, 138, 347, 443-444
IBM New User's Forum, 347, 353-354
IBM Object Technology Forum, 138, 347-348
IBM OS/2 Service Pak, 139, 348-349
IBM OS/2 Support Forum, 349
IBM PowerPC Forum, 140, 350
IBM Storage Systems Forum, 141, 351, 428
IBM Systems/Utilities Forum, 141, 354
IBM ThinkPad Forum, 142, 351
IBM Users Network, 142, 352, 354
Information Management Forum, 355
The Intel Forum, 188, 406
Intel Corporation, 87, 143, 357, 405, 422
Internet Forum, 143
Intuit Forum, 143-144, 276
JDR Microdevices, 92, 144, 369-370
Kodak CD Forum, 144, 373
Lan Technology Forum, 145, 375
The Laser's Edge, 188
Lexmark Forum, 88, 147, 380
Logitech Forum, 88, 147, 321, 381
Lotus Communications Forum, 147
Lotus Press Release Forum, 148, 382
Lotus Technical Library, 148, 382
The Mac Zone/PC Zone, 62, 189
Macintosh Communications Forum, 149, 422
Macintosh Community Club Forum, 149
Macintosh Entertainment Forum, 150
Macintosh File Finder, 150
Macintosh Forums, 150-151
Macintosh Hardware Forum, 151
Macintosh Hypertext Forum, 151, 429
Macintosh Multimedia Forum, 151-152, 429
Macintosh New Users Help Forum, 152
Macintosh Systems Forum, 152
Macmillan Publishing Forum, 43, 153, 394
MacNav Support Forum, 153
Macromedia Forum, 154, 429
magazines
    LAN Magazine, 144-145
    PC Computing, 173-174, 473-474
    PC Direct UK Magazine Forum, 174, 568
    PC Magazine UK Forum, 174-175, 568-569
    PC Magazine UK Online, 175, 569, 603
    PC MagNet, 475, 603
    PC MagNet Editorial Forum, 175, 603-604
    PC MagNet Utilities/Tips Forum, 176, 476, 604
    PC Week Forum, 177-178, 478, 604, 605
    PC World Online, 178, 395-396, 478
Media Vision Forum, 154, 400, 430
Micrografx Forum, 154-155
Microsoft Applications Forum, 155, 409
Microsoft Connection, 156, 410
Microsoft DOS Forum, 410-411, 427
Microsoft Fox Users Forum, 158, 225, 411-412

Microsoft Knowledge Base, 158, 412
Microsoft Languages Forum, 412
Microsoft Mail and Workgroups Forum, 158-159, 412-413
Microsoft Sales and Information Forum, 159, 413
Microsoft SQL Server Forum, 159, 221, 413-414
Microsoft TechNet Forum, 159-160, 414
Microsoft Windows Forum, 160-161, 415
Microsoft Windows Fun Forum, 161, 297, 415
Microsoft Windows Multimedia Forum, 297-298, 415-416
Microsoft Windows News Forum, 161, 416
Microsoft Windows NT SNA Forum, 161, 416
Microsoft Windows Shareware Forum, 162, 417
MicroStation Forum, 57, 163, 418
MicroWarehouse, 163, 418
Mobile Computing, 164, 420
Modem Games Forum, 164, 298
Multimedia Services, 165
National Computer Security Association (NCSA), 439
NCR/ATT Forum, 166, 440-441
NCSA InfoSecurity Forum, 441, 508-509
networks, *see* networks
Newton Developers' Forum, 27, 166, 456
NeXT Forum, 166-167, 456
Novell Client Forum, 167, 456-457
Novell Connectivity Forum, 167, 457
Novell Developer Info Forum, 167-168, 457
Novell Developer Support Forum, 168, 457-458
Novell DSG Forum, 168
Novell Files Database, 168-169
Novell Information Forum, 169
Novell Library Forum, 169
Novell NetWare 2.x Forum, 169-170
Novell NetWare 3.x Forum, 170
Novell NetWire, 170-171
Novell Network Management Forum, 171
Novell OS/2 Forum, 171
Novell Technical Bulletin Database, 171-172, 227
Oracle Forum, 172
Other Banyan Patchware Forum, 172-173
Packard Bell Forum, 173, 471
PC Catalog, 61, 173, 473
PC Contact Forum, 174
PC Plug and Play Forum, 176, 321-322, 476-477
PC Plus/PC Answers Online, 176-177, 569
PC Publications, 177, 477
Powersoft Forum, 178, 221
programming, *see* programming
Santa Cruz Operation Forum, 505-506
security
    National Computer Security Association (NCSA), 99, 165
    NCSA Info Security Forum, 166

Sierra Online, 180, 517-518
Small Computer Book Club, 520
Smith Micro Forum, 180, 521-522
Softdisk Publishing, 180-181, 523-524
SOFTEX, 181
software, *see* software
Speakeasy Forum, 182
Spinnaker Software Forum +, 182
Standard Microsystems Forum, 182
SunSoft Forum, 182-183, 535-536
Support On Site, 183, 228
Sybase Forum, 183, 537
Symantec AntiVirus Prod. Forum, 537-538
Symantec Applications Forum, 183-184
Symantec CPS DOS Forum, 184
Symantec CPS WinMac Forum, 184
Symantec Dev. Tools Forum, 184-185
Symantec FGS Forum, 185
Symantec Norton Util Forum, 185
Symantec Ntwrk Products Forum, 185
SynOptics Forum, 186
Tandy Model 100 Forum, 186, 543
Tandy Professional Forum, 186, 543
TAPCIS Forum, 543
Telecommunications Forum, 187, 545-546
Texas Instruments Forum, 187, 549
Texas Instruments News, 187-188, 549
TIMESLIPS Forum, 189
Toshiba Forum, 189, 557
Toshiba GmbH Forum, 189-190, 557
UK Computing Forum, 190, 570
UK Sports Clips, 54
UKSHARE Forum, 190
Ultimedia Hardware Plus Forum, 190-191
Ultimedia Tools Series A Forum, 191, 573
Ultimedia Tools Series B Forum, 191
Ultimedia Tools Series C Forum, 191-192
UNIX Forum, 192, 574-575
UnixWare Forum, 192-193
UserLand Forum, 193
VAX Forum, 193, 237, 577
vendor support
    Amiga Vendor Forum, 24-25, 107
    Apple II Vendors' Forum, 27, 109
    CADD/CAM/CAE Vendor Forum, 57, 58
    CD-ROM Vendors Forum, 64, 116
    Graphics Vendors C Forum, 84, 132, 317
    Graphics A Vendor Forum, 129, 313-314, 320
    Graphics B Vendors Forum, 129-130, 314, 320-321
    IBM OS/2 Vendor Forums, 139-140, 349
    LAN Vendor Forum, 145, 375-376
    Macintosh Vendor Forums, 152-153
    MIDI Vendor Forums, 164, 419
    Modem Vendor Forum, 165

computers – databases

Novell Vendor Forums, 172
PC Vendor Forums, 177, 477-478
Unix Vendor A Forum, 192, 575
Vines 4.x Patchware Forum, 39, 194
Vines 5.x Patchware Forum, 40, 194
viruses
    McAfee Virus Forum, 154
Vobis AG Computer Forum, 581
Wang Support Forum, 195, 584
WinCIM Support Forum, 195
Windows 3rd Party A Forum, 195, 406-407
Windows 3rd Party App B Forum, 195-196, 407
Windows 3rd Party App. D Forum, 196, 407
Windows 3rd Party App. G Forum, 196, 408
Windows 3rd Party E Forum +, 196-197, 407-408
Windows Sources Forum, 197
WinNT Forum, 197, 408
Wolfram Research Forum, 197-198
Working-From-Home Forum, 199, 307, 593
WPCorp Files Forum, 199
WRQ/Reflection Forum, 199
WUGNET Forum, 200
Zenith Data Systems Forum, 200, 598
Ziff Bendata Forum, 200
Ziff Cobb Applications Forum, 200-201
Ziff Computer Shopping Forum, 201
Ziff Editor's Choice, 201, 202
Ziff Executives Online Forum, 202
Ziff Newsbytes, 202
Ziff Software Center, 202-203
Ziff-Davis Press Booknet, 203
ZiffNet Designer Templates, 203
ZiffNet File Folder, 203-204
ZiffNet Membership & Benefits, 204
ZiffNet Reviews Index, 204
ZiffNet Support Forum, 204-205
ZiffNet Surveys, 205
Ziffnet Zshare Online Newsletter, 205
ZiffNet/Mac Download Forum, 205
ZiffNet/Mac File Finder, 206
Computers/Technology Menu, 119-120, 206
Consumer Forum, 48, 208, 424
consumer issues
    Consumer Forum, 208
    New Car Showroom, 446-447
conventions (Electronic Convention Center), 208, 254-255
Cook's Online Forum, 208-209, 333-334
Corel Forum, 81, 120, 209
Country Music, 209
The Court Reporter's Forum, 377, 551
CP/M Forum, 120, 209-210
Crafts, 210, 334
Creative Labs, 120-121, 210, 434

crime
    Safetynet Forum, 210-211, 282-283, 490, 505
    Time Warner Crime Forum, 211, 556, 580
    see also public safety
Crosstalk Forum, 121, 211
CSI Forth Net Forum, 94, 121, 211
CTOS/Pathway Forum, 121-122, 212, 443
cultural issues (African American Art and Culture Forum), 16-17, 29, 212
current events
    Associated Press Online, 32-33, 259, 447-448
    Global Crisis Forum, 212-213, 310, 360, 424
    Hollywood Hotline, 311
    Issues Forum, 213, 342, 366-367, 485, 496-497
    National Public Radio (NPR), 213-214, 307, 439-440
    News Source USA, 214, 226, 448, 454
    NewsGrid, 214, 226, 449
    NewsNet, 214-215, 226-227, 449-450, 455
    Newspaper Archives, 215, 450
    Reuters News Pictures Forum, 213, 451, 483, 500
    U.S. News & World Report, 215, 452
    U.S. News Forum, 215-216, 452
    U.S. News Women's Forum, 216
    UK News Clips, 216
    UK Newspaper Library, 216
    White House Forum, 217, 312, 454, 586
    see also news
customer service
    Aldus Online Customer Support, 525
    Detroit Free Press Store, 217, 233
    see also computers, vendor support
Cyber Forum, 122, 217, 580

D

D&B Dun's Canadian Market, 219
D&B Dun's Canadian Market Identifiers, 48-49, 245
D&B Dun's Electronic Business Directory, 49, 219, 245-246, 273, 363
D&B Dun's Market Identifiers, 49, 220, 246, 273-274, 363-364
Da Vinci Forum, 122, 220
Data Access Corp. Forum, 122, 220-221
databases
    Amiga File Finder, 106-107
    Computer Library Online, 90, 119, 222
    D&B Dun's Canadian Market Identifiers, 245, 272-273
    Digital Database, 465
    Digitalk Database, 126-127, 238-239, 521
    Executive Service Option, 222-223, 267, 280
    Global Report, 51, 223, 281, 310-311
    Graphics File Finder, 131, 315

Health Database Plus, 324, 327
Human Sexuality Databank, 342
IBM DB2 Database Forum, 136-137, 223, 345
IBM File Finder, 137, 223-224, 346, 353
Information Management Forum, 396
InvesText, 224, 363, 365-366
IQuest, 224, 355, 366, 498
Knowledge Index, 225, 303-304, 373, 499
Law Research Center, 379
Legal Research Center, 376, 380
Lotus Technical Library, 148
Macintosh File Finder, 150
Magazine Database Plus, 355-356, 395
Microsft Access Forum, 409
Microsoft Access Forum, 155, 225
Microsoft Fox Users Forum, 158, 225, 411-412
Microsoft Knowledge Base, 158, 412
Microsoft Software Library, 102
Microsoft SQL Server Forum, 159, 221, 413-414
News Source USA, 214, 226, 448, 454
NewsGrid, 214, 226, 449, 455
NewsNet, 214-215, 226-227, 449-450, 455
Novell Files Database, 458
Novell Technical Bulletin Database, 171-172, 227, 461-462
PaperChase-MEDLINE Forum, 401-402, 471
Powersoft Forum, 178, 221, 486
PRC Publishing, 61, 85, 221-222
Rare Diseases Database, 241, 242
Standard Indus. Class., 52, 227, 530
Support Directory, 76, 536
Support On Site, 183, 228, 536-537
Thomas Register Online, 228, 278, 554-555
Ticker/Symbol Lookup, 278, 555, 583
TRADEMARKSCAN, 558
TRW Bus. Credit Reports, 565
UK Company Library, 53-54, 229, 570
UK Newspaper Library, 571-572
UK Newspaper Library, 216
ZeffNet Reviews Index, 204
Ziff Editor's Choice, 201-202, 599-600
ZiffNet Designer Templates, 203
ZiffNet File Finder, 608-609
ZiffNet File Folder, 203, 204
ZiffNet/Mac File Finder, 206, 611
DataEase International Forum, 123, 229
Dataquest Online, 73, 229
DB2 (IBM DB2 Database Forum), 223, 345
DEC Equipment, *see* **digital equipment**
DECPCI Forum, 123-124, 231
DELL Forum, 124, 232
Delrina Forum, 124, 232

demographics
State-County Demographics, 227-228, 232, 531-532
SUPERSITE Demographics Forum, 228, 233, 397, 536
desktop publishing
Aldus Forum, 21
Aldus Online Customer Support, 22
Aldus Special Programs Forum, 22
FontBank Online, 287, 565-566
Ventura Software Forum, 193-194, 577
Detroit Free Press, 233, 370, 439, 484, 535
Detroit Free Press Store, 217, 233, 370-371
Diabetes Forum, 234, 323, 342-343
Diabilities Forum, 378
DiagSoft QAPlus Forum, 124-125, 234-235, 509, 541
Dial-A-Mattress, 40, 235, 399
dictionaries (American Heritage Dictionary), 22-23, 235-236, 249
Digital Database, 465
Digital Equipment Corporation, 68, 125, 236, 433-434, 589-590
DEC PC Forum, 123, 231
DEC Users Network Main Menu, 123, 231
DECPCI Forum, 231
Digital NT Support Forum, 125, 236-238
Digital PC Integration Forum, 125-126, 230-231, 238
Digital PC Store, 126, 229-230, 238, 466
VAX Forum, 193, 237, 577
digital media rights (Electronic Frontier Foundation Forum), 103-104, 360-361
Digital NT Support Forum, 125, 236-238, 590
Digital PC Integration Forum, 125-126, 230-231, 238
Digital PC Store, 126, 229-230, 238, 466
Digitalk Database, 14, 126-127, 238-239, 521
Digitalk Forum, 28, 127, 239, 521
Digtal NT Support Forum, 68
Dinosaur Forum, 239-240, 506
directories
D&B Dun's Electronic Business Directory, 245-246, 273, 363
Member Directory (CompuServe), 240, 402-403
PRC Publishing, 487
Support Directory, 536
disabilities
Disabilities Forum, 240
Health/Fitness, 18
Disabilities Forum, 240, 257, 433
diseases (Rare Diseases Database), 18, 241-242, 493
Disney (Florida Today Forum), 242, 285-286
Dissertation Abstracts, 242, 250, 498

Dividends and Splits, 243-274
dolls (Collectibles Forum), 70
DOS
    Microsoft DOS Forum, 101, 410-411, 427
    Symantec CPS DOS Forum, 184
Dr. Dobb's Forum, 127, 243-244, 488, 576
Dr. Neuhaus Forum, 127-128, 244, 271, 420-421, 497-498
Dreyfus Corporation, 244-245, 364, 438
Dun and Bradstreet
    D&B Dun's Canadian Market Identifiers, 48-49, 219, 245, 272-273
    D&B Dun's Electronic Business Directory, 49, 219, 245-246, 273, 363
    D&B Dun's Market Identifiers, 49, 220, 246, 273-274, 363-364
Dvorak Development Forum, 78, 128, 246, 440

E

E*TRADE Securities, 247-248, 274-75, 364-365, 532-533
E*TRADE Stock Market Game, 248, 275, 294, 583
e-mail
    Lotus Communications Forum, 89, 147, 247, 381, 382, 445
    Microsoft Mail and Workgroups Forum, 158-159, 247, 412-413
    see also communications
Earth Forum, 248, 265
economy (Finance), 248-249, 275
    see also finances
education
    ADD Forum, 249
    Computer Training Forum, 100, 119, 250
    Dissertation Abstracts, 242, 250, 498
    Education Forum, 206, 250-253, 545
    Education Research Forum, 207, 251, 253
    ERIC-Education Resources Information Center, 251, 266
    Foreign Language Forum, 359
    Grolier's Academic American Encyclopedia, 252, 317
    IBM New User's Forum, 100
    Students' Forum, 252, 534
    Univ of Phoenix, 252
Education Forum, 206, 250-253, 545
Education Research Forum, 207, 251, 253
Ei Compendex Plus, 28, 253-254, 258, 486
Eicon Technology Forum, 128, 254, 522, 597
Electronic Books, 79, 128-129, 254, 601
Electronic Convention Center, 208, 254, 255
Electronic Frontier Foundation Forum, 103-104, 237
electronic games, *see* **games**
Electronic Tax Return Filing, 255, 544

electronics
    computers
        The Escort Store, 207
        The Heath Company, 207
    Electronic Convention Center, 208
    Electronic Frontier Foundation Forum, 237
    The Escort Store, 305
    The Heath Company, 552
    Siemens Automation, 255-256, 517
    Stac Electronics Forum, 256, 529-530
EMI Aviation Services, 19, 256, 564
emotional problems, *see* **mental health**
employment (Classified Ads), 68, 257
Encounters Forum, 257-258, 471-472, 568
encyclopedias (Grolier's Academic American Encyclopedia), 252, 317
engineering
    The CompuServe Practice Forum, 551
    Ei Compendex Plus, 28, 253-254, 258, 486
    Engineering Automation Forum, 57, 103, 129, 258
English, *see* **language**
Enhanced Adventure, 15, 255, 259
entertainment
    Air Traffic Controller game, 20-21
    All-Music Guide, 22, 434
    Associated Press Online, 32-33, 259
    Broadcast Professionals Forum, 546-547
    Entertainment Center, 263, 294-295
    Entertainment Drive Center, 64, 259, 263, 428
    Hollywood Hotline, 260, 311, 336
    Macintosh Entertainment Forum, 80, 150, 384, 391
    Marilyn Beck/Smith Hollywood, 304, 396-397
    Movie Reviews
    Music Hall, 435
    Music Industry Forum, 438, 501
    Music Vendor Forum, 501-502
    Music/Arts Forum, 436
    New Country Music, 436-437, 447
    Rocknet Forum, 260, 437, 501-502
    Roger Ebert's Movie Reviews, 426, 500-502
    Seattle Film Works, 426
    Showbiz Quiz, 260, 298, 427, 516-517, 547, 564-565
    ShowBiz-Media Forum, 261, 517
    Sight and Sound Forum, 34, 261, 518
    Soap Opera Summaries, 522-523
    Society of Broadcast Eng., 523
    Stein Online, 64, 261, 532
    The Absolut Museum, 52
    UK Entertainment Reviews, 261-262, 570
    Video Games Forum, 262
    Video Games Publishers Forum, 262
    Warner Bros. Song Preview, 437-438, 495
    The Whiz Quiz, 548-549, 554, 565
    You Guessed It!, 262-263, 597-598
    see also celebrities; music

Entertainment Center, 263, 294-295
Entertainment Drive Center, 64, 259, 263, 428
Entrepreneur Magazine, 263-264, 519
The Entrepreneur's Forum, 53, 551-552
Entrepreneur's Small Business Forum, 50
Entrepreneur Small Business Square, 50, 264-265, 519-520
environmental issues
    Earth Forum, 248, 265
    Ei Compendex Plus, 253-254, 258, 486
Epic MegaGames, 265-266, 295-296, 513
ERIC-Education Resources Information Center, 251, 266
The Escort Store, 207, 305, 552
Executive News Service, 50, 267, 280, 359, 448
Executive Service Option, 222-223, 267, 280

F

Family Handyman Forum, 269-270, 302, 336
family issues
    ADD Forum, 472
    Genealogy Forum, 269, 301-302, 329-330
    Missing Children Forum, 420
    Retirement Living Forum, 500, 523
Fantasy/Role-Playing Adventure, 270, 296, 503
fashion
    Americana Clothing, 69, 514
    Brooks Brothers Online Store, 46, 69, 514
    Glamour Graphics Forum, 270, 309, 313, 481-482
    JC Penney, 515
    Shoppers Advantage Club, 70, 241, 512, 515-516
faxes
    Dr. Neuhaus Forum, 127-128, 244, 271, 420-421, 497-498
    Intel Corporation, 405, 422
    The Intel Forum, 553
field computing (HP Handhelds Forum), 87, 134, 271-272, 339-340
Figi's Inc., 272
films
    Roger Ebert's Movie Reviews, 272, 426, 500-502
    Seattle Film Works, 426, 507-508
    Showbiz Quiz, 427
Finance, 248-249, 275
finances
    The Business Wire, 52, 451-452, 550
    Consumer Forum, 48, 208, 424
    D&B Dun's Electronic Business Directory, 49, 219, 245-246, 273, 363
    D&B Dun's Market Identifiers, 49, 220, 246, 273-274, 363-364
    Electronic Tax Return Filing, 255, 544
    Executive News Service, 50, 267, 280, 359, 448
    Executive Service Option, 222-223, 267, 280
    Finance, 248-249, 275
    Financial Forecasts, 275-276, 279, 281, 358-359, 365
    Financial Forums, 50-51, 279-280
    Global Report, 51, 223, 281, 310-311
    H&R Block, 319, 544
    Intuit Forum, 143-144, 276, 361
    Intuit Personal Tax Forum, 361-362, 544
    investments
        D&B Dun's Canadian Market, 219
        D&B Dun's Canadian Market Identifiers, 48-49, 272-273
        Dividends and Splits, 243-274
        Dreyfus Corporation, 244-245, 364, 438
        E*TRADE Securities, 274-275, 364-365, 532-533
        E*TRADE Stock Market Game, 248, 275, 294, 583
        Financial Forecasts, 275-276, 279, 281, 358-359, 365
        Financial Forums, 50-51, 279-280
        InvesText, 224, 363, 365-366
        Market Highlights, 397, 533
        Securities Screening, 277, 508, 533
        Securities Symbols Lookup, 277-278, 508, 533-534
        Single Issue Price Hist, 278, 519, 534
        Ticker/Symbol Lookup, 278, 555, 583
        UK Historical Stock Pricing, 54, 571
        Vestor Stock Recommendation, 278-279, 534, 577
    IRS Tax Forms and Documents, 366, 545
    LDC Spreadsheet Forum, 145-146
    Microsoft Excel Forum, 157, 411
    Mortgage Calculator, 276-277, 424-425
    News-A-Tron, 277, 449, 454-455
    OTC NewsAlert, 51, 281-282, 359-360, 450, 468-469
    TRW Bus. Credit Reports, 565
    UK Company Library, 53-54, 229, 570
Financial Forecasts, 275-276, 279, 281, 358-359, 365
Financial Forums, 50-51, 279-280
Fine Art Forum, 30-31, 67, 282, 423
fire fighting, *see* public safety
fish
    Aquaria/Fish Forum, 28-29, 283, 331
    Pet Products/Reference Forum, 25
fitness
    Health and Fitness Forum, 59
    martial arts (Health and Fitness Forum), 59
    see also health & fitness
Flight Simulation Forum, 285, 518, 527
Florida
    Florida Forum, 285
    Florida Today Forum, 242, 285-286, 557-558

flowers
    800 Flowers, 11, 307-308, 286
    FTD Online, 302-303
    Walter Knoll Florist, 286-287, 309, 583-584
FontBank Online, 287, 565-566
food
    Adventures in Food, 15, 287, 513
    Bacchus Wine and Beer Forum, 39, 590
    Cook's Online Forum, 208-209, 333-334
    Ei Compendex Plus, 28, 253-254, 258, 486
    Omaha Steaks International, 61, 466
    Virginia Diner, 306, 308, 580
    Zagat Restaurant Guide, 598
Ford Motor Company, 35-36
Foreign Language Forum, 266-267
freemasons, 398-399
freeware
    Microsoft Windows Shareware Forum, 417
    ZiffNet FREE UTILS Forum, 609
FTD Online, 302-303
furniture (Dial-A-Mattress), 40, 235, 399

G

Game Forums and News, 293, 296, 518-519
Game Publishers Forums, 80, 293, 296-297
games
    Air Traffic Controller, 20-21, 293-294
    Brøderbund Software, 113
    Chess Forum, 65, 294, 332-333
    Commodore Art/Games Forum, 71, 117
    E*TRADE Stock Market Game, 248, 275, 294, 583
    Enhanced Adventure, 15, 255, 259
    Entertainment Center, 263, 294-295
    Epic MegaGames Forums, 265-266, 295-296, 513
    Fantasy/Role-Playing, 270, 296, 503
    Flight Simulation Forum, 285
    Game Forums and News, 293, 296, 518, 519
    Game Publishers Forums, 80, 293, 296-, 297
    Macintosh Entertainment Forum, 150, 384, 391
    MegaWars I and II, 297, 402
    Microsoft Windows Fun Forum, 161, 297, 415
    Microsoft Windows Multimedia Forum, 297-298, 415-416, 430
    Modem Games Forum, 164, 298, 422-423
    Multi-Player Games Forum, 427
    Showbiz Quiz, 260, 298, 427, 564-565
    SNIPER! game, 70, 299, 522, 584
    Sports Forum, 299
    Sports Simulation Forum, 299
    STAGEII, 299, 300, 530
    Video Game Publishers Forum, 262, 300, 578-579
    Video Games Forum, 262, 300, 579
    You Guessed It!, 262-263, 300-301
    see also simulators; sports
Gardening Forum, 301, 338, 484-485
Gateway 2000 Forum, 91, 301, 320
Genealogy Forum, 269, 301-302, 329-330
general information
    Grolier's Academic American Encyclopedia, 317
    Information USA, 311-312, 356, 495-496
    Intelligence Test, 357, 548
    IQuest, 366, 498
    Knowledge Index, 373, 499
    Magazine Database Plus, 395
    Masonry forum, 398-399
    Online Surveys, 467, 537
    Participate, 305, 437, 472, 479, 485-486
    Speakeasy Forum, 506, 528
    UK Forum, 571
    The Whiz Quiz, 548-549, 554
German
    Dr. Neuhaus Forum, 244, 420-421, 497-498
    Toshiba GmbH Forum, 557
    Vobis AG Computer Forum, 581
    WordPerfect GmbH Forum, 462-463, 591-592
gifts
    Alaska Peddler, 21
    The Gift Sender, 305-306, 308, 552
    see also shopping
Glamour Graphics Forum, 270, 309, 313, 481-482
Global Crisis Forum, 212-213, 310, 360, 424
Global Report, 51, 223, 281, 310-311
The 'GO GRAPHICS' Tutorial, 86, 188, 549
Golden CommPass Support, 311, 468
government
    Census Bureau Online Service, 47-48, 65, 531-532
    Information USA, 311-312
    Members of Congress, 312, 403
    White House Forum, 217, 312, 454, 586
    see also politics
Graphcs Plus Forum, 316
Graphics A Vendor Forum, 129, 313-314, 320
Graphics B Vendors Forum, 129-130, 314, 320-321
Graphics Corner Forum, 130, 314, 482
Graphics Developers Forum, 82, 130-131, 314-315
Graphics File Finder, 82, 131, 315
Graphics Forums, 83, 131, 313-316
Graphics Gallery Forum, 83, 131-132, 316, 482
Graphics Plus Forum, 83-84, 132, 482-483
Graphics Support Forum, 84, 316-317
Graphics Vendors C Forum, 84, 132, 317
Grolier's Academic American Encyclopedia, 252, 317
Gupta Forum, 318

H

H&R Block, 319, 544
HamNet Forum, 319, 493
handheld computers (HP Handhelds Forum), 134
Handicapped User's Database, 319-320
Hayes Forum, 133, 322, 421
Hayes Online, 87, 90, 133, 322, 421
health & fitness
    ADD Forum, 14-15, 472
    CCML AIDS Articles, 17-18, 63, 322-323
    Diabetes Forum, 234-323, 342-343
    Disabilities Forum, 378, 240, 257, 433
    Handicapped User's Database, 319-320
    Health and Fitness Forum, 59, 283-284, 323, 325-326, 398
    Health and Vitamin Express, 324, 326
    Health Database Plus, 324, 327, 401
    Health/Fitness, 18, 240-241, 326-328
    HealthNet, 284, 327-328, 528-529
    Holistic Health Forum, 284, 324-325, 335-336
    Human Sexuality Databank, 325, 510
    Medical News/Research, 400
    PaperChase-MEDLINE Forum, 325, 401-402, 471, 499
    Rare Diseases Database, 18, 241-242, 493
    see also mental health
Health and Fitness Forum, 59, 283-284, 323, 325-326, 398
Health and Vitamin Express, 324, 326
Health Database Plus, 324, 327, 401
Health/Fitness, 18, 240-241, 326-328
HealthNet, 284, 327-328, 528-529
The Heath Company, 207, 552
Help
    CompuServe Help Forum, 75, 77, 328
    Computer Club Forum, 328-329
    Macintosh New Users Help, 386, 393
history
    Archive Photos Forum, 29, 329, 480-481
    Genealogy Forum, 269, 301-302, 329-330
    Global Crisis Forum, 310
    JFK Assassination Forum, 330, 370
hobbies
    800 Flowers, 11
    The Absolut Museum, 550
    Artist Forum, 29, 30
    Astronomy Forum, 33, 546
    Canon Net Menu, 59, 332, 481
    Canon Support Forum, 60, 332, 481
    Chess Forum, 65, 294, 332-333
    Collectibles Forum, 70, 243, 333, 531
    Comics/Animation Forum, 71, 333
    Cook's Online Forum, 208-209, 333, 334
    Crafts, 210, 334

    Dinosaur Forum, 506
    Gardening Forum, 301, 338, 484-485
    Motor Sports Forum, 425
    Outdoor Forum, 304-305, 469
    Photography Forum, 58, 334-335, 483
    Quality Paperbacks, 491, 493-494
    Recreational Vehicle Forum, 425, 560-561
    Sailing Forum, 505, 597
    Scuba Forum, 242-243, 506-507
    Space Exploration Forum, 526
    The Absolut Museum, 52
    TrainNet Forum, 335, 558-559
    Walter Knoll Florist, 583-584
    Worldwide Car Network, 593
    see also entertainment; recreation; sports
Holistic Health Forum, 284, 324-325, 335-336
Hollywood Hotline, 260, 311, 336
Home Forum, 334, 336-338
homes issues
    Family Handyman Forum, 269-270, 302, 336
    Home Forum, 334, 336-338
    Homefinder By AMS, 338, 494
    Mortgage Calculator, 276-277, 424-425
Home-Based Business, 337
horticulture (Gardening Forum), 338
hotels, 13
    ABC Worldwide Hotel Guide, 339, 559
    Inn and Lodging Forum, 338-339, 356-357, 560
    UK Accommodation & Travel Service, 562, 569-570
HP Handhelds Forum, 87, 134, 271-272, 339-340
HP Omnibook Forum, 134, 340
HP Peripherals Forum, 134-135, 340
HP Specials, 135, 340-341
HP Systems Forum, 135, 341
HSX Adult Forum, 42, 303, 341, 509
HSX Open Forum, 303, 341, 509-510
human behavior
    HSX Adult Forum, 42, 303, 341, 509
    HSX Open Forum, 303, 341, 509-510
    Human Sexuality Databank, 342
human rights (Issues Forum), 213, 342, 366-367, 496-497
Human Sexuality Databank, 325, 342, 510
hyperactivity (ADD Forum), 14-15

I

IBM Applications Forum, 78, 135-136, 345, 352
IBM CAD/CAM Forum, 136, 345
IBM Communications Forum, 73, 136, 352, 353, 421-422
IBM DB2 Database Forum, 136-137, 223, 345
IBM File Finder, 137, 223-224, 346, 353
IBM Hardware Forum, 137, 321, 346, 353

IBM Image Plus Forum, 137
IBM ImagePlus Forum, 84, 346
IBM Languages Forum, 95, 138, 346, 347
IBM LMU2 Forum, 138, 347, 443-444
IBM New User's Forum, 100, 347, 353-354
IBM Object Technology Forum, 138, 347-348
IBM OS/2 Developers Forum, 95, 138-139, 348
IBM OS/2 Service Pak, 139, 348-349
IBM OS/2 Support Forum, 100, 349
IBM OS/2 Users Forum, 101, 349
IBM OS/2 Vendor Forum, 139-140, 349
IBM Personal Software Products, 140, 350
IBM PowerPC Forum, 140, 350
IBM Programming Forum, 95-96, 140, 350
IBM Software Forum, 141
IBM Software Solutions Forum, 351
IBM Storage Systems Forum, 141, 351, 428
IBM Systems/Utilities Forum, 141, 354
IBM ThinkPad Forum, 142, 351
IBM Users Network, 142, 352, 354
Ideas and Inventions Forum, 354-355, 362
Information Management Forum, 142-143, 355, 396
Information USA, 311-312, 356, 495-496
Inn and Lodging Forum, 338-339, 356-357, 560
Intel Corporation, 87, 143, 357, 405, 422
The Intel Forum, 188, 406, 553
intelligence
    Intelligence Test, 357-548
    Mensa Forum, 404
international interests
    Bilingual Education, 41
    Financial Forecasts, 358-359
    Japan Forum, 357-358, 369
    Political Debate Forum, 358, 450-451, 485, 567
    see also languages
Internet
    Electronic Frontier Foundation Forum, 103-104, 360-361
    Internet Forum, 143, 361
Intuit Forum, 143-144, 276, 361
Intuit Personal Tax Forum, 361-362, 544
inventions
    Ideas and Inventions Forum, 354-355, 362
    Patent Research Center, 362, 376-377, 473, 499-500
investements, see finances, investments
IQuest, 224, 355, 366, 498
IRS Tax Forms and Documents, 366, 545
Issues Forum, 213, 342, 366-367, 485, 496-497

J–K

Japan Forum, 357-358, 369
JC Penney, 369, 515
JDR Microdevices, 92, 144, 369-370

JFK Assassination Forum, 330, 370
Journalism Forum, 371, 594

Knowledge Index, 225, 303-304, 373, 499
Kodak CD Forum, 144, 373, 480, 487-488

L

labor unions (Air Line Pilots Association), 20, 37
LAN Magazine, 90, 144-145, 375, 444
Lan Technology Forum, 145, 375, 444
LAN Vendor Forum, 145, 375-376, 444-445
languages
    American Heritage Dictionary, 22-23, 235-236, 249
    Bilingual Education, 41
    Foreign Language Forum, 266-267, 359
    German
        Dr. Neuhaus Forum, 127-128, 244, 497-498
        Toshiba GmbH Forum, 189-190, 557
        Vobis AG Computer Forum, 194, 581
        WordPerfect GmbH Forum, 198, 591-592
    programming, see computers, programming
    Vobis AG Computer Forum, 89
laptop computers
    HP Handhelds Forum, 271-272, 339-340
    Tandy Model 100 Forum, 186
    Toshiba Forum, 189, 557
    Toshiba GmbH Forum, 189, 190
The Laser's Edge (laser discs), 62, 188, 553
LDC Spreadsheet Forum, 145, 146, 377
LDC Word Processing Forum, 146, 377, 378
LDC Words & Pixels Forum, 85, 146-147, 378
LEAP (League for Engineering Productivity), 57
Legal Forum, 376, 379-380
legal issues
    The Court Reporter's Forum, 377
    Legal Forum, 376, 379-380
    Legal Research Center, 376, 379-380
    Patent Research Center, 376-377, 473, 499-500
    TRADEMARKSCAN, 558
Legal Research Center, 376, 379-380
Lexmark Forum, 88, 147, 380
Literary Forum, 271, 380, 381, 594-595
Logitech Forum, 88, 147, 321, 381
Lotus Communications Forum, 89, 147, 247, 381-382, 445
Lotus Press Release Forum, 148, 382
Lotus Technical Library, 148, 382

M

The Mac Zone/PC Zone, 62, 388, 189, 553
Macintosh Applications Forum, 148, 383, 389
Macintosh CIM Support Forum, 149, 383, 389-390
Macintosh Communications Forum, 383, 390, 422
Macintosh Community Club Forum, 149, 384, 390

Macintosh Developers Forum, 96, 150, 384, 390-391
Macintosh Entertainment Forum, 80, 150, 384, 391
Macintosh File Finder, 150, 385, 391
Macintosh Forums, 150-151, 385, 391, 392
Macintosh Hardware Forum, 89, 151, 385, 392
Macintosh Hypertext Forum, 151, 385-386, 392, 429
Macintosh Multimedia Forum, 151-152, 386, 392-393, 429
Macintosh New Users Help, 386
Macintosh New Users Help Forum, 152, 393
Macintosh Systems Forum, 152, 386-387, 393
Macintosh Vendor Forums, 152-153, 387, 393-394
Macmillan Publishing Forum, 43, 153, 394
MacNav Support Forum, 153, 387, 394
Macromedia Forum, 154, 394-395, 429
MacWAREHOUSE, 92, 387-388, 395
Magazine Database Plus, 355,-356, 395
magazines
    Entrepreneur Magazine, 263-264, 519
    The Entrepreneur's Forum, 551-552
    Florida Today Forum, 557-558
    LAN Magazine, 375, 444
    Lan Technology, 375
    Lan Technology Forum, 444
    Magazine Database Plus, 355-356, 395
    News Source USA, 226
    PC Computing, 173-174, 473-474, 601-602
    PC Contact Forum, 602
    PC Direct UK Magazine Forum, 602
    PC Magazine UK Forum, 174-175, 568-569, 602-603
    PC Magazine UK Online, 175, 475, 603
    PC MagNet, 475, 603
    PC MagNet Editorial Forum, 603-604
    PC MagNet Programming Forum, 175-176, 476, 604
    PC MagNet Utilities/Tips Forum, 176, 476, 604
    PC Plus/PC Answers Online, 176-177, 477, 569
    PC Publications, 477
    PC Week Forum, 177-178, 478, 604-605
    PC World Online, 178, 395-396, 478
    U.S. News & World Report, 215, 452, 567
    U.S. News Forum, 215-216, 452, 567
    U.S. News Women's Forum, 452-453, 591
    Windows Sources Forum, 197, 589
    Ziff Editor's Choice, 599-600, 607
    Ziff Executives Online Forum, 607
    ZiffNet Reviews Index, 609-610
    ZiffNet/Mac Download Forum, 610-611
    see also publications, 177
maps (Weather Maps), 396, 562-563
Marilyn Beck/Smith Hollywood, 304, 396-397
Market Highlights, 397, 533

market research
    SUPERSITE Demographics, 228, 536
    SUPERSITE Demographics Forum, 233, 397
marketing (PR and Marketing Forum), 16, 397-398, 486-487, 489
martial arts (Health and Fitness Forum), 59, 283-284, 323, 325-326, 398
Masonry forum, 398-399
McAfee Virus Forum, 102, 154, 399
Media Newsletters, 45-46, 399-400
Media Vision Forum, 154, 400, 430
Medical News/Research, 400
Medicare (Retirement Living Forum), 17, 400-401
medicine
    ADD Forum, 14-15
    CCML AIDS Articles, 17-18, 63
    Health Database Plus, 327
MegaWars I and II, 297, 402
Member Assistance, 75, 402
Member Directory, 240, 402-403
Member Recommendation, 403
Members of Congress, 312, 403
Membership Changes, 403-404
Mensa Forum, 404
mental health
    ADD Forum, 249
    Disabilities Forum, 257, 378
    see also support groups
Message Handling Service Hub, 404-445
Metropolitan Museum of Art, 30, 404-405
Micrografx Forum, 85, 154-155, 405
Microsft Access Forum, 409
Microsoft 32-bit Languages Forum, 79, 96, 101, 408-409
Microsoft Access Forum, 155, 225
Microsoft Applications Forum, 155, 409
Microsoft BASIC Forum, 96-97, 155-156, 409-, 410
Microsoft Connection, 156, 410
Microsoft DevCast Forum, 97, 156, 410
Microsoft Developers Relations Forums, 27-28, 156-157, 234, 406
Microsoft DOS Forum, 101, 410-411, 427
Microsoft Excel Forum, 157, 411
Microsoft Foundation Classes Forum, 97, 157, 411
Microsoft Fox Users Forum, 158, 225, 411-412
Microsoft Knowledge Base, 158, 412
Microsoft Languages Forum, 412
Microsoft Mail and Workgroups Forum, 158-159, 247, 412-413
Microsoft Sales and Information Forum, 102, 159, 413
Microsoft Software Library, 79, 102, 413
Microsoft SQL Server Forum, 159, 221, 413-414
Microsoft TechNet Forum, 159, 160, 414
Microsoft WIN32 Forum, 97-98, 160, 414

Microsoft Windows Extensions Forum, 98, 160, 414-415
Microsoft Windows Forum, 103, 160-161, 415, 586-587
Microsoft Windows Fun Forum, 161, 297, 415
Microsoft Windows Multimedia Forum, 297-298, 415-416, 430
Microsoft Windows News Forum, 161, 416, 587
Microsoft Windows NT SNA Forum, 161, 416
Microsoft Windows Objects Forum, 98, 162, 416-417
Microsoft Windows SDK Forum, 98-99, 162, 417
Microsoft Windows Shareware Forum, 162, 417, 512
Microsoft Word Forum, 163, 418
MicroStation Forum, 57, 163, 418
MicroWarehouse, 93, 163, 418
MIDI Vendor Forums, 164, 419, 430-431, 435
MIDI/Music Forum, 25, 388, 419, 431, 434-435
Military Forum, 419-420
Missing Children Forum, 66, 420
Mobile Computing, 164, 420
Modem Games Forum, 164, 298, 422-423
Modem Vendor Forum, 165, 423
modems
    Dr. Neuhaus Forum, 127-128, 244, 271, 420-421, 497-498
    Hayes Forum, 133, 322, 421
    Hayes Online, 87, 90, 133, 322, 421
    IBM Communications Forum, 73, 136, 352-353, 421-422
    Intel Corporation, 143, 357, 405, 422
    The Intel Forum, 188, 553
    Macintosh Communications Forum, 149, 383, 390, 422
    Modem Games Forum, 164, 298, 422-423
    Modem Vendor Forum, 165, 423
modern art (Fine Art Forum), 30-31, 67
money, *see* **finances**
Mortgage Calculator, 276-277, 424-425
motor homes (Recreational Vehicle Forum), 58-59
Motor Sports Forum, 36, 425
Movie Reviews, 426
movies, *see* **films**
MS-DOS, *see* **DOS**
Multi-Player Games Forum, 427
multimedia
    Autodesk Multimedia Forum, 34-35, 56, 111, 428
    Creative Labs, 434
    Entertainment Drive Center, 64, 259, 263, 428
    IBM Storage Systems Forum, 141, 351, 428
    Intel Corporation, 143
    Macintosh Hypertext Forum, 151, 385-386, 392, 429
    Macintosh Multimedia Forum, 151-152, 386, 392-393, 429
    Macromedia Forum, 154, 394-395, 429
    Media Vision Forum, 154, 400, 430
    Microsoft Windows Multimedia Forum, 297-298, 415-416, 430
    MIDI Vendor Forums, 164, 419, 430-431, 435
    MIDI/Music Forum, 25, 388, 419, 431, 434-435
    Multimedia Services, 165, 431, 433
    Ultimedia Hardware Plus Forum, 431-432
    Ultimedia Tools Series A Forum, 432
    Ultimedia Tools Series B Forum, 432
    Ultimedia Tools Series C Forum, 432
Multimedia Services, 165, 431, 433
museums (Metropolitan Museum of Art), 30, 404-405
music
    All-Music Guide Forum, 22, 330-331, 434
    Country Music, 209
    Creative Labs, 120-121, 210, 434
    MIDI Vendor Forums, 164, 419, 430-431, 435
    MIDI/Music Forum, 25, 388, 419, 431, 434-435
    Music Hall, 435
    Music Industry Forum, 435-436, 438, 501
    Music Vendor Forum, 501-502
    Music/Arts Forum, 436
    New Country Music, 436-437, 447
    Rocknet Forum, 260, 437, 501-502, 578
    Warner Bros. Song Preview, 437-438, 495, 584
Music Hall, 435
Music Industry Forum, 435-436, 438, 501
Music Vendor Forum, 436, 501-502
Music/Arts Forum, 436

N

National Computer Security Association (NCSA), 99, 165, 439
National Public Radio (NPR), 213-214, 307, 439-440
NavCIS (Dvorak Development Forum), 78, 128, 246, 440
NCAA Collegiate Sports Network, 440
NCR/ATT Forum, 166, 440-441
NCSA InfoSecurity Forum, 166, 441, 508-509
networks
    3Com Online Information Service Menu, 11, 104
    ACI US Forum, 441
    APPC Info Exchange Forum, 26, 107-108, 441-442
    Artisoft Forum, 31, 109, 442
    Ask3Com Forum, 32, 109
    Banyan Forum, 39, 112, 442
    Cabletron Systems Forum, 55, 113, 442-443
    Cabletron Systems Menu, 55, 113-114, 443
    CTOS/Pathway Forum, 121-122, 212, 443
    Digital Equipment Corporation, 589-590
    Eicon Technology Forum, 597

Hayes Online, 87, 90, 133
IBM LMU2 Forum, 138, 347, 443-444
Intel Corporation, 87, 143, 357
LAN Magazine, 90, 144-145, 375, 444
Lan Technology Forum, 145, 375, 444
LAN Vendor Forum, 145, 375-376, 444-445
Lotus Communications Forum, 89, 147, 247, 381-382, 445
Message Handling Service Hub, 404, 445
Microsoft Mail and Workgroups Forum, 158-159, 247
Novell Client Forum, 167, 456-457
Novell Connectivity Forum, 167, 457
Novell Developer Info Forum, 167-168, 457
Novell Developer Support Forum, 168, 457-458
Novell DSG Forum, 168, 458
Novell Files Database, 168-169, 458
Novell Information Forum, 169, 458-459
Novell Library Forum, 169, 459
Novell NetWare 2.x Forum, 169-170, 459
Novell NetWare 3.x Forum, 170, 459-460
Novell NetWare 4.x Forum, 460
Novell NetWire, 170-171, 460
Novell Network Management Forum, 171, 461
Novell OS/2 Forum, 461, 468
Novell Technical Bulletin Database, 171-172, 227, 461-462
Novell Vendor Forums, 172, 462
Other Banyan Patchware Forum, 469
Standard Microsystems Forum, 182, 445-446, 530-531
Sybase Forum, 183, 537
Symantec Ntwrk Products Forum, 185, 540
SynOptics Forum, 186, 446, 540
Thomas-Conrad Forum, 555
Vines 4.x Patchware Forum, 39, 91, 194, 579
Vines 5.x Patchware Forum, 40, 91, 194, 579
WRQ/Reflection Forum, 199, 595

new age
Encounters Forum, 568
Holistic Health Forum, 324-325, 335-336
New Age Forum, 446
Speakeasy Forum, 182, 506, 528

New Age Forum, 446
New Car Showroom, 36, 446-447
New Country Music, 436-437, 447
New York NewsLink Forum, 447
news
Associated Press Online, 32-33, 259, 447-448
Bilingual Education, 41
The Business Wire, 451-452
Detroit Free Press, 233, 370, 439, 484, 535
Detroit Free Press Store, 233, 370-371
Executive News Service, 50, 267, 280, 359, 448
Executive Service Option, 267-280

Financial Forecasts, 275-276, 279, 281, 358-359, 365
Foreign Language Forum, 266-267
Global Crisis Forum, 212-213, 310, 360, 424
Global Report, 281, 310-311
Lotus Press Release Forum, 382
National Public Radio (NPR), 213-214, 307
New York NewsLink Forum, 447
News Source USA, 214, 226, 448, 454
News-A-Tron, 277, 449, 454-455
NewsGrid, 214, 226, 449, 455
NewsNet, 214-215, 226-227, 449-450, 455
Newspaper Archives, 215, 450
NWS Aviation Weather, 463
OTC NewsAlert, 51, 281-282, 359-360, 450, 468-469
Political Debate Forum, 450-451, 485, 567
Reuters News Pictures Forum, 213, 451, 483, 500
Syndicated Columns, 540
U.S. News & World Report, 215, 452, 567
U.S. News Forum, 215-216, 452, 567
U.S. News Women's Forum, 216, 452-453, 591
UK News Clips, 216, 453, 571
UK Newspaper Library, 216, 453
UK Sports Clips, 453-454
Weather Maps, 585
Weather Reports, 563, 585
What's New, 306-307
Ziff Newsbytes, 202, 600, 607
see also current events

News Source USA, 214, 226, 448, 454
News-A-Tron, 277, 449, 454-455
NewsGrid, 214, 226, 449, 455
newsletters
Media Newsletters, 45-46, 399-400
Ziffnet Zshare Online Newsletter, 205, 610

NewsNet, 214-215, 226-227, 449-450, 455
Newspaper Archives, 215, 450, 455-456
newspapers
Florida Today Forum, 285-286
Floriday Today Forum, 242
News Source USA, 226
Newspaper Archives, 215, 450, 455-456
Syndicated Columns, 451, 540
The Sysop Forum, 13, 59, 554
UK Newspaper Library, 571-572

Newton Developers Forum, 27, 166, 456
NeXT Forum, 166-167, 456
notebook computers
Toshiba Forum, 189
Toshiba GmbH Forum, 189-190

Novell Client Forum, 167, 456-457
Novell Connectivity Forum, 167, 457
Novell Developer Info Forum, 167-168, 457
Novell Developer Support Forum, 168, 457-458
Novell DSG Forum, 168, 458

Novell Files Database, 168-169, 458
Novell Information Forum, 169, 458-459
Novell Library Forum, 169, 459
Novell NetWare 2.x Forum, 169-170, 459
Novell NetWare 3.x Forum, 170, 459-460
Novell NetWare 4.x Forum, 460
Novell NetWire, 170-171, 460
Novell Network Management Forum, 171, 461
Novell OS/2 Forum, 171, 461, 468
Novell Technical Bulletin, 171-172
Novell Technical Bulletin Database, 227, 461-462
Novell Vendor Forums, 172, 462
nutrition
    Health and Vitamin Express, 324, 326
    Sundown Vitamins, 516, 535, 581
NWS Aviation Weather, 37-38, 463

O

object-oriented programming (Digitalk Database), 14, 126-127, 238-239, 465, 521
Official Airline Guide, 19-20, 465-466, 558, 560
OLE (Microsoft), 98
Omaha Steaks International, 61, 466
Online Surveys, 304, 467, 537
Oracle Forum, 172, 467
OS/2
    Golden CommPass Support, 311, 468
    IBM OS/2 Developers Forum, 138-139, 348
    IBM OS/2 Service Pak, 139, 348-349
    IBM OS/2 Support Forum, 100, 349
    IBM OS/2 Users Forum, 101, 349
    IBM OS/2 Vendor Forum, 139-140, 349
    Novell OS/2 Forum, 171, 461, 468
OTC NewsAlert, 51, 281-282, 359-360, 450, 468-469
Other Banyan Patchware Forum, 172-173, 469
Outdoor Forum, 304-305, 469

P

Packard Bell Forum, 173, 471
palmtop computers (HP Handhelds Forum), 87, 134
PaperChase-MEDLINE Forum, 325, 401-402, 471, 499
paranormal experiences (Encounters Forum), 257-258, 471-472, 568
Participate, 305, 437, 472, 479, 485-486
Patent Research Center, 362, 376-377, 473, 499-500
PC Catalog, 61, 173, 473
PC Computing, 173-174, 473-474, 601-602
PC Contact Forum, 174, 474, 602
PC Direct UK Magazine Forum, 174, 474, 568, 602
PC Magazine UK Forum, 174-175, 474-475, 568-569, 602-603

PC Magazine UK Online, 175, 475, 569, 603
PC MagNet, 475, 603
PC MagNet Editorial Forum, 175, 475-476, 603-604
PC MagNet Programming Forum, 94, 175-176, 476, 604
PC MagNet Utilities/Tips Forum, 176, 476, 604
PC Plug and Play Forum, 176, 321-322, 476-477
PC Plus/PC Answers Online, 176-177, 477, 569
PC Publications, 177, 477
PC Vendor Forums, 177, 477-478
PC Week Forum, 177-178, 478, 604-605
PC World Online, 178, 395-396, 478
PCs
    DEC PC Forum, 123, 231
    IBM PowerPC Forum, 140
    The Mac Zone/PC Zone, 553
    PC Plug and Play Forum, 321-322, 476-477
    PC Plus/PC Answers Online, 569
    PC Vendor Forums, 177, 477-478
Personality Profile, 478-479, 488, 496
Pet Products/Reference Forum, 25, 283, 479, 578
pets
    Aquaria/Fish Forum, 28-29, 283, 331
    Pet Products/Reference Forum, 25, 283, 479, 578
    Time Warner-Dogs & Cats Forum, 25-26, 556
philosophy
    New Age Forum, 446
    Religion Forum, 465
    see also religion
Photo-CD (Kodak CD Forum), 144, 480, 487-488
photography
    Archive Photos Forum, 29, 329, 480-481
    Canon Net Menu, 59, 332, 481
    Canon Support Forum, 60, 332, 481
    Detroit Free Press, 233, 484
    Glamour Graphics Forum, 270, 309, 313, 481-482
    Graphcs Plus Forum, 316
    Graphics Corner Forum, 130, 314
    Graphics Gallery Forum, 83, 131-132, 316, 482
    Graphics Plus Forum, 83-84, 132, 482-483
    Kodak CD Forum, 373
    Photography Forum, 58, 334-335, 483
    Quick Picture Forum, 491
    Reuters News Pictures Forum, 213, 451, 483, 500
Photography Forum, 58, 334-335, 483
physics (Ei Compendex Plus), 486
plants
    Gardening Forum, 301, 338, 484, 485
    Walter Knoll Florist, 583-584
    see also flowers
Political Debate Forum, 358, 450-451, 485, 567
politics
    Global Crisis Forum, 212-213, 310, 360, 424
    Issues Forum, 213, 342, 366-367, 485, 496-497
    Political Debate Forum, 358, 450-451, 485, 567
    White House Forum, 217, 312, 454, 586
    see also government

pollution (Ei Compendex Plus), 28
Powersoft Forum, 178, 221, 486
PR and Marketing Forum, 16, 397-398, 486-487, 489
PRC Publishing, 61, 85, 221-222, 487
President of the U.S. (White House Forum), 217
programming
    CASE-DCI Forum, 60, 93, 115
    CSI Forth Net Forum, 94, 121, 211
    Digital Database, 126-127
    Digitalk Database, 14, 238-239, 465, 521
    Digitalk Forum, 28, 239, 521
    Dr. Dobb's Forum, 127, 243-244, 488, 576
    Graphics Developers Forum, 314-315
    IBM Languages Forum, 95, 138, 346,-47
    IBM OS/2 Developers Forums, 95, 138-139
    IBM Programming Forum, 95-96, 140, 350
    Macintosh Applications Forum, 389
    Macintosh Developers Forum, 96, 150, 384, 390-391
    Microsoft 32-bit Languages Forum, 79, 96, 101, 408-409
    Microsoft BASIC Forum, 96-97, 155-156, 409-410
    Microsoft DevCast Forum, 97, 156, 410
    Microsoft Developers Relations Forum, 27-28, 234, 406
    Microsoft Foundation Classes Forum, 97, 157, 411
    Microsoft Languages Forum, 412
    Microsoft WIN32 Forum, 97-98, 160, 414
    Microsoft Windows Extensions Forum, 98, 160, 414-415
    Microsoft Windows Objects Forum, 98, 162, 416-417
    Microsoft Windows SDK Forum, 98-99, 162, 417
    PC MagNet Programming Forum, 94, 175-176, 476, 604
    Software Development Forum, 525-526
    Ziff Cobb Programming Forum, 94, 201, 599, 606
psychic experiences (Encounters Forum), 257-258, 471-472, 568
psychology (Personality Profile), 478-479, 488, 496
Public Brand Software (PBS) Applications Forum, 178-179, 488-489, 605
Public Brand Software (PBS) Home Forum, 179, 489, 605
public relations (PR and Marketing Forum), 16, 397-398, 486-489
public safety, 210-211
    Missing Children Forum, 66, 420
    Safetynet Forum, 282-283, 490, 505
    Time Warner Crime Forum, 211, 556, 580
publications (PC Publications), 177
    see also magazines

publishing
    Macmillan Computer Publishing, 43
    Macmillan Publishing Forum, 153, 394
    Media Newsletters, 45-46, 399-400
    PRC Publishing, 61, 85, 487
    Time Warner Bookstore, 62
    Ziff-Davis Press Booknet, 601

Q

Quality Paperbacks, 43-44, 466-467, 491, 493-494
Quick Picture Forum, 86, 491

R

radio
    HamNet Forum, 319, 493
    National Public Radio (NPR), 213-214, 307, 439-440
Rare Diseases Database, 18, 241-242, 493
real estate (Homefinder By AMS), 338, 494
Recording Industry Forum, 436
recreation
    Adventures in Travel, 494
    California Forum, 58
    Recreational Vehicle Forum, 58-59, 425, 495, 560-561
    see also hobbies
relationships (Personality Profile), 478-479, 488, 496
religion
    Issues Forum, 213, 342, 366-367, 496-497
    Religion Forum, 66, 465, 497
    SDAs On-Line, 497, 507
    see also philosophy
research
    Canopus Research Forum, 114-115
    Dissertation Abstracts, 242, 250, 498
    Education Research Forum, 251, 253
    Health Database Plus, 324, 401
    InvesText, 365-366
    IQuest, 224, 355, 366, 498
    Knowledge Index, 225, 303-304, 373, 499
    Legal Research Center, 376, 379-380
    market research (SUPERSITE Demographics Forum), 228, 233, 397, 536
    Medical News/Research, 400
    medical research (Health Database Plus), 327
    Online Surveys, 304
    PaperChase-MEDLINE Forum, 325, 401-402, 471, 499
    Patent Research Center, 362, 376-377, 473, 499-500
    The Sysop Forum, 554
    Wolfram Research Forum, 591

Retirement Living Forum, 17, 400-401, 500, 523
Reuters News Pictures Forum, 213, 451, 483, 500
rights
    digital media (Electronic Frontier Foundation Forum), 237, 360-361
    human rights (Issues Forum), 366-367, 496-497
Rocknet Forum, 260, 437, 501-502, 578
Roger Ebert's Movie Reviews, 272, 426, 500-502

S

safety, *see* public safety
Safetynet Forum, 210-211, 282-283, 490, 505
Sailing Forum, 42-43, 505, 597
Santa Cruz Operation Forum, 505-506
scanners
    HP Handhelds Forum, 271-272, 339-340
    Logitech Forum, 147, 321, 381
science
    Astronomy Forum, 331-332, 546
    Dinosaur Forum, 239-240, 506
    Ei Compendex Plus, 253-254, 258
science fiction (Speakeasy Forum), 182
Scuba Forum, 242-243, 335, 506-507
SDAs On-Line, 497, 507
Sears, 507, 515
Seattle Film Works, 426, 507-508
securities, *see* finances
Securities Screening, 277, 508, 533
Securities Symbols Lookup, 277, 278, 508, 533-534
security (computers)
    National Computer Security Association (NCSA), 99, 165-166
sexuality
    HSX Adult Forum, 42, 303, 341, 509
    HSX Open Forum, 303, 341, 509-510
    Human Sexuality Databank, 325, 342, 510
shareware
    ASP Shareware Forum, 32, 109-110, 510
    Epic MegaGames, 265-266, 295, 513
    Microsoft Windows Shareware Forum, 162, 417, 512
    Public Brand Software (PBS) Applications Forum, 178-179
    Shareware Depot, 179, 510-513
    Shareware Registration, 179-180, 511
    UKSHARE Forum, 190, 511, 572-573
    Ziffnet Zshare Online Newsletter, 205, 610
    ZiffNet/Mac Download Forum, 205, 388-389, 610-611
Shareware Depot, 179, 510-513
Shareware Registration, 179-180, 511
Shop-at-home, 511-512, 515
Shoppers Advantage Club, 70, 241-512, 515-516

shopping
    800 Flowers, 11, 307-308
    Adventure in Food, 287
    Adventures in Food, 15, 513
    Airline Services Unlimited, 21, 513-14, 559
    Alaska Peddler, 21, 308, 514
    Americana Clothing, 23, 69, 514
    Brooks Brothers Online Store, 46, 69, 514
    Detroit Free Press Store, 217, 233, 370-371
    Dial-A-Mattress, 399
    Digital PC Store, 229-230, 238, 466
    The Escort Store, 207, 305, 552
    Figi's Inc., 272
    800 Flowers, 286
    FTD Online, 302-303
    The Gift Sender, 305-308, 552
    The Heath Company, 207, 552
    IBM Personal Software Products, 140
    JC Penney, 369, 515
    The Laser's Edge, 62, 188, 553
    The Mac Zone/PC Zone, 62, 189, 553
    MacWAREHOUSE, 92, 387-388, 395
    Metropolitan Museum of Art, 30
    MicroWarehouse, 93, 163
    Omaha Steaks International, 61, 466
    PC Catalog, 61, 173
    Quality Paperbacks, 43-44, 466-467, 491, 493-494
    Sears, 507, 515
    Seattle Film Works, 426, 507-508
    Shareware Depot, 179, 510-513
    Shop-at-home, 511-512, 515
    Shoppers Advantage Club, 70, 241, 512-515, 516
    Sierra Online, 180, 517-518
    Small Computer Book Club, 44
    Softdisk Publishing, 180-181, 523-524
    SOFTEX, 99, 181, 524
    The Store, 553-554
    Sundown Vitamins, 516, 535, 581
    Sunglasses/Shavers & More, 516, 535
    The Mac Zone/PC Zone, 388
    Time Warner Bookstore, 44, 62, 555-556
    Virginia Diner, 306, 308, 580
    Walter Knoll Florist, 286-287, 309, 583-584
    WORLDSPAN Travelshopper, 563-564, 593
    Ziff Computer Shopper Forum, 201, 599, 606-607
    Ziff-Davis Press Booknet, 203
    ZiffNet Designer Templates, 203, 608
Showbiz Quiz, 260, 298, 427, 516-517, 547, 564-565
ShowBiz-Media Forum, 261, 517
Siemens Automation, 255-256, 517
Sierra Online, 180, 517-518
Sight and Sound Forum, 34, 261, 518

simulators – software

simulators
    Air Traffic Controller, 293-294
    Flight Simulation Forum, 285, 518, 527
    Game Forums and News, 293, 296, 518-519
    Sports Simulation Forum, 299, 529
Single Issue Price Hist., 278, 519, 534
small business
    The Entrepreneur's Forum, 53
    Entrepreneur's Small Business Forum, 50
Small Computer Book Club, 44, 520
Smalltalk/V
Smalltalk/V users
    Digitalk Database, 14, 126-127, 238-239, 465, 521
    Digitalk Forum, 28, 127, 239, 521
Smith Micro Forum, 180
Smith Micro Products, 521-522
SNA
    Eicon Technology Forum, 128, 254, 522, 597
    Microsoft Windows NT SNA Forum, 416
SNIPER! game, 70, 299, 522, 584
Soap Opera Summaries, 522-523, 547
Social Security (Retirement Living Forum), 17, 400-401, 500, 523
Society of Broadcast Eng., 46, 523, 547-548
Softdisk Publishing, 180-181, 523-524
SOFTEX, 99, 181, 524
software
    ACI US Forum, 104, 441
    Adobe Forum, 524
    Aldus Forum, 21, 105, 524-525
    Aldus Online Customer Support, 22, 105-106, 525
    Aldus Special Programs Forum, 22, 106, 525
    anit-virus
        McAfee Virus Forum, 102, 154, 399
        Symantec AntiVirus Prod. Forum, 537-538
    application development (Digitalk Forum), 127
    Artisoft Forum, 31, 109, 442
    ASP Shareware Forum, 32, 109-110
    Atari Computing Forum, 33-34, 110
    Autodesk AutoCAD Forum, 110-111
    Autodesk Retail Products Forum, 111
    Blyth Software Forum, 42, 112-113
    Brøderbund Software, 46, 113
    business
        ACI US Forum, 14
        BASIS Internation Forum, 40
    CAD
        Autodesk AutoCAD Forum, 34, 55-56
        Autodesk Retail Products Forum, 35, 56
        Cadence Forum, 56-57
        MicroStation Forum, 57
    CADD/CAM/CAE Vendor Forum, 114
    Cheyenne Software Forum, 66
    Clarion Software Forum, 67, 116
    Crosstalk Forum, 211
    Data Access Corp. Forum, 122, 220-221
    desktop publishing (Ventura Software Forum), 577
    DiagSoft QAPlus Forum, 541
    finance (Intuit Forum), 143-144, 276
    graphics
        Adobe Forum, 15, 81, 104-105
        CADD/CAM/CAE Vendor Forum, 57-58, 81, 114
        Corel Forum, 81, 120, 209
        The 'GO GRAPHICS' Tutorial, 86, 188
        Graphcs Plus Forum, 316
        Graphics A Vendor Forum, 129, 313-314, 320
        Graphics B Vendors Forum, 129-130, 314, 320-321
        Graphics Corner Forum, 130
        Graphics Developers Forum, 82, 130-131, 314-315
        Graphics File Finder, 82, 131
        Graphics Forums, 83, 131, 313, 315-316
        Graphics Gallery Forum, 83, 131-132, 316
        Graphics Plus Forum, 83-84, 132
        Graphics Support Forum, 84, 316-317
        Graphics Vendors C Forum, 84, 132, 317
        IBM Image Plus Forum, 137
        LDC Words & Pixels Forum, 85, 146-147, 378
        Micrografx, 85
        Micrografx Forum, 154-155, 405
        MicroStation Forum, 163
        PRC Publishing, 61, 221-222
        Venture Software Forum, 86, 193-194
    IBM Personal Software Products, 140, 350
    IBM Software Forum, 141
    IBM Software Solutions Forum, 351
    LDC Spreadsheet Forum, 145-146, 377
    LDC Word Processing Forum, 146, 377-378
    Logitech, 88, 147, 381
    Lotus Press Release Forum, 148
    Macintosh Applications Forum, 148
    Microsoft Access Forum, 155, 225, 409
    Microsoft Excel Forum, 157, 411
    Microsoft Software Library, 79, 102, 413
    Microsoft Windows Forum, 160-61, 415
    Microsoft Windows Fun Forum, 161
    Microsoft Windows Shareware Forum, 417
    Microsoft Word Forum, 163, 418
    Oracle Forum, 467
    Public Brand Software (PBS) Application Forum, 178-179, 488-489, 605
    Public Brand Software (PBS) Home Forum, 179, 489, 605
    Shareware Depot, 179
    Shareware Registration, 179-180
    Sierra Online, 180, 517-518
    Softdisk Publishing, 180-181

SOFTEX, 181, 524
Software Development Forum, 525-526
Software Pub. Assoc. Forum, 181, 526
Software Publisher Online, 181-182, 526
Spinnaker Software Forum, 528
Spinnaker Software Forum +, 182
spreadsheets
    LDC Spreadsheet Forum, 145-146, 377
    Microsoft Excel Forum, 157, 411
The Store, 553-554
SunSoft Forum, 182-183
Support On Site, 183, 228, 536-537
Symantec Applications Forum, 183-184, 538
Symantec CPS DOS Forum, 184, 538
Symantec CPS WinMac Forum, 184, 538-539
Symantec Dev. Tools Forum, 539
Symantec FGS Forum, 539
Symantec Norton Util Forum, 539-540
Symantec Ntwrk Products Forum, 185, 540
SynOptics Forum, 186
UKSHARE Forum, 190
Ultimedia Tools Series A Forum, 191, 573
Ultimedia Tools Series B Forum, 191, 573-574
Ultimedia Tools Series C Forum, 191-192, 574
UnixWare Forum, 575
UserLand Forum, 193, 576
Ventura Software Forum, 193, 194
WinCIM Support Forum, 195
Windows 3rd Party App B Forum, 195-196
Windows 3rd Party App G Forum, 196
Windows 3rd Party E Forum +, 196-197
Wolfram Research Forum, 197-198
word processing
    LDC Word Processing Forum, 146, 377-378
    Microsoft Word Forum, 163, 418
    WordPerfect GmbH Forum, 198, 462-463, 591-592
    WordPerfect Users Forum, 198, 463, 592
    WordStar Forum, 198-199, 592-593
WPCorp Files Forum, 463
Ziff Cobb Applications Forum, 200-201, 606
Ziff Software Center, 202-203, 600-601, 607-608
Software Development Forum, 525, 526
Software Pub. Assoc. Forum, 181, 526
Software Publisher Online, 181-182, 526
sound (Sight and Sound Forum), 261, 518
space
    Flight Simulation Forum, 527
    Space Exploration Forum, 526-527
    Space Flight Forum, 527
Speakeasy Forum, 182, 506, 528
spelling (American Heritage Dictionary), 22-23
Spinnaker Software Forum, 528
Spinnaker Software Forum +, 182

sports
    HealthNet, 528-529
    Motor Sports Forum, 425
    NCAA Collegiate Sports Network, 440
    Outdoor Forum, 469
    Sailing Forum, 505
    Scuba Forum, 242-243, 335, 506-507
    Sports Forum, 299, 529
    Sports Simulation Forum, 299, 529
    UK Sports Clips, 453-454, 529, 572
spreadsheets
    LDC Spreadsheet Forum, 377
    Microsoft Excel Forum, 411
    ZiffNet Designer Templates, 608
Stac Electronics Forum, 256, 529-530
STAGEII, 299-300, 530
Standard Indus. Class., 52, 227, 530
Standard Microsystems Forum, 182, 445-446, 530-531
State-County Demographics, 227-228, 232, 531-532
statistics
    Census Bureau Online Service, 47-48, 65, 531-532
    State-County Demographics, 227-228, 232, 531-532
    SUPERSITE Demographics Forum, 233
Stein Online, 64, 261, 532
stock market
The Store, 553-554
student newspapers (The Sysop Forum), 13, 59
Students' Forum, 252-534
subscriptions
    Detroit Free Press, 535
    Detroit Free Press Store, 217, 233, 370-371
Sundown Vitamins, 516, 535, 581
Sunglasses/Shavers & More, 516, 535
SunSoft Forum, 182, 183, 535-536
SUPERSITE Demographics, 228, 536
SUPERSITE Demographics Forum, 233, 397
Support Directory, 76, 536
support groups
    ADD Forum, 472
    Diabetes Forum, 323
    Disabilities Forum, 378, 433
    Handicapped User's Database, 319-320
    HSX Adult Forum, 303, 341
    HSX Open Forum, 303, 341
    Mensa Forum, 404
Support On Site, 183, 228, 536-537
Sybase Forum, 183, 537
Symantec AntiVirus Prod. Forum, 537, 538
Symantec Applications Forum, 183, 184, 538
Symantec CPS DOS Forum, 184, 538
Symantec CPS WinMac Forum, 184, 538-539
Symantec Dev. Tools Forum, 184-185, 539

Symantec FGS Forum, 185, 539
Symantec Norton Util Forum, 185, 539-540
Symantec Ntwrk Products Forum, 185, 540
Syndicated Columns, 451, 540
SynOptics Forum, 186, 446, 540
The Sysop Forum, 13, 59, 554
system integration (DiagSoft QAPlus Forum), 124-125

T

Tandy CoCo Forum, 116
Tandy Color Computer, 70
Tandy Model 100 Forum, 186, 543
Tandy Professional Forum, 186, 543
TAPCIS Forum, 186-187, 543
taxes
    Electronic Tax Return Filing, 255, 544
    H&R Block, 319, 544
    Intuit Personal Tax Forum, 361-362, 544
    IRS Tax Forms and Documents, 366, 545
telecommunications (IBM Communications Forum), 73
Telecommunications Forum, 187, 545-546
Telephone Access Numbers, 76, 546
television
    Broadcast Professionals Forum, 45, 546-547
    Soap Opera Summaries, 522-523, 547
    Society of Broadcast Eng., 46, 523, 547-548
testing
    Benchmarks and Standards, 41
    Benchmarks and Standards Forum, 112, 548
    Intelligence Test, 548
Texas Instruments Forum, 187, 549
Texas Instruments News, 187-188, 549
The Absolut Museum, 52
Thomas Register Online, 228, 278, 554-555
Thomas-Conrad Forum, 555
Ticker/Symbol Lookup, 278, 555, 583
Time Warner Bookstore, 44, 62, 555-556
Time Warner Crime Forum, 211, 556, 580
Time Warner-Dogs & Cats Forum, 25-26, 556
TIMESLIPS Forum, 41-42, 189, 556
Toshiba Forum, 189, 557
Toshiba GmbH Forum, 189-190, 557
tourism (Official Airline Guide), 19-20
TRADEMARKSCAN, 53, 558
TrainNet Forum, 335, 558-559
travel, 13
    ABC Worldwide Hotel Guide, 339, 559
    Adventures in Travel, 16, 494
    Air France, 18-20, 559
    Air Line Pilots Association, 484
    Airline Services Unlimited, 21, 559
    California Forum, 494-495
    EMI Aviation Services, 19, 256, 564
    Florida Forum, 285
    Florida Today Forum, 242, 285-286, 557-558
    Inn and Lodging Forum, 338-339, 356-357, 560
    Official Airline Guide, 19-20, 465-466, 558, 560
    Recreational Vehicle Forum, 58-59, 425, 495, 560-561
    The Travel Forum, 306
    Travel Britain Online, 561
    Travel Forum, 561
    Travelers Advantage, 561, 564
    UK Accommodation & Travel Service, 569-570
    VISA Advisors, 472-473, 562, 581
    West Coast Travel, 563, 585
    WORLDSPAN Travelshopper, 309, 563-564, 593
trivia
    Showbiz Quiz, 260, 298, 427, 516-517, 547, 564-565
    STAGEII, 299-300, 530
    The Whiz Quiz, 548-549, 554-565
    You Guessed It!, 300-301, 597-598
TRW Bus. Credit Reports, 565

U

U.S. News & World Report, 215, 452, 567
U.S. News Forum, 215-216, 452, 567
U.S. News Women's Forum, 216, 452-453, 591
UFOs (Encounters Forum), 257-258, 568
UK, *see* United Kingdom
Ultimedia Hardware Plus Forum, 190-191, 431-432
Ultimedia Tools Series A Forum, 191, 432, 573
Ultimedia Tools Series B Forum, 191, 432, 573-574
Ultimedia Tools Series C Forum, 191-192, 432, 574
Ultmedia Hardware Plus Forum, 573
United Kingdom
    British Books in Print, 43-45
    British Trade Marks, 45, 47
    PC Direct UK Magazine Forum, 174, 474, 568, 602
    PC Magazine UK Forum, 174-175, 474-475, 568-569, 602-603
    PC Magazine UK Online, 175, 475, 569, 603
    PC Plus/PC Answers Online, 176-177, 477, 569
    Travel Britain Online, 561
    UK Accommodation & Travel Service, 562, 569-570
    UK Company Library, 53-54, 229, 570
    UK Computing Forum, 190, 570
    UK Entertainment Reviews, 261-262, 570
    UK Forum, 562, 571
    UK Historical Stock Pricing, 54, 571
    UK News Clips, 216, 453, 571
    UK Newspaper Library, 216, 453, 571-572
    UK Professionals Forum, 54, 572

UK Sports Clips, 54, 453-454, 529, 572
UKSHARE Forum, 190, 511, 572-573
Univ of Phoenix, 252, 480, 574
UNIX (Santa Cruz Operation Forum), 505-506
UNIX Forum, 192, 574-575
Unix Vendor A Forum, 192, 575
UnixWare Forum, 192-193, 462, 575
user groups
    WordPerfect Users Forum, 592
    WordStar Forum, 592-593
    WUGNET Forum, 575, 589, 595
User Profile Program, 76-77, 329, 576
UserLand Forum, 193, 576

V

VAX Forum, 193, 237, 577
vendor support
    Accounting Vendor Forum, 13, 47
    Amiga Vendor Forum, 24-25, 107
    Apple II Vendors' Forum, 27, 109
    CADD/CAM/CAE Vendor Forum, 57-58, 81, 114
    CD-ROM Vendors Forum, 64, 116
    Graphics A Vendor Forum, 129, 313-314
    Graphics B Vendors Forum, 314
    Graphics Vendors C Forum, 84, 132, 317
    IBM OS/2 Vendor Forums, 139-140
    The Intel Forum, 188, 406, 553
    LAN Vendor Forum, 145, 375-376, 444-445
    Macintosh Vendor Forums, 152-153, 387, 393-394
    MIDI Vendor Forums, 164, 419, 430-431, 435
    Modem Vendor Forum, 165, 423
    Music Vendor Forum, 436, 501-502
    Novell Vendor Forums, 172, 462
    PC Vendor Forums, 177, 477-478
    Smith Micro Forum, 180
    Smith Micro Products, 521-522
    Software Publisher Online, 181-182
    Spinnaker Software Forum, 528
    Stac Electronics Forum, 529-530
    Standard Microsystems Forum, 530-531
    SunSoft Forum, 182-183, 535-536
    Support Directory, 536
    Sybase Forum, 183, 537
    Symantec AntiVirus Prod. Forum, 537-538
    Symantec Applications Forum, 183-184, 538
    Symantec CPS DOS Forum, 538
    Symantec CPS WinMac Forum, 184
    Symantec Dev. Tools Forum, 184-185, 539
    Symantec FGS Forum, 185
    Symantec Norton Util Forum, 185
    Symantec Ntwrk Products Forum, 185
    SynOptics Forum, 186
    TAPCIS Forum, 186-187
    Thomas-Conrad Forum, 555
    TIMESLIPS Forum, 189, 556
    Toshiba GmbH Forum, 557
    Ultimedia Hardware Plus Forum, 190-191
    Ultimedia Tools Series A Forum, 191, 432, 573
    Ultimedia Tools Series B Forum, 191, 432, 573-574
    Ultimedia Tools Series C Forum, 191-192, 432, 574
    Ultmedia Hardware Plus Forum, 573
    Unix Vendor A Forum, 192, 575
    UnixWare Forum, 192-193, 462, 575
    UserLand Forum, 193, 576
    Video Game Publishers Forum, 262, 578-579
    Wang Support Forum, 584
    Windows 3rd Party A Forum, 195, 406-407, 587
    Windows 3rd Party App B Forum, 195-196, 407, 587-588
    Windows 3rd Party App. D Forum, 196, 407, 588
    Windows 3rd Party App G Forum, 196, 408, 588-589
    Windows 3rd Party E Forum +, 196-197, 407-408, 588
    WinNT Forum, 408, 590-591
    Wolfram Research Forum, 197-198, 591
    WordPerfect GmbH Forum, 462-463
    WPCorp Files Forum, 199, 592, 594
    WRQ/Reflection Forum, 199, 595
    Ziff Bendata Forum, 200, 605-606
Venture Software Forum, 86, 193-194, 577
Vestor Stock Recommendation, 278-279, 534, 577
veterinarians (Pet Products/Reference Forum), 25
Video Game Publishers Forum, 262, 300, 578-579
Video Games Forum, 262, 300, 579
Vines 4.x Patchware Forum, 39, 91, 194, 579
Vines 5.x Patchware Forum, 40, 91, 194, 579
violence, *see* **crime**
Virginia Diner, 306, 308, 580
virtual reality (Cyber Forum), 122, 217, 580
viruses (McAfee Virus Forum), 102, 399
VISA Advisors, 472-473, 562, 581
Vobis AG Computer Forum, 89, 194, 581

W

Walter Knoll Florist, 286-287, 309, 583-584
Wang Support Forum, 195, 584
Warner Bros. Song Preview, 437-438, 495, 584
weather
    NWS Aviation Weather, 37-38, 463
    Weather Maps, 396, 562-563, 585
    Weather Reports, 563, 585
West Coast Travel, 563, 585
What's New, 77, 306-307, 585-586
White House Forum, 217, 312, 454, 586
The Whiz Quiz, 548-549, 554-565
WinCIM Support Forum, 77, 195-586

Windows
- CIS Navigator Windows Support Forum, 67
- Microsoft WIN32 Forum, 97-98
- Microsoft Windows Extensions Forum, 160
- Microsoft Windows Forum, 103, 160-161, 415, 586-587
- Microsoft Windows Fun Forum, 161, 297
- Microsoft Windows Multimedia Forum, 415-416
- Microsoft Windows News Forum, 161, 416, 587
- Microsoft Windows SDK Forum, 98-99, 162, 417
- Microsoft Windows Shareware Forum, 162, 417
- SDK extensions, 98
- Symantec CPS WinMac Forum, 538-539
- WinCIM Support Forum, 77, 195, 586
- Windows 3rd part App. D Forum
- Windows 3rd Party App B Forum, 195-196, 587-588
- Windows 3rd Party App. D Forum, 196, 588
- Windows 3rd Party App. G Forum, 196, 588-589
- Windows 3rd Party E Forum +, 196-197, 588
- Windows Sources Forum, 197, 589
- WUGNET Forum, 200, 575, 589, 595

Windows NT
- Digital Equipment Corporation, 68, 125, 236, 433-434, 589-590
- Digital NT Support Forum, 68, 125, 236, 237-238, 590
- Microsoft Windows NT SNA Forum, 161, 416
- WinNT Forum, 197, 408, 590-591

Windows Sources Forum, 197, 589
wine and beer (Bacchus Wine and Beer Forum), 39, 590
WinNT Forum, 197, 408, 590-591
Wolfram Research Forum, 197-198, 591
women's issues (U.S. News Women's Forum), 216, 452-453, 591
word processing
- LDC Word Processing Forum, 377-378
- Microsoft Word Forum, 163, 418
- WordPerfect GmbH Forum, 198, 462-463, 591-592
- WordPerfect Users Forum, 198, 463, 592
- WordStar Forum, 198-199, 592-593

WordPerfect GmbH Forum, 198, 462-463, 591-592
WordPerfect Users Forum, 198, 463, 592
WordStar Forum, 198-199, 592-593
Working-From-Home Forum, 199, 307, 593
WORLDSPAN Travelshopper, 309, 563-564, 593
Worldwide Car Network, 36-37, 593
WPCorp Files Forum, 199, 463, 592, 594
writing
- Journalism Forum, 371, 594
- Literary Forum, 271, 380-381
- *see also* literature

WRQ/Reflection Forum, 199, 595
WUGNET Forum, 200, 575, 589, 595

X–Y–Z

X.25 (Eicon Technology Forum), 128, 254, 522, 597

yachts (Sailing Forum), 42-43
You Guessed It!, 262-63, 300-301, 579-598

Zagat Restaurant Guide, 598
ZeffNet Reviews Index, 204
Zenith Data Systems Forum, 200, 598
Ziff Bendata Forum, 200, 598, 605-606
Ziff Cobb Applications Forum, 200-201, 598-599, 606
Ziff Cobb Programming Forum, 94, 201, 599, 606
Ziff Computer Shopper Forum, 599, 606-607
Ziff Computer Shopping Forum, 201
Ziff Editor's Choice, 201-202, 599-600, 607
Ziff Executives Online Forum, 202, 600, 607
Ziff Newsbytes, 202, 600, 607
Ziff Software Center, 202-203, 600-601, 607-608
Ziff-Davis Press Booknet, 203, 601, 608
ZiffNet
- PC Computing, 173-174, 473-474, 601-602
- PC Contact Forum, 174, 474, 602
- PC Direct UK Magazine Forum, 174, 474, 568, 602
- PC Magazine UK Forum, 174-175, 474-475, 568-569, 602-603
- PC Magazine UK Online, 175, 475, 569, 603
- PC MagNet, 475, 603
- PC MagNet Editorial Forum, 175, 475-476, 603-604
- PC MagNet Programming Forum, 94, 175-176, 604
- PC MagNet Utilities/Tips Forum, 176-476, 604
- PC Week Forum, 177-178, 478, 604-605
- Public Brand Software (PBS) Application Forum, 488-489, 605
- Public Brand Software (PBS) Applications Forum, 178-179
- Public Brand Software (PBS) Home Forum, 179, 489, 605

ZiffNet Electronic Books, 128-129
ZiffNet Designer Templates, 203, 608
ZiffNet File Finder, 608-609
ZiffNet File Folder, 203-204
ZiffNet FREE UTILS Forum, 609
ZiffNet Membership & Benefits, 204, 609
ZiffNet Reviews Index, 609-610
ZiffNet Support Forum, 204-205, 610
ZiffNet Surveys, 205, 610
Ziffnet Zshare Online Newsletter, 205, 610
ZiffNet/Mac Download Forum, 205, 388-389, 610-611
ZiffNet/Mac File Finder, 206, 389, 611

New Riders's Official CompuServe Yellow Pages
REGISTRATION CARD
NRP

Fill out this card to receive information about future CompuServe books and other New Riders titles!

Name _____ Title _____

Company _____

Address _____

City/State/ZIP _____

I bought this book because: _____
_____

I purchased this book from:
☐ A bookstore (Name _____)
☐ A software or electronics store (Name _____)
☐ A mail order (Name of Catalog _____)

I purchase this many computer books each year:
☐ 1–5   ☐ 6 or more

I currently use these applications: _____
_____
_____
_____

I found these chapters to be the most informative: _____
_____

I found these chapters to be the least informative: _____
_____

Additional comments: _____
_____

☐ I would like to see my name in print! You may use my name and quote me in future New Riders products and promotions. My daytime phone number is:_____

New Riders Publishing 201 West 103rd Street • Indianapolis, Indiana 46290 USA

Fold Here

New Riders Publishing
201 West 103rd Street
Indianapolis, Indiana 46290
USA

PLACE STAMP HERE

WANT MORE INFORMATION?

CHECK OUT THESE RELATED TITLES:

	QTY	PRICE	TOTAL

A Guide to Multimedia. This title focuses on teaching you how to integrate popular, affordable, multimedia technologies. This is your guide to integrating sound, video, and animation into eye-popping presentations. *A Guide to Multimedia* also discloses valuable tips and techniques for planning and developing multimedia presentations. ISBN: 1-56205-082-6. _____ $29.95 _____

A Guide to CD-ROM. This is the complete guide to selecting, installing, and using CD-ROMs in business and at home! Learn how CD-ROMs work and what to look for when purchasing a CD-ROM drive. This title also covers where to get CD-ROM titles for any use—from research to games! You'll also learn how to install and share CD-ROMs on networks and workstations. ISBN: 1-56205-090-7. _____ $29.95 _____

Ultimate Windows 3.1. This book and 3-disk set is the ultimate guide to Windows 3.1. This title is organized for easy reference with all related information presented in one place rather than spread throughout the book. *Ultimate Windows 3.1* also covers all of the newest and most popular Windows hardware including sound boards, video accelerators, scanners, VGA-TV technology and CD-ROM drives. *Ultimate Windows 3.1* also gives you all the information you need about Windows 3.1 and MS DOS 6! ISBN: 1-56205-125-3. _____ $39.95 _____

Inside MS-DOS 6. This book and disk combination features expert advice on how to use MS-DOS 6 with today's advanced computers. This book features expert DOS 6 hard disk and memory management tips and secrets, as well as the most complete virus coverage of any DOS 6 book available. Learn the strengths, weaknesses and workarounds of the new DOS 6 utilites. ISBN: 1-56205-132-6. _____ $39.95 _____

Name _____

Company _____

Address _____

City _____ State ____ ZIP _____

Phone _____ Fax _____

☐ Check Enclosed   ☐ VISA   ☐ MasterCard

Card # _____ Exp. Date _____

Signature _____

Prices are subject to change. Call for availability and pricing information on latest editions.

Subtotal _____

Shipping _____

$4.00 for the first book and $1.75 for each additional book.

Total _____

Indiana residents add 5% sales tax.

New Riders Publishing 201 West 103rd Street • Indianapolis, Indiana 46290 USA

Orders/Customer Service: 1-800-428-5331
Fax: 1-800-448-3804

------- Fold Here -------

New Riders Publishing
201 West 103rd Street
Indianapolis, Indiana 46290
USA

PLACE
STAMP
HERE

GO AHEAD. PLUG YOURSELF INTO
MACMILLAN COMPUTER PUBLISHING.

Introducing the Macmillan Computer Publishing Forum on CompuServe®

Yes, it's true. Now, you can have CompuServe access to the same professional, friendly folks who have made computers easier for years. On the Macmillan Computer Publishing Forum, you'll find additional information on the topics covered by every Macmillan Computer Publishing imprint—including Que, Sams Publishing, New Riders Publishing, Alpha Books, Brady Books, Hayden Books, and Adobe Press. In addition, you'll be able to receive technical support and disk updates for the software produced by Que Software and Paramount Interactive, a division of the Paramount Technology Group. It's a great way to supplement the best information in the business.

WHAT CAN YOU DO ON THE MACMILLAN COMPUTER PUBLISHING FORUM?

Play an important role in the publishing process—and make our books better while you make your work easier:

- Leave messages and ask questions about Macmillan Computer Publishing books and software—you're guaranteed a response within 24 hours
- Download helpful tips and software to help you get the most out of your computer
- Contact authors of your favorite Macmillan Computer Publishing books through electronic mail
- Present your own book ideas
- Keep up to date on all the latest books available from each of Macmillan Computer Publishing's exciting imprints

JOIN NOW AND GET A FREE COMPUSERVE STARTER KIT!

To receive your free CompuServe Introductory Membership, call toll-free, **1-800-848-8199** and ask for representative **#597**. The Starter Kit Includes:

- Personal ID number and password
- $15 credit on the system
- Subscription to CompuServe Magazine

HERE'S HOW TO PLUG INTO MACMILLAN COMPUTER PUBLISHING:

Once on the CompuServe System, type any of these phrases to access the Macmillan Computer Publishing Forum:

GO MACMILLAN **GO BRADY**
GO QUEBOOKS **GO HAYDEN**
GO SAMS **GO QUESOFT**
GO NEWRIDERS **GO ALPHA**

Once you're on the CompuServe Information Service, be sure to take advantage of all of CompuServe's resources. CompuServe is home to more than 1,700 products and services—plus it has over 1.5 million members worldwide. You'll find valuable online reference materials, travel and investor services, electronic mail, weather updates, leisure-time games and hassle-free shopping (no jam-packed parking lots or crowded stores).

Seek out the hundreds of other forums that populate CompuServe. Covering diverse topics such as pet care, rock music, cooking, and political issues, you're sure to find others with the same concerns as you—and expand your knowledge at the same time.

WINDOWS TITLES

ULTIMATE WINDOWS 3.1
FORREST HOULETTE, JIM BOYCE, RICH WAGNER, & THE BSU RESEARCH STAFF

The most up-to-date reference for Windows available!

Covers 3.1 and related products
ISBN: 1-56205-125-3
$39.95 USA

INSIDE WINDOWS NT
FORREST HOULETTE, RICHARD WAGNER, GEORGE ECKEL, & JOHN STODDARD

A complete tutorial and reference to organize and manage multiple tasks and multiple programs in Windows NT.

Windows NT
ISBN: 1-56205-124-5
$34.95 USA

WINDOWS FOR NON-NERDS
JIM BOYCE & ROB TIDROW

This helpful tutorial for Windows provides novice users with what they need to know to gain computer proficiency...and confidence!

Windows 3.1
ISBN: 1-56205-152-0
$18.95 USA

INTEGRATING WINDOWS APPLICATIONS
ELLEN DANA NAGLER, FORREST HOULETTE, MICHAEL GROH, RICHARD WAGNER, & VALDA HILLEY

This book is a no-nonsense, practical approach for intermediate- and advanced-level Windows users!

Windows 3.1
ISBN: 1-56205-083-4
$34.95 USA

To Order, Call 1-800-428-5331

GRAPHICS TITLES

INSIDE CORELDRAW! 4.0, SPECIAL EDITION
DANIEL GRAY

An updated version of the #1 best-selling tutorial on CorelDRAW!

CorelDRAW! 4.0
ISBN: 1-56205-164-4
$34.95 USA

CORELDRAW! SPECIAL EFFECTS
NEW RIDERS PUBLISHING

An inside look at award-winning techniques from professional CorelDRAW! designers!

CorelDRAW! 4.0
ISBN: 1-56205-123-7
$39.95 USA

CORELDRAW! NOW!
RICHARD FELDMAN

The hands-on tutorial for users who want practical information now!

CorelDRAW! 4.0
ISBN: 1-56205-131-8
$21.95 USA

INSIDE CORELDRAW! FOURTH EDITION
DANIEL GRAY

The popular tutorial approach to learning CorelDRAW!...with complete coverage of version 3.0!

CorelDRAW! 3.0
ISBN: 1-56205-106-7
$24.95 USA

To Order, Call 1-800-428-5331

OPERATING SYSTEMS

INSIDE MS-DOS 6.2, 2E

NEW RIDERS PUBLISHING

A complete tutorial and reference!

MS-DOS 6.2
ISBN: 1-56205-289-6
$34.95 USA

DOS FOR NON-NERDS

MICHAEL GROH

Understanding this popular operating system is easy with this humorous, step-by-step tutorial.

Through DOS 6.0
ISBN: 1-56205-151-2
$18.95 USA

INSIDE SCO UNIX

STEVE GLINES, PETER SPICER,
BEN HUNSBERGER, & KAREN WHITE

Everything users need to know to use the UNIX operating system for everyday tasks.

SCO Xenix 286, SCO Xenix 386, SCO UNIX/System V 386
ISBN: 1-56205-028-1
$29.95 USA

INSIDE SOLARIS SunOS

KARLA SAARI KITALONG,
STEVEN R. LEE, & PAUL MARZIN

Comprehensive tutorial and reference to SunOS!

SunOS, Sun's version of UNIX for the SPARC workstation, version 2.0
ISBN: 1-56205-032-X
$29.95 USA

To Order, Call 1-800-428-5331

NETWORKING TITLES

#1 Bestseller!

INSIDE NOVELL NETWARE, THIRD EDITION
DEBRA NIEDERMILLER-CHAFFINS & DREW HEYWOOD

This best-selling tutorial and reference has been updated and made even better!

NetWare 2.2, 3.11 & 3.12
ISBN: 1-56205-257-8
$34.95 USA

MAXIMIZING NOVELL NETWARE
JOHN JERNEY & ELNA TYMES

Complete coverage of Novell's flagship product…for NetWare system administrators!

NetWare 3.11
ISBN: 1-56205-095-8
$39.95 USA

NETWARE: THE PROFESSIONAL REFERENCE, SECOND EDITION
KARANJIT SIYAN

This updated version for professional NetWare administrators and technicians provides the most comprehensive reference available for this phenomenal network system.

NetWare 2.x & 3.x
ISBN: 1-56205-158-X
$42.95 USA

NETWARE 4: PLANNING AND IMPLEMENTATION
SUNIL PADIYAR

A guide to planning, installing, and managing a NetWare 4.0 network that best serves your company's objectives.

NetWare 4.0
ISBN: 1-56205-159-8
$27.95 USA

To Order, Call 1-800-428-5331